INVINCIBLE

TRUEMAN'S *Specific* Series®

NTA

UGC-NET/SET

ENGLISH

INVINCIBLE

TRUEMAN'S *Specific* Series®

NTA

UGC-NET/SET

For JRF and Eligibility Test for Assistant Professor

(and Ph.D/M.Phil Entrance Exams)

Code No. : 30

ENGLISH

New Syllabus

With

Previous Years' Papers

By

B.P. PANIGRAHI

Dr. SAVITA YADAV

Authentic & Dependable

Produced and Published by

Danika Publishing Company

(Publishers of Trueman's *Specific* Series)

4352/4C, Ansari Road,

Daryaganj, New Delhi - 110002

Ph.: 011-23242482, 41501988

e-mail: danikabooks@yahoo.com

Can be had from

Invincible Publishers

2nd Floor, SAS Tower, Medicity, Sector 38,

Gurugram (Haryana)

ISBN : 9788189301897

New Edition : 2025

Price : Rs. 600/-

Data Processing :
Inhouse

Printed at :
Dhruv Printers
New Delhi.

Subject to New Delhi Jurisdiction only

PUBLISHERS' NOTE

The present work is a humble attempt to satisfy the needs of students appearing for UGC NET/SET Examinations. Syllabus and Guidelines for Paper II have been given in the book. After theory and MCQs, model papers are provided for practice. We have also incorporated questions asked in previous NET examinations. The book in the present form shall serve as a reliable evocative book for those preparing for NET/SET examinations.

Any suggestions for the improvement shall be thankfully acknowledged.

— With Best Wishes

CONTENTS

This Book Covers

- Chronology of historical events and literary works
- Multiple choice questions
- New Model Papers
- Previous Years' Papers

UGC-NET NEW SYLLABUS

The Test will consist of two papers as given below:

Paper	Marks	Number of Questions	MCQs	Duration
I	100	50	The questions will be generic in nature, intending to assess the teaching/research aptitude of the candidate. It will primarily be designed to test reasoning ability, comprehension, divergent thinking and general awareness of the candidate.	03 hours All the questions will be compulsory.
II	200	100	This will be based on the subject selected by the candidate.	

The Test will be conducted in Computer Based Test (CBT) mode only.

The candidates who desire to appear in the test may see the detailed **Information Bulletin** for UGC-NET which will be available on the website **www.nta.ac.in** and **www.ntanet.nic.in**.

SYLLABUS

Unit –I : Drama

Unit –II : Poetry

Unit –III : Fiction, short story

Unit –IV : Non-Fictional Prose

NOTE: The first four units must also be tested through comprehension passages to assess critical reading, critical thinking and writing skills. These four units will cover all literatures in English.

Unit –V : Language: Basic concepts, theories and pedagogy. English in Use.

Unit –VI : English in India: history, evolution and futures

Unit –VII : Cultural Studies

Unit –VIII : Literary Criticism

Unit –IX : Literary Theory post World War II

Unit –X : Research Methods and Materials in English

UNIT
I-IV

- DRAMA
- POETRY
- FICTION, SHORT STORY
- NON-FICTIONAL PROSE

CHAUCER TO SHAKESPEARE

The period from Chaucer to Shakespeare may be divided into three parts:

1. The Age of Chaucer
2. The Post–Chaucer period
3. The Renaissance period

In this chapter, we shall discuss the characteristics and literary works of these periods in brief along with the life and works of William Shakespeare.

PRE-CHAUCERIAN AGE

Literature is not something like a dormant volcano which keeps sleeping for ages to erupt suddenly, nor is it comparable to anything mechanical such as found around us these days; it is, as quoted by Emile Legouis, like a river which is shaped gradually by numerous tributaries and streams which keep it flowing. This is especially true with reference to English literature of Chaucer's times. The literature preceding the Age of Chaucer (1340-1400) cannot be termed as English Literature because of two theoretical reasons: we find no span of time when language remained persistently single from first to last; secondly, there has not been the continuity of written works handed down from generation to generation. Despite these pedagogical limitations, the literature produced or acquired is by no means inferior in its content and quality from thematic or stylistic perspective.

Generally speaking we can divide the Pre-Chaucerian literature into two main parts: Anglo Saxon and Anglo Norman.

Anglo Saxon's Literature

By the end of 5th century, a many Teutonic tribes from the neighbor invaded Britain where Brythons of Celtic race had already settled. These locals were already Christianized by Romans. The invaders came from two directions: Engle_land (Germanic) invaders settled in Northumbria and Merice, whereas Saxons (Scandinavian and Icelanders) and Jutes invaded the Southeast part of Britain and the food resources kept them there forever. By the next couple of centuries they transformed into the local settlers. These settlers brought with them the tales, inspirations and folklore of their parent culture which haphazardly inspired the literature if there was any in infancy. Their tales and inspirations marked the spirit of paganism in contrast to the Christian inspiration and religious zeal of the native people. The invaders' values match exactly with the spirit of their contemporary parent culture in those times. For example, German Hagen Epic of ***Nibeungen Lied*** and ***Edda and prose sagas of*** Scandinavia and Iceland depict the similar flare which was found in the invaders taste. Their tales relating the contests between savage men and god warfare reflect the similar spirits.

Anglo Saxons did not affect the later English literature as much as it contributed the English vocabulary. We find Germanic and Franco Latin roots in English words even today.

By themes, most of the literature concerned with the contests between savage men, gods' warfare, religious travelogues and monks' fervor. In Latin prose of that age, we find treatises mostly written by courtiers to administer the savage tribes.

In poetry the most influential piece is a Long poem of 6000 lines Beowulf which truly represents the pagan spirit of the age. This poem relates the heroics of a strong godlike hero who kills the giant Grendel in fierce fights. At times the pieces in the poem appear with the emotional grandeur as powerful as are found in the Greek tale of Hercules. Beowulf is such a forceful piece that it still survives though in fragments. Apart from Beowulf, the other mentionable pieces are Caedmon's "Paraphrase of Scriptures" and Cynewuf's "Elene", a series of poems relating to Christ.

In prose, we find Aldhem with his Book of Riddles; the venerable Bede wrote many treatises but the most valuable work was Ecclesiastical History of England. Alcuin also wrote treatises, letters and a few poems. Last but not the least, the monks and clerks added a flare of Saxon Chronicles which show the religion as an important segment of Anglo Saxon's lives.

Marsh observes, *"Anglo Saxon Literature, so far from being the mother, was not even the nurse of the infant genius who opened its eyes to the sun of England."*

Anglo Norman's Literature

Anglo Norman era starts with the French conquest of Britain in 1066. The conquest in those times meant a complete change of status quo in all the forms of life from geographical to social level. William 1 the conqueror brought with him a complete change of set up so comprehensive that changed the themes, and even modes of literature. The French brought with them "the Norman feudalism with its lordly barons and degraded serfs; its castles, moats and drawbridges; its Wambas and Robin Hoods; its troubadours or wandering minstrels; men of no small esteem and importance; and its armour clad knights, — chivalrous defenders of ladies, brave champions in the battle or tournament." For nearly three hundred years the slow amalgamation of ruling Normans and enslaved Saxons, with the fusion of their languages resulting in English, was in progress. Literally no big name whose work survives, quoted or even remembered today, however potentially Anglo Norman era is so important that according to Emile Legouis: "no knowledge of Anglo Saxon is needed in order to understand Chaucer; but it is impossible to understand the origin of his work without knowing something of the French poetry which preceded it."

Generally speaking we can divide Anglo Norman literature into three categories: The Latin writings of numerous monks and historians, Norman French, and Semi Saxon.

The Latin writings of numerous monks and historians:

- Walter Map or Mape wrote stories of King Arthur, De Nugis Curialium (trifles of courtiers)
- Geoffrey of Monmouth wrote History of Britons (preserving the tales of King Arthur)
- Ralph Higden wrote 24 miracle plays titled as "Chester Plays", also wrote polychronicon (in 7 books).

Norman French

- Wace wrote "Brut d'Angleterre" a versified history of Britons.

Semi Saxon: (Morley calls it the transitional English)

- Layamon wrote the "Brut" (a superior translation and enlargement of Wace's poem).
- Orm or Ormin wrote "Ormulum".
- Romances in poetry by Nichoas of Guildford.

ANGLO-SAXON LITERATURE

Anglo-Saxon literature (or **Old English literature**) encompasses literature written in Anglo-Saxon (Old English) during the 600-year Anglo-Saxon period of Britain, from the mid-5th century to the Norman Conquest of 1066. These works include genres such as epic poetry, hagiography, sermons, Bible translations, legal works, chronicles, riddles, and others. In all there are about 400 surviving manuscripts from the period, a significant corpus of both popular interest and specialist research.

Some of the most important works from this period include the poem *Beowulf*, which has achieved national epic status in Britain. The *Anglo-Saxon Chronicle* is a collection of early English history. The poem *Cædmon's Hymn* from the 7th century is one of the oldest surviving written texts in English.

Anglo-Saxon literature has gone through different periods of research—in the 19th and early 20th centuries the focus was on the Germanic roots of English, later the literary merits were examined, and today the interest is with paleography questions and the physical manuscripts themselves such as dating, place of origin, authorship, and looking at the connections between Anglo-Saxon culture and the rest of Europe in the Middle Ages.

A large number of manuscripts remain from the 600 year Anglo-Saxon period, with most written during the last 300 years (9th–11th century), in both Latinand the vernacular. Old English literature is among the oldest vernacular languages to be written down. Old English began, in written form, as a practical necessity in the aftermath of the Danish invasions—church officials were concerned that because of the drop in Latin literacy no one could read their work. Likewise King Alfred the Great (849–899), wanting to restore English culture, lamented the poor state of Latin education:

"So general was [educational] decay in England that there were very few on this side of the Humber who could...translate a letter from Latin into English; and I believe there were not many beyond the Humber" (Pastoral Care, introduction).

King Alfred noted that while very few could read Latin, many could still read Old English. He thus proposed that students be educated in Old English, and those who excelled would go on to learn Latin. In this way many of the texts that have survived are typical teaching and student-oriented texts.

In total there are about 400 surviving manuscripts containing Old English text, 189 of them considered major. These manuscripts have been highly prized by collectors since the 16th century, both for their historic value and for their aesthetic beauty of uniformly spaced letters and decorative elements.

Not all of the texts can be fairly called literature, such as lists of names or aborted pen trials. However those that can present a sizable body of work, listed here in descending order of quantity: sermons and saints' lives (the most numerous), biblical translations; translated Latin works of the early Church Fathers; Anglo-Saxon chronicles and narrative history works; laws, wills and other legal works; practical works on grammar, medicine, geography; lastly, but not least important, poetry.

Nearly all Anglo-Saxon authors are anonymous, with some exceptions.

Research in the 20th century has focused on dating the manuscripts (19th-century scholars tended to date them older than modern scholarship has found); locating where the manuscripts were created—there were seven major scriptoria from which they originate: Winchester, Exeter, Worcester, Abingdon, Durham, and two Canterbury houses Christ Church and St. Augustine; and identifying the regional dialects used: Northumbrian, Mercian, Kentish, West Saxon (the latter being the main dialect).

Old English Poetry

Old English poetry is of two types, the heroic Germanic pre-Christian and the Christian. It has survived for the most part in four manuscripts. The first manuscript is called the *Junius manuscript* (also known as the *Caedmon manuscript*), which is an illustrated poetic anthology. The second manuscript is called the *Exeter Book*, also an anthology, located in the Exeter Cathedral since it was donated there in the 11th century. The third manuscript is called the *Vercelli Book*, a mix of poetry and prose; how it came to be in Vercelli, Italy, no one knows, and is a matter of debate. The fourth manuscript is called the *Nowell Codex*, also a mixture of poetry and prose.

Old English poetry had no known rules or system left to us by the Anglo-Saxons, everything we know about it is based on modern analysis. The first widely accepted theory was by Eduard Sievers (1885) in which he distinguished five distinct alliterative patterns. The theory of John C. Pope (1942) uses musical notations which has had some acceptance; every few years a new theory arises and the topic continues to be hotly debated.

The most popular and well known understanding of Old English poetry continues to be Sievers' alliterative verse. The system is based upon accent, alliteration, the quantity of vowels, and patterns of syllabic accentuation. It consists of five permutations on a base verse scheme; any one of the five types can be used in any verse. The system was inherited from and exists in one form or another in all of the older Germanic languages. Two poetic figures commonly found in Old English poetry are the Kenning, an often formulaic phrase that describes one thing in terms of another, e.g. in Beowulf, the sea is called the *swan's road* and Litotes, a dramatic understatement employed by the author for ironic effect.

Old English poetry was an oral craft, and our understanding of it in written form is incomplete; for example, we know that the poet (referred to as the *Scop*) could be accompanied by a harp, and there may be other aural traditions we are not aware of.

Poetry represents the smallest amount of the surviving Old English text, but Anglo-Saxon culture had a rich tradition of oral story telling, just not much was written down or survived.

The Poets

Most Old English poets are anonymous; twelve are known by name from Medieval sources, but only four of those are known by their vernacular works to us today with any certainty: Caedmon, Bede, Alfred, and Cynewulf. Of these, only Caedmon, Bede, and Alfred have known biographies.

Caedmon is the best-known and considered the father of Old English poetry. He lived at the abbey of Whitby in Northumbria in the 7th century. Only a single nine line poem remains, called *Hymn*, which is also the oldest surviving text in English:

Now let us praise the Guardian of the Kingdom of Heaven the might of the Creator and the thought of his mind, the work of the glorious Father, how He, the eternal Lord established the beginning of every wonder. For the sons of men, He, the Holy Creator first made heaven as a roof, then the Keeper of mankind, the eternal Lord God Almighty afterwards made the middle world the earth, for men.—(Caedmon, *Hymn*, Leningrad manuscript)

Aldhelm, bishop of Sherborne (d. 709), is known through William of Malmesbury who said he performed secular songs while accompanied by a harp. Much of his Latin prose has survived, but none of his Old English remains.

Cynewulf has proven to be a difficult figure to identify, but recent research suggests he was from the early part of the 9th century to which a number of poems are attributed including *The Fates of the Apostles* and *Elene* (both found in the Vercelli Book), and *Christ II* and *Juliana* (both found in the Exeter Book).

Heroic Poems

First page of Beowulf, contained in the damaged Nowell Codex.

The Old English poetry which has received the most attention deals with the Germanic heroic past. The longest (3,182 lines), and most important, is *Beowulf*, which appears in the damaged Nowell Codex. It tells the story of the legendary Geatish hero Beowulf who is the title character. The story is set in Scandinavia, in Sweden and Denmark, and the tale likewise probably is of Scandinavian origin. The story is biographical and sets the tone for much of the rest of Old English poetry. It has achieved national epic status, on the same level as the Iliad, and is of interest to historians, anthropologists, literary critics, and students the world over.

Beyond *Beowulf*, other heroic poems exist. Two heroic poems have survived in fragments: *The Fight at Finnsburh*, a retelling of one of the battle scenes in *Beowulf* (although this relation to *Beowulf* is much debated), and *Waldere*, a version of the events of the life of Walter of Aquitaine. Two other poems mention heroic figures: *Widsith* is believed to be very old in parts, dating back to events in the 4th century concerning Eormanric and the Goths, and contains a catalogue of names and places associated with valiant deeds. *Deor* is a lyric, in the style of *Consolation of Philosophy*, applying examples of famous heroes, including Weland and Eormanric, to the narrator's own case.

The *Anglo-Saxon Chronicle* contains various heroic poems inserted throughout. The earliest from 937 is called *The Battle of Brunanburh*, which celebrates the victory of King Athelstan over the Scots and Norse. There are five shorter poems: capture of the Five Boroughs (942); coronation of King Edgar (973); death of King Edgar (975); death of Prince Alfred (1036); and death of King Edward the Confessor (1065).

The 325 line poem *Battle of Maldon* celebrates Earl Byrhtnoth and his men who fell in battle against the Vikings in 991. It is considered one of the finest, but both the beginning and end are missing and the only manuscript was destroyed in a fire in 1731. A well known speech is near the end of the poem:

Thought shall be the harder, the heart the keener, courage the greater, as our strength lessens. Here lies our leader all cut down, the valiant man in the dust; always may he mourn who now things to turn away from this warplay. I am old, I will not go away, but I plan to lie down by the side of my lord, by the man so dearly loved.—(*Battle of Maldon*)

Old English heroic poetry was handed down orally from generation to generation. As Christianity began to appear, retailers often recast the tales of Christianity into the older heroic stories.

Wisdom Poetry

Related to the heroic tales are a number of short poems from the Exeter Book which have come to be described as "Wisdom poetry". They are lyrical and Boethian in their description of the up and down fortunes of life. Gloomy in mood is *The Ruin*, which tells of the decay of a once glorious city of Roman Britain (Britain fell into decline after the Romans departed in the early 5th c.), and *The Wanderer*, in which an older man talks about an attack that happened in his youth, where his close friends and kin were all killed; memories of the slaughter have remained with him all his life. He questions the wisdom of the impetuous decision to engage a possibly superior fighting force: the wise man engages in warfare to *preserve* civil society, and must not rush into battle but seek out allies when the odds may be against him. This poet finds little glory in bravery for bravery's sake. *The Seafarer* is the story of a somber exile from home on the sea, from which the only hope of redemption is the joy of heaven. Other wisdom poems include *Wulf and Eadwacer*, *The Wife's Lament*, and *The Husband's Message*. King Alfred the Great wrote a wisdom poem over the course of his reign based loosely on the neoplatonic philosophy of Boethius called the *Lays of Boethius*.

Classical and Latin Poetry

Several Old English poems are adaptations of late classical philosophical texts. The longest is a 10th century translation of Boethius' *Consolation of Philosophy* contained in the Cotton manuscript. Another is *The Phoenix* in the Exeter Book, an allegorization of the *De ave phoenice* by Lactantius.

Other short poems derived from the Latin bestiary tradition such as *The Panther*, *The Whale* and *The Partridge*.

Christian Poetry

Saints' Lives

The Vercelli Book and Exeter Book contain four long narrative poems of saints' lives, or hagiography. In Vercelli are *Andreas* and *Elene* and in Exeter are *Guthlac* and *Juliana*.

Andreas is 1,722 lines long and is the closest of the surviving Old English poems to *Beowulf* in style and tone. It is the story of Saint Andrew and his journey to rescue Saint Matthew from the Mermedonians. *Elene* is The story of Saint Helena (mother of Constantine) and her discovery of the True Cross. The cult of the True Cross was popular in Anglo-Saxon England and this poem was instrumental.

Guthlac is actually two poems about English Saint Guthlac (7th century). *Juliana* is the story of the virgin martyr Juliana of Nicomedia.

Biblical Paraphrases

The Junius manuscript contains three paraphrases of Old Testament texts. These were re-wordings of Biblical passages in Old English, not exact translations, but paraphrasing, sometimes into beautiful poetry in its own right. The first and longest is of *Genesis*. The second is of *Exodus*. The third is *Daniel*.

The Nowell Codex contains a Biblical poetic paraphrase, which appears right after *Beowulf*, called *Judith*, a retelling of the story of Judith. This is not to be confused with Aelfric's homily *Judith*, which retells the same Biblical story in alliterative prose.

The Psalter Psalms 51-150 are preserved, following a prose version of the first 50 Psalms. It is believed there was once a complete psalter based on evidence, but only the first 150 have survived.

There are a number of verse translations of the Gloria in Excelsis, the Lord's Prayer, and the Apostles' Creed, as well as a number of hymns and proverbs.

Christian Poems

In addition to Biblical paraphrases are a number of original religious poems, mostly lyrical (non-narrative).

The Exeter Book contains a series of poems entitled *Christ*, sectioned into *Christ I*, *Christ II* and *Christ III*.

Considered one of the most beautiful of all Old English poems is *Dream of the Rood*, contained in the Vercelli Book. It is a dream vision of Christ on the cross, with the cross personified, speaking thus:

"I endured mucn hardship up on that hill. I saw the God of hosts stretched out cruelly. Darkness had covered with clouds the body of the Lord, the bright radiance. A shadow went forth, dark under the heavens. All creation wept, mourned the death of the king. Christ was on the cross."—(*Dream of the Rood*)

The dreamer resolves to trust in the cross, and the dream ends with a vision of heaven.

There are a number of religious debate poems. The longest is *Christ and Satan* in the Junius manuscript, it deals with the conflict between Christ and Satan during the forty days in the desert. Another debate poem is *Solomon and Saturn*, surviving in a number of textual fragments, Saturn is portrayed as a magician debating with the wise king Solomon.

Other Poems

Other poetic forms exist in Old English including riddles, short verses, gnomes, and mnemonic poems for remembering long lists of names.

The Exeter Book has a collection of ninety-five riddles. The answers are not supplied, a number of them to this day remain a puzzle, and some of the answers are obscene.

There are short verses found in the margins of manuscripts which offer practical advice There are remedies against the loss of cattle, how to deal with a delayed birth, swarms of bees, etc. the longest is called *Nine Herbs Charm* and is probably of pagan origin.

There are a group of mnemonic poems designed to help memorise lists and sequences of names and to keep objects in order. These poems are named *Menologium*, *The Fates of the Apostles*, *The Rune Poem*, *The Seasons for Fasting*, and the *Instructions for Christians*.

Specific features of Anglo-Saxon Poetry

Simile and Metaphor

Anglo-Saxon poetry is marked by the comparative rarity of similes. This is a particular feature of Anglo-Saxon verse style, and is a consequence of both its structure and the rapidity with which images are deployed, to be unable to effectively support the expanded simile. As an example of this, the epic Beowulf contains at best five similes, and these are of the short variety. This can be contrasted sharply with the strong and extensive dependence that Anglo-Saxon poetry has upon metaphor, particularly that afforded by the use of kennings.

Elaboration

It is also a feature of the fast-paced dramatic style of Anglo-Saxon poetry that it is not prone, in the way that, say, Celtic literature of the period was, to overly elaborate decoration. Where typically a Celtic poet of the time might use 3 or 4 similes to make a point, typically an Anglo-Saxon poet might reference a kenning, before moving swiftly on.

Old English Prose

The amount of surviving Old English prose is much greater than the amount of poetry. Of the surviving prose, sermons and Latin translations of religious works are the majority. Old English prose first appears in the 9th century, and continues to be recorded through the 12th century.

Christian Prose

The most widely known author of Old English was King Alfred, who translated many books from Latin into Old English. These translations include: Gregory the Great's *The Pastoral Care*, a manual for priests on how to conduct their duties; *The Consolation of Philosophy* by Boethius; and *The Soliloquies* of Saint Augustine. Alfred was also responsible for a translation of the fifty Psalms into Old English. Other important Old English translations completed by associates of Alfred include: *The History of the World* by Orosius, a companion piece for Augustine of Hippo's *The City of God*; the Dialogues of Gregory the Great; and the *Ecclesiastical History of the English People* by Bede.

Elfric of Eynsham, wrote in the late 10th and early 11th century. He was the greatest and most prolific writer of Anglo-Saxon sermons, which were copied and adapted for use well into the 13th century. He also wrote a number of saints lives, an Old English work on time-reckoning, pastoral letters, translations of the first six books of the Bible, glosses and translations of other parts of the Bible including Proverbs, Wisdom and Ecclesiasticus.

In the same category as Aelfric, and a contemporary, was Wulfstan II, archbishop of York. His sermons were highly stylistic. His best known work is *Sermo Lupi ad Anglos* in which he blames the sins of the British for the Viking invasions. He wrote a number of clerical legal texts *Institutes of Polity* and *Canons of Edgar.*

One of the earliest Old English texts in prose is the *Martyrology*, information about saints and martyrs according to their anniversaries and feasts in the church calendar. It has survived in six fragments. It is believed to date from the 9th century by an anonymous Mercian author.

The oldest collection of church sermons are the *Blickling homilies* in the Vercelli Book and dates from the 10th century.

There are a number of saint's lives prose works. Beyond those written by Aelfric are the prose life of Saint Guthlac (Vercelli Book), the life of Saint Margaret and the life of Saint Chad. There are four lives in the Julius manuscript: Seven Sleepers of Ephesus, Saint Mary of Egypt, Saint Eustace and Saint Euphrosyne.

There are many Old English translations of many parts of the Bible. Aelfric translated the first six books of the Bible (the Hexateuch). There is a translation of the Gospels. The most popular was the *Gospel of Nicodemus*, others included "..the *Gospel of Pseudo-Matthew, Vindicta salvatoris, Vision of Saint Paul* and the *Apocalypse of Thomas*".

One of the largest bodies of Old English text is found in the legal texts collected and saved by the religious houses. These include many kinds of texts: records of donations by nobles; wills; documents of emancipation; lists of books and relics; court cases; guild rules. All of these texts provide valuable insights into the social history of Anglo-Saxon times, but are also of literary value. For example, some of the court case narratives are interesting for their use of rhetoric.

Secular Prose

The *Anglo-Saxon Chronicle* was probably started in the time of King Alfred and continued for over 300 years as a historical record of Anglo-Saxon history.

A single example of a Classical romance has survived, it is a fragment of a Latin translation of *Apollonius of Tyana* by Philostratus (220 AD), from the 11th century.

A monk who was writing in Old English at the same time as Aelfric and Wulfstan was Byrhtferth of Ramsey, whose books *Handboc* and *Manual* were studies of mathematics and rhetoric.

Aelfric wrote two neo-scientific works, *Hexameron* and *Interrogationes Sigewulfi*, dealing with the stories of Creation. He also wrote a grammar and glossary in Old English called *Latin*, later used by students interested in learning Old French because it had been glossed in Old French.

There are many surviving rules and calculations for finding feast days, and tables on calculating the tides and the season of the moon.

In the Nowell Codex is the text of *The Wonders of the East* which includes a remarkable map of the world, and other illustrations. Also contained in Nowell is *Alexander's Letter to Aristotle*. Because this is the same manuscript that contains *Beowulf*, some scholars speculate it may have been a collection of materials on exotic places and creatures.

There are a number of interesting medical works. There is a translation of Apuleius's *Herbarium* with striking illustrations, found together with *Medicina de Quadrupedibus*. A second collection of texts is *Bald's Leechbook*, a 10th century book containing herbal and even some surgical cures. A third collections is known as the *Lacnunga*, which relies of charms, incantations, and white magic.

Anglo-Saxon legal texts are a large and important part of the overall corpus. By the 12th century they had been arranged into two large collections (see *Textus Roffensis*). They include laws of the kings, beginning with those of Aethelbert of Kent, and texts dealing with specific cases and places in the country. An interesting example is *Gerefa* which outlines the duties of a reeve on a large manor estate. There is also a large volume of legal documents related to religious houses.

Historiography

Old English literature did not disappear in 1066 with the Norman Conquest. Many sermons and works continued to be read and used in part or whole up through the 14th century, and were further catalogued and organised. During the reformation, when monastic libraries were dispersed, the manuscripts were collected by antiquarians and scholars. These included Laurence Nowell, Matthew Parker, Robert Bruce Cotton and Humfrey Wanley. In the 17th century begun a tradition of Old English literature dictionaries and references. The first was William Somner's *Dictionarium Saxonico-Latino-Anglicum* (1659). Lexicographer Joseph Bosworth began a dictionary in the 19th century which was completed by Thomas Northcote Toller in 1898 called *An Anglo-Saxon Dictionary*, which was updated by Alistair Campbell in 1972.

Because Old English was one of the first vernacular languages to be written down, nineteenth century scholars searching for the roots of European "national culture" (see Romantic Nationalism) took special interest in studying Anglo-Saxon literature, and Old English became a regular part of university curriculum. Since WWII there has been increasing interest in the manuscripts themselves— Neil Ker, a paleographer, published the ground breaking *Catalogue of Manuscripts Containing Anglo-Saxon* in 1957, and by 1980 nearly all Anglo-Saxon manuscript texts were in print. J.R.R. Tolkien is credited with creating a movement to look at Old English as a subject of literary theory in his seminal lecture *Beowulf: The Monsters and the Critics* (1936).

Old English literature has had an influence on modern literature. Some of the best-known translations include William Morris' translation of *Beowulf* and Ezra Pound's translation of *The Seafarer*. The influence of the poetry can be seen in modern poets T. S. Eliot, Ezra Pound and W. H. Auden. Much of the subject matter and terminology of the heroic poetry can be seen in *The Hobbit*, *The Lord of the Rings* and many others.

Quotes

Jorge Luis Borges, from *The Aleph, and Other Stories, 1933-1969* (1969):

"I knew that at home, on a certain top shelf, I had copies of Sweet's Anglo-Saxon Reader and the Anglo-Saxon Chronicle. When the students came the next Saturday morning, we began reading these two books. We skipped grammar as much as we could and pronounced the words like German. All at once, we fell in love with a sentence in which Rome (Romeburh) was mentioned. We got drunk on these words and rushed down Peru Street shouting them at the top of our voices. And so we set out on a long adventure. I had always thought of English literature as the richest in the world; the discovery now of a secret chamber at the very threshold of that literature came to me as an additional gift. Personally, I knew that the adventure would be an endless one, and that I could go on studying Old English for the rest of my days."

THE AGE OF CHAUCER

This was the age, when the seeds of modern age were being endropped. Unrest and transition were the common features of this age. Geographical discoveries and the revolt against medieval traditions led towards the process of transition, which dates back to the second half of the fourteenth century. In the religious world, there was a serious outburst of unorthodoxy. Wyclif and his followers were making an organised attack upon the Church. In town and country alike, doctrines were being preached, in which a future age was to familiarize under the name of Protestantism. The Church was not the only medieval institution that was attacked. The working classes were stirring and had begun to display a spirit of independence hitherto unknown. A period of economic discontent was followed by an open revolt – a revolt which marked the downfall of the manorial system. But, there were constructive as well as destructive forces at work. Political and military events were contributing to the growth of a national consciousness, the former in a negative manner by minimising the extent of Papal influence, the latter, more positively, by stimulating the pride of the English people.

CHARACTERISTICS OF CHAUCER'S AGE

John Wyclif : An Evidence of Chaucer's Age

Among the great contemporaries of Chaucer, few deserve more attention than John Wyclif, for he was one of the first Englishmen to challenge the authority of the Catholic Church; and in doing so, he anticipated Martin Luther, by nearly one hundred and fifty years. Like his famous successor, he came to the conclusion that clerical pretensions had raised a barrier between man and God; and both, by pen and in pulpit, he endeavoured to break it down. Free access to the Bible was what the spiritual life required.

1. **Question Mark on Church Supremacy.** The prestige of the Church was, in truth, beginning to decline. Politically, intellectually and spiritually, its influence had diminished. Until the reign of John, it was the clergy more than any other class who ensured good government. For, they had held the balance between the despotic inclinations of the King on the one hand and the anarchical tendencies of the nobility on the other. But for reasons, which we need not discuss here, this patriotic policy had been hindered during the thirteenth century. Then came the birth of Parliament, and the people began to fight their own political battles.

2. **Environment Oriented Towards Economy.** The fourteenth century opened brightly for Industrial England. There had been no repetition of the anarchy of Stephen's reign, when so barren was the land that – to use the words of a contemporary writer– "you might as well have tilled the sea." The material prosperity of the working classes had steadily increased. Both with regard to food and clothing, the English labourer was better off than his fellows on the continent. He had, moreover, another important reason for self-congratulation which requires a word or so of explanation, for, one cannot follow the trend of economic events during this period without referring, however briefly, to the curious medieval system of land tenure.
3. **Progressive Spirit**. A final illustration of the progressive spirit animating society at his time may be found in the growth of national sentiments. What were the conditions which favoured that development? It will perhaps be remembered that in dealing with the psychology of the Teutonic people, a prominent trait was found, i.e., their power of adaptation. Since this pliability enabled them to readily absorb the characteristics of races wholly alien to themselves, it is not surprising that this fusion was still more rapid when different branches of the parent stock encountered one another.
4. **The Hundred Years' War.** The accession of Edward III marked the beginning of that struggle with France popularly known as "The Hundred Years' War"– a title which explains itself. To narrate the causes which occasioned this mighty conflict would be unnecessary, for we are only concerned with historical events in so far as they have some direct bearing on the literature of the period. What does it call for notice is the brilliant start which England made.

   In the very year in which Chaucer was born, there occurred the great sea fight off Sluys. This battle has a two-fold interest. It was the first of an almost unbroken series of victories which lasted nearly twenty years and included the familiar name of Crecy and Poitiers; further it was one of the earliest of those naval successes, which in the years to come, Blake and Nelson were to make so typically English. But in the importance of its results, Sluys cannot, of course, compare with Crecy – the battle which Froissart has described in such a vivid and picturesque language.
5. **Degradation of Pope's Status.** In the fourteenth century, the Papacy met with a series of misfortunes, of which the English kings were not slow to avail themselves. The temporal overlordship of the Pope was definitely repudiated. Nor was this all. He lost also the important advantages of being able to fill the bishopries with his own nominees. By these and other measures, the Parliaments of Edward III and his successors began that process of separation from Rome, which the work of Henry VIII completed. Such then, briefly, are the main political and social tendencies of the time in which Chaucer and Langland lived and wrote – a transitional age, with the old feudalism slowly losing its pristine vigour and utility, with a great Church, rich in its traditions of intellectual and moral guidance, exhibiting signs of decadence and enfeeblement; yet with no clear ideals as yet, or only dimly lined ideals, as to what form of social reconstruction was to take their place.

Geoffrey Chaucer

Geoffrey Chaucer was the "father of English poetry" and the greatest narrative poet of England. With his emergence the old literative poetry died. The exact date of his birth is uncertain, but most scholars fix it at 1340. Geofferey's early life was spent in London during his most plastic years, and the impressions of the city and its teeming life were likely to make an ineffaceable impression on his imagination. Chaucer symbolises, as no other writer does, the Middle Ages. He stands in much the same relation to the life of his time, as Pope does to the earlier phases of the eighteenth century, and Tennyson to the Victorian era; and its place in English literature is ever more important than theirs, for he is the first great poet in English; the first to make English composite language a thing compact and vital.

Background and the First Phase of Chaucer

Chaucer was born in London to a family of wine merchants. He was brought up in a middle class background, which is a crucial aspect of his writing and the times he lived in. The name 'Chaucer', itself, shows its stand for *chaufe aire* (i.e. a "chafe wax"), and suggests a foreign lineage. It is probable that his grandfather was one Robert le Chaucer, collector of wine dues in the Port of London. On his death, the widow remarried Richard le Chaucer. His stepson John was a vintner like his stepfather, acting also as King's butler to Edward III, whenever that monarch crossed the water. John Chaucer married Agnes, niece of Hugo de Compton; and it is probable that Geoffrey Chaucer was their son. In 1357, Chaucer was appointed to the household of Elizabeth, countess of Ulster, and wife of Lionel, third son of Edward III, and from items of her expenditure that have survived, we gather that she provided the youth with red black breeches, and shoes. Two years later, he was captured by the French, while on a military expedition to France, and the King paid a ransom for his release. He became subsequently a personal attendant of the King – a "beloved valet," as he was called, or as we should say today, a gentleman-in-waiting. From this position, he ascended to that of esquire, where he was concerned with helping to entertain the court and any strangers that might come along. In this way his social qualities were sharpened, a characteristic that left ample impression on his later poetry.

On Diplomatic Mission. From 1370 to 1378, he went on a diplomatic mission abroad-during the later part of the time to Italy. These journeys, especially the Italian ones, affected in marked fashion, his literary work. During this period, he obtained from the corporation of London a life lease of the Gatehouse at Aldgate, where he lived for a number of years. Later he became the comptroller of customs in the port of London.

End of the Journey. We pass now to the last period of Chaucer's life. His fortunes at this time declined. He lost Court favour in 1386 and became relatively poor. For the next few years, he was however more free to turn to literary work. A slight improvement in his position occurred in 1389 when he was made clerk of the Works: looking after the repairs and alterations at the palace of Westminster, the Tower, and St. George's Chapel, Windsor. In 1391, however, he was superseded in these activities, and lived on pension for the remaining years of his life. A literary hint sent to Henry IV, titled *Complement to his Purse*, had facilitated matters in this direction. His great work '*The Canterbury Tales*' was written almost entirely during the later years of this period, when he made splendid use of his knowledge of men and affairs. The finest part of the Canterbury Tales is the prologue, the noblest story is probably and the Knight Tales. He died in 1400 and was buried in St. Benet's Chapel in Westminster Abbey. During the last few months of his life, he had taken a house in the garden of St. Mary's, Westminster. In 1868, a stained glass window, symbolising his life and work, was erected by Dean Stanley, over against his grave.

The Salient Features of the Age of Chaucer or the Late 14th Century

The fourteenth century brightly opened for industrial England but the glory was overtaken by plague, the Black Death (1348-49), as a result most of the laborers escaped death, left the country. The prestige of the Church was, in truth, beginning to decline, and, then came the birth of parliament. The literary moment of the age clearly reflected by five famous poets, in which, Langland, voicing the social discontent, preaching the equality of men and the dignity of labor; Wyclif, giving the Gospel to the people in their own tongue; Gower criticizing the vigorous life and plainly afraid of its consequences; Mandeville romancing about the wonders to be seen abroad; and Chaucer, sharing in all the stirring life of the times, and reflecting it in literature as no other but Shakespeare had ever done.

There is little to record about the prose which includes Chaucer's Treatise on the Astrolabe; Wyclif's Bible, but Mandeville's Travels and Travellers keeps its place as the first English prose classic. The greatest gift of the age was "the heroic couplet Chaucer introduced into English verse, the rhyme royal he invented", and its example is The Canterbury Tales which shows, Chaucer's Age is still characteristically medieval, marked the persistence of chivalry. In this Age, for the first time, the major poets wrote poetry in the native language, and make it a rival to the dominant French; as a result, literature came to be written which was read alike by all the classes of the literate. Chaucer write:

Through me men gon into that blysful place
Of hertes hele and dedly woundes cure;
Through me men gon unto the welle of grace

"With Chaucer was born our real poetry" (Arnold) who has "a fondness for long speeches and pedantic digression...long explanation when none were necessary" (Albert). Chaucer was much occupied by divers official duties which all helped to increase his knowledge of humanity and of affairs, and gave him that intimate, sympathetic acquaintance with men and women which was the raw stuff of his final accomplishment—The Canterbury Tales, an immense work of one hundred and twenty-eight tales, which covers the whole life of England, through 32 characters. The Canterbury Tales (c.1387-1400) is a cycle of linked tales told by a group of pilgrims who meet in a London tavern before their pilgrimage to the shrine of St Thomas a Becket in Canterbury. The Canterbury Tales had been essentially romantic, and so had never attempted to the study of men and women as they are so that the reader recognizes them, not as ideal heroes, but as his own neighbors. The work ends with a kindly farewell form the poet to his reader, and so "*here taketh the makere of this book his leve*" In The Canterbury Tales it appears that he did not have a very high opinion of woman, but we find a remark respectable to women when he says about the Squire, Knight's son:

"and born him well, as of so litel space;
in hope to standen in his lady grace."

The critics have found the seed of the novel in The Canterbury Tales which is famous for the ten syllable rhyming couplets, which makes him, as Ward points out, "the first painter of character" that is why "Chaucer is to be regarded as English first story-teller as well as first modern poet," cries W.J. Long. The Canterbury Tales had been essentially romantic, and so had never attempted to the study of men and women as they are so that the reader recognizes them, not as ideal heroes, but as his own neighbors. The work ends with a kindly farewell form the poet to his reader, and so

"here taketh the makere of this book his leve."

The most important thing that Chaucer did for English poetry was to bring a healthy realism to it. He brought poetry closer to nature, and or reality. He began as his contemporaries did, with dream visions and allegorical works. But gradually he reached the conclusion that nothing could be as nature herself. He comes to look upon the world of man. He set about reproducing it in his work. He became a painter of life in words. Chaucer's broad and humane vision of life helped him in his portraiture of life. Sympathizing with the follies of men and women of average standards, he never riles and rants in his writings. He lets his character's speak for themselves. He is the pioneer of that set of people who look upon the world with indulgent, tolerant and amused eyes.

Chaucer is by universal consent the first great English humorist. His is a healthy humour like that of Shakespeare and Fielding that depends for its effect on strong commonsense. Chaucer had a sound mind and was capable of playing with humanity. He had so much sorrow in his life that could get down in his heart and weaken his intelligence or dim is sight. Chaucer had a free and open mind. He was not afraid, on occasion, of questioning even the ways of God to men. In The Knights's Tale, he shows his poignant awareness of the baffling problem of pain and evil in the world. Chaucer found English a dry, uncouth brick but left it marble—beautiful and full of liquid luster. He found it a dialect and made it a Standard English of his own day. In his works, he appears as a great picture painter, as an observer whose aim was to see and not to reform, and as a representative of his century.

He was a great reformer and observer of men and had an extraordinary insight into human nature. "Chaucer sees things", writes Legouis, "as they are, and paints them as he sees them." He saw all sorts of men—rogues, hypocrites and posers—and had a soft corner in his heart for all of them. All of Chaucer's characters are true to life and cause willing suspension of disbelief. Chaucer considered the first poet of English literature. In his poetry we find the great qualities of simplicity, clarity, melody and harmony which arouse fellow feeling and brotherly affection in the heart of the reader. Chaucer's characters are a description of eternal principles" says Blake. They are not for one age but for all ages.

The world which Chaucer had created in the geography of imagination is as fresh as ever or even fresher than the world in which we live. There is no doubt about Chaucer's help to dramatist. Shakespeare is borrowing of a plot for one of his complicated plays, Troilus and Cressida from Chaucer's Troilus and Cressida. Chaucer's The Prologue may be described as "a novel of miniature". It has an unrivalled richness and variety in the characterization, an abundant fund of humour, and a full representation of real life. He had the sweetness of Goldsmith, the compassionate realism and humour of Fielding, and the high chivalrous tone of Scott. Thus we follow the point of Chesterton, that "There was ever a man who was more of a Maker than Chaucer." Shakespeare and Milton were the greatest sons of their country; but Chaucer was the father of his country.

The period of ruin and reconstruction:

With the Norman conquest of England in 1066, began a new era in English history. The Normans represented the civilization of France which was the literary centre of all Europe. They brought them law, culture, and the strong impulse to share in the great world's work which attracted the Anglo Saxon. They turned naturally to the cultured and progressive Norman's for their literary models. The Normandy imported into England a French literary ideal which seemed to crush the native tongue which was spoken by the down-trodden and the vanquished race. But so tenaciously the common people clung to their own speech that in the end their native tongues absorbed almost the whole body of French words and became ultimately the language of the whole of England. This new language was quite different from the language used in Anglo-Saxon poetry; it was colored by the French ideals.

No knowledge of Anglo-Saxon poetry is needed in order to read Chaucer. But it is impossible to understand Chaucer's work without knowing something of the French poetry which preceded it. The most important contribution of the Normans conquest can be traced in the aristocratic note in Middle English poetry. The old Anglo- Saxon democratic spirit ended with and there began a literature of high society from Chaucer.

The historical background (1350-1450). The age of Chaucer includes the greater part of the reign of Edward III and the long French wars associated with his name; the accession of his grandson Richard II and the revolution of 1399, the deposition of Richard and the foundation of the Lancastrian dynasty. From the literary point of view of greater importance are the social and intellectual movements of the period; the terrible plague called the Black Death, brining poverty, unrest and revolt among the peasants, and the growth of the spirit of inquiry, which was strongly critical and found expression in the teachings of Wycliff and the Lollards, and in the stern denunciations of Langland.

Chaucer lived and wrote in a world where the half shadows of the middle Ages were only beginning to scatter before the clear dawn light of modern culture. He, first of all men in England , reacted to the stimulation and emancipating movement called the renaissance, as it stirred in the souls of men beyond the Alps and his artistic consciousness escaped from the rigid bonds, the cramping conventionalities, the narrow inhibitions of the Middle Ages. From them he emerged into the world of living actualities that he exhibits in his powerful later word. In this sense, he was far beyond his age.

Literary Features of the Age. The standardizing of English: With Chaucer, the English language has shaken down to a kind of average – to the standard of the East Midland speech, the language of the capital city and of the universities –French and English have amalgamated to form the standard English tongue, which attains to its first full expression in the works of Chaucer.

A Modern Note. The real modern note begins to be apparent at this period. There is a shaper spirit of criticism, a more searching interest in man's affairs and a less ch llike faith in, and a less complacent acceptance of the established order. The vogue of the romance, though it has by no means gone, is passing and in Chaucer it is derided. The freshness of the romantic ideal is being superseded by the more acute spirit of the drama which even at this early time is faintly foreshadowed. Chaucer is regarded as the first English short story teller and the first English modern poet. He attempted the mew realistic task of portraying men and women as they were and described them so that the readers could recognize them as their own acquaintances. His characters have, for this reason, become a permanent treasure of English literature. Chaucer is the first great English writer to bring the atmosphere of romantic interest about the man and woman and the daily work of one's own world which is the aim of nearly all modern literature, another more modern feature is that the age of anonymity is passing away with Chaucer.

Prose. The age of Chaucer begins the foundation of an English prose style. Earlier specimens of prose were mainly experimental or purely imitative. But in the prose works of Malory and Mandeville, we get both original and individual prose. The English tongue is now ripe for a prose style. The language is setting to a standard; Latin and French are losing grip as popular prose mediums and the growing desire for an English bible exercises as steady pressure in favor of a Standard English prose.

Scottish Literature. For the first time in English literature, in the person of Barbour (1316-1395) Scotland supplies a writer worthy of note. This is only the beginning, for the tradition is handed on to the powerful groups of poets of the succeeding period.

Medieval Chivalry. Chaucer's England was predominantly medieval in spirit. And the most outstanding feature of the Middle Ages was chivalry. Chaucer's Knight is a true representative of the spirit of medieval chivalry which was a blend of love, religion, and bravery. He has been a champion of not fewer than fifteen battles in the defense of

Christianity. Even the tale that he tells is, like him, imbued with the spirit of medieval chivalry-though nominally it has the ancient Greece for its setting and has for its two important characters the two Greek heroes who are said-to have flourished in an unspecified period of history. Chaucer almost completely medievalizes this story to enable us to have a taste of the chivalry of his age.

We must, however, point out here that the spirit of true chivalry was breathing its last in the age of Chaucer. The Knight, in fact, is a representative of an order which was losing its ground. The true representative of the new order is his young son, the Squire, who has as much taste for revelry as for chivalry. He is "a lover and a lusty bachelor." He is singing and fluting all the day and love-struck as he is, he sleeps "no more than a nightingale." However, we justly wonder if he could have proved himself another Arcite or another Palamon. At any rate, he truly represents the marked change in the world of chivalry which was fast coming over the age of Chaucer.

A Cross-section of Society. *The Canterbury Tales* gives us a fairly authentic and equally extensive picture of the socio-political conditions prevailing in England in the age of Chaucer. Each of the thirty pilgrims hails from a different walk of life, and among themselves they build up an epitome of their age. Each of them is a representative of a section of society as well as an individual. Even though the chief events of the age are not dealt with exhaustively by Chaucer, the thirty pilgrims provide us with the taste of life in the England of Chaucer. Chaucer was not a reformer but a delineator of reality. Legouis remarks "What he has given is a direct transcription of daily life, taken in the very act," as it were, and in its most familiar aspects. Chaucer's work is the most precious document for whoever wishes to evoke a picture of life as it then was...."

Trade, Commerce, and Craft. For the first time in history the trading and artisan sections of society were coming to their own in the age of Chaucer. With the fast expansion in trade and commerce merchants had become prosperous and so had the craftsmen whose goods they traded in. We are told by Chaucer that the Haberdasher, the Carpenter, the Weaver, the Dyer, and the Tapicer were well clothed and equipped. Their weapons were not cheaply trimmed with brass, but all with silver. They were so respectable-looking that

Well seined each of them a fair burgeus
To sitten in a yeldhalle, on a days.

They were no longer despised by the nobility. The Merchant is a typical representative of his class, and the forefather of Sir Andrew Freeport, the merchant who is a member of the Spectator Club as delineated by Addison and Steele in the eighteenth century. His character-sketch as done by Chaucer exudes prosperity. He is always talking about the increase in his income and knows well how to make money in the market place. The countrymen and merchants have always made the two most common objects of humour and satire. But Chaucer lets the Merchant go without much of satire, perhaps in recognition of the importance that his class had gained in his age.

Medicine. Chaucer's portrait of the Doctor of Physic is fairly representative of the theory and practice of medicine in his age. The knowledge of astronomy (rather astrology) was a must for a physician as all the physical ailments were supposed to be the consequences of the peculiar configurations of stars and planets. That is why the Doctor, too, was, "grounded in astronomy." However, "his study was but little on the Bible" perhaps because he had not much time to spare from his professional studies. He had amassed a fortune in the year of the great plague and was keen to keep it with him:

He fcepte that he wan in pestilence.
For gold in phisik is a cordial,
Therefore he lovede gold in special.

Gold in the form of a colloidal solution was administered as a tonic fay physicians. However, Chaucer has a sly dig at the Doctor in his reference to his gold-loving nature.

The Church. Through the ecclesiastical characters in *The Canterbury Tales* Chaucer constructs a representative picture of the condition of the Church and her ministers in his age. The Church had then become a hotbed of profligacy, corruption, and rank materialism. The Monk, the Friar, the Summoner, the Pardoner, and the Prioress are all corrupt, pleasure-loving, and materialistic in outlook. They forget their primary duty of guiding and edifying the masses and shepherding them to the Promised Land. The Monk is a fat sporting fellow averse to study and penance. The Friar is a jolly beggar who employs his tongue to carve out his living. The Prioress bothers more about modish etiquette than austerity. The Pardoner is a despicable parasite trading in letters of pardon with the sinners who could ensure a seat in heaven by paying hard cash. The Summoner is, likewise, a depraved fellow. These characters fully signify the decadence that had crept into the Church. The only exception is the "Poor Parson' apparently a follower of Wyclif who revolted against the corruption of the Church.

The New Learning. Though Chaucer's age was essentially medieval, yet some sort of a minor Renaissance was evident. The French and Italian contemporary writers influenced considerably the course of English literature and thought. Petrarch arid Boccaccio, the two Italian writers, in particular, exerted this influence. The seeds of humanistic culture of the ancient Greeks, too, can be identified in this age. The "Clerk of Oxenford" represents the "new" intellectual culture which had percolated into fourteenth-century England long before the Renaissance. He is an austere scholar who prefers twenty books of Aristotle's philosophy on his bed's head to gay clothes and musical instruments.

Literary Works

(1) *A prayer to the virgin, A.B.C.* which is declared by many to be his first extant poem.

(2) He made a translation of the famous *'Roman de la Rase'*.

(3) Before 1369, he had struck out a line of graceful and tender sentiment in the *'Complaint unto Pite'*.

(4) It was followed by the *Book of the Duchess* in 1369 – the Duchess being the wife of Chaucer's patron, John of Gaunt. On returning to England from Italy, he wrote *'Troilus'* and *'Criseyde'*, 1380-83, founded on the *Filostrato of Boccaccio*.

(5) He wrote also *'The story of Griselda (The Clerk's Tale)'*. The story of the patient Griselda had fascinated Petrarch, and became immeasurably popular. Indeed, it had been seized upon by the ballad writers, in the same way as *Guy of Warwick;* and the unhappy fortunes of this peasant girl excited the widest interest. Like King Cophetua, Walter, Marquis de Lalune weds a peasant girl whom he had met while on a hunting expedition. The marriage turns out to be an unhappy, once the Marquis treats her with brutality; and ultimately, shorn of her rich clothes, she is sent back to her father.

(6) *The Legend of Good Women* deals with the poet as wishing to make reparation for past errors. He regrets having translated the *Romance of the Rose*; he upbraids himself for the stigma he has cast on women in his picture of Cressida. So here he vows he will treat honourably of true and good women.

His choice of good women is not free from critical exception, as he elects to lead off with Cleopatra, who despite her charms and brilliance can scarcely pose as "a model of all the virtues!" Yet, perhaps, he realise this. Anyhow, he adds this whimsical comment:

"Now, ere I find a man thus true and stable,
And woll for love his death so freely take,
I pray God let our hedes never ake."

(7) Some of his works are in English such as The Canterbury Tales, The Miller, The Reeve, The Cook, The Wife of Bath, The Merchant, The Friar, The Nun Priest. The Book of the Duchess, The House of the Fame, The Parliament of Fouls and The Pardoner. The Prologue is supposed to have been written in 1388.

English Literature and Chaucer

According to Emerson. "A great poet, who appears in illiterate times, absorbs into his sphere, all the lights, which are anywhere radiating. Every intellectual jewel, every flower of sentiment, it is his fine office to bring to his people, and he comes to value his memory equally with his invention. He is therefore, little solicitous whence have been derived; whether through translation, whether through tradition, whether by travel to distant countries, whether by inspiration; from whatever sources, they are equally welcome to his uncritical audience. But Chaucer is a huge borrower. . . He steals by this apology– that what he takes has no worth where he finds it, and the greatest where he leaves it. It has come to be practically a sort of rule in literature, that a man, having once shown himself capable of original writing, is entitled, therefore, to steal from the writings of others at discretion. Thought is the property of him who can entertain it, and of him who can adequately place it. A certain awkwardness marks the use of borrowed thoughts; but, as soon as we have learned what to do with them, they become our own."

This Emerson's appeal is a sound criticism. The supreme question after all is, not where does the tap-root of genius draw its nourishment, but what is the culminating expression of that nourishment? What blossom is forthcoming? Genius has an alchemy of its own that can transmute the baser metals, it may steal on occasion, into pure gold. Such was the way of that other splendid borrower, Shakespeare; and Chaucer is less unblushing in his literary thefts than him.

The Canterbury Tales (1386-95)

The Canterbury Tales place us in the heart of London. The Canterbury Tales is a collection of twenty four Tales, mostly inverse, introduced by 'The General Prologue'. It is the story of a group of thirty people who travel as pilgrims to Canterbury (England). The pilgrims who come from all layers of the society tell stories to each other to kill time while they travel to Canterbury.

There is a disquisition on table manners in the Prologue. Each guest brought his own knife, but for common use, there were no forks. At the beginning and at the end of dinner, every one washed his hands obviously a desirable proceeding. On to the rush-strewn floor, the guests flung the bones and scraps of meat. The difficulties presented by gravy were met by the meat– which was served by a carver at a side table – being laid upon thick slices of bread which absorbed the gravy. Every guest had a napkin, and the proper use of the napkin was an elaborate ritual in itself.

The picture of the average merchant has a familiar ring about it:

"A Merchant was there with a forked berd, In mottelee, and hye on horse he sat;

Upon his heed a Flaundryssh bevere hat;

His bootes clasped faire and fetisly
His resons he spak ful solempnely,
Sownynge always th'encress of his wynnyng.
This worthy man ful wel his wit bisette;
Ther wiste no wight that he was in dette."

The bever hat still survives in the "topper," and the business instincts of the gentleman express themselves with no radical difference today.

Chaucer accepts the current class divisions between "gentles" and "churls." Neither he nor Langland ignore distinctions of rank; and although rich and poor, cultured and rude jostle one another in the procession, yet he is well aware that some of the Tales might displease the "gentles" among his readers as he offended the "gentles" in the poem. Yet, he adds with the tolerance of the artist:

"... I must rehearse,
All of their tales, the better and the worse, or else prove false to some of my design."

The Doctor of Physic

In Chaucer's Doctor of Physic, we have an excellent picture of the medieval medicine man, with his herbal remedies and his knowledge of astronomy or what we should call astrology. In common with the physicians of the day, Chaucer indicates that his medical studies had drawn him away from his profession: "His studie was but litel on the Bible". Chaucer gives a sly dig at him for his fee-loving propensities:

"For gold in phisik is a cordial,
Therefore he lov'ede gold in special."

The supposed medicinal value of the metal, so common not only in the Middle Ages by a century or so later, is here touched upon.

Such was the London in which Chaucer was brought up.

The Form of the Canterbury Tales

Chaucer was a representative poet. His realism is seen in "*The Canterbury Tales*" which is represented as a mirror to the life of the age. In the field of literature, Chaucer worked as a social chronicler.

Of this work, about 17,000 lines are in verse, with two stories – *The Tale of Melibeus* and *The Parson's Tale*-in prose. The verse consists of rhymed couplets. It forms a compromise between the old and new prosody. He does not care for alliteration or dogged rhyme, and chooses the form of "heroic" verse with rhymed couplets and five accented syllables.

Knight's Tale

In the *Knights' Tale*, we have much more than a typical romance; we have a presentment, with rare artistic skill of the finer elements in medieval romance, avoiding, as the author of Gawayne does, many of the vain repetitions and dull meanderings found in so many of them, and the whole clarified and sharpened by that sure sense of character, of which Chaucer alone of his age possessed the secret.

We have, in Sir Thopas, the baser and more foolish kind of romances, burlesqued; the coarse, the pungent humour of the *Fabliau*; and the wrangle with the Summoner jostle with tales of pathos, such as the Clerk's.

Tragedies and Comedies

There are tragedies as well as comedies in the tales: some are grave and subdued, others ablaze with colour and merriment; but the thread of honest and kind laughter runs through them all, serious and gay, alike. What is central in the Knight Tale is a concern with the right ordering of the elements that make up a personal total soul essentially a concern with justice.

There is nothing of the dreamer about Chaucer – nothing of the stern moralist and social reformer. Like Shakespeare, he makes it his business, in *The Canterbury Tales*, to paint life as he sees it, and leaves others to draw the moral.

John Gower

John Gower was a person of shrewd business instincts, with a large amount of landed property in East Anglia. Some authorities have inclined to prove him as a lawyer, but M.G.C. Macaulay, his most exhaustive biographer, suggests that he made his money as a merchant; judging by the way, in which he speaks of "City", and the number of merchants with whom he was in personal communication. However that may be, it is clear that about middle life, he is concerned entirely with the management of his estates and the writing of books. His sympathies were aristocratic and conservative, and the Peasants' Revolt horrified him exceedingly, not, merely as an upholder of law and order, but as a landlord with vested interests.

(1) **Gower's Literary Works.** His chief works were *Speculum Hominis*, written in French; the *Vox Clamantis*, written in Latin; and the *Confessio Amantis*, written in English. The first is a poem of some 30,000 lines, somewhat in the nature of a morality. The Vices and Virtues are classified, and a picture of society is drawn. For its improvement Gower looks to the intervention of the Blessed Virgin. Historically, the work is of small value, but, as in Langland and Chaucer, there are interesting sidelights of city life.

(2) His another work the **Vox Clamantis** written in Latin was occasioned by the Rising of 1381. It consists of seven books; the first book describing the wilderness in which this medieval Baptist cries. In later books, he pictures the common people as having lost their reason and being transformed into wild beasts. Poor Tyler is suggested as an elephantine boar, later on as a jay who has learnt to speak (*Way = a jay* in A. S.) Throughout the poem, politics and theology are intermingled, the later books dealing with man's responsibility towards man. The author divides people into three classes: clerk, soldier, and ploughman; he criticises the clergy as freely as Langland does – a significant testimony to the corruption of the Medieval Church. And the satirical touch that wealth and wisdom for them are not synonymous, is worthy of Carlyle.

(3) **The Confessio Amantis** written in English was completed around 1390, and was written in the days when he believed in Richard. Later on, he substitutes the name a Henry IV for Richard II.

"This book upon amendement
I send unto mine owen lord
Which of Lancaster is Henry named:"

It is clear, from the drift of the poem, that the writer is opposed to social reform. He uses a number of stories with the definite intention of telling the people what are the rudiments of good morality. In telling the stories he is clear and straightforward, more so than Chaucer, whose delight in humanity causes him to dally with certain sides of his subject. Gower points the moral "to adorn a tale"; and if the result is less satisfying, less rich in dramatic material, than with the author of The Canterbury Tales, yet the poem has merit all its own– like the merit of Pope's didactic verse.

(4) His last writing, his *Traite*, deals with love and marriage, and consists of a number of ballads, exhibiting many of the qualities shown in his earlier work, with greater power of technique, though, perhaps less imagination in treatment. It was written about 1397, possibly on the occasion of his second marriage, and is addressed to married people.

POST–CHAUCER PERIOD

(The period of Renaissance, 1400-1600)

Chaucer's age was followed by the period of Renaissance. Renaissance ("rebirth") is the name applied to the period of European history, following the Middle Ages; it is commonly said to have begun in Italy in the late fourteenth century and to have continued in western Europe through the fifteenth and sixteenth centuries. In this period, the arts of painting, sculpture, architecture, and literature reached an eminence not exceeded by any civilization in any age. The development came late to England in the sixteenth century, and did not have its flowering until the *Elizabethan* and *Jacobean* periods. In fact, Milton (1608–1674) is said to be the last great Renaissance poet.

Many attempts have been made to define "the Renaissance," as though one essence underlay the complex features of the culture of numerous countries over several hundred years. It has been described as the birth of the modern world out of the ashes of the dark ages; as the discovery of the world and the discovery of man; as the era of untrammeled individualism in life, thought, religion and art. Recently, some historians, finding that these attributes were present in various people and places in the Middle Ages, and also that many elements long held to be medieval survived into the Renaissance, have denied, that the Renaissance ever existed. It is true that history is a continuous process, and that "periods" are invented not by God but by historians; but the concept of a period is a convenience, if not a necessity, of historical analysis, and one is able to identify, during the span of the Renaissance, a number of events and discoveries which in the course of time altered radically the views, productions, and manner of life of the intellectual classes.

All these events may be regarded as putting a strain on the relatively closed and stable world of the great civilization of the later Middle Ages, when most of the essential truths about man, the universe, religion, and philosophy were held to be well known and permanently established. The full impact of many of these Renaissance developments did not make itself felt until the later seventeenth and the eighteenth centuries, but the very fact that they occurred in this period indicates the vitality, the audacity, and the restless curiosity of many men of the Renaissance, whether scholars, thinkers, artists, or adventurers.

Thomas Hoccleve

Thomas Hoccleve (c. 1369–c. 1426), was a personal friend of Chaucer and a clerk in the Exchequer. He was an English verse maker of that period. He wrote on Chaucer,

Simple is my goost, and scars my letterure,
Unto your excellence for to write
Myn inward love, and yit in aventure
Wyl I me putte, thogh I can but lyte.

Mi dere maistir – God his soule quyte!–
And fadir, Chaucer, fayn wolde han me taght;
But I was dul, and lerned lyte or naught.
Allas! my worthy worthi honorable,
This landes verray tresor and richesse,
Deth, by thi deth, hath harme irreparable
Unto us doon; hir vengeable duresse
Despoiled hath this land of the swetnesse of rethorik; for un-to Tullius
Was never man so lyk a-monges us.
She myghte han taried hir vengeance a while
Til that sum man had egal to the be;
Nay, lat be that! sche knew wel that this yle
May never man forth brynge lyk to the,
And hir office needes do mot she:
God bad hir so, I truste as for the beste;
O maister, maister, God thi soule reste!

Literary Career and Works

Hoccleve's first for which a date is known with certainty is Letter of Cupid, which was published in 1402. A translation and adaptation of the popular French poet Christine de Pisan's Epistre au Dieu d'Amours (1399), the poem was one of Hoccleve's most popular works. It was an example of courtly poetry in the manner of the lines of the Roman de la Rose.

His next poem was La Mile Régle ('The Male Regimen'; 1406'). In this autobiographical poem, Hoccleve complains of the hardships of his life, many of which, he confesses, he brought on himself. He describes his physical ailments, financial strains and moral failings quite accurately. Hoccleve's principal work, De Regimine Principum (The Regiment of Princes, 1411-12) was written for the future King Henry V, when he was Prince of Wales. This homily is written in the form of a seven-line stanza. Consisting of advice to the prince on the proper conduct of a monarch, the poem was Hoccleve's most successful work. The poem's prologue includes a lengthy dialogue between Hoccleve and a beggar and an address to Chaucer.

Hoccleve's poem was written at a time, when England was still feeling the consequences of the deposition of Richard II, which haunted the usurper's reign by raising questions about the legitimacy of the Lancastrian line. It was dedicated to Prince Henry, who eased to be a prince, when he ascended the throne on 21st March, 1413, as Henry V. The poem begins with a 2000-line prologue, which sets the poem in the context of a complaint about the author's overdue annuity. Hoccleve reminds the Prince of delinquent payments due to him and therefor the poem can also be considered as a personal petition, a critique of the current regime or even a work of propaganda.

John Lydgate

John Lydgate (c. 1370–1451) was a monk at the Benedictine Monastery of Bury St. Edmunds, in Suffolk. Perhaps his most interesting piece of work is his *London Lackpenny,* an agreeable and lively set of verses describing the woes of a poor man in Westminster Hall and about the London Streets, where he sees much to attract him, but can avail himself of no allurements or purchases for lack of funds. His learning overweighed his muse, and the naive admission of Occleve, "But I was dulle," might well have been uttered by Lydgate also. He imitated with more labour than skill, Chaucer's favourite metres, and his treatment of romantic themes but he floundered about disastrously in his cadences, admitting ruefully, "I took none head neither of short nor long."

Possibly, no unfair description of Lydgate would be to call him an accomplished scholar with a fair knack of verse-making, and a fluency that considerably outruns the knack.

Literary Career and Works

Lydgate's only prose work, The Serpent of Division was written in 1422. His three most important works are the long poems, *The Troy Book* (1412-20), *The Siege of Thebes* (1420-22) and *The Fall of Princes* (1431-38). The Troy Book was written at the behest of The Prince of Wales, later King V. It is an attempt to recount the story of the Trojan War. Lydgate's poem is a translation and expansion of Guido delle Colonne's Historia destructionis Troiae, a Latin prose account written in 1287.

The Siege of Thebes falls about midway in Lydgate's career and was completed before the death of Henry V. The work is based on some version of the French Roman de Thebes (c. 1175). The main body of the work is an elaborate 4540-line exemplum chronicling the disastrous careers of a series of deeply flawed kings: Oedipus, his sons Eteocles and Polynices and finally Creon.

The work is also related to Chaucer's Canterbury Tales. Lydgate imagines himself joining Chaucer's pilgrims in Canterbury and narrates a tale that is meant to be a companion piece to *The Knight's Tale. The Falle of Princes* charts the rise and fall of the fortunes of famous people.

The text is based on a similar work by Boccaccio. It begins with the Fall of Adam and Eve and ends eight books later, with the account of the capture of King John of France at the Battle of Poitiers in 1356. Containing 36365 lines, this is Lydgate's longest work In addition to these works, Lydgate also wrote courtly poems. *The Complaint of the Black Knight, The Floure of Courtesy* and *The Temple of Glas* (1403), *Saints' Lives* (The Man of Lav's Tale), devotional poems (The Life of Our Lady and The Dance of Death) and occasional pieces: He probably died at the monastery of Bury St Edmunds.

Stephen Hawes

Stephen Hawes. (d. 1523) Post Chaucer scholars such as Occleve, Lydgate, Hawes, affect one and all in the same way. Their work had literary merit of a fitful kind, but it was sadly lacking in spontaneity, original impulse, and sincerity. Among these scholars, Stephen Hawes was a man of culture with a taste for travel and remarkable memory. He wrote loyal verse to congratulate Henry VII on his accession. He had a gift for phrases which lighten up his prolix muse from time to time, for instance these lines:

"Be the day weary, or be the day long, At length it draweth to Evensong."

And an aptitude for allegory, less happy in pleasure-conferring qualities. The French aspects of Chaucer's genius attracted him chiefly, and he followed the author of the *Romaunt of the Rose* rather than that of the *Canterbury Tales.*

Literary Career and Works

Hawes' most popular work was the long allegorical poem, *The Passetyme of Pleasure* (1509). The main theme of the poem was the education and pilgrimage of the knight Graunde Amoure. The poem was written in rime royal and contained about 5800 lines, divided into forty-five chapters.

His other notable work was the allegorical The Example of Vertu. It was mostly written in the seven-line Chaucerian stanza, except the description of the arming of the hero, where decasyllabic couplets are used and it was divided into 14 chapters. Hawes can be labelled as a Chaucerian only in prosody and not in content.

Like Chaucer, he employed rime royal and decasyllabic couplets in his work According to A C Ward, "Hawes looked upon himself as a follower of Chaucer, though he was in fact a belated medievalist using verse as a medium for sermonical allegories uneasily wedded to chivalrous romance."

John Skelton (1460–1529)

John Skelton was a Norfolk cleric, a remarkable scholar, and at one time tutor to Henry VIII. He attacked abuses of the day, both in the Church and Court, with an uncompromising rigour worthy of John Knox. When Wolsey was at the height of his power, Skelton did not hesitate to criticise him severely, as in his satire *Why Come ye not to Court?* There is no advance in beauty of workmanship. In fact, Skelton neglected beauty quite openly, striving for some fresh metrical form of expression to suit his subject matter.

But at any rate, we are outgrowing the imitative period, for Skelton was an original force, albeit a rough and undisciplined one. Beginning, as most young poets do, in the conventional and imitative vein, he soon broke away, and his later work, despite all its uncouthness, had an individual flavour, refreshing to meet with, after the tameness of his predecessors. He was a moralist, with a message for his generation, that he was determined to make as effective as possible.

"For tho' my rime be ragged,
Tattered and jagged,
Rudely rain-beaten,
Rusty and moth-eaten;
If ye take well therewith,
It hath in it some pith"

His most popular work was the quaint *Boke of Philip Sparrow*, celebrating the death of the pet bird of Mistress Joan Scrope; his most outspoken was the Hogarthian sketch *The Tunning* (brewing) of *Flynour Rummyng*–recounting the brewing and subsequent ritual of a certain broach of ale, by a rural alewife and her friends. He had a liking for brief, jerky metres : e.g.

"Mistress Gertrude with womanhood endued."

Literary Career and Works

Skelton found a patron in the learned Countess of Richmond, Henry VII's mother, for whom he wrote of Mannes Lyfe the Pereggmacioun, a translation, a lost translation of Guillaume de Deguilleville's Pélerinage de la vie humaine. He also wrote an elegy of the death if the noble prince Kynge Edwards the forth.

John Skelton also served as the tutor to Henry VIII for five years. Based on his experiences, he wrote a satire of court life entitled Bowge of Courts, which was published in 1499. His other famous works include Colin Clout (1521) which was directed against the power of Cardinal Wolsey, Phyllyp Sparrow (1505) the lament of a Norwich school girl for her pet bird killed by a cat and Ballade of the Scotgzsshe Kynge (1513), a celebration of the victory at Flodden.

Skelton's famous Magnficence (1516), is an allegory in which the generous prince Magnificence is first destroyed by his own ill-advised generosity then restored by Goodhope, Perseverance and related virtues. Skelton's repetition of short two beat lines with accents became known as the skeltonic meter.

Scottish Literature in the 14th and 15th Century

Scotland had won hardly and desperately, her war of independence, and this fact had served as trumpet call to the imaginative minds of the age.

John Barbour

John Barbour led the way with his patriotic poem– *Bruce* (c.1376), a poem recalling, in its noble apostrophe to Freedom, the famous lines of Shelley in the *Masque of Anarchy*. The rough material of poetry was there, all that was needed was something of the fine culture that had already made its way into England, to fashion and grace it.

James I (1394–1437)

About this time JAMES I, a cultured and accomplished prince, returned from his years of captivity in England and the influence he exercised on national verse was just what was needed. His own poem, *The King's Quair*, was one of no small beauty and power. Imitative, it is true, of Chaucer and of the head. He wrote with power because he loved Lady Jane Beaufort, not because he fancied himself a versifier of Chaucer' school.

Robert Henry Son (1430–1506)

Robert Henry Son (1430–1506) was a "school master in Dunformline". Like his royal predecessor, a faithful admirer of Chaucer Henryson, he showed real first-hand observation of nature and an insight born of no mere literary accomplishment, into the simple and ordinary aspects of lowly life. There was a quaint charm about his description of why he added to Chaucer's story of *Troilus* and *Cressida*. One winter's night, he told us, he sat by the fire reading Trioses, and comforting himself with some hot drink.

Literary Career and Work

Henryson's main work include Works a version of *Aesop's Fables* (usually entitled *The Morall fabillis of Esope the Phrygian*), *The Testament of cresseid*, a follow-on to Chaucer's Troilus and Criseyde, and (but also seen as his own, a poem in its own right), *Robene and Makyne* and *Makyne* and *Orpheus and Eurydice,* a version of the classic tale.

In *The Testament of cresseid*, Henryson takes up the story of Chaucer's heroine in *Troilus and Criseyde* and decides to provide his own interpretation to the story. He purports to describe, "the fatal desteny of fair Cresscid, that ended wretchedly."

The poem is made up of three basic parts, the prologue, tale and the epilogue. The prologue begins with an account of the weather by the poet himself, who decides to pass the time on a miserable day by reading Chaucer's Troilus and Criseyde. The author then decides to occupy himself by writing his own tale.

The Tale of Cresseid describes her exclusion after her betrayal of Troilus and abandonment by the lustful Diomede. She blasphemes both Venus and Cupid and rails against them for her ruin.

The God punishes her with leprosy, which destroys her looks and condemns her to penury. She is forced to lead life as a leper and beg for alms. During one of her begging encounters, she meets Troilus. She then laments her infidelity and bequeaths her body to the toads and worms and her royal ring to Troilus.

In contrast to Chaucer's poem, Henryson's poem ends with Cresseid's death. Chaucer, by the end of his tale, destroys any confidence the audience might have in courtly love. But Henryson rearranges fate to suit his purposes: his Troilus lives rather than dies and his Cresseid dies due to the infidelity.

William Dunbar (1465–1530)

After Henryson, comes William Dunbar, a poet of striking undisciplined power, and one of the great names in Scottish Literature. He was the Burns of the fifteenth century, with something of that poet's passion for beauty, native humour, and force of expression. He was not like Burns, moreover, in character: sensual and head-strong.

Literary Career and Works

Dunbar's chief allegorical poems are *The Goldyn Targe*, a courtly dream-vision poem that celebrates the victory of love over the golden shield of reason and The Thrissil an the Rois, a prothalamium celebrating the marriage of James IV and Margaret Tudor. Dunbar's most well-known is Lament for the Makers, an elegy dedicated to the distinguished writers who had preceded him, including Geoffrey Chaucer, John Gower and John Lydgate. Although written in a ballad form, the poem is actually a meditation on serious moral and religious issues. It focuses on death as a great leveler and comments on transience of human nature.

The Dawn of the Renaissance

(a) Renaissance in Italy and Germany. There was a stirring of fresh life, a kindling of new desires in Italy and Germany. In each country, the horizon was aglow with promise – a promise that spoke according to the personality of each nation. In Italy, the Renaissance thrills through the senses; in Germany, it speaks through the intellect. Thus is it that from the first awakening assumed in Germany a religious character; it merged at once into the Reformation. In Italy, it was different: the old ecclesiasticism became paganised. "The Gods descend from Olympus and live once more amongst men". Pagan influences were needed: though the sudden transition from a starved asceticism to a rich, pulsing life could not be accomplished without moral disasters. Perhaps, no more significant illustration of difference in outlook can be given than in the portal of the Cathedral at Basle had depicted the dead rising from graves and donning hurriedly their garments, so as to appear decently clad at the Last Judgement. After the Renaissance, as Jusserand has reminded us, a naked woman was wrought in bronze upon the tomb of a Pope. All that was beautiful and, through the eyes of the Renaissance, also divine. The human body, so long despised and ill-treated, came into its kingdom and was glorified: "Beauty is Truth, Truth is Beauty."

(b) Renaissance in England. It has been pointed out, the fifteenth century dawned upon an England that had outlived the energising idealism of the twelfth century. The vigorous vitality of that era had been paralysed by the wasteful futilities of the Hundred years War with France, and divided counsels at home. Feudalism, that had been a power in Norman times in evolving order and Solidarity out of anarchy and confusion, survived now only as a spent force. No longer did it suit the needs of the nation. The plaint of Langland, the anathema of Wycliff, bear witness to the general unrest and disorganisation. The sterility of English literature after Chaucer testifies to the lowered vitality of the time. Yet once again is the old saying justified that it is darkest before the dawn.

But, while Italy was on fire with the new sunrise, it was still for England merely a streak of light upon the horizon.

The Medieval Church, in place of welcoming the cleansing changes of a Wyclif, opposed all remedies for curing her of her sick condition. Nor were their kings any more farseeing. Henry IV helped to stiffen the automatic power of the Church by passing the Act that practices should be burned to death. Henry V persecuted the Lollards with relentless vigour. But in vain, did they try to prop up the tottering edifice of medieval thought. They could hold back for a while the oncoming tide; to give fresh life to what was moribund was beyond their power; so England stood:

"Between two words, one dead,
The other powerless to be born".

Invention of Printing. The invention of the printing press, coupled with the discovery some time before, of a way of transforming linen rags into paper, made the multiplication and circulation of books a very different matter from what it had been in the Middle Ages.

Sir Thomas Malory

Of Sir Thomas Malory; very little is definitely known. He, an unknown writer, was suddenly made famous by Caxton. He may have belonged to a Worcestershire family of that name who fought with both, Lancaster and York, in the Wars of the Rose, one member of parliament in 1444-5; several families in Yorkshire and also in the Midlands aspire to have him for an ancestor, but no trace of a Thomas can be found who lived about that time. Professor Kitteridge in "*Who was Sir Thomson Malory?*" traces him to a certain Sir Thomson Malory of Newbold Revell in Warwickshire, who succeeded to the family estates about 1434. John Bale (1495–1563) the historian, in his *Account of the lives of Eminent writers of Great Britain,* says, he was a Welshman. The one thing certain is, that he wrote the *Morte d'Arthur,* which comprises twenty-one books compiled from a variety of sources. According to Bale, the first four books are founded on Robert de Borron's *Romance of Merlin*; Book V from *Morte d' Arthur* manuscript in Lincoln Cathedral Library ; Book VI from the french Romance of Lancelot; Book VII is not identified; Books VIII-X from the *Romance of Tristan* by Luce de Gasc; Books XI-XXI are Lancelot, interpolations.

Caxton

Caxton's personality is an interesting one: it may be seen in his various preface. These reflect a kindly and simple nature, with a pleasant admixture of keen humour to take off the flatness.

His style was uncertain, for he was not clear, how far to draw upon foreign tongues. But he had a ready instinct for good Saxon prose, and his prose was far more readable and attractive than some of the prose written about this time. One of his pleasantest qualities was the confidential note, which he struck – a note, that was later on to be the distinctive note of the English Essay. At present English prose is still in the experimental state: like, to a lesser extent, the verse. But poetry was to have a glorious career, before English to be reckoned.

For nearly fifty years after the death of Caxton, the book trade in English was directed, for the most part, by two men, Jan Wynkyn de Worde (d.1534), and Richard Pynson (d.1530); but the admirable start made by Caxton was scarcely maintained by his successors. Classical learning took a very low place, and until 1543 no Greek book was printed in England. Religious literature of a mediocre kind could be had in abundance, there was a steady market for these, and the contemporary poets like Skelton and Hawes had the gratification of finding some of their work printed. For any advance in the development of English literature we must look, however, not to the printer but to a wealthy nobleman, Lord Berners, who did admirable work as a translator.

Fabyan and Hall

Robert Fabyan (d. 1513) did useful work as a chronicler of London history, despite his tendency to accept all the fabulous tales of national origin, first made by Geoffrey of Monmouth. Edward Hall (d.1547), is a man of more scholarly attainment. He chronicled the story of the House of Lancaster and York, and carried the story down to 1532. He had an eye for characterisation; and some of his work attracted Shakespeare, who made fairly generous use of it in his plays dealing with Plantagenet England.

Henry VII

Henry VII had done much to encourage the New Learning. Mention of him usually recalls the memory of shrewd and sagacious statesman, a man with a genius for practicability and cautious common sense. For the rest, he does not impress himself upon us as a figure of the Renaissance. But there were two Henrys: and one of them especially marked in earlier year was a kindly, art-loving student, somewhat reserved perhaps, but with flashes of humour, and an ardent, romantic temperament. We may recall the delight which Malory's Legends afforded him; the pleasure it gave him to surround himself with the best scholars of the day; the careful eduction he bestowed upon his children. He lacked the open, genial bearing of his successor; yet his tastes were as fully filled with the New Learning as were those of his son.

Assuredly a man of the Renaissance, he wrote lyrics and composed music, was an expert on various instruments himself, and ranged over most subjects in science and philosophy, with an eager interest characteristic of the time. There was nothing of his father's parsimony about him. Erasmus was made heartily welcome and Holbein invited to stay, the clever foreigner was welcome at court. England at length was coming into line with the Southern nations.

Sir Thomas More

Among the most remarkable of the time was Sir Thomas More; he was the son of Sir John More, a justice of the King's Bench, who had his residence in the heart of the City, and it was here, in Milk street, that Thomas was born in 1478. As a child, he attended St. Anthony's School in Threadneedle Street, at that time considered to be a school of high repute. From here, he followed the useful custom in those days of becoming attached to some great household. Thomas More was particularly fortunate in his parton, Cardinal Morton, the Archbishop of Canterbury, who quickly discovered his young retainer's promise, remarking: "Whoever liveth to try it, shall see this child here waiting at table prove a marvelous man."

At the age of twenty-one, More was a Member of Parliament, and when a proposal was made four years later, by King Henry VII for a subsidy for the marriage portion of his daughter Margaret, who was to be James IV of Scotland, more openly opposed the demand of the King. As his opposition influenced Parliament to the extent of their refusing the subsidy he had at once to bear the wrath of the displeased monarch: "A beardless boy has disappointed the King's purpose!"

Writings of Thomas More. In 1510, *Life of Pico of Mirandola,* from the incomplete History of Richard III (written in Latin c. 1513), has been called the first book in classical

English prose; it is sometimes said to have been based on a Latin work by Archbishop Morton, not extant.

Utopia was first printed in 1516 at Louvain; a second edition appeared in 1517. It was then revised by More and printed in 1518. It was also reprinted in Paris and Vienna. It did not appear in English, till translated by Ralph Robison, after More's death in 1551.

More's other Latin works include epigrams, a translation of Lucian's dialogues and pamphlets against the Lutherans.

Amongst his English controversial works, the most important is the *Dyaloge against Lutheranism* and Tyndale in five books.

He also wrote much English as well as Latin verse.

Utopia: or, to give the full title, *The Discourses of Raphael Hythloday, of the Best state of a Commonwealth.*

This satire, on the social and political evils of the age, was written in Latin in two parts. Though printed at Louvain, Basle, Paris, and Vienna, no English edition appeared till Robinson's translation in 1551. Gilbert Burnet made a better translation in 1684, and Burnet's is the one used.

Erasmus and More

More's friend Erasmus was a man of equal ability, but quite other in temperament and character. More's humour is genial, Erasmus is bitterly satirical. Erasmus' brilliance is clear-cut and cold, More's is softened with a kindliness of heart. His severities as chancellor, whatever we may think of them, were certainly not the expression of his real nature. The best part of More was seen in his family life at Chelsea, and in the *Utopia*. His tenderness of heart extended to animals – a trait rare indeed in those times. "God", says he, "has given them life that they may live. . . . How can we find more pleasure in seeing a dog run after a hare than in seeing a dog run after another dog?"

It is interesting to note both More's Utopia and Erasmus' *Christian Primer* were written about the same time, and embody the ideals of the new learning as applied to social and political life; ideal defined by a modern historian as "the art of living together in civil society and of securing the common weal of the people". Erasmus had little of More's fine humanity and delicacy of feeling, but intellectually he was at one with him. He urged the importance of the Golden Rule, and suggested that kings should refrain from entering into any avoidable war. It was best for them to seek the good of their people, not a mere section, but the good of the whole community. A king's claim to the throne should rest upon the goodwill of the nation, he should tax them as little as possible, and what taxation there is should fall upon the wealthy, not the poorer classes.

William Tyndale

William Tyndale (born c. 1484), a small, thin, earnest man of extreme pertinacity, was educated at Oxford and Cambridge, and later acted as tutor in a Gloucestershire family. He was an ardent supporter of Luther, and although he did not lack friends in London, found it necessary to go abroad to work at his translation of the New Testament, from Greek into English. This he completed at Hamburg, and the translation was finally printed at Worms, three years after Luther's translation of the New Testament into German. He was helped in his work by one William Roy, a Minorite educated at Cambridge. Tyndale had no special affection for his collaborator, about whom he remarked dryly: "As long as he had gotten no money, somewhat I could rule him; but as soon as he had gotten his money he became like himself again. Nevertheless, I suffered all things till that was ended which I could not do alone ... when that was ended took my leave and bade him farewell for our two lives, and as men say, a day longer." The translation, coming as it did from one associated so closely with "the arch heretic" Luther, was denounced by Cuthbert Tunstal at St. Paul's cross, and publicly burnt.

More was selected to do battle against Tyndale. He criticised his text, for its avoidance of certain Catholic terms such as grace, confession, and penance. Tyndale defended his exclusion of these words, on the ground that a false meaning had become attached to them. More frankly admitted, however, that the English ought to have the Bible in their own tongue, and disposed of the argument that some might come to harm that way, by saying that "to keep the whole commodity from any people because of harm that by their own folly and fault may come to some part, were as though an unlicensed surgeon should . . . cut off a man's head by the shoulders to keep him from toothache."

Whatever may be thought of Tyndale's substitution of such words as congregation, elder, knowledge, penance, for church, priest, confession, penance, the rhythmic grace and verbal charm of his version has not been questioned.

'Bible' in English

The first complete version of the Bible in English was made by Wyclif in 1382, though Wyclif himself was responsible probably only for the Gospels. The introduction of printing signalised the rapid multiplication of summaries of various portions of the Bible, and in 1525, Tyndale's translation of the New Testament was first issued. To Miles Converdale, however, belongs the privilege of rendering the first complete English Bible in 1535, a Bible based on the Swiss-German version. Tyndale's translation, however, being freely used so far as it went.

Thomas Wyatt

Thomas Wyatt was born in 1503, entered St. John's college, Cambridge, at the age of twelve, and took his degree at fifteen.

He was at one time, like Chaucer, esquire to the King. He travelled to Italy on several occasions, and was the first to introduce the sonnet into England. His friend Surrey praised his handsome appearance where "force and beauty met." He was an accomplished swordsman, and could bandy words as well as the rapier; a fine linguist, an agreeable musician, a brilliant talker, it is small wonder that he became a favourite with Henry VIII. His letters to his son have the weighty wisdom of Chesterfield's utterances.

Thomas Wyatt's Contribution as a Sonneteer in Elizabethan Age

Wyatt was the first English poet to introduce and handle sonnet into English literature. Before him, there was nothing to guide him in the field of sonnet writing. He had to depend solely on his intellect and Italian resources. His was a pioneering attempt to introduce sonnet. The existing forms of the lyric were suitable only for composing songs. He felt the need for a medium for self-expression which could be more sophisticated having greater appeal to the educated mind. There is very large agreement among the critics that Wyatt's sonnets lack intrinsic merits and are the worst part of his poetry. Only three critics maintain that some of his sonnets do possess merit and are of the opinion that critics like Tillyard and C.S. Lewis have not been fair to Wyatt. They maintain that Wyatt has not made any considerable contribution to sonnets. Unlike their views, J.W. Lever says:

"He contributed significantly to the Elizabethan poetry"

C.S. Lewis has called the age of Wyatt as Drab Age of English Poetry rather dead whose poetic structure was infused by the skillful merits of Thomas Wyatt. He has embodied two elements: a native and foreign, a quality lacking in most Elizabethan poets. Wyatt wrote in all 31 sonnets, out of which, the first 19 are, by and large, translations from the Italian. These poems follow the originals in all poetic characteristics except for a few subtle differences. The most prominent difference is that they end in a couplet, not to found in Patriarch or his imitators. The couplet gave a logical ending to his sonnet and changed the balance and rhyme of the poem. Wyatt also introduced some other metrical technical changes. The majority of lines are decasyllabic while the lines in Italian sonnets are nine syllables. In some sonnets, he attempted to follow the original he translated. His careful patterning of the translation, word for word and stress by stress cleared the way for the emergence of a contemporary English style. From Patriarch, he translated the following poem:

"The long love that in my thought I harbor/ And in mine heart does keep his residence"

Wyatt soon realized that Italian versification could not be transferred to English. J.W. Lever remarks, "The texture of English weakened intolerably the delicate Italian rhymes". He kept experimenting with the originals and modified them lightly and greatly to come up with a style most suited to his native language. As the sonnet evolved in the hands of Wyatt, two more changes occurred in the sonnet form. The octave came to be divided into clear-cut quatrains. The sestet had already been divided into two parts, one of four lines and the second of the final couplet. He began to ridicule the cult of adulation for the sonnet heroine. As he furthered more translations, he began to introduce his own attitude of skepticism towards women, as evident from the following sonnet:

"Who so list to hunt? I know where is a hind!/But as for me, alas! I have may no more"

The sonnet voices the lover surrender. His pursuit, long and tedious, has brought to the conclusion that his mistress is incapable of love with life-long companionship. He compares her to a female deer. For beauty, the hind is matchless and irresistibly tempting but it fails to understand what love is. These sentiments are quite the opposite of those expressed by Petrarch. With this sonnet, Wyatt's experimentation with the sonnet form comes to an end. He ceases to be a translator and becomes almost original, though he makes Petrarchan sonnet as the basis of his own. His own vigorous personality transformed the Petrarchan medium and founded a new form consisting of three quatrains of decasyllables and the final couplet. Form and content interpenetrated closely reflecting a view of life almost directly antithetical to that of Petrarch as in:

"Once I am sure you will, or no: and if you will,/ Then leave your bourds"

The poet is restless and wants a quick reply but he is not imposing any restriction on her. If she refuses, she may well go and find another man. The two sonnets "who so list to hunt" and "Farewell love" reflect Wyatt's self-assurance and technical control. The first one is based on Petrarchan sonnet, but the second one is original. A critic has summed up the achievement of Wyatt in the sonnet in the following words: 'We may see his work into three periods: the early phase of a suitable medium, the middle-period of mature love sonnets and the final phase of public life in which his interest for love declined and he chose social topics as themes of his personal poetry'. He was true poet and man of his age and responded vigorously to his age. He experienced many ups and downs in his political career. He loved truth and did not compromise with his self-respect. It was this attitude that ultimately enabled him to discard the romantic notion of love that the lover should be true to the beloved despite her disdain. He rejected this medieval concept of courtly love and created his own concept of love. However, he showed that Petrarchan form of sonnet could be modified to five expressions to complex personal experience and could be used to the tradition of his own nation. This achievement of his has entitled him to be one of the pioneers of Elizabethan poetry.

Henry Howard

Wyatt's friend and disciple, Henry Howard, Earl of Surrey, was born about 1517. More hot-blooded than his friend, he was continually getting into trouble as a young man, and made several visits to the Fleet Prison. His whole career was a chequered one; in fighting, sonneteering, and roystering. He spent his days, and fell at last a victim to Henry's arbitrary power, being beheaded, on a pretext of treason, in 1547. He was more dashing and indiscreet than his friend, but equally with him, had an open, ingenuous disposition, charm of manner, and a cultured mind.

Henry excelled his friend as a metrist, and showed little of the awkwardness that mars much of Wyatt's verse. But it must be remembered that if the disciple excelled his master in ease and assurances, the master had the advantage of having opened up the way. In the work of these men, we mark for the first time a more personal note in English poetry, for the great characteristic of medieval verse is its impersonal character. Conventional it still is, and often stiff in expression; but a more individual tone is now imparted to it.

Each care decays, and yet my sorrow springs!

George Gascoigne

George Gascoigne (c. 1525–1577) was an interesting figure of the time and had been held responsible for the first English prose comedy. *The Supposes* (from Ariosto), the first regular verse satire; *The Steel Glass*, the first prose tale (from Bandello); the first translation from Greek tragedy; *Jocasta*, the first critical essay, *Notes of Instruction*. Whether this be correct or not, he was undoubtedly a man of considerable culture, was a well-known figure at Court and in political circles, and was, as befitted a man of breeding and education, a fairly extensive traveller. He was a tolerable metrist and had a nice turn for fantasy, as may be seen by his collection of verse, *Flowers, Herbs, and Weeds*. His *Lullaby of a Lover* was a pleasant specimen of original power.

Turberville, Googe and Tusser

These men were all agreeable verse-writers rather than genuine poets; happy occasionally in their phrasing and fancies, but uninspired and mediocre on the whole. It is best to regard them as indirectly helping the development of English poetry by their translation work. This indirectly served to strengthen and enrich the language, and therefore, gave the original men of the age, better material on which to exercise their craft.

"The green that you did wish me wear
Aye for your love,
And on my helm a branch to bear
Not to remove,
Was ever you to have in mind
Whom Cupid hath my feire assigned.
As winter's force cannot deface
This branch his hue,
So let no change of love disgrace
Your friendship true;

Your were mine own, and so be still
So shall we live and love our fill.

Then I may think myself to be
Well recompensed,
For wearing of the tree that is
So well defenses
Against all weather that doth fall
When wayward winter spits his gall."

Thomas Sackville

Thomas Sackville, 1st Earl of Dorset was an English statesman, poet and dramatist. He wrote first English drama in blank verse, *Gorboduc*. His *Mirror for Magistrates* gave a powerful picture of the underworld where the poet describes his meeting with famous Englishman who had suffered misfortune. This work is not all from Sackville's pen but the Prologue and design are his, and the Prologue has a Dantesque intensity about it, and a power of allegorising, unequalled save in the pages of Spenser.

Sir Philip Sidney

Philip Sidney was born on 30th November 1554, in the beautiful historic mansion of Penshurst, in Kent-Sir Henry Sidney, his father, being engaged at this time, in the thankless task of governing Ireland. His mother, Lady Mary Dudley, was a daughter of the duke of Northumberland, the nobleman whose schemes as queen-maker cost him his head, and it was at this tragic period of their family history that Sidney's life began.

After Oxford, Sidney found it an easy matter to enter Queen Elizabeth's Court, his uncle, the Earl of Leicester, being at the time the Queen's favourite; and it was he who introduced him to the all-powerful man of the day, Sir William Cecil, afterwards Lord Burghley.

Literary Works of Sidney

His literary works occurred between the years 1578 and 1582, though nothing was published till his death. *The Arcadia* appeared in 1590, in an unfinished state, and appeared again in 1598, complete. About 1580 *Apologie for Poetrie* was written. In 1591, this work was named *Defense of Poesie. The Astrophel* and *Stella* Sonnets appeared in 1593, numbering one hundred and eight, and eleven songs.

Less brilliant than Marlowe, less witty than Lyly, inferior to Spenser in glamour, and excelled many others.

'Arcadia': Of his Arcadia and its remarkable influence, mention is made elsewhere. Here may be noted the discerning critique – *The Defense of Poesie* – where he uttered those poignant simple words that go to the roots of all poetry: "I never heard the old story of Percy and Douglas, that I found not my heart moved more than with a trumpet."

His quick and sensitive imagination, enabled him to pluck out the very soul of song. "It is not riming and versing that maketh a poet, no more than a long gowne maketh an advocate, Who though he pleaded in armour should be an advocate and no soldier."

But his most remarkable literary work was to be found in the series of sonnets, *Astrophel and Stella,* first published after his death. There was undoubtedly a personal element in these love verses, Sidney (Astrophel) having been in love with Penelope Devereux (Stella), who afterwards made an unhappy marriage, but allowance must be made for a poet's fancy, and there is no need to treat them as entirely autobiographical.

Some illustrations from his works are given hereunder: But, if some of his work seems more literary in inspiration than original and first hand; if, as compared with

Spenser, the lines on occasion drag somewhat nervelessly, there are rare flashes of beauty, fine notes of passion, unforgettable phrases.

We recall such lines as:
"Fool! said my Muse, look in thy heart and write";

such verses as:
"Doubt you, to whom my Muse, these notes intendeth,
Which now my breast overcharged to music lendeth,
To you, to you! all song of praise is due:
Only in you my song begins and endeth;

such melodious things as:
"Ring out your bells, let mourning shows be spread;
For Love is dead";
and the even more familiar:
"My true love hath my heart, and I have his."

Sidney and Spenser

By some Sidney has been lauded, as co-equal with Spenser, by others as cold and artificial. The open-minded student cannot fail to realise the injustice of both these verdicts. As a many-gifted personality, he was probably second to none; as a poet, he was certainly inferior to Spenser in power of expression and in range.

A man of exquisite culture with a delicate palate for all that is fine in literature, he knew precisely what to say, but lacked at times the executive power to say it in the right way. This was largely due to need of experience in writing; and his later verses were greatly superior to his earlier efforts.

Literary Career and Works

It at Kent that he published his first publicly-released (1579) poetic work, *The Shepheardes Calendar* (1579), to positive reviews. It was dedicated to Philip Sidney. In imitation of the classical poet Virgil, the Shepheardes Calendar (1579) consists of a series of eclogues (short poems usually cast as pastoral dialogues), in which various characters, in the guise of innocent and simple shepherds, discuss life and love, formulating weighty and often satirical opinions on questions of the day. The twelve eclogues correspond to twelve months of English calendar.

Through his poetry, Spenser hoped to secure a place at court, which he visited in Walter Raleigh's company to deliver his most famous work, *The Faerie Queene* (Book 1-3, 1590; Book 4-6, 1596). He offered Elizabeth The Faerie Queene in an attempt to gain her favour. In recognition for his poem, Elizabeth awarded Spenser £ 100. However, he earned the ire of Lord Burghley, who he lampooned in the text Of Mother Hubbard's Tale for preventing the payment of the sum promised by the Queen. As a result of this, he had to return to Ireland in early 1591 without further preferment,

In 1596, Spenser wrote a prose pamphlet titled, A View of the Present State of Ireland. It was in dialogue form from the standpoint of the Anglo-Irish chronicles, the pamphlet argued that Ireland would never be totally 'pacified' by the English until its indigenous language and customs had been destroyed, if necessary by violence. Two years later, in September 1598 Spenser was appointed Sheriff of Cork, but his tenure was: short-lived. He was driven from his home by the native Iris) forces during the Nine Years War. He took up lodging in King' Street and it was here that he died in January 1599. He buried in Westminster Abbey.

The Drama and the Earlier Renaissance

An articulate story, presented in action, may be termed as drama. Upon English literature, the drama is incomparably the greatest force of the time: it inspired grandest poetry as well as sweetest lyrics; it gave variety, flexibility, and clarity to our prose. It inspired poetry, because the exigencies of the stage demanded word pictures that should conjure up clearly and vividly the scene suggested; because the exigencies of acting demanded the eloquent exhibition of elemental emotions and swift transition of mood; because the exigencies of individualising demanded nice distinction of diction. Philosophic reflection, poignant introspection, joyousness of heart, agony of spirit; all these things clamoured for utterance in the drama. Elizabethan poetry voiced them all. The drama made for intensity of expression; it made also for extensity.

The origins of the drama have always been deeply rooted in the religious instincts of mankind. This is true of the Greek, Indian, Chinese, Egyptian, and of the modern Christian drama. The ancient Greek drama never lost its kinship with the religious ceremonies of the people. Dionysus, God of Life and Death, the God of Wine, and of the Fertile Earth, was the father of Greek Comedy and Tragedy. The production of a play was a sacred function that every citizen had a right to attend. The Roman drama was an offshoot of the Greek, but in the days of the late empire it fell into a degraded and corrupt state. So, when Christianity became the state religion, the theatre was heartily frowned upon. But it was as futile to hope to suppress the drama as to suppress laughter and tears, and before long, the Church was found utilising the very tendencies she had endeavoured to crush, so that it is true to say, the "cradle of the drama" in Europe, and more particularly in England, "rested on the altar." The clergy were obliged to find some method of teaching and explaining to the ignorant masses the doctrinal truths of religion. The services of the Church were in Latin, and even if the Bible had been accessible to the laity, few could read it. Hence, in very early times, the Gospel stories were illustrated by a series of living pictures in which the performers acted the story in dumb show.

TYPES OF DRAMA, ELEMENTS OF DRAMA

Let us consider a few popular types of drama:

- **Comedy.** Comedies are lighter in tone than ordinary works, and provide a happy conclusion. The intention of dramatists in comedies is to make their audience laugh. Hence, they use quaint circumstances, unusual characters, and witty remarks.
- **Tragedy.** Tragic dramas use darker themes, such as disaster, pain, and death. Protagonists often have a tragic flaw – a characteristic that leads them to their downfall.
- **Farce.** Generally, a farce is a nonsensical genre of drama, which often overacts or engages slapstick humor.
- **Melodrama.** Melodrama is an exaggerated drama, which is sensational and appeals directly to the senses of the audience. Just like the farce, the characters are of a single dimension and simple, or may be stereotyped.
- **Musical Drama.** In musical dramas, dramatists not only tell their stories through acting and dialogue, but through dance as well as music. Often the story may be comedic, though it may also involve serious subjects.

Examples of Drama in Literature

Example 1: Much Ado About Nothing (By William Shakespeare)

Much Ado About Nothing is the most frequently performed Shakespearian comedy in modern times. The play is romantically funny, in that love between Hero and Claudio is laughable, as they never even get a single chance to communicate on-stage until they get married.

Their relationship lacks development and depth. They end up merely as caricatures, exemplifying what people face in life when their relationships are internally weak. Love between Benedick and Beatrice is amusing, as initially their communications are very sparky, and they hate each other. However, they all of sudden make up, and start loving each other.

Example 2. Oedipus Rex (By Sophocles)

Tragedy. Sophocles' mythical and immortal drama Oedipus Rex is thought to be his best classical tragedy. Aristotle has adjudged this play as one of the greatest examples of tragic drama in his book, Poetics, by giving the following reasons:

- The play arouses emotions of pity and fear, and achieves the tragic catharsis.
- It shows the downfall of an extraordinary man of high rank, Oedipus.
- The central character suffers due to his tragic error called hamartia; as he murders his real father, Laius, and then marries his real mother, Jocasta.
- Hubris is the cause of Oedipus' downfall.

Example 3. The Importance of Being Earnest (By Oscar Wilde)

Farce. Oscar Wilde's play, The Importance of Being Earnest, is a very popular example of Victorian farce. In this play, a man uses two identities: one as a serious person, Jack (his actual name), which he uses for Cesily, his ward, and as a rogue named Ernest for his beloved woman, Gwendolyn.

Unluckily, Gwendolyn loves him partially because she loves the name Ernest. It is when Jack and Earnest must come on-stage together for Cesily, then Algernon comes in to play Earnest' role, and his ward immediately falls in love with the other "Ernest." Thus, two young women think that they love the same man - an occurrence that amuses the audience.

Example 4. The Heiress (By Henry James)

Melodrama. The Heiress is based on Henry James' novel the Washington Square. Directed for stage performance by William Wyler, this play shows an ungraceful and homely daughter of a domineering and rich doctor. She falls in love with a young man, Morris Townsend, and wishes to elope with him, but he leaves her in the lurch. The author creates melodrama towards the end, when Catherine teaches a lesson to Morris, and leaves him instead.

Function of Drama

Drama is one of the best literary forms through which dramatists can directly speak to their readers, or the audience, and they can receive instant feedback of audiences. A few dramatists use their characters as a vehicle to convey their thoughts and values, such as poets do with personas, and novelists do with narrators. Since drama uses spoken words and dialogues, thus language of characters plays a vital role, as it may give clues to their feelings, personalities, backgrounds, and change in feelings. In dramas the characters live out a story without any comments of the author, providing the audience a direct presentation of characters' life experiences.

Mysteries

The term *Mystery* is applied to the stories taken from the Scripture narrative, while *Miracles* are plays dealing with incidents in the lives of saints and martyrs.

The history of the English drama is rooted in lay as well as in religious history. It may be well at this point to sketch the main lines of development, before dealing in greater detail with the early plays that merged gradually into Elizabethan drama.

Pausing then, to consider the lines of development shown by the drama from Plantagenet times down to the era of Elizabeth, we find certain distinctive stages, whilst underlying the entire movement is a twofold appeal.

Miracle Plays

Drama is obviously inherent in the very ritual of the Church, and the Mass itself was a factor in dramatic development. The seasons of the year suggested the subject matter of plays: Christmas, Easter, stories derived from the Bible, called *Mysteries*, stories from the lives of the Saints, called *Miracle Plays*. Early in the Middle Ages the clergy celebrated Holy Days– Christmas, Easter, etc.— by playing scenes from the life of Christ.

The first positive stage in the development of the drama is marked by the performance of these stories in the church.

On the whole, miracle plays proved more popular than mysteries, probably on account of their fresher subject-matter. Each big town had its own cycle of plays– e.g. York, Chester, Coventry. One of the earliest examples of the miracle play has been preserved in an Orleans M S, and concerns St. Nicholas. It is written in Latin, with old French refrains.

The *Office of the Shepherds* was performed on Christmas Eve. A cradle was placed on the alter and beside it an image of the Virgin Mary. A number of the clergy represented the shepherds and entered the church carrying crooks and having with them real sheep and dogs. Some of the shepherds pretend to go to sleep, while others watch their flocks. Suddenly a choir-boy, dressed as an angel, mounts the pulpit and, preceded by blasts from the trumpeters, announces the birth of Christ. Immediately a choir of singers in the clerestory sing "Glory to God in the Highest." The shepherds proceed up the church to the altar where other priests show them the child and bid them announce his birth to the people. The shepherds adore the Child and his Mother and march through the church singing a hymn of praise.

Morality Play

Morality play, also called morality, an allegorical drama popular in Europe especially during the 15th and 16th centuries, in which the characters personify moral qualities (such as charity or vice) or abstractions (as death or youth) and in which moral lessons are taught.

Western theatre: Morality plays

Together with the mystery play and the miracle play, the morality play is one of the three main types of vernacular drama produced during the Middle Ages. The action of the morality play centres on a hero, such as Mankind, whose inherent weaknesses are assaulted by such personified diabolic forces as the Seven Deadly Sins but who may choose redemption and enlist the aid of such figures as the Four Daughters of God (Mercy, Justice, Temperance, and Truth).

Morality plays were an intermediate step in the transition from liturgical to professional secular drama, and combine elements of each. They were performed by quasi-professional groups of actors who relied on public support; thus the plays were usually short, their serious themes tempered by elements of farce. In the Dutch play He estbatement den appelboom ("The Miraculous Apple Tree"), for example, a pious couple, Staunch Goodfellow and Steadfast Faith, are rewarded when God creates for them an everbearing apple tree with the property that whoever touches it without permission becomes stuck fast. This leads to predictable and humorous consequences.

The most famous of the French morality plays is *Nicolas de la Chesnaye's Condemnation des banquets* (1507), which argues for moderation by showing the bad end that awaits a company of unrepentant revelers, including Gluttony and Watering Mouth. Among the oldest of morality plays surviving in English is *The Castle of Perseverance* (c. 1425), about the battle for the soul of Humanum Genus. A plan for the staging of one performance has survived that depicts an outdoor theatre-in-the-round with the castle of the title at the centre. Of all morality plays, the one that is considered the greatest, and that is still performed, is Everyman.

English Comedy and Humour

Of more importance at this period, was the development of English comedy, as exemplified by *Ralph Roister Doister* (c. 1566), and *Gammer Gurton's Needle* (1575), plays rich in English humour; the first (the better of the two) showing a keen sense of dramatic movement.

The Wakefield Cycle

The Wakefield cycle consists of thirty-two plays commencing with the Creation.

The usual series of plays follow: *Noah; Abraham and Isaac; Jacob and Esau;* the Old Testament prophecies of Christ; Pharaoh; *The taxing of the world* by Caesar Augustus; the *Annuciation, Salutation, and Nativity; the Visit of the Wise Men, the flight into Egypt, the Slaughter of the Innocents, the Purification, Jesus among the Doctors, John the Baptist, the Last Supper, three plays on the Passion and the Crucifixion, Harrowing of Hell, the Resurrection, the Appearance of Christ to the Disciples, the Ascension, Doomsday, the Raising of Lazarus, and the Hanging of Judas.*

The Chester Plays

The Chester Plays show a more serious and didactic purpose than the other cycles. The plays of which there are twenty-five, were acted by the trade companies of the city on Monday, Tuesday, and Wednesday in Whitsun week from 1268 to 1577, and again in 1600. The series commences with the *Fall of Lucifer*, acted by the Tanners, next came the *Creation and the Fall.* The *Creation* was rendered more realistic by sending into the crowd as many strange animals as could be obtained, and by sending a flight of pigeons into the air.

The Coventry Plays

A complete cycle of plays have been preserved, which are said to have been acted at Coventry, on the Festival of Corpus Christi. This, however, rests on uncertain evidence, and if the plays belong to Coventry, it is thought probably they were acted by the Grey Friars of the town and were not connected with the trade guilds. The M.S. Dates from the time of Henry VI (c. 1468), and consists of forty-two plays which were, however, not all acted in one year the custom being to perform the first twenty-eight in one year, and the remainder the next year.

The Interludes

The Interludes of John Heywood stand midway between the moralities and the regular drama, since in the Interlude the allegorical characters have disappeared. The morality was a sermon in disguise; the Interlude aimed at amusement and entertainment. It is possible that Interludes of music, jesting and story-telling, had always to a greater or lesser extent accompanied feasts and banquets, but it was left to John Heywood, in the reign of Henry VIII, to give the Interlude a definite place not only in literature but in the evolution of the drama. Heywood was born in North Mimms in Hertfordshire, he was Roman Catholic and a friend of Sir Thomas More, who obtained for him his position at Court, as a producer of entertainments of the king's pleasure. This he kept through the reign of Edward VI and Queen Mary. On the death of Queen Mary, he is said to have fled from the country. He died in exile sometime between 1577 and 1587. An Interlude by Heywood is *The Mery Play between the Pardoner and the Frere,* printed in 1533, but which was written before 1521.

English Tragedy

The first English tragedy was written by Thomas Sackville and Thomas Norton, and was acted by the Gentlemen of the Inner Temple before Elizabeth, on the Banqueting Day of the Grand Christmas festival of the Inner Templars, January 18, 1561.

The argument of the play is as follows: "Gorboduc, King of Britain divided his realms in his lifetime to his sons Ferrex and Porrex. The sons fell to dissension. The younger killed the elder. The mother, that more dearly loved the elder, for revenge killed the younger. The people moved with the cruelty of the fact, rose in rebellion, and slew both father and mother. The nobility assembled, and most terribly destroyed the rebels; and afterwards for want of issue of the Prince, whereby the succession of the crown became uncertain they fell to civil war, in which both they and many of their issues were slain, and the land for a long time almost desolate and miserably wasted."

The story is divided into five acts, Norton wrote the first, second, and third, and Sackville the fourth and fifth. The action takes place behind the scenes, and each act ends with a chorus, in mitation of the tragedies of Seneca. It departs from the classical model in the use of dumb show and is written in blank verse—first used by Surrey in translating a part of Virgil's *A Eneid,* and now for the time applied to the drama.

First Regular English Comedy 'Ralph Roister Doister'

The first regular English comedy, based on the model of the Latin comedy, was produced in 1541 or earlier. The play is usually attributed to Nicholas Udall, headmaster of Eton from 153 to 1541. Udall was born in Hampshire in 1506. He was educated at Corpus Christi College, Oxford, and came under the influence on the teaching of More, Colet, and Erasmus. Udall and a number of other young men were arrested in 1527 by order of Wolsey, for possessing Tyndale's translation of the New Testaments and Luther's Tracts. The students saved their lives by making a public recantation. After leaving Oxford, Udall seems to have became a schoolmaster in the North. In 1533 Udall was in London, and shortly afterwards was appointed headmaster of Eton, where he remained until 1541.

It was the custom at public schools to act Latin plays on special occasions. The idea seems to have occurred to Udall to substitute an English play for the usual comedy from Plautus of Terence, Hence the production of *Ralph Roister Doister.*

The Towneley Plays

These were acted at Woodkirk, near Wakefield, and are sometimes known as the Wakefield Plays, deriving their first title from the fact that the M.S. volume containing the text was discovered in the library of Towneley Hall in Lancashire. Some of the plays may have been acted by the two fairs which were held annually at Woodhirk. Five of the plays are almost identical with plays in the York cycle, and some of them were acted by the trade guilds of Wakefield.

The second Shepherd's play is prefaced by a comic interlude that has been described as the first farce in the English language.

The shepherds are out in the fields on Christmas Eve, they begin to grumble at the weather, their heavy taxes:

"We are so lamed
We are made hand–tamed
With these gentlery men".
Of the trials of matrimony :
"We silly wed-men dree mickle woe".

SOME FAMOUS DRAMATISTS OF THE AGE

John Lyly

He was born in 1554. The plays of Lyly were written after the publication of *Euphues*, and were acted by "the children of Paul's before her Majesty." In character, they were mythological or pastoral, and approximated to the Maseque, rather than to the narrative drama of Marlowe.

They were written in prose intermingled with verse, and whereas the verse is almost wholly charming, the prose is often marred by the fantastic conceits, that weary the reader of *Euphues*. Nor had Lyly that sense of the theatre displayed by many of his contemporaries, who lacked his sense of literary form and polished wit.

George Peele

George Peele, of Devonshire origin, the son of James Peele, citizen and salter of London, was born about 1558, and as a free scholar, was educated at Christ's Hospital from 1566-70. In March of the following year, he went to Broadgate Hall, Oxford, and completed his degree in arts in 1579.

His works are: *The Arraignment of Paris*, 1584; *Edward I, 1593; The Battle of Alcazar, 1594; The Old Wives' Tale, 1595* – the only known copies of this are one in the British Museum and one in the library at Bridgewater House; *David and Fair Bathsheba*, 1599; and an earlier play now lost, entitled *The Hunting of Cupid*, supposed to have been written about 1591. Among other works may be mentioned *Polyhymnia*, 1590, a poem in blank verse; *The Honour of the Garter*, 1593; *The Fall of Troy*, published with *A Farewell to Norris and Drake*, 1589 ; and a thumb book 1¼ X 1, with two lines on a page.

George Peele left behind him some half dozen plays, richer in poetic beauty than any of his group, save Marlowe. His earliest work is *The Arraignment of Paris*; his most notable, perhaps, *David and Bathsheba*.

Thomas Kyd

Thomas Kyd (1558-95) was the son of a London notary, and received his education at Merchant Taylor's School. A dramatist and translator, he achieved great popularity with his first work *The Spanish Tragedy*, which was translated into German and Dutch, and in which Jonson is supposed by some to have been his collaborator. The record of his life and works is uncertain.

Putting aside his translation of *Cornelia*, *The Spanish Tragedy* is his only known play; and although its ranting style roused the contempt of Shakespeare, yet there are touches of genuine force behind the extravagances; and even extravagance is better than lifelessness.

Robert Greene

His plays comprise *Orlando Furioso, Friar Bacon and Friar Bungay, Alphonsus King of Aragon, Looking Glass for London and England (with Lodge), and George-a-Greene, the Pinner of Wakefield*. Among his other works the most important are *Pandosto*, from which Shakespeare took the plot for *The Winter's Tale: Penelope's Web*, and his partly autobiographical *Groat's Worth of Wit bought with a Million of Repentance*.

Christopher Marlowe

We pass to the greatest of the band, to the great protagonist of Elizabethan drama-Christopher Marlowe.

Tamburlaine is a Scythian shepherd, obsessed with the idea, that his mission in life is to be "the scourge of God" and a terror to the world till "Immortal Jove says, Cease, Tamburlaine!" He pursues and overcomes the mightiest monarchs of the Eastern world with the bloodthirstiness of a savage beast: captive kings drag his chariot to the field of battle for further conquest, and with their queens imprisoned in cages; at length rashing out their brains, rather than exist for further indignity. Yet, Tamburlaine is possessed of a personal magnetism that cannot be withstood:

"Sooner shall the sun fall from his sphere
Than Tamburlaine be slain or overcome"

says the Persian warrior sent to quell him.

Tamburlaine was succeeded by *The Tragical History of Doctor Faustus*, in which the dramatist gives an old medieval legend a glowing Renaissance setting. The story of the alchemist who sells his soul to the Devil never lost its fascination, and in late years Faustus became more of the heartless sensualist than the headstrong magician. It was in this form that Goethe found the story and turned it to his own use. In the ancient legend the Faustus barters his soul in return for some years of gaiety and pleasure. Marlowe's Fausus desires pleasure also, but incidentally only, it is every form of joy that he would drink of freely. He is a genuine incarnation of the Renaissance spirit, and has nothing of that calculating, introspective nature peculiar to Goethe's gentleman.

'Faustus' was followed by *The Jew of Malta*, a play rich in fine episodes, and with a glorious opening, but lacking the grip and imaginative appeal of the earlier plays. *Edward ll*, his last play, is from the technical point of view also his best. Lacking the intensity and rhythmic beauty of the earlier plays, it shows rare skill of construction, while the characterisation is wholly admirable. To some extent no doubt it inspired Shakespeare's *Richard II*, and the abdication scene is obviously modelled on Marlowe's.

Marlowe's other work for the stage is almost negligible. *The Massacre of Paris* survives, it is true, in a fragmentary and corrupt condition, but this dramatisation of contemporary French history is strangely lacking in power and interest. *The Tragedy of Dido*, written in conjunction with Nash and published, bears little impress of Marlowe's greatness, and is supposed to be an early work, greatly altered and added to, by his collaborator. A great portion of *Henry VI* is from Marlowe's pen, and more happily reminiscent. But the outstanding work, putting aside the four plays above discussed, is the fragmentary *Hero* and *Leander*, a poem of singular freshness and beauty.

The Prose and Earlier Renaissance

The English Novel. The eager, inquisitive spirit that flamed up at the Renaissance could not exhaust itself entirely in the expansion of English poetry, or even in the creation of the romantic drama; for in achieving this it realised also the compelling interest of everyday actualities.

The favourite story-teller of Chaucer's time had been the Minstrel. It was he, who first familiarised the common folk with the legends of Arthur and his Knights, of Charlemagne, with such verse tales as *Gawain and the Green Knight,* and the popular *Guy of Warwick.* Needless to say, the art of story-telling in the minstrels' hands was of a rough and crude kind. They broadened and coarsened the Arthurian Romances to suit the taste of their primitive-minded hearers; but in doing so, introduced a contemporary note, interlarding their tales with ridicule of the decadent medieval church, and thus giving that flavour or actuality, which paved the way for the Novel of Elizabeth's time.

While they were doing this, our first great realistic poet, Chaucer, was helping with finer artistry to create a distaste for the high-falutin medieval romance. He effected this directly in *Troilus* and *Cressida,* an ancient romance treated as a genuine character study; indirectly in his epic of contemporary life, *The Canterbury Tales.*

Here, then, in Chaucer's time is the first stage in the development of the novels from the old romance that had its inspiration in the songs of the minstrel.

William Painter's Collection. There was no more popular book than William Painter's collection of Italian stories. He was the Clerk of the Ordnance in the Tower, and his translation not merely inspired the Romantic drama but interested English reader in Italian fiction specifically, and the art form of the Novel generally. Thus he paved the way, for the English novel as well as providing a background for the English drama.

Painter's volume had been ransacked to furnish the playhouses of London. Shakespeare borrowed from him generously in *Romeo* and *Juliet, and The Merchant of Venice*; and Beaumont and Fletcher themselves only less liberally of his stories.

Growth and Development of English Prose in the Elizabethan Age

Although the Elizabethan age is called The Golden Age of English poetry and drama, it should also be regarded as a glorious age of English prose, for English prose was set on the track of glory by such great prose writers as Lyly, Greene, Lodge, Nashe, Deloney and Dekker with Sir Philip Sidney on the forefront.

At the outset, the Elizabethan prose turned to be translation of foreign books, especially the Italian Novella or Short romantic stories like Palace of Pleasure by William, Tragical Discourses by Geoffrey Fenton. Petite Palace by George Petite, an original writing published in 1576, was a collection of legendary tales. The most interesting of the early Elizabethan prose fiction was The Adventures of Master FJ by George Gascoigne. It was published in 1573.

Of the original prose writers of the Elizabethan age, John Lyly was the most famous. In 1578, the publication of his curious book, Euphues, the Anatomy of Wit and its sequel entitled Euphues and his England in 1580 created a sensation. Although the books contained love stories with thin plots, they were intended to be read as books of conduct for aristocratic youths. Through these two books Lyly introduced an inimitable and unique style known as Euphuism marks him as a pioneer. The beauty of the style lies in the perfect use of balanced phrases, intricate alliteration, classical allusion, and ornate epithets.

Sir Philip Sidney's Arcadia, the first pastoral romance in English, was modeled on the Spanish pastoral Romance. Sidney's Arcadia may better be called a piece of poetry in the form of prose. However, it could exert great influence upon the drama of the age.

In imitation of Lyly, Robert Greene wrote short novels – Mamillia (1583), The Mirror of Modesty and The Card of Fancy. His most popular romance Pandosto provided Shakespeare with the plot of The Winter's Tale. Pandosto is marked by better narratives, shorter soliloquies and lesser Euphuism than other books. Greene modeled his Menaphon (1589) on Sidney's Arcadia. Perhaps the best of Greene's Euphuistic romance is To His Love published in 1589.

Thomas Lodge became famous for his euphuistic romance Rosalinde, the source of Shakespeare's As You Like It. Although Lodge imitated Greene's style of romantic tale, he surpassed his master by introducing masculine material borrowed from Chaucer.

Thomas Dekker was famous for his realistic portrayal of contemporary life. His prose works include Bellman of London; Lantern and Candlelight; The Seven Deadly Sins of London; News from Hell brought by the Devil's Carrier, all published between 1606 and 1608. We should note that Dekker's characters are all idealized vagabonds.

Thomas Nash should be regarded as the first writer of what is called travelogue for his famous book The Unfortunate Traveler or The Life of Jack Wilton. The story relates the life of Jack Wilton, a page in the reign of Henry VIII who becomes an adventurer.

Thomas Deloney is remembered for his famous prose work Gentle Craft, Jack of Newbery and Thomas of Reading. These books tell the stories of weavers and shoemakers of his time.

As the age was intellectually very sound, it inspired a number of scholars to write non-fictional prose, Raphael Holinshed wrote his famous Chronicles which is a compilation of English, Scottish, and Irish history deriving from a variety of earlier sources. Thomas North published his scholarly translation of Plutarch's Lives. Both the books were the source of Shakespeare's history plays. In this age Richard Hakluyt published his Principal Navigations, Voyages, (Traffiques) and Discoveries of the English Nation.

There was another great scholar who contributed a great deal to the enrichment of English prose. He was Francis Bacon (1561-1626). He was the first to introduce in English the literary genre, known as the Essay, innovated by the French philosopher Montaigne. Bacon was both a scholar and a creative genius with a unique style of his own. Bacon was the first to introduce the intellectual, impersonal, reflective essays in a style which is inimitable. Brevity is the soul of Bacon's essay. The words chosen by him are crisp and pithy. His sentences though small, speak volumes. It may be said that the Elizabethan intellectual prose finds its culmination in Bacon.

Richard Hooker's masterly work Of the Laws of Ecclesiastical Policy is one of the greatest of the non-fictional prose works of the Elizabethan age. It began appearing volume by volume in 1594 and continued till the author's death. It was the first book in England which used English for a serious philosophic discussion. Hooker was a Protestant who combined the piety of a saint with the simplicity of a child. His purpose in writing the book was to defend the Church of England and to support certain principles of Church government.

A basic characteristic common to almost all Elizabethan prose is the nearness of their prose to poetry. It is colourful, blazing, rhythmic, indirect, prolix, and convoluted. The Renaissance spirit of humanism, liberalism and romanticism found full play in the growth and development of English prose in the Elizabethan Age.

The Elizabethan Prose Writers

The Elizabethan prose writers, who distinguished themselves in prose fiction, were John Lyly, Robert Greene, Thomas Lodge, Sir Philip Sidney, and Thomas Nash.

(1) **John Lyly (1554–1606).** John Lyly was the pioneer of the English novel, the first stylist in prose, and the most popular writer of his age. A young Kentish man, with slender financial resources and very few friends, he had the good fortune to attract the attention of Lord Burghley, who become his patron.

In 1579, Lyly published the first part of his famous fiction, *Euphues*, the *Anatomy of Wit*, which was received with general delight and approbation.

In the structure of his work, Lyly was Spanish, but there was much more moralising in Lyly, than in Guevara, and more sentiment. That, no doubt, was another reason for his popularity. From Lyly to the present day, the most popular writers of fiction had always been sentimental and didactic.

There were witty turns of speech in Lyly worth remembering:

"It is a blind goose that cometh to the fox's sermon."

"Thou must halt cunningly to beguile a cripple."

"The best charm for an aching tooth is to pull it out and the best remedy for love is to wear it out"

Sayings like these recall the modern apothems of George Eliot.

The style is marked by the constant use of antithesis and alliteration, which at times becomes mannered to a wearisome extent, but often gives agreeable force and pungency to the matter:

. . . Where salt doth grow nothing else can breed.
Where friendship is built no offence can harbour."

A defect in Lyly's prose style was his excessive fondness for classical authorities– a fondness that overburdened his prose with a torrent of allusions, comical rather than impressive. Fickleness and constancy, when mentioned, brought with them interminable lists of mythological ladies and gentlemen remarkable for these characteristics. He was not content with an illustration: an allusion with him was synonymous with cataloguing.

Major Works

- Euphues: The Anatomy of Wit (1578)
- Campaspe (1580)
- Mother Bombie (1594)
- Gallathea (1592)
- The Woman in the Moon (1597)
- Euphues and his England (1580)
- Sappho and Phao (1584; acted 1582)
- Endymion (1591)
- Midas (1592)
- Love's Metamorphosis (1601)

(2) **Robert Greene (1558–1592).** Robert Greene, who succeeded Lyly, if less brilliant, attains a greater simplicity in his later writings. He was a happy-go-lucky Bohemian, who had no patron, and lived on his wits. His first novel was poor and imitative, but in *Pandosto (1580),* from which Shakespeare took his Winter's Tale, he showed real originality. The most considerable factor made by Greene to the development of the novel is found in his pamphlets rather than in his conventional fiction, for here he writes from personal knowledge of the "underworld" of his day. Especially vivid is his *Life and Death of Ned Browne,* a notorious cut-purse, wherein he anticipates the "low life" scenes of Defoe and Smollett.

Major Works

- Mamillia (1587)
- Euphues: His Census to Philautus (1587)

- Pandosto: His Censure to Philautus (1588)
- The History of Orlando Furioso (1590)
- A Looking Glass for London and England (with Thomas Lodge) (1590)
- The Scottish History of James of Fourth (1590)
- The Comical History of Alphonsus, King of Aragon (1590)
- A Groatsworth of Wit Bought with a Million of Reprentance (1592)
- Philomela (1592)
- A Quip for an Upstart Courtier (1592)
- Honourable History of Friar Bacon and Friar Bungay (1594)

(3) **Thomas Lodge (1558–1625).** Another writer of fiction to be noted is Thomas Lodge, the studious friend of Greene. He travelled much in the earlier years of his life, and while journeying he wrote several romances; one entitled *Rosalynde* (1590), which inspired Shakespeare's *As you Like it.*

Lodge also derived from Lyly, but not in the same way as did Greene. Lodge had travelled, as did many young men of that time, over distant seas, looking for opportunities abroad rather than at home to advance him. These did not come, but during the long journeys by sea he wrote several romances; one entitled *Rosalynde* being of special interest to us, far from it Shakespeare, with a quick eye for a good story evolved the plot of *As you like it.*

Far removed were his prefaces from the simpering, deprecating prefaces of Lyly. He had his own little way with critics. If they did not like his books, let them hold their peace, otherwise he will throw them overboard to feed cods. This was swashbuckling with a vengeance.

Major Works

- An Alarum Against Usureres (1584)
- Scillaes Metamorphosis (1589)
- Rosalynde: Euphues Golden Legacie (1590)
- The Wounds of Civil War (1594)
- A Looking Glass for London and England (1594, with Robert Greene)
- A Margarite of America (1596)
- A Treatise of the Plague (1603)

(4) **Sir Philip Sidney (1554–1586).** Sidney's contribution to English literature on French influences more considerably affected Sidney than his predecessors. Perhaps he was of all of them the least touched by the magic of Italy, though he was a great admirer of Spanish literature. For example, we are taking here Pamela's prayer from Sidney's "*Arcadia*".

"Kneeling down, even where she stood, she thus said: O All-seeing Light, and eternal Life of all things, to whom nothing is either so great, that it may resist, or so small that it is condemned; look upon my misery with thine eye of mercy, and let thine infinite power vouchsafe to limit out some proportion of deliverance unto mee, as to thee shall seem most convenient. Let not injuries, O Lord, triumph over me; and let my faults by thy hand bee corrected and make not mine unjust Enemy the ministers of thy Justice. But yet, my God, if, in thy wisdom, this be the aptest chastisement for my inexcusable folly; if this low bondage be fittest for my over-high desires; if the pride of my enough humble heart, be thus to be broken, O Lord, I yeeled unto thy will, and joyfully embrace what sorrow thou wilt have me suffer. Only thus much let me crave of thee... let calamity be the exercise, but not the overthrow of my virtue; let their power prevail, but not prevaile to destruction: let my greatness be their prey:

let my pains be the sweetnesse of their revenge: let them, if so it seem good unto thee, vexe me with more and more punishment. But, O Lord, let never their wickednesse have such a hand, but that I may carry a pure minde in a pure body. And pausing, a while: And, O most gracious Lord, said shee, what ever become of me, preserve the vertuous Musidorus."

(5) **Thomas Dekker (1572–1632).** Dekker, whose dramatic work had already been noticed, also essayed fiction. But although he had shown some measure of Nash's gaiety and shrewdness of observation in the "Picaresque" stories which he essayed, it was as a dramatist and writer of prose, other than fiction, that he was most entitled to remembrance. With the close of the Elizabethan period, the first period of the English novel came to an end. During the next century, French romance, of the extravagant and artificial order, came into fashion for the class who cared about fiction.

(6) **Thomas Nashe (1567–1601)** was an English Elizabethan pamphleteer, playwright, poet and satirist. He was the son of the minister William Nashe and his wife Margaret (née Witchingham). While staying in the household of Archbishop John Whitgift at Croydon, in October 1592 he wrote an entertainment called *Summer's Last Will and Testament*, a "show", with some resemblance to a masque. In brief, the plot described the death of Summer, who, feeling himself to be dying, reviewed the performance of his former servants and eventually passed the crown on to Autumn. The play was published in 1600. Nashe is widely remembered for three short poems, all drawn from this play and frequently reprinted in anthologies of Elizabethan verse: "Adieu, farewell, earth's bliss," "Fair summer droops" and "Autumn hath all the summer's fruitful treasure." Nashe may also have contributed to *Henry VI, Part 1*, the play later published under Shakespeare's name as the first part of the *Henry VI* trilogy. Many scholars believe that Shakespeare himself, who was just starting out as a writer, only contributed some scenes to the play. Gary Taylor believes that Nashe was the principal author of the first act. Nashe subsequently promoted the play in his pamphlet *Pierce Penniless*. In 1593 Nashe published *Christ's Tears Over Jerusalem*, a pamphlet dedicated to Lady Elizabeth Carey. Despite the work's apparently devotional nature, it contained satirical material which gave offence to the London civic authorities and Nashe was briefly imprisoned in Newgate. The intervention of Lady Elizabeth's husband Sir George Carey gained his release. In 1597 Nashe co-wrote the play *The Isle of Dogs* with Ben Jonson. The work caused a major controversy for its "seditious" content. The play was suppressed and never published. He was alive in 1599, when his last known work, *Nashes Lenten Stuffe*, was published, and dead by 1601, when he was memorialised in a Latin verse in *Affaniae* by Charles Fitzgeoffrey.

Literary Career and Works

Martin Marprelate was the pseudonym, under which appeared several Puritan pamphlets (1588-89) satirising the authoritarianism of the Church of England under Archbishop John Whitgift. Nashe is believed to have written several satiric pamphlets, of which *An Almond far a Parrot* (1590) can be attributed to him with conviction. Nashe's most significant work is his picaresque tale *The Unfortunate Traveller or The Life of Jack Wilton* (1594). It is an account of the wild overseas adventures of a youngster called jack Wilton. This work is considered to be the precursor of the picaresque novel and is also sometimes known as the first English historical novel; His other works are *Pierce Penniless: His Supplicatian to the Devil* (l592), *The Terrors of the Night* (1594) and *Summer's Last Will and Testament* (1600).

Nashe was involved in a bitter pamphlet war with Gabriel Harvey, whom he also abuses in Pieree Penniless. Harvey further attacked Nashe's Pieree Penniless in Pieree's Supererogation (1593), which Nashe in turn countered with Have with You to Sagfron Walden (1596). This 'war' controversy finally ended in June 1599, when Archbishop Whitgift and Bishop Bancroft decreed that "All Nashe's books and Doctor Harveye's books be taken away wheresoever they may be found and that none of their books be ever printed thereafter." Nashe died at the age of 34, in 1601.

Major Works

- The Anatomy of Absurdity (1589)
- Preface to Greene's Menaphon (1589)
- An Almond for a Parrot (1590)
- Pierce Permiless (1592)
- Summer's Last Will and Testament (play performed 1592, published 1600)
- Christ's Tears over Jerusalem (1593)
- Terrors of the Night (l594)
- The Unfortunate Traveller (1594)
- Have with You to Saffron-Walden (1596)
- Isle of Dogs (1597)

Non-fictious Prose

During the fifteenth century, Latin was the vehicle of prose, and works of importance were almost entirely written in that tongue. There names alone stand out before the time of Caxton, as makers of English – Reginald Pecock, Sir John Fortcscue, and the Paston Family.

Reginald Pecock

Pecock's personality is a remarkable one. He was a Welshman by birth, and an Oxonian by training. Having taken orders, he soon distinguished himself as an opponent of Lollardy. His zeal brought, in his wake numerous foes, and as the most effective attack against an enemy was the change of heresy, this heresy hunter was charged himself by his political foes of heretical tendencies. He escaped death by recantation, of errors he had never held, and died finally in imprisonment. One of his offences was that he wrote in English, another that he urged the use of reason in confuting arguments. This is the line he adopted in the Repressor, but his learning excited both jealousy and suspicion; and the one argument in strong favour was to suppress by merely citing adverse authorities. That Pecock abjured at this time, was sufficient to damn him, in an age when the faintest show of tolerance towards a heretic, even if it took the innocent form of quietly pointing out his errors and trying to dissuade him by the method of what Arnold called "sweet reasonableness".

THE STYLE OF THE PROSE

Roger Ascham

Roger Ascham is known as a distinguished writer, a fine classical scholar, and an entertaining correspondent. He was born at Kirby Wiske, near Thirsk in Yorkshire, in the year 1515, and died in 1568. He became a student of St. John's College, Cambridge, in 1530 and soon obtained his fellowship, notwithstanding his well known sympathy with the Reformed doctrines. Later, he was appointed University Reader in Greek, and in

1546, University Orator. Amongst "past-times" for gentlemen, he gives cock fighting an important place, but Ascham's chief interests were music, writing and archery.

His first work to attract attention, *Toxophilus*–devoted to archery, one of his favourite recreations– he published in 1545, and dedicated it to Henry VIII. In 1548, his reputation gained for him the position of tutor, to the Lady Elizabeth at Cheshunt.

The years 1550–53 were lived on the Continent, chiefly at Augsburg; he was then secretary to Sir Richard Morysin or Morison, who held the post of ambassador to Charles V. When he returned to England, he obtained the Latin secretaryship to Queen Mary. This prominent post, being given to a Protestant, has occasioned great surprise. His extreme care and tact helped him to escape suffering in any way for his opinions.

On the accession of Elizabeth, who was once his pupil, he remained at Court and became the Queen's tutor, as well as secretary. These posts were held by Ascham until the end of his life.

Ascham, a sturdy old scholar of the more formal type, was a Puritan in his taste, and opposed to the new taste for romance, by an undoubted pioneer of good, direct English prose.

In an age so saturated with rhetoric and ornate conceits, it is a great tribute to Ascham that he should have achieved a prose at once simple and straightforward, yet never bald nor unmusical.

Literary Works

1. *Toxophilus*, published 1545
2. *Schoolmaster*, published 1570, after his death.
3. *Report of Germany*
4. *Two hundred and ninety-five letters*, Latin and English, partly official and partly personal.

Professor Saintsbury calls his prose "a gocart to habituate the infant limbs of English prose to orderly movement." It is no unfair description.

Sidney and Prose

Sir Philip Sidney brought forward the prose another stage. Considering him here as a stylist, he put aside the elaborate affectations of Lyly, and while not free from mannerism, struck a happy comparison between the straightforward simplicity of Ascham and the lightly-coloured complexity of euphuism. His prose at its best is both simple and melodious, strong and sweet, and he achieves for prose much what Spenser did for verse.

"The poet both not only show the way, but giveth so sweet a prospect into the way as will entice any man to enter into it. Nay, he doth, as if your journey should lie thro' a fair vineyard, at the very first give you a cluster of grapes, that full of that taste you may long to pass further."

Hooker

The aim of Hooker was to give us a prose that should be at once simple and impressive. Sidney had combined simplicity with cadence. Hooker gave to the cadence a finer and more sustained rhythm. In point of time he is the forerunner of Lyly, but he certainly carried prose style to a higher stage of development, and if less powerful an influence in his day than either Lyly or Sidney, exerted in the long run a more potent one.

Theological literature very rarely lends itself to literary excellences. For a few modern theologians can it be said that they had the art of saying well what they had to say. But

Hooker will be remembered not merely as that first vernacular defender of the English Church, but as a writer of fine, eloquent prose.

Sir Walter Raleigh

Sir Walter Raleigh, one of the most versatile, brilliant, and daring spirits of his time, whose achievements give a colour to the period in which he lived, was born near Budleigh Salterton in 1552. His father had married the widow of Otho Gilbert, thus Walter Raleigh was the half- brother of Sir Humphrey Gilbert, the explorer, who took possession of Newfoundland, oldest British colony, in 1583.

Remarkable, as was Raleigh's physical activity, no less restless was his mind. When imprisonment gave enforced leisure to the one, the other part of him went a-roving.

He was a verse-writer of distinction – does not Gabriel Harvey speak of his "fine and sweet invention"? And wrote a fine sonnet that was appended to the first edition of the *Faerie Queene* and many poems signed "Ignoto," published in *England's Helicon.*

As to his prose, perhaps his most notable achievement was the *History of the World*, a serious, discursive review of the past and present very popular for its treatment of Biblical history and early times, but disliked by James, "for being too saucy in censuring Princes." It is rich in fine passages of eloquent prose and is also an interesting piece of self-revelation. Its chief defect, an entire lack of humour, is felt at times, but is largely counterbalanced by the picture it presents of a restless, adventurous and ambitious spirit, with a rich sense of the fullness of life and a tragic appreciation of its ironies.

"Even such is time that takes on trust
Our Youth, our joys, our all we have,
And pays us but with rust and dust."

Literary Works

1. *Fight about the Islet of the Azores,* appeared in 1591.
2. *A Discovery of the Empire of Guiana,* 1596.
3. *History of the world,* written during his imprisonment, 1612.
4. *Verses* found in his Bible in the Gatehouse in Westminster, 1618.
5. *Cynthia,* lost until part of it was published by Dr. Hannah in 1885.
6. *The Pilgrimage,* supposed to be written in 1603.
7. *Poems on Sir Philip Sidney,* 1591, without his signature.
8. *The Lie* first appeared in print in 1608.
9. *Nymph's Reply, the Prerogatives of Parliaments, The Cabinet Council,* published by Milton in 1658.
10. *The Discoveries.* " Perfect piece of writing."
11. *Advice* to his son.

William Webbe

The Rules to be Observed in Scottish Poetry (1585), by James the First, is a book of not much importance, but William Webbe's *Discourse of English Poesie* (1586) is of greater value.

Webbe was an enthusiastic admirer of Spenser– "the mightiest English poet that ever lived." With the poetry of Chaucer's age however, he is not closely acquainted, and in his excursion into the poetry of the past, he displays no particular acumen.

Webbe's value lies less in his argumentative disquisition than in his power of appreciation. He has a natural taste for fine verse, and it is on the appreciative side of criticism, not the judicial, that he claims recognition.

Earlier Renaissance

Michelet summed up the Renaissance in "the discovery of the world and the discovery of man". With the latter aspect, the culture, and art of the movement are necessarily concerned. The richly veined humanity of the Italian Renaissance sufficiently emphasized this side: on the other, the revolution wrought in astronomy and the art of navigation introduced a new world as dazzling and surprising in its vast possibilities as the imaginative world opened by Michael Angelo and Shakespeare.

The Call of the Sea

The sense of curiosity and the craving for adventure and so long restricted to the tortuous word-spinning and crusading zeal of the Middle Ages, received a tremendous stimulus that soon found expression in maritime discovery and commercial enterprise. The adventurous sea-man was to open up not merely new countries but a new literature. Yet, the Call of the Sea was no new note in our literature; the white surf thunders grimly through *Beowulf*, and carries its desolating grandeur throughout the whole of Saxon poetry. After the Norman conquest when the English were becoming more civilised, and the seaman adventure was merged into the bartering merchant, the Call of the Sea is lost in other cries, and even Chaucer's Shipman fails to carry conviction. But with the Renaissance, once again we can hear the roar of the ocean and can taste the salt brine.

The adventurous spirit in English literature, hitherto, had been practically confined to that extra-ordinary mixture of outrageous fable and genuine travel entitled the *Travels of Sir John Mandeville*; that had sufficed during the late Middle Ages to satisfy the craving for wonders beyond narrow seas. It really mattered very little that there was "no such person" – indeed it took several ventures to find that out, so distinct is its impress of a genial, curious, broad–minded personality revealed in this mosaic of many men's wanderings, for its enormous popularity testified not merely to the love of the marvellous but to the passion for knowledge about the other countries, which is characteristically English.

The serious recording of voyagers, however, was a thing not begotten in England. It came, as might be expected, from Spain and Italy. Peter Martyr of Aughina catechised the navigators of the time.

Literary improvements of the period are given below :

1. One of the earliest names in the new literature of the sea is that of **Richard Eden**, an industrious compiler of Spanish achievements, with the laudable object of inspiring his country to go on and do likewise. He further published a book on the *Art of Navigation,* 1581. In his style, he is clear and unpretentious, and as an interpreter of maritime discovery, he is worthy of a place of honour.
2. Meanwhile, in 1553, Sir Hugh Willoughby had perished in his voyage to the North– East, an account of which was written in Latin by Clement Adams and translated later by Hakluyt.
3. After this came the remarkable voyages of Sir JOHN HAWKINS in 1562,1564, 1567. On the third occasion, he wrote an account of his experiences in a brisk and forcible style, made nonetheless attractive by the occasional vein of philosophic meditation.

4. In 1576 George Gascoigne wrote a preface to a Discourse of a *Discoverie, for a new passage to Cathay*, attributed to Sir Humphrey Gilbert. The tract was written primarily to convince Gilbert's brother who looked upon the project as a wild and foolish thing.
5. In Marlowe, we find it perhaps at its height. Marlowe's restless imagination and insatiable curiosity seized hungrily on the stuff of travel for his plays, and did not Stow declare that Drake was "as famous in Europe and America as Tamburlaine was in Asia and Africa."
6. There is the spirit of Hawkins and of Drake in Tamburlaine and Faust; it is hard to imagine *The Tempest* and *Pericles of Shakespeare*, with their vivid descriptions, without the sea chronicler of the time, or the stirring speeches of Othello, with no Hakluyt to give colour and substance to the romantic visions of the poet.

   Throughout this great era of drama and of poetry, the Call of Sea persists; and from Spenser's *Faerie Queen* to the *New Atlantis* of Bacon, and the *Paradise Lost* of Milton, we may trace its spell. With the decline of the Renaissance, it dies down as a stimulus to our literature; and the matter-of-fact, common-sense attitude of the eighteenth century found its plenary inspiration elsewhere. Nonetheless, the spirit of adventure had its own triumph even in that age, and the stirring exploits that had stirred into flame the genius of Marlowe, descended on that brilliant, home-loving journalist, Defoe. So, a literature that started with *Tamburlaine* ended with *Robinson Crusoe.*

HEIGHTS OF THE RENAISSANCE

"An over-faint quietness", wrote Sir Philip Sidney in 1581, "should seem to strew the house for poets." Hitherto the scholar and courtier, had ruled domain of fantasy with pleasing and graceful though not, with very vital results. But the words were no sooner uttered than force came into poetry that speedily dispersed the "over-faint quietness". Spenser came at a crucial moment in English poetry. The spell of Italy had taken hold of our senses, without gripping the heart and conscience. Ascham's suspicion of the novel, and his hostile attitude towards Italian influence, did at any rate represent one side of national feeling. The revival of letters had merged into the Protestant Revolution; but the influence of Germany and Italy were hitherto antagonistic forces in English literature. It is impossible not to feel that the verse of Surrey, and of Gascoigne, reflect *only* in part national character and temperament. Now in Spenser, the Puritan side and the artistic side are merged and reconciled. Spenser is the child of the Renaissance and the Reformation. On one side we may regard him with Milton as "the sage and serious Spenser," on the other he is the humanist, alive to the finger-tips with the sensuous beauty of southern romance.

Edmund Spenser (1552–1599)

He is considered as one of the greatest poets and is recognized as one of the premier craftsmen of Modern English verse in its infancy. His best known work is 'The Faerie Queene', which is an epic poem and allegory celebrating the Tudor dynasty and Elizabeth I.

He used a distinctive verse form, called the spenserian stanza in most of his works. The stanza's main meter is iambic pentameter with a final line in iambic hexameter.

In "Merry London, my most kindly nurse," in his own words, Edmund Spenser was born about 1552. His father (of a Lancashire family related to the noble house of Spenser) was a journeyman cloth-maker, and was living in London before 1550. Of his mother,

Elizabeth, nothing is known. His eduction began as a "spending of the money of Robert Nowell," and at Merchant Taylor's School opened in 1561. In 1569, he matriculated at Pembroke Hall, Cambridge, and in 1576, took his degree of M.A. There is little doubt, judging from work he did at this time, that he showed remarkable ability. His Miscellany published by Dr. Jan van der Noodt, called *"A Theatre for Worldlings"*, showed considerable promise, but was only later, acknowledged by Spenser.

Literary Works

(1) *The Shepherd's Calendar,* entered at Stationers' Hall December 5, 1579.
(2) *Colin Clout's Come Home Again,* published 1595.
(3) *Faerie Queene,* first three books published, 1590.
(4) *Faerie Queene,* second three books published, 1596
(5) Two Cantas of some following books of the *Faerie Queene,* 1609.
(6) *Complaints,* nine miscellaneous poems appeared early in 1591. One of these, *Minopotmos, or Fate of the Butterfly,* had already been issued in 1590.
(7) *Prospopoia* or more often called *Mother Hubbuard's Tale,* a satire. This is amongst the collection.
(8) *Daphnaida,* an elegy, 1592.
(9) *Amoretti,* and *Epithalamion,* 1595.
(10) *Prothalamion,* a "Spousal" Ode, privately printed in 1596.
(11) *Four Hymns,* now lost, in 1596.
(12) *Astrophel,* an Arcadian elegy on Sir Philip Sidney's death, 1596. This same year, he wrote his prose treatise, *View of Ireland.*

Song Writers and Sonneteers

The formal modifications, characterising the Shakespearean form of sonnets, were first of all introduced by Daniel and Drayton.

(I) Drayton's sonnet, *A Parting,* is a magnificent piece of verse, sure in its handling, at once strong and restrained in its expression of passion.
(II) Daniel's work, though less masterly, is skilful and pleasing always, occasionally touching great heights; but Daniel, no less than Drayton, did for Shakespeare's sonneteering, much what Marlowe did for his blank verse. They showed the way, his genius did the rest.
(III) Around Spenser are number of verse writers, who, while influenced large by him, and to a less extent by Sidney, in their choice of subject, have yet sufficient creative power of their own to make us realise the richness of the poetic wealth now to our hand.
  (a) There is GILES FLETCHER, graceful and fantastic; the many sided THOMAS LODGE, whose madrigals are unexcelled for dainty sweetness;
  (b) WILLIAM PERCY, to whose scholarly gifts, might be added the more dubious accomplishment of copious ale-drinking, and whose work is suggestive of contemporary French as well as the usual Italian influences;
  (c) The mysterious "J.C." with his pretty aphoristic gift displayed in six-line stanzas.
(IV) There are also NICHOLAS BRETON, versatile in moods and methods, but at his happiest in sentimental conceits; and HENRY CONSTABLE, whose sonnets have no small measure of Spenser's sensuous charm.

(V) Michael Drayton is one of the most astonishing writers of his time. His versatility was amazing and there is scarcely any side of poetic craftsmanship which he could not tackle with success. His literary life opens in 1591, with the *Harmony of the Church*; his sacred verse not pleasing, he reappears in 1593 with the *Shepherd's Garland*, an experiment in pastoral verse. Then came the *Barons' War*, and *England's Heroical Epistles*, while in later life the colossal *Polyolbion*, inspired by patriotic sentiment. As an historical poet he may be regarded as the Scott of his age, and his *Ballad of Agincourt* is a splendid specimen of its kind. Quite in another key is the quaint and fantastic *Nymphidia*; while his satirical gift is well illustrated in short poems like *The Owl* and *The man in the Moon*.

Satire In English

Though there is satirical fancy, of course, to be found in English poetry, from Saxon times onwards, but the first definite satirist is Skelton. Gaseoigne's *Steel Glass* is less clumsy; and he is followed by Joseph Hall with his *Virgidemiarum*; Lodge's satires are not equal to his romantic work, but Hall, though far inferior in general literary power, is a better artist in the domain of satire; and is interesting as a social historian. Donne is so much more than a satirist and his writings have so many striking points of interest that he is best considered in dealing with the late Renaissance period.

Spenser's Lyric School.

Spenser's lyric school is famous for the sudden flowering of the lyric during second half of the sixteenth century, specially in terms of the persistent study of foreign poetry and the growing popularity of music. Some components of this school have been discussed below–

(1) Such brilliant musicians as Byrd, Tallis, and Dowland needed articulate expression for their sweet lute melodies. The gift of song no doubt was dormant in many an Elizabethan verse-writer. It needed some outside stimulus to call it forth; and assuredly at no time in our history, has there been so rich a company of singers; some already famous in other directions as dramatists or novelists, many quite unknown save for their "short swallow flights of song".

(2) William Byrd is the earliest of these singers, but his verse is characterised by its quaint moralising, rather than by any flight of fancy. Lighter in texture are the songs of John Dowland, famed for his "heavenly touch upon the lute." In the last years of the sixteenth century, he published two volumes of "Songs and Airs." Take this charming snatch from the first volume (1597);

"Dear, if change, I'll never choose again;
Sweet, if you shrink, I'll never think of love;
Fair, if you fail, I'll judge all beauty vain;
Wise, if too weak, more wits I'll never prove.
Dear, sweet, fair, wise! Change, shrink, nor
be not weak;
And, on my faith, my faith shall never break."

(3) Campion distinguished himself in three capacities, putting aside him, fame as a musician. He wrote masques, among the best of their kind; displayed this nimble wit and scholarship in Latin verse, and discussed in prose form, the values of music and poetry.

Campion's songs are light as thistledown, and float away in the air. Of his sonneteering we have already spoken.

(4) Following these came John, Daniel, Robert Jones, Thomas Morley, and in the early years of the seventeenth century a crowd of names, about whom, in many cases, little is known, save for the gay and tender lyrics ascribed to them.

INDIVIDUALISTIC CHARACTER OF RENAISSANCE

(1) **Psychological Legacy.** The psychological legacy of the Renaissance and Reformation movement was twofold: a splendid access of self-confidence, and an irrepressible faculty for self-expression whether in action or in literature. Man believed in himself, trusted in his powers, dared the Fates as he had never done before. In Shakespeare's time just as in Chaucer's, the gay and jocund crowds and put against the dark, mysterious background of the unknown. Chaucer's privy thief called Death remains yet a gaunt sinister figure. But in Shakespeare's day there is one difference. The helplessness of man in the hands of the inscrutable. Fate which was strongly and constantly present to the medieval mind, carries no longer the same appeal. Chaucer faced the tragic issues of life with a kind of stoical reticence, as if to say, "The less said of these things the better. Accept them we must, we can't help ourselves, why dwell on them?" This was not the way of Shakespeare, he faced them boldly, and although he had too tenacious a grasp of the concrete facts of life to cry "Peace" where there was no peace, yet throughout his plays, there breathes a sturdy self-reliance and sense of human responsibility.

(2) **Self Reliance and Self-Expression.** Self-reliance, was a characteristic of the age. Self-expression was another.

Just as a man relied on himself; believed in his own powers, and buoyed with hope, though enterprise too perilous to attempt; so did the Elizabethan give amplest expression to passion and instinct. After the self-repression and austerity of the Middle Ages, they exulted in their new-found freedom, like men let out of the Old Bastille. In literature and life alike, they were impatient of rule and convention, caring only to give expression to their own special characteristics. To be different from your neighbour; to borrow whatever style in dress or in letters seemed best to suit your disposition. That was the aim. Naturally, this led to some excesses.

Alongside of the coarseness, the violence, the brutality, may be found splendid endurance, exalted passion, and a broad and tolerant humanity. The people, who loved the crude delights of the cockfight and the bear garden, delight nonetheless in the self-questioning of a Hamlet and the sentimental refinements of a Faerie Queene. It was an age of intense curiosity, and exuberant joy of life.

The aggrandisement of wealth, the discovery of other worlds, the acquisition of knowledge; these matters which our more prosaic age seeks after with cooler calculation, and more scientific precision, were sought after by the Elizabethans in the eager, idealising, adventurous spirit of youth. Life was a glorious adventure; and knowledge itself a fantastic game. His literary career starts in 1590. Since then he was under dramatic apprenticeship and experiments. During this period be wrote – "Men are fools that wish to die"– that was the burden of Elizabethan song. To suck the marrow out of life; to find out all that was worth knowing; to realise all that was worth the feeling, such as the ideal of Shakespeare's age.

Shakespeare's exact birth–date is inferred to have been 23 April 1564. He had the usual grammar school education with some knowledge of Latin and less of Greek. He was married and became father of a child before he was twenty one; and then he approached a theatrical company in which he began as an actor, and later came to be a leading share-holder. In the next twenty years he composed thirty– seven plays, two narrative poems, about 150 sonnets and some lyrics. His only son had died in 1600; he saw his two daughters well married, made his will in March 1616, and died a month later on April 23, 1616. *Man's tragedy*, strong in lyric beauty though lacking the grandeur and breadth of the later tragedies; while *The Merchant of Venice* (1594) though in a form a comedy, is in sombre framework of tragic irony, relieved by a golden thread of romance.

For the rest, he writes in buoyant spirits a social extravaganza, *Love's Labour's Lost* (1591); a rollicking farce, the *Comedy of Errors* (1592); a sentimental romance. *Two Gentlemen of Verona* (1591); and a fantastic romance, *A Midsummer Night's Dream* (1594–95).

Marlowe probably had a share in the *Henry VI* plays; he frankly inspired *Richard III* and *Richard II; King John* being the first of the domination of Marlowe.

After 1595 he become perfect in dreamy writing. There are three historical plays here, finer in quality than those preceding, the two plays of *Henry IV (1597) and Henry V* (1598). *Henry V* is the more showy, and has been well described as a "National Anthem in five acts", but the *Henry IV* plays are far richer in humour and psychological power. Of the comedies, *The Taming of the Shrew (1595)* and *The Merry Wives of Windsor* (1598) are cast in the early farcical vein, though the handling is easier and stronger; *Much Ado about Nothing* (1599) is on a higher plane of wit; while in *As You Like It* (1600) and *Twelfth Night* (1600), humour and romance blend in perfect proportion.

Meanwhile, in 1594, a fresh essay in poetry was signalised.

The majority of the sonnets were written probably in 1594, when Shakespeare had gained the patronage of the Earl of Southampton. The popularity of the sonnet was then at its height. And already we have seen, what men like Daniel and Drayton, Spenser and Sidney made of it. The form he chose was not the Italian form, and consisted of three decasyllabic quatrains, each rhyming alternately and rhyming couplet to conclude. Although unequal in power and beauty, they show a far maturer touch than that displayed in the splendid though undisciplined *Venus and Adonis* and *Tarquin and Lucrece*.

Tragedy predominates after 1600 and we reach here the culminating point of Shakespeare's power as a dramatist. The romances of the period, *All's Well that Ends Well* (1595), *Measure for Measure (1604)* and *Troilus and Cressida* (1603), are essentially tragedies, set in a key of forced comedy; they are rich in poetry, but leave a confused and unpleasant impression upon the mind.

Incomparably greater are the tragedies. Starting in grave measured style with *Julius Caesar* (1601), he rose to greater heights of drama and reflective poetry in *Hamlet* (1602); while in *Othello* (1604), *King Lear* (1605), and *Macbeth* (1606)– that superb trilogy of plays– imaginative subtlety and passionate intensity make these dramas the most superb and compelling in English literature.

The last period opens with tragedy; *Antony and Cleopatra* (1608). With weaker dramatic grip than its immediate predecessors, but fully as ripe in the strength of its characterisation. *Coriolanus* (1609), *Timon Athens* (1608) are only fitfully great, the three latter, perhaps only Shakespearean in part : but when in the eventide of his career he turned again to his first love, romance, we get *Cymbeline* (1610), *The Tempest* (1611) and *The Winter's Tale* (1611).

The tragic period has left behind it a legacy of spiritual power and imaginative subtlety, that make the last works of the dramatist, a fitting paean of farewell.

JACOBEAN TO RESTORATION PERIOD

JACOBEAN AND PURITAN PERIODS

The reign of James I (in Latin, "Jacobus"), 1603–1625, followed the Elizabethan Age. This was the period in prose writings of Bacon, Donne's sermons, Burton's *Anatomy of Melancholy,* and the King James translation of the Bible. It was the period also of Shakespeare's greatest tragedies and tragicomedies, and of major writings by other notable poets and playwrights, including Donne, Ben Jonson, Drayton, Beaumont and Fletcher, Webster, Chapman, Middleton, and Massinger.

The first half of the 17th century is known as the Puritan Age, for Puritanism was the dominant force during this period. It is also called the Age of Milton, for Milton was the greatest poet of this period. As first King James I and then Charles I ruled England during these years, it is also referred to as the Jacobcan Age (adjective from 'James') or the Caroline Age (adjective from Charles). It is an age of transition. By this time, the Renaissance impulse had exhausted itself, the Elizabethan zest for life was gone, and the Elizabethan exuberance and optimism had been succeeded by a mood of apprehension, disillusionment and defeat.

Here, the important point to note is that the Jacobean age ended with the end of James I, while Puritan age remained upto mid-seventeenth century. In the broadest sense, Puritanism may be regarded as the renaissance of the moral sense of man. The Greco-Roman Renaissance of 15th and 16th centuries was largely pagan and sensuous. It did not touch the moral nature of man, it did nothing for his religious, political and social emancipation. The Puritan movement, on the other hand, was the greatest movement for moral and political reform. Its aims were :(1) religious liberty, *i.e.,* that men should be free to worship according to their conscience, and (2) that they should enjoy full civil liberty. The Puritans wanted to make men honest and to make them free. They insisted on the purity of life.

During this period, criticism of the church and the court increasingly became more vocal and wide spread and resulted ultimately in the civil war and the beheading of Charles I. The critical temper of the age is reflected in its literature poetry, prose and drama. It was an age of transition in which the old order collided with the new, and writers, like Donne, were virtually suspended between two worlds, the old world of Decay, and the new world of Progress.

Literary Trends of Puritan Age

The chief literary trends of the New Age may be summarised as follows:

(1) **Dominance of Satire.** As **R.G. Cox** points out, there is an increase in scepticism, introspection, self-consciousness, and self-criticism. In literature, this results in a growing emphasis in satire and realism. Satire is everywhere, in prose, in poetry and on the stage. *Joseph Hall* claims to be the first English satirist. *Marston* is a great satirist, and Donne's poetry is not only satirical, but often, cynical and brutal in tone. The professed aim of the *Ben Jonsonian Comedy* is satirical *i.e.*, to laugh folly out of court. Ben Jonson represents the typical antithesis to Shakespeare. Romance and imaginative exuberance in him, are replaced by classical self-control and realism.

(2) **Realism in Love-Poetry.** The Elizabethan love-poetry was largely Petrarchan. There were also the medieval and platonic strains in Elizabethan love-poetry. In the new age, love-poetry is characterised by increasing realism. Thus Donne emphasises that, to be a satisfactory relationship, love should be a mutual passion. Claims of the body are recognised, and woman is no longer treated as a goddess, but as a creature of flesh and blood.

(3) **Development of New Style.** The language of poetry had grown too poetic, and a conventional and stereotyped phraseology was used by poet after poet. Classical mythology was freely exploited for decoration and imagery. In the new age, there is development of new styles: the older rhetorical method in verse, with its copiousness and formal elaboration, gives way to a more concentrated manner, following more closely the diction and rhythms of speech, to what were called at the time, "strong lines", and to what became known later as "metaphysical" wit. In prose, there is a reaction away from Ciceronian eloquence, as a model towards the packed terseness of Seneca and Tacitus.

(4) **The Metaphysical Trend.** There are marked changes in style and interest. Metaphysical elements were the main agents of change and the dominant moulders of the new tradition, as are seen in John Donne and Ben Jonson. Of the two, Donne's originality is, by far, the more spectacular. One aspect of Donne's originality, in fact, is that he gave to the short lyric something of the flexibility, the urgent and profound expressiveness, that came to be developed in dramatic blank verse. However, Jonson's non-dramatic verse does not show such an obvious originality or such a decisive breach with contemporary fashion as Donne's; yet his different modification of the Elizabethan manner is almost equally significant. Even his songs have a greater neatness and point; they are more economical in method, and the best of them achieves a striking sureness of movement, a king of controlled *elan*, which is different from the limpid Elizabethan flow.

(5) **Abundance of Religious Poetry.** Besides the metaphysical poets and the Caroline lyricists, religious poetry also occupies an important place in the literature of this period. John Donne is the greatest of the religious poets of the century and following his example, the metaphysical style is used for religious poetry by such religious poets as *George Herbert, Henry Vaughan, Richard Crashaw*; and many others.

(6) **A Unique Element of Epic Poetry.** It was an age of short lyrics rather than of long poems. However, Milton's epics were an exception. In this connection, one is reminded of Daniel's *The Civil Wars* and *Drayton's Polyolbion.* But they are long narrative poems, rather than epics in the classical style. Similarly, Spenser's *Fairy Queen* is a "romantic epic" or an "epical romance", rather than a classical epic of the type of the epics of Homer and Virgil. Later in the 17th century, Abraham Cowley (*Davide*) and D' Avenant (*Gondibart*) also tried their hand at the epic. But, none of them could succeed. It was left for Milton to achieve this goal,

and in the cosmic sweep and range of his epic, to surpass even the ancients. Therefore it would be correct to say that, "the English epic begins and ends with Milton."

(7) **Prose of Matter Rather Than Manner.** The prose of the earlier half of the seventeenth century is even more varied than its verse, and the lines are harder to distinguish. This is partly because of the more varied functions that prose has to serve – practical, informative, persuasive, rhetorical, artistic – functions, which, at this time, were not clearly distinguished and some of which overlap those of verse; and partly because there was, as yet, no prose of everyday use, as a norm, from which significant variations could be made for special purposes. In some respects, nevertheless, the age shows developments in prose, roughly parallel to those in the domains of poetry. If we move forward from renaissance period, the new concern is with matter, rather than manner, a desire for more concentration and weight, and a preference for the epigrammatic terseness of Seneca or Tacitus.

(8) **Logical and Straight Forward Style.** Character-writing or character is a prose "*enre*", which encouraged pithy and epigrammatic writing, rather than elaboration and amplification, and it is cultivated by a number of writers. One of the most popular forms of prose-writing is the sermon. Prose is used for science and philosophy, for history and travel, for biography, for diary and letter, for pamphleteering and 'journalism'. On the whole, the movement is towards a simpler, clearer, more logical and more straight - forward prose style. The general concern of the new age is intellectual, and both, prose and poetry, display this concern.

(9) **Degeneration of Drama.** The exhaustion of the Renaissance impulse results in the drying up of the creative vein, and literature becomes decadent. This degeneration is best reflected in the Drama of the New Age. Sensationalism, a morbid preoccupation with disease and death, the exploitation of crude physical horrors and unnatural themes, such as incest, and growing obscenity and immorality of the plays, are all symptoms of this decadence, This degenerated drama died a natural death with the closure of the theatres, in the 1640's.

Poetry of the Jacobian and Puritan Periods

(A) General Trends

(1) **Revolt Against Elizabethan Tradition.** The leaders of this revolt were Ben Jonson and John Donne. Both of them were forceful personalities who attracted staunch followers and founded schools. The first, Ben Jonson – the founder of the classical school which reached its full flowering in the poetry of Dryden and Pope – was primarily a dramatist. As a poet, he profoundly influenced the Caroline lyricists. The other is John Donne. His poetry is remarkable for its concentrated passion, intellectual agility and dramatic power. He is given to introspection and self-analysis; he writes of no imaginary shepherds and shepherdesses, but of his own intellectual, spiritual and amorous experience. His early satires, his *Songs and Sonnets, his Holy Sonnets etc.*, are all different expressions of his varied experiences. His poetry is marked with a tone of realism, even cynicism, but it is always forceful and startling. He is the founder of the so-called "Metaphysical school" of poetry, of which *Richard Crashaw, George Herbert, Henry Vaughan and Abraham Cowley* are the other leading poets.

(2) **The Metaphysical School.** Emergence of the metaphysical school was a special characteristic of this age. Literally, "Meta" means "beyond" and "physics" means "physical nature". It was Dryden who first used the word, "Metaphysical", in connection with Donne's poetry and wrote, "*Donne affects the metaphysics*", and **Dr. Johnson** confirmed the judgment of Dryden. Ever since, the word "*Metaphysical*" has been used for Donne and his followers. However, the term is an unfortunate one, for it implies a *process of dry reasoning, a speculation about the nature of the universe,* the problems of life and death, etc. Milton's *Paradise Lost,* Pope's *Essay on Man* and even, Tennyson's *In Memoriam,* may be called metaphysical poems, for they are concerned with the nature of things. Donne's poetry is not metaphysical in the true sense of the world. A metaphysical poem is long, while Donne's poems are all short. His poetry does not expound any philosophical system of the universe, rather it is as much concerned with his emotions and personal experiences, as any other poetry. No doubt, there is much intellectual analysis of "emotion" and "experience", but this by itself cannot be called metaphysical. The poetry of the school of Donne is not metaphysical, as far as its content is concerned. But as **Grierson** puts it, "*Donne is metaphysical not only by virtue of his scholasticism, but by his deep reflective interest in the experiences of which his poetry is the expression, psychological curiosity with which he writes of love and religion.*"

In other words, Donne's poetry may be called "metaphysical", only in as far as its technique or style is concerned. It is heavily overloaded with "*conceits*", which may be defined as the excessive use of over- elaborated similes and metaphors, drawn from the most far-fetched, remote and unfamiliar sources. The peculiarity of the metaphysicals lies in the fact that (1) They use figures of speech excessively. (2) Their similes and metaphors are far-fetched and are often drawn from the most unfamiliar sources. (3) Their figures are elaborated to the farthest limit (4) The relationships they perceive are occult. They are not obvious on the face of nature. (5) Their images are logical and intellectual, rather than sensuous or emotional.

(3) **Cavalier of Caroline Lyric.** The Caroline lyrics, like the Elizabethan lyrics, were published in miscellanies and anthologies, as *Wits Recreation* (1641), *Wit Restored* (1658), *Parnassus Biceps* (1656), etc. The miscellanies have preserved for us the best songs and lyrics of even the lesser known poets. It is the result of conscious effort. It is artificial. It is a work of art characterised by finish, polish and elegance of language, but lacking that spontaneity and absence of effort which characterised the Elizabethan lyric. It has formal finish and perfection, but is wanting, in natural ease and warmth of emotion. It mirrors the mood and temper of the age. It is often coarse, licentious and indecent, thus reflecting the coarseness and indecency of the court and the courtly circles to which most of the poets of this school belonged. The poets of this school, again and again find the various beauties of nature united in the beauty of their respective beloveds. The Cavalier poets are great lovers of nature. They observe nature minutely and describe it with feeling. Concrete, visual images, drawn from the homelier and simpler objects and forces of nature, abound in their lyrics.

The Caroline lyric is charming, but there is something trivial and unsubstantial about it. In this respect again, it reflects the triviality and frivolity of the life of those times.

(4) **Wit.** "Wit" denotes a kind of verbal expression which is brief, deft, and intentionally contrived, to produce a shock of comic surprise. This surprise is usually the result of an unforeseen connection, or distinction between words or concepts, which frustrates the listener's expectation only to satisfy it in a different way. For example, Donne often begins his poems abruptly, as in *The Canonisation*:

For God's sake hold thy tongue, and let me love.

Elsewhere, he begins on a bitter note :

When by thy scorne, o' murderers, I am dead.

–and then proceeds to tell her what terrors his ghost would cause to her after his death. Donne's witticism too, has a similar purpose, *i.e.*, to startle and surprise. His wit is not merely, "*what oft was thought, but never so well expressed.*" "*The King's real and his stamped face*", and the passage about the Phoenix in *the Canonisation* etc. are relevant examples. Donne surprises and arrests attention, both by the content and style of his poetry.

(5) **Satire.** There was an unprecedented rise of the spirit of satire in the last decade of the 16th and opening one of the 17th century. The exhaustion of the Renaissance spirit, religious, and political controversies, uncertainty as regards the accession to the throne, the uncouthness and unpopularity of James I, his extravagance and immorality, the clash between the old and the New Philosophies, all contributed to a growing sense of disillusionment and defeat, self-introspection and self-criticism. It was but natural, that satire could flourish under the circumstances. Men felt, that the times were out of joint, eyes were focussed on the many ills of society, and so, satire had its heyday. Donne is the greatest of the satirist of the period, others being *John Marston, Joseph Hall, Ben Jonson, etc.*

(B) Poets of Puritan Age

(1) **Satirists of the Age.** As both *Saintsbury* and *Leishman* notice, most of the Elizabethan and early 17th century satirists are harsh, because they believed that the harsh and unpleasant nature of satire needed a correspondingly harsh versification. In this way, the satiric effect was heightened. Most of the satirists believed that they were imitating *Horace, Juvenal* and *Persius,* but with a few occasional exceptions, it seems that all they really succeeded in reproducing, what was the imaginary harshness of the verses of these poets. They had been taught that the model satirist was Persius, and that his chief characteristics were harshness of style and hardness of conceit. This supposedly indispensable harshness, some of them, notably Donne, deliberately cultivated.

(I) **John Donne.** Donne has left behind him only five formal satires, all belonging to the early years of his poetical career, but the satiric vein penetrates even those lyrics of his which are not professedly satiric. In his satires, what strikes the eye at first sight, is their extremely rugged nature. Donne's satires are notorious for their harshness, unevenness and unpleasantness.

The satiric vein in Donne, overflows the five formal *Satyres* and it is to be found everywhere in his poetry, whether the early *Songs* and *Sonnets, the Elegies,* or the later religious poetry. All aspects of contemporary London life, life at court, its immorality and indecency, women and their inconsistency, love and its follies, the greed, hypocrisy and dishonesty of

London lawyers, and the folly and cupidity of their clients, in short, a thousand contemporary vices and affectations, find a satirical treatment in the poetry of Donne. Despite some shortcomings, Donne must be ranked very high as a satirist. We must agree with **K. D. Gransden's** view that *in any literary history of England, Donne's satires must be described as important landmarks.*

(II) **Joseph Hall (1574-1656).** He considered himself the first satirist in English poetry, and made the boastful claim :

"I first adventure, follow me who list
And be the second English satirist"

The claim of Hall was evidently wrong, for satire had also been written by Langland, Skelton, Gascoigne and Spenser. Hall was certainly not the first satirist of England. But he was a powerful satirist, the first to write satires on the classical model. In his *Vergidemiarum,* he attacked the extravagance in dress and the foppishness of courtiers. He mocked at the conceits of the sonneteers and condemned the rant and bombast which Marlowe had introduced into drama, as also the buffoonery of the clowns. He was bold enough to satirise even writers, who stood head and shoulder above him. He was full of force, vehemence and fire.

(III) **John Marston (1575-1634).** He was even more virulent, and surpassed Hall, in fury and declamatory intensity. He published a book of *Satires and The Scourge of Villainy* in 1598. He was one of the most abusive and obscene of Elizabethan satirists. Under the pretence of teaching morals, Marston allowed himself to become extremely coarse, rough and boorish. He pretended to imitate Juvenal. He denounced lewd verse, but he himself was the most obscene of Elizabethan satirists.

(IV) **George Wither (1588-1667).** He was bitterly opposed to the evils prevalent in the court. His *Abuses Spirit and Whipt* appeared in 1653 and landed him in jail, for in it, he had dared to satirise those in power at the court.

(V) **Ben Jonson (June 1572-Aug. 1637).** He was a playright, poet and literary critic of the seventeenth century. He popularised the comedy of humours. He is best known for satirical plays, like *Every man in His Humour, Volpone* or *The Foxe.* He is generally regarded as the second most important English dramatist, after William Shakespeare, during the reign of James I. It was Ben Jonson's object, to expose the follies of his times, and thus bring about social reform.

"I'll strip the ragged follies of the time
Naked, as at their birth, and with a whip of steel,
Print wounding lashes in their iron ribs".

(2) **Metaphysical Poets.** John Donne was the founder of the so called "Metaphysical" school of poetry, and he is the greatest of the poets of this school. Some important poets of this school are the following:

(I) **John Donne (1572-1631).** In Donne's poetry, there is always an "*intellectual analysis of emotion*". Every lyric arises out of some emotional situation, and the emotion concerned is analysed thread-bare. Like a clever lawyer, Donne gives arguments in support of his point of view. Thus, in *Valediction : Forbidding Mourning,* he proves that true lovers need not mourn at the time of parting; in *The Canonisation* he establishes that lovers are saints of love; and in *The Blossome* he argues against the *Petrarchan* love-tradition. This imparts to his poetry, a *hard intellectual tone*, but it also results in that, *"unification of sensibility"*, for which **T. S. Eliot** praised the metaphysical poetry so highly.

(II) **George Herbert (April 1593-March 1633).** The range of Herbert's poetry is limited; he wrote only on religious themes, and nearly all his poems are comparatively short lyrics. Their quality, however, both in content and technique, invites the adjective "great". Many of Herbert's poems are direct colloquies with God, expressed in a conversational tone of remarkable intimacy. He uses a very wide variety of metrical forms. No less than one hundred and sixteen of his poems are written in forms, which he does not repeat. His poetry expresses the combination of intellect and sensibility and the flexibility of attitude characteristic of metaphysical wit; but his use of imagery and conceit differs considerably from that of Donne. He does not draw his images from scientific or scholastic learning, as Donne often does, but from familiar, everyday sources. Like Donne, he surprises the reader into a new understanding; but he does this, not by outlandish comparisons, but by the contrast between the dignity of his subject-matter and the familiarity of the image used to illustrate it, as in *Affliction.*

(III) **Thomas Carew (1595-1640).** Carew's poetry combines the influences of Donne and Jonson, and he is fully aware of his debt, to both. His *Elegie upon the Death of the Dean of Pauls, Dr. John Donne,* is not only a fine poem, but a remarkable demonstration of critical insight; and his poem *To Ben Jonson* records the awareness of the value of careful artistry which the Cavaliers learnt from him. He praises Donne in *The Elegie,* for doing away with the classical impediments, his own work is strewn with classical references. His debt to Donne is to be seen in his analysis of feelings and flexibility of attitude; his ability to sustain and elaborate poetic arguments; his vivid phrases and conceits (sometimes actually borrowed from Donne); and sometimes, his achievement of that fusion of feeling, thought and image, which is characteristic of Donne.

(IV) **Richard Crashaw (1613-1649).** The main body of Crashaw's poetry appeared in *Steps to the Temple* (1664), a collection of religious poems, to which, a section of secular poems, *The Delights of the Muses,* was attached. The title *Steps to the Temple* recalls Herbert, but Crashaw was utterly unlike Herbert as a poet.

Though Crashaw's work is clearly related to the metaphysical tradition, it diverges very considerably from it, being greatly influenced by Italian poetry. His feeling is expressed in verse of great sensuousness, and we find the poet, whose secular "love poems", were of an essentially idealistic nature, unrelated to any real amorous experience, frequently using the language of erotic poetry, to express religious emotion.

(V) **Henry Vaughan (1621-1695).** His greatest work is *Silex Scintillans,* a collection of religious poems. The influence of George Herbert, which Vaughan acknowledged, is obvious enough in the abundant borrowings of themes, titles, metrical forms and phrases from *The Temple.* But, what Vaughan borrows, he makes it his own. In many poems, he contrasts the inconstancy of man towards God, with the constancy of natural creation. Later, Vaughan looks upon nature as expressing the mind and will of God. Thus, the image of nature which in his earlier poems had been largely ornamental, becomes, in his sacred poems, the means of expressing a living, central experience; a means by which the thought is illustrated, developed and communicated. In these poems, in fact, Vaughan's new found seriousness of purpose makes him a true metaphysical poet, handling imagery, diction and movement, in the authentic metaphysical way.

(VI) **Andrew Marvell (1621-1678).** Marvell's handing of verse is masterly. His work reveals the successful assimilation and fusion of the two great poetic influences *Donne* and *Herbert,* of the early seventeenth century. It combines the passionate, probing intellectuality of Donne, with the clarity and poise of Jonson.

In the nineteenth century, Marvel was admired for his delight in nature and his skill in natural description and with good reason. His *The Garden* is full of sensuous delight. In the poem, grass comes to life and thinks.

T.S. Eliot wrote that the special quality of Marvell's verse is the, "*quality of a civilization, of a traditional habit of life.*" The most immediately obvious of these qualities is Marvell's handling of verse. His skill is such that he is able to combine the idiomatic speech-quality of Donne with an elegant polish, a balanced ease, which point forward to Pope. This technical assurance, however is not mere facility; it expresses a remarkable urbanity of tone – a sense of assured critical detachment, which has nothing to do with complacency, but is based on firmly held values. Marvell is assured in manner, because his spiritual and cultural standards are sure.

(VII) **Abraham Cowley (1618-1667).** Though, Cowley wrote in the metaphysical manner, in so far as he used conceits, puns, arguments, and so on, but his mind was radically different from Donne's. He lacked intensity of passion and depth of insight. His wit is a matter of ingenuity, and his images are usually decorative and fanciful, rather than a means of exploiting experience or resolving conflict. He lacks the fusion of thought and feeling which produces the characteristic metaphysical intensity, and the experiences he conveys, are less complex. The Augustan tendency in Cowley made him so popular in his own time and well into the eighteenth century. In 1647, a collection of his love verses was published, titled 'The Mistress. Inspite of the trouble of the time, on his return to England in 1656, he published a volume of his collected potential works. This volume included, 'The Pindarique Odes', 'The Davideis, 'The Mistress and some Miscellanies. This section of this work opens with the famous aspiration:

"What shall I do to be forever known,
And make the coming age my own?"

(3) **Cavalier of Caroline Lyric and Lyricists.** The term *'Cavalier' or Caroline* is used for a group of mid 17th century poets, who sided with King Charles I against the Parliament. These Cavalier or Caroline poets were the followers of Ben Jonson, and may properly be called the *'Sons of Ben'*, though some of them also display the influence of John Donne. The more important poets of this schools are Herrick, Carew, Lovelace, Suckling, Waller and Denham. We would first consider their works separately, and then examine some distinctive features of the Caroline lyric.

(I) **Robert Herrick (1591-1674).** Robert was a great Cavalier poet. His lines are fresh, with the authentic feeling for nature and the countryside, and have a rare sweetness and simplicity of tone. He was a graduate of Cambridge and spent a good many years in London, in the company of poets and wits, "the sons of Ben". He accepted the Vicarship of Dean Prior in Devonshire in 1629. Here he lived, feeling exiled from London, yet learning to make most of the simple country life around him. The Puritan victory cost him his living and he was back in London in 1648, in which year he published the collection of lyrics, by which he is still remembered – *Hesperides.*

There is little of the exaggerated sophistication of the Cavaliers in Herrick's lyrics. In his sweetness and freshness, he is closer to the Elizabethans, than other lyricists of the age. He is perhaps nearer than any other English poet, to the tone of the early Greek and Latin lyric poets. Within the radius of his parish, he found any number of wonderful trifles to write about : he sings of flowers, brooks, and other beauties of Nature. His touch is light and graceful. He feels, thinks and writes lightly. It is his style which places him beyond time and change. "For expressions, as accurately cut as jewels, and for melody, as clearly articulated as a peal of bells, Herrick is unrivalled". *He is the perfect artist in slight verse, as Milton is in a grander poetry.*

(II) **Richard Lovelace (1617-1657).** In half a dozen of Lovelace's songs, the braggadocio of the Cavalier is transmuted into the chivalry and loyalty of the knight errant. English chivalry lives forever in his song, *To Lucasia, on Going to the Wars.* Although he was an ardent admirer of Ben Jonson, he is nevertheless, neither so correct as Carew, nor so natural as Suckling.

His verse exhibits the more serious side of Cavalier life, its courage and elegance, and reminds us that any cause may evoke the best in a man, if he believes in it whole-heartedly. His important works are songs *To Lucasta, On Going to the Wars,* and *To Althea, from Prison,* in which he sings of the liberty he still can feel, though in prison:

"Stone walls do not a prison make,
Nor iron bars a cage."

The lines have become proverbial.

(III) **John Suckling (1609-41).** Throughout his poetry, there runs a vein of hard cynicism, which he had learned from Donne. He excels Carew in what he borrows, but, unlike Carew, he never tries to follow Donne, in his nobler flights. So, far from copying Donne's high serious manner, he makes fun of it. He begins one of his songs, with a line from Donne's serious poem, *Love's Deity,* simply to emphasize the frivolity of what follows; and in another, after a couplet in Donne's heavy manner, he breaks into something like a chuckle.

He was one of King Charles' courtiers and a notorious gambler. He sided with the king, and was forced to flee to France where, it is thought, he committed suicide. His poems exhibit the gay, devil may-care tone of Cavalier life. The most famous of them are *A Doubt of Martyrdom; The Constant Lover,* in which he expressed surprise at his having loved one woman, "three whole days together."

It is this light, flippant tone, which characterises Suckling. He does not take care to polish his verses, and mocks at Carew for doing so. **Legouis** praises him for his ability to write, "charming verses on nothing", and **Congreve** (*in Way of the World*) calls him, "natural, easy Suckling."

(IV) **Thomas Carew (1595-1640).** Although, *The Poems* (1640), are full of borrowings from Donne's *Songs and Sonnets*, Carew's literary debt to Donne, is in reality, very small. "He uses the same thoughts in a different manner and for a different end. In fact, Carew was not really a "metaphysical" poet. In his *Elegy upon Death of Dr. Donne,* which is still the best short estimate of Donne's place in English poetry, while praising Donne for his "genial fancy" and "masculine expression", he admits that as regards language he must yield precedence to writers:

.... whose tuned chime
More charms the outward sense.

He himself always tried to make his verse melodious, and industriously avoided any appearance of effort. In his polish and refinement, in his logical order, he is the disciple of Ben Jonson.

Among his best songs are *To Celia; The Rapture; Ask Me No More.* Like other Cavalier poets, he again and again reminds the girls, that time plays tricks with beauty and youth, and that, they had better take their joy in the present. Again and again, he finds all the beauties of nature united in his mistress. He is the most indecent and licentious of the poets of this school, as well as the most perfect and refined in his style and versification.

(V) **Edmund Waller (1606-87).** Waller's long life, links up two periods, separated by a political convulsion and a literary revolution. Throughout his life he wrote verse, but only occasional verse. He did not pride himself upon inventiveness. The aim, which he set before himself in his youth, was like that, which the young Pope proposed to follow. "Methought", he is reported to have said, "I never saw a good copy of English verse; they want smoothness; then I began to essay". Thought in his poems matters little. Elegance, correctness, a certain studious grace, something cold and stilled, belong to them all. It is Thomas Carew, whom he most resembles. The love-songs he sings in honour of his beloved, recall Carew's more decent verses, by their regularity of structure, and their adroitness. His well-known poems – *The Bud; Go, Lovely Rose* and *On a Girdle* – are some of the finest love-lyrics of the period.

(VI) **John Denham (1615-69).** He is among the earliest pioneers of classicism. *"His strength is praised by Pope in the same line as Waller's sweetness."* The renown which Denham attained by a small literary production, is proof of the appetite of the age for regulated poetry. He owed his fame, save for a few occasional poems, to his half-descriptive, half-didactic *Copper's Hill,* which appeared in 1642. It has been called the first example of local description, but in the main, it is a meditation inspired by a place of many historical memories, *Near the Thames, Windsor Forest, The ruins of an Abbey,* which recall destruction of the monasteries, and *Runymede Field,* where Magna Carta was signed. What is described there has a moralizing turn. More than half a century later, Pope was inspired by it to write his *Windsor Forest.*

(VII) **Sir William Davenant (1606-68).** He did not write any lyrics, but it is proper to consider him at this stage, for like the Caroline lyricists, he too was a supporter of the king and went into exile with him, where he was subjected to the same influences as the lyricists. He is known for his epical romance *Gondibert.* He is one of those early classical poets who exercised considerable influence on the Restoration writers. The heroic tragedy of the Restoration era owes its inspiration to his *The Siege of Rhodes. "In it are to be found the germs both of the English Opera and of the Heroic Tragedy"* (**Legouis**). Both, his poetry and drama, are characterised by the ascendancy of the French influence.

(4) **Milton and Epic Poetry.** In Milton's poetry, there is a nice fusion of elements, both of the renaissance and the reformation. He was the child, both of the Renaissance and the Reformation. His childhood was spent at a time when the Renaissance was in the ascendancy. His youth witnessed the rise of puritanism, and his old age marked the consummation of the Puritan ideals. So, Milton's poetry is a link between the Age of the Renaissance and the Puritan Age. He is both, a belated Elizabethan and a fervent disciple of the Reformation.

Milton's works fall naturally into four periods.

(I) **The College Period.** His college poems, Latin and English, are for the most part simply a youngman's experimental work, and are of little importance. But, the *Ode on the Morning of Christ's Nativity,* is an exception. It is written on a Biblical subject, but glows with imagination and is full of pagan imagery, thus revealing a fusion of the Renaissance and Reformation influences.

(II) **The Horton Period.** To this period belong four minor poems. These poems are *L' Allegro* and *Il Penseroso* (1633), *Comus* (1634), and *Lycidas* (1637). From them, we now learn that he began to write chiefly under the inspiration of the learning and art of the Renaissance; that the Puritan element was at first, quite subordinate; and that it gradually gained in strength and depth, till it became at last, the dominant element. Thus, in *L' Allegro* and *Il Penseroso,* with their charming contrasted pictures of man, nature and art ,as seen through the medium of the mood, in the one case of gladness, and in the other of melancholy, there is little that is characteristically Puritan, and a good deal that is really un-Puritan; for the poet dwells frankly upon the pleasures of romance and rustic sports, upon the beauty of Church architecture and music – all of which things, were to the religious fanatic, objects of uncompromising hatred.

Then, *Comus,* on the literary side, belongs to the Renaissance; it is an example (and the finest example in our literature) of that type of drama which is called *the Masque,* which had been brought from Italy, and which had ever since been extremely popular at court and among the nobility in England.

Finally, in *Lycidas* we have a puritanism, which is political and ecclesiastical, as well as spiritual and ethical. An elegy on the death of Milton's college friend, Edward King, *Lycidas,* like Spenser's *Astrophel,* is in the conventional style of the classical pastoral-elegy. In form, therefore, it belongs with *Comus* to the Renaissance. But the religious accent in it throughout is unmistakably Puritan, while its famous attack upon the corrupt church and the hireling clergy of the time openly proclaims Milton's adherence to the Puritan cause.

(III) **The Period of Religious and Political Controversies.** Milton, in his 31st year, threw himself into the fierce controversies of the hour, and thus, in his own words, embarked, "on a troubled sea of noises and hoarse disputes". The ambition to write a great epic poem had already taken shape in his mind, but this he laid aside in order that he might give all his strength and industry to the performance of what he conceived to be a great public duty. Involved in political and religious controversies, he thus turned from poetry entirely; and for the next twenty years, continued active as a writer of prose. This was a great loss to poetry.

(IV) **The Period of the Great Epics.** In *Paradise Lost, Milton,* he produced the greatest English epic. It is in this stupendous masterpiece of intellectual energy and creative power that the full significance of the combination of the Renaissance and Reformation elements becomes apparent.

In *Paradise Regained,* the poet is completely dominated by Puritanism. There is hardly any action in this epic, the entire space being taken up by the spiritual conflict between good and evil.

The "dramatic poem" *Samson Agonistes* crowns the labours of these closing years. In this, as in *Paradise Lost,* Milton applies the form of classical art to the treatment of a Biblical subject, for the work is fashioned strictly upon the principles of Greek tragedy, while the matter, mood, tone and outlook are strictly Herbraic and Biblical.

From a study of the works of Milton, it is obvious that Milton represents not only the highest, but the completest type of Puritanism. But it should never be forgotten, that the culture of the Renaissance was never totally exterminated by his puritanical bent of mind.

In Milton's poetry, *the Puritanical strain is apparent in following manners* (a) in the choice of religious subjects, especially in the later poems, (b) the sense of responsibility and moral exaltation, (c) the fondness for preaching, and lecturing, which, in *Paradise Lost,* is a positive weakness, and (d) the narrowness of outlook, strongly Puritanical, seen in his outbursts against his opponents (as in *Lycidas*), in his belief regarding the inferiority of women, and in his scorn for the "miscellaneous rabble". *The Renaissance elements are seen in his love of beauty, his classical learning, and his use of classical forms of poetry.*

Prose of Puritans

(1) **The Character-writers.** During Jacobian and Puritan periods, the most popular exercise of the essayist was the delineation of character. Bacon, no doubt, founded a genre, but he had practically no successors. The character writers of the early 17th century drew their inspiration from the Greek writer *Theophrastus.* These character-writers also have a close affinity with the satirists in verse, like Joseph Hall, who did in poetry what the character-writers did in prose. *John Earle, Thomas Overbury, George Herbert* and, later in the century, *Thomas Fuller,* are the greatest of the writers in this genre.

(I) **John Earle's** *Microcosmography* was first published in 1628. As the title indicates, Earle regards each character as microcosm of the macrocosm, *i.e.*, a representation in brief of the humanity at large. The book, containing fifty-five characters, was immediately popular and ran into several editions. The characters lack variety, the writer's experience was limited to the university and so the university type predominates. However, the essayist has shown great skill in the treatment of character in his chosen field.

Earle does not make the display of his wit and skill, his chief concern. His wit is not mere play with words; it is real wisdom. Often it is pungent and biting. Like other character-writers of the day, he is not concerned wholly with manner, but is concerned with matter also. His sketches are truthful, life-like. He never loses touch with truth and reality. His work is marked with perfect sincerity. His characters have universality and so, appeal even upto this day. He is greatest of the character writers of the school of Theophrastus.

(II) **Sir Thomas Overbury** (1581-1613) is known for the twenty one prose sketches, which he added to the first edition of his poem *The Wife* (1614). Overbury's characters are much inferior to those of Earle. His style is hopelessly artificial; he sacrifices matter to manner. His style abounds in far-fetched and fantastic conceits, and in this way, his concern with manner, pushes out truth and reality. However, his characters become concrete and solid, as each one of them is given some trade and occupation, and has the virtues of that occupation.

(III) While other character-writers followed the tradition of Theophrastus, **George Herbert** (1593-1633) breaks from this tradition, since his work *The Country Parson,* does not deal with a number of different characters, but all the thirty-seven essays in the book have the country parson as the central figure. Each essay deals with a different aspect of his personality. His work has unity of design, which makes it different from Theophrastus' characters.

His work is entirely free from the prevailing vices of the period : there is no extravagant display of wit, *i.e.*, writer's skill in the use of words. Even Earle is not entirely free from this artificiality; but Herbert is.

There are real and life-like presentations of the life and character of a parson. The work is stamped with the sincerity of its writer.

(IV) **Thomas Fuller** (1608-1661) is the greatest man who ever touched the character sketch. His *Holy and Prafane State* (1641) is one of the greatest books in this *genre.* It is just a character-study of the virtuous and the vicious types, with the virtuous, pre-dominating.

The style of his essays is discursive and diffuse, even garrulous, instead of being condensed and pithy, as in the case of other character-writers. Thirdly, a whole wealth of amusing anecdotes, used to illustrate some particular trait of character, is scattered all over the essays. There is wit in him; but it is not something artificial, a mere word-play. His wit is also wisdom.

All these qualities make Fuller's work, a thing apart in literature. In the personal, intimate atmosphere of his essays, may be likened with Lamb alone, in the whole range of the English essay.

(2) **Melancholy of Robert Burton.** Burton is one of those eccentrics who stand alone, but whose works still enjoy considerable popularity. Burton suffered from melancholia and gloom, he was a learned writer and for his amusement he collected all the allusions to melancholy which he could find in the Latin and Greek works he had studied. The result was the enormous volume *Anatomy of Melancholy* (Published in 1621) which at once ran into several editions. It is a pillage from all known books; but a sort of unity is introduced by the personality of the collector. His melancholy is different from romantic melancholy; it is a kind of sickness, near allied to madness. His style is heavy and cumbersome, heavily overloaded with Latin quotations, expression and allusions. There is too much of word-play resulting from a childish joy in words. Long chains of synonyms are constantly used.

(3) **Sir Thomas Browne (1605-82).** Sir Thomas Browne was a man of wide and varied learning and his learning is reflected in his writings. He was a doctor by profession and a mystic by temperament. The mystic vein runs through his works, and everything is coloured by his personal experiences. *Religio Medici* and *Hydrataphia* are his chief works.

In *Religio Medici* (1635), the religion of a doctor, his most personal work, he reveals his complex soul. He frequently generalises on the vanity of glory, and the nearness of death. His greatest work *Hydrotaphia or Urn Burial* (1658) was inspired by the discovery of some fifty Roman Urns in the neighbourhood of his residence. It shows Browne's vast erudition regarding the various ancient modes of burial.

Browne is one of the greatest stylists in English literature. It is as an artist, that he excels. As compared with his contemporaries, his sentences are short, clearly outlined, and modern and restrained in construction. He had a passion for harmony, and naturally chooses the most melodious words, which make his sentences musical. The poetry of few poets is as musical, as is the prose of Browne. His love of the lofty and sublime leads him to use long, learned terms and quotations. This makes him rather difficult. There is over-abundant use of such references and allusions, as are not likely to be familiar to the average reader. His style is heavily Latinised. There are too many Latin words and Latin constructions. He frequently coins words according to his need.

Browne has an important place in the history of the English essay. He is an artist with words and his style is highly-wrought, ornate and gorgeous.

(4) **Pamphleteering of John Milton.** It was an age of political and religious pamphleteering. A pamphleteer aims at presenting his point of view to the people, or to attack that of his opponents. Milton, too, behaved in same manner and wrote a number of pamphlets to support the Republican and Puritan cause. Of these, *Aeropagetica* is among the immortal classics of English prose.

Of all the prose-writings of Milton, the greatest is *the Aeropagetica* (1644), the poet's noble and inspired defence of the liberty of press and free expression. Though Milton frequently rises to the heights of eloquence, his prose is marred by serious faults such as long, shapeless, tortuous and involved sentences, which are difficult to follow; both, the vocabulary and syntax are heavily Latinised; too many classical and Biblical allusions; quotations from Latin sources; and over-condensation and concentration, that is why, sometimes, he is aphoristic.

But, when all is said, *Aeropagetica* remains a great work. One frequently comes across inspired passages in which Milton rises to the height of eloquence. Frequently, we get admirable imagery and poetic cadences. Such passages make Milton one of the great masters of English prose.

(5) **Biographies of Izaak Walton.** The most delightful and the most endearing literary figure of the period is Izaak Walton. He is a delightful biographer. His biographies of Donne, Hooker, George Herbert, etc., are among the most charming biographies, ever written in the English language. He knew his subjects intimately and narrates their life-histories accurately. He relates only such facts as he has painstakingly verified, and therein, lies the value of his book. His biography of *John Donne* is our most reliable source for knowing the facts of the great poet's life. **Walton** writes with all the intimacy of personal acquaintance. He was cheerful, optimistic, good-natured and shrewd and his writings derive their charm from his personality, and outlook on life.

Even more popular is his *The Compleat Angler.* It is inspired by his optimism and love of nature, and the charm of his personality runs through it like fragrance. It is in the form of the dialogue between the angler and his pupil. It is a transformed pastoral. "*It is perhaps the only book on an art or craft which ranks as literature, and it seems to have won its place without seeking* **(Legouis)**". The work is a minor classic of the English language.

Drama of Puritans

1. **George Chapman (1559-1634).** Chapman, known for his translation of Homer, had enough of classical learning, but he did not have the classical spirit. He lacked the good sense and reason of the humanists. He has left behind him, a number of tragedies, on subjects taken from contemporary French history, and a number of comedies, based on English life. However, his plays are now little read; as a dramatist he does not have any high merit. His best known tragedy is *Bussy D' Ambois,* a revenge tragedy, with a French theme. Both, the character and events of the play, are historical. But, they lack life and reality. The play degenerates into melodrama.

   Literary Career and Works

   Chapman's first published work was The Shadow of Night (1594). This long poem was divided into two parts, the Hymnus in Nootem and the Hymnus in Cynthiam. These contained hymns dedicated to Night and Cynthia, the Greek Goddess of Moon. His second work, Ovid's Banquet of Sense (1595) parodied the genre of the erotic narrative poem such as Shakespeare's Venus and Adonis.

   Chapman's reputation was further cemented by his continuation of Christopher Marlowe's Hero sand Leander (1598) and his translations of Homer. John Keats effusively praised Chapman's translation of Homer in his famous poem On First Looking into Chapman's Homer. Apart from Homer, Chapman also translated the Georgics of Virgil and the works of Hesiod. Chapman began writing for the stage around 1595. His first extant play, The Blind Beggar of Alexandria was produced in 1596. His most famous comedy was All Fools, based on two classical Roman comedies by Terence, the Heauton Timorumenos and the Adelphoe.

   His best known tragedy was Bussy D'Ambois, based on the career of a protégé of brother of Henry III of France. Bussy is portrayed as a malcontent in a world of courtly intrigue.

   Despite his success as a dramatist, Chapman lived in dire financial straits. He was imprisoned for debt in 1600. He died in poverty in London around 1634.

   Major Works

   - The Shadow of Night (1594)
   - Ovid's Banquet of Sense (1595)
   - The Blind Beggar of Alexandria (1596)
   - A Humorous Day's Mirth (1597)
   - All Fools (1605)
   - Bussy D'Ambois (1607)
   - The Revenge of Bussy D'Ambois (1610)
   - The Iliads of Homer (1611)
   - Caesar and Pompey (1613)
   - The Whole Works of Homer (1616)
   - The Crown of All Homer's Works (1624)

2. **Ben Jonson (1572-1637).** Ben Jonson, a classicist, was a disciple of the ancients, one who resolutely tried to reform the English stage. In some sense, Ben Jonson is more original than Shakespeare. While Shakespeare accepted with a smile, the shortcomings of his stage, Ben Jonson raised his voice against them and tried to reform the English stage, on the model of the ancients. He is a

voluminous writer and has written numerous comedies, historical tragedies, and court-masques. He was profoundly learned and had studied not only the prominent writers of the past, but also the mediocre and the little-known ones. He had also studied closely and patiently, contemporary life and society, and we find the evidence of his wide learning, scattered all over his works.

(a) **His Comedies.** His early comedies *Every man in His Humour (1598) and Every Man Out of His Humour, Cynthia's Revels (1601),* and *The Poetasters (1602)* are immature, as far as their plot-construction is concerned. Each one of his characters is the representative of some "humour". The scene of Jonson's comedies is real, familiar London, rather than romantic Venice or the forest of Arden or the shores of Ilyria. The purpose of the writer is to satirise the follies and foibles, the weaknesses and vices of contemporary society, and his satire is generally coarse and brutal.

His later and maturer comedies *Volpone, the Fox* (1605), *Epicone, or the Silent Woman* (1609), *The Alchemist (1610),* and *The Bartholomew Fair,* are among the most remarkable works of the English Renaissance. These comedies show types of human folly and weakness, but they are also powerfully constructed.

Jonson was a moralist. His aim is ferocious satire, to "strip naked the ragged follies of the time," and "to whip them with a whip of steel", and such corrective and satiric aims exclude laughter. There is little laughter in his comedies, in contrast with Shakespeare, in whose comedies, there is laughter, more laughter and nothing, but laughter. However, his *Epicone, or the Silent Woman* is an exception. It is a delightful farce; its chief aim being to produce loud laughter. *Bartholomew Fair* is a satire on Puritans and "Jonson certainly wrote nothing more entertaining, than this play."

(b) **His Tragedies.** *Sejanus* (1603) and *Catiline* (1611) are the two great tragedies of Jonson. They are steeped in the dramatist's learning. Inspired by the success of Shakespeare's *Julius* Ceaser, Jonson, too, goes to Roman history, but chooses his subject from a little-known period. He is learned and accurate, throughout, there are no such anachronisms or historical blunders, as spoil the historical plays of Shakespeare, but he fails to make his characters live. He is correct and learned, full of vigorous and exact touches, but he fails to infuse life into the dry bones of history as Shakespeare does, both in his Roman and English history plays.

(c) **His Masques.** That, Ben Jonson was a great poet, is made clear by the numerous *Masques* which he wrote for the Court of King James I. The best of these masques are : (I) *The Satyr,* (II) *Masque of Beauty,* (III) *The Masque of Queens,* and (IV) *Cupid.* The masques are remarkable for their pageantry and spectacle, for their mingling of allegory, mythology and fairy tale, and for the exquisite lyrics and songs that abound in them.

3. **John Marston (1575-1634).** John Marston, besides being a dramatist, was also a satirist and published his *Scourge of Villainy* in 1598. His dramas, both tragedies and comedies, are also marked by ferocious satire. The best of his tragedies are (1) *Antonio's Revenge,* and (2) *Antonio and Mellida.* Both these tragedies are the direct descendants of the *Spanish Tragedy.* They are in the Senecan tradition, and are characterised by coarseness, brutality and violence. They reveal the cynicism, and pessimism of the dramatist. They lack originality and are frankly imitative. There is greater coarseness in him than in any other writer.

The best of his comedies are (a) *The Malcontant* (1601), and (b) *The Dutch Caurtesan* (1604). They are ill-constructed, coarse and licentious. The dramatist's genius is revealed only in particular passages and scenes.

Marston collaborated with Jonson and Chapman in the writing of the play *Eastward Ho* (1605), which is among the best of the Renaissance comedies. The play is known (I) for its vigour, (II) for its realism, (III) for its light-heartedness, and (IV) for its decency. The life of the goldsmiths of those days and their apprentices have been realistically delineated. The action moves on merrily, without any structural or moral obstacles. It is the story of a good apprentice who marries his master's daughter. The play is worth reading, even today. It is realism with a moralising touch.

Literary Career and Works

Marston's literary career began as a poet in 1598. His first known works are Books of Ovidian eroticism and poetic satire, The Metamorphosis of Pigmalion's Image and The Scourge of Villanie A year later, Marston began working as a playwright for Philip Henslowe. He wrote all his plays before taking holy orders in 1609. Histriomastix is considered as his first play.

His other popular plays are Antonio and Mellida (which deals with the 'comic crosses of true love' faced by Antonio, son of the good Duke Andrugio, and Mellida, daughter of the wicked Duke Piero), Malcontent (a satirical comedy which is centered on a supplanted Duke who returns to his Dukedom in disguise) and The Dutch 'Courtesan (story of two friends, Freevill and Puritan Malheureux, and their turbulent relationship with the passionate Dutch Courtesan Franceschina).

Probably under the influence of his father-in-law, Marston became a reader at the Bodleian library at Oxford in 1609 and was made a dcacon on 24th September and a priest on 24th December, 1609 A few years later, he was assigned the living of Christchurch, Hampshire. Marston died on 24th June, 1634 in London.

Major Works

- The Metamorphosis of Pigmalioris Image and Certaine Satyres (1598)
- The Scourge of Villanie. Three Bookes of Satyres (1599)
- Histriomastix (1599)
- Antonio and Mellida (1599-1600)
- Antonio's Revenge (1600)
- Jacke Drums Entertainment: Or, The Comedie of Pasquill and Katherine (1600-01)
- What You Will (1601)
- The Malcontent (1604)
- Parasitaster, or The Fawn (1604)
- Eastward Ho (by Marston, George Chapman, and Ben Jonson, 1604-1605)
- The Dutch Courtesan (1605)
- The Spectacle presented to the Sacred Majesties of Great Britain and Denmark as They Passed through London (1606)
- The Entertainment of the Dowager-Countess of Darby (1607)

4. **Thomas Dekker (1570-1641).** Dekker was optimistic and gay. His cheerfulness and gaiety is surprising, if we take into account the general decadence and

gloom of the period. The best known plays of Dekker are: (1) *The Shoe-maker's Holiday* (1599), which gives us realistic pictures of the followers of the craft and has been directly inspired by Deloney's *The Gentle Craft.* (2) *The Honest Whore* (1604) gives us a glimpse of the underworld of London and records the trials and experiences of a whore or prostitute who is determined to lead an honest life. It might be called a domestic drama, as far as the main plot is concerned.

While he has merits of a high order, he cannot be ranked with the greatest. His plays are ill-constructed and marred by much coarseness and licentiousness.

Literary Career and Works

Dekker started his literary career in the 1590s. In the year 1599, Dekker produced two plays, *Old Fortunatus* (1599), a morality play based on German legend and *The Shoemaker's Holiday* (1599), a comedy centered on Simon Eyre, a shoemaker. The plot of the second play derives from Thomas Deloney's story. Dekker's most famous and successful play was The Honest Whore (1604-1605). It is the story of a prostitute Bellafront, who redeems herself.

Dekker also wrote successful pamphlets such as The Wonderful Year (1603), a graphic account of London beset by plague. He further provided accounts of London underworld in pamphlets, The Seven Deadly Sins of London (1606) and The Belman of London (1608). The Gull's Hombook (1609), the Roaring girl (1610) written with Thomas Middleton. Thomas Dekker died in 1632, being heavily in debt.

Major Works

- Old Fortunatus (1599)
- The Shoemaker's Holiday (1599)
- The Honest Whore (1604-05)
- The Wonderful Year (1603)
- The Seven Deadly Sins of London (1606)
- The Belman of London (1608)
- The Gull's Hombook (1609)
- The Roaring Girl (1610)

5. **Thomas Heywood (1575-1650).** Thomas Heywood, a prolific dramatist, cared more for quantity than quality. He himself claimed to have written more than 200 plays, only a few of which have come down to us. He is the most important exponent of the domestic drama, a form of drama which deals with infidelity committed within the family circle, as a result of which, family ties are broken and tragedy takes place. Thomas Heywood's *A Woman Killed with Kindness* (1603) is the masterpiece of this type of drama.

Another of his important plays is *The Four 'Prentices of London.'* The play flatters the citizens of London. Its theme is the Quixotic exploits of four youths who go out in the manner of knights of chivalry and have glorious exploits and do heroic deeds in remote countries.

Literary Career and Works

Heywood's first play was perhaps The Four Prentices of London, a tale of four apprentices, who become knights and travel to Jerusalem. Most of Heywood's significant plays were written between 1600 and 1620. In 1633, in the preface to his play The English Traveller, Heywood claimed to have written 220 plays.

Heywood's most popular play was a domestic tragedy A Woman Killed with Kindness. It is the story of a happy marriage broken when Anne, the wife is seduced by her husband's friend.

The title of the play is taken from a proverb in Shakespeare's The Taming of a Shrew. Heywood also wrote a number of pamphlets and poems. During the late years of his career, he devoted himself to writing non-dramatic works. He was called 'Prose Shakespeare' by Charles Lamb. He died in 1641 and was buried in St James's Church in the Clerkenwell section of London.

Major Works

- A Woman Killed with Kindness (1602-03)
- An Apology for Actors, Containing Three Brief Treatises (1612)
- The Royal King and the Loyal Subject (1615-18)
- The English Traveller (1623)
- A Mayden-Head Well Lost (1634)
- A Challenge for Beautie (1636)
- Loves Maistresse or The Queens Masque (1636)

6. **Thomas Middleton (1570-1627).** Middleton depicts, like Thomas Heywood, the life of London citizens, but instead of flattering them, he ridicules their follies and weaknesses. His pictures are marked by his cynicism and have licentious implications, but are not as brutally obscene as the dramas of Heywood. His light farcical comedies like *A Mad World, My Masters and a Chaste Maid in Cheapside* are remarkable for their vivacity and close acquaintance with London life and justify **Legouis'** remark, that Middleton is, "the most modern of the humorists of the Renaissance." *Women Beware Women* is the best of his tragedies. The scene is laid in Italy and deals with the life of a famous Italian courtesan. Middleton is today remembered mainly for his *The Witch* which has striking resemblances with Shakespeare's *Macbeth.* Another of the plays which was immensely popular at the time is *A Game of Chess;* it is a curious political allegory directed against Spain. *The Changeling,* another of his masterpieces, is a powerful play and it would have ranked with the tragedies of Shakespeare, had it not been disfigured by a coarse and worthless secondary plot.

Middleton is one of the most original of the dramatists of his time and his greatest skill lies in making even improbable situations, convincing and real. He is a satirist who exposes evil and vice. His dramas have a moral tendency, for in them, vice never remains unpunished.

Literary Career and Works

Middleton's comedies deal with London life in the tradition of Dekker and Heywood. His earliest surviving independent play, Blurt, Master Constable was printed in 1602. As a playwright he was frequently commissioned to write pageants and civic entertainments. His famous comedies of intrigue were, A Trick to Catch the Old One (1605), A Mad World, My Masters (1605) and A Chaste Maid in Cheapside (1611). His play A Game at Chess (1625) an allegory about England and Spain's political tension was anti-Spanish in tone. It drew the ire of the Spanish ambassador and prompted James I to suppress the play.

His most famous tragedy was Women Beware Women (1625) which depicts the degeneration of Bianca, wife of Leantio, after the Duke of Florence seduces her in presence of her husband. Middleton also wrote a highly successful tragedy in collaboration with William Rowley in 1622, titled The Changeling. The heroine of this play was Beatrice Joanna, who in her quest to escape marriage to a man she dislikes, ends up getting entangled in the vicious schemes of her servant De Flores (who also loves her). Middleton died of natural causes at Newington Butts and was buried there on 4th July 1627

Major Works

- The Phoenix (1603-04)
- The Honest Whore, Part 1 (1604), co-written with Thomas Dekker
- Michaelmas Term (1604)
- A Trick to Catch the Old One (1605)
- A Mad World, My Masters (1605)
- The Bloody Banquet (1608-09); co-written with Thomas Dekker.
- A Chaste Maid in Cheapside (1611)
- More Dissemblers Besides Women (1614)
- A Fair Quarrel (1616). Co-written with William Rowley.
- The Old Law (1618-19). Co-written with William Rowley and perhaps a third collaborator, who may have been Philip Massinger or Thomas Heywood.
- Anything for a Quiet Life (1621). Co-written with John Webster.
- The Changeling (1622). Co-written with William Rowley.
- Women Beware Women (1625)
- A Game at Chess (1625)

7. **Cyril Tourneur (1575-1625).** These are two of the early 17th century dramatists, who put new life into melodrama at a time, when Shakespeare was abandoning tragedy to write his Last Plays or Dramatic Romances.

Tourneur's masterpieces are:

1. *The Revenger's Tragedy* (1607)
2. *The Atheist's Tragedy* (1611)

Both the tragedies are set in Italy, in a coarse and brutal world of crime and vice, from which there is no escape and which knows no pity. The theme is revenge and punishment, and the action moves swiftly, clearly and with intensity. They are revenge tragedies in the tradition of *The Spanish Tragedy.*

8. **John Webster (1575-1624).** John Webster, one of the greatest figures in post-Shakespearean drama, is one of those dramatists whose plays are of interest, even today. His two masterpiece are:

1. *The White Devil* (1611)
2. *The Duchess of Malfi* (1614)

The White Devil is one of a series of studies of famous Italian courtesans which had been appearing during the previous few years.

It is based on the life of the celebrated Italian courtesan, Vittoria.

On the other hand, *The Duchess of Malfi,* Webster's masterpiece, is a more closely knit play, but its appeal is the same.

It is a powerful play, but it must be called a melodrama, and not a high tragedy, because Webster substitutes for psychology, "a search for pathos inherent in situations and even in material effects."

Webster was a painstaking artist who tried to write pure tragedy of the classical type, but could create only a masterpiece of melodrama. He stands for the, "*triumph of melodrama raised to the level of true poetry.*" According to **Jfor Evans,** his play suffers from a number of coincidences, improbabilities, and forced effects, "and then, weaknesses and excesses of dramatic structure", are quite apparent.

"The moral world of Webster is different from that of Shakespeare" and Love is the sole theme of the tragedy, and evil, though punished in the end, is present everywhere, throughout the action.

Literary Career and Works

Webster was employed as a playwright in the theatre company of Phillip Henslowe. His literary career began with collaborative works with writers such as Dekker, Rowley, Ford and Heywood. Between 1602 and 1605, he collaborated on 5 plays, including Caesar's Fall, Lady Jane, Westward Ho! and Northward Hal. Webster's first individually written play was The Devil's Law Case, a tragicomedy.

This was followed by his two most famous plays, The White Devil and The Duchess of Maw, among the finest of all Jacobean tragedies. Both of them are revenge tragedies. The White Devil is centered on Vittoria Corombona and the Duke of Brachiano, who are in an adulterous relationship. The Duke murders Vittoria's husband and his own wife. After the murders, both of them get married. However, justice is restored at the end with both the Duke and Vittoria getting killed at the hands of Isabella's (Duke's slain wife) avengers. The Duchess of Mal?, on the other hand, revolves around a widowed Duchess, who marries her steward, Antonio Bologna secretly without her brothers' knowledge.

When the Duchess' brothers, Cardinal and Ferdinand become aware of her secret marriage, they both get her and Antonio killed. However, here too justice prevails with the death and downfall of the evil characters at the end of the play. Webster died sometime around November, 1634. Elizabethan theatre rapidly declined after his death.

Major Works

- Caesar's Fall (1602, collaboration with Michael Drayton, Thomas Dekker, Thomas Middleton and Anthony Munday)
- Lady lane (1602, collaboration with Heywood and other)
- Westward Ho (1604, collaboration with Thomas Dekker)
- Northward Ho (1605, collaboration with Dekker)
- The White Devil (1608-09)
- The Devil's Law Case (1610)
- The Duchess of Malfi (1613)
- Anything For a Quiet Life (1621, collaboration with Middleton)
- The Fair Maid of the Inn (1625, collaboration with Massinger and Ford)
- A Cure for a Cuckold (1625, collaboration with Heywood)

9. **John Fletcher (1579-1625) and Francis Beaumont.** The names of these two dramatists are associated together. Though they also worked separately, yet produced some of their finest plays in collaboration. Their masterpieces are:

a. *Faithful Shepherdess* – a pastoral play, full of charming passages and showing the lyrical talents of the poets.

b. *The Scornful Lady* – an excellent domestic comedy.

c. *The Knight of the Burning Pestle* – one of the most amusing and nimble paradise of the chivalrous romance of knight-erranty, the craze for which was widespread in the London middle-class at that time.

d. *The Maid's Tragedy and a King and No King – A King and No King* is a tragi-comedy. The scene is laid in a far off country. The play represents incestuous love and hovers on the brink of tragedy. However, the end is happy for the lovers are discovered to be no brother and sister, and are happily married in the end.

The plot is closely knit and well-constructed and the scenic and dramatic qualities of the work are surprising. The language is harmonious and the working is graceful.

10. **Philip Massinger (1583-1640).** Massinger was a prolific writer who has a number of plays to his credit. The best of them are:
    a. *A New Way to Pay Old Debts* – one of his most charming and successful comedies. It is a realistic comedy of the Jonson type.
    b. *The Roman Actor* – a tragedy full of violence, tumult and crime.
    c. *The Maid of Honour* – the most classical of his plays, one, in which, a simple plot is smoothly unfolded and one, which has unity of action and regular construction. But, the characters and situation are stereotyped and artificial. There is imitation and no invention.

    Philip Massinger's work combines within itself, the qualities, both of Fletcher and Jonson.

11. **John Ford (1586-1639).** Ford had a melancholy and morbid temperament, and gloom, tragedy and bloodshed had a strange fascination for him. Gloom, unrelieved even by a single ray of light, is his chief characteristic. A sense of fatality hangs over his tragedies; tragedy seems to be pre-destined, and in this respect, he shows his affinity with the Greeks.

    Ford's masterpiece is *It is Pity. 'She is a Whore'* is incest. It is the story of the love of a brother for his sister and its tragic consequences. "Not only does Ford show incestuous, sinful love, he even glorifies it and romanticises it." When the sister refuses herself to her brother, he kills her and re-appears with her heart on the point of his dagger, "*so that the morbid and the melodramatic are combined.*"

    Literary Career and Works

    Ford's first published work was an elegy, he wrote on the Earl of Devonshire in Fame's Memorial (1606). Before he started writing dramatic works, Ford wrote poems such as Christ's Bloody Sweat (1613), and two prose essays published as pamphlets, The Golden Mean (1613) and A Line of Life (1620).

    His first venture in dramatic work may well have been in the writing or revising of A Bad Beginning Makes a Good Ending, which was acted by the King's Men at court in 1612-1613. However, he came to limelight with his collaborative work with Thomas Dekker and William Rowley, The Witch of Edmonton in 1621.

    His reputation as a playwright rests on the plays Tis Pity She's a Whore (1624) and The Broken Heart; The 'Lover' Melanchobl (1628). Revolving around the theme of incest, Tis Pig; She's a Whore centers on the siblings Giovanni and Annabella, who insist on the rightness of their incestuous passion for each other, regardless of structures of religion, family and society. The Broken Heart, on the other hand, depicts Penthea, a noble and virtuous heroine, who is forced by her brother to leave her love, Orgilus and marry Bassanes. Ford died in 1639.

    Major Works

    - Christ's Bloody Sweat (1613)
    - The Witch of Edmonton (1621), with Thomas Dekker and William Rowley
    - The Sun's Darling (1624), with Dekker

- Tis Pity She's a Whore (1624)
- The Lover's Melancholy (1628)
- The Broken Heart (1628)
- Love's Sacrifice (1632)
- Perkin Warbeck (1629-34)
- The Fancies Chaste and Noble (1635-36)
- The Lady's Trial (1638)

12. **James Shirley (1596-1666).** According to **Charles Lamb**, Shirley is, *"the last of a great race."*

    His best tragedies are : (1) *The Traitor, and* (2) *The Cardinal* – his masterpiece. The first tragedy is a close imitation of Tourneur's *The Revenger's Tragedy,* and the second is based on Webster's Duchess of Malfi. Both are tragedies of bloodshed and horror.

    His best comedies are : (1) *The Welding.* (2) *The Changes,* (3) *The Lady of Pleasure* – his masterpiece. It foreshadows Restoration *Comedy of Manners.*

    His comedies show greater originality than his tragedies, for they paint society, its manners and fashion, its literary crazes, and all these had changed with years. In spite of its inferior wit and vigour, the *Lady of Pleasure* foreshadows **Sheridan's** *School for Scandal.*

    Shirley also wrote a number of tragic - comedies towards the end of his career, in which he exploited Spanish themes. The influence of Spain was growing, and Shirley freely exploits it in his romantic comedy, *The Imposture.*

RESTORATION PERIOD

The Restoration and the Eighteenth Century, 1660-1785

- The Restoration period begins in 1660, the year in which King Charles II (the exiled Stuart king) was restored to the English throne.
- England, Scotland, and Wales were united as Great Britain by the 1707 Act of Union.
- The period is one of increasing commercial prosperity and global trade for Britain.
- Literacy expanded to include the middle classes and even some of the poor.
- Emerging social ideas included politeness a behavioral standard to which anyone might aspire and new rhetoric of liberty and rights, sentiment and sympathy.

Religion and Politics

- The monarchical restoration was accompanied by the re-opening of English theatres (closed during Cromwell's Puritan regime) and the restoration of the Church of England as the national church.
- Church and state continued to be closely intertwined. The Test Act of 1673 required all holders of civil and military offices to take the sacrament in the Anglican Church and deny transubstantiation; those who refused (e.g., Protestant Dissenters and Roman Catholics) were not allowed to attend university or hold public office.
- King Charles II, though he outwardly conformed to Anglicanism, had Catholic sympathies that placed him at odds with his strongly anti-Catholic Parliament.
- Charles had no legitimate heir. His brother James (a Catholic) was next in line to the throne. Parliament tried to force Charles to exclude his brother from the line of succession. Charles ended this "Exclusion Crisis" by dissolving Parliament.

- The Exclusion Crisis in a sense created modern political parties: the Tories, who supported the king, and the Whigs, who opposed him.
- Once crowned, King James II quickly suspended the Test Act. In 1688, the birth of James's son so alarmed the country with the prospect of a new succession of Catholic monarchs that secret negotiations began to bring a new Protestant ruler from Europe to oust James.
- In 1688, William of Orange and his wife Mary (James's daughter) landed in England with a small army and seized power—an event known as the Glorious or Bloodless Revolution.
- James II fled to exile in France. For over 50 years his supporters (called Jacobites, from the Latin *Jacobus*, for James) mounted unsuccessful attempts to restore the Stuart line of Catholic kings to the British throne.
- Queen Anne, another of James II's daughters, was the next monarch (1702-1714). Anne's reign was a prosperous time for Britain, as the War of the Spanish Succession (1702-1713) created new trade opportunities.
- England, Scotland, and Wales were united as Great Britain by the 1707 Act of Union.
- As Anne, like Mary, had no heirs, the succession was settled upon the royal house of Hanover. A long line of King Georges (I-IV) ensued, which is why the eighteenth century is also known as the Georgian period.
- We now associate the term "Whig" with liberalism and "Tory" with conservatism, but the principles behind these two parties remained fluid and responsive to political circumstance throughout the period.
- Robert Walpole, a Whig politician who served under both King George I and George II, held a parliamentary seat from 1701 until 1742. Walpole was the first man to be described as a "prime" minister.
- During King George III's long rule (1760-1820) Britain became a major colonial power. At home and abroad, George III's subjects engaged with a new rhetoric of liberty and radical reform, as they witnessed and reacted to the revolutions in France and America.

The Context of Ideas

- The court of King Charles II championed the right of England's social elite to pursue pleasure and libertinism.
- King Charles II authorized two new companies of actors. Women began to appear on stage in female roles.
- Dogmatism, or the acceptance of received religious beliefs, was widely regarded as dangerous.
- Charles II approved the Royal Society for London for the Improving of Natural Knowledge (1662). The Royal Society revolutionized scientific method and the dispersal of knowledge.
- The specialized modern "scientist" did not exist; Royal Society members studied natural history (the collection and description of facts of nature), natural philosophy (study of the causes of what happens in nature), and natural religion (study of nature as a book written by God).
- The major idea of the period (founded on Francis Bacon's earlier work) was that of empiricism.
- Empiricism is the direct observation of experience, which infers that experience (including experimentation) is a reliable source of knowledge. John Locke, George

Berkeley, and David Hume all pursued differing interpretations of empiricism, and the concept itself had a profound impact on society and literature.

- Writers (including women such as Mary Astell) began to advocate for improved education for women during this period.
- Around 1750, the word "sentiment" evolved to describe social behavior based in instinctual feeling. Sentiment, and the related notions of sensibility and sympathy, all contributed to a growing sense of the desirability of public philanthropy and social reforms (such as charities for orphans).
- Increased importance was placed on the private, individual life, as is evident in literary forms such as diaries, letters, and the novel.

Conditions of Literary Production

- The Stage Licensing Act (1737) established a form of dramatic censorship in which the Lord Chamberlain pre-approved and licensed all plays for performance in London.
- Censorship of other print material changed radically with the 1710 Statute of Anne, the first British copyright law not tied to government approval of a book's contents.
- Copyrights were typically held by booksellers.
- The term "public sphere" refers to the material texts concerning matters of national interest and also to the public venues (including coffeehouses, clubs, taverns, parks, etc.) where readers circulated and discussed these texts.
- Thanks to greatly increased literacy rates (by 1800, 60-70 percent of adult men could read, versus 25 percent in 1600), the eighteenth century was the first to sustain a large number of professional authors. Genteel writers could benefit from both patronage and the subscription system; "Grub Street" hacks at the lower end of the profession were employed on a piecework basis.
- Women published widely.
- Reading material, though it remained unaffordable to the laboring classes, was frequently shared. Circulating libraries began in the 1740s.
- Capital letters began to be used only at the beginnings of sentences and for proper names, and the use of italics was reduced.

Literary Principles

Literature from 1660 to 1785 divides into three shorter periods of 40 years each, which can be characterized as shown below.

- 1660-1700 (death of John Dryden): emphasis on "decorum," or critical principles based on what is elegant, fit, and right.
- 1700-1745 (deaths of Jonathan Swift, Alexander Pope in 1744): emphasis on satire and on a wider public readership.
- 1745-1784 (death of Samuel Johnson): emphasis on revolutionary ideas.
- England's Augustan age was modeled on that of Rome, when Augustus Caesar re-established stability after civil war following Julius Caesar's assassination. English writers, following the restoration of King Charles II, felt themselves to be in a similar situation, in which the arts (repressed under Cromwell) could now flourish.
- English writers endeavored to formulate rules of good writing, modeled on classical works, but with a new appeal to the passions, in simple, often highly visual, language. This embrace of new (*neo*) aims and old models is called "neoclassicism."
- Horace's phrase, *ut picture poesis* (meaning "as in painting, so in poetry") was interpreted to mean that poetry ought to be a visual as well as a verbal art.

- Augustan poets began the century's focus on nature, by examining the enduring truths of human nature.
- The classical genres from which Augustan writers sought to learn included epic, tragedy, comedy, pastoral, satire, and ode. Ensuring a good fit between the genre and its style, language, and tone was crucial.
- Augustan writing celebrates wit, or inventiveness, quickness of thought, and aptness of descriptive images or metaphors.
  - The heroic couplet (two lines of rhymed iambic pentameter) was the most important verse form of Pope's age, for it combined elegance and wit. Poets also continued to use blank verse (unrhymed iambic pentameter, not closed in couplets).
  - Not just aristocrats and classically educated scholars wrote verse: ordinary people also began to write poetry, often featuring broad humor and burlesque, thereby creating a distinction between high and low verse.

Restoration Literature, 1600-1700

- Dryden was the most influential writer of the Restoration, for he wrote in every form important to the period occasional verse, comedy, tragedy, heroic plays, odes, satires, translations of classical works – and produced influential critical essays concerning how one ought to write these forms.
- Restoration prose style grew more like witty, urbane conversation and less like the intricate, rhetorical style of previous writers like John Milton and John Donne.
- Simultaneously, Restoration literature continued to appeal to heroic ideals of love and honor, particularly on stage, in heroic tragedy.
- The other major dramatic genre was the Restoration comedy of manners, which emphasizes sexual intrigue and satirizes the elite's social behavior with witty dialogue.

Eighteenth-Century Literature, 1700-1745

- The Augustan era of writers like Swift, Defoe, Pope, Addison, and Steele was rich in satire and new prose forms that blended fact and fiction, such as news, criminal biographies, travelogues, political allegories, and romantic tales.
- Early eighteenth-century drama saw the development of "sentimental comedy" in which goodness and high moral sentiments are emphasized, and the audience is moved not only to laughter, but also to sympathetic tears.
- The theatre business boomed; celebrity performers flourished; less important were the authors of the plays.
- James Thomson's poems on the seasons, beginning with "Winter" (1726), carried on the earlier poetic tradition of pastoral retreat and began a new trend of poetry focused on natural description.

The Emergence of New Literary Themes and Modes, 1740-1785

- Novelists became better known than poets, and intellectual prose forms such as the essay proliferated.
- The mid-eighteenth century is often referred to as the "Age of Johnson" after the renowned essayist Samuel Johnson, who in 1755 wrote one of the first English dictionaries to define word meanings by employing quotations taken from the best English writers, past and present.
- By the 1740s the novel rose to dominate the literary marketplace, with writers like Henry Fielding, Samuel Richardson, and Laurence Sterne defining the form and its modes of representing the private lives of individuals.

- The late eighteenth century saw a medieval revival, in which writers venerated and imitated archaic language and forms. One important development of this movement was the Gothic novel, which typically features such forbidden themes as incest, murder, necrophilia, atheism, and sexual desire.
- Late eighteenth-century poetry tends to emphasize melancholy, isolation, and reflection, in distinction to the intensely social, often satirical verse of earlier in the period.

Continuity and Revolution

- Some critics place the end of the eighteenth century at 1776 (linking it to the American Revolution); others at 1789 (the beginning of the French Revolution); still others at 1798 (the publication of Wordsworth and Coleridge's *Lyrical Ballads*).
- Later Romantic writers, who valued the idea of originality, also prized the meaning of "revolution" which signified a violent break with the past and often represented their work as offering just such a break with tradition. However, changes to literary forms and content occurred much more gradually than this use of the word "revolution" might suggest.

Literary Trends of Restoration Period

The chief literary trends of this period may be summarised as:

(1) **Rise of Neo-Classicism.** In the literature of the Restoration era, we note a sudden breaking away from old standards, just as society broke away from the restraints of Puritanism. The break with the past was almost absolute. Post-restoration literature is a converse of the previous Elizabethan Age. It is called Classical or Neo-classical, as opposed to the Elizabethan Romanticism.

(2) **Imitation of the Ancients.** Lacking the genius of the Elizabethans, the authors of the time turned to the great classical writers, in particular to the Latin writers, for guidance and inspiration. This habit, quite noticeable during the time of Dryden, deepened and hardened during the age of Pope so much so, that the later poet laid down as a final test of excellence :

> *" Learn hence for ancient rules a just esteem,*
> *To copy Nature is to copy them".*

Dryden himself was a noted classical scholar, and his translations of the classics, specially those of Virgil, are classics in their own way. Countless such other translations of ancient classics were made during the age.

(3) **French Influence.** On the literature of this period, it was the French influence which predominated. Charles II, and the literary men who accompanied him, had passed most of their time in France, and when they returned to England, they brought with them a new admiration for French literature, renounced old ideals and standards, and demanded that English poetry and drama should follow the style to which they had grown accustomed, in the gaieties of Paris life. The influence of French comedy is seen in the coarseness and indecency of the restoration comedy of Manners, of Dryden, Wycherly and Congreve; the combined influence of French and classical models of tragedy is seen in a *new genre*, the heroic tragedy. This type is well represented by Dryden's *Tyranic Love. All for love* is also heroic in spirit, though not written in the heroic measure. The foreign influence is also responsible for the growth and popularity of the *Opera* in Restoration England.

(4) **Realism and Formalism.** The Restoration Literature developed realism in a marked degree. This tendency was, at first, thoroughly bad. Later, this tendency to realism became more wholesome. While it neglected much that is romantic and interesting to youth, it led to a keener study of the practical motives which govern human action.

There was a reaction against the excesses and extravagances of both, the Elizabethans and the 'metaphysicals', headed by Donne. This reaction resulted in a marked tendency towards directness and simplicity of expression and to this excellence tendency, English literature is greatly indebted. The Restoration writers brought back the tendency to regard established rules for writing, to emphasise close reasoning rather than romantic fancy, and to use short clear-cut sentences, without an unnecessary word. Emphasis was laid on a 'correct adherence' to the rules of the ancients, as interpreted by the French.

(5) **An Age of Prose and Reason.** This tendency towards formalism and preciseness, this avoidance of enthusiasm or the exaltation of reason over passion, would justify us in calling this period, an 'age of prose and reason'. In Dryden's age, English prose begins definitely to find its feet, and a prose style is gradually evolved, which is admirably suited to the miscellaneous needs of everyday life. The critical temper of the age, the growth of science, and religious and political controversies, all fostered the rise of prose.

(6) **The Decline of the Lyric and Rise of Satire.** During this period, lyric spirit is largely on the decline and outside Dryden, there is very little lyric poetry of any worth. The bulk of the poetic output is narrative and argumentative, its purpose being to convince or persuade and not to inspire. The best poetry of the era is satirical. Dryden's *Absalom and Achitophel* is an excellent example of political satire, and his *Mreflecknoe,* that of personal satire. *The Rehearsal,* which parodies the literary vices of the time, is the finest literary satire in the language.

(7) **Perfection of the Heroic Couplet.** Another significant contribution of the age is growth and perfection of the heroic couplet. Chaucer had also used the couplet, but he cared more for the thought than for the form . But with the Restoration writers, form became all-important. Dryden made the couplet the prevailing literary fashion. Soon it became the order of the day, and excluded all other forms of versification. It was dominant in England for a full century, gradually it lost its freshness and vigour, and grew more and more mechanical and monotonous.

Restoration Poetry

(1) **John Dryden.** Dryden was a great 'Hawed poet', according to J.R. Lowell. He is the greatest of the poets who link up the Renaissance with the Neo-classical age. He has the classical passion for perfection of form – clarity, symmetry, obedience to rules, proportion, logic reasoning, architectural instinct – but he has also the Elizabethan flights of fancy and imagination, as well as their emotional ardour. He perfects the verse-form of the new poetry – the Heroic Couplet – but in his hands, it still retains that freedom and flexibility which disappeared in the hands of the poets of the next generation. He returns to blank verse towards the end of his career. He does not apply the unities regularly. He mingles comedy with tragedy. He shows an appreciation, greater than that of any of his contemporaries, of the great Elizabethan masters of poetry. Thus, he is nearer to the true classics than the poets of the next generation, referred to

as the pseudo-classics. His is a mixed art, *"in which the soundest and the truest liberties of the romantics are grafted on to a general background of order and choice"* (**Legouis**). His classicism is made of a restrained and self-disciplined romanticism.

Dryden made his mark as a satirist with the publication of *Absalom and Achitophel in* 1861. It was followed in quick succession by *The Medal Mac Flecknoe* and *Absalom and Achitophel, part II,* written in collaboration with Nahum Tate.

In the Heroic Couplet, which he perfected, Dryden gave to his followers, a fitting medium for satire and in his satirical portraits, he set an example, which was followed by all those who took part in political controversies. The satires put him at the head and front of the English men of letters. His satire is not so sly as that of Chaucer, but it is distinguished by the same good nature. There is no malice in it. He began with writing a Tory pamphlet and within a very short time, became the supreme satirist of England. He imparted epic grandeur and sublimity to political satire, which in the hands of his contemporaries, was coarse and brutal.

(2) **Samuel Butler.** Next, in order of merit among the Restoration satirists, is Samuel Butler. He was a Royalist and in his powerful satire *Hudibras,* he has satirised Puritanism, in what may be called doggerel verse, largely on the pattern of the comic doggerel of Skelton.

Hudibras is a long and witty mock-epic, aimed at the Puritans. It describes the adventures of a fanatical justice of peace, Sir Hudibras, a blusterous, ignorant, repulsive, looking Puritan knight, and of his squire Ralpho.

In *Hudibras* and *Ralpho,* the extreme types of Puritans, Presbyterians and Independents are mercilessly satirised.

Hudibras, at its best, is a burlesque, echoing Rabelais and Cervantes. It is not a regular satire, but a mock heroic poem full of scornful irony, low buffoonery, and witty epigrams. It is undoubtedly the greatest satire outside Dryden's *Absalom* and *Achitophel* and remains the masterpiece of satire in the grotesque manner.

(3) **Other Poets of the Restoration.** The other poets of the age may be dismissed summarily. The poets of the court of Charles II and James II were, in their own age, considered true poets, for they followed the prevailing fashion– classicism, the result of the imitation of French models. However, now they are little read or cared for. From an analysis of their poetry, we discern three main themes – (1) love and gallantry (2) abstract argumentation (3) philosophic ardour. Love poems, didactic poems, pindaric odes are produced in large numbers. There is much argumentation and reasoning, and passion and imagination are chilled by this cold atmosphere. Passion is scarce in the poetry of that time, and feeling exceptional; scarce also is the heat of strong imagination.

Restoration Prose

(1) **Abraham Cowley.** In the field of essay, Abraham Cowley (1618-67) is the greatest figure. He writes personal essay in the tradition of Montaigne. Just as Bacon is the founder of the Aphoristic essay, Cowley may be said to be the founder in England, of the *Personal essay* such, as that of Montainge. He is a pure essayist, "*one who has the true essay manner, and one who leads directly to Addison* and *Charles Lamb.*" His essay *On Myself* is the perfect example of what an essay should be – elegant, fresh, confidential, "constructed with as much care as a sonnet."

His essays are short familiar talks on moral subjects, strewn with anecdotes, and of a remarkably easy movement. The personal touch is present everywhere and constitutes the main charm of his eleven short, familiar talks, collectively called *The Essays.* There are also classical reminiscences and allusions and the style has the virtues of measure and order. His sentences are short and simple. He thus stands at the opposite pole to Sir Thomas Browne.

(2) **John Dryden.** The credit for creating the modern prose style must go to Dryden. It was he who forged a prose style, suitable for everyday needs of life, a flexible style which can easily adapt itself to any idea. Dryden was essentially a poet and a dramatist : his prose-work consists of numerous epistles, dedications, prefaces, introductions, etc. which he wrote for his poetic and dramatic works. Among the best of his prose works are : (1) *Essay of Dramatic Poesy* – His prose masterpiece. *(2) Essay on Satire. (3) Preface to Fables* and *(4) Essay on Epic Poetry.*

Dryden had a clear understanding of the essentials of a sound prose style. His sentences are logically linked up one with the other. Within the sentence, the words must follow a natural order or sequence, which is the order of thought. There is close connection between words and ideas. He steers a middle way between Bacon and Sir Thomas Browne and thus becomes the father of modern English prose.

Dryden's prose has a simplicity, a suppleness of movement, an ease and grace, which make it almost perfect. However, Dryden is still at fault in the building of the whole work : there are still digressions and superfluities, there are still frequent wanderings from the main thought.

Despite such shortcomings, our debt to Dryden is great. He did much towards fashioning a prose, both balanced and clear, suited to the everyday needs of life.

(3) **John Bunyan (1628-1688).** Among the religious writers of the period, one great name is that of John Bunyan. He was a tinker by profession and so did not have the benefit of any university education. His style, his very personality, was shaped entirely by one work, *The Bible.* His chief works are : (1) *Grace Abounding (1666)* – is an autobiography. *(2) The life and Death of Mr. Badman (1680). (3) The Pilgrim's Progress (1678)* – his masterpiece.

The Pilgrim's Progress narrates the pilgrimage of its hero, Christian, to the Eternal City, the vicissitudes, and dangers he suffers on the way, and the courage and fortitude, with which he faces them.

Much of the charm of this admirable work comes from its style which has only one model, *The Bible.* Bunyan feels and perceives with greatest keenness, and succeeds in communicating to his readers his feelings and perceptions.

The Pilgrim's Progress makes such interesting reading, that it has been called the precursor of the English novel.

Restoration Criticism

(1) **John Dryden.** It was **Dr. Johnson** who first called Dryden, *"the Father of English Criticism as the writer who first taught us to determine upon principles the merit of composition,"* and critic after critic has agreed with his estimate. Not that there was no criticism in England before Dryden. There had been critics like Sir Philip Sydney and Ben Jonson. But they were critics merely by chance; their critical works were merely occasional utterances on the critical art.

The earlier criticism was "magisterial" or dogmatic. They claimed to lay down rules for the guidance of poets and writers, rules which were dogmatically asserted. Dryden, on the other hand, is never magisterial or pontific; he is "sceptical"; he does not lay down the rules, he rather sets out to discover the rules for his guidance in writing plays, as well as in judging of those written by others.

It was Dryden who inaugurated the era of descriptive criticism. He was qualified for this function by his wide reading and learning. It is in his criticism that literary analysis, the dominant concern of the modern critic, emerges for the first time.

He is also a pioneer in the field of *'historical criticism.'* Critics upto the time had a very rudimentary sense of literary history. Dryden, on the other hand, shows a well-developed historical sense.

He recognises that the temperament of the French and the English differ and hence the literatures of the two countries are bound to be different. Indeed, he is the father of *'Comparative Criticism'* in England. *In the Essay* there is constant weighing and balancing of the qualities of the English drama, as against those of the French.

He is also the pioneer of liberal classicism. He has great respect for classical rules. He had read Aristotle, Horace, the Italian and French critics and has great respect for them, and has profited much from his study of both, the ancient and modern critics.

His criticism suffers from well marked faults. He is often prejudiced in favour of his own country, and his age; often his criticism is in the nature of special pleading, sometimes he commits errors of fact or conveniently ignores awkward facts. He is guilty of many inconsistencies, and is often vague and desultory. But, despite these faults, he will always be known as a great English critic.

(2) **Thomas Rhymer (1641-1713).** According to **Macaulay**, Rhymer was the worst critic that ever lived. His chief critical works are three: (1) His preface to his own translation of the French writer Rapin's *Reflections on Aristotle's 'Poetics'*, published in the year 1677, (2) *The Tragedies of the Last Age* (1678), and (3) *A Short View of Tragedy,* which appeared in 1692.

From these works, we find that Rhymer was a man of remarkable learning, for his age and country. He lacked true critical judgment and this faculty of critical judgment is an inborn faculty. Much of his criticism is prejudiced, violent, vituperative and abusive.

In the history of literary criticism, Rhymer, despite all his absurdity and folly, has a secure place, for he has to his credit the distinction of a double or even a triple, first. Says **George Watson,** "Rhymer's *Tragedies of the Last Age* is the first critical book in English which is altogether concerned with analysing the works of other Englishmen. And its main sequel, *A Short View of Tragedy,* is the first pure example of literary history in English. Thirdly, he is the first English critic to quote abundantly in the course of his practical criticism, and though his comments on quotations are merely generalised insults, they are at least particular in their application. Again and again, he poses the right questions, though he fails to give the right answers. He has a strong sense of history, wide reading and erudition, so much so, that Dryden was impressed enough by him, to reply to his savage attack on Shakespeare. He is a genius, but a perverse genius, who, despite all his gifts, fails to think rightly and judge correctly.

(3) **John Dennis (1658-1734).** In his own age, nobody paid any special attention to John Dennis. The critics of the romantic school were not much attracted by him, but in modern times, a sort of reaction has taken place in his favour.

In the Pamphlet entitled, "*Usefulness of the Stage to the Happiness of Mankind, to Government and to Religion*," Dennis replies to Jeremy Collier (see-below) and his standpoint, throughout, is ethical. He had the good taste to appreciate Dryden, and in his attack on Pope, he has the intelligence enough to point out some of his real weaknesses.

He judges Shakespeare by Rhymer's principle of poetic justice, finds a painful disregard of poetic justice in his plays, and so condemns Shakespeare.

Dennis is an advent of 'Rules' and the imitation of the ancients. He accepts the dictum : "To follow nature is to follow them." His critical doctrines are mostly derived from Aristotle and Horace, as well as from their French imitators.

(4) **Jeremy Collier (1650-1726).** No account of literary criticism during the Restoration age can be considered complete, without a mention of Jeremy Collier's *A Short View of the Profaneness and Immorality of the English Stage*. This frontal attack on the indecency and licentiousness of Restoration drama did much to focus attention on the many vulgarities and obscenities of the contemporary drama. The attack was so effective that dramatists were compelled to take note of it. As a result of Collier's attack, the Restoration drama was considered as something worthless, below the notice of decent people, all through the 18th and the 19th centuries, and it is only in the modern age that it has come to be regarded as literature once again.

Restoration Drama and Prose

The Restoration of King Charles II to the English throne in 1660 brought a new change in English literature. Previously closed theatres were opened again. New groups of writers began to write plays.

During the restoration period, we also notice some development in prose work John Dryden wrote his critical work named Essay on Dramatic Poesy. In this work, Dryden compares English drama with French drama. He points out the limitations of French drama and considers English drama to be superior to French drama. He has written it in a clear, reasonable and balanced way. His popularity as a critic is also very great.

John Bunyan wrote two allegorical prose works, namely The Pilgrims Progress and The Holy War. The first allegorical story presents Christian's difficult journey to the heaven. Its best metaphor is 'life is a journey'. The English language has borrowed some phrases and words from this work and they are commonly used in day-to-day conversation, such as Vanity Fair, Slough of Despond, Mr. Great Heart. In the second work he has presented his own experience of the civil war. Bunyan sets an example of writing prose in clear and simple style.

John Locke's prose was also clear, earnest and without ornament, though it lacks the balance in its sentences which gives Bunyan's style its charm. But Locke's Essay on the Human Understanding is one of the most important works of English philosophy. It gave a new direction of thought, not only in England but in other countries of Europe.

Samuel Pepys famous diary is also considered as a prose work. His diary could not be read until 1852, because it was written in secret signs. It gives the true picture of the social life of that time and describes some events of the time in detail. His diary, which presents himself as a hero, is very interesting and colorful work.

The Restoration Drama

We generally notice two kinds of developments in this period, namely the Heroic plays and the Comedy of Manners. These plays were quite different from Elizabethan plays in some ways. Heroic plays showed the heroic virtues in noble men, and the women were described as wonderfully beautiful. The tragic drama of this period was made up of heroic plays which were mainly written in heroic couplet. The main character in these plays was torn between the patriotic duty to their country and their duty as a lover. In these dramas we find brave heroes, beautiful women, a great deal of shouting and nonsense things.

John Dryden was a famous dramatist of restoration period. He was a genius who had perfect command over stagecraft. His plays were greatly successful on the stage. His best heroic plays were The Conquest of Granada and Aurengzebe which he had used the rhymed form. The second one is about the struggle for empire in India. His famous play All for Love deals with the tragic love of Antony and Cleopatra and was written in blank verse. It is supposed that he wrote this play by improving Shakespeare's play Antony and Cleopatra. Of the tragedies by other dramatist, there are three best heroic plays written by Thomas Otway. They include Don Carlos, The Orphan and Venice Preserved. The last one was his well- received and best play.

A new type of comedy called the Comedy of Manners appeared the end of the seventeenth century. This comedy was unique in itself. It was written in prose. These plays were witty, difficult, bright and heartless. They showed the life and manners of the upper-class society of the day. They laughed at the fashionable society, their witty and fine conversation, and their immoral behaviors. It was introduced by Sir George Etheregе. It was mainly confined to the rich, courtly and fashionable circle of London. Generally, people from the country are ridiculed for their humbleness and lack of sophistication.

George Etherege wrote The Man of Mode (1696) which shows the immoral manners of the society. William Wycherley, was a satirical dramatist. His best works were The Country Wife and The Plain Dealer.

One of the famous dramatists who wrote Comedy of Manners was William Congreve. His plays are not as coarse as the earlier plays. His Old Bachelor was a perfect comic picture of the hypocritical society. It is about an old man who pretends to hate women, but marries a bad one. The Double Dealer is about angry lovers. Love for Love is funnier and contains clever speeches and interesting, but foolish, characters. His best play is The Way of the World. It truly represents the comedy of manner of restoration period. When this play was not well received, Congreve gave up writing plays in disgust.

John Vanbrugh a professional architect wrote three successful comedies. They are The Relapse, The Provoked Wifeand The Confederacy. Then much later, another two dramatists Goldsmith and Sheridan wrote this type of comedy, Sheridan's important satirical play is The Critic which attacks drama and literary criticism in a funny way.

Restoration Drama

(1) **John Dryden.** Dryden began his dramatic career with *Wild Gallant,* a comedy after the prevailing fashion of the Restoration comedy of wit, or the comedy of manners. It was an utter failure and Pepys pronounced it, "as poor a thing as I ever saw in life". *His only significant contribution in this field is the creation of a pair of light-hearted lovers who carry on a flirtation without too much modesty certainly, and with a remarkable absence of refinement, but at the same time with some genuine affection for one another.* This pair first makes its appearance in the *Wild Gallant,*

and is later perfected and refined in *The Maiden Queen.* It should also be noted that Dryden's lovers are, for the most part, free from the brutal heartlessness and cruelty of those of Etherege and other restoration writers of comedy.

Dryden's heroic plays even the best of them, like *The Tyrranic Love, Conquest of Granada, Aurengzebe, etc.*, reveal the heroic kind at its best and worst. He was a man of genius, who had perfect mastery over stage craft, and so, despite their many artificialities, extra ordinary absurdities and improbabilities, and indecencies, his plays were immensely successful on the stage, and this was his first object.

However, though the faults of the heroic drama were veiled by the force of Dryden's genius, they easily exposed this genre to ridicule in the hands of lesser playwrights.

Dryden himself was getting bored with the heroic couplet, and in *Aurengzebe* (1675) he bade good-bye to his "long loved mistress Rhyme", and turned to the blank-verse of Shakespeare and Milton. He now came out, alongwith many other blank verse plays, with *All for Love* (1878) and *Don Sebastian* (1690), the two plays, on which, his fame as a dramatist chiefly rests, and which, of all his plays, are better equipped for competition for a place among the dramas of all time. Of the two, *All for Love* is generally considered superior.

Dryden's genius was not dramatic, and he had no "effective call" in that direction. He took to play writing because it was the shortest literary cut to fame and fortune.

His plays suffer from a number of weaknesses. Since he wrote for money, he had to cater to the public taste. He had to please to live. Hence it is that, in general, he is so indecent and coarse, that most of his plays are regarded as unreadable, and except for *All for Love,* have been confined only to the shelves of scholars. He had no understanding of the human heart, and this has adversely affected his characterisation.

Dryden's limitations are so glaring that they have obscured *his real greatness as a dramatist.* But, his mastery over his craft was such, that on the boards, his plays acted well and his faults were forgotten. Many of its satiric touches distinguish it from the comedy of manners which, in the main, is not satirical.

An Essay of Dramatic Poesy

Dryden's An Essay of Dramatic Poesy was probably written in 1666 during the closure of London theatres due to plague. It was published in 1688, the essay can be seen as a defence of drama as an art form. The essay is structured as a dialogue/debate between four speakers – Eugenius, Crites, Lisideius and Neander.

These stand for William Davenant, Robert Howard, Roger Boyle and Dryden respectively. The essay begins with a reference to a naval battle between the British and Dutch on 3rd June, 1665, in the English Channel.

Four speakers named above observe this battle from a barge floating on Thames. After the battle gets over and the English navy wins, the four speakers begin discussing English drama. Eugenius literally means 'a well-bom genius'. He favours the modems over the ancients, arguing that the moderns have excelled over the ancients because of having learned and profited from their example. The name Crites comes from the Greek word 'critic' or one who is able to express a reasoned judgement on something. He argues in favour of the ancients and applauds the observance of the three unities in drama. He considers Ben Jonson as the greatest English playwright because he followed the ancients' example by adhering to the unities.

Lisideius' name is probably based on the (royal emblem of France, the fleurdelis. He argues in favour of the modern day French playwrights. He believes that French drama is superior to English drama because of their adherence to the classical unities, because of their focus on one plot and one character and because of their use of narration.

The name Neander literally means 'the new man'. He favours the modems, but does not disparage the ancients. He states that English are best at 'The lively imitation of nature' (human nature), conceding that while French poesy is beautiful, it is also lifeless like a 'statue'. He critiques 'the barrenness of the French plots' and praises the 'variety and copiousness of the English plays'. Neander also goes on to defend the genre of tragicomedy since it increases the effectiveness of both tragic and comic elements by way of contrast. He indicates his preference for Shakespeare over Ben Jonson.

Shakespeare "had the largest and most comprehensive soul," while Jonson was "The most Earned and judicious writer which any theater ever had." Before Dryden, the English had no native criticism on drama.

Dryden's essay thus breaks new ground and makes serious efforts to develop a theory of drama by discussing ancient, contemporary French and English drama and by comparing the works of various individual English dramatists and the foreign dramatists.

Major Works

- The Indian Emperor (tragedy, 1665)
- Annus Mirabilis (poem, 1667)
- The Enchanted Island (comedy), 1667, an adaptation with William D'Avenant of Shakespeare's The Tempest
- Secret Love, or The Maiden Queen (1667)
- An Essay of Dramatick Poesie (1668)
- An Evening's Love (comedy, 1668)
- Tyrannick Love (tragedy, 1669)
- The Conquest of Granada (1670)
- Marriage a La Mode (1672)
- Aureng-zebe (1675)
- All for Love (1678)
- Oedipus (heroic drama), 1679, an adaptation with Nathaniel Lee of Sophocles' Oedipus
- Absalom and Achitophel (1681)
- The Medal (1682)
- Threnodia Augustalis (1685)
- A Song for St Cecilia's Day (1687)
- Amphitryon (1690)
- Don Sebastian (1690)

- Love Triumphant (1694)
- The Works of Virgil (1697)
- Alexander's Feast (1697)
- Fables, Ancient and Modern (1700)

(2) **William Congreve (1670-1729).** Congreve, the supreme master of the comedy of manners, wrote all his comedies, before he was thirty. During the last years of his life, he gave up writing for the stage and spent the rest of his time as a popular social figure, largely supported by government pensions.

Congreve's first play is *Old Bachelor,* a perfect piece of comic portraiture remarkable for a young man of twenty-three. It was an immediate success. His next play was the *Double Dealer,* not as successful as the *Old Bachelor.*

Two years after the *Double Dealer,* Congreve came out with his next play *Love for Love* (1695), which is wholly comic from first to last. It was a great success. Congreve realised the mistake of mixing tragic seriousness with cynic mirth and in the new play, he rectified that error by presenting pure comedy.

By general consent, Congreve's best comedy is the *Way of the World.* As a work of art and as a pure comedy of manners, it is considered to be the best of the comedies in this *genre.* The *Way of the World* is a classic of English comedy because of its many artistic excellences, such as flashes of wit, and brilliant, sparkling dialogues. Construction, characterization, dialogues, are alike, brilliant.

His plays are a faithful reflection of the upper-class life of his day, but their undoubted immorality is saved from being objectionable by brilliant wit, a hard finish and a total lack of realism.

(3) **John Vanbrugh (1664-1726).** His best comedies are : (1) *The Relapse* (1696), (2) *The Provok'd Wife* (1697), *and* (3) *The Confederacy* (1705). Vanbrugh's plays lack the art and elegance of Congreve's, but they are full of energy and genial humour. He is fond of farcical situations, and his characters are often mere caricatures, but his plots, though often immoral, are soundly constructed. In his hands, comedy comes down from the higher level to the lower depths of farce. His plots are designed, not as those of Congreve for the expression of fancies of the mind, but for the elaboration of sex-situations. In intellectual force, Vanbrugh's work is on a lower plane than Congreve's, but by way of compensation, he has a more genial humour and a genius for farcical situations, which Congreve did not have.

(4) **George Farquhar (1677-1707).** The main plays of Farquhar are *Love in a Bottle, The Recruiting Officer* and *The Beaux Stratagem.* His plots are more carefully constructed than those of Congreve, but he lacks the wit of Congreve. He breaks away from the tradition of the true comedy of manners. Vanbrugh had already broken away from it by broadening its boundaries and sweetening its humours. With Farquhar, the break becomes complete. The artificial element is still to be found in the earlier plays, but in the latter ones, he sets aside the gallants and fops, and deals with humble folk, and with a more diversified life. In his rapidly developing humanity, and his growing respect for moral standards, Farquhar looks forward to the dramas of Steele and other dramatists of the succeeding age. He is a connecting link of great significance.

(5) **Thomas Otway (1652-85) –** Thomas Otway wrote a number of heroic plays. His reputation rests on two plays : *The Orphan* and *Venice Preserved.* Otway strikes

the note of deep pathos which is its distinguishing feature. The play has a calmness of tone and absence of rant unusual in its day. *Venice Preserved* is his finest work. Here the tragedy is on a grander scale than in *The Orphan,* and the characters are skilfully handled– especially those of Jaffer and Pterre. The play has a rugged and sombre force, and reveals a considerable skill in working out a dramatic situation.

Otway has the genuine passion which Dryden often lacked and his tragedies are not marred by such distortions of human life and character, as abound both, in Dryden and in the Jacobean dramatists. His tragedies are the forerunners of the sentimental tragedy of the turn of the century.

(6) **Nathaniel Lee (1653-92) –** He wrote many tragedies, of which the prominent ones are *Nero (1674). Sophonisha (1676), The Rival Queens (1677),* and *Mithridates (1678).* Lee rejoiced in ambitious subjects, in the splendour of his settings and in great historical personages. In the plays of Lee, construction is weak, the psychology almost always rudimentary, and the style is full of bombast and conceit, exhibiting bad taste. As a result, "During his own time Lee's name became a byword to distinguish a kind of wild, raving style, which in part, at least, seems to have been a product of his madness. But he can write well when the spirit is in him; he has a command of pathos, and all through his work he has touches of real poetic quality".

(7) **Nikholas Rowe (1674-1718) –** Rowe was made Poet Laureate in 1715. His best known plays are *Temerlane* (1702), *The Fair Penitent* (1703), and the popular *Jane Shore* (1714). **Johnson** says of him, "His reputation comes from the reasonableness of some of his scenes, the elegance of his diction, and the suavity of his verse." His tragedies are the best extant examples of the *She-tragedy,* which succeeded the Heroic-tragedy.

AUGUSTAN AGE: 18TH CENTURY LITERATURE

THE AGE OF 18TH CENTURY

The period of 18th century is known by a variety of names.

(1) **The Augustan Age.** The original Augustan Age was the brilliant literary period of Vergil, Horace, and Ovid under the Roman emperor Augustus (27 B.C. – A. D. 14). Since the eighteenth century, however, the term has also been applied to the period in England from approximately 1700 to 1745, on the ground that the leading writers of the period (such as Pope, Swift, Addison, and Steele) greatly admired the Roman Augustans, themselves drew the parallel between the two ages, and deliberately imitated their literary forms and subjects, their emphasis on social concerns, and their ideals of moderation, decorum, and urbanity. The poet Goldsmith was the first to call it, "The Augustan Age".

(2) **Neo-classical Age (The Age of Pope and Dr. Johnson).** The period of English history from 1700 to 1798, commonly referred to as the Pseudo-classical or Neo-classical age, may conveniently be divided into two; *The early half, from 1700-1740,* may be called the Age of Pope, for Pope was the leading poet and man of letters of the period, *the later half of the century from 1740-1798* may be called the Age of Dr. Johnson, for Dr. Johnson was its leading literary figure. During this time, first Queen Anne and then the three Grorges ruled over England. Matthew Arnold refers to the period as, "Our admirable and indispensable 18th century", for the age saw the rise of the social Essay and the Novel, and the development of the modern prose style. As during the Restoration Era, in this age also, the French influence pre-dominated and neo-classicism became more rigid and stringent.

(3) **The Age of Prose and Reason. Matthew Arnold** called the age, *"the age of prose and reason."* The age chronicled the triumph of English prose. The new interests of the age, arising from the changed political and social condition, demanded expression through pamphlets, magazines, and newspapers. The result is the development of prose, a development which astonishes us by its rapidity and excellence. (The greatest names in the period are the names of prose writers—*Addison, Steelse, Swift, Defoe Gibbon and Burke*. Indeed, *Poetry itself becomes prosaic, for it is used not for creative works of imagination, but for ethical essays, for satire, and for criticism.*) It is used for purposes which are suitable for prose and not for poetry. It is polished and refined in the hands of Pope, but it lacks fire, passion, enthusiasm—qualities proper to poetry. It does not appeal to the imagination, rather it seeks to please us by its realism, wit and common sense.

A hard intellectuality and rationality — prosaic qualities — reign supreme, even in the poetry of the era.

LITERARY TRENDS OF THE AGE

(A) Literary Trends In First Half of The 18th Century

Literary trends of first half of the 18th century may be expressed in following heads :

(1) **Dominance of Prose and Realism.** The 18th century society had been changed completely. Barbarity and corruption were prevalent in society. Women's condition was worst. Under these circumstances 'straight forward and realistic approach' replaced 'beauty and imagination' from literature. Consequently prose was used frequently. Poets are guided by, *"Cold reason"* and not by the, *"fine madness"* which, as *Dryden* points out, should possess a poet's brain. Their eyes do not roll with fine frenzy.

(2) **The Rise of the Novel.** In the field of literature the most important phenomenon is the complete collapse of drama and the rise of the novel. Expansion of education and the rise of a new class of readers and publishers, the new patrons of literature, the circulating libraries and the increased leisure, enjoyed even by the lower sections of society, all contribute to the popularity of the novel. This new kind of prose fiction reflects the life of the middle classes and is distinguished from the earlier romances by its realism. There is not even one dramatist of outstanding merit in the age, while we have four outstanding novelists – Fielding, Richardson, Smollett and Sterne – writing practically at the same time.

(3) **Emergence of the Social Essay.** Another outstanding feature of the literature of the age is the emergence of the social essay and the, *"middle style"* in prose. *Addison's* prose is the model of the middle style. We now find a prose suitable for miscellaneous purposes – for newspaper and political work, for the essay, for history and biography. We can very well say that with Addison begins the modern era in English prose. In the hands of *Addison* and *Steele* the Essay takes a great stride forward. They use it for the improvement of social manners and morals. In political prose, *Swift* is the outstanding figure : and in religious writing his *Tale of a Tub* has a similar importance.

(4) **Claim of Having Classical Approach.** The age was classical. For the writers of the period claimed that the classical writers of ancient Greece and Rome were their models and that they were imitating the ancient classics. They insisted on beauty of form, and definiteness of expression which they found were the leading traits of their models. They were guided by reason, good sense, and wit; they wanted order and balance and every kind of excess and irregularity was abhorrent to them. *Thus they were classics, for they claimed to follow the classical qualities of moderation, tolerance, and good sense.*

(5) **Pseudo-classicism.** But in reality, they were not *classical* but *'pseudo-classics'* or sham or false classics. As **H. Grierson** in his *The Background to English Literature* establishes, the hallmark of the ancient classical literature is a harmonious balance between from and substance. This harmonious balance of form and substance is distributed in the Age of Pope. The writers of the period care for form, not for the weight of matter; they care only for manner, for artistic finish and polish, but not for genuine poetic inspiration. The content, thought and feeling, is subordinated to form.

(6) **Critical Approach.** The French influence predominated during the period. *"The artificiality, the polish and the refinement of social life infected literature also. The general tendency of literature was to look at life critically, to emphasise the intellect rather than imagination, the form of, rather than the content of, a sentence.* They had a great regard for *"correctness"* and for the avoidance of extremes.

(7) **Literature of the Town.** The literature of this period was *the literature of the town and the fashionable upper circles of the city of London.* The writers claimed to follow *"nature"* but the nature they follow is *"human nature"* as revealed by the fashionable circles of London. It does not deal with *"nature"* that fascinates us in Wordsworth and Shelley.

(8) **Lack of Epic Dramatic and Lyric Poetry.** Drama and epic, the grandest forms of poetry, were beyond the reach of the writers of this period. They lacked lyric intensity and could not write lyrics. They excel only in one kind of poetry, *i.e., Satiric,* which is certainly not the highest or the best kind of poetry. This prevalent tendency to satire results from the unfortunate union of politics with literature. Nearly every writer of the day was used by the two political parties to hurl satires over the heads of each other. No doubt, the satires of Pope, Swift and Addison have rare brilliance and are the best in the language, but they cannot be called great literature. These giants were capable of far better things than those which occupied them all their lives.

(9) **The Use of Only One Metre – the Heroic Couplet.** *Heroic Couplet* is the only verse form which they perfected and in which they excelled. It was used with rare brilliance and effect for satirical and intellectual poetry. But excessive refinement led to monotony and rigidity in the hands of the followers of Pope.

(B) Literary Trends in Later Half of the 18th Century

Following are the chief characteristics of literature of later period.

(1) **The Classical Tradition.** The poets of the period, like Gray, eminently represent the persistence of classical dogma. The classical age was an age of prose and reason. The poetry of the age is as prosaic as it was in the hands of Pope. The poets are still dominated by the classical tradition, they adhere to the closed couplet and show a marked dislike for blank verse. Their critical doctrines are those of the previous age; and much of their work is marred by Augustan prejudices. Periphrasis, personifications, rhetorical declamations, and other artifices of the Augustans continue to be used.

(2) **The Romantic Spirit.** However, there is a strong tendency among writers of the rising generation to abandon the practice of the school of Pope, and seek fresh subjects, fresh forms, and fresh modes of feeling and expression. Emotion, passion and imagination invade poetry more and more to the destruction of the old intellectuality and narrow principles. The dead hand of the past still checks and retards the new spirit, but it is markedly present in the works of a number of poets like Gray, Collins, Blake, Young, Cowper, etc.

(3) **A Return to Nature.** A real feeling for the world of leaves and flowers. This feeling for nature was shown as early as Thomson's *Seasons* (1730), it grew stronger and reached its culmination in the poetry of Wordsworth. Poets gradually turned away from the "town" and took more and more interest in country life. The works of poets, *like Gray, Cowper, Burns and Crabbe,* show a marked sympathy for the poor the down-trodden.

(4) **Increasing Preference for simplicity.** *There is a distinct break-away from the artificial "poetic diction" of Pope and his school,* and an increasing preference for simplicity and force in language. *There is a rejection of the conventional "heroic couplet"* and an adoption of other verse forms.

(5) **Revival of Colourful Middle Ages.** *In their search for fresh themes, writers turn to supernatural stories and legends.* There is a revival of interest in the past, especially in the colourful Middle Ages. The magic and mystery commonly associated with the Dark Age inspire and thrill a growing number of poets.

(6) **Emphasis on Individual Interests.**

Emphasis is now laid on individual inspiration, intuition and imagination, and not on the classic rules of composition.

(7) **Transition from Pseudo-classicism to Romanticism:** The age of Johnson is remarkable for the transition from the Pseudo-classicism of the early 18th century to the Romanticism of the opening years of the 19th. It witnessed the rise of those new tendencies which came to their own with the turn of the century. Writers, like Gray, Johnson, *etc.*, may still cling to the classical tradition, but they are definitely men of the past; the future lies with the new spirit. Even the poetry of such writers reflects the rising trends.

Poetry in The Augustan Age

The Augustan era in English poetry is noted for its fondness for wit, urbanity, and classical (mostly Roman) forms and values. Named for the Augustan period or "Golden Age" in Roman poetry, the English Augustans both translated and modeled their own verse after poets such as Virgil, Horace, and Propertius. This period is marked by the end of the Restoration era at its beginning, approximately 1690, and by the death of Alexander Pope in 1744. Thc Augustans were eventually overshadowed by the growth of English Romanticism. Practitioners of Augustan models included Pope, John Dryden, John Gay, Jonathan Swift, and Samuel Johnson. These poets are famous for their long verse narratives or mock epics, which are often satirical and imitate classical models. Prime examples include The Rape of the Lock by Pope and MacFlecknoe by Dryden. These poems take features found in classical epics-invocations to deities, grandiose speeches, battles, divisions into cantos-and apply them to trivial subjects (in MacFlecknoe, lambasting the work of a minor poet; in The Rape of the Lock, a clandestine haircut). These conventions would have been well-known to readers of the day, and the juxtaposition between high rhetoric and low subject matter adds to the humor of the poem. Pope and Dryden were masters of the heroic couplet a verse form first introduced by Geoffrey Chaucer in the fourteenth century.

POETRY OF THE AGE

(A) Classicism

(1) **Alaxander Pope.** Pope is the poet who represents best the early 18th century. Its literary merits and defects are alike conspicuous in his verse and he stands immeasurably above the numerous versifiers who may be said to belong to his school. Pope was the child of his age. The literary characteristics of the age are emphasis on wit and good sense, a genius for satire, a regard for correctness and the avoidance of extremes. The poets are not inspired by passion or enthusiasm : wit takes precedence over imagination, nature is concealed by artifice. All these merits and demerits of the age are faithfully represented by the poetry of Pope. It

was an age of, "prose and reason" and even the poetry of the age is prosaic. A hard intellectuality and rationality, qualities proper to prose, mark the poetry of Pope. His themes too are prosaic – criticism, moral philosophy and satire – which require critical analysis and discussion. He is the most "correct" of English poets. Indeed, as **Johnson** points out, Pope wrote for his age, and he exhibits extraordinary art in ministering to the tastes of the age. Its critical, commonplaces are admirably summed up by him in his *Essay on Criticism;* and his *Essay on Man* summarises the current Ethical Code. His satires throw a flood of light not only on the characters of the poetasters of Grub Street, but also on the decline of educational and literary standards, and on the pedantry and corruption in high places. **Leslie Stephen** is, therefore, right when he says that not writer reflects, *"so clearly and completely the spirit of his own days."*

However, it is to be noted that Pope describes only the life of the upper classes of the city of London. The life of the lower sections of society, life of the dwellers in the countryside – shepherds, farmers, etc., is ignored. Even the life of the upper classes has been dealt with only superficially. He deals only with the surface glitter, and ignores the reality behind.

His works may be summarised in three periods of his carrier :

(i) The first period of his career lasts from 1704-1713. The more important works of this period are :

(a) The Pastorals, (b) Windsor Forest, (c) Essay on Criticism, (d) The Rape of the Lock, (e) Some minor poems – The Temple of Fame, The Messiah, etc.

(ii) The second period, extending from 1713 to 1725, *is the period of the great Homer translations.* The translation of the *Illiad* was begun in 1717, and was completed by 1720. The *Odyssey* appeared in 1725 and 1726. It was translated with the help of two classical scholars, Fanton and Broome. The two translations were perfectly successful and brought Pope immense wealth and popularity.

In this middle period, Pope created some original poetry. The two pieces, *Elosia to Abelard, and the Elegy to the Memory of an Unfortunate Lady* are Popes' chief achievements in emotional poetry. He rises to true poetic greatness towards the close of the *Elegy.*

(iii) The last and the greatest period of Pope's poetic output, from 1725-1740, may also be called the *Twickenham or the Horation period.* During this period, the poet was writing his masterly satires on the hack-writers of Grub Street, carrying of his war of words with them. The masterpieces of this great period are :

(a) The Dunciad, (b) Moral Essays, including *The Essay on Man. (c) The Limitations of Horace and the Epistle to Dr. Arbuthnot. (d) Two Dialogues, entiled 1758.*

(2) **Matthew Prior (1664-1721).** His contribution to satire is noteworthy. His parody of Dryden's *The Hind and the Panther* entitled *Story of the Country Mouse,* and his satire on contemporary philosophy, entitled *Alima, The Progress of the Mind,* in which he traces the advance of the soul from the ankles to the head, are among the best of his satires. However, Prior is best known not for his satire, but for his numerous poems for children. He recalls Samuel Butler in his handing of the octosyllabic couplets.

(3) **John Gay (1685-1732).** He showed a better talent for satire than Prior. His most important work *The Beaggr's Opera* is a satire on the Italian opera so popular in the age. *Trivia, or the Art of Walking the Streets in London* is a parody of *The Georgics of* Virgil. It is the most famous of the fashionable, "town eclogues," written also by such other poets as Swift, Lady Mary Wortley Montague, and some others. Gay's satire is mostly impersonal and good-natured and gay. A delightful, refreshing irony marks all his satire.

Literary Career and Works

Gay had a deep love for literature and began his career as a poet and ballad-lyric writer. He had a quirky sense of humour and a talent for writing satirical and ironic pieces. His first published poem was a parody, Wine. His first play was The Mohawks which was never produced. His second play, The Wifi of Bath, was produced at Drury Lane, a prominent theatre, in 1713. His poem Rural Sports first appeared in 1713. It was an evocative work that described in detail the country side and dealt with hunting and fishing. This poem was dedicated to Alexander Pope who was his lifelong supporter and a close friend.

He found his first big success in 1714 with the play, The Shepherd Week, a series of six mock classical poems drawn from rural English life. The purpose of writing this was to ridicule the Arcadian pastorals of Ambrose Philips. In 1716 his poem Trivia or, The Art of Walking on the Streets of London, was published. This poem was highly appreciated for its vivid descriptions of London and is considered to be his finest poem.

Though he produced many great works of literature over his long and productive career, his ballad opera The Beggar's Opera is the best known of his works. The ballad opera parodied the King's government and his Chief Minister, Robert Walpole. He used the symbols of highwaymen and thieves to depict the moral degradation of the society.

He died at the age of 47 on 4th December, 1732 in London)

(4) **Edward Young (1683-1765).** Edward Young was one of the first imitators of Horace in the eighteenth century. **Sherburn** writes of him, "The first Horatian satires to achieve real success were the seven that Edward Young published in 1725-28, as *Love of Fame, the Universal Passion.* Practically all of Pope's satires post-dated those of Young, which were highly praised.

(5) **Dr. Johnson (1709-84).** Dr. Johnson comes next only to Pope among the verse satirists of the eighteenth century. His two verse-satires are *London (1738)* and *The Vanity of Human Wishes* is according to **Edmund Gosse,** "a much finer and more accomplished production." Johnson's style is heavy-handed and serious, and his attitude, too, is Juvenalian in its pessimism and noble disdain.

Literary Career and Works

At Oxford, Johnson translated Pope's Messiah in Latin, which was published in 1731. In 1734, he managed to complete a translation of Father Jeronymo Lobo's Account of Abyssinia, which became his first published book. In May 1738, Johnson's first major work, the poem 'London Imitation of the Third Satire a fluvenal, was published anonymously. This was followed by his works, Lify of Mr Richard Savage, The Vanigr of Human Wishes (Imitation of The Tenth Satire of juvenal) and the play Irene.

Johnson's most monumental work, A Dietianaiy of the English Language was begun in 1746, when a group of publishers approached him to create a dictionary of English language. He worked for 9 years on this work, which was finally published in 1755. This work established his literary reputation.

Johnson's other important works are hisvsatirical Rasselas, Prince of Abyssinia, The Life of Ascham, Notes to Shakespeare and The Fountains: A Fairy Tale. He is also known for hislessays for the periodicals, The Rambler (1750-52) and The Idler (1758-60) and The Lives of the Poets (1779-81). In 1762, when George III came to the throne, Johnson was provided with a pension of £ 300 per year. During his late years, Johnson published his A Journgl to the Western Islands of Scotland and Prayers and Meditations.

He died in 1784 at the age of 75 and was buried in Westminster Abbey.

> **LONDON**
>
> **Imitation of the Third Satire of Juveual**
>
> - The full title of the Poem is London—*Imitation of the Third Satire of Juvenal.*
> - Johnson transforms Juvenal's' cultural satire into a political one with its focus on the corruption in the court of King George II.
> - It is a satire which addresses the condition of 18th century England, marked by various changes on the personal and public front.
> - Johnson utilises the figure of Thales to develop his socio-political critique of the metropolitan space, represented by London. The poem begins with Thales leaving London for the countryside.

(B) The Pre-Romantics

The period 1730-70 marks the beginning of movement from one distinct school or convention of English poetry towards another. To the first the epithet *Pseudo-Classical* is usually applied, and to the second the epithet *Romantic.* From as early as 1730, there were poets, including Thomson, Cowper, Collins and Gray, who formed a bridge, as it were between the two schools, and whose works have certain characteristics of both. These poets called Pre-romantics, have been discussed bellow : -

(1) **Gray.** Gray is the central figure in that drift away from the dominant school of Classicism towards the rising school of Romanticism, which began with the publication of Thomson's *The Seasons* in 1730, and which reached its culmination with the publication of the *Lyrical Ballads* in 1798.

In the early poetry of Gray there is nothing romantic. In these early years of his career he was a complete classicist. His early odes-*Ode to Eton, Ode to Spring* and *Ode* to *Adversity* are examples of his classicism.

The famous *Elegy* marks a transition from the early period of classicism to the later period of Romanticism. It has many classical touches. It is the masterpiece of the *"Il Penseroso"* school then in fashion and has summed up for all English readers and for all times the poetry of the tomb. It has also an abundance of and for all times the poetry of the tomb. It has also an abundance of personifications and other artifices of the classics. Despite its many conventional touches it is *"Romantic in its mood, and stands as a transition between his period of classicism and his more highly imaginative poetry."* We may add that besides *its romantic mood, The Elegy is also romantic in its true, humanitarian note and its feeling for nature.* In its subjective tone, in its vague aspirations, fondness for solitude and gloomy meditation, it is quite different from other poems of the fashionable school.

The two *Pindaric odes* show Gray well on the way towards romanticism. *"The two odes, specialty 'The Bard', are the most imaginative poetry Gray ever produced, and were distinctly in advance of the age."* In these *Odes,* Gray does no longer follow his age, *he strikes out ahead of it and helps to mould its literary tostes.* From this time, the people began to regard his as a romantic and looked for wild and extravagant production from his hand. But besides these works Gray, the romantic, is still unable to free himself from the shackles of classicism.

This freedom came with his translations from, and adaptations of, Norse and Welsh mythology and poetry. In *The* Fatal *Sisters, The Descent of Odin, and The Triumphs of Owen,* Gray is strictly a romantic.

Gray could not harmonise these two contrary tendencies as was done by Keats at a later date. But there is no denying the fact that he was a precursor of romanticism, one who gave the romantic impulse, *"a practical poetic form"* for the first time and expressed its chief features in his poetry.

An Elegy Written in a Country Churchyard

- Thomas Gray's Elegy Written in a Country Churchyard was first published in 1751.
- The Elegy is usually said to have been inspired by the death of Clay's friend, Richard West in 1742.
- The poem consists of 128 lines divided into 32 quatrains including three stanzas devoted to the epitaph.
- The poem invokes the classical idea of memento mori, a Latin phrase, which states plainly to all mankind, 'remember that you must die.'
- The speaker of the poem sees a country churchyard at sunset, which impels him to meditate on the nature of human mortality.
- The speaker muses on the inevitability of death.
- The speaker also deals with the futility of all human ambitions and aspirations since 'the paths of glory lead but to the grave.
- Both the rich and the poor desire to be remembered after death. The dying man desires some dear person to shed tears on his death as a mark of mourning.
- According to W.V. Moody and R.M. Lovett, "the Elegy is the finest power of that literature of melancholy which Gray may be said to be haunted by a Hamlet like melancholy and sense of frustration."

(2) **Collins.** Gray and Collins, the two greatest precursors of the Romantic Revival in England, have always been grouped together in literary history. There are, no doubt, certain superficial reassembles between the two poets. In their own times, the two stood close together as lyric poets and apart from the other poets of their day. Both of them were violently criticised in their own age as poets, who sought for "new beauties." Both of them wrote Odes at a time when lyric poetry was not in fashion, and both avoided the satirical and social poetry which was the reigning taste of the day.

Collins was certainly superior to Gray in lyrical and emotional content. His Odes are superior to those of Gray. There is no doubt that in his Eclogues, Collins is inferior to the other poetic compositions of Gray. It has been said that, "Collins of *The Odes,* at his best, is the poet of all time in general and no time in particular : the Collins of the *Eclogues* is everywhere the poetaster of the eighteenth century." *The Odes* of Collins retrieve his position and make him superior to Gray in respect of lyricism and emotional power.

But Gray is the superior to Collins in architectural design and ornament in poetry. It does not mean that Collins has no design or ornament but, as a finished workman, Collins is often open to reproach. It is worth noting that both, Gray and

Johnson, blame him on just the same grounds. Collins structure and decision are often obscure and unintelligible. His images, word and phrases are often carelessly chosen. These defects are not found in Gray.

Gray and Collins are the two last lyrical poets of England whose art is consciously directed and held in check by the Pseudo-classic school of the early 18th century. Both of them were also alive to the rising school of romanticism, but in both, to a very great extent, the romantic impulse was suppressed by their much greater art-consciousness and the spirit of Greek and Roman Literature.

Literary Career and Works

His first verses were published in a six penny pamphlet on The Royal Nuptials. His Persian Eclogues (1742) were published when he was only 17. This was followed by Verses Humbly Addressed to Sir Thomas Hanmer in 1743. In 1749, he also published the Elegy on Thomson, and the Dirge in Cymbeline. In the beginning of 1750, he composed the Ode on the Popular Superstitions of the Highlands. Collins is also well-known for his twelve odes- Ode to Fear, Ode to Pity, Ode on the Poetical Character, Ode for Music, Ode to Evening, Ode to Mercy, Ode to Simplicity, Ode Written In The Beginning of The Year 1746, Ode to Liberty, Ode to a Lady on the Death of Colonel Ross, Ode to Peace and The Manners An Ode.

Collins died on 12th June 1759.

(3) **James Thomson (1700-48).** A typical transitional poet, James belongs to the first half of the eighteenth century. He began writing when Pope was at the height of his popularity, yet he broke away from the tradition of his schools to explore, "fresh woods and pastures." His *The Seasons* published in 1730 is an important landmark in the history of English poetry. He bade good-bye to the heroic couplet, and used other measures – the blank verse and the Spenserian stanza. Spenser and Milton, rather than Dryden and Pope, are his masters. *The Seasons* is the first really important poem in which Nature becomes the central theme. Its historical significance is great, for its influence was wide and all-pervasive. It was widely imitated by scores of poets. From this time onwards, Nature became increasingly prominent in English poetry.

Thomson's *Castle of Indolence* (1748) is in Spenserian stanzas as captures much of the luxuriant, imaginative colour of the Elizabethan poet. Thomson anticipates the romantics in his love of nature in his treatment of new subjects, in his strong imagination, and in his giving up of the heroic couplet. But his diction often degenerates into typical neo-classical bombast and artificiality.

Literary Career and Works

Thomson went to London in 1725 where he earned his living as a tutor. He published his masterpiece, a long blank verse poem in four parts, called The Season. The first part Winter appeared in 1726, but its dedication procured only 20 guineas, not a patron. The poem was very well received, however, and it was followed by Summer (1727) and Spring (1728). The poems were applauded and imitated. Thomson's belief that the scientist and poet must collaborate in the service of God, as revealed through nature, found its best expression into the memory of Sir Isaac Newton (1727). The whole poem The Seasons including Autumn, was published in 1730.)

(4) **Oliver Goldsmith (1728-74).** Goldsmith was the contemporary of **Dr. Johnson,** as **Thomson** was that of Pope. He was as essentially a conservative. In literary theory, as Dr. Johnson, of whose "Club" he was an eminent member. He has left behind him two important poems, *The Traveller* (1764) and *The Deserted Village* (1770), and

both are in heroic couplets. The first poem is didactic and is concerned with the description and criticism of the various places and people of Europe which Goldsmith visited as a tramp. The second poem is rich in natural descriptions, and is vibrant with a peculiar note to sentiment and melancholy which fore-shadows nineteenth century romantics. The substance of both the poems foreshadows the rising romanticism of the day, but the diction is artificial and pompous in the pseudo-classical tradition of the past.

Literary Career and Works

For some years, he worked as an apothecary's assistant, school usher, physician and as a hack Writer. However, he soon rose to fame with his Enquiry into the Present State of Polite Learning in Europe. Goldsmith also came to the notice of Samuel Johnson's, who invited Goldsmith to join his exclusive Turk's Head Club. Through Johnson's patronage, Goldsmith began to publish his first master works, including the novel The Vicar of Wakefield.

His other works include The Citizen of the World (a collection of essays, 1762), An Elegy on the Death of a Mad Dog (ironic poem, 1766), The Goad-Natured Man (comic play, 1768), She Stoops to Conquer (a farce, 1773) and The Deserted Village (a poem on rural population and the Enclosure Movement, 1770).

Goldsmith died on 4th April, 1774, after suffering from kidney disease.

(5) **William Cowper (1731-1800).** He is another of the great pre-romantics. "He", says **Compton-Rickett,** "is a blend of the old and the new, with much of the form of the old and something of the spirit of the new." In his satires he imitated the manner of Pope, but his greatest poem *The Task is* all his own. It is written in blank verse, and contains the famous line: *"God made the country and man made town,"* which indicates his love of Nature and humble humanity. However, the classical element in him puts down the new and the romantic. "There is a tenderness in poems *like My Mother's Picture,* that not even Goldsmith in his verse can quite equal; while his fresh and intimate nature-pictures point to a stage in the development of poetic naturalism, more considerable than we find in Thomson and his immediate successors". He is the first to strike that democratic knot which reaches its full flowering in the poetry of Wordsworth.

(6) **George Crabbe (1754-1832).** He continued the neo-classic tradition as far as his diction is concerned and was decisively dubbed as, "a Pope in worsted stocking", for this reason. In his masterpiece *the Village,* which is mostly descriptive of the miseries of the poor villagers, he is an uncompromising realist. He showed much concern for the humble humanity living in the lap of nature, but it was left for Wordsworth to glorify their simplicity and humility. Crabbe's excessive boldness as a realist alienates him both, from the polish of the neo-classical school, and the romanticism of the rising school. But by his plain and realistic treatment of the life of the villagers, he served to focus attention on their miseries. He occupies an important place in the naturalistic reaction against Pope and his school.

Literary Career and Works

In 1780, he travelled to London to gain a foothold in the literary establishment. After months of virtual destitution, he wrote a pleading letter to the highly influential statesman and philosopher, Edmund Burke, who, admiring Crabbe's writing, helped him have his long poem, The Library published. Burke helped him greatly in advancing his literary career and guiding his career in the church. Burke introduced him to the literary and artistic society of London, including Sir Joshua Reynolds and Samuel Johnson.

Crabbe is best known for his poem, The Village, written as a protest against Oliver Goldsmith's The Deserted Village. The poem concentrated on the poverty and bleakness of life in the region of Suffolk, a fishing village.
His other poems include poems (1807), The Borough (1810), Tales in Verse (1834). In 1814, Crabbe became Vicar of Trowbridge in Wiltshire, where he remained till his death. He died on 3rd February, 1832.

(7) **Robert Burns (1759-96).** He was a Scottish peasant who took to poetry and became the truly national poet of Scotland. His *Poems, chiefly in the Scottish Dialect (1786)* sky-rocketed him to fame. All these poems reflect the spirit of romanticism in their spontaneity, humour, pathos, love of nature and her lowly creatures, including the sons of the soll. Sometimes, indeed, Burns tries to write in the "correct" manner of the Angustan school, but in such poems he is unimpressive and insipid. Burns was influenced a great deal by the spirit of the French Revolution. His love and sympathy extended even to the lower animals, whom he studied minutely and described feelingly, says **Hudson,** "he is the mouthpiece of the growing faith in Liberty, Equality and Fraternity."

Literary Career and Works

Most of Burns' early poetry was written in song form to well-known Scottish tunes, the first being Handsome Nell, a tribute to Nelly Kirkpatrick of Dalrymple. Burns' first published work of poetry was Poems, Chiefly in the Scottish Dialect in 1786. This is also known as Bums's Kilmarnock Volume. This was intended to raise money for his emigration to West Indies, but it became so successful that Burns cancelled his plans of moving there. The Kilmarnock Volume was a mixture of several poems, Scots poems such as *The Twa Dogs, Scotch Drink, The Holy Fair, An Address to the Deil, The Death and Dying Words of Poor Maillie, To a Mouse and To a Louse*; six gloomy and histrionic poems in English and verse letters addressed to friends.

(8) **William Blake (1757-1827).** Blake was the first to introduce the romantic note of mysticism in English poetry. In his poetry we are very close to Wordsworth. Though he is a transitional poet or a precursor of the Romantic Revival, in many ways he is even more romantic than the romantic poets. He is best known for his three thin volumes – *Poetical Sketches (1783), Songs of Innocence (1789)* and *Songs of Experience* (794), which contain some of the most precious gems of English lyricism. He had vision of a world regenerated by a gospel of universal brotherhood, "transcending law". He loves Nature, but all Nature for him is, "afire with God", she is for him, "a window to God". He may not spiritualise Nature, but he comes very near to doing so. With Blake, we are on the very threshold of the romantic era.

(9) **The Churchyard School.** A renewed interest in the poetry of the old English masters, more specifically, Spenser and Milton are among the special features of medieval revival. Under the inspiration of Milton's *Penseroso,* there grew up a school or cult of melancholy and the poets of this school are known as *"the churchyard school of poets"* Gray's *Elegy Written in a Country Churchyard* is the best and the most popular poem of this school. In this connection mention may also be made of *Edward Young* who in his *Night Thoughts* imparted the romantic touch of melancholy to the poetry of the period, for it became a fashion to imitate Young and write, like him, in a melancholy vein.

(10) **"The Ode" in the 18th Century.** There are two important forms of the ode : *(I) The Pindaric Ode (II) The Horation Ode.*

(I) ***The Pindaric Ode.*** Pindar (6th to 5th century B.C.) was the greatest lyric poet of ancient Greece. He was the father of the *Pindaric* or *"Choric"* Ode. They were written generally in honour of the gods or to sing the triumphs or victories of rulers or athletes. Hence they are also known as *"triumphal"* odes. A Pindaric ode has a fixed stanza- structure or pattern. The number of stanzas may vary, but they are invariably arranged in groups of three, each group being called *a triad.* The first stanza in each triad is called a *"trophe"*. It was chanted by the dancing chorus as it proceeded in one direction, the second stanza in each *triad* is called an *"ante-strophe"*–it was chanted by the chorus as it returned. The third stanza in each triad is called an *"epode"*, and was sung when the chorus was stationary. Pindar's odes range from one triad to thirteen in length. Gray's fame as a writer of odes rests largely on the two *Pindaric Ode – The Progress of Poesy* and *The Band.*

(II) ***The Horation or "Personal" Ode.*** This kind of ode has been named after the Latin poet, Horace, who imitated Pindar, but with far reaching differences. The Horatian ode consists of a number of stanzas with a more or less *regular metrical structure* but without any division into triads of the Pindaric. It may be rhymed or unrhymed. This kind of ode is light and personal (not choric) without elaboration and complexity of the Pindaric. Many of the finest English odes are of this lighter sort. Some notable example are: *Collin's Ode to simplicity and Ode to Evening; Gray's Eton Ode* and *Ode to Spring; Wordworth's Ode to Nightingale.*

PERIODICAL ESSAY AND PROSE SATIRE

The Periodic Essay. The 18th century social life and its conditions produces a peculiar kind of essay, called 'Periodicals', because it was not published in a book form like other types of essays, say *The Essays* of Bacon, but was published in journals and magazines which appeared *"periodically', i.e.,* after fixed intervals of time. It differs from other types of the essay in as much as its aims were deliberately social, *i.e.,* the improvement of the manners and morals of the people. Therefore, it is also called the *Social Essay.*

Important Periodical Essayists are :

(I) **Steele and Addison.** The aim of the periodical essay, as handled by Steele and Addison, was in the words of **Davis Daiches,** "frankly educative." The two co-workers set the tone for the periodicals to come, and made it a landmark in the literary history of England. According to **Courthope,** *The Tatler* and *The Spectator* were the first organs in which an attempt was made to give form and consistency to the opinions arising out of the social contact between different classes.

Addison excluded politics, religious controversy, and pedantry, but he embraced every topic of literary, social, or moral interest. Therefore, both Addison and Steele may be regarded as great periodical essayists of the period because of their epoch making works.

(II) **Dr. Johnson.** About a hundred papers of Dr. Johnson were contributed to *The Idler,* which appeared between 1758 and 1760. These essays are lighter and shorter than those published in the periodical *The Rambler. The Rambler* appeared twice a week, between 1750 and 1752. Dr. Johnson as an essayist was much more serious in purpose than was Steele. His lack of humour and unrelieved gravity coupled with his ponderous English make his *Rambler* paper quite a heavy reading. This accounts for the lack of popularity of *The Rambler,* and it could not survive for long.

As a prose writer, Dr. Johnson is known for his *Preface to his Dictionary,* his essays and articles contributed to various periodicals, his philosophical novel *Resselas*, and his critical works *Lives of the poets* and *preface to Shakespeare*. Dr. Johnson was the great Cham or literary dictator of his age and an accepted arbiter of taste. His style, though vigorous and direct, is too heavy and learned and for want of a better name is called 'Johnsonese' which Chambers's Dictionary defines as "Johnsonian style idiom, diction or an imitation of it - ponderous English, full of antitheses, balanced triads, and words of classical origin." He lacked the true essay manner and so, does not stand very high as an essayist. However, his prose-style merits a more detailed consideration.

(III) **Edward Cave and Ralph Griffith.** A significant development in the later half of the 18th century was the creation of the "*magazine*" variously called *The Review* and the digest. It was an anthology of interesting and significant material which had already appeared in recent newspapers or periodicals. The first of such magazines was Edward Cave's monthly. *The Gentleman's Magazine* made a modest beginning in 1731. The vogue of the magazine caught on and many magazines, including *The Magazine of Magazines* (1750-51), appeared and disappeared. *The Magazine* was in course of time more and more devoted to the criticism of books. The first of the periodicals devoted largely to literary criticism was Ralph Griffith's *Monthly Review* (1749-1845). These reviews are the fore-runners of the literary reviews of the 19th century.

(IV) **Oliver Goldsmith** is the most important of the essayist of the later 18th century. From 1757 to 1792, he contributed to no fewer than ten periodicals, including *The Monthly Review*. His own periodical *The Bee* (1759) ran to only eight weekly numbers, *The Citizen of the World* (1762) – Goldsmith's best work – is a collection of essays which originally appeared in *The Public Ledger* as the "*Chinese Letters*" (1760-61). He did much to revive the popularity and prestige of the periodical. He avoids bitterness, coarseness, pedantry and stiffness. His style lacks the boldness of the aristocratic manner, and it escapes the tendency of his generation to follow Johnson into excessive heaviness of diction and balanced formality and of sentence structure. Johnson's friend and admirer, Goldsmith, was made of the stuff which enters into the composition of a true essayist. He is the last inheritor of Addison and Steele. He had the true essay manner. He started his career as an essayist with his contributions to *The Bee* (1759), a weekly which did not survive for long. Among these essays the best known is the tender prose-poem, *The City Night piece,* which may be regarded as the finest specimen of his art in this field. "These essays of Goldsmith in *The Bee* are a real success: he has understood the true ethos of periodical essay and has produced papers which are short, light, witty, and yet informative, including a wide variety of subject-matter."

But, his art reaches perfection in the essays contributed to *The Public Ledger* (1760-61) and later published under the title – *The Citizen of the World*. These essays are in the form of a series of letters supposed to have been written by a Chinaman during his visit of observation and study to the capital England.

(V) **Biographers and Letter Writers.** The eighteenth century produced a number of biographers, autobiographers, and writers of letters. **James Boswell** (1740-95), the biographer of Dr. Johnson, has the pride of place among them. His work is as massive as the great Johnson himself. His *Life of Johnson* is a unique work of its kind. Boswell's biography of Dr. Johnson has immortalised him as well as the great Doctor. Among the autobiographers, mention may also be made of Gibbon, Lord Harvey and John Wesley.

Lady Mary Worley Montagu, Cowper, Chesterfield, Gilbert White, Gray and Horace Walpole were some of the famous letter-writers of the eighteenth century. Lord Chesterfield's *Letter to His Son* has a universal interest and so has become immortal. In this connection, mention may also be made of **Dr. Johnson's** *Letter to Lord Chesterfield* which gave a knock-out blow to the system of patronage.

(VI) **The Historians.** The eighteenth century was a great age of historical writing. **Edward Gibbon** (1737-94) – The writer of the monumental *The Decline and Fall of the Roman Empire* – was the greatest of the historiographers of the age. His attitude is entirely rational. His style is dignified and somewhat ponderous. He can effectively combine harmony and majesty with logic and precision.

(VII) **Fdmund Burke (1729-97).** Burke was the greatest orator of the age. He dealt with the pressing political problems facing the British Empire. His works concerning Indian and American affairs and the French Revolution are written in well-reasoned, brilliant and rhetorical prose which cannot fail to impress even the most indifferent reader.

(C) Prose-Satire

(1) **Addison.** Addison's aims were frankly and degradedly reformative and corrective, and he laughs at the follies of the age in order to correct and improve them. He is more concerned with social reform and moral instruction than with pure entertainment. The characteristic humour of Addison is satiric, and we come across satire everywhere in the pages of the *Spectator Papers.* As a matter of fact, Addison is one of the greatest satirists in the English language.

As a satirist, Addison is neither malicious nor ferocious nor virulent. He ridicules to correct and improve and not to degrade, slander or insult. Neither is his satire universal, like that of Swift, who laughs bitterly at mankind as a whole. Addison ridicules the follies and frivolities, weaknesses and absurdities of his age, but never virtue and good sense. Feminine vanity, coquetry, triviality, and their craze for fashion is most frequently satirised. He regards women as another name for triviality, but he never means to insult them or degrade them.

As Courthope points out, irony is the very essence of Addison's humour and satire. Irony may be defined as the use of language with a meaning opposite to what the words apparently convey. Irony may also be defined as the simulated adoption of another's point of view. The ironist praises highly what he, reality, seeks to expose and ridicule. In short, irony is an indirect means of exposure and ridicule, and satirists make good use of it as an instrument.

The difference between the satire of Swift and that of Steele and Addison is due mainly to two causes. The first and fundamental cause is the difference between the men in character. Swift's satire was savage because there was savagery in his own nature; whereas Steele was the most genial and kind-hearted of men, and though there may have been some taint of malice in Addison, he was essentially good-natured. The second and subsidiary cause was the difference in the circumstances in which the satires were produced. Swift's great satires were substantive works; and even the shorter, occasional papers were, for the most part, independent of their surroundings. But the papers of Steele and Addison had to conform to the general tone of the periodicals to which they were contributed. We cannot imagine the Yahoos in *The Spectator.* The spirit of the papers on Mandonella spread over *The Tatler* and from it transmitted to *The Spectator,* in place of the raillery about puffs and patches and furbelows and Picts and Salamanders.

(2) **Swift.** Swift, in his satires, lashes with rare Zeal at all kind of aberrations and departures from the normal. In a *Tale of a Tub,* he lashes at the follies and corruptions of religion and in the *Battle of the Books,* it is the literary affectations and hypocrisy that come under his lash. In the *Gulliver's Travels,* he strips the whole of humanity with a mad glee and shows that man is a filthy creature filled all over with excrements. He uses all the known stylistic devices, allegory, digression, fable, irony, etc. as instruments of his satire. He knew that satire conveyed indirectly is more effective than the direct one, and so often invests it with a double meaning. In *The Tale of a Tub,* the story of the three brothers dividing their father's coat, is a brilliant allegorical cloak to hide the satire on religions intolerance and pretension. *The Meditations upon a Broomstick and The Battle of the Book* are both complete, long drawn out metapors, right from the beginning. The whole of *The Gulliver's Travels* is a story with a double meaning. Swift is a master of the art of story-telling and it is a measure of his greatness, that the greatest of the children's classics is also one of the greatest and bitterest of satires in the language.

Irony is the most potent weapon of satire in the armoury of Jonathan Swift. Irony is the used of language with an opposite or at least different tendency. Thus, in *The Battle of the Books,* Swift does not tell us that Bentley, the keeper of the Kings's Library, was very rude to Boyle. Rather, he praises him for his courtesy. Irony is like homeopathic treatment. It was such a simulated attitude which Swift used to expose the hypocrisy and pretension of Paridge, the almanac-maker. A very similar attitude was adopted by in *A Modest Proposal to Irish Parents,* containing his calibrated advice that children should be pickled and eaten to save the cost and trouble of brining them up. In *The Battle of the Books,* we get this type of irony in the accounts of Momus and the Goddess of Criticism, helping the moderns in their war with the ancients, as well as in the march of Wotton and Bentley in search of some isolated ancients. In *The Gulliver's Travels,* every aspect of English life, English professions, politics, religion, habits, institutions, has been ironically treated.

In the beginning of *The Battle of the Books*, mankind is likened to the Commonwealth of Dogs, and human quarrels are said to be motivated by the same reasons– a bone or a female is always at the root of it. These are examples of imagery in his satires.

In some way, swift's satire comes to have an element of the comic in it. In *The Battle of Books,* we get the humorous picture of the pot-bellied Bentley who, "endeavouring to climb up, is obstructed by his own unhappy weight, and tendency towards his centre", in fact all the moderns have a mighty "pressure about their posteriors and their heels", which always keeps them down. This humorous vein runs throughout the description of the fighting between the ancients and the moderns.

Thus, both, the bulk of Swift's satire and its quality, make him undoubtedly the prince of English satirists.

ROMANTIC PERIOD

The limits of the Romantic Period in English literature are usually set either at 1789 (the beginning of the French Revolution) or 1798 (the publication of Wordsworth and Coleridge's *Lyrical Ballads*) and 1832, when Scott died and the passage of the Reform Bill signaled the political preoccupations of the Victorian era, for some characteristics of the thought and writings of this great literary period. Major writers of the time, in addition to Wordsworth and Coleridge, were the poets Blake, Byron, Shelley, Keats, and Landor, the essayists Lamb, Hazlitt, De Quincey, and Leigh Hunt, and the novelists Jane Austen and Sir Walter Scott.

SOCIAL BACKGROUND

The last decade of the 18th century and the opening decades of the 19th constitute an era of revolutionary social changes, economic, political, religious and literary. This rapid social change which took place between 1776 and 1832 resulted from a variety of causes.

(1) It arose from the writings of the French intellectuals, writings which circulated freely in England, from the spread of interest in scientific discoveries and their possible practical applications, from the American example in setting up a constitution without hereditary legislators, from the philosophical speculations as to the perfectibility of man.

(2) The progress of social change was accelerated by the French revolution (1789-1799) and the war with France (1793) which followed, and which lasted till 1815, the year of *The Battle of Waterloo.* The forces generated by the Revolution shook the very fabric of European society, including English society.

(3) The period from 1789 to 1832 in English social history is a period of revolutionary social change which was destined to transform the entire economy and social structure of the country. A series of scientific inventions rapidly gave England a new and vastly revolutionary industry – the making of cheap cloth by mass production methods. The resulting social conditions, both rural and urban, were appalling; England was soon sharply divided between capital and labour, and the masses of workers had little protection from exploitation by the wealthy mill owners.

(4) The result of this social misery was that a wave of protest and minor revolts took place in the early years of the 19th century. Other forces from abroad were also string the masses to demand social and political reforms. A whole literature of democracy soon came into being and it was eagerly read everywhere. A series of reform bills were introduced in parliament to rectify some of the inequalities and miseries caused by the political and social upheavals.

(5) As a result of the various measures of social reform, a new and numerous middle class steadily gained political power and "poor laws" and "peoples' charters" slowly raised the standards and increased the civil rights of the masses of Englishmen. The individual felt a little more free and he lived better. Art and literature, which had fled from reality during the turbulent years, were to compromise with reality and the new middle-class society by mid-century.

(6) The century opened in the midst of widespread disturbance caused by the French Revolution and the events which had followed. A change in English thought was completed by the long struggle with Napoleon.

(7) England was being rapidly transformed from an agricultural and mercantile nation into an industrial one. The far-reaching social changes caused by this transformation made political reorganization an imperative necessity. Chartism (1837-49) died out under the influence of improved industrial conditions; but the extension of the franchise, though delayed, came in time, and *the reform Acts of* 1867 and 1884–85 register the steady onward sweep of English democracy.

(8) At the beginning of this period, the social consciousness was deeply stirred; the old sharp dividing lines between class and class began to be obliterated; increasing attention was given to the claims of the masses as against those of the privileged few; humanitarianism spread, and the sphere of legislation was enlarged to include the amelioration of the conditions of labour and of the poor. Some advancement was made towards the breaking up of social conventions and the increase of freedom of thought and action and, more important still, a movement began for the emancipation of women.

(9) The development of popular education, though very slow, was yet another significant accompaniment, partly cause and partly effect, of democratic progress. Ideas and speculations which would have been limited to the aristocracy of culture became the common property of the common man.

(10) It was a starting period of the application of science to life, in the factory, the railway, the steamship, and in the multitudinous uses of electricity. The result was a complete transformation of the world. No less complete was the revolution effected in the domain of thought. In matter, spirit alike literature was profoundly effected by this "march of mid" and the new ideas which it brought in its train.

(11) New Knowledge and old dogmas came into fierce conflict; the ancient system of thought was shaken of its foundations; traditional landmarks were swept away; intelligent men of all sects and classes were deeply stirred by the spirit of speculation and unrest. Hence the scepticism, the continual heart-searchings, the widespread melancholy which are among the persistent features of the literature of the period, and the strenuous morel spirit which makes it so different as a whole from the literature of the age of Elizabeth or of the first half of the 18th century. Hence, too, strong reaction against the domination of science in many quarters, the religious revivals initiated in the High Church movement: and outside the Church itself the unceasing protest of some of the greatest poets and prose writers against the materialism to which science seemed to lead.

(12) The revolt against eighteenth century realism and "common sense" found expression in the wild *phantasmagories* of Blake, and in the strange dream world of Coleridge. The revulsion from the Augustan indifference to the Middle Ages led, through the forgeries of Chatterton and the epic chants of the pseudo-Ossian, to Scott, for whom it was reserved to create the life of the past on a vast scale, and with an unparalleled illusion of truth".

ROMANTICISM

Definition

The term 'Romanticism" has been variously defined by various writers. :

(1) **Pater,** calls it the "addition of strangeness to beauty".

(2) **Watts Dunton** defines it as, "the renaissance of wonder".

(3) **Goethe,** the German poet-critic, contrasts Romanticism with Classicism and says, "Romanticism is disease, Classicism is health."

(4) **Abercrombie,** on the other hand, stresses the subjective element of romanticism and writes, "Romanticism is a withdrawal from outer experience to concentrate upon inner experience." He points out that vagueness, indefiniteness, and a tendency to disregard reality are essential elements of the Romanticism.

(5) **Heines, Beers and Phelps** define it as, "the re-awakening of the Middle ages."

(6) **Victor Hugo** considers the democratic spirit as the most significant aspect of romantic art and describes it as, "Liberalism in Literature."

(7) **Herford** calls it extra-ordinary development of imaginative sensibility.

(8) **Legouis and Cazamian** emphasis both, the emotional and imaginative aspects of romanticism and call it, *"an accentuated predominance of emotional life, provoked and directed by the exercise of imaginative vision."*

All such definitions are, however, unsatisfactory and partial, for they emphasise one or the other element of this type of literature instead of giving a composite view. But in real sense, romanticism is characterised by–

(a) An expression of the inner urges of the soul of the artist.

(b) Spontaneous outflow of powerful passions.

(c) Extraordinary expression of the wonder, mystery and beauty of the universe.

(d) A penchant of satisfaction.

(e) Love for nature.

(f) Expression of the inherent dignity and nobility of man.

(g) Simplicity and a revolt against all artificiality.

(h) An interest in the past and experiment with old metres and poetic forms.

The First Romantics

It is generally supposed that the English romantic movement began in 1798, with the publication of *The Lyrical Ballads.* But it is a mistake to assign any definite date to it. It was not a sudden outburst, but the result of long and gradual growth and development. The poets of the romantic school– Wordsworth, Coleridge, Shelley, Keats, etc.– were not even the first romantics of England, for the Elizabethan literature is essentially romantic in spirit. It is also full of that sense of wonder and mystery, that love of daring and adventure, that curiosity and restlessness which we associate with the poets of the early 19th century. "The romantic quest is for the remote and the distant", says **Albert**, and in this sense, "the Elizabethans were our first romantics."

A Gap of Augustan Age

However it may be, the romantic spirit suffered a total decline and eclipse during the Augustan age. The Augustan literature was mainly intellectual and rational, deficient in emotion and imagination. It dealt exclusively with the artificial life of the upper classes of the city of London, and its form and diction was as artificial as its theme. It had no feeling for nature and no feeling for those who lived outside the narrow confines of the fashionable London society. It confined itself only to the heroic couplet, to the utter disregard of the music and melody of a host of ancient English metres. The romantic movement began as a reaction against the dry intellectuality and artificiality of the Pseudo-classics.

The Pre-Romantics: Return to Nature

This played a very prominent part in the revival of romanticism. Suffocated with the cramped and crowded city atmosphere, people longed for the freshness of Nature. Even when Pope was at the height of his powers; there were poets, like *Thomas Parnell and Lady Winchilsea,* who showed in their poetry a genuine sense for natural beauty and charms of rural life. However, it was in *The Seasons (1730) of Thomson* that nature came into its own for the first time. The seeds sown by Thomson grew and flourished in the poetry of such poets as *Gray, Collins, Burns, Cowper and Crabbe.* These poets, who have been rightly called the precursors of the romantic movement, show a genuine feeling for nature and for the simple humanity living in her lap. But the dead hand of the past restrains them from giving a free and frank expression to their feelings.

Mystricism of Blake

Blake was the first to introduce a romantic note of mysticism in English poetry. His poems are "extraordinary compositions, full of unearthly visions, charming simplicity and baffling obscurity." For him all nature is, " a window to God."

The Medieval Revival

The poets of the middle Ages stirred the imagination of the romantics who turned back to these ages for theme and inspiration. **Bishop Percy's** *Reliques of Ancient English Poetry (1765)* fired the imagination of the people and stimulated interest in the medieval balled literature. It attained wide popularity and proved a great power in spreading romantic tastes. It was an epoch-making work which served to inspire *Coleridge* and *Scott* and later on *Keats.* Equally far-reaching was the influence of **Chatterton's** *Rowley Poems.* The publication of **James Macpherson's** *Ossian* in 1700 ushered in the Celtic spirit of the North into the English romantic movement. The *Ossianic* poems are in matter and spirit wildly romantic. They are filled with supernaturalism steeped in that melancholy and sentimentalism which was now invading literature from all sides. They explain the medievalism of romantics like Coleridge, Scott and Keats.

The "Lyrical Ballads"

A long step forward in the history of romanticism was taken with the publication of the *Lyrical Ballads* in 1798. It was now for the first time that the two friends– *Wordsworth* and *Coleridge*– emphasised the aims and objectives of new poetry. The enunciate the theory and methods of the new poetry, gave a new consciousness and purpose to the movement, and thus opened a new chapter in the history of English Romanticism.

The second Generation of the Romantics

Keats, Shelley and *Byron* belong to the second generation of the romantic poets. They began to compose mainly after 1815, by which date the elder romantics had given the best which they had to give. All the three were rejected by society: this rejection caused them much sorrow and suffering, and these are those who attribute their early deaths to this fact.

ROMANTIC POETRY

(1) **Wordsworth (1770-1850).** Wordsworth was the first of the great Romantics to be influenced profoundly by the French Revolution which had far reaching impact on his life and poetry. But its ideals– *Liberty, Equality and Fraternity* were not new to him. The societies with which he had been most familiar in his youth were essentially democratic. As **Hudson** tells us, it was during his second visit to France in 1791 that he fell violently in love with *Annette Vallon,* and this emotional connection must have coloured, to some extent at least, his intellectual attitudes. He also became intimate with a "band of military officers" of strongly revolutionary sentiments, and in his many discussions with them the "zeal which yet had slumbered, now in opposition burst like a Polar summer." *His tenderness, meekness, gallantry, and utter devotion* to the cause of the people are celebrated in glowing language in *The Prelude.* He returned to England towards the close of 1792. He found the conservative opinion in the country strongly against the Revolution. He was still unshaken in his faith and wrote firmly in its defence. But before long he was torn by a conflict of loyalties. His moral nature received a terrible shock when England declared war upon France. He loved his country, but was convinced that she was wrong and rejoiced when her armies met with disaster. The course of events in France brought him little relief. When the Republicans in France still professing to act upon the principles of liberty, equality, and fraternity, entered upon a policy of military aggression, his "general feelings" were turned into bitterness.

By 1802, his disillusionment with France was complete. From this time onward, he travelled farther and farther away from the political faith of his youth. Gradually, he become a Tory among the Tories, and the march of events in England only served to make him the more narrow and obstinate in his conservatism. It was for this reason that *Browning* went to the extent of calling him the *"Lost leader"* and *Shelley* called him a *"Moral Eunuch"*.

Nature really comes to her own, for the first time, in the poetry of Wordsworth. He is variously called the "harbinger of Natures", the "high priest of nature" and the "worshipper of nature", for he was the poet of nature *Par excellence* and his chief originality is to be found in his poetry of nature. From his very boyhood the external world was the most important formative influence on him. It was Wordsworth, who for the first time in English poetry, penetrated beneath the outward manifestations of nature and gave to her a separate life and soul of her own. Faith in the goodness of nature, an advocacy of the "return to nature" from the artificiality of the cities, is the theme of his poetry.

Poem Summary

The Prelude affords one of the best approaches to Wordsworth's poetry in general and to the philosophy of nature it contains. However, the apparent simplicity of the poem is deceptive; comprehension is seldom immediate. Many passages can tolerate two or more readings and afford new meaning at each reading. Wordsworth, it will be recalled, likened his projected great philosophical work to a magnificent Gothic cathedral. And he explained (in the Preface to The Excursian) that The Prelude was like an antechapel through which the reader might pass to gain access to the main body of the structure.

The poem begins in his boyhood and continues to 1798. By the latter date, he felt that his formative years had passed, that his poetic powers were mature, and that he was ready to begin constructing the huge parent work. Alternating with his almost religious conviction, there is an unremitting strain of dark doubt through the poem. The poem itself therefore may be considered an attempt to stall for time before going on to what the poet imagined would be far more difficult composition. As he tells the reader repeatedly, his purpose was threefold: to provide a reexamination of his qualifications, to honor Coleridge, and to create an introduction to The Recluse.

It was actually finished in 1805 but was carefully and constantly revised until 1850, when it was published posthumously. It had been remarked that Wordsworth had the good sense to hold back an introductory piece until he was certain that what it was to introduce had some chance of being realized. Moreover, The Prelude contained passages which promised to threaten the sensibilities of others, as well as himself, during the rapidly changing course of events after 1805. The year 1805 is the approximate date of his conversion to a more conservative outlook. However, his later-year recollection was that this change occurred some ten years earlier, and he tries in his revisions to push the date back.

The 1805 original draft was resurrected by Ernest de Selincourt and first published in 1926. A comparison of it with the 1850 (and final) version shows the vast change the work underwent. Some passages in the earlier version do not appear at all in the later; others are altered almost beyond recognition. The 1805 draft contains the clearest statement of Wordsworth's philosophy and is fresher and more vigorously written. The toned-down work as published in 1850 represents the shift of his thought toward conservatism and orthodoxy during the intervening years. The student is likely to find the 1850 version much more accessible for the purpose of reading the whole poem. Yet on the whole, critics tend to prefer the 1805 version when citing actual lines from the poem.

The only action in the entire poem is an action of ideas. Similarly, it would be inaccurate to speak of the poem has having a plot in any standard sense. Its "story" is easily summarized. The poem falls rather naturally into three consecutive sections: Books 1-7 offer a half-literal, half-fanciful description of his boyhood and youthful environment; Book 8 is a kind of reprise. Books 9-11, in a more fluid and narrative style, depict his exciting adventures in France and London. Books 12-14 are mostly metaphysical and are devoted to an attempt at a philosophy of art, with the end of the last book giving a little summary.

Each of these three "sections" corresponds roughly to a phase in Wordsworth's poetic development and to a period in his life. The first dates from the time of his intuitive reliance on nature, when he wrote simple and graceful lyrics. The second represents his days of hope for, and then disappointment with, the Revolution, and his adoption of Godwinian rationalism, during which he wrote the strong and inspiring sonnets and odes. The last coincides with his later years of reaction and orthodoxy, when he wrote dull and proper works such as The Excursion and Ecclesiastical Sonnets. The Prelude is critically central to his life work because it contains passages representing all three styles.

In the last analysis, The Prelude is valuable because it does precisely what its subtitle implies: It describes the creation of a poet, and one who was pivotal in English letters. In fact, The Prelude was so successful in its attempt that there was nothing left to deal with in The Recluse. Wordsworth could reach the high level of abstraction needed for a true philosophical epic only sporadically, in some of the shorter lyrics and odes, and could not sustain the tone.

(2) **Coleridge (1772-1834).** The French revolution had a great impact on coleridge. The first effect was to distract his attention from his studies. Soon after the fall of Bastille,

Coleridge entered Cambridge. He failed to concentrate on his books. *Plato, Aeschylus* and the other prescribed text-books were pushed aside and Coleridge and his few conversation-loving friends freely discussed the pamphlets of the day.

At the close of 1796, Coleridge wrote an, *Ode on the Departing Year.* At the end of this ode, Coleridge seems to be reversing his earlier position and with drawing from the Revolution. *His farmer enthusiasm now seems to have cooled down, and he washes his hands off, "the evil thing".*

The *Ode of France* was the last of the poems produced by Coleridge under the influence of the French Revolution. *Thenceforth, he turned into a warm patriot, and eventually a strong conservative.*

(3) **Byron (22 January, 1788-19 April, 1824).** Lord Gordon Byron was more completely a child of the French Revolution than either Wordsworth or Coleridge. In his hands English poetry became, for the first time, European, as he was much interested in Weimar, Florence, Venice, Rome and Paris, as in London. In him we find complete fulfillment of the cosmopolitanism of the revolutionary philosophy. Byron published Hours of Idleness, collection of poems in heroic couplet. Byron complete of Childe Harold's Pilgrimage during his two years tour of the continent.

Major Works

English Bards and Scotch Reviewers

- Published anonymously in 1809, English Bards and Scotch Reviewers was Byron's first major work after his volume Hours of Idleness.
- It was a satirical poem written in heroic couplets.
- It was modeled on Alexander Pope's satirical verse.
- The foundation for English Bards was» a poem called British Bards, written by Byron in October 1807. In January 1808, after the Edinburgh Review published a scathing review of Byron's book of poems Hours of Idleness; Byron was, so incensed that he revised his original satire and renamed it English Bards and Scotch Reviewers.
- The work is an attack on contemporary writers and critics.
- The poem is a vindication of the Augustan ideals of wit, reason and propriety, which Byron felt had been devalued by his contemporaries.
- Byron draws a contrast between past and present and argues that modern writers, with few exceptions, have neglected their great heritage from Shakespeare, Milton, Dryden and Pope. It is an attack on the excesses of the contemporary writers: Wordsworth, Coleridge, Southey, Mrs Radcliff and others. 'X '
- C.H. Herford called Byron's English Bards as "The last angry, reverberation of the literary satire of Dryden and Pope. He termed it an Inverted Dunciad where the "novice falls upon the masters of his day, as the Augustan master upon the nonentities of his and emulates Pope's stiletto with a vigorous bludgeon".

Childe Harold's Pilgrimage: Summary

- Byron's Childe Harold's Pilgrimage written in four cantos was published between 1812 and 1818.
- It is a semi-autobiographical poem that focuses on a nobleman disillusioned with sensory pleasures and embarking on a search for entity.
- The Childe of the poem's title is a medieval title for a young man, who is eligible for knighthood.
- It is this poem, which introduced the concept of the Byronic hero- a brooding, solitary man, who is an outcast or outlaw.

- Byron envisioned Childe Harold's Pilgrimage as a poetic travelogue of his experiences in Portugal, Spain, Greece and Albania. In his 'Preface' to the poem, Byron stated that the poem "was written, for the most part, amidst the scenes which it attempts to describe. It was begun in Albania and the parts relative to Spain and Portugal were composed from the author's observations in those countries. Thus, it may be necessary to state for the correctness of the descriptions".
- The poem also reflects Byron's political views, particularly his support for Greek independence from Turkey and the Convention of Cintra in which the English politicians allowed enemy French soldiers captured in battle to return to France with their loot intact.
- The poem is written in Spenserian stanzas.

(4) **Shelley (4 August, 1792-8 July, 1822).** Shelley represents the influence of the idealistic aspect of the Revolutionary philosophy.

He was a reformer as well as a prophet. He was optimistic about the dawn of a golden age, a millennium in which justice, goodness, peace, truth and beauty would reign supreme, and "*evil, tyranny, lust and the whole Satanic crew will be annthilated*". He wanted the West Wind to be, "the trumpt of his prophesy":

"O, Wind,
If winter comes, can spring be far behind?"

All his major poetry expresses not only his intense passion for reforming the world, but also his prophecy of a, "golden age".

Queen *Mab* is the poet's cry against war, marriage, government and religion, *i.e.*, against all those forces of evil which weigh down humanity; *Alastor* represents the wanderings of the hero, a mere shadow of Shelley, in search of ideal Beauty. In *The Revolt of Islam,* he denounces all the forces of tyranny and oppression represented by kings and priests, who dominate the world and rule selfishly from one corner to another. In the *Masque of Anarchy* he exhorts the people of England to rise against the tyrants for, "Ye *are many– they are few". Hellas is a triumphant song celebrating the victory of Good over Evil. Prometheus Unbound* is a passionate outburst of indignation against celestial tyranny. It represents the victory of good over evil, of love hate, of freedom over slavery, and of reason over superstition.

Major Works

A Defence of Poetry

- Shelley's A Defence of Poetry was originally written in 1821 in response to Thomas Love Peacock's The Four Ages of Poetry.
- Shelley begins his essay by distinguishing between reason and imagination. He defines reason as logical thought and imagination as perception, arguing that "Reason respects the differences and imagination the similitudes of things".
- Shelley states that Poetry is the 'expression of the imagination' of the poet. Poets, using their imagination, 'imagine and express' the 'indestructible order'.
- A poem, for him is, "The very image of life expressed in its eternal truth...the creation of actions according to the unchangeable forms of human nature, as existing in the mind of the Creator"; while Poetry is 'a mirror which makes beautiful that which is distorted'.
- Poets, for Shelley, are "not only the authors of language and of music...they are the institutors of laws and the founders of Civil Society." They are the 'unacknowledged legislators of the world'. Poets have the power to transform society.

- Gerald Lucas states that Shelley believes poetry to be divine, since it "Provides the seed for all of humanity's creations: religions, institutions, politics, philosophy and technology."
- Shelley says that poetry both pleases and instructs. It gives both pleasure and wisdom.
- Poetry as a whole, he argues, 'is ever-accompanied with pleasure' and it 'lifts the veil from the hidden beauty of the world'. Poetry's primary purpose is to focus on revealing the beauty in the world that is apparently hidden from people.

Ode to the West Wind: Summary

- Shelley's Ode to the West Wind was written in 1819 and published in the Prometheus Unbound volume in 1820.
- The poem is written in terza rima a verse form consisting of stanzas of three lines (tercets); the first and third lines rhyming with one another and the second rhyming with the first and third of the following tercet.
- In his note to the poem, Shelley wrote, "This poem was conceived and chiefly written in a wood that skirts the Arno, near Florence and on a day when that tempestuous wind, whose temperature is at once mild and animating, was collecting the vapours, which pour down the autumnal rains. They began, as I foresaw, at sunset with a violent tempest of hail and rain, attended by that magnificent thunder and lightning peculiar to the Cisalpine regions".
- The poem is addressed to the West Wind. The speaker of the poem appeals to the West Wind to infuse him with a new spirit and a new power to spread his ideas.
- The West Wind is personified both as a 'Preserver' and a 'Destroyer'.
- The speaker describes the effects of the West Wind on land, air and water.
- The speaker wants to be like the wind's lyre and implores the wind to blow his thoughts over the universe so that they might become seeds to cause a new birth. He wants to be an agent of change and spread his revolutionary ideas.
- Ian Lancashire states that in this poem, Shelley invokes Zephirus, the West Wind, to free his 'dead thoughts' and words, "As from an unextinguished hearth / Ashes and sparks", in order to prophesy a renaissance among humanity, 'to quicken a new birth'. He hopes that his 'spark-like, potentially very thoughts and words' will 'enlighten humanity and liberate it from intellectual and moral imprisonment'

(5) **John Keats (31 Oct. 1795-23 Feb. 1821).** John Keats was wholly unaffected by the great upheaval in France and Europe. His love of nature is frankly sensuous. He does not draw imaginary scenes, but writes from actual conteplation. It is the stationary objects which he can describe best. Like the Greeks, he excels in creating statuesque effect; *he habitually personifies the objects and forces of nature.* Thus in the second stanza of *The Ode to Autumn,* the four different activities typical of the season have been vividly humanised. The description has the richness, clarity and firmness of a Greek sculptor. There is nothing more charming in Keats' treatment of Nature. In the presence of nature all considerations of the past and the future were obliterated. There is no "irritable reaching after fact and reason but a complete abandonment to the pleasures of the moment. This negative capability enables him to enjoy the present the beauty of the hour forgetful of all pains of life. Like shelley he does never look before and after, and pine for what is not; the joys of the moment are enough for him. Though Keats has left behind a number of long narrative poems– *Endymion, Isabella, Lamia, Hyperion,* etc. his genius was essentially odaic. It is in his six great Odes that Keats is at his best. These *Odes* are a things apart in literature

and they shall last as long as English literature and language are read and admired. In *The Ode to Nightingale* the poet enjoys the immortal Beauty of the Nightingale's song, in *The Ode to Autumn* the mellow fruitfulness of nature in that season of golden mists, and in *The Grecian Urn* his imagination is fired by the perfect beauty of a piece of Greek sculpture.

Ode to a Nightingale

- Keats' Ode to a Nightingale was composed in 1819.
- Charles Brown, a friend with whom Keats was living when he composed this poem, wrote about its composition: "In the spring of 1819 a nightingale had built her nest near my house. Keats felt a tranquil and continual joy in her song and one morning he took his chair from the breakfast table to the grass-plot under a plum-tree, where he sat for two or three hours. When he came into the house, I perceived he had some scraps of paper in his hand and these he was quietly thrusting behind the books. On inquiry, I found those scraps, four or five in number, contained his poetic feeling on the song of our nightingale".
- The speaker begins with a declaration of his heartache. So, exquisite is the song of the nightingale in the shadowy forest that it makes the speaker's heart ache with joy and numbs his senses like a drug. The singing kindles in him a desire for a drought of wine, greenery, country dances, the music of Southern France and days spent in the Sunshine.
- He longs to disappear into the dim forest with the nightingale and fade away. In the world of the nightingale, he would forget about the afflictions of the world-weariness, fever, worries, old age.
- The speaker tells the nightingale to fly away and says that he will follow, not through alcohol (Not charioted by Bacchus and his pards), but through poetry, which will give him 'viewless wings'.
- Surrounded by the nightingale's song, the speaker thinks that the idea of death seems richer than ever and he longs to 'cease upon the midnight with no pain.' By the end of the poem, the speaker realises that the nightingale is immortal. The song of the nightingale that he is listening to was also heard in ancient times by emperors and peasants.
- He comes back to a realisation of his own state and consciousness. He realises that he cannot escape even with the help of his imagination. At the end of the poem, the speaker wonders whether he has had a true insight or experience or whether he has been daydreaming.
- In Keats' ode, the song of the nightingale is a symbol of an that outlasts mortal life.

(6) **Hellenism in Romantic Poetry.** The word *"Hellenism"* comes from *'Hellenses'*, meaning inhabitants of Hallas or ancient Greece. Hellenism, therefore, implies a love of ancient Greek way of life, of Greek art, culture, literature and mythology, as well as the attempt to express this love in one's writings.

Romantic poets, such as Byron, Shelley and Keats, were mostly influenced by Hellenism. Hellenic notes in the works of these poets are being discussed below.

(a) **George Gordon Byron (1788-1824).** He is regarded as one of the greatest British poets and he also joined the Greek war of Independence, fighting the Ottoman Empire. He was also a leading figure in the Romantic movement. His best known works are –

Don Juan. A satiric poem having 16,000 lines of verse. It has 16 complete cantos and an unfinished 17th cantos. Though criticized for its immonal content, it was also immensely popular.

Hours of Idleness. It was the first volume of poetry published in 1807 when he was 19 years old.

Childe Harold's Pilgrimage. A lengthy narrative poem in four cantos written in spenserian stanza. The poem describes the travels and reflections of a world weary young man. The title comes from the term 'Childe', a medieval title for a young man who was a candidate for knighthood.

Other major work includes 'The Walks in Beauty', 'The Bride of Abydos', 'Tale : A Lale', 'The prisoner of Chillon', The Just Kiss of Love'.

Byron's *Isles of Greece'* we have a fine appreciation of the great deeds done by the Greeks in the past.

(b) **Shelley.** Shelley in his *Hymn of Pan* recovers the ideas and feelings for Pan, one of the gods (Apollo) of ancient Greece. In Shelley's *To the Night and The Cloud,* although the subjects are not taken from ancient Greek life, the treatment of Nature is very Greek. The old Greeks were myth-makers. They delighted in making myths or stories out of the forms and processes of nature, as Shelley does out of the two natural phenomena– the night and the cloud. It is not mere personification of nature-objects that we find in these two poems. The Night and the Cloud appear before us as playful maidens, loving, tender and also fierce. They are represented in a highly humanised form just as the ancient Greeks would have represented them.

(c) **Keats.** Keats is will known among all the Romantic poets for hellenic notes are most pronounced in his poetry. His *Endymion, Hyperion, Lamia, Grecian Urn, Psyche all have themes borrowed from the Greeks. The Grecian Urn* is a monument of the poet's power of entering imaginatively into another world. The readers feel that they have been transported entirely to the Hellenic world of beauty, love, festivity and ritual. It is permeated through and through with the Greek spirit. It may also be mentioned that the *'Ode'* form which he made particularly his own and in which he excels all other English poets, is typically a Greek verse form. In his worship of Beauty not of nature alone, but of all Beauty– Keats justifies the remark of Shelley that he was a Greek.

ROMANTIC PROSE AND ESSAYS

(1) **Charles Lamb.** Charles Lamb (1775-1834) has been called *the Prince of English Essayists,* for his essays touch perfection. Lamb was one of the most autobiographical of English essayists and his essays at every step reflect his good nature, his charity, his simplicity, innocence and boundless kindliness. He takes the readers freely into his confidence and chats with them frankly as with an intimate friend. He communicates with his readers about his friends, relatives, joys and sorrows, likes and dislikes. It is possible from a study of *the Essays of Elia* to reconstruct the whole of his life from beginning to end. *Dream Children, My Relations, Christ Hospital,* etc., are all replete with a hundred self-revelations. Even in his essay *The Convalescent,* he tells us of his own selfishness during an illness and how the arrival of the letter of his editor made him conscious of the outer world and of his duties as a writer.

There is an element of exaggeration in Lamb's humour. His frequent exaggerations make the readers smile. Many examples of such humorous exaggerations can easily be quoted from his essay: *Poor Relations, Christ Hospital, The Convalescent,* and a number of other essays.

This humour invariably and exquisitely mingles with pathos and thus heightens the charms of his essays. The close of the *Dreams Children* is remarkable for its blend of humour and pathos. This every blend is also seen in *Old China,* in *Poor Relations* and in other essays. His Prose style is closely modelled upon that of the great Elizabethans.

However, this does not mean that Lamb was a mere borrower or a servile imitator. He was so thoroughly saturated with his reading that the antique style of his favourite authors had become a part and parcel of his being, and when he took to writing he could not help reflecting their mannerism and turns of expression.

An important quality of Lamb's style is his extensive and over-abundant use of allusions and quotations. He was a widely read man not only in the Elizabethans, but also in *The Bible* and the classics. His style is full of quotations from *The Bible,* and allusions to Biblical events and stories. In *Christ Hospital* alone there are numerous allusions. In *The Old and New School Master* there are references to Achilles and his hiding with women, and to the Sirens and their fatal song.

Another important quality of his style is iteration (repetition). Sometimes we get from him a perfect riot of whimsical metaphors, as in the beginning of the essay on *Poor Relations.*

Lamb is an artist with words, not easily satisfied. He revises and re-revises with great care his effort being to say what he has to say in the best of words possible.

Lamb's style is quaint and mannered. Quotations abound in the two volumes of *Elia,* and their text, probably, contains many less conspicuous reminiscences of sentences and phrases which have been left unnoticed or unidentified. Whole text is cast in forms which recalls the manner of the seventeenth century prose-writers.

(2) **Hazlitt (1778-1830).** Hazlitt stands in the very first rank of the English essayists. He has been repeatedly bracketed with Lamb. His work is frequently marked by a *flavour* of bitterness and by prejudice. His essays, contributed largely to *The Morning Chronicle, The Examiner,* and *The London Magazine* may broadly be divided into two categories: (1) *Critical Essays,* and (2) *Miscellaneous Essays.* The best of his work as an essayist is to be found in the essays of the second class, though his criminal essays, too, are remarkable for their rare insight and penetrations. The Miscellaneous Essays, including such volumes as (1) *Table Talk* (2) *Sketches* and *Essays* (3) *Winter, Slow,* reveal the wide range and variety of his interests.

In whatever he did or said Hazlitt was an enthusiast. *A rare gusto marks his essays and is one of their chief sources of power.* Whatever he has to say, he says forcefully and enthusiastically. His essays reveal the zest of his enjoyment of life and nature.

Hazlitt's *Essays* are autobiographical in character. He belongs to the group of personal essayists and is in the direct tradition of Montaigne who was his model. Like Sir Thomas Browne, he constantly uses the "I", takes the readers into his confidence, and pours out to them a hundred different aspects of his rich, varied personality. In essays like "My first Acquaintance with Poets," "Farewell to Essay-Writing," "On Living to Oneself", "On Going a Journey", etc., we come nearest to the heart to Hazlitt.

Hazlitt has that garrulousness of the personal essayist which imparts to the essay a rare human interest and charm. However, sometimes, he tends to become "degressive" and "*discursive.*" Thus in the essay on *"The Indian Juggler"*, he wanders off the point and becomes prolix and repetitive.

As regards Hazlitt's *Critical Essays,* it would be sufficient to point out that they too are characterised by the same qualities of sincerity, originality and independence. He is a critic of the romantic school. His criticism is personal appreciation. He does not judge a writer by line and rule, but he gives his own impression of him.

Hazlitt's prose-style is one of the glories of literature. He thought for himself and tried to say things in his own way. He tried to be as clear and forceful as possible. He had a rare command over words, understood their full significance, and could define them accurately and precisely. His *expository style* is seen at its best in the opening of his essay "On poetry".

He was a romantic essayist and his essays show more feeling and imagination than moral purpose. But they reveal that he is neither a shallow optimist nor a pessimist. That is why the appeal of his essays has been universal. His energy and enthusiasm have been infectious, and his influence has been felt all through the 19th century.

(3) **De Quincy (1785-1859).** De Quincy made his name by writing his "*Confessions of an English Opium Eater.*" Most of his essays were written for the *Black Wood's Magazine* and *The London Magazine.* By "essay" De Quincy meant history or philosophy in the making. His essays are literary attempts at the various subjects with which they deal. *The English mail coach, Murder Considered as a Fine Art, The knocking at the Gate in 'Macbeth', Literature,* etc., are some of his some of his finest essays.

As a literary critic De Quincy showed great penetration. He came into intimate contact with some of the greatest men of the age– Coleridge, Wordsworth, Lamb and Hazlitt. His critical essays on these great contemporaries show his literary acumen and clarity of understanding. His power of illuminative suggestion is best seen in his essays on *The Knocking at the Gate in 'Macbeth'.*

De Quincy's most memorable achievement is the recreation for the 19th century of that impassioned or poetic prose which the seventeenth century had known and the 18th had forgotten. The whole of *The Confessions* is written such poetic prose; not only the sound and rhythm are those of poetry, but the language used is also highly figurative. His skill in the use of such figurative language is also seen in his essay on literature.

Too much emphasis on the sound of words at the cost of their meaning makes De Quincy unsubstantial and vapoury. His matter is often trivial and superficial. But he lacks a back-bone of thought and so falls below the highest standards.

Everywhere in his works he displays a deplorable incapacity to concentrate. Needles digressions and the introduction of a lot of irrelevant matter spoil the effect of the best of his works. His essay on literature is remarkable free from these defects.

De Quincy's humour is generally flat and ineffective and so his works are often dreary and dull. It is only rarely, as in the essay on, "Murder Considered as a Fine Art" that his humour is successful.

ROMANTIC NOVELS

(1) **Sir Walter Scott (1771-1832).** The Minstrelsy of the Scottish Border is a collection of Border ballad compiled by Walter Scott, Which was published in three volumes. As a novelist, Scott is the creator of a world of events and characters. His novels are pieces of reconstructed history, invested with life and flavoured with humanity. Scott is the father of the historical novel in the English language. He is the real creator of, as well as the master-artist in this form of fiction. Scott came to his work as a novelist after achieving popularity as a poet. A lover of nature, of medievalism, of feudalism, and of romanticism, Scott brought to his work as a novelist, his entire personality. He blended into a unity fact and fancy, and history and romance. It is true that Scott alters the facts of history and changes the sequence of events in the interest of his art. With his *Waverly* (1814), Scott gave birth to a new kind of fiction– the Historical Novel. For nearly twenty years after he published novels in quick succession. *Guy Mannering* (1815), *The Heart of Midlothian* (1817), *Rob Roy* (1818), *The Bridge of Lemmermoor* (1819), *Ivanhoe* (1820), *Quentin Durward* (1823), *Red Gauntlet* (1824), *The Talisman* (1825) are some of his well-known novels. From Soctt's stray observations in the prefaces to some of his novels like *Ivanhoe* and *Quentin Durward,* we may conclude that he viewed history as centrifugal and the novel as centripetal. He seems to have regarded history as related to the historical novel in the same way as the architect's elevation is related to the perspective view of an artist.

(2) **Bulwer Lytton (1803-1873).** In Bulwer Lytton's novels such as *Rienzi* and *The Last Days Pompeil,* historical fiction attains maturity. In them we find the historical spirit distinctly guiding the novelist's art. Bulwer Lytton does not merely gather historical details to give scenery and romantic atmosphere to his novels. He attempts to reconstruct the history of the time completely and to present that history in relation to individual life. In the opinion of Cross no historical novel had has so many readers as *The Last Days of Pompeii.*

(3) **Thackeray (1811-1863).** Thackeray's *Henry Esmond* takes the historical novel a stage further. Here we have the imaginative interpretation of history. By allowing such things as conscience, hesitation and doubt, and conflict between love and duty to come into the novel and dwell there side by side with geographical realism. Thackerary makes the historical novel, the novel, of the soul. In doing this he has completed the works of his predecessors in historical fiction. As **Bliss Perry oserves:** "*Scott and Dumas made history the bondmaiden of romance; Bulwer made historical investigation the companion of romance: Thackeray made history the master of romance. These are the three stages of the evolution of the historical novel.*"

(4) **Maria Edgeworth (1768-1849).** Maria Edgeworth published her first novel *Castle Rockrent* in 1800, and it was followed by *The Absentee* and *Belinda.* Her work has a unique importance in the history of the English novel for she is the founder of the Regional novel in England. She gives to her novels a local habitation and name, and her characters are conditioned by the fact that they live in a particular locality which has its own traditions and distinctive way of life. Her characters are generally rounded life-like figures which live long in the memory once you are acquainted with them.

(5) **Miss Burney (1752-1840).** Miss Burney preceded Jane Austen by several years: her masterpieces *Evelina* was published in 1778, when Jane was but three years

old; – *Cecilia* came four years later, and *Canilia* in 1796, the same year in which *Pride and Prejudice* was written, though it was not published till 1813. There is no doubt that Jane owed much to her predecessor, but her gifts were far greater. Miss Burney's cleverness consists in the portrayal of feeling in a young girl's sensitive mind, her stories are stories of country life and simple everyday activity. Miss Burney had her vogue only for a short while as she dealt with contemporary manners. The only one of her novels which is still read is *Eveline,* but it is not to be compared with any of Jane Austen's novels, which are for all time. Jane is far ahead of Miss Burney in the field Shakespeare. Jane Austen is also as far ahead of Fanny Burney in the use of simple, direct English as well as she is in construction and effect.

(6) **Jane Austen (1775-1817).** Austen's greatest novels are *Sense and Sensibility (1811), Pride and Prejudice (1813), Northanger Abbey and Persuasion (1818), Mansfield Park (1814)* and *Emma (1816).*

Jane Austen (1775-1817) is regarded as modern novelist, for she is the leading exponent of what **Robert Liddell** calls "the pure novel", for she delights us by the formal qualities of her composition, by her study of the relation between the characters or of their relation to a central theme.

She has her own interpretation of life to offer, and her matter, her design is always subordinated to this end. She was the last, and the finest flower of that century. But she is entirely free from 18th century sentimentality, indeed sentiment is often the object of her satire. She does not also indulge in the crude horseplay and buffoonery of the 18th century novelist. She does not indulge in any direct moralising. She uses, irony as her weapon, as the instrument of her comic vision.

The main emphasis in Jane Austen's works is on manners which she regards an moral in microcosm. The standards by which manners, and morals, are to be judged are both explicit and implict in her novels. Self-command, a just consideration of others, knowledge of the heart, and a principle of right derived from education, are the standards by which she judge her characters.

Her method of character-delineation is superb, but what gives her characters their value is the fact that it is through them that the novelist presents her view of life which is *"a highly serious criticism of life expressed in terms of comedy".* "Comedy deals with the conflict between illusion and reality" and this is also the conflict in the novels of the Jane Austen. She shatters the follies and illusions of mankind and thus makes it know the truth. Overall she was a great novelist of 18th century, distinct from her contemporary novelists and is included under the list of modern novelists.

VICTORIAN PERIOD

INTRODUCTION

The beginning of the Victorian Period is dated sometimes as 1832 (the passage of the first Reform Bill) and sometimes as 1837 (the accession of Queen Victoria); it extends to the death of Victoria in 1901. The year 1870 is often used to divide "early Victorian" from "late Victorian." Much writing of the period, whether imaginative of didactic, in verse or in prose, reflected current social, economic, and intellectual problems–for example, the industrial revolution and its effects on the economic and social structure; rapid urbanization and the deterioration of rural England; massive poverty, growing class tensions, and pressures toward political and social reform; and the impact on philosophy and religious fundamentalism of he theory of evolution, and of the rapid extension of "positivism" (the method of investigation and proof developed in the physical sciences) into all areas of speculation and inquiry. It was an age of immense and variegated and often self critical literary activity. The derogatory connotations of the term "Victorian" in our time–sexual priggishness, narrow-mindedness, respectability, complacency–are based on the actual attitudes and values of many members of the rapidly expanding Victorian middle class; but current attacks on these attitudes merely echo the attacks by numerous men of letters within the age itself. The most eminent poets were Tennyson, Browning, and Arnold; the most prominent distinguished of many excellent novelists (this was the greatest age of English fiction) were Dickens, Thackeray, George Eliot, Meredith, Trollope, Hardy, and Sumel Butler.

TRENDS IN THE VICTORIAN NOVEL

(1) **Feilding Tradition with Loose Plots.** For one thing, the Victorian novel continues to be largely in the Fielding tradition. The plot is generally loose and ill-constructed. The main outline of the victorian novel is the same.

(2) **A Mixture of Strength and Weakness.** The Vicrtorian novel is an extraordinary mixture of sentiment, flashy melodrama and lifeless characters. There is much that is improbable and artificial in character and incident.

(3) **Entertainment Value.** The Victorian Novel makes interesting reading. The novelists may not construct a compact plot, but they tell the story so well. They are so entertaining, that children still love to read and enjoy a novel of Dickens or Thackeray. The readers' attention is not allowed to flag even for a single moment. They do not like to give it up unfinished.

(4) **Panoramic Value.** Novels like *Vanity Fair, David Copperfield* etc., are not like most modern novels, concentrated wholly on the life and fortunes of a few principal characters; they also provide panoramas of whole societies. In the Victorian novel, Cecil says, "*A hundred different types and classes, persons and nationalities, jostle each other across the shadow screen of our imagination*".

(5) **Immense Variety.** The Victorian novelists have capacity of varied moods. Their range of mood are as wide as their range of subject. They write equally for the train journey and for all time; they crowd realism and fantasy, thrills and theories, knock out farce and effects of pure aesthetic beauty, check by jowl on the same page; they are Mr. Galsworthy and Mr. Huxley and Mrs. Woolf, Mrs. Christs and Mr. Wood house, all in one. A book like *David Coperfield* is a sort of vast schoolboy hamper of fiction with sweets and sandwiches, pots of jam with their greased paper caps, cream and nuts and glossy apples, all packed together in a heterogeneous deliciousness.

(6) **Imaginative Rendering of Reality.** Not only have the Victorian novelists width and range of subject and mood, not only are they entertaining story-tellers, they have also creative imagination in ample measure. Their imagination works on their personal expertness and transform and transmutes them. The act of creation is always performed. Dickens is, "the romancer of London streets", and Thackeray too, transports us to an entirely new world, call it vanity fair or Thackeray-land or what you will. The creative imagination of the Victorian novelist works on the setting of his story and transforms it.

(7) **Humour.** The creative imagination is also seen in the humour of the Victorian novelists. Each of the great Victorian novelists is a humorist, and each is humorist in a style of his own. They have created a number of immortal figures of fun, each is comic in his own different way. There are hundreds of fine jokes and witty remarks spread all over the Victorian novel.

(8) **Characterisation.** *The Victorians are all able to make their character live.* Their characters may not always be real, there may be much in them that is improbable and false, but they are amazingly and indomitably alive. They are wonderfully energetic and vital. A Victorian novel a crowd of breathing, crying, living, laughing people. It has a crowded canvas, crowded with living, breathing individuals.

(9) **Lack of High Artistic standard.** The Victorian novel lacks uniformity. It is extremely unequal; it is an extra-ordinary mixture of strength and weakness. It is technically faulty. This is so because it is still in its infancy, it is considered as a light entertainment, and not a serious work of art, and the laws of its being have not yet evolved.

(10) **Lack of Liberalism.** The Victorian novels shows a definite decline from the earlier English novel. Any lapse from virtue is shrouded in an atmosphere of, "drawing the blinds and lowering the voice." Free and uninhibited treatment of the animal side is tacking. The Victorian novel presents only a particle, one sided view of life.

First Generation Victorian Novels

The main features of the first generation novels are as follows:

Themes

One of the prominent features, that the novel of the early Victorian era had, was the concern with the 'condition of England question'.

They chose for their themes the specific contemporary problems of the Victorian society caused by the predominance of industrialisation and utilitarianism and wrote about them sometimes as satirists, sometimes as humanists and sometimes as moralists.

Imaginative Rendering of Reality

In spite of the fact that they were conscious of the havoc caused by the industrial revolution, the presence of mass poverty and accumulation of riches in a few hands, yet they believed like the common Victorians that these evils would prove to be temporary and that on the whole, England was growing prosperous, which was evident from the enormous increase in material wealth and there was no reason why this progress should not continue indefinitely.

Characterisation

A significant shift in the English Novel in its movement from the 18th to the 19th century was the change of emphasis from action to character. They gave primacy to the character as opposed to Neo-classical novelists who gave more importance to action.

Loose Plots

The early Victorian novel, unlike both the novel of the preceding era as well as the following novel of the later phase of the Victorian period, was rather formless.

One of the reasons was the new reading public (the masses of middle and lower middle class) for whom they were being written. Like the Elizabethan drama, the novel in the early Victorian phase was written more for any entertainment than for any artistic purpose. But in spite of that, it contained the large purpose of offering a picture and criticism of contemporary life. The second and real cause of the lack of organisation in these novels was that they were serialised in the monthly and weekly magazines. Quite often, a novel took 25 serials to complete in the magazine.

First Generation Novelists

The early Victorian or first generation novelists comprised of Charles Dickens, Anthony Trollope, Mrs Gaskell, Bronte Sisters and William Thackrey etc. Although there were several more novelists of the time, only the ones mentioned here have survived the test of time and are considered representative of the early phase of the Victorian fiction in England.

Second Generation Victorian Novels

The later Victorian novels or the second generation novels were published in 1860s and 70s.

Main features of second generation Victorian novels are as follows:

Main Themes

The novelists of the later Victorian era, were not entertainers and reformers as were their elders. Instead, they were more serious composers with greater involvement in the deeper passions of life particularly love.

Moreover, their main concern was with the rural England, which was being destroyed by industry and commerce rather than the city working class and its masters, the mill-owners etc. They depicted the tragedy of transition from the agrarian way of life to the industrial order.

Lack of High Artistic Standard

The second generation Victorian novelists were more 'literary' and less 'popular' than the first generation. They had more academic favours in their writings and more poetic imagination. They did not have the breadth and variety (with the exception of Middlemarch) of the early novelists but they certainly had greater depth of characterisation and greater intensity of presentation.

Focus on Rural Background

Another change that took place in the English novel around the year 1860, was the shift in its focus from city with it industrialism and utilitarianism to the village with its vision of destruction under the threat of the new scientific rationalism and evolutionism, which started new ethics and human relations inspired by Darwinian concepts of 'struggle for existence' and 'survival of the fittest'.

These new ideas made the novelists look at human society from a new perspective, not as a static Biblical model existing in the dynamic tension between good and evil, but as an evolutionary process of human nature, society and civilisation, growing on the Darwinian principles.

Growth of Intellectualism

Another significant change that took place in the Victorian age, was the shift towards intellectualism. Although Dickens and Thackeray were 'educated' enough to grasp the cross current of ideas in their time, but were not 'learned' in the sense Meredith and other later Victorian novelists were. The novelists of the later Victorian Age were more learned than their predecessors.

Second Generation Novelists

George Eliot, George Meredith, Thomas Hardy, George Butler and R.L. Stevenson etc. were all major novelists of the 2nd generation who started publishing their novels around the end of the 50s or later.

THE VICTORIAN NOVELISTS

(1) **Charles Dickens (1812-1870).** Dickens was regarded as a Radical, even in his own days. He was a social reformer who was dissatisfied with the slow course of legislation : one who wanted to bring about rapid and radical changes to give liberty and voice to the majority of the people. But he never desired a political revolution of a thorough kind.

Dickens' remedy for various social evils is private benevolence. He distrusts legislation; he has also no faith in charitable institutions.

As a social reformer, he expresses the conscience of his age, which despite all its shortcomings, he accepted and loved.

He is the best of all the English novelists. Previous to his day, the novelists only wrote of the life and adventures of the rich and aristocratic sections of society. *Dickens was the first to introduce to the reading public life of the poor and the oppressed.* His *Oliver Twist* (1838) is a powerful indictment of the education of poor children of his day.

Dickens is pre-eminently the novelist to nowhere does this note ring clearer and truer than in *David Copperfied.*

In David Copperfied he treats particularly of evils of child labour and the reform of schools. No one can be more tender than Dickens in protecting the innocence of childhood and the purity of young womanhood, in the latter case he comes once more into line with Shakespeare and Scott.

To write of Charles Dickens at all is to presuppose his humour; it was the supreme quality of his genius. It was as a humourist that Dickens made his name. *Pickwick Papers* abounds in farce, now quite distinct from, and now all but blending with, the higher characteristics of Humour. At his worst, he is capable of facetiousness as in *Nicholas Nickleby.* The scene between little David Copperfield and the waite, in Chapter V of *David Copperfield*, seems to **Gissing**. In the celebrated Mrs. Gamp, the same perfect method of idealisation, as in Shakespeare's Falstaff, is used in converting into a source of pleasure things in life repel or nauseate. And in both cases, the sublimation of character and circumstance is affected by a humour that seems unsurpassable. Consider Spenlow and Jorkins in *David Copperfield* and Tadgers in *Martin Chuzzlewit.* Dickens had remarkable acquaintance with the Inn Waiter : read the Waiter's autobiography in *Somebody's Luggage.*

Inseparable from the gift of humour is that of pathos of which Dickens has an abundance, the earliest instance being that of the death of the chancery prisoner in the *Pickwick Papers.* He is at his best in bringing out the pathos of child-life. We see how closely the truly pathetic and quick observation are allied in Dickens. *Little Dorrit* is strong in both, pathos and humour. Pathos of a graver and subtler kind is the distinguishing note of *Great Expectations.* Perhaps, however, his best pathos is seen in *The Cristmas Book.* He continues the work of two writers whom he always held dear, Goldsmith and Sterne. Goldsmith's sweetness and Sterne's sensitive humanity had no small part in forming Dickens. There is a foretaste of Dickens' humour is Moses, the son of Goldsmit's Vicar of Wakefield. *"Dickens is truly and profoundly, national; of humour the very incarnation, he cannot, think of his counter without sunny smile."*

Dickens as Short Story Writer

Dickens also wrote many colourful, sad, funny and witty novellas and short stories of the Victorian era. Some of his prominent short stories are:

- A Holiday Romance Charming four short stories presented through the point of view of four children.
- A Message From the Sea It is a story about nautical adventure and mystery story that begins with a message in a bottle.
- Doctor Mari Gold A short story about a street peddler who finds happiness with his adopted deaf-mute daughter.
- Mrs. Lirriper's Legacy. A short story of how Mrs Lirriper and her friend send stories to her son at school.
- Master Humphrey's. Clock A story of a lonely man who decides to start a club, where the members would read out their stories to others.
- Mudfog and Other Sketches. Collection of short stories-Public Life of Mr Tulrumble, The First Meeting of Mudfog, The Pantomime of Life.
- Mudfog Junctional. Collection of short tales revolving around Victorian railway station.
- Sketches of Young Couples Collection of short story focusing on couples. A parody of social relations between the sexes.
- Somebody's Luggage. Story about a waiter who stumbles upon some luggage and' tries to identify its owner. Dickens wrote short stories throughout his career, he mixes humour with macabre imagery to create vivid illustrations of the lives of ordinary people. Designed to uncover social injustices and promote reform in his own time, the endearing characterisations and moving situations presented in short stories have appealed to audiences up to the present day.

Major Works

Christmas Books

- A Christmas Carol (1843)
- The Chimes (1844)

- The Cricket on the Hearth (1845)
- A The Battle of Life (1846)
- The Haunted Man and the Ghost's Bargain (1848)

Short Story Collections

- Sketches by Boz (1836)
- The Mudfog Papers (1837)
- Reprinted Pieces (1861)
- The Uncommercial Traveller (1860-1869)

IMPORTANT CHARACTERS IN DICKENS' NOVELS

Name of Character	Name of Novel	Name of Character	Name of Novel
Artful Dodger	Oliver Twist	Abel Magwich	Great Expectations
Bentley Drummle	Great Expectations	Blathers	Oliver Twist
Bumble	Oliver Twist	David Crimple 'Crimp'	Martin Chuzzlewit
Edward Murdstone	David Copperfield	Jaggers	Great Expectations
Kit Nubbles	Old Curiosity Shop	Noddy Boffin	Our Mutual Friend
Quebec Bagnet	Bleak House	Rob the Grinder	Dombey and Son
Sleary	Hard Times	Sloppy	Our Mutual Friend
Stephen Blackpool	Hard Times	Thomas Gradgrind	Hard Times
Uriah Heep	David Copperfield	Harold Skimpole	Bleak House
Mr Wopsle	Great Expectations	Polly Toodle	Dombey and Son
Silas Wegg	Our Mutual Friend	Dick Swiveller	The Old Curiosity Shop
Mr Sowerberry	Oliver Twist	Pumblechook	Great Expectations
Sophia (Sophy) Wackles	The Old Curiosity Shop		

(2) **Charles Reade (1814-1884).** Charles Reade visited prison and studied the law business, banking, even life between the decks on an ocean steamer. He also knew the life of the gold-diggers in Australia. He poured his experience and his reading into his novels. As a novelist of social reform he ranks very high. He needs documentation to the novel as a weapon for the social reformer.

His masterpiece, *The Cloister and the Hearth* (1861) is a historical romance. Reade was a poet at heart, and this helped him to produce *Cloister and the Hearth* which contains true, "Renaissance of wonder, in its pages. It is Reade's passport to immortality.

(3) **Wilkie Collins (1824-1889).** Wilkie Collins with an admirable grasp of the market brought Gothicism up-to-date. He was influenced by Poem, Richardson and Dickens. It was he who handed over the detective story from Poem to the author of Sherlock Holmes.

His formula for a successful novel was "Make' em laugh; make' em cry; make' em wait." "In *The Woman in White* he whirled his theatrical characters through a fantastic plot, broken by a series of climaxes, preçeded breathtaking suspense, seeking and finding the depths of depravity below the apparently rosy surface of middle-class life" **(Dinna Neil)**. His most important contribution to the Victorian novel was the detective novel of crime and mystery. We still remember him and read him at least for two of his novels, *The Woman in White* (1860) and *The Moonstone. "They are the most brilliant detective novels ever written."* **(Walter Allen)**

(4) **Richard Blacknore (1825-1900).** The one single novel on which rests the fame of Blacknore is *Lorna Doone* (1869), "The scene of this fascinating romance is laid in Exmoor in the seventeenth century. The story abounds in romantic scenes

and incidents; its descriptions of natural scenery are unsurpassed; the rhythmic language is at times almost equal to Poetry; and the whole tone of the book is wholesome and refreshing. Altogether it would be hard to find a more delightful romance in any language, and it well deserves the place it has won as one of the classics of our literature" **(W.J. Long).**

(5) **Anthony Trollope (1815-82).** Anothony Trollope is regarded as a, "garrulous male Jane Austen unware of the stress and storm of the world." His superiority to his contemporaries is mainly nagative, he did not make their mistakes. His positive superiority resolves itself into one quality – he observed the surface of life more accurately than they did. His greatness depends on his power to use his observation to make a new world in his creative imagination."

The almost idolatrous admiration of Trollope in the nineteen-thirties and forties was inspired by his perfect studies of English clerical life, *The Warden* (1855), *Brachester Tower* (1857), *Doctor Thorne* (1859) and *The Last Chronicle of Barcel* (1867). These novels reflect the Cathedral world that is peculiarly English. *The Warden* is his masterpiece.

He is the novelist of the middle and upper-middle classes. With urbane familiarity and shrewd observation he presents an accurate, detailed picture of their quiet, uneventful lives in a matter-of-fact way which gives his work the appearance of chronicles of real life. His main concern is with character rather than with plot. The framework of his a series of parallel stories moving with the leisureliness of everyday life. His style, efficiently direct, simple, and lucid, is seen to particular advantage in his dialogue. A vein of easy satire runs through many of his novels, and he makes skilful use of pathos.

(6) **Thomas Love Peacock (1785-1868).** Thomas Love Peacock stands alone and apart from the whole sequence of English novelists this career overlapped Jane. Austen's at the one end his son-in-law Meredith's at the other. He has been imitated but he has never been seriously rivalled. His work exists in a purity, his disciples have not been able to match; his limits were narrow and strict, and to attempt to broaden them is merely to destroy the delicately poised world they contain. In this way Peacock achieved perfection, and more than once. *Headlong Hall, Nightmare Abbey, Crotchet Castle are* among the more important of his novels. They are full of "sublimely comic passages in which a congeries of events is explained and the future forecast in terms of a single overriding theory. His novels form a comic dramatization of the intellectual notions of his age. For anything comparable in our time we would need to imagine a novelist intellectually powerful enough to satirize in one book the exponents of, say, Marxism, psycho-analysis, the psychology of Jung, logical positivism, neo-catholicism, existentialism, Christianity, science, abstract painting. Peacock's intellectual ability, together with the neutral position he himself seems to hold, makes him a devastating critic of the theories of his, and since the counterparts of those theories always exist he remains a formidable critic whose work, because of his insight into the implications of the ideas he satirizes, is permanently topical **(Walter Allen).**

(7) **Charles Kingsley (1819-1875).** Charles Kingsley, a novelist of the second rank, belonged to the Romantic school and that particular side of the Romantic school which followed in the wake of Scott. He wanted in the novel stirring episodes, varied excitement, and a past that seemed richer in colour than the drab futilities of contemporary Victorian Cathedral towns. "He is a capital writer for boys and in any case is best enjoyed in the uncritical days of youth. But his strong anti-

catholic sentiment and horror of celibacy and ascetic life become rather troublesome obsessions in his stories" **(Compton-Rickett).**

Westward Ho, published in 1855, is the most important of his novels. It is a patriotic tale of adventure, Jesuit intrigue, and naval enterprise. The action is set in the age of Queen Elizabeth. The Elizabethan setting of *Westward Ho* brings the partisanship more prominently forward and this spirited story with its patriotic note would have been all the better had Kingsley been less anxious to idealise our attractive but not over-squeamish old sea dogs, Hawkins and Drake, and to paint in such lurid colours the catholic Spaniard.

(8) **Mrs. Elizabeth Gaskell (1810-1865).** She is one of those novelits who have effectively used the novel as an instrument of social reform. Her early novels *Mary Barton* (1948) and *North and South* (1865) depict industrial life, her object being the amelioration of the condition of labourers and workers.

She was made an interesting study of female life and psychology in her masterpiece *Cranford* (1853). Life of women spending their time in tea-drinking, stale gossip, and basking in the sun is presented faithfully and psychologically. In her next novel, *Ruth,* Mrs. Gaskell deals with an ethical and moral subject. *"All deals however hidden and long passed by have their eternal consequences",* is the theme of this novel.

Ruth becomes a study of inner life. The novel *"announces the approach of the psychological novel in a restrictive sense."* Mrs. Gaskell, "did not posses the clearness of vision, the equipment of knowledge, and the breadth of horizon required for completely satisfying the definition of the psychological novel. What she did in part was fully accomplished by George Eliot" **(Cross).**

Major Works

Novels

- Mary Barton (1848)
- Cranford (1851-53)
- Ruth (1853)
- North and South (1854-55)
- Sylvia's Lovers (1863)
- Wives and Daughters: An Everyday Story (1865)

Novellas

- The Moorland Cottage (1850)
- Mr Harrison's Confessions (1851)
- The Old Nurse's Story (1852)
- Lizzie Leigh (1855)
- My Lady Ludlow (1859)
- Round the Sofa (1859)
- Louis the Witch (1861)
- A Dark Night's Work (1863)
- Cousin Phillips (1864)

Short Stories

- Libbie Marsh's Three Eras (1847)
- The Sexton's Hero (1847)
- Christmas Storms and Sunshine (1848)
- Hand and Heart (1849)
- The Well of Pen-Morfa (1850)
- The Heart of John Middleton (1850)
- Disappearances (1851)
- Bessy's Troubles at Home (1852)
- My French Master (1853)
- The Squire's Story (1853)
- Half a Life-time Ago (1855)
- Company Manners (1854)
- The Poor Clare (1856)
- The Doom of the Griffiths (1858)

- Right at Last (1858)
- The Cage at Cranford (1863)
- The Grey Woman (1861)
- Crowley Castle (1863)

Non-Fiction

- An Accursed Race (1855)
- French Life (1864)
- The Life of Charlotte Bronte (1857)

(9) **The three Bronte Sisters.** The three Bronte Sisters Charlotte, Emily, Anne– made notable contribution to the English novel during the early part of the Victorian era.

Their chief novels are the following:

Charlotte Bronte (1816-1855)

Victorian novelist Charlotte Bronte was born in Thornton, Yorkshire in 1816. She was the third child of Rev Patrick Bronte and his wife Maria. Charlotte and her sisters studied at the Clergy Daughters' School at Cowan Bridge. The conditions at this school were so appalling that two of her sisters Maria and Elizabeth, died of consumption. After their deaths, Charlotte was sent back home. She later continued her education at the school at Roe Head, but she left school the following year to teach her sisters at home. She returned to Roe Head School in l835 as a governess.

Literary Career and Works

In 1846, a collection of poems by Charlotte Bronte and her sisters, Emily and Ann Bronte was published under the male pseudonyms of Currer Bell, Ellis and Acton Bell respectively. Charlotte's first novel, the autobiographical Iane Eyre was published in 1847. This novel traced the life and development of the plain, but intelligent Jane Eyre from her traumatic childhood to adulthood. Charlotte herself wrote about the protagonist of the novel, "I will show you a heroine as plain and as small as myself'. Jane Eyre was followed by Shirley in 1848 and Vilette in l853.

Charlotte married her father's curate, Rev Arthur Bell Nicholls in 1854. Though her father was initially opposed to the match, he later agreed to the marriage. Charlotte herself was apathetic towards the match. Shortly after getting married, she became pregnant and was diagnosed with pneumonia. She died of the disease in 1855.

Major Works

- Poems by Currer, Ellis and Acton Bell (1846)
- Jane Eyre (1847)
- Shirley (1849)
- Villette (1853)
- The Professor (her first Written novel published posthumously in 1857) ,

The influence of Charlotte's novels has been immense. Charlottle's combination of romance and satiric realism had been the mark of nearly all the women novelists for a century. Her fruitful innovation were the presentation of a tale through the sensibility of a child or young woman, her lyricism and the picture of love from a woman's stand point.

Jane Eyre

- It was published in 1847, Charlotte Bronte's Jans Eyre is a bildungsroman that focuses on the growth and development of Iane Eyre from a rebellious 8 years old orphan to a mature thirty year old married woman.

- The novel is written in first person with the older Jane recalling her life from her childhood.
- The novel is partly based on experiences in Charlotte's own life. Charlotte herself was plain and small like Jane. The death of Helen Burns in the novel recalls the deaths of her sisters at Cowan Bridge. John Reed's decline into alcoholism and dissolution is modelled upon the life of Charlotte Bronte's brother Branwell. Jane's experiences as a governess are based on Charlotte's own years as a governess.
- Charlotte describes five distinct stages in the development of Iane, each linked to a particular place: Jane's childhood at Gateshead, her education at the Lowood School, her time as Adele's governess at Thornfield, her time with the Rivers family at Morton and at Marsh End (also called Moor House), and her reunion with and marriage to Rochester at Ferndean.
- The novel also contains Gothic elements, focusing on the dark and mysterious. The episode of the Red Room, the madwoman in the C attic, the shadowy corridors of Thornfield all add to the Gothic element.
- Bertha Mason, Rochester's first wife, who turns insane, is considered as Jane's double. Richard Juplit states that "Locked away in a hidden room of Thornfield, Bertha's only freedom comes when her keeper falls into a drunken sleep and she can sneak around the house and create havoc. Bertha is locked as tightly in her secluded room as Jane is locked into her subordinate life."
- Coming at the end of the novel, the most famous line in Jane Eyre is 'Reader, I married him.'

Emily Bronte (1818-1848)

One of the three Bronte sisters, Emily was born in Thornton, Yorkshire in 1818. Emily's father was Irish clergyman Patrick Bronte and her mother Maria Barnwell.

Her mother died when she was just three years old. Emily attended the Clergy Daughters' School at Cowan Bridge between 1824 and 1825 but after the death of her elder sisters, Maria and Elizabeth in 1825, she was withdrawn from the school and thereafter educated largely at home by her father, her aunt, her elder sister Charlotte. In 1835, Emily enrolled at Miss Wooler's School at Roe Head, Mirfield where her sister, Charlotte was teaching, but she soon returned home when she became homesick and ill.

There after she worked as a governess at Law Hill Hall in Halifax, West Yorkshire. In 1840 Emily and Charlotte planned to open their own school but did not succeed in their plan.

Literary Career and Works

She wrote under pseudonym Ellis Bell, who wrote poems and produced but one novel Wuthering Heights (1847) a highly 'imaginative work of passion and hate set on the Yorkshire moors. Emily Bronte was perhaps the greatest of three Bronte sisters but the record of her life is extremely meagre and her single novel darkens rather than solves the mystery of her spiritual existence.

Emily's only novel, Wuthering Heights was published in 1847. Heathcliff is the main character in the novel, and the whole plot revolves around him from the time when he arrives at Wuthering Heights as a dark and dirty foundling and until he ends his days as a powerful landlord of both Wuthering Heights and Thrushcross Grange. His almost inhuman devotion to Catherine Earnshaw is the moving force in his life. The story of the novel is narrated by Lockwood, a gentleman from London. Emily caught a severe cold at the funeral of her brother, Branwell and died of tuberculosis a year after her novel was published.

Anne Bronte (1820-1849)

The youngest member of the Bronte literary family was also an English novelist and poet. She was born on 17th January, 11820 in Thornton, Yorkshire, England. Soon after her birth, her father Patrick Bronte and family moved to the village of Hawarth where her father was appointed perpetual curate. Anne's mother died of cancer when she was barely one. After her mother's death Anne and her sisters were raised by their aunt Elizabeth Branwell.

Literary Career and Works

Anne's first novel, Agnes Grey, a story about the life of a governess, appeared in 1847. It was based on Anne's recollections of her experience with the children of the Ingham family and the Robinson family.

In July, 1848, Thomas Newby marketed Anne's second book, The Tenant of Wildfell Hall to an American publisher as the latest work of Currer Bell, affirming that 'to the best of his knowledge' the Bells were one person.

Smith, Elder and Co., who had been promised Currer's next book, were alarmed and furious. Charlotte and Anne saw only one way to prove, beyond doubt, that Currer, Ellis and Acton Bell were separate people. They went to London to reveal their identities to the publishers.

Emily flatly refused to go with them 'and was adamant that the secret must go no further. The Tenant of Wildfell was partially based on Anne's observations of her brother, Branwell. However, even though, Anne's second novel proved a success, her hopes of becoming a renowned writer was darkened by the death of her brother Branwell in September of 1848 and Emily in December of 1848. Anne Bronte was herself diagnosed with tuberculosis and died at Scarborough in 1849.

(10) **George Eliot (1819-1880).** *She stands at the gateway between the old novel and the new no unworthy heir to Thackeray and Dickens and no unworthy foreunner of Hardy and Henery James.* She was essentially a novelist of intellectual life. She contributed to the English novel an air of sobriety, sternnes and seriousness which it had not attained in the hands of the early Victorian novelists. *Adam Bede, Silas Marner, Middlemarch, Romola, etc., are among her greatest novels.*

George Eliot did not care much for plot–construction, at least of the traditional kind; she was governed not by the story but by her idea.

In fact, the laws conditioning the form of George Eliot's novel are the same laws condition those of Henery James and Wales and Conrod and Arnold Bennet. Hers are the first examples in English of the novelin its mature form; in them it structurally comes of age."

The early novels of George Eliot, *Adam Bede, Mill on the Floss, and Stlas Marner* are concrete in the presentation of the life of the Midland countries of Warwickshire and Derbyshire, which she had intimately known. Realism and faithful portraiture of life and character known to her the hallmarks of her novels. In her later novels beginning with *Romola* and upto Daniet Deronda, she laid her store of experience which she had also exhausted in *Adam Bede, Mill on the Floss and Silas Marner* and turned to political experiences of other people (*Felix Holt*), *problems of racial integration* (*Daniel Deronda*) and presentations of life in Florence during the fifteenth century. "But when she left familiar grounds for unknown and untrodden fields, she faltered, and failed, and it is only once again in *Middlemarch* that she could hold out a gleam of her former glory, for this novel, like her earlier work, is also a faithful picture of the life of the Midlands and of her people, such as the Garths and the Vinceys".

George Eliot is more successful in the presentation of scenes of pathos. She could depict moving incidents which touch the crore of our heart. Her tragedies are heart-rending. "George Eliot completed the work of Wordsworth. He dealt with the pathos of pastoral life in a spirit of measureless humanity, she mingled its pathos with humour and produced the greatest dramatic effect."

"George Eliot's style is lucid, and, to begin with, simple, but later in reflective passages, it is often overweighted with abstractions. Her dialogue is excellent for the revelation of character, and her command of the idiom of ordinary speech enables her to achieve a fine naturalness. Only rarely does she rise to the impassioned poetical heights of the Brontes, but her earlier novels, particularly *The Mill on the Floss,* are full of fine descriptions of the English countryside, and her faculty fornatural description she never lost entirely" **(E. Albert).** And **Cazamian** writes, "Her style, through many a page; through whole chapters and episodes, has the indefinable quality they suggests a lesson in psychology, ethics or history."

Major Works

Novels

- Adam Bede (1859)
- The Mill on the Floss (1860)
- Silas Mamet (1861)
- Romola (1863)
- Felix Holt, the Radical (1866)
- Middlemarch (1871-72)
- Daniel Deronda (1876)

Poetry

- The Spanish Gypsy (a dramatic poem) (1868)
- Agatha (1869)
- The Legend of Arion (1874)
- Brother and Sister (1869)
- Armgart (1871)
- Jubal (1874)
- A Minor Prophet (1874)
- A College Breakfast Party (1879)
- The Death of Moses (1879)

SHORT DESCRIPTION OF ELIOT'S MAJOR WORKS

Name of Novel	Description
Adam Bede	Eliot's first novel, Adam Bede is a pastoral novel set in the rural community of Loamshire, England, in the summer of 1799. The novel revolves around a love triangle between beautiful, but thoughtless Hetty Sorrel, Captain Arthur Donnithorne, the young squire, who seduces her, Adam Bede, her unacknowledged lover and Dinah Morris, Hetty's cousin, a fervent Methodist lay preacher. Eliot took the plot of Adam Bede from the death of Mary Voce, who was executed in 1802 for killing her child. Eliot's aunt Samuel visited Voce in jail and converted her. The character of Adam was inspired by Eliot's own father and the character of Dinah was drawn from her Methodist Aunt Samuel.

Name of Novel	Description
The Mill on the Floss' (1860)	It is Eliot's most autobiographical novel. The story of the protagonist, Maggie Tulliver is partially based on Eliot's own life and the character of Tom is based on Eliot's brother, Isaac. Eliot draws on her own experiences with a once-beloved but rigid and controlling brother to depict the relationship between Maggie and her brother Tom.
Silas Marner	Eliot's third novel published in 1861, Silas Marner is a realistic novel centering on a humble weaver-Silas who renounces religion after members of his church blame him for the theft of a pouch of coins.
Romola	Published in 1863, Romola is a historical novel set in Florence during the 1490s Renaissance. It explores late 15th century Florentine religion and politics through the eyes of the beautiful, highly educated Romola and Tito, her witty, cultured and entirely amoral husband.
Felix Holt	Felix Holt is a social and political novel set during the time of the Reform Act of 1832. The action is set in Treby Magna, a town caught up in the transition from the old England of rural farmland associated with a rigid class structure to the new England of manufacturing associated with the breakdown of that structure. It narrates the story of Harold Transome, heir to Transome Court, who comes to claim his inheritance and campaign for a Radical seat in Parliament and Felix Holt, working-class heir to a quack patent medicine business who returns to the town to stir the new electorate to a sense of worth.
Middlemarch	Subtitled A Study of Provincial Life, Eliot's Middlemarch was first published in 1871 and 1872, as a serial novel in eight parts. It represents the spirit of nineteenth-century England through the common people, and their perspective on change. The heroine of the novel, Dorothea is an excessively religious and pious girl. Who marries a man- Mr Casaubon, who cannot satisfy her emotionally or mentally. Virginia Woolf called Middlemarch "The magnificent book, which with all its imperfections, is one of the few English books written for grown-up people".
Daniel Deronda	This novel was Eliot's most controversial novel since it dealt with the position of Jews in British and European society. The novel begins with the meeting of Daniel Deronda and Gwendolen Harleth in the fictional town of Leubronn, Germany.

(11) **William Makepeace Thackeray (1811-1863).** While in his own age, Thackeray was regarded by **Anthony Trollope** as one of the greatest of English novelists, by **W.E. Bronwell** one of the few great novelists of the world, but in the 20th century **Walter Allen** regards his view of life as, "trival", and **Arnold Kettle** regards the ending of *vanity fair as "the feeblest of ending."* One, in the decline of his popularity is his great concern with the Sephemeral customs, traditionals, ideals, and way of life, of his own age. Otherwise it was Thackeray who perfected the fielding–novel. He was the first to impart to the scale panoramic English novel a coherent plot and structure. His novels mark an immense advance over Fielding as far as plot–construction is concerned.

Thackeray is realistic, but his realism does not mean a photographic reproduction. There is selection and accentuation in the manner of the true artist and the selection is determined and conditioned by his moral purpose.

He was the first English novelist who used the novel to express "a conscious, considered criticism of life". He tells us the truth about contemporary society. Generalising from particular experiences of his life, he gives to his readers a complete philosophy of life. *His creative power shows itself not in transforming the facts he has observed about life, but in arranging them in a symmetrical order.* Thackeray was the first to use the novel for satiric purposes on such a large, extended scale.

Thackerary imparted to the novel epic grandeur, sweep and dignity. His novels are all built on a grand scale; they present the sweeping panorama of contemporary life. Thus *Vanity Fair* is built on a vast scale, its action ranges over the whole of Western Europe and over a period of fifteen years. The novel thus has the grandeur, the vastness, the sweep and movement of an epic. Like the epic, it brings out the very spirit of the age.

His Characters are extremely vital and varied. They are visualised dramatically, as well as by the use of telling names, words and phrases. They are universal types standing for certain permanent traits common to all ages and countries. But, at the same time, they are also suitable representatives of particular institutions and organisations of their own age.

Thackeray was a conscious artist with a turn for technical experiment. In other novels of his, he mainly follows the convention of Fielding. They have a conventional 'hero', 'a villain', "intrigue' and finally 'marriage'. But in *Vanity Fair* he breaks free from convention altogether. The novel has an operatic symmetry. For the contrasted characters and careers of the two girls, Rebecca and Amelia, illustrate the same laws. *"The structural scheme of Vanity Fair is Thackeray's greatest technical achievement"* **(David Cecil).** Herein lies his greatest claim to originality and recognition.

His method of narration is unique, **Whibley** says, *"He plays the same part in his book as is played in a Greek Tragedy by a Chorus of tiresome elders".*

Irony is the keynote of Thackeray's attitude. If Thackeray is out to expose, this irony is bitter; if to illustrate those domestic affections which he thought the most amiable of human impulses, it is almost dissolved in sentiment".

For all these reasons, Thackerays may be regarded as a greatest novelist of second rank.

Vanity Fair

It was published serially in London in 1847 and 1848, Thackeray's Vanigz Fair is subtitled A 'Navel Without a Hero. It is a satirical novel of manners. The title of the novel is derived from John Bunyan's allegorical story The Pilgrim's Progress, where Vanity Fair is the name of a stop in a town called Vanity. The heroine of the novel, Rebecca Sharp or Becky is a strong-willed young woman obsessed with status and wealth. Another important character in the novel is Amelia Sedley, who is an exact opposite of Becky.

Amelia's goodness and sweetness is contrasted with Becky's wit and physical charm. While Amelia clings to ideals, Becky is amoral. Vanity Fair follows the fortunes of two contrasting but inter-linked lives: through the retiring Amelia Sedley and the brilliant Becky Sharp, Thackeray examines the position of women in an intensely exploitative male world.

Contemporary reviewers and novelists appreciated the brilliance of the novel. John Forster Wrote, "Vanity Fair is the work of a mind at once, accomplished and subtle which has enjoyed opportunities of observing many and varied circles of society... his genteel characters .... have a reality about them."

(12) **George Meredith (1828-1909)**. George Meredith is the founder of psychological novels. He is also the founder of the "lyrical-comical" novel. His chief novels are : *The Shaving of Shagpot, The Ordeal of Richard Feverel, Evan Harringtion, Rhoda Fleming, The Egoist, Diana of the Crossways,* etc.

Meredith was not a good narrator, and he hardly pretended to tell a story. Like Browning, instead of presenting his tale in plain, clear narrative, he prefers to give it to using flashes and half lights, as it is seen from different points of view. He plays round his story, seeming to miss a hundred strong situations for which the reader actually hungers. But this is his strategy of novel-writing."

Often it seems that the novelist has no hold over his plots. His plots are merely pegs to hand his dramatic scenes upon. He himself explained his method of story telling in the following words : "My method has been to prepare my readers for a comical exhibition of the personal and the into give the scene in the fullest of their blood and brain under stress of a fiery situation.

Meredith was essentially a psychological novelist. He was interested in the study of mental processes and analysis of motives.

He was opposed to Realism and the realistic school of novelists who aimed at the production of life with scrupulous minuteness and fidelity. He does not reproduce life, he does not decorate it, he does not idealize it, but he exemplifies it in types and situations of unusual meaning and power.

His novels have a hard intellectual tone. He was opposed to sentimentalism or softness of every kind. The egoism of Willoughby in *The Egoist* is treated as a queer exhibition of sentimentalism. Meredith exposed and ridiculed these manifestations of sentimentalism in his novel. He subjected them to the hammer blows of the comic spirit.

The novels of Meredith are comedies in spirit and are based on his concept of the comic spirit. He explains what he considers to be the essence of the comic spirit in the very opening sentences of *The Egoist.*

It is essentially a satiric spirit – a spirit of intelligence, reason, commonsense working against tradition or prejudice, social stupidity or individual folly.

His novels develop under the influence of the comic spirit, ridiculing and satirising folly, stupidity, egoism sentimentality, wherever these vices are found. The comic spirit, thus conceived, is exactly the spirit, not merely of *The Egoist,* but of the great bulk of Meredith's prose as well, and the fact that there is often a strong infusion of tragedy no more alters the character of his novels than 'he presence of Shylock transforms *The merchant of Venice* into a tragedy. Meredith's comic spirit is very closely akin to Ben Jonson's comedy and it plays the same role as it does in Ben Jonson's comedies.

Meredith's novels express his optimistic attitude towards life and his faith in evolution.

Meredith's characters, both male and female, are drawn from aristocratic and upper middle class society. He concentrates on the inner life of his characters rather than on the externals. He always probes deep into the hearts of his characters and studies their motives in undertaking a particular line of action. In The Egoist, there is enough of psychological analysis and dissection of the motives of Clara who is unwilling to marry Willoughby.

In his novels wit and poetry exist side by side, and each irradiates the other. It is this combination which gives Meredith his special place in the history of the English novel.

(13) **Thomas Hardy (1840-1928).** Hardy is one of the greatest novelist in the whole range of English Literature.

His first novel, the *Desperate Remedies* appeared in 1871, and thereafter novels after novels flowed from his pen in quick succession. His last novel *Jude The Obscure,* which was published in 1895, was vehemently criticised as being immoral. This hostile reception made him give up novel-writing for good, for exclaimed he, "a man would be a fool to deliberately stand up to be shot at". *The Mayer of Casterbridge, The Return of the Native, Tess of the d' Urbervillies and Jude The Obscure* are regarded by universal consent as his masterpieces, and they have been compared to the four great Shakespearean tragedies.

He is a regional novelist. He is the creator of *"Wessex",* a small tract of country consisting of six odd counties in South England. Wessex heaths and woodlands have an epic grandeur and his principal characters have the greatness of epic heroes and heroines. He has thus imparted a new emphasis and significance to the regional novels which had already been dignified by the Brontes.

He constantly inquires about the why and where of things and constantly attacks accepted beliefs. *Mans's predicament in the universe is the theme of Thomas Hardy's novels.* He has no faith in the benevolent and omnipotent God of Christianity. He conceives of the First Cause as blind, indifferent and unconscious. Man suffers not owing to any fault of his, but owing to the imperfections of he powers on high.

To Thomas Hardy must go the credit of having democratised the English novel. The heroes and heroines of the great Hardian tragedies are all drawn from the lowest rand of life. Henchard, the hero of *The Mayor of Casterbridge,* is a haytrusser. Tess is a milkmaid, Giles is a cider-maker and pine planter, Gabriel Oak is a shepherd, and Crym is a furze-cutter. He has thus completely broken away from tradition and his novels do not suffer in any way. Hardy's tragedy is as great an *apotheosis* of the human spirit as the tragedy of Shakespeare.

He was the first English novelist who dared to make a woman who had sinned, or who was an adulteress, the heroine of his novels. Tess is a woman with a past, yet Hardy had made her the heroine of *Jude the Obscutre,* is an adulterness. Hardy thus shocked Vietorian notions of morality and was vehemently criticised as being immoral and a corrupter of the people. His books were burnt. But he did not yield, he rather choose to give up novel-writing when the bitter attacks of his critics were too much for him.

Thomas Hardy was a master of the art of characterisation. Some of his characters are among the immoral figures of literature. He chose his characters from the lower strata of society. His female characters are better and more forceful than his male characters, because women are more elemental, "nearer to nature" than men. His range of characterisation is limited. All his important characters belong to Wessex and to the lower strata of society. He deals with the universal passions of man and so his characters are universal in their interest. They appeal to people in all ages and countries. One has to think only of Henchard, Clym, Tess Eustacia, Giles, Marty South, etc., to realise the truth of this statement.

Hardy's characters may be divided into two broad classes – major and minor. His major characters include such unforgettable and forceful figures as – Henchard, Farfrae, Elizabeth-Jane, Clym, Eustacia, Giles, Marty Sough, Bathsheba, Gabriel Oak, Tess, Angel Clare, Sue, Sue, Jude, etc. His minor character are sons of the soil, real children of the earth. They are the representatives of antiquity. They are the main source of humour in his novels. They provide a norm by which to judge the main characters of his novels. Often they are the spokesmen of Hardy himself and express his views on life. They appear in groups and generally remain in the background. When they are absent, as from *Tess*, even the best of his novels lose something owing to their absence.

Harrdy's novels have an architectural finish and symmetry. The architectonics of Hardy have been praised by all who have studied him.

But his plots are old-fashioned. They are all love stories. The wrong man meets the wrong woman or vice-versa and thus the complications arise leading the characters to their doom. The "eternal triangle" is always there.

His style is the best suited for his purposes. It is a poetic style. He has an almost Shakespearean felicity of expression and has the rare, and invaluable knack of using the best work for his purpose. His rustics speak their own dialect, but they use it most forcefully and effectively. He instinctively chooses the best possible vehicle of expression for them and himself.

His form is conventional, but as far as his matter is concerned he is entirely a modern. He is a modern in his views of God and religion and in his free and frank treatment of sex.

Conclusively, Hardy occupies an important place in the development of English novel.

Major Works

- Tess of the d'Urbervilles (1891)
- Far From the Madding Crowd (1874)
- The Mayor of Casterbridge (1886)
- Jude the Obscure (1895)
- The Return of the Native (1878)
- Under the Greenwood Tree (1872)
- The Wood Landers (1887)
- A Pair of Blue Eyes (1873)
- The Oxford Book of Gothic Tales
- Great Short Stories-Quick Roads
- Desperate Remedies (1871)
- The Trumpet Major John Love Day (1880)
- Wessex Tales (1888)
- The Fiddlers of the Reels and Other
- A Laodicean : Story of Today (1881)
- The Best Horror Stories
- The Three Strangers and Other Stories
- Towns Men

The Return of the Native

Thomas Hardy was a master of the art of characterisation. Some of his characters are among the immortal figures of literature. He chose his characters from the lower strata of society. Hardy's female characters are more forceful than his male characters because women are more elemental 'nearer to nature' than men. However his major characters are portrayed with a psychological insight, the minor ones being used only to provide some comic relief.

The plots of Hardy's novels are constructed with great skill and reveal his inventive powers. But they are often marred by elements of improbability, casualty and excessive use of coincidences.

In presenting human life as a tragedy, Hardy may be said to be expressing his pessimism and his gloomy view of life. His disgust at the modern life and civilisation may said to be responsible for his loss of faith and growth of pessimistic outlook.

Hardy as Short Story Writer

Hardy was prolific not only as novelist and poet but also as a writer of short stories. He began publishing short stories in periodicals in 1874 and continued to do so for over thirty years in total over fifty short stories ranging from the brief narratives to the long novellas 'The Romantic Adventures of a Milk Maid'.

He published the main body of his short stories in three volumes Wessex Tales (1888), A Group of Nobel Dames (1891) and Life's Little Ironics (1894). He collected the remaining stories under the title A Changed Man and other Tales in 1913. Unlike anything else Hardy wrote A Group of Noble Dames is a story cycle in which the speakers forced indoors by inclement weather tell tales of the 18th century Dorset aristocracy.

Hardy's stories are a condensed but more intense version of the novels and as such give a fascinating precis of Hardy's outlook upon and understanding of the world in which psychological factors are prominent.

The continuing popularity of Hardy's novels owes much to their richly varied yet always accessible style and combination of romantic plots and convincingly presented characters. Many of his novels have been adopted also.

VICTORIAN POETRY (1837-1901)

The Victorian Age

The Victorian (1837-1901) Age is named after the reign of Queen Victoria, who ruled from 1837 to 1901. She was the first English monarch to see her name given to the period of her reign while still living. Vast social, political and technological changes occurred during this age. It was one of the most prosperous periods in the history of England, a period of industrial development and colonial expansion. It is also sometimes known as the Age of Reform because of the plethora of reforms, which took place during this period.

It was an age of democracy. The major democratic movement in Britain during Queen Victoria's reign was directed towards expanding the voting population for parliamentary elections. Victoria came to the throne 5 years after the passage of the 1832 Reform Bill, which reduced property requirements for voting and holding office in Britain and increased the number of individuals entitled to vote. However, the 1832 Reform Act still failed to extend the vote beyond those owning property. As a result of this, People's Charter was drawn up for the London Working Men's Association (LWMA) by Thomas Lovett and Francis Place in 1838, which demanded votes for all men, equal electoral districts; abolition of the requirement that Members of Parliament be property owners; payment for MPs; annual general elections and the secret ballot. This movement known as the Chartist Movement of 1838, became important for working class agitators for social reform.

The 1867 Reform Bill (extended right to vote to all settled male tenants) and 1884 Reform Bill (which gave working men in rural England the same rights as those in the boroughs) achieved further democratisation of British politics and by the end of the 19th century universal male suffrage became almost a reality. However, women were still deprived of the right to vote.

Apart from social and political reforms, reforms also took place on the economic front. The most important of these was the repeal of the Corn Laws in 1846. The Corn Laws were a series of statutes enacted between 1815 and 1846, which kept corn prices' at a high level to protect British farming from foreign competition. These laws were repealed by Prime Minister Robert Peel in 1846.

The Victorian age was also characterised by the triumph of the middle classes, with their belief in progress, their opposition to governmental interference in trade and economics, their moral prudery, their religious faith and their observance of external superficial norms for behaviour.

Several movement and reforms took place during this period, which influenced the literature. There was tremendous growth in publication of periodicals and also the emergence of children's literature as a genere. Dramatic monologue emerged as a poetic form in the poems of Robert Browning. Charles Dickens, George Eliot, the Bronte sisters were storytellers and their novels reflected the Victorian period.

Literary Movements of the Victorian Age

Apart from social, political and economic reforms, Victorian age also witnessed a few literary movements.

A notable few are described in brief below:

Oxford Movement. Oxford movement was a 19th century movement centred at the University of Oxford that sought renewal of Roman Catholic thought and practice within the Church of England. Immediate cause of the movement was the change that took place in the relationship between the State and the Church of England.

The igniting factor was the proposal of the Whig government to suppress half the Anglican bishoprics and to re-dispose their incomes, without first consulting the church. This created a wave of opposition, spearheaded by John Keble, John Henry Newman and others.

John Henry Newman dated the beginning of the Oxford movement to Keble's Assize Sermon of July 1833, on National Apostasy. Other figures associated with this movement were Richard Hurrell Froude, Frederick Faber, Isaac Williams, Charles Marriott, Bernard Dalgairns, William Ward and Edward Bouverie Pusey. Although, it was primarily a religious movement, its main connection with literature was the series of doctrinal papers setting forth the aims and teachings of the movement. These were named as the Tracts for the Times.

Aesthetic Movement. The Aesthetic movement was launched during the later part of the 19th century and emphasised aesthetic values over moral or social themes in literature and other arts. It was a reaction against utilitarian philosophies, predominance of scientific thinking and the widespread belief of the middle classes that art should have a moral purpose. The movement drew upon the formula of '1' Art pour 1 'art' Art for art's sake-articulated most memorably by the French novelist Théophile Gautier in his 1836 preface to Mademoiselle lie Maupin. Gautier was one of a number of French writers and artists of the period, who argued that art should be evaluated with reference to its own criteria.

While, the historical roots of the movement can be traced back to Immanuel Kant's Critique of Judgement (1790), the movement was brought into England by Walter Pater, who in The Renaissance (1873) remarked that 'The love of art for its own sake'. He believed that art produced pleasurable sensations that added up to an impression of beauty.

The most important and the most known writer of late Victorian period associated with this movement was Oscar Wilde. Wilde felt very strongly about elegance and richness and it was this very coherence of philosophy that held the Aesthetic Movement together and gave it a lasting influence.

Pre-Raphaelite Movement/Brotherhood. Pre-raphaelites were a group of artists, poets and painters first formed in 1848, who rejected the dramatic, artificial mannerist painting styles succeeding Raphael and Michelangelo (hence the term 'Pre-Raphaelite') and aimed to create more genuine, humble representations of their subjects.

The Pre-Raphaelite Brotherhood was formed by three Royal Academy students Dante Gabriel Rossetti, who was a gifted poet as well as a painter, William Holman Hunt and John Everett Millais. They were later joined by William Michael Rossetti, James Collinson, Thomas Woolner and FG Stephens.

The Pre-Raphaelite/Brotherhood was based on the following principles:

- To have genuine ideas to express.
- To study nature attentively.
- To sympathise with what is direct and serious and heartfelt in previous art.
- To defy all conventions of art.

The ideals of this group of painters and artists were taken over by a literary movement, which included Dante Gabriel Rossetti, Christina Rossetti, William Morris and Algernon Charles Swinburne. In poetry, the movement came in the shape of a revolt against contemporary poetry of the kind of Tennyson's, which was full of tradition and involved in the immediate, mundane problems of contemporary society. The 'Pre-Raphaelites also started a periodical called The Germ (1850), which outlined their aesthetic theories. The most famous literary work associated with the Pre-Raphaelites was DG Rossetti's poem, The Blessed Damazel.

The Scottish poet and critic Robert Buchanan criticised the Pre-Raphaelite school of poetry and termed it as fleshly school of poetry. It was a term of abuse coined by him to attack the explicit nature of subject matter as well as erotic imagery in the poetry of poets such as Rossetti, Swinburne and William Morris.

Buchanan identified Rossetti as the leader of this group whose followers had taken a vow. "To appreciate fleshiness as the distinct and supreme end of poetic and pictorial art; to state that poetic expression is greater than poetic thought and by inference that the body is greater than the soul and sound superior to sense and that the poet, properly to develop his poetic faculty, must be an intellectual hermaphrodite, to whom the very facts of day and night are lost in a whirl of aesthetic terminology."

Three Phases of the Victorian Age

The Victorian period is often divided into three main phases-early (1837-1848); mid (1848-1870) and late (1870-1901).

Early Victorian Phase

The Early Victorian period was a period of turbulence, marked by economic, political and social difficulties.

Important events during this phase were the Chartist Movement and Repeal of the Corn Laws. This period also saw large scale expansion of railways. Literature of this period focused on the concerns of the new emerging middle and working class. IS Mill and Thomas Carlyle are writers that belong to this phase.

Mid Victorian Phase

The second phase of Victorian age was a period of economic prosperity and colonial expansion. Contrary to the first phase, this was a much stable stage. This phase witnessed the Great Exhibition of 1851, the first international exhibition of manufactured products.

It was organised by Henry Cole and Prince Albert and held in a purpose-built Crystal Palace in Hyde Park, London. This phase of Victorian age saw the appearance of scientific works such as Charles Darwin's The Origin of Species (1859) and The Descent of Man (1871) which challenged long held religious assumptions. Works of Charles Dickens and George Eliot belong to this phase.

Late Victorian Phase

The third phase of Victorian period was a period of scepticism, when people began to question Britain's Empire building activities. An important topic of debate during this phase was the proposed Home Rule for Ireland.

Literature of this period was marked by the Decadent Movement, who aspired to set literature and art free from the materialistic pre-occupations of industrialised society. Writers associated with this movement were Oscar Wilde, Arthur Symons and Ernest Dowson. These writers took a cue from French writers such as Baudelaire and Gautier and showed interest in perversity, ennui boredom art for art's sake, transgressive modes of sexuality, artificiality and decay.

(1) **Lord Alfred Tennyson (1808-1892).** Tennyson is a representative poet, one who represents his age not in fragments but completely, in all its manifold variety and complexity.

But even more typical are the content and quality of his poems. His *Locksley Hall,* 1842, is full of the restless spirit of "young England" and of its faith in science, commerce, and the progress of mankind. In *The Princess* the poet graples with one of the rising questions of the day—that of the higher education of women and their place in the fast changing conditions of modern society; *Maud* quivers with the patriotic passion of the time of the Crimean War and with the general ferment which followed this war. It also reflects the mammon worship of the day. In the **Idylls of the King** it is a series of twelve narrative poems on the celetic legends of King Arthur and his Knights of the round table. While the medieval machinery is retained, the old story is turned into a parable, the lessons of which have a direct bearing upon contemporary life. *Both politically and socially he stands out as, on the whole, the poetic exponent of the cautious spirit of Victorian liberalism.*

Tennyson was essentially the poet of law and order as well as of progress; he was quite as firmly opposed to 'raw haste', rash experiments, and everything that savoured of revolution. *"Tennyson's poetry is often the vehicle of he spreling democratic sympathies of Victorian England."* Recluse and aristocratic as he was, he was profoundly interested in common people and common things; and it is not the least significant feature of his work as a whole that along with *The Princess, Maud. The Idylis of the King,* it contains such things as *The May Queen, Enoch Arden, Dora.*

A careful student of science and philosophy, he was-deeply impressed by the far reaching meaning of the new discoveries and speculations by which the edifice of old thought was being undermined. He represents the Victorian spirit of compromise when he writes:

Let knowledge grow from more to more
Bust more of reverence in us dwell.

The "two voices – science and religion – of that century are perpetually heard in his work; in *In Memoriam* which is a requiem for the poet's beloved Cambridge friend Arthur Henry Hallam we may read of the great conflict of the age between doubt and faith; while in many later poems as in *The Ancient Sage,* we may see how the poet challenged the current materialism and asserted the eternal verities of God and immortality.

He was a great artist because of being a minute observer of Nature, which furnished him with a store of poetic description and imagery; a scholarly apprecater of all that is most picturesque in the literature of the past; an exquisite preciser in the use of words and phrases; and the picturesqueness and aptness of similes. He has an avoidance of he commonplace (by the use of clever, roundabout expression.) His use of repetition and assonance; the expressive harmonies of his rhythm; and the subtle melody of his dicition. Also proves his artistic abilities in poetry writing.

In his word-painting, Tennyson follows the example of Keats. Nearly all Tennyson's poems, even the simplest, abound in ornate description of natural and other scenes. They show exactness of observation and a rare loveliness of epithet; but they lack the intense insight, the ringing, romantic note, of the best efforts of Keats. Often his art degenerates into artifice, and manner into mannerism.

Tennyson is a great and original nature-poet and in his nature-poetry the impact on him of contemporary science can best be studied. His view of Nature is full of the brutal struggle for existence. He finds Nature, *"red in tooth and claw."*

Modern critics believe that the best of Tennyson is not to be found in his longer and more ambitious poems, but in his lyrics. He wrote lyrics of many kinds. *In Memorian* is a long elegy composed to many short lyrics. The elegy was peculiarly suited to Tennyson's melancholy and reflective temper. He also wrote a number of lyrical poems dealing with classical subjects. *Tithonus* is an example.

Tennyson has expressed himself on various matters, political, social, religious and ethical, but his philosophy is neither great nor inspiring. *To-day, he is valued not as a thinker, but as a consummate literary artist.* **Alfred Tennyson.** After Samuel Roger's refusal, Tennyson was appointed to the position of Poet Laureate in 1850. He held the position until his own death in 1892, by far the longest tenure of any laureate before or since.

Major Works

- Poems, Chiefly Lyrical (1830)
- Poems (1832)
- Poems, 2 volumes (1842)
- The Princess: A Medley (1847)
- In Memoriam (1850)
- Ode on the Death of the Duke of Wellington (1852)
- Maud and Other Poems (1855)
- Idylls of the King (1859)

- Enoch Arden etc (1864)
- The Holy Grail and Other Poems (1869)
- Queen Mary: A Drama (1875)
- Harold (1876)
- Becket (1879)
- Demeter and Other Poems (1889)
- The Death of Oenone, Akbar's Dream and Other Poems (1895).

(2) **Robert Browning (1812-1889).** Browning was gifted with an almost unlimited power of imagination which was always exerted upon real things. He treats of visible realities – the experiences of men and women – and this makes him a dramatic poet; he also treats of invisible realities, *i.e.*, the spiritual and the abstract, and this makes him a philosophical poet.

The most marked feature of Browning's poetry is his profound interest in character. *He is a great master of the art of representing the inner side of human beings, their mental and moral qualities.* He catches his characters in a cool moment of introspection or of guarded self-revelation, and he lets us see in their minds the causes and results of previous actions as few other poets have been able to do. But, he was lacking in some of the most essential qualifications of the dramatist.

He presents not only single characters in solitude, but also groups of characters, and he can make each describe how be feels and thinks. He emphasises antithetical attributes in a character, a little over much. In the department of narrative poetry, he takes a high rank. His descriptions of scenery and natural objects are extraordinary vivid.

His lyrics have a charm of their own which marks them of from all others. The best of his lyrics are love-lyrics in which he treats of all shades and varieties of love – married love, love triumphant and love unsuccessful, passionate love and abnormal love.

Browning frequently expresses his views on human life. He was not a profound philosopher. But he had more of the air of a profound philosopher than a poet ought to wear. He is striving to utter in his writings some truth too deep for ordinary language. He seems to come as one preaching a new revelation, as having a "message" which he alone can deliver.

He is an optimist to the core. He is not mere ascetic, protesting against art and culture as well as folly. He finds all things good, though virtue is the best. Imperfection is due to an inability to see things in their -proper relation to each other. *In Abt Vogler, Rabi Ben Ezra* and *the Epilogue to Asolando* we have that fullest and the most uncompromising statement of this faith.

Browning is the very, 'antithesis of Pope'. *He is careful of the thought, but careless of expression.*

He is one of the greatest metrical artists in the English language. He invented a large variety of verse-forms and used them with consummate success. His use of the gortesque is usually artistically justified. *As one critic has said, he is the greatest poet of the grotesque in the English language.* Finally, we may conclude about him that he *was astonishingly great but also astonishingly faulty, and his faults have come in the way of the appreciation of his real greatuess.*

Major Works

- Pauline; A Fragment of a Confession (1833)
- Paracelsus (1835)
- Strafford (play) (1837)
- Sordello (1840)
- Bells and Pomegranates Number I: Pippa Passes (play) (1841)
- Bells and Pomegranates Number II: King Victor and King
- Charles (play) (1842)
- Bells and Pomegranates Number III: Dramatic Lyrics (1842)
- Bells and Pomegranates Number IV: The Return of the
- Druses (play) (1843)
- Bells and Pomegranates Number V: A Blot in the Scutcheon (Play) (1843)
- Bells and Pomegranates Number VI: Colombe's Birthday (play) (1844)
- Bells and Pomegranates Number VII: Dramatic Romances and Lyrics (1845)
- Men and Women (1855)
- Dramatic Personae (1864)
- The Ring and the Book (1868-69)

My Last Duchess (1842): Summary

This poem is based on historical events involving Alfonso, the Duke of Ferrara, who lived in the 16th century. The Duke is the speaker of the poem. He tells us he is entertaining an emissary who has come to negotiate the Duke's marriage (he has recently been widowed) to the daughter of another powerful family. As he shows the visitor through his palace, he stops before a portrait of the late Duchess, apparently a young and lovely girl. The Duke begins reminiscing about the portrait sessions, then about the Duchess herself. His musings give way to a diatribe tirade on her disgraceful behaviour: he claims she flirted with everyone and did not appreciate his 'gift of a nine-hundred-years-old name'. As his monologue continues, the reader realises with ever-more chilling certainty that the Duke in fact caused the Duchess' early demise.

My Last Duchess comprises rhyming pentameter lines. The lines do not employ end-stops; rather, they use enjambment-that is, sentences and other grammatical units do not necessarily conclude at the end of lines. Consequently, the rhymes do not create a sense of closure when they come, but rather remain a subtle driving force behind the Duke's compulsive revelations.

The Duke is quite a performer: he mimics other's voices, creates hypothetical situations and uses the force of his personality to make horrifying information seem merely colorful. Indeed, the poem provides a classic example of a dramatic monologue: the speaker is clearly distinct from the poet and audience is suggested but never appears in the poem and the revelation of the Duke's character is the poem's primary aim).

(3) **Matthew Arnold (1822-1883).** Arnold is regarded as the greatest elegiac poet of England. *Rugby Chapel, Thyrsis, Scholar Gypsy, Dover Beach, etc.*, are some of his finest elegies.

Matthew Arnold is mainly a writer of personal expressions of grief; but he also *philosophises* over the fate of humanity in general.

As a matter of fact, Matthew Arnold's elegies are an expression of his inherent pessimism and sense of lonelines. Various factors combined to make him a frustrated individual. His elegies are an expression of this inner gloom. He seizes every possible opportunity to express his pessimistic view of life. His expressions of grief have been called, "*the Virgillian cry of horror over the mournfulness of human destiny.*" But it is to be noted that his lamentations are always characterised by classical self-control, dignity and decorum.

Rugby Chapel, for example, is a personal elegy in which the poet mourns the death of his father. It shows Arnold's elegiac genius at its best.

In *Thyrsis,* a great pastoral elegy, he mourns the death of his friend and Oxford companion, Arthur Clough. The expression of grief gains in intensity by the poet's self-control and the elegy ends on a note of calm acceptance, consolation and serenity, which reminds one of the end of Tennyson's *In Memorian* or Shelley's Adnais. There is, in the words of Compton-Rickett, "No winning, no luxury of grief, no sentimental pessimism. Neither is there any joy, and real peace. It is the serenity of a troubled but brave spirit." And this is true not only of *Thyrsis* but also of the other elegies penned by him.

Dover Beach (1867): Summary

Arguably Matthews Arnold's most famous poem, Dover Beach manages to comment on his most recurring themes despite its relatively short length. Its message like many of his other poems is that the world's mystery has declined in the face of modernity. However, that decline is here painted as particularly uncertain, dark and volatile. One night, the speaker of Dover Beach sits with a woman inside a house, looking out over the English Channel near the town of Dover. They see the lights on the coast of France just twenty miles away and the sea is quiet and calm.

When the light in France suddenly extinguishes, the speaker focuses on the English side, which remains tranquil. He trades visual imagery for aural imagery, describing the 'grating roar' of the pebbles being pulled out by the waves. He finishes the first stanza by calling the music of the world an 'eternal note of sadness.' The next stanza flashes back to ancient Greece, where Sophocles heard this same sound on the Aegean Sea and was inspired by it to write his plays about human misery.

Stanza three introduces the poem's main metaphor, with: "The Sea of Faith/ Was once, too, at the full, and round Earth's shore." The Phrases suggests that faith is fading from society like the tide is from the shore. The speaker laments this decline of faith through melancholy diction. In the final stanza, the speaker directly addresses his beloved who sits next to him, asking that they always be true to one another and to the world that is laid out before them. He warns, however, that the world beauty is only an illusion, since it is in fact a battle field full of people fighting in absolute darkness.

What also makes the poem particularly powerful is that his romantic streak has almost no tinge of the religious. Instead, he speaks of the 'Sea of Faith' without linking it to any deity or heaven. This 'faith' has a definite humanist tinge-it seems to have once guided decisions and smoothed over the world' problems, tying everyone together in a meaningful way. It is no accident that the sight inspiring such reflection is that of untouched nature, almost entirely absent from any human involvement. In fact, the speaker's true reflection begins once the only sign of life the light over France extinguishes. What Arnold is expressing is an innate quality, a natural drive towards beauty.

(4) **Arthur Hugh Clough (1819-1961).** Clough was a life long friend and college companion of Arnold and his death was the subject of Arnold's elegy *Thyrsis.* Clough resembles his friend in may respects. **F.L. Lucas** calls him, "a half hewn matthew Arnold, left lying in the quarry." However, in his inquiries and analyses he does not approach the dignity and stature of Arnold. For one thing, he does not have the single-midedness and emotional integrity of his friend. His is not an unrelieved pessimism – in the *Bothie* the dominant note is that of high spirits and holiday tranquility. **G.D. Klingopulos** observes, "*Clough's work is not by any means entirely somebre much is humorous and faintly satirical.*" For example, "*say Not the Struggle Naught Availeth*", a usual anthology piece, puts forward an optimistic message of action and hope for the best. "During the dark years of the Second World War the poem was used by Sir Winston Churchill for a morale-boosting text. It contains in *Ulysses*-like terms what is called the philosophy of action, not stoic endurance which characterises Arnoldian attitude." Comparing the two poets, **Huge Walker** writes, "Clough is the more hopeful poet of the two. Arnold lays the whole stress upon courageous endurance, the doing of duty in spite of the certainly of defeat. Clough sees all the western land bright in he sunshine, and the tide breading in else-where, if not here."

Clough's *Dipspchus* is a good example of the Victorian conflict between its two spiritual voices – science and religion. But as is usual with Clough, the note of seriousness in the poem is often broken by salies of wit and humour.

(5) **James Thomson (1834-1882).** James Thomson in *The City of Dreadful Night* and the shorter Insomnia strikes a note of the intensest, nightmarish pressimism. In him we come across unrelieved pessimism, largely subjective. As a young boy he was fed on Calvinistic doctrines, in which, under the influence of science, he later on lost faith. Absolute despair, unrelieved by any, "silver lining", was the outcome. He himself was subject to insomnia and at night he often felt lonely and gloomy; and his personal experience and melancholy give a touch of reality to ghastly, horrible pictures he draws in the poem mentioned above. His pessimism does not have the brooding energy of Stoic fortitude of Arnold's or Clough's. In the words of Hugn Walker, "his pessimism was founded on the conviction that there was no hope for humanity any more than of himself, and that the appearance of progress was a mere illusion."

As a man, Thomson was not altogether an unalloyed melancholiac lost to all sense of humour, fun, or humanitarianism. He definitely had more sides to his personality. He was, says Compton Rickett, "in his happier moments, an affectionate and steadfast friend, a delightful companion, and an unselfish worker in the cause of humanity."

(6) **Edward Fitzgerald (1809-1888).** Edward Fetzerald is chiefly known for his verse transition of the Persian Rubaiyat of Omar Khayyam. This work, says David Daiches "puts an altogether more attractive face on pessimism. Thomson alternated between hedonism and despair; Fitzerald expressed a hedonism grounded on skepticism." Fitzerald's pessimism is inherent in his acceptance of the evanescence of life and its purposelessness. This acceptance makes him cry a halt to all maddening activity and prompts him to devote, whatever time has been granted to him in this world, to sensual pleasures. His pessimism is the cause of his Epictureanism; eat, drink and be merry, for human life is sort and may end at any moment. "His paradise is earthly, somewhat befogged, but overflowing with orientals splendour and luxury" wine, women and music are the chief objects of his pleasure.

Fatalism like that of the orient is an important ingredient in Fiazgerald's pessimism. After all he may be summed up as renowned poet of the age.

The Differences: Uniqueness of 'In Memoriam'–

However, the distinctive nature of In Memoriam and its real greatness are thrown into sharp relief by the differences between Tennyson's elegy, and the other elegies. While the other three elegies are in the pastoral convention and the poets mourn their loss in the guise of shepherds mourning the death of another shepherd, Tennyson does not follow the pastrol convention. He mourns in his own person, his expression of grief is direct, and so it is more poignant and effective. It has a greater ring of sincerity. Not only is Tennyson's grief more intense and poignant, it is also deeper and more lasting. It lasts for over seventeen years while the grief of the other three the poets is of a much shorter duration. The passage of time does not weaken the poet's grief. It only grows calmer, but deeper, Thirdly, "In Memoriam is a much more ambitious work than either of the other elegies. It is much longer, consists of 131 elegiac lyrics carefully arranged to from an integrated whole."

An Epitome of the Age. Not only is *In Memoriam* superior as an expression of grief, it is superior in another respect also. As **Percival** points out, besides the elegy, there also runs a theology; It is also an expression of the poet's view of God, Nature, immortality of the soul, and the mystery of life and death. It traves the way of the soul from grief and despair, through the conquest of that despair, to ultimate hope and joy. It is a record of Tennyson's spiritual troubles, and as his spiritual troubles are also those of his age, *In Memoriam* is a valuable social document, a faithful record of the doubts and uncertainties, hopes and aspirations, of the times in which it was written. Evolutionary science had given a knock out blow to the traditional theories of creation, and faith both in God and Nature was shaken. *In Memoriam* reflects this loss of faith. If God is merciful and if he has a holy plan, why is there so much of suffering, such brutal struggle for existence, and pain and death? Thus in Tennyson's breast, and in the age, there was a conflict between science and religion. God's omnipotence and His love were hard to reconcile with the fact of suffering, Tennyson's plea is for a compromise between science and religion, and he stresses that such a reconciliation can be possible only through faith, and not through knowledge. The best and most lyrical parts of In Memoriam and those in which he becomes the voice of the human race and deals with problems which exercised his age and which have always exercised mankind. In short, "In Memoriam" is an epitome of its age, which the other elegies are not. In this respect, Tennyson's elegy stands alone in the whole range of literature.

(7) **The Pre-Raphaelite Poets.** It was in 1848, that a Pre-Raphaelite brotherhood was formed in England by three young painters, including Dante Gabriel Rossetti. 'hese young artists aimed at a return to older principles in painting, but as Rossetti and many of his followers were gifted writers, their work gave rise to a literary movement which advocated a close study of nature and a revival of the spirit and methods of the early Italian masters. But as the movement Progressed, it developed a literary manner of its own which, through not strictly Pre-Raphaelite in character, is still given that name for want of a better name. Among the notable poets of this school are D.G. Rossetti, William Morris and Suinburne.

(a) **D.G. Rossetti (1828-1882).** Truth to Nature, distinctness of details, vividness and profusion of images, warmth of loudness of colour- these are the leading characteristics of the Pre-Raphaelites, and Rossetti's Poetry has all these qualities.

He may be called "the Apostle of Beauty". He had great artistic gifts; his poetry is richly coloured, his verse is curiously and skillfully wrought, but his work is not entirely wholesome, manly or sincere. His poetic world lies beyond the limits of our ordinary experience – a shadowy world ruled by mystery, wonder, beauty and love, and lit by another light than that of common day. His poems are full of sensuous pictures of feminine beauty.

As a result of this tendency to describe feminine beauty, Rossetti was criticised as a 'fleshly' poet but it must be said that he is not sensual, but sensuous. Besides, he usually combines physical beauty with spiritual beauty; there is in him a love of mysticism as is reflected in The Blessed Demozel, and this saves him from the charge of being "fleshly". His love of beauty, along with his supernaturalism, makes him an essentially romantic poet.

The extreme fondness for elaboration of detail, and the outlook upon Nature not as a rhythmic pageant of colour, but as study in still life, is specially noticeable in the poetry of Rossetti. He thinks and feels in pigments, as a painter.

His passion for beauty governed also his choice of words an phrases and made him lover of melody and music, He aims at "the pure gold of a perfect phrases" and is a great melodist. His style is marked by an abundant use of symbois. The House of Life, his masterpiece, has the time of passionate love, treated in a symbolic manner. The chief Pre-Raphaelite trait, *i.e.*, pictorial quality, is also an essential feature of his style.

His poetry shows no contact with the political or social condition of his age. He has written several medieval poems. The Staff and Script is a tale of medieval chivalry. Sister Helen deals with the medieval belief in magic, ghost and hell-fire. In Such poems as The King's Tragedy and The White Ship he touches the popular ballad with all its rough simplicity and naivete; and if he fails to realise the hearty humanity that touches Scott's best work, he is more faithful to the conventions of the old ballad form. Again, he has essayed in poems like The Bride's Prelude and Rose Mary to reproduce that sensuous atmosphere which gave such richness of effect to Keats' The Eve of St. Agnes and Lamia; and his success here is unquestioned.

For him the supernatural had an intense reality. His supernaturalism is suggestive and psychological, not crude like Scott's.

Conclusively, he is admired for his pictorial qualities, supernaturalism and his own pre raphaelite trend.

(b) **A.C. Swinburne (1837-1909).** Swinburne's most popular works are Atlanta in Calydon and Songs before Sunrise. Music and melody, and pictorialism are the two leading qualities of his poetry. Melodic splendour is the most obvious thing about his poetry, but the full value of its significancee is not always realised. All great poetry, must necessarily charm both the eye and the ear; these are the avenues by which it seeks to hold the imagination of the reader. To concede melodic beauty to a poet is really only to save in other words that he is a poet, and the question therefore in Swinburne is one of degree, not of kind. "And it is here that the emphatic quality of Swinburne's music is appreciated for he is the most musical of our poets" (Composing-Rickett). In many of our poets the pictorial faculty is quite as dominant, sometimes, as in Rossetti's case everything is subordinate to the melodic.

"I would never have believed," said a distinguished critic "that there could be such music in words, and especially in the English language." "Just as Rossetti made thought pictorially sensuous, Swinburne has made thought musically sensuous. He is not merely melodic – Shelley was gloriously melodic – he harmonic; Shelley's music is the music of the lute; Swinburne's the music of a full orchestra; his melodies are rich and complex, with a sweeping grandeur that no other poet has equalled, much less excelled" (Comption - Rickett).

VICTORIAN ESSAY AND PROSE

(1) **R.L. Stevenson (1850-94).** Stevenson was the foremost essayist since Lamb, a poet, a novelist and a short story-writer. He touched everything and adorned what he touched. The gift of essay-writing was inborn in him. *An Inland Voyage, Travels with a Donkey, Familiar Studies of Men* and *Books, Memories* and *Portraits*, etc., are some his finest collections of essays.

His essays are highly autobiographical. The personal note is one of the most important characteristics of his writings, They reveal his charming personality. From his essay- On the Books that Have Influenced Me' we know of the various books that he read and enjoyed and that went into the making of his personality. He was always a moralist, and a profound ethical note is another important characteristic of his essays. He ridicules crime in many of the essays as in the Dynamiter. His morality finds expression in the most unexpected places, but this ethical note is most prominent in the Old Morality and Christmas Sermons. Another important quality of Stevenson is his love of the heroic. He believed, "It is better to live and be done with it, than to die daily in the sick room". His love of the heroic and the self-sacrificing is reflected in most of his writings.

He was a conscious artist who mastered his calling as a craft. Before he took to writing, he laboured hard to cultivate his style. He had a remarkable gift of condensing his meaning into a striking phrase. This makes him one of the most memorable and quotable of the English essayists. He bestowed great care on the choice of his words and systematically and laboriously studied their sounds. But he is never affected and never subordinates meaning to sound.

(2) **Thomas Carlyle (1795-1881).** His first important volume was the extraordinary Sartor Resartus (1833), a kind of autobiography of an imaginary German professor. The astonishing style and the unusual opinions expressed in it made it rather a startling production. The French Revolution (1837) which followed gave fire and intensity to history, while political tracts of great insight, and literary merit appeared in Past and Present (1843) and Later day Pamphlets (1850). The later years of his life were occupied with two immense historical works, Oliver Cromwell's Letters, and Speeches (1845) and The Life of Frederick (1865). Hero and Hero-worship is another of his important works.

For more than a generation, Carlyle was revered, both as teacher and a prophet. By his admirers he was called "the Sage of Chelsea", and he maintained his reputation by means of books, letters, and conversation. He was much concerned with contemporary social and political affairs, as well as with the more personal concerns of religion and private morals.

A later generation finds it somewhat difficult to accept Carlyle's teachings. His writings abound in words, and a rather confusing amount of good advice. In the main, he lays down a few simple rules of conduct, such as the cultivation of hard work, the necessity for personal inquiry into religious and other opinions, and the relief of the poor and oppressed. Though it now seems to amount to very little,, we must remember that by its influence Carlyle's teaching died do an immense amount of good. His robust faith in himself and in the ultimate good of all things was like a tonic in a time of wavering faith and increasing pessimism.

Major Works

- Signs of the Times (1829)
- Sartor Resartus (1831-34)
- The French Revolution (1837)
- Charitism (1840)
- On Heroes and Hero Worship and the Heroic in History (1841)
- Past and Present (1843)
- The Life of John Sterling (1851)
- History of Friedrich II (1858)
- The early kings of Norway (1875)
- Reminiscences of my Irish Journey in 1849 (1882)

(3) **Lord Babingtin Macaulay (1800-59).** Macaulay offers a curious a curious contrast to Carlyle. The latter was the preacher, the idealist, and the sage; the former was the hard-headed man of affairs, taking the world as it came, and offering no remedies to cure its evils. In his prose we find no struggle, exaltation, and despair such as we find in the prose of Carlyle. Instead, we observe a brisk details. We should not the copious vocabulary, the clever variations of the sentences, and the swiftly moving rhythm. His History of England had an enormous popular success, which was due to his selection of telling incident, his clear and rapid narrative and clean cut, assured manner of statement. As a historian, he was inclined to Whig views, and he is prone to exaggeration.

(4) **John Ruskin (1819-1900).** Ruskin was born of affluent parents, but his views on life were not in keeping with his social position in it. In art he was equally unconventional; in particular, he was a strong supporter of Turner, the landscape-painter. His total amount of books, pamphlets, articles and lectures were so numerous that we can name only a few of them His first and longest book was Modern Pointers, begun in 1843 and completed in 1860. It expounded Ruskin's ideas upon art and life in general. Shorter works on art were *The Seven Lamps of Architecture* (1849) and *The Stones of Venice* (1851–58). Among his articles and lectures are *The Two Paths* (1869), *Unto this Last. (1860), The Crown of Wild Olive* (1964) and *Sesame and Lilies* (1865).

Ruskin was an idealist, far in advance of his time. He spent much of his money and nearly all his life preaching to people who were largely indifferent to his efforts. He died in the Lake District, a disappointed man.

Several features of this remarkable prose style are at once apparent: the enormous sentence, rolling along like a torrent; the cunning use of semi colons, dividing the sentence into convenient lengths; the strong rhythm, which in places is almost metrical, and the studied loveliness of epithet, which becomes quite poetical in hits effect, As an piece of descriptive writing it is gorgeous and almost dazzling in its effect.

Ruskin had another style, which he employed chiefly in his numerous lectures, It has all his care and poetical effect, but it is severely simple. Frequently its diction is suggestive of *The Bible.*

Major Works

- Poems (1835-1846)
- The Poetry of Architecture: Cottage, Villa etc. (1837-1838)
- The King of the Golden River, or The Black Brothers (1841)
- Modern Painters (Volumes 1-9)(1853-1860)
- Review of Lord Lindsay's "Sketches of the History of Christian Art" (1847)
- The Seven Lamps of Architecture (1849)
- Letters to the Times in Defense of Hunt and Millais (1851)
- Architecture and Painting (1854)
- The Elements of Drawing, in Three Letters to Beginners (1857)
- Unto This Last: Four Essays on the First Principles of Political Economy (1860)
- The Flamboyant Architecture of the Somme (1869)
- The Queen of the Air: Being a Study of the Greek Myths of Cloud and Storm (1869)
- Verona and its Rivers (1870)
- Fors Clavigera: Letters to the Workmen and Labourers of Great Britain (Volumes 1-4)(1871-80)
- Love's Meinie (1873)
- Review of Paintings by James McNeill Whistler (1878)
- Bible of Amiens (1885)
- Proserpina: Studies of Wayside Flowers while the Air was Yet Pure among the Alps and in the Scotland and England, Which My Father Knew (1886)
- Praeterita: Outlines of Scenes and Thoughts Perhaps Worthy of Memory in My Past Life (1885-1889).

TRENDS IN VICTORIAN DRAMA

(1) It was under Ibsen's influence that serious drama from 1890 onward ceased to deal with themes remote in time or place. Ibsen had taught men that drama, if its themes remote in time or place, Ibsen had taught men that drama, if it was to live a true of its own, must deal with human emotions, with things near and dear to ordinary men and women. Hence melodramatic romanticism and the treatment of remote historic themes alike disappeared in favour of treatment of actual English life, first of aristocratic life, then of middle–class lives, and finally of labouring conditions, So far as choice of subject–matter is concerned, the break between the drama of romantic period and the naturalistic drama of the late 19th and 20th century is complete.

(2) With the treatment of actual life, the drama became more and more a drama of ideas, which are sometimes veiled in the main action and are some times did actively set forth. The ideas were for the most part revolutionary, so that the drama came to form an advanced battle ground for a rising school of young thinkers.

(3) Romantic love, too, came in for its particular onslaughts, with the tearing off of those veils of prudety with which the Victorians had covered the facts of sex, the new dramatistic came to take a definitely scientific view of life, Social convention,

common standards of existence, seemed as nothing compared with this tremendous fact; Ann tracks down the father of her children in *Man and Superman,* and her sister, Ann Leets in *Mr. Granville Barker's* play, throws over Lord John Car[for the plebeian John Abud.

(4) The class-war, which has found its expression in actual life, was freely dealt with by the newer school, cynically, yet profoundly, by men such as *Mr. Bernard Shaw,* seriously by men such as *Mr. Galsworthy.*

(5) The inner quality of the modern theatre was intensified greatly by the recent investigations of psychologists, The new study of the "soul" interested many, and none more than the dramatists, In their plays, therefore, they sought ever more subtly and delicately to depict the most intricate aspects of the human spirit.

(6) To express almost inexpressible ideas, emotions, instincts, which the psychologists have defined for us, the new writers found that ordinary direct words were insufficient. *This accounts for the extensive use of symbolism in modern drama.* The dramatists found precisely the same difficulty which faced the mystics of countless, centuries before, and they came to employ the same methods for the explaining of their purposes.

(7) With the increased inwardness, must be accounted, too, a tendency on the part of some of our living dramatists to make their protagonists not men, but unseen force. Social forces are used as dramatic personages for the purpose of making wider and larger the sphere of drama. The tendency is most pronounced in the plays of Mr. Galsworthy. It is one of the chief tendencies which separates the earlier romantic theatre from the later naturalistic play.

(8) It is perfectly natural that the age should be satiric, Satire will always flourish in a society which has become over-civilized, where the artificial life rendered necessary to city existence has driven men, emotionally and morally, to be cut off from elemental conditions and primitive impulses. All signs indicate that this satire will continue to be marked feature of modern drama.

(9) **Role of George Bernard Shaw as a Dramatist.** No account of the revival of English drama can be complete without a consideration of the contribution of Bernard Shaw. Shaw is a peculiar mixture of Ibsen and Wycherley. His aim is as serious, his analysis is as deep, as that of any of the more serious dramatists, yet he clockes that seriousness of purpose with a gaiety and a wit which has rarely been equalled in any time. We may call Shaw's plays comedies of purpose. They aim at being as laughable as Congreve's as stinging as Jonson's, as profound as Ibsen's. There is no earlier comedy in English comparable to those of Shaw; he has brought to the English stage a type of drama entirely new–a type, however, which few could follow. Unquestionably, critics of hundred years hence will regard his plays as one of the most notable contributions to the theatre in our time, but it is probable that they will had only one or two other dramatists with whom to compare him. The comedy of purpose, if it is not to drift into mere sentimentalism, demands a genius not only of a high, but also of a peculiar kind.

MODERN PERIOD

The term "modern" is, of course, highly variable in its temporal reference, but it is frequently applied to the literature written since the beginning of World War I in 1914. This half-century has been one of the outstanding periods in English and American literature. It has been marked by persistent and multi-dimensioned experiments in subject matter and form, and has produced major achievements in all the literary genres. The poets include Yeats, Frost, Eliot, Wallace Stevens, Auden, Robert Graves, Robert Lowell, and Dylan Thomas; the novelists, Conrad, Joyce, Lawrence, Virginia Woolf, E.M. Forster, Ernest Hemingway, F. Scott Fitzgerald, and William Faulkner; the dramatists, G.B. Shaw, Sean O' Casey, Eugene O' Neill, Tennessee Williams, and Samuel Beckett; and the critics, T.S. Eliot, I.A. Richards, F.R. Leavis, Lionel Trilling, and the American *New Critics.*

SOCIAL BACKGROUND

Following were the social factors which influenced the shaping of the literature of modern period—

(1) The end of rural England, and the increasing urbanisation of the country.

(2) Emergence of new psychological theories presented a new concept of human behaviour. Freud emphasised the power of the unconscious to affect conduct. Intellectual convictions, he pointed out, were rationalisations of emotional needs. Human beings are not so rational as they are supposed to be; their conduct is not guided and controlled by the conscious, rather it is at the mercy of the forces lying buried deep within the unconscious.

(3) As a result of the teaching of modern psychology, man is no longer considered as self responsible or rational in his behaviour.

(4) The rise of the scientific spirit and rationalism led to a questioning of accepted social beliefs, conventions and traditions. In matters of religion it gave rise to scepticism and agnosticism.

(5) Sexual renunciation has ceased to be a theme of literature, interest in sex-perversion has grown, and there is a free and frank discussion of sex. Victorian taboos on sex are no longer operative. There is a break up of the old authoritarian pattern in family relationships, the assessment of the relative roles of the sexes has changed, woman has come to her own, and the notion of male superiority has suffered a serious blow.

(6) The First World War strained the authoritarian pattern of family relationships and increased tensions and frustrations. The reaction of the post-war world has been to suspect all manifestations of authority. It may be called an era of revolt against authority. Political and religious scepticism, general disillusionment, cynicism, irony, etc., have become the order of the day.

(7) Despite the revival efforts for Christianity even in the orthodox forms, as in the works of T.S. Eliot and Graham Greene, the 20th century under the impact of science and rationalism has witnessed a gradual weakening of religious faith. Religious controversies no longer exercise any significant influence on public issues. Moral and ethical values are no longer regarded as absolute.

(8) The First World-War resulted in the search for a "system" or "pattern" in Politics and Economy. Consequently, Marxism and the concept of economic planning emerged.

(9) A phenomenal rise in literacy and increasing number of cheap and commercial literature (including books, magazines etc.,) have changed the taste of common people. There has been an increase in vulgarity, brutality and careness. Human relationships have been coarsened and cheapened; man has become incapable of finer and subtler emotional responses.

(10) Vigorous experiments are being made in the field of music and other fine arts and literature, but this is a symptom of the break-done of cultural continuity rather than of cultural vigour.

LITERARY TRENDS OF MODERN PERIOD

(A) Poetry

Literary trends in modern poetry may be summarised as follows:

(1) **Complex and Many sided. Twentieth** century poetry is a curious mixture of the traditional and the experimental, of the old and the new. It is complex and many-sided.

(2) **Poetry of Revolt.** Modern poetry is a poetry of revolt against tradition, and as such there is much in it that is experimental, ephemeral, and puerile. This is why **Roy Campbell** describes modern poetry as, "an epidemic of intellectual and emotional diarrhoea", and **A.C. Ward** finds it, "eccentric, way-ward, in derail and commonplace".

(3) **Realism In Poetry.** The poet turns away from the decadent romantic tradition: a tradition which still persists in Georgian poetry. This revolt is best exemplified in the poetry of T.S. Eliot. The poet sees life in its naked realism, and even the most prostatic and commonplace subjects are considered suitable.

(4) **Debris of War.** After the war, poems appear in an ever increasing number on the destructive means of warfare.

(5) **The Language of Everyday Life.** The imagery and vocabulary of the modern poet reflect the influence of science and scientific inventions. Realism in subject matter has led the modern poet to reject the highly ornate and artificial poetic style of the romantics in favour of a language which resembles closely the language of everyday life. Modern poetry is characterised by the use of colloquial diction, speech rhythms and prosaic words.

(6) **Delight in the Sensuous Beauty of Nature.** For the modern poet, nature is a box of toys which delights his heart and which is very dear to him. A deep feeling of love and joy in nature is a prominent characteristic of such poets as W.H. Davis, Walter De La Mare, Edmund Blunden, etc. But the modern poet does not spiritualise nature, like Wordsworth, nor does he intellectualise her, like Shelley. Rather, he is content to render her through the senses, and his rendering of her is remarkable for its realism, and precision in detail. However, Eliot does not write of nature of the countryside. His poetry is strictly urban.

(7) **The Humanitarian Spirit.** Nor does the modern poet love nature alone; he also loves and feels for the lower animals living in the lap of nature. He is moved by their suffering and makes a forceful plea for a more humane treatment of the dumb creation. Indeed, humanitarianism– a deepened sense of pity for the poor and the suffering– is a leading characteristic of modern poetry. Gibson in particular is the champion of the under dog and the down rodden. Davidson, Masefield, etc., are other poets who take pains to glorify and reveal the heroism of the mean, obscure, and squalid existence of the have-nots.

(8) **Disillusionment.** The new poetry is realistic and the poet's consciousness of the grim realities of life has shattered all illusions and romantic dreams. The pessimism of the modern poet is more poignant and heart-rending, even more than the pessimism of Hardy, because it arises out of the contemplation of the stark realities of life, and there is nothing sentimental about it. Eliot regards man as "hollow" and 'stuffed" and in *The Crazy-jane Poems* Of W. B. Yeats, "human sorrow becomes an elemental passion, profound, eternal and burning like a flame." As a matter of fact, the modern poet sees life as a whole, wants to face it squarely, and has no wish to escape from it into a world of dreams. He looks at life without the spectacle of romance, and paints it as he finds it in all its ugliness, and in all its misery and headache. Nor has he lost his capacity for laughter. Even in the works of the most pessimistic of poets, we find wit, satire, humour, grim jests and jokes.

(9) **The Religious Note.** The influence of science and the spirit of rationalism not mean that religion is not longer a source of inspiration in the new poetry. In T.S. Eliot and Francis Thompson, we find a revival of Christian mysticism. Masefield's *The Everlasting Mercy* has a religious theme and there are many fine devotional lyrics scattered all over his works. Even today there are mystical poets in the tradition of Blake and Wordsworth. Thus D.H. Lawrence has his mystic, "religion of blood", and speaks of strange dark gods. W.B. Yeats is a mystic visionary in whose poetry the gods and fairies of Celtic mythology live again, and T.S. Eliot finds the still point in the supernal.

(10) **The Metaphysical Note.** There has been a revival of interest in the poetry of Donne and the other Metaphysical Poets of the 17th century. **Grierson's** edition of Donne's poems was published in 1912, and ever since English poetry has reflected more and more the intellectual qualities of Donne's poetry. Eliot has done much to bring about this metaphysical revival.

(11) **The Romantic Note.** Despite its stark realism in theme and treatment, there also runs a vein of romanticism in modern poetry. Much of Georgian and Edwardian poetry is in the romantic strain. We find this strain of romance in the poetry of walter De La Mare, John Masefield, Edward Thomas, etc. Robert Bridges has left behind him some fine love lyrics, and W.B. Yeats has been called the greatest love poet of the 20th century.

(12) **Symbolism.** In France, this note of romance is struck by the French symbolists, Laforgue, Verlaine, Mellarme, etc. Under the influence of French symbolists, poets like Yeats and Eliot make extensive use of symbolism to communicate their vision and sensations, often too complex and intricate to be conveyed in any other way. Such use of symbolism often results in ambiguity and obscurity.

(13) **Poetic Techniques.** The modern poet is constantly experimenting with new verse forms and poetic techniques. The use of slang and colloquialism has become

common, the language and rhythm of poetry approximate more and more to those of common speech, the bonds of metre have been loosened, and the use of *verse libre* has become increasingly common.

(14) **The Age of Innovations.** Modern period was the age **Innovations.** *Impressionism, imagism and Surrealism* are some innovations in 20th century poetry. The impressionists seek to convey the vague, fleeting sensations passing through their minds by the use of a novel imagery and metaphor. The imagists, headed by Ezra Pound, aim at clarity of expression through the use of hard, accurate and definite images to convey their intellectual and emotional complexes. The Surrealists try to express whatever passes in the subconscious, or even the unconscious, without any control or selection by the conscious. These innovations have influenced the art of poets and verse writers of the age.

(B) Novel

English novel has got its immense popularity at the turn of the 19th century. It has eclipsed poetry and drama, it is the only literary form which has competed successfully with the radio and the cinema, and it is in this *genre* that work of the greatest merit is being produced. Chief literary trends of modern novel may be summarised in following ways,

(1) A prominent feature of the modern English novel is its immense variety and complexity. Novels are being written practically on all possible themes and subjects. A number of different trends are to be noticed.

(a) There are the traditionalists like *H.G. Wells, Arnold Bennett* and *Galsworthly* who, while they propound new ideas and open out new vistas to the human mind, still follow the Victorian tradition, as far as the technique of the novel is concerned.

(b) There are innovators, like *Henry James, Joseph Conrad, James Joyes,* and *Virginia Woolf,* who have revolutionised the technique of the novel with their probings into the subconscious.

(c) While *H.G. Wells* fully exploits modern science in his scientific romances, novelists of purpose or novelists of social reform, like *Galsworthy,* make the novel form a vehicle for the discussion of the baffling socio-economic problems of the day. Along with above discussed trends biographical novels, regional novels, satirical novels, sea-novels, detective novels, war-novels and novels of humour, also continue to flood the market and the list is by no means exhaustive.

(2) The modern novel is realistic. It deals with all the facts of contemporary life, the pleasant as well as the unpleasant, the beautiful as well as the ugly, and does not present merely a one-side view of life.

(3) The modern novel presents realistically the doubts, the conflicts and the frustrations of the modern world. It is, therefore, pessimistic in tone.

(4) The theories of psychologists, like *Freud* and *Havelock Ellis,* new biological theories and methods of birth control, and the boredom, frustration and brutality caused by the war, go far to explain the pre-occupation of the contemporary novel with sex-themes.

(5) The modern novel has evolved as a serious art form. It is compact in body and integrated in form and everything superfluous is careful avoided. It is very well constructed, having nothing loose or rambling about it.

(6) Story seems to have died out of the 20th century English novel. For the Victorian novelist life easily fell into the mould of a story; but for the novelist of today it refuses to do so. It is like a sentence that sets out confidentially. It has grasp of origins but not of ends. It is like an incomplete sentence and, its incompleteness is a reflection of the incompleteness of a whole region of thought and belief.

(7) The modern novelist rejects his characterisation as superficial. He has realised that it is impossible to give a psychologically true account of character by such means. He propose deep into the sub-conscious, even the unconscious, and loses himself in the complexities and subtleties of inner life; instead of depicting a conflict between different personalities, he depicts the individual at war with himself.

(8) The modern novels is predominantly psychological. The psychologist shock the foundations of human thought by their revolutionary discoveries in the field of Psychology. They revealed that human consciousness has very deep layers and buried under the conscious, are the subconscious and the unconscious. Novelists like *Henry James, Joseph conrad, James Joyce, Virginia Woolf, Dorothy Richardson, Elizabeth Bowen* have made the English novel extremely psychological in nature.

(9) The impact of the new psychology on plot and character has already been noticed above. Its impact has been equally far-reaching on the theme of the novel. There is a shift in the theme of the modern novelist. The individual is more important for him than society. Both *Lawrence* and *Forster* consider "the great society" as the enemy of the individual and want it to be reformed. Conrad's chief personages are all lonely souls and betrayal is the major theme of his novels.

(10) New influences, specially the Russian and the American, are daily widening its horizons and renewing its vigour and vitality. New experiments are being widening its horizons and renewing its vigour and vitality. New experiments are being conducted, some temporary and fleeting, others, of a more permanent significance. The caravan of the English novel goes on, everchanging, becoming and growing.

(C) Drama

(1) There is the naturalistic prose drama, dealing with contemporary social problems, focussing attention on them, discussing them from various angles, and in this way provoking thought on these problems. Shaw and Galsworthy are the chief exponents of this realistic prose drama.

(2) Despite the efforts of the major Victorian poets, there was not tradition of poetic drama at the beginning of the 20th century. But, later, it came in modern trend and became, common.

(a) By 1920, there were signs of a rebirth, but the atmosphere in which realistic, naturalistic drama throve was uncongenial to a play in verse.

(b) At the *Abbey Theatre* Dublin, **W.B. Yeats** attempted to revive poetry on the stage but he lacked the essential qualities of the dramatist.

(c) **Stephen Philips** (1864-1915) is a more important figure in the history of poetic drama. He wrote a number of blankverse plays, including *Herod, Ulysses, The Son of David,* and *Nero,* but he had little popular appeal.

(d) **Masefield** (1878-1967), too, experimented in poetic drama but had only limited success while **Gordon Bottomely** (1874-1948), who wrote a number of quite powerful poetical plays, saw hope for this form only in the amateur.

(e) It was also during this period that **John Drinkwater** (1882-1937), began his career with poetic dramas, and achieved popularity with such plays as *The Stonm, The God of Quiet,* and *X = 0 : A Night of the Trojan War.*

(f) But the true poetic drama was that of **J.M. Synge** (1871-1909) which, though not is verse, had all the qualities which the others lacked.

(g) **Lord Dunsany's** career as a dramatist began in 1909 with the staging of *The Glittering Gate.* One of the best exponents of the One-act play, he merit inclusion in our consideration of poetic drama (although he writes in prose) by virtue of the romance on which his plays are built and his ability to create a most powerful atmosphere, often of the East.

(h) **T.S. Eliot,** both through his theory and practice, provided a powerful stimulus to English Poetic Drama, and **Christopher Fry** (1907-2005) contributed to it the "Theatre of Words", and the "Comedy of moods."

Literary Criticism

(1) New discoveries in psychology, anthropology, sociology, economic, etc., have brought about a revolution in critical methods with the result that modern criticism is quite different from criticism in the 19th century. Critics like I.A. Richards, T.S. Eliot, F.R. Leavis, William Empson, have provided entirely new interpretations of old writers, and presented them in an entirely new light.

(2) However, at the turn of the century there were two traditions– the Mathew Arnold tradition of intellectual, abstract or scientific criticism, and the aesthetic, impressionistic tradition of Walter Pater– that held the day. Difference between these two traditions are as follows.

(a) While Arnold made "high seriousness" and "criticism of life" the tests of poetry, Pater's criticism aesthetic or impressionistic;

(b) While Arnold made art subservient to life, Pater advocated the theory of "art for art's sake".

(c) Arnold's influence was an all-pervasive and continuing one. That is why Eliot once remarked that we seem still to be living in the critical tradition of Arnold. Pater, on the other hand, has been a source of inspiration for the *"Bloomsbury group"* of critics, as E.M. Forster, Virginia Woolf, Lytton Strachy, and Clive Bell.

According to these critics, the enjoyment of art and the appreciation of beauty is the greatest good of human life, and art, therefore, must be freed from the shackles of morality. Their criticism is impressionistic, they assess a work of literature on the basis of the pleasure that it affords them.

(3) Literary criticism is largely academic, the work of distinguished university professors. They are eminent scholars, they painstakingly collect facts, biographical, historical and social, and evaluate a writer on the basis of these facts, but they lack a precise point of view. Chief among these scholar-critics are– *George Saintsbury, Edward Dowden, A.C. Bradley, Oliver Elton, W.B. Ker, W.J. Courthope,* etc.

(4) There is another group of scholars who devote their attention to textual-emendation. Distinguished scholars, like *Furness, Dover Wilson, Gregg, Pollard,* try to reach an authentic version of old texts.

(5) After World War I, English insularity was broken and ideas and influences from Europe began to flow in and affect the course of literary criticism in England.

First, there was the influence of Marx and his concept of class struggle. Writers were analysed and interpreted in terms of class-conflict. For example, **David Daiches** in his book *Society and Literature* shows how economic trends are reflected in literature; **Christopher Caudwell** studies Shakespeare, Milton, Wordsworth, Coleridge, and the other romantics, against the background of social and economic changes. Aestheticism of Pater is thus rejected and literature is viewed as a social activity reflecting the changing social and economic patterns.

(6) There was the potent influence of the Italian critic Benedetto Croce. According to his theory, vivid picture are constantly rising in the mind of the poet, and he must express them spontaneously and fully as they arise in his mind, without any attempts at organisation. *This is known as Expressionism.*

(7) Expressionistic writing is bound to be broken and fragmentary in keeping with the fragmentary and chaotic nature of the vague sensation fleeting through the consciousness of the poet. The teaching of Croce had a far-reaching impact on creative and literary activity in England.

(8) Closely allied with Expressionism is the French theory of *Surrealism.* Surrealism attributes artistic creation of dreams and the influence of spirits who inspire the artist with his forms and images. Herbert Read is one of those critics whose works reveal the influence of this creed.

(9) English criticism is strengthened by the teachings of modern psychology, specially those of **Freud, Jung** and **Bergson**. Freud believed that suppression of the sex-instinct result in frustration and neurosis, and art is but a sublimated expression of this neurosis. Psychological theories were used for an analysis and interpretation of past writers and their works. Thus *Hamlet* has been interpreted in the light of Freud's theory of the *Oedipus complex.* The motives and processes that lead to a particular work of art were studied and thus new dimensions were added to literary criticism.

(10) The impact of literature on the mind of the readers is sought to be explained in Psychological terms. **I.A. Rechards** is the most outstanding of the critics of the psychological school. According to him, the pleasure of literature arises from the fact that it brings about a healthy equilibrium between the instincts and impulses of the readers.

(11) After the World War II, the most potent single influence was that of the "New *Critics."* The term was first used by J.E. Spingarn, and though the New Criticism had its origin in the writings of T.E. Hulme, it is now mainly an American movement. Its chief exponents in America are Kenneteh Burke, John Crowe Ransome, Allen Tate, Richard Blackmur, Cleanth Brooks, etc. In Englandits leading representatives are I.A. Richards, T.S. Eliot, F.R. Leavis, William Empson etc.

(12) The New Critics are opposed to the biographical, historical, sociological, and comparative approach of conventional criticism. All such considerations are regarded as extrinsic and irrelevant, and a work of art is judged solely on its own merits.

MODERN POETRY

(1) **Rudyard Kipling** (1865-1936). Kipling is an imperialist who celebrates the British empire and the white man's burden in his poetry, as well as in his novels. He was essentially the poet of soldiers and sailors; and many of his poems are written on the exploits of British soldiers in foreign lands. The language he uses is the

language actually used by the British soldiers. "By making the uneducated British fighting man articulate, Kipling brought a new element into English poetry." *Departmental Ditties (1886), Barrack Room Ballads* (1892), *The Seven Seas* (1896), *The Five Nations* (1903) and *Inclusive Verse* and *Poems* (1830) contain the best of his poetry.

He is the poet of England and the laureate of her empire. Imperialism finds a clear and unabashed voice in him. He exulted in the achievements of his countrymen in founding the Empire and did not care to emphasis the harsh and cruel means they adopted to colonies foreign lands. He is proud of the achievement of England and constantly harps on the white man's burden. He is narrowly nationalistic in his outlook.

Kipling shows great skill as a craftsman and a motorist, but he lacks that intensity of vision which results in great poetry.

(2) **Thomas Hardy** (1840-1928) Thomas Hardy OM : Order of Merit, was one of the two great pessimistic poets of The Edwardian era poetry is the final expression of the disillusionment resulting from the advance of science and the disintegration of faith and traditional values.

The pessimism, which is a characteristic feature of Hardy's fiction, also marks his poetry. His poems reveal his consciousness of the miseries and sufferings of human life. As in his novels, so in his poetry his theme is the human predicament and the suffering which is caused to him by the imperfections of the power that rules on high. Destiny strews joy and pain with a nerveless and purposeless hand and this aimlessness makes human life, " a strange orchestra of victim shriek and pain." However, his pessimism is not an unrelieved one for he believes that human lot can be made endurable through tact, mutual sympathy, and wise social reform. Some of his works are 'Far From the Madding Good', 'The Mayor of Casterbridge.

(3) **A.E. Houseman** (1859-1936). Housemen Joins Hardy in the run of pessimistic poets of edwardian era. His poetry bears of close affinity to that of Hardy. His poetic output was small. He produced *A Shropshire Lad* (1896), *Last Poems* (1922), and *More Poems,* (1936). The predominant mood in his poetry is one of "cultured ironical disillusionment with life", though underlying this tragic view there is a warm appreciation of the beauties of nature, particularly in *A Shropshire Lad which* depicts the country life of the Welsh border. The poems of Housemen have the polished ease and restraint which might be expected of so fine a classical scholar. They are concise, sometimes epigrammatic in expression yet always perfectly easy to understand. Music came to him under the stress of emotion, but it was controlled by his scholarly sense for metre."

It is Housemen's love of Nature that relieves much of the gloom and tedium of his pessimism. His nature-poetry is refreshing.

(4) **Robert Bridges** (1844-1930). Bridges was essentially an artist and artistic subjects like Beauty, Love and Nature are the themes of his poetry.

He learnt the art of poetry very painstakingly. He is a great artist with words; the stamp of The artist's pen is on every line of his verse.

As a lyric poet, he lacked the force and intensity of Shelley's lyrics. He had too much of artistic reserve and self-control to soar aloft on the wings of lyric fancy. His lyrics are marked with artistic beauty, but the fire of passion and the heat of emotion do not kindle them. His best love poetry is contained in "*The Growth of Love*", a sonnet-sequence. *Awake My Heart, to be Loved, Awake are his famous love lyrics. Among these Awake* is one of the finest love-lyrics in the English language.

Bridges is the poet of joy and optimism. According to him, earthly beauty is only a reflection of heavenly beauty. Beauty is not merely an earthly vision of womanly grace, but the manifestation of divine beauty and perfection in human life.

Bridges is also a great lover of the beauty of nature. His enjoyment of Nature is personal and first hand and his expression of her beauty is simple and direct, unaffected by any artificial glow of imagination.

He was a great metrical artist. "His effort was to naturalise classical metres in England. He threw fresh light on the laws and secrets of English versification and provoked considerable interest in the study of English prosody.

(5) **Gerald Manley Hopkins** (1844-89). Hopkins was a great religious poet of the 20th century, an age essentially irreligious. He embraced the Roman Catholic in 1866. His early poetry reveals his love of religion, nature and God. He glorifies God and his own soul. *The Wreck of he Deutschland,* 1875, his longest and most difficult poem, recounts the death of five nuns who went down in the ship of that name. It is a poem marked with tragic pathos. His last poems *That nature is a Heraclitear Fire and Of the Comfort of the Resurrecion* show that he regained his lost faith in God. He sees all Nature consumed into ashes while his soul alone remains imperishable like an "immortal diamond". It has been said, "that the poet in Hopkins was strangled by the priest." But the poetry of Hopkins, while glorifying God, is not without an acute sensibility for the beauties of Nature. His appreciation of nature is deep and heartfelt, more specially, his early poetry reveals a sensuous love of nature.

Hopkins was a great artist with words as well as a great rhythmic innovator. He believed that poetry needed a language distinct from that of prose, a language rich in suggestion both to the senses and the intellect. He freely used archaic and colloquial words. He used compound epithets such as, "drop-of blood", "foam-dapple cherry", and his imagery is short and precise.

(6) **John Masefield (1878-1967).** John Masefield was a Georgian poet. He succeeded Robert Bridges as poet Laureate in 1930. His early poetry was written in the style and manner of Kipling and is marked with a note of action and adventure. It was his *Salt Water Ballads*_(1902) which brought out fully his genius as a poet. *Ballads and Poems* (1910) show an advance in technical skill. *The Everlasting Mercy* (1911) is his first really great narrative poem. It was followed by *The Widow in the Bye Street* (1912), *The Daffodil Fields* (1913) *and Lollingdown Down* (1917). *Dauber* (1913) is an autobiographical poem describing the life of a youth who runs away to sea, and it contains many reminiscences of the poets' early life. *Reynard the Fox* (1919), a vigorous narrative poem, is " a little Odyssey of fox-hunting." It contains many true Chaucerian sketches of human figure.

His poetry is charged with his democratic sympathy for the downtrodden, the poor and the suffering. He is essentially a poet of the people. Another important feature of his poetry is his stark realism, and sometimes it becomes coarse and brutal, ugly and sordid.

He is also a romanticist and a lover of beauty, and best of his poems are those in which we get glimpses both of romance and beauty as in poems like *'The Seekers'* and *'Cargoes'*.

Mesefield is a great sea-poet and few poets have been able to capture the atmosphere and life of sea, the ships, and sailors, as vividly and realistically as he has done in poems like *Dauber* and *Sea-Fever.* He loves the English landscape and his poetry gives a many-sided picture of rural England.

Masefield's poetry suffers from many faults – a coarse brutal realism expressed in slangy and violent phraseology is his besetting sin. But, on the whole, he is a great poet and he deserves all praise for his narrative poems, his democratic feelings of sympathy; his love for nature, and his appreciation of the beauties of the countryside.

(7) **Walter De La Mare (1873-1956).** He is among the poets of the Georgian period. He is essentially the poet of the fairyland creating in his poetry a world of dreams, fantasies and imagination, a world which appeals to children as well as to grown up people. In *The Listeners and Other Poems* (1912), *Peacock Pie* (1913), *The Fleeting and Other Poems* (1933), *Collected Poems* (1902–18)' *Poems for Children* (1930), *Bells and Grass* (1941), *The Traveller,* (1946) we have some of the finest poetry of the era.

He is formally and by profession a children's poet. He has very successfully captured the joy and pleasures of childhood in his *Songs of Childhood.*

His Poetry is the note of fantasy. He gives his fancy free reign, and throws to the winds the laws of logic and probability. He is the laureate of the fairyland. Fairies, ghosts and phantoms haunt his poems. He provides an escape from the problems of life into the world of the fairies. In *The Listerners* and *The Mocking Fairy,* the haunting atmosphere is expectancy grips the readers who read spell-bound upto the very end.

He is also a master artist and a superb craftsman. His verses have a cadence and subtlety of rhythm which linger, rise and fall like the tremulous fall of a snow-flake. All this wizardry of music and technical perfection is achieved without the least sign of artifice or labour. It has the ease and effortlessness of he highest art.

(8) **James Elroy Flecker (1884-1995).** Flecker is essentially the poet of the East, dwelling lovingly in a world of oriental grandeur and magnificence. He was fascinated by the exotic novelty and illusive romanticism of the east, which he has depicted in one poem after another.

He is the master of jewelled phrase and gem-like verse. He is a great and inspired artist with words – "He has full command over his language and versification." "He delights in the very names of exotic things and distant places, and master as he is of dazzling phrase and supple rhythm, he seldom fails to evoke an answering delight in the reader."

(9) **W.H. Davies (1871-1940).** Davies is a great poet of Nature and rural life. He presents the sights and scenes of nature as well as the life of the innocent country people living in the lap of nature. He has immortalised himself through his *The Autobiography of a Super Tamp* (1908). It was after the loss of a leg while attempting to board a train that he turned to poetry for a living and produced a few volumes of verses, which at once caught the public eye, and brought fame and recognition to the poet.

Davies is essentially a lyric poet. His lyrics are short and spontaneous. Most of Davies poems are shorter than those of any other modern poet. Out of 400 poems in his *Collected Poems,* two hundred and seventy are only of three stanzas or even less. His lyrics are characterised by, spontaneity and simplicity.

The world of his poetry is a world of vivid description of natural beauty. Of intense joy, a world of sunrises, cows and sheep, owls and cuckoos, butterflies and squirrels. Davies may not be very accurate and precise in his nature-descriptions. He does not seek to portray Nature with the eye of a scientific observer. But he communicates successfully his own joy in nature, and inspires his readers with his own zest for Nature. There is something infectious about the freshness of nature in his poetry.

There is a note tender sympathy in Davies' poems for animals and children. He has a sense of the tramp's comradeship with the horse, the cow, the sheep, the cuckoo and the butterfly.

Literary Career and Works

Davies wrote his first poem entitled Death. In his Poet's Pilgrimage (1918) Davies recounts the time when, at the age of 14, he was left with orders to sit with his dying grandfather.

Davies's view of his own disability was ambivalent. In his poem The Fog, published in the 1913 Foliage, a blind man leads the poet through the fog, showing the reader that one who is handicapped in one domain may well have a considerable advantage in another.

For his poetry Davies drew extensively on his experiences with the seamier side of life, but also on his love of nature. By the time of his prominent place in the Edward Marsh Georgian Poetry series, he was an established figure. He is generally best known for the opening two lines of the poem Leisure, first published in Songs of Joy and Others in 1911 : What is the life if, full of care/We have no time to stand and stare ..."

His first collection, The Soul's Destroyer (1905), established many of the key features of Davies's verse: pastoralism and sympathy for the underdog.

Between 1905 and 1939, he published several volumes of poetry. In 1908, his Autobiography of a Super-Tramp was published, which described his experiences of a vagrant life. It was written in bildungsroman mode, Davies begins his autobiography by relating the story of his childhood in Wales, where he was raised by his grandparents after his father died and his mother abandoned her children.

Davies also produced 4 novels, including The True Traveller (1912) and The Adventures of Johnny Walker, Tramp (1926); other prose works included Beggars (1909), Nature (1.914) and My Birds and My Garden (1933). He wrote two poems about his experience. One is called Sheep.

(10) **John Drinkwater (1882-1937).** John Drinkwater's *Collected Poems* show that he is an intellectual interested not in lyrics and songs, but in elegiac and meditative verse. His poems exhibit his gravity and earnestness, his sanity and rigorous discipline. He is a self-conscious artist, who writes in the "cold ink of thought", rather than in the "red blood of a fired brain." "His work is always controlled in emotion and expression. There is little of the *furor poeticus,* and his language and imagery shows him to be a deliberate, careful craftsman of rather limited gifts." His imagery shines not as a star or a flower, but like a jewel, a priceless gem of art. "He speculates, meditates, ruminates, but only rarely illuminates, other than as the glow-worm illuminates himself and his own surroundings."

However, John Drinkwater will be remembered not for his longer, reflective poetry, but for his nature poetry. He represented and celebrated "the English countryside, its streams and pools and woods, its birds and cattle and flowers, its shepherds and gypsies, with a cultured pastoral fancy untroubled by any urgencies." Few modern poets equal Drinkwater in the appreciation of nature.

(11) **W.B. Yeats (1865-1939).** Yeats was an Irish man, but he takes his place among the great English poets of the age.

He is great by virtue of the bulk and variety of his poetry, and critics have agreed that very few of his poems can be regarded as definitely inferior. His work is uniformly good even though he writes on such varied subjects as ancient legend, mythology, folklore, politics, history, love, and constantly makes new myths of his own. His creative range is immense, he writes with perfect ease and mastery on themes taken from every possible sphere of life, and a high standard of performance is maintained throughout.

The period of poetic activity in his case extended over fifty years. His early poetry is romantic while the later one is realistic both in theme and treatment. He began writing verse in the thinned out romantic, Pre-raphaelite tradition. His early poems are frankly escapist and are heavily over-hung with Pre-Raphaelite tapestry. His use of Irish mythology and folklore took all Europe by storm and it had a rare fascination for those who were fed up with the hackneyed classical myths and legends.

He has been called by **Graham Hough** and others, *"the last of the great romantics"* , but he became dissatisfied with this romanticism and discarded it more and more as he aged. His later poetry is characterised by stark, naked realism, even brutality and coarseness, and with a masculine vigour and force. In keeping with modern realistic trends, there is greater and greater approximation to speech rhythms and colloquial diction. The poetry of the rich and complex *The Tower* and *The* Winding Stair volumes is a majestic utterance which stimulates and lifts up the readers by its very urgency, intensity and immediacy.

His poetry is a battle-ground for the clash of opposites. The antimonies of the human and the non-human, of the spiritual and the physical, the sensuous and the artistic, physical decay and intellectual maturity, the past and the present, the personal and the impersonal, power and helplessness, are for ever appearing and reappearing in his poetry. In the early poetry, such opposites are merely rendered, but in his later poetry, according to David Daiches, there is also an attempt at reconciling them.

Yeats was a symbolist from the beginning to the end of his carrier, so **Arther Symons** regarded him as the chief exponent of the Symbolist Movement in England.

With age and experience, Yeats acquired full command over his material and widened the scope of the lyric. Thus in the brief, *Leda and the Swan* the poet succeeded in compressing whole ages of history from the remote antiquity down to the present age. The admirable and effective poem *The Second Coming* owes its intensity to Yeats' prophetic vision.

Cleanth Brooks regards him as a great myth-maker and his *Vision as "the most ambitious attempt made by any poet of our time to set up a myth".*

The charge of obscurity has sometimes been brought against Yeats. There is no doubt a vein of mysticism running through Yeats' poetry and mysticism by its very nature is incapable of rational exposition. Yeats was a conscious artist. He selects his words with reference both to their sense and sound. As an artist, he had the creative gift and the inward conviction and his so-called arrogance arises from his assurance. He may sometimes seem coarse and brutal, but his very brutality is an expression of his integrity of purpose.

He kept away from the *Verse libre* and other technical innovations of his day, but he used the traditional metres and stanza-forms with consummate skill. He freed the English lyric from the tyranny of he limbic and manipulated the stress, pause and cadence of the long line with great mastery and self-confidence. The octosyllabic couplet he made particularly his own and brought out its full colloquial possibilities. He had a Donne-like command over stanza-structures and made his stanza patterns correspond with the movement of thought and emotion. The sudden shifts in tone and mood, often within the same line, further indicate Yeats' affinity with Donne and his school.

He may not be a Shakespeare, a Dante, or a Milton, but he must certainly rank with the greatest poets of all times.

(12) **Imagist Poets.** The reaction against Georgian trend is represented by a group of poets who called themselves 'Imagists' for their aim was to represent real life in images that were clear, precise and exact. The founder of this school, **T.E. Hulme** (1833-1917) and his most illustrious disciple **Ezra Pound** insisted that, "poetry should restrict itself to the world perceived by the senses and to the presentation of its themes in a succession of concise, clearly visualized, concrete images, accurate in detail and precise in significance. They defined poetry, "as the presentation of visual situation in the fewest possible concrete words, lightened of the lightened of the burdens of conventional adjectival padding and unhampered by general ideas or philosophical or moral speculations. The new rhythms of the Imagists bore a close affinity to those of everyday speech and were quite different from conventional verse-patterns.

Ezra Pound and **Edith Sitwell** are the two most original and prominent poets of this school. Their poetry is still read and enjoyed.

(13) **Rupert Brooke (1987-1915).** Brooke was soldier-poet. He gave expression to patriotic fervour in his sonnets, particularly in the *Soldier.* When the war came in 1914, Brooke hailed it with enthusiasm. He wrote a number of war sonnets expressing his patriotic enthusiasm and noble resolve to serve his country. He himself enlisted as a soldier, and went to war for the sake of his dear motherland. He was killed in action in 1915, and in popular imagination he was canonized. "It is natural, though unprofitable, to speculate is to what might have been Rupert Brook's place in English poetry if he had lived on. The marks of greatness in his poems are few, but such marks there are. He saw the world with a clear eye and recorded what he was with directness and clarity. Yet, however poetic in himself, Rupert Brooke was more important as the occasion for poetry in other "*the war-time revival of English poetry, had its origin in Brooke aloue*" **(A.C. Ward).**

(14) **Miss Edith Sitwell (1887-1964).** The early poetry of Edith Sitwell partakes fully of the gloom and frustration generated by the war. Her long poem *The Sleeping Beauty* is a highly-wrought work of art, glowing with colour and imagery. She was considerably influenced by the second world war and her memorable war poems *Songs of the Cloud* (1945) and *The Canticle of the Sun* (1949) bring out the impact of the second war on the poetess. "Later Edith Sitwell developed into one of the major religious and metaphysical poets of the period under the stressful and sobering influences of the troubled nineteen thirties and the ensuing second world war. *The Song of the Cloud* (1945) though containing mainly poems written from 1919 onward, also includes a number of pieces from her early and middle period, and shows her progress from the fantastical to the spiritual – a progress which, in the light of her poetry as a whole, can be seen as orderly and inevitable" (A.C. Ward).

(15) **T.S. Eliot (1888-1965).** He dominated the English literary scene and tried his hand at poetry, at drama, at criticism, both literary and social, and at journalism, and achieved eminent success in each of these field. He has become a part and parcel of the English literary tradition which he has modified and enriched for the benefit of the coming generations.

One of his greatest achievements consists in his having given expression to the dominant anxieties and feelings of his age. Through the medium of his poems he has rendered the torturing impact of a great metropolis on the human soul, the anguish, the ennui, the boredom, the neurosis which such a life generates. But he is not merely a representative poet, he is also a critic of his age. He universalises contemporary predicament, and shows it to be a part of the human predicament in every age and country. His poetry is a curious mixture of tradition and individual talent. The English Metaphysical tradition, the French Symbolist movement, the poetry of Dante, Existential philosophy, the philosophies of the orient, Hindu, Buddhist and others, Christian tradition and theology, and ancient myths and legends, are only a few of the many influences which have gone into the making of his poetry. He called himself a "Classicist in literature." He was a conscious artist who, like the classics, achieved formal perfection through carefully studied means.

His poetry is a poetry of revolt against the decadent and exhausted, almost dead, poetry of his day; it marks a complete break from the thinned out romantic tradition. He was that architect of the English language, who tried to restore to it life and vitality bringing it into contact not only with current speech but also with European literary tradition.

The use of conversational rhythms and imagery drawn from urban life, the use of symbols, the juxtaposing of the past and the present in his poetry, etc., are some of the ways in which he communicates his sense of the modern predicament.

He forged new measures to express the complexity and intricacy of modern life. The traditional lambic metre was loosened and made more and more flexible till it could express the changing tempo of the modern mind, the clash of opposite thoughts and feelings within the soul, as well as the jaring sounds and incoherent noises of urban life. Eliot's view of life was essentially religious. He has given impetus to a number of poets to experiment with new forms and evolve new techniques.

Literary Career and Works

Eliot met Ezra Pound in 1914. Pound became his literary mentor who got his poems published and aided him in receiving critical acclaim. Eliot's first major poem The Love Song of I Abcred Prufrock was published at-Pound's insistence in Poetry: A Magazine of Verse after Pound persuaded the magazine editor-Harriet Monroe. The poem was later published in a separate book as part of Eliot's first published collection of poetry Prafroek and Other Observations in 1917. This famous modernist poem examined the fragmented and tormented psyche, emotionally and physically sterile character of the prototypical modern man. The title of this 'song' comes from Rudyard Kipling's poem The Lave Song of Har Dyal. Although the title refers to the poem as a 'love song', the poem is actually anti-romantic in tone, reflecting on Prufrock's failure as a lover.

The poem's well known opening lines contain a conceit that compares evening to a patient lying upon the table

Let us go then, you and I,
When the evening is spread out against the sky
Like a patient etherised upon a table;

Eliot's next major work– the 434 lime modemist landmark poem The Wasteland was first published in The Criterion. Eliot dedicated the poem to Pound and referred to him as *il miglior fabbro* or *the better craftsman.* This phrase emphasised Pound's hand in editing and shaping the poem. Although, criticised for being too obscure and complex, The Wasteland reflects Eliot's disillusionment with the moral and spiritual decay in post-World War Europe. Apart from writing poetry, Eliot also served as literary editor of the feminist magazine, the Egoist.

He was also a notable modern critic known for his essays Tradition and the Individual Talent and Hamlet and His Problems, both published in 1920.

In Tradition and Individual Talent, Eliot defined poetry as 'not a turning loose of emotion, but an escape from emotion; 'not the expression of personality, but an escape from personality'. Eliot's plays Murder in the Cathedral (1935), The Family Reunion (1939), The Cocktail Party (1949), The Confidential Clerk (1954), and The Elder Statesman (1959) were published in one volume in 1962.

In 1948, he was awarded Nobel Prize in Literature for his pioneer contribution to poetry. He died on 4th January, 1965, in London.

Major Works

Poetry

- Prufrock and Other Observations (1917)
- The Love song of J Alfred Prufrock
- Portrait of A Lady
- Aunt Helen

Poems (1920)

- Gerontion
- Sweeney Among the Nightingales
- Mr Eliot's Sunday Morning Service
- A Cooking Egg
- The Waste Land (1922)
- The Hollow Men (1925)
- Ariel Poems (1927-1954)
- The Journey of the Magi (1927)
- Ash Wednesday (1930)
- Four Quartets (1945)

Plays

- Sweeney Agonistes (published in 1926, first performed in 1934)
- The Rock (1934)
- Murder in the Cathedral (1935)
- The Family Reunion (1939)
- The Cocktail Party (1949)
- The Confidential Clerk (1953)
- The Elder Statesman (first performed in 1958, published in 1959)

(16) **W.H. Auden (1907-1973).** Auden studied the life of the common man and the social problems confronting him in the post-war world. He was disgusted with the outdated social order and advocated violent social reforms for bringing about a more just social order. He advocated revolutionary reforms along communistic lines for the regeneration of the downtrodden and the miserable sections of society. His early poetry, written during the inter-war period, expresses his sense of the, *"hollowness of the disintegrating post-war civilization"*.

Later, Auden came under the influence of Freud and his psychological approach to the problems of human life. He now advocated sympathetic understanding of the problems of the weaker sections of society, rather than a sentimental sympathy for them.

As an artist and experimentator, Auden showed considerable intellectual curiosity and receptiveness to new ideas and suggestions. He was influenced in many ways by Eliot, Owen, Hopkins and the French symbolists.

Major Works

- Poems (1930)
- The Operators An English Study (1932, dedicated to Stephen Spender)
- The Dance of Death (1933, play dedicated to Robert Medley and Rupert Doone)
- Poems (1934; contains Poems [1933 edition], The Oratam [1932 edition] and The Dance of Death)
- The Dog Beneath the Skin (1935; play with Christopher Isherwood, dedicated to Robert Moody)
- Look, Stranger! (1936, Us Edn. On this Island, 1937) (dedicated to Erika Mann)
- For the Time Being (1944)
- The Age of Anxiety A Baroque Eclogue (1947, dedicated to John Betjeman)
- The Shield of Achilles (1955)
- The Enchfed Flood or The Romantic Iconography of the Sea (1950, dedicated to Alan Ansen)

(17) **Stephen Spender (1909-1995).** He is interested in the uplift of the masses, and has constantly advocated social reform on Communistic lines. *Poems* (1933) clearly indicate the same Marxist attitude as that of Auden. In the poems of this volume we have the vision of a future world from which death, despair and decay have been completely wiped out. The old world, *"where shapes of death haunt human life"*, must go and the young comrade must, *"advance got rebuild...advance to rebel"*, giving up, *"dreams...of heaven after our world."* They must be governed and dominated by, *"the palpable and obvious love of man for man."* They must work for a world in which none would die of hunger and, *"Man shall be man."*

Spender is "an artist of fine sensibilities and considerable technical accomplishment", and his work is widely admired today for his lyricism, sensuous imagery, psychological penetration, introspective insight, and his advocacy of the inherent dignity and nobility of the individual.

Literary Career and Works

Spender's early poetry, Poems (1933) was inspired by themes of social struggle. His poem Vienna (1934) was written in praise of the 1934 uprising of Viennese socialists, while Trial of a Judge (1938) was an anti-Fascist drama in verse. His autobiography, World within World (1951), was a recreation of the political and social atmosphere of the 1930s. He also tried his hand at novel writing. His first novel The Temple was not published until 1988 because of its frank portrayal of homosexuality. Spender also wrote works of literary and social criticism such as The Destructive Element (1935), The Creative Element (1953), The Making of a Poem (1962) and Love-Hate Relations: English and American Sensibilities (1974).

He died at the age of 86.

Major Works

- Poems, 1933
- Vienna, 1934
- Trial of a Judge, 1938
- The Edge of Being, 1949
- World within World, 1951
- The Generous Days, 1969
- Love-Hate Relations, 1974
- The Thirties and After, 1978
- Collected Poems 1928-1985, 1985
- Dolphins, 1994

(18) **Cecil Day Lewis (1904-1972).** "Cecil Day Lewis gives perhaps the clearest expression to the revolutionary doctrines shared by a number of his poetic friends, like Auden and Spender." In the **Magnetic Mountain,** he makes a frontal attack on the existing social order and makes a fervent appeal for a revolution which would usher in a more just social system. In the early poetry of Day Lewis, the influence of T.S. Eliot and Auden is clearly perceptible. But Day Lewis, in spite of the influence of Auden, "is a more human poet". His poetry is not intellectual in tone. He does not exhibit, "the same restless intellect and acquisitiveness of knowledge as does Auden". He is a great lover of the beauty of nature, and his love of nature is clearly brought out by his later lyrics. "Day Lewis was an open air poet, above all a poetry of the wind and of bird-song, of everything that shared and inspired his own nervous vitality **(A.S. Collins).**

(19) **Dylan Thomas (1914-1953).** Dylan Thomas is closely associated with the revival of religious poetry in the forties. He is also recognised as the father of the new romantic poetry of the poetry. His poetry is strongly emotional in tone, full of fervour and vigour. It is vital, and vividly colourful and musical. "The depth and intensity of his passion, his verbal gift, the technical skill which underlies his metrical experiments, all suggest that Dylan Thomas has the making of a great poet".

Dylan Thomas is a difficult poet, for his poetry is packed with metaphor symbolic imagery, often difficult to grasp. A number of his earlier poems are obscure because of their metaphor and imagery, and above all their use of personal symbols. His attempt to push into the service of his muse every Biblical, Freudian or folk-image, makes him obscure and difficult. He is a poet for the learned few, and not for the average reader. In this respect he is true disciple of T.S. Eliot.

MODERN NOVEL

(1) **Henry James (1843-1916).** He was a prolific writer who has left behind him a number of novels, short stories, essays, articles and critical tracts. *The Portrait of a Lady and The Ambassadors are* his masterpieces.

He developed his theory of the novel in his famous critical work *The Art of Fiction* (1884). According to James, the main business of the novelist is to give his impressions of life in such a manner as to create an illusion of reality in his work. In his view the novelist is an *impressionist,* competing with, "his brother the painter in his attempt to render the look of things, the look that conveys their meaning, the colour, the relief, the expression, the surface, the substance of the human spectacle." James believed that a novel should not be used for preaching of imparting moral lessons.

Henry James departed from the Victorian tradition, in as much as he paid no attention to the construction of his plots. There is very little action in the novels of James. He is concerned more with the study of mental processes than with the emotions of the human heart.

He evolved the technique of presenting his story "through the consciousness of a single character, thus discarding the ubiquity and omniscience of traditional novelist". He is the first of the impressionists.

Literary Career and Works

He met his cousin Mary Temple, who impressed him very much. She was young and zealous. She was fond of reading (George Eliot). He portrayed her in many of his works in The Portrait of a Lady as Isabel Archer, The Wings of the Dave as Milly Theale, The Awkward Age as Nanda and The Golden Bowl as Maggie Verver. In 1848, the review of Henry James first book appeared in the North American Review. His first story The Story of a Year appeared in the Atlantic Monthly in March 1865. In 1866, his story Poor Richard was praised by the author William Dean.

He settled in England. In Europe, he met many great writers and artists. In his book Partial Sketches, he wrote these experiences. He wrote biography of Nathaniel Hawthorne in 1897. He wrote his first great novel The Portrait of a Lady (1881). It got great success. It is called a master piece and is a story of a young, spirited American woman 'affronting her destiny. The novel is an account of the limits of self-sufficiency which makes it stand as a great American novel and a critique of American exceptionalism." He died of TB in 1870 in the age of 24.

(2) **George Moore (1852-1933).** George Moore was a realist, his aim being to paint life realistically. In the view of Walter Allen, he took over the "naturalistic novels" from France and tried to popularise it in England. He was an Irishman who, early in his life, came under the influence of Zola and Flaubert, from whom he learned the subtle art of presenting the reality of things in an impartial and impersonal manner. In his novels like *A Modern Lover* (1813), *A Mummer's Wife* (1885), *Spring Days* (1888) and Esther Waters (1894), he made a sympathetic study of the poor people and their miserable existence. His realism often grows morbid and oppressive, for his novels present a lose and realistic study of the sordid side human life bringing to view the misery and suffering of the poor and the down-trodden. The sympathy of the novelist is always with those whose lot is to suffer.

(3) **George Gissing (1857-1903).** Gissing was essentially a realist, like Moore, interested in the study of the people and their mean and squalid existence. However he did not sympathise with the poor as did George Moore. He simple focussed the attention of social reformers on the miseries of the underdog and the socially alienated. His pictures of the sordid and seamy side of life have been drawn convincingly. He exhibited a rare skill in his unflinching realism, concrete detail, and a graphic description of the poor in an urban industrialised society. But he could not achieve the detachment of Moore; he was subjective and often coloured his accounts of the poor with his own personal experiences. His main works are *The nether World* (1889), Grub *Street* (1891), and *The House of Cobwebs* (1906).

The Private Papers of henry Ryecraft is autobiographical in character and presents realistic studies of the squalid and savage people whom he had personally known, but without much sympathy with their unhappy lot. However he is more sympathetic to women; the range of his female characters is considerably greater than that of his men. This makes *The Odd Women and In the year of the* Jubilee, his most successful novels.

(4) **Samuel Butler (1835-1902).** Butler, "the literary bad boy of the Victorians", whom he scandalized almost as badly as his namesake had scandalized the Puritans, and for the same reason, because he understood neither their idealism nor the moral earnestness from which it sprang.

The fame of Samuel Butler rests chiefly on three novels, *Erewhon* (1872), and its equal *Erewhon Revisited,* and *The Way of All Flesh (1903),* which is his best known work. In these novels Butler blazed a new trail which ran counter to the prevailing tendencies of the Age. Bulter's book (*The Way of All Flesh*) was dominated by his opinions and prejudices. His book sprawled over several generations and suffered a major fracture half-way through. He often contented himself with basic summary of both scene and conversation.

Butler exercised considerable influence on the younger novelists who were bent flouting Victorian taboos and conventions. *As a scientific rationalist,* Butler subjected the sentimental sanctions of the home and Parental love and filial duty to a chilly anthropological scrutiny, and as an evolutionist he traced the ancestry of his central character to show how the dominant was all the more thorough by being reinforced by Butler's antipathy to Christian faith in general and the Church of England in particular. Butler is an original thinker and a great iconoclast, though not a great technician.

(5) **Rudyard Kipling (1865-1936).** He was a prolific and versatile writer. He was a poet, a journalist, a novelist and a teller of tales. He was both a realist and a romancer. He was a realist in his setting and character, which are however romantically treated. Realism is the basis of his romance. He is an impressionist whose pictures of reality are coloured by his own personal impression, and so are tinged with romance. Instead of finding romance in the past and the Middle Ages, he finds romance in the present realities of life. *"He is the romancer of he present, of the modern social order, on which shines from afar a light as resplendent as that which shone on medieval society, for it is the same light of the imagination. Kipling feels the presence of romance in shot and shell as well as in bow and arrows, and in red coats as well as in buff jerkins"* **(W.L. Cross).**

Kipling was an imperialist and his tales are so many glorifications of the British rule and British empire. "His insistent proclamation of the superiority of the white races, of Britain's undoubted mission to extend through her imperial policy the benefits of civilization to the rest of the world, his belief in progress and the value of the machine, found an echo in the hearts of many of his readers" **(E. Albert).** This accounts for his contemporary popularity.

(6) **Arnold Bennett (1867-1931).** Bennett was essentially a realist and a regionalist, and his realism is well brought out in the vivid and real pictures of the pottery districts of England or in his study of the Five Towns. *The Old Wive's Tale, Clayhanger, Imperial Palace,* etc., are among his better known novels. Bennett became an interpreter of the life an society of a particular region, the Five Towns, which he knew well. But it is to his credit that like a true artist he maintained an air of impartiality and detachment in the presentation of the life

of this region. He did not aim at any propaganda or moral preaching through the medium of his art, A charming Dickens-like humour plays over all, and makes the reading enjoyable. The impression of drabness dullness, and sordidness that might be-created from the study of his realistic pictures of the life of Five Towns is further removed by his addition of romance, specially the romance of love. Besides finding romance in love, Bennett, like Kipling, finds romance in the ordinary things of life. He refused to identify romance, "with the merely picturesque or the merely extraordinary" God had endowed him with the ability of "evoking the beauty and romance of the romance of the ordinary lives of ordinary folk and it is one of the most attractive features of his best novels".

Major Works

- A Man from the North, 1898
- Anna of the Five Towns, 1902
- The Grand Babylon Hotel, 1902
- The Old Wives' Tale, 1908
- Clayhanger, Family 1910
- The Card, 1911
- These Twain, 1915
- Riceyman Steps, 1924
- The Journals of Arnold Bennett, 1932-1933
- Leonara (1903)
- A Great Man (1904)
- Teresa of Watling Street (1904)
- Sacred and Profane Love (1905)
- The Glimpse (1909)
- The Honey Moon (1910)
- The Price of Love (1914)
- The Lions' Share (1916)

(7) **H.G. Wells (1866-1946).** Wells was a prolific writer and thinker, who produced novels pamphletes, histories, stories and romances with unceasing regularity. His novels such as *The Time Machine, The First Men in the Moon, The Food of the Gods, The Island of Dr. Moreau,* deal with scientific subjects in an imaginative way. He had his own ideas about the nature and function of fiction. For him the novel was not a mere matter of relaxation and entertainment. He considered it as a powerful instrument of moral and social suggestion and propaganda. In his hands, the novel became an instrument of social, political and educational discussion, criticism and reform.

He did not remain in the world of scientific fantasies for long, and soon drifted away from the world of scientific dreams to the wider field of social life. He became a social critic and attacked social evils with the vehemence of an inspired reformer. In the *History of Mr. Polly* he exposed educational impostures and in *Tono Bungay* he attacked modern commercialism. His method as a social reformer is different from that of Charles Dickens. Whereas Dickens attempted to gain his object of social reform through persuasion, Wells adopted a more aggressive attitude. Writes **A.C. Ward** : "When he (Wells) laughed at abuses he was a second Dickens; when he grew fretful over them, he became a second-rate edition of himself. And he was perhaps the first of that army of propagandist writers that, more particularly in the nineteen-thirties, endeavoured to hector rather than to persuade and convince."

(8) **Joseph Conrad (1857-1924).** Conrad was a Pole by birth; he did not know a word of the English language till he was over twenty, and yet, he wrote in English with distinction. He was the contemporary of such traditional novelists as Arnold Bennett, H.G. Wells and Galsworthy, and yet his work is entirely different from theirs. He is a great technical innovator.

His experiences on the sea and in many lands made him a man of no single specially the Malayan Archipelago. His character are drawn from many nations. Malays, Borneans, Swedes, and other Europeans living in the East, the Negroes, the Germans and the Dutch, and people of many other lands move across his pages and are painted with deep insight and sympathy. They have national differences, and yet basically they are the same.

He was a great romantic, yet at the same time a great realist. Romantic-realism is the key-note of his work. He did not invent his plots. He was almost incapable of such invention. His material was reality, subjected to the transmuting processes of a lively imagination. Seeds of fact planted in his mind germinated into a 'romantic-realistic' novel or tale.

The organic unity of his novels is amazing. Character, setting, and language, all contribute to the total effect aimed at by the novelist. His aim was to render the human soul, and with this end in view he adopts the impressionistic technique. He addressed to the philosophical purpose of awakening *that feeling of unavoidable solidarity which binds men to each other and all mankind to the visible world."*

He was much concerned with the problem of Evil, all of the above and he saw Evil within man, as well as in the environment in which he lived and had his being. In his philosophy, it is only Fidelity, the sense of solidarity with the human race, which can enable him to wage a successful war against Evil and overcome it.

Sea and Seamen. One of his main themes is the corrupting effect of the East on the white men who live there, and Nature in her Eastern guise is a complex power, working through men and things.

But, *he did not organise his plots well;* Too often he delayed *he is a novelist of extreme situations;* he does not explore human relationships; the action and interaction of character is rare in him; many of his stories are merely melodramatic and sensational; he offers few triumphs of feminine portraiture; his novels are deficient in his love-interest; and the unrelieved gloom of his tragedies, his depressing philosophy of life, makes his novels cheerless reading, and repels and horrifies. *But these limitations do not count for much, when we remember the astonishing range and variety of his achievement.*

Major Works

- An Out Cast of the Islands (1896)
- Heart of Darkness (1899)
- Lord Iim (1900)
- Nigger of the Narcissus (1897)
- Youth
- Nostromo (1904)
- The Secret Agent (1907)
- Under Western Eyes (1911)

(9) **Somerset Maugham (1874-1965).** Maugham is one of the prominent novelists and short story writers of the 20th century. *The Moon and Six Pence, Of Human Bondage, Cackes and Ale,* and *The Razor's Edge,* are among his masterpieces. These novels bring out his interest not only in his own country but also in other countries like Italy, France, India and the South Seas. The settings of his novels are cosmopolitan; they are not confined to any one country or climate.

Maugham is interested in three problems – the problem of renunciation and materialistic craze for possession, the problem of love, and the human predicament, the futility and meaninglessness of human life. In his view renunciation of worldly power and pelf is the ultimate solution to all our problems, cares and worries. In his treatment of Love, Maugham presents the tragedy of love rather than its triumph. Love does not come out successful and happy in his novels. Everywhere we come across the tragedy of love. Life seems to Maugham, "a tale told by an idiot, full of sound and fury, signifying nothing". *Of Human Bondage* is his final judgement on the meaninglessness and loneliness of human life. *"It is one of the most moving accounts of loneliness in our language"* **(W. Allen).**

Maugham's greatness lies in his thought. As a thinker he is original and provoking. He makes us think about life and its problems. He gives jerks to our self-complacent ideologies, and forces us to view life in a philosophic way. He convinces us that, *"art, unless it leads to right action, is no more than the opium of the intelligentsia"*.

(10) **E.M. Forster (1879-1970).** E.M. Forster is one of the prominent novelists and short story writers of the 20th century. "As a novelist Forster is rather difficult to understand, partly because of the symbolism that works its way through his work, and partly because of the manner in which he seeks to impart his message. As a novelist he is often delightful and always baffling and ambiguous, and he has always stood apart from his contemporaries" **(Walter Allen).** *Passage to India* is his masterpiece and his best known novel.

E.M. Forster is a symbolist, and what could not be expressed adequately through words is suggested by Forster through symbols. In *The Longest Journey,* Forster employs the symbol of the Train, representing salvation and the a passing away of evil and wickedness. In *Howard's End* motor car is the symbol of the rush and recklessness of modern fast moving civilization. It is a symbol indictment of our civilization with its feverish rush and activity. In *A Passage to India,* the symbolism is represented in the very title. "Passage" is symbolic of "link" or "connection", and by giving the title *A Passage to India,* the author advocates and link or connection between the Anglo-Indians and the natives of India. **Glen O. Allen** is of the view that the three fold division of the novels symbolises three attitudes towards life; the path of activity, the path of knowledge and the path of devotion. Forster was a social critic and reformer who used symbolism as a means of his social purpose. In so doing, he added poetry to the English novel.

Major Work

Novels

- Where Angels Fear to Tread (1905)
- The Longest Journey (1907)
- A Room with a View (1908)
- Howards End (1910)

- A Passage to India (1924)
- Maurice (written in 1913-14, published posthumously in 1971)

Short Stories

- The Celestial Omnibus (and other stories) (1911)
- The Eternal Moment and other Stories (1928)
- The Gentleman in the Parlour: A Record of a Journey From Rangoon to Haiphong (1930)

(11) **D.H. Lawrence (1885-1930).** D.H. Lawrence is one of the most disputed geniuses in the history of the modern English novel. His has been excessively praised as well as excessively abused. His pre-occupation with sex has resulted in his being condemned as a sex-maniac, and there are many who still regard him as a turner out of cheap sex novels. His novels like *The Rainbow* and *Lady Chatterley's Lover* were proscribed on grounds of immorality, his *Sons and Lovers* was condemned as a mass of sexuality and mother-love, and the controversy raised as a consequence has come in the way of a fair and impartial assessment of his worth as a novelist. Let us examine the merits and demerits of Lawrence as a novelist and thus form an impartial estimate of our own of his true place and significance in the history of the English novel.

He has made significant contribution to the development of the English novel. His work is continuous with the richest tradition of the English Novel, but at the same time, his work modifies that tradition by adding something new. *He altered the dimensions of the English novel, and revealed its hidden possibilities.* His novels are something new, and not mere copies of earlier novels.

(12) **Aldous Huxley (1894-1963).** Huxley's works present satirically the disillusionment and frustration with contemporary social life. *Chrome yellow* (1921), his first novels, "is something of a youthful firework display." *Point Counter Point* (1928) is a serious novels representing satirically the conflict between passion and reason, and the foolishness of sticking to only one point of view without ever caring to look at the other side of the picture. This novel adopts a special technique which may be called, " the musicalization of fiction." It is rich in witty and satirical epigrams. In *The Brave New World* (1932) Huxley satirises a scientific utopia in which everything is controlled and conditioned by considerations of scientific uniformity. The severe critic of this scientifically organised world is the savage John who pleads for greater freedom of the individual and for spiritual life. The satire lies in the fact that he fails to persuade the inhabitants of this scientific world to five up to his ideal of a free, spiritual life.

Huxley, in his 'Jesting Pilate', recounts his experiences traveling through six countries (India, Burma, Malaya, Japan, China and America).

Huxley is a novelist with a mission and a message. In *Point Counter Point;* he lays emphasis on synthesis and harmony between sense and reason. In *Eyeless in Gaza* we have the message of non-attachment. He does not mortify the flesh. He lays emphasis on the fact that the spirit is determined by the body. He say's "Sooner or later very soul is stifled by the sick body, sooner or later there are no more thoughts but only pain and vomiting apustupor. The spirit has no significance; there is only the body." Huxley will always live as a thought-provoking and stirring writer of our times.

(13) **James Joyce (1882-1941).** He is one of the prominent novelists of the 20th century. He is the main exponent of the stream of consciousness novel and his *Ulysses* is the finest example of the use of this technique in modern fiction. In Joyce, "*the twentieth century passion for experiment in literary form reached its climax.*" *Dubliners, A portrait of the Artist as a Young Man, and Finnegans Wake* are among his more important works.

In Dubliner (1914), a collection of short stories, he throws light on the life of the slum-dwellers of Dublin. The stories are objective and realistic in character and are written in a simple and direct style. *A Portrait of the Artist as a Young Man* (1916) is an autobiographical work and the artist Dedalus, the chief protagonist, stands for the novelist. "As a revelation of Joyce's power to explore the psychology of his own nature with detachment and scientific curiosity, A *Portrait of the Artist as a Young Man* is unparalleled in a period rich in self-analysis. Pride and sensuality struggle for the possession of the soul of Stephen Dedalus, who, having rejected the help of religion, seeks to escape into tranquility through the impersonality of art" **(Diana Neill).**

Ulysses(1922) is Joyce's masterpiece. In this novel the stream of consciousness technique finds its best exposition. The novel is set in Dublin and seeks to represent and reconstruct Dublin life in all its sordid realism. It narrates in a rambling manner the wanderings of Leopold Bloom and Stephen Dedalus through the city of Dublin, on one particular day. The novel is extremely formless, loose and incoherent. It is *the reductional absurdum* of the extreme subjective method. **Diana Neill** says rightly that, "the book is unintelligible and its formal complexities have left readers baffled and confused. However, its style is marked with rare ingenuity, witticism and satirical flashes. The novel has been called a 'comic epic' in which the novelist went deeper and farther than any other novelist in his handling of the interior monologue and the stream of consciousness technique. *Ulysses* may be little read today, but Joyce's greatness as an artist cannot be questioned.

In *Finnegan's Wake (1939),"* "Subtlety and complexity produce incomprehensibility. It is a study of he history of the human race from its earliest beginnings, as seen through the incoherent dreams of one Mr. Earwicker. The use of an inconsecutive narrative and of a private vocabulary adds to the confusion, but it cannot conceal the poetic fervour, the power and brilliant verbal skill of the work." **(E. Albert).**

(14) **Dorothy Richardson (1873-1957).** Dorothy though considered less important today than Virginia Woolf, yet she influenced her and the subsequent women novelists considerably with her novel. *Pointed Roofs* (1915). It was something new which Dorothy Richardson did in this novel. She endeavoured to give both the subjective and the objective biography of a character – a young women named Miriam Henderson. The description is entirely subjective. It is the stream of Miriam's consciousness that Miss Richardson reproduces without any interference on her own part. Her novel is truly feminine and she comes closest of all English novelists. To reality and accuracy in her study of the mind of a woman. No novelist has succeeded so well in presenting feminine psychology.

Major Works

- Pointed Roofs (1915)
- Backwater (1916)
- Honeycomb (1917)
- The Tunnel (1919)

- Interim (1920)
- Deadlock (1921)
- Revolving Lights (1923)
- The Trap (1925)
- Oberland (1927)
- Dawn's Left Hand (1931)
- Clear Horizon (1935)
- Pilgrimage (4 vols.) (1938)
- Journey to Paradise : Short Stories and Autobiographic Sketches (1989)

(15) **Katherine Mansfield (1888-1923).** She was brought up in New Zealand and was a writer of short stories and during her life-time, five volumes of her stories were published. She was an impressionist in her art and sought to portray objectively, "the significant moment in human relationship, the curious and subtle adventure and the poignant ironies of contrasting human emotions." She studied life objectively and, "understood characters widely divergent from herself in both temperaments and accidentals." In her stories, she has tried to present the weariness and frustrations of modern English life. "Her stories are marked with a note of somberness and are characterised with a haunting sense of pathos." *The Prelude,To the Bay, The Fly, The Garden Party,* represent at its best the subtle psychological art of Katherine Mansfield.

(16) **Mrs. Virginia Woolf (1882-1941).** Mrs. Woolf belongs to the school of "stream of consciousness" novelists. She is one of those great English novelists of the 20th century who had the courage to break free from tradition, and then to give a new direction, a new form and a new spiritual awareness, to the English novel. She began writing in the established tradition of the novel; her first two novels, *The Voyage Out* and *Night and Day* are largely traditional. But soon she realised the inadequacy of the traditional novel, and adopted the stream-of-consciousness technique in the *Jacob's Room,* her third novel. Her art rapidly matured and her next two novels *Mrs. Dalloway* and *To the Lighthouse* represent the very consummation of the novel of subjectivity.

Major Works

Novels

- The Voyage Out (1915)
- Night and Day (1919)
- Jacob's Room (1922)
- Mrs Dalloway (1925)
- To the Lighthouse (1927)
- Orlando (1928)
- The Waves (1931)
- The Years (1937)
- Between the Acts (1941)

Biographies

- Flush: A Biography (1933)
- Roger Fry: A Biography (1940)

Non-Fiction Books

- Modern Fiction (1919)
- A Room of One's Own (1929)
- On Being III (1930)
- Three Guineas (1938)

Imparted Form and Balance to the Novel of Subjectivity

She is not one of the architects of the "stream-of-consciousness novel", she is not its originator, but it is in her novels that "the stream-of-consciousness" technique finds its balance. She has succeeded in imposing form and order on the chaos inherent in the novel of subjectivity. In this way, as **R.L. Chambers** puts it, she has brought this particular *genre* of the novel out of the realm of "stunt literature", and has made it an acceptable and coherent art form. She was also one of the most forceful and original theorists of, "the stream-of-consciousness novel", and by her exposition of the aesthetics of this kind of novel, she did much to throw light on its technique and to bring out its superiority to the conventional novel.

Her novels need some painstaking on the part of the reader, but if followed imaginatively, they have the power to illuminate and transform. Giving an estimate of her achievement, **G.S. Frazer** in his book *The Modern Writer and His World* writes, "She offers us a lyrical abstraction from the pain with which she felt the world; the quality of her mind and spirit has a distinction that will make some readers always grateful to accept the offering." She may not be one of the greatest of English novelists, but there can be no denying the fact that, "She is a delicate and subtle artist, who upheld spiritual and aesthetic values in a coarse, materialistic age." Her influence has been profound and all-pervasive, so much so that **R.A. Scott-James** writes, *"After her, in her own country, the serious novel could never again be just what it had been before."*

(17) **Elizabeth Bowen (1899-1973).** She is a prominent novelist of exceptional individuality. She is a close follower of the technique of Virginia Woolf. *The Heat of the Day and Last September* are her chief novels. Like Mrs. Woolf, she is interested in the study of the human heart. She studies life around her with an artistic detachment, and presents her impressions of life in a delicate, subtle style characterized by feminine sensitiveness. She presents the social comedy of manners with an ironically sympathetic understanding. She may not attain the extraordinary fullness of Virginia Woolf and her characters may not react to London life with the same intensity as does Mrs. Dalloway. "But our senses are always being appealed to by an observer who is more obviously feminine than Virginia Woolf; physical details of the body, careful appraisal of dress, match the insight into feminine moods' **(Collins),** Like Virginia Woolf, she was achieved greater success in the depiction of her women that her men.

MODERN AGE DRAMA

The drama which had suffered steep decline during the Victorian Age was revived with great force at the beginning of the 20th century and the course of six decades has witnessed many trends and currents in the 20th-century drama.

The drama of Modernist Movement in England was much less innovative in technique than it was its poetry and novel.

History of Modern Drama in English Literature

English Drama during the Modernist Period (1845-1945) A.D. falls into three categories:

1. The first and the earliest phase of modernism in English Drama is marked by the plays of G.B. Shaw (read Summary of Candida) and John Galsworthy, which constitute the category of social drama modeled on the plays of Ibsen and.
2. The 2nd and the middle phase of Modernist English drama comprise the plays of Irish movement contributed by some elites like Yeats. In this phase, the drama contained the spirit of nationalism.
3. The 3rd and the final phase of the Modernist English Drama comprise plays of T.S. Eliot and Christopher Fry. This phase saw the composition of poetic dramas inspired by the earlier Elizabethan and Jacobean tradition.

The three categories reflect the three different phases as well as the three different facets of the Modern English Drama.

Modern Drama Characteristics

- **Realism.** Realism is the most significant and outstanding quality of the Modern English Drama. The dramatists of the earlier years of the 20th century were interested in naturalism and it was their endeavor (try) to deal with real problems of life in a realistic technique to their plays.

  It was Henrik Ibsen, the Norwegian dramatist who popularised realism in Modern Drama. He dealt with the problems of real life in a realistic manner of his play. His example was followed by Robertson Arthur Jones, Galsworthy and G. B. Shaw in their plays.

  Modern drama has developed the Problem Play and there are many Modern Dramatists who have written a number of problem plays in our times. They dealt with the problems of marriage, justice, law, administration, and strife between capital and labor in their dramas.

  They used theatre as a means for bringing about reforms in the conditions of society prevailing in their days. Henrik Ibsen's play A Doll's House is a good example of problem play. The problem play was a new experiment in the form and technique and dispensed with the conventional devices and expedients of theatre.
- **Play of Ideas.** Modern Drama is essentially a drama of ideas rather than action. The stage is used by dramatists to give expression to certain ideas which they want to spread in the society.

  The Modern Drama dealing with the problems of life has become far more intelligent than ever it was in the history of drama before the present age. With the treatment of actual life, the drama became more and more a drama of ideas, sometimes veiled in the main action, sometimes didactically act forth.

MODERN DRAMA

(1) **Galsworthy (1867-1933).** He was one of those prominent artists who discussed the various problems of modern life in one work after another. His plays are so many pieces of criticism of contemporary life. *Justice, Strife Silver Box, Loyalties, The Mob, The Eldest Son,* all focus attention on some one problem or the other.

He is the critic and interpreter of contemporary English life. In his plays we have a thread-bare discussion of the problems of marriage, sex-relationship, labour disputes, administration of law, solitary confinement, cast or class prejudices. These social problems are treated by Galsworthy in the context of society and social relationships.

His depiction of the contemporary society and its problems is realistic and penetrating. He is a thought-provoking writer. He was faithful to life as he saw it. "His realism did not end in his material. It also extended to his artistic method. He did not aim at stagey-effects or theatricality. His settings and details of local colour were strictly realistic.

He deals with the problems of life with impartiality. He is an artist who takes a detached view of the problems he deals with, and examines them in all their facets. The warm sympathy of the dramatist is evident in almost all his plays, and numerous examples maybe cited at random. *Justice, Strife, Silver Box, etc.,* all reveal the sympathy of the dramatist for the poor and the oppressed. He considered the present social organisation and conventions as responsible for this suffering, and hence he wanted to reform our social life. But he was not a propagandist like Shaw. Therefore, he suggested reform in his dramas, in a hushed and muffled tone.

His prominent characters are drawn from the middle class or the lower strata of society. They range from the accidental thief and the middle-class Member of Parliament, to the workman and the company director, the charwoman and the Colonel's wife.

Galsworthy is a great craftsman and dramatic artist. His plots are faultlessly constructed, and have dramatic effectiveness. He manges his plots with economy, restraint and concentration.

He is a great dramatist who has created numerous tense and dramatically effective scenes, situations and characters. But he lacks the gift of humour; the atmosphere of his plays is too serious and tragic for the taste of the average reader and play-goer. Therefore, he could never achieve the popularity, which was achieved by his great contemporary, GBS.

(2) **Noel Coward (1899-1973).** During the early decades of the twentieth century, there was a revival of the Comedy of Manners, a kind of Comedy practised by the Restoration dramatists like Etherege, Wycherley and Congreve. In this new Comedy of Manners, as in the Restoration one, wit and sparkling dialogues were the chief sources of interest. The new comedy had a short life. It suffered a setback after the World War II, for the social conditions of the period after 1945 were not conductive to the display of light-hearted wit. "The Comedy of Manners is a tender plant and will not bloom if cold winds are blowing."

Noel Coward is known for his social comedies or comedy of Manners. "His unerring sense of theatrical effect, his wit and dance of dialogue, his sparkling presentation of the hurly-burly of the bright young moderns and their disillusioned and fantastic elders, play goers in play after play" **(Collins).** His best comedies are *The Rat Trap* (1924), *The Vortex* (1924), *Fallen Angles* (1925), *Easy Virtue* (1925), *Bitter Sweet* (1929), *Private Lives* (1930), etc.

(3) **John Drinkwater (1882-1937).** Among the dramatists who popularised historical plays, the name of Bernard should certainly be placed at the top. His *Ceasar and Cleopatra* and *St. Joan* are historical plays which have been a source of inspiration to others. But it was **John Drinkwater** (1882-1937) who really made a significant contribution to historical drama by his four plays Abraham Lincoln (1918) *Mary Stuart* (1921-22) *Oliver Cromwel* (1922) and *Robert E. Lee* (1923). In each one of these plays there is a central dominating personality standing heads and shoulders over "the multiplicity of individually delineated characters", and this personality is by and large true to history. These historical plays of Drinkwater are not merely chronicle plays focussing attention on event and external happenings, taken from history, but the plays of ideas, discussing problems of human life in a dramatic form. For example, in *Abraham Lincoln* the problem set forth is whether a hero like Lincoln should pursue his ideals with unflinching determination of yield to external pressure and give up war for ensuring peace.

(4) **Clifford Bax (1886-1962).** Another prominent figure is the author of several historical plays such as *Mr. Pepys* (1926), *Socrates* (1930), *The Venetian* (1931), *The Immortal Lady* (1931), and *The Rose without a Thorn* (1932). The *Rose without a Thorn* is his best play. In it we have neither the exuberant lyricism of the

Venetian nor the philosophical intensity of *Socrates.* In this play the, "author has set himself to develop characters within a pattern, based on historic fact, but shaped by his imagination. This play is assuredly one of he most important and beautifully constructed historical dramas of our times." In the opinion of **Allardyce Nicoll.** "*Mr. Bax is one of those dramatists of this generation whose plays will live. His effective treatment of character, his skillful wielding of material, and his delicate sense of style give prime distinction to his work*".

(5) **Sean O'Casey (1880-1964).** He was an expressionist. He, the Irish dramatist was interested in the presentation of the life of the slums of Dublin bringing out all the sordidness, drunkenness and misery of the Irish men and women. The background to his plays is provided by the "slums of Dublin, crowded, noisy tenements where women quarrelled and loafers drank, and the tragic violence of civil was ever at hand" **(A.S. Collins).**

In the plays of O'Casey the tragedy and comedy of Irish life is well brought out in dialogues which are vivid, racy and rhythmical. Comedy and tragedy constantly fuse and mingle. "Comedy is seldom long absent, yet one can never forget the grim, underlying sadness." He draws what he sees with a ruthless objectivity and an impressionistic vividness of detail.

According to **A.S. Collins,** "Few writers have so intimately fused realism and pathos, tragedy and comedy, for his world is a basically comic one whose atmosphere is a sky laden with fate ever ready to strike almost at random and, therefore, it is a most pitiable world."

(6) **T.S. Eliot (1888-1965).** Eliot's fame as dramatist rests entirely upon the *Murder in the Cathedral* (1935), and four plays in contemporary setting, which followed each other in quick succession. These plays are: *(1) The Family Reunion (1939), (2) The Cocktail Party (1949), (3) The Confidential Clerk (1953), and (4) The Elder Statesman (1958).* His purpose in writing these plays was to bring about a revival of poetic drama. The bulk of his dramatic out put is small, but its quality, and its impact on the entire course of modern English drama, would justify us in calling Eliot, the Shakespeare of the modern drama.

MODERN ESSAY AND PROSE

(1) **E.V. Lucas (1868-1938).** Among the 20th century essayists, **Lucas** is one who is generally regarded as the true inheritor of the manner of Lamb. He is one of the most prolific essayists of our age. He worked long as a journalist and contributed mostly to the *Punch.* His most representative and popular collection of essays is entitled *The Character and Comedy* (1907).

Lacus has followed in the footsteps of Lamb. He has Lamb's humanity, his all-embracing sympathy, his humour and whimsicality and his confidential tone, as well as his pensive yearning for the beauty and charm of the old things and personalities. But he has wisely eschewed the many extravagances of Lamb as well as his many mannerisms of style. He has the virtues of Lamb without his faults.

Lucas has displayed a remarkable accurate power of observation and an equally remarkable capacity for discovering beauty and mystery in the commonplace things and objects of life. **Edmund Gosse,** in his brief article on "*The Essays of Mr. Lucas*", has observed: "The essay does not achieve genuine success unless it is written in the language spoken today by those who employ it with the maximum of purity and grace. It should be a model of current, cultivated ease of expression and a mirror of the best conversation. The essays of Mr. Lucas fulfil this requirement." Lucas writes a pure, chaste, lucid and clear prose, which has effortless ease, spontaneity, conciseness and compactness. He is one of those essayists who have fully exploited the poetic possibilities of English prose to describe the beauty and glory of the familiar and the common.

(2) **G.K. Chesterton (1874-1936).** He is a writer of versatile genius and his essays reveal, "an extraordinary range of mind; there was no subject on which he could not have found something original, and if possible challenging, to say, from the fundamental basis of morals to the proper way of eating cheese. And on each page, of course, is the hard-hitting power of his style. He is eloquent, provocative, splendidly graphic and admirably humorous.

Originality and ingenuity in thought and approach are the leading characteristics of his essays. Often he makes use of witty paradox which delights and surprises as well as provokes thought. His style is highly brilliant, self-conscious and idiosyncratic, replete with alliteration, balance, antithesis and paradox. He constructs his sentences with great ingenuity, which offers a constant challenge to the reader and at times have an air of verbal, if not intellectual, puzzle. *The Uses of Diversity; Tremendous Trifles, etc.*, are among the more popular of his collections of essays.

(3) **Hilaire Belloc (1870-1953).** He is another versatile and prolific essayist of the 20th century. His reputation as an essayist rests securely on several volumes, a few among which are entitled as *Something, Nothing, Everything.*

Belloc himself observes, and also makes his readers observe, novelty in the real and familiar things of everyday life, and he also presents the hackneyed problems so concretely and cleverly as to charge them with an altogether new significance. His range of mood, theme, and subject is very wide. He can be playful and garrulous as in his essay on "*Cheese*", but he can be tenderly, even lyrically, emotional as in "*The Good Woman*", and between these he can play on all possible shades and gradations.

In his prose style, it is his transparent clarity which strikes our attention most immediately. He is a master at once of the simple, chaste, direct and homely manner, relying mostly on familiar word and precise epithets, on sentences which are generally simply and brief and which follow each other in quick succession, and have an artless pattern and rhythmical effect; and also on the grand sonorous prose which generally comes at the crucial moments when emotion rises to a higher pitch. His rapidity of movement from one mood to another in the same essay is remarkable.

(4) **A.G. Gardiner (1865-1946).** He was a journalist and essayist of the school of Montaigne and Lamb. He is better known to his readers by his pen name *Alpha of the Plough,* which he adopted in response to the invitation of the editor of *the Star* to which he contributed a number of his essays. He was a prolific essayist and his best collections of essays are entitled *The Pillars of Society, Pebbles on the Shore, Leaves in the Wind, etc.* He brings out the significance of the most trivial things and communicates knowledge and wisdom in an entirely informal, modest, intimate and delightful manner. Herein lies the secret of Gardiner's greatness as a personal essayist.

Gardiner's style is easy, clear, lucid and flexible. He modulates his prose to his changing moods, chatty, reflective, enthusiastic and observant. His vocabulary is drawn from the common everyday speech and his language is dignified and yet mostly within the comprehension even of the moderately read readers. "But when he has to render his impressions of the beauty, mystery and sublimity of nature his words are clothed with beauty, colour and picturesqueness, the sentences have amplitude and rhythm and the images become more frequent, vivid and of refreshing charm and grace." He has no mannerism, no trace of any effort to be striking, yet he always selects the precise and vivid world and uses it with the most telling effect. He is one of the greatest stylists in the English language.

(5) **Robert Lynd (1879-1949).** He followed the footsteps of Lamb, Stevenson and Goldsmith. A large range and variety of mood and emotion is possible for him. He may be light-hearted, humorous, whimsical and amusingly philosophical, reflective, retrospective and frankly personal and autobiographical. For Lynd, as for any genuine essayist any subject, is a good enough peg to hang his personal thoughts, reflections, humours and emotions on. He has always something delightful and thought-provoking to say, but more important than what he says, is the manner of saying it. In his essays, it is manner of saying things which constitutes the man charm.

His style has all the ease, range and liveiness of conversation. An effortless ease and a natural flow of words are the distinguishing features of his style. The language is equally beautiful and dignified throughout; it has no purple patches, no heightening of colour. "Its colours meet and blend together to producer that unity of tone and atmosphere which is the soul of a true essay as much as of a lyric."

(6) **Max Beerbohm (1872-1956).** He was who won wide popularity by his *Zuleika Bobson* (1911) was delightful essayist and witty parodist, who was never tired of exposing the follies and fobles of his great contemporaries. Commenting on his achievement as an essayist, A.C. Ward writes: "Max Beerbohm brushes lightly, delicately, wittily over the surface of life, with great tenderness for all that he has enjoyed and unfailing humour. In his observations and in his style, there is "nothing too much", but there is always just enough. In an age of hurry he never hurried; in a machine age he preserved in his writings and drawings the delicate craft work of a more leisured endless strenuous time; in an age when most people could write moderately well, but few had anything to write about, he was perfect both in manner and matter."

CONTEMPORARY PERIOD

INTRODUCTION

The period after World War II was that of devastation, hopelessness and multitudes of problems of 'displaced persons'. There were millions of displaced persons some had fled willingly, others were deported as undesirable minorities. The Allies did what they could to feed and house the refugees and to reunite families that had been forcibly torn apart but the obstacles were enormous. Most of the countries were in ruins, fields, forests and vineyard were ripped to pieces. Apart from US and Allies such as Canada and Australia, the European powers such as Britain and France had precious little to spare. Britain had largely bankrupted itself fighting the war. Pestilence, war, famine and death-so familiar during the Middle Ages-appeared again in the modern world. War also acted as an agent to accelerate the weakening of European Empire. In many countries social change also sped up with the help of science and technology.

The shared suffering and sacrifice of the war years strengthened the belief in most democracies that government had an obligation to provide basic care for all citizens. The Labour Government in Britain moved rapidly to establish a welfare state. Established political orders-fascist and conservative came under challenge as people looked for new ideas and leaders.

CONTEMPORARY ENGLISH LITERATURE

Literature in the United Kingdom after World War II cannot be generalised under any specific genere. The only clear group is the Angry Young Men, a group of dramatists and novelistists who in the 1950s expressed their discontent with traditional English society in anti-establishment works that have also been described as 'Kitchen Sink Realism'.

When we talk about contemporary literature and the start date of this label, we have to acknowledge World War II and the surrounding events. The horrors of the war, including bombs, ground wars, genocide and corruption, are the pathways to this type of literature. It is from these real-life themes that we find the beginning of a new period of writing.

Working of contemporary literature reflects a society's social and/or political viewpoints, shown through realistic characters, connections to current events and socio-economic messages. The writers are looking for trends that illuminate societal strengths and weaknesses to remind society of lessons they should learn and questions they should ask. The idea of utopian existence and ideals of modemism were left far behind. Most of the literature in this period is not escapist in nature.

So when we think of contemporary literature, we cannot simply look at a few themes or settings. Since society changes over time, so do the content and messages of this writing.

According to Dr Valerie Morrison, while the modern writer "focused on the objects of his or her culture, contemporary writers and artists are more intent on describing people's emotional states". Contemporary writers believe in lack of order or prevalence of chaos as a defining characteristic of the present world.

Same characteristics of contemporary literature are:

- Lack of resolution.
- Focus on the personal, rather than the social.
- Cynicism about the role of art and literature.
- Realistic settings.
- Subversion of traditional gender roles.
- A blurring line between the natural and the artificial/constructed.
- Lack of any possibility for a greater action.

Novel Writing in Contemporary Period

After 1945 when novelists faced the task of explaining the new historical reality and the position of individuals in the post-war order, most novelists realised that this entailed making a choice between traditional literary models and experimental modernist models.

Post modernism or contemporary was born out of this dilemma. Post-modemism can thus said to be a new cultural atmosphere in which the writer is inevitably aware of this open choice between tradition and experimentation. Post-war novelists cannot escape the shadow of either Modernism or Victorianism, so some produced a synthesis which is the real characteristic of post modernistic novel writing. But this synthesis was slow to come.

In the period between 1945-1953; a nostalgic look at the lost pre-war past was combined with a look at the new-reality faced by generation growing up in the 1940s often in provincial surroundings.

In early 1950 brought a new interest in the present possibly as a reaction against the nostalgic backward look at an essentially phoney world from which many, mostly lower middle and working classes, were excluded. In these novels, the margins of culture moved to the centre, expressing, a generalised discontent which.was paralleled in the plays of

Angry Young Men and also in some poetical works. Novelists of this period are too many we will discuss them and their works one by one).

AMERICAN LITERATURE

The literary historian Malcolm Cowley described the years between the two world wars as a "second flowering" of American writing. Certainly American literature attained a new maturity and a rich diversity in the 1920s and '30s, and significant works by several major figures from those decades were published after 1945. Faulkner, Hemingway, Steinbeck, and Katherine Anne Porter wrote memorable fiction, though not up to their prewar standard; and Frost, Eliot, Wallace Stevens, Marianne Moore, E.E. Cummings, William Carlos Williams, and Gwendolyn Brooks published important poetry. Eugene O'Neill's most distinguished play, *Long Day's Journey into Night*, appeared posthumously in 1956. Before and after World War II, Robert Penn Warren published influential fiction, poetry, and criticism. His *All the King's Men*, one of the best American political novels, won the 1947 Pulitzer Prize. Mary McCarthy became a widely read social satirist and essayist.

Not only did a new generation come out of the war, but its ethnic, regional, and social character was quite different from that of the preceding one. Among the younger writers were children of immigrants, many of them Jews; African Americans, only a few generations away from slavery; and, eventually, women, who, with the rise of feminism, were to speak in a new voice.

The Novel and Short Story Realism and "Metafiction"

Two distinct groups of novelists responded to the cultural impact, and especially the technological horror, of World War II. Norman Mailer's *The Naked and the Dead* (1948) and Irwin Shaw's *The Young Lions* (1948) were realistic war novels, though Mailer's book was also a novel of ideas, exploring fascist thinking and an obsession with power as elements of the military mind. A sequel, *Closing Time (1994),* was an elegy for the World War II generation. Kurt Vonnegut, Jr., in *Slaughterhouse-Five* (1969), described the Allied firebombing of the German city of Dresden with a mixture of dark fantasy and numb, loopy humour. Later this method was applied brilliantly to the portrayal of the Vietnam War—a conflict that seemed in itself surreal—by Tim O'Brien in *Going After Cacciato* (1978) and the short-story collection *The Things They Carried* (1990).

In part because of the atomic bomb, American writers turned increasingly to black humour and absurdist fantasy. Many found the naturalistic approach incapable of communicating the rapid pace and the sheer implausibility of contemporary life. A highly self-conscious fiction emerged, laying bare its own literary devices, questioning the nature of representation, and often imitating or parodying earlier fiction rather than social reality. Russian-born Vladimir Nabokov and the Argentine writer Jorge Luis Borges were strong influences on this new "metafiction."

In an important essay, "The Literature of Exhaustion" (1967), John Barth declared himself an American disciple of Nabokov and Borges. After dismissing realism as a "used up" tradition, Barth described his own work as "novels which imitate the form of the novel, by an author who imitates the role of Author." Donald Barthelmemocked the fairy tale in *Snow White* (1967) and Freudian fiction in *The Dead Father* (1975). Barthelme was most successful in his short stories and parodies that solemnly caricatured contemporary styles, especially the richly suggestive pieces collected in *Unspeakable Practices, Unnatural Acts* (1968), *City Life* (1970), and *Guilty Pleasures* (1974).

Thomas Pynchon emerged as the major American practitioner of the absurdist fable. His novels and stories were elaborately plotted mixtures of historical information, comic-book fantasy, and counter-cultural suspicion. The underlying assumption of Pynchon's fiction was the inevitability of entropy—*i.e.*, the disintegration of physical and moral energy.

Other influential portraits of outsider figures included the Beat characters in Jack Kerouac's *On the Road* (1957), *The Dharma Bums* (1958), *Desolation Angels* (1965), and *Visions of Cody* (1972); the young Rabbit Angstrom in John Updike's *Rabbit, Run* (1960) and *Rabbit Redux* (1971); Holden Caulfield in J.D. Salinger's.

Though writers such as Barth, Barthelme, and Pynchon rejected the novel's traditional function as a mirror reflecting society, a significant number of contemporary novelists were reluctant to abandon Social Realism, which they pursued in much more personal terms. In novels such as *The Victim* (1947), *The Adventures of Augie March* (1953), *Herzog* (1964), *Mr. Sammler's Planet* (1970), and *Humboldt's Gift* (1975), Saul Bellow tapped into the buoyant, manic energy and picaresque structure of black humour while proclaiming the necessity of "being human." With the publication of *Ravelstein* (2000), his fictional portrait of the scholar-writer Allan Bloom, and of *Collected Stories* (2001), Bellow was acclaimed as a portraitist and a poet of memory.

Four other major Jewish writers—Bernard Malamud, Grace Paley, Philip Roth, and Isaac Bashevis Singer—treated the human condition with humour and forgiveness. Malamud's gift for dark comedy and Hawthornean fable was especially evident in his short-story collections *The Magic Barrel* (1958) and *Idiots First* (1963). While Roth was known best for the wild satire and sexual high jinks of *Portnoy's Complaint* (1969), a hilarious stand-up routine about ethnic stereotypes, his most-lasting achievement may be his later novels built around the misadventures of a controversial Jewish novelist named Zuckerman, especially *The Ghost Writer* (1979), *The Anatomy Lesson* (1983), and, above all, *The Counterlife* (1987). Like many of his later works, from *My Life as a Man* (1974) to *Operation Shylock* (1993), *The Counterlife* plays ingeniously on the relationship between autobiography and fiction. His best later work was his bitter, deliberately offensive story of a self-destructive artist, *Sabbath's Theater* (1995). They evolved from fantastic tales of demons and angels to realistic fictions set in New York City's Upper West Side, often dealing with the haunted lives of Holocaust survivors. These works showed him to be one of the great storytellers of modern times.

Another great storyteller, John Cheever, long associated with *The New Yorker* magazine, created in his short stories and novels a gallery of memorable eccentrics. He documented the anxieties of upper-middle-class New Yorkers and suburbanites in the relatively tranquil years after World War II. In sharp contrast, Nelson Algren (*The Man with the Golden Arm* [1949]) and Hubert Selby, Jr.(*Last Exit to Brooklyn* [1964]), documented lower-class urban life with brutal frankness. Similarly, John Rechy portrayed America's urban homosexual subculture in *City of Night* (1963).

Southern Fiction

Post-World War II Southern writers inherited Faulkner's rich legacy. Three women—Eudora Welty, Flannery O'Connor, and Carson McCullers, specialists in the grotesque—contributed greatly to Southern fiction. O'Connor, writing as a Roman Catholic in the Protestant South, created a high comedy of moral incongruity in her incomparable short stories. Welty, always a brilliant stylist, first came to prominence with her collections of short fiction *A Curtain of Green* (1941) and *The Wide Net, and Other Stories* (1943). She also published *Reflections in a Golden Eye* (1941), *The Member of the Wedding* (1946), and *The Ballad of the Sad Café* (1951), all later adapted to the stage or screen. Other fine storytellers in the Southern tradition include Elizabeth Spencer, whose short fiction was collected in *The Southern Woman* (2001), and Reynolds Price, whose best novels were *A Long and Happy Life* (1961) and *Kate Vaiden* (1986).

William Styron's overripe first novel, *Lie Down in Darkness* (1951), clearly revealed the influence of Faulkner. In two controversial later works, Styron fictionalized the dark side of modern history: *The Confessions of Nat Turner* (1967) depicted an antebellum slave revolt, and *Sophie's Choice* (1979) unsuccessfully sought to capture the full horror of the Holocaust. Inspired by Faulkner and Mark Twain, William Humphrey wrote two powerful novels set in Texas, *Home from the Hill* (1958) and *The Ordways* (1965). Equally impressive were the novels and stories of Peter Taylor, an impeccable Social Realist, raconteur, and genial novelist of manners who recalled a bygone world in works such as *The Old Forest* (1985) and *A Summons to Memphis* (1986).

African American Literature

Black writers of this period found alternatives to the Richard Wright tradition of angry social protest. James Baldwin and Ralph Ellison, both protégés of Wright, wrote polemical essays calling for a literature that reflected the full complexity of black life in the United States. In his first and best novel, *Go Tell It on the Mountain* (1953), Baldwin portrayed the Harlem world and the black church through his own adolescent religious experiences. Many considered his novel *Invisible Man* (1952) the best novel of the postwar years.

Later two African American women published some of the most important post-World War II American fiction. In *The Bluest Eye* (1970), *Sula* (1973), *Song of Solomon* (1977), *Beloved* (1987), *Jazz* (1992), and *Paradise* (1998), Toni Morrison created a strikingly original fiction that sounded different notes from lyrical recollection to magic realism. Like Ellison, Morrison drew on diverse literary and folk influences and dealt with important phases of black history—*i.e.*, slavery in *Beloved* and the Harlem Renaissance in *Jazz*. African American men whose work gained attention during this period included Ishmael Reed, whose wild comic techniques resembled Ellison's; James Alan McPherson, a subtle short-story writer in the mold of Ellison and Baldwin.

New Fictional Modes

The horrors of World War II, the Cold War and the atomic bomb, the bizarre feast of consumer culture, and the cultural clashes of the 1960s prompted many writers to argue that reality had grown inaccessible, undermining the traditional social role of fiction. Writers of novels and short stories therefore were under unprecedented pressure to discover, or invent, new and viable kinds of fiction. One response was the postmodern novel of William Gaddis, John Barth, John Hawkes, Donald Barthelme, Thomas Pynchon, Robert Coover, Paul Auster, and Don DeLillo—technically sophisticated and highly self-conscious about the construction of fiction and the fictive nature of "reality" itself. These writers dealt with themes such as imposture and paranoia; their novels drew attention to themselves as artifacts and often used realistic techniques ironically. Other responses involved a heightening of realism by means of intensifying violence, amassing documentation, or resorting to fantasy.

In his World War II novel, *The Naked and the Dead* (1948), Mailer wrote in the Dos Passos tradition of social protest. Feeling its limitations, he developed his own brand of surreal fantasy in fables such as *An American Dream* (1965) and *Why Are We in Vietnam?* (1967). As with many of the postmodern novelists, his subject was the nature of power, personal as well as political. When he returned to fiction, his most effective work was *Harlot's Ghost* (1991), about the Central Intelligence Agency. His final novels took Jesus Christ (*The Gospel According to the Son* [1997]) and Adolf Hitler (*The Castle in the Forest* [2007]) as their subjects.

In her early work, especially *A Garden of Earthly Delights* (1967) and *them* (1969), Joyce Carol Oates worked naturalistically with violent urban materials, such as the Detroit riots. Among her later works was *Blonde: A Novel* (2000), a fictional biography of Marilyn Monroe. While Mailer and Oates refused to surrender the novel's gift for capturing reality, both were compelled to search out new fictional modes to tap that power.

The surge of feminism in the 1970s gave impetus to many new women writers, such as Erica Jong, author of the sexy and funny *Fear of Flying* (1974), and Rita Mae Brown, who explored lesbian life in *Rubyfruit Jungle* (1973).

The Influence of Raymond Carver

Perhaps the most influential fiction writer to emerge in the 1970s was Raymond Carver. His self-destructive characters were life's losers, and his style, influenced by Hemingway and Samuel Beckett, was spare and flat but powerfully suggestive. It was imitated, often badly, by minimalists such as Frederick Barthelme, Mary Robison, and Amy Hempel. Another strong male-oriented writer in a realist mode who emerged from the 1960s counterculture was Robert Stone. His *Dog Soldiers* (1974) was a grimly downbeat portrayal of the drugs-and-Vietnam generation, and *A Flag for Sunrise* (1981) was a bleak, Conradian political novel set in Central America. In leisurely, good-humoured, minutely detailed novels, Richard Russo dealt with blue-collar losers living in decaying Northeastern towns in *The Risk Pool* (1988), *Nobody's Fool* (1993), and *Empire Falls* (2001), but he also published a satiric novel about academia, *Straight Man* (1997). Deborah Eisenberg, Amy Bloom, Antonya Nelson, and Thom Jones also helped make the last years of the 20th century a fertile period for short fiction.

Multicultural Writing

The dramatic loosening of immigration restrictions in the mid-1960s set the stage for the rich multicultural writing of the last quarter of the 20th century. Her story *The Shawl* (1980) concerns the murder of a baby in a Nazi concentration camp. David Leavitt introduced homosexual themes into his portrayal of middle-class life in *Family Dancing* (1984). At the turn of the 21st century, younger Jewish writers from the former Soviet Union such as Gary Shteyngart and Lara Vapnyar dealt impressively with the experience of immigrants in the United States.

Novels such as N. Scott Momaday's *House Made of Dawn*, which won the Pulitzer Prize in 1969, James Welch's *Winter in the Blood* (1974) and *Fools Crow* (1986), Leslie Marmon Silko's *Ceremony* (1977), and Louise Erdrich's *Love Medicine* (1984), *The Beet Queen* (1986), and *The Antelope Wife* (1998) were powerful and ambiguous explorations of Native American history and identity.

Some of the best immigrant writers, while thoroughly assimilated, nonetheless had a subtle understanding of both the old and the new culture. These included the Cuban American writers Oscar Hijuelos (*The Mambo Kings Play Songs of Love* [1989]) and Cristina Garcia (*Dreaming in Cuban* [1992] and *The Agüero Sisters* [1997]); the Antigua-born Jamaica Kincaid, author of *Annie John* (1984), *Lucy* (1990), the AIDS memoir *My Brother* (1997), and *See Now Then* (2013); the Dominican-born Junot Díaz, who won acclaim for *Drown* (1996), a collection of stories, and whose novel *The Brief Wondrous Life of Oscar Wao* (2007) won a Pulitzer Prize; and the Bosnian immigrant Aleksandar Hemon, who wrote *The Question of Bruno* (2000) and *Nowhere Man* (2002). Chinese Americans found an extraordinary voice in Maxine Hong Kingston's *The Woman Warrior* (1976) and *China Men* (1980), which blended old Chinese lore with fascinating family history. Her first novel, *Tripmaster Monkey: His Fake Book* (1989), was set in the bohemian world of the San Francisco Bay area during the 1960s.

During the 1990s some of the best energies of fiction writers went into autobiography, in works such as Mary Karr's *The Liar's Club* (1995), about growing up in a loving but dysfunctional family on the Texas Gulf Coast; Frank McCourt's *Angela's Ashes* (1996), a vivid portrayal of a Dickensian childhood amid the grinding conditions of Irish slum life; Anne Roiphe's bittersweet recollections of her rich but cold-hearted parents and her brother's death from AIDS in *1185 Park Avenue* (1999); and Dave Eggers's *A Heartbreaking Work of Staggering Genius* (2000), a painful but comic tour de force, half tongue-in-cheek, about a young man raising his brother after the death of their parents.

Poetry

The post-World War II years produced an abundance of strong poetry but no individual poet as dominant and accomplished as T.S. Eliot, Ezra Pound, Wallace Stevens, Robert Frost, or William Carlos Williams, whose long careers were coming to an end. The major poetry from 1945 to 1960 was Modernist in its ironic texture yet formal in its insistence on regular rhyme and metre.

Formal Poets

The leading figure of the late 1940s was Robert Lowell, who, influenced by Eliot and such Metaphysical poets as John Donne and Gerard Manley Hopkins, explored his spiritual torments and family history in *Lord Weary's Castle* (1946).

Experimentation and Beat Poetry

By the mid-1950s, however, a strong reaction had developed. Poets began to turn away from Eliot and Metaphysical poetry to more-romantic or more-prosaic models such as Walt Whitman, William Carlos Williams, Hart Crane, and D.H. Lawrence. A group of poets associated with Black Mountain College in western North Carolina, including Charles Olson, Robert Creeley, Robert Duncan, Edward Dorn, and Denise Levertov, treated the poem as an unfolding process rather than a containing form. Olson's *Maximus Poems* (1953–68) showed a clear affinity with the jagged line and uneven flow of Pound's *Cantos* and Williams's *Paterson.* Other Beat poets included Lawrence Ferlinghetti, Gregory Corso, and Gary Snyder, a student of Eastern religion who, in *Turtle Island* (1974), continued the American tradition of nature poetry.

The openness of Beat poetry and the prosaic directness of Williams encouraged Lowell to develop a new autobiographical style in the laconic poetry and prose of *Life Studies* (1959) and In her poetry Plath joined an icy sarcasm to white-hot emotional intensity. Another poet influenced by Lowell was John Berryman, whose *Dream Songs* (1964, 1968) combined autobiographical fragments with minstrel-show motifs to create a zany style of self-projection and comic-tragic lament. Deeply troubled figures, Sexton, Plath, and Berryman all took their own lives.

"Deep Image" Poets

Through his personal charisma and his magazine *The Fifties* (later *The Sixties* and *The Seventies*), Robert Bly encouraged a number of poets to shift their work toward the individual voice and open form; they included Galway Kinnell, James Wright, David Ignatow, and, less directly, Louis Simpson, James Dickey, and Donald Hall. Yet, like their Hispanic models, they were also political poets, instrumental in organizing protest and writing poems against the Vietnam War. Kinnell was a Lawrentian poet who, in poems such as "The Porcupine" and "The Bear," gave the brutality of nature the power of myth.

New Directions

James Wright's style changed dramatically in the early 1960s. He abandoned his stiffly formal verse for the stripped-down, meditative lyricism of *The Branch Will Not Break* (1963) and *Shall We Gather at the River* (1968), which were more dependent on the emotional tenor of image than on metre, poetic diction, or rhyme. In books such as *Figures of the Human* (1964) and *Rescue the Dead* (1968), David Ignatow wrote brief but razor-sharp poems that made their effect through swiftness, deceptive simplicity, paradox, and personal immediacy. Another poet whose work ran the gamut from prosaic simplicity to Emersonian transcendence was A.R. Ammons.

Both daily life and an exposure to French Surrealism helped inspire a group of New York poets, among them Frank O'Hara, Kenneth Koch, James Schuyler, and John Ashbery. Whether O'Hara was jotting down a sequence of ordinary moments or paying tribute to film stars, his poems had a breathless immediacy that was distinctive and unique. Koch's comic voice swung effortlessly from the trivial to the fantastic.

Bishop, Elizabeth: first four stanzas of "Manuelzinho" Other impressive poets of the postwar years included Elizabeth Bishop, whose precise, loving attention to objects was reminiscent of her early mentor, Marianne Moore. In *The Changing Light at Sandover* (1982), James Merrill, previously a polished lyric poet, made his mandarin style the vehicle of a lighthearted personal epic, in which he, with the help of a Ouija board, called up the shades of all his dead friends, including the poet Auden. In a prolific career highlighted by such poems as *Reflections on Espionage* (1976), "Blue Wine" (1979), and *Powers of Thirteen* (1983), John Hollander, like Merrill, displayed enormous technical virtuosity.

Autobiographical Approaches

With the autobiographical knots and parables of *Reasons for Moving* (1968) and *Darker* (1970), Mark Strand's paradoxical language achieved a resonant simplicity. He enhanced his reputation with *Dark Harbor* (1993) and *Blizzard of One* (1998). Other strongly autobiographical poets working with subtle technique and intelligence in a variety of forms included Philip Levine, Charles Simic, Robert Pinsky, Gerald Stern, Louise Glück, and Sharon Olds. Levine's background in working-class Detroit gave his work a unique cast, while Glück and Olds brought a terrific emotional intensity to their poems. With the sinuous sentences and long flowing lines of *Tar* (1983) and *Flesh and Blood* (1987), C.K. Williams perfected a narrative technique founded on distinctive voice, sharply etched emotion, and cleanly observed detail.

That decade also enabled some older poets to become more loosely autobiographical and freshly imaginative, among them Stanley Kunitz, Robert Penn Warren, and W.S. Merwin. The AIDS crisis inspired *My Alexandria* (1993) by Mark Doty, *The Man with Night Sweats* (1992) by Thom Gunn, and a superb memoir, *Borrowed Time* (1988), and a cycle of poems, *Love Alone* (1988), by the poet Paul Monette. With razor-sharp images and finely honed descriptive touches, Louisiana-born Yusef Komunyakaa emerged as an impressive African American voice in the 1990s. He wrote about his time as a soldier and war correspondent in Vietnam in *Dien Cai Dau* (1988) and received the Pulitzer Prize in 1994 for his volume of new and selected poems *Neon Vernacular* (1993).

Drama – Miller, Williams, and Albee

Two post-World War II playwrights established reputations comparable to Eugene O'Neill's. Arthur Miller wrote eloquent essays defending his modern, democratic concept of tragedy; despite its abstract, allegorical quality and portentous language, *Death of a Salesman* (1949) came close to vindicating his views. Miller's intense family dramas were rooted in the problem dramas of Henrik Ibsen and the works of the socially conscious ethnic dramatists of the 1930s, especially Clifford Odets, but Miller gave them a metaphysical turn.

Though his work was uneven, Tennessee Williams at his best was a more powerful and effective playwright than Miller. Creating stellar roles for actors, especially women, Williams brought a passionate lyricism and a tragic Southern vision to such plays as *The Glass Menagerie* (1944), *A Streetcar Named Desire* (1947), *Cat on a Hot Tin Roof* (1955), and *The Night of the Iguana* (1961).

Miller and Williams dominated the post-World War II theatre until the 1960s, and few other playwrights emerged to challenge them. Then, in 1962, Edward Albee's reputation, based on short plays such as *The Zoo Story* (1959) and *The American Dream* (1960), was secured by the stunning power of *Who's Afraid of Virginia Woolf?*

The Off-broadway Ascendancy

The centre of American drama shifted from Broadway to Off-Broadway and Off-Off-Broadway with works such as Jack Gelber's *The Connection* (1959). American playwrights, collaborating with the Living Theatre, the Open Theatre, and other adventurous new companies, were increasingly free to write radical and innovative plays. David Rabe's *The Basic Training of Pavlo Hummel* (1971) and *Sticks and Bones* (1972) satirized America's militaristic nationalism and cultural shallowness.

Amiri Baraka (Le Roi Jones) and Ed Bullins inspired an angry black nationalist theatre. Baraka's *Dutchman* and *The Slave* (1964) effectively dramatized racial confrontation, while

Bullins's *In the Wine Time* (1968) made use of "street" lyricism. Maria Irene Fornés's *Fefu and Her Friends* (1977) proved remarkable in its exploration of women's relationships. Shepard's earlier work, such as*The Tooth of Crime* (1972), was rooted both in the rock scene and counterculture of the 1960s and in the mythic world of the American West.

Other important new voices in American drama were the prolific Lanford Wilson, Pulitzer winner for *Talley's Folly* (1979); John Guare, who created serious farce in *The House of Blue Leaves* (1971) and fresh social drama in *Six Degrees of Separation* (1990); and Ntozake Shange, whose "choreopoem" *For Colored Girls Who Have Considered Suicide/When the Rainbow Is Enuf* moved to Broadway in 1976.

The anguish of the AIDS epidemic proved a dark inspiration to many gay playwrights, especially Tony Kushner, who had gained attention with *A Bright Room Called Day* (1991), set in Germany in 1932–33; he won Broadway fame with his espically ambitious two-part drama *Angels in America* (1991–92), which combined comedy with pain, symbolism with personal history, and invented characters with historical ones. A committed political writer, Kushner often focused on public themes. *The American Plan* (1990), and *Take Me Out* (2002), the last about a gay baseball player who reveals his homosexuality to his teammates. Donald Margulies dealt more directly with Jewish family life in *The Loman Family Picnic* (1989). He also explored the ambitions and relationships of artists in such plays as *Sight Unseen* (1992) and *Collected Stories* (1998).

Literary and Social Criticism

Until his death in 1972, Edmund Wilson solidified his reputation as one of America's most versatile and distinguished men of letters. The novelist John Updikeinherited Wilson's chair at *The New Yorker* and turned out an extraordinary flow of critical reviews collected in volumes such as *Hugging the Shore* (1983) and *Odd Jobs* (1991). Gore Vidal brought together his briskly readable essays of four decades—critical, personal, and political—in *United States* (1993). Alfred Kazin wrote literary history (*An American Procession* [1984], *God and the American Writer* [1997]) and autobiography (*Starting Out in the Thirties* [1965], *New York Jew* [1978]), while Irving Howe produced studies at the crossroads of literature and politics, such as *Politics and the Novel* (1957), as well as a major history of Jewish immigrants in New York, *World of Our Fathers* (1976). His criticism reflected the inward turn from politics toward "moral realism" that coincided with the Cold War. But the cultural and political conflicts of the 1960s revived the social approach among younger students of American literature, such as Henry Louis Gates, Jr., who emerged in the 1980s as a major critic, theorist, and editor of black writers in studies such as *Figures in Black* (1987) and *The Signifying Monkey* (1988).

Literary Biography and the "New Journalism"

The waning of the New Criticism, with its strict emphasis on the text, led not only to a surge of historical criticism and cultural theory but also to a flowering of literary biography. Major works included Leon Edel's five-volume study of Henry James (1953–72), Mark Schorer's *Sinclair Lewis: An American Life* (1961), Richard Ellmann's studies of James Joyce (1959) and Oscar Wilde (1988), R.W.B. Lewis's revealing biography of Edith Wharton (1975), Joseph Frank's five-volume biography of Dostoyevsky (1976–2002), Paul Zweig's brilliant study of Walt Whitman (1984), and Carol Brightman's exhaustive life of Mary McCarthy (1992).

One positive result of the accelerating complexity of post-World War II life was a body of distinguished journalism and social commentary. John Hersey's *Hiroshima* (1946) was a deliberately controlled, unemotional account of atomic holocaust. Ralph Ellison's essays on race and culture in *Shadow and Act* (1964) and *Going to the Territory* (1986) were immensely influential. Norman Mailer's "new journalism" proved especially effective in capturing the drama of political conventions and large protest demonstrations. The novelist Joan Didion published two collections of incisive social and literary commentary, *Slouching Towards Bethlehem* (1968) and *The White Album* (1979). Robert M. Pirsig's *Zen and the Art of Motorcycle Maintenance* (1974) defied all classification. Pirsig equated the emotional collapse of his central character with the disintegration of American workmanship and cultural values.

Theory

The major New Critics and New York critics were followed by major but difficult academic critics, who preferred theory to close reading. European structuralism found little echo in the United States, but post structuralist theorists such as Michel Foucault, Roland Barthes, and Jacques Derrida found a welcome in the less-political atmosphere, marked by skepticism and defeat, that followed the 1960s. Four Yale professors joined Derrida to publish a group of essays, *Deconstruction and Criticism* (1979). Two of the contributors, Paul de Man and J. Hillis Miller, became leading exponents of deconstruction in the United States. The other two, Harold Bloom and Geoffrey H. Hartman, were more interested in the problematic relation of poets to their predecessors and to their own language.

Philosophers Richard Rorty and Stanley Cavell and critic Richard Poirier found a native parallel to European theory in the philosophy of Emerson and the writings of pragmatists such as William James and John Dewey. Emulating Dewey and Irving Howe, Rorty emerged as a social critic in *Achieving Our Country* (1998) and *Philosophy and Social Hope* (1999). Other academic critics also took a more-political turn. Stephen Greenblatt's work on Shakespeare and other Elizabethan writers and Edward Said's essays in *The World, the Text, and the Critic* (1983) were influential in reviving historical approaches to literature that had long been neglected. Said's *Orientalism* (1978) and *Culture and Imperialism* (1993) directed attention to the effects of colonialism on the arts and society.

All these methods yielded new dimensions of critical understanding, but in less-adept hands they became so riddled with jargon or so intensely political and ideological that they lost touch with the general reader, with common sense itself, and with any tradition of accessible criticism. Reactions against theory-based criticism set in during the 1990s not only with attacks on "political correctness" but also with a return to more informal and essayistic forms of criticism that emphasized the role of the public intellectual and the need to reach a wider general audience.

The 1990s also saw the emergence of several talented women playwrights. Paula Vogel repeatedly focused on hot-button moral issues with humour and compassion, dealing with prostitution in *The Oldest Profession* (1981), AIDS in *The Baltimore Waltz* (1992), pornography in *Hot 'n' Throbbing* (1994), and the sexual abuse of minors in *How I Learned to Drive* (1997). She later adapted George and Ira Gershwin's *Porgy and Bess* in 2012, and her *Father Comes Home from the Wars (Parts 1, 2 & 3)*, produced in 2014, placed Homer's *Odyssey* in the context of the American Civil War. Other well-received works included Heather McDonald's *An Almost Holy Picture* (1995), a one-man play about the spiritual life of a preacher; poet Naomi Wallace's *One Flea Spare* (1995), set in London during the Great Plague of 1665; and Margaret Edson's *Wit* (1995), about the slow, poignant cancer death of a literary scholar whose life has been shaped by the eloquence and wit of Metaphysical poetry.

BRITISH LITERATURE AFTER 1945

Increased attachment to religion most immediately characterized literature after World War II. This was particularly perceptible in authors who had already established themselves before the war. W.H. Auden turned from Marxist politics to Christian commitment, expressed in poems that attractively combine classical form with vernacular relaxedness. Christian belief suffused the verse plays of T.S. Eliot and Christopher Fry. While Graham Greene continued the powerful merging of thriller plots with studies of moral and psychological ambiguity that he had developed through the 1930s, his Roman Catholicism loomed especially large in novels such as *The Heart of the Matter* (1948) and *The End of the Affair* (1951). Evelyn Waugh's *Brideshead Revisited* (1945) and his *Sword of Honour* trilogy (1965; published separately as *Men at Arms* [1952], *Officers and Gentlemen* [1955], and *Unconditional Surrender* [1961]) venerate Roman Catholicism as the repository of values seen as under threat from the advance of democracy.

Fiction

The two most innovatory novelists to begin their careers soon after World War II were also religious believers—William Golding and Muriel Spark. In novels of poetic compactness, they frequently return to the notion of original sin—the idea that, in Golding's words, "man produces evil as a bee produces honey." Concentrating on small communities, Spark and Golding transfigure them into microcosms. In Golding's first novel, *Lord of the Flies* (1954), schoolboys cast away on a Pacific island during a nuclear war reenact humanity's fall from grace as their relationships degenerate from innocent camaraderie to totalitarian butchery. In form and atmosphere, *Lord of the Flies* has affinities with George Orwell's examinations of totalitarian nightmare, the fable *Animal Farm* (1945) and the novel *Nineteen Eighty-four* (1949).

The stylized novels of Henry Green, such as *Concluding* (1948) and *Nothing* (1950), also seem to be precursors of the terse, compressed fiction that Spark and Golding brought to such distinction. This kind of fiction, it was argued by Iris Murdoch, a philosopher as well as a novelist, ran antiliberal risks in its preference for allegory, pattern, and symbol over the social capaciousness and realistic rendition of character at which the great 19th-century novels excelled.

While restricting themselves to socially limited canvases, novelists such as Elizabeth Bowen, Elizabeth Taylor, and Barbara Pym continued the tradition of depicting emotional and psychological nuance that Murdoch felt was dangerously neglected in mid-20th-century novels. In contrast to their wry comedies of sense and sensibility and to the packed parables of Golding and Spark was yet another type of fiction, produced by a group of writers who became known as the Angry Young Men. But the most inspired fictional cavalcade of social and cultural life in 20th-century Britain was Angus Wilson's *No Laughing Matter* (1967), a book that set a triumphant seal on his progress from a writer of acidic short stories to a major novelist whose work unites 19th-century breadth and gusto with 20th-century formal versatility and experiment.

From the late 1960s onward, the outstanding trend in fiction was enthrallment with empire. The first phase of this focused on imperial disillusion and dissolution. In his vast, detailed *Raj Quartet* (*The Jewel in the Crown* [1966], *The Day of the Scorpion* [1968], *The Towers of Silence* [1971], and *A Division of the Spoils* [1975]), Paul Scott charted the last years of the British in India; he followed it with *Staying On* (1977), a poignant comedy about those who remained after independence. Three half-satiric, half-elegiac novels by J.G. Farrell (*Troubles* [1970], *The Siege of Krishnapur* [1973], and *The Singapore Grip* [1978]) likewise spotlighted imperial discomfiture. Then, in the 1980s, postcolonial voices made themselves audible. For Rushdie, as *Shame* (1983), *The Satanic Verses* (1988), *The Moor's Last Sigh* (1995), and *The Ground Beneath Her Feet* (1999) further demonstrate, stylistic miscellaneousness—a way of writing that exhibits the vitalizing effects of cultural cross-fertilization—is especially suited to conveying postcolonial experience. (*The Satanic Verses* was understood differently in the Islamic world, to the extent that the Iranian leader Ayatollah Ruhollah Khomeini pronounced a fatwa, in effect a death sentence [later suspended], on Rushdie.) However, not all postcolonial authors followed Rushdie's example. Vikram Seth's massive novel about India after independence, *A Suitable Boy* (1993), is a prodigious feat of realism, resembling 19th-century masterpieces in its combination of social breadth and emotional and psychological depth. Kazuo Ishiguro's spare, refined novel *An Artist of the Floating World* (1986) records how a painter's life and work became insidiously coarsened by the imperialistic ethos of 1930s Japan. Novelists such as Buchi Emecheta and Ben Okri wrote of postcolonial Africa, as did V.S. Naipaul in his most ambitious novel, *A Bend in the River*.

Widening social divides in 1980s Britain were also registered in fiction, sometimes in works that purposefully imitate the Victorian "Condition of England" novel (the best is David Lodge's elegant, ironic *Nice Work* [1988]).

Just as some postcolonial novelists used myth, magic, and fable as a stylistic throwing-off of what they considered the alien supremacy of Anglo-Saxon realistic fiction, so numerous feminist novelists took to Gothic, fairy tale, and fantasy as counter effects to the "patriarchal discourse" of rationality, logic, and linear narrative. Having distinguished herself earlier in a realistic mode, as did authors such as Drabble and Pat Barker, Doris Lessing published a sequence of science fiction novels about issues of gender and colonialism, *Canopus in Argos—Archives* (1979–83).

Typically, though, fiction in the 1980s and '90s was not futuristic but retrospective. As the end of the century approached, an urge to look back—at starting points, previous eras, fictional prototypes—was widely evident. The historical novel enjoyed an exceptional heyday. Beryl Bainbridge, who began her fiction career as a writer of quirky black comedies about northern provincial life, turned her attention to Victorian and Edwardian misadventures: *The Birthday Boys* (1991) retraces Captain Robert Falcon Scott's doomed expedition to the South Pole; *Every Man for Himself* (1996) accompanies the Titanic as it steamed toward disaster; and *Master Georgie* (1998) revisits the Crimean War.

Many novels juxtaposed a present-day narrative with one set in the past. A.S. Byatt's *Possession* (1990) did so with particular intelligence. It also made extensive use of period pastiche, another enthusiasm of novelists toward the end of the 20th century. In addition to the interest in remote and recent history, a concern with tracing aftereffects became dominatingly present in fiction. Most subtly and powerfully exhibiting this, Ian McEwan—who came to notice in the 1970s as an unnervingly emotionless observer of contemporary decadence—grew into imaginative maturity with novels set largely in Berlin in the 1950s (*The Innocent* [1990]) and in Europe in 1946 (*Black Dogs* [1992]).

Poetry

The last flickerings of New Apocalypse poetry—the flamboyant, surreal, and rhetorical style favoured by Dylan Thomas, George Barker, David Gascoyne, and Vernon Watkins—died away soon after World War II. The preeminent practitioner of this style was Philip Larkin, who had earlier displayed some of its qualities in two novels: *Jill* (1946) and *A Girl in Winter* (1947). In Larkin's poetry (*The Less Deceived* [1955], *The Whitsun Weddings* [1964], *High Windows* [1974]), a melancholy sense of life's limitations throbs through lines of elegiac elegance. Suffused with acute awareness of mortality and transience.

In contrast to the rueful traditionalism of their work is the poetry of Ted Hughes, who succeeded Betjeman as poet laureate (1984–98). In extraordinarily vigorous verse, beginning with his first collection, *The Hawk in the Rain* (1957), Hughes captured the ferocity, vitality, and splendour of the natural world. This realization, along with strong regional roots, is something Hughes had in common with a number of poets writing in the second half of the 20th century. The work of Geoffrey Hill (especially *King Log* [1968], *Mercian Hymns* [1971], *Tenebrae* [1978], and *The Triumph of Love* [1998]) treats Britain as a palimpsest whose superimposed layers of history are uncovered in poems, which are sometimes written in prose.

Britain's industrial regions received attention in poetry too. In collections such as *Terry Street* (1969), Douglas Dunn wrote of working-class life in northeastern England. Harrison's social and cultural journey away from that world by means of a grammar school education and a degree in classics provoked responses in him that his poetry conveys with imaginative vehemence and caustic wit: anger at the deprivations and humiliations endured by the working class; guilt over the way his talent had lifted him away from these.

Also from Yorkshire was Blake Morrison, whose finest work, "The Ballad of the Yorkshire Ripper" (1987), was composed in taut, macabre stanzas thickened with dialect. Morrison's work also displayed a growing development in late 20th-century British poetry: the writing of narrative verse. An especially ambitious exercise in the narrative genre was Craig Raine's *History: The Home Movie* (1994), a huge semifictionalized saga, written in three-line stanzas, chronicling several generations of his and his wife's families. The defining characteristic of this school was a poetry rife with startling images, unexpected but audaciously apt similes, and rapid, imaginative tricks of transformation that set the reader looking at the world afresh.

From the late 1960s onward Northern Ireland, convulsed by sectarian violence, was particularly prolific in poetry. From a cluster of significant talents—Michael Longley, Derek Mahon, Medbh McGuckian, Paul Muldoon—Seamus Heaney soon stood out. Born into a Roman Catholic farming family in County Derry, he began by publishing verse—in his collections *Death of a Naturalist* (1966) and *Door into the Dark* (1969)—that combines a tangible, tough, sensuous response to rural and agricultural life, reminiscent of that of Ted Hughes, with meditation about the relationship between the taciturn world of his parents and his own communicative calling as a poet. Since then, in increasingly magisterial books of poetry—*Wintering Out* (1972), *North* (1975), *Field Work* (1979), *Station Island* (1984), *The Haw Lantern* (1987), *Seeing Things* (1991), *The Spirit Level* (1996)—Heaney has become arguably the greatest poet Ireland has produced, eventually winning the Nobel Prize for Literature (1995). Present and past coalesce in Heaney's verses: Iron Age sacrificial victims exhumed from peat bogs resemble tarred-and-feathered victims of the atrocities in contemporary Belfast; elegies for friends and relatives slaughtered during the outrages of the 1970s and '80s are embedded in verses whose imagery and metrical forms derive from Dante.

Drama

Apart from the short-lived attempt by T.S. Eliot and Christopher Fry to bring about a renaissance of verse drama, theatre in the late 1940s and early 1950s was most notable for the continuing supremacy of the well-made play, which focused upon, and mainly attracted as its audience, the comfortable middle class. The most accomplished playwright working within this mode was Terence Rattigan, whose carefully crafted, conventional-looking plays—in particular, *The Winslow Boy* (1946), *The Browning Version* (1948), *The Deep Blue Sea* (1952), and *Separate Tables* (1954)—affectingly disclose desperations, terrors, and emotional forlornness concealed behind reticence and gentility. In 1956 John Osborne's *Look Back in Anger* forcefully signaled the start of a very different dramatic tradition. Also working within this tradition was John Arden, whose dramas employ some of Bertold Brecht's theatrical devices. Arden wrote historical plays (*Serjeant Musgrave's Dance* [1959], *Armstrong's Last Goodnight* [1964]) to advance radical social and political views and in doing so provided a model that several later left-wing dramatists followed.

An alternative reaction against drawing-room naturalism came from the Theatre of the Absurd. Some of Beckett's themes and techniques are discernible in the drama of Harold Pinter. Characteristically concentrating on two or three people maneuvering for sexual or social superiority in a claustrophobic room, works such as *The Birthday Party* (1958), *The Caretaker* (1960), *The Homecoming* (1965), *No Man's Land* (1975), and *Moonlight* (1993) are potent dramas of menace in which a slightly surreal atmosphere contrasts with and undermines dialogue of tape-recorder authenticity. Joe Orton's anarchic black comedies—*Entertaining Mr. Sloane* (1964), *Loot* (1967), and *What the Butler Saw* (1969)—put theatrical procedures pioneered by Pinter at the service of outrageous sexual farce (something for which Pinter himself also showed a flair in television plays such as *The Lover* [1963] and later stage works such as *Celebration* [2000]). Orton's taste for dialogue in the epigrammatic style of Oscar Wilde was shared by one of the wittiest dramatists to emerge in the 1960s, Tom Stoppard. In plays from *Rosencrantz and Guildenstern Are Dead* (1966) to later triumphs such as *Arcadia* (1993) and *The Invention of Love* (1997), Stoppard set intellectually challenging concepts ricocheting in scenes glinting with the to-and-fro of polished repartee. The most prolific comic playwright from the 1960s onward was Alan Ayckbourn, whose often virtuoso feats of stagecraft and theatrical ingenuity made him one of Britain's most popular dramatists. Ayckbourn's plays showed an increasing tendency to broach darker themes and were especially scathing (for instance, in *A Small Family Business* [1987]) on the topics of the greed and selfishness that he considered to have been promoted by Thatcherism, the prevailing political philosophy in 1980s Britain.

Irish dramatists other than Beckett also exhibited a propensity for combining comedy with something more sombre. Their most recurrent subject matter during the last decades of the 20th century was small-town provincial life. Brian Friel (*Dancing at Lughnasa* [1990]), Tom Murphy (*Conversations on a Homecoming* [1985]), Billy Roche (*Poor Beast in the Rain* [1990]), Martin McDonagh (*The Beauty Queen of Leenane* [1996]), and Conor McPherson (*The Weir* [1997]) all wrote effectively on this theme.

Playwrights who had much in common with Arden's ideological beliefs and his admiration for Brechtian theatre—Edward Bond, Howard Barker, Howard Brenton—maintained a steady output of parable-like plays dramatizing radical left-wing doctrine. David Edgar developed into a dramatist of impressive span and depth with plays such as *Destiny* (1976) and *Pentecost* (1994), his masterly response to the collapse of communism and rise of nationalism in eastern Europe.

Hare also wrote political plays for television, such as *Licking Hitler* (1978) and *Saigon: Year of the Cat* (1983). Trevor Griffiths, author of dialectical stage plays clamorous with debate, put television drama to the same use (*Comedians* [1975] had particular impact). Dennis Potter, best known for his teleplay *The Singing Detective* (1986), deployed a wide battery of the medium's resources, including extravagant fantasy and sequences that sarcastically counterpoint popular music with scenes of brutality, class-based callousness, and sexual rapacity. Potter's works transmit his revulsion, semireligious in nature, at what he saw as widespread hypocrisy, sadism, and injustice in British society. His masterpieces, though, are dramatic monologues written for television—*A Woman of No Importance* (1982) and 12 works he called *Talking Heads* (1987) and *Talking Heads 2* (1998). In these television plays, Bennett's comic genius for capturing the rich waywardness of everyday speech combines with psychological acuteness, emotional delicacy, and a melancholy consciousness of life's transience.

The 21st Century

As the 21st century got under way, history remained the outstanding concern of English literature. Although contemporary issues such as global warming and international conflicts (especially the Second Persian Gulf War and its aftermath) received attention, writers were still more disposed to look back. Bennett's play *The History Boys* (filmed 2006) premiered in 2004; it portrayed pupils in a school in the north of England during the 1980s. Although *Cloud Atlas* (2004)—a far-reaching book by David Mitchell, one of the more ambitious novelists to emerge during this period—contained chapters that envisage future eras ravaged by malign technology and climactic and nuclear devastation, it devoted more space to scenes set in the 19th and early 20th centuries. In doing so, it also displayed another preoccupation of the 21st century's early years: the imitation of earlier literary styles and techniques. There was a marked vogue for pastiche and revisionary Victorian novels (of which Michel Faber's *The Crimson Petal and the White* [2002] was a prominent example). McEwan's *Atonement* (2001) worked masterly variations on the 1930s fictional procedures of authors such as Elizabeth Bowen. In *Saturday* (2005), the model of Virginia Woolf's fictional presentation of a war-shadowed day in London in *Mrs. Dalloway* (1925) stood behind McEwan's vivid depiction of that city on Feb. 15, 2003, a day of mass demonstrations against the impending war in Iraq. Heaney continued to revisit the rural world of his youth in the poetry collections *Electric Light* (2001) and *District and Circle* (2006) while also reexamining and reworking classic texts, a striking instance of which was *The Burial at Thebes* (2004), which infused Sophocles' *Antigone* with contemporary resonances. Although they had entered into a new millennium, writers seemed to find greater imaginative stimulus in the past than in the present and the future.

INDIAN LITERATURE

Contemporary Indian Literature which is only one and a half centuries old is marked by amazing variables in both the literatures and the regions through which it was produced.

Before delving deeply into the exceedingly diversified genre of contemporary Indian literature, it is of tremendous importance to comprehend the fraternal terms of 'modern', 'modernity' and 'modernisation' in the Indian context. These three terms in the modern context are quite significant and highly condensed terms for historical experiences. Keeping in mind the chronological pattern, the twentieth century is considered to be more modern than the nineteenth century, but that does not exclude the 19th century from contemporary literature in India genre. The criterion involved here is not qualitative, but rather simplistic. Furthermore, anything which is fashionable today is considered modern whether it is desirable or not.

However, the more significant aspect of modernity is a value-based approach. Particular attitudes and ideas are conceived more progressive and hence it is natural to condition them as modern as opposed to what existed before. The chronological sense is in a way implicit in this concept. The Indian context of contemporary literature bears an essential relation with the social and political history of the country during the mid-19th century, which indeed had marked a breakthrough. English education had gradually disseminated in India during the first half of the 19th century, but its effect is seen manifestly in Indian literary creation only in the second half of the century. A new approach towards literature had emerged in the major languages. There indeed had existed an unambiguous novelty in form and content, mostly in both literatures, as form and content are always cohesively bound together.

Language in Contemporary Indian Literature

The distinct Indian flavour was back in the English language and thus the works of the modern Indian writers reflected the Indianised English. Be it Salman Rushdie, Shahshi Tharoor or Amitav Ghosh the deconstruction of the British of English was quite evident. The regional languages were freely used in the prose forms; thus once again breaking, restructuring and adding a new twist and dimension to the traditional narrative patterns. Hindi, Gujarati, Bengali, Telugu, Tamil, Kannada, Marathi writers adhered to the 'modern' and 'post modern' idiom of writing. For instance, Mulk Raj Anand's work is replete with Hindi and Punjabi words like '*haanaai*', '*saalamhuzoorii*', '*shabashshabash*' **(Coolie).** Most path breaking is Arundhati Roy's use of untranslated malyalam words in day to day conversations in her **The God of Small Things** like '*chacko sir vannu*', 'she is very beautiful sundarikutty', '*oower, orkunniley, kushambi.*

As far as poetry was concerned, it did not necessarily rhyme. Rather rhyme was done away with consciously to bring forth the discordance in the life of modern man. Both Indian English and regional poems deliberately distanced themselves from rhythm.

Themes in Contemporary Indian Literature and Post-Colonialism

Post independence, India was faced with a number of crises including social, political and economic. The society was in a continuous state of flux. This time the writers were no more eulogising their nation. Rather they were bringing to the forefront the reality through their works. Both verse and prose were time and again emphasising on the dominant crises. In order to establish a new narrative, to break away from the colonial mind set, contemporary Indian writers adapted new narrative patterns to put through their notions.

Experimentation in Contemporary Indian English Literature

Making a move from the 18th or 19th century, that had indeed sowed the budding phase of then referred contemporary Indian literature, writers belonging to contemporary India are additionally very conscious about their own culture and traditions. Hence can be witnessed a massive body of vernacular language and literature flourishing in it. While some of the authors pen in English, most of them continue to write in their colloquial languages. The philosophy and thought behind their works exhibit influences of western thoughts and principles. It is quite laudable that these authors have been successful enough to maintain the unique flavour of their region in their works and tinge it further with a modern dimension The literary genre of the contemporary Indian literature are manifold. Present Indian readers have novels, plays, short stories, literary criticism, science fiction and poetry to choose from.

Contemporary Indian Regional Literature

Besides the Indian English Literature, the regional literature of the subcontinent reflected significant changes as well. For instance, in Marathi literature changes were creeping in after 1800 which was the period of intellectual fervour and reformist didactism. Many English books were translated in Marathi. Ram Ganesh Gadkari and Prahlad Keshav are also shared the stage with stalwarts like, Mohan Agashe, Sriram Lagoo, Kashinath Ghanekar, Prabhakar Panshikar started playing many immortal characters written by geniuses like Vasant Kanetkar, Kusumagraj, **Vijay Tendulkar**. This movement in drama was suitably supported by Marathi films which did not become a roaring success. There were pioneers like V. Shantaram and Dadasaheb Phalkeand Marathi cinema had a tremendous impact on contemporary film industry.

Modern Marathi poetry commenced with the works of Jyotibha Phule but the later poets like Keshuta Balakavi, Ravi Kiran Mandal wrote poetry inspired by romantic and Victorian English tradition. But the major paradigmatic shift occurred in the mid forties with the poetry of Mardhekar and in the nineties in the hands of Abhidhanantar and Shabadavedh. The Little Magazine movement which became powerful in the fifties because of radical and path breaking writings gained momentum in the nineties too in the hands of Manya Joshi, Hemant Divate and Sachin Ketkar.

Similar developments were also witnessed in the South Indian literary circles. In the 19th century the south Indian literature was inspired by European genres but in the end of the century things started to change with the help of modern writers like VVS Aiyar and Subhramania Bharati who started developing new forms. Modern south Indian literature boasts of great stalwarts who have left their imprint on the mind of numerous readers the world around.

Indian Contemporary Literatures and Post- Colonialism

Contemporary writers like Jhaver Chand Meghani, Dharamvir Bharati, Mulk Raj Anand, Arundhati Roy, Vikram Seth, Jhumpa Lahiri and Amitav Ghosh have won international awards and put India firmly on the world‘s literary map. The two most famous names are the Mumbai born Salman Rushdie who received a booker price for his Midnight‘s Children and the Keralan author Arundhati Roy who also bagged a booker for her God of Small Things. Other important writers are Shashi Deshpandewhose A Matter Of Time revolves around the problems in the middle class household when the husband leaves; Rohinton Mistry‘s Family Matters and Fine Balance where he deals with Indian society keeping Mumbai as the background. R.K. Narayan is another renowned south Indian writer who scaled great heights with his works revolving around the south Indian small towns of Malgudi. His chief works are Swami and his Friends, The Financial Expert, The Guide, Waiting for the Mahatma and Malgudi Days. Kamala Markandaya‘s Nector in a Sieve describes the heart wrenching struggle of a south Indian woman against the ravages of time and the destructive forces of nature.

Kaka Saheb Kalelkar is another celebrated writer in pre-independent India. His philosophical writings demonstrate his vast erudition, his commentary on the *Bhagavad Gita*, his essays on culture, his travelogues, his translation of Gitanjali had won him applauding appreciation from all quarters. The other eminent personalities that contributed to the literature world redefining contemporary Indian literature during this period comprise: Vempalli Gangadhar, K.K. Munshi, Joy Somnath, Khushwant Singh and many others.

List of Postmodern Literature

Some well known examples of postmodern literature, in chronological order, include:

Finnegans Wake (1939) by James Joyce [50]

At Swim-Two-Birds (1939) by Flann O'Brien

Pierre Menard, Author of the Quixote (1939) by Jorge Luis Borges

The Third Policeman (1941, published 1967) by Flann O'Brien

The Cannibal (1949) by John Hawkes

The Ginger Man (1955) by J. P. Donleavy

The Recognitions (1955) by William Gaddis

The Comforters (1957) by Muriel Spark
Naked Lunch (1959) by William Burroughs
The Sot-Weed Factor (1960) by John Barth
Catch-22 (1961) by Joseph Heller
The Lime Twig (1961) by John Hawkes
Mother Night (1961) by Kurt Vonnegut
Pale Fire (1962) by Vladimir Nabokov
The Man in the High Castle (1962) by Philip K. Dick
The Bell Jar (1963) by Sylvia Plath V. (1963) by Thomas Pynchon
Cat's Cradle (1963) by Kurt Vonnegut
Hopscotch (1963) by Julio Cortázar
Albert Angelo (1964) by B. S. Johnson
Wide Sargasso Sea (1966) by Jean Rhys
Sputnik Sweetheart (1999) by Haruki Murakami
The Crying of Lot 49 (1966) by Thomas Pynchon
Lost in the Funhouse (1968) by John Barth
Do Androids Dream of Electric Sheep? (1968) by Philip K. Dick
The Left Hand of Darkness (1969) by Ursula Le Guin
Slaughterhouse-Five (1969) by Kurt Vonnegut
Yellow Back Radio Broke-Down (1969) by Ishmael Reed
The French Lieutenant's Woman (1969) by John Fowles
Ada or Ardor: A Family Chronicle (1969) by Vladimir Nabokov
Moscow-Petushki (1970) by Venedikt Erofeev
The Atrocity Exhibition (1970) by J. G. Ballard
The Obscene Bird of Night (1970) by José Donoso
Another Roadside Attraction (1971) by Tom Robbins
Double or Nothing (1971) by Raymond Federman
Fear and Loathing in Las Vegas (1971) by Hunter S. Thompson
The Monster at the End of This Book (1971) by Jon Stone
Invisible Cities (1972) by Italo Calvino
Mumbo Jumbo (1972) by Ishmael Reed
Chimera (1972) by John Barth
Crash (1973) by J. G. Ballard
Breakfast of Champions (1973) by Kurt Vonnegut
Gravity's Rainbow (1973) by Thomas Pynchon
The Magus (1973) by John Fowles
Alphabetical Africa (1974) by Walter Abish
The Last Days of Louisiana Red (1974) by Ishmael Reed
J R (1975) by William Gaddis
The Illuminatus! Trilogy (1975) by Robert Shea and Robert Anton Wilson
The Dead Father (1975) by Donald Barthelme
Dhalgren (1975) by Samuel R. Delany
Options (1975) by Robert Sheckley
The Alteration (1976) by Kingsley Amis
Even Cowgirls Get the Blues (1976) by Tom Robbins
Almost Transparent Blue (1976) by Ryu Murakami
Ratner's Star (1976) by Don DeLillo
Ceremony (1977) by Leslie Marmon Silko
A Scanner Darkly (1977) by Philip K. Dick
The Public Burning (1977), by Robert Coover
Life: A User's Manual (1978) by Georges Perec
The Twyborn Affair (1979) by Patrick White
If on a winter's night a traveler (1979) by Italo Calvino
Mulligan Stew (1979) by Gilbert Sorrentino
How German Is It (1980) by Walter Abish
Coin Locker Babies (1980) by Ryu Murakami
Nikopol Trilogy (1980–1993) by Enki Bilal
Kindred (1979) by Octavia Butler
Housekeeping (1980) by Marilynne Robinson
Still Life with Woodpecker (1980) by Tom Robbins
VALIS (1981) by Philip K. Dick
Sixty Stories (1981) by Donald Barthelme
Lanark: A Life in Four Books (1981) by Alasdair Gray
The Transmigration of Timothy Archer (1982) by Philip K. Dick
Mantissa (1982) by John Fowles
Waterland (1983) by Graham Swift
Brilliant Creatures (1983) by Clive James
The Name of the Rose (1983) by Umberto Eco
Neuromancer (1984) by William Gibson
Miss Peabody's Inheritance (1983) by Elizabeth Jolley
Nights at the Circus (1984) by Angela Carter
Jitterbug Perfume (1984) by Tom Robbins
Blood and Guts in High School (1984) by Kathy Acker
Dictionary of the Khazars (1984) by Milorad Pavic
Democracy (1984) by Joan Didion

Foxybaby (1985) by Elizabeth Jolley
Oranges Are Not the Only Fruit (1985) by Jeanette Winterson
Fantasia: An Algerian Cavalcade (1985) by Assia Djebar
Less Than Zero (1985) by Bret Easton Ellis
The New York Trilogy (1985–86) by Paul Auster
White Noise (1985) by Don DeLillo
A Maggot (1985) by John Fowles
Hard-Boiled Wonderland and the End of the World (1985) by Haruki Murakami
The Infinite Deadlock (1985–1988) by Dmitry Galkovsky
Watchmen (1986–87) by Alan Moore and Dave Gibbons
The Well (1986) by Elizabeth Jolley
Memoirs of Many in One (1986) by Patrick White
Kisses of the Enemy (1987) by Rodney Hall
Moon Tiger (1987) by Penelope Lively
Women and Men (1987) by Joseph McElroy
Beloved (1987) by Toni Morrison
The Mezzanine (1988) by Nicholson Baker
Foucault's Pendulum (1988) by Umberto Eco
Braschi's Empire of Dreams (1988) by Giannina Braschi
Wittgenstein's Mistress (1988) by David Markson
Tracks (1988) by Louise Erdrich
London Fields (1989) by Martin Amis
The Sandman (1989–1996) by Neil Gaiman
The Black Book (1990) by Orhan Pamuk
Haroun and the Sea of Stories (1990) by Salman Rushdie
My Cousin, My Gastroenterologist (1990) by Mark Leyner
The Things They Carried (1990) by Tim O'Brien
Almanac of the Dead (1991) by Leslie Marmon Silko
Omon Ra (1991) by Victor Pelevin
Maus (1991) by Art Spiegelman
The Gold Bug Variations (1991) by Richard Powers
American Psycho (1991) by Bret Easton Ellis
What a Carve Up! (1991) by Jonathan Coe
Generation X: Tales for an Accelerated Culture (1991) by Douglas Coupland
Snow Crash (1992) by Neal Stephenson
Vurt (1993) by Jeff Noon
A Frolic of His Own (1994) by William Gaddis
Astronautilía Hvezdoplavba (1995) by Jan Kresadlo
Galatea 2.2 (1995) by Richard Powers
The Tunnel (1995) by William H. Gass
Reservation Blues (1995) by Sherman Alexie
The Wind-Up Bird Chronicle (1995) by Haruki Murakami
Infinite Jest (1996) by David Foster Wallace
Chapayev and Void (1996) by Victor Pelevin
Fight Club (1996) by Chuck Palahniuk
Mason & Dixon (1997) by Thomas Pynchon
Underworld (1997) by Don DeLillo
In the Miso Soup (1997) by Ryu Murakami
Transmetropolitan (1997-2002) by Warren Ellis and Darick Robertson
Yo-Yo Boing! (1998) by Giannina Braschi
Glamorama (1998) by Bret Easton Ellis
Zero Degree (1998) by Charu Nivedita
Koolaids: The Art of War (1998) by Rabih Alameddine
My Name Is Red (1998) by Orhan Pamuk
Tomcat in Love (1998) by Tim O'Brien
Generation "?" (1999) by Victor Pelevin
The Rings of Saturn (1999) by W. G. Sebald
Q (1999) by Luther Blissett
Motherless Brooklyn (1999) by Jonathan Lethem
White Teeth (2000) by Zadie Smith
Morning and Evening (2000) by Jon Fosse
An Invisible Sign of My Own: A Novel (2000) by Aimee Bender
The Blind Assassin (2001) by Margaret Atwood
Austerlitz (2001) by W. G. Sebald
Everything Is Illuminated (2002) by Jonathan Safran Foer
You Shall Know Our Velocity (2002) by Dave Eggers
Kafka on the Shore (2002) by Haruki Murakami
2666 (2004) by Roberto Bolaño
After Dark (2004) by Haruki Murakami
On Beauty (2005) by Zadie Smith
Lunar Park (2005) by Bret Easton Ellis
Against the Day (2005) by Thomas Pynchon
Never Let Me Go (2005) by Kazuo Ishiguro
Lullabies for Little Criminals (2006) by Heather O'Neill
What Is the What (2006) by Dave Eggers
The Last Novel (2007) by David Markson
The City & the City (2009) by China Miéville

Generation A (2009) by Douglas Coupland
Inherent Vice (2009) by Thomas Pynchon
Z213: Exit (2009) by Dimitris Lyacos
1Q84 (2009–2010) by Haruki Murakami
Witz (2010) by Joshua Cohen
The Pale King (2011) by David Foster Wallace
United States of Banana (2011) by Giannina Braschi
Home (2012) by Toni Morrison
Middle C (2013) by William H. Gass
Bleeding Edge (2013) by Thomas Pynchon
Taipei (2013) by Tao Lin
A Brief History of Seven Killings (2014) by Marlon James
With the People from the Bridge (2014) by Dimitris Lyacos

DAME ROSE MACAULAY

- *Southey in Portugal* (1945)
- *Evelyn Waugh* (1946)
- *Pleasure of Ruins* (1953)
- *Letters to a Friend 1950–52* (1961)
- *Letters to a Sister* (1964)
- *They Went to Portugal Too* (1990)

ELIZABETH BOWEN

- *The Heat of the Day* (1949)
- *Eva Trout* (1968)
- *The Demon Lover and Other Stories* (1945) *Ivy Gripped the Steps and Other Stories* (1946,)
- *Stories by Elizabeth Bowen* (1959) *A Day in the Dark and Other Stories* (1965)
- *The Collected Stories of Elizabeth Bowen* (1980)
- *The Bazaar and Other Stories* (2008) - edited by Allan Hepburn

Non-fiction books

- *Bowen's Court* (1964)
- *Anthony Trollope: A New Judgement* (1946)
- *Why Do I Write?: An Exchange of Views between Elizabeth Bowen, Graham Greene and V.S. Pritchett* (1948)
- *Collected Impressions* (1950)
- *The Shelbourne* (1951)
- *A Time in Rome* (1960)
- *Afterthought: Pieces About Writing* (1962)

REBECCA WEST

- *The Return of the Soldier* (1918), *The Judge* (1922), *The Thinking Reed* (1936), *The Fountain Overflows* (1956), *This Real Night* (1984), *Cousin Rosamund* (1985), *The Birds Fall Down* (1966), *Sunflower* (1986), *The Sentinel* (2002),

Non-fiction

- *The Meaning of Treason* (1949)
- *The New Meaning of Treason* (1964)
- *Family Memories: An Autobiographical Journey* (1987)
- *The Selected Letters of Rebecca West* (2000)
- *Survivors in Mexico* (2003)
- *Woman as Artist and Thinker* (2005)
- *The Essential Rebecca West: Uncollected Prose* (2010)

GRAHAM GREENE

- *The Heart of the Matter* (1948)
- *The Third Man* (1949),
- *The End of the Affair* (1951)
- *Twenty-One Stories* (1954)
- *Loser Takes All* (1955)
- *The Quiet American* (1955)
- *The Human Factor* (1978)
- *Doctor Fischer of Geneva* (1980)
- *Monsignor Quixote* (1982)
- *The Last Word* (1990)

Bibliography

- *A Question of Upbringing* (1951)
- *At Lady Molly's* (1957)
- *The Military Philosophers* (1968)
- *Books Do Furnish a Room* (1971)
- *Temporary Kings* (1973)
- *Hearing Secret Harmonies* (1975)

Partial bibliography of other novels, plays, and works:

- *John Aubrey and His Friends* (1948)
- *Two Plays: The Garden God, The Rest I'll Whistle* (1971)
- *O, How the Wheel Becomes It! (novel)* (1983)
- *The Fisher King* (1986)
- *Some Poets, Artists & 'A Reference for Mellors'*, 2005
- *The Acceptance of Absurdity.* Anthony Powell & Robert Vanderbilt: Letters 1952 - 1963.

Edited by John Saumarez Smith & Jonathan Kooperstein. Maggs Brothers, London 2011

Diaries

- *Journals 1982–1986* (1995)
- *Journals 1987–1989* (1996)
- *Journals 1990–1992* (1997)

GEORGE BERNARD SHAW

Full length plays

- *Saint Joan*
- *The Apple Cart*
- *Too True to Be Good*
- *On the Rocks*
- *The Simpleton of the Unexpected Isles*
- *The Millionairess*
- *Geneva*
- *In Good King Charles's Golden Days*
- *Buoyant Billions*

Short plays

- *A Village Wooing*
- *The Six of Calais*
- *Cymbeline Refinished*
- *Farfetched Fables*
- *Shakes versus Shav*
- *Why She Would Not*

ANTHONY POWELL

- *A Question of Upbringing* (1951)
- *A Buyer's Market* (1952)
- *The Acceptance World* (1955)
- *Books Do Furnish a Room* (1971)
- *Temporary Kings* (1973)
- *Hearing Secret Harmonies* (1975)

Partial bibliography of other novels, plays, and works:

- *John Aubrey and His Friends* (1948)
- *Two Plays: The Garden God, The Rest I'll Whistle* (1971)
- *O, How the Wheel Becomes It! (novel)* (1983)
- *The Fisher King* (1986)
- *A Writer's Notebook*, 2001
- *Miscellaneous Verdicts. Writings on Writers 1946-1989*, 1990
- *Under Review. Further Writings on Writers 1946-1989*, 1991
- *Some Poets, Artists & ´A Reference for Mellors´*, 2005

CHRISTOPHER FRY

- *A Phoenix Too Frequent* (1946)
- *The Firstborn* (1946)
- *The Lady's Not for Burning* (1948)
- *Thor, With Angels* (1948)
- *The Lark* (1955), adapted from Jean Anouilh's play
- *Tiger At The Gates* (1956), adapted from Jean Giraudoux's play
- *Crown of the Year* (1958), music by Michael Tippett
- *Duel of Angels* (1958), adapted from Jean Giraudoux's play *Pour Lucrèce*
- *Curtmantle* (1961)
- *One Thing More (or Caedmon Construed)* (1986)
- *A Ringing of Bells* (2001)

ARTHUR MILLER

Stage plays

- *All My Sons* (1947)
- *Death of a Salesman* (1949)
- *The Crucible* (1953)
- *A View from the Bridge* (1955)
- *A Memory of Two Mondays* (1955)
- *The Last Yankee* (1991)
- *The Ride Down Mt. Morgan* (1991)
- *Broken Glass* (1994)
- *Mr Peter's Connections* (1998)
- *Resurrection Blues* (2002)
- *Finishing the Picture* (2004)

Radio plays

- *The Story of Gus* (1947)

Screenplays

- *The Hook* (1947)
- All My Sons *(1948)*
- Death of a Salesman *(1985)*
- The Crucible *(1995)*
- Mr. Peters' Connections (1998)
- *Assorted fiction*Focus *(novel, 1945)*
- Presence: Stories *(short stories, 2007)*

Non-fiction

- *Situation Normal* (1944), *In Russia* (1969), *In the Country* (1977), *Chinese Encounters* (1979), *Salesman in Beijing* (1984), *Timebends: A Life*, Methuen London (1987) CollectionsMartin, Robert A. (ed.), "The theater essays of Arthur Miller, Steven R Centola,

TENNESSEE WILLIAMS

Plays

Apprentice plays

- *You Touched Me* (1945)
- *Stairs to the Roof* (1947)

Major plays

- *A Streetcar Named Desire* (1947).
- *The Night of the Iguana* (1961)
- *The Eccentricities of a Nightingale* (1962)
- *The Milk Train Doesn't Stop Here Anymore* (1963)
- *The Mutilated* (1965)
- *The Seven Descents of Myrtle* (1968, aka *Kingdom of Earth*)
- *In the Bar of a Tokyo Hotel* (1969)
- *Will Mr. Merriweather Return from Memphis?* (1969)
- *The Notebook of Trigorin* (1980)
- *Something Cloudy, Something Clear* (1981)
- *A House Not Meant to Stand* (1982)
- *In Masks Outrageous and Austere* (1983)

Novels

- *The Roman Spring of Mrs. Stone* (1950) *and the World of Reason* (1975)

Screenplays and teleplays

- *The Glass Menagerie* (1950)
- *A Streetcar Named Desire* (1951)
- *The Rose Tattoo* (1955)
- *Boom!* (1968)
- *The Loss of a Teardrop Diamond* (2009; screenplay from 1957)

Short stories

- *The Resemblance Between a Violin Case and a Coffin* (1951)
- *Hard Candy: A Book of Stories* (1954)
- *One Arm and Other Stories* (1967)
- *Eight Mortal Ladies Possessed: a Book of Stories* (1974)
- *It Happened the day the Sun Rose, and Other Stories* (1981)

Poetry

- *In the Winter of Cities* (1956)
- *Androgyne, Mon Amour* (1977)

SAMUEL BECKETT

Theatre

- Human Wishes (published 1984)
- Eleutheria (written 1947 in French; published in French 1995, and English 1996)
- En attendant Godot (published 1952, performed,1953) (Waiting for Godot, pub. 1954, perf. 1955)
- as Spiel, 1963; English version 1964)
- Come and Go (first performed in German, then English, 1966)
- Rockaby (first performed 1981)
- Ohio Impromptu (first performed 1981)
- Catastrophe (Catastrophe et autres dramatiques, first performed 1982)
- What Where (first performed 1983)

Radio

- All That Fall (broadcast 1957)
- From an Abandoned Work (broadcast 1957)
- Embers (broadcast 1959)

Television

- Eh Joe with Jack MacGowran (broadcast 1966)
- Beginning To End with Jack MacGowran (1965)
- Ghost Trio (broadcast 1977)
- Beckett Directs Beckett (1988/92)

Cinema

- Film (1965)

Novels

- Dream of Fair to Middling Women (written 1932; published 1992)
- L'innommable (1953); The Unnamable (1958)
- Comment c'est (1961); How It Is (1964)
- Mercier and Camier (written 1946, published 1970); English translation (1974)

Short prose

- "L'Expulsé", written 1946, in Nouvelles et Textes pour rien(1955); "The Expelled" Stories and Texts for Nothing(1967)
- "As the Story was Told" (1990)
- The Complete Short Prose: 1929-1989,
- Gontarski. New York: Grove Press, 1995

Non-fiction

- Three Dialogues (with Georges Duthuit and Jacques Putnam) (1949)

Poetry collections

- Whoroscope (1930)
- Echo's Bones and other Precipitates (1935)
- Poèmes (1968, expanded 1976, 1979, 1992)

- Poems in English (1961) Translation collections and long works
- Anna Livia Plurabelle (James Joyce, French translation by Beckett and others) (1931)
- Negro: an Anthology (Nancy Cunard, editor) (1934)

SIR WILLIAM GOLDING

Poetry

- Poems (1934)

Drama

- The Brass Butterfly (1958)

Novels

- Lord of the Flies (1954)
- The Inheritors (1955)
- The Paper Men (1984)
- Rites of Passage (1980)
- Close Quarters (1987)
- Fire Down Below (1989)
- The Double Tongue (posthumous publication 1995)

Non-fiction

- The Hot Gates (1965)
- A Moving Target (1982)
- An Egyptian Journal (1985)

HENRY MILLER

- Tropic of Cancer , Tropic of Capricorn , Sexus (The Rosy Crucifixion,) Black Spring , Plexus (The Rosy Crucifixion), The Colossus of Maroussi , Quiet Days in Clichy , Nexus (The Rosy Crucifixion)

LAWRENCE DURRELL

Novels

- Cefalu (1947; republished as The Dark Labyrinth in 1958)
- White Eagles Over Serbia (1957)
- The Alexandria Quartet (1962)
- Nunquam (1970)
- The Avignon Quintet (1992)
- Monsieur: or, The Prince of Darkness (1974)
- Livia: or, Buried Alive (1978)
- Quinx: or, The Ripper's Tale (1985)
- Judith (2012, written 1962-c. 1966)
- Caesar's Vast Ghost (1990)

Poetry

- Cities, Plains and People (1946)
- On Seeming to Presume (1948)
- The Suchness of the Old Boy (1972)
- Collected Poems: 1931-1974 Edited by James A. Brigham (1980)
- Selected Poems of Lawrence Durrell Edited by Peter Porter (2006)

Drama

- Bromo Bombastes, under the pseudonym Gaffer Peeslake (1933)
- Sappho: A Play in Verse (1950)
- An Irish Faustus: A Morality in Nine Scenes (1963)
- Acte (1964)

Humour

- Esprit de Corps (1957)
- Stiff Upper Lip (1958)
- Sauve Qui Peut (1966)

Letters and essays

- A Key to Modern British Poetry (1952)
- Lawrence Durrell and Henry Miller: A Private Correspondence (1962) edited by George Wickes
- Letters to Jean Fanchette (1988), edited by Jean Fanchette

ANGUS WILSON

Novels

- The Old Men at the Zoo (1961)
- Late Call (1964)
- No Laughing Matter (1967)
- As If By Magic (1973)
- Setting the World on Fire (1980)

Short story collections

- The Wrong Set (1949)
- Such Darling Dodos (1950)
- A Bit Off the Map (1957)
- Death Dance (selected stories, 1969)

Play

- The Mulberry Bush (1955)

DAME MURIEL SPARK

Novels

- The Comforters (1957)
- Robinson (1958)
- Memento Mori (1959)
- The Ballad of Peckham Rye (1960)
- The Bachelors (1960)
- The Prime of Miss Jean Brodie (1961)

- The Girls of Slender Means (1963)
- The Mandelbaum Gate (1965)
- The Public Image (1968)
- The Driver's Seat (1970)
- Not to Disturb (1971)
- The Hothouse by the East River (1973)
- The Abbess of Crewe (1974)
- The Takeover (1976)
- Reality and Dreams (1996)
- Aiding and Abetting (2000)
- The Finishing School (2004)

E. M. FORSTER

Short Stories

- Collected Short Stories (1947)
- "The Story of a Panic"
- "The Other Side of the Hedge"
- "The Celestial Omnibus"
- "Other Kingdom"
- "The Curate's Friend"
- "The Road from Colonus"
- "The Machine Stops"
- "The Point of It"
- "Mr Andrews"
- "Co-ordination"
- "The Story of the Siren"
- "The Eternal Moment"
- "Ansell"
- "Albergo Empedocle"
- "The Classical Annex"
- "The Torque"
- "The Other Boat"

Film scripts

- A Diary for Timothy (1945) (directed by Humphrey Jennings, spoken by Michael Redgrave)

LIBRETTO

- Billy Budd (1951) (with Eric Crozier; based on Melville'snovel, for the opera by Benjamin Britten)

Collections of essays and broadcasts

- Abinger Harvest (1936)
- Two Cheers for Democracy (1951)
- The Prince's Tale and Other Uncollected Writings (1998)

Literary criticism

- Aspects of the Novel (1927)
- The Feminine Note in Literature (posthumous) (2001)
- The Creator as Critic and Other Writings

Biography

- Goldsworthy Lowes Dickinson (1934)
- Marianne Thornton, A Domestic Biography (1956)
- Travel writingAlexandria: A History and Guide (1922)
- Pharos and Pharillon (A Novelist's Sketchbook of Alexandria Through the Ages) (1923)
- The Hill of Devi (1953)

Miscellaneous writings

- Selected Letters (1983-85)
- Commonplace Book (facsimile ed. 1978; edited by Philip Gardner, 1985)
- Locked Diary (2007) (held at King's College, Cambridge)
- Arctic Summer (2003)

H.G. WELLS

- 1953 - Peter Pan, an animated film produced by Walt Disney adapted from the play.
- 2003 - Peter Pan, a live action film released by Universal Pictures, Columbia Pictures and Revolution Studios, directed by P. J. Hogan, starring Jeremy Sumpter as Peter and Jason Isaacs as Hook.
- 1991 - Hook, a live-action sequel directed by Steven Spielberg, starring Robin Williams as the adult Peter Banning,Dustin Hoffman as Hook and Julia Roberts as Tinker Bell.
- 2002 - Return to Never Land, an animated sequel to the 1953 Disney film.
- 2015 - Pan, a live-action origin film directed by Joe Wright, released by Warner Bros., starring Levi Miller as Peter, Hugh Jackman as Blackbeard and Garrett Hedlund as Hook.

Oscar Wilde

- The Ballad of Reading Gaol (1898, poem)

J. B. PRIESTLEY

- Novels : Three Men in New Suits (1945)
- Bright Day (1946)
- Jenny Villiers (1947)
- Festival at Farbridge (1951)
- Low Notes on a High Level (1954)
- Lost Empires (1965)
- It's an Old Country (1967)

- The Image Men Vol. 1: Out of Town (1968)
- The Image Men Vol. 2: London End (1968)
- The Other Place (1952) (Short Stories)
- Snoggle (1971) (Novel for children)
- The Other Window (1975) (A screenplay written in collaboration with Jacquetta Hawkes as part the Shadows television series)
- The Carfitt Crisis (1975) (Two novellas and a short story)
- An Inspector Calls (1945)
- The Linden Tree (1947)
- Last Holiday (1950, wrote story, screenplay and produced the film)
- His play The Thirty-first of June was first produced in Toronto in 1957.
- The Thirty-first of June: A Tale of True Love, - BBC radio dramatisation; one and a half hours
- Literature and Western Man (1960)
- Charles Dickens and his world (1969)

Social and political works

- The Prince of Pleasure and his Regency (1969)
- The Edwardians (1970)
- The English (1973)

Autobiography and essays

- Journey Down a Rainbow (1955)
- Margin Released (1962)
- The Moments and Other Pieces (1966)

W. SOMERSET MAUGHAM

- Dirty Gertie from Harlem U.S.A.(1946). Unauthorized film version of "Miss Thompson" with an all-black cast, directed bySpencer Williams.
- The Razor's Edge (1946) featuring Tyrone Power and Gene Tierney. Based on the book of the same name.
- Of Human Bondage (1946) version starring Eleanor Parker.
- Quartet (1948) Maugham appears as himself in introductions. Based on four of his short stories.
- Trio (1950) Maugham appears as himself in introductions. Another collection based on short stories.
- Encore (1951) Maugham appears as himself in introductions. A third collection of Maugham short stories.
- The Letter (1969) starring Eileen Atkins. Based on play of the same name. (Made for television.)
- Theatre (1978) starring Vija Artmane. Based on the novel of the same name.
- The Letter (1982) featuring Lee Remick, Jack Thompson and Ronald Pickup. Based on play of the same name. (Made for television.)
- The Razor's Edge (1984) with Bill Murray. Based on the novel by the same name.
- Up at the Villa (2000) starring Kristin Scott Thomas and Sean Penn, directed by Philip Haas. Based on the novella of the same name.
- Being Julia (2004) featuring Annette Bening. Based on the novel Theatre.
- The Painted Veil (2006) with Naomi Watts and Edward Norton. Based on the novel of the same name.

W. H. AUDEN

Books

- The Collected Poetry of W. H. Auden (New York, 1945; includes new poems) (dedicated to Christopher Isherwood andChester Kallman).
- The Age of Anxiety: A Baroque Eclogue (New York, 1947; London, 1948; verse; won the 1948 Pulitzer Prize for Poetry) (dedicated to John Betjeman).
- Collected Shorter Poems, 1930-1944 (London, 1950; similar to 1945 Collected Poetry) (dedicated to Christopher Isherwood and Chester Kallman).
- The Enchafèd Flood (New York, 1950; London, 1951; prose) (dedicated to Alan Ansen).
- Nones (New York, 1951; London, 1952; poems) (dedicated to Reinhold and Ursula Niebuhr)
- The Shield of Achilles (New York, London, 1955; poems) (won the 1956 National Book Award for Poetry)
- Collected Longer Poems (London, 1968; New York, 1969).
- Secondary Worlds (London, New York, 1969; prose) (dedicated to Valerie Eliot).

- City Without Walls and Other Poems (London, New York, 1969) (dedicated to Peter Heyworth).
- A Certain World: A Commonplace Book (New York, London, 1970; quotations with commentary) (dedicated to Geoffrey Grigson).
- Epistle to a Godson and Other Poems (London, New York, 1972) (dedicated to Orlan Fox).
- Forewords and Afterwords (New York, London, 1973; essays) (dedicated to Hannah Arendt).
- Thank You, Fog: Last Poems (London, New York, 1974) (dedicated to Michael and Marny Yates).

Film scripts and opera libretti

- The Rake's Progress (1951, with Chester Kallman, libretto for an opera by Igor Stravinsky).
- Elegy for Young Lovers (1956, with Chester Kallman, libretto for an opera by Hans Werner Henze).
- The Bassarids (1961, with Chester Kallman, libretto for an opera by Hans Werner Henze based on The Bacchae of Euripides).
- Runner (1962, documentary film narrative for National Film Board of Canada)
- Love's Labour's Lost (1973, with Chester Kallman, libretto for an opera by Nicolas Nabokov, based on Shakespeare's play).

STEPHEN SPENDER

Poetry collections

- Poems of Dedication (1947)
- The Edge of Being (1949)
- Collected Poems, 1928-1953 (1955)
- Selected Poems (1974)
- Recent Poems (1978)
- Collected Poems 1928-1985 (1986)
- Dolphins (1994)
- New Collected Poems, edited by Michael Brett, (2004)
- An Elementary Classroom

Drama

- Trial of a Judge (1938)
- Rasputin's End (opera libretto, music by Nicolas Nabokov, 1958)
- The Oedipus Trilogy (1985)

Novels and short story collections

- The Burning Cactus (1936, stories)
- The Backward Son (1940)
- Engaged in Writing (1958)
- The Temple (written 1928; published 1988)

Criticism, travel books and essays

- The Destructive Element (1935)
- Poetry Since 1939 (1946)
- The God That Failed (1949, with others, ex-Communists' testimonies)
- Love-Hate Relations (1974)
- Eliot (1975; Fontana Modern Masters)
- W. H. Auden: A Tribute (edited by Spender, 1975)
- The Thirties and After (1978)
- China Diary (with David Hockney, 1982)

DYLAN THOMAS

- The Collected Poems of Dylan Thomas: The New Centenary Edition. Ed. with Introduction by John Goodby. London: Weidenfeld and Nicolson, 2014.
- Under Milk Wood, ed. Walford Davies and Ralph Maud. London: Dent, 1995
- 1972: Under Milk Wood, starring Richard Burton, Elizabeth Taylor, and Peter O'Toole
- 2009: Nadolig Plentyn yng Nghymru/A Child's Christmas in Wales, 2009 2014

LOUIS MACNEICE

Poetry collections

- Holes in the Sky (1948)
- Collected Poems, 1925-1948 (1949)
- Ten Burnt Offerings (1952)
- Autumn Sequel (1954)
- Visitations (1957)
- Solstices (1961)
- The Burning Perch (1963)
- Selected Poems (1988s, 2009)
- Collected Poems (2007)

Plays

- The Dark Tower and other radio scripts (1947)
- Goethe's Faust (1949, published 1951, a translation)
- The Mad Islands [1962] and The Administrator [1961] (1964, radio)
- Persons from Porlock [1963] and other plays for radio (1969)

- One for the Grave: a modern morality play [1958] (1968)
- Selected Plays of Louis MacNeice, ed. Alan Heuser and Peter McDonald (1993)

Books (fiction)

- Roundabout Way (1932, as "Louis Malone")
- The Sixpence That Rolled Away (1956, for children)

Books (non-fiction)

- Astrology (1964)
- Varieties of Parable (1965, criticism)
- Selected Prose of Louis MacNeice, ed. Alan Heuser (1990)

SIEGFRIED SASSOON

Poetry collections

- Collected Poems (Faber and Faber: 1947)
- Common Chords (privately printed: 1950/1951)
- Emblems of Experience (privately printed: 1951)
- The Tasking (privately printed: 1954)
- Sequences (Faber and Faber: 1956)
- Lenten Illuminations (Downside Abbey: 1959)
- The Path to Peace (Stanbrook Abbey Press: 1960)
- Collected Poems 1908-1956 (Faber and Faber: 1961)
- The War Poems ed. Rupert Hart-Davis (Faber and Faber: 1983)
- Meredith (Constable: 1948) - Biography of George Meredith

AMERICAN AND OTHER NON-BRITISH LITERATURES

AMERICAN LITERATURE

1. Henry Wordsworth Longfellow (1807-1882)

Longfellow is known for his verse and poetries. His earlier works are not as much important as his later works are, some hackneyed minor pieces of his earlier works that have been parodied to death, are *Excelsior*, *The Village Blacksmith* or *The Psalm of Life*. But it is as unfair to judge Longfellow by these, as it would be better to judge Tennyson by *The May Queen*, *The Brook* or *The Supposed Confession of a Second-rate Sensitive Mind*.

The first insistent impression conveyed to us by Longfellow's verse is its deft and delicate grace. For example, he praises night as,

"Thou layest thy fingers on the lips of care,
And they complain no more".

His briefer pieces throughout his long career ripple with graceful fancies; and if these are not always fresh enough to fill the "loosely-hanging sails", they are often sufficiently animated to give an agreeable vitality and dainty movement to the verse.

It is this gift that delights us in his touching lines on Hawthorne, with its happy allusiveness : "The unfinished window in Aladdin's tower, unfinished must remain" and that lifts out of the commonplace the myriad little pictures of Nature scattered throughout his writings.

"Morn on the mountain, like a summer bird,
Lifts up her purple wing".

He is not at his best as a sonneteer, for the magical felicity that blends thought and expression into an harmonious pattern was beyond him. His sonnets too often are merely things of shreds and patches and the few glimmering threads of gold are not sufficient recompense for the abundance of honest, yet unattractive fustian. But even here his grace of fancy has come to the poet's rescue more than once and such sonnets as to *Shakespeare* and *The Tides* have certainly some claim to affection and remembrance.

"I saw the long line of the vacant shore,
The seaweed and the shells upon the sand,
And the brown rocks left bare on every hand
As if the ebbing tide would flow no more.
Then heard I, more distinctly than before,
The ocean breathe and its great breast expand,
And hurrying came on the defenceless land

The insurgent waters with tumultuous roar.
All thought and feeling and desire, I said,
Love, laughter and the exultant joy of song,
Have ebbed from me for ever ! Suddenly o'er me
They swept again from their deep ocean-bed,
And in tumult of delight and strong
As youth and beautiful as youth, upbore me".

Though he was not a great proseman, his little romances, *Hyperion* and *Kavanagh*, are well worth reading for the delightful fancies with which they abound, to say nothing of flashes of humour that never see light in his verse.

Sometimes, he reminds us curiously of Holmes, while delivering detached sayings. A few detached sayings, are as follows :-

"Silence is a great peacemaker".
"In youth all doors open outward; in old age they all open inward".
"When looking for anything lost, begin by looking where you think it is not".
(All are taken from Kavanagh.)

There is also a singing quality in Longfellow's verse that is often underrated. His melodies may have nothing in them of the opulent splendour of Swinburne's or the haunting sweetness of Tennyson's; the music is thinner. But music it is, none the less, pleasant and appealing in its note.

Longfellow's poems lend themselves to a musical setting better than do most poets, because he did not pack them with too much music. They are just musical enough to crave the complement of a sister art to bring out their full charm. Tennyson, Shelley, Swinburne, lose rather than gain by a musical setting, for they have all the music they need. They very perfection of their art stands in their way as song-writers. Longfellow's cruder art and homelier methods give him the advantage here.

Longfellow is at bottom a moralist, as nearly all American writers are; and it is this in combination with his homely sentiment that its urgency at times spoiled his art. It was a source of his strength as well as of his weakness; especially when informed by the genial, buoyant spirit of the man. His tolerant charity is reflected in everything that he wrote. Poe had said some very bitter things about him, but after Poe's death, when someone commented on this to Longfellow, his only reply was : "He is dead; I am alive and writing: that is an end of the matter".

In spite of his didactic tendency, there is no obtrusion of the personal point of view; in fact, he is an impersonal often as Emerson himself. This is well exhibited in his lyrics, where most poets give expression to their minds and idiosyncrasies, but Longfellow's lyrics are local, not personal, as we shall see if we run over the titles: *The Bridge, The Belfry at Bruges, The Lighthouse, The River Charles & C.* The emotions he expresses are general, not particular. This may blunt at times the interest we feel in his work. The sunshine is so evenly distributed that we long peevishly for a storm or momentary eclipse. But it adds to the charm of the engaging friendliness of which I have spoken. What could be better in its intimate ease, than the prelude to the pleasant *Tales of a Wayside Inn* :

"One Autumn night in Sudbury town,
Across the meadows bare and brown,
The windows of the wayside Inn
Gleamed red with firelight through the leaves
Of woodbine, hanging from the eaves,
Their crimson curtains rent and thin.
As ancient is this hostelry

As any in the land may be,
Built in the old Colonial day,
When men lived in the grander way,
With ampler hospitality;
A kind of old Hobgoblin Hall,
Now somewhat fallen to decay,
With weather-stains upon the wall,
And stairways worn and crazy doors,
And creaking and uneven floors,
And chimneys huge and tiled and tall.
A region of repose it seems
A place of slumber and of dreams,
Remote among the wooded hills !"

A word must be said in conclusion as to the wide range over which his benignant spirit passes. As the poet of American life, he touches on one side the Indian epic of Hiawatha; on the other, the doings of his Puritan ancestry in *Evangeline* and *The Courtship of Miles Standish.*

As a scholar and translator he did much to familiarise the reader with French, Spanish, German and Italian poets. His own genius was more akin to the German than to any other European people; he is especially happy in dealing with Richter; and his cosmopolitan interests contributed greatly to the appreciation of Longfellow on the Continent.

Another aspect of his work is revealed in his concern with children and child life. He has been fitly called "The Children's Poet"; and his simple directness, his tenderness, his unpretentious sentiments are at their best here.

There is no poet more readily understood and loved by children than he is. The *Tales of a Wayside Inn* can be appreciated by both young and old, but *The Wreck of the Schooner Hesperus, Pegasus in Pound, The leap of Roushan Beg, The Three Kings, The Emperor's Bird's Nest* —to mention a few only—have a peculiar appeal for children. Indeed, who can doubt that the man who wrote *The Children's Hour* knew how to warm young hearts and fire young imaginations ?

After all, Longfellow's appeal lies chiefly in his intimate simplicity and tender humanity. He does not deal with recondite aspects of human life, but with the universal emotions of love, pity, faith and hope. Whether in his domestic pictures, in his unpretentious moralities, his picturesque narratives, or his lyrics of everyday life, there is a direct and engaging friendliness and a sweet sanity of outlook that, though easily ridiculed, are matters for grateful remembrance. The very titles he gave to his collections of verse are eloquent of this homely simplicity — *Voices of the Night, The Seaside and the Fireside, In the Harbour.*

And thus we come back to Longfellow's power of dealing with simple, human characteristics. His faults and Limitations as a literary artist are clear enough—I am not concerned to dispute them. But Longfellow is emphatically not to be dismissed as some have tried to do, as merely a facile writer of commonplace sentimentalities. He was a versatile scholar who did much to develop the culture of young literary America; a vigorous ballad writer with peculiar force and charm when the sea is his subject; a narrative poet of abundant force and clarity; above all, a kindly and gracious personality, whose kindliness and graciousness diffused themselves over everything that he wrote. If not a great poet, he was a genuine one, with a power of swift and direct appeal to thousands whom our greater poets would have left cold.

Major Works

- Voices of the Night (1839)
- 'Evangeline' (1847)
- 'Poems on Slavery (1842)
- 'Belfry of Bruges' (1845)
- 'Hyperion' and 'Kavanagh'
- Hymn of the Night
- The Arrow and the Song
- The Building of the Ship
- Morituri Salutamugs
- Pilgrimage Beyond the Sea (1835)
- 'The Song of Hiawatha' (1855)
- 'The Spanish student (1843)
- 'The Golden Legend' (1851)
- A Psalm of Life (Poem)
- The Bridge
- The Arsenal at Springfield
- The Village Black Smith

2. John Greenleaf Whittier (1807–1892)

If we consider the intensity of imagination and emotional power, Whittier ranks higher as a poet than Longfellow. Taking him at his best and selecting a score of poems from the hundreds that he wrote, Whittier is assuredly one of the greater poets of America, with a virility that can only be matched by the rarer ballad writers of English Literature. The strength of his imaginative sympathies though, does not make him superior than other American poets, but his artistic skill is not commensurate with his native endowment. It is only by fine flashes here and there in the considerable body of his verse that we realise that his art matches his inspiration. Sometimes, as in that lovely idyll, *Snowbound* or in the passionate lament over Daniel Webster's attitude towards the Abolitionist problem, Whittier rises to the heights of great poetry. But his emotions, though intense, have little plasticity; his imagination, though deep, is narrow and restricted. Given a cause that touched him to the quick, like Anti-Slavery or certain aspects of New England life, he can rise to the occasion. Unfortunately, he has written a great deal of verse that though workmanlike and agreeable, lacks distinction and fire; and has neither the simple, sentimental charm of Longfellow's ordinary verse nor the intellectual suggestiveness that reconciles one to some extent to the rough artistry of Emerson and Thoreau.

Snowbound, Randolph of Roanoke, Moloch in State Street, Ichabod, Barbara Frietchie, Maud Muller, The Henchman, The Barefoot Boy, Taking the Bees and *Proem* are poems, full of tenderness, strength and passionate scorn for the tyrant and the base.

Here is an illustration:

Ichabod

So fallen ! So lost ! the light withdrawn
Which once he wore !
The glory from his gray hairs gone
For evermore !
Revile him not, —the Tempter hath
A snare for all;
And pitying tears, not scorn and wrath,
Befit his fall.
O, dumb be passion's stormy rage,
When he who might
Have lighted up and led his age,
Falls back in night.

Scorn ! would the angels laugh, to mark
A bright soul driven

Friend-goaded, down the endless dark,
From hope and heaven !
Let not the land once proud of him
Insult him now,
Nor brand with deeper shame his dim
Dishonored brow.
But let its humbled sons, instead,
From sea to lake,
A long lament, as for the dead,
In sadness make.

Of all we loved and honoured, nought
Save power remains, —
A fallen angel's pride of thought,
Still strong in chains.
All else is gone; from those great eyes
The soul has fled :
When faith is list, when honour dies,
The man is dead !
Then, pay the reverence of old days
To his dead fame :
Walk backward, with averted gaze,
And hide the shame !

We may add also the beautiful hymn, *Dear Lord and Father of Mankind*, than which no lovelier expression of Quaker spirit exists in our sacred verse.

"Drop Thy still dews of quietness,
Till all our strivings cease —
Take from our souls the strain and stress;
And let our ordered lives confess
The beauty of Thy Peace.

Breathe through the pulses of desire
Thy coolness and Thy balm;
Let sense be dumb, its heats expire;
Speak through the earthquake, wind and fire,
O still small voice of calm".

Poem

(To introduce the first collected edition of his poems)

I love the old melodious lays
Which softly melt the ages through,
The songs of Spencer's golden days,
Arcadian Sidney's silvery phrase,
Sprinkling our noon of time with freshest morning dew.

Yet vainly in my quiet hours
To breathe their marvellous notes I try;
I feel them, as the leaves and flowers
In silence feel the dewy showers,
And drink with glad, still lips the blessing of the sky.

The rigour of a frozen clime,
The harshness of an untaught ear,
The jarring words of one whose rhyme
Beat often Labour's hurried time,
Or Duty's rugged march through storm and strife, are here.

Of mystic beauty, dreamy grace,
No rounded art the lack supplies;
Unskilled the subtle lines to trace,
Or softer shades of Nature's face,
I view her common forms with unanointed eyes.

Nor mine the seer-like power to show
The secrets of the heart and mind;
To drop the plummet-line below
Our common world of joy and woe,
A more intense despair or brighter hope to find.

Yet here at least an earnest sense
Of human right and weal is shown;
A hate of tyranny intense,
And hearty in its vehemence,
As if my brother's pain and sorrow were my own.

O freedom ! if to me belong
Nor mighty Milton's gift divine,
Nor Marvell's wit and graceful song,
Still with a love as deep and strong
As theirs, I lay, like them, my best gifts on thy shrine.

Major Works

- Snow Bound
- Moloch in State Street
- Maud Muller
- The Henchman
- Taking the Bees
- Randolph of Roanoke
- Ichabod
- Barbara Frietchie
- The Barefooted Boy
- Dear Lord and Father of Mankind

3. Walt Whitman (1819-1892)

Walt Whitman was born on May 31, 1819, in West Hills, on Long Island, New York. He was the second son of Walter Whitman, a house-builder, and Louisa Van Velsor. In the 1820s and 1830s, the family, which consisted of nine children, lived in Long Island and Brooklyn, where Whitman attended the Brooklyn public schools.

At the age of twelve, Whitman began to learn the printer's trade and fell in love with the written word. Largely self-taught, he read voraciously, becoming acquainted with the works of Homer, Dante, Shakespeare, and the Bible.

Whitman worked as a printer in New York City until a devastating fire in the printing district demolished the industry. In 1836, at the age of seventeen, he began his career as teacher in the one-room schoolhouses of Long Island. He continued to teach until 1841, when he turned to journalism as a full-time career.

He founded a weekly newspaper, The Long-Islander, and later edited a number of Brooklyn and New York papers, including the Brooklyn Daily Eagle. In 1848, Whitman left the Brooklyn Daily Eagle to become editor of the New Orleans Crescent for three months.

After witnessing the auctions of enslaved individuals in New Orleans, he returned to Brooklyn in the fall of 1848 and co-founded a "free soil" newspaper, the Brooklyn Freeman, which he edited through the next fall. Whitman's attitudes about race have been described as "unstable and inconsistent." He did not always side with the abolitionists, yet he celebrated human dignity.

In Brooklyn, he continued to develop the unique style of poetry that later so astonished Ralph Waldo Emerson. In 1855, Whitman took out a copyright on the first edition of Leaves of Grass, which consisted of twelve untitled poems and a preface. He published the volume himself, and sent a copy to Emerson in July of 1855. Whitman released a second edition of the book in 1856, containing thirty-two poems, a letter from Emerson praising the first edition, and a long open letter by Whitman in response. During his lifetime, Whitman continued to refine the volume, publishing several more editions of the book. Noted Whitman scholar, M. Jimmie Killingsworth writes that "the 'merge,' as Whitman conceived it, is the tendency of the individual self to overcome moral, psychological, and political boundaries. Thematically and poetically, the notion dominates the three major poems of 1855: 'I Sing the Body Electric,' 'The Sleepers,' and 'Song of Myself,' all of which were 'merged' in the first edition under the single title Leaves of Grass but were demarcated by clear breaks in the text and the repetition of the title."

At the outbreak of the Civil War, Whitman vowed to live a "purged" and "cleansed" life. He worked as a freelance journalist and visited the wounded at New York City-area hospitals. He then traveled to Washington, D. C. in December 1862 to care for his brother, who had been wounded in the war.

Overcome by the suffering of the many wounded in Washington, Whitman decided to stay and work in the hospitals; he ended up staying in the city for eleven years. He took a job as a clerk for the Bureau of Indian Affairs within the Department of the Interior, which ended when the Secretary of the Interior, James Harlan, discovered that Whitman was the author of Leaves of Grass, which Harlan found offensive. After Harlan fired him, he went on to work in the attorney general's office.

In 1873, Whitman suffered a stroke that left him partially paralyzed. A few months later he travelled to Camden, New Jersey, to visit his dying mother at his brother's house. He ended up staying with his brother until the 1882 publication of Leaves of Grass (James R. Osgood), which brought him enough money to buy a home in Camden.

In the simple two-story clapboard house, Whitman spent his declining years working on additions and revisions to his deathbed edition of Leaves of Grass (David McKay, 1891-92) and preparing his final volume of poems and prose, Good-Bye My Fancy (David McKay, 1891). After his death on March 26, 1892, Whitman was buried in a tomb he designed and had built on a lot in Harleigh Cemetery.

Along with Emily Dickinson, he is considered one of America's most important poets.

Selected Bibliography

Poetry

- Leaves of Grass (David McKay, 1891)
- Good-Bye, My Fancy (David McKay, 1891)
- Leaves of Grass (James R. Osgood, 1881)
- Passage to India (J.S. Redfield, 1870)
- Leaves of Grass (J.S. Redfield, 1870)
- Leaves of Grass (William E. Chapin, 1867)
- Drum Taps (William E. Chapin, 1865)

- Sequel to Drum Taps (William E. Chapin, 1865)
- Leaves of Grass (Thayer & Eldridge, 1860)
- Leaves of Grass (Fowler & Wells, 1856)
- Leaves of Grass (self-published, 1855)

Prose

- Complete Prose Works (David McKay, 1892)
- November Boughs (David McKay, 1888)
- Memoranda During the War (self-published, 1875)
- Democratic Vistas (David McKay, 1871)
- Franklin Evans; or, The Inebriate (New World, 1842)

Texts

Year	Title
1892	Specimen Days [Death of a Pennsylvania Soldier]
1892	Specimen Days [Hospitals Closing]
1892	Specimen Days [Manhattan from the Bay]
1892	Specimen Days [February Days]
1855	Preface, Leaves of Grass
1891	A Backward Glance O'er Travel'd Roads
2019	The First Edition of Leaves of Grass, 1855
2019	An Advertisement for Walt Whitman's 1855 Leaves of Grass
2019	Walt Whitman's Notes on Leaves of Grass
2019	A Draft of Walt Whitman's Elegy for Abraham Lincoln

4. Nathaniel Hawthorne (1804-1864)

Nathaniel Hawthorne, born on July 4, 1804 in Salem, Massachusetts was an American short story writer and romance novelist who experimented with a broad range of styles and genres. He is best known for his short stories and two widely read novels: The Scarlet Letter (mid-March 1850) and The House of Seven Gables (1851). Along with Herman Melville and Edgar Allan Poe much of Hawthorne's work belongs to the sub-genre of Dark Romanticism, distinguished by an emphasis on human fallibility that gives rise to lapses in judgement that allow even good men and women to drift toward sin and self-destruction. Dark Romantics tends to draw attention to the unintended consequences and complications that arise from well-intended efforts at social reform. Melville dedicated his epic novel, Moby-Dick to Hawthorne: "In token of my admiration for his genius." Hawthorne's lesser-known poems exemplify Dark Romanticism; some of his darkest works, including his ghost stories and tales involving the supernatural, fall within the genre of Gothic Literature.

Young Hawthorne was a contemporary of fellow Transcendalists: Ralph Waldo Emerson, Henry David Thoreau, and Louisa May Alcott, Hawthorne was part of this prominent circle of Massachusetts writers and philosophers. The Transcendentalists believed in the "inherent goodness of both people and nature." I would encourage you to think of them as intellectual hippies of the early 19th century (the movement sprang forth in the 1820s and 1830s). Hawthorne was a founding member of Brook Farm, a utopian experiment in communal living – though he is not portrayed as a deep believer in its ideals. As Hawthorne matured, he drifted further and further from some of the transcendental principles. In fact, his later writing, produced after greater experience in the world, demonstrated an increasing disdain for the Transcendental Movement. He notably fictionalized the experiences of Brook Farm in his satirical novel The Blithedale Romance (1852).

I think it's important to mark Hawthorne's migration from a young Transcendental idealist to a Dark Romanticwriter. At one level it's a remarkable journey because the older man comes to embrace the opposite inclinations of his youth; that rather then being inherently good, people were deeply fallible, prone to lapses in judgement and they difted easily to sin. Furthermore, some of their greatest sins were committed under the umbrella of good intentions. On another level, the journey is common-place, as almost all individuals discover that the journey of life tempers their youthful idealism. But there is also a personal history the weighed heavily on Hawthorne. He had two stern forefathers in his patrilineal heritage, his great-great-great grandfather and his great-great-grandfather John Hathorne. So he knew well that men could, cloaked in the countenance of goodness and piety, commit great sin. Here is Hawthorne describing them both (starting with the great-great-great grandfather):

He was a soldier, legislator, judge; he was a ruler in the Church; he had all the Puritanical traits, both good and evil. He was likewise a bitter persecutor; as witness the Quakers, who have remembered him in their histories, and relate an incident of his hard severity towards a woman of their sect, which will last longer, it is to be feared, than any record of his better deeds, although these were many. His son, too, inherited the persecuting spirit, and made himself so conspicuous in the martyrdom of the witches, that their blood may fairly be said to have left a stain upon him. So deep a stain, indeed, that his dry old bones, in the Charter Street burial-ground, must still retain it, if they have not crumbled utterly to dust!

Hawthorne was acutely aware of his ancestors' sins, so ashamed that he was actually born "Hathorne" and added the "w" to hide his true lineage.

With knowledge of these biographical details, the reader can easily see the influence of his ancestors not only rise up in his drift into Dark Romanticism, but also in his writing, which was often set in colonial New England and heavily weighted with the moral complexity of his Puritan background (and perhaps the deeds of his ancestors in those communities). Which brings us to his most acclaimed work. The Scarlet Letter, a work rife with moral complexity.

The Scarlet Letter was one of the first mass-produced novels in America and became an instant best seller, selling over 2,500 copies in the first two weeks. It has been praised for its sentimentality and moral purity by the likes of D. H. Lawrence, who said that there could be no more perfect work of the American imagination.Though Edgar Allan Poe -- a fellow author in the Dark Romantic Movement and influential literary critic -- wrote negative reviews of Hawthorne's stories. Poe did not admire stories that were allegorical and moral in nature so his criticism was in form. Though even he begrudgingly acknowledged that Hawthorne's style "is like purity itself." Hawthorne's highest regarded short stories include My Kinsman, Major Molineaux (1832), Young Goodman Brown (1835), Feathertop (1852), and The Minister's Black Veil.

Now I am going to break from my biographical narrative to add a personal note. After a lifetime of reading, Nathaniel Hawthorne has emerged as one of my absolute favorite authors of all time. If you are not having fun while reading Hawthorne you are doing it wrong! For instance, My Kinsman, Major Molineaux is a comic short story and should be enjoyed as such (it does have a "tragic" ending). It's the story of a young "hayseed" on his first visit to the "big city" and he suffers the embarrassments one would expect and few extras thrown in for good measure. It could inspire a Monty Python skit. I think there is a secret to understanding and appreciating Hawthorne's body of work. And I will share that with you. But be warned; he is not a cheap date! You will have to work hard before you can truly love this writer.

The price of admission is that one must read and study over the introductory chapter to The Scarlet Letter, The Custom-House. Then read the Preface to the Second Edition and then -- sorry -- read The Custom-House again. As much as it will not feel like it at the time, if you are a high school student, and your English teacher has asked you to specifically read The Custom-House, it's because he or she loves you and cares about your education (which as Twain famously pointed out, should not be confused with your schooling). You will know that you truly understand those two introductory chapters when you realize the Nathaniel Hawthorne was a mid-1850s Bad Ass who explicitly, purposely, and repeatedly "stuck it to the man", even after, heck especially after they asked him to stop! I also do not think you can properly understand The Scarlet Letter without understanding The Custom-House (and also marking the sins of Hawthorne's forefathers). I assure you, the effort is worth the reward. [And I do offer belated apologies to my sophomore English teacher for my essay entitled, "Why I Hate English Class," which I tendered like a smart-aleck after my first bout with The Custom-House way back in 1981.]

5. Edgar Allan Poe (1809–1849)

His Work. A brilliant though erratic critic, with a naturally fine literary palate and a bundle of prejudices; an ingenious versifier with flashes of greatness and a master craftsman in the romance of horror. Thus, briefly we may sum up the work of this unhappy man of genius. As a writer of fiction he belongs to the Gothic school; only he achieves with remarkable skill what Mrs. Radcliffe, Horace Walpole, Maturin and Monk Lewis did in cruder and more stumbling fashion; revels as they did in the eerie side of things; but he is a professional artist in horrors, while they were well-meaning amateurs succeeding only by fits and starts and more or less accidentally, in the art of blood-curdling. Maturin, in his Eastern Romances, approaches the closest to Poe in grim power; but a wide gulf divides *Vathek* from masterly studies like *The Pit and the Pendulum and the Fall of the House of Usher.*

In certain respects, Poe resembles his greater contemporary, Hawthorne. He brings to bear upon his work an analytical intellect, a prying imagination. Like Hawthorne he is attracted towards the night side of things and is fascinated by pathological problems. But here the likeness ends. Poe externalised his horrors; Hawthorne spiritualised them. Hawthorne stimulates our imagination; Poe sears it. In constructive power, Poe is superior; he has a more meticulous mind a more masculine genius. But the beauty, the delicacy, the essential sanity of Hawthorne is without his range. Even while he grips he disgusts you. There is the reek of the charnel-house in the majority of his tales and his intensely morbid pre-occupation with pain and death oppress one like a miasma. His most agreeable work lies in the direction of the puzzle story. Here his ingenuity and power of ratiocination mark him out as the pioneer of the modern detective story. He is the protagonist of Gaboriau and Du Boisgobey, Anna K. Green and Conan Doyle. Of their kind, nothing could well be better done than his *Murder in the Rue Morgue, his Mystery of Marie Roget,* or *The Gold Bug.* On a somewhat lower plane come his pseudo-scientific tales such as *The Descent into the Maelstrom;* but even here he open a new field in fiction which has since his time been more fully exploited by Jules Verne and Mr. H. G. Wells.

His studies in morbid psychology exhibit yet a third side of his genius; and if he is excelled here in range and delicacy by his successor, Hawthorne, yet he certainly prepared the way; and putting aside the "spiritual clamminess" which R.H. Hutton found in his tales, the hunting intensity with which he can depict a guilty conscience, or trace the growth of some terrible obsession, as in the *Tell-Tale Heart*, is horribly effective and arresting.

Poe's work, therefore, when viewed in relation to certain developments in the later fiction of the age, is of undeniable interest, even apart from its intrinsic merit. It is a pity that he wasted his genius so much in the merely gruesome; for his imagination was strong enough to disperse with those adventitious horrors. I do not find fault with him, as some do, because he elected to deal with problems of mental pathology; I blame him because he treats them too little as an artist, too much as a scientist.

As a poet, there is not a single American man of letters, who is his peer in sheer artistry. There is greater artistry in his verse than in his prose and if the imagination shown is less flexible, less adventurous, it is also less rank, less variable. Its range is narrow; but in that range its effectiveness is remarkable.

In *Israfel* and *To Helen*, he has achieved a fantastic beauty and melodic cadence, that of its kind has never been equalled in American Literature. Elsewhere in his tenuous body of verse he has shown himself a cunning master of verbal harmonics and three at least of his poems—*The Raven, The Bells and Annabel Lee* —have taken captive the popular imagination to an extraordinary extent. Nevertheless, we cannot but feel the presence, more or less, of a certain strain of affectation and pretentiousness in his verse, which, although not impairing the universal sweetness of his music, debar one from classing it with the romantic lyrics of poets like Shelley, Keats and Tennyson. The debatable border line between Art and Artifice finds Poe nearly always on the wrong side. Sometimes as in *Annabel Lee and The Bells,* faintly so; at others, as in *The Haunted Palace* and the over-praised *Raven,* markedly so. Of course, many readers do not feel this. To them there is something peculiarly haunting and compelling in Poe's imaginative power; nor do they feel any jarring note. But excepting *Israfel,* which seems to me quite the most magically perfect thing that Poe ever wrote, there is no poem that is not spoiled, however, slightly, by some touch of tinsel.

There is the touch of tinsel even in *Helen,* with its elusive charm and fine phrasing. It occurs in the third line (the italics are mine) :

"Helen, thy beauty is to me
Like those Nicean barks of yore
That gently, o'er a perfumed *sea,*
The weary, way-worn wanderer bore
To his own native shore".

Why "perfumed" ? This boudoir word strikes an artificial note and will not compensate even for such felicities as :

"The glory that was Greece
And the grandeur that was Rome".

Sometimes the touch of tinsel shows itself, not in a word or a phrase, but in the palpable effort on the part of the writer to intensify his effects. This is the weakness of *The Raven* : the effects are not subtle enough; the shadows are accentuated with too obvious a care to achieve the impressive. To a less extent *The City in the Sea,* with its admirable opening, suffers from over-elaboration. To compare with a fantasy that is perfect in its romantic art, let the reader turn to Tennyson's *Lady of Shalott* after reading Poe's verse and he will realise the difference.

Apart from its fitful, though genuine romantic beauty and admirable, though not perfect artistic cunning Poe's verse is singularly limited in its scope. He never touches the broad, general interests of life and thought and has nothing of the benign sanity of Longfellow, the tender humanity of Whittier or the naked force of Whitman. Yet he is an attractive and influential poet in his own way and as a proseman one of the few original forces in American letters. Had his breadth and sanity of outlook been at all commensurate with his shaping and imaginative faculty, he would have had no peer in the literature of his country.

The Haunted Palace

In the greenest of our valleys
By good angels tenanted,
Once a fair and stately palace —
Radiant palace — reared its head.
In the monarch Thought's dominion—
It stood there !
Never seraph spread a pinion
Over fabric half so fair !

Banners yellow, glorious, golden,
On its roof did float and flow
(This—all this—was in the olden
Time long ago),
And every gentle air that dallied,
In that sweet day,
Along the ramparts plumed and pallid,
A winged odour went away.

Wanderers in that happy valley,
Through two luminous windows, saw
Spirits moving musically,
To a lute's well-tuned law,
Round about a throne where, sitting
(Porphyrogene !)
In state his glory well befitting,
The ruler of the realm was seen.

And all with pearl and ruby glowing
Was the fair palace door,
Through which came flowing, flowing, flowing,
And sparkling evermore,
A troop of Echoes, whose sweet duty
Was but to sing,
In voices of surpassing beauty,
The wit and wisdom of their king.

But evil things, in robes of sorrow,
Assailed the monarch's high estate.
(Ah, let us mourn !— for never morrow
Shall dawn upon him desolate !)
And round about his home, the glory
That blushed and bloomed
Is but a dim remembered story
Of the old time entombed.

And travellers now, within that valley,
Through the red-litten windows see
Vast forms, that move fantastically
To a discordant melody,
While, like a ghastly rapid river,

Through the pale door
A hideous throng rush out for ever
And laugh —but smile no more.

The City in the Sea

Lo ! Death hath reared himself a throne
In a strange city lying alone
Far down within the dim west
Where the good and the bad and the worst and the best
Have gone to their eternal rest.
There shrines and palaces and towers
(Time-eaten towers that tremble not !)
Resemble nothing that is ours.
Around, by lifting winds forgot,
Resignedly beneath the sky
The melancholy waters lie.

No rays from the holy heaven come down
On the long night-time of that town;
But light from out the lurid sea
Streams up the turrets silently—
Gleams up the pinnacles far and free—
Up domes— up spires — up kingly halls
Up lanes— up Babylon-like walls—
Up shadowy long -forgotten bowers
Of sculptured ivy and stone flowers—
Up many and many a marvellous shrine
Whose wreathed friezes intertwine
The viol, the violet and the vine.
Resignedly beneath the sky
The melancholy waters lie.
So blend the turrets and shadows there
That all seem pendulous in air,
While from a proud tower in the town
Death looks gigantically down.

There open fanes and gaping graves
Yawn level with the luminous waves
But not the riches there that lie
In each idol's diamond eye—
Not the gaily-jewelled dead
Tempt the waters from their bed.
For no ripples curl, alas !
Along that wilderness of glass—
No swellings tell that winds may be
Upon some far-off happier sea—
No heavings hint that winds have been
No seas less hideously serene.

But lo, a stir is in the air !
The wave—there is a movement there
As if the towers and thrust aside,

In slightly sinking, the dull tide—
As if their tops had feebly given
A void within the filmy heaven.
The waves have now a redder glow—
The hours are breathing faint and low—
And when, amid no earthly moans,
Down, down that town shall settle hence,
Hell rising from a thousand thrones,
Shall do it reverence.

Israfel

In Heaven a spirit doth dwell
"Whose heart-strings are a lute";
None sing so wildly well
As the angel Israfel,
And the giddy stars (so legends tell),
Ceasing their hymns, attend the spell
Of his voice all mute.

Tottering above
In her highest noon,
The enamoured moon
Blushes with love,
While, to listen, the red levin
(With the rapid Pleiades, even
Which were seven),
Pauses in Heaven.

And they say (the starry choir
And the other listening things)
That Israfel's fire
Is owing to that lyre
By which he sits and sings—
The trembling living wire
Of those unusual strings.

But the skies that angel trod,
Where deep thoughts are a duty—
Where Love's a grown-up God—
Where the Houri glances are
Imbued with all the beauty
Which we worship in a star.

Therefore, thou art not wrong,
Israfel, who despisest
An unimpassioned song;
To thee the laurels belong,
Best bard, because the wisest !
Merrily live and long.

The ecstasies above
With thy burning measures suit—

Thy grief, thy joy, thy hate, thy love,
With the fervour of thy lute—
Well may the stars be mute !

Yes, Heaven is thine; but this
Is a world of sweets and sours;
Our flowers are merely—flowers,
And the shadow of thy perfect bliss
Is the sunshine of ours.

If I could dwell
Where Israfel
Hath dwelt and he where I,
He might not sing so wildly well
A mortal melody,
While a bolder note that this might swell
From my lyre within the sky.

The Note of Realism in American Fiction. The later years of the nineteenth century witness a change in the character of American fiction. Hitherto the romantic note had predominated; but just as in England realistic stories of town and country life gradually grew more and more numerous and relegated romantic adventure to the background, so in America the note of realism becomes gradually insistent. The change was ushered in by no great names as in England and few would prefer the milk-and-water sentimentalities of *The Wide, Wide World* of ELIZABETH WETHERELL and *The Lamplighter* of MARIA S. CUMMINS to the flamboyant excitement of Cooper and Melville.

6. Ralph Waldo Emerson (1803–1882)

Emerson is the articulate conscience of New England. There is something curiously impersonal about his writings. Despite the gracious, subtly distinctive personality that emerges from his chit-chat in letters and from the reports of friends, we, who have never known him in the flesh, think of him as a Voice rather than as a Man. We can picture the shy, critical, brooding Hawthorne from his tales and essays; can actualise sharply and distinctly the genial philosopher of the *Breakfast Table,* the placidly observant Thoreau. But Emerson ? We gather from the table talk of friends that he was gentle, benignant, humorous and we may reasonably infer that there was a forcefulness about his presence or Carlyle would not have so warmly welcomed him.

But as we turn over the pages of his lectures and essays, we find ourselves merely listening to an oracular voice uttering words of gnomic wisdom, in clear but almost expressionless tones.

In his basic attitude towards life, he is certainly a mystic : that is obvious to the most superficial reader. But the mysticism has no warmth or ecstasy about it. It has a cold, astringent quality, very agreeable to some temperaments, but disconcerting to the fervent enthusiast. When Low ell said he had a "Greek head on right Yankee shoulders", he gave us the clue to his character. For Emerson is only half a mystic; his intellect approved this relation with the unseen world, the world of spirit; having approved it, the practical, critical American side of him came uppermost. When he bade us "hitch" our "wagon to a star", many of us saw in this adjuration merely the mystical moralist; nor realised that the monition showed quiet as fully the practical moralist. He is quite as emphatic about the wagon as about the star. The Idealist who is always looking at the star moved Emerson to mild reproach; though he was tolerant enough with his reforming friends. "We are little wild here .....numberless projects of reform," he wrote, adding characteristically, "I am gently mad myself."

So gentle, so clam, so temperate is his method that we do not realise at once the extent of his spiritual radicalism.

The Mystic. Unless we grasp the mystical side of Emerson's nature, we shall be apt to lose ourselves in the steady hailstorm of pithy sayings, apparently unelated with one another. His central doctrine may be found in his Essay on the *Over Soul.* This world of ours is permeated with a spiritual being—Soul. What, then is Soul ? It is a universal spiritual tidal life that overflows into individual lives, working independently of our own efforts, when one we have allowed it ingress. It is a life that makes for righteousness. We are possessed of it. Our individualities indeed, are like islands lapped round by an infinite sea. Those who admit its influence are linked to one another by a social solidarity of spirit; and everyone may admit the influences and should do so, for our own individual strength depends on it. Every man may be his own philosopher. So let us unbar our private door and let in God.

In a fine saying he tells us, "I conceive of a man as always spoken to from behind and unable to turn his head and see the speaker. In all the millions who have heard the voice, none ever saw the face."

The purpose of life, then, in Emerson's view is to acquaint man with the character of his own powers. And he must be always open to fresh impressions and beware of the stereotyped mind. "I want to say what I feel and think with the proviso that tomorrow, perhaps, I shall contradict it all."

And this mystical attitude towards life in general, he carries into its various departments. He is a mystic in his critical valuations. No one would have more thoroughly endorsed Milton's saying that "a good book is the precious life blood of a master spirit." He valued writers for their vitalising powers. He loved those who, to use his own quaint phrase, could make his "top spin." The great man is forceful hero to Carlyle; he is an illuminating seer to Emerson. Yet each acclaimed him for his dynamic influence. "The unstable estimate of men," said Emerson, "crowd to him whose mind is filled with truth as the heaped waves of the Atlantic follow the moon."

In temperament, Emerson is akin to the Quakers. Anger and violence he passes on one side. As a thinker, he has no wish to storm the reader with philosophic artillery; merely to surround him and permeate him like an atmosphere.

His thought is not original, his texts are familiar enough, but he gives them freshness by his handling.

The Moralist. Yet, the practicality of the man is quite as insistent as his mysticism. He believes absolutely in the paramount importance of conduct. His mysticism is concerned not in making for spiritual exaltation, but for moral stability. With Emerson, as with Matthew Arnold, "Conduct is three-fourths of life."

"Every man takes care," says he, "that his neighbour shall not cheat him, but a time comes when he begins to care that he shall not cheat his neighbour. Then all goes well. He has changed his market cart into a chariot of the sun."

Right thinking and clean living, according to Emerson, go together. The average moralist says, "Live straight and don't waste time in searching for intellectual truth." Emerson says, "Live straight and you'll think straight." Morality to him implies health of mind and body; "Character is the habit of action from the permanent vision of truth." Here we see the link that binds the moralist to the mystic. The obedience to the universal spirit is no blind fatalism with Emerson, it is conscious effort on man's part; let him identify himself with the sublime order of things and he will do "with knowledge what the stars do by structure," fulfil the law of their being. Thus, by understanding ourselves and indentifying ourselves with the great forces of the universe we become rulers of others. Emerson takes pains to show that the moral law of the universe is as clear as the physical law; and will affect the soul of man just as gravitation and chemical forces affect his body.

Yet, Emerson had little sympathy with dogmatic religion :

"We are all very sensible," he says, "It is forced on us every day, that churches are outgrown; that the creeds are outgrown... The Church is not large enough for the man; it cannot inspire the enthusiasm which is the parent of everything good in history... For that enthusiasm you must have something greater than yourselves and not less. But in churches every healthful and thoughtful mind finds itself in something less; it is checked, cribbed, confined."

"The Jewish *cultus* is declining : the Divine, or as some will say, the truly Human, hovers, now seen, now unseen, before us."

"Swedenborg and Behmen, both, failed by attaching themselves to the Christian symbol instead of to the moral sentiment, which carries innumerable Charistianities, humanities, divinities, in its bosom. What have I to do with arks and passovers, ephahs and ephods ? ...Good for Orientals, these are nothing to me. The more learning you bring to explain them, the more glaring the impertinence. Of ail absurdities, this of some foreigner proposing to take away my rhetoric and substitute his own and amuse me with pelican and stork instead of thrush and robin, palm-trees and shittim-wood instead of sassafras and hickory, seems the most useless.

"If a man claims to know and speak of God and carries you backward to the phraseology of some old mouldered nation in another country, in another world, believe him not."

Again :

"I object, of course, to the claim of miraculous dispensation— certainly not to the *doctrine* of Christianity. This claim impairs, to my mind, the soundness of him who makes it and indisposes us to his communion... It is contrary to that law of Nature which all wise men recognise; namely, never to require a larger cause than is necessary to the effect.

"The word miracle, as it is used, only indicates the ignorance of the devotee, staring with wonder to see water turned into wine and heedless of the stupendous fact of his own personality. Here he stands, a lonely thought, harmoniously organised into correspondence with the universe of mind and matter. What narrative of wonders coming down from the thousand years ought to charm his attention like this ?.... It seems as if, when the Spirit of God speaks so plainly to each soul, it were an impiety to be listening to one or another saint. Jesus was better than others, because he refused to listen to others and listened at home.

"It is so wonderful to our neurologists that a man can see without his eyes, that it does not occur to them that it is just as wonderful that he should see with them; and that is ever the difference between the wise and the unwise the latter wonders at what is unusual, the wise man wonders at the usual.

"Far be from me the impatience which cannot brook the supernatural, the vast; far be from me the lust of explaining away all which appeals to the imagination and the great presentiments which haunt us. Willingly I too say, Hail ! to the unknown awful powers which transcend the ken of the understanding.

"It is not the incredibility of the fact, but a certain want of harmony between the action and the agent.

The most satisfying point about Emerson's thought is not its optimism but its crisp practicality. What is the good of telling a man or woman whose life has been blighted by another's baseness that evil has no real existence ? What consolation is afforded by telling the victim to cancer that "all's right with the world" ? it is not Browning's optimism, but his courage and grit that inspire his readers : it is not Emerson's optimism, but his cool common-sense and sensitiveness to spiritual values, that count for those who construe his pages. His views on the problem of Evil will appeal to those in basic affinity with him. They cannot touch others. At the best his generalisation is but a cheery guess, for which he gives no intellectual justification. But the common-sense helpfulness of such lines as these is quite obvious :

"Some of the ills you have cured,
And the sharpest you still have survived,
But what torments of pain you endured
From the Evil that never arrived."

To do him justice, it should be said that Emerson, despite the tenacity of his own convictions never attempted propagandist work. Like Newman, he disliked controversies and held that they were for the most part futile. As early as 1838 he had written :

"I do not gladly utter any deep convictions on the soul in a company where I think it will be contested. No, nor unless I think it will be welcomed. Truth has already ceased to be itself if polemically said".

"Unless I think it will be welcomed." The words are significant and illustrate the man's whole attitude : its strength as well as its limitations.

Emerson's was a high-minded and finely moulded nature. Among the moral counsellors of the age, he will always hold a distinguished place, for the spiritual delicacy of his monitions and the practical wisdom of his ethics.

7. Henry David Thoreau (1817–1862)

Henry David Thoreau, (born July 12, 1817, Concord, Massachusetts, U.S.-died May 6, 1862, Concord), American essayist, poet, and practical philosopher, renowned for having lived the doctrines of Transcendentalism as recorded in his masterwork, Walden (1854), and for having been a vigorous advocate of civil liberties, as evidenced in the essay "Civil Disobedience" (1849).

Early Life

Thoreau was born in 1817 in Concord, Massachusetts, the third child of a feckless small businessman named John Thoreau and his bustling wife, Cynthia Dunbar Thoreau. Though his family moved the following year, they returned in 1823. Even when he grew ambivalent about the village after reaching adulthood, he never grew ambivalent about its lovely setting of woodlands, streams, and meadows. In 1828 his parents sent him to Concord Academy, where he impressed his teachers and so was permitted to prepare for college. Upon graduating from the academy, he entered Harvard University in 1833. There he was a good student, but he was indifferent to the rank system and preferred to use the school library for his own purposes. Graduating in the middle ranks of the class of 1837, Thoreau searched for a teaching job and secured one at his old grammar school in Concord. He found that he was no disciplinarian and resigned after two shaky weeks, after which he worked for his father in the family pencil-making business. In June 1838 he started a small school with the help of his brother John. Despite its progressive nature, it lasted for three years, until John fell ill.

Friendship With Emerson

Ralph Waldo Emerson settled in Concord during Thoreau's sophomore year at Harvard, and by the autumn of 1837 they were becoming friends. Emerson sensed in Thoreau a true disciple-that is, one with so much Emersonian self-reliance that he would still be his own man. Thoreau saw in Emerson a guide, a father, and a friend.

With his magnetism Emerson attracted others to Concord. Out of their heady speculations and affirmatives came New England Transcendentalism. In retrospect, it was one of the most significant literary movements of 19th-century America, with at least two authors of world stature, Thoreau and Emerson, to its credit. Essentially, it combined romanticism with reform. It celebrated the individual rather than the masses, emotion rather than reason, nature rather than man. Transcendentalism conceded that there were two ways of knowing, through the senses and through intuition, but asserted that intuition transcended tuition. Similarly, the movement acknowledged that matter and spirit both existed. It claimed, however, that the reality of spirit transcended the reality of matter. Transcendentalism strove for reform yet insisted that reform begin with the individual, not the group or organization.

Literary Career

In Emerson's company Thoreau's hope of becoming a poet looked not only proper but feasible. Late in 1837, at Emerson's suggestion, he began keeping a journal that covered thousands of pages before he scrawled the final entry two months before his death. He soon polished some of his old college essays and composed new and better ones as well. He wrote some poems-a good many, in fact-for several years. A canoe trip that he and his brother John took along the Concord and Merrimack rivers in 1839 confirmed in him the opinion that he ought not be a schoolmaster but a poet of nature.

As the 1840s began, Thoreau formally took up the profession of poet. Captained by Emerson, the Transcendentalists started a magazine, The Dial. Its inaugural issue, dated July 1840, carried Thoreau's poem "Sympathy" and his essay on the Roman poet Aulus Persius Flaccus. The Dial published more of Thoreau's poems and then, in July 1842, the first of his outdoor essays, "Natural History of Massachusetts." Though disguised as a book review, it showed that a nature writer of distinction was in the making. Then followed more lyrics, and fine ones, such as "To the Maiden in the East," and another nature essay, remarkably felicitous, "A Winter Walk." The Dial ceased publication with the April 1844 issue, having published a richer variety of Thoreau's writing than any other magazine ever would.

In 1840 Thoreau fell in love with and proposed marriage to an attractive visitor to Concord named Ellen Sewall. She accepted his proposal but then immediately broke off the engagement at the insistence of her parents. He remained a bachelor for life. During two periods, 1841-43 and 1847-48, he stayed mostly at the Emersons' house. In spite of Emerson's hospitality and friendship, however, Thoreau grew restless; his condition was accentuated by grief over the death of his brother John, who died of tetanus in January 1842 after cutting his finger. Later that year Thoreau became a tutor in the Staten Island household of Emerson's brother, William, while trying to cultivate the New York literary market. Thoreau's literary activities went indifferently, however, and the effort to conquer New York failed. Confirmed in his distaste for city life and disappointed by his lack of success, he returned to Concord in late 1843.

Move to Walden Pond

Back in Concord Thoreau rejoined his family's business, making pencils and grinding graphite. By early 1845 he felt more restless than ever, until he decided to take up an idea of a Harvard classmate who had once built a waterside hut in which one could read and contemplate. In the spring Thoreau picked a spot by Walden Pond, a small glacial lake located 3 km (2 miles) south of Concord on land Emerson owned.

Early in the spring of 1845, Thoreau, then 27 years old, began to chop down tall pines with which to build the foundations of his home on the shores of Walden Pond. From the outset the move gave him profound satisfaction. Once settled, he restricted his diet for the most part to the fruits and vegetables he found growing wild and the beans he planted. When not busy weeding his bean rows and trying to protect them from hungry groundhogs or occupied with fishing, swimming, or rowing, he spent long hours observing and recording the local flora and fauna, reading, and writing A Week on the Concord and Merrimack Rivers (1849). He also made entries in his journals, which he later polished and included in Walden. Much time, too, was spent in meditation.

Out of such activity and thought came Walden, a series of 18 essays describing Thoreau's experiment in basic living and his effort to set his time free for leisure. Several of the essays provide his original perspective on the meaning of work and leisure and describe his experiment in living as simply and self-sufficiently as possible, while in others Thoreau described the various realities of life at Walden Pond: his intimacy with the small animals he came in contact with; the sounds, smells, and look of woods and water at various seasons; the music of wind in telegraph wires-in short, the felicities of learning how to fulfill his desire to live as simply and self-sufficiently as possible. The physical act of living day by day at Walden Pond is what gives the book authority, while Thoreau's command of a clear, straightforward, elegant style helped raise it to the level of a literary classic.

Thoreau stayed for two years at Walden Pond (1845-47). In the summer of 1847 Emerson invited him to stay with his wife and children again, while Emerson himself went to Europe. Thoreau accepted, and in September 1847 he left his cabin forever.

Midway in his Walden sojourn Thoreau had spent a night in jail. On an evening in July 1846 he encountered Sam Staples, the constable and tax gatherer. Staples asked him amiably to pay his poll tax, which Thoreau had omitted paying for several years. He declined, and Staples locked him up. The next morning a still-unidentified lady, perhaps his aunt, Maria, paid the tax. Thoreau reluctantly emerged, did an errand, and then went to collect huckleberries. A single night, he decided, was enough to make his point that he could not support a government that endorsed slavery and waged an imperialist waragainst Mexico. His defense of the private, individual conscience against the expediency of the majority found expression in his most famous essay, "Civil Disobedience," which was first published in May 1849 under the title "Resistance to Civil Government." The essay received little attention until the 20th century, when it found an eager audience with the American civil rights movement. To many, its message still sounds timely: there is a higher law than the civil one, and the higher law must be followed even if a penalty ensues. So does its consequence: "Under a government which imprisons any unjustly, the true place for a just man is also a prison."

Later Life and Works

When Thoreau left Walden, he passed the peak of his career, and his life lost much of its illumination. Slowly his Transcendentalism drained away as he became a surveyor in order to support himself. He collected botanical specimens for himself and reptilian ones for Harvard, jotting down their descriptions in his journal. He established himself in his neighbourhood as a sound man with rod and transit, and he spent more of his time in the family business; after his father's death he took it over entirely. Thoreau made excursions to the Maine woods, to Cape Cod, and to Canada, using his experiences on the trips as raw material for three series of magazine articles: "Ktaadn [sic] and the Maine Woods," in The Union Magazine (1848); "Excursion to Canada," in Putnam's Monthly (1853); and "Cape Cod," in Putnam's (1855). These works present Thoreau's zest for outdoor adventure and his appreciation of the natural environment that had for so long sustained his own spirit.

As Thoreau became less of a Transcendentalist, he became more of an activist-above all, a dedicated abolitionist. As much as anyone in Concord, he helped to speed fleeing slaves north on the Underground Railroad. He lectured and wrote against slavery; "Slavery in Massachusetts," a lecture delivered in 1854, was his hardest indictment. In the abolitionist John Brown he found a father figure beside whom Emerson paled; the fiery old fanatic became his ideal. By now Thoreau was in poor health, and, when Brown's raid on Harpers Ferryfailed and he was hanged, Thoreau suffered a psychic shock that probably hastened his own death. He died, apparently of tuberculosis, in 1862.

Legacy

In terms of material success, Thoreau lived a life of repeated failures. He had to pay for the printing of A Week on the Concord and Merrimack Rivers; when it sold a mere 220 copies, the publishers dumped the remaining 700 on his doorstep. Walden (the second and last of his books published during his lifetime) fared better but still took five years to sell 2,000 copies. And yet Thoreau is regarded as both a classic American writer and a cultural hero of his country. This opinion of his greatness stems from the power of his principal ideas and the lucid, provocative writing with which he expressed them.

Thoreau's two famous symbolic actions, his two years in the cabin at Walden Pond and his night in jail for civil disobedience, represent his personal enactment of the doctrines of New England Transcendentalism as expressed by his friend and associate Emerson, among others. In his writings Thoreau was concerned primarily with the possibilities for human culture provided by the American natural environment. He adapted ideas garnered from the then-current Romantic literatures in order to extend American libertarianism and individualism beyond the political and religious spheres to those of social and personal life. "The life which men praise and regard as successful is but one kind. Why," Thoreau asked in Walden, where his example was the answer, "should we exaggerate any one kind at the expense of the others?" In a commercial, conservative, expedient society that was rapidly becoming urban and industrial, he upheld the right to self-culture, to an individual life shaped by inner principle. He demanded for all men the freedom to follow unique lifestyles, to make poems of their lives and living itself an art. In a restless, expanding society dedicated to practical action, he demonstrated the uses and values of leisure, contemplation, and a harmonious appreciation of and coexistence with nature. Thoreau established the tradition of nature writing later developed by the Americans John Burroughs and John Muir, and his pioneer study of the human uses of nature profoundly influenced such conservationists and regional planners as Benton MacKaye and Lewis Mumford. More important, Thoreau's life, so fully expressed in his writing, has had a pervasive influence because it was an example of moral heroism and an example of the continuing search for a spiritual dimension in American life.

8. Oliver Wendell Holmes (1809–1894)

There is no more genial, more agreeable personality in American letters than Oliver Wendell Holmes; and the versatile ease with which he could turn from verse to table-talk and from table-talk to fiction, are not the least of his attractions. As essayist he has neither the distinction of Emerson, the freshness of Thoreau, nor the vigorous staying power of Lowell. Yet, at his best, as in *The Breakfast Table Series* and *Elsie Venner*, there is an ease and a play of charming fancy about his work, that gives him quite a distinctive place among American prosemen. He is an adept in the art of allusive chit-chat. No American writer can talk in print so intimately or with such discursive wisdom as he. He has mastered the art of buttonholing; and his easy-jacket, carpet-slipper style admirably suits the play of humour and fancy which he brings to bear upon all manner of subjects.

The very title of his famous series of chatters is significant of the man : *The Breakfast Table Series.*

He is an Autocrat, Poet and a Professor of the Breakfast Table. Not a time many of us would select for philosophy and dialectics, however, airily and playfully conducted. We recall sympathetically "Elia's" eloquent plea for lying a-bed mornings and digesting our dreams and say "Amen" to his comment that "Jokes came in with candlelight" His strenuous, healthy and sanguine temperament bids us start the day well, with a clear head and a bright heart. And that is why, despite superficial resemblances between his chit-chat and that of Lamb, there is a basic difference of temperament between them.

If not a deep thinker, he is invariably a clear and vigorous one and carries the epigrammatic power of Emerson and Thoreau with a more light-hearted air. Occasionally he can be as serious and as suggestive as the Concord Oracle himself, for instance when he observes :

"Sin has many tools, but a lie is the handle which fits them all."

Or :

"Faith always implies the disbelief of a lesser fact in favour of greater".

But more often he is content to be blithe and flippant, as in

"We never tell our secrets to people who jump for them".

"Memory is a net, one finds it full of fish when he takes it form the book, but a dozen miles of water have run through it without sticking".

(Of the Red Indian)

"A few instincts of legs flourishing a tomahawk".

But the graceful flippancies of Holmes are the most palatable when turned into verse. There his literary deftness, his underlying tenderness, his worldly sagacity, blend with the happiest results.

The Old Man Dreams

O for one hour of youthful joy !
Give back my twentieth spring !
I'd rather laugh a bright-haired boy
Than reign a grey-beard king !

Off with the wrinkled spoils of age !
Away with learning's crown !
Tear out life's wisdom-written page,
And dash its trophies down !

One moment let my life-blood stream
From boyhood's fount of flame!
Give me one giddy, reeling dream
Of life all love and fame !

— My listening angel heard the prayer,
And calmly smiling, said,
"If I but touch thy silvered hair,
Thy hasty wish hath sped.

"But is there nothing in thy track
To bid thee fondly stay,
While the swift seasons hurry back
To find the wished-for day ?"

—Ah, truest soul of womankind !
Without thee, what were life !
One bliss I cannot leave behind :
I'll take —my —precious —wife !

—The angel took a sapphire pen
And wrote in rainbow dew,
"The man would be a boy again,
And be a husband too !"

—"And is there nothing yet unsaid
Before the change appears ?
Remember, all their gifts have fled
With those dissolving years."

Why, yes; for memory would recall
My fond paternal joys;
I could not bear to leave them all :

I'll take—my—girl—and —boys !

The smiling angel dropped his pen,—
"Why, this will never do;
The man would be a boy again,
And be a father too !"

And so I laughed,—my laughter woke
The household with its noise,—
And wrote my dream, when morning broke,
To please the grey-haired boys.

The Last Blossom

Though young no more, we still would dream
Of beauty's dear deluding wiles;
The leagues of life to greybeards seem
Shorter than boyhood's lingering miles.

Who knows a woman's wild caprice ?
It played with Goethe's silvered hair,
And many a Holy Father's "niece"
Has softly smoothed the papal chair.

When sixty bids us sigh in vain
To melt the heart of sweet sixteen,
We think upon those ladies twain
Who loved so well the tough old Dean.

We see the Patriarch's wintry face,
The maid of Egypt's dusky glow,
And dream that Youth and Age embrace,
As April violets fill with snow.

Tranced in her lord's Olympian smile
His lotus-loving Memphian lies,—
The musky daughter of the Nile
With plaited hair and almond eyes.

Might we but share one wild caress
Ere life's autumnal blossoms fall,
And Earth's brown, clinging lips impress
The long cold kiss that waits us all !

My bosom heaves, remembering yet
The morning of that blissful day
When Rose, the flower of spring, I met,
And gave my raptured soul away.

Flung from her eyes of purest blue,
A lasso, with its leaping chain
Light as a loop of larkspurs, flew
O'er sense and spirit, heart and brain.

Thou com'st to cheer my waning age,
Sweet vision, waited for so long !
Dove that would seek the poet's cage
Lured by the magic breath of song !

She blushes ! Ah, reluctant maid,
Love's drapeau rouge *the truth has told;*
O'er girlhood's yielding barricade
Floats the great Leveller's crimson fold !

Come to my arms !—Love heeds not years,
No frost the bud of passion knows—
Ha ! what is this my frenzy hears ?
A voice behind me uttered, —Rose !

Sweet was her smile,—but not for me;
Alas, when woman looks too kind,
Just turn your foolish head and see,—
Some youth is walking close behind !

In his higher flights, Holmes is less satisfactory; that ingenuity of his, so telling in the lighter verse—such piece as *The Deacon's Masterpiece* or *The One-Hoss Shay*—gives a touch of artificiality to poems like *The Chambered Nautilus*; the graceful sentiment which touches with sufficient tenderness *The Last Leaf*, grows too riotous in a lyric like *Under the Violets*. These things are assuredly not without charm, but they are insufficiently strong and simple for great poetry. One has only to compare Hood's treatment of young girl's death with Holmes to appreciate the difference.

Holmes never mastered the art that conceals art : and thus he is at his best when he reminds us of our own Praed, where a delicate artificiality is a charm and not a blemish.

The most poetic thing Holmes ever wrote is his novel, *Elsie Venner* : the scientific problems raised in that remarkable book have a stimulating effect on the writer's imagination, that is nowhere else manifest. More of the twilight atmosphere of Hawthorn would no doubt have heightened the tragic romance of the *Snake Woman*—it is a little too clear- out and definite; but there are passages in the book that reach a very high level of imaginative beauty.

On the whole, Holmes is at his best when he appears before us —to use a phrase Thackery applied to himself —as the "week-day preacher." Bred in an intellectual atmosphere, there is nothing academic about his thought. His fresh adventurous mind scorns the narrow groove. He might have demurred to Bernard Shaw's contention that the medical profession is an organised conspiracy to defraud the laity (though we can imagine him chuckling at its daring impudence), but he was strongly in favour of the idea underlying Shaw's sally —

"You can't keep gas in a bladder and you can't keep knowledge tight in a profession—special knowledge will leak out and general knowledge leak in."

His general outlook may be gauged by his statement, that

"The great thing is not so much where we stand as in what direction we are moving." —"To reach the port of heaven we must sail sometimes with the wind; sometimes against it".

We may regard Holmes in literature as we regard the shrewd family physician in daily life. For serious crises we call in the expert, as at such times the family physician may prove unequal to the emergency. But in the ordinary run of life, all we need is sound counsel on hygienics and, perhaps, an occasional alternative mixture to keep us fit. There we find the value of Holmes. He knows our little infirmities well and can adapt himself to our moods and fancies. He knows that what does all of us good at times, is a picnic of ideas and none can prepare that meal more adroitly and more palatably than the "Autocrat."

9. James Russel Lowell (1819-1891)

James Russell Lowell, (born Feb. 22, 1819, Cambridge, Mass., U.S.-died Aug. 12, 1891, Cambridge), American poet, critic, essayist, editor, and diplomat whose major significance probably lies in the interest in literature he helped develop in the United States. He was a highly influential man of letters in his day, but his reputation declined in the 20th century.

A member of a distinguished New England family, Lowell graduated from Harvard in 1838 and in 1840 took his degree in law, though his academic career had been lacklustre and he did not care to practice law for a profession. In 1844 he was married to the gifted poet Maria White, who had inspired his poems in A Year's Life (1841) and who would help him channel his energies into fruitful directions.

In 1845 Lowell published Conversations on Some of the Old Poets, a collection of critical essays that included pleas for the abolition of slavery. From 1845 to 1850 he wrote about 50 antislavery articles for periodicals. Even more effective in this regard were his Biglow Papers, which he began to serialize June 17, 1846, and the first series of which were collected in book form in 1848. In these satirical verses, Lowell uses a humorous and original New England dialect to express his opposition to the Mexican War as an attempt to extend the area of slavery. The year 1848 also saw the publication of Lowell's two other most important pieces of writing: The Vision of Sir Launfal, an enormously popular long poem extolling the brotherhood of man; and A Fable for Critics, a witty and rollicking verse evaluation of contemporary American authors. These books, together with the publication that year of the second series of his Poems, made Lowell the most popular new figure in American literature.

The death of three of Lowell's children was followed by the death of his wife in 1853. Henceforth his literary production comprised mainly prose essays on topics of literature, history, and politics. In 1855 his lectures on English poets before the Lowell Institute led to his appointment as Smith professor of modern languages at Harvard University, succeeding Henry Wadsworth Longfellow. After a yearlong visit to Italy and Germany in 1855-56 to study, he held this professorship for the next 20 years. In 1857 he married Frances Dunlap, who had cared for his only remaining child, Mabel; and in that year he began his four years' editorship of the new Atlantic Monthly, to which he attracted the major New England authors. Lowell wrote a second series of Biglow Papers for the Atlantic Monthly that were devoted to Unionism and that were collected in book form in 1867. After the American Civil War he expressed his devotion to the Union cause in four memorial odes, the best of which is "Ode Recited at the Harvard Commemoration" (1865). His essays such as "E Pluribus Unum" and "Washers of the Shroud" (1862) also reflect his thought at this time.

Disillusioned by the political corruption evident in President Ulysses S. Grant's two administrations (1869-77), Lowell tried to provide his fellow Americans with models of heroism and idealism in literature. He was editor with Charles Eliot Norton of North American Review from 1864 to 1872, and during this time appeared his series of critical essays on such major literary figures as Dante, Chaucer, Edmund Spenser, John Milton, William Shakespeare, John Dryden, William Wordsworth, and John Keats. These and other critical essays were collected in the two series of Among My Books (1870, 1876). His later poetry includes The Cathedral (1870), a long and ambitious but only partly successful poem that deals with the conflicting claims of religion and modern science.

President Rutherford B. Hayes rewarded Lowell's support in the Republican convention in 1876 by appointing him minister to Spain (1877-80) and ambassador to Great Britain (1880-85). Lowell won great popularity in England's literary and political circles and served as president of the Wordsworth Society, succeeding Matthew Arnold. After his second wife died in 1885, Lowell retired from public life.

Lowell was the archetypal New England man of letters, remarkable for his cultivation and charm, his deep learning, and his varied literary talents. He wrote his finest works before he was 30 years old, however, and most of his subsequent writings lack vitality. The totality of his work, though brilliant in parts, ultimately suffers from a lack of focus and a failure to follow up on his undoubted early successes.

OTHER NON-BRITISH LITERATURES

Meanwhile, during the time when Whatman was sounding a new note in literature, a number of lesser writers were continuing the elder tradition of verse. Among these, may be mentioned – NATHANIEL PARKER WILLIS (1806-1867) a facile writer whose sentimental verse, now almost forgotten, was nonce as popular as the verse of Tom Moore; CHARLES FENNO HOFFMAN (1806-1884), less popular and singularly unequal, but a sweet singer at his best; and Dr. THOMAS WILLIAM PARSON of Boston (1819-1892), who belongs to the considerable school of scholarly verse-writers; he was strongly affected by the Dante Revival and no poem that he wrote is happier in its dignity and grace than the Line on a Bust of Dante.

Two figures of greater literary importance are BAYARD TAYLOR (1825-1878) and SIDNEY LANIER (1842-1881). Taylor was an illustrious traveller, who live abroad for two years, seeing a good deal of the democratic life both of Germany and Italy. His first success was made in travel-letters and he always excelled in these, but he was an effective ballad-writer; his *poem of the Orient* (1834) being among his best. His life was one of tragic and varied interest; he essayed much, but perhaps he will best be remembered for his fine translation of Goethe's Faust (unfinished) and his delightful *Travel Chat.*

Lanier— a musician, solder, poet and critic— fought for the South in the American War, and emerged from his harrowing experiences, broken in health. His skill as a musician is exhibited in his verse, notably *The Marshes of Glynn, Sunrise* and Corn. He died of consumption in North Carolina, after a vain search for climes to restore his health. A less considerable figure in American letters than Taylor, he is, if not a more accomplished, yet a more original poet.

Among the ballads evoked by the Civil War, there is none better than the familiar *Maryland, My Maryland,* by JAMES RIDER RANDALI.

It is not practicable to discuss here the later development of American verse. All that needs to be said is that democratic ideals have entered more and more intimately into the poetry of the age and although no poets of commanding power haversian, Yet such names as THOMAS BAILEY ALDRICH (1836-1896) and RICHARD WATSON GILDER (1844-1909) are sufficient indication of the sound technical accomplishment and imaginative fervour to be found among a large number of latter-day poets.

A Canadian verse-writer of originality and power appears in WILLIAM BLISS CARMAN (1861). His first work, *Low Tide on Grand Pre,* was published in 1893 and at once made its mark. He is especially happy as a song-writer, *Behind the Arras, Ballads of Lost Haven.*

R. K. Narayan (1906-2001). R.K. Narayan obtained his bachelor's degree from Mysore University and devoted almost whole of his life as a writer. He started by writing short stories which appeared in 'The Hindu'; and he also worked as a Mysore Correspondent of 'Justice', a newspaper from Madras.

Narayan is the true master of humour, irony, realism, romance and artistry. His stories are set in South India, where, like Thomas Hardy's Wessex, he created a famous town of Malgudi. Some critics, however, hold that he lacks true pathos, genuine depth of feeling, realistic description of poverty and misery—the elements which make a novelist really great.

Narayan accepts the social system prevailing in the country and portrays it realistically without making an attempt to castigate the ills of the society. He deals with the middle class which he knows very intimately, as also the plight of the underdog. It is sad that he makes no attempt to present India in an exotic light for the sake of foreign readers.

Novels. Swami and Friends (1935), Bachelor of Art (1973), The Dark Room (1938), The English Teacher (1945) The Guide (1958), The Painter of Signs (1976).

Story Collections. Malgudi Days, Dodu and Other Stories, Cyclone and Other Stories, Gods, Demons and Others (1964).

Autobiography. My Days (1974), My Dateless Diary (1960).

Ramayana. It is an English version of the Tamil epic by Kamban.

The Emerald Route (1978). It is a travelogue wherein his younger brother R.K. Laxman, the famous cartoonist, has given the sketches.

Arun Kolatkar (1932-2004). He was a poet from Maharashtra. His first book of English poetry, Jejuri, is a collection of 31 poems. This book won commonwealth writer's prize in 1977. His Marathi verse collection 'Bhijki Wahi' won a Sahitya Akademi Award in 2005.

Manohar Malgaonkar (1913-2010). He has portrayed the heroism of Indian independence, as well as the good qualities of the old Indian aristocracy in his novels some of his works are, 'Distant Drums', 'The Princess', 'A Bend in the Ganges', 'The Devil's Wind', 'Dead and Living Cities'.

Anita Desai (born in 1937). She had been short listed three times for the booker prize. She received the Sahitya Akademi Award in 1978 for her novel 'Fire on the mountain'. She won the British Guardian prize for 'The village by the sea'.

Mulk Raj Anand (1905-2004). He was an Indian writer, who with his works, depicted the poorer castes in traditional Indian society. His first main novel Untouchable was published in 1935, it exposed the day to day life of the helpers members of India's untochable caste. Some of his novels are 'Untouchable' (1935), 'Coolie' (1936), Two leaves and Bud' (1937).

Aurobindo Ghosh (1872-1950). He was an Indian nationalist, freedom fighter, philosopher and poet. His main literary works are 'The Life Divine', 'Synthesis of Yoga', 'Savitri : en epic poem'. Sri Aurobindo was one of the first Indians to create a literary corpus in English. Most of his works include translation of India scriptures and also on the yoga system and philosophy which he had introduced.

Henry Louis Vivian Derozio (1809-1931). He was an Indian poet and a radical thinker. He was one of the first Indian eductors to disseminate Western leaving and science among the young men of Bengal. Some of his main works are, 'Song of the Hinduestanee Mistrel', 'Chorus of Brahmin', 'To the Pupils'.

Nirad C. Chaudhuri (1897-1999). He was a Bengali English writer. He was awarded the Sahitya Akademi Award in 1975 for his biography on Max Muller called 'Scholar Extraordinary', by the Sahitya Akademi. He was honoured with the title of 'Commander of Order of the British Empire' by Queen Elizabeth in 1992. He became the first and only Indian to be selected for Duff Cooper Memorial Award, for his work 'The Continent of Circe', in 1965.

His masterpiece 'The Autobiography of an unknown Indian' was published in 1951. His prose was highly influenced by Sanskrit and the older version of Bengali language. His other works include: 'A Passage to England', 'To live or not to live', 'The Hand, Great Anarch', 'The East is East and West is West'.

Toru Dutt (1856-1877). She was an Indian poet who wrote in English. She left behind an impressive collection of prose and poetry. Her two novels, 'The unfinished Bianca', or 'the young Spanish maiden', written in English and 'Le Journal Le Mademoiselle d'Rivers', written in French, were based outside India, with non-Indian protagonists.

RHETORIC AND PROSODY

RHETORIC AND RHETORICAL CRITICISM

(1) Development of Rhetoric

In his *Poetics* Aristotle defined poetry as a mode of *imitation*—a fictional representation of human beings thinking, feeling, acting and interacting—and focused his discussion on such elements as plot, character, thought and diction within the work itself. In his *Rhetoric* Aristotle defined rhetorical discourse as the art of discovering all the available means persuasion in any given case and focused his discussion on the various ways in which the orator deploys devices for achieving intellectual and emotional effects on an audience that are needed to persuade them to accede to his point of view. Later classical rhetoricians concurred with this definition of rhetoric as the art of persuading an audience and (still following Aristotle's lead) analysed the text of a rhetorical discourse into "invention" (the finding of arguments or proofs) "disposition" (the arrangement of such matters) and "style" (the choice of words figures and rhythms that will most effectively express this material). They also discriminated three main categories of oratory, each of which uses characteristic devices to achieve its distinctive effects :

(i) **Deliberative**—to persuade an audience (such as a legislative assembly) to approve or disapprove of a matter of public policy and to act accordingly.

(ii) **Forensic** —to achieve (for example, in a judicial trial) condemnation or approval of a man's actions.

(iii) **Epideictic** —"display rhetoric" used on ceremonial occasions to amplify the praise (or sometimes, the blameworthiness) of a person or group of persons.

Horace, in his versified *Art of Poetry,* declared that the aim of a poet is either to instruct or to delight a reader, or preferably to do both. Such *pragmatic criticism,* which breaks down Aristotle's distinction between poetry and rhetoric, in one or another form dominated literary theory from late classical time through eighteenth century; discussions of poetry absorbed and expanded upon the terms of traditional rhetoric and a poem was regarded mainly as a deployment of artistic means for achieving effects upon the reader or audience. The triumph in the early nineteenth century of *expressive* theories of literature (which conceive a work primarily as the expression of the feelings, temperament, and mental powers of the author himself), followed by the dominance, beginning in the 1920s, of *objective* theories of literature (which maintain that a work must be considered as an object in itself, independently of the mental qualities of the author and the response of a reader) served to diminish and sometimes to eliminate, rhetorical considerations in literary criticism. (*See Criticism.*)

Since the late 1950s, however, there has been strong revival of interest in literature as a public act involving communication between author and reader and this has led to the development of a *rhetorical criticism* which, without departing from a primary focus on the work as such, undertakes to analyse those elements within a poem or a prose narrative which are there primarily for the reader's sake. As Wayne Booth has said in the Preface to his influential book *The Rhetoric of Fiction* (1961), his subject is "the rhetorical resources available to the writer of epic, novel or short story as he tries, consciously or unconsciously, to impose his fictional world upon the reader". A number of recent critics of prose fiction and of narrative and non-radioactive poems have devoted special attention to an author's use of variety of means—especially the authorial presence or *voice* that he projects —in order to inform, to achieve imaginative consent and to engage the interests and guide the emotional responses of the reader to whom, whether deliberately or not, his literary work is inevitably addressed.

(2) Rhetorical Figures

It is convenient to list under this heading, some common figures of speech which depart from standard or "literal", language mainly by the arrangement of their words to achieve special effects and not, like metaphors and other *tropes*, by a radical change of meaning in the words themselves.

(I) **Apostrophe.** An *apostrophe* is directly addressed either to an absent person or to an abstract or inanimate entity. Keats begins his "Ode on a Grecian Urn" by apostrophising the urn: "Thou still unravished bride quietness"; and in his fine poem,"Recollections of Love", Coleridge turns suddenly from thoughts of his beloved to apostrophise the River Greta :

But when those meek eyes first did seem
To tell me, Love within you wrought
O Greta, dear domestic stream!

Has not, since then, Love's prompture deep,
Has not Love's whisper evermore
Been ceaseless, as thy gentle roar?
Sole voice, when other voice sleep,
Dear under-song in clamor 's hour.

(II) **Invocation.** If such an address is to a god or muse to assist the poet in his composition, it is called an *invocation*; so Milton invokes divine guidance at the opening of *Paradise Lost :*

And chiefly Thou, O Spirit, that dost prefer
Before all temples th' upright heart and pure,
Instruct me.....

(III) **Rhetorical Question.** A *rhetorical question* is a question asked, not to evoke an actual reply, but to achieve an emphasis stronger than a direct statement. The figure is most used in persuasive discourse and tends to impart an oratorical tone to a speech. When "fierce Thalestris" in Pope's *The Rape of the Lock asks* Belinda,

Gods! shall the ravisher display your hair,
While the fops envy and the ladies stare?

she does not stay for an answer, which is obviously "No!" (By far the most common rhetorical question is one that won't take "Yes" for an answer.) Shelley's "Ode to the West Wind" closes with the most famous rhetorical question in English :

O, Wind,
If Winter comes, can Spring be far behind?

(IV) **Chiasmus.** *Chiasmus* is a sequence of two phrases or clauses which are parallel in syntax, but with a reversal in the order of the words. So, in this line from 'Pope', the verb first precedes, then follows the adverbial phrase :

Works without show and without pomp *presides*

The effect is sometimes reinforced by alliteration and other similarities in sound, as in Pope's summary of common fate of coquettes in marriage :

A *fop* their passion, but their prize a *sot.*

In Yeats's "An Irish Airman Foresees His Death", the chiasmus consists in a reversal of the position of the same phrase :

The years to come seemed *waste of breath,*
A *waste of breath* the years behind.

(V) **Zeugma.** *Zeugma* in Greek means "yoking"; in the most common present usage, it is applied to expressions in which a single word stands in the same grammatical relation to two or more other words, but with some alteration its meaning from one instance to the next. Here are various instances of zeugma in Pope :

Or stain *her honour or her new brocade.*
Obliged *by hunger and request of friends.*
To rest, the cushion and soft Dean invite.

To achieve the maximum of concentrated verbal effects within the tight limits of the *closed couplet,* Pope exploited all these language patterns with supreme virtuosity. He is the English master of the rhetorical figures, as Shakespeare is of the metaphorical figures.

PROSODY

Signifies the systematic study of versification, that is, of the principles and practice of *meter, rhyme* and *stanza.* Sometimes the term "prosody" is extended to include also the study of sound effects such as *alliteration, assonance, euphony* and *onomatopoeia.*

(1) Meter

In all sustained spoken English we feel a *rhythm,* in the sense of a recognisable though variable pattern in the beat of the stresses in the stream of sound, if this rhythm is structured into a recurrence of regular—that is, approximately equal —units, we call it *meter.* Compositions written in meter are known as *verse.*

(A) **Determining the Meter.** The meter of a line of verse is determined by the pattern of stronger and weaker stresses in its component syllables. (What the ear detects as a strong stress is not an absolute quantity, but is relative to the degree of stress in the adjacent syllables; the degree of perceived stress is determined primarily by the relative loudness of the pronunciation of the syllable and to a lesser extent, by its relative pitch and duration.

There are three factors that determine where the stresses (in the sense of the relatively stronger stresses or "accents") will fall in line of verse :

(1) Most important is the "word accent" in polysyllabic words; in the noun "accent" itself, for example, the stress falls on the first syllable.

(2) There are also many monosyllabic words in the language and on which of these—in a sentence or a phrase — the stress will fall depends on the grammatical function of the word (we normally put stronger stress on nouns, verbs and adjectives, for example, than on articles or prepositions) and also on

the "rhetorical accent" or the emphasis we give a word because awe want to enhance its importance in a particular utterance.

(3) Another determinant of stress is the "metrical accent" which is an expected pulsation, in accordance with the stress pattern which was established earlier in the matrical line or passage.

(B) **Wrenched Accent.** If matrical accent enforces an alteration of the normal word accent, we get a *wrenched accent.* Wrenching may be the result of a lack of metrical skill; it was, however, conventional in the *folk ballad* (For example, "fair ladie", "far countree") and is sometimes deliberately used, as in Byron's *Don Juan* and in the verses of Ogden Nash, for comic effects.

(C) **Degree of Stress.** It is possible to distinguish various degrees of relative stress in English speech, but the most common and generally useful fashion of analysing and classifying the standard English meters is to distinguish only two categories of stress in syllables—weak stress and strong stress—and to group the syllables into metric feet according to the patterning of these two stresses. A *foot* is the combination of a strong stress and the associated weak stress or stresses which make up the recurrent metric unit of a line. The relatively stronger-stressed syllable is called, for short, "Stressed"; the relatively weaker-stressed syllables are called "light" or a "slack" or simply "unstressed."

(D) **Four Standard Feet.** The four standard feet distinguished in English are :

(i) **Iambic** (the noun is "lamb") : a light followed by a stressed syllable.

The cur few tolls the knell of par ting day.

Gray, "Elegy in a Country Churchyard")

(ii) **Anaplastic** (the noun is "anapest") : two light syllables followed by a stressed syllable.

The As syrian came down like a wolf on the fold.

(Byron, "The Destruction of Sennacherib")

(iii) **Trochaic** (the noun is "trochee") : a stressed followed by a light syllable.

There they are, my fifty men and women.

(Browning, "One Word More")

Most trochaic lines lack the final syllable-in the technical term, such lines are *catalectic.* So in Blake's "The Tiger" :

Tiger! tiger! burning bright
In the forest of the night.

(iv) **Dactylic** (the noun is "dactyl") : a stressed syllable followed by two light syllables.

Eve, with her basket, was
Deep in the bells and grass.

(Ralph Hodgson, "Eve")

Iambs and anapests, since the strong stress is at the end, constitute a "rising meter"; trochees and dactyls, with the strong stress at the beginning, constitute a "falling meter". Iambs and trochees, with two syllables, are called "duple meter"; anapests and dactyls, with three syllables, are called "triple meter". It should be noted that the iamb is by far the commonest English foot.

(E) **Feet as Occasional Variant :**—Two other feet, often distinguished, occur only as occasional variants from standard feet :

(i) **Spondaic** (the noun "spondee") : two successive syllables with approximately equal strong stresses, as in the first two feet of this line :

Good strong thick stupefying in cense smoke.

(Browning, "The Bishop Orders His Tomb")

(ii) **Pyrrhic** (the noun is also "pyrrhic") : two successive syllables with approximately equal light stresses, as in the second and fourth feet in this line :

My way is to begin with the be gin ning

(Byron, *Don Juan*)

Some traditional metrists do not admit the existence of a true pyrrhic, on the grounds that the prevailing metrical accent —in this instance, iambic—always imposes a slightly stronger stress on one of the two syllables.

(F) **Naming of a Metric Line.** A metric line is named according to the number of feet composing it :

monometer : one feet
dimeter : two feet
trimeter : three feet
tetrameter : four feet
pentameter : five feet
hexameter : six feet (an *Alexandrine* is a line of six iambic feet)
heptameter : seven feet (a *fourteener* is a line of seven iambic feet ; it tends to break into a unit of four feet followed by a unit of three feet)
octameter : eight feet

(G) **Method of Describing the Meter.** To describe the meter of a line we name – (a) the predominant foot, and (b) the number of feet it contains. In the illustrations above, for example, the line from Gray's "Elegy" is "iambic pentameter," and the line from Byron's "The Destruction of Sennacherib" is "anapestic tetrameter."

(H) **Scansion.** To scan a passage of verse is to go through it line by line, analysing the component feet and also indicating where any major pauses fall within a line. Here is a *scansion*, signified by conventional symbols, of the first five lines from Keats's *Endymion* : the passage was chosen because it exemplifies a flexible and variable rather than a highly regular metrical pattern.

(i) A thing of beauty is a joy forever:
(ii) Its loveliness increases; // it will never
(iii) Pass into nothingness,// but still will keep
(iv) A bower quiet for us // and a sleep
(v) Full of sweet dreams and health and qui et breath ing.

The prevailing meter is clearly iambic and the lines are iambic pentameter. As in all fluent verse, however, there are "variations" upon the basic iambic foot :

(vi) The closing feet of lines 1,2 and 5 end with an extra light syllable and are said to have a *feminine ending.* Line 3 and 4, in which the closing feet, since they are standard iambs, end with a stressed syllable, are said to have masculine endings.

(vii) In lines 3 and 5, the opening iambic feet have been "inverted" to from trochees. (These initial positions are the most common place for such inversions in iambic verse).

(viii) I have marked the second foot in line 2 and the third foot of line 3 and line 4, as pyrrhics (two light stresses). This is a procedure with which competent readers often disagree : some will feel enough of a metric beat in all these feet to mark them as iambs; others will mark still other feet (for example, the third foot of line 1) as pyrrhics also. And some metric analysts prefer to use symbols measuring two degrees of strong stress and will indicate a difference in the feet, as follows :

Its loveliness increases.

Notice, however, that these are differences in nuance rather than in essentials : the readers agree that the prevailing pulse of Keats's versification is iambic throughout.

(I) **Metric Movement of Keats's Passage.** Two other elements are important in the metric movement of Keats's passage :

(i) ***End - Stopped and Run on Lines***. In lines 1 and 5, the pause in the reading — which occurs naturally at the end of syntactic phrase or clause-coincides with the end of the line; such lines are called end-stopped. Lines 2 through 4, on the hand, are called *run- on lines* (or in French term, they exhibit *enjambement*— "a striding over"), because the pressure of the incompleted syntactic unit toward closure carries on over the end of the verse-line

(ii) ***Caesura***. When a strong phrasal pause falls within a line, as in lines 2, 3 and 4, it is called a *caesura,* indicated in the quoted passage by the conventional symbol //. The management of these internal pauses is important for giving variety and for providing rhetorical emphases in the long pentameter line.

(J) **Function of Scansion.** To understand the function of such scansion, we must realise that it is an abstract scheme which deliberately omits notation of many physical attributes of the actual reading of a poem that contribute to its movement and total impression. It does not specify, for example, whether the component words in a metric line are short words or long words or whether the strong stresses fall on short vowels or long vowels; nor does it give any indication of the "intonation" or voice melody- the overall rise and fall of the pitch and loudness of the voice - which we use to bring out the meaning and rhetorical effect of these poetic lines. We deliberately omit such details in order to lay bare the essential metric skeleton; that is, the fall of the stronger stresses in the syllabic sequence. Moreover, an actual reading of a poem, if it is a skillful reading, will not accord mechanically with the scansion. That is, there is a difference between the scansion, as an abstract metrical paradigm or norm and the oral "performance" of a poem; and in fact, no two readers will perform the same lines in precisely the same way. But the metric norm indicated by the scansion is sensed as an implicit understructure of pulses and the interplay of an expressive performance, sometimes with and sometimes against this underlying structural pattern, helps to give tension and vitality to our experience of a poem.

(K) **Kinds of Meters.** We should note, finally, that various kinds of English versification differ from the syllable-and stress type already described :

(i) **Strong stress meters.** In this native English meter, only the strong stresses count in the scanning and the number of intervening light syllables is indeterminate and variable. There are usually four stressed syllables in a line. This was the meter of Old English poetry and of many Middle English poems, until Chaucer popularised the syllable and stress meter. In the opening passage, for example, of *Piers Plowman* (latter fourteenth century) the four strong stresses (always divided by a medial caesura) are often reinforced by alliteration (see *alliterative meter*); the light syllables, which vary in number, are recessive and do not assert their individual presence :

In a somer seson, // whan soft was the sonne,

I shope me in shroudes, // as I a shepe were,
In habits like an heremite, // unholy of workes,
Went wyde in this world, // wonders to here.

This type of meter still survives in traditional children's rhymes and was revived as an artful literary meter by Coleridge in *Christabel,* in which each line has four strong stresses and the number of syllables in a line may vary from four to twelve.

What G. M. Hopkins called his *sprung rhythm* is a variant of strong-stress meter : each foot, as he describes it, begins with a stressed syllable, which may stand alone or else be associated with from one to three (occasionally even more) light syllables. Two six-stress lines from Hopkins' "The Wreck of the *Deutschland"* indicate the variety of the rhythms in this meter and also exemplify its most striking feature : the great weight of the strong stresses, and the frequent juxtaposition of strong stresses at any point in the line. The stresses in the second line were marked in a manuscript by Hopkins himself; they indicate that in complex instances, his metric decisions may be rather arbitrary :

The sour scythe cringe and the blear share come.
Our hearts charity's hearth's fire, our thoughts' chivalry's throng's Lord.

A number of modern metrists, such as T. S. Eliot and Ezra Pound, skillfully interweave both strong-stress and syllable-and-stress meters in some of their versification.

(ii) **Quantitative meters.** These, in English, are written in imitation of Greek and Latin versification, in which the metrical pattern is not determined by the stress, but by the "quantity (duration of pronunciation) of a syllable and the foot consists of a combination of "long" and "short" syllables. Sidney, Spenser and other Elizabethan poets experimented with this meter in English, as did Coleridge, Tennyson, Longfellow and Robert Bridges later on. The strong accentual character of English, however, as well as the indeterminateness of the syllabic duration, makes it impossible to sustain a purely quantitative meter in that language.

In *free verse,* the component lines have no (or at least only occasional) units of recurrent stress - patterns.

(2) Rhyme

In English versification, the standard rhyme consists in the identity, in rhyming words, of the last stressed vowel and of all the speech sounds following that vowel : *late-fate; follow -swallow.*

(a) **End and Internal Rhymes.** *End rhymes,* by far the most frequent type, occur at the end of a verse-line. *Internal rhymes* occur within a verse-line, as in Swinburne's

Sister, my sister, O *fleet sweet* swallow.

A stanza from Coleridge's *The Ancient Mariner* illustrates the patterned use both of internal rhymes (within line 1 and 3) and of an end rhyme (lines 2 and 4) :

In mist or *cloud,* on mast or *shroud,*
It perched for vespers *nine,*
Whiles all the *night,* through fog- smoke *white,*
Glimmered the white moon-*shine.*

The numbered lines in the following stanza of Wordsworth's "The Solitary Reaper" are followed by a column which, in conventional fashion, marks the sequence of the terminal rhyme elements by a sequence of the letters of the alphabet :

(i) Whate'er her theme, the maiden sang	*a*
(ii) As if her song could have no *ending;*	*b*
(iii) I saw her singing at her *work,*	*c*
(iv) And o'er the sickle *bending—*	*b*
(v) I listened, motionless and *still;*	*d*
(vi) And as I mounted up the *hill,*	*d*
(vii) The music in my heart I *bore,*	*e*
(viii) Long after it was heard no *more.*	*c*

(b) **Masculine and Feminine Rhymes.** Lines 1 and 3 do not rhyme with any other line. Both, in lines 5 and 6, and lines 7 and 8, the rhyme consists of a single stressed syllable and is called a *masculine rhyme* : still-hill, bore-more. In lines 2 and 4, the rhyme consists of a stressed syllable followed by an unstressed syllable and is called *feminine rhyme* : ending- bending.

A feminine rhyme, since it involves two syllables, is also known as a *double rhyme.* A rhyme involving three syllables is called a *triple rhyme.* Such rhymes, since they coincide with surprising patness, usually have a comic quality. In *Don Juan* Byron often uses triple rhymes such as comparison-garrison and sometimes intensifies the comic effect by permitting the pressure of the rhyme to force a distortion of the pronunciation; thus he addresses the husbands of learned wives :

But —Oh! ye lords of ladies intellectual
Inform us truly, have they not hen pecked you *all?*

This maltreatment of words, in which the poet seems to surrender helplessly to the exigencies of a triple rhyme, thoroughly exploited by Ogden Nash :

Farewell, farewell, you old rhinocerous,
I'll stare at something less prepocerous.

(c) **Perfect and Imperfect Rhymes.** If the correspondence of the rhymed sounds is exact, it is called *perfect rhyme,* or else "full" or true "rhyme." Until recently, almost all the English writers of serious poems have limited themselves to perfect rhymes, except for an occasional *poetic license* such as *eye-rhymes* or words whose endings are spelled alike and in most instances were once pronounced alike, but now have a different pronunciation : prove-love, daughter-laughter. Many modern poets, however, deliberately supplement perfect rhyme with *imperfect rhyme* (also known as "partial", "near" or "slant rhyme"). This effect is fairly common in folk poetry such as children's verses and it was employed occasionally by various writers of art lyrics such as Thomas Vaughan and William Blake. Hopkins and Yeats, however, were the first important poets fully to exploit partial rhymes, in which the rhymed vowels are either approximate or quite different and occasionally even the rhymed consonants are similar rather than identical. Wilfred Owen constructs the following six-line stanza with two sets of partial rhymes :

The centuries will burn rich loads
With which we groaned,
Whose warmth shall lull their dreamy lids,
While songs are crooned.
But they will not dream of us poor lads
Lost in the ground.

In his poem "The Force that through the Green Fuse Drives the Flower", Dylan Thomas uses, most effectively, such distantly approximate rhymes as (with masculine endings) trees-rose, rocks-wax, tomb-worm and (with feminine endings) flower-destroyer-fever.

(d) **Making Ends Meet in Verse.** The passages quoted will illustrate some of the many effects of the device that has been called "making ends meet in verse" — the pleasure of the expected but varying chime; the reinforcement of syntax and rhetorical emphasis when a strong masculine rhyme concurs with the end of a clause, sentence or stanza; the sudden grace of movement which may be lent by a feminine rhyme; the broadening of the comic by a pat coincidence of sound; the sometimes haunting effect of the limited consonance in partial rhymes. Cunning artificers in verse make it more than an auxiliary sound effect; they use it to enhance or contribute to the meaning of the words. When Pope satirized two contemporary pedants in the lines,

Yet ne'er one sprig of laurel graced these ribalds,
From slashing Bentley down to piddling Tibalds,

the rhyme, as W. K.Wimsatt has said, demonstrates "what it means to have a name like" that, with its implication that the scholar is as graceless as his appellation. And in one of its important functions, rhyme ties individual lines into the pattern of a *stanza.*

(3) Stanza

A stanza (Italian for "stopping place") is a grouping of the verse-lines in a poem. Usually the stanza of any given poem is marked. By a recurrent rhyme scheme, stanzas are also uniform in the number and lengths of the component lines. Some unrhymed poems, however, are divided into stanzaic units (for example, Collins' "Ode to Evening"), and some rhymed poems are composed of variable stanzas (for example, the *irregular ode*).

Of the great variety of English stanza forms, many have no special names and must be described by specifying the number of lines, the type and number of *feet* in each line and the pattern of the *rhyme.* Some stanzas, however, have been used so frequently that they have been given the convenience of a name, as follows :

(a) **Couplet.** A *couplet* is a pair of rhymed lines. The *octosyllabic couplet* has lines of eight syllables, usually consisting of four iambic feet. So in Marvell's "To His Coy Mistress" :

The grave's a fine and private place,
But none, I think, do there embrace.

Iambic pentameter couplets are called *heroic couplets* (discussed in a separate entry).

(b) **Triplet.** The *terct,* of *triplet,* is a stanza of three lines with a single rhyme. The lines may be the same length (as in Robert Herrick's "Upon Julia's Clothes", written in tercets of iambic tetrameter), or else of varying lengths. In Richard Crashaw's "Wishes to His Supposed Mistress", the lines of each tercet are successively in iambic dimeter, trimeter, and tetrameter :

Who e'er she be
That not impossible she
That shall command my heart and me.

(c) **Terza Rima.** *Terza rima* is composed of tercets which are interlinked, in that, each is joined to the one following by a common rhyme: *a b a, b c b, c d c* and so on. Dante composed his *Divine Comedy* in terza rima; but although Sir Thomas Wyatt introduced the form early in the sixteenth century, it has not been a common meter ion English, in which rhymes are much harder to find than in Italian. Shelley, however, used it brilliantly " Ode to the West Wind," and it occurs also in the poetry of Milton, Browning, and T.S. Eliot.

(d) **The Quatrain.** The *quatrain* or four line stanza is the most common in English versification, and is employed with various meters and rhyme schemes. The *ballad stanza* (in alternating four and three foot lines) is one common quatrain and the *heroic quatrain*, in iambic pentameter rhyming *a b a b*, is the stanza of Gray's "Elegy Written in a Country Churchyard."

(e) **Rhyme Royal.** *Rhyme royal* was introduced by Chaucer in *Troilus and Criseyde* and other narrative poems; it is believed to take its name, however, from its later use in the verses of King James-I of Scotland. It is a seven line, iambic pentameter stanza, rhyming *a b a b b c c.*

(f) **Ottava rima.** *Ottava rima*, as the Italian name indicates, has eight lines; it rhymes *c b a b a b c c.* Like terza rima and the sonnet, it was brought from Italian into English by Sir Thomas Wyatt. Although employed by a number of earlier poets, it is peculiarly the stanza which helped Byron discover what he was born to write, the satiric poem *Don Juan* :

Juan was taught from out the best edition,
Expurgated by learned men, who place,
Judiciously, from out the schoolboy's vision,
The grosser parts; but, fearful to deface
Too much their modest bard by this omission,
And pitying sore his mutilated case,
They only add them all in an appendix,
Which saves, in fact, the trouble of an index.

(G) **Spenserian Stanza.** *Spenserian stanza* is a still longer form devised by Edmund Spenser for *The Faerie Queene* – nine lines, the first eight iambic pentameter and the last iambic hexameter (an *Alexandrine*), rhyming *a b a b b c b c c.* Enchanted by spenser's gracious movement and music, many poets have attempted the form in spite of its difficulties.Its greatest successes have been in poems which, like *The Faerie Queene*, move in a leisurely way, with ample time for unrolling the richly textured stanzas : James Thomson's "The Castle of Indolence", Keats's "The Eve of St. Agnes", Shelley's "Adonais" and the narrative section of Tennyson's "The Lotus Eaters".

(H) **French Stanza Forms.** There are also various elaborate stanza forms imported from France, such as the rondeau, the villanelle and the triolet, containing intricate repetitions of rhymes and lines, which have been used mainly, but not exclusively, for *light verse.* Their revival by W. H. Auden, William Empson and other poets is a sign of renewed interest in high metrical artifice. Dylan Thomas' "Do not go gentle into that good night" is a villanelle; that is, it consists of five tercets and quatrain, all on two rhymes and with systematic later repetitions of lines 1 and 3 of the first tercet.

LITERARY COMPREHENSION

I. I was angry with my friend:
I told my wrath, my wrath did end.
I was angry with my foe:
I told it not, my wrath did grow.

And I watered it in fears,
Night and morning with my tears
And I sunned it with smiles,
And with soft deceitful wiles.

And it grew both day and night
Till it bore an apple bright.
And my foe beheld it shine,
And he knew that it was mine

And into my garden stole
When the night had veiled the pole;
In the morning glad I see
My foe outstretched beneath the tree.

1. What is your impression of the poet's attitude towards Christian forgiveness?

Ans. There is of course a subtle play of Christian themes of sin and forgiveness in the poem, but the mocking, ironical tone of the narrator gives it significance much beyond that. A parallel between the forbidden "tree of knowledge" and the poet's "poison tree" is rather too easy to draw and to confine its meaning merely to an exploration of the imperative and liberating power of Christian forgiveness would be to severely under read it. The poem is unmistakably about the ramifications of repressed anger and hypocrisy, a vice condemned in almost all Christian scriptures, and to that extent, the poet's attitude can be called Christian.

2. How does the poet feel at his foe's death ?

Ans. On the very first reading itself, what strikes us as peculiar and mysterious in the poem is the poet's tone. The simplicity of the first stanza seems to be dissolving in a more knowing and yet, more unfeeling voice as we progress towards the end and the end comes almost unexpectedly, leaving the reader in an aura of mystery, awe and incompleteness. The poet's or rather the narrator's, "gladness" at the death of his foe is not certainly the final message. There seems an inherent irony built into the poem throughout and the irony suddenly becomes manifold and dissipated as the extended metaphor stops.

3. Comment on the significance of the title of the poem.

Ans. The title of the poem is at once a condensed metaphor of the theme and an allusion to the forbidden "tree of knowledge". Apparently it is also the only, or the most appropriate title for this poem. However, this tree is not only the representation of the narrator's growing inner wrath, it is also something external, something conspicuous, the fruits of which "shine" in the open. Hence, the tree also stands for the hypocrisy, the deceitful curtesy of the narrator. Here do we recognize the full significance of the tree as a metaphor – something seductive and dangerous.

4. Do you think the poem is a confession of the poet's hypocrisy ?

Ans. A confession of hypocrisy it certainly is, but the tone is not repentant enough to make it obvious. There is mention of "tears" and "fears" which would have brought the poem closer to a confessional but for the conclusive lines. The narrator's gladness at his enemy's demise project all his fears and tears to be ultimately paying. The wrath consequently proves fatal to his enemy but does no harm to the narrator. Obviously, the confession is not a Christian confession of sinfulness. It is not a light-hearted sharing of a sense of triumph either. It is a straightforward and unmixed narration of a truth or truism in action

---

II. Who are these coming to the sacrifice ?
To what green altar, O mysterious priest,
Lead'st thou that heifer lowing at the skies,
And all her silken flanks with garlands dressed ?
What little town by river or sea shore,
Or mountain-built with peaceful citadel,
Is emptied of this folk, this pious morn ?
And, little town, thy streets for evermore
Will silent be; and not a soul to tell
Why thou art desolate, can e'er return.

1. Why does the poet say that the "little town" will remain "desolate" for ever ?

Ans. The stanza depicts a pagan sacrifice, a procession of simple folks led by the priest and the animal to be sacrificed. However, the entire scene has been depicted as transfixed for ever. There is no progress in the action. Here it appears, the poet is contemplating a sculpture or a piece of painting, and lamenting the process by which art renders things eternal. The people represented in the piece of art have been rendered static and wherever they might have come from they cannot go back. Interestingly the poet imagines a little town which must have been emptied of these people and it is going to remain empty for ever, as the people have fallen into the eternal trap of art.

2. What impression do you get of the poet's tone ?

Ans. The poet's voice borders on the mournful and the pensive, contemplating a scene that is frozen and silent. Its vocabulary suggests a loss, even a desolation, entailed in the process of contemplating eternity. There is an intense, sympathetic voice, juxtaposed with dense visual and spatial imagination which makes the stanza highly romantic and highly philosophical at once.

3. There is a series of questions in the stanza. Who are they addressed to ?

Ans. The questions are more rhetorical than curious. However, they give a sense of immediacy and intensity to the stanza. It is through these questions that the poet depicts the piece of art he is contemplating. So, though it might seem at the first instance that the poet is asking questions to the "mysterious priest", on repeated reading one cannot overlook the brilliance of these questions as a device to tease the readers' imagination.

4. What category do you think the poem should be put into ?

Ans. This poem, as is seen from this stanza, is a highly imaginative one contemplating on the painful process of immortalization through art. The theme is philosophical, without being moral or didactic, the flow is smooth and melodious without being strained and the voice of melancholy is evocative without being depressed. In a way the poem is Romantic for its far-fetched imagination and amoral theme. However it has nothing of the impassioned self-consciousness of the Romantics.

III. Though the goblins cuffed her and caught her,
Coaxed and fought her,
Bullied and besought her,
Scratched her, pinched her black as ink,
Kicked and knocked her
Mauled and mocked her,
Lizzie uttered not a word;
Would not open lip from lip
Lest they should cram a mouthful in :

But laughed in heart to feel the drip
Of juice that syrupped all her face,
And lodged in dimples of her chin,
And streaked her neck which quaked like curd.

1. Do you think the poem is written for children ?

Ans. The name 'Lizzie', the strangeness of the narrative and the restless rhyme, all point towards children's literature as that of Lewis Caroll, but its nasty ramifications stretch far beyond childhood and childish intransigence into the realm of sexual threat. The implied spiritual message of resisting evil, which is at once seductive and dangerous, also cannot be overlooked. Moreover, the poem is also about female self-assertion in the face of male dominance. Hence, though the poem has everything that children would like, it has as many things to make adult readers think.

2. What impression do you get of the goblins ?

Ans. The very word goblin reminds us of the small, ugly, mischievous creature of fairy tales. The narrative of the poem confirms it while adding further significance to it. They seem to be bent upon feeding Lizzie the mysterious juice for no apparent purpose. Thus, they stand for the kind of "motiveless malignity", ruthlessness and nastiness, that are attributed to evil.

3. Why does Lizzie keep her mouth shut ?

Ans. The way Lizzie keeps her mouth shut might remind us of any intransigent child, but the adult knowingness with which she laughs in her heart projects her as much more than a child. That she knew the taste of the syrup that she would die not to eat and also enjoyed it in heart, makes the apparent tyranny of the goblins seem ridiculous and trivial. Her mouth kept shut despite all kinds of threat and lure is a symbol of spiritual self-control and also of female self-assertion.

4. Can the poem be categorized as metaphysical ?

Ans. The term metaphysical has been so variously used by poets and critics that one cannot overlook its vagueness while applying it to particular poetic pieces. There is hardly any conceit in the poem as is often found in the metaphysical school, there is no violent bringing together of far-fetched ideas. However, the poem is not merely about physicality, its suggestiveness stretches it far beyond the physical images given in the narrative and hence it is metaphysical. Categories for literature are not watertight compartments more so in case of poetry.

IV. And as the smart ship grew
In stature grace and hue
In shadowy silent distance grew the iceberg too.
Alien they seemed to be:
No mortal eye could see
The intimate welding of their later history....

1. Can you relate the poem to any historical event ?

Ans. As soon as one reads the stanza, one is reminded of all those great and famous ships which had drowned in the sea after striking some hidden iceberg, more particularly of the Titanic. The last line almost confirms our guess that the poem is about a historical event, such as the drowning of the Titanic.

2. Do you think the poet is a fatalist ? Justify your answer.

Ans. The poet unmistakably appears to be a fatalist by asserting that the ship's drowning was pre-destined. "The intimate welding of their "later history" sounds typically fatalistic and passimistic. The line "No mortal eye could see" is a reflection on man's ignorance of destiny that works beyond his powers.

3. Do you think the poet sees nature as complicit with man's gloomy fate ?

Ans. The poem is about the sinking of a great ship and also a pessimistic assertion of its inevitability. There is hardly much description of nature, save the growing iceberg. If the iceberg is taken as a representation of nature, then that the poet sees it as complicit with man's sad fate is obvious. However, it is dubious to take the iceberg as a representation of nature without any clue.

4. Comment on the phrase "smart ship".

Ans. The phrase "smart ship" is not merely an ironical understatement of its "later history" but also a comment on the futility of all those grand human aspirations that destiny undoes. A ship is a symbol of man's victory over sea, or nature, and calling it smart might at first seem an appreciation of man's achievement. It is only when we are aware of its sad end that we realize the irony implicit in it.

V. Cold, delicately as the dark snow,
A fox's nose touches twig, leaf;
Two eyes serve a movement, that now
And again now, and now, and now
Sets neat prints in the snow,
Between trees.........

Across clearings, an eye,
A widening deepening greenness,
Brilliantly concentratedly,
Coming about its own business

Till, with a sudden sharp hot stink of fox
It enters the dark hole of the head.
The window is starless still; the clock ticks,
The page is printed.

1. What is the fox looking for ?

Ans. Even though there is no explicit mention of what the fox is looking for, it is obvious to imagine that it is looking for its food. However, the poem is not certainly about a fox searching its food. The fox is a metaphor, a metaphor for man's intellectual hunting for appropriate creative expressions. The touching of "twig, leaf" is a part of the process of creativity.

2. Do you think the poem is written in the symbolist tradition ?

Ans. There is a significant difference between a poem's being symbolic and its being in the symbolist tradition. The poet doesn't follow the symbolist tradition as such. The poem is an extended metaphor, comparing the fox with human intellect, and all the imageries are built upon this parallel.

3. Do you think the poet draws a parallel between animal and human activity ?

Ans. The poet, of course, draws a parallel between animal and human activity; however it is not a simple comparison between man and animal nature. The parallel is drawn as a metaphor and there seems to be no intention on part of the poet to compare human being with animals as such. In this poem, the animal and its animality loose importance in the face of what they have been compared to.

4. Explain the significance of the concluding line.

Ans. The concluding line "The page is printed" bears almost the entire load of the poem's significance. It is at its conclusion that we realize that the fox is not a fox and that its searching for food in a dark wood is only a metaphor for the creative process through which the intellect has to go, in order to find expression.

VI. On St. Valentine's Day, 1989, the last day of her life, the legendary popular singer Vina Apsara woke sobbing from a dream of human sacrifice in which she had been the intended victim. Bare-torsoed men resembling the actor Christopher Plummer, had been gripping her by the wrists and ankles. Her body was splayed out, naked and writhing, over a polished stone bearing the graven image of the snakebird Quetzalcoatl. The open mouth of the plumed serpent surrounded a dark hollow scooped out of the stone, and although her own mouth was stretched wide by her screams the only noise she could hear was the popping of flashbulbs; but before they could slit her throat, before her lifeblood could bubble into that terrible cup, she awoke at noon in the city of Guadalajara, Mexico, in an unfamiliar bed with a half-dead stranger by her side, a naked mestizo male in his early twenties, identified in the interminable press coverage that followed the catastrophe as Raul Paramo, the playboy heir of a well-known local construction baron, one of whose corporations owned the hotel.

She had been perspiring heavily and the sodden bedsheets stank of the meaningless misery of the nocturnal encounter. Raul Paramo was unconscious, white-lipped, and his body was galvanized, every few moments, by spasms which Vina recognized as being identical to her own dream writhings. After a few moments he began to make frightful noises deep in his windpipe, as if someone were slitting his throat, as if his blood were flowing out through the scarlet smile of an invisible wound into a phantom goblet. Vina, panicking, leapt from the bed, snatched up her clothes, the leather pants and gold-sequinned bustier in which she had made her final exit, the night before, from the stage of the city's convention centre. Contemptuously, despairingly, she had surrendered herself to this nobody, this boy less than half her age, she had selected him more or less at random from the backstage throng, the lounge lizards, the slick, flower-bearing suitors, the industrial magnates, the aristotrash, the drug underlords, the tequila princes, all with limousines and champagne and cocaine and may be even diamonds to bestow upon the evening's star.

1. Why was Vina perspiring when she woke up ?

Ans. Vina was perspiring as she had just woken up from a fearful nightmare. However, she was perspiring also because she had woken up at noon in the city of Mexico, where St. Valentine's Day may be expected to be hot at that time. There seems to be a connection between the heat of the atmosphere and the internal heat of her excitation.

2. What impression do you get of Vina's profession ?

Ans. The profession of a popular public figure such as of Vina has been exposed with ruthless precision in these passages. Not only being a popular singer she cannot hide from the public eye, but she cannot also share with them her loneliness. Thus, she is wary of both, the public and herself and treats both of them with contempt. Vina's behaviour may seem only natural when juxtaposed with the real life story of many popular female singers in the West, and that is how she becomes a representative of her profession.

3. Comment on the term 'aristotrash'.

Ans. The word "aristotrash' is a portmanteau word, a word formed by fusing two words with different meanings into one, in order to pack both their meanings into one word. Here the word also bears severe compression of both, Vina's feeling of contempt for such people and a comment on their moral disposition.

4. Comment on the significance of Vina's dream.

Ans. Vina's dream is not only a reflection of her anxiety, her feeling of insecurity and her loneliness, but also an intuition of her imminent death. Moreover, its erotic suggestions indicate that her dream is also a reflection of "the meaningless misery of the nocturnal encounter". If can be observed from the very appropriateness of this phrase to describe both, her sexual act with a stranger and her experience of the nightmare. A similar parallelism between death and sexual act (or love making) can be seen in the fact that the day of reference is both, "St. Valentine's Day" and "the last day of her life."

VII. Hemingway was trembling and Goethe clutched his arm: "Calm down, Ernest! Calm down, my friend. I understand you. What you've just been telling me reminds me of my dream. It was my last dream, after that I had no more or else they were confused and I could no longer distinguish them from reality. Imagine a small puppet theatre. I am behind the scenes, I control the puppets and recite the text. It is a performance of *Faust*. My *Faust*. Did you know that *Faust* is at its most beautiful when performed as a puppet play ? That's why I was so happy that no actors were present and I alone recited the lines, which on that day sounded more beautiful than ever before. And then, I suddenly glanced at the seats and saw that the theatre was empty. That puzzled me. Where was the audience? Was my *Faust* so boring that everyone had gone home ? Was I not even worth booing ? Bewildered, I turned round and I was aghast: I expected them out front, and instead they were at the back of the stage, gazing at me with wide open, inquisitive eyes. As soon as my glance met theirs, they began to applaud. And I realized that my *Faust* didn't interest them at all and that the show they wished to see was not the puppets I was leading around the stage, but me myself! Not *Faust*, but Goethe! And then I was overcome by a sense of horror very similar to what you described a moment ago. I felt they wanted me to say something, but I couldn't. My throat felt locked tight, I put down the puppets and left them lying on the brightly lit stage that nobody was watching. I tried to maintain a dignified composure, I walked silently to the coat-rack where my hat was hanging, I put it on my head and without a glance at all those curiosity-seekers, I left the theatre and went home. I tried to look neither to the right nor the left and especially not behind me, because I knew, they were following. I unlocked the heavy front door and slammed it behind me. I found an oil lamp and lit it. I lifted it with my shaking arm and went to my study, hoping that my rock collection would help me forget this unpleasant episode. But, before I had time to put the lamp down on the table, I happened to glance at the window. Their faces were pressed against the glass. Then I realized that I would never get rid of them, never, never. I realized that the lamp was lighting up my face, I saw it by those wide-open eyes that were scrutinizing me. I put out the lamp and yet I knew that I shouldn't have done so; now they realized that I was trying to hide from them, that I was afraid of them and this was sure to incite them all the more. But by now, my fear was stronger than my reason and I ran off into the bedroom, pulled the covers off the bed, threw them over my head, stood in the corner of the room, and pressed myself against the wall....'

1. Why was Hemingway trembling ?

Ans. Hemingway seems to be trembling with emotion and excitation. Peculiarly the fictional Hemingway described here behaves very similar to the way American novelist Earnest Hemingway behaved at times. In fact, as we read the entire passage we realize that it is the same historical Hemingway, put in a fictional situation where he could be talking about his anxiety at being persecuted by the public to Goethe, one who had died long before even Hemingway was born.

2. Why does Goethe leave the theatre ?

Ans. Goethe is intolerably weary of the fact that the public for whom he had been performing the puppet show is not only indifferent to his art, but also obtrusively interested in his own private self. He is embarrassed of being watched by an audience directly, without the clothing of his art and in disgust with the intrusive public leaves the theatre. The passage shows the longing for privacy of an author and his helplessness after once having been famous. The irony is implicit that the real puppet is Goethe himself and his life a ludicrous puppet show.

3. What do you know about the friendship of Goethe, the famous French poet, and Hemingway, the American Nobel Laureate ?

Ans. Hemingway and Goethe were historically born in different ages and there was no possibility of their being friends. This is a fictional piece in which the author imagines Goethe and Hemingway talking like contemporaries. By doing so, he deliberately shows the agonies of an author, regardless of time and space.

4. Comment on the genre of the prose passage. Do you think it is a part of Goethe's biography ?

Ans. This prose passage is not a part of any biography for the very impossibility of its being true. It seems to be a piece of post modernist fiction in which reality and imagination, history and fiction have been freely juxtaposed without an apology. Moreover, it is also a philosophical discussion about the comparative importance of an author and his work. It shows the predicament of an author at being treated as a book himself, at the dissipation of his identity as an individual in his public self.

VIII. She sought to answer such arguments by the familiar if oblique method of finding the gipsy life itself rude and barbarous; and so, in a short time, much bad blood was bred between them. Indeed, such differences of opinion are enough to cause bloodshed and revolution. Towns have been sacked for less, and a million martyrs have suffered at the stake rather than yield an inch upon any of the points here debated. No passion is stronger in the breast of man than the desire to make others believe as he believes. Nothing so cuts at the root of his happiness and fills him with rage as the sense that another rates low what he prizes high. Whigs and Tories, Liberal party and Labour party – for what do they battle except their own prestige ? It is not love of truth but desire to prevail that sets quarter against quarter and makes parish desire the downfall of parish. Each seeks peace of mind and subserviency rather than the triumph of truth and the exaltation of virtue - but these moralities belong and should be left to the historian, since they are as dull as ditch water.

1. Why does the female character argue and with whom ?

Ans. The female character seems to be arguing with one or more of the gypsies about relative merits of their lives. She argues because she thinks that in order to prove the merit of her own life, she must demean the gypsy life and speak of it with contempt.

2. Why are the Whigs and Tories at odds with one another ?

Ans. The Whigs and Tories, like any two rivals groups, are at odds with each other because they find prestige and self-respect only in putting themselves against something that they find as opposite in belief or method to themselves. They are not really interested in who is wrong and who is right, the entire focus of their effort being the downfall of their opponents.

3. Does the author mean that it is only the historians who seek truth ?

Ans. The author describes here the general psyche that leads to feuds, rather than his own opinion, though the description couldn't be entirely without an authorial opinion. The fact, that people think "triumph of truth and the exaltation of virtue" belong to the historian, is ironical again. If all battles for truth and all quests for virtue in human history are sheer attempts at self-aggrandizement than the historian's finding, such "moralities" is ironical. The historian can only record history, but cannot reconstruct it. Hence what he reconstructs is fiction and not history. That makes morality itself fictional, a part of history that never happened.

4. Why do people fall out according to the author ?

Ans. People fall out in asserting their differences of opinion, and in this feud what matters the least is who is on the right side; the only matter of concern being who is on one's own side and who is on the opposite side. Towns are destroyed, martyrs are killed and human blood is shed like water – all for the sake of proving oneself right. This reflects man's love neither for truth nor for virtue, but an irrational and idiotic intransigence, a stagnant and putrid mind.

IX. At nine o'clock in the morning, towards the end of November, the Warsaw train was approaching Petersburg at full speed. It was thawing, and so damp and foggy that, it was difficult to distinguish anything ten paces from the line to right or left of the carriage windows. Some of the passengers were returning from abroad, but the third-class compartments were most crowded, chiefly with people of humble rank, who had come a shorter distance on business. All of course were tired and shivering, their eyes were heavy after the night's journey, and all their faces were pale and yellow to match the fog.

In one of the third-class carriages, two passengers had, from early dawn, been sitting facing one another by the window. Both were young men, not very well dressed, and travelling with little luggage; both were of rather striking appearance, and both showed a desire to enter into conversation. If they had both known what was remarkable in one another at that moment, they would have been surprised at the chance which had so strangely brought them opposite one another in a third-class carriage of the Warsaw train. One of them was a short man about twenty-seven, with almost black curly hair and small, grey, fiery eyes. He had a broad and flat nose and high cheek bones. His thin lips were continually curved in an insolent, mocking and even with a malicious smile. But the high and well–shaped forehead redeemed the ignoble lines of the lower part of the face. What was particularly striking about the young man's face was its death-like pallor, which gave him a look of exhaustion in spite of his sturdy figure, and at the same time an almost painfully passionate expression, out of keeping with his coarse and insolent smile and the hard and conceited look in his eyes. He was warmly dressed in a full, black, sheepskin-lined overcoat, and had not felt the cold at night, while his shivering neighbour had been exposed to the chill and damp of a Russian November night, for which he was evidently unprepared. He had a fairly thick and full cloak with a big hood.

1. Why were the third-class compartments most crowded ?

Ans. The third-class compartments were most crowded because it charged less for travelling and suited the "people of humble rank". This is an indirect comment on the fact that the people belonging to the lower strata of economic life are the most numerous in Russia as elsewhere. The impression of poverty is reinforced when we find the two characters being described "not very well dressed, and travelling with little luggage."

2. What impression do you get of the description of the physiognomy of the characters.

Ans. The author is persistent and particular about the physiognomy of the characters. The countenance of the characters as described in these passages is not merely an introduction to their appearance, it is also an introduction to what the characters actually are, their economic, social and moral condition. The physiognomy is a mirror of personality. The 'smile' is 'malicious', the 'look' is 'conceited' and 'the high and well-shaped forehead redeemed the ignoble lines of the lower part of the face."

3. What do you mean by 'death-like pallor' in this passage.

Ans. The face being described as having a "death-like pallor" is a condensed expression of its exhaustion, its suffering the severe cold of the November night in Russia and also its sickness. The expression "death-like" juxtaposes at once pity and contempt, on part of the observer and suffering and indifference on part of the character.

4. In which century is the narrative set according to you ?

Ans. The narrative is most probably set in 19th century Russia. That it is the description of a train journey, rules out the possibility of the setting being prior to 19th century. However everything starting from the attire and appearance of the characters to the overcrowded train travelling from Poland to Russia gives the impression of a setting that cannot be modern. It is the time when train was one of the chief means of travelling between countries and that is suggestive of the later part of the 19th century.

X. So, it was in Paris I walked with the policeman and talked with him, and found him everywhere, in shop windows, with big bulging eyes and each eye a wonder to see. I saw eyes in Paris bookshop, windows such as I have never seen anywhere, small eyes, big eyes, green eyes, white-feathery eyes, lathery eyes, parroty eyes, pepper eyes and progressive eyes – red eyes for the red and all the world grew into Red beauty – (and, this you will find, in rue Racine) – and green eyes and scarlet eyes, soutane and sepulchre beads and biblical eyes – you find them just behind in smutty shops with big squares and courtyards and bright red geraniums at the bay windows – sooty eyes bespeaking of paradise, yellow eyes Luxembourg, eyes of the young, eyes of children and lovers and of the autumnal falling leaves – everywhere you see eyes in Paris, and they all had colours and I loved them. I lived in rue Servandoni later – and had two eyes there that had needle connection and logic was its palaetiology. For, on the point of the needle, was my love born – and it started stitching my tatterment. Oh, the love-needle, the pertinence, the power, and the purity of the stitching needle. My heart was made into a Hindu sack with prayer-verses on the top as of Benares – and I counted the doubtful beads. I was virtuous and I took on assigned form. The needle stitched and stitched me, and I took on a white and wandlike shape. I became a magician of looks, and I gave eyes to many. I opened a shop of Hindu eyes – I the policeman– and Oh, what a chatter and a clamour was there. God, God is my business, I cried – Hindu gods. Four annas a hundred tricks – standing on the nose and breathing through the umbilical stitch, practising celibacy through baths and kundalini – etc., etc., – eating milk and nuts to walk in the air, eating bitter neem leaves and sherbet for swallowing nails and toothbrushes and broken glass – for telling the future – motor cars, mansions and marriages, and all, fortunes – I opened such a shop. The trade was good. I did much business. The Municipal Council of Perpignan —for I had moved there by now– voted me a certificate of fine conduct. And all the virgins came to my confessions. I dealt in potions that increased physiological virginity – gave no scratches or itches or leucorrhoea – You touched me and you were cured. It was wonderful. And God was the message they got. I was virtuous and good. And I grew big. I became fashionable. Newspapers spoke of me. I was the policeman of God, and my certificates hung on all my four walls. I was given the *Legion d'Honneur.* II class, God seemed to speak to me from the heavens every night – and all day all night the logical needle stitched my sores, and when I woke up, I had a good bath and I looked so fresh and young. I could walk the Promenade des Anglais with the agility of a tennis player. They said, here goes the Policeman of God – and later they came and sate me by them in chaiseslongues, and as the sun poured on me tender and golden, I became a legitimate divinity. I had fruits and flowers offered to me, and I was right happy. I was God.

1. Why is the narrator walking with the policeman ?

Ans. The narrator is walking with the policeman who is neither a real policeman as such nor outside himself. It is only when we read the entire passage that we realize that the policeman is the narrator himself. The policeman here is at once a symbol of vigilance and duty. It reminds one of voltaire : "Civilization is the crossroad where the policeman stands".

2. What is the narrator's occupation ?

Ans. The narrator calls himself the 'Policeman of God', which at once shows the narrator's pride in his occupation as a Hindu priest or 'holy man' and the author's sarcastic irony. This prose piece is a biting satire on all such fake 'holy men' who find recognition and material prosperity abroad as representatives of God by manipulation of Hindu rituals and superstitions.

3. What do you mean by "physiological virginity" ?

Ans. The 'physiological virginity' is another ascerbic irony, which exposes the falsehood of both the narrator and of those so-called-virgins who came to him. He dealt in potions that helped in avoiding the physical signs of not being a virgin and thus "increased physiological virginity". That virginity was physiological in the same way that the narrator practised celibacy through baths and kundalini. Such practices also reflect the severe distortion in meaning of words such as purity, virginity and virtuosity in the modern society, particularly the West.

4. Comment on the tone of voice the author adapts in this passage.

Ans. The tone of voice is sarcastic and full of ironical undertones. The boasting of "*Legion d'Honneur*", the metaphor of "a Hindu sack with prayer-verses on the top as of Benares" for the narrator's heart, the awarding of "the certificate of fine conduct", the expression "legitimate divinity" and the concluding sentence, "I was God" – every small detail in the passage is sarcastic and ironical. However it is not a simple irony. It is not deliberate on part of the narrator and even the author, having an autobiographical narrator, makes no effort to make the irony obvious. It is an indirect, subtle, and complex irony interspersed with symbols.

ADDITIONAL COMPREHENSION

PASSAGE 1

I have often noticed that we are inclined to endow our friends with the stability of type that literary characters acquire in the reader's mind. No matter how many times we reopen "King Lear," never shall we find the good king banging his tankard in high revelry, all woes forgotten, at a jolly reunion with all three daughters and their lapdogs. Never will Emma rally, revived by the sympathetic salts in Flaubert's father's timely tear. Whatever evolution this or that popular character has gone through between the book covers, his fate is fixed in our minds, and, similarly, we expect our friends to follow this or that logical and conventional pattern we have fixed for them.... Any deviation in the fates we have ordained would strike us as not only anomalous but unethical. We would prefer not to have known at all our neighbor, the retired hot-dog stand operator, if it turns out he has just produced the greatest book of poetry his age has seen.

1. The passage argues that
   (A) "stability of type" is more common in reallife than in literature
   (B) it is a waste of time to reread works of literature
   (C) people never really betray each other the way that fictional characters do
   (D) we expect humans to act as consistently as fictional characters do
2. The passage calls into question the concept of
   (A) mimesis (B) catharsis
   (C) hamartia (D) inmediasres
3. The passage refers explicitly to
   (A) Crime and Punishment
   (B) Don Quixote
   (C) Madame Bovary
   (D) Anna Karenina
4. The passage appears in a work in which a
   (A) man falsely believes himself to be a medieval knight
   (B) woman is made to wear a red letter on her bodice
   (C) man remains youthful while a portrait of him ages
   (D) man becomes obsessed with his landlady's twelve-year-old daughter

ANSWERS

1. (D) 2. (A) 3. (C) 4. (D)

PASSAGE 2

Let others better mould the running mass
Of metals, and inform the breathing brass,
And soften into flesh a marble face;
Plead better at the bar; describe the skies,
And when the stars descend, and when they rise.
But, Rome! 'tis thine alone, with awful sway,
To rule mankind, and make the world obey,
Disposing peace and war thy own majestic way;
To tame the proud, the fettered slave to free:
These are imperial arts, and worthy thee.

1. Which of the following most accurately describes the passage?
   (A) The speaker argues that the fate of empires can be discovered by interpreting celestial events.
   (B) The speaker defends himself as a loyal citizen but expresses regret over the state of the arts in Rome.
   (C) The speaker compliments Greek culture for its achievements in art and science, and singles out administration as a Roman art.
   (D) The speaker deplores the widespread use of slaves in the ancient world.
2. As used in line 6, "sway" most nearly means
   (A) power (B) resolve
   (C) wisdom (D) tact
3. Line 9 presents an example of
   (A) anaphora
   (B) apostrophe
   (C) chiasmus
   (D) periphrasis
4. Which of the following words or phrases has been omitted as understood after "worthy" (line 10) ?
   (A) of (B) before
   (C) beside (D) according to

5. Which line of the translated passage is an Alexandrine?
(A) 2 (B) 3
(C) 5 (D) 8

6. The passage is from
(A) Chapman's translation of Homer
(B) Dryden's translation of Virgil
(C) Sandys' translation of Ovid
(D) Longfellow's translation of Dante

ANSWERS

1. (C) 2. (A) 3. (C) 4. (A) 5. (D) 6. (B)

PASSAGE 3

When Eleanor laid her head on her pillow that night, her mind was anxiously intent on some plan by which she might extricate her father from his misery; and, in her warm-hearted enthusiasm, self-sacrifice was decided on as the means to be adopted. Was not so good an Agamemnon worthy of an Iphigenia? She would herself personally implore John Bold to desist from his undertaking; she would explain to him her father's sorrows, the cruel misery of his position; she would tell him how her father would die if he were thus dragged before the public and exposed to such unmerited ignominy; she would appeal to his old friendship, to his generosity, to his manliness, to his mercy; if need were, she would kneel to him for the favour she would ask;—but before she did this, the idea of love must be banished.... She could not be understood as saying, Make my father free and I am the reward. There would be no sacrifice in that;—not so had Jephthah's daughter saved her father;—not so could she show to that kindest, dearest of parents how much she was able to bear for his good.

1. The passage indicates that Eleanor
(A) has no respect for John Bold
(B) fears that her father dislikes John Bold
(C) wants to be a heroine by saving her father
(D) secretly mistrusts her father

2. Eleanor is characterized by her propensity to
(A) see herself as the object of everyone's romantic intentions
(B) excuse her father's shortcomings as charming foibles
(C) see plots and schemes behind apparently chance circumstances
(D) compare herself to figures from the Bible and classical literature

3. According to Eleanor, "sacrifice" (lines 4 and 18) should involve
(A) eliminating the possibility of marriage so that her actions appear disinterested

(B) relinquishing her dowry to repay the money owed John Bold
(C) pretending to admire qualities in John Bold that he does not have
(D) risking death to secure her father's independence

4. The style of the passage features
(A) apostrophe
(B) soliloquy
(C) stream of consciousness
(D) ekphrasis

5. Which of the following verbs is used in a way that is no longer idiomatic?
(A) "laid" (line 1)
(B) "extricate" (line 3)
(C) "implore" (line 7)
(D) "were" (line 14)

6. The two characters mentioned in line 6 belong to the house of
(A) Atreus
(B) David
(C) Thebes
(D) Athens

7. Jephthah and Agamemnon are associated because both of them
(A) murdered their daughters in an angry rage
(B) banished their daughters for insulting them
(C) abdicated in favor of their daughters
(D) had their daughters put to death to fulfill a religious vow

ANSWERS

1. (C) 2. (D) 3. (A) 4. (D) 5. (D) 6. (A) 7. (D)

PASSAGE 4

I stretched thy joints to make thee even feet,
Yet still thou run'st more hobbling than is meet;
In better dress to trim thee was my mind,
But nought save homespun cloth i'th'house I find.
In this array 'mongst vulgars may'st thou roam.
In critic's hands beware thou dost not come,
And take thy way where yet thou art not known;
If for thy father asked, say thou hadst none;
And for thy mother, she alas is poor,
Which caused her thus to send thee out of door.

1. The speaker is comparing
(A) a father's and a mother's love
(B) disabled and able-bodied people
(C) homemade clothing and manufactured cloth
(D) a book and a child

2. The word "feet" in line 1 refers to
(A) a person's height
(B) lengths of fabric
(C) metrical units of poetry
(D) arduous tasks

3. As used in line 5, "vulgars" refers to
(A) immoral people
(B) people of different races
(C) common people
(D) dead languages

4. In line 8, "If for thy father asked" is best understood to mean
(A) before your father asks
(B) when your father is asked
(C) because your father asked
(D) if you are asked who your father is

5. Lines 8-10 are best interpreted to mean that

(A) the author resents her parents for failing to provide for her
(B) the author acknowledges her mother's sacrifices in rearing her alone
(C) the author lacks the means to craft her work skillfully before publishing it
(D) embarrassment has motivated the author to hide her humble origins

6. The poem is written in
(A) heroic couplets
(B) terzarima
(C) ballad measure
(D) blank verse

ANSWERS

1. (D) 2. (C) 3. (C) 4. (D) 5. (C) 6. (A)

PASSAGE 5

He talked of fore-grounds, distances, and second distances—side-screens and perspectives—lights and shades;—and Catherine was so hopeful a scholar, that when they gained the top of Beechen Cliff, she voluntarily rejected the whole city of Bath, as unworthy to make part of the landscape. Delighted with her progress, and fearful of wearying her with too much wisdom at once, Henry suffered the subject to decline, and by an easy transition from a piece of rocky fragment and the withered oak, which he had placed near its summit, to oaks in general, to forests, the inclosure of them, waste lands, crown lands and government, he shortly found himself arrived at politics; and from politics, it was an easy step to silence.

1. The passage is based on the eighteenth-century concept of the
(A) picturesque (B) grotesque
(C) sublime (D) fortunate fall

2. As used in line 3, "hopeful" most nearly means
(A) optimistic (B) anxious
(C) gullible (D) promising

3. In line 12, the "inclosure of [forests]" refers to which of the following practices?
(A) The attempt to make a group of trees appear like a bower or habitation of some kind
(B) The claiming of once-common land as private property
(C) The separation of forests from adjacent lands used exclusively for agriculture
(D) The segregation of a certain species of trees, such as oak, from other kinds of trees

4. The tone of the narrator is best described as one of
(A) matter-of-factness
(B) political stridency
(C) amused detachment
(D) sympathetic identification with Catherine

ANSWERS

1. (A) 2. (D) 3. (B) 4. (C)

PASSAGE 6

What happens to a dream deferred?
Does it dry up
like a raisin in the sun?
Or fester like a sore —
And then run?
Does it stink like rotten meat?
Or crust and sugar over—
like a syrupy sweet?
Maybe it just sags
Like a heavy load.
Or does it explode ?

1. The questions in the poem convey a sense of
(A) suspicion (B) melancholy
(C) outrage (D) resolve

2. The lines employ all of the following poetic devices EXCEPT
(A) alliteration (B) simile
(C) parallelism (D) oxymoron

3. The dream is "deferred" (line 1) because
(A) one does not at present have time to pursue it
(B) one does not at present have the technology to achieve it
(C) fulfilling it is not profitable
(D) prejudice prevents its fulfillment

4. The final italicized line is different from the others in that it
(A) marks a shift of voice from one speaker to another
(B) moves from predicting the future to reporting on the present
(C) moves from rhetorical questions to a standard interrogative
(D) presents the dream not as passive but as active, even violent

5. The poem provided the title for a play by
(A) James Baldwin
(B) MayaAngelou
(C) August Wilson
(D) Lorraine Hansberry

ANSWERS

1. (C) 2. (D) 3. (D) 4. (D) 5. (D)

PASSAGE 7

I happened soon after to attend one of his Sermons, in the Course of which I perceived he intended to finish with a Collection, and I silently resolved he should get nothing from me. I had in my Pocket a Handful of Copper Money, three or four silver Dollars, and five Pistoles in Gold. As he proceeded I began to soften, and concluded to give the Coppers. Another Stroke of his Oratory made me asham'd of that, and determin'd me to give the Silver; and he finish'd so admirably, that I emptied my Pocket wholly into the Collector's Dish, Gold and all. At this sermon there was also one of our Club, who being of my Sentiments respecting the Building in Georgia, and suspecting a Collection might be intended, had by Precaution emptied his Pockets before he came from home; towards the Conclusion of the Discourse however, he felt a strong Desire to give, and apply'd to a Neighbor who stood near him to borrow some Money for the purpose.

1. The passage shows the speaker struggling with competing impulses toward
(A) selfishness and altruism
(B) bigotry and tolerance
(C) vindictiveness and forgiveness
(D) deception and honesty

2. The progression in the passage from copper to silver to gold parallels the
(A) main character's growing impatience with the length of the sermon
(B) main character's increasing faith in religious dogma
(C) increasing power of the sermon to alter the main character's will
(D) growing rate of inflation during the period in which the passage was written

3. Which of the following verbs is used in the passage in a way that is no longer idiomatic?
(A) "happened" (line 1)
(B) "perceived" (line 2)
(C) "resolved" (line 3)
(D) "concluded" (line 7)

4. The passage is taken from
(A) Thomas Paine's *The Age of Reason*
(B) Thomas Jefferson's *Notes on the State of Virginia*
(C) Olaudah Equiano's *Interesting Narrative*
(D) Benjamin Franklin's *Autobiography*

ANSWERS

1. (A) **2.** (C) **3.** (D) **4.** (D)

PASSAGE 8

It was she who used to come between me and my paper when I was writing reviews. It was she who bothered me and wasted my time and so tormented me that at last I killed her. You who come of a younger and happier generation may not have heard of her—you may not know what I mean by the..... I will describe her as shortly as I can. She was intensely sympathetic. She was immensely charming. She was utterly unselfish. She excelled in the difficult arts of family life. She sacrificed herself daily.... In short she was so constituted that she never had a mind or a wish of her own, but preferred to sympathize always with the minds and wishes of others. . . . And when I came to write I encountered her with the very first words. The shadow of her wings fell on my page; I heard the rustling of her skirts in the room. Directly, that is to say, I took my pen in my hand to review that novel by a famous man, she slipped behind me and whispered: "My dear, you are a young woman. You are writing about a book that has been written by a man. Be sympathetic; be tender; flatter; deceive; use all the arts and wiles of our sex. Never let anybody guess that you have a mind of your own...." And she made as if to guide my pen. I now record the one act for which I take some credit to myself.... I turned upon her and caught her by the throat. I did my best to kill her. My excuse, if I were to be had up in a court of law, would be that I acted in self-defence. Had I not killed her she would have killed me.

1. The passage mainly concerns the
(A) unresolved murder of a beautiful woman
(B) jealous rivalry that undermines a happy marriage
(C) importance of civility in professional interactions between men and women
(D) interior conflict between a writer's need for independence and her internalized norms of femininity

2. The name of the figure that completes line 6 is the
(A) Angel in the House
(B) Madwoman in the Attic
(C) Lady of the Lake
(D) Belle of the Ball

3. In her effects on the speaker, the figure described is implicitly contrasted with a
(A) Fate (B) Fury
(C) Gorgon (D) Muse

4. The passage has most directly influenced which of the following?
(A) Psychoanalytic criticism
(B) Feminist criticism
(C) New Criticism
(D) New Historicism

5. The passage is by
(A) Mary Wollstonecraft
(B) Mary Shelley
(C) Edgar Allan Poe
(D) Virginia Woolf

ANSWERS

1. (D) 2. (A) 3. (D) 4. (B) 5. (D)

PASSAGE 9

When my grave is broke up again
Some second guest to entertain
(For graves have learn'd that woman-head
To be to more than one a bed),
And he that digs it, spies
A bracelet of bright hair about the bone,
Will he not let us alone,
And think that there a loving couple lies,
Who thought that this device might be some way
To make their souls, at the last busy day,
Meet at this grave, and make a little stay?

1. Lines 1-2 refer to the
(A) practice of using existing graves to accommodate new corpses
(B) belief that after death the soul could transmigrate into another body
(C) custom of burying some material possessions in the grave along with the deceased
(D) time when the poet will be buried in a plot next to that of his mistress

2. In line 3, "woman-head" is best understood to mean a woman's
(A) physical remains
(B) spiritual rebirth
(C) frustrated aspirations
(D) characteristic behavior

3. Lines 1-4 allude to
(A) sexual inconstancy
(B) religious heresy
(C) feminine vanity
(D) political iconoclasm

4. In line 9, "this device" refers to the poet's
(A) having his family crest on his coffin
(B) pretending to have married his mistress before she died
(C) having tied some of his mistress' hair around his wrist
(D) writing the poem as a way of eternalizing his love

5. In line 10, "the last busy day" refers to the day
(A) that the poem was written
(B) that the poet and his mistress agreed to part
(C) that the poet visited the grave of his mistress to mourn her untimely death
(D) of judgment for the souls of the living and the dead

6. The lines are the opening of
(A) "Song: To Celia " by Ben Jonson
(B) "The Relic" by John Donne
(C) "The Altar" by George Herbert
(D) "Home Burial" by Robert Frost

ANSWERS

1. (A) **2.** (D) **3.** (A) **4.** (C) **5.** (D) **6.** (B)

PASSAGE 10

I saw the best minds of my generation destroyed by madness, starving hysterical naked,
dragging themselves through the negro streets at dawn looking for an angry fix,
angelheaded hipsters burning for the ancient heavenly connection to the starry dynamo in the machinery of night,
who poverty and tatters and hollow-eyed and high sat up smoking in the supernatural darkness of cold-water flats floating
across the tops of cities contemplating jazz,
who bared their brains to Heaven under the El and saw Mohammedan angels staggering on tenement roofs illuminated,
who passed through universities with radiant cool eyes hallucinating Arkansas and Blake-light tragedy among the scholars
of war

1. The poetic form of the excerpt most reflects the influence of
(A) Carl Sandburg
(B) Walt Whitman
(C) Langston Hughes
(D) Robert Frost

2. The last three lines exhibit the rhetorical structure called
(A) antithesis
(B) anaphora
(C) apostrophe
(D) chiasmus

3. The reference to "the El" in line 5 helps develop a thematic link between
(A) sanity and insanity
(B) poverty and materialism
(C) race and gender
(D) the celestial and the urban

4. The reference to Blake in line 6 reinforces the idea of the poem as
(A) apocalyptic vision
(B) personal confession
(C) political advocacy
(D) ascetic restraint

5. The phrase "scholars of war" (line 6) is used to
(A) refer to advanced students of combat history
(B) signal contempt for cutthroat competition in academia
(C) allude to military-industrial funding for academic research
(D) condemn communist sympathizers in the government

6. The author is
(A) JackKerouac
(B) William Burroughs
(C) Bob Dylan
(D) Allen Ginsberg

ANSWERS

1. (B) **2.** (B) **3.** (D) **4.** (A) **5.** (C) **6.** (D)

UNIT V

LANGUAGE: BASIC CONCEPTS, THEORIES AND PEDAGOGY ENGLISH IN USE

ENGLISH LANGUAGE LEARNING THEORIES

INTRODUCTION

The language teacher, not being a theoretician, usually depends on the research done by linguists, psycho-linguists and socio-linguists. The teacher practices the theories put forward by the theoreticians, including linguists and educationalists, in the class. These theories which eventually lead to methods help the teacher to create techniques to teach a foreign language in the classroom effectively. Thus language theories guide a teacher to select and follow an approach to the teaching of any new language.

A modern psychological approach to language is based on moves around two basic theories: behaviourist and cognitive theories of language. Both the theories try to provide an explanation to language learning and present different answers. Behaviourists consider language learning as a process of conditioning and the expected goal in learning is achieved by a series of stimulus and responses. According to behaviourists, learning takes place due to the relationship between stimulus and learners' responses to it. Learner, as a result of this conditioning, will be able to give the expected response and then it can be said that he has learned. Thus practicing the lesson should be important activity of the language learner. Behaviourists believe that these responses of the learners to the stimulus are automatic and not a result of any deliberate thought. During 1930s and 40s, linguists were influenced by Behaviourism and which resulted in the publication of teaching materials based on behaviourist theory.

Cognitive theorists say that each learner has a cognitive structure into which any new learning is absorbed. Cognitive theory is also called 'mentalistic' because all cognitive interpretation of language learning rests upon the neuro-psychological base of thought. Cognitive theoreticians consider language learning as a 'meaningful process'. Cognitive theory validates Experiential Language Learning because there the learner will understand the new input and connect it with previous inputs or experiences.

Language Learning Strategies

Learning strategies are used by the learners to help one to acquire, to take input, (Rewrite) and use the information, to make ones learning, quick, simple, more effective which can be passed on to new situations. A learner wants to learn English language to communicate in English fluently and correctly. He needs English in business in a restaurant, to ask directions, etc. Using learning strategies will not enable him to use the language in such situations. Using different learning strategies in a reasonable course of time will enable the learner to use the language successfully. Linguists call it a 'strategy chain', a set of interconnected and supportive strategies. Language autonomy can be acquired with the help of learning strategies. Managing one's own learning process is a must for autonomy. Self-efficacy also can be improved by learning strategies.

There are six major learning strategies: cognitive, mnemonic, metacognitive, compensatory, affective and social.

1. **Cognitive.** Learners already have many of information. He is always updating this information with new information which he collects from various sources. Cognitive strategy helps learners to make an association with the previous and new knowledge or information. Analysing, guessing, inductive and deductive reasoning, rearranging the information and taking regular notes of the information are examples of cognitive strategies.
2. **Mnemonic strategy.** Mnemonic strategy assists learners to connect a newly learned knowledge with what they have already learned and know. These are useful for remembering knowledge in a systematic way in different ways. Examples are by sounds as in rhyming, by body movement as learners follow teachers' command, particular point in a black board or page. Mnemonic strategy connects old & newly learned knowledge stimulus-response manner. This drawback does not prevent learners to use Mnemonic strategy to learn vocabulary items and grammar principles.
3. **Metacognitive strategy.** Many types of Metacognitive strategies exist. (i) They assist learners to manage themselves as learners, (ii) In knowledge seeking process, (iii) Choose particular tasks for learning. This strategy will help the learner to focus on his area of interest his needs and the best style of learning. Each learning style approach helps to learn a language. Learner can select the learning style which suits him best. Metacognitive strategy helps a learner to select the right resource and fix a goal for language learning. If the goals are not clear the learning process will be obstructed. Metacognitive strategy also helps the learner to handle particular language tasks. Selecting resources to solve these particular tasks also come under this Metacognitive strategy.
4. **Compensatory Strategies.** Guessing the meaning or idea while listening and reading fills a learning gap. Likewise compensatory or communicative strategies assist learners while speaking and writing. Using synonym and gesturing is a strategy for speaking and use of synonym will fill the knowledge gaps while writing. Cohen (1977) thinks that this strategy is suitable for language use only. Little (1999) and Oxford (1990) are of the opinion that this strategy suits both language use and language learning.
5. **Affective strategies.** A learner can identify his feelings like anger, unhappiness and anxiety and s/he can be aware of such situations which produce such feelings. Such in language learning process positive attitudes and beliefs can increase the learner's motivation and will improve his language learning.
6. **Social strategies.** Social strategies are an integral part of communicative language learning. Social strategies help students to know about the culture of the target language speaking people. Using this strategy learners can learn with others discuss problem questions, etc.

Rubin (1975) believes that the following properties will make a good learner if s/he is a willing and accurate guesser, has a strong drive to communicate, willing to make mistakes, practice, monitors his or her own and others' speech, and pays attention to meaning

A learner can be taught with different learning strategies. The result depends on cultural back ground and contents of the teacher's material.

Characteristics and Features of Language

Language is, today, an inseparable part of human society. Human civilization has been possible only through language. It is through language only that humanity has come out of the stone age and has developed science, art and technology in a big way. Language is a means of communication, it is arbitrary, it is a system of systems. We know that Speech is primary while writing is secondary.

Language is human so it differs from animal communication in several ways. Language can have scores of characteristics but the following are the most important ones: language is arbitrary, productive, creative, systematic, vocalic, social, non-instinctive and conventional. These characteristics of language set human language apart from animal communication. Some of these features may be part of animal communication; yet they do not form part of it in total.

Language is Arbitrary. Language is arbitrary in the sense that there is no inherent relation between the words of a language and their meanings or the ideas conveyed by them. There is no reason why a female adult human being be called a woman in English, aurat in Urdu, Zen in Persian and Femine in French. The choice of a word selected to mean a particular thing or idea is purely arbitrary but once a word is selected for a particular referent, it comes to stay as such. It may be noted that had language not been arbitrary, there would have been only one language in the world.

Language is Social. Language is a set of conventional communicative signals used by humans for communication in a community. Language in this sense is a possession of a social group, comprising an indispensable set of rules which permits its members to relate to each other, to interact with each other, to co-operate with each other; it is a social institution. Language exists in society; it is a means of nourishing and developing culture and establishing human relations.

Language is Symbolic. Language consists of various sound symbols and their graphological counterparts that are employed to denote some objects, occurrences or meaning. These symbols are arbitrarily chosen and conventionally accepted and employed. Words in a language are not mere signs or figures, but symbols of meaning. The intelligibility of a language depends on a correct interpretation of these symbols.

Language is Systematic. Although language is symbolic, yet its symbols are arranged in a particular system. All languages have their system of arrangements. Every language is a system of systems. All languages have phonological and grammatical systems, and within a system there are several sub-systems. For example, within the grammatical system we have morphological and syntactic systems, and within these two sub-systems we have systems such as those of plural, of mood, of aspect, of tense, etc.

Language is Vocal. Language is primarily made up of vocal sounds only produced by a physiological articulatory mechanism in the human body. In the beginning, it appeared as vocal sounds only. Writing came much later, as an intelligent attempt to represent vocal sounds. Writing is only the graphic representation of the sounds of the language. So the linguists say that speech is primary.

Language is Non-instinctive, Conventional. No language was created in a day out of a mutually agreed upon formula by a group of humans. Language is the outcome of evolution and convention. Each generation transmits this convention on to the next. Like all human institutions languages also change and die, grow and expand. Every language then is a convention in a community. It is non-instinctive because it is acquired by human beings. No body gets a language in heritage; he acquires it because he an innate ability.

Language is Productive and Creative. Language has creativity and productivity. The structural elements of human language can be combined to produce new utterances, which neither the speaker nor his hearers may ever have made or heard before any, listener, yet which both sides understand without difficulty. Language changes according to the needs of society.

Finally, language has other characteristics such as Duality referring to the two systems of sound and meaning, Displacement which means the ability to talk across time and space, Humanness which means that animals cannot acquire it,Universality which refers to the equilibrium across humanity on linguistic grounds,Competence and Performance which means that language is innate and produced is society and furthermore, language is culturally transmitted. It is learnt by an individual from his elders, and is transmitted from one generation to another. Thus using J. Firth's term, language is a 'polysystametic'. It is also open to be studied from multifaceted angles.

Dialect, Sociolect, Idiolect

Different situations and different people create varieties in the way the language is spoken. The variety is divided into three distinct features: the dialect, sociolect and idiolect.

Dialect is a variety in spoken language. This language has its own vocabulary, grammar and pronunciation. A sector in dialect is the regional dialect; where the geographical position of a country effects the language spoken. An example is the difference between the Yorkshire dialect and Cockney dialect. There is also a difference between the Urban and Rural Areas. The vocabulary changes in a dialect, for example in Northern Ireland, the word 'wee' is used instead of the word 'little' that is used in Standard English.

There is also a change in grammar. An example can be that in the Black Vernacular English, there is no use of the verb 'to be' - 'he playing!'. In the regional dialects, there is non-standard grammatical form. An example can be the fact that they have missing plurals ex. 'she bought five chocolate'. The pronunciation is also diverse, where words such as dance and chance, change their ways of being said.

On the other hand, sociolect means that different groups of people have distinct styles of language use. These are created to mark an identity and induces a sense of belonging. There are several factors that influence the style of language including:

- socio-economic status (ex. language of high class is different from that of low class)
- age (ex. adults and teens do not have the same style of language)
- occupation (ex. certain professions such as lawyer or doctor have their very own jargon and sentence structure)
- gender (ex. men tend to use slang and swear words more than woman)

Subsequently, idiolect is how individuals use language differently. This obviously depends on the region where you are from, the socio-economic background ,gender , age, occupation and education given. Although sociolects speak the same language, the manner is different. Everyone has his own voices, phrases and personality which effect the language spoken.

To conclude, a language as it is spoken by many, takes different forms and is used in different ways in order to satisfy every situation.

Theories, Approaches, Methods and Techniques

Edward Anthony, an American applied linguist, defines language learning theories, approaches, methods and techniques as follows:

An *approach* is a set of correlative assumptions dealing with the nature of language (i.e. linguistic) and the nature of language teaching and learning; it describes the nature of the subject matter to be taught; it is more theoretical and forms the basis of any method to be formulated; an approach is axiomatic.

A *method* is an overall plan for the orderly presentation of language material; no part of the method evolved contradicts the principles of the approach on which it is based; a method is more procedural; within any approach, there can be several methods.

A *technique* represents implementation; it is the actual implementation of a method in the classroom. It is the particular way of doing things to accomplish an immediate objective. Techniques must be consistent with a method, which in turn must be in harmony with an approach (1963:66).

So English language or any language learning approaches and methods have their sources and routes on language learning theories like behaviourism, cognitivism, structuralism, transformationalism and semanticism.

The Origin of Language

Yesterday we discussed the gulf that separates the creative use of language by humans from the inborn signals of animals. Bees returning from their first flight out of the hive know perfectly how to perform their complex nectar dances. With humans, the precise form of language must be acquired through exposure to a speech community. Words are definitely not inborn, but the capacity to acquire and language and use it creatively seems to be inborn. Noam Chomsky calls this ability the LAD (Language Acquisition Device). Today we will ask two questions: how did this language instinct in humans originate? And how did the first language come into being?

Concerning the origin of the first language, there are two main hypotheses, or beliefs. Neither can be proven or disproved given present knowledge.

(1) **Belief in divine creation.** Many societies throughout history believed that language is the gift of the gods to humans. The most familiar is found in Genesis 2:20, which tells us that Adam gave names to all living creatures. This belief predicates that humans were created from the start with an innate capacity to use language. It can't be proven that language is as old as humans, but it is definitely true that language and human society are inseparable. Wherever humans exist language exists. Every stone age tribe ever encountered has a language equal to English, Latin, or Greek in terms of its expressive potential and grammatical complexity. Technologies may be complex or simple, but language is always complex. Charles Darwin noted this fact when he stated that as far as concerns language, "Shakespeare walks with the Macedonian swineherd, and Plato with the wild savage of Assam." In fact, it sometimes seems that languages spoken by preindustrial societies are much more complex grammatically than languages such as English (example: English has about seven tense forms and three noun genders; Kivunjo, a Bantu language spoken on the slopes of Mount Kilimanjaro, has 14 tenses and about 20 noun classes.) There are no primitive languages, nor are any known to have existed in the past-even among the most remote tribes of stone age hunter-gatherers.

Nevertheless, it is impossible to prove that the first anatomically modern humans possessed creative language. It is also impossible to disprove the hypothesis that primitive languages might have existed at some point in the distant past of Homo sapiens development.

(2) **Natural evolution hypothesis.** At some point in their evolutionary development humans acquired a more sophisticated brain which made language invention and learning possible. In other words, at some point in time humans evolved a language acquisition device, whatever this may be in real physical terms. The simple vocalizations and gestures inherited from our primate ancestors then quickly gave way to a creative system of language – perhaps within a single generation or two. /Mention the hypothesis about rewiring the visual cortex of the brain into a language area./ According to the natural evolution hypothesis, as soon as humans developed the biological, or neurological, capacity for creative language, the cultural development of some specific system of forms with meanings would have been an inevitable next step.

This hypothesis cannot be proven either. Archeological evidence unearthed thus far, seems to indicate that modern humans, Homo sapiens, emerged within the last 150,000 years. By 30,000, BC all other species of humanoids seem to have been supplanted by Homo sapiens. Could the success of our species vis-a-vis other hominids be explained by its possession of superior communicative skills? Speaking people could teach, plan, organize, and convey more sophisticated information. This would have given them unparalleled advantage over hominid groups without creative language. Of course, no one knows whether other species of humanoids--Homo erectus and Homo neanderthalis -- used creative language. Perhaps they also did. In any case, Homo sapiens, "the wise human," should perhaps really be called Homo loquens, "the speaking human" because language and humans are everywhere found together, whereas wisdom among humans is much more selectively distributed.

Invention hypotheses. Moving on to our second question, if humans acquired the capacity for language either by divine gift or by evolution, then exactly how might humans have devised the first language? There are several hypotheses as to how language might have been consciously invented by humans based on a more primitive system of hominid communication. Each hypothesis is predicated on the idea that the invention of language and its gradual refinement served as a continuous impetus to additional human mental development. None of the invention hypotheses I will mention is convincing and most sane linguists agree that the origin of language is still a mystery. But the inventive, sarcastic names given these hypotheses by their critics prove that even linguists can at times be creative.

First, there are four imitation hypotheses that hold that language began through some sort of human mimicry of naturally occurring sounds or movements:

(1) **The "ding-dong" hypothesis.** Language began when humans started naming objects, actions and phenomena after a recognizable sound associated with it in real life. This hypothesis holds that the first human words were a type of verbal icon, a sign whose form is an exact image of its meaning: crash became the word for thunder, boom for explosion. Some words in language obviously did derive from imitation of natural sounds associated with some object: Chinook Indian word for heart--tun-tun, Basque word for knife: ai-ai (literally ouch-ouch). Each of these iconic words would derive from an index, a sign whose form is naturally associated with its meaning in real space and time.

The problem with this hypothesis is that onomatopoeia (imitation of sound, auditory iconicity) is a very limited part of the vocabulary of any language; imitative sounds differ from language to language: Russian: ba-bakh=bang, bukh= thud. Even if onomotopoeia provided the first dozen or so words, then where did names for the thousands of naturally noiseless concepts such as rock, sun, sky or love come from?

(2) **The "pooh-pooh" hypothesis** holds that the first words came from involuntary exclamations of dislike, hunger, pain, or pleasure, eventually leading to the expression of more developed ideas and emotions. In this case the first word would have been an involuntary ha-ha-ha, wa-wa-wa These began to be used to name the actions which caused these sounds.

The problem with this hypothesis is that, once again, emotional exclamations are a very small part of any language. They are also highly language specific. For instance, to express sudden pain or discomfort: Eng. ouch; Russ. oi.; Cherokee eee. Thus, exclamations are more like other words in that they reflect the phonology of each separate language. Unlike sneezes, tears, hiccoughs or laughter, which are innate human responses to stimuli, the form of exclamations depends on language rather than precedes language. Also, exclamations, like most other words are symbols, showing at least a partially arbitrary relationship between sound and meaning.

(3) **The "bow-wow" hypothesis** (the most famous and therefore the most ridiculed hypothesis) holds that vocabulary developed from imitations of animal noises, such as: Moo, bark, hiss, meow, quack-quack. In other words, the first human words were a type of index, a sign whose form is naturally connected with its meaning in time and space.

But, once again, onomotopoeia is a limited part of the vocabulary of any language. The linguistic renditions of animal sounds differ considerably from language to language, although each species of animal everywhere makes essentially the same sound:

(a) Dog:bow-wow; Chinese:wu-wu; Jap.wan-wan Russ gaf-gaf, tyaff-tyaff;

(b) Cat-meow, Russ.myaoo, Chin--mao, Jap.nya-nya purr in French is ron ron.

(c) Pig: oink-oink; Russ. hryu-hryu; Chin.--oh-ee-oh-ee; Jap. bu-bu.

(d) Russian rooster: kukareiku. Japanese kokekoko

(e) Russian owl:ukh; Cherokee goo-ku Spanish, Japanese – no special word

Thus, the human interpretation of animal sounds is dependent upon the individual language, and it seems unlikely than entire vocabularies derived from them.

(4) A somewhat different hypothesis is the "ta-ta" hypothesis. Charles Darwin hypothesized (though he himself was sceptical about his own hypothesis) that speech may have developed as a sort of mouth pantomime: the organs of speech were used to imitate the gestures of the hand. In other words, language developed from gestures that began to be imitated by the organs of speech--the first words were lip icons of hand gestures.

It is very possible that human language, which today is mostly verbal, had its origin in some system of gestures; other primates rely on gesture as an integral part of communication, so it is plausible that human communication began in the same way. Human gestures, however, just like onomotopoeic words, differ from culture to culture. Cf. English crossing the finger for good luck vs. Russian "fig" gesture; nodding for yes vs. for no in Turkish and Bulgarian; knocking on wood vs. spitting over the left shoulder three times.

A second set of hypotheses on language origin holds that language began as a response to some acute necessity in the community. Here are several necessity hypotheses of the invention of language:

(1) **Warning hypothesis.** Language may have evolved from warning signals such as those used by animals. Perhaps language started with a warning to others, such as Look out, Run, or Help to alert members of the tribe when some lumbering beast was approaching. Other first words could have been hunting instructions or instructions connected with other work. In other words, the first words were indexes used during everyday activities and situations.

(2) **The "yo-he-ho" hypothesis.** Language developed on the basis of human cooperative efforts.

The earliest language was chanting to simulate collective effort, whether moving great stones to block off cave entrances from roving carnivores or repeating warlike phrases to inflame the fighting spirit.

It is fairly certain that the first poetry and song came from this aspect of beginning speech. Songs of this type are still with us: Volga boatmen, military marching chants, seven dwarfs working song.

Plato also believed that language developed out of sheer practical necessity. And Modern English has the saying: Necessity is the mother of invention. Speech and right hand coordination are both controlled in the left hemisphere of the brain. Could this be a possible clue that manual dexterity and the need to communicate developed in unison?

(3) A more colorful idea is the lying hypothesis. E. H. Sturtevant argued that, since all real intentions or emotions get involuntarily expressed by gesture, look or sound, voluntary communication must have been invented for the purpose of lying or deceiving. He proposed that the need to deceive and lie – to use language in contrast to reality for selfish ends-- was the social prompting that got language started.

There are no scientific tests to evaluate between these competing hypotheses. All of them seem equally far-fetched. This is why in the late 19th century the Royal Linguistic Society in London actually banned discussion and debate on the origin of language out of fear that none of the arguments had any scientific basis at all and that time would be needlessly wasted on this fruitless enquiry. Attempts to explain the origin of language are usually taken no more seriously today either. Recently, comedian Lily Tomlin came up with her own language invention hypothesis: she claimed that men invented language so that they could complain.

Each of the imitation hypotheses might explain how certain isolated words of language developed. Very few words in human language are verbal icons. Most are symbols, displaying an arbitrary relationship of sound and meaning.

And each of the necessity hypotheses might explain how involuntary sounds made out of need in certain contexts might have come to be manipulated as words for an object even out of context. However, the extended use of natural indexes still leaves unexplained the development of grammar--the patterns in language which have definite structural functions but no specific meaning. The creative, generative aspect of human language that we call grammar is language's most unique feature. Where did grammar come from? There is nothing like grammar (patterns with definite functions yet no set meaning) in animal systems of communication.

In isolated instances it can be shown that a grammatical pattern developed from chance lexical combinations:

(a) suffix -hood from OE word haeda= state. childhood, boyhood, puppyhood.

(b) Continuous action: form of verb to be + main verb comes from a locative phrase I am working > I am at working-- cf. the song I'm a working on the railroad.

But these are isolated instances. How language developed a complex grammar remains a complete mystery. This means that how language developed is equally a mystery. We simply don't know how language may have actually evolved from simple animal systems of sounds and gestures.

Hypotheses regarding Language Diversity

Regardless of whether language was a special gift from the gods, a natural evolutionary acquisition, or an ingenious, conscious human invention made at some specific moment in our species' distant past, the fact remains that language does exist. And since so many languages exist today, a second question arises: Was there one or more than one original language? Was there one or more than one invention of language? There are about 5,000 languages spoken on Earth today. We know that there were even more spoken in the past, when most people lived in small bands or tribes rather than in large states.

There are two age-old beliefs regarding the origin or the world's present linguistic diversity.

(1) The oldest belief is that there was a single, original language. The idea of a single ancestor tongue is known today as monogenesis. In Judeo-Christian tradition, the original language was confused by divine intervention, as described in the story of the Tower of Babel in Genesis. There is a similar story from the Toltecs of pre-Columbian Mexico, who tell of the building of the great pyramid at Cholula, and the dispersal of the builders by an angry god. And similar stories are found in other parts of the world.

It may be interesting to note here that people who believe in a single origin for language have different hypotheses as to what that first language may have been.

(a) A Basque scholar claimed that the first language was Basque.

(b) A German philologist of the last century maintained that German was the first language and that all other languages are inferior corruptions of it. Other European linguists conferred the same exalted status on Greek or Sanskrit.

(c) One Swedish philologist claimed that in the Garden of Eden God spoke Swedish, Adam spoke Danish and the serpent spoke French.

(2) There is a second hypothesis of human origin and, consequently, of the origin of human language: the hypothesis of parallel evolution. This hypothesis holds that, as humans evolved parallel in more than one location; each group developed its own unique language. The hypothesis of the multiple origin of humankind is sometimes called the Candelabra theory. The candelabra hypothesis tends to be favored in East Asia and by a smaller number of scientists in the West. The hypothesis of multiple linguistic origins that often goes along with this hypothesis is known as polygenesis. Each of the original languages then would then have diverged into numerous forms. The major language families of today would be descended from these separate mother tongues.

(3) Scientific monogenesis: The Mother Tongue theory.

Theories of monogenesis do not necessarily derive from religious belief. Many modern scholars believe in a theory of monogenesis that has come to be called the Mother Tongue Theory. This theory holds that one original language spoken by a single group of Homo sapiens perhaps as early as 150 thousand years ago gave rise to all human languages spoken on the Earth today. As humans colonized various continents, this original mother tongue diverged through time to form the numerous languages spoken today. Since many scientists believe that the first fully modern humans appeared in Africa, the mother tongue theory is connected with a more general theory of human origin known as the Out of Africa theory. Currently, the theory of evolutionary monogenesis tends to be favored by a group of linguists working in the United States.

Regardless of the origin of language, the fact remains that there are over 5,000 mutually unintelligible forms of human speech used on Earth today. And, although many are radically different from one another in structure--the differences are superficial since each and every one of these languages can be used creatively.

Languages do not differ in terms of their creative potential but rather in terms of the level upon which particular distinctions are realized in each particular language. What is expressed concisely in one language requires a phrase in another language. (Examples of aspect and evidentiality; also words like Swahili mumagamagama "a person who habitually loses things" and Russian zajchik "the rainbow reflection from glass." Linguists study how each particular language structures the expression of concepts. Such cross-language comparisons fall under a branch of linguistics called language typology.

If the structural diversity of human languages is superficial, then why in language typology important? Why do so many linguists spend so much time studying language diversity?

(1) First, to try to trace the original mother tongue (or mother tongues). Linguists who compare modern languages try to reconstruct ancient languages are called comparative linguists.

(2) Second, because languages change more slowly than the environment in which they are spoken, languages contain all sorts of indications of bygone culture. For historians and anthropologists, language provides a special window into the past: ursus/bear/ medved; time/tide/vremya. Study a language--any language--and you will learn much about the history of the people who speak that language. You will also be taking a crucial step toward understanding the contemporary culture of the speakers. Linguists who study language from this cultural standpoint are called anthropological linguists.

Remember that – contrary to the hypothesis of linguistic determinism – studying a language will not help you predict the future for the people who speak that language. The future will happen with little regard for language structure, and language will be shaped by that future, not the other way around.

And this is why will we spend the next four weeks studying the morphology, syntax and phonology of diverse languages. And during the second half of the course we will return to questions of language in society and the connection between language and the brain.

Grammar-Translation Method

Medieval scholastic theories produced the grammar-translation method, which was the only teaching method for several centuries. Howatt's 'A History of English Language Teaching' gives a detailed account of the factors that contributed to the grammar-translation method.

The origins of the grammar-translation method do not lie in an attempt to teach languages by grammar and translation; these were taken for granted anyway. The original motivation was reformist. ... The grammar-translation method was an attempt to adopt these traditions to circumstances and requirements of schools (1984:279)

Howatt says that the method used by individual learners to read and understand a book in a foreign language using dictionary, grammar texts, etc was taken to schools to teach a foreign language or languages. Literary classics were the source textbooks for teaching foreign languages in the grammar-translation methods, because they were the models of good writing correct grammar. Grammar-translation method was practiced in both east and west for many centuries. In India it was for Persian and Sanskrit and in the west it was for Latin and Greek. Franz Ahn and H.G. Ollendorff are the major successful practitioners of this method. Franz Ahn designed courses for German and then in English, Spanish, Italian and Russian languages. Ollendorff designed the textbooks in a graded linguistic syllabus for the first time.

The learner studies the grammar of the L2 in detail. In the second stage, this knowledge of the grammar will be utilised to translate from the mother tongue into the L2. Later he can use the same method to translate from L2 to L1. 34

The first language is maintained as the reference system in the acquisition of the second language (Stern 1983).

GT method gives more importance to translating sentences and parts of lessons. Teachers give sentences and parts of lessons to students to translate from L1 to L2 and L2 to L1. It is assumed that the learner will be able to translate precisely and learn L2. Bilingual word lists, dictionaries are of much help to teach vocabulary. Learners also memorize words of L2 and its meaning in L1. The flaw of GT method is, it gives least importance to speaking and listening skills. Teachers base their teaching entirely on 'text' and they follow each unit. Communication skills or pronunciation skills are not taken into consideration and literary language is focussed upon. Learners' involvement, application of innovative technique of teachers to meet the needs of the learners are not considered. The entire focus is on writing and reading. Teachers use L1 or mother tongue profusely to explain lessons in L2. Another drawback is even though the texts are written by well known authors they are not from the academic teaching field. For example, to teach English, works of text excerpts of well known authors like, Dickens, Hardy, Shakespeare, Tennyson, Burke are commonly used. Texts in the foreign language are translated into native language orally and in writing and ideally their literary and cultural significance is discussed, although in many classes because of the limitation in the time available, this is done very perfunctorily, if at all (Rivers 1968)

Structural-oral-situational Approach

Structural-oral-situational approach or S-O-S approach is the proposition and practice of diligently taken grammatical structures of English in successful, relevant situations. Formally it is practiced through speech. In the next stage focus was on reading and writing. Language is considered as structural elements for sending meaningful messages. Teaching lessons are chosen and classified by qualified teachers or linguists. Classification will decide which should come in the beginning and which should follow the first and whichshould follow the third, etc. It is difficult to do anything at any stage, if it is adaptable and suitable many places(Mackey, 1965). In order to classify structural elements, teaching experts take special note of the following points.

(a) Frequency of structural elements in the language of the user.
(b) Are the classified structures beneficial to acquiring Language.
(c) The feasibility of the teaching and learning in the classrooms.
(d) Which structural elements can be taken together for the purpose of meeting the students' needs.

Additionally, vocabulary of the L2also are chosen and classified. 2000-3000 words which are frequently used by the native speakers and written texts and which are necessary for teaching English are diligently chosen to prepare the vocabulary list.

S-O-S approach is based on the conviction that 'language is primarily speech' L2 is taught in the same way as the learners picked up their L1. As they learned their mother tongue, learners first learn by listening, then speaking, then reading and finally writing. Methodologists who advocate SOS believe that Language is a set of habits. They are also influenced by the operant conditioning theories of BF Skinner. Skinner believed that learning language is a habit formation and more use of a language will reinforce it. 'The learners learn to manipulate structures to a point of automatic response to a language stimulus (Rivers, 1964:31)'. Frisby (1957) summarises Palmer's views of language learning process to; first the learner will receive knowledge or resources with knowledge, secondly he will store them into his memory by repeating them and finally he will use them according to the suitability of the situation. SOS approach includes pattern-drilling and memorisation. This may be due to the influence of the behavioural psycho or stimulus-response theory of learning formulated by Skinner.

Direct Method

Direct Method during its initial stages was called natural method. Linguists wanted learners to learn English Language as they learnt their first language or in other words, as a child learns a language. Direct method can be aptly defined as follows. "The direct method originated in a desire to do something that the schools of the time were not doing, and could not do, namely to teach first languages as practical skills for everyday purposes of social survival questions of educational value and worthwhileness were irrelevant. What mattered was the ability to communicate effectively in ordinary life" (Howatt, 1984). 'Direct' suggests that this method intends to teach without translation, grammar or dictionary. Every human being has the ability to communicate in the necessary situations. Most proper and successful way to acquire language is by conversation drills. Maria Dakowska (2005) deems the basic principles of direct method as learning language in a situational context by connecting new words to related contexts for getting suitable meanings.

Direct method gives importance to correct pronunciation. In a Direct Method class, new teaching units were introduced orally. Words were selected based on its usefulness in the given situations. Meaning was taught using objects, pictures, gestures etc. Grammar is learned inductively.

Communicative Language Teaching (CLT)

Communicative Language Teaching (CLT) focuses on the learner's role, and the importance of meaning. Communicative competence is given prominent position in the process of language learning. CLT deals with most of the aspects of language learning compared to the conventional and modern language teaching methods. Howat talks about the two different types of CLT:

There is, in a sense, a 'strong' version of communicative approach and a 'weak' version. The weak version which has become more or less standard practice in the last ten years stresses the importance of providing learners with opportunities to use their English for communicative purposes and, characteristically, attempts to integrate such activities to wider programmes of language teaching... The 'strong' version of Communicative Language Teaching on the other hand, advances the claim that language is acquired through communication, so that it is not merely a question of activating an existing but inert knowledge of the language, but of stimulating the development of the language system itself. If the former could be described as 'learning to use' English the latter entails using English to learn it. The two basics of communication is giving a message and completing the information space. Successful communication depends on listener's willingness and ability to understand". (1984:279)

Savingnon (1983:8) says, 'We make the best use we can of the symbolic system we know, The meaning we convey depends on others who share an understanding of these symbols and who may or may not interpret them as we intend". Maria Dakowska (2005:93) gives the following key factors or parameters of the communicative situations.

PARAMETERS FOR COMMUNICATIVE SITUATIONS

The setting	The time and place of communication
The participants	The social roles of the speakers and the addressees or audience
The purpose	The communicative goal which can be further subdivided into smaller functions
The key	Tone, manner or spirit in which the speech act is performed
The content	The topic of communication may determine the use of specialized language
The channel	The two main channels are activation and visual

Canal and Swaine (1980) say that communication competence is made of grammatical, socio-linguistic and strategic competence. The Aim of teaching should be for the betterment of the communicative competence. The facilitator (teacher) using CLT methodology should take into consideration the communication requirements of students. The students should be allowed to interact with target language speakers. On the other hand, students' mother tongue and the skills used in it should be amply used. Primary purpose of Communicative Language Teaching is to allow the students to experience target language and use it in different contexts. Widdowson (1978: 31) says "meanings do not exist, readymade in the language itself: they are worked out. We are given linguistic clues to what propositions are expressed and what acts are performed, and on the basis of these clues we make sense of the sentences".

Principles of Communicative Method

The initiation and implementation of the Communicative Language Teaching is a step forward in the language teaching pedagogy. The following are some important principles underlying Communicative Language Teaching:

1. Communicative Language Teaching is student-focused: Students' participation and involvement during the English Language teaching class is the most important factor. In CLT learner is the centre of action or activities. Teacher's role is secondary. (Richards and Rodgers, 1986). The teacher is a facilitator or guide and he involves in the Communicative Language Teaching with the learner in equal terms. The learner can do, involve, negotiate or change the lessons or other components of their task in the target language.
2. The aim of Communicative Language Teaching is the effective target language learning. Considering this the teaching materials of classroom activities should be made relevant, authentic and meaningful. This will make the learner to understand better and to remember the already learned or done activities. The lessons or activities planned or designed should be open ended and give

opportunities for students to think, have original independent ideas or answers. It should be reality based, relevant, interesting and related to modern civilization lessons and be ideal for CLT. These will make successful learning possible in CLT class. Johnson's suggests,

The attempts to make information gaps in the classroom, thereby producing communication, viewed as the bridging of the information gap, has characterised much recent communicative methodology. (1979: 201)

This information gap in the CLT should be provided to students as pictures, puzzles, games, audio or video clips, etc.

3. Culture content of the syllabus should be identical to the culture of learners and target language users. Communication and culture are inter-related. So if the classroom activities and lessons like passages, pictures, posters, film clippings, games, puzzles and objects reflect the culture relevant to the learner of target language, they can promote learning via communication.
4. Observing the speaker is important for the listener to comprehend his message in full. The speaker's body language expressions are very important, in addition to his verbal messages. This property of learner-listener observation makes video an integral part of Communicative Language teaching methodology. Subtitles, printed scripts, graphics, print or hand written notes can be used to arrive at successful communication.
5. A Communicative Language Teaching text book should focus on context. It should be skill-oriented, it should be rich, colourful and illustrated with pictures, photographs, cartoons, drawing, maps, charts, etc. Passages should be interesting, real, original and useful. Tasks for teaching all aspects of learning should be there. Tasks should promote problem solving, interaction, planning in advance, making presentation, short speeches, etc.

Task based Language Learning

Long (1985:89) defines task as any job undertaken by somebody for himself or for other people. It can be buying a ticket, reserving a seat in the theatre and similar other jobs anybody does in his or her everyday life, personally or professionally. Richards (1986: 289) defines a pedagogical task as a performance done as a result of 'processing or understanding language'. Watching a play and later enacting it is an example of a pedagogical task. Practicing or doing variety of tasks will enhance language learning and can be considered as successful task completion. It also will increase the communication skill of the student. Language is practised for learning communication and not for the sake of the language. Breen (1987:23) defines pedagogical task as any language learning attempt which has a definite aim, suitable content and a planned procedure. Doing the task should enhance language learning. Tasks can be done individually, in pair or as a group activity.

Skehan (1998) considers meaning as the basis of a task. Learners have to invent, find out or guess the meaning and he cannot depend on meanings provided by others. The tasks which are given to the learning should be similar to real life incidents. Prominence should be given to the successful completion of the task. Task evaluation is done on the basis of outcome.

Ellis (2003 : 16) expects a task to be like a real work activity, which involve in productive oral and written skills like any other language learning process.

David Nunan (2007 : 4) defines a task as a classroom work, which helps students to understand, manipulate and communicate in the target language. Students should acquire grammatical knowledge, while being involved in a task. For meaning expression, conveying meaning is preferred to manipulation. A task should be complete, independent and should have 'a beginning, middle and an end'.

A Task Framework

A task used in the task based language teaching is similar to or identical to any activity which a person does in his or her routine life. Halliday (1985) divides real world tasks, into three general activities. He calls them three 'macro functions of language. People use language to buy or sell or exchange goods and perform and get service. This is transactional or service macro function. We as social human beings use language to interact with others. This is known as the interpersonal or social macro functions. We use language to write or read, i.e., for enjoyment and entertainment and this according to Halliday is the aesthetic macro function of language.

Day to day activities or real-world tasks are brought into the classroom for learning and they are presented as pedagogical task. Tasks are planned and implemented in the classroom, not for repeating what they do outside but to use as a learning method. In the beginning the learners will reproduce learning with or without changes, but later this will make them capable of creating language expressions selecting from the texts and other materials developed for doing the tasks. David Nunan says, "...Language classrooms are unnatural by design, and that they exist precisely to provide for learners the kinds of practice opportunities that do not exist outside the class room." (2007: 22). According to David Nunan principles of task based language leaching can be defined as following (2007)

Principles of Task based Language Teaching

1. **Scaffolding.** Teacher has an important role in the learner-centred task-based language teaching. Learning materials and study units support and back the learning process. Teacher will facilitate a favourable atmosphere where learning takes place. The task to be introduced is higher than the learner's existing knowledge. All the teaching or implementation of the steps of the task should be done carefully and in time.
2. **Dependency.** Each lesson is a chain of different tasks. Each task precedes another and is succeeded by another. Each task is a natural continuation of the preceding task. In each task there are sub activities like listening or observing the tasks repeatedly and manipulating and then creating new language expressions.
3. **Recycling.** Learners should be given more opportunities for learning a particular lesson by taking more time. This time period will give him opportunities for going through or face varied linguistic and experiential environments. The learner will see how a piece of learning material which he did not understand initially works in conjunction with other closely related linguistic items. From the different opportunities society give for example, in a restaurant, theatre or super market, the learner can learn how to express like and dislike, such as yes or no questions, making preferences, etc.
4. **Active Learning.** The Major idea of experiential learning is 'learning by doing'. Learners can build up their learning and knowledge instead of waiting for the teacher to transfer it to them. Experiential learning provides immense opportunities for the learners in the class, they can 'use' the language by way of role play, memorisation of dialogues, developing storylines, completing chart, etc. Using audio and video input, listening to teachers and fellow students will

help to complete their learning tasks. Experiential learning doesn't reject the teacher. Teacher has a major role –giving input, explaining etc. But real class time should be student focussed and not teacher dominated.

5. **Integration.** Language teaching, especially second language teaching was based on synthetic approach, where lexical, grammatical and phonological items were taught separately. Communicative activities did not consider their effect and by 1980 they argued for a meaning based approach instead of the form based or synthetic approach. Due to this conflict an attempt has been made to integrate both the formal and functional aspects of teaching where communication's role was stressed because 'communication is learning'.
6. **Reproduction is learning.** In regular tasks, students repeat or reproduce what is provided by the teachers and teaching materials. These tasks are provided for the purpose of teaching forms, functions and meanings. These tasks can be considered as the pre-tasks which were followed by creative tasks where students connecting these expressions and familiar components create original and new ideas, usages and sentences. They will reach a level where they can generate creative language.
7. **Reflection.** In task-based language teaching, each teaching task is based on a distinct teaching strategy. Students who understand this strategy were better learners. Because of the change in the focus from language content to learning process, a reflective learner can learn better.

Experience Based Language Teaching

It is difficult for a language teacher trainer to teach or train the teacher trainees because they are new and inexperienced in the profession of teaching. It is difficult for the new teacher to anticipate problems which his students may have. The new teacher will find it difficult to know in advance which aspect of language learning is difficult for his students.

But an experienced teacher knows the aspects of language lesson which troubles the students and he knows how much time is required for a student to understand a lesson unit. Language teachers, who are experienced, teach target languages in a flexible manner. Each class they take makes them a better teacher and they will improve their materials, techniques etc so that the later classes were more didactic, memorable and enjoyable. Every experience each language teacher acquires helps him to use innovative techniques to teach difficult grammar points, solve the problem in pronouncing difficult words, the phrases the students misused, etc. easily. Experience helps language teachers to use or modify or sometimes abandon certain teaching techniques. These strategies can be recollected and used in a future class in the similar way or with changes as the situation requires. As per the teaching situation the teacher selects the most suitable teaching strategy to use in that particular class. Experienced language teachers teach in a flexible manner in the class rooms and it can be elaborated in cognitive psychology term 'schema' theory. Medin and Ross say as follows:

(a) A schema refers to one's knowledge about the word (as opposed to information that is in the world).

(b) It is general, encoding information about a particular type of situation rather than about one particular situation.

(c) It is structured, meaning that it includes not only a set of facts, but also how the facts are related. This allows inferences to be made.

(d) Its structure allows it to be used in the comprehension of types of situations (1992: 346)

Another aspect of schema theory is that they produce expectations of what is going to happen, it helps us to understand any unusual happening and it will help us to foresee what is going to happen. Language teachers draw from their memory bank and refine them to introduce in the most suitable way in the class, everyday.

Language teachers improve their teaching skills on the job. A teacher may ask for opinion and get some materials from other teacher. He may collect the necessary materials from the library. Text books from other countries may not be acceptable wholly because of cultural difference. In such case the teacher will revise, modify and change the materials to suit the students' cultural background. Breen and Litlejohn (2000: 9) say "the actual syllabus is a compromise between the original syllabus and teacher's response to student's needs that is revealed in the classroom".

A well experienced Language teacher has the ability to utilize all teaching skills, and achieve the set goal. The success of this effort will make the students to trust such teachers because they know that any activity done in the class was useful to them.

Activity Based Language Teaching

"By engaging in activities that generate feelings of involvement, urgency and excitement, language students find themselves forgetting their inhibitions and expressing themselves more readily in the target language". (Rose M. Senior, 2006 : 182). Activities that allow students to enjoy and be entertained are very effective. Activity based language learning with games and other task is part of the communicative approach. If the games and tasks are selected and prepared carefully to suit the students, they are very much relevant. Further these games and fun not only reduce the inhibitions of the students but releases their tension and nervousness. Since they have to gain language proficiency in a short time, this is more relevant in the case of adult learners. Also students preparing for college education do not have much time and are much pressurised. Language teachers in schools find that highly energetic young boys can be streamlined by using activity based language teaching. Teachers can streamline this extra energy to language learning, which is very productive. Communicative games, role-playing, going around the classroom, to interact with others to complete the game, competitive activities where students can encourage their team mates, chanting, singing or giving dictations, making imaginary telephone conversations, students line up according to age and height, move to another location where there is more space and etc., are some of the contents of activity based education.

There is a risk of confusing fun with learning. Several educationalists recognized it. According to Ormrod (2000: 601) "Excitement and entertainment should not be thought of as goals in and of themselves. Rather, they are means to a more important goal: achieving instructional goals".A feeling of lightness and fun will make language learners tension free and will create an atmosphere for better language learning.

Collaborative Learning

Entire stake holders, including students and teachers, in English language education can collaborate for the following reasons: (i) to experiment with additional methods of teaching, (ii) encouraging an atmosphere of Co-operation or collaboration among learners instead of competition for which is practiced by the traditional teaching approaches, (iii) collaborative learning will create a situation where all stake holders benefit in equal quantity and terms by sharing information and knowledge, making it a win-win situation, (iv) placing the learner at the centre of the learning process instead of the traditional teacher centered process. (Nunan, Introduction. 2003 : 1)

All students are varied and study in his/her own way. These differences in the students' style of learning might be considered for choosing the right learning experiences. Nunan (2003 : 2) says, "At each stage in the curriculum process, be it planning, implementation or evaluation, information about learners (and, where feasible, from learners) will be used to guide the selection content, learning experiences and the means of assessing outcomes".

Learner centred curriculum and traditional curriculum agrees on planning, implementation and evaluation. Intense participation of the students in the decision-making method, which includes deciding the subjects of the curriculum and the teaching method, which was hither to done by the teacher only, there is a collaborative effort, and that makes learner centred approach distinct and more significant.

A meaningful and effective collaboration between the learners and teacher can result in the following situation. (i)It can improve the learning of the students in addition to their learning about their learning. (ii) It may improve their knowledge about the target language, about themselves as learners and about (their) learning. (iii) It will improve their communication skills. (iv) Learner has to deal with, understand and adjust with the differences between group needs and individual needs during language learning process, 'both in social, procedural terms as well as linguistic, content terms'. Learner will come to know that the curriculum subjects and learning methods are very much connected. Also he will know that the decision-making tasks are really communicative actions.

Collaborative learning will help students 'to acquire common learning goals'. It encourages co-operation on the other hand traditional teaching methods pave way for competition. Meanwhile collaborative learning will give opportunities for learners to have occasions for a very healthy competition like competing with other groups and pairs of his class. The successes or failures here will not be personal and in this can they can have the benefits of competition like facing challenges, putting more effort, having a competitive spirit etc and avoid the ill effects of traditional competitive classroom practices. Stevens, Madden, Slavin and Farnish (1987) came to a conclusion that learners using cooperative style outperformed learners who got traditional instruction, in linguistic, grammatical and communication skills. The findings "support the link between the communicative approach to foreign language instruction and cooperative learning in small groups. The study demonstrates how to forge a link between the content and process of instruction"

In tasks where learners negotiate for meaning or are required to negotiate for meaning are significantly appropriate for the development of target language.

Bassano and Christison (1988) suggest three areas in which cooperative learning can be significant. They are: "(i) classroom environment and social tasks; (ii) process tasks such as peer tutoring and goal setting and (iii) progress monitoring and evaluative tasks". They are of the opinion that classrooms and social tasks are ideally suitable for creating cooperation which will lead to better learning. They also suggest that learners can handle responsibilities like, arranging and maintaining of the classroom, keeping the attendance records, making announcements regarding any matters and get feedbacks regarding discipline matters. These duties are in addition to the more important work they have to do, they are: choosing the task activities, setting the goal for each task, developing the materials for pre, main and post tasks, assessing themselves and others and finally creating and maintaining progress charts.

Armstrong gives a list of five advantages of collaborative teaching approaches.

1. Team teaching permits team members to take advantage of individual teacher strengths in planning for instruction and in working with learners.
2. Team teaching spurs creativity because teachers know they must teach for their colleagues as well as for their learners.
3. Team learning facilitates individualized instruction because it is possible to provide learning environments involving close personal contact between teacher and learner.
4. Team teaching provides for better sequencing and pacing of increments of instruction because perceptions of an individual teacher must be verified by at least one other team member.
5. Team teaching builds program continuity over time. Team teaching programs abide. Specific teachers within a team do not.

EXPERIENTIAL LEARNING

Experience is transformed into or used to acquire knowledge. Experiential learning is a conceptual basis for task-based language teaching. Learning experience is used as a language learning content by reliving that experience orally and/or writing their learning intensely.These experiences can be artificially created by asking or allowing them to do different tasks which themselves will promote language learning. 'Learning by doing' is the central idea and the learner's active participation is a must and it is possible if the teacher provides them with interesting tasks, which is related to the everyday life, culture, etc. David Kolb (1984) believes that experiential learning has its roots in subjects like social psychology, humanistic education, developmental education and cognitive theory. Learners make use of what they already know and can do to acquire new knowledge and do new skills. Learners "do this by making sense of some immediate experience, and going beyond the immediate experience through a process of reflection and transformation."

Another theorist of experiential learning Kohonen provides the following maxims for action for experiential learning.

(a) Encourage the transformation of knowledge within the learner rather than transmission of knowledge from the teacher to the learner.
(b) Encourage learners to participate actively in small, collaborative groups.
(c) Embrace a holistic attitude towards subject matter rather than a static, atomistic and hierarchical attitude.
(d) Emphasize process rather than products, learning how to learn, self-enquiring, social and communication skills.
(e) Encourage self-directed rather than teacher-directed learning.
(f) Promote intrinsic rather than extrinsic motivation.

Kohonen (1992: 37) believes that any learning is a part of personal growth. Experiential learning is based on, this maxim, learning a new language is learner's prerogative and responsibility. Experiential language learning enhances learner's ability for self-direction.

The learner brings in his/her own personal experiences and thereby adds to the content and learning process instead of waiting for the teacher to do it. All this prove that experiential learning is ideally learner-centred and the learner sidelines the teacher and becomes an independent and self-directed person.

David Kolb and Experiential Learning

David Kolb's 'learning cycle is based on in the concept of 'experience' and his definition of 'learning' has influenced many linguists. Kolb defines, "Learning is the process whereby knowledge is created through the transformation of experience." He considers experience as the base for the generation of knowledge and likes to "suggest through experiential learning theory a holistic integrative perspective on learning that combines experience, perception, cognition, and behaviour." He calls his experiential learning model as 'Lewinian Experiential Learning Model'. He creates his own learning theory based on this model. Kolb talks of two aspects in his learning cycle. Concrete and immediate experiences help in producing meaning and validating the learning method.

Immediate personal experience is the focal point for learning, giving life, texture, and subjective personal meaning to abstract concepts and at the same time providing a concrete, publicly shared reference point for testing the implications and validity of ideas created during the learning process.

Since Kolb's model rests on action research and laboratory teaching, feedback is necessary. The Process of aim-directed action and evaluation of the consequences of this action originates from these feedbacks.

All levels in this model fit into different forms of adaptation to different 'learning styles'. Each learner's learning ability and learning style corresponds to each level mentioned above. Kolb writes:

Learners, if they are to be effective, need four different kinds of abilities –concrete experience abilities, reflective observation abilities, abstract conceptualization abilities, and active experimentation abilities. That is, they must be able to involve themselves fully, openly, and without bias in new experiences. They must be able to reflect on and observe their experiences from many perspectives. They must be able to create concepts that integrate their observations into logically sound theories, and they must be able to use their theories to make decisions and solve problems.

So, each part of the circle refers to varied abilities of learners which are required for successful action and thinking. In Kolb's learning cycle, experience is very much subjective and it moves to the rear and correlates to various levels which refer to learners' varied learning abilities. Elkjaer believes that "Kolb has won such a prominent position in many educational researchers' practice and research... is because he says something that feels intuitively correct, namely that it is important to base teaching on participants' own experiences." Experiences for Kolb are a closed circle of the actions and thinking of learners.

Kolb considers learning as a process of creating knowledge. To know more about this learning, human knowledge should be explored to find out the types and the methods through which the knowledge was acquired. Knowledge creation happens, whether small or big, in all spheres. Interaction between 'social' and 'personal' knowledge creates knowledge. Social knowledge is the 'the civilized objective accumulation' of the learners' cultural experience. Personal knowledge is collection of each individual learner's 'subjective' experience. Thus knowledge is created by the close interaction among the objective and subjective experiences in a 'process called learning.

David Kolb (1984: 3-4) considers learning especially experiential learning as a lifelong process. EL is based on social psychology, philosophy and cognitive psychology. He says,

The experiential learning model pursues a framework for examining and strengthening the critical linkages among education, work, and personal development. It offers a system of competencies for describing job demands and corresponding educational objectives and emphasizes the critical linkages that can be developed between the classroom and the 'real world' with experiential learning methods.

EL model considers workplace as a place for learning that can enhance and add knowledge. It can facilitate the development of the human personality through meaningful action and career development prospects.

The present research used the experiential learning methods promoted by David Kolb and Kohenen elaborately. ELM was considered to be the most appropriate for the selected respondents as the candidate require 'familiar experiences' to enhance their expression skills.

UNIT VI

ENGLISH IN INDIA: HISTORY, EVOLUTION AND FUTURES

ENGLISH IN INDIA

Introduction

Human beings are different from other animals in the sense that they can speak and understand language. Language is specific for human beings. It is the major medium of expressing thoughts and emotion so human beings need to learn a language.

Language is the reflection of human history through the ages. It is not only the preservation of thought, but also the presentation of the manners of its people. It is the most living medium for communicating the general facts and feelings of everyday life. Thus, it is the expression of the human mind which leads us on to a quite different kind of value. To express something means to utilize the thoughts and determined by the expression, and this expression of human persona in either written or spoken words is called language.

The way of expressing our thoughts or letting others know what is in our minds, what we are thinking about or feeling or what we desire, is what we call 'speech' or 'language'. But the question arises, how one associates the meaning of the „language or to make it clear, how one learns a language. We cannot tell what is passing in the mind of another, nor can others know what is in our minds, except by means of a symbol, an image, picture, a statue, a sign, or by means of certain sounds. A symbol stands for something and those who are familiar with the symbol and the particular way of using it recognize and understand it. A picture or a statue or a colour may have a meaning for everybody.

The present study primarily aims the evaluation of the curriculum in the subject of Compulsory English at the U.G. level, in the affiliated colleges to the universities in Maharashtra especially in Marathwada region. The present research focuses on the Curriculum and Teaching of ESL at U.G. level. Responses will be collected in the form of answers to the questions asked in the questionnaire prepared for present study.

The thesis is divided into four chapters viz.:

1. ESL in India: A historical perceptive.
2. Curriculum Design (ESL) : The present Scenario
3. The Efficacy and Implementation of E.S.L. Curriculum.
4. Conclusion.

Today, Language plays an important role in human life. Everyone makes use of it, be he a beggar or a king. From birth to death, we are surrounded by it. Language is a means of communication. It is very difficult to think of a society without language. It is the medium by which thoughts convey from one person to another. Different linguists have defined language differently, stressing its various characteristics. Edward Sapir defines, "Language is purely human and non-instinctive method of communicating ideas, emotions and desires by means of a system of voluntarily produced symbols".

According to O.Jesperson, "Language is a set of human habits, the purpose of which is to give expression to thoughts and feelings" (Pahuja 12).

In the words of Bloch and Trager, "A language is a system of arbitrary vocal symbols by means of which a social group co-operates." (Bist 01).

Noam Chomsky in Syntactic Structures defines: "A language is a set (finite or infinite) of sentences, each finite in length and constructed out of a finite set of elements".

In other word, we can say that language is the flesh and blood of our culture. We can t imagine a word without language. There will be little communication among the people except by signs and gestures. Most of the activities will stop and all teaching and learning will come to an end. The progress of mankind will be blocked without language.

English a Pedant Language in World

English is the mother tongue of 300 million people in the world. The countries where English is the native or first language are the United Kingdom, the United States of America, Canada, Australia, New Zealand and South Africa. Some other countries like India, Pakistan, Africa, France, and the Soviet Union, etc. use English as a second or foreign language.

Thus English is spoken by 700 million people in the world, which is next only to the Chinese language. But there is a distribution of the speakers of the two languages. Whereas Chinese is restrained mostly to the Chinese subcontinent, English is used in all parts of the world. The speaker of English will be understood in all countries.

English is one of the six official languages of the U.N.O. It is also the link language of commonwealth countries. It has created a better understanding among the nations of the world and has been responsible for cultural give and take. It has facilitated mobility of teachers and students from one country to another. It has opened worldwide, chances for employment, and becomes an international language on world map. English can be described as a window on the rapid progress of technology and scientific knowledge that is constantly taking place in the world.

English is the key to the storehouse of knowledge. Most of this knowledge is not as yet available in Indian languages. The Kothari Education Commission has rightly stressed that English would play a vital role in higher education as an important library language. The commission has said that no student should be considered as qualified for the degree, in particular, a master s degree, unless he has acquired a reasonable proficiency in English.

U.G.C. recommended: "English is a language which is rich in literature, humanistic, scientific and technical. If under sentimental urges, we should give up English, we would cut our self off from the living stream of ever growing knowledge"(Mishra 8).

English is a link language in India. It is the only language which is understood by the educated people all over the country. The trade correspondence from one state to another is mostly conducted in English. Without knowledge of English, there will be no dialogue between persons from different states. In the absence of English a person from Mysore will not be able to communicate with a person from Kerala, nor will a Bengali share his thoughts with a Punjabi. Thus, English is a unifying factor and helps national integration. In the struggle for independence, English played a significant role in bringing together our national leaders from various regions of the country by enabling them to share their thoughts in it.

Today English is an international language, and it is also a link language. In these days we recognize it as a library language because we get the treasure of tremendous knowledge through ancient books, and most of these ancient books present in English.

Due to the all reasons we can say that English is a pedant language. English is the language that links the different nations, states, communities. The importance of English has been increased today. English language introduces us to the civilization of other foreign countries, especially the western culture. It is through this language that we have shared the wisdom of the west and the west has shared with us our intellectual and spiritual heritage.

It is again through English that our national consciousness was aroused by the writings of John Stuart-Mill, Raja Roy, Lincoln, Ravindranath Tagore and Ruskin. Modern Indian literature has been greatly influenced by English literature. It is only through English that Tagore, Gandhi and Nehru have communicated our aspirations to the world outside.

Most people in India need English for communicating purposes. We have, therefore, to impart them the language skills. In short English has become an important element of contemporary Indian culture.

Curriculum and Teaching in English

Curriculum is the content material of education. In fact, it is the curriculum on which the structure of education is based. Unless the curriculum is scientifically organized and properly planned, education cannot be successful. Curriculum serves the same purpose as that of a timetable for a railway traveller and of the knowledge of the road for a pedestrian. It is of interest, both to the teachers and the students. It gives an idea to the student of the things, that he has to study, and to the teacher, of the things that he has to teach.

Curriculum is the basis of all the activities of the school. It is the life blood of the educational programme. Unless the curriculum is nicely planned, it is not possible to utilize the precious years of the lives of the students that are spent in the school.

It is the means, through which the aim of education is achieved. It gives an idea to the teacher and the students of what to do, how to do, and when to do. It is the tool in the hands of the teacher through which he can mould the lives of the student. Prof. Cunningham has rightly remarked: "It is a tool in the hands of the artist (teacher) to mould his material (pupils) according to his ideal (objective) in his studio (school)".

Today the concept of curriculum has assumed a new outlook. This concept is broad based. It consists of the totality of experiences that the pupil receives through the many fold activities that go into the school, in the class-room, library, laboratories, workshops, and playgrounds, and in the numerous contacts between the teachers and the pupils. It is neither dogmatic nor rigid in its formation and structure. It is neither uniform nor it is standardized to conform to a prescribed pattern. It is characterized by variety and elasticity and is tailored to the needs of the students of different age levels. It gives the students an increasing awareness of the environment around them so that they may in the efficiency in the fabric of community life. The curriculum is varied and has the element of elasticity. All these things are there in order to fulfil the needs and requirements of the students. In fact the education is to be moulded according to the needs of the students and so the curriculum has to be constructed accordingly.

Belonging to the Latin language, the word curriculum means the 'racecourse' or a 'runway', which one runs to reach a goal. Interpreted accordingly, a curriculum is the instructional and the educative programme by following which the pupils achieve their goals, ideals and aspiration of life. It is a curriculum through which the general aims of a school receive concrete expression. The curriculum consists of those pupils experiences and activities that come under the guidance of the school. However, it should not be considered as synonym with courses of study or academic subjects of instruction. The courses of study do list much of the content and indicate many activities, but they form only the part of the curriculum. Instead of including academic subjects only it includes the totality of experiences that a pupil receives through the manifold activities that go on in the school, in the classroom, library, laboratory, workshop, playgrounds and in the numerous informal contacts between teachers and pupils.

In this sense the whole life of the school becomes the curriculum which can touch the life of the students at all points help in the evolution of a balanced personality. Much of the functioning of the curriculum is contributed by teachers and pupils and is not recorded in any textbooks, syllabus or courses of study. The Curriculum is an inclusive term and should not be used as synonym for one of its subdivisions. It consists of the contents and activities which the school employs for the purpose of training the students. It is a recognized, simplified and purposely selected portion of information and experience. In a limited sense curriculum is a systematic arrangement of courses designed to meet the needs of pupils. In a broader sense it includes the complete school environment involving all the courses, activities, readings and associations furnished to the pupils in the school. It is a total situation available to the teacher through which he makes behaviour changes.

The curriculum has been defined as all the experiences that the pupils have while under the direction of the school; it includes classroom and extra class-room activities, work as well as play. All such activities should promote the needs and welfare of the individuals and of society. The curriculum has been defined by various thinkers and educationists in various ways. All these definitions have the element of the modern concept in them.

In India, the requisites of the curriculum have been properly realized. Government of India has been given a thought to the construction of scientific curriculum.

Teaching has been defined in different ways. It is a process by which 'One person helps others to achieve knowledge, skill and attitude'. This is the traditional concept of teacher dominated affair. But the famous Brazilian educationist Paulo Freire considered this concept oppressive as it robs the learning group of self, particularly in adult education, where the teacher cannot assume the role of judge, ideologue and doctor. Freire has made a significant contribution to the field of adult literacy.

Education is not a process of depositing by a teacher in a bank of passive minds, but a dialogue between the learner and co-coordinator. In the same way teaching is often thought of as something that comes rather naturally to people who know their subject. In general, it is thought that it is a simple process that produces simple outcomes. But teaching is an intriguing, important and complex process. It takes place in a complicated social institution, which is filled with diverse people.

In teaching process one cannot just know the subject and teach it, because the subject themselves are ever changing. The physics of 1989 is not the physics of 1979. The art of today is not the art of 1930. It is true that teaching is the process by which teacher and students create a shared environment, including sets of values and beliefs which in term colour their view of reality. The social movements now shaping the world were not imagined by the best minds of a generation ago. The teacher must learn to control five processes of teaching ; first- making and using knowledge, second shaping the school, third- teaching with strategy, fourth-creating interpersonal climates and fifth and last controlling a teaching personality.

Mahatma Gandhi had always impressed upon the teaching community said that there is a need to develop inner urges and make learning as a means for broader perspectives of life. Dr. Ivan Illich, Director, centre for International Documentation, Carnavce, Maxico advocated thought his writings that a teacher is a co-learner in adult education settings. This concept is widely accepted to a different degree, popularly termed as a feedback mechanism. The teacher cannot depend for the whole life upon what he learns once a while.

Rabindra Nath Tagore had nicely put it as a teacher can never truly teach unless he is still learning himself. A lamp can never light another lamp unless it continues to burn its own flame. The teacher who has come to the end of his subject, who has no living traffic with his knowledge, but merely repeats his lessons to his students, cannot lead their minds; he cannot quicken them.

In short, teaching is a process which can t learn on one side. The teacher cannot just pour the knowledge in the student s mind. If the students are not interested in learning, the teacher can t go ahead without the proper cooperation of students, and a well designed curriculum.

How English became a Subject in India

The history of the English language in India dates back to the arrival of the British. However, they did not concentrate their attention on the education (Teaching and learning of English) from the very beginning. Their first attention was trade.

The British traders became the rulers of India. The Missionaries started schools and English was one of the subjects being taught. Gradually, the teaching of English developed. In order to win over the people, the British decided to open educational institutions. Such education helped them to create new office worker such as a clerk in offices, so they developed such educational institutions in Calcutta, Madras, and Bombay. They also opened Banaras Sanskrit College. Though there were institutions of classical learning. Provision was made for the teaching of English also. Such was the early beginning of the English in India.

In 1813 the charter of the East India Company was renewed, and an educational clause was added to it. Through this clause the Governor-General must devote not less than 1, 00,000 rupees annually to the education of Indians.

The clause was written as under:

" .... that a sum of not less than one lack of rupees in each year shall be set apart and applied to the revival and improvement of literature and the encouragement of the learned natives of India, and for the introduction and promotion of knowledge of the sciences among the inhabitants of the British territories in India" (Aslam 6).

This clause was the foundation of English education in India. The clause clearly mentioned that the money would be spent on promoting 'literature' (by which they meant English literature) and for 'encouragement of learned natives of India'. Which means it would be spent on promoting English literature only and then implementing the charter Act of 1813, a General Committee of Public Instruction was set up in Calcutta. The committee started its work with an Orientalist policy, rather than a western oriented one, in this committee the majority of the members were Indians. During this period, there was an increasing demand for the teaching of English. To meet this demand Raja Ram Mohan Roy and others established the Hindu College in 1817. Soon the missionaries too opened few colleges and schools.

In 1823 the General Committee of Public Instruction was set up. And in 1834 Macaulay was invited to preside over the committee. He strongly recommended that the spread of western learning could only be possible through the medium of the English language. The view was welcomed by all the members. Woods Dispatch (1854) which is often described as the MagnaCarta of English education in India confirmed the opinion of Macaulay. In the year 1824 Raja Ram Mohan Roy wrote a letter to Viceroy Lord Amberest. In that letter Roy request them or demanding that please introduce the English to Indian people then they will refer the British literature.

In the year 1817 Merole first started English and he first established the Hindu College in Calcutta. This time Western literature, European literature and classical English literature were started for teaching, and there was included two other languages which were translated in English, it was Latin and Greek language.

In 1831 English teaching was first started by the Kings College London University. In the colleges and university first time Greek, Latin, Mathematics and theology these subjects were taught. In the year 1894, Oxford introduced English literature as a subject of study, only at the end of the 19th century Indian people had already accepted that English literature as a subject study. During the British period, education was a source and a path on which British Government would use educated Indian persons to run the British administrative machinery smoothly. Vocationalisation of education and establishment of professional colleges could not come under the provision of educational institutions. Mass education was totally neglected. Lord Macaulay was against the spread of Indian culture through education on the contrary, he wanted a class of persons- Indians in blood and colour, but English in tastes – in opinions, in moral and in intellect. His narrow minded views were accepted by British rulers on the ground that it would save British revenue. The controversy of the time gave rise to westernization of Indian education and Indianisation of Indian education was thrown away. In a few days the schools and colleges increased by leaps and bounds. In them English was given a predominant position and the vernaculars (native language) began to be neglected. Then Indian education commission (1882) expressed its dissatisfaction at the exclusive use of English as the medium of instruction and education. The Indian universities Commission (1902) also raised its voice against the neglect of vernaculars. However the Calcutta University commission (1917) tried to adjust the claims of both English and vernaculars, by giving them different fields.

The dominance of English given by Macaulay continued till the independence of India. After the independence, the position of English in India underwent a change. Meanwhile, a new angle was given to education from two sources of different character. One was from the Christian missionaries and the other from a "semi-rationalist" movement. The Christian missionaries had started their educational activities as early as 1542, upon the arrival of St.Francis Xavier. Afterwards, the movement spread throughout the land and exercised a lasting influence on Indian education. It gave a new direction to elementary education through the introduction of instruction at regular and fixed hours, a broad curriculum, and a clear-cut class system. By printing books in different vernacular languages the missionaries stimulated the development of Indian languages. The study of vernaculars went hand in hand with the teaching of western subjects through the medium of English, known in India as „English education .

Lord Macaulay, who in his famous minutes clearly favoured the western education in India through the medium of English, according to him English must be taught in the Indian schools. He said, "English stands pre-eminent even among the languages of the west—whoever knows that language has ready access to all the vast intellectual wealth which all the wisest nations of the earth have created and hoarde in the course of ninety generation" (Ibid 7).

After it many minutes, dispatches and commissions - for instance Lord Auckland s Minutes of 1839, Wood s Dispatch of 1854, and Hunter Commission of 1882 had Suggested different changes to make English education in India a permanent feature of instruction in the Indian educational institutions.

THE INTRODUCTION TO INDIAN WRITING IN ENGLISH LITERATURE ESSAY

Any opinions, findings, conclusions or recommendations expressed in this material are those of the authors and do not necessarily reflect the views of UK Essays.

The seed of Indian Writing in English was sown during the period of the British rule in India. Now the seed has blossomed into an ever green tree, fragrant flowers and ripe fruits. The fruits are being tasted not only by the native people, but they are also being 'chewed and digested' by the foreigners. It happened only after the constant caring, pruning and feeding. Gardeners' like Tagore, Sri Aurobindo, R.K. Narayan, Raja Rao – to name only a few, looked after the tender plant night and day. In modern time, it is guarded by a number of writers who are getting awards and accolades all over the world.

Indian English Literature is an honest enterprise to demonstrate the ever rare gems of Indian Writing in English. From being a singular and exceptional, rather gradual native flare-up of geniuses, Indian Writing has turned out to be a new form of Indian culture and voice in which India converses regularly. Indian Writers – poets, novelists, essayists, and dramatists have been making momentous and considerable contributions to world literature since pre-Independence era, the past few years have witnessed a gigantic prospering and thriving of Indian English Writing in the global market.

Indian English Literature has attained an independent status in the realm of world Literature. Wide ranges of themes are dealt within Indian Writing in English. While this literature continues to reflect Indian culture, tradition, social values and even Indian history through the depiction of life in India and Indians living elsewhere, recent Indian English fiction has been trying to give expression to the Indian experience of the modern predicaments. There are critics and commentators in England and America who appreciate Indian English novels. Prof. M.K. Naik remarks "â€¦one of the most notable gifts of English education to India is prose fiction for though India was probably a fountain head of story-telling, the novel as we know today was an importation from the west".

India's substantial contribution to world literature is largely due to the profusely creative literary works generated by Indian novelists in English. Their works contemplated and deliberated on multifarious range of issues like nationalism, freedom struggle, social realism, individual consciousness and the like. This literary movement being fortified by the overwhelming output by novelists and distinguished itself as a remarkable force in world fiction. This has been achieved by novelists who sought to prove their inner creative urges in English language, which is indeed an alien tongue for them. It is to the credit of these novelists that they have overcome the hurdles of writing in a foreign language and have been evolved a distinctive style for themselves by mastering the intricacies of the language and assimilating in it the hues and flavors of the Indian – sub continent. Raja Rao famously argued in 1938, in the preface to his novel Kanthapura, for using English, but English adapted to Indian conditions:

English is not an alien language to us. It is the language of our intellectual make-up – like Sanskrit or Persian was before – but not of our emotional make-up. We are all instinctively bilingual, many of us in our own language and in English. We cannot write like the English. We should not. We can only write as Indians. Our method of expression will someday prove to be as distinctive and colorful as the Irish or the American.

The struggle for independence was a mighty and momentous movement sweeping the entire nation and exerting tremendous impact on the sense of national consciousness among the literary fraternity. Thus the lucid description of the freedom struggle showcased images of the awakened Indians who sought to regain their freedom from the grueling and torturous regime of the Britishers. Apart from these reflections, the writers were able to propagate their point of view, which ultimately helped to motivate and guide the masses. Thus the fixation on religious aestheticism was replaced by concerns on socio - political issues. The joy of accomplishing the grandiose feat of obtaining Independence was abruptly marred by the horrendous and traumatic partition of 1947. The horrors, tragic consequences and partition like the large scale migration, reckless looting and merciless massacres were portrayed by the writers in their works which captured the interest, and imagination of the reader, the Indian English novels began to prove its mark in the global literary scenario. East-West conflict, multi-culturalism, social realism, gender issues, comic aspect of human nature, ecological concerns, magic realism, diasporic writings and the like became the themes of the post-Independent writers.

English has acquired a rare privilege and popularity in India especially among the elite and the middle classes. It is increasingly being used by writers to give shape to the conflicting dilemmas and issues that confront the human psyche. It has definitely become a convenient medium to express the intrinsic talents of the writers. Moreover the Indian English writers use it with enviable ease and gaining mastery of a foreign tongue to articulate the vagaries and vicissitudes of an individual's consciousness in a realm of its own aptly substantiate the expansiveness and verve of the Indian English writer.

Indian writing in English has commended unstinted admiration in both home and abroad, is now in its full swing. It has carved out a new track, a new vision - a vision that is replete with an un answering faith and hope, myths and traditions, customs and rites etc. If we dive deep into the works of the Indian stalwarts of English fictions, it is revealed that their works are not an imitation of English literary pattern but highly original and intensely Indian in both theme and spirit. They have given a new shape and color to English literature in the same way as the Australians and Americans have evolved their own literature in their respective countries.

Indian English literature is two hundred years old. Sri Aurobindo stands like a huge oak spreading its branches over these two centuries. The contribution of Sri Aurobindo as a perfect writer and craftsman is undoubtedly great. He is the first poet in Indian English writing who has given the re - interpretation of myths. Sri Aurobindo envisages spiritual humanism. What Sri Aurobindo points out to the philosophers of today is that human life, body and mind are the evolved forms of super mind. Aurobindo's famous works "The Human Cycle and The Ideal of Human Society" taken together to give a complete picture of Aurobindo's version of the future possibilities of man and shows the humanistic trend in his thought. In the Human cycle, the poet - philosopher offers us a social philosophy of history illuminated by a splendid spiritual vision of future. It is self-evident that Indian English drama could not secure a firm foothold and build s tradition of its own about which M.K. Naik says:

"Owing to the lack of a firm dramatic tradition nourished on actual performance in a live theatre, early Indian English drama in Bengal, as elsewhere in India, grew sporadically as mostly closet drama; and even later, only Sri Aurobindo, Rabindranath Tagore and Harindranath Chattopadhyaya produced a substantial corpus of dramatic writing."

Rabindranath Tagore (1861-1941) is a celebrated name in the sphere of English literature. His creative genius is so much accounting and his literary output is so much rich and varied that the phrase 'myriad-minded', which Mathew Arnold had used for Shakespeare, can aptly be used for him also. He won Nobel Prize for literature in 1913, for his immortal poetic work Gitanjali (1913). Besides being a great universal poet, the genius Tagore is also a novelist, dramatist, Short-Story writer, musician, philosopher, painter, educationalist, reformer and critic in every field and had earned a niche for himself. The setting of his novel is representative and reflective, their characters are natural, realistic, full-blooded and life-like. The socio-religious culture of Bengal is brilliantly portrayed in his novels. Through his novels he brings out some of the problems of the woman of his age. Different kinds of human relations are portrayed and analysed through the different social settings. Some of his novels deal with the modern problems of our society and the interest in them centers round the psychological development of characters under the compelling stress of circumstances. To his credit, there is a long list of poems and plays, both in Bengali and English which had made his place among the world's greatest writers. In Iyengar's words;

As the years passed, he became more and more a legendary figure; in his flowing bead and immaculate white robes he was truly in the line of the great Rishi of Upnishadic times, and indeed he was truly in the line of the great bearing witness to the triune Reality, seeing the way showing it to others.

Tagore neither does nor adheres to the conventional narrative method, nor does he use the principles of organic, consequential plot - structure. He also tries through his novels, to focus the attention on some of the bitter truths and cruel customs of the lives and society as well. His novels amuse, perplex and bring out the real literary pleasures. Tagore has written thirteen novels of which nine are translated into English. The translated works are Gora, The Home and The World (1910), The wreck (1921), Binodini (1964) and many more. Tagore wrote his first original dramatic piece when he was twenty - Valmiki Pratibha (1881) and stated that his works sought to articulate "the play of feeling and not of action." Tagore's dramas used more philosophical and allegorical themes. Tagore's plays also are important to Bengali literature. All of his plays have been repeatedly staged and re-interpreted over the years. His most famous play, perhaps, is Raktakaravi (1926) ("Red Oleanders") - the name of a red flower. It tells of a king who lives behind an iron curtain while his subjects have cruelty and death delivered upon them at the slightest pretext. People are forced to work in the mines so that the kleptocratic king and his cronies may render themselves even wealthier. The play follows the heroine Nandini, who leads the people and finally the king himself towards the destruction of this artifact of subjugation. However, this ultimate victory is preceded by numerous deaths, most importantly that of Ranjan, Nandini's lover, and Kishore a young boy devoted to her. Tagore devoted much effort to Raktakaravi (1926), with (at least) eleven extant revisions. Tagore's Chandalika (1938) was modeled on an ancient legend describing how Gautama Buddha's discipline asks water of a tribal girl.

K.S. Venkataramani (1892-1952) is an Indo-Anglian writer of the pre-Independence era brilliantly focuses on the stupendous impact of Mahatma Gandhi in general. He is a novelist and Short-Story writer. He interweaves the centrality of the novel keeping in view the Gandhian ideology of a self-sufficient, morally and economically integrated village community as the elemental unit of the superstructure of the Indian society. He wrote two novels Murugan, The Tiller (1927), Kandan, The Patriot (1934) and his collection of short stories are Jatadharan and other stories (1937).

Bhabani Bhattacharya (1906-1988) is one of the novelists of the older generation of Indo - Anglian writers. He is endowed with a transparently positive vision of life, explored and expressed artistically in his novels. He throws that the novel must have a social purpose, his stories abound in social and historical realities, quite often bitter and gruesome, such as the Bengal Famine of 1943, the tragedies of freedom struggle and partition, and the evils of poverty, corruption, ignorance, superstition, exploitation, greed etc. Bhattacharya affirms that an artist should inevitably be concerned with truths and social reality. In his first six novels, Bhattacharya has treated culture with different angles. His first five novels are set against Indian social sense in the perspectives of world shaking historical events, whereas the sixth one has its setting both in India and

America's Hawaii Island and deals with the theme of spiritual quest. His novels are So Many Hungers (1947), Music for Mohini (1952), He Who Rides Tiger (1955), The Goddess Named Gold (1960), and Shadow From Ladakh (1966), A Dream of Hawaai (1978).

Post-Independent India has been making quick strides in the field of science and technology. There has been an admirable economic growth in India in recent times. So, the novel proved to be an effective medium for the reflection of the spirit of the age, encompassing the bitter and sweet realities of the period. The great proliferation of the Indian English novel also owes its credit to the sudden increase of interest in the new literature of post colonial nations by the west.

The Indian English fiction has had a meteoritic growth during the dawn of the millennium year and the writing in all genres of literature has gained momentum, particularly the Indian novel, the doyens of the Indian writing like R.K.Narayan, Mulk Raj Anand, and their ilk promoted the conventional mode of writing. The crusaders of the contemporary and modern era include Salman Rushdie, Amitav Ghosh, Vikram Seth and many more. They elucidate and substantiate strength of the emerging modern voice of India, which has the vibrancy and energy of a gushing artesian along with an unmatched resolve to experiment and explore new avenues of writing novels. A host of contemporary post - colonial writers like Rushdie, Arundati Roy, Meena Alexander, Anita Nair and Jhumpa Lahiri have initiated the process of decolonizing the 'Colonial English' and using it as a medium to express Indian thoughts and sensibilities with a distinctive Indian style.

The freedom movement spearheaded by Gandhi inspired a flurry of activity in the literary world. The need for an autonomous, independent country lead to an explosion of creativity, which sought to appeal to the masses to take up the cudgels and oust the Britishers from the Indian soil. Therefore, there was a flourish of novels in both regional and as well as in the national stream. This burst of energy in regional literature, laid the ground work of fine - tuning and enhancing the vibrancy and the scope of the Indian English Fiction.

The dual combination of independent movement and nationalist consciousness gave much impetus and spur to the outflow of novels in which affection for motherland was the crux and this served to invoke the patriotic sentiments of the masses. Raja Rao's Kanthapura(1938), K.S.Venkataramani's Kandan, The Patriot (1934) and Mulk Raj Anand's Untouchable(1935), Coolie (1936), The Sword and the Sickle(1942), revolved around the varying themes of the independence struggle. Post - Independent India also produced number of novels involving the causes and aftermaths of the freedom movement. The novels that belong to this category include Nayantara Saghal's A Time to be Happy(1952), Khwaja Ahmed Abbas' Inquilab(1955), R.K.Narayan's Waiting for the Mahatma(1955) etc.

The triumvirs Mulk Raj Anand, Raja Rao and R.K.Narayan were the novelists who stabilized and fortified the Indian English Fiction with their ample works and unique literary style. Thus, it was aptly noted by William Walsh regarding the afore mentioned writers:

> Distinguished not only for their own work but as the inaugurators of the form itself since it was they who defined the area in which the Indian novel in English was to operate, drew the first models of its characters and themes and elaborated its particular logic. Each used its own version of an English freed from the foggy taste of Britain. (walsh, 62)

The majority of Mulk Raj Anand's (1905-2004) novels brings to the limelight the inequalities of society and trials and tribulations of the less fortunate. Untouchable (1935), Coolie(1936), The Village(1939), and The Private Life of an Indian Prince(1953) addresses the evils existing in the society in the Marxist terms. His novels also give a graphic description of the daily existence of his characters, their tale of woe, sweat and misery.

Untouchable (1935) targets the evil of casteism and brings to the surface the issue of segregation of people on the basis of their profession. In Coolie (1936), he presents a poverty-stricken protagonist, Munoo who portrays the hollowness of the society and the curse faced by the proletariat. He was instrumental in bringing about an awareness of the inequality that existed in India. He also advocated solutions for the issues. Both novels are: "a plea for downtrodden, the poor and the outcast, who face economic hardship and emotional humiliation in a rigid social structure".

R.K. Narayan (1906-2001) is another celebrity author who enjoys a unique position in the crowded literary scene of Indian Fiction. He is undoubtedly the master of portraying the socio-comic aspects of the ordinary Indian's family and idiosyncrasies of human which form the crux of his novels. The greatest merit of his language and style lives in its simplicity. His subtle use of ironic humor explores the oddities of human nature and juxtaposing it with a dose of harmless humor. His fiction revolves around the imaginary sleepy South Indian town of Malgudi but expresses an outlook which has universal appeal. His famous novels are The Bachelor of Arts and The Painter of signs (1933). Swami and Friends (1935), The English Teacher (1945), Waiting for Mahatma (1955), The Guide (1958), The Sweet Vendor (1967). The vividness in character portrayal is balanced by ironic humor, which is his characteristic style. His writing has stretched across seven decades and occupies a remarkable position in the history of Indian English Fiction. Narayan has gained mastery of the art of portraying characters and nuances of the English language.

Raja Rao's (1908-2006) reputation as a novelist of metaphysics and philosophy is amply justified by his substantial contribution in upholding these themes in his novels. Women in Raja Rao's novels suffer from domestic injustice and tyrannical tradition, but the writer suggests no way out of their dilemma. His women characters, who are a little ambitious, end up playing the devoted role of a wife like Savitri in The Serpent and the Rope (1960). Indian culture being rooted into his consciousness fails him to offer any concrete solution to the besetting women's issue. He analysis modern India from a different perspective and elevates Hindu orthodoxy to a grand metaphysic. His work The Serpent and the Rope(1960) abounds with various themes. It is the story of an intellectual Rama who is in quest of personal enlightment and seeks inspiration and revelation from eastern and western metaphysics. He has a French wife and his association with Savithri brings to the forefront the contemplation of the Feminine Principle and endeavors to correlate the eastern and western views. The later works by Raja Rao includes The Cat and The Shakespeare (1956) and Comrade Kirillov (1976). Kanthapura (1938) by Raja Rao emphasizes the influence of the Gandhian movement by highlighting the 1920's and the Gandhi - Irwin Pact of 1931. He focuses a small village through which he explores the impact of the freedom movement on the villagers and also captures their roles in the struggle for Independence. Rao uses his novels to spread the Gandhian message and as propaganda against social evils.

Mulk Raj Anand (1905-), R.K.Narayan (1906-2000) and Raja Rao (1909-) became the trinity of Indian writing in English. Speaking of The Big Three, Walsh said:

"It is these three writers who defined the area in which the Indian novel was to operate. They established its assumptions; they sketched its main themes, freed the first models of its characters and elaborated its particular logic. Each of them used an easy, natural idiom which was unaffected by the opacity of a British inheritance. Their language has been freed of the foggy taste of Britain and transferred to a wholly new setting of brutal heat and brilliant light."

The sudden spirit of creative writing in the eighties reflects the sense of awareness of the plurality of the nation. It transcends the east-west conflict and portrays the new Post Colonial India with its evolving outlook, which is essentially a blend of tradition and modernism. It reveals the cosmopolitan outlook of the new generation who strives to strike a balance between the inherited traditional values and imbibed foreign culture. The treatment and technique of the novel is Trans-national and Trans - continental. Salman Rushdie, Amitav Ghosh and Upamanya chatterjee are the writers who reigned supreme with their momentous work. Their works delve into the hurdles faced by newly independence nation, which at times a harsh depiction of reality. These writers have made bold attempts to recapture the altered perceptions of Post - colonial India and the use of revolutionary narrative technique has elevated their position among the writers of Indian Fiction in English.

Salman Rushdie (1947) was born and brought up in Bombay and later went to England for higher education. Thus, his roots and early education in India combined with the exposure to higher education in a foreign country, has played a stupendous role in shaping the mind of this writer. His novels abounds with myths, symbols and motifs. The arrival of his best novel Midnight Children(1981) shook the very foundation of the complacency of the Indian English Fiction. The language, style theme and narrative technique employed by Rushdie is entirely novel and highly innovative. He initiated a trend which cared very less about the continental method of writing novels. Incredible imagination, amazing comic sense and absolute word-play are the hallmarks of Rushdie's works. Midnight's Children(1981), the novel has three parts and based on the crucial role by history in the narrative, it can be categorized as the growth of the characters during pre-Independence, partition and post-Independence. His works abounds with the lavish use of symbols and fantasy. Rushdie will always be remembered for his dare devil techniques, narrative spanning generations, depiction of characters with eccentricities, experimentation with style, abundant usage of allegory, symbols and thinly veiled disguise of real life people and political overtones.

A Suitable Boy(1993), by Vikram seth was the cynosure of all eyes on its publication. Seth delves in detail on the social milieu of post-Independent India. The novel portrays the concerns of the middle aged lady, Mrs.Rupa Mehra, who embarks on a mission suitable groom for her daughter Lata and succeeds when she meets the young Haresh Kanna. Though match making is the novel's theme, the major attraction of the novel is the depiction of social panorama of India which encompasses cultural arena, politics in academics circles and the like also form an integral part of the novel. Inexhaustible. It is also remarkable that the theme and technique of novels in Indian literature during this period found based on social upset, poverty, untouchability, exploitation, social movement, political movement etc. Iyengar observes,

Some of the best studies of social life are, naturally enough, in the regional languages; and it is not easy to translate the racy idioms of every day speech into English. This is particularly true of life in the country side, the seaside, the hillside where life has, perhaps, changed very little indeed during the last two thousand years. Urban life in India attracts the novelists by its excitement, perversions, sophistications and violent alternations between affluence and poverty, splendor and squalor; but the interior, the areas of obscurity and inaccessibility have their attractions too, and sometimes bring out the best in the creative novelist.

Women novelists have played a crucial and momentous role in enhancing the quality and quantity of the Indian English Fiction. They have further added the woman's perspective and feministic dimensions to the novels. These rich contributions have widened the spectrum of issues deliberated in the novel. In the past, the work by the Indian women authors has always been undervalued because of some patriarchal assumptions. Indian societies gave priorities to the work of male experiences. In those days, women used to write about a women's perception and experiences within the enclosed domestic arena.

On the other hand, male authors used to deal with heavy themes. Thus, it was assumed that their work would get more priority and acceptance in the society. During the eighteenth century, these factors led towards the decline of Indian women writing. And with all these factors, production of women's literature declined further. In the nineteenth century, more and more women actively participated in India's reformist movement against the British rule. It again led to the women's literature. At that time, their write - ups mainly concentrated on the country's freedom struggle. Over the years, the world of feminist ideologies began to influence the English literature of India.

The contributions by women writers cannot go unnoticed. In fact the works by women writers constitute a major segment of the contemporary Indian writing in English. Today women are seen establishing their identity in almost all walks of life and they have heralded a new consciousness in the realm of literature too. Anees Jung in her book Unveiling India states her ideology in the following words:

In the complex pantheon of diversities, the Indian woman remains the point of unity unveiling through each single experience a collective unconscious prized by a society that is looked in mortal combat with the power and weakness of age and time. She remains the still centre, like the centre the potter's wheel, circling to create new forms, unfolding the continuity of a racial life, which in turn has encircled and helped her acquire a quality of concentration.

Among the women writers Sarojini Naidu, the great poetess charmed the readers with her writings. Feminism themes have also been used by authors like Nayantara Sahgal and Rama Mehta. Regional fiction theme has been aptly used by Kamala Das, Anita Nair and Susan Viswanathan. Novelists like Kamala Markandaya and Anita Desai captured the spirit of Indian cultures and its traditional values. During 1990's India became a popular literary nation as a number of women authors made their debut in this era. Chitra Banerjee Divakaruni, Suniti Namjoshi and Anuradha Marwah Roy used realism as main theme of their novels. The novels of authors like Namita Gokhale or Shobha De are really out - spoken. Most of these female novelists are known for their bold views that are reflected in their novels. Basically, these are the novels of protest and an outburst of reservations and contaminations. Unlike the past, where the works of women novelists were given less priority and were actually undervalued, classification of feministic or male writings hardly makes any sense today.

In the twentieth century, women's writing was considered as a powerful medium of modernism and feminist statements. The last two decades have witnessed phenomenal success in feminist writings of Indian English literature. Today is the generation of those women writers who have money and are mostly western education. Their novels consist of the latest burning issues related with women as well as those issues that exist in the society since long. The publishers feel that the literature actually survives because of these types of bold topics and commercials used by the women novelists. They describe the whole world of women with simply stunning frankness. Their write - ups give a glimpse of the unexplored female psyche, which has no accessibility. The majority of these novels depict the psychological suffering of the frustrated housewife. At this pint of time, it is essential to quote Virginia Woolf,

It is probable, however, that both in life and in art, the values of women are not the values of man. Thus, when a woman comes to write a novel, she will find that she is perpetually wishing to alter the established values - to make serious what appears insignificant to a man, and trivial what is to him important.

Since long, feminism has been used by the women novelists. Their novels reflect that the present age women have realized that she is not helpless and is not dependent.

They feel that a woman is an equal competent just like a man. Today a woman has also become a direct money earner and she is not only confined to household works. The women of modern era think on different lines and that is what is depicted in the novels of the Indian women authors. These facts are incorporated by the women writers. Indian women writers explore the feminine subjectivity and apply the theme that ranges from childhood to complete womanhood. These women writers say that feminism means putting an end to the silent sufferings of women.

Women writers in India are moving forward with their strong and sure strides, matching the pace of the world. We see them bursting out in full bloom spreading their own individual fragrances. They are recognized for their originality, versatility and the indigenous flavor of the soil that they bring to their work. Indian women writers like Kamala Markandaya, Bharathi Mukherjee ,Anita Desai, Nayantara saghal and many more have played a pioneering role in conveying the readers a wild range of indigenous Indian issues, punctuated by a strong feministic outlook. It is amazing to note that these writers have climbed the ladder of success in a slow and painful way. Thus, this new voice of emerging modern India succeeded in drawing the attention of the public towards the pressing problems of gender inequality, social evils, and encroachment of land by foreign nationals and exploitation of women in a patriarchal society.

Kamala Markandaya (1924-2004) was brought up in South India, but her works do not confine to provincial characters and themes. Kamala's oeuvre explores a multitude of issues and the choices of themes exhibit her potential to approach the subject with appreciable maturity and good organisation. Her works are a realistic delineation of the double pulls that the Indian women is subjected to, between her desire to assert herself as an individual and her duty in the capacity of a daughter, wife and mother. She also points out how the socio-economic conditions affect the women most. Nectar in the Sieve (1954) is her first novel, which delineates the tragic outcomes of penury, natural calamities and intruding modernization with its horrendous aftermaths. It is a well constructed novel on the classical mode on the theme of hunger and starvation. Some Inner Fury (1955) and Possession (1963) and The Golden Honey Comb (1977) are her popular novels, wherein she gives a clear and economical account of the life style of the peasants, the middle classes and the aristocracy and also focuses on the conflicting East - West relations. Kamala's ability to depict her social observations comes to the force in A Handful of Rice (1966). In Pleasure City (1982), Kamala concentrates on the intrusion of modernity in a traditional world and its consequences. The routine life of the fisher folk with its simplicity and awareness of the complexity of unknown dangers in the sea and the like are portrayed vividly by Kamala. The characterization in the novel is a testimony to Kamala's caliber to etch characters realistically and humorously.

Nayantara Saghal (1927) is another popular woman novelist who dominated the Post - Independence scenario of an Indian novel in English. She dealt with issues concerning women that later became major issues in the feminist movement launched in the sixties. With delicate sensitivity, she exposes the prejudices women face in the male-dominated society. Sahgal has a limited world of feminist id

in the language class should be the important strategies of teaching English as a second language. This is evident from what Littlewood has to say:

"Foreign language learners need opportunities to develop the skills, by being exposed to situations... the learners need to acquire not only reportoire of linguistic items, but reportoire of strategies for using them in concrete situations".

Littlewood further writes elaborately on the significance of meaning or semantic options, as language is essentially a system of meaning potential i.e. it consists of sets of semantic options available to the language users that relate what the user can do in terms of social behaviour, what the user can say in terms of grammar. Littlewood writes:

"Students must also learn to relate language to the social meaning that it carries and to use it as a vehicle for social interaction. To this end, it is necessary to increase their sense of performing in a meaningful social context, rather than simply responding to promote... with the necessary linguistic form and the necessary links between form and meaning".

Howatt distinguishes between a 'strong' and 'weak' version of this approach as:

"There is in a sense, a 'strong' and 'weak' version of the communicative approach. The weak version which has become more or less standard practice in the last ten years, stresses the importance of providing learners with opportunities to use their English for communicative purposes and characteristically, attempts to integrate such activities into a wider program of language teaching...The 'strong' version of communicative teaching, on the other hand, advances the claim that language is acquired through communication, so that it is not merely a question of activating an existing but inert knowledge of the language, but of stimulating the development of the language system itself. If the former could be described as 'learning to use' English, the latter entails 'using English to learn it".

Summarising the main characteristics of the communicative approach Richards and Rodgers asserts:

" (i) Language is a system for the expression of meaning.

(ii) The primary function of language is for interaction and communication.

(iii) The structure of language reflects its functional and communicative uses.

(iv) The primary units of language are not merely its grammatical and structural features, but categories of functional and communicative meaning as exemplified in discourse".

An important aspect of communicative approach which has attracted attention of the applied linguists is the syllabus model. Wilkins's notional- syllabus was one of the very first syllabus models, which specified the semantic-grammatical categories and the categories of communicative function that learners need to express. But it was soon criticized by linguists as merely replacing functions. According to Richards and Rodgers "it specified products rather than communicative processes".

The roles of the learner and the teacher as visualised in CLT are different from those found in the traditional second language classrooms. Breen and Candlin describe the learner's role within CLT in the following terms:

"The role of the learner as negotiator-between the self, the learning process, and the object of learning, emerges from and interacts with the role of joint negotiator within the group and within the classroom procedures and activities, which the group undertakes. The implication for the learner is that he should contribute as much as he gains, and thereby learn in an interdependent way".

Thus, it is the co-operative approach to learning which Breen and Candlin stress in CLT. Students interact primarily with each other rather than with the teacher.

Breen and Candlin further describe the role of the teacher in CLT which is essentially as two-fold:

"The teacher has two main roles: the first is to facilitate the communication process between all participants in the classroom, and between these participants and various activities and texts. The second is to act as an independent participant within the learning-teaching group. The latter role is closely related to the objectives of the first role and arises from it. These roles imply a set of secondary roles for the teacher; first, as an organiser of resources and as a resource himself, second as a guide within the classroom procedures and activities... A third role for the teacher is that of a researcher and learner with much to contribute in terms of appropriate knowledge and abilities, actual and observed experience of the nature of learning and organizational capacities".

Thus, the CLT teacher's primary role is to organize the classroom as a setting for communication and communicative activities. The teaching materials are also designed to promote communicative language use. Richards and Rodgers consider three kinds of instructional materials currently used in CLT and label these as: 'text-based, task-based, and realia'.

Michael Swan argues against the belief that the traditional structure-based courses neglect the teaching of functions, notions and skills. He writes:

"It is quite false to represent older courses as concentrating throughout on form at the expense of meaning, or as failing to teach people to do things with language".

However, Swan concedes that we have, by and large, gained more than we have lost from the communicative approach in that it has helped us to analyse and teach the language of interaction. We can benefit from the innovative language teaching methodologies only if "we can keep our heads, recognize dogma for what it is, and try out the new techniques without giving up useful older methods simply because they have been proved wrong".

Richards and Rodgers catalogue some of the important questions which are raised by the applied linguists and pedagogues alike regarding the communicative approach as:

" (i) can the communicative approach be applied at all levels in a language programme?
(ii) is communicative approach equally suited to ESL and EFL situations?
(iii) does communicative approach require grammar-based syllabuses to be abandonded or merely revised?".

To conclude, the communicative approach takes into account all the four basic linguistic skills viz. listening, speaking, reading, writing and also the conversational skill where the social context of utterances play the significant role.

UNIT VII

CULTURAL STUDIES

CULTURAL STUDIES

INTERDISCIPLINARY FIELD

Cultural studies, interdisciplinary field concerned with the role of social institutions in the shaping of culture. Cultural studies emerged in Britain in the late 1950s and subsequently spread internationally, notably to the United States and Australia. Originally identified with the Center for Contemporary Cultural Studies at the University of Birmingham (founded 1964) and with such scholars as Richard Hoggart, Stuart Hall, and Raymond Williams, cultural studies later became a well-established field in many academic institutions, and it has since had broad influence in sociology, anthropology, historiography, literary criticism, philosophy, and art criticism. Among its central concerns are the place of race or ethnicity, class, and gender in the production of cultural knowledge.

Cultural studies is a field of theoretically, politically, and empirically engaged cultural analysis that concentrates upon the political dynamics of contemporary culture, its historical foundations, defining traits, conflicts, and contingencies. Cultural studies researchers generally investigate how cultural practices relate to wider systems of power associated with or operating through social phenomena, such as ideology, class structures, national formations, ethnicity, sexual orientation, gender, and generation. Cultural studies views cultures not as fixed, bounded, stable, and discrete entities, but rather as constantly interacting and changing sets of practices and processes. The field of cultural studies encompasses a range of theoretical and methodological perspectives and practices. Although distinct from the discipline of cultural anthropology and the interdisciplinary field of ethnic studies, cultural studies draws upon and has contributed to each of these fields.

Cultural studies was initially developed by British academics in the late 1950s, 1960s, and 1970s, and has been subsequently taken up and transformed by scholars from many different disciplines around the world. Cultural studies is avowedly and even radically interdisciplinary and can sometimes be seen as antidisciplinary. A key concern for cultural studies practitioners is the examination of the forces within and through which socially organized people conduct and participate in the construction of their everyday lives. As a result, Cultural Studies as a field of research is not concerned with the linguistically uncategorized experiences of individuals, or, in a more radical approach, holds that individual experiences do not exist, being always the result of a particular social-political context.

Cultural studies combines a variety of politically engaged critical approaches drawn including semiotics, Marxism, feminist theory, ethnography, critical race theory, post-structuralism, postcolonialism, social theory, political theory, history, philosophy, literary theory, media theory, film/video studies, communication studies, political economy, translation studies, museum studies and art history/criticism to study cultural phenomena in various societies and historical periods. Cultural studies seeks to understand how meaning is generated, disseminated, contested, bound up with systems of power and control, and produced from the social, political and economic spheres within a particular social formation or conjuncture. Important theories of cultural hegemony and agency have both influenced and been developed by the cultural studies movement, as have many recent major communication theories and agendas, such as those that attempt to explain and analyze the cultural forces related and processes of globalization.

During the rise of neo-liberalism in Britain and the US, cultural studies both became a global movement, and attracted the attention of many conservative opponents both within and beyond universities for a variety of reasons. Some left-wing critics associated particularly with Marxist forms of political economy also attacked cultural studies for allegedly overstating the importance of cultural phenomena. While cultural studies continues to have its detractors, the field has become a kind of a worldwide movement that is to this day associated with a raft of scholarly associations and programs, annual international conferences, publications and students and practitioners from Taiwan to Amsterdam and from Bangalore to Santa Cruz. Somewhat distinct approaches to cultural studies have emerged in different national and regional contexts such as the United States, Canada, Australia, New Zealand, Latin America, Asia, Africa and Italy.

Characteristics

In his 1994 book, *Introducing Cultural Studies*, Ziauddin Sardar lists the following five main characteristics of cultural studies:

- The aim of cultural studies is to examine cultural practices and their relation to power. For example, a study of a subculture (such as white working class youth in London) would consider their social practices against those of the dominant culture (in this example, the middle and upper classes in London who control the political and financial sectors that create policies affecting the well-being of white working class youth in London).
- The objective of cultural studies includes understanding culture in all its complex forms and analyzing the social and political context in which culture manifests itself.
- Cultural studies is a site of both study/analysis and political criticism/action. (For example, not only would a cultural studies scholar study an object, but s/he would connect this study to a larger, progressive political project.)
- Cultural studies attempts to expose and reconcile constructed divisions of knowledge that purport to be grounded in nature.
- Cultural studies has a commitment to an ethical evaluation of modern society and to a radical line of political action.

History

As Dennis Dworkin writes, "a critical moment" in the beginning of cultural studies as a field was when Richard Hoggart used the term in 1964 in founding the Centre for Contemporary Cultural Studies (CCCS) at the University of Birmingham in the UK, which was to become home for the development of the intellectual orientation that has become known internationally as the "Birmingham School" of cultural studies. CCCS at the university thus became the world's first institutional home of cultural studies.

Hoggart appointed Stuart Hall as his assistant, and Hall was effectively directing CCCS by 1968. Hall formally assumed the directorship of CCCS in 1971, when Hoggart left

Birmingham to become Assistant Director-General of UNESCO. Thereafter, the field of cultural studies became closely associated with Hall's work. In 1979, Hall left Birmingham to accept a prestigious chair in Sociology at the Open University in the UK, and Richard Johnson took over the directorship of the Centre.

In the late 1990s, "restructuring" at the University of Birmingham led to the elimination of CCCS and the creation of a new Department of Cultural Studies and Sociology (CSS) in 1999. Then, in 2002, the University of Birmingham's senior administration abruptly announced the disestablishment of CSS, provoking a substantial international outcry. The immediate reason for disestablishment of the new department was an unexpectedly low result in the UK's Research Assessment Exercise of 2001, though a dean from the university attributed the decision to "inexperienced 'macho management.'" The RAE, a holdover initiative of the Margaret Thatcher-led UK government of 1986, determines research funding for university programs.

There are numerous published accounts of the history of cultural studies.

STUART HALL'S DIRECTORSHIP OF CCCS AT BIRMINGHAM

Beginning in 1964, after the initial appearance of the founding works of British Cultural Studies in the late 1950s, Stuart Hall's pioneering work at CCCS, along with that of his colleagues and postgraduate students including Paul Willis, Dick Hebdige, David Morley, Charlotte Brunsdon, John Clarke, Richard Dyer, Judith Williamson, Richard Johnson, Iain Chambers, Dorothy Hobson, Chris Weedon, Tony Jefferson, Michael Green and Angela McRobbie, gave shape and substance to the field of cultural studies. Many cultural studies scholars employed Marxist methods of analysis, exploring the relationships between cultural forms (the superstructure) and that of the political economy (the base). By the 1970s, the work of Louis Althusser radically rethought the Marxist account of "base" and "superstructure" in ways that had a significant influence on the "Birmingham School." Much of the work done at CCCS studied youth subcultural expressions of antagonism toward "respectable" middle-class British culture in the post-WWII period. Also during the 70s, the politically formidable British working classes were in decline. Britain's manufacturing industries were fading and union rolls were shrinking. Yet millions of working class Britons backed the rise of Margaret Thatcher. For Stuart Hall and his colleagues, this shift in loyalty from the Labour Party to the Conservative Party had to be explained in terms of cultural politics, which they had been tracking even before Thatcher's victory. Some of this work was presented in the cultural studies classic, *Policing the Crisis*, and in other later texts such as Hall's *The Hard Road to Renewal: Thatcherism and the Crisis of the Left* and *New Times: The Changing Face of Politics in the 1990s*.

To trace the development of British Cultural Studies, see, for example, the work of Richard Hoggart, E. P. Thompson, Raymond Williams, Stuart Hall, Paul Willis, Angela McRobbie, Paul Gilroy, David Morley, Charlotte Brunsdon, Richard Dyer, and others.

Cultural Studies in the Late-1970s and Beyond

By the late 1970s, scholars associated with The Birmingham School had firmly placed questions of gender and race on the cultural studies agenda, where they have remained ever since. Also by the late 1970s, cultural studies had begun to attract a great deal of international attention. It spread globally throughout the 1980s and 90s. As it did so, it both encountered new conditions of knowledge production, and engaged with other major international intellectual currents such as poststructuralism, postmodernism and postcolonialism. The wide range of cultural studies journals now located throughout the world, as shown below, is one indication of the globalization of the field.

Developments Outside the UK

In the US, prior to the emergence of British Cultural Studies, several versions of cultural analysis had emerged largely from pragmatic and liberal-pluralist philosophical traditions. However, when British Cultural Studies began to spread internationally in the late 1970s, and to engage with feminism, poststructuralism, postmodernism and race in the late 70s and 1980s, critical cultural studies (i.e., Marxist, feminist, poststructuralist, etc.) expanded tremendously in US universities in fields such as communication studies, education, sociology and literature. *Cultural Studies*, the flagship journal of the field, has been based in the US since its founding editor, John Fiske, brought it there from Australia in 1987.

A thriving cultural studies scene has existed in Australia since the late 1970s, when several key CS practitioners emigrated there from the UK, taking British Cultural Studies with them, after Margaret Thatcher became Prime Minister of the UK in 1979. A school of cultural studies known as "cultural policy studies" is one of the distinctive Australian contributions to the field, though it is not the only one. Australia also gave birth to the world's first professional cultural studies association (now known as the Cultural Studies Association of Australasia) in 1990. Cultural studies journals based in Australia include *International Journal of Cultural Studies*, *Continuum: Journal of Media & Cultural Studies* and *Cultural Studies Review*.

In Canada, cultural studies has sometimes focused on issues of technology and society, continuing the emphasis in the work of Marshall McLuhan, Harold Innis, and others. Cultural studies journals based in Canada include *Topia: Canadian Journal of Cultural Studies*.

In Africa, human rights and Third World issues are among the central topics treated. Cultural Studies journals based in Africa include the *Journal of African Cultural Studies*.

In Latin America, cultural studies has drawn on thinkers such as José Martí, Ángel Rama and other Latin American figures, in addition to the Western theoretical sources associated with cultural studies in other parts of the world. Leading Latin American cultural studies scholars include Néstor García Canclini, Jésus Martín-Barbero, and Beatriz Sarlo. Among the key issues addressed by Latin American cultural studies scholars are decoloniality, urban cultures, and post-development theory. Latin American cultural studies journals include the *Journal of Latin American Cultural Studies*.

Even though cultural studies developed much more rapidly in the UK than in continental Europe, there is a significant cultural studies presence in countries such as France, Spain and Portugal. The field is relatively undeveloped in Germany, probably due to the continued influence of the Frankfurt School, which is now often said to be in its third generation, which includes notable figures such as Axel Honneth. Cultural studies journals based in continental Europe include the *European Journal of Cultural Studies*, the *Journal of Spanish Cultural Studies*, *French Cultural Studies*, and *Portuguese Cultural Studies*.

In Germany, the term *cultural studies* specifically refers to the field in the Anglo-sphere especially British Cultural Studies to differentiate it from the German Kulturwissenschaft which developed along different lines and is characterized by its distance from political science. However, Kulturwissenschaft and cultural studies are often used interchangeably, particularly by lay persons.

Throughout Asia, cultural studies has boomed and thrived since at least the beginning of the 1990s. Cultural studies journals based in Asia include *Inter-Asia Cultural Studies.* In India the Centre for Study of Culture and Society, Bangalore and the Department of Cultural Studies at The English and Foreign Languages University Hyderabad at two major institutional spaces for Cultural Studies.

ISSUES, CONCEPTS AND APPROACHES

Marxism, Feminism, Race and Culture

As noted above, Marxism has been an important influence upon cultural studies. Those associated with CCCS initially engaged deeply with the structuralism of Louis Althusser, and later in the 1970s turned decisively toward Antonio Gramsci. Cultural studies has also embraced the examination of race, gender, and other aspects of identity, as is illustrated, for example, by a number of key books published collectively under the name of CCCS in the late 1970s and early 80s, including *Women Take Issue: Aspects of Women's Subordination* (1978), and *The Empire Strikes Back: Race and Racism in 70s Britain* (1982).

Gramsci and Hegemony

To understand the changing political circumstances of class, politics and culture in the United Kingdom, scholars at The Birmingham School turned to the work of Antonio Gramsci, an Italian thinker, writer and communist party leader of the 1910s, 20s and '30s. Gramsci had been concerned with similar issues: why would Italian laborers and peasants vote for fascists? What strategic approach is necessary to mobilize popular support in more progressive directions? Gramsci modified classical Marxism, and argued that culture must be understood as a key site of political and social struggle. In his view, capitalists used not only brute force (police, prisons, repression, military) to maintain control, but also penetrated the everyday culture of working people in a variety of ways in their efforts to win popular "consent." It is important to recognize that for Gramsci, historical leadership, or "hegemony," involves the formation of alliances between class factions, and struggles within the cultural realm of everyday common sense. Hegemony was always, for Gramsci, an interminable, unstable and contested process.

Scott Lash writes:

In the work of Hall, Hebdige and McRobbie, popular culture came to the fore... What Gramsci gave to this was the importance of consent and culture. If the fundamental Marxists saw power in terms of class-versus-class, then Gramsci gave to us a question of *class alliance.* The rise of cultural studies itself was based on the decline of the prominence of fundamental class-versus-class politics.

Edgar and **Sedgwick** write:

The theory of hegemony was of central importance to the development of British cultural studies [particularly The Birmingham School. It facilitated analysis of the ways subordinate groups actively resist and respond to political and economic domination. The subordinate groups needed not to be seen merely as the passive dupes of the dominant class and its ideology.

Structure and Agency

The development of hegemony theory in cultural studies was in some ways consonant with work in other fields exploring agency, a theoretical concept that insists on the active, critical capacities of subordinated peoples (e.g. the working classes, colonized peoples, women). As Stuart Hall famously argued in his 1981 essay, "Notes on Deconstructing 'the Popular'," "ordinary people are not cultural dopes." Insistence on accounting for the agency of subordinated peoples runs counter to the work of traditional structuralists. Some analysts have however been critical of some work in cultural studies that they feel overstates the significance of or even romanticizes some forms of popular cultural agency.

Cultural studies often concerns itself with agency at the level of the practices of everyday life, and approaches such research from a standpoint of radical contextualism. In other words, cultural studies rejects universal accounts of cultural practices, meanings, and identities.

Judith Butler, an American feminist theorist whose work is often associated with cultural studies, wrote that the move from a structuralist account in which capital is understood to structure social relations in relatively homologous ways to a view of hegemony in which power relations are subject to repetition, convergence and rearticulation brought the question of temporality into the thinking of structure. It has marked a shift from a form of Althusserian theory that takes structural totalities as theoretical objects to one in which the insights into the contingent possibility of structure inaugurate a renewed conception of hegemony as bound up with the contingent sites and strategies of the rearticulation of power.

Globalization

In recent decades, as capitalist culture has spread throughout the world via contemporary forms of globalization, cultural studies has generated important analyses of local sites and practices of negotiation with and resistance to Western hegemony.

Cultural Consumption

Cultural Studies criticizes the traditional view of the passive consumer, particularly by underlining the different ways people *read,* receive and interpret cultural texts, or appropriate other kinds of cultural products, or otherwise participate in the production and circulation of meanings. On this view, a consumer can appropriate, actively rework or challenge the meanings circulated through cultural texts. In some of its variants, then, cultural studies has thus shifted the analytical focus from (traditional understandings of) production to consumption, which is nevertheless understood as a form of production (of meanings, of identities, etc.) in its own right. Stuart Hall, John Fiske, and others have been influential in these developments.

A special 2008 issue of the field's flagship journal, *Cultural Studies*, examined "Anti-Consumerism" from a variety of cultural studies angles. As Jeremy Gilbert noted in his contribution to this issue, cultural studies must grapple with the fact that "we now live in an era when, throughout the capitalist world, the overriding aim of government economic policy is to maintain consumer spending levels. This is an era when 'consumer confidence' is treated as the key indicator and cause of economic effectiveness."

The concept of "text"

Cultural studies, drawing upon and developing semiotics, uses the concept of *text* to designate not only written language, but also television programs, films, photographs, fashion, hairstyles, and so forth; the texts of cultural studies comprise all the meaningful artifacts of culture. This conception of textuality derives especially from the work of the pioneering and influential semiotician, Roland Barthes, but also owes debts to other sources, such as Juri Lotman and his colleagues from Tartu–Moscow School. Similarly, the field widens the concept of "culture." "Culture," for a cultural studies researcher, includes not only traditional high culture (the culture of ruling social groups), but also everyday meanings and practices, which have, as noted above, become a central focus of cultural studies. Cultural studies even approaches sites and spaces of everyday life, such as pubs, living rooms, gardens and beaches, as "texts."

Jeff Lewis summarized much of the work on textuality and textual analysis in his cultural studies textbook and a post-9/11 monograph on media and terrorism. According to Lewis, 'textual studies' use complex and difficult heuristic methods and require both powerful interpretive skills and a subtle conception of politics and contexts. The task of the cultural analyst, for Lewis, is to engage with both knowledge systems and texts, and observe and analyse the ways the two interact with one another. This engagement represents the critical dimensions of the analysis, its capacity to illuminate the hierarchies within and surrounding the given text and its discourses.

Academic Reception

Cultural studies has evolved through the confluence of various disciplines—anthropology, media and communication studies, literary studies, education, geography, philosophy, sociology, politics and others. While some have accused certain areas of cultural studies of meandering into political relativism and a kind of empty version of "postmodern" analysis, others hold that at its core, cultural studies provides a significant conceptual and methodological framework for cultural, social and economic critique. This critique is designed to "deconstruct" the meanings and assumptions that are inscribed in the institutions, texts and practices that work with and through, and produce and re-present, culture. Thus, while some scholars and disciplines like to dismiss cultural studies for its methodological openness and rejection of disciplinarity, its core strategies of critique and analysis have had a profound influence throughout areas of the social sciences and humanities. Cultural studies work on forms of social differentiation, control and inequality, identity, community-building, media, and knowledge production, for example, has had a substantial impact. Moreover, the influence of cultural studies has become increasingly evident in areas as diverse as translation studies, health studies, international relations, development studies, computer studies, economics, archaeology, and neurobiology, as well as across the range of disciplines that initially shaped the emergence of cultural studies, including literature, sociology, communication studies, and anthropology.

Cultural studies has also diversified its own interests and methodologies, incorporating a range of studies on media policy, democracy, design, leisure, tourism, warfare and development. While certain key concepts such as ideology or discourse, class, hegemony, identity and gender remain significant, cultural studies has long engaged with and integrated new concepts and approaches such as deconstruction and postmodernism. The field thus continues to pursue political critique through its engagements with the forces of culture and politics.

The Blackwell *Companion to Cultural Studies,* edited by leading cultural studies scholar Toby Miller, contains essays that analyze the development of cultural studies approaches within each of a wide range of disciplines across the contemporary social sciences and humanities.

Literary Scholars

Many cultural studies practitioners work in departments of English or Comparative Literature. Nevertheless, some traditional literary scholars such as Yale professor Harold

Bloom have been outspoken critics of cultural studies. On the level of methodology, these scholars dispute the theoretical underpinning of the movement's critical framework.

Bloom stated his position during the September 3, 2000 episode of C-SPAN's *Booknotes*, while discussing his book *How to Read and Why*:

There are two enemies of reading now in the world, not just in the English-speaking world. One [is] the lunatic destruction of literary studies...and its replacement by what is called cultural studies in all of the universities and colleges in the English-speaking world, and everyone knows what that phenomenon is. I mean, the...now-weary phrase 'political correctness' remains a perfectly good descriptive phrase for what has gone on and is, alas, still going on almost everywhere and which dominates, I would say, rather more than three-fifths of the tenured faculties in the English-speaking world, who really do represent a treason of the intellectuals, I think, a 'betrayal of the clerks'."

Marxist literary critic Terry Eagleton is not wholly opposed to cultural studies, but has criticised aspects of it and highlighted what he sees as its strengths and weaknesses in books such as *After Theory* (2003). For Eagleton, literary and cultural theory have the potential to say important things about the "fundamental questions" in life, but theorists have rarely realized this potential.

Sociologists

Cultural studies has also had a substantial impact on sociology. For example, when Stuart Hall left CCCS at Birmingham, it was to accept a prestigious professorship in Sociology at the Open University in Britain. The subfield of cultural sociology, in particular, is disciplinary home to many cultural studies practitioners. Nevertheless, there are some differences between sociology as a discipline and the field of cultural studies as a whole. While sociology was founded upon various historic works purposefully distinguishing the subject from philosophy or psychology, cultural studies has explicitly interrogated and criticized traditional understandings and practices of disciplinarity. Most CS practitioners think it is best that cultural studies neither emulate disciplines nor aspire to disciplinarity for cultural studies. Rather, they promote a kind of radical interdisciplinarity as the basis for cultural studies.

One sociologist whose work has had a major influence upon cultural studies is Pierre Bourdieu. Bourdieu's work makes innovative use of statistics and in-depth interviews. However, although Bourdieu's work has been highly influential within cultural studies, and although Bourdieu regarded his work as a form of science, cultural studies has never embraced the idea that it should aspire toward "scientificity," and has marshalled a wide range of theoretical and methodological arguments against the fetishization of "scientificity" as a basis for cultural studies.

Two sociologists who have been critical of cultural studies, Chris Rojek and Bryan S. Turner, argue in their article, "Decorative sociology: towards a critique of the cultural turn", that cultural studies, particularly the flavor championed by Stuart Hall, lacks a stable research agenda, and privileges the contemporary reading of texts, thus producing an ahistorical theoretical focus. Many, however, would argue, following Hall, that cultural studies has always sought to avoid the establishment of a fixed research agenda; this follows from its critique of disciplinarity. Moreover, Hall and many others have long argued against the misunderstanding that textual analysis is the sole methodology of cultural studies, and have practiced numerous other approaches, as noted above. Rojek and Turner also level the accusation that there is "a sense of moral superiority about the correctness of the political views articulated" in cultural studies.

UNIT VIII

LITERARY CRITICISM

LITERARY THEORY AND CRITICISM

REQUIREMENTS OF A GOOD POETRY

1. **Recurrent rhythms.** Although the rhythm of a poem may vary from the mechanical beat of its meter, there is always a recurring beat that unifies the poem and makes it one. This rhythm is in harmony with the thought. Sadness and contemplation, for example, demand a slower beat.

   Break, break, break,

   On thy cold gray stones, O sea!

   Happiness and swiftness of the other hand demand rapid movement.

   The road was a ribbon of moonlight over the purple moor,

   And the highwayman came riding —

2. **Imaginative use of language.** Prose is used basically to communicate ideas and facts, as Poetry stirs our feelings and imaginations. It shows us such relationships, that we had never dreamed that they existed. It puts into words, that which we have often felt, but have never before expressed.

   I never saw a moor,
   I never saw the sea;
   Yet know I how the heather looks,
   And what a wave must be.
   I never spoke with God,
   Nor visited in Heaven;
   Yet certain am I of the spot
   As if the chart were given.

3. **Poetic machinery.** A poet takes full advantage of the less subtle aspects of poetry such as rhymes, figures of speech and stanzaic patterns to emphasize his imagery, pinpoint the emotional reactions sought and increase the pleasure of the reader.

4. **Condensed utterance.** A poet will express his thoughts in minimum of words. He requires concentration on the part of the reader, a willingness to re-read and re-read, until the full import of the words is realised. He makes each word carry a much heavier load of meaning than can be expected of the same word in prose. He expects a word or phrase to evoke a vivid mental image or specific emotional reaction.

After the reader has read the best in poetry, he feels that he has grown mentally and emotionally. He feels that he has met the poet and understood him.

DEFICIENCIES IN POETRY

1. Instead of the rhythms subtly harmonizing with the thought pattern, the meter in these poems drowns all the other things out and the regular beat of the lines comes through without variation.

And now I see the end of all I sought
Oh why, Oh why should it have come to nought !

2. A poem should contain sentiment, true feeling, but when the poet pulls at our heart strings and brings forth sorrow or sympathy beyond that called for by the situation, the poem suffers – as does the reader.

    Stay awhile and shed two dozen tears
    For this poor thief o'ercome with fears
    That any one of number of ills
    Could rob him so quickly of his skills.

3. A poem should help to make the reader a better person through leading him to a more sensitive understanding of men and ideals. The moment the poet, however, delivers a lethal blow and than makes certain that the reader understands by drawing the obvious moral, the poet has killed the suggestiveness that must be part of a poem for it to be good.

    Therefore dear reader now you know
    A truth that has ever been so—
    The hopes of those that practice sin
    Must ever be found among the might have been.

4. A poet can convey much through the pictures he evokes in the minds of the reader. These images, however, must harmonise with the thought, the mood, the sentiment. Unless the poet is deliberately planning to evoke laughter, he can easily cause a reader to smile instead of feel sad by bringing the forth wrong type of imagery.

    Like poor fish turning brown in the frying pan
    Jerry allowed the sun to turn his pallor to tan.

5. Instead of the lines singing, as in great poetry or even following a too regular beat, as in limericks or verse, too often the lines in poor poetry will lose all meter and sound like prose.

    Therefore dear reader I know what I say
    Allan fought much too hard on that Monday

6. Even in his use of words to be rhymed, the poet must be fully aware of the lift that his lines must give the reader's spirit. If he uses too many obvious rhymes, the reader soon feels that the thought is just as obvious. He must learn to use these very sparingly–

    love — above moon - June day —say might — right

7. The essence of poetry is its economy of words. If the poet uses too many words to express an idea, if he repeats himself needlessly or if he adds words to fill out a line, he is not writing at the highest levels.

FIGURES OF SPEECH

The figures of speech are those forms of expression that are different from the ordinary modes in order to emphasise or make the meaning more effective. In the hands of a skilled craftsman, these devices can enhance the value of the written material. When misused these devices can destroy the worth of the material. The following are the figures of speech, most frequently used in poetry.

1. **The simile.** A directly expressed comparison. It usually contains the words *like* or *as.* The successful simile can evoke an ever-expanding vivid image in the mind

of the reader. An effective simile must have an element of surprise in it; it must be appropriate; it should realise the emotional reaction anticipated by the poet–as idle as "a painted ship upon a painted ocean

Similes, however, may be misused.

Trite (commonplace) Simile : red as arose innocent as a child.

Exaggerated Simile : as powerful as ten men.

Inappropriate Simile : as silently as a ghoul, my love glided into my heart.

Her hair dropped round her pallid cheeks, like seaweed on a clam.

2. **The metaphor.** A comparison which is implied rather than stated. It does not contain the words *like* or *as*.

   Trite metaphor : pearly teeth, icy stare, clammy hands.

   Exaggerated Metaphor : one who is the *right hand of justice.*

   Appropriate Metaphor : The Lord is my shepherd. A spring of love gushes from his heart.

   Mixed Metaphor : The bitter taste of her remarks acted as a fuse that set off my anger.

   This is a big step forward in our jet-propelled push forward.

   He will take a backseat in our eyes if he remains forever self-centered.

   You will have to learn to steer a steady course as the sands of time fly by.

3. **Personification.** The figure of speech in which we give human qualities to inhuman things or objects.

   The wind sings a varied song.

   This intensifier must be used with caution by the poet. Too often, it can lead to sentimentalism rather than heightened reality.

   Inappropriate Personification : Nature cried in torrents when I failed the test.

4. **Hyperbole.** Intentional exaggeration. In the hands of a skilled humorist, this can be a most powerful device. Used occasionally, it can involve the reader very quickly in the author's ideas.

   My thoughts threaten to shake down the goodness that is left in the world and leave all to evil and ruin.

5. **Apostrophe.** The figure of speech in which the absent are addressed as though they were present, the living, as well as the dead, objects, as well as human beings. Again, this can be a device highly charged with emotion.

   Blow, blow thou winter wind
   Thou art not so unkind
   As man's ingratitude

   This device can be so easily abused, leading to overcharged words that do not arouse the reader's imagination.

   Come forth, all former graduates of Lafayette High...

   Kindness, fill her heart with goodness, not fear.

6 **Inversion.** The figure of speech in which words are presented out of their natural or expected order.

   Of arms and a man I sing

   This device is frowned upon by most of the modern serious poets. However, it is a crutch that is much overused by the beginner and those who are striving for effects that are beyond the words and thoughts that they are using.

7. **Onomatopocia.** Formation of words to represent natural sounds. A most effective device in appealing to the sense of sound.
Shrill bugles *buzzing* of the bees
Whirring wings
As with the other figures of speech, this device can be effective or most inappropriate.
Inappropriate : The buzzing of the babies in their cribs.
8. **Alliteration.** Repetition of initial consonant sounds, rhyming of initial consonants.
furrow followed free
Alliteration gives a sense of continuity. It is one of the oldest devices in the language and one that is most effective if it is not overused.
9 **Assonance.** Repetition of vowel sounds, the pairing of the same vowel sounds without regard for consonants.
and *screen* from *seeing* and *leave* in sight
This is a device used to give tonal values to lines. It is difficult to introduce and not easily sensed by the reader.

OTHER DEVICES OF POETRY

1. **Rhyme.** The word reserved for rhymes occurring at the end of lines.
To the seas and and the *streams*
In their noonday *dreams*
Masculine Rhyme : The rhyme ends with accented syllables.
She tried and tried in *vain*
To bring that ease from *pain* ...
Feminine Rhyme : A rhyme in two syllables, the first of which as accented.
sweater—letter
Rhymes add music to the lines and are a source of pleasure for the reader if the poet does not resort to misuse. The major fault is found in hackneyed rhymes, ones that have been much over-used–
bright —light flower—hour gold —old
2. **Poetic language.** The fashion has long since come and gone, but many writers don't seem to be aware of this change in styles. They still insist on using old-fashioned words that were once considered elegant and poetic. Some such words are–
ope for open oft for often yclept (called)
Sometimes in the Literature Test one of the choices offered for the missing line of poetry can be eliminated because it relies on these words whereas the other three choices use more modern, direct words.

THE RHYTHMS OF POETRY

The basis of poetic rhythm is in the repetition of accented syllables. These syllables are followed by unaccented ones in an ordered fashion to create the tempo of the lines. For the sake of identification, a line of poetry has been arbitrarily said to consist of a number of feet.

1. **The iambus.** The iambic foot contains an unaccented first syllable and an accented second syllable.
   de táil con fér
2 **The trochee** : The trochaic foot contains an accented first syllable and an unaccented second syllable.
   spéll ing màs ter
3 **The dactyl.** The dactylic foot begins with an accented syllable, which is followed by two unaccented syllables.
   family tech ni cal
4. **The anapest.** The anapestic foot begins with two unaccented syllables, which are followed by the accented syllable.
   un re formed non be liéf

THE LINES OF POETRY

Poetry lines are named according to the number of feet they contain. The most common ones are as follows :

Dimeter A line of two feet
Raise her | gently |
Trimeter A line of three feet
On high | our flag | is flown |
Tetrameter A line of four feet
of all | the men | I e'er | have known |
Pentameter A line of five feet
When I | consi | der how | my light | is spent |
Hexameter A line of six feet
When I | have felt | the weight | of days | and years | pushing |

The lines of poetry are usually named after the type of foot that is found most frequently in it. Therefore, we speak of an iambic pentameter or a trochaic trimeter. The most common line in the English language is the iambic pentameter. The dactylic hexameter, while much used in Latin and French, has proved too long for English.

You should be able to identify lines in this fashion, since very often, in a Literature Test, you are asked to choose a missing line of poetry and one or more of those suggested may be defective, lacking a foot or using a different type of foot.

STANZA SETTING

1. **Free Verse.** The rhythm is determined by the subject matter. The lines do not follow a regular meter, but vary from thought to thought. Rhyme is usually not used.
   Pile the bodies high at Austerlitz and Water loo.
   Shovel them under and let me work—
   I am the grass; I cover all.
   Walt Whitman and Carl Sandburg have helped to establish this as a staple in the repertory of the modern poet. Free verse is a modern form and therefore the images and the language used by the poet tend to be modern.
2. **Blank Verse.** Each line contains ten syllables. The predominant bear is iambic. The lines are unrhymed. Blank verse is written in unrhymed iambic pentameter.

This has been most popular among the best and the poorest technicians. If each line is a complete thought, then it is *end stop*. If the ideas flow from one line to the next, then it is *enjambed*. The pause within the line is called the *caesura*.

Here we may reign secure and in my choice
When I was young and thought I knew all truths

3. **Heroic Couplet.** Two lines of rhymed iambic pentameter.

    Know then thy self, presume not God to scan;
    The proper study of mankind is man.

4. **Quatrain.** Any four-line stanza. The best known of the quatrains is in the old English ballads. The most frequent ballad quatrain consisted of alternating iambic tetrameter and iambic trimeter lines rhyming *xaya* : that is, the second and fourth lines only would usually rhyme.

    The king sits in Dumferling town,
    Drinking the blood-red wine ;
    "Oh where will I get a good sailor,
    To sail this ship of mine".

5. **Sonnet.** A 14 line stanza usually in iambic pentameter. The Italian sonnet has a thought division. The first eight lines, the octave, will present an idea or state a thesis; the last six lines, the sestet, will apply the idea or give the example that proves the truth in the thesis. The Italian sonnet is also called Petrarchan or the Miltonic after the Italian master who originated the form and the great English writer who used it as the vehicle for some of his greatest poetic realizations. The Shakespearean sonnet consists of three quatrains and a concluding summarising couplet.

STYLE IN LITERATURE

Style is the way in which we write. It is, however, a great deal more than freedom from obvious faults, such as prolixity and obscurity. "Style is the body to which thought is the soul and through which it expresses itself".

Of the soul the body form doth take;
For soul is form and doth the body make.

The Elements of Style. A good style is an essential part of a good story, A good style is one that is suitable for its purpose. There are two main elements of style - (1) Choice of ideas, and (2) Expression ideas, though, in the best styles, the two are inseparably interwoven.

Choice of Ideas. The writer's aim is to impart information. For him, there is scarcely any choice : the facts are there and he has merely to state them. But as soon as he wishes to interest or amase, persuade or sadden, a writer has to select his facts. He may merely state general principles; he may illustrate general principles by particular cases. Not that detail is always desirable; Macaulay has pointed out that Milton, instead of giving exact details, uses "dim intimations", So that Heaven and Hell, angels and devils are for us remoter and sublime, shrouded in mystery.

He, above the rest
In shape and gesture proudly eminent,
Stood like a tower. His form had yet not lost.
All her original brightness, nor appeared
Less than Archangle ruined and the excess
Of glory obscured.

Thus, he does not give us a clear picture of Satan; but, we can see this in Keat's *Autumn*—

Sometimes whoever seeks abroad may find,
Thee sitting careless on a granary floor,
Thy hair soft-lifted by tyhe winnowing wind;
Or on a half- reap'd furrow sound asleep,
Drowsed with the fume of poppies.

Keats has the power of visualisation; he makes us see Autumn because he himself sees her more clearly than if she were actually a living person before him. "This power of visualation varies immensely in individuals; some of us have a bright mental image of our uncle or the cook as soon as we have their names, others can with difficulty recall whether their noses turn up or down. But none of us can hope to equal Chaucer and Dickens, whose "slightest sketches have startling aliveness".

The Expression of Ideals

The charm of all writing is a nice mingling of the familiar and the unfamiliar. Good style is mainly a matter of prefect use of contrast and similarity, new and the old.

In the sphere of expression, repetition - either of idea or of phrase - is perhaps the simplest. The great poets can get from it an exquisite music and a wonderful suggestiveness. Take Tennyson's *Break, break, break.*

Break, break, break,
On thy cold gray stones, O sea!
And I would that my tongue could utter
The thoughts that arise in me.

O well for the fisherman's boy,
That he shouts with his sister at play!
O well for the sailor lad
That he sings in his boat on the bay!

And the stately ships go on
To their haven under the hill;
But O for the touch of a vanish'd hand,
And the sound of a voice that still!

The Spenserian Style

The Spenserian style is the style of a lover of beautiful sights and sounds, rather than that of a thinker of profound thoughts. Take the following stanza from the *Faerie Queen-*

The sigtht of whom, though now decayed and mard,
And eke but hgardly seene by candle-light,
Yet, like a Diamond of rich regard,
In doubtful shadow of the darksome night,
With starrie beames about her shining bright,
These merchants fixed eyes did so amaze,
That what through wonder and what through delight,
A while on her they greedily did gaze,
And did her greatly like and did her greatly praise.

Thus we find that in this style, there is the easy, unhasting, untiring pace—a pace largely due to the metre. It has a great contrast with the heroic-couple of Pope, a form where at the end of every two lines we seem to have reached the end of the poem !

The Elizabethan Sonneteer's Style

The Elizabethan sonneteers adopt the style of the conventional amorist. Some of them go so far as to borrowing both sentiments and phrasing from foreign poets; nearly all of them address similar calmly preferred appeals to similar inexorable mistresses, "The lady's eyes are always stars, her cheeks always roses, her lips always cherries".

Conceited Style

A figure of speech or 'conceit' is twisted and turned and squeezed till the last drop of sense is extracted. Thomas Campion's "There is garden in her face" is a case in point. Conceits were not, of course, confined to love-poems: they are found almost ever where in Elizabethan verse; Shakespeare's *Richard II* and his early plays are full of them.

The Metaphysical Style

It is said that the metaphysical style began with Donne and the ordinary metaphors and similes had become common places; they were to a man with an imagination, what plain, unfigurative speech is to us. When he felt truly poetical, his mind 'jumped off' from the ordinary analogies and comparisons to something more remote. At his best, a metaphysical poet is sublimely daring.

The weakness of a metaphysical poet was when his imagination failed to work, he used his ingenuity instead. There is extravagance in language which lacks the charm of the earlier Elizabethan excesses, because it is less spontaneous.

Euphuistic Style

Euphuism has been derived from Lyly's work. We get Euphuism with its elaborate cross-alliteration, its play on words, its antitheses, its endless comparisons drawn from "unnatural natural history".

"Though Aeneas were too *fickle* to Dido, yet Troylus was too faithful to Cresside; though others seem counterfeit in their deeds, yet, Lucilla, persuade yourself, that Euphues will be always current in his dealings".

Arcadian Style

The term 'Arcadian' is from Sidney. Arcadianlism lies in its laboured elegance, in its compound words, in its comparisons of the natural to the artificial and in its idyllic pastoralism—

"There were...meadows enamelled with all sorts of eye-pleasing flowers; thickets which, being lined with most pleasant shade, were witnessed so to by the cheerful disposition of many well-turned birds; each pasture stored with sheep, feeding with sober security, while the pretty lambs with bleating oratory craved the dam's comfort".

The Epigrammatic Style

The epigrammatic style was taken up and modified by the writers of Characters (1614 and later). They gave it a more familiar tone and increased the number and audacity of the conceit, until they came to write what may almost be called metaphysical prose.

"A gallant is one that was born and shapt for his c'oathes; and if *Adam* had not faine, had liv'd to no purpose .....

A Cooke : The Kitchen is his Hell and hee the Divell in it, where his meate and he frye together.

Architectural Prose Style

The prose that owed a great deal to Bacon in vocabulary and in sentence structure, but more to Latin, is the architectural prose. In this style, the writer used his words to build great arches and pinnacles of sound' Milton's was of this order; so was Browne's. "But Browne had in addition much of the subtlety of thought, the old imagination of the best metaphysical poets".

"Afflictions induce callosities; miseries are slippery or fall like snow upon us, which not with- standing is no unhappy stupidity. To be ignorant of evils to come and forgetful of evils past, is a merciful provision in nature, whereby we digest the mixture of our few and evil days and, our delivered senses not relapsing into cutting remembrance, our sorrows are not kept raw by the edge of repetitions... man is a noble animal, splendid in ashes and pompous in the grave, solemnizing nativities and deaths with equal lustre, nor omitting ceremonies of bravery in the infamy of his nature".

The Gentlemanly Style

Dryden's prose is the gentlemanly style of prose, full of a cultured common sense and an easy mastery of the language.

"But enough of this; there is such a variety of game springing up before me, that I am distracted in my choice and know not which to follow. 'Tis sufficient to say according to the proverb, that *here is God's plenty*. We have our forefathers and great-grand-dames all before us as they were in Chaucer's days".

Johnsonian Style

Doctor Johnson was a sturdy classicist. He had read widely among the Elizabethans and Jacobeans and *Browre* was one his favourite writers. His style was apt to be mechanically balanced and rather heavy, but it was nervous, manly and forcible, rhetorical in the best sense.

Hollingworth suggests about the prose-style of Burke, Gibbon, Scott, Macaulay and Lamb as follows :-

Dr. Johnson was not, of course, the sole early representative of the *re-action- Burke* brought back some of the old wild audacity of imagination; *Gibbon*, who owed not a little to Johnson, brought a certain gorgeousness of diction and rhythm and more than the old fullness of thought and learning — but Johnson was by far the most influential. He remained the Dictator in letters, at least as far as Academies for young Ladies were concerned, till well on into the next century; even *Scott* not infrequently falls into the veriest Johnsonese and *Macaulay* owes most of his characteristic virtues as well as most of his characteristic faults to the Doctor.

By the time Scott died, English prose had almost achieved the infinite variety of the Elizabethan period. There was the whimsical style of *Lamb*, which owed something to many writers-especially to Browne— but yet remained intensely original, allusive, humorous, pathetic, full of quaint imaginings and irrelevant relevancies, a style to which something is owed by almost every subsequent writer of such essays as are primarily works of art.

De Quincey's Prose-poetry Style

De Quincey's prose-poetry style aimed deliberately at introducing into prose, the imagination and the magniloquence at that time generally associated only with verse. His style is the parent of Ruskin's purple patch and some sort of relation to Pater's and

Wilde's and Galsworthy's aesthetic styles. Mark the following extract from De Quincey's work—

"Vain prayer ! Empty adjuration ! Profitless rebellion against the laws which season all things for the inexorable grave! Yet not the less we rebel again and again; and though wisdom counsels resignation, yet our human passions, still cleaving to their object, force us into endless rebellion".

Grotesque Style of Carlyle

In contrast to the simple style of Landor, Carlyle's style is grotesque, disjointed, vivid, full of queer compounds and queer words, odd inversions and odder omissions of the less important parts of speech. His style is perhaps overloud, over-emphatic, but thoroughly alive

"Johnson's youth was poor, isolated, hopeless, very miserable ...The largest soul that was in all England; and provision made for it of four pence-half penny a day ? Rude, stubborn, self help here; a whole world of squalor, rudeness, confused misery and want, yet of nobleness and manfulness withal.

Dicken's Prose Style

To some extent, akin to Carlyle's style, Dickens has the mastery of grotesque and the force, but there is nothing of the merely eccentric in his prose. He believes in detailed description. "Whereas Carlyle's influence on style has been almost wholly bad—even Meredith learnt as many faults as virtues from him —Dickens has formed a good model for hundreds of beginners and has taught much to many, such as Chesterton, who are not beginners.

The New Cryptic Style

The new cryptic style has an application to thought and speech of new realism. Side by side with it, the realism of description continues which borrows some of its neighbour's economy of words Mark the following extracts, one from Meredith and the other from Sinclair Lewis.

1. She begged a day's delay; which would enable her, she said, to join them in dining at the Blachington's and seeing dear Lakelands again. "I was invited, you know". She spoke in childish style and under her eyes she beheld her father and mother exchange loops.
2. Under the rolling clouds of prairie a moving mass of steel. An irritable clink and rattle beneath a prolonged roar. The sharp scent of oranges cutting the soggy smell of unbathed people and ancient baggage.

Towns are planless as scattering of paste board boxes on an attic floor. The stretch of faded gold stubble, broken clumps of willows encircling white housed and red barns.

CRITICISM

Criticism is the branch of study concerned with defining, classifying, expounding and evaluating works of literature. Theoretical criticism undertakes to establish, on the basis of general principles, a coherent set of terms, distinctions and categories to be applied to the consideration and interpretation of works of literature, as well as the "criteria" (the standards or norms) by which these works and their writers are to be evaluated. The earliest great work of theoretical criticism was Aristotle's *Poetics*; recent influential books in English are I.A. Richard's **Principles of Literary Criticism* (1924) and Northrop Frye's

Anatomy of Criticism (1957). *Practical criticism* or "applied criticism", concerns itself with the discussion of particular works and writers; in an applied critique, the theoretical principles controlling the analysis and evaluation are left implicit or brought in only as the occasion demands. Among the major works of applied criticism in England are the literary essays of Dryden, Dr. Johnson's *Lives of the Poets,* Coleridge's chapters on the poetry of Wordsworth in *Biographia Literaria* and his lectures on Shakespeare, Matthew Arnold's *Essays in Criticism* and T.S. Eliot's *Selected Essays.*

Practical Criticism

Practical criticism is sometimes distinguished into impressionistic and judicial criticism :

I. **Impressionistic criticism.** It attempts to represent in words the felt qualities of a particular work and to express the attitudes and feelingful responses (the "impression") which the work directly evokes from the critic as an individual. As Hazlitt put it in his essay, "On Genius and Common sense": "You decide from feeling and not from reason; that is, from the impression of a number of things on the mind ...though you may not be able to analyse or account for it in the several particulars". And Walter Pater later said that in criticism "the first step toward seeing one's object as it really is, is to know one's own impression as it really is, to discriminate it, to realise it distinctly" (Preface to *Studies in the History of the Renaissance*). At its extreme this mode of criticism becomes, in Anatole France's phrase, "the adventures of a sensitive soul among masterpieces".

II. **Judicial criticism.** On the other hand, judicial criticism attempts not merely to communicate, but to analyse and explain the effects of a work in terms of its subject, organisation and techniques and to base the critic's individual judgements on general standards of literary excellence. Rarely are the two modes of criticism sharply distinct in practice, but good examples of primarily impressionistic commentary can be found in Longinus (see the characterisation of the *Odyssey* in his essay *On the Sublime),* Hazlitt, Pater (the locus classicus of impressionism is his description of Leonardo's *Mona Lisa* in *The Renaissance*) and in the critical essays of E.M Forster and Virginia Woolf.

Type of Criticism

I. **Mimetic criticism.** It views the literary work as an imitation or reflection or representation of the world and human life and the primary criterion applied to a work is that of the "truth" of its representation to the objects it represents; or should represent. This mode of criticism, which first appeared in Plato and (in a qualified way) in Aristotle, is characteristic of modern theories of literary realism.

II. **Pragmatic criticism.** It views the literary work as something which is constructed in order to achieve certain effects on the audience (effects such as aesthetic pleasure, instruction or special feelings) and it tends to judge the value of the work according to its success in achieving that aim. This approach, which dominated literary discussion from Roman times through the eighteenth century, has been revived in recent *rhetorical criticism,* which emphasises the artistic strategies by which an author engages and influences the responses of his readers to the matters represented in a literary work.

III. **Expressive criticism.** It regards the literary work primarily in relation to the author himself. It defines poetry as an expression or overflow or utterance of feelings or as the product of the poet's imagination operating on his perceptions, thoughts and feelings; it tends to judge the work by its sincerity or genuineness or adequacy to the poet's individual vision or state of mind; and it often looks in the work for evidences of the particular temperament and experiences of the author who, consciously or unconsciously, has revealed himself in it. Such views were developed mainly by Romantic critics and remain widely current in our own time.

IV. **Objective criticism.** It approaches the literary work as something which stands free from poet, audience and the environing world. It describes the literary product as a self-sufficient object or integer or as a world-in-itself, which is to be analysed and judged by "intrinsic" criteria such as complexity, coherence, equilibrium, integrity and the interrelations of its component elements. This is the characteristic approach of a number of important critics since the 1920s, including the *new critics* and the *Chicago school* of criticism.

(5) **Textual criticism.** A basic literary enterprise, which the ordinary reader takes for granted, is textual criticism; its aim is to establish as closely as possible what an author actually wrote, by assaying and correcting the sources of error and confusion in various printings of a work.

(6) **Other varieties of criticism.** It is also common to distinguish types of criticism which bring to bear upon literature various special areas of knowledge and theory, in the attempt to explain the influences which determined the particular characteristics of a literary work. Accordingly, we have "historical criticism", "biographical criticism", "sociological criticism" (an important subspecies is "Marxist criticism"), "psychological criticism" (a subspecies is "Freudian criticism") and *archetypal* or myth criticism.

UNIT IX

LITERARY THEORY POST WORLD WAR II

POST-WAR ENGLISH LITERATURE 1945-1990

HISTORICAL BACKGROUND 1945-1990

The history of Britain in the post-war period is undoubtedly a history of decline. In the last fifty years Britain has tried to maintain a leading role in the world, based on its heroic defence of democracy in World War II and its links with the Commonwealth countries, the ex-colonies of the now lost British Empire. Yet a succession of economic crises, the predominance of the USA and its "Cold War" politics, and the Franco-German project of a United Europe have forced Britain to partly abandon its pretences to world leadership. Arguably, Britain now occupies an uncomfortable secondary position among the world's nations, under the powerful shadow of its former colony, the USA, and lacking a firm pro-European stance.

Ten Prime Ministers –four Labour, six Conservative– headed the British Government between 1945 and 1990. Labour ruled the country for seventeen years, the Conservatives for twenty-eight, including the eleven years under Margaret Thatcher, the longest-serving Prime Minister of this century (1979-1990). Despite frequent changes of Government, history has run its own course, shaping an economic, social and cultural new order beyond the control of the politics and ideology of either Labour or Conservatives.

The history of Britain in the period 1945-1990 can be roughly divided into two parts :

(1) The period 1945-1963 saw the establishment by Labour governments of the Welfare State, the beginnings of the dismantling of the Empire –supported by an optimistic faith in the capacity of the Commonwealth to maintain the links between Britain and its ex-colonies– and the birth of Harold Wilson's "affluent society".

(2) From 1963 (the year of the Profumo scandal) onwards, the British were progressively disappointed by their own institutions, and started to harbour serious doubts about Britain's capacity to retain its role as world leader. The imperialist attitude still maintained by Britain in the disastrous Suez crisis (1957) opened a breach in the Commonwealth, whereas Britain's subordination to American Cold War politics through NATO showed that the country could no longer maintain an independent position in international politics.

After 1963 a constant state of economic unrest brought the fall of one government after another. Britain was faced with the loss of its Empire, France's reluctance to grant it membership of the European Economic Community, and also major conflicts at home, especially those caused by strained industrial relations and the situation in Northern Ireland.

Thatcher's successful lightning war in the Falklands (1982) elevated Britain's morale for a while. This victory helped her to stay in power for two more terms of office, during which her liberal politics brought about the illusion of the recovery of a lost economic splendour. In fact, the gap between rich and poor grew, while Thatcher's alliance with Reagan's America jeopardised Britain's position in Europe. After forcing Thatcher's resignation in 1990 over the issue of Europe, the Conservatives led by **John Major** continued her economic policies while strengthening the Government's pro-European stance.

1. Literature 1945-1990: Cultural Context

Four main trends define the evolution of post-war English Literature within the cultural context of the period in Britain:

(a) the intensive commercialisation of the book market,

(b) the expansion of literary criticism and literary theory, brought about by the departments of English of the universities, old and new,

(c) the popularisation of audio-visual narrative media, which is often said to be a direct cause of the alleged decline of Literature, and

(d) the growth of English Literature written by women and by post-colonial writers.

Despite the frequent apocalyptic warnings concerning the decline of Literature, the list of prominent contemporary writers in English is, in fact, remarkably long. At any rate, although it cannot be denied that more books are sold than ever, it is important to note that Literature is but a segment of a much larger book market.

The Book Market in Britain

Literature is published in Britain by a small number of publishing houses that are currently undergoing an as yet unfinished process of merger, often with other publishing houses based in the USA. These gigantic conglomerates have made the survival of the smaller, independent houses difficult and are forcing the market to march in directions that have more to do with **multinational business** than strictly with Literature.

The trend is to publish more and more titles each year in smaller editions, with only a few reaching substantial sales figures. Most Literature is published initially in **hardback format**, that is to say, in editions with hard covers and good quality paper that are designed to last. Hardbacks cost between £15.00 and £25.00 and are bought mainly by public libraries and those readers who can afford them.

Hardbacks are expected to have a year-long run in the bookshops, after which a **paperback edition** is issued, usually by a different, specialised publishing house. Paperbacks are editions with paper of inferior quality and soft covers, and cost between £5.00 and £7.00; their relatively low price means that they may reach a large readership.

However, the choice of new titles is limited also by the **selling policies** of the main chains, which usually keep new books on display for only a very short period, so as to be able to display and sell a large number of new titles.

It is easy to see that prospective readers need **reliable guides** to find their way among so many new titles. The problem is that literary journalists and reviewers are no longer very influential – the market for Literature is not animated by literary debates but, rather, by advertising, the media coverage of publicity surrounding authors and books, and also by television and film adaptations.

Universities, which support their own circuits –conferences, specialised journals, academic presses– and university teachers (often themselves writers or editors) maintain a readership for literary works that find a less favourable reception among the general reading public. Best-seller lists show, nonetheless, a remarkable **mixture of literary works and popular literature** of the type usually disregarded by the universities.

Yet, many prejudices regarding the **commercialisation of Literature** still survive. There is still the opinion that Literature is somehow tainted by the touch of money. Martin Amis, one of the main contemporary novelists, was heavily criticised when he was offered a £1 million advance for his novel, *The Information* (1996). Amis argued that he had as much right as other people to sell his talent for money, but this did not convince his detractors. In contrast, novelists such as Frederick Forsythe or John Le Carré measure their success by the number of books they sell, seemingly accepting commercial success as compensation for the literary critics' neglect of their work.

The Relationship between Literature and the Universities

The universities have played a rather ambiguous role in the evolution of contemporary Literature in Britain.

(1) On the one hand, many contemporary writers and editors (especially of poetry) are also university lecturers, so that it is safe to say that Literature is influenced by the **literary criticism** and the **literary theory** produced by the universities. Most writers –including the so-called popular novelists and playwrights– hold university degrees in English and are therefore familiar with both the classics of Literature and contemporary literary theory.

The rub is that the Literature produced by this fusion of writer and university teacher runs the risk of excluding, in Virginia Woolf's famous phrase, the **common reader**, if such a common reader still exists. The academic novel, a genre popularised by David Lodge and Malcolm Bradbury, gives an insight into the tortuous relationship between Literature inside the university and the world outside it, but it seems at times a private joke that the uninitiated cannot grasp.

(2) On the other hand, university departments of English face the problem of what to do with the literature that the British common reader massively reads –from Ruth Rendell to Ken Follett– while also trying to accommodate in their syllabi the Literature produced by the minorities (women and post-colonial writers, mainly), without neglecting the latest trends in literary theory, often imported from abroad.

One way of bridging the gap between Literature and popular taste is through **literary prizes**. The Booker Prize –the main award given to novels in English–ensures that the attention of many buyers and readers is drawn to novels purportedly selected on the basis of their undeniable literary merit by informed judges. However, prizes like this are now being questioned from various sides: some unpopular choices have worried book sellers, who have accused the judges of being elitist; on the other hand, much that is popular and of good quality is excluded from the Booker, which has never, for example, selected a **genreÿÿnovel** (science-fiction, fantasy, horror, thriller, romance and other genres).

Adaptations of Literary Works for Television and the Cinema

The main bridge towards the common reader's pocket is now the television or film adaptation. Even though film and television are regarded with hostility by many literary purists, in fact, they have provided a **new field for writing**; many novelists and playwrights combine their literary work with writing original or adapted screenplays.

Indeed, instead of undermining the book market, adaptations have proved to be one of its greatest boons. Famous television adaptations, such as that of Evelyn Waugh's *Brideshead Revisited*, or film adaptations such as that of Jane Austen's *Emma*, have opened new markets for both contemporary Literature and the classics.

Not even poetry has been left unaffected by this phenomenon. Thanks to the popularity of the film *Four Weddings and a Funeral* (1994), in which a poem by W. H. Auden is read in a crucial, emotive scene, an anthology of Auden's poems edited for the occasion became the surprise best-seller of the year.

The Minorities in English Literature: Women and Post-colonial Writers

Feminism and post-colonialism are two other important issues in post-war English literature.

(1) **Women writers** are not a novelty in English Literature, nor can it be said that they have been systematically discriminated against by literary criticism. Thus, for the influential critic **F. R. Leavis**, Jane Austen and George Eliot (Mary Anne Evans) are an undeniable part of the Great Tradition in the English novel. However, the rise of 1960s **feminism** and successive waves (or feminisms) have forced post-war female writers in English to take a position for or against feminism, especially as this has played an important role in academic literary criticism. Some of the most important female writers, such as Angela Carter or Fay Weldon, have based their literary careers precisely on their ambiguity concerning feminism.

(2) Writers born in the ex-colonies of the British Empire –and also writers of other nationalities within the United Kingdom: Welsh, Scottish, Northern Irish– have used English to express the experience of colonization. **New national literatures in English** have been born in the post-war period, mainly in Africa, Asia and the Caribbean. The work of **migrant writers** from the ex-colonies who now live in Britain (first or second generation, that is, immigrants or born of migrant parents in Britain) has also forced literary critics to question the meaning of the adjective 'English' in the phrase 'English Literature'.

To sum up, there is no denying that the book market for Literature in Britain is rich and thriving, despite the apocalyptic pessimism of some. The variety of literary and extra-literary texts –that is, of texts likely to enter the university syllabus or not– is certainly remarkable. The classics of the past share the same cultural space with the new products of post-war literature, whether traditional or experimental. And the new voices of women (feminist or not) and post-colonial writers have joined a culture in constant expansion.

2. The English Novel 1945-1990

The history of the post-war novel in English, and also that of drama and poetry, cannot be understood without reference to the coexistence in the first half of the twentieth century of Modernism and the more traditional approaches to literature inherited from the Victorian period.

The Modernist writers reacted against realism in fiction and the remains of Romantic sentimentalism in poetry by introducing technical innovations that could be used to look at reality from the point of view of the irrational, the subconscious, the anti-sentimental, or the highly individualistic. In drama, the revolution followed other lines, with G. B. Shaw's introduction to the English stage of the naturalistic drama developed by Ibsen. Modernism can be said to enter the English stage precisely at the time of Shaw's death in 1950, when Samuel Beckett's plays challenged the hegemony of naturalism and the artificial, well-made play.

After 1945, when novelists faced the task of explaining the new historical reality and the position of the individual in the new post-war order, most realized that this entailed making a choice between traditional literary models that seemed more suitable for transmitting an accurate portrait of the individual in a changing society, and experimental, Modernist models that seemed more suitable for explaining the disjunction between the individual consciousness and the problematic flow of contemporary history.

Post-modernism was born out of this dilemma. **Post-modernism** can thus be said to be a new cultural atmosphere in which the writer is inevitably aware of this open choice between **tradition** and **experimentalism**, rather than a continuation of Modernism or a reaction against it. Post-war novelists cannot escape the shadow of either Modernism or Victorianism and must accommodate both in their work. Some have produced a new **synthesis** –which is what is really characteristic of post-modernism– while others have openly acknowledged their allegiance to either literary tradition or experimentation.

As far as the post-war novel is concerned, the post-modernist synthesis was relatively slow to come, if it came at all, for there seemed to be a need to first define the **new contours of social reality** after the war before resuming the project of Modernism.

Traditionalism: Between the Past and the Present

In the period between 1945 and 1955, a **nostalgic look** at the lost pre-war past was combined with **a look at the new reality** faced by the generation growing up in the 1940s, often in provincial surroundings.

Novels such as **Evelyn Waugh's** *Brideshead Revisited* (1945) and **L.P. Hartley's** *The Go-Between* (1953) analyse the present by looking backwards, searching for the flaws that cause the desolation of the individual speaking in the present.

This return to a personal past shows, above all, why innocence has been the main casualty of war, and suggests that despite its apparent placidity, the best that the pre-war world could offer in social terms was inherently corrupt.

The idea that civilisation contains the seeds of corruption is perhaps best expressed in **William Golding**'s *Lord of the Flies* (1954). In this novel Golding does not examine a particular moment of the recent past, but childhood, as the site where adult civilised values are implanted, only to find there sheer brutality.

The early 1950s brought a **new interest in the present**, possibly as a reaction against the nostalgic backward look at an essentially phoney world from which many –above all, the lower middle and working classes– were excluded. Leaving aside the beginnings of the post-colonial novel, what happened in the 1950s novel is that the margins of culture moved to the centre, expressing a generalised discontent, which was paralleled in the plays of the Angry Young Men and some of the poetry of The Movement.

At the time, this discontent was defined as political discontent, but it would seem now, rather, to be lower middle-class frustration at being denied a place in the vanished world of the upper classes portrayed by pre-war Literature.

Thanks to the new educational opportunities opened up by post-war Labour governments, new lower middle-class and working class writers, who often came from places other than London, found themselves in a cultural world in which they were simultaneously strangers and also the rising new stars.

William Cooper's *Scenes from Provincial Life* (1950) was the mirror in which the new writers found an appropriate model to narrate the discontent of the post-war generation. Novels such as **Kingsley Amis**'s *Lucky Jim* (1954), **John Waine**'s *Hurry on Down* (1953), **John Braine**'s *Room at the Top* (1957), **Allan Sillitoe**'s *Saturday Night, Sunday Morning* (1958), **Keith Waterhouse**'s *Billy Liar* (1958), or **David Storey**'s *This Sporting Life* (1960), dramatise the position of the individual who is aware of the new chances for upward social mobility and who either benefits from them –hence Jim's luck– or sees them slip from his grasp, whether by choice or because the social structure is still too rigid.

What is relevant is that through these novels a world that had been neglected by pre-war fiction entered the course of the English novel, often in close alliance with the **Free Cinemaÿÿmovement** of the 1960s, which frequently found its inspiration in these novels and the plays of the Angry Young Men. Both films and novels portray an England that is no longer the heroic country of World War II but a country struggling to understand its own contradictions.

Fantasy, Realism and Experimentalism

The period 1945-1960 also saw the entrance of **fantasy** into the English novel on a large scale. The novels of these years preceded the new wave of fantasy writers in the 1960s, including **J.G. Ballard** and **Michael Moorcock**, who questioned the boundaries between fantasy and the mainstream or realistic novel.

Orwell's political dystopian fantasies, *Animal Farm* (1945) and *Nineteen Eighty-Four* (1949), **Mervyn Peake**'s Gothic *Gormenghast* trilogy (*Titus Groan*, 1946; *Gormenghast*, 1950; and *Titus Alone*, 1959), **John Wyndham**'s science-fiction novel *The Day of the Triffids* (1951) and **J.R.R. Tolkien**'s trilogy *The Lord of the Rings* (*The Fellowship of the Ring*, 1954; *The Two Towers*, 1954; and *The Return of the King*, 1955) exemplify this trend.

Orwell's use of fantasy suggests that far from being escapist, fantasy can be a way of expressing the anxieties caused by history in an alternative way. Peake himself drew the inspiration for his bizarre gallery of characters in *Gormenghast* from the horror of the Belsen concentration camp, which he had visited.

The idea of the long chronicle criss-crosses fantasy and realism in the novel, for the trilogy and other even longer sequences, now typical only of fantasy, were the format chosen by, among others, **Anthony Powell** (*The Music of Time*, 1951-75, 12 volumes), **C.P. Snow** (*Strangers and Brothers*, 1940-70, 11 volumes), **Olivia Manning** (*The Balkan Trilogy*, 1960-62), **Paul Scott** (*The Raj Quartet*, 1966-75, 4 volumes) and **Lawrence Durrell** to narrate contemporary life.

Durrell's ***Alexandria Quartet*** (*Justine*, 1957; *Balthazar*, 1958; *Mountolive*, 1959; and *Clea*, 1960) and his ***Avinyon Quintet*** (1974-85) question the very idea of the chronicle by returning repeatedly to the same events, which are narrated in each volume from the point of view of a different character.

Reality, Durrell suggests, cannot be apprehended from a single point of view and is necessarily mediated by the consciousness through which it is filtered –a point that had already been made by the Modernists.

As Durrell's work shows, the **experimentalism** derived from Modernism found a new, if clearly minority, vein in the novel of the late 1950s, especially in the novels of **Samuel Beckett** and **Nigel Dennis**.

Experimentalism greatly expanded in the 1960s and 1970s without, however, displacing the work of **realists** such as **Graham Greene** from its position of pre-eminence. At what precise moment the Modernist experiments in technique became post-modernist is a matter of dispute. Writers such as **Henry Green**, **Lawrence Durrell** and **Wyndham Lewis** seem to bridge the gap between the two periods, whereas others alternate realism with experimentalism.

Anthony Burgess's *The Clockwork Orange* (1962), **Doris Lessing's** *The Golden Notebook* (1962) and **John Fowles's** *The French Lieutenant's Woman* (1969) are outstanding novels outside the realistic framework, but they were written nonetheless by novelists who were also proficient in the writing of more traditional realistic novels.

A number of novelists heavily influenced by the French "nouveau roman"–**Andrew Sinclair**, **Julian Mitchell**, **Christine Brooke-Rose**, **John Berger**–chose experimentalism rather than realism in the 1960s and 1970s.

The Post-modern Novel

Nonetheless, it could be said that the distinguishing mark of the English **post-modern novel** is its reluctance to totally abandon realism and its interest in creating a synthesis with other narrative modes, such as fantasy, autobiography and historiography. At any rate, it is essential to understand that the coexistence of widely diverging novelistic genres is the main characteristic of the post-war English novel and, perhaps, of post-modernism itself.

This may be due to a pragmatic approach to the world of Literature, an approach that precludes confrontations of the kind that took place between the Modernists and the Edwardian traditionalists. Possibly, novelists are aware, above all, of the increasing popularity of the **audio-visual narrative** media, which compete with the novel, and would rather secure a place in the cultural marketplace for the novel in general than for any particular kind of novel.

A look at the English novel of the period 1975-1990 reveals a healthy state of affairs, despite the constant warnings about decaying standards. It may be true that there are not as many memorable characters as in the Victorian novel, but there are certainly novels that are memorable for their **complex architecture** and, often, for their **wry humour**.

Nothing much can be said to unify the work of contemporary English novelists except the writers' reluctance to see their work as part of any identifiable school, movement or trend.

Women novelists, such as **Angela Carter** or **Fay Weldon**, challenge feminist tenets in their work, thus questioning the idea that women's novels are necessarily feminist novels.

The work of other novelists such as **Kazuo Ishiguro** or **Salman Rushdie** –and indeed the remarkable group of Scottish novelists, including, among others, **Alasdair Gray**, **James Kellman**, **Janice Galloway** and **Iain Banks**– has forced literary critics to consider whether the English novel is written by the English at all.

English novelists such as **Martin Amis**, **Julian Barnes**, **Graham Swift**, **Peter Ackroyd**, **Alan Hollinghurst** and **Ian McEwan**, who started their careers in the late 1970s, are currently pursuing their individual projects. The work they produce is regarded as **literary fiction**, as opposed to that of more popular writers, yet literary fiction is not as radically different from fiction without literary ambitions as might be expected. In fact, much of the literary fiction of the 1980s and 1990s uses elements drawn from popular fiction; alternatively, it could be said that it has turned experimental techniques into devices to produce eminently readable novels.

This may explain why the lists of best-selling novels in Britain are now as likely to feature the latest Ishiguro, Rushdie or Amis as the latest book by any of the more popular writers, from **Terry Pratchett** to **Ruth Rendell**.

The post-war English novel is **polyphonic**, as it gathers many different voices. If there is anything that defines the English novel of the last fifty years it is its protean essence: thanks to its flexibility, the novel can now accommodate the experiences of different social classes, different genders, different nationalities and different literary projects, from realism to experimentalism.

The novel is certainly conditioned by the market forces that dictate literary fashions and make or break literary reputations, yet there is still room in the book market for very personal projects, provided they find enough readers to sustain them.

Contemporary novels in English do not seem to be at the ideological centre of contemporary culture –which has shifted to the **media**– but in all their variety they provide a comprehensive, highly critical and often pessimistic portrait of the realities and the fantasies that shape the world of the individual in the late twentieth century.

Drama in England 1945-1990

Although both novels and plays can be said to be narrative genres, there is an obvious difference between them: a play can only reveal all its literary potential when it is performed on a stage. There are, thus, two possibilities when considering the evolution of drama in a particular period:

(1) considering plays as published texts, (2) considering plays in performance.

The history of post-war drama involves important changes in the way plays are performed. These changes are interdependent with the changes in the way plays are written: the innovations introduced by the plays require **new acting styles**, **new theatres**; the evolution of acting styles and new trends in the management of theatres also encourage the writing of **innovative plays**.

West End Theatre and the New English Drama

The recent history of English drama can be summarised as the rise of a strong **opposition to** the mainstream play that dominated **the West End theatres** of London. Paradoxically, after decades in which constant innovations inspired by revolutions in both the form and the content of contemporary drama in English have led to the establishment of solid alternatives to the West End, the success of the playwrights who sustained the **new English drama** can be measured by their now habitual presence in West End theatres. As happens in the field of the novel, in which literary fiction coexists with popular fiction in the best-seller lists, mainstream theatre has expanded to include everything commercially successful, whether experimental or traditional.

At the end of World War II the **theatre industry** was in a very delicate position. Many theatres had been destroyed, there was a shortage of actors and managers, and more worrying still, films were becoming increasingly popular, which led to many theatres being converted into cinemas. Later, the stage was to face further competition from television.

In the decade after the war, the West End theatres in London were dominated by a consortium of business interests, popularly known as **The Group,** which ensured the predominance of metropolitan over provincial tastes, the success of musicals (often imported from the USA) and the dependence of drama on the star system. Repertory companies working in provincial theatres and touring companies from the capital satisfied the craving for theatre outside London.

The tastes of West End audiences were conservative and the main **innovations** in drama came from **amateur clubs**, which were free from the pressures of business. Actor-managers with their own companies, such as **Laurence Olivier**, contributed to enlivening post-war theatre by offering alternatives to the habitual West End fare, alternatives based mainly on the classics.

What could be seen in most West End theatres were so-called **well-made plays**, originating in late nineteenth-century French theatre. These were plays that centred on an upper-class hero undergoing a crisis, which would mark his progression from ignorance to knowledge, bound by a plot fixed by the unities of time, place and action. Ibsen had added naturalism to the well-made play, thus opening the way for the drama of social and political content written by **G.B. Shaw** in England. By the 1940s, the well-made play was sounding too artificial –the twist endings too contrived– and naturalism, especially in acting, was gaining ground.

The main playwrights of the time were **Noël Coward**, **Terence Rattigan** and **J.B. Priestley**, though the more experimental plays in verse by **T.S. Eliot** and **Christopher Fry** also enjoyed considerable success.

Absurdist Drama and Social and Political Drama

By the 1950s, the time was ripe for a reaction against West End drama. Almost simultaneously, the West End stage faced two challenges:

(a) one posed by the **minimalist, absurdist drama** of Samuel Beckett's *Waiting for Godot* (1955),

(b) the other by the **socially critical theatre** of John Osborne's *Look Back in Anger* (1956).

Beckett proposed a reflection on the form of drama, drawing the audience's attention to the artificiality of speech, plot and characters on the stage. **Osborne** invited the audience to consider the new sense of social alienation of the rising lower middle-class, also shattering conventions as to the decorum so far observed on the English stage.

Look Back in Anger also secured the financial survival of George Devine's **English Stage Company** at the Royal Court, Chelsea. This company exerted an enormous influence as it specialised in staging work by new dramatists, among them **N.F. Simpson**, **Arnold Wesker**, **Anne Jellicoe** and **John Arden**.

It was also in the 1950s that **Harold Pinter** presented his masterpiece, *The Birthday Party* (1958). Pinter, still regarded today as the main figure of the English stage, set with this absurdist play an apolitical alternative to Osborne's theatre.

Pinter is perhaps Beckett's main disciple, though he lacks the latter's physiological, existentialist preoccupations. Yet Pinter's plays are unmistakably his own. His anti naturalistic, minimalist, often violent dramas, in which silence occupies the dramatist's attention as much as speech, speak above all of the impossibility of communication. His characters move in a void, in a bizarre world best defined by the adjective **Pinteresque**.

New Theatre Companies and The Arts Council

Between 1956 and 1966 there was an extraordinary transformation of the English theatre. These years saw not only the emergence of many new playwrights, but also the establishment in 1960 of the London branch of the **Royal Shakespeare Company**, directed by **Peter Hall**, and of the new **National Theatre** company led by **Laurence Olivier**. Hall would replace Olivier when the National Theatre moved to the new South Bank complex in the 1970s.

The figure of the **director** steadily grew in importance and so did the companies formed around them. **Joan Littlewood's Theatre Workshop**, a company that in 1953 moved to the **Theatre Royal**, located in a suburb of London, was the most outstanding example of the cohesion then sought between director, actors and authors.

Littlewood's Workshop had much in common with **Brecht's Berliner Ensemble**, the foreign company that most deeply influenced the development of drama in England. The idea of creating permanent companies like Brecht's appealed to actors, directors and authors alike, who saw the advantages of collaboration over individualism.

In addition, Brecht's **political and experimental theatre** offered a useful synthesis that attracted many followers. Brechtian drama also encouraged the use of new architectural styles for new play houses – less formal, with less marked differentiation between audience and stage – and a much more open acting style, with a new emphasis on the possibilities of body language.

The problem was that Brecht's state-supported company inspired British directors to look to the Government for support through the **Arts Council**. And this brought instability to the English stage. Between 1946 and 1956 the patronage of the Arts Council was limited; it was assumed that local councils should support drama as they were empowered by a 1948 act to spend a percentage of taxes on the arts.

However, given the lack of interest among local councils, between 1957 and 1964 grants rose steadily, and from 1964 onwards it can be said that the Arts Council became a victim of its own success as subsidies became more and more necessary to keep afloat not only fringe theatres but also the national companies.

A series of measures aimed at obtaining patronage from other sources, such as industry, local councils, private investors or even the trade unions, proved unable to counteract the centralisation of patronage. Thus, the work of the Arts Council, while positive in that it encouraged new initiatives, was also negative, for it created an artificial situation in which it was impossible to know what audiences really wanted, unlike in the field of literary fiction, which was practically untouched by state patronage.

Theatre from the Mid-1960s Onwards

By the mid-1960s the distinctions between experimental and established theatre were becoming blurred: conventional plays such as **Robert Bolt**'s *A Man for All Seasons* were praised by the critics; Osborne's more demanding plays were staged in the West End. Samuel Beckett and Harold Pinter continued writing their minimalist drama, increasingly focusing on the meaning of silence.

The so-called "**kitchen-sink**" playwrights, those interested, like **Arnold Wesker**, **Brendan Behan** and **Shelagh Delaney**, in the daily dramas of the lower-middle and working classes, had somehow lost momentum. Despite their efforts, it is difficult to say to what extent they succeeded in creating a genuine working-class theatre in England.

The late 1960s also brought the **end of stage censorship**: the rule of the Lord Chamberlain was abolished in 1968. This gave younger authors a greater freedom of language and allowed them to go much further than the **Angry Young Men** or the working-class dramatists in their virulent social criticism.

Several new trends thus merged in the mid-1960s with the rise of the second wave of new dramatists, who still dominate the English stage today. **Tom Stoppard** brilliantly continued the tradition of experimentalism first set up by Beckett and Pinter with *Rosencrantz and Guildenstern are Dead* (first presented at the Edinburgh Festival Theatre in 1965), responding to their minimalism with a rich, luxuriant use of dialogue.

The ludicrous and the outlandish, influenced by Antonin Artaud's theatre of cruelty and Eugene Ionesco's absurdist drama, inspired the disruptive, carnivalesque work of **N.F. Simpson**, **Joe Orton** and **David Rudkin**. This was anti-middle class drama for the middle classes, and the limits of upward mobility seemed to be the centre of interest for the new playwrights' often satirical portrait of English society.

The new social realists of the 1970s –**Peter Nichols**, **David Storey**, **Simon Gray**– fused social satire with G. B. Shaw's problem plays to offer a bleak portrait of suburbia, also shared by more conventional plays, such as the comedies of **Alan Ayckbourn**.

More committed to the political left was the work of **Edward Bond**, **Howard Brenton**, **David Hare**, **David Edgar**, **Trevor Griffiths**, **Peter Barnes** and **John Arden**, among others, which flourished in the smaller theatres under the influence of Brecht's example but later came to be accepted by the West End.

Apart from the experimentalists and the politically committed playwrights, the English stage has sustained an important number of more traditional dramatists, such as **Alan**

Ayckbourn, **Michael Frayn**, **Christopher Hampton**, **James Saunders**, **Anthony Shaffer**, **Peter Shaffer**, **John Mortimer**, **John Whiting** and **Robert Bolt**. Not only they, but also others such as Harold Pinter and Tom Stoppard, have divided their time between writing original plays and writing for the screen –both film and television– and, alternatively, adapting novels for the stage. Presumably, this mixed **allegiance to the stage and the screen** will also bring in new ideas about their work, for it will have to be reassessed.

It seems simply inappropriate to draw rigid dividing lines between plays and screenplays when both are produced by the same writer. As for the English stage, although in need of new blood, it cannot be said to be in decline, despite the competition from television and the cinema. Each seems to have found its place in the global map of entertainment, perhaps at the expense of blunting their political and artistic edges.

English Poetry 1945-1990

The history of post-war poetry is initially the history of the poets' constant fluctuations towards and away from **T.S. Eliot** and **W. H. Auden**. Eliot's Modernist experimentalism and Auden's rational, moralising, politically committed poetry offered post-war poets two eloquent alternatives that could not be ignored. Yet, post-war poetry was also influenced by the remarkable integration of the poet and the academic world.

The market for poetry is limited and this has forced poets to seek other means of securing financial support. Thus, most English poets hold university positions as lecturers or writers in residence, frequently in American universities. Otherwise, their professional occupations are related to publishing or literary journalism.

Poets who are professional writers, and these are very few, usually combine poetry with other genres. Contemporary poets live and work, therefore, in a much more limited cultural territory than novelists or playwrights. This does not mean, however, that contemporary poetry is uniform in tone and content –quite the contrary; post-war poetry is as varied as post-war novels and post-war drama.

Post-war poetry also reflects the breakdown of the unity of English. Other **varieties of English** spoken in and outside England have entered contemporary poetry, questioning the privileged position held by standard English, which is often denounced as an instrument of cultural imperialism.

This common interest in vindicating other varieties of English for poetry links the work of followers of **Modernism**, such as David Jones and Basil Bunting, with that of **social realists** such as Douglas Dunn and Tony Harrison.

Outside England, the poets of **Northern Ireland**, led by Seamus Heaney, have fused English with local poetical traditions, whereas the **post-colonial poets** – including first and second-generation immigrants as well as poets living outside Britain – have introduced **new rhythms** and **speech patterns** into English poetry.

Romantic and Other Singular Poets

After Auden's exile, **Dylan Thomas** became the main poet living in Britain. His new romanticism exerted an immediate influence on the poets of the 1940s, from **W.S. Graham** and **George Barker** to the poets of **The Apocalypse**. These mixed Thomas' example with the influence of French Surrealism, which was especially strong in the work of **David Gascoyne**.

The poets of The Apocalypse, a movement that soon came to be known as **New Romanticism** –**Henry Treece**, **J.F. Hendry**, **Nicholas Moore**, **Norman MacCaig**, **Vernon Watkins**– preferred to follow the example of Thomas' highly sensitive, personal and subjective poetry to Auden's more rational approach in their search for a poetical language capable of expressing the anxieties endured by the individual trapped by the horrors of contemporary history.

The work of the Second World War poets, especially **Keith Douglas** and **Alun Lewis**, also addressed this question. Paradoxically, unlike in World War I, when civilians were at a safe distance from the front line, Hitler's raids over

England forced civilians to face violent mass destruction. As a consequence, both civilians and combatants expressed in their poetry similar horrors.

The 1940s, however, also saw the beginnings of the careers of **Stevie Smith** and **R.S. Thomas**. Possibly thanks to their relative isolation from the main channels of poetical activity, each developed throughout their long career a unique, singular poetical voice. Smith's feminine but wry, almost minimalist verse contrasted with Thomas' poetry about his difficult relationship with God and his links with his native rural Wales.

The Movement and The Group

The 1950s were almost totally monopolised by the emergence of **The Movement**, a group of poets (which was not a unified school in any sense) gathered around **Stephen Spender's** journal *Horizon* and anthologised by **D.J. Enright** and **Robert Conquest**. The group included **Kingsley Amis**, **John Waine** –both also novelists– **Enright** himself, **Elizabeth Jennings**, **John Holloway**, **Thom Gunn**, **Donald Davie** and, above all, its main figure, **Philip Larkin**.

The poets of The Movement were products of the expansion of education brought about by the Labour government: often of lower middle-class origin, they had been helped by scholarships to enter Oxford or Cambridge, and were later employed as lecturers of English in the new universities. As scholars, they were indebted to the work of the English critic **F.R. Leavis** and to **American New Criticism**, though some of them –especially Larkin– rejected foreign influences on English poetry.

The poetry of The Movement mocked the excesses of New Romanticism and was characterised by its urbanity, civility and decorum, and by a restrained use of emotion. It was a poetry aimed at maintaining with the reader a "level-toned and civilised conversation, often of a fairly literary kind" (Corcoran 1993: 82).

Apart from The Movement, the 1950s saw the birth of other movements, such as **The Group**, organized by **Philip Hobsbaum** and **Edward Lucie-Smith**. The Group, founded in 1952, included poets such as **Peter Porter**, **Peter Redgrove**, **George MacBeth** and **Alan Brownjohn**.

The Group had no common pattern, no manifesto, but it acted as an **open forum** where poets could read each other's work, and thus foreshadowed the now popular writing workshops.

Foreign Influences and the Underground Poets

Other poets who started their careers in the 1950s, such as **Donald Davie**, **Charles Tomlinson** and **Thom Gunn**, showed a much greater enthusiasm towards **American poetry**. For them, American poetry seemed more in touch with the rough rhythms of contemporary life than the urbane poetry of The Movement. Gunn himself eventually emigrated to America, like Auden.

The interest in incorporating foreign poetical influences into English poetry was also shared by **Ted Hughes** and **Geoffrey Hill**. Despite their very different styles, both sensed that the historical realities of post-war Europe demanded a more vigorous poetry than anything The Movement could offer.

Yet, instead of looking towards America, they looked towards their **native North England** and towards the work of other **European poets**, especially from the 1960s onwards, when translation became an essential activity in English poetry. Hughes has become one of the main poetical voices in English thanks to his celebration of the dark rhythms of nature and his valuation of the animal world above the rational, destructive impulses of human civilization.

By the 1960s English poetry came clearly under the influence of the American poets (especially **Robert Lowell** and **Sylvia Plath**), whose work seemed to better dramatise the individual's disintegration in the chaotic post-war world. The "academic-administrative verse" of The Movement –in the critic A. Alvarez's words– seemed unable to carry the weight of this disintegration, and so the younger poets drifted towards other currents coming from abroad through translation, and also towards Underground experimental poetry.

The **Underground** brought a renewal of poetry in performance, associating it with rock music, festivals, happenings and anti-Vietnam war protest, but it was by nature ephemeral.

It had its high point in England in the 'International Poetry Incarnation' at the Albert Hall in June 1965 and in Michael Horovitz's Penguin anthology *Children of Albion: Poetry of the 'Underground' in Britain* (1969).

Social Realists and Neo-modernists

With the work of **Douglas Dunn** and **Tony Harrison** the 1960s England of the lower middle class found its poetical voice. Theirs is a poetry that speaks about the difference between the centre and the margins (social, cultural and geographical), written by people displaced from their origins –Scotland and the Midlands, respectively– by the new educational opportunities opened up by comprehensive schools and the newly built universities of the early 1960s.

Yet the **social realism** of Dunn and Harrison does not exclude the **neo-modernism** of poets such as **Christopher Middleton**, **Roy Fisher** and **J.H. Prynne**, whose work runs parallel to the development of new trends within literary theory, such as post-structuralism, and who seem interested above all in making room in poetry for commenting on poetry itself.

The Northern Irish poets

The first group of Northern Irish poets, headed by **Seamus Heaney**, is completed by **Michael Longley** and **Derek Mahon**.

Heaney's first book, *Death of a Naturalist* (1966), made it possible for other poets to express their problematic sense of Irishness, often as a burden imposed on their personal, poetical sensibilities by the political circumstances in Northern Ireland. Heaney fused the tradition of English poetry with the Irish poetical tradition, thus finding a new language for Northern Ireland. His poetry deals with the historical confrontation between Britain and Ireland from the point of view of the sensitive individual facing it, rather than as a political issue.

Longley and Mahon followed Heaney's example and adapted Irish tradition to contemporary needs marked by history. Longley shows an interest in using historical, classical and mythical events to comment on the present, whereas Mahon shows a greater scepticism as to the force of poetry in difficult historical conditions such as those of Northern Ireland.

The second generation of Northern Irish poets –**Paul Muldoon**, **Tom Paulin**, **Ciaran Carson**– have found themselves forced to either accept or reject Heaney's powerful figure. They have shown an interest in a strong sense of orality rooted in the vernacular and the contemporary (Carson being the one most interested in recovering the lost sense of orality in poetry), rather than in historical issues.

Regionalists, Women and Post-colonial Poets

The 1970s were marked by the steady rise of the poetry of **regionalism** – poetry based on geographical variants of English other than the standard – and the progressive decentralisation of publishing. The polarisation of England between a poorer North and a richer South inspired poets to cut their ties with the metropolis.

Both **Neil Astley**'s Bloodaxe Press (1978) in Newcastle and **Michael Smith's** Carcanet Press (late 1960s), first based in Oxford then in Manchester, published new poets, kept the old ones in print, and translated foreign works, thus animating the market for poetry outside London.

New poetry marked by region, gender or race –often antagonistic to the idea of London as the dominant cultural or political system– emerged in the 1970s. In addition, an important number of poets started publishing: women poets such as **Medbh McGuckian**, **Liz Lochhead**, **Anneÿÿ Stevenson**, **Sylvia Kantaris**, **Carol Rumens**, **Denise Riley** and **Wendy Cope**; and post-colonial poets such as **John Aggard**, **James Berry**, **Linton Kwesi Johnson**, **Grace Nichols** and **E.A. Markham**. In the 1980s, possibly the most important post-colonial poetical voice to be heard was that of **David Dabydeen**.

The 'Martian School of Poetry' and Other Poetical Voices

From the 1970s onwards these main trends continued. The more recent innovations are those of **Craig Raine**'s '**Martian school of poetry**'–christened thus because of his poem "A Martian Sends a Post-card Home". Both Raine and Christopher Reid have shown a keen interest in representing reality from a fresh, slightly ironic or parodic point of view.

On the other hand, poets such as **James Fenton**, **Andrew Motion**, **Peter Reading** and **Blake Morrison** have been using verse to produce a new narrative poetry, which has also attracted Raine.

Like Craig's Martians, the narrators of these poems are often strangers or aliens in their communities –a feature shared by many contemporary novels. This is a poetry of circumstance, of a time, place and society in which the poet must show his/her power to mimic the **voice of the outsider**, as in Blake Morrison's *The Ballad of the Yorkshire Ripper* (1987).

The newest wave of poets, including **Michael Hoffman**, **John Ash**, **Simon Armitage**, **Tony Curtis**, and **Glyn Maxwell**, are, like the novelists, following their own individual projects, keeping their own singular poetical territories afloat in a crowded cultural marketplace.

It is certainly difficult to assess the role of poetry in the post-war period. As can be seen, this is a rich field in English literature. The permanence of the novel at the centre of contemporary culture worries contemporary novelists, despite the undeniable popularity of the novel as a genre. On the other hand, the lack of popularity of poetry, which occupies a clearly marginal position in the contemporary world, does not seem to worry literary critics or poets to the same extent. Perhaps this is as it should be, for poetry has never been a genre enjoyed by many. Post-war poetry can be said to be written and read by a much larger circle than, for instance, Elizabethan poetry, but it is nonetheless a small circle.

UNIT X

RESEARCH METHODS AND MATERIALS IN ENGLISH

HIGHER EDUCATION RESEARCH METHODOLOGY-LITERATURE METHOD

RESEARCH

The English noun 'research' comes from the Middle French 'recerche' (16th century) which goes back to the Latin 'circare' (to go around, to wander, ...). Research is an investigation conducted an aim to solve a problem. It is similar to the Science projects one conducts in Schools, wherein one attempts to learn something by way of experimenting. In order to start a research, one must have a question, a need to and an answer to something. As depicted by Cambridge Dictionary, "a detailed study of a subject, especially in order to discover 'new information or reach a (new) understanding".

Research is a careful and detailed study into a specific problem, concern, or issue using the scientific method.

Research is undertaken within most professions. More than a set of skills, research is a way of thinking: examining critically the various aspects of your day-to-day professional work; understanding and formulating guiding principles that govern a particular procedure; and developing and testing new theories that contribute to the advancement of your practice and profession. It is a habit of questioning what you do, and a systematic examination of clinical observations to explain and find answers for what you perceive, with a view to instituting appropriate changes for a more effective professional service.

Very little research in the field is pure in nature, i.e., very few people do research in research methodology person. Most research is applied research, which has wide application in many disciplines. Every profession uses research methods in varying amounts in many areas. They use the methods and procedures developed by research methodologists in order to increase understanding in their own profession and to advance the professional knowledge base. It is through the application of research methodology that they strengthen and advance their own profession. Examine your own field. You will find that its professional practice follows procedures and practices tested and developed by others over a long period of time.

It is in this testing process that you need research skills, the developments of which fall in the category of pure research. As a matter of fact, the validity of young findings entirely depends upon the soundness of the research methods and procedures adopted by you. Within any profession, where you directly or indirectly provide a service, such as health (nursing, occupational therapy, physiotherapy, community health, health promotion and public health), education, psychology or social work, the application of research can be viewed from four different perspectives:

Research is one of the ways to find answers to your questions. When you say that you are undertaking a research study to find out answers to a question, you are implying that the process being applied:

- is being undertaken within a framework of a set of philosophies;
- uses procedures, methods and techniques that have been tested for their validity and reliability;
- is designed to be unbiased and objective.

Types of Research

If you examine a research endeavour from the perspective of its application, there are two broad categories: pure research and applied research.

Pure Research. It involves developing and testing theories and hypotheses that are intellectually challenging to the researcher but may or may not have practical application at the present time or in the future. Thus such work often involves the testing of hypotheses containing very abstract and specialised concepts. Pure-research is also concerned with the development, examination, verification and refinement of research methods, procedures, techniques and tools that form the body of research methodology.

Examples of pure research include developing, a sampling technique that can be applied to a particular situation; developing a methodology to assess the validity of a procedure; developing an instrument, say, to measure the stress level in people; and finding the best way of measuring people's attitudes.

Applied Research. The knowledge produced through pure research is sought in order to add to the existing body of knowledge of research methods to give rise to the Applied research. In other words, the research techniques, procedures and methods that from the body of research methodology are applied to the collection of information about various aspects of a situation, issue, problem or phenomenon so that the information gathered can be used in other ways — such as for policy formulation, administration and the enhancement of understanding of a phenomenon.

Characteristics of Research

Philosohical orientation is a stem from one of the several paradigms and approaches in research - positivist, interpretive, phenomenology, action or participatory, feminist, qualitative, quantitative - and the academic discipline in which one has been trained. Chief characteristics of a research can be summarised as the following:

- **Validity.** It can be applied to any aspect of the research process. It ensures that in a research study correct procedures have been applied to find answers to a question.
- **Reliability.** It refers to the quality of a measurement procedure that provides repeatability and accuracy.
- **Unbiased and Objective.** It means that you have taken each step in an unbiased manner and drawn each conclusion to the best of your ability without introducing your own vested interest. The author makes a distinction between bias and subjectivity.
- **Subjectivity.** It is integral part of your way of thinking that is 'conditioned by your educational background, discipline, philosophy, experience and skills, e.g. a psychologist may look at a piece of information differently from the way in which an anthropologist or a historian looks at it. Bias, on the other hand, is a deliberate attempt to either conceal or highlight something.
- **Controlled.** The concept of control implies that, in exploring causality in relation to two variables, you set up your study in a way that minimises the effects of other factors affecting the relationship.

ENGLISH LITERATURE METHODOLOGY

Literature research methodology is to read through, analyze and sort literatures in order to identify the essential attribute of materials. Its significant difference from other methodologies is that it does not directly deal with the object under study, but to indirectly access to information from a variety of literatures, which is generally referred to as "non-contact method." Literature materials are the crystallization of wisdom, are the ocean of knowledge, have important values for the development of human society, history, culture and research scholars. Education researches shall fully share information, conduct literature researches to grasp sources of relevant researches and scientific developments and to understand what our predecessors have achieved and the progress made by other researchers. However, in the ocean of knowledge of such a vast amount of information, how should we choose representative literatures?

HOW TO CHOOSE REPRESENTATIVE RESEARCH LITERATURES

As we write dissertations, we often encounter the problem of what materials are representative literatures.

The Root of the Problem

The root of this problem, for researchers, is the lack of qualitative analysis of the literatures.

"Literature research methodology" include non-structured qualitative analysis and structured quantitative analysis. They access to and process information contained in literatures from different perspectives. Generally speaking, literatures are descriptions of the nature, functions and characteristics of objects. These qualitative descriptions seldom show the variable relationship of research subject, so researchers tend to apply logical reasoning to explore the logical relations among objects rather than the quantity relationship.

In general, qualitative analysis is to classify information contained in literatures, to select typical examples to re-organize and come to conclusion on the basis of qualitative description. The qualitative analysis of literatures has special values in distinguishing the past trends and forecasting future models.

Qualitative research of literatures does not focus on the quantity and completeness of literature materials. It focuses on personal literature researches and chooses small samples or characteristics of cases according to the interests of the researches and subject requirements.

Qualitative analysis is to study whether the objects under researches have certain nature or to study chance reasons and process analysis. The base of qualitative analysis is philosophy method. It compares the similarities and differences between things through reasoning, sums up the types of things and grasps the rules of things. The common reasoning process of qualitative analysis is as follows: what is the problem? What is the definition of the concept? What are the facts? What is the reason? What is the conclusion of the study? Qualitative analysis commonly applies seven methods, respectively,: causal analysis, comparative analysis, conflicts analysis, the results and functional analysis, induction and deduction, analysis and synthesis and scientific abstract method.

Strategies to Overcome the Problem

There are three strategies to overcome this problem, to talk with scholars, to identify the grade of literatures and to enhance theory knowledge.

After we have collected as many literatures as possible related to our research subject, we must sort them out and analyze to determine what representative research literatures are and what general references are. In the determination of the representative literatures, several principles must be followed: One is purpose: Literature materials must be pertinent, valuable for the subject under research, are the theoretical base or background information of the research subject and are typical examples. Researchers could use these materials to find out the past trends and to predict future relevant to these materials. The second is. Authority: The author of the literature has reputation or is representative in this research field, or is academic leader, or authority editor of key discipline research bases, and has published articles in national famous magazines. The authority of literature can also be known by identifying how many times the literature has been cited. Under normal circumstances, only literature with authority could earn trust and be given references. The third one is effectiveness. Research materials are valuable for the research subject. The values are reflected through being good for abstracting, being beneficial for obtaining arguments, being conducive to the formation of research thoughts. Therefore, research data must be accurate, comprehensive, profound and typical, not out of date. The stronger the effectiveness is, the more likely the true scientific conclusions could be achieved. The literature then is representative. The fourth one is reliability: The reliability of literature includes authenticity of the literature and the reliability of the contents. When researchers refer to certain literature, they must first make sure whether these literatures are authentic, or fakes or modified, especially for historical documents describing issues. Because the formation time of them is far from our times, it is hard to determine its authenticity. After identifying the authentity of literatures, we must also verify whether the facts or data recorded in the literature are reliable, such as whether the literature faithfully records the truth and whether the concepts and date in the literature and data are accurate, and so on.

Then, how to choose representative research literatures? The following ways could be applied.

To Interview Scholars

To interview scholars and ask them to recommend representative research literatures is a rather direct and efficient way. For example, one of my teachers recommends us to read several books which are all valuable for education researches, which are *Encyclopedia for Education Researches, Education Researches Handbook, and Education Researches Comments.* These literatures are valuable for us to conduct education researches are representative.

To Identify the Grade of Literatures

Under the premise of identifying the grade of literature, we should first explain how to identify the authenticity of literatures. Methods of identifying literature include two ways, respectively, external audit and internal audit. External audit is to identify the authenticity of literatures. We should identify the authenticity of the version by comparing the book's presentation style with contemporary publications on the other hand, we can also examine whether the contents of the book describe the facts that occur after the book is written since. We should also identify the authenticity of authors. Three ways are generally used. The first one it to analyze other works of the author to know the language styles of the author and then check whether the literature on hand has same language style. The second is to analyze whether the style of the literature is consistent. The third is whether the idea of literature and logical point of view is consistent. Internal audit refers to the identification of the authenticity of contents. Main methods include: first, mutual prove of words. If there are inconsistencies between the events described, we should verify it. Secondly, we could use real object to literature in words. We could check whether the text description is consistent with physical evidence. The third is to compare the contents of the documents with historical background to see if it's consistent with the contemporary political and cultural background. The fourth is to study of the life, point of view, basic thoughts of the author and the specific environment when the literature is formed to determine objectivity and tends of the author. In short, internal audit and external audit both make comparison to identify the authenticity of contents in order to collect quality literature.

To identify the authenticity of the documents, we can grade collected materials. According to the content processing ways, education literature could be divided into zero grade, first grade, second grade and third grade. Zero grade literature is usually called the first-hand literature and is the first description of events or experiences and is written by persons who experience the event and is the most primitive original documents, not published or modified, such as the letter, draft, discussion draft, or original record. First grad literature generally refers to works of the record of the incident, research results, new knowledge and new technology monographs, papers, investigation reports and other literature. Literature is also referred to as a secondary literature, is the evidence description reports or materials processed once by actual witnesses and participants in the events. It includes books, newspapers, periodicals, research reports, and government publications and so on. The second grade literature is also known as the retrieval of documents. It refers to literatures that process and sort books and papers to summarize the main points and to put them in system with some methods, such as the bibliography, titles, abstracts, indexes and other publications. Such documentation will be distributed in a systematic literature, entries. Third grade literature is also known as the reference literature. It systematically sorts the first grade literature and make summary based on the second grade literatures. Such literature is different from the original literature, and also different from the secondary literature. It has subjective nature and reflects the authors opinion on the first grade literature and is the comprehensive research results of many first grade literature, such as the dynamic synthesis of educational research, teaching thematic commentary, teaching progress report, which is therefore called as the third grade literature.

To Enhance Theory Knowledge

How to choose representative research literature? On this issue, we must not only mater above-mentioned points; we should also study the fundamental theory knowledge of literature methodology. How are we going to collect the literature? To find valuable literatures for certain research subject in the vast literature ocean, we must master effective method to collect the documents. First of all, researchers should determine the scope and nature of the research subject and fix the direction of the search. Secondly, researchers must know education journals and periodicals both at home and abroad, understand domestic and foreign types of educational books, pictures, audio and video, electronic data and statistics overview and know from where could these materials be obtained. Finally, researchers must be familiar with literature index and directory classification method and master the basic skills of literature retrieval.

Then, we must sort and analyze the large number of literatures collected. How to handle it? The sorting of the literature refers to the process in which researchers conduct creative analysis, comparison and summarizing of literatures that are collected and are identified. Through this kind of reasoning, researches form scientific understanding of research subject. The specific methods of literature sorting mainly apply logical analysis, judging, reasoning, synthesis and dialectical thinking, etc., to make fact judgment from the materials or to summarize some rules or principles to sort these materials.

After sorting literatures, we should analyze the literatures. As raised by a scholar, literature research methods include non-structured qualitative analysis methods and structured quantitative analysis. Non-structured qualitative analysis has been illustrated. Structured quantitative analysis is also known as content analysis. Content analysis is to systematically and objective quantitative literature contents and to make description. For example, when a reader wants to buy a book, he or she will first look at the directory, read an article and take a look at the keywords. These are a kind of intuitive content analysis. Some educators have conducted researches on *Education Science* by Kaiipob. It is found that Kaiipob mentioned "the transfer of knowledge" more than 100 times and only mentioned "the development of intelligence" only 10 times. Therefore, he put forward that Kaiipob's education science is a education science of imparting knowledge. This study is the use of the content analysis. The characteristics of content analysis are intuitive, objective, systematic, and quantitative. The nature of content analysis is to describe literature in words by data, which is good for formal hypothesis application, for scientifically sampling, and for the application of computers to do literature researches. Content analysis is mainly used in trend analysis, comparative analysis and intention analysis.

SUMMARY

For the problem of how to choose representative research literatures, we make the following summary.

1. To master fundamental theory knowledge, including qualitative analysis, literature grade identifying, literature collection methods, literature sorting and contents analysis.
2. To identify representative literatures based on fundamental knowledge
   (a) The literatures written by experts or scholars from national key discipline research bases
   (b) Comment literatures used by discipline annul report or discipline development status meeting
   (c) Literatures written by discipline leading scholars
   (d) Literatures often cited
   (e) Literature of time effectiveness reflecting the current development of research fields
   (f) Comments by experts on relevant issues of literature and timely learn the authority of literatures.

MATERIALS AND TOOLS OF RESEARCH

The materials of literary research are manuscripts and printed books. By manuscripts we mean all the works of an author whether written in his own hand-writing' or in the writings of others. Printed books and manuscripts include all the texts, letters, diaries, journals, memoirs and reviews and critical comments and criticism by the author.

In science the basic tools are observation and experiment. In literature, too, the basic tools are observation and experiment." Of course, we do not make experiments in the way a physicist does. In this respect we are nearer to sociology and history.

MATERIALS

Manuscripts can be divided into two broad divisions: manuscripts in cursive writing before the introduction of the printing machine in England and manuscripts when the spellings were modernised in the eighteenth century and a uniformity was reached in the shape of the letters.

The problems that the Old English and Middle English manuscripts pose are the following :

(a) Old English is almost foreign even to the native English speakers.

(b) Spellings of Old English words are also strikingly different from those of New English words.

(c) There was no uniformity in the shape of the written symbols (graphemes). For example the letters *a or b* could be written in many ways.

(d) Though Middle English is very near to New English, many of its words are obsolete and some of them have changed semantically.

(e) The syntax of Middle English is also different in many cases. For example, the pronouns its and his were interchangeable and two negatives made a sentence negative.

(f) The authors in most cases wanted to remain anonymous and never dated the texts.

New English manuscripts pose little problems excepting these two :

(a) A large number of manuscripts arc unsigned.

(b) The writing is illegible when the writer is in a hurry or tired.

Editions. Caxton set up his printing machine in 1476. It is unnecessary here to record the books he printed and published.

We have only to know that the introduction of the press was revolutionary. Uptill then a book was copied by scribes. The work was tedious, time-taking and in most cases boring. Secondly, the scribes made mistakes while copying and the result was that the manuscripts differed considerably. Now the press made the work easier and more accurate. However printed editions are not always reliable and pose before the research student or scholar the following problems :

(a) There is a considerable difference between a manuscript and a printed edition.

(b) The number of an edition or reprint is seldom printed.

(c) The year of publication is rarely recorded.

(d) Polemical articles do not bear the authors' names.

(e) There are pirated editions and forged manuscripts.

Paper. The paper of a text is also a part of the materials of research. The study of the paper is important for determining the date of a text and ascertaining its genuineness. A paper expert will tell us the age of a paper after examining its quality and watermark. Once we have come to know the date of the paper of a text we can safely assume that the text was written after the date. If a forgerer presents a manuscript claiming that it was written in the thirteenth century, we can examine its genuineness by determining the date of the paper.

Ink. Ink is the third important part of the materials. To take a simple example, if some one comes with a manuscript written with a ball-point pen and claims that it belongs to the nineteenth century, we will at once say that he is cheating us because ball-point pens did not exist at that time. A book on the history of ink will tell us kinds of ink which were used in different ages.

The complex nature and size of materials has made literary research a really difficult and also interesting form of investigation for the discovery of truth.

Finding materials. The nature of finding materials depends on the topic. If we are to edit a text, say Milton's *Paradise Lost,* we have to look for the manuscripts, the different editions, critical commentaries and relevant criticism. Suppose we are writing a doctoral dissertation on W.B. Yeats's use of myths.

We need not consult the manuscripts. We have to study books on Irish mythology, the books discussing myths in general, all the works of Yeats and critical works on Yeats.

But how to know the titles of books, their authors and places of publication? The best source is, of course, *Cambridge Bibliography of Literature.* The other useful general bibliography is PMLA bibliography which is published every year. *Oxford History of English Literature, Pelican Guide to English Uterature, A Literary History of America* and *A Literary History of England* contain useful bibliography. *The English Novel* and *The English Poetry* edited by A.E. Dyson contain bibliography on the more important British novelists and poets and, in addition, contain useful introduction to each of the selected authors. Nowadays critical books on authors contain selected bibliography which includes both primary and secondary sources. For more recent books (he best is *Hooks in Print* which is published every year. The research student can find materials there in three ways : authorwise, titlewise and subjectwise.

All university libraries have adopted the decimal system of classification. It is easy to locate books where there is the open system after consulting the cards which are indexed titlewise and authorwise and which are stored in drawers in the entrance hall. Some prestigious libraries have computerised the system. The great benefit is that a reader after necessary payment can collect information about the books on the subject in these libraries. Journals are a very useful part of bibliography. Every library displays the recent arrivals on a board. For the old issues the research student should go to the reference section or the archives where journals are kept.

The libraries of national importance maintain the manuscripts of old authors. For the living authors, the best sources are the authors themselves or their trustees. In England, the manuscripts of most of the authors upto the nineteenth century are preserved in the university or public libraries. Since writing in English began in India in the last quarter of the nineteenth century (we are not concerned with books in Sanskrit, Arabic. Persian, Urdu, Hindi and the regional languages here) manuscripts can be located in the houses of the authors or their inheritors. The best way, therefore, is to contact the authors or their trustees for the study of manuscripts. In England and America, too, research students or scholars approach the authors or their trustees to consult manuscripts for copyright reasons.

LITERARY RESEARCH

When you think of research, do you picture scientists in lab coats with test tubes and experimental rats? That is a common. But, as a student, you may have been asked to do literary research, and are probably confused about what that means and how to get started. Well, here we go!

The first thing to think about is that 'literary' relates to literature. Research usually means finding something new: a substance, a formula, or an invention. So, literary research means finding something new within a literary work. It really is that simple. Just like a lab scientist, you are being asked to take what is already there and find a new way to interpret the information, and then discuss it.

The first thing to do is get familiar with what research articles and papers look like. You can find many articles online by simply searching for the title of a work and adding 'academic articles' to your search terms. The research librarian at your school or public library should also be an excellent source for help. This might seem time consuming, but you can't expect to write something if you have no idea what the finished product should look like.

Literary Research is of four kinds:

1. Bibliography and Textual Criticism
2. Biographical
3. Theoretical
4. Interpretive.

TOOLS OF RESEARCH

The basic tools; observation and experiment, are common to all kinds of research. Here we are concerned with the special tools of literary research, although some of them are used in natural and social sciences. The tools of literary research are:

(a) **Bibliography.** Hit-word bibliography usually means a list of books and articles on a given subject or an author. In literary research the term means "the science of books" and has a wider denotation. We may divide bibliography into four kinds:

(i) Historical bibliography deals with the history of book production which includes the history of writing, printing, binding, illustrating, publishing and selling. By a successful use of historical bibliography we determine the date of a text. It is a well known fact that there has been a gradual development in the process of making paper, science of printing and art of writing. The historical bibliography is equally useful in editing a text, determining its authenticity and attributing it to an author.

(ii) Bibliothecal bibliography helps us locate books and journals in a library. Primarily concerned with library science and history of library it gives an idea about the classification and location of important libraries. Nowadays all modern libraries use the decimal system of classification and arrange cards author-wise and title-wise alphabetically. The reference section is maintained separately and there is the archives where old journals and manuscripts are housed.

In modern times knowledge has fairly advanced and no subject can be studied in isolation. The research student should not confine himself to the topic research nor limit his knowledge to the subject of specialisation but study books related to his research, though they may belong to other subjects. Some prestigious libraries prepare a list of books available on a subject but the list must not be considered final and the research student should make use of bibliothecal bibliography. Now some libraries have computerised the information system but we must know that computers cannot surpass the human brain. It is the human brain that feeds data to computers. Internet has its own limitations.

(iii) Enumerative bibliography helps the research student know the books he actually needs. The standard bibliographies, *Cambridge Bibliography of English Literature* and *MIA Bibliography* published every year help the student prepare a working bibliography. The other useful source is *Books in Print* published every year and maintained by every university library. (For details read the section Finding Materials in this very chapter)

(iv) Practical bibliography is concerned with the methods of work of student and author — reading, research, compilation of notes and bibliography, preparation of the manuscript, typing of the research paper or the thesis.

Bibliography is usually divided into two main divisions : Primary sources and secondary sources.

The Primary Sources consist of all the writings of an author — literary texts (poems, plays, novels, essays), autobiography, diary, journals, letters and memoirs. The letters, diaries, journals and reminiscences of his close friends and contemporaries are also included in the primary sources. Some scholars include standard biographies in the list of primary sources. The important point to note is that we include only those materials in the list of primary sources, which give us a first hand knowledge of the author.

The Secondary Sources include books on the works of the author. These are usually critical books, research papers notes, reviews, comments and unpublished theses. The main difference between the two is that the primary sources are the subject of investigation and the secondary sources help us understand, analyse and interpret the primary sources. Both are important but our main concern is always the primary sources.

(b) **Note system.** Notes provide facts for future reference. Note taking helps students concentrate attention during lectures and study of books. Different people have different reasons for taking notes, and to a considerable extent the reason dictates the way in which the notes should be taken. There is no hard and fast rule. However, in literary research a technique has been developed for taking notes, which is generally known as note-system.

Lecture notes. There are basic differences between college lectures and university lectures. First of all the university lecturer speaks much faster because he expects his students to take down only bare facts. Since he assumes more general knowledge and expects his students to spend more time in the university library, he is more selective, and unless he enlarges upon a special aspect, he will not give facts. Indeed he will refer to source material, perhaps even write the title of books and journals, names of authors and the uncommon or technical words on the blackboard. In fact he, in most cases, does not try to "teach" the post-graduate or M.Phil, or Ph.D. students' everything there is to know on the subject; instead he guides them. This means that the research student has to concentrate more and be more selective in the classroom. Usually, besides a few facts or quotations, the lecturer provides a valuable structure and references which are worth-noting.

The best way to take lecture notes is to note the main points of argument in the hall and immediately after the lecture, because the contents of the lecture are still fresh in memory, to enlarge it and compare it with the notes of the class fellows to ascertain that all the points have been taken down.

MULTIPLE CHOICE QUESTIONS

1. The Norman Conquest of England in the Battle of Hastings is an important landmark in the history of English literature. It occurred in the year
   (A) 1066 (B) 1076
   (B) 1065 (D) 1075

2. Beowulf, the only important piece of literature surviving since the old English period is a/an
   (A) lyrical ballad (B) prose narrative
   (C) Anglo-saxon epic (D) classical epic

3. Out of the four chief dialects that flourished in the pre-Chaucerian period, the one that became the standard English in Chaucer's time is
   (A) the Northern (B) the East-Midland
   (C) the West-Midland
   (D) the Southern

4. Which of the following is not one of the features of French literature that the Normans imported to England ?
   (A) Clarity of expression
   (B) Varied verification
   (C) Gloom and other-worldly attitude
   (D) Varied moods and themes

5. Which of the following was a characteristic feature of Medieval literature ?
   (A) A large body of personal literature
   (B) Realism in representation of time and space
   (C) Absence of alliteration in poetry
   (D) The popular genre of the bird and the beast fable

6. Which of the following statements is incorrect regarding medieval literature ?
   (A) Allegory was frequent and usual
   (B) The dream-vision convention was prevalent.
   (C) Chaucer exploited the dream-vision convention in *The Canterbury Tales.*
   (D) There was often an undercurrent of moral and dialectic strain.

7. The poet who was born in the reign of Edward III, lived through that of Richard II and died in the reign of Henry IV was
   (A) Trevelyan (B) Chaucer
   (C) Boccaccio (D) Langland

8. The Black Death that swept over England, when Chaucer was about nine years old is another name for
   (A) the Great Plague
   (B) the Great Flood
   (C) the Great Drought
   (D) the Great Revolt

9. There were three important medieval institutions. Which of the following was not one of them ?
   (A) Feudalism
   (B) Chivalry or Knight-errantry
   (C) The Church (D) Slavery

10. In Chaucer's times the Peasant Revolt resulted in the
    (A) dethronement of the king
    (B) demolition of church as an institution
    (C) end of serfdom
    (D) rise of nationalism

11. The spirit of new learning in the transitional period from the medieval to the modern was chiefly the influence of
    (A) French Renaissance
    (B) Italian Renaissance
    (C) German Renaissance
    (D) All of the above

12. The two French writers who considerably influenced Chaucer in his early literary career were

(A) De Lorries and De Meung
(B) Dante and Boccaccio
(C) Blanche and De Lorris
(D) Blanche and Gower

13. *The Book of the Duchess* by Chaucer is a

(A) lengthy allegory on the death of his patron's wife
(B) short lyrical story of the Duchess of Wales
(C) long narrative story of an adulterous Duchess
(D) tribute to his beloved and her beauty

14. Which of the following works of Chaucer bears close resemblance to Dante's *Divine Comedy* ?

(A) *The Romaunt of the Rose*
(B) *The Parliament of Fowls*
(C) *The House of Fame*
(D) *Troilus and Criseyde*

15. Which of the following works of Chaucer contains passages that have been directly taken from Dante ?

(A) *The House of Fame*
(B) *The Parliament of Fowls*
(C) *The Canterbury Tales*
(D) *Legend of Good Women*

16. *Troilus and Criseyde* by Chaucer shows great influence of *Filostrato* by

(A) Dante (B) De Lorries
(C) De Meung (D) Boccaccio

17. *Troilus and Criseyde* and *Pandorus* reveal maturity of Chaucer's narrative skills and his dexterity in handling the

(A) Heroic Couplet (B) Rhyma Royal
(C) Free Verse (D) Blank Verse

18. The very idea of *The Canterbury Tales* is believed to have been taken from Boccaccio's

(A) *Recamerone*
(B) *Filostrato*
(C) *Confessio Amantis*
(D) *Polychronicon*

19. The poem by Chaucer, known to be the first attempt in English to use the Heroic Couplet is

(A) *The Complaint unto Pity*
(B) *The Romance of the Rose*
(C) *The Legend of Good Women*
(D) *Troilus and Criseyde*

20. Who has remarked that "Chaucer found English a dialect and left it a language" ?

(A) Legouis (B) Hadow
(C) Lang (D) Lowes

21. Hudson has rightly said that under the influence of Chaucer in English poetry, the rhyme gradually displaced

(A) free verse (B) alliteration
(C) prose narrative (D) None of these

22. Chaucer used *ottava rhyma*, the eight syllabic line rhyming in couplets, in

(A) *The Prologue*
(B) *The Canterbury Tales*
(C) *The Book of the Duchess*
(D) *Troilus and Criseyde*

23. In *Prologue and Canterbury Tales,* Chaucer employed the

(A) Ottava Rhyma (B) Rhyma Royal
(C) Heroic Couplet (D) Both (A) and (C)

24. The *rhyma royal* which Chaucer so effectively used in *Troilus and Criseyde* is arranged in stanzas consisting ten-syllabic lines and having

(A) seven lines in each stanza
(B) five lines in each stanza
(C) eight lines in each stanza
(D) nine lines in each stanza

25. In the *Prologue to the Canterbury Tales,* the fading chivalry of Middle Ages is represented by the aged knight, while the budding chivalry of Chaucerean times is represented by

(A) the friar (B) the squire
(C) the parson (D) Wyclif

26. Chaucer's physician in the *Doctor of Physique* was heavily dependent upon
(A) church (B) astrology
(C) modern Science (D) sorcery

27. Chaucer has been criticized for presenting an incomplete picture of his times, because
(A) he overemphasises the rights of the lower class
(B) he exaggerates the courtly benevolence
(C) he writes for the court and cultivated clas- ses and neglects the suffering of the poor
(D) he supports the Lollardy and the Peasant Revolution too fervently

28. Who among the following has been called *The Morning Star of the Renaissance* ?
(A) Shakespeare (B) Spenser
(C) Chaucer (D) Marlowe

29. Chaucer's *Canterbury Tales* is a story of
(A) nineteen pilgrims
(B) twenty-four pilgrims
(C) thirty-nine pilgrims
(D) thirty-four pilgrims

30. Who among the following has been called by Spenser as "*The Well of English Undefiled*" ?
(A) Chaucer (B) Langland
(C) Shakespeare (D) Thomas More

31. Chaucer introduced the Heroic Couplet in English verse and invented the
(A) Ottava Rhyma (B) Blank Verse
(C) Sonnet (D) Rhyma Royal

32. One of the main drawbacks of *Troilus and Criseyde* is
(A) lack of coherence
(B) long and tiresome speeches
(C) complex characters
(D) the unmistakable personal accent

33. The character of *Criseyde* is
(A) a superficial portrait of a haughty woman
(B) a psychological study of a complex woman
(C) the true representative of a typical medieval woman
(D) the reflection of frailty of women in Chaucer's times

34. *Pandorus* is a/an
(A) negative character
(B) literary genius
(C) comic character
(D) obnoxious rogue

35. John Gower's *Confessio Amantis,* "an encyclopedia of the art of love", was written in
(A) Latin
(B) French
(C) English (East-Midland dialect)
(D) Anglo-Saxon

36. *The Vision of William Concerning Piers, the Plowman* is the only extant poem of
(A) John Gower (B) Lydgate
(C) W. Langland (D) Higden

37. Four anonymous poems contained in one manuscript of about 1370 were found which give us good examples of medieval allegories. Which of the following is not one of them ?
(A) Sir *Gawayn and the Green Knight*
(B) *Patience*
(C) *Pearl* (D) *Pardon*

38. The poet, known entirely for *Bruce*, the supreme national poem of Scotland, is
(A) John Gower (B) John Barbour
(C) Langland (D) John Wycliffe

39. One of the earliest works in English prose was the translation that appeared in 1377 of the French *Travels* of Sir John Mandeville. It was the work of a French physician,
(A) John of Trevisa
(B) Jean de Bourgone
(C) De Lorris (D) De Meung

40. The contemporary of Chaucer who is regarded the most original and powerful prose writer of his times is
(A) John Wycliffe (B) John of Trevisa
(C) W. Langland (D) John Gower

41. In the *Canterbury Tales* the fictional inn, where the pilgrims meet is

(A) Canterbury (B) Tabard
(C) Wessex Hall (D) Princetown

42. Chaucer shows almost a modern attitude in his
(A) realism
(B) rejection of conventions
(C) humour (D) All of these

43. Arnold criticizes Chaucer for lacking in
(A) coherence
(B) high seriousness
(C) the lyric quality
(D) verisimilitude

44. Whose followers are known as Lollards ?
(A) Martin Luther King
(B) John Wycliffe
(C) John of Trevisa
(D) William Langland

45. William Caxton pointed the first book in English in 1474. Name the book.
(A) *To Gentlemen of Verona*
(B) *The Bible*
(C) *History of Troy*
(D) *Utopia*

46. In which month did the pilgrims march towards Canterbury ?
(A) April (B) March
(C) June (D) May

47. Which of the following took place during 1455-85 ?
(A) The War of Roses
(B) The Battle of Hastings
(C) The Norman Conquest
(D) The Peasant Revolution

48. When did Henry VII, the patron of education come to throne ?
(A) 1456 (B) 1468
(C) 1473 (D) 1485

49. Which of the following is a prose story by Chaucer ?
(A) *Tale of Melibens*
(B) *The Parson's Tale*
(C) *The Parliament of Fowls*
(D) Both (A) and (B)

50. Who is regarded as the first translator of the Bible into English ?
(A) Thomas More (B) John Wycliffe
(C) William Tyndale (D) William Langland

51. In Chaucerean period, the Hundred Years' War was a collective name for the long succession of feuds and skirmishes between
(A) England and Scotland
(B) England and Ireland
(C) England and France
(D) England and Germany

52. What was the prize for the best story-teller among the pilgrims in the *Canterbury Tales*?
(A) A free horse ride
(B) A free supper
(C) A book of the Bible
(D) All of the above

53. What is the true import of the Clerk's tale in the *Canterbury Tales* ?
(A) That man can make his own fortune.
(B) That adversity is the best teacher.
(C) As you sow, so you reap.
(D) That man must learn to endure adversity with courage and understanding.

54. Which of the following was not a consequence of the *Battle of Agincourt* (1415) ?
(A) England's Supremacy in Europe was established.
(B) English nationalism was on a high tide
(C) The general condition of the people improved.
(D) Henry V became a symbol of national glory.

55. Which war in England paved the way for the enlightened and powerful Tudor rule ?
(A) The War of Roses
(B) The Battle of Agincourt
(C) The Battle of Hastings
(D) The Anglo-French Wars

56. The new Grammar Schools of 15th century England were a result of

(A) diversion of funds from going to monasteries to education
(B) royal patronage of educational institutions
(C) the War of Roses
(D) the ascent of Henry VII

57. William Caxton set up the first printing press of England in 1475 at
(A) London (B) New South Wales
(C) Scotland (D) Westminister

58. *A Letter of Cupid* and *The Regimine of Princes* are 15th century works of
(A) John Lydgate
(B) Alexander Barclay
(C) Stephen Hawes
(D) Thomas Occleve

59. *London Lack Penny*, a short and lively story of the misery of a poor rustic who visits London in quest of justice, is attributed by most to the doubtful authorship of
(A) Occleve (B) Skelton
(C) Lydgate (D) Hawes

60. The invention of the genre, the Eclogues is attributed to
(A) Stephen Hawes
(B) William Dunbar
(C) Alexander Barclay
(D) Gaulin Douglas

61. Who among the following was not one of the Scottish Chaucereans ?
(A) King James I (B) John Skelton
(C) Robert Henryson
(D) William Dunbar

62. *The Thistle and the Rose* and *The Golden Targe* are two allegories of
(A) Gawin Douglas (B) Robert Henryson
(C) William Dunbar (D) Thomas Occleve

63. The most remarkable ballads of the 15th century included
(A) *The Nut-Brown Maid*
(B) *Chevy-chase*
(C) *Mort D' Arthur*
(D) Both (A) and (B)

64. The *Paston Letters* are considered among the important works of the 15th century, because
(A) of their great literary merit
(B) of their value as reliable social chronicles
(C) of their innovative style and form
(D) of poverty of the age in prose writing

65. "It is the first book in English in poetic prose". Which book of 15 century, printed by Caxton, has been referred to here?
(A) *Mort D' Arthur*
(B) *The History of Troy*
(C) *The Bible*
(D) *The Palace of Honour*

66. The drama in England evolved through four well-marked stages till the end of 16th century. Which of the following was not one of them ?
(A) The religious plays
(B) The morality plays
(C) The comedy of humours
(D) The interludes

67. *Everyman* (1490) is an important extant example of
(A) religious play (B) morality play
(C) interlude (D) artistic drama

68. The origin of English drama is attributed to
(A) the ballad
(B) the Chaucerean School
(C) the Lituogy (a religious ceremony of the church)
(D) the royal clowns

69. *The Satire of the Three Estates,* remarkable for its reformist zeal, was written by
(A) John Bales (B) Sir John Lindsay
(C) Thomas Sackville
(D) Thomas Norton

70. The best of John Heywood's interludes or farces was
(A) The Four P's
(B) Ralph Roister Doister
(C) Grammar Gurtan's Needle
(D) King Jehan

71. Which of the following, written by Nicholas Udall, has the credit of being the first English comedy of the classical school ?
(A) *The Four P's*
(B) *Gorbuduc*
(C) *Ralph Roister Doister*
(D) *Jocasta*

72. The first tragedy of the Senecan School to be written in England was *Gorbuduc or Ferrex and Porrex* by
(A) Thomas Sackville
(B) Thomas Norton
(C) Thomas Kyd
(D) Both (A) and (B)

73. An important Senecan tragedy by George Gascoigne was
(A) *Spanish Tragedy*
(B) *Jocasta*
(C) *The Mirror of Magistrates*
(D) *King Jehan*

74. Who among the following was the first to use blank verse in English drama ?
(A) Sackville (B) Gascoigne
(C) Shakespeare (D) Marlowe

75. The first English playhouse called *The Theatre* was founded in the suburbs of London in
(A) 1476 (B) 1526
(C) 1576 (D) 1626

76. Which of the following is not one of the dominant forms of poetry of fifteenth century England ?
(A) Allegory (B) Sonnet
(C) Eclogue or pastoral poetry
(D) Ballad

77. The greatest shortcoming of 15th century poetry was
(A) poverty of themes
(B) immoral note
(C) poor versification
(D) All of the above

78. The most voluminous of Chaucerians who has written more than 1,40,000 lines is
(A) Hawes (B) Barclay
(C) Skelton (D) Lydgate

79. Who among the following satirised the vice of the clergy in his *Book of Colin Clout* ?
(A) Lydgate (B) Skelton
(C) Occleve (D) Dunbar

80. The poet who thought Chaucer was too lenient on the immoral Cressyde and relegated him to object poverty in the *Testament of Criseyde* was
(A) Dunbar (B) Wycliffe
(C) King James I (D) Henryson

81. The prose works of Sir Thomas More included
(A) *The Life of John Picus*
(B) *The Game and Play of the Chess*
(C) *The History of Richard III*
(D) Both (A) and (C)

82. Who among the following is well-known for his *Morte D' Arthur* ?
(A) Malory (B) Norton
(C) Fisher (D) Kyd

83. Long called the *Prologue to the Canterbury Tales,* the prologue to modern fiction because of its
(A) realism
(B) narrative unity
(C) far-fetched imagery
(D) humour

84. Who among the following has been called, *the morning star of Reformation* ?
(A) Wycliffe (B) Malory
(C) Chaucer (D) Caxton

85. What is the significance of the name, the War of the Roses ?
(A) England and France both had the same national flower, the rose.
(B) The war occurred in the season of roses.
(C) The rival fractions in the war were symbolised by red and white roses respectively.
(D) Rose symbolised the bloodiness of the war.

86. The first translator of Virgil into English was
(A) Chaucer (B) Lydgate
(C) Douglas (D) Gower

87. In which year was More's *Utopia* published?
(A) 1416 (B) 1441
(C) 1476 (D) 1516

88. Ralph Robinson's translation of More's *Utopia* appeared in
(A) 1551 (B) 1581
(C) 1521 (D) 1611

89. *Utopia* is also known by the name
(A) *An Unknown Island*
(B) *The Strange Country*
(C) *The World of Imagination*
(D) *The Kingdom of Nowhere*

90. The *Tale of Melibens* in the Canterbury Tales was told by
(A) the owner of the Inn
(B) Chaucer himself
(C) the Clerk
(D) the Parson

91. The authorised version of the Bible is based on the translation made by
(A) Tyndale (B) Sir Pope John Paul
(C) Wycliffe (D) All of the above

92. The Spanish Armada was defeated in
(A) 1465 (B) 1488
(C) 1535 (D) 1588

93. *The Ways of Perfect Religion* was written by
(A) John Wycliffe
(B) John Fisher
(C) John of Trevisa
(D) Lydgate

94. Luther's Wittenberg theses were published in
(A) 1398 (B) 1417
(C) 1517 (D) 1598

95. Earl of Surrey was executed in
(A) 1496 (B) 1527
(C) 1547 (D) 1596

96. Who ascended the throne of England in 1558 ?
(A) Henry VIII (B) Mary
(C) Edward VI (D) Elizabeth I

97. Both *The Prince* of Machiavelli and *The Courtier* of Castiglione are representatives of the Renaissance spirit in the sense that
(A) both exemplify free-thinking and vigorous life
(B) both advocate worldly success by questionable means
(C) both revive interest in sculpture and painting
(D) both inculcate a pride in patriotism

98. The expeditions of Columbus to America and Vasco da Gama to India in the last decade of the fifteenth century may be attributed to
(A) intellectual curiosity
(B) man's mastery over the sea
(C) lust for wealth
(D) spiritual quest

99. Who strengthened the monarchy after the War of the Roses in England ?
(A) Edward II (B) Henry VII
(C) Henry VIII (D) Elizabeth I

100. Who among the following was a fifteenth century educationist and reformer ?
(A) Roger Ascham (B) Martin Luther
(C) Machiavelli (D) Drayton

101. Why did Henry VIII quarrel with the Pope ?
(A) Because of the Pope's corrupt and high-handed practices
(B) Because the Pope spied for other empires
(C) Because the Pope did not grant him divorce from queen Catherine
(D) Because of the general anticlerical sentiment

102. Calvin, whose followers in England have been called "the spiritual ancestors of the great puritan movement of the 17th century", was a
(A) German physician

(B) Italian reformer
(C) Spanish physician
(D) French reformer

103. More's *Kingdom of Nowhere* was inspired by
(A) Machiavelli's *The Prince*
(B) Plato's *Republic*
(C) *The Bible* (D) Virgil's *Aeneid*

104. Who has been called *the first of the modern pacifists ?*
(A) Tyndale (B) Ascham
(C) More (D) Surrey

105. Who is known for *The Schoolmaster*, which contains his advice to teachers on the teaching of Latin ?
(A) Roger Ascham (B) Thomas Wyatt
(C) Martin Luther (D) John Wycliffe

106. Who completed the translation of the Bible begun by William Tyndale ?
(A) Roger Ascham (B) Thomas Cranner
(C) Erasmus (D) Miles Coverdale

107. The *English Prayer Book*, adopted as the official prayer book in 1549, was largely the work of
(A) Wycliffe (B) Tyndale
(C) Cranner (D) Erasmus

108. Who introduced the sonnet form to England ?
(A) Petrarch (B) Wyatt
(C) Spenser (D) Shakespeare

109. Besides the sonnet form, what else was introduced by Wyatt to England ?
(A) The Italian *terza rima*
(B) The *ottava rima*
(C) The elegy
(D) Both (A) and (B)

110. Who made the first use of the unrhymed ten-syllabled line in English poetry through his translations of Virgil ?
(A) Thomas Wyatt
(B) Thomas Sackville
(C) The Earl of Surrey
(D) None of the above

111. Queen Elizabeth ascended the throne of England in
(A) 1545 (B) 1556
(C) 1558 (D) 1561

112. Which church was made a reality by Elizabeth in England ?
(A) The Anglican
(B) The Catholic
(C) The Protestant
(D) None of the above

113. The rhetoric exuberance associated with John Lyly and his contemporaries owed its inspiration ultimately to
(A) Machiavelli (B) Plato
(C) Virgil (D) Cicero

114. Gaveston, a mixture of Machiavelli and Tamburlaine, is a character from
(A) *Dr. Faustus* (B) *Edward II*
(C) *Fairy Queen* (D) *Arcadia*

115. The term 'euphuism' owes its origin to the famous character of *Euphues* of
(A) Marlowe (B) Sidney
(C) Lyly (D) Nash

116. An alternative name for Lyly's *Euphues* is
(A) *Bestiary*
(B) *The Unfortunate Traveller*
(C) *The Winter's Tale*
(D) *The Anatomy of Wit*

117. Which Rennaissance poet was killed at the battle of Zutphen ?
(A) Sidney (B) Sackville
(C) Lyly (D) Nash

118. One of the dominant characteristics of Sidney's *Arcadia* is
(A) pathos (B) pathetic fallacy
(C) euphuism
(D) concrete imageries

119. The Elizabethan love for picturesque description was inherited from
(A) Greece (B) Germany
(C) France (D) Italy

120. One of important critical and prose works of the Elizabethan period is Sidney's *Apology for Poetry*, published posthumously in

(A) 1585 (B) 1586
(C) 1595 (D) 1596

121. *The Defence of Ryme* (1503) was written by

(A) Philip Sidney (B) Samuel Daniel
(C) Robert Greene (D) Thomas Dekker

122. *Pandosto,* which supplied the plot of Shakespeare's *The Winter's Tale*, is one of the best romances of

(A) Cicero (B) Marlowe
(C) Greene (D) Nash

123. Who among the following is best known as the creator of a new genre, the picaresque novel ?

(A) Lily (B) Greene
(C) Deloney (D) Nash

124. *Laws of Ecclesiastical Polity* has been said to be "one of the first masterpieces of English prose". Who was its author ?

(A) Wycliffe (B) Richard Hooker
(C) Thomas Dekker (D) Bishop Andrews

125. The *Authorised Version* of *The Bible* (1611) was the work of

(A) Tyndale and Coverdale
(B) Bishop Andrews
(C) Forty-seven scholars
(D) Richard Hooker

126. The great essayist who had once said that the vernaculars "would one day play the bankrupt with books" is

(A) Bacon (B) Johnson
(C) Steele (D) Raleigh

127. In Bacon's *New Atlantis*, the place where scientists devote themselves to the advancement of knowledge is

(A) Wemberley (B) Solomon's House
(C) the Royal Society
(D) Spain

128. Bacon had borrowed the term *Essay* from the French writer

(A) De Meung (B) Goethe
(C) Montaigue (D) De Lorris

129. Bacon published the first edition of this *Essays* in

(A) 1589 (B) 1597
(C) 1612 (D) 1625

130. "Virtue is like precious odours, more fragrant when they are incensed or crushed". This is a typical extract from

(A) Pope (B) Lamb
(C) Johnson (D) Bacon

131. The greatest demerit of Bacon as an essayist, when compared to Montaigne or Lamb, is

(A) his excessive indulgence in himself
(B) his over pragmatic notions
(C) his lack of personal touch
(D) disjointed thoughts

132. "Nakedness is uncomely, as well in mind as in body." This statement is an example of Bacon's

(A) immorality (B) prudence
(C) philosophical bent
(D) love for attire

133. Who is called the first great stylist in English prose ?

(A) Lyly (B) Sidney
(C) Bacon (D) Dryden

134. *The Civil Wars* published in 1595 and based on the *War of the Roses* is the most characteristic work of

(A) Samuel Daniel
(B) Michael Drayton
(C) Edmund Spenser
(D) Earl of Surrey

135. Drayton is regarded as the first to poetise geography in his

(A) *The Baron's War* (B) *Polyolbion*
(C) *New Atlantis* (D) *Miscellany*

136. Who is the hero in Spenser's *Fairy Queen*?

(A) Prince Arthur
(B) Prince Edward

(C) Henry VII
(D) Spenser himself

137. The knights undertake dangerous adventures in each book of *The Fairy Queen* in order to
(A) protect their religion
(B) protect their countrymen
(C) win the favour of their lady love
(D) usurp the throne

138. *The Fairy Queen* apparently follows the style of
(A) Homer's *Odyssey*
(B) Virgil's *Aeneid*
(C) Dante's *Divine Comedy*
(D) Ariosto's *Orlando Furioso*

139. Which of the following had the aim "to fashion a gentleman or noble person in virtuous and gentle discipline" ?
(A) *The Baron's War*
(B) *The Fairy Queen*
(C) *Shepherd's Calender*
(D) *Essays* (1612)

140. The first book of *The Fairy Queen* is believed to be an allegory of the struggle between the protestant church and the Roman Catholic church, Lady Una in it represents
(A) Queen Elizabeth
(B) Queen Catherine
(C) Queen Mary of Scots
(D) None of the above

141. In *The Fairy Queen,* Elizabeth and the Red-Cross Knight stands for
(A) the Protestant Church
(B) the Catholic Church
(C) the Protestant and the Catholic Church respectively
(D) the Catholic and the Protestant Church respectively

142. Sans Foy and Sans Loy in *The Fairy Queen* are
(A) all powerful knights
(B) holy knights
(C) wicked knights
(D) friends of the Red-Cross knight

143. Error and Orgoglio in *The Fairy Queen* are
(A) holy angels
(B) fallen angels
(C) sorcerers
(D) monsters

144. Which character of Spenser represents Queen Mary of Scots ?
(A) Lady Una (B) Duessa
(C) Abessa (D) Archimego

145. Who called Spenser, "the poets' poet" ?
(A) Bacon (B) Johnson
(C) Lamb (D) Arnold

146. Who praised Spenser in the words, "no man was ever born with a greater genius or more knowledge to support it" ?
(A) Milton (B) Dryden
(C) Fletcher (D) Byron

147. Though Wyatt had imported the Sonnet from Italy, and Surrey had invented the English form of it, the Sonnet proper remained neglected till the publication of Sidney's
(A) *Arcadia*
(B) *Apology for Poetry*
(C) *Astrophel and Stella*
(D) None of the above

148. Name the book which contained 88 sonnets of Spenser.
(A) *Micellany*
(B) *Shepherd's Calender*
(C) *Arcadia* (D) *Amoretti*

149. Three quatrains followed by a couplet, linked together by an artistic arrangement of lines. This is the description of a
(A) Petrarchan sonnet
(B) Spenserian sonnet
(C) Shakespearean sonnet
(D) All of the above

150. Who among the following is not one of the "silver poets" of 16th century, referred to thus by Gerald Bullet ?
(A) Wyatt (B) Sidney
(C) Davies (D) Spenser

151. Tottel's *Miscellany* (1557) contained the songs and sonnets of
(A) Wyatt and Surrey
(B) Wyatt and Raleigh
(C) Surrey and Sidney
(D) Sidney and Spenser

152. Which of the following causes accounts for the popularity of Elizabethan drama ?
(A) Novels were few and could be enjoyed only by the educated.
(B) National themes and sentiments were dramatized.
(C) Drama was the best way for the author to earn money.
(D) All of the above

153. *Campaspe*, *Endymion*, *Hudibras*, *Love's Metamorphosis* and *The Woman in the Moon* are the best works of John Lyly, who wrote mostly
(A) tragedies (B) comedies
(C) chronicle plays (D) poetic plays

154. The best known play of George Peele is
(A) *Tamburlaine*
(B) *Edward I*
(C) *The Old Wive's Tale*
(D) *The Woman in the Moon*

155. Who among the following University Wits is primarily known for his *Friar Bacon* and *Friar Bungey* ?
(A) Lyly (B) Peele
(C) Greene (D) Kyde

156. Thomas Kyd's *The Spanish Tragedy* shows conspicuous influence of
(A) Seneca (B) Ariosto
(C) Homer (D) Virgil

157. *The Spanish Tragedy* is historically important because it foreshadows Shakespeare's
(A) *King Lear* (B) *Hamlet*
(C) *Macbeth* (D) *Othello*

158. One of the University Wits, who was killed in a tavern brawl at the age of 29, was
(A) Kyd (B) Greene
(C) Lyly (D) Marlowe

159. Marlowe's tragedies are all
(A) tragedies of royal people
(B) love tragedies
(C) one-man tragedies
(D) revenge plays

160. Who coined the phrase, "Marlowe's mighty line" ?
(A) Ben Jonson (B) Samuel Johnson
(C) R.L. Stevenson (D) Richard Steele

161. One of the elements that Marlowe introduced into English tragedy is
(A) blank verse
(B) internal struggle
(C) supernatural characters
(D) a unified plot

162. The *Jew of Malta* is the story of insatiable passion for
(A) power (B) woman
(C) wealth (D) exotic land

163. The Dutch Scholar who is known for his works like *Wolloquis* and *In Praise of Folly* is
(A) Boccaccio (B) Machiavelli
(C) John Colet (D) Erasmus

164. The 16th century author of two significant works, *The Mirror of Magistrates* and *Induction*, is
(A) Wyatt (B) Gascoigne
(C) Sackville (D) Sidney

165. Who is credited for introducing the first English comedy, *The Supposes*, the first verse satire, *The Steel Glass,* and the first translation from the Greek tragedy *Jocasta*?
(A) Sackville (B) Gascoigne
(C) Erasmus (D) Philip Sidney

166. The Spenserian poet who had said that he became "irrecoverably a poet" by reading the *Faerie Queen* when a boy, is
(A) Dryden (B) Fletcher
(C) Moore (D) Cowley

167. *I first adventure, follow me who list*
And be the second English satirist
Who acclaimed himself to be the first English satirist in these words ?

(A) Joseph Hall (B) Shakespeare
(C) John Donne (D) John Marston

168. Which of the following is not one of the satirical works of Ben Jonson ?
(A) *Every Man in His Humour*
(B) *Every Man out of His Humour*
(C) *Alchemist*
(D) None of the above

169. The Italian *novella* became common in English translation after the middle of the
(A) 14th century (B) 15th century
(C) 16th century (D) 17th century

170. In which of the following, Naples has been described as a place "of more pleasure than profit and yet of more profit than pity" ?
(A) *Euphues* by Lyly
(B) *Pandosto* by Greene
(C) *The Adventures of Master F.J.* by Gascoigne
(D) *Rosalynde* by Lodge

171. *The Unfortunate Traveller* by Thomas Nashe is a typical
(A) love tragedy
(B) pastoral romance
(C) revenge play
(D) picaresque novel

172. The two gentlemen in the *Two Gentlemen of Verona* are
(A) Douglas and Calvin
(B) Valentine and Proteus
(C) Henry Bailey and Avenant
(D) Lovelace and Herric

173. Who among the following wrote only tragedies ?
(A) Shakespeare
(B) Thomas Kyd
(C) Christopher Marlowe
(D) Thomas Nash

174. Which of the following poems celebrates Spenser's love ?
(A) *Amoretti*
(B) *The Fairie Queene*
(C) *The Ruins of Time*
(D) *Epithalamion*

175. Who among the following is Shakespeare's 'Fair Vestal', Spenser's 'Gloriana' and Raleigh's 'Cynthia' ?
(A) The English throne
(B) Queen Mary
(C) Queen Elizabeth
(D) Eve

176. "The lunatic the lover and the poet
Are of imagination all compact"
These words of Shakespeare have been extracted from
(A) *Love's Labour Lost*
(B) *Hamlet*
(C) *Henry IV*
(D) *Midsummer Night's Dream*

177. Sidney's *Apologie for Poetrie* is an answer to
(A) Nash (B) Plato
(C) Gosson (D) Aristotle

178. Who is referred to as the pioneer of picaresque novel in English?
(A) Kyd (B) Nashe
(C) Greene (D) Lyly

179. Who popularised the inductive method for arriving at through his *Novum Organum* ?
(A) Ben Jonson (B) Francis Bacon
(C) Addison and Steele
(D) Dr. Johnson

180. Bacon defined the essay as
(A) "receptacle for detached thoughts"
(B) "disposed meditations"
(C) "leisurely talk of a philosopher over the dinner table"
(D) Both (A) and (B)

181. "Marlowe's mighty line" – this phrase refers to his
(A) blank verse (B) weighty diction
(C) compact style (D) imagery

182. On whose tomb the following lines have been inscribed ?
"Good friend for Jesus' sake forebeare

To dig the dust enclosed heare;
Bleste be the man that spares these stones,
And curst be he that moves my bones"

(A) Marlowe's (B) Sidney's
(C) Shakespeare's (D) Milton's

183. The one that traces the genealogy of a Shoemaker is

(A) *Cobbler*
(B) *Shoemaker's Holiday*
(C) *School of Abuse*
(D) *The Gentle Craft*

184. How many tales were actually planned by Chaucer for his *Canterbury Tales*, but how many could be complete ?

(A) 120 planned, 20 completed
(B) 124 planned, 24 completed
(C) 20 planned, 20 completed
(D) 134 planned, 30 completed

185. The *Tales* are all in verse except two. Which are the ones in prose ?

(A) Chaucer's Tale of Milibee
(B) Doctor's Tale
(C) Knight's Tale
(D) Squire's Tale

186. There is one tale in *The Canterbury Tales* which is a shrewd satire on unequal marriages. Which one is that ?

(A) The Nun's Priest's Tale of the Cock Chanticleer and the Fox
(B) The Merchant's Tale of January and May
(C) The Wife of Bath's Tale
(D) The Knight's Tale

187. Name the longest tale in *The Canterbury Tales.*

(A) The Wife of Bath's
(B) The Franklin's
(C) The Knight's
(D) The Cook's

188. An interesting work of this period is a verse debate of two birds who advocate their relative merits. What is the name of the poem, which is often found in the school anthologies in India ?

(A) *Ormulum*
(B) *The Owl*
(C) *Cuckoo Song*
(D) *The Cricket and the Grass-hopper*

189. Sir Gawayn *and the Green Knight* is

(A) a romance (B) an epic
(C) a fairy tale (D) a verse drama

190. In the 15th century, Scottish poetry flourished in England. Given below are four poets. Only one of them is not a Scottish poet. Who is that ?

(A) John Skelton (B) John Barbour
(C) William Dunbar (D) Gawin Douglas

191. About *Tottel's Miscellany* a character in Shakespeare's play says, "I had rather than forty shillings I had my Book of Songs and Sonnets here." Who is the speaker and in which play ?

(A) Slender in *The Merry Wives of Windsor*
(B) Caliban in *The Tempest*
(C) Rosalind in *As You Like It*
(D) Don Pedro in *Much Ado About Nothing*

192. Who of the following is considered the founder of English prose ?

(A) King Arthur
(B) King Alfred
(C) Chaucer (D) Aelfric

193. Who is the author of *Book of Philip Sparrow*?

(A) Philip Sidney (B) Lydgate
(C) John Skelton (D) Chaucer

194. Name of Sackville's blank verse tragedy

(A) *A Georgeous Gallery of Gallant Inventions*
(B) *Gorboduc*
(C) *Gorboduc or Ferrex and Porrex*
(D) *Steel Glass*

195. Name the author of *Book of Martyrs* (1563)?

(A) Hugh Latimer (B) Bishop Ridley
(C) John Foxe (D) John Knox

196. Given below are the title of some famous ballads. Mark the one which is called "a little epic". It describes the gallant fight between two lords, Percy of Northumberland and Douglas of Scotland.

(A) *Chevy Chase*
(B) *Sir Patrick Spens*
(C) *Robin Hood and the Curtal Friar*
(D) *Lochinvar*

197. Which month figures in the prologue to *Canterbury Tales* ?

(A) March (B) March-April
(C) April (D) May

198. Identify the love lyric among the following:

(A) *Handlying Sin* (B) *Alison*
(c) *Sir Patrick Spens* (D) *Ormulum*

199. A noteworthy work produced under the French influence in England was Layamon's voluminous poem of about 30,000 lines, named Brut. What is this book about ?

(A) It is a legendary history of Britain
(B) It is the story of Brutus
(C) It is King Arthur's quest
(D) It is a long pastoral poem

200. What is the subject of Gower's *Confessio Amentis* ?

(A) Love
(B) Moral teachings
(C) Adventure
(D) Confession of a sinner

201. Into how many periods can we divide Chaucer's works ?

(A) Two - French and English
(B) Three - French, English and Italian
(C) Four - French, English, Italian and Latin
(D) One - English only

202. Who in Shakespeare's *Hamlet* mumbles a song from the "Book of Songs and Sonnets" known as *Tottel's Miscellany* ?

(A) Hamlet himself
(B) One of the two clowns, a grave-digger
(C) Polonius
(D) Gertrude

203. Name the castle where Spenser lived and finished the first three books of *Fairy Queen*.

(A) Leicester House
(B) Kilcolman
(C) Lord Grey's Castle
(D) Harvey House

204. William Shakespeare was born on

(A) 26 April 1563 (B) 23 April 1564
(C) 23 April 1563 (D) 3 May 1564

205. Identify the first English comedy written by a headmaster of Eton.

(A) *Grammar Gurton's Needle*
(B) *Ralph Roister Doister*
(C) *The Pour Ps*
(D) *Wit and Science*

206. Who wrote the introductory Sonnet to Spencer's *Fairy Queen* ?

(A) Spencer himself
(B) Leiscester
(C) Sir Philip Sidney
(D) Sir Walter Raleigh

207. He was a musician in the court of Henry VIII. His aim was to amuse and not moralise. His interludes were hilarious and they paved the way for comedy. Name the writer and his work.

(A) Bishop Bale – *King John*
(B) John Heywood – *The Four Ps*
(C) Skeleton – *Magnificence*
(D) Lyndsay – *Satire of the Three Estates*

208. Name the dramatist of *Campaspe*, *Endymion*, *Love's Metamorphoses*.

(A) John Lyly
(B) Robert Greene
(C) Thomas Lodge
(D) Thomas Nash

209. "The fault, dear Brutus, is not in our stars, But in ourselves that we are underlings." Who said this and in which play ?

(A) Cassius in *Julius Caesar*
(B) Antony in *Julius Caesar*
(C) Caliban in *The Tempest*
(D) Antony in *Antony and Cleopatra*

210. Whom would you assign the line "Drink to me only with thine eyes." ?
(A) John Lyly
(B) William Shakespeare
(C) Ben Jonson
(D) Thomas Nash

211. One contemporary of Jonson had a bitter and extravagant style. In his *Poetaster* Jonson gives him a purge which makes him vomit his learned and bombastic words. Who is this poet ?
(A) George Chapman
(B) Thomas Dekker
(C) Marston
(D) Tournier

212. About whom these words are uttered:
"Cover her face; mine eyes dazzle:
She died young."
(A) Juliet in *Romeo and Juliet* (Shakespeare)
(B) Duchess in *The Duchess of Malfi* (Webster)
(C) Cordelia in *King Lear (*Shakespeare)
(D) Anne in *A Woman Killed with Kindness* (Thomas Heywood)

213. Name the famous pair of writers who gained popularity by their joint ventures.
(A) Ben Jonson and George Chapman
(B) George Chapman and Marston
(C) Tournier and Webster
(D) Beaumont and Fletcher

214. "Farewell ! Othello's occupation's gone", What does this cry signify ?
(A) There were no dramatists left after Ben Jonson
(B) The dramatists were taking other occupations
(C) The British Parliament closed the theatre as Puritans came to power
(D) People preferred poetry

215. Name the play in which Shakespeare and Fletcher collaborated.
(A) *Henry VIII*
(B) *Griselda*
(C) *The Two Noble Kinsmen*
(D) *The Maid's Tragedy*

216. How would you classify *The Knight of the Burning Pestle* by Beaumont and Fletcher?
(A) Comedy
(B) Tragedy
(C) Tragi-comedy
(D) Farce

217. This public place was made famous and immortal by Shakespeare, Seldon, Donne, Beaumont, Fletcher and Ben Jonson. Name it.
(A) The Friday Street Club
(B) Mermaid Tavern
(C) Bread Street Tavern
(D) Will's Coffee House

218. Who wrote the book *England from Noah to Elizabeth?*
(A) Daniel
(B) Michael Drayton
(C) William Warner
(D) Christopher Marlowe

219. In the first three plays of Marlowe each of the heroes is consumed by a burning passion which leads to his doom. In *The Jew of Malta*, it is the greed for riches; in *Dr. Faustus* it is inordinate thirst for knowledge. Which passion is depicted in his *Tamburlaine* ?
(A) Thirst for bloodshed
(B) Homicidal instinct
(C) Lust
(D) Thirst for power

220. Barabas is ruined by Christians. He plans a revenge by resorting to incredible cruelties until he falls into a cauldron of boiling water prepared for his enemies. This is in short, the story of a play by Marlowe. Identify the play.
(A) *Edward II*
(B) *The Jew of Malta*
(C) *The Massacre of Paris*
(D) *Dido*

221. How many books are contained in *The Shepherd's Calender*?
(A) 12 (B) 10
(C) 7 (D) 11

222. In *The Shepherd's Calender*, England is represented as a big sheep-farm ruled by
(A) Queen Elizabeth
(B) Shepherd Queen Lisa
(C) Shephered Queen Elisa
(D) Mother Nature

223. Which poem of Spenser was praised by Coleridge for its "Swan-Like Movement" ?
(A) *Ephithalamion*
(B) *Prothalamion*
(C) *Amoretti*
(D) *Astrophel*

224. Edmund Spenser is considered the best poet of Elizabethan age. Identify his period.
(A) 1551–1560 (B) 1552–1599
(C) 1557–1590 (D) 1552–1596

225. When did Spenser's *Shepherd's Calendar* appear ?
(A) 1579 (B) 1580
(C) 1570 (D) 1596

226. In which of Shakespeare's plays the following lines appear :
"Blow, blow, thou winter wind
Thou art not so unkind
As man's ingratitude..." ?
(A) *All's Well That Ends Well*
(B) *As You Like It*
(C) *Antony and Cleopatra*
(D) *King Lear*

227. Which work records Spenser's experiences of his first visit to England in 1589-90 when he was introduced by Sir Walter Raleigh to the Queen ?
(A) *Astrophel*
(B) *Colin Clout's Come Home Again*
(C) *Prothalamion*
(D) *Amoretti*

228. Who wrote the romance *Rosalynde* which supplied the plot for Shakespeare's *As You Like It* ?
(A) Greene (B) Lodge
(C) Lyly (D) Nash

229. Edmund Spenser dedicated his *Shepherd's Calender* to his friend describing him as "the distinguished and virtuous gentleman most worthy of all titles both of learning and chivalry." Who was this friend ?
(A) Sir Walter Raleigh
(B) Leicester
(C) Harvey
(D) Sir Philip Sidney

230. *Arcadia,* a pastoral romance, was written by its author to entertain
(A) the queen
(B) his friend Spenser
(C) his daughter
(D) his sister, the Countess of Pembroke

231. Given below are some of early tragedies. Out of these one was full of "horror". However, it became popular and remained so till the end of the century. Ben Jonson refers to it in his *Everyman in his Humour*. Identify it.
(A) *Dr. Faustus* by Marlowe
(B) *The Jew of Malta* by Marlowe
(C) *Spanish Tragedy* by Kyd
(D) *Gorboduc* by Thomas Norton and Thomas Sackville

232. The first printed collection of William Shakespeare's plays was brought out by Heming and Condell who asserted that they did the work "in order to keep the memory of so worthy a friend and fellow alive." What is this first edition now called ?
(A) *Heming and Condell's Edition*
(B) *Everyman's Shakespeare*
(C) *First Folio*
(D) *Authentic Shakespeare*

233. How many plays are attributed to Shakespeare in toto ?
(A) 37 (B) 36
(C) 21 (D) 154

234. Which of the following books marks the beginning of Shakespeare's success ?
(A) *Love's Labour Lost*
(B) *The Merchant of Venice*
(C) *Venus and Adonis*
(D) *Sonnets*

235. In 1609 an unusual event took place which gave a theme to Shakespeare for one of his enchanting plays. An English ship disappeared, and all aboard were given up for lost. However, a year later the sailors came back. They had been ship-wrecked on the unknown Bermudas and were terrified by mysterious noises which they thought came from the devils. This account was used by Shakespeare in
(A) *The Tempest*
(B) *The Winter's Tale*
(C) *Two Gentlemen of Verona*
(D) *As You Like It*

236. Name the theatre in which Shakespeare had shares.
(A) The Blackfriars
(B) The Theatre
(C) The Universe
(D) The Rose

237. Shakespeare depended primarily on two sources for his legendary and historical plays. Which is the most important one?
(A) King Arthur's legend
(B) Holinshed's *Chronicles*
(C) Plutarch's *Lives*
(D) Legends of Charlemagne

238. How many sonnets has Shakespeare written in toto?
(A) 150 (B) 160
(C) 120 (D) 130

239. Name the picaresque romance which is considered by some critics as the first Elizabethan novel.
(A) *Rosalynde* by Lodge
(B) *Euphues's Golden Legacy* by Lodge
(C) *Jack of Newbury* by Deloney
(D) *Jack Wilton or The Unfortunate Traveller* by Nash

240. Queen Elizabeth, it is said, desired to see Falstaff in love. So at her behest Shakespeare wrote a comedy titled :
(A) *Taming of the Shrew*
(B) *Comedy of Errors*
(C) *Merry Wives of Windsor*
(D) *Measure for Measure*

241. In which play does Shakespeare introduce us to the world of fairies, with the roguish imp of folklore, Puck ?
(A) *The Tempest*
(B) *As You Like It*
(C) *Twelfth Night*
(D) *A Midsummer Night's Dream*

242. In which play does Forest of Arden figure ?
(A) *A Midsummer Night's Dream*
(B) *Macbeth*
(C) *As You Like It*
(D) *The Merry Wives of Windsor*

243. Assign the locales correctly to their plays :

a.	Birnam Woods	1.	*As You Like It*
b.	Forest of Arden	2.	*Merry Wives of Windsor*
c.	Windsor Forest	3.	*Romeo and Juliet*
d.	Capulet's Orchard	4.	*Macbeth*

Codes:

	a	b	c	d
(A)	1	2	3	4
(B)	4	1	2	3
(C)	1	3	4	2
(D)	2	1	3	4

244. Winter's Tale is based on
(A) Greene's *Pandosto*
(B) Lodge's *Rosalynde*
(C) Plutarch's *Lives*
(D) An old English folklore

245. Name the writer of the Elizabethan period who completed Marlowe's *Hero and Leander* and collaborated with Jonson and Marston in *Eastward Ho*!

(A) Thomas Dekker
(B) George Chapman
(C) John Webster
(C) Thomas Heywood

246. Which of Ben Jonson's work is a seething satire on false poets of the age ?
(A) *Volpone, The Fox*
(B) *Poetaster*
(C) *Cynthia's Revel*
(D) *Epicoene or The Silent Woman*

247. Who among the following was a friend of Edmund Spenser and offered hints for the interpretation of Spenser's *The Fairie Queene* indicating a plan of 12 books in all that was never completed ?
(A) Bacon (B) Daniel
(C) Drayton (D) Raleigh

248. Philoclea and Pamela in 'The Arcadia' are the daughters of
(A) Pyrocles (B) Basilius
(C) Musidorus (D) Eurachus

Match the following lists using the codes given below.

249. List I / **List II**
a. *Doctor of Physique* 1. Wycliffe
b. *Chevy Chase* 2. Chaucer
c. *Bruce* 3. 15th Century Ballad
d. The Morning star of English Reformation 4. John Barbour

Codes:

	a	b	c	d
(A)	1	2	3	4
(B)	4	3	2	1
(C)	2	3	4	1
(D)	3	1	2	4

250. List I
a. *Vox Clamantis*
b. *Piers, the Plowman*
c. *Sir Gawayn and the Green Knight*
d. *Polychronicon*

List II
1. William Langland
2. John of Trevisa
3. John Gower
4. Anonymous

Codes:

	a	b	c	d
(A)	3	2	4	1
(B)	3	1	4	2
(C)	2	3	1	4
(D)	2	1	4	3

251. List I / **List II**
a. 1384 1. Death of Chaucer
b. 1400 2. Death of Lydgate
c. 1449 3. Death of Surrey
d. 1547 4. Death of Wycliffe

Codes:

	a	b	c	d
(A)	1	2	3	4
(B)	2	3	1	4
(C)	4	1	3	2
(D)	4	1	2	3

252. List I / **List II**
a. 1066 1. The War of Roses
b. 1415 2. Battle of Agincourt
c. 1455 3. Norman Conquest
d. 1571 4. Battle of Lepanto

Codes:

	a	b	c	d
(A)	3	2	1	4
(B)	1	4	3	2
(C)	2	3	1	4
(D)	4	1	2	3

253. List I / **List II**
a. *London Lack Penny* 1. Occleve
b. *A Letter of Cupid* 2. Lydgate
c. *The Passtyme of Pleasure* 3. Barclay
d. *Ship of Fools* 4. Stephen Hawes

Codes:

	a	b	c	d
(A)	2	1	4	3
(B)	4	2	3	1
(C)	1	3	2	4
(D)	3	4	1	2

254. List I

a. *The Fables*
b. *The Palace of Honour*
c. *The Thistle and the Rose*
d. *The King's Quair*

List II

1. King James I
2. William Dunbar
3. Gavin Douglas
4. Robert Henryson

Codes:

	a	b	c	d
(A)	1	4	2	3
(B)	4	3	2	1
(C)	4	2	1	3
(D)	2	1	4	3

255. List I / **List II**

a. *Everyman* — 1. Farce
b. *The Four P's* — 2. Tragedy
c. *Grammar Gurton's Needle* — 3. Morality Play
d. *Jocasta* — 4. Comedy

Codes:

	a	b	c	d
(A)	1	4	2	3
(B)	4	3	2	1
(C)	3	1	4	2
(D)	2	4	1	3

256. List I

a. 1558 b. 1588
c. 1611 d. 1576

List II

1. Construction of first play house in London.
2. Ascent of Elizabeth
3. Defeat of the Spanish Armada
4. Authorised version of the Bible accepted.

Codes:

	a	b	c	d
(A)	2	3	4	1
(B)	1	2	3	4
(C)	4	1	2	3
(D)	3	4	1	2

257. List I / **List II**

a. Martin Luther — 1. England
b. Machiavelli — 2. Germany
c. Roger Ascham — 3. Italy
d. Dunbar — 4. Scotland

Codes:

	a	b	c	d
(A)	1	2	3	4
(B)	4	3	2	1
(C)	2	1	3	4
(D)	2	3	1	4

258. List-I / **List II**

a. *Ars Poetica* — 1. Sidney
b. *Poetics* — 2. Horace
c. *Apology for Poetry* — 3. Daniel
d. *Defence of Ryme* — 4. Plato

Code:

	a	b	c	d
(A)	1	2	3	4
(B)	2	4	1	3
(C)	3	1	4	2
(D)	4	3	2	1

259. List I / **List II**

a. Thomas Nash — 1. Poet's Poet
b. Spenser — 2. The morning star of English drama
c. Marlowe — 3. One of the greatest of literary plagiarists
d. Shakespeare — 4. Young Juvenal

Codes:

	a	b	c	d
(A)	1	2	3	4
(B)	4	3	2	1
(C)	4	1	2	3
(D)	1	3	2	4

260. List I / **List II**

a. Tragedy — 1. *King Lear*
b. Comedy — 2. *As You Like It*
c. Historical play — 3. *Henry IV*
d. Romance — 4. *The Tempest*

Codes:

	a	b	c	d
(A)	1	2	3	4
(B)	4	3	2	1
(C)	1	3	2	4
(D)	3	4	1	2

261. List I **List II**

a. *The Kingdom of Nowhere* — 1. George Foxe
b. *The Temple of Glass* — 2. William Dunbar
c. *Dance of the Seven Deadly Sins* — 3. Thomas Moore
d. *Book of Martyrs* — 4. John Lydgate

Codes:

	a	b	c	d
(A)	1	3	2	4
(B)	2	1	4	3
(C)	4	2	3	1
(D)	3	4	2	1

262. List I **List II**

a. Thomas Middleton — 1. *Twefth Night*
b. Ben Jonson — 2. *Women Beware of Women*
c. Shakespeare — 3. *The Masque of Beauty*
d. Philip Massinger — 4. *A New Way to Pay Old Debts*

Codes:

	a	b	c	d
(A)	2	3	1	4
(B)	3	2	1	4
(C)	4	3	1	2
(D)	1	4	2	3

263. List I **List II**

a. *The Owl and the Nightingale* — 1. Ben Jonson
b. *Cuckoo and the Nightingale* — 2. George Peele
c. *Volpone* — 3. Anonymous
d. *The Old Wive's Tale* — 4. Anonymous

Codes:

	a	b	c	d
(A)	3	1	2	4
(B)	4	2	3	1
(C)	3	4	1	2
(D)	3	2	4	1

264. List I

a. *The Mourning Bride*
b. *The Gentleman Dancing Master*
c. *The Sullen Lovers*
d. *Don Carlos*

List II

1. William Wycherly
2. Thomas Otway
3. William Congreve
4. Thomas Shadwell

Codes:

	a	b	c	d
(A)	1	2	3	4
(B)	2	3	1	4
(C)	3	1	4	2
(D)	3	2	1	4

265. List I **List II**

a. Bobadill — 1. Bunyan
b. Videna — 2. Jonson
c. Mephistopheles — 3. Sackville
d. Apollyon — 4. Marlowe

Codes:

	a	b	c	d
(A)	2	3	4	1
(B)	3	4	1	2
(C)	4	1	2	3
(D)	1	2	3	4

266. List I **List II**

a. *The Relapse* — 1. Nathaniel Lee
b. *The Rival Queens* — 2. John Vanbrugh
c. *The Confederacy* — 3. William Congreve
d. *Cleomenes* — 4. John Dryden

	a	b	c	d
(A)	1	4	4	2
(B)	3	1	4	1
(C)	2	1	2	4
(D)	4	2	3	2

267. List I **List II**

a. *The Man of Mode, or Sir Fopling Flutter* 1. George Farquhar

b. *Love for Love* 2. George Etheredge

c. *Aurengzeb* 3. William Congreve

d. *The Beaux Stratagem* 4. John Dryden

Codes:

	a	b	c	d
(A)	2	1	3	4
(B)	2	3	4	1
(C)	4	1	2	3
(D)	1	3	4	2

268. List I **List II**

a. 1660 1. Church of England restored

b. 1662 2. England and Scotland unite

c. 1688 3. Charles II restored

d. 1707 4. Glorious Revolution

Codes:

	a	b	c	d
(A)	3	1	4	2
(B)	2	3	1	4
(C)	4	1	3	2
(D)	1	2	3	4

269. List I **List II**

a. 1660 1. *The Battle of the Books*

b. 1682 2. *Astraea Redux*

c. 1687 3. *Religio Laici*

d. 1704 4. *Principia*

Codes:

	a	b	c	d
(A)	3	2	1	4
(B)	4	3	2	1
(C)	1	4	3	2
(D)	2	3	4	1

270. List I **List II**

a. 1611 1. Cromwell becomes land protector

b. 1616 2. Accession of Charles I

c. 1625 3. Death of Shakespeare

d. 1653 4. King James' Bible Published

Codes:

	a	b	c	d
(A)	3	2	1	4
(B)	4	3	2	1
(C)	1	2	3	4
(D)	2	3	4	1

271. Which of the following is untrue about puritanism ?

(A) Frequent satirical references to puritans are found in Shakespearean plays.

(B) The puritans rejected the Anglican church.

(C) They considered beauty and pleasure as traps of evil.

(D) The puritans insisted on the purity of body more than the purity of soul.

272. A civil war broke out in England between the king and the parliament in

(A) 1603 (B) 1628

(C) 1640 (D) 1688

273. Who among the following is not one of the religious poets of the Jacobean period ?

(A) George Herbert (B) A. Cowley

(C) Henry Vaughan (D) Crashaw

274. The decaying drama of the Age of Milton died a natural death with the closure of the theatres in

(A) 1603 (B) 1628

(C) 1640 (D) 1688

275. "He it is who in his own time and ever afterwards provided a typical antithesis to Shakespeare". Whom does this statement refer to ?

(A) Christopher Marlowe

(B) Ben Jonson

(C) Philip Sidney

(D) George Chapman

276. Which of the following is not a work of Ben Jonson ?

(A) *Volpone, the Fox*

(B) *The Alchemist*

(C) *Epicone, or the Silent Woman*

(D) *Scourge of Villainy*

277. Who did Marston collaborate with in writing the play *Eastward Ho* (1605) ?
(A) Ben Jonson
(B) George Chapman
(C) Thomas Dekker
(D) Both (A) and (B)

278. Who tried to give a glimpse of the underworld of London in his *The Honest Whore* ?
(A) Thomas Dekker
(B) John Marston
(C) George Chapman
(D) Ben Jonson

279. *A Woman Killed with Kindness* was written by one of the most important exponents of domestic drama,
(A) John Webster
(B) Thomas Heywood
(C) Thomas Middleton
(D) Philip Massinger

280. *The Revenger's Tragedy* and *The Atheist's Tragedy*, both the masterpieces of Cyril Tourneur are set in
(A) Italy (B) Germany
(C) France (D) London

281. Webster's *The White Devil* is based on the life of the celebrated Italian courtesan
(A) Elizabeth (B) Vittoria
(C) Philoclea (D) None of these

282. Whom does the Duchess marry in Webster's *The Duchess of Malfi* ?
(A) Bassanio (B) Malvolio
(C) Antonio (D) Mortimer

283. *The Masid's Tragedy* and *A King and No King* are the works of
(A) Beumont and Fletcher
(B) Philip Massinger
(C) Ford and Shirley
(D) Thomas Middleton

284. *The Cardinal* and *The Lady of Pleasure* are the masterpieces of a playwright whom Charles Lamb called, "the last of a great race". Name him.
(A) Massinger (B) John Ford
(C) Webster (D) James Shirley

285. The leaders of the metaphysical school were
(A) Ben Jonson and John Donne
(B) John Donne and Henry Vaughan
(C) George Herbert and Abraham Cowley
(D) Henry Vaughan and Abraham Cowley

286. "For God's sake hold thy tongue and let me love." Such abrupt beginnings are a characteristic feature of
(A) Ben Jonson (B) John Donne
(C) Shakespeare (D) Spenser

287. The term "Metaphysical", in connection with Donne's poetry, was first used by
(A) Cowley (B) Dr. Johnson
(C) Herbert (D) Dryden

288. Who among the following stated his objective as follows:
"I'll strip the ragged follies of time Naked, as at their birth, and with a whip of steel, print wounding lashes in their iron ribs" ?
(A) John Donne
(B) Henry Vaughan
(C) Ben Jonson
(D) John Milton

289. Regarding the poetry of which metaphysical poet, Coleridge commented that "nothing can be more fine, manly and unaffected" ?
(A) Richard Crashaw
(B) G. Herbert
(C) Thomas Carew
(D) Andrew Marvell

290. *The Elegie* in praise of John Donne was written by
(A) Henry Vaughan
(B) Thomas Carew
(C) Abraham Cowley
(D) Andrew Marvell

291. Regarding which metaphysical poet T.S. Eliot says that the special quality of his verse is "the quality of civilization, of a traditional habit of life" ?

(A) Robert Herrick
(B) Richard Lovelace
(C) Abraham Cowley
(D) Andrew Marvell

292. The poets who sided with King Charles I against the parliament are called
(A) Cavalier poets
(B) Caroline poets
(C) Metaphysical poets
(D) Both (A) and (B)

293. The collection of lyrics, *Hesperides,* published at London in 1648 was prepared by
(A) Robert Herrick
(B) Richard Lovelace
(C) John Denham
(D) John Suckling

294. Who among the following is known for his epical romance *Gondibert* ?
(A) Denham (B) D'Avenant
(C) Waller (D) Suckling

295. *L'Allegro*, *Il Penseroso*, *Comus* and *Lycidas* are the four immortal poems of
(A) D'Avenant (B) Denham
(C) Milton (D) Lovelace

296. Which of the following is not one of the songs of Thomas Carew ?
(A) *To Celia* (B) *The Rapture*
(C) *The Bud* (D) *Ask Me No More*

297. Milton's *Comus* is an example of that type of drama which is called the
(A) Farce (B) Masque
(C) Romance (D) Revenge tragedy

298. Milton wrote one of his treatises against an order of parliament which passed a censorship on books. Name it.
(A) *Comus* (B) *L'Allegro*
(C) *Areopagitica* (D) *Il Penseroso*

299. Compared to *Paradise Last*, *Paradise Regained* is less significant and more
(A) liberal (B) puritan
(C) religious (D) secular

300. Which critic found Milton's poetry harsh and unequal with little music ?
(A) William Hazlitt
(B) Alfred Tennyson
(C) Samuel Johnson
(D) Mathew Arnold

301. Who called Milton "the mighty-mouthed inventor of harmonies" ?
(A) Arnold (B) Dryden
(C) Johnson (D) Tennyson

302. The character writers of the early 17th century mostly followed the Greek writer
(A) Theophrastus (B) Homer
(C) Plato (D) None of these

303. The voluminous work of Robert Burton which had considerably influenced Dr. Johnson and Charles Lamb is
(A) *Holy and Profane State*
(B) *Microcosmography*
(C) *Anatomy of Melancholy*
(D) *The Complete Angler*

304. *Holy and Profane State*, one of the greatest works of character sketch, was written by
(A) Thomas Fuller (B) Robert Burton
(C) Thomas Overbury
(D) John Earle

305. How many characters does George Herbert's *The Country Parson* deal with in its thirty-seven essays ?
(A) Thirty-seven (B) Three
(C) Twenty (D) One

306. Thomas Browne, the greatest prose writer of the puritan age, was by profession
(A) a cobbler (B) a doctor
(C) a hunter (D) a pamphleteer

307. What is the most significant contribution of Izaak Walton to the literary world ?
(A) *Biography of John Donne*
(B) *Hydrotaphia*
(C) *The Complete Angler*
(D) *Religio Medici*

308. Who wrote *Hydrotaphia or Urn Burial* (1658) inspired by the discovery of some fifty urns in the neigbourhood ?
(A) Milton
(B) Izaak Walton
(C) Thomas Browne
(D) Thomas Fuller

309. *Bussy D' Ambois*, *Caesar and Pompey* and *The Tragedy of Philip Cabot* are some of the best known tragedies of
(A) John Marston
(B) George Chapman
(C) Thomas Heywood
(D) Thomas Dekker

310. *The Witch* and *Game at Chess* are the last plays of
(A) Beaumont (B) Tourneur
(C) Middleton (D) Webster

311. One of the greatest contemporaries of Bacon, whose last book *Ecclesiastical Polity* was published in 1597, was
(A) Raleigh (B) Hooker
(C) Dekker (D) Middleton

312. Who authored the series of *characters* (1614), written from the point of view of the courtier and are epigrammatic and witty ?
(A) Thomas Overbury
(B) Samuel Butler
(C) John Earle (D) Francis Bacon

313. *Ode of Wit* is a small masterpiece of
(A) Andrew Marvell
(B) George Herbert
(C) Abraham Cowley
(D) John Pope

314. *The Definition of Love* and *To His Coy Mistress* are the famous poems of
(A) Abraham Cowley
(B) Henry Vaughan
(C) John Donne
(D) Andrew Marvell

315. *Hudibras* is a famous work of
(A) Dryden (B) Butler
(C) Donne (D) Bacon

316. Dr. Faustus makes a deal of surrendering his soul in return for 24 years of life with
(A) Eunuchus
(B) Mephistopheles
(C) Bobadill
(D) Brainworm

317. In Jonson's *Every Man in His Humour* who is the jealous husband ?
(A) Kitley Merchant
(B) Edward Knowell
(C) Mathew
(D) Stephen

318. *The Pilgrim's Progress* which has been called "the holy grail of puritanism" was written by
(A) John Milton (B) Burton
(C) Bunyan (D) Buccanan

319. Who has been called an opportunist for statements like "A mixture of lie doth ever add pleasure" ?
(A) Jonson (B) Dr. Johnson
(C) Donne (D) Bacon

320. The play by Marston that foreshadows Shakespeare's *The Tempest* is
(A) *The Dutch Courtesan*
(B) *The Malcontent*
(C) *Antonio's Revenge*
(D) *Antonio and Mellida*

321. In 1660, which marks the beginning of the Restoration Age, who among the following was restored to the English throne ?
(A) James II (B) Edward II
(C) Charles II (D) Henry V

322. In the Restoration era almost the entire England was divided into two parties :
(A) the *Whigs* and the *Tories*
(B) the *Democrats* and the *Republicans*
(C) the Catholics and the *Protestants*
(D) the *Conservatives* and the *Liberals*

323. Which period "marks the real moment of birth of our modern English prose", according to Arnold ?
(A) The Elizabethan
(B) The Jacobean

(C) The Puritan
(D) The Restoration

324. Poetry in the Restoration period was predominantly
(A) lyrical (B) satirical
(C) sentimental (D) philosophical

325. *Absalom and Achitophel* and *Mc Flecknoe* are the best satires of
(A) Dryden (B) Congreve
(C) Pope (D) Wycherly

326. An important element in Dryden's satire is his dexterity in handling the
(A) blank verse
(B) sonnet form
(C) heroic couplet
(D) None of the above

327. A satire by Dryden, chiefly personal in content and not very great as a work of art, but still immensely popular in its times was
(A) *Absalom and Achitophel*
(B) *The Medal*
(C) *Mc Flecknoe*
(D) *Hudibras*

328. Whose essay *On Myself* has been hailed as the perfect example of what a personal essay should be ?
(A) Cowley (B) Bacon
(C) Dryden (D) Bunyan

329. Who is credited for creating the modern prose style through his essays like *Essay on Satire* and *Essay on Epic Poetry* ?
(A) Bacon (B) Bunyan
(C) Dryden (D) Cowley

330. *Grace Abounding* is the autobiography of
(A) J, Collier
(B) A. Cowley
(C) John Milton
(D) John Bunyan

331. Who set a new trend in literary criticism through his *Examen of the Silent Woman* ?
(A) Milton (B) Bunyan
(C) Dryden (D) Bacon

332. Dryden emphasized three virtues for which the poet should arouse admiration. Which of the following is not one of them ?
(A) Valour (B) Justice
(C) Duty (D) Love

333. What does Dryden mean by the term "concernment" ?
(A) Duty (B) Sanity
(C) Compassion (D) Infatuation

334. Dryden's *All for Love* is a transitional play, showing the features of both, the heroic play and the
(A) sentimental tragedy
(B) sentimental comedy
(C) restoration comedy
(D) comedy of humours

335. The finest examples of the sentimental tragedy or the she-tragedy are *The Fair Penitent* and *Jane Shore* by
(A) Dryden
(B) Nicholas Rowe
(C) William Congreve
(D) Wycherly

336. Congreve achieved immediate success with his first play
(A) *Double Dealer*
(B) *Love for Love*
(C) *Old Bachelor*
(D) *The Way of the World*

337. Mrs. Millamant and Mirabel are the famous characters of
(A) *Love for Love*
(B) *The Beaux Stratagem*
(C) *The Provok'd Wife*
(D) *The Way of the World*

338. The Restoration comedies such as *The Relapse*, *The Provok'd Wife* and *The Confederacy* are the works of
(A) Congreve (B) Vanbrugh
(C) Farquhar (D) Otway

339. Who wrote comedies such as *Love in a Bottle* and *The Recruiting Officer* in the Restoration Age ?

(A) Otway (B) Wycherley
(C) Vanbrugh (D) Farquhar

340. The contemporary of Dryden whose reputation lies chiefly on heroic plays such as *The Orphan* and *Venice Preserved* is
(A) Nathaniel Lee
(B) Thomas Otway
(C) Nicholas Rowe
(D) George Farquhar

341. The Great Fire that destroyed a major part of London occurred in
(A) 1606 (B) 1636
(C) 1665 (D) 1696

342. Who wrote *A Satyre Against Mankind* in 1675?
(A) Wycherley (B) Rochester
(C) Dryden (D) Katherine Philips

343. The Glorious Revolution that forced James II to flee occurred in
(A) 1688 (B) 1689
(C) 1690 (D) 1691

344. Newton's *Principia* was published in
(A) 1677 (B) 1687
(C) 1697 (D) 1707

345. Who wrote the *Essay Concerning Human Understanding* in 1690 ?
(A) Bacon (B) Dryden
(C) Congreve (D) Locke

346. Who is the 17th century author of *The Indian Emperor* ?
(A) Etheredge (B) Shadwell
(C) Dryden (D) Otway

347. *She Would If She Could* (1668) was written by
(A) Congreve (B) Farquhar
(C) Etheredge (D) Vanbrugh

348. Which poem of Dryden was written in celebration of Charles II's restoration ?
(A) *Absalom and Achitophel*
(B) *Annus Mirabilis*
(C) *Astrae Redux*
(D) *Conquest of Granada*

349. Who wrote 'Pindaric Odes' which influenced 18th century poetry ?
(A) Herbert
(B) Andrew Marvell
(C) John Donne
(D) Abraham Cowley

350. To whom will you assign these lines :
"*Death, be not proud*", and
"*For God's sake, hold thy tongue and let me love*" ?
(A) Robert Herrick
(B) John Donne
(C) George Herbert
(D) Henry Vaughan

351. Who said this about Donne : "for not keeping of accent Donne deserved hanging" ?
(A) T.S. Eliot
(B) Ben Jonson
(C) S.T. Coleridge
(D) Robert Southey

352. Only one line "Death thou shall be dead" sums up the whole spirit of his writing. Whose ?
(A) Ben Jonson
(B) John Donne
(C) George Herbert
(D) Crawshaw

353. Which of the following poems of Herbert is considered a predecessor of Bunyan's *Pilgrims's Progress* ?
(A) The Pilgrimage
(B) The Church Porch
(C) The Gifts of God
(D) The Altar

354. How is George Herbert's poetry described ?
(A) Turbulent
(B) Revolt against tradition
(C) Serene and quiet
(D) Boisterous

355. Who is the author of *The Temple* ?
(A) John Donne
(B) Andrew Marvell

(C) Abraham Cowley
(D) George Herbert

356. In its broadest sense the Puritan Movement is regarded as
(A) a second Renaissance of the moral nature of man
(B) a religious movement
(C) a movement by narrow-minded and gloomy dogmatists
(D) a struggle for liberty

357. Under whom was the Commonwealth established in 1648 ?
(A) Charles I
(B) Richard Cromwell
(C) Thomas Cromwell
(D) General Monk

358. Given below are four important writers. Three belong to the Puritan period, one does not. Identify him.
(A) John Donne
(B) George Herbert
(C) Francis Bacon
(D) John Milton

359. In what lies the peculiarity of the Cavaliers?
(A) Open rebellion against Puritan ideals
(B) Lighter vein and gaiety, yet religiousness
(C) Licentiousness and triviality
(D) All of the above

360. To whom do we assign these charming poems – 'Corinna's Maying', 'Gather Ye Rose Buds While Ye May', 'To Daffodils' ?
(A) Robert Herrick
(B) Thomas Carew
(C) Sir John Suckling
(D) Sir Richard Lovelace

361. Some poets of the Puritan age called themselves the "Sons of Ben". Who among following is among them ?
(A) Robert Herrick
(B) Thomas Carew
(C) Andrew Marvell
(D) All of the above

362. The poet regarded as the link between the Renaissance and the Classical age is
(A) Cowley (B) Denham
(C) Waller (D) All of these

363. Dr. Johnson begins his *Lives of the Poets* with
(A) Edmund Spenser
(B) Edmund Waller
(C) Abraham Cowley
(D) John Donne

364. To whom do we assign these lines wherein the poet argues that since everything in nature drinks, why shouldn't we ?
"Fill up the bowl, then fill it high,
Fill all the glasses there – for why
Should every creature drink but I ?
Why, man of morals, tell me why ?"
(A) Umar Khayyam
(B) Abraham Cowley
(C) Edmund Waller
(D) John Donne

365. Who wrote *Cooper's Hill* (1642) ?
(A) Edmund Waller
(B) Abraham Cowley
(C) John Dryden (D) Denham

366. Who is author of the famous lines :
"Stone walls do not a prison make,
Nor iron bars a cage" ?
(A) Sir Richard Lovelace
(B) Sir John Suckling
(C) Abraham Cowley
(D) Edmund Waller

367. Who wrote the following lines ?
"He that would hope to write well hereafter in laudable things, ought himself to be a true poem; that is a composition and pattern of the best and most honorable things."
(A) John Milton
(B) Sir Richard Lovelace
(C) Ben Jonson
(D) John Dryden

368. "Thy soul was like a star and dwelt apart;
Thou hast a voice whose sound was like the sea-
Pure as the naked heavens, majestic free;"
The above lines are from *Sonnet on Milton*. Who wrote the sonnet ?
(A) S.T. Coleridge
(B) Robert Browning
(C) William Wordsworth
(D) None of the above

369. John Milton wrote a poem when he was at Cambridge, which still remains one of his best. Name it.
(A) *L'Allegro*
(B) Il *Penseroso*
(C) *On the Morning of Christ Nativity*
(D) *Lycidas*

370. John Milton was born in
(A) 1607 (B) 1608
(C) 1600 (D) 1601

371 How many books are there in *Paradise Regained*?
(A) Ten (B) Two
(C) Four (D) One

372. Who is the hero of *Paradise Regained* ?
(A) The Puritan Church
(B) Christ
(C) Satan
(D) None of the above

373. What is the theme of *Paradise Regained* ?
(A) The upliftment of man
(B) The fall of man
(C) The temptation of Jesus Christ
(D) Praise of Puritan Church

374. What do "L' Allegro" and "Il Penseroso" mean ?
(A) The cheerful man
(B) The play-house
(C) The pensive man
(D) (A) and (C) respectively

375. Who said that the sonnet in Milton's hand "became a trumpet" ?
(A) Dr. Johnson
(B) Lord Tennyson
(C) S.T. Coleridge
(D) William Wordsworth

376. The plot of *Samson Agonistes* is taken from
(A) *The New Testament*
(B) *The Book of Judge*
(C) *Greek Mythology*
(D) Plutarch's *Lives*

377. Milton's *Samson Agonistes* is a tragedy on the Greek model. Whom does he follow here?
(A) Sophocles (B) Seneca
(C) Euripides (D) Aristotle

378. What is the literary form used in *Samson* ?
(A) Iambic pentameter
(B) Blank verse
(C) Prose
(D) Spencerian stanza

379. Who out of the following visited Samson in the Philistine prison ?
(A) Manoa, his father
(B) Delila, his wife
(C) Harapha, the braggart
(D) All of the above

380. Who is the hero of *Paradise Lost* ?
(A) God (B) Satan
(C) Jesus Christ (D) Adam

381. How many books are contained in *Paradise Lost* ?
(A) 10 (B) 4
(C) 14 (D) 12

382. When was *Paradise Lost* published ?
(A) 1640-41 (B) 1667
(C) 1663 (D) 1658

383. In Book III of *Paradise Lost* Satan comes to the earth. Where does he alight first ?
(A) In the Garden of Eden
(B) On the Sun
(C) On Mount Niphates
(D) None of the above

384. Who directs Satan to the earth in *Paradise Lost* ?

(A) Sun (B) Gabriel
(C) Raphael (D) Uriel

385. Name the angel who comes down to carry out the decree of God after the Fall.

(A) Raphael (B) Gabriel
(C) Michael (D) Son of God

386. What form does Satan take when he comes to tempt Christ in *Paradise Regained* ?

(A) Serpent
(B) An aged man in rural weeds
(C) An Angel
(D) None of the above

387. A story begins thus : "As I walked through the wilderness of this world I lighted on a certain place where was a den (Bedford Jail) and laid me down in that place to sleep; and, as I slept, I dreamed a dream." Identify the book and its author.

(A) John Bunyan – *Pilgrim's Progress*
(B) Dante – *Divine Comedy*
(C) John Bunyan – *The Holy War*
(D) John Milton – *Paradise Lost*

388. A critic, Taine, says, "Next to the Bible, the book most widely read in England is ..."

(A) *Fairy Queen*
(B) *Religio Medici*
(C) *Unto This Last*
(D) *Pilgrim's Progress*

389. The journey in *Pilgrim's Progress* is undertaken in

(A) two stages
(B) five stages
(C) twelve stages
(D) ten stages

390. Sir Thomas Browne's *Religio Medici* became an immediate success. It was translated into Latin, French, German, Dutch and Italian and was reprinted about eight times during the author's life-time. What is the theme of the work ?

(A) The religion of a doctor
(B) Doctors are not atheists
(C) Religion is not incompatible with science
(D) All of the above

391. One work of Sir Thomas Browne deals with number five. Which one ?

(A) *Hydriotaphia*
(B) *The Garden of Cyrus*
(C) *Religio Medici*
(D) *Christian Morals*

392. A prose writer of the Puritan age is known for his rhetorical and rhythmical style, rich fancy and classical learning. His book *Holy Living and Holy Dying* is admired for its pictorial quality but criticized for its Latinism. Name the writer.

(A) Jeremy Taylor
(B) Thomas Hobbes
(C) Edward Hyde
(D) Izaak Walton

393. Who is the leviathan of Hobbes' work *Leviathan* ?

(A) A legendary sea monster
(B) The state
(C) England
(D) None of the above

394. When was Coverdale's *Great Bible* issued?

(A) 1540 (B) 1610
(C) 1560 (D) 1604

395. One of the following prose works of the Puritan period influenced Dr. Johnson, Sterne, Charles Lamb. Name it.

(A) Sir Thomas Browne's – *Vulgar Errors*
(B) Robert Bacon's – *Anatomy of Melancholy*
(C) Francis Bacon's – *Essays*
(D) Izaak Walton's – *The Compleat Angler*

396. Some Protestants who had fled from Mary's reign of persecution and had settled in Geneva also translated the Bible. What is this translation known as ?

(A) Bishop's Bible

(B) Vulgate
(C) Calvinistic Bible
(D) Geneva Bible

397. Which critic refers to Milton's "the grand style" ?
(A) William Wordsworth
(B) Dr. Samuel Johnson
(C) Mathew Arnold
(D) S.T. Coleridge

398. Right or wrong, good or bad are concepts which according to Thomas Hobbes are
(A) elevating
(B) necessary for social uplift
(C) determined by self-interest
(D) determined by God

399. Spot the book written in the form of a dialogue between Piscator (fisherman) and Venator (hunter).
(A) Thomas Fuller's – *Worthies of England*
(B) Clarendon's – *History of Rebellion*
(C) Izaak Walton's – *Compleat Angler*
(D) John Selden's – *Table-Talk*

400. The first regular English journal was started in 1622 by
(A) Thomas Archer
(B) Nicholas Burne
(C) Addison and Steele
(D) Both (A) and (B)

401. The theatres which were closed in 1642 were reopened in
(A) 1652 (B) 1660
(C) 1662 (D) 1670

402. Who may be regarded as representative of Dryden himself in his *Essay of Dramatic Poesy ?*
(A) Neander (B) Eugenius
(C) Crites (D) None of these

403. The first Poet Laureate in England was
(A) Milton (B) Dryden
(C) Jonson (D) Pope

404. *A Game of Chess,* a political satire by Middleton is set in
(A) England (B) Scotland
(C) Spain (D) Italy

405. Dryden's *Absalom and Achitophel* dealt with the people's plan to prevent James from coming to the throne and make Duke of Manmonth the King, which is known as
(A) the Royal conspiracy
(B) the Protestant drill
(C) the Popish plot
(D) All of the above

406. Regarding whom Dr. Johnson said that he "found English of brick and left it of marble" ?
(A) Milton
(B) Shakespeare
(C) Ben Jonson
(D) Dryden

Match the following lists using the codes given below.

407. List I — **List II**
a. *The Changeling* — 1. Herbert
b. *Oh, Shakespeare* — 2. Middleton
c. *Affliction* — 3. Vaughan
d. *The Retreat* — 4. Milton

Codes:

	a	b	c	d
(A)	3	4	2	1
(B)	2	4	1	3
(C)	4	1	2	3
(D)	3	2	4	1

408. List I — **List I**
a. *On Arriving at the Age of Twenty three* — 1. Marvell
b. *Pindarique Odes* — 2. Cowley
c. *The Rehearsal Transposed* — 3. Milton
d. *The Infant Mortyrs* — 4. Crashaw

Codes:

	a	b	c	d
(A)	3	2	1	4
(B)	1	3	4	2
(C)	4	1	2	3
(D)	2	4	3	1

409. List I — **List II**

a. *All Fools* — 1. Thomas Dekker

b. *The Shoemaker's Holiday* — 2. John Fletcher

c. *The Faithful Shepherdess* — 3. Thomas Middleton

d. *Moll Cutpurse* — 4. G. Chapman

Codes:

	a	b	c	d
(A)	2	3	4	1
(B)	1	4	2	3
(C)	4	1	2	3
(D)	3	2	4	1

410. List I — **List II**

a. Ben Jonson — 1. *The Devil's Law Case*

b. Beaumont and Fletcher — 2. *Cynthia's Revels*

c. Heywood — 3. *Philaster*

d. Webster — 4. *The Captives*

Codes:

	a	b	c	d
(A)	1	2	3	4
(B)	4	3	2	1
(C)	1	4	3	2
(D)	2	3	4	1

411. List I — **List II**

a. Philip Massinger — 1. *The Witch of Edmonton*

b. John Ford — 2. *A Kind of No King*

c. John Marston — 3. *Antonio's Revenge*

d. Beaumont and Fletcher — 4. *The City Madam*

Codes:

	a	b	c	d
(A)	4	1	3	2
(B)	2	3	1	4
(C)	4	1	2	3
(D)	3	2	4	1

412. List I — **List II**

a. Thomas Kyd — 1. *Cymbeline*

b. Ben Jonson — 2. *Cornelia*

c. George Chapman — 3. *The Staple News*

d. Shakespeare — 4. *Eastward Ho*

Codes:

	a	b	c	d
(A)	1	4	2	3
(B)	3	2	4	1
(C)	2	3	4	1
(D)	4	1	3	2

413. List I

a. *The History of Richard III*

b. *The Advancement of Learning*

c. *Leviathan*

d. *Good Thought and Bad Times*

List II

1. Thomas Hobbes
2. Thomas More
3. Francis Bacon
4. Thomas Fuller

Codes:

	a	b	c	d
(A)	1	2	4	3
(B)	2	3	1	4
(C)	3	1	2	4
(D)	4	2	3	1

414. List I

a. *Sylva and Sylvaram*

b. *The Scholemaster*

c. *The Ways of Perfect Religion*

d. *Holy Living*

List II

1. Francis Bacon 2. Roger Aschem
3. John Fisher 4. Jeremy Taylor

Codes:

	a	b	c	d
(A)	4	3	2	1
(B)	3	2	1	4
(C)	2	1	3	4
(D)	1	2	3	4

415. List I

a. *Edward the First*

b. *The Unfortunate Traveller*

c. *The Wounds of Civile War*
d. *The Tragedy of Dido, the Queen Carthage*

List II

1. Thomas Nash
2. Thomas Lodge
3. George Peele
4. Christopher Marlowe

Codes:

	a	b	c	d
(A)	3	1	2	4
(B)	4	2	3	1
(C)	1	3	4	2
(D)	2	4	1	3

416. List I

a. *Leviathan*
b. *Essay Concerning Human Understanding*
c. *The Decline and Fall of the Roman Empire*

List II

1. John Locke 2. Thomas Hobbes
3. Edward Gibbon

Codes:

	a	b	c
(A)	2	3	1
(B)	2	1	3
(C)	3	2	1
(D)	3	1	2

417. List I

a. *The Universal Passion*
b. *Ama, or the progress of the Mind*
c. *Preface to Shakespeare*

List II

1. Dr. Johnson 2. Edward Young
3. Mattew Prior

Codes:

	a	b	c
(A)	1	2	3
(B)	3	2	1
(C)	2	3	1
(D)	1	3	2

418. List I

a. *Dissection of a Coquette's Heart*
b. *The Progress of Error*
c. *The Rosciad*

List II

1. Joseph Addison 2. William Cowper
3. Charles Churchill

Codes:

	a	b	c
(A)	1	2	3
(B)	2	3	1
(C)	3	2	1
(D)	1	3	2

419. List I

a. *The Vanity of Human Wishes*
b. *Cooper's Hill*
c. *The School for Scandal*

List II

1. Descriptive poetry 2. Verse satire
3. Play

Codes:

	a	b	c
(A)	2	3	1
(B)	2	1	3
(C)	3	1	2
(D)	3	2	1

420. List I **List II**

List I	List II
a. Captain Absolute	1. *School for Scandal*
b. Tony	2. *The Rivals*
c. Lady Teazle	3. *She Stoops to Conquer*

Codes:

	a	b	c
(A)	2	1	3
(B)	1	3	2
(C)	2	3	1
(D)	1	2	3

421. Which Age was referred by Saintsbury *The Peace of the Augustans?*

(A) The Age of Milton
(B) The Age of Dryden
(C) The Age of Pope
(D) The Age of Tennyson

422. In the 18th century the status of women was
(A) moderately high (B) very high
(C) low (D) that of a slave

423. Who was the first to call the age of Pope and Johnson as "the Augustan Age"?
(A) Steele (B) Goldsmith
(C) Johnson (D) Burke

424. Who called the Augustan Age as the "age of prose and reason" ?
(A) Johnson (B) Addison
(C) Swift (D) Arnold

425. In the Age of Pope which kind of poetry dominated the other kinds?
(A) Epic poetry (B) Lyric poetry
(C) Satiric poetry (D) Romantic poetry

426. The first important work of Pope which appeared in 1711 is
(A) *The Rape of the Lock*
(B) *The Pastorals*
(C) *The Dunciad*
(D) *An Essay on Criticism*

427. Which classical scholar had helped Pope in the translation of *The Odyssey* into English ?
(A) Fenton (B) Broome
(C) Addison (D) Both (A) and (B)

428. Who has said, "If Pope be not a poet, where is poetry to be found" ?
(A) Dr. Johnson (B) Arnold
(C) Wordsworth (D) Coleridge

429. "True wit is nature to advantage dressed
What oft was thought, but never so well expresed."
This couplet is a famous quote from
(A) Swift (B) Pope
(C) Dryden (D) Shakespeare

430. Which mock epic by Pope was a devastating attack on a number of poetasters and hack writers of Grub Street?
(A) *The Rape of the Lock*
(B) *The Dunicad*
(C) *Epistle to Arbuthnot*
(D) *Moral Essays*

431. The *Two Treatises of Government* published in 1689-90 was written by
(A) John Locke (B) Francis Bacon
(C) Alexander Pope (D) Dyden

432. Who among the following was associated with *The Tatler*?
(A) Lamb (B) Johnson
(C) Richard Steele (D) Arnold

433. In Pope's poetry which of the following has been most meticulously maintained?
(A) Emotional appeal
(B) Nature worship
(C) Satirical tone
(D) Correctness of form and expression

434. Atticus is a character in which of the following satires of Pope ?
(A) *The Epistle to Arbuthnot*
(B) *The Rape of the Lock*
(C) *The Dunciad*
(D) *Epistles of Horace Imitated*

435. The character Atticus is a caricature of
(A) Addison (B) Steele
(C) Johnson (D) Bacon

436. Who was first crowned the hero of the Dunceland in *Dunciad* ?
(A) Arbuthnot (B) Atticus
(C) Theobald (D) Cibber

437. Who wrote a parody on Dryden's *The Hind and the Panther*, entitled *Story of the Country Mouse*?
(A) John Gay (B) Matthew Prior
(C) Edward Young (D) Dr. Johnson

438. *London* and *The Vanity of Human Wishes* are the two verse-satires by
(A) John Pope (B) Dr. Johnson
(C) Edward Young (D) Matthew Prior

439. Which poetic work of Thomas Gray has been hailed as a mark of transition between the classical school and the romantic school?
(A) *Ode to Eton*
(B) *Ode to Spring*

(C) *The Descent of Odin*
(D) *The Elegy*

440. Which of the following pre-romantic poets wrote *The Seasons* ?
(A) Collins (B) Gray
(C) Thomson (D) Goldsmith

441. Thomson's '*Castle of Indolence*' has been written in
(A) Blank verse (B) Free verse
(C) Spenserian Stansa
(D) Sonnets

442. The two most important poems by Oliver Goldsmith are
(A) *The Taks* and *The Traveller*
(B) *The Traveller* and *The Deserted Village*
(C) *The Deserted Village* and *The Task*
(D) *The Task* and *The Revolt of Islam*

443. Who is known for his piercing lyric such as *My Love is Like a Red, Red Rose* and *A Found Kiss and then We Sever* ?
(A) Blake (B) Gray
(C) Cowper (D) Burns

444. Which poem by Cowper, written in blank verse contains the famous line "God made the country and man made town" ?
(A) *The Task*
(B) *The Village*
(C) *Songs of Experience*
(D) *The Deserted Village*

445. Collin's *Ode to Simplicity* and *Ode to Evening*, Gray's *Eton Ode* and *Ode to Spring* and Wordsworth's *Ode to Nightingale* are written in the form of
(A) Pindaric ode (B) Horatian ode
(C) Petrachan ode (D) Spenserian ode

446. In the first number of *The Tatler*, Steele announced that the activities of the new journal will be based upon the
(A) history of England
(B) men of letters
(C) literature of the age
(D) clubs

447. About a hundred papers of Dr. Johnson were contributed between 1758 and 1760 to
(A) *The Spectator* (B) *The Tatler*
(C) *The Idler* (D) *The Rambler*

448. Edward Cave's monthly, which made a modest beginning in 1731, was named
(A) *The Magazine*
(B) *The Gentleman's Magazine*
(C) *The Review*
(D) *The Monthly Review*

449. Oliver Goldsmith's own periodical which ran to only eight weekly numbers was named
(A) *The Bee*
(B) *The Wrangler*
(C) *The Public Ledger*
(D) *Coverley Papers*

450. *The Citizen of the World* by Goldsmith originally appeared in
(A) *The Spectator*
(B) *The Rambler*
(C) *The Public Ledger*
(D) *The Monthly Review*

451. *The Vision of Mirza* and *Public Credit* are popular allegories by
(A) Goldsmith (B) Addison
(C) Steele (D) Johnson

452. Sir Roger De Coverley was
(A) the publisher of "Coverley Papers"
(B) the patron of Addison
(C) the famous imaginary old man of Addison's essays
(D) the owner of the Spectator Club

453. Addison has often been hailed as the pioneer of
(A) the essay form
(B) the modern novel
(C) prose friction
(D) the middle style

454. Who called Addison's prose as "Attic" and "Asiatic" ?
(A) Johnson (B) Steele
(C) Arnold (D) Addison himself

455. *Preface to Shakespeare* and *Lives of the Poets* are the chief critical works of

(A) Steele (B) Pope
(C) Johnson (D) Burke

456. In which of his works Jonathan Swift imitates and ridicules the solemn style and manner of a princely pious moral essayist?

(A) *A Tale of a Tub*
(B) *Gulliver's Travels*
(C) *A Modest Proposal*
(D) *Meditation on a Broomstick*

457. The five letters by Swift, published in 1724 and presenting a public indignation at English indifference to Ireland, were named

(A) *The Drapier's Letters*
(B) *The Belles Lettres*
(C) *A Tale of a Tub*
(D) None of the above

458. Which of the following by Swift is more popularly known as *Gulliver's Travels* ?

(A) *Travels into Remote Parts of the Universe*
(B) *Travels into Remote Nations of the Universe*
(C) *Travels into Remote Parts of the World*
(D) *Travels into Remote Nations of the World*

459. In the land of Houyhnhms, Gulliver tries to identity himself with the

(A) Yahoos
(B) horses
(C) lilliputians
(D) human beings

460. Who wrote the *Cooper's Hill* published first in 1642 ?

(A) Cowper (B) Anne Finch
(C) Denham (D) Pope

461. Who wrote the *Moral Essays* in which the four Epistles were addressed to carefully selected figures : Martha Blount, Lords Cobham, Bathurst and Burlington ?

(A) Robert Walpole
(B) Jonathan Swift
(C) Joseph Addison
(D) John Pope

462. The author of *Winter* and *Summer,* who wrote an elegy on Newton after his death in 1727, was

(A) Pope (B) Thomson
(C) Dennis (D) Addison

463. "I shall be ambitious to have it said of me, that I have brought philosophy out of closets and libraries, schools and colleges, to dwell in club and assemblies, at Tea-Tables, and in Coffee-Houses." Who made this statement?

(A) Richard Steele (B) Joseph Addison
(C) James Thomson (D) Dr. Johnson

464. Sir Roger de Coverley, the imaginary old man of *Coverley Papers* is a

(A) city merchant
(B) army officer
(C) rich man-about-town
(D) Tory country squire

465. Besides Sir Roger de Coverley, which of the following characters is/are also associated with Addison ?

(A) Sir Andrew Freeport
(B) Captain Sentry
(C) Will Honeycomb
(D) All of the above

466. As a contributor to *The Spectator* Steele was mostly a censorious critic of

(A) poetry (B) drama
(C) prose fiction (D) satire

467. Which of the following is Addison's once highly esteemed and financially successful venture into tragedy ?

(A) Catos
(B) *The London Merchant*
(C) *Lady Jane Grey*
(D) None of the above

468. Besides Marlowe, who else wrote a tragedy by the name *Tamerlaine* ?

(A) Addison (B) Steele
(C) Gay (D) Nicholas Rowe

469. Calista and Lothario are characters of a long-admired tragedy by Nicholas Rowe. Name the play.
(A) *Jane Shone*
(B) *Tamerlaine*
(C) *The Fair Penitent*
(D) *Lady Jane Grey*

470. *Three Hours After Marriage* is a collaborative satire jointly written by
(A) Pope and Gay
(B) John Gay, Alexander Pope and John Arbuthnot
(C) Pope, Arbuthnot and George Lillo
(D) Gay, Pope and George Lillo

471. The publication of Defoe's *The Life and Strange Surprising Adventures of Robinson Crusoe* marked a new beginning in the history of prose fiction in
(A) 1716 (B) 1719
(C) 1721 (D) 1723

472. Which Lady Character is the narrator in Defoe's *The Fortunate Mistress* ?
(A) Roxana (B) Moll Flanders
(C) Clarissa (D) None of these

473. *A Journal of the Plague Year* and *Memoirs of a Cavalier* are historical novels by
(A) Henry Fielding
(B) Samuel Richardson
(C) Daniel Defoe (D) Diderot

474. *The History of a Young Lady* is the subtitle of
(A) *Moll Flanders* (B) *Pamela*
(C) *Clarissa* (D) None of these

475. The protagonist of *Pamela* is
(A) Mr. B (B) Colonel Jacques
(C) Lovelace (D) John Belford

476. Who rapes Clarissa in Richardson's novel ?
(A) Belford (B) Howe
(C) Lovelace (D) All of these

477. The third epistolary novel of Richardson, which was praised by Jane Austen and George Eliot above his other novels, was
(A) *Pamela*
(B) *Clarissa*
(C) *The Apprentice's Vade Mecum*
(D) *The History of Sir Charles Grandison*

478. Who was so enraged by Richardson's *Pamela* that he wrote an antipathetic satire on it the subsequent year, called *Shamela*?
(A) Smolett (B) Fielding
(C) Sterne (D) Charlotte Lennox

479. Parson Adams is a character in
(A) *Tom Jones*
(B) *The Life of Jonathen Wild the Great*
(C) *Joseph Andrews*
(D) *Miscellanies*

480. Who has been called "a Foundling" by its author ?
(A) Shamela (B) Joseph Andrews
(C) Jonathan Wild (D) Tom Jones

481. Henry Fielding's sister and the author of *David Simple* is
(A) Charlotte (B) Mary Wortley
(C) Sarah (D) Arabella

482. Who is the author of *The Female Quixote : or the Adventures of Arabella* ?
(A) Tobias Smollett
(B) Sterne
(C) Charlotte Lennox
(D) Henry Brooke

483. *Roderick Random* has as its hero a well-born and educated Scot exposed to the "selfishness, envy, malice and base indifference of mankind" in England. Who is its author ?
(A) Richardson (B) Smollett
(C) Fielding (D) Sterne

484. Commodore Hawser Trunnion, a wonderfully exaggerated reflection on Smollett's naval experience, is a character in
(A) *The Adventures of Peregrine Pickle*
(B) *The Expedition of Humphrey Clinker*

(C) *The Adventures of Roderick Random*
(D) *Ferdinand Count Fathom*

485. *A Sentimental Journey through France and Italy* is a peculiar parody of conventional travel-book, written by
(A) Tobias Smollett
(B) Lawrence Sterne
(C) Henry Fielding
(D) Sheridan

486. The philosophical tale *The Vicar of the Wakefield* is written by
(A) Lawrence Sterne
(B) Oliver Goldsmith
(C) Samuel Richardson
(D) Joseph Addison

487. What is the subtitle of Goldsmith's Semi-autobiographical poem *The Traveller* ?
(A) *A Song to David*
(B) *The Citizen of the World*
(C) *A Prospect of Society*
(D) *The Good-Natur'd Man*

488. *London : A Poem of 1738* and *The Vanity of Human Wishes* are poems by Johnson written in imitation of
(A) Sophocles (B) Spenser
(C) Juvenal (D) Milton

489. Johnson contributed the *Idler* papers to
(A) *The Rambler*
(B) *The Universal Chronicle*
(C) *The Spectator*
(D) *The Coverley Papers*

490. Which of the following journals was established by Johnson himself ?
(A) *The Idler* (B) *The Spectator*
(C) *The Review* (D) *The Rambler*

491. Who called Dr. Johnson as "the Hero as Man of Letters" ?
(A) Thomas Carlyle (B) Boswell
(C) Arnold (D) Eliot

492. The last of Johnson's great works was
(A) *Dictionary of the English Language*
(B) *The History of Rasselas*
(C) *Lives of the Poets*
(D) *Life of Mr. Richard Savage*

493. Who is known for his novels of mystery and terror, such as *The Castle of Otranto* ?
(A) Horace Walpole (B) Tobias Smollett
(C) Mrs. Radcliffe (D) Mathew Lewis

494. The 18th century author of *The Rivals, The School for Scandal* and *The Critic* is
(A) Goldsmith (B) Steele
(C) Johnson (D) Sheridan

495. Mrs. Malaprop is a character from Sheridan's
(A) *The Rivals* (B) *The Critic*
(C) *The School for Scandal*
(D) None of the above

496. Which play by John Gay was praised by Ifor Evans as one of those plays "which are permanent and have success, whenever they are competently, revived to intelligent audiences" ?
(A) *The Careless Husband*
(B) *The Beggar's Opera*
(C) *The Fatal Dowry*
(D) *The Tragedy of Jane Shore*

497. The first periodical that appeared in Europe was
(A) *The Tatler* (B) *The Spectator*
(C) *Gazetta* (D) *The Review*

498. Which of the following was the name of the first daily newspaper that began in 1702 ?
(A) *Gazetta*
(B) *The Daily Courant*
(C) *The Daily Digest*
(D) *The Daily Review*

499. Regarding which of his books Jonathan Swift had reportedly exclaimed, "What a genius I had when I wrote that book" ?
(A) *The Battle of the Book*
(B) *Meditation on a Broomstick*
(C) *A Tale of a Tub*
(D) *Gulliver's Travels*

500. Which of the following books was authored by John Arbuthnot ?

(A) *The Battle of the Book*
(B) *The Jockey's Intelligence*
(C) *Nocturnal Reverie*
(D) *The Art of Political Lying*

501. Mr. Marwood and Mrs. Millament are characters from
(A) *Mac Fleckhoe*
(B) *The Way of the World*
(C) *Epistle to Dr. Arbuthnot*
(D) None of the above

502. The story of Robinson Crusoe was inspired by the real life experience of a seaman, Alexander Selkirk, who spent four years on the deserted island of
(A) Borneo
(B) Lagado
(C) Juan Fernandez
(D) None of the above

503. What is the name of Squire Allworthy's nephew who conspires against him ?
(A) Thwackum (B) Blifil
(C) Patridge (D) Square

504. What is the name of Vicar Wakefield's second daughter ?
(A) Deborah (B) Olivia
(C) Cordelia (D) Sophia

505. The characters such as Moll White, Will Wimble and Tom Touchy are creations of
(A) Henry Fielding
(B) Jonathan Swift
(C) Joseph Addison
(D) Daniel Defoe

506. Who gave a satirical caricature of Dr. Johnson in the character of Pemposo in *Ghost* ?
(A) William Cowper
(B) Oliver Goldsmith
(C) Charles Churchill
(D) Matthew Prior

507. Which 18th century critic has criticised *Paradise Lost* for its lacking in human interest?
(A) Dr. Johnson
(B) Mathew Arnold
(C) Oliver Goldsmith
(D) Richard Steele

508. The second part of *Absalom and Architophel* contains a seething attack on
(A) Shaftesbury (B) Thomas Shadwell
(C) John Marston (D) Titus Oates

509. Who among the following is another satirist of Dryden's times?
(A) Samuel Butler (B) Samuel Pepys
(C) Roger North (D) John Bunyan

510. Who wrote *Ode on Mrs. Killigrew, Song on St. Cicilia's Day* and *Alexander's Feast* ?
(A) John Bunyan (B) John Dryden
(C) William Temple (D) Ben Johnson

511. Given below are names of journals with which Richard Steele was associated. Identify the one which he did not edit.
(A) *London Gazette* (B) *Guardian*
(C) *Spectator* (D) *Tatler*

512. Steele and Addison collaborated in editing three of the following four journals. Identify the one which they did not edit together.
(A) *The Tatler*
(B) *The Spectator*
(C) *The Whig Examiner*
(D) *The Guardian*

513. Name the imaginary old bachelor who edited *The Tatler*.
(A) Sir Roger de Coverley
(B) Isaac Bickerstaff
(C) Sir Andrew Freeport
(D) Berkley

514. How long did *The Tatler* last ?
(A) Less than 2 years
(B) Four years
(C) 1 year & 7 months
(D) 3 year & 2 months

515. When was *The Spectator* launched ?
(A) March 1711 (B) April 1712
(C) January 1711 (D) April 1709

516. What was the periodicity of the journal *The Spectator* ?
(A) Weekly (B) Daily
(C) Fortnightly (D) Monthly

517. While launching *The Spectator* one of its editors declared that the aim was to bring "philosophy out of closets and libraries, schools and colleges, to dwell in clubs, and assemblies, at Tea-Tables and Coffee-Houses." Who said this ?
(A) Joseph Addison (B) Richard Steele
(C) Jonathan Swift (D) Sir Coverley

518. Where do we meet Sir Andrew Freeport, Will Honeycomb, Captain Sentry ?
(A) In Richard Steele's works
(B) In *The Tatler*
(C) In *The Spectator*
(D) In *The Daily Courant*

519. Point out how the term 'Augustan Age' originated ?
(A) Pope referred to it so
(B) The inclination of literary men was towards Latin literature
(C) Dryden referred to it so
(D) Dr. Johnson wrote "What was said of Rome, adorned by Augustus, may be applied by an easy metaphor to English poetry embellished by Dryden".

520. During the Elizabethan age poetry and drama flourished. Which genre marked the Augustan age ?
(A) Essay
(B) Novel
(C) Biography, diary, journal, magazine
(D) All of the above

521. Which of the following was Daniel Defoe's contribution to English literature ?
(A) *The True-Born Englishman*
(B) *Robinson Crusoe*
(C) *The Shortest Way With the Dissenters*
(D) All of the above.

522. Of the following journals identify the one started by Defoe.
(A) *Athenian Gazette*
(B) *The Observator*
(C) *The Review*
(D) *The English Post*

523. How would you classify the following works of Daniel Defoe : Moll Flanders, Roxana, Colonel Jack, Captain Singleton, A Journal of The Plague Year and memoirs of a Cavalier ?
(A) Reports (B) Prose writings
(C) Adventure (D) Fiction

524. Which out of the following is correctly matched ?
(A) Captain Singleton 1. a priest
(B) Moll Flanders 2. a prostitute
(C) Colonel Jack 3. a valiant solider
(D) Cavalier 4. a prince

525. Who is Robinson Crusoe's companion on the island ?
(A) Friday (B) Captain Singleton
(C) Jack (D) The goat

526. Samuel Johnson wrote two satires in verse in imitation of Juvenal. Name one of them.
(A) *Minstrel*
(B) *The Lives of Poets*
(C) *The Vanity of Human Wishes*
(D) *Ossian*

527. What is the subject matter of Samuel Johnson's *London* ?
(A) Oppression of the poor
(B) Arrogance of the rich
(C) Cry against French fashions
(D) All of the above

528. Which one of the following is Oliver Goldsmith's poetic work ?
(A) *The Deserted Village*
(B) *The Traveller*
(C) *Retaliation*
(D) All of the above

529. Who said, "A book should help us either to enjoy life or to endure it" ?

(A) Boswell (B) Pope
(C) Dr. Johnson (D) Addison

530. Which work of the 18th century begins with the reign of Trajan in A.D. 98 and ends with the fall of the Byzantine Empire in 1453 ?
(A) Edward Gibbon's *History*
(B) John Locke's *Essays Concerning Human Understanding*
(C) Edmund Burke's *A Vindication of Natural Society*
(D) Edward Gibbon's *The Decline and Fall of the Roman Empire*

531. Who, of the following, can be called the first poet of the Romantic Revival ?
(A) John Gray (B) Thomson
(C) Pope (D) Wordsworth

532. Which of the following does not mark the romantic revival ?
(A) Revolt against the bondage of rule and custom
(B) Return to intellect, philosophy and classical ideals
(C) Renewed interest in medieval ideals
(D) Intense human sympathy

533. Who wrote the following books : *She Stoops to Conquer, Vicar of the Wakefield, The Deserted Village, The Traveller* ?
(A) Oliver Goldsmith
(B) James Boswell
(C) Dr. Johnson
(D) William Cowper

534. Where do we meet Croaker, a laughable character ?
(A) *The Vicar of Wakefield*
(B) *The Citizen of the World*
(C) *The Good Natured Man*
(D) *She Stoops to Conquer*

535. One castaway utters, "I am the monarch of all I survey." Identify the poet and the poem.
(A) Goldsmith, *The Deserted Village*
(B) William Cowper, *Alexander Silkirk*
(C) Thomas Gray, *Ode on Eton*
(D) Jonathan Swift, *Gulliver's Travels*

536. Who is the author of such charming pieces, which are included in school syllabi in India, as: *John Gilpin, Alexander Silkirk, Table Talk* ?
(A) Thomas Gray
(B) Thomson
(C) Oliver Goldsmith
(D) William Cowper

537. Who wrote these lines :
"Piping down the valleys wild,
Piping song of pleasant glee,
On a cloud I saw a child,
And he laughing said to me:" ?
(A) William Cowper
(B) Thomas Gray
(C) William Blake
(D) George Crabbe

538. Who of the following wrote in Scottish dialect ?
(A) William Blake
(B) Robert Burns
(C) William Cowper
(D) James Thomson

539. *Songs of Innocence* and *Songs of Experience* were written by
(A) William Cowper
(B) William Collins
(C) William Blake
(D) Thomas Percy

540. When was Black's *Poetical Sketches* published ?
(A) 1783 (B) 1780
(C) 1804 (D) 1770

541. Who is the author of *Roderick Random* (1748), *Peregrine Pickle* (1751), *Humphrey Clinker* (1771) ?
(A) Tobias Smollett
(B) Lawrence Sterne
(C) Richardson
(D) Henry Fielding

542. This is a picaresque novel modelled on *Gil Blas*, the picaresque romance by the French writer Le Sage. Name the novel.

(A) *Roderick Random* - Smollett
(B) *Jonathan Wild* - Fielding
(C) *Sir Charles Grandison* - Richardson
(D) *A Sentimental Journey* - Sterne

543. Whom does Roderick, Smollett's hero in *The Adventures of Roderick Random*, marry after a series of adventures and misadventures?
(A) Amelia
(B) Emily Gauntlet
(C) Narissa
(D) Miss Tabitha

544. Which is the longest novel of Smollett ?
(A) *Humphrey Clinker*
(B) *Peregrine Pickle*
(C) *Ferdinand Count Fathom*
(D) *Sir Launcelot Greaves*

545. Which of Smollett's novels relates the adventures of a Welsh family through England and Scotland ?
(A) *Humphrey Clinker*
(B) *Sir Launcelot Greaves*
(C) *Roderick Random*
(D) *Peregrine Pickle*

546. What is the family status of Smollett's Humphrey Clinker and Henry Fielding's Joseph ?
(A) Rich prospective sons-in-law
(B) Sons of rich men
(C) Servants
(D) None of the above

547. Who wrote *A Sentimental Journey* ?
(A) Tobias Smollett
(B) Lawrence Sterne
(C) Henry Fielding
(D) Jane Austen

548. What is the exact title of *Tristam Shandy* ?
(A) *The Life of Tristam Shandy*
(B) *The Life and Opinions of Tristam Shandy*
(C) *Tristam Shandy, Gentleman*
(D) *The Life and Opinions of Tristam Shandy, Gentleman*

549. Noted below are some peculiarities of *Tristam Shandy*. Three are correct, one is not. Identify it.
(A) Tristam, the titular hero was born only after the book is half-way through and he is heard of no more after that.
(B) The opinions expressed are his father's.
(C) His name means "most auspicious".
(D) The real hero is uncle Toby.

550. Sterne's *A Sentimental Journey* is an autobiography. In order to illustrate his sentiments he refers to the story of
(A) Anchises and Aphrodite
(B) Aeneas and Lavinia
(C) Aeolus and Odysseus
(D) Aeneas and Dido

551. Henry Mackenzie's *The Man of Feeling*, and Henry Brooke's *The Fool of Quality* are
(A) gothic novels
(B) sentimental novels
(C) romantic novels
(D) picaresque novels

552. Gothic novels are
(A) novels of mystery and terror
(B) novels written under the French influence
(C) novels of revolt
(D) novels of romantic adventures

553. Who is accredited for having introduced horror in fiction ?
(A) Mrs. Radcliffe with *Mysteries of Updolpho* (1794)
(B) Horace Walpole with *Castle of Otranto* (1765)
(C) Clara Reve with *The Old English Baron* (1777)
(D) Gregory Lewis with *The Monk* (1795)

554. Who wrote *Caleb Williams* ?
(A) Thomas Holcroft
(B) Hannah More
(C) William Godwin
(D) Clara Reeve

555. Whose writings influenced the revolutionary novels of the 18th century ?

(A) Hobbes (B) Locke
(C) Rousseau (D) Descartes

556. Who is the heroine of Ann Radcliffe's *Mysteries of Updolpho* ?

(A) Julia
(B) Emily de St. Aubert
(C) Madame Cheron
(D) Matilda de Villaneqas

557. What is common about these novels: *Caelebs in Search of a Wife, Evelina, Simple Story, Emma, The Old English Baron?*

(A) They are all Gothic novels
(B) They are all sentimental novels
(C) They are all written by women
(D) They are all Romantic novels

558. What is common about : *The Monk* by Methew Gregory Lewis, *Dr. Faustus* by Marlow and *Vathek* by William Beckford ?

(A) They are full of mysteries
(B) They are romantic
(C) The heroes bargain their souls to the devil
(D) Nothing is common

559. Identify the correct match of the works with the authors:

(A) Sir Walter Scott	1. *The Castle of Indolence*
(B) J. Thomson	2. *Castle Dangerous*
(C) Horace Walpole	3. *Castle Rackrent*
(D) Maria Edgeworth	4. *The Modern Giselda*

560. Given below are the novels in which the hero-heroine pairs appear. Which of them is correctly matched ?

(A) *The Castle of Otranto*	1. Theodore-Isabella
(B) *Roderick Random*	2. Roderick-Narcissa
(C) *Joseph Andrews*	3. Lord Orville-Evelina
(D) *Evelina*	4. Joseph-Fanny

561. Whom did Dr. Johnson call his "little character monger" ?

(A) Fanny Burney
(B) Oliver Goldsmith
(C) James Boswell
(D) Mrs. Ann Radcliffe

562. Who are the "Four Wheels of the Novel Wain," as Saintsbury calls them ?

(A) Richardson, Fielding, Golding, Sterne
(B) Fielding, Richardson, Smollett, Johnson
(C) Smollett, Sterne, Burney, Golding
(D) Richardson, Fielding, Smollett, Sterne

563. An author sums up the human condition thus, "human life is everywhere a state, in which much is to be endured and little to be enjoyed." Who said this and where ?

(A) Alexander Pope - *Essay on Man*
(B) Oliver Goldsmith - *The Vicar of Wakefield*
(C) Albert Camus - *The Stranger*
(D) Dr. Johnson - *Rassellas*

564. Which term describes best the English novel of 1700-1800 ?

(A) The Sentimental School
(B) The Gothic School
(C) The Revolutionary School
(D) All of the above

565. In how many volumes *Pamela* was published?

(A) Four (B) Two
(C) One (D) Five

566. Which novel is not written by Richardson ?

(A) *Pamela, or Virtue Rewarded*
(B) *Clarissa, or The History of a Young Lady*
(C) *Rob Roy*
(D) *Sir Charles Grandison*

567. Identify the correct match of the male characters with their female counterparts :

(A) Pamela	1. Mr. B.
(B) Clarissa	2. Sir Charles Grandison
(C) Harriet Byron	3. Lovelace
(D) Evelina	4. Fanny

568. Who kills Lovelace in a duel in *Clarissa* ?
(A) John Belford (B) Mr. B.
(C) Morden (D) Sir Charles

569. Which is Henry Fieldings first novel ?
(A) *Jonathan Wild*
(B) *Joseph Andrews*
(C) *Amelia*
(D) *Tom Jones*

570. The full title of henry Fielding's novel *Tom Jones* is
(A) *The History of Tom Jones*
(B) *Tom Jones*
(C) *Tom Jones, a Foundling*
(D) *The History of Tom Jones, a Foundling*

571. In which novel do we meet Mr. Snap ?
(A) *Tom Jones* (B) *Jonathan Wild*
(C) *Amelia* (D) *Joseph Andrews*

572. Who is regarded as the "Father of English Novel" ?
(A) Daniel Defoe
(B) Samuel Richardson
(C) Samuel Pepys
(D) John Bunyan

573. When fifty, this writer of elegant epistles was approached by publishers to write a series of model letters. Who was he ?
(A) Daniel Defoe
(B) Samuel Pepys
(C) Samuel Richardson
(D) Oliver Goldsmith

574. Which of his novels is called "a comic epic in prose" by Henry Fielding ?
(A) *Joseph Andrews*
(B) *Tom Jones*
(C) *Amelia*
(D) *Jonathan Wild*

575. Joseph Andrews has Abraham Adam as a companion during his adventures. Who accompanies Tom Jones after he takes to the road ?
(A) Squire Booby (B) Blifil Allworthy
(C) Partridge (D) Jonathan Wild

576. Of the total 555 papers of the *Spectator* over 500 were written by Addison and Steele. Who contributed the rest ?
(A) Pope (B) Berkley
(C) Swift (D) All of the above

577. Who praised Addison's style as "the model of the middle style" ?
(A) Alexander Pope (B) Jonathan Swift
(C) Dr. Samuel (D) Boswell

578. Which genre developed simultaneously in England, France and Germany in the 18th Century ?
(A) Drama (B) Epic Poetry
(C) Prose (D) Novel

579. In part I of *Gulliver's Travels*, Gulliver, a ship's surgeon, lands in Lilliput, the land of dwarfs. Where does he land in part II of the book ?
(A) Laputa (B) Lagado
(C) Brobdingnag (D) Houyhnhnms

580. One of the following poems is written by Oliver Goldsmith. Identify it.
(A) *On the Death of a Favourite Cat*
(B) *Elegy Written in The Country Churchyard*
(C) *Elegy on The Death of a Mad Dog*
(D) *Elegy*

581. Name the poem which exposes the weaknesses of Catholic, Lutheran and Calvinist beliefs as opposed to the Anglican.
(A) *Gulliver's Travels*
(B) *Tale of a Tub*
(C) *Journal to Stella*
(D) *Drapier's Letters*

582. Who wrote the famous *Life of Johnson* ?
(A) Edmund Burke
(B) Oliver Goldsmith
(C) James Boswell
(D) Joseph Addison

583. Who is Samuel Johnson's *Rasellas*, the hero of *Rasellas* ?
(A) A legendary hero
(B) An Arthurian Knight
(C) Son of the Emperor of Abyssinia
(D) A Scottish Chieftain

584. Which French dramatist influenced Restoration Comedy ?
(A) Moliere (B) Corneille
(C) Racine (D) None of these

585. Where do we meet Sir Roger Coverly ? In
(A) *The Tatler*
(B) *Gulliver's Travels*
(C) *The Spectator*
(D) *The Rape of The Lock*

586. *Absalom and Architophel* is written in
(A) blank verse
(B) Spenserian stanza
(C) heroic couplet
(D) mixed versification

587. With whom do we associate Liliput ?
(A) Joseph Addison
(B) Jonathan Swift
(C) Samuel Johnson
(D) Alexander Pope

588. Dryden wrote *Religio Laici* and defended the Church of England. Then after his conversion to Catholic faith he wrote another poem to defend the Catholic Church against the Church of England. Name the latter work.
(A) *The Hind And the Panther*
(B) *Annus Mirabilis*
(C) *Astraea Redux*
(D) *Alexander's Feast*

589. Who wrote '*The Seasons*' ?
(A) William Wordsworth
(B) Ambrose Philip
(C) James Thomson
(D) Thomas Gray

590. Name Dryden's literary venture which brought failure.
(A) *Marriage a la Mode* (comedy)
(B) *All For Love* (tragedy)
(C) *Conquest of Grenada* (heroic play)
(D) *Wild Gallant* (comedy)

591. Which of the following is not written by Dryden ?
(A) *The Medal*
(B) *MacFlecknoe*
(C) *Absalom* : *Absalom*
(D) *Religio Laici*

592. Pope translated only half of
(A) *Iliad* (B) *Odyssey*
(C) *Aenid* (D) *Ovid*

593. What is the span of the so-called Age of Dryden ?
(A) 1631 - 1700
(B) 1640 - 1702
(C) 1600 - 1700
(D) None of these

594. Identify Dryden's critical pieces.
(A) *Essay of Dramatic Poesy*
(B) *Defence of the Epilogue*
(C) *Dedication to Examen Poeticum*
(D) All of the above

595. Who among the following wrote plays which are known as 'sentimental comedy' ?
(A) Congreve (B) Jonson
(C) Goldsmith (D) Dryden

596. *Essay on Criticism* by Pope shows influence of
(A) Boleau
(B) Dryden
(C) Horace
(D) Both (A) and (C)

597. "The wife bolth out her husband. She shuts herself in Eden with Satan, Adam is left outside." Who commented thus on the immorality prevalent in the 18th century ?
(A) Dr. Johnson
(B) Victor Hugo
(C) Pope
(D) Goldsmith

598. A fictitious character whom the satiric voice speaks to, such as Arbuthnot in Pope's *Epistle to Dr. Arbuthnot* is called
(A) The second voice
(B) The adversarous
(C) The silent narrator
(D) The addressee

Match the following lists using the codes given below.

599. List I **List II**

a. 1701 1. The Peace of Utrecht
b. 1702 2. Union of England and Scotland
c. 1707 3. Anne Succeeds
d. 1713 4. War of Spanish Succession begins

Codes:

	a	b	c	d
(A)	1	2	3	4
(B)	4	3	1	2
(C)	2	3	1	4
(D)	4	3	2	1

600. List I **List II**

a. *The Way of the World* 1. Anne Finch
b. *Miscellany Poems* 2. Daniel Defoe
c. *The Beaux Stratagen* 3. Congreve
d. *Robinson Crusoe* 4. Farquhar

Codes:

	a	b	c	d
(A)	1	3	2	4
(B)	3	1	4	2
(C)	2	4	1	3
(D)	4	2	3	1

601. List I **List II**

a. *The Lying Lover* 1. Jonathan Swift
b. *The Campaign* 2. Steele
c. *Sermons* 3. John Tillotson
d. *Journal to Stella* 4. Addison

Codes:

	a	b	c	d
(A)	2	4	3	1
(B)	2	3	4	1
(C)	4	1	3	2
(D)	4	3	2	1

602. List I **List II**

a. *The Tender Husband* 1. Lady Winchilsea
b. *The Drapier's Letters* 2. Jonathan Swift
c. *The Spleen* 3. Steele

Codes:

	a	b	c
(A)	1	2	3
(B)	3	2	1
(C)	3	1	2
(D)	2	1	3

603. List I **List II**

a. *Pastorals* 1. Mathew Prior
b. *Alma* 2. Lady Winchilsea
c. *A Nocturnal Reverie* 3. Alexander Pope

Codes:

	a	b	c
(A)	3	2	1
(B)	1	2	3
(C)	2	3	1
(D)	3	1	2

604. List I **List II**

a. *Alexander's Feast* 1. John Dryden
b. *Hudibras* 2. Alexander Pope
c. *Windsor Forest* 3. Samuel Butler

Codes:

	a	b	c
(A)	1	3	2
(B)	1	2	3
(C)	3	2	1
(D)	3	1	2

605. List I **List II**

a. *The Rape of the Lock* 1. The Summit of the Alps
b. *The Deserted Village* 2. Lady Arabella
c. *The Traveller* 3. Auburn

Codes:

	a	b	c
(A)	1	3	2
(B)	2	3	1
(C)	3	1	2
(D)	1	2	3

606. List I | List II

a. Pastoral elegy 1. *The Rape of the Lock*
b. Mock epic 2. *The Traveller*
c. Didactic poem 3. *The Deserted Village*

Codes:

	a	b	c
(A)	1	2	3
(B)	2	3	1
(C)	3	2	1
(D)	3	1	2

607. List I | List II

a. 1719 1. *Gulliver's Travels*
b. 1726 2. *Tom Jones*
c. 1749 3. *Robinson Crusoe*

Codes:

	a	b	c
(A)	3	1	2
(B)	3	2	1
(C)	1	3	2
(D)	1	2	3

608. List I | List II

a. Dr. Primrose 1. *The Way of the World*
b. Peachum 2. *The Vicar of the Wakefield*
c. Mirabell 3. *The Beggar's Opera*

Codes:

	a	b	c
(A)	3	1	2
(B)	2	1	3
(C)	3	2	1
(D)	2	3	1

609. List I | List II

a. Lamb 1. 1785-1859
b. Hazlitt 2. 1778-1830
c. De Quincey 3. 1774-1834

Codes:

	a	b	c
(A)	1	2	3
(B)	3	2	1
(C)	2	3	1
(D)	2	1	3

610. List I | List II

a. Coleridge 1. 1772-1834
b. Wordsworth 2. 1788-1824
c. Shelley 3. 1770-1850
d. Keats 4. 1792-1822
e. Byron 5. 1795-1821

Codes:

	a	b	c	d	e
(A)	1	3	2	4	5
(B)	3	2	4	1	5
(C)	3	1	4	5	2
(D)	1	3	4	5	2

611. *Reflections on the Revolution in France and on the Proceedings in Certain Societies in London Relative to that Event*, published in 1790 was the work of
(A) Gibbon (B) Burke
(C) Coleridge (D) Paine

612. The fall of the prison of Bacfille, that marks the beginning of the French Revolution, occurred on
(A) June 14, 1789 (B) June 14, 1798
(C) July 14, 1789 (D) July 14, 1798

613. "Man is born free, but alas! he is everywhere in chains" – these are the famous words of
(A) Plato (B) Socrates
(C) Hobbes (D) Rousseau

614. Who wrote the *Ode to France* under the influence of the French Revolution ?
(A) Coleridge (B) Blake
(C) Shelley (D) Byron

615. In which of his poems Shelley denounces all the forces of tyranny and oppression represented by kings and priests ?
(A) *Alaster* (B) *Queen Mab*
(C) *Adonais*
(D) *The Revolt of Islam*

616. "O Wind, if winter comes, can spring be far behind ! These famous words of Shelley have been taken from
(A) *The Cloud*
(B) *Ode to West Wind*
(C) *Isabella*
(D) *The Eve of St. Agnes*

617. Though Keats was the least affected by the French Revolution directly, which of his works has been said to be bearing revolutionary implications ?
(A) *Ode to Autumn* (B) *Endymion*
(C) *Hyperion* (D) *Psyche*

618. *Grongar Hill*, a piece of vigorous landscape painting, was written by the pre-Romantic poet
(A) James Thomson
(B) John Dyer
(C) Lady Winchilsea
(D) Thomas Paruel

619. Wordsworth has described various stages of his association with Nature. In which stage did he hear "The still sad music of humanity" ?
(A) The boyish stage
(B) The initial stage
(C) The final stage
(D) All the stages

620. In which of his poems Wordsworth tells the scholar to do away with books and make Nature his teacher ?
(A) *Tables Turned*
(B) *Tintern Abbey*
(C) *The Solitary Reaper*
(D) *The Prelude*

621. Who uses the 'pansies' as the symbol of sad thoughts and 'violets' of modesty and innocence in one of his poems ?
(A) Wordsworth
(B) Coleridge
(C) Keats (D) Shelley

622. "And it is my faith
That every flower enjoys the air it breathes."
Who holds this faith ?
(A) Wordsworth (B) Coleridge
(C) Keats (D) Shelley

623. What has been addressed as a "cloud of fire", an "unembodied joy", "a golden glow-worm", "a rose empowered in green leaves" and a "poet hidden in the light of thought" ?
(A) West Wind (B) Pansy
(C) Skylark (D) Nightingale

624. Who has been said to combine *Pantheism* and *Platonism* in his nature poetry ?
(A) Keats (B) Shelley
(C) Byron (D) Coleridge

625. Shelley writes in *Adonais,*
"A portion of the loveliness
Which once he made more lovely."
Who does "he" refer to in these lines ?
(A) Himself (B) Keats
(C) Wordsworth (D) Coleridge

626. Which of the nature poets has been said to be endowed with "organic sensibility" ?
(A) Wordsworth (B) Coleridge
(C) Shelley (D) Keats

627. Who wrote the "Isles of Greece", a fine appreciation of the great deeds done by the Greeks in the past ?
(A) Byron (B) Shelley
(C) Keats (D) Leigh Hunt

628. Whom does the Greek god Pan fight with in Shelley's *Hymn of Pan* ?
(A) Titans (B) Apollo
(C) Zeus
(D) All of the above

629. "Hallas", a frequent theme in Romantic Poetry is
(A) a Greek god
(B) an ancient Greek sculptor
(C) the oldest poet of Greece
(D) the ancient name of Greece

630. Which of the following poems of Keats bears the mark of Hellenism ?
(A) *Endymion* and *Hyperion*
(B) *Lamia* and *Grecian Urn*
(C) *Ode to Nightingale* and *Psyche*
(D) All of the above

631. The most important ballad collection of the eighteenth century was *Reliques of Ancient English Poetry*. Who made this admirable collection ?

(A) Thomas Chatterton
(B) Rowley
(C) Bishop Percy
(D) James Macpherson

632. The *Ossianic Poems* which explore the world of Celtic antiquity was written by
(A) Bishop Percy
(B) Byron
(C) Macpherson
(D) Coleridge

633. Porphyro and Madeline are the lovers in
(A) *La Belle Dame Sans Merci*
(B) *The Eve of St. Agnes*
(C) *The Eve of St. Mark*
(D) *Isabella*

634. Who was called by Keats as "The Egotistical Sublime" ?
(A) Wordsworth (B) Shelley
(C) Byron (D) Coleridge

635. Who has been referred to as "the high priest of romanticism" ?
(A) Wordsworth (B) Keats
(C) Blake (D) Coleridge

636. In which of his poems coleridge wrote,
"O Lady ! we receive but what we give
And in our life alone does Nature Live" ?
(A) *Kubla Khan*
(B) *The Ancient Mariner*
(C) *Christabel*
(D) *The Dejection Ode*

637. "Abundantly and enchantingly sensuous" – this phrase was attributed to Keats by
(A) Shelley (B) Leigh Hunt
(C) Arnold (D) Eliot

638. "Beauty is Truth, Truth Beauty – that is all
Ye know on earth, that's all ye need to know"
These famous lines have been taken from one of the famous odes of Keats. Name it.
(A) *Ode to Nightingale*
(B) *Ode on a Grecian Urn*
(C) *Ode to Autumn*
(D) *Ode to Psyche*

639. Prior to Keats who else was an endowment of what has been called the "Negative capability" ?
(A) Wordsworth
(B) Milton
(C) Spenser
(D) Shakespeare

640. Regarding whom does Symonds write, "In none of his greatest contemporaries was the lyrical faculty so paramount" ?
(A) Keats (B) Spenser
(C) Shelley (D) Coleridge

641. *Frankenstein*, a proto-science fiction was written by
(A) P.B. Shelley
(B) Mary Shelley
(C) Charles Lamb
(D) Mary Lamb

642. Who is Frankenstein in Mary Shelley's novel?
(A) A monster
(B) An evil spirit
(C) The feeling of irrational fear personified
(D) The scientist

643. In which of his poems Wordsworth records his impressions of a manufacturing district of Northern England ?
(A) *Prelude*
(B) *Lyrical Ballads*
(C) *The Excursion*
(D) *The Ruined Cottage*

644. The historic drama *The Fall of Robespierre* published in 1794 was written by Coleridge and
(A) Crabbe (B) Southey
(C) Wordsworth (D) Burns

645. Who is the author of *The Book of the Church* and *Sir Thomas More ?*
(A) Priestly (B) Burns
(C) Southey (D) Godwin

646. Which of the following is a pro-revolutionary poem by Southey ?

(A) *The Fall of Rabespierre*
(B) *Joan of Arc*
(C) *Walt Tylor*
(D) *The Constitution of Church and State*

647. Coleridge's *Biographia Literaria* was published in
(A) 1801 (B) 1808
(C) 1817 (D) 1827

648. Who introduces as a narrator a country parson exploring "the simple annals" of his parish leafing, in his poem *The Parish Register* (1807) ?
(A) Southey (B) Burns
(C) Crabbe (D) Austen

649. Lady Catherine is the famous character of Austen's
(A) *Pride and Prejudice*
(B) *Persuasion*
(C) *Mansfield Park*
(D) *Emma*

650. Who wrote *The Entail* (1822), a tragic fiction?
(A) Scott (B) Ferrier
(C) Edgeworth (D) Galt

651. Who is the author of *The Absentee, Ormond* and *Castle Rackrent* ?
(A) Walter Scott
(B) Edgeworth
(C) Galt
(D) Susan Ferrier

652. *Marmion, The Lady of the Lake* and *Rokeby* are the well-known poems of
(A) Raleigh (B) Hunt
(C) Ferrier (D) Scott

653. The first two cantos of *Childe Harold* which made Byron instantaneously famous were published in
(A) 1810 (B) 1811
(C) 1812 (D) 1814

654. *Sardanapalus* and *The Two Foscari* are the verse tragedies of
(A) Shelley (B) Byron
(C) Keats (D) Southey

655. Who was expelled from the Oxford University for his undergraduate pamphlet *The Necessity of Atheism* ?
(A) Byron (B) Keats
(C) Shelley (D) Coleridge

656. Which of the following written in 1821 and published posthumously in 1840 bears Shelley's most confidential proclamation of the social function of poetry and the prophetic role of the poet ?
(A) *A Defence of Poetry*
(B) *The Triumph of Life*
(C) *Hellas*
(D) *The Mask of Anarchy*

657. "Here lies one whose name was writ in water." This was chosen as his own epitaph by
(A) Shelley (B) Byron
(C) Keats (D) Shakespeare

658. Who wrote *An Essay on the Principles of Human Action* (1805) from which Keats drew considerably ?
(A) Coleridge (B) Scott
(C) Hazlitt (D) Hunt

659. Hazlitt presented a sharp and witty criticism of his literary and political contemporaries in 1825, in his compilation
(A) *Spirit of the Age*
(B) *Essays on the Principles of Human Action*
(C) *New Pygmalion*
(D) None of the above

660. Who established his literary reputation as 'Elia', the author of a series of essays mostly contributed to the 'London Magazine' ?
(A) Hazlitt (B) Charles Lamb
(C) De Quincey (D) Crabbe

661. Who is the author of the celebrated and once notorious work, *The Confessions of an English Opium Eater,* published in the *London Magazine* in 1821 ?
(A) Byron (B) Lamb
(C) De Quincey (D) Coleridge

662. *Maid Marion* and *The Misfortunes of Elphin* are the novels written by
(A) De Quincey (B) T.L. Peacock
(C) S. Glowry (D) Hazlitt

663. Who wrote a poem by the name *The Shepherd's Calender* that was published in 1827 ?
(A) William Cobbet
(B) Robert Bloomfield
(C) John Clare (D) Hopkins

664. "But Europe at that time was thrilled with joy
France standing on the top of golden hours
And human nature seeming born again".
These lines regarding the French Revolution are of
(A) De Quincey (B) Shelley
(C) Wordsworth (D) Sir Walter Raleigh

665. "Liberty the soul of Life shall reign | Shall throb in every pulse, shall flow through every vein."
Who wrote the above lines about the French Revolution ?
(A) Thomas Paine
(B) S.T. Coleridge
(C) William Godwin
(D) Robert Southey

666. "Men of England, wherefore plough
For the lords who Day ye low ?
Wherefore weave with toil and care
The rich robes you tyrants wear ?"
These revolutionary thoughts hailed from
(A) Byron (B) Shelley
(C) De Quincey (D) Walter Scott

667. John Murray and William Gifford were the publisher, and editor respectively of
(A) *Quarterly Review*
(B) *The Edinburgh Magazine*
(C) *The London Magazine*
(D) *New Monthly Magazine*

668. About which magazine Scott had said, "No genteel family can pretend to be without it" and Carlyle had remarked that it was "a kind of Delphic Oracle and voice of the inspired for the great majority of what is called the intelligent public" ?
(A) *Edinburg Review*
(B) *The London Magazine*
(C) *Fraser's Magazine*
(D) *The Westminister Review*

669. In which chapter of the *Biographia Literaria* does Coleridge make a subtle distinction between *imagination* and *fancy* ?
(A) Chapter I (B) Chapter VII
(C) Chapter XIII (D) Chapter XX

670. Who in his critical work *Specimens of English Dramatic poets who wrote about the time of Shakespeare,* endeavoured to spread the knowledge of older English playwrights?
(A) Hazlitt (B) Coleridge
(C) Leigh Hunt (D) Lamb

671. Who wrote the essays, *Note on the knocking at the Gate in Macbeth* and *Murder considered as one of the Fine Arts* ?
(A) Charles Lamb
(B) William Hazlitt
(C) Thomas De Quincey
(D) Leigh Hunt

672. Whose fame as an essayist rests on *Imaginary Conversations* ?
(A) De Quincey (B) Hunt
(C) Scott (D) Landor

673. The credit of pioneering the historical novel is often attributed to
(A) Godwin (B) Scott
(C) Austen (D) Southey

674. Which of the following attempts at historical fiction was made prior to Scott's popularization of the genre ?
(A) *The Scottish Chiefs* by Jane Porter
(B) *The Castle of Otranto* by Horace Walpole
(C) *Recess* by Sophia Lee
(D) All of the above

675. In which of his novels Scott represented that Shakespeare died in 1590 without writing his tragedies ?
(A) *Kenilworth* (B) *Red Gauntlet*
(C) *Woodstock* (D) *Abbot*

676. In which one of Austen's novels Fanny visits her parents' home at apartments after an absence of more than 10 years ?
(A) *Emma* (B) *Persuasions*
(C) *Pride and Prejudice*
(D) *Mansfied Park*

677. Where does Darcy propose Elizabeth in the *Pride and Prejudice* ?
(A) Hunsford Parsonage
(B) The village ball
(C) Germany
(D) None of the above

678. In which novel of Austen, John Dashwood, the henpecked husband, appears ?
(A) *Northanger Abbey*
(B) *Emma*
(C) *Sense and Sensibility*
(D) *Mansfield Park*

679. Which work of Jane Austen is a satire directed against Gothic Romance and stormy passions ?
(A) *Pride and Prejudice*
(B) *Mansfield Park*
(C) *Emma*
(D) *Northanger Abbey*

680. Who wrote blank-verse tragedies such as *Cain, Manfred, Marino Faliero* and *The Deformed Transformed* ?
(A) Swinburne (B) Coleridge
(C) Scott (D) Byron

681. Who wrote the tragedy *John Woodvil*, that was originally given the title *'Pride's Care'* ?
(A) Lamb (B) Hazlitt
(C) De Quincey (D) Hunt

682. "The churchyard school of poets" means
(A) the poets who wrote only about the church
(B) the poets who wrote poetry chiefly of melancholic strain
(C) the poets who wrote for the reformation of the church
(D) All of the above

683. Who among the following has been called a "Ploughman Poet" ?
(A) Blake (B) Gray
(C) Thomson (D) Burns

684. *Tom Jones* by Henry Fielding was dedicated to
(A) Richardson (B) Defoe
(C) G. Lyttleton (D) Bishop Percy

685. Whom did T.L. Peacock satirise in his *Nightmare Abbey* ?
(A) Shelley (B) Keats
(C) Coleridge (D) Both (A) and (C)

686. "It is a truth universally acknowledged that a single man in possession of a good fortune, must be in want of a wife". Which novel of Jane Austen begins with this sentence ?
(A) *Pride and Prejudice*
(B) *Sense and Sensibility*
(C) *Emma*
(D) *Mansfield Park*

687. *The Times* which acquired this name in 1788 was earlier known as
(A) *Daily Universal Register*
(B) *The Daily Digest*
(C) *The Tatler*
(D) *The Rambler*

688. Who among the following had written, "Hell is a city much like London" ?
(A) Byron (B) Shelley
(C) Thomson (D) Lamb

689. Many critics have hailed the publication of the *Lyrical Ballads* as the beginning of the Romantic Period. In which year was it published?
(A) 1796 (B) 1797
(C) 1798 (D) 1799

690. The Romantic writers were influenced by the idealism of German philosophers such as

(A) Kant and Rousseau
(B) Rousseau and More
(C) More and Hegel
(D) Kant and Hegel

691. Who among the following had called Wordsworth, a 'Moral Eunuch'?

(A) Byron (B) Browning
(C) Shelley (D) Arnold

692. Who emphasized the use of the "language really used by men" for poetry ?

(A) Coleridge (B) Wordsworth
(C) Shakespeare (D) Pope

693. The mariner in "The Ancient Mariner" kills a bird. Identify the bird among the following.

(A) Albatross (B) Swan
(C) Penguin (D) Flemingo

694. Who made a scathing attack on the contemporary literary scene and the 'Edinburgh Review' through his satire, *English Bards and Scotch Reviewers* ?

(A) Shelley (B) Byron
(C) Scott (D) Hazlitt

695. "I awoke one morning and found myself famous" - who commented thus on his sudden success as a poet ?

(A) Milton (B) Shelley
(C) Keats (D) Byron

696. Regarding whom did Charlotte Bronte say, "The passions are perfectly unknown to her: she rejects even a speaking acquaintance with that stormy sisterhood."

(A) Jane Austen
(B) Lady Caroline Lamb
(C) Mary Shelley
(D) Emile Bronte

697. "For thy sake, tobacco, I would do anything but die". Who has been quoted here ?

(A) Byron (B) Coleridge
(C) Lamb (D) De Quincey

698. Who hastened the death of Keats according to Shelley's *Adonais* ?

(A) The Government
(B) The brutal reviewers
(C) His beloved
(D) Poetry

699. Who expressed his dislike for poetry "that has a palpable design upon us" in one of his letters ?

(A) Addison (B) Arnold
(C) Wordsworth (D) Keats

700. "It is no small thing to have so loved the principle of beauty as to perceive the necessary relation beauty with truth, and of both with joy". Who is Arnold talking about in this sentence ?

(A) Shakespeare (B) Wordsworth
(C) Keats (D) Tennyson

701. Who called Keats "a Greek" for his preoccupation with Hellenism in poetry ?

(A) Arnold (B) Shelley
(C) Eliot (D) None of these

702. Which book, though not literature, exercised an enormous influence in England during the beginning of 19th century ?

(A) *Communist Menifesto*
(B) Robert Burns's *Poems*
(C) Thomas Paine's *Rights of Man*
(D) All of the above

703. Who formed "Pantisocracy on the banks of Susquehanna " ?

(A) Coleridge & Southey
(B) Wordsworth & Southey
(C) Coleridge & Wordsworth
(D) Richardson & Steele

704. Who wrote : "Bliss was it in that dawn to be alive | But to be young was very heaven." ?

(A) S.T. Coleridge
(B) William Wordsworth
(C) Walter Scott
(D) Joseph Lancaster

705. Three of the following are called "Lake poets." Identify who is not.
(A) William Wordsworth
(B) Lord Byron
(C) S.T. Coleridge
(D) Robert Southey

706. The age of Romanticism was
(A) 1800-1850 (B) 1770-1850
(C) 1760-1820 (D) 1771-1832

707. Name the woman novelist whose pictures of Irish life suggested to Walter Scott the idea of writing Scottish romances.
(A) Fanny Burney (B) Hannah More
(C) Jane Porter (D) Maria Edgeworth

708. Who writes novels of haunted castles, bandits, trapdoor and horror ?
(A) Maria Edgeworth
(B) Walter Scott
(C) Fanny Burney
(D) Mrs. Anne Radcliffe

709. Where do we meet Hermes, Lycious, Appolonius ?
(A) *Lamia* (B) *Endymion*
(C) *Hyperion* (D) None of these

710. The story of *Lamia* is taken from
(A) Plutarch
(B) Homer (Chapman's Homer)
(C) Lemprier's Dictionary
(D) Philostratus

711. Keat's *Endymion* has
(A) 3,000 lines (B) 4,000 lines
(C) 2500 lines (D) 4,500 lines

712. Which is the pair of lovers Endymion does not meet in Keat's *Endymion* ?
(A) Venus and Adonis
(B) Romeo and Juliet
(C) Glaucus and Scylla
(D) Arcthusa and Alpheus

713. Who wrote the famous *Preface to the Lyrical Ballads* ?
(A) Coleridge (B) Southey
(C) Wordsworth (D) Byron

714. When were the *Lyrical Ballads* published ?
(A) 1797 (B) 1798
(C) 1800 (D) 1801

715. The *Lyrical Ballads* opens with
(A) *Kubla Khan*
(B) *Ode to Duty*
(C) *Rime of the Ancient Mariner*
(D) *Immortality Ode*

716. The *Lyrical Ballads* closes with
(A) *Kubla Khan*
(B) *Immortality Ode*
(C) *Christabel*
(D) *Lines Written above Tintern Abbey*

717. Who was the third person with Coleridge and Wordsworth at Quantock Hills when the *Lyrical Ballads* were composed ?
(A) Robert Southey
(B) Walter Scott
(C) Dorothy Wordsworth
(D) Mary Lamb

718. William Wordsworth was born in
(A) 1770 (B) 1771
(C) 1768 (D) 1769

719. Who of the following is known for his Hellenic Spirit ?
(A) Lord Byron (B) P.B. Shelley
(C) Southey (D) John Keats

720. Who wrote :
"Our Sweetest songs are those
That tell our saddest thoughts" ?
(A) P.B. Shelley
(B) Robert Southey
(C) Cardinal Newman
(D) S.T. Coleridge

721. How do we classify Shelley's *Prometheus Unbound* ? As
(A) an epic
(B) a legendary story
(C) mythological story
(D) a lyrical drama

722. Who wrote this : "He prayeth Well, who loveth well | Both man and bird and beast" ?

(A) William Wordsworth
(B) S.T. Coleridge
(C) Leigh Hunt (D) Cardinal Newman

723. Name the journal to which Southey contributed regularly.
(A) *The Quarterly Review*
(B) *The Blackwoods Magazine*
(C) *The Edinburgh Review*
(D) *The Westminister Review*

724. Sir Walter Scott collected Scottish ballads, and published them along with his own, in
(A) *The Lay of the Last Minstrel*
(B) *Marmion*
(C) *Minstrelsy of The Scottish Border*
(D) *The Lord of The Isles*

725. How old was Byron when he published *Hours of Idleness*, a collection of poems in heroic couplet ?
(A) 19 (B) 29
(C) 18 (D) 30

726. When *Hours of Idleness* was criticised by the Edinburgh Review, Lord Byron retaliated by writing a satiric piece. What was the title of this satire ?
(A) *The Vision of Judgement*
(B) *Mazeppa*
(C) *The Giaour*
(D) *English Bards and Scotch Reviewers*

727. How many cantos could Byron complete of *Childe Harold's Pilgrimage* during his two years tour of the continent ?
(A) All four (B) First two
(C) One and three (D) Only one

728. The first two cantos of *Childe Harold* take a reader to
(A) Spain (B) Portugal
(C) Greece and Albania
(D) All of the above.

729. What is the tone of the ending of the second canto of *Childe Harold* ?
(A) Joyous (B) Melancholy
(C) Self-pitying (D) Optimistic

730. In which canto does the description of the "Battle of Waterloo" appear ?
(A) Canto I
(B) It is an independent poem
(C) Canto III
(D) Canto IV

731. Who is the hero of *Childe Harold* ?
(A) Nature
(B) An unnamed traveller
(C) A legendary king
(D) The poet himself

732. "Michael", "The Solitary Reaper," "To a Highland Girl" - all these poems depict
(A) the poet's joy at the beauty of nature
(B) simple common folk
(C) poet's awe at the spiritual presence
(D) deep sense of music

733. What was Wordsworth's professed aim in the *Lyrical Ballads* ?
(A) Purge poetry of all conceit
(B) Simplicity of diction
(C) Make it intelligible to common people
(D) All of the above

734. Which work inspired Coleridge's *Kubla Khan* ?
(A) Holinshed's *Chronicle*
(B) Plutarch's *Lives*
(C) *Travels in Scotland*
(D) Purchas's *Pilgrimage*

735. The name of the prisoner of Chillon was
(A) Beppo (B) Giaour
(C) Francois de Bonnivard
(D) Pasha

736. The *Vision of Judgment* is
(A) an attack on Jeffrey, the editor
(B) satire on Southey
(C) satire on a young man of Seville
(D) satire on society

737. *Don Juan* has
(A) 5 cantos (B) 15 cantos
(C) 16 cantos (D) 20 cantos

738. Who is Haidee in *Don Juan* ?
(A) Wife of Don Alfonso
(B) Daughter of an old pirate
(C) Princess of Constantinople
(D) A Duchess

739. Where do we find these lines ?
"Man's love is of man's life a thing apart,
"Tis woman's whole existence...." ?
(A) *Don Juan* (B) *Beppo*
(C) *Childe Harold* (D) *Lara*

740. Where do we meet these characters ? Don Alfonso, Julia, Sultana ? In
(A) *Lara* (B) *Don Juan*
(C) *Childe Harold* (D) *Beppo*

741. When he wrote Queen Mab, Shelley was only
(A) 19 (b) 18
(C) 21 (D) 22

742. Which of Shelley's poems has a story from Greek mythology ?
(A) *Prometheus Unbound*
(B) *Alastor*
(C) *Queen Mab*
(D) *Julian and Maddalo*

743. Which poem was inspired by the Greek proclamation of independence, followed by Greek revolt against Turkish rule ?
(A) *Epipsychidion* (B) *Queen Mab*
(C) *Hellas* (D) *Prometheus*

744. Who is Adonais of the poem *Adonais* ?
(A) Lord Byron (B) John Keats
(C) Shelley himself
(D) None of the above

745. We meet characters such as Asia, Hercules, Jupiter in
(A) *Hellas* (B) *Prometheus Unbound*
(C) *Adonais* (D) *Queen Mab*

746. In which novel Scott projects Scotland under Robert Bruce, King and national hero ?
(A) *Quentin Durward*
(B) *Kenilworth*
(C) *Castle Dangerous*
(D) *St. Ronan's Well*

747. Which of the following is not written by Walter Scott ?
(A) *The Black Dwarf*
(B) *The Legend Montrose*
(C) *The Talisman*
(D) None of the above

748. What is the background of Ivanhoe ?
(A) The first crusade of Constantinople
(B) Contemporary life in the Scottish span of St. Ronan's Well
(C) Enmity of Saxon and Norman
(D) Wales under Henry II

749. Who wrote the following: *Castle Rackrent, the Absentee, Ormond* ?
(A) Fanny Burney
(B) Jane Poster
(C) Thomas Peacock
(D) Maria Edgeworth

750. This woman novelist wrote "Scotch" novels: *Thaddeus of Warsaw* and *The Scottish Chiefs*. Who is she ?
(A) Jane Porter
(B) Susan Ferrier
(C) Marry Russell Mitford
(D) Maria Edgeworth

751. Who wrote *Headlong Hall, Maid Marian, Melincourt, Nightmare Abbey, Misfortunes of Elphin, Crotchet Castle and Gryll Grange*?
(A) Thomas Peacock
(B) G.P.R. James
(C) George Meredith
(D) Charles Lever

752. One of the following was not associated with the 'Edinburgh Review'. Identify him.
(A) Sidney Smith
(B) William Blackwood
(C) Henry Brougham
(D) Francis Jeffrey

753. One of the characters of Jane Austen remarks, "A lady's imagination is very rapid;

it jumps from admiration to love, from love to matrimony in a moment." Who said this and in which novel ?

(A) Mr. Woodhouse in *Emma*
(B) Darcy in *Pride and Prejudice*
(C) Catherine in *Nothanger Abbey*
(D) None of the above

754. His sonnet was rejected by a magazine *Gem*, on the plea that it would "shock mothers". At this he wrote to a friend, "I am born out of time .... When my sonnet was rejected, I exclaimed 'Hang the age, I will write for antiquity.' Who is he ?

(A) Thomas Peacock (B) Hazlitt
(C) Charles Lamb (D) Leigh Hunt

755. This patriotic song is often prescribed for school anthologies in India :

"Breathes there the man,
With soul so dead
Who never to himself hath said,
'This is my own, my native land."
Who is the poet ?

(A) Robert Southey
(B) Walter Scott
(C) Lord Byron
(D) William Wordsworth

756. Where do we find Bingley ?

(A) *Pride and Prejudice*
(B) *Sense and Sensibility*
(C) *Mansfield Park*
(D) *Persuasion*

757. When was the unfinished dream poem 'Kubla Khan' published ?

(A) 1816 (B) 1810
(C) 1820 (D) 1821

758. Read the line : "About thirty years age, Miss Maria Ward of Huntingdon, with only seven thousand pounds, had the good luck to captivate Sir Thomas Bertram......". This is the beginning of a novel by Jane Austen. Which one ?

(A) *Mansfield Park*
(B) *Emma*
(C) *Sense and Sensibility*
(D) *Northanger Abbey*

759. "It is a truth universally acknowledged, that a single man in possession of a good fortune, must be in want of a wife." Which of Jane Austen's novels begins with these words ?

(A) *Sense and Sensibility*
(B) *Northanger Abbey*
(C) *Pride and Prejudice*
(D) *Emma*

760. Which of Scott's novels depicts the conflict between the Puritans, the Covenanters, and the royal forces under Claverhouse" ?

(A) *Old Morality*
(B) *Castle Dangerous*
(C) *Heart of Midlothian*
(D) *Talisman*

761. "Which novel, begun in 1895, but put aside, is Walter Scott's first novel ?

(A) *Ivanhoe* (B) *Waverley*
(C) *Kenilworth*
(D) *Peveril of The Peak*

762. All, except one, of the following poems are written by Coleridge. Mark the one which is not.

(A) "Frost at midnight"
(B) "Hymn Before Sunrise in The Vale of Chamouni"
(C) "Ode to Night"
(D) "Ode on Dejection"

763. Who wrote :

"My hopes are with the Dead; anon
My place with them will be
And I with them shall travel on
Through all futurity;
Yet leaving here a name, I trust,
That will not perish in the dust" ?

(A) S.T. Coleridge
(B) Robert Southey
(C) Lord Byron
(D) Shelley

764. Who was appointed Poet Laureate in 1813?
(A) Robert Southey
(B) William Wordsworth
(C) Lord Byron
(D) Lord Tennyson

765. Which of these ballads and short tales are written by Robert Southey ?
(A) *The Battle of Blenheim*
(B) *Bishop Hatto*
(C) *Inchcape Rock*
(D) All of the above

766. Who wrote the popular nursery tale *Three Bears* ?
(A) Sir Walter Scott
(B) Lord Byron
(C) Robert Southey
(D) Charles Lamb

767. What, according to Wordsworth, is the power of nature ?
(A) To teach (B) To elevate
(C) To soothe and console
(D) All of the above.

768. Name Wordsworth's spiritual autobiography.
(A) *Tintern Abbey* (B) *The Recluse*
(C) *The Prelude* (D) *Immortality Ode*

769. In which poem do these lines occur:
"For oft when on my couch I lie
In vacant or in pensive mood
They flash upon that inward eye
When is a bliss of solitude"?
(A) *To Daffodils*
(B) *The Daffodils*
(C) *The Solitary Reaper*
(D) None of the above

770. Who wrote *Lectures on Shakespeare* and *Biographia Literaria* ?
(A) S.T. Coleridge
(B) Samuel Johnson
(C) Alexander Pope
(D) Lord Byron

771. What is Coleridge's *Anima Poetae* ?
(A) A treatise on poetry
(B) Biographies of poets
(C) Table-talk and notes
(D) Lectures

772. Following poems are written by Shelley, except one. Identify the one not written by him.
(A) *Ode to the West Wind*
(B) *To a Skylark*
(C) *Ode to the Nightingale*
(D) *The Cloud*

773. Who is the author of *Story of Rumini* ?
(A) John Keats (B) Leigh Hunt
(C) George Darley (D) Macaulay

774. Where were *Lyrical Ballads* written ? In
(A) Cumberland Hills
(B) Cambridge
(C) Quantock Hills
(D) Hawshead

775. Who wrote *Frankenstein* ?
(A) Mary Shelley
(B) Mary Wollstonecraft
(C) Miss Edgeworth
(D) Mrs. Radcliff

776. Who is Elia of Charles Lamb's *Essays of Elia* ?
(A) His friend
(B) His patron
(C) An Italian clerk with whom he had worked in the South Sea House
(D) An imaginary figure

777. *Essays of Elia* first appeared in
(A) *London Magazine*
(B) *Gem*
(C) *Blackwood's Magazine*
(D) *Edinburgh Review*

778. *Tales from Shakespeare* were written at the suggestion of
(A) Shelley (B) Leigh Hunt
(C) Godwin (D) De Quincey

779. Whom does Lamb describe as "an archangel a little damaged" ?
(A) Shelley (B) Coleridge
(C) Wordsworth (D) Keats

780. Who is not a member of the "Cockney school" out of the following ?
(A) Hazlitt (B) De Quincey
(C) Lamb (D) Leigh Hunt

781. Who wrote letter to *Mr. Gifford, The Round Table, Table Talk, The Spirit of the Age* ?
(A) William Hazlitt (B) Leigh Hunt
(C) Charles Lamb (D) De Quincey

782. Which is Thomas De Quincey's best known work ?
(A) *Confessions of an Opium Eater*
(B) *The English Mail Coach*
(C) *Literature of Knowledge* and *Literature of Power*
(D) *Surpiria De Profundis*

783. Who is the author of *Imaginary Conversations* ?
(A) De Quincey
(B) Landor
(C) William Cobbet
(D) Hazlitt

784. Who started and edited *Political Register*, a weekly newspaper ?
(A) De Quincey
(B) Leigh Hunt
(C) William Cobbet
(D) Lamb

785. Who had said that he had "a smack of Hamlet" in himself ?
(A) Byron (B) Keats
(C) Shelley (D) Coleridge

786. Who is the author of *Emile* that had influenced the Romantic Movement ?
(A) Balzac (B) Kant
(C) Diderot (D) Rousseau

787. Who had said that "truth is always strange; stranger than fiction" ?
(A) Coleridge (B) Johnson
(C) Byron (D) Hazlitt

788. Scott's novels are set in
(A) Scotland (B) Italy
(C) England (D) All of these

789. Who wrote what are known as 'Waverley novels' ?
(A) Hazlitt (B) Hardy
(C) Scott (D) Peacock

790. The *Reform Bill* was passed in the year
(A) 1812 (B) 1832
(C) 1820 (D) 1840

791. Regarding which character did Jane Austen say that she was a "heroine whom no one but myself will much like "?
(A) Elizabeth Bennet
(B) Mrs. Bennet
(C) Emma
(D) None of the above

792. The celebrated twentieth century novelist Woolf had died by drowning herself. Which Romantic poet had died a similar death ?
(A) Keats (B) Byron
(C) Coleridge (D) Shelley

793. Who had refused to accept the post of poet laureate in 1813 as a result of which it had gone to Robert Southey ?
(A) Wordsworth (B) Scott
(C) Cowper (D) Byron

Match the following lists using the codes given below.

794. List I | **List II**

List I	List II
a. 1789	1. Flight of Louis XVI
b. 1791	2. Execution of Louis XVI
c. 1793	3. The fall of Bastille

Codes:

	a	b	c
(A)	1	2	3
(B)	3	2	1
(C)	2	3	1
(D)	3	1	2

795.

List I	List II
a. *The Rights of Man*	1. Blake
b. *The Marriage of Heaven and Hell*	2. Burke
c. *Political Justice*	3. Paine
d. *America*	4. Godwin

Codes:

	a	b	c	d
(A)	3	2	4	1
(B)	3	4	1	2
(C)	1	3	4	2
(D)	1	2	4	3

796. List I **List II**

a. *Camilla* 1. Wollstonecraft
b. *The Wrongs of Woman* 2. Burney
c. *Castle Reckrent* 3. Edgeworth
d. *The Lady of the Lake* 4. Scott

Codes:

	a	b	c	d
(A)	1	2	3	4
(B)	2	1	3	4
(C)	1	2	4	3
(D)	2	1	4	3

797. List I **List II**

a. 1801 1. Restoration of Louis XVIII
b. 1814 2. Union of British and Irish parliaments
c. 1815 3. Battle of Waterloo

Codes:

	a	b	c
(A)	3	1	2
(B)	3	2	1
(C)	2	3	1
(D)	2	1	3

798. List I **List II**

a. 1802 1. Blackwood's *Edinburgh Magazine*
b. 1809 2. *Edinburgh Review*
c. 1817 3. *Westminister Review*
d. 1824 4. *Quarterley Review*

Codes:

	a	b	c	d
(A)	1	4	2	3
(B)	2	3	1	4
(C)	2	4	1	3
(D)	1	3	2	4

799. List I **List II**

a. Scott 1. *Alastor*
b. Byron 2. *Guy Mannering*
c. Shelley 3. *The Shepherd's Calender*
d. Clare 4. *The Corsair*

Codes:

	a	b	c	d
(A)	4	2	1	3
(B)	2	4	3	1
(C)	4	2	3	1
(D)	2	4	1	3

800. List I **List II**

a. *The Antiquery and Old Mortality* 1. Galt
b. *Northanger Abbey* 2. Ferrier
c. *Marriage* 3. Jane Austen
d. *The Entail* 4. Scott

Codes:

	a	b	c	d
(A)	3	4	2	1
(B)	4	3	2	1
(C)	4	1	2	3
(D)	3	4	1	2

801. List I **List II**

a. *Annals of the Parish* 1. Galt
b. *Rob Roy* 2. Cobbett
c. *Manfred* 3. Scott
d. *Rural Rides* 4. Byron

Codes:

	a	b	c	d
(A)	1	3	4	2
(B)	3	1	4	2
(C)	1	3	2	4
(D)	3	1	2	4

802. List I **List II**

a. Poetry 1. Sheridan
b. Drama 2. De Quincey
c. Essays 3. Cowper

Codes:

	a	b	c
(A)	1	2	3
(B)	3	1	2
(C)	2	3	1
(D)	3	2	1

803. List I **List II**

a. Spiritualisation 1. Keats
b. Intellectualisation 2. Shelley
c. Sensualisation 3. Coleridge
d. Supernaturalisation 4. Wordsworth

Codes:

	a	b	c	d
(A)	4	1	2	3
(B)	1	4	3	2
(C)	4	2	1	3
(D)	1	3	4	2

804. List I **List II**

a. *Dream Children* 1. De Quincey
b. *Table Talk* 2. Charles Lamb
c. *The English Mail Coach* 3. Hazlitt

Codes:

	a	b	c
(A)	1	2	3
(B)	3	2	1
(C)	2	1	3
(D)	2	3	1

805. List I **List II**

a. *The Convalescent* 1. Lamb
b. *The Indian Juggler* 2. Hazlitt
c. *The Knocking at the Gate in Macbeth* 3. De Quincey

Codes:

	a	b	c
(A)	1	2	3
(B)	2	3	1
(C)	3	1	2
(D)	2	1	3

806. List I **List II**

a. *Seven Lamps of Architecture* 1. Charlotte Bronte
b. *Villette* 2. Ruskin
c. *The Newcomers* 3. Thackeray

Codes:

	a	b	c
(A)	1	2	3
(B)	3	2	1
(C)	2	1	3
(D)	3	1	2

807. List I **List II**

a. Robert Browning 1. *The Last Chronical 1of Barset*
b. Trollope 2. *Men and Women*
c. Meredith 3. *The Ordeal of Richard Feverl*

Code:

	a	b	c
(A)	2	3	1
(B)	2	1	3
(C)	3	1	2
(D)	3	2	1

808. List I **List II**

a. *Phineas Finn* 1. Hardy
b. *The Subjection of Women* 2. Trollope
c. *The Return of the Native* 3. J.S. Mill

Codes:

	a	b	c
(A)	1	2	4
(B)	2	1	3
(C)	1	3	2
(D)	2	3	1

809. List I **List II**

a. *Edwin Drood* 1. Arnold
b. *The Egoist* 2. D.G. Rossetti
c. *Literature and Dogma* 3. Meredith

Codes:

	a	b	c
(A)	2	3	1
(B)	2	1	3
(C)	3	1	2
(D)	3	2	1

810. List I **List II**

a. *Harold, Becket, The Cup* 1. Tennyson
b. *Pippa Passes, Asolando* 2. Arnold
c. *Balder Dead, New Poems* 3. Browning

Codes:

	a	b	c
(A)	1	2	3
(B)	1	3	2
(C)	2	1	3
(D)	2	3	1

811. What was the age of Queen Victoria when she rose to the throne ?
(A) 15 (B) 17
(C) 18 (D) 21

812. When was Darwin's *Origin of Species* published?
(A) 1859 (B) 1869
(C) 1879 (D) 1889

813. In 1830, Tennyson published his first collection of poems, entitled
(A) *Poems, 1830*
(B) *Poems, Chiefly Lyrical*
(C) *Dramatic Lyrics*
(D) *The Priness*

814. Who is the author of *On Heroes and Hero Worship* ?
(A) Tennyson (B) Dickens
(C) Carlyle (D) Thackeray

815. In which of the novels of Dickens, the portagonist remembers how he had been "a child's Tom Jones, a harmless creature" in his boyhood ?
(A) *Great Expectations*
(B) *Hard Times*
(C) *Pickwick Papers*
(D) *David Copperfield*

816. Thackeray complained in the preface to one of his novels that "Since the author of Tom Jones was burried, no writer of fiction among us has been permitted to depict to his utmost power a man". Name the novel
(A) *The Rose and the Ring*
(B) *Pendennis*
(C) *Vanity Fair*
(D) *The three Georges*

817. In which novel of Dickens Sir Leicester Deadlock appears ?
(A) *David Copperfield*
(B) *Hard Times*
(C) *A Tale of Two Cities*
(D) *Bleak House*

818. Mr. Brooke fails to get himself elected to the new parliament in
(A) *Pickwick Papers*
(B) *Middlemarch*
(C) *Silas Marner*
(D) *Great Expectations*

819. In which one of the works of Carlyle do we find a theorizing German central character with a mediating and explicitly English, editor?
(A) *Sartor Resartus*
(B) *Live of Schiller*
(C) *Felix Holt*
(D) *Past and Present*

820. Dicken's *A Tale of Two Cities* shows considerable influence of Carlyle's
(A) *Sarter Resartus*
(B) *The French Revolution*
(C) *Past and Present*
(D) None of the above

821. Dicken's first full-scale work of fiction was
(A) *Sketches by Boz*
(B) *Pickwick Papers*
(C) *Nicholas Nickelb*
(D) *Master Humphrey's Clock*

822. What is the subtitle of Dickens's *Oliver Twist*?
(A) *The Posthumous Papers*
(B) *The Old Curiosity Shop*
(C) *The Parish Boy"s Progress*
(D) *Our Mutual Friend*

823. Dickens uniquely transferred his concern with the modern condition of England out of London in his succinct and often bitter satire on the effects of the industrial revolution in northern England, named

(A) *Oliver Twist*
(B) *The Mystery of Edwin Drood*
(C) *Hard Times*
(D) *Little Dorrit*

824. Which of the following is Dicken's last work, an unfinishable, obsessive, mystery story?
(A) *Our Mutual Friend*
(B) *The Mystery of Edwin Drood*
(C) *David Copperfield*
(D) *A Tale of Two Cities*

825. *Mary Barton* which dramatizes the urban ills of the late 1840s, an era marked by industrial conflict, was written by
(A) Harriet Martineau
(B) Carlyle
(C) Trollope
(D) Elizabeth Gaskell

826. Margaret Hale is the central woman character in Gaskell's
(A) *Sylvia's Lovers*
(B) *Cranford*
(C) *North and South*
(D) *Ruth*

827. Which of the following novels by Gaskell is a set at the time of Napoleonic wars and its plot hinges on the disappearance of a lover who is carried off by a press gang enforcing recruitment into the navy ?
(A) *Sylvia's Lovers*
(B) *Wives and Daughters*
(C) *Cranford*
(D) *Mary Barton*

828. *Yearst : A Problem,* serialized in *Fraser's Magazine* was written by
(A) Disraeli (B) Kingsley
(C) Gaskell (D) Dickens

829. Whose early novels such as *Vivian Grey, The Young Duke, Contarini Fleming* and *Alrey* have been satirized as "Silver-fork fiction" by Dickens in *Nicholas Nickleby ?*
(A) Kingsley (B) Gaskell
(C) Thackeray (D) Disraeli

830. In which of the following novels by Disraeli the opinions of the super-sophisticated, multicultered Jew, Sidonia, in many ways provide the clue to the quality of Disraeli's own arguments ?
(A) *The Young Duke*
(B) *Sybil : Or The Two Nations*
(C) *Coningsby : Or The New Generation*
(D) *Tancred : Or The New Crusade*

831. Whose *History of England*, a monumental work in five volumes, was published between 1848 and 1861 ?
(A) Disraeli (B) Carlyle
(C) Kingsley (D) Macaulay

832. Becky Sharp and Amelian Sedley are characters from Thackeray's
(A) *Vanity Fair*
(B) *The History of Henry Esmond*
(C) *The Adventure's of Philip*
(D) *Book of Snobs*

833. In which of Thackeray's Novels the portagonist is an Indian Army Officer ?
(A) *Henry Esmond*
(B) *Pendennis*
(C) *The Newcomers*
(D) *Vanity Fair*

834. In which of his novels Trollope caricatured his mother as a genteel scribbler, Lady Carbury ?
(A) *Doctor Thorne*
(B) *La Vendee*
(C) *Henry Esmond*
(D) *The Way We Live Now*

835. Which of the following is not a novel by Trollope ?
(A) *Can You Forgive Her* ?
(B) *The Eustance Diamonds*
(C) *Phineas Finns*
(D) *The Professor*

836. In Charlotte Bronte's *Jane Eyre* Jane rejects the proposal of
(A) Rochester

(B) St. John Rivers
(C) Patrick
(D) Both (A) and (B)

837. What is the subtitle of *Jane Eyre* of Charlotte Bronte ?
(A) *The Unfortunate*
(B) *An Autobiography*
(C) *The Independent Woman*
(D) None of the above

838. Who is the narrator in Charlotte's *Villette* ?
(A) Lucy Snowe
(B) Shirley Keeldar
(C) Nelly
(D) Helen Graham

839. The often impercipient, would-be misanthrope Lockwood is the primary narrator in
(A) *Jane Eyre*
(B) *The Tenant of Wildfell Hall*
(C) *Agnes Grey*
(D) *Wuthering Heights*

840. Tennyson's *'In Memorium'* expresses his deep sense of bereavement at the death of his friend and critic
(A) Mathew Arnold
(B) Arthur Hallam
(C) Swinburne
(D) Christina Rossetti

841. Which of the following is a deeply ambiguous narrative poem, one which moves uncertainly from a present-day prologue to a story set in an undefined medieval past, and attempts to explore the pressing contemporary subject of women's higher education, written by Tennyson ?
(A) *In Memorium*
(B) *Maud*
(C) *The Princess*
(D) *The Idylls*

842. "The old order changeth, yielding place to new, And God fulfills himself in many ways...." This is an extract from Tennyson's
(A) *St. Simeon Stylites*
(B) *Break, break, break*
(C) *Enoch Arden*
(D) *Morte d' Arthur*

843. Tennyson succeeded Wordsworth as the Poet Laureate in
(A) 1843 (B) 1847
(C) 1850 (D) 1860

844. Which of Tennyson's love poems begins starkly with the words 'I hate' ?
(A) *Ode on the Death of the Duke of Wellington*
(B) *Maud*
(C) *The Idylls of the King*
(D) *Enoch Arden*

845. The radical Victorian poet who wrote *Poems and Ballads* (1866) and *Songs before Sunrise* (1871) is
(A) Tennyson (B) Browning
(C) William Morris (D) Swinburne

846. Which of the following is not written by Morris?
(A) *The Earthly Paradise*
(B) *Goblin Market*
(C) *A Dream of John Ball*
(D) *News from Nowhere*

847. Who is the author of *Goblin Market,* an extraordinary poem in its times, the spiritual message in which stretches from childish fears to sexual threat and female self-assertion ?
(A) Morris (B) Swinburne
(C) Mazzini (D) Rossetti

848. Which of the following is not written by Christina ?
(A) *Sing Song : A Nursery Rhyme Book*
(B) *The Princes's Progress and Other Poems*
(C) *Aurora Leigh: A Poem in Nine Books*
(D) *A Pageant and Other Poems*

849. *Aurora Leigh: A Poem in Nine Books*, written by Elizabeth Barrett Browning is a
(A) blank-verse novel

(B) verse satire
(C) play in sonnets
(D) mock epic

850. Elizabeth Barrett Browning's husband also wrote a verse novel. Name it.
(A) *Strafford*
(B) *The Ring and the Book*
(C) *Men and Women*
(D) *Dramatis Personae*

851. "She thanked me – good ! but thanked
Somehow–I know not how – as if she ranked
My gift of a nine-hundred-years-old name
With anybody's gift. Who'd stoop to blame
This sort of trifling ? "
This is an extract from Robert Browning's
(A) *Dramatis Personae*
(B) *My Last Duchess*
(C) *Dramatic Lyrics*
(D) *Men and Women*

852. Which of the following by Robert Browning is a children's poem ?
(A) *The Lost Leader*
(B) *Two in the Campagna*
(C) *Childe Roland to the Dark Tower Came*
(D) *The Pied Piper of Hamelin*

853. Robert Browning's tragedy *Strafford* had been conceived and written in the mid-1830s at the earnest request of one of the great victorian actors.
(A) W.C. Macready (B) Bulwer-Lytton
(C) Douglas Jerrold (D) Charles Dickens

854. Verse dramas like *Queen Mary* and *Becket* were written by
(A) Robert Browing
(B) Elizabeth Barrett Browning
(C) Alfred Tennyson
(D) W.C. Macready

855. Who is the author of the popular nautical melodrama, *Black-Eyed Susan : or All in the Downs ?*
(A) Douglas Jerrold
(B) Robert Browning
(C) Matthew Arnold
(D) Dion Boucicault

856. The Irish author of *The Collear Bawn,* Arrah-na-Pogue, *and The Shaughraun* is the only mid-victorian playwright who found favour with twentieth century producers and audiences. Name the dramatist.
(A) Tennyson (B) Browning
(C) Boucicault (D) Jerrold

857. *The Moonstone*, a multiple narrative which subtly explores the nature of detection and the vagaries of memory observation, is the masterpiece of
(A) Elizabeth Braddon
(B) William Wilkie Collins
(C) Charles Reade
(D) None of the above

858. Which of the following is not written by Collins ?
(A) *The Woman in White*
(B) *No Fame*
(C) *Armadale*
(D) *The Double Marriage*

859. Elizabeth Braddon achieved immediate popular acclaim with her gripping, almost breathless novel
(A) *Dianna of the Crossways*
(B) *Lady Chatterley's Lover*
(C) *Lady Audley's Secret*
(D) *No Thoroughfare*

860. *The Egoist*, which has long been most admired for the substantial dialogue scenes and the tense comedy of English upper class manners, was written by
(A) Christina Rossetti
(B) Dante Gabriel Rossetti
(C) Mari Ann Evans
(D) George Meredith

861. Whose first published works of fiction, the three *Scenes of Clerical Life* were acclaimed by reviewers ?
(A) George Meredith
(B) George Eliot

(C) Charles Dickens
(D) Thackeray

862. Queen Elizabeth was so pleased to read a novel by Mari Ann Evans that she commissioned two paintings of scenes from it. Name the novel.
(A) *Middlemarch*
(B) *Silas Marner*
(C) *Adam Bede*
(D) *Mill on the Floss*

863. In which of George Eliot's novels Maggie Tulliver appears as the central woman character ?
(A) *Middlemarch* (B) *Silas Marner*
(C) *Daniel Deronda* (D) *Mill on the Floss*

864. *Middlemarch* published in 1871-72 which is very closely related to the determining spirit of the age, is set in the years
(A) 1829-32 (B) 1839-42
(C) 1849-52 (D) 1859-62

865. Whom does Dorothea marry in the end in *Middlemarch* ?
(A) Casaubon (B) Lydgate
(C) Ladislaw (D) Fred Vincy

866. Who is the first lover of Dorothea, whom she rejects, in Middlemarch
(A) Baulstrode (B) Fred
(C) Casaubon (D) Chewtham

867. It is George Eliot's most cosmopolitan novel, dealing with the contrast between the sensibilities of a pampered and limited English aristocracy and these of despised, but intense, Jewish outsiders. Which novel are we referring to ?
(A) *The Spanish Gipsy*
(B) *Daniel Deronda*
(C) *Romola*
(D) *Felix Holt, the Radical*

868. The leading philosopher and ardent advocate of the extension of democracy who wrote the essay *On Liberty is*
(A) George Eliot
(B) Matthew Arnold
(C) John Stuart Mill
(D) Thomas Hughes

869. Who wrote *Culture and Anarchy*, playfully dividing English society into three constituent classes: a Barbarian aristocracy, a Philistine bourgeoisie and an unlettered 'Populace' ?
(A) J.S. Mill
(B) Matthew Arnold
(C) A.H. Clough
(D) Ruskin

870. "O born in days when wits were fresh and clear,
And life ran gaily as the sparkling Thames;
Before this strange disease of modern life,
With its sick hurry, its divided aims,
Its heads o'ertaxed, its palsied hearts, was rife"
This is an extract from Arnold's
(A) *Scholar Gipsy*
(B) *Empedocles of Etna*
(C) *Tom Brown's Schooldays*
(D) *Rugby Chapel*

871. In which of his poems Arnold returns to the contours of the Oxfordshire landscape, but now imbues them with reminiscences of the Greek and Roman pastoral tradition ?
(A) *Scholar Gipsy*
(B) *Thyrsis*
(C) *Empedocles of Etna*
(D) *Amours de Voyage*

872. *Amours de Voyage*, a sequence of verse letters is the best known poetry of
(A) Arthur Hugh Clough
(B) Mathew Arnold
(C) Alfred Tennyson
(D) John Hopkins

873. In 1860, A.H. Clough had started a series of essays in 'Cornhill Magazine', concerning the economic and social integrity of mid-Victorian England, but was obliged to stop it soon. In 1862, it appeared as a book, entitled

(A) *Modern Painters*
(B) *The Stones of Venice*
(C) *Unto this Last*
(D) *The Christian Year*

874. Who is the author of volumes of essays such as *Modern Painters, Stores of Venice, etc.* ?
(A) A.H. Clough
(B) Matthew Arnold
(C) Hopkins
(D) Ruskin

875. What is the title of Ruskin's digressive and evasive autobiography ?
(A) *Essays on Myself*
(B) *Praeterita*
(C) *Loss and Gain*
(D) *Apologia Pro Vita Sua*

876. The Oxford Movement in the Victorian period started in the early
(A) 1830s (B) 1840s
(C) 1850s (D) 1860s

877. One of the most articulate and influential disciples of the Oxford Movement, who authored some 150 works and most notably *The Hair of Redclyffe and The Trial*, is
(A) J.M. Neale
(B) C.M. Yonge
(C) Henry Newman
(D) John Keble

878. A dominant figure amongst the regional leaders of the Oxford Revival, who wrote the novel *Loss and Gain* is
(A) John Keble
(B) Robert Bridges
(C) G.M. Hopkins
(D) J.H. Newman

879. Which of the following is not a novel by Lewis Caroll, alias Reverend Charles Lutwidge Dodgson ?
(A) *Condensation of Determinants*
(B) *Euclid and his Modern Rivals*
(C) *Alice's Adventures in Wonderland*
(D) *The Ring and the Book*

880. Who wrote *The Importance of Being Earnest*, mocking at the mid-victorian confidence and earnestness ?
(A) Oscar Wilde
(B) Dickens
(C) G.B. Shaw
(D) Carlyle

881. Who is the author of *The Women of England*, that outlines the role of female sex as being of service to the male members of the family ?
(A) J.S. Mill
(B) Robert Owen
(C) Mrs. Ellis
(D) A.C. Swinburne

882. What was the original title given to Charles Lamb's John Woodwill ?
(A) *The Humble Cow*
(B) *Pride's Cure*
(C) *The Reformed Transformed*
(D) *Atlanta in Calydon*

883. The professor of poetry at Oxford who is considered as the father of the Oxford Movement in England is
(A) G.K. Chesterton
(B) Henry Newman
(C) John Keble
(D) Charles Kingsley

884. Who wrote in his book *The Victorian Ages in Literature* : " The Oxford Movement was, out of the very roots of its being, a rational movement, almost a rationalist movement"?
(A) Henry Newman
(B) G.K. Chesterton
(C) Lockhart
(D) Newman

885. *Apologia Pro Vita Sua* is the spiritual autobiography of
(A) Henry Newman
(B) Lewis Caroll
(C) John Keble
(D) Lockhart

886. A name connected with the Oxford Movement, he is the author of the novel *Fabiola*. Identify him from among the following :
(A) W.G. Ward
(B) Henry Newman
(C) Cardinal Wiseman
(D) Charlotte Young

887. "Man for the field and woman for the hearth
Man for the sword and for the needle she,
Man to command and woman to obey
All else confusion"
This is an extract from Tennyson's poem, in which he displays Victorian conservatism. Name the poem.
(A) *The Mary Queen*
(B) *The Northern Farmer*
(C) *Village Wife*
(D) *The Princess*

888. "To strive, to seek, to find and not to yield"- this famous statement is an extract from Tennyson's poem
(A) *The Princes*
(B) *Ulysses*
(C) *In Memorium*
(D) *The Northern Cobbler*

889. "God is law, say the wise : O soul, and let us rejoice | For it He thunders by law the thunder is yet his voice." Tennyson thus reflects his attitude to God in his
(A) *Higher Pantheism*
(B) *In Memorium*
(C) *Locksley Hall*
(D) *Maud*

890. "Ah love, let us be true
To one another ! for the world which seems
To lie before us like a land of dreams,
So various, so beautiful, so new
Hath really neither joy, nor love, nor light
Nor certitude, nor peace, nor help for pain";
This passage showing Arnold's pessimism has been extracted from his poem
(A) *Rugby Chapel*
(B) *Dover Beach*
(C) *The Scholar Gipsy*
(D) *Sohrab and Rustam*

891. Arnold reflects his despair at common human testing in the following lines:
"Most men eddy about
Here there — eat and drink
Are raised aloft, are hurl'd in the dust
Striving blindly, achieving nothing
And then they die — perish."
In which poem do these lines occur ?
(A) *The Scholar Gipsy*
(B) *Dover Beach*
(C) *Rugby Chapel*
(D) *In Isolation*

892. "Thou shalt have one God only; who
Would be at the expense of two ?
No graven images may be
Worshipped, except the currency "
Which poem of A.H. Clough contains these lines ?
(A) *Orat*
(B) *The Latest Decalogue*
(C) *Dipsychus*
(D) *Easter Day*

893. "Unborn tomorrow and dead yesterday
Why fret about them if today be sweet ?"
Who has thus hedonistically rejected the apprehensions of Arnold ?
(A) James Thomson
(B) A.H. Clough
(C) D.G. Rossetti
(D) Edward Fitz-Gerald

894. Morris and Swinburne belonged to the school of poetry which rejected didacticism or moralisation as one of the aims of poetry. What is this school called as ?
(A) Edwardian School
(B) Pre-morden School
(C) Pre-Raphaelite School
(D) None of the above

895. Who is the author of poems such as *The Blessed Domozel, Sister Helen, A last Confession* and *Rose Mary*?
(A) Swinburne (B) Tennyson
(C) Morris (D) Rossetti

896. *Sigurd the Volsung* an epic of the old Northern warrior who had defied death and fate, is written by
(A) William Morris
(B) Rossetti
(C) Swinburne
(D) W.H. Hunt

897. Who criticised the pre-Raphaelite poetry severely in his essay, The *Fleshly School of Poetry – D.G. Rossetti*?
(A) A.H. Clough
(B) Robert Buchanan
(C) Hugh Walker
(D) Mathew Arnold

898. In poems such as *Fra Lippo Lippi* and *Andrea Del Sarto*, Browning reflects his love for
(A) Greece (B) Spain
(C) Italy (D) None of the above

899. *The White Ship, Sister Helen and Eden Bower* are D.G. Rossetti's famous
(A) novels (B) elegies
(C) sonnets (D) ballads

900. Who gave up the criticism of art for criticism of society, saying, "no one could go on painting pictures in a burning house"?
(A) Rossetti (B) Ruskin
(C) Carlyle (D) Arnold

901. Who wrote in his book, *Sign of the Times,* "it is the Age of Machinery in every outward and inward sense of that word "?
(A) Carlyle (B) Ruskin
(C) Arnold (D) Thomson

902. Who expressed aptly the sense of Victorian predicament in the following lines :
"Between two worlds, one dead,
The other powerless to be born"?
(A) Tennyson (B) Browning
(C) Arnold (D) Hopkins

903. Who has severely criticised the social and industrial conditions of the Victorian age in his *Past and Present*?
(A) Ruskin (B) Carlyle
(C) Browning (D) Hopkins

904. The author of *Sybil*, who most assiduously cultivated the social novel, is
(A) Ruskin (B) Carlyle
(C) Disraeli (D) Dickens

905. "I'm not denyin' the women are foolish .... God Almighty made them to match men". Who has been quoted here ?
(A) Elizabeth Gaskell
(B) Charlotte Bronte
(C) Emily Bronte
(D) George Eliot

906. The famous author of *The Picture of Dorian Gray* who was sentenced to two years' jail on charges of homosexual practice is
(A) Arthur Symons
(B) Oscar Wilde
(C) John Davidson
(D) Aubrey Beardsley

907. The leader of the Decadent Movement, he joined hands with Henry Highland in bringing out a periodical *The Yellow Book.* Identify him from among the following:
(A) Aurey Beardsley
(B) Arthus Symons
(C) Oscar Wilde
(D) Earnst Dowson

908. The Poet who wrote *Barrack Room Ballads* and *The Seven Seas* is
(A) W.E. Henley
(B) G.M. Hopkins
(C) Rudyard Kipling
(D) Alice Meynell

909. Alfred Tennyson wrote *In Memoriam* at the death of
(A) Hallam
(B) Wordsworth
(C) Byron
(D) P.B. Shelley

910. *The Princess* (1847) is written in a
(A) romantic style
(B) epic style
(C) mock-heroic style
(D) comic style

911. From which poem of Tennyson the following lines have been taken :
"There lives more faith in honest doubt,
Believe me, than in half the creed."
(A) *In Memoriam*
(B) *Maud*
(C) *The Idylls of The King*
(D) *Dora*

912. *In Memoriam* was published in
(A) 1855 (B) 1850
(C) 1854 (D) 1860

913. How many poems are there in *The Idylls of the King* ?
(A) 12 (B) 11
(C) 10 (D) 15

914. The last poem written by Tennyson in anticipation of his death is
(A) *Locksley Hall*
(B) *Maud*
(C) *The Dreamer*
(D) *Oenone*

915. Identity the poet about whom it can be said that he is the greatest poet among English critics and the greatest critic among English poets.
(A) Coleridge
(B) Dryden
(C) Matthew Arnold
(D) Dr. Johnson

916. Which Poem of Arnold contains these lines:
"Hath neither joy, nor love, nor light,
Nor certitude, Nor peace, Nor help for pain"?
(A) *Dover Beach*
(B) *The Scholar Gipsy*
(C) *Rugby Chapel*
(D) None of these

917. Who said about Tennyson, that he is, "decidedly the greatest poet of our living poets"?
(A) P.B. Shelley
(B) William Wordsworth
(C) Keats
(D) Matthew Arnold

918. Who propagated the idea of "high seriousness" and "grand style" in poetry ?
(A) Byron (B) Spenser
(C) Matthew Arnold (D) Scott

919. Who advocated "disinterestedness" in literary criticism ?
(A) T.S. Eliot
(B) Aristotle
(C) Matthew Arnold
(D) None of the above

920. Which one of the following poems is the most difficult and obscure, written by Robert Browning ?
(A) *Sordello*
(B) *The Pied Piper*
(C) *The Lost Leader*
(D) *The Lost Mistress*

921. Robert browning is first and foremost a
(A) philosopher
(B) moralist
(C) preacher
(D) satirist

922. Identify the poem, written by Alfred Tennyson, which contains the following line:
"To strive, to seek, to find, and not to yield."
(A) *Maud*
(B) *Ulysses*
(C) *In Memoriam*
(D) *Locksley Hall*

923. One of the Victorian poets, who was interested in "incidents in the development of the soul," is
(A) Alfred Tennyson
(B) Swinburne
(C) Matthew Arnold
(D) Robert Browning

924. The longest poem in the English language, Written by Robert Browning is
(A) *The Last Ride Together*
(B) *The Ring and The Book*
(C) *The Lost Leader*
(D) *Evelyn Hoe*

925. Which one of the following poems written by Browning contains the following lines ?
"O World as God had made it !
.... and lone is duty."
(A) *Sordello*
(B) *Adrea Del Sarto*
(C) *The Gardian Angel*
(D) *The Last Ride Together*

926. *Maud* was written by
(A) Browning
(B) Altred Tennyson
(C) Mathew Arnold
(D) A.H. Clough

927. Who wrote *The Cry of The Children* ?
(A) Robert Browning
(B) Elizabeth Barrett Browning
(C) Alfred Tennyson
(D) P.B. Shelley

928. Who said about Shakespeare :
"Others abide our question. Thou art free. We ask and ask- | Thou smilest and art still, out-topping knowledge ....
(A) Robert browning
(B) Alfred Tennyson
(C) Matthew Arnold
(D) Clough

929. Matthew Arnold is best known for
(A) poetry (B) drama
(C) novel (D) criticism

930. "Poetry is a criticism of life" - the poet who advocated this idea is
(A) Matthew Arnold
(B) Robert Browning
(C) Tennyson
(D) Clough

931. "In the domain of criticism we are still living in the age of Matthew Arnold" - who voiced this idea about Arnold ?
(A) Geoffrey Tillotson
(B) T.S. Eliot
(C) F.R. Leavis
(D) Wismatt

932. Mathew Arnold's *Culture and Anarchy* is a revolt against
(A) politics
(B) Manchesterdom
(C) poverty
(D) ruler

933. 'Men and Women' is a collection of poems written by
(A) William Blake
(B) John Keats
(C) Robert Browning
(D) Rabinder Nath Tagore

934. Maggie is a character in George Eliot's novel. What is the name of that novel ?
(A) *Middlemarch*
(B) *The Mill on The Floss*
(C) *Adam Bede*
(D) *Silas Marner*

935. Who introduced George Eliot to G.H. Lewes?
(A) Herbert Spencer
(B) Milton
(C) William Blake
(D) Sidney

936. George Eliot wrote under the pseudonym of a man. Who was the man ?
(A) G.H. Lewes
(B) G.B. Shaw
(C) G. Tillotson
(D) W. Allen

937. *The Mill on The Floss* (1806), a novel by George Eliot is looked upon as a
(A) historical novel
(B) spiritual autobiography
(C) regional novel
(D) picaresque novel

938. Identify the novelist who is known as, "a novelist of civilization".
(A) Thomas Hardy
(B) George Eliot
(C) Henry James
(D) Virginia Woolf

939. Name the poet who wrote, *The Darkling Thrush.*
(A) John Keats
(B) Thomas Hardy
(C) P.B. Shelley
(D) William Wordsworth

940. Who wrote *The Preface to the Essays* ?
(A) Matthew Arnold
(B) Ruskin
(C) Thomas Hardy
(D) Carlyle

941. "On judicatis Terram," third essay in *Unto This Last*, Ruskin has borrowed the title from the masterpiece of a great writer. Name of that writer is
(A) Aristotle (B) Dante
(C) Plato (D) Goethe

942. The Reform Bill in which the power was passed from aristocracy to the middle classes, came into being in
(A) 1832 (B) 1836
(C) 1833 (D) 1838

943. *Vanity Fair* is a novel by
(A) George Eliot
(B) Thomas Hardy
(C) Dickens
(D) Thackeray

944. Identify the novel in which Dickens said : "No words can express the agony of my soul."
(A) *David Copperfield*
(B) *Hard Times*
(C) *A Tale of Two Cities*
(D) *Great Expectations*

945. *Bleak House*, a serious novel by Dickens and an attack on the legal system, was published in
(A) 1846 (B) 1853
(C) 1859 (D) 1841

946. Pip is a character in one of Dickens' novels. Name of the novel is
(A) *David Copperfield*
(B) *Hard Times*
(C) *Bleak House*
(D) *Great Expectations*

947. Which novelist of the Victorian age, besides Dickens, is known for his brilliant irony and social spirit?
(A) Thackeray
(B) Kingsley
(C) G.K. Chesterton
(D) Huxley

948. *Sonnets from the Portuguese* has been written by
(A) Tennyson
(B) Browning
(C) Mrs. Browning
(D) Shakespeare

949. Who wrote *Ballads and Sonnets* ?
(A) Mrs. Browning
(B) Dante Gabriel Rossetti
(C) Tennyson
(D) William Wordsworth

950. Alfred Tennyson was appointed Poet Laureate in
(A) 1855 (B) 1850
(C) 1854 (D) 1857

951. The poems : 'Palace of Art' and 'A Dream of Fair Women' were written by
(A) Rossetti (B) Browning
(C) Arnold (D) Alfred Tennyson

952. The musical quality of Tennyson's poetry was superb and unsurpassed. Who is the poet who voiced the idea that Tennyson's poetry is musical except one word "scissors" ?

(A) R.C. Jebo
(B) Harold Nicolson
(C) Arnold
(D) T.S. Eliot

953. The subject of *In Memoriam* remained in Tennyson's mind for

(A) sixteen years
(B) seventeen years
(C) fifteen years
(D) twelve years

954. *The Earthly Paradise* (1868-1870) is a collection of

(A) poems
(B) poems and stories
(C) stories in verse
(D) stories in prose

955. Identify the last victorian poet.

(A) Dante Gabriel Rossetti
(B) Swinburne
(C) Mrs. Browning
(D) Alfred Tennyson

956. *Pickwick Papers* was published in

(A) 1832 (B) 1839
(C) 1834 (D) 1836

957. *Henry Esmond* (1852) by Thackeray is a

(A) religious novel
(B) historical novel
(C) regional novel
(D) stream-of consciousness novel

958. Name the writer who said about himself : "I have no brains above my eyes,
I describe what I see."

(A) Thackeray
(B) Dickens
(C) George Eliot
(D) Thomas Hardy

959. 'Lydgate' is a character in George Eliot's one of the novels. The novel is

(A) *Adam Bede*
(B) *Silas Marner*
(C) *Middlemarch*
(D) *The Mill on the Floss*

960. Which of the following works si the fruit of ratiocination

(A) *David Copperfield*
(B) *Pere Gorlot*
(C) *Madame Bovary*
(D) *Moby Dick*

961. Who wrote *The Cloister and The Hearth* (1861), one of the best historical novels of victorian age ?

(A) Charles Reade (B) Thackeray
(C) George Eliot (D) Anthony Trollope

962. Name of the novelist who wrote *Jane Eyre* (1847) is

(A) Emily Bronte
(B) Charlotte Bronte
(C) Thackeray
(D) Anthony Trollope

963. *Life of Charlotte Bronte*, one of best biographies is written by

(A) Mrs. Gaskell
(B) Charles Reade
(C) Anthony Trollope
(D) George Eliot

964. Who wrote *Essays on Milton* ?

(A) Carlyle (B) Macaulay
(C) Charles Reade (D) Mrs. Gaskell

965. Ruskin's English may be called

(A) Johnsonian
(B) Shakespearean
(C) Chaucerean
(D) Spenserian

966. A great critic-poet of Victorian age wrote against materialism and mechanization, the forces that were spilling the moral and spiritual foundation of the Victorian society, the man is

(A) Browning (B) Tennyson
(C) MathewArnold (D) P.B. Shelley

967. When did Victoria become the queen of England ?
(A) 1836 (B) 1837
(C) 1839 (D) 1832

968. *Unto this Last* contains
(A) 3 essays (B) 4 essays
(C) 7 essays (D) 2 essays

969. The duration of Queen Victoria's reign was
(A) 60 years (B) 75 years
(C) 64 years (D) 65 years

970. In the last decade of the nineteenth century the comedy of manners was revived in the works of
(A) Wilde (B) Jones
(C) Pinero (D) All of these

971. *Lady Windermere's Fan* and *Woman of No Importance* are the famous plays of
(A) G.B. Shaw
(B) Oscar Wilde
(C) J.M. Synge
(D) W.B. Yeats

972. Which of the following is G.B. Shaw's first play?
(A) *Widower's House*
(B) *Man and Superman*
(C) *Mrs. Warren's Profession*
(D) *Murder in a Cathedral*

973. The Norwegian dramatist who apparently influenced G.B. Shaw's plays is
(A) Henrik Ibson
(B) J.M. Synge
(C) John Galworthy
(D) Oscar Wilde

974. Who produced a collection of plays, *Plays Pleasant and Unpleasant,* in 1898 ?
(A) Gladstone
(B) Galsworthy
(C) G.B. Shaw
(D) Henrik Ibsen

975. What is Mrs. Warren's profession in G.B. Shaw's *Mrs. Warren's Profession* ?
(A) Tailor (B) Sweeper
(C) Housemaid
(D) Prostitute

976. Francis Thompson, whose greater poetry was published between 1983 and 1897 was influenced by
(A) Miltonic diction
(B) Romantic poetry
(C) metaphysical poets
(D) art for art's sake

Match the following lists using the codes given below.

977. List I **List II**
a. 1830 1. Opium War
b. 1837 2. Victoria's accession
c. 1840 3. Death of George IV

Codes:

	a	b	c
(A)	1	2	3
(B)	3	2	1
(C)	2	3	1
(D)	2	1	3

978. List I **List II**
a. *Poems, Chiefly Lyrical* 1. Carlyle
b. *Sketches by 'Boz'* 2. Tennyson
c. *Sartor Resartus* 3. Dickens

Codes:

	a	b	c
(A)	1	2	3
(B)	3	2	1
(C)	2	3	1
(D)	2	1	3

979. List I **List II**
a. *Master Humphrey's Clock* 1. Cobbett
b. *Sordello* 2. Browning
c. *Rural Rides* 3. Dickens

Codes:

	a	b	c
(A)	3	2	1
(B)	1	2	3
(C)	2	1	3
(D)	2	3	1

980. List I **List II**

a. 1854 1. Crimean War
b. 1864 2. Geneva Convention
c. 1870 3. Death of Dickens

Codes:

	a	b	c
(A)	1	2	3
(B)	2	3	1
(C)	3	2	1
(D)	1	3	2

981. List I **List II**

a. *A Christmas Carol* 1. Thackeray
b. *The Tenant of Wildfell Hall* 2. Dickens
c. *Berry Lyndon* 3. Anne Bronte

Codes:

	a	b	c
(A)	1	2	3
(B)	3	2	1
(C)	2	1	3
(D)	2	3	1

982. List I

a. *Eros and Psyche*
b. *The Daffodil Fields*
c. *Bells and Grass*
d. *Memoirs of a Fox-hunting Man*

List II

1. Siegfried Sassoon
2. Walter de la Mare
3. John Masefield
4. Robert Bridges

Codes:

	a	b	c	d
(A)	3	2	1	4
(B)	2	1	4	3
(C)	4	3	2	1
(D)	1	4	3	2

983. List I

a. *Major Barbara*
b. *The Tragedy of Pompey the Great*
c. *The Feast of Bachhus*
d. *The Silver Box*

List II

1. John Galsworthy
2. G.B. Shaw
3. Masefield
4. Robert Bridges

Codes:

	a	b	c	d
(A)	1	4	3	2
(B)	4	1	2	3
(C)	2	3	4	1
(D)	3	2	1	4

984. List I

a. *The Apple Cart*
b. *Good Friday*
c. *The Return of Ulysses*
d. *The Forsyte Saga*

List II

1. Robert Bridges
2. John Galsworthy
3. G.B. Shaw
4. Masefield

Codes:

	a	b	c	d
(A)	4	1	3	2
(B)	3	4	1	2
(C)	1	2	4	3
(D)	2	1	3	4

985. List I

a. *Back to Methuselah*
b. *Escape*
c. *A Woman of No Importance*
d. *The Constant Wife*

List II

1. John Galsworthy
2. Oscar Wilde
3. Somerset Maugham
4. G.B. Shaw

Codes:

	a	b	c	d
(A)	1	2	3	4
(B)	2	3	4	1
(C)	3	4	1	2
(D)	4	1	2	3

986. List I

a. *The Doctor's Dilemma*
b. *Jack Straw*
c. *An Ideal Husband*
d. *The Star Turns Red*

List II

1. G.B. Shaw
2. Somerset Maugham
3. Oscar Wilde
4. Sean O'Casey

Codes:

	a	b	c	d
(A)	1	2	3	4
(B)	2	3	4	1
(C)	3	4	1	2
(D)	4	1	2	3

987. List I

a. *Pygmalion*
b. *The Birthday Party*
c. *When We Are Married*
d. *Justice*

List II

1. Harold Pinter
2. G.B. Shaw
3. John Galsworthy
4. J.B. Priestley

Codes:

	a	b	c	d
(A)	4	2	1	3
(B)	2	4	3	1
(C)	1	2	3	4
(D)	2	1	3	4

988 List I

a. *The Country House*
b. *Red Roses for Me*
c. *The Dark Lady of the Sonnets*
d. *Caesar's Wife*

List II

1. G.B. Shaw
2. John Galsworthy
3. Sean O'casey
4. Somerset Maugham

Codes:

	a	b	c	d
(A)	3	2	4	1
(B)	4	3	1	2
(C)	2	3	1	4
(D)	1	4	2	3

989. List I	**List II**
a. *Flower Wilderness*	1. John Galsworthy
b. *Immaturity*	2. Henry Arthur Jones
c. *The Liars*	3. G.B. Shaw
d. *Strife*	4. Somerset Maugham

Codes:

	a	b	c	d
(A)	1	2	3	4
(B)	1	3	2	1
(C)	3	4	2	2
(D)	4	1	3	4

990. List I

a. *Time and the Conways*
b. *Everybody's Political What is What*
c. *Salome*
d. *The Care Taker*

List II

1. Harold Pinter
2. Oscar Wilde
3. J.B. Priestley
4. G.B. Shaw

Codes:

	a	b	c	d
(A)	3	4	2	1
(B)	2	3	1	4
(C)	1	2	4	3
(D)	4	1	3	2

991. Who is the portagonist in Samuel Butler's *'The Way of All Flesh"* ?

(A) Beckett (B) Earnest
(C) Flabby (D) Diego

992. At the dawn of mordernism the contrast between generations and attitudes has been pointedly portrayed in *You can Never Tell* of

(A) Galsworthy (B) G.B. Shaw
(C) Ibsen (D) Sinclair

993. Whose novel *Robert Elsmere* appeared in 1888 and sold about 40,000 in its first year of publication in England and about 10,000 in America ?

(A) Mrs Humphry Ward
(B) Samuel Butler
(C) W.H. White
(D) Mrs. Gaskell

994. Who is better known as Mark Rutherford for his *Autobiography of Mark Rutherford*?

(A) Walter Pater (B) Gissing
(C) W.H. White (D) Conan Doyle

995. *Studies in the History of Renaissance* which provoked widespread public debate due to his supposed advocacy of aesthetic hedonism, was written by

(A) W.H. White (B) Moore
(C) Walter Pater (D) Hardy

996. In whose sprawling poetic drama, *The Dynasts,* the delusions and ambitions of humankind are watched over by choric forces, who from their extended perspectives undercut any assumption of heroic action ?

(A) J.M. Synge (B) G.B. Shaw
(C) W.B. Yeats (D) Thomas Hardy

997. Hintock Wood is presented as somehow expressive of the "unfulfilled intention which makes life what it is" in Hardy's

(A) *The Return of the Native*
(B) *The Woodlanders*
(C) *Jude the Obscure*
(D) *Tess of the D'Urbervilles*

998. In which one of Hardy's novels Arabella Donn, the central female character, is presented as both crude and exploitative, unlike his other heroines ?

(A) *The Return of the Native*
(B) *Two on a Tower*
(C) *Jude the obscure*
(D) *The Woodlanders*

999. The writer who under the French influence started a series of attacks on literary censorship, especially Muddies, in the ending decades of the Victorian period is

(A) Walter Pater
(B) George Moore
(C) J.M. Synge
(D) G.B. Shaw

1000. Moore's most memorable and popular work written is his autobiographical comedy

(A) *Hail and Farewell*
(B) *The Brook Kerith*
(C) *A Modern Lover*
(D) *A Dramas in Muslin*

1001. The narrator in *The Private Papers of Henry Ryecroft* announces, "I am no friend of the people as a force, by which the tenor of the time is conditioned, they inspire me with distrust, with fear; as a visible multitude, they make me shrink aloof, and often move to abhorrence." Who is the author of this novel?

(A) George Gissing
(B) George Moore
(C) R.L. Stevenson
(D) H.G. Wells

1002. Sherlock Holmes was introduced to the reading public in 1887 by Sir Arthur Conan Doyle's

(A) *The Lost World*
(B) *Micah Clarke*
(C) *A Study in Scarlet*
(D) *The Exploits of Bregadier Gerard*

1003. *Dracula*, a masterpiece of horripilation, is written by

(A) Conan Doyle (B) Stevenson
(C) Bram Stoker (D) J.M. Barrie

1004. R.L. Stevenson's *Kidnapped* and its sequel *Catriona* are set in 18th century

(A) England (B) Ireland
(C) Italy (D) Scotland

1005. The author of *Kim* (1901) was born in Bombay and in most of his writings, presented a kaleidoscopic view of India. Name the author
(A) Rudyard Kipling
(B) E.M. Fooster
(C) R.L. Stevenson
(D) Joseph Conrad

1006. The Polish seafarer, who often wrote stories and in many of his works presented colonialism as both brutal and brutalizing, is
(A) R.L. Stevenson
(B) Rudyard Kipling
(C) Joseph Conrad
(D) Oscar Wilde

1007. "The conquest of the earth, which mostly means taking it away from those who have a different complexion or slightly flatter noses then ourselves, is not a pretty thing when you look at it too much." This is an extract from Conrad's
(A) *The Secret Agent*
(B) *Under Western Eyes*
(C) *An Outpost of Progress*
(D) *Heart of Darkness*

1008. One of the most influential of Oscar Wilde's plays, a tragedy, was written in French and was translated into English in 1894 by Lord Alfred Douglas. Name the play
(A) *Vera : or, The Nihilists*
(B) *Salome*
(C) *The Duchess of Padua*
(D) *A Florentive Tragedy*

1009. The contemporary of Oscar Wilde who wrote such plays as *Trelawny of the 'Wells'* and *The Second Mrs. Tanqueray was*
(A) G.B. Shaw
(B) John Galsworthy
(C) A.W. Pinero
(D) H. Ibsen

1010. The admirer of Ibsen who wrote the essay *The Quintessence of Ibsenism* is
(A) G.B. Shaw
(B) A.W. Pinero
(C) H.G. Wells
(D) W.B. Yeats

1011. Shaw's early plays which fell 'victim to Lord Chamberlain's censorship include
(A) *The Philanderer*
(B) *Mrs. Warren's Profession*
(C) *Widower's Houses*
(D) Both (A) and (B)

1012. Who wrote a sequence of plays concerned with the ancient hero Cuchulain, beginning with *On Baile's Strand* in 1903 ?
(A) William Sharp
(B) W.B. Yeats
(C) J.M. Synge
(D) E.G. Craig

1013. Who wrote *Riders to the Sea,* a short poetic play which suggests the perennial failure of those who work with and on the sea ?
(A) R.L. Stevenson
(B) Joseph Canrad
(C) J.M. Synge
(D) W.B. Yeats

1014. The remote Mayo coastline, on which the play is set, serves to confine an isolated rural community, one which is disturbed by the arrival of a fugitive, a supposed parricide. Which play of J.M. Synge are we referring to ?
(A) *Riders to the Sea*
(B) *The Tinker's Wedding*
(C) *The Well of the Saints*
(D) *The Playboy of the Western World*

1015. One of the most interesting stage works of J.M. Barrie, it moves from the Mayfair drawing room of Lord Loam to a desert island where the sterling qualities of Loam butler declare themselves. Name the play
(A) *Peter Pan*
(B) *The Little Minister*

(C) *The Admirable Crichton*
(D) *Dear Brutus*

1016. In which one of Barriers plays the plot moves round the mysterious disappearance and reappearance of its title character on a Hebridean island ?
(A) *Mary Rose*
(B) *Dear Brutus*
(C) *Peter Pan*
(D) *The Admirable Crichton*

1017. His own affection for France and the French tradition gave him, as the Parisian episodes in *The Old Wives Tale* suggest, a usefully detached perspective on his own birth place. Who are we talking of ?
(A) Arnold Bennett
(B) H.G. Wells
(C) G.B. Shaw
(D) J.M. Barrie

1018. The sections dealing with Sophia Scales's Paris *Pension* and with the two sister's sojourn at Buxton serve to ramify the idea of the hotel as a no man's land of comfort, tidiness and impersonality. Name the novel being referred to
(A) *Grand Babylon Hotel*
(B) *Imperial Palace*
(C) *Clayhanger*
(D) *The Old Wive's Tale*

1019. Which one of the fictional works of Bennett centres on the limited ambitions and perceptions of a suburban bookseller, his wife and his barely literate servant ?
(A) *Hilda Lessways*
(B) *Riceyman Steps*
(C) *These Twain*
(D) *Clayhanger*

1020. The portagonist, a tyrannical exile on a Pacific island, is also a post-Darwinist Frankenstein, torturing and metamorphizing animals in his 'House of Pain' only to be destroyed as his horrid creations revert to their brutal types. In which novel of H.G. Wells does he appear?
(A) *The War of the Worlds*
(B) *The Time Machine*
(C) *Tono Bungay*
(D) *The Island of Dr. Moreau*

1021. In which novel of H.G. Wells, the nation and the society are seen as ruled by stupidity, "like the leaden goddess of the Dunciad, like some fat, proud flunkey, like pride, like indolence, like all that is darkening and heavy and obstructive in life" ?
(A) *The History of Mr. Polly*
(B) *Kipps*
(C) *The New Machiavelli*
(D) *Ann Veronica*

1022. A detailed study of individual repression and expression is presented in *Mary Olivier : A Life*, a novel which traces the expanding consciousness of a middle-class girl, the youngest child in a family of boys. Who is its author?
(A) H.G. Wells
(B) Arnold Bennett
(C) May Sinclair
(D) Virginia Woolf

1023. *Where Angels Fear to Tread, The Longest Journey, A Room with a View* are the first three novels of
(A) H.G. Wells (B) May Sinclair
(C) Arnold Bennett (D) E.M. Forster

1024. In which of his novels, published posthumously, E.M. Forster probes contemporary taboos, mainly homosexuality ?
(A) *Howards End*
(B) *Maurice*
(C) *A Room with a view*
(D) *A Passage to India*

1025. Forster presents great, and often implied, narrative play with the novel's terse epigraph, 'Only Connect' in
(A) *Howards End*
(B) *A Passage to India*
(C) *The Longest Journey*
(D) *Where Angels Fear to Tread*

1026. Forster's most ambitious and persuasive novel, *A Passage to India*, was published in 1924 following a period in which he had acted as secretary and companion to
(A) Maharaja of Dewas Junior
(B) Maharaja of Dewas Senior
(C) Maharaja of Gwalior Junior
(D) Maharaja of Gwalior Senior

1027. In which one of his novels, Chesterton's anti-centralist, anti-authoritarian, anti-theoretical prejudices serve to shape a Utopian romance about an independent London ruled from an indistinguished inner suburb?
(A) *The Man Who Was Thursday*
(B) *The Napolean of Notting Hill*
(C) *The Trumpet Major*
(D) *Remembrance of Things Past*

1028. Who wrote *The Ballad of Reading Gaol* after his term of imprisonment with hard labour for two years ?
(A) G.B. Shaw
(B) Oscar Wilde
(C) W.B. Yeats
(D) Charlotte Mew

1029. Whose allusive short stories, the first of which appeared in 1894 in one of the celebrated anthologies, *The Yellow Book,* dealt with defeat, and unrequited love ?
(A) A.E. Houseman
(B) Oscar Wilde
(C) Charlotte Mew
(D) None of the above

1030. Wessex, a place in England, is invariably associated with one of the dominant novelists of the modern period. Name him.
(A) H.G. Wells (B) D.H. Lawrence
(C) Thomas Hardy (D) Oscar Wilde

1031. Who wrote in his essay, *The Celtic Twilight,* "I have desired, like every artist, to create a little world out of the beautiful, pleasant and significant things of this marred and clumsy world" ?
(A) W.B. Yeats
(B) G.K. Chesterton
(C) H.G. Wells
(D) Thomas Hardy

1032. Volumes of poetry written by W.B. Yeats include
(A) *The Wild Swans at Coole*
(B) *The Tower*
(C) *The Winding Stair and other Poems*
(D) All of the above

1033. Which of Yeats's poems opens with the words "Between extremities/Man runs his course" ?
(A) *The Celtic Twilight*
(B) *The Tower*
(C) *Vacillation*
(D) *Lapis Lazuli*

1034. Yeats expressed his system of art and symbols in his highly speculative essay,
(A) *The Celtic Twilight*
(B) *A Vision*
(C) *The Dawn*
(D) *On Poetry*

1035. "A Shudder in the loins engenders there
The broken wall, the burning root and tower
And Agamemnon dead."
This is an extract from Yeats's
(A) *The Tower*
(B) *Sailing to Byzantium*
(C) *Leda and the Swan*
(D) *The Second Coming*

1036. "Things fall apart; the centre cannot hold". This is how opens Yeats's prophetic poem,
(A) *Vacillation*
(B) *The Second Coming*
(C) *Sailing to Byzantium*
(D) *The Hound of Heaven*

1037. "Consume my heart away; sick with desire
And fastened to a dying animal
It knows not what it is; and gather me
Into the artifice of eternity."
Which poem of Yeats ends with these lines?

(A) *Sailing to Byzantium*
(B) *The Tower*
(C) *Lapis Lauli*
(D) *Leda and the Swan*

1038. Name the poet who was killed in 1915 at the battle of Laos, But his *Marlborough and Other Poems* of 1916 ran through six editions in its first year of publication ?
(A) Edward Thomas
(B) Rupert Brooke
(C) C.H. Sorley
(D) George Herbert

1039. One of the most influential autobiographies dealing with soldier's experiences of the war was Robert Graves'
(A) *Sherston's Progress*
(B) *Goodbye to All That*
(C) *Memoirs of an Infantry Officer*
(D) None of the above

1040. Who wrote a trilogy on war experience including *Memoirs of a Fox Hunting Man, Memoirs of an Infantry Officer* and *Sherston's Progress* ?
(A) Sigfried Sassoon
(B) Robert Graves
(C) Edward Thomas
(D) C.H. Sorley

1041. Who wrote war poems such as '*Break of Day in the Trenches*', '*Louse Hunting*' and '*Dead Man's Dump*' ?
(A) Wilfred Owen
(B) Isaac Rosenberg
(C) Sigfried Sasson
(D) None of the above

1042. The great admirer of Keats who wrote a poem, *The Parable of the Old Man and the Young*, peculiarly turning the story of Abraham and Isaac in the final couplet, is
(A) Sigfried Sassoon
(B) Isaac Rosenbery
(C) Wilfred Owen
(D) C.H. Sorley

1043. Who in his pithy essay *Art and Life,* had argued that "the correspondence between art and life which we so habitually assume is not at all constant and requires much correction before it can be trusted" ?
(A) Ellen Wilkinson
(B) Richard Bloomsbury
(C) E.M. Forster
(D) Roger Fry

1044. The first English newspaper, devoted exclusively to Women's interests, founded in 1903, was
(A) *Daily Mail*
(B) *Daily Express*
(C) *Daily Mirror*
(D) *Daily Vision*

1045. Who wrote the essays, 'Modern Fiction' and 'Mr. Bennett and Mrs. Brown' ?
(A) Noel Coward
(B) Dorothea Richardson
(C) Virginia Woolf
(D) Lytton Starchey

1046. The club formed in 1920, centered around Leslie Stephen's two daughters, their husbands, their friends and neighbours, was named
(A) the Bloomsbury Group
(B) the Memoir Club
(C) the Stephen's Club
(D) Eminent Victorians

1047. A "coherence in things" is what Mrs. Ramsay recognizes in a visionary moment of tranquility as "a stability.... something..... immune from change." Which novel of Virginia Woolf is being referred to in these lines ?
(A) *Mrs. Dalloway*
(B) *The Waves*
(C) *Between the Acts*
(D) *To the Lighthouse*

1048. In her longest novel, Woolf stresses the nature of a local awareness of the sequential passage of time from the 1880s to the 1930s and explores the consequences and

processes of waiting, learning and ageing. Name the novel.
(A) *The Years*
(B) *The Voyage Out*
(C) *A Room of One's Own*
(D) *Orlando*

1049. In which of her novels, Woolf apparently seeks to both dissolve and define character in a fanciful connection of English history and shifting gender ?
(A) *A Room of One's Own*
(B) *Mrs. Dalloway*
(C) *The Years*
(D) *Orlando*

1050. Who wrote succinct narratives as *In a German Pension, Bliss, and other Stories* and *The Garden Party and other Stories* ?
(A) Marcel Proust
(B) Virginia Woolf
(C) Katherine Mansfield
(D) Victoria Sackville-West

1051. Katherine Mansfield draws significantly on the landscapes and flora of her native country, as in *The Aloe.* What was her native country ?
(A) England (B) USA
(C) Russia (D) New Zealand

1052. The American philosopher and psychologist who coined the phrase "stream of consciousness" is
(A) Marcel Proust
(D) Sigmund Freud
(C) Henry James
(D) Bertrand Russell

1053. Prior to Proust, who had pioneered the technique of 'Stream of consciousness' in France?
(A) Rousseau (B) Balzac
(C) Dujardin (D) Moupassant

1054. *Pilgrimage*, Dorothy Richardson's sequence of novels, contained how many volumes in toto ?
(A) 7 (B) 13
(C) 17 (D) 21

1055. Who proposed to give "new, really new feelings, a whole new line of new emotion, which will get us out of the emotional rut" in a series of essays in 1920s ?
(A) Woolf
(B) Mansfield
(C) Richardson
(D) Lawrence

1056. In which of his essays Lawrence proclaimed the novelist to be superior to the saint, the scientist, the philosopher and the poet ?
(A) *The Man who Died*
(B) *Why the Novel Matters*
(C) *Victorian Prose*
(D) *Surgery for the Novel - or a Bomb*

1057. At the opening of the novel the Brangwen family farm, divided from the sprawling mining village by a canal, seems to be on "the safe side of civilization", and the male members of the family are mystically linked by a "blood-intimacy" to the fertility of the soil they till. Which novel of Lawrence is being referred to here ?
(A) *The Rainbow*
(B) *Sons and Lovers*
(C) *Women in Love*
(D) *Lady Chatterley's Lover*

1058. In which novel of Lawrence, Gerald Crich, the son of a colliery owner and the efficient masterer both of his men and of animal resistance, conceives of a world in which "the will of man was the determining factor"?
(A) *Sons and Lovers*
(B) *The Rainbow*
(C) *Women in Love*
(D) *Kangaroo*

1059. Gerald Crich appears in which of the following novels of D.H. Lawrence ?
(A) *The Plumed Serpent*

(B) Dante
(C) Laforgue
(D) Pound

1071. Whose account of contemporary French Poetry, *The Symbolist Movement in Literature* (1899), had impressed Eliot in his early career ?
(A) Laforgue
(B) Arthur Symons
(C) F.H. Bradley
(D) Ezra Pound

1072. In which of his essays Eliot argued that "no poet, no artist of any art, has his complete meaning alone" ?
(A) *Tradition and the Individual Talent*
(B) *The Use of Poetry and Use of Criticism*
(C) *The Metaphysical Poets*
(D) *Twentieth Century Poetry*

1073. "... Sang within the bloody wood
When Agamemnon cried aloud
And let their liquid shiftings fall
To stain the stiff dishonoured shroud."
This is an extract from Eliot's
(A) *The Waste Land*
(B) *The Love Song of J. Alfred Prufrock*
(C) *Sweeny Among the Nightingales*
(D) *Gerontion*

1074. "Words Strain
Crack and sometimes break, under the burden,
Under the tension, slip, slide, perish,
Decay with imprecision, will not stay in place,
Will not stay still"
This is an extract from Eliot's
(A) *East Coker*
(B) *The Waste Land*
(C) *Journey of the Magi*
(D) *Burnt Norton*

1075. Eliot's verse-comedies include
(A) *The Cocktail Party*
(B) *The Confidential clerk*
(C) *The Elder Statesman*
(D) All of the above

1076. *Valmouth*, *Santal*, *The Flower beneath the Foot*, *Sorrow in Sunlight* and *Concerning the Eccentricities of Cardinal Pirelli* are the last five completed novels of
(A) Edith Sitwell
(B) James Joyce
(C) Ronald Firbank
(D) Wilfred Owen

1077. Who wrote the anthology of poems *Facade* in 1922 ?
(A) Wilfred Owen
(B) Edith Sitwell
(C) John Masefield
(D) T.S. Eliot

1078. Edith Sitwell's volumes of poetry include
(A) *Street Songs*
(B) *Green Song*
(C) *The Song of the Cold*
(D) All of the above

1079. The collection of twelve stories finished in 1905 by James Joyce at the outset of his literary career, but which was published in 1914, was entitled
(A) *Finnegans Wake*
(B) *Dubliners*
(C) *Ulysses*
(D) *Of Human Bondage*

1080. Which work of Joyce Eliot was referring to when he described certain portions of it as "almost the finest I have read: I have lived on it ever since I have read it" ?
(A) *Finnegan's Wake*
(B) *Ulysses*
(C) *A Portrait of the Artist as a Young Man*
(D) *Of Human Bondage*

1081. The adolescent Stephen is the protagonist in Joyce's
(A) *Finnegan's Wake*
(B) *Ulysses*

(C) *A Portrait of the Artist as a Young Man*
(D) *Of Human Bondage*

1082. Which of Joyce's novels follows the extraordinary vagaries of Bloom's mind as he shops, lusts, cooks, eats, relieves himself in the privy, and goes about his business?
(A) *Ulysses*
(B) *A Portrait of the Artist as a Young Man*
(C) *Finnegan's Wake*
(D) *Of Human Bondage*

1083. The thought and actions, in *Ulysses*, of the three principal characters, are interwoven with the diverse life of Dublin on a single day, *i.e.,*
(A) 16 May 1901
(B) 16 June 1901
(C) 16 May 1904
(D) 16 June 1904

1084. *Sweeny Agonistes,* published in 1932, was an experiment in modern playwriting by
(A) James Joyce
(B) Sean O'Casey
(C) J.B. Priestley
(D) T.S. Eliot

1085. Who wrote the plays *Heartbreak House* and *Saint Joan* ?
(A) T.S. Eliot
(B) G.B. Shaw
(C) Henrik Ibsen
(D) W.B. Yeats

1086. In which of O'Casey's plays the theme of deception and self-deception is played ironically back in a revolutionary, urban setting?
(A) *The Shadow of a Gunman*
(B) *Playboy of the Western World*
(C) *The Plough and the Stars*
(D) *The Silver Tassie*

1087. Who in the immediately post-war years achieved success with *The Vortex*, a high-flown exploration of the condition of a drug-addict fermented by his slovenly mother's adulteries ?
(A) Sean O'Casey
(B) J.B. Priestly
(C) Noel Coward
(D) R.C. Sheriff

1088. Which of the following plays of Coward is a study of the miserable marriage of a playwright and his novelist-wife ?
(A) *Bitter Sweet*
(B) *The Rat Trap*
(C) *Private Lives*
(D) *Cavalcade*

1089. Which of the following is not written by Noel Coward ?
(A) *The Vortex*
(B) *Design for Living*
(C) *Cock-a-Doodle Dandy*
(D) *The Queen Was in the Parlour*

1090. One of the plays of Noel Coward, written in five days in 1941, ran for 1,997 performances in the West End of London as well as touring the provinces. Name the play.
(A) *Cavalcade*
(B) *The Rat Trap*
(C) *Bitter Sweet*
(D) *Blithe Sprit*

1091. Who during the Second World War, established his reputation as a novelist with *The Good Companions* and *Angel Pavement* ?
(A) Robert Graves
(B) J.B. Priestly
(C) Herbert Read
(D) R.C. Sheriff

1092. Which of the following is among the best known plays of J.B. Priestly ?
(A) *Time and Conways*
(B) *When We Are Married*
(C) *An Inspector Calls*
(D) All of the above

1093. Who in his highly coloured autobiography, *Goodbye to All That,* describes a sense of alienation from post-war student life in Oxford ?
(A) Herbert Read

(B) Robert Graves
(C) Wilfred Owen
(D) Stephen Spender

1094. Who is the author of *Journey's End,* that combines realism with the kind of restraint which is expressive of far more the stiff-upper-lip heroics of idealized British Officers ?
(A) R.C. Sheriff
(B) J.C. Powys
(C) J.B. Priestley
(D) Robert Graves

1095. The military officer who wrote an epic of suffering and comradeship, *In Parenthesis,* is
(A) David Jones
(B) Stephen Spender
(C) John Cowper Powys
(D) William Gerhardie

1096. Who wrote the vast and idiosyncratic novel. *A Glastonbury Romance* (1932) ?
(A) Compton-Burnett
(B) Henry Green
(C) John Cowper Powys
(D) Noel Coward

1097. A sense of disillusionment and an amused superciliousness runs through Gerhardie's two first, and best, novels, *Futility : A Novel on Russian Themes* and
(A) *Fifth Column*
(B) *The King's Quair*
(C) *The Criterion*
(D) *The Polyglots*

1098. *Party Going,* with a seemingly unpromising subject of the four-hour delay experienced by set of smart party-goes, is a remarkable novel written by
(A) L.G. Gibbon
(B) Robert Green
(C) Henry Green
(D) David Jones

1099. In which of Henry Green's novels Dupret, the son of a factory owner walks through the artisan streets as he remarks on their air of "terrible respectability on too little money" ?
(A) *Loving* (B) *Living*
(C) *Party-Going*
(D) None of the above

1100. Gibbon made a wide ranging representation of working-class life and working-class perception in her remarkable triology collectively known as
(A) *A Scots Quair*
(B) *A King's Quair*
(C) *Pack My Bag*
(D) *Travels in London*

1101. Which of the following is not included in Lewis Grassie Gibbon's triology *A Scots Quair*?
(A) *Sunset Song*
(B) *Cloud House*
(C) *Remote People*
(D) *Grey Granite*

1102. In which novel of Gibbon, Chris's communist son Ewan is fired by the idea that he is himself History: " A Hell of a thing to be History! – not a student, a historian, a tinkling reformer, but LIVING HISTORY ONESELF..." ?
(A) *Sunset Song*
(C) *Cloud House*
(C) *Dolores*
(D) *Grey Granite*

1103. Who after disowning her first published work, *Dolores*, wrote eighteen novels describing an enclosed, circumscribed and dying historical world, drab in its consistency ?
(A) L.G. Gibbon
(B) Ivy Compton-Burnett
(C) Bertic Wooster
(D) Koestler

1104. In which novel of Compton-Burnett, Miles Mowbray serenely expounds the principle that his three unmarried daughters have the life they ought to have: "A life in the family home, with the protection and provision that is fit for them" ?

(A) *Men and wives*
(B) *Parents and Children*
(C) *A Father and his Fate*
(D) *A House and its Head*

1105. P.G. Wodehouse introduced his most famous characters, Bertie Wooster and his man Jeeves in an unremarkable story in the collection

(A) *A Handful of Dust*
(B) *The Man with Two Left Feet and Other Stories*
(C) *My Man Jeeves and Other Stories*
(D) None of the above

1106. Novels such as *Decline and Fall*, *A Handful of Dust*, *Vile Bodies* and *Black Mischief* were written by

(A) Henry Green
(B) P.G. Wodehouse
(C) Christopher Isherwood
(D) Evelyn Waugh

1107. Which novel of Evelyn Waugh is set in the tattering African Kingdom of Azania ?

(A) *A Handful of Dust*
(B) *Vile Bodies*
(C) *Black Mischief*
(D) *Decline and Fall*

1108. Which novel of Evelyn Waugh explores the painful collapse the illusions and complacencies of a rural feudalism, represented by Tony Last, and exposes the surface values and cynicism of the thoroughly modern and essentially metropolitan "bright young things" ?

(A) *A Handful of Dust*
(B) *Vile Bodies*
(C) *Decline and Fall*
(D) *Black Mischief*

1109. Charles Ryder is the narrator and protagonist in Evelyn Waugh's

(A) *Helena*
(B) *Brideshead*
(C) *Remote People*
(D) None of the above

1110. *Men at Arms, Officers and Gentlemen* and *Unconditional Surrender* constitute the ambitious trilogy of Evelyn Waugh,

(A) *The Loved One*
(B) *Eyless in Gaza*
(C) *Sword of Honour*
(D) None of the above

1111. *Point Counter Point*, as suggested by its title, attempts to investigate an analogy with musical counterpoint by offering glimpses of diverse experience which seem to be observed simultaneously. Identify its author from among the following

(A) P.G. Wodehouse
(B) Evelyn Waugh
(C) D.H. Lawrence
(D) Aldous Huxley

1112. Aldous Huxley's most celebrated book is a Utopian, or rather Dystopian, fantasy

(A) *Crome Yellow*
(B) *Barren Leaves*
(C) *Antic Hay*
(D) *Brave New World*

1113. In *Brave New World* the calender is dated AF, which stands for

(A) after Falstaff
(B) after Ford
(C) after France
(D) after Fleming

1114. A. Huxley described his experiences of India in the travel book

(A) *Jesting Pilate*
(B) *Remote People*
(C) *Travels in Arabia Deserts*
(D) None of the above

1115. Apart from his collaborative experiments with drama, he is also remembered for his two most individual works of fiction, *Mr. Norris Changes Trains* and *Goodbye to Berlin* ?

(A) W.H. Auden

(B) *Women in Love*
(C) *The Virgin and the Gipsy*
(D) *The Rainbow*

1060. Which of the following travel books was/were written by Lawrence ?
(A) *Sea and Sardina*
(B) *Mornings in Mexico*
(C) *Etrusean Places*
(D) All of the above

1061. Much of Lawrence's best poetry, concentrated, stark and unrhymed appeared in the volume of 1923,
(A) *Georgian Poetry*
(B) *Pansies*
(C) *Peacock Pie*
(D) *Birds, Beasts and Flowers*

1062. Who was appointed the Poet Laureate in 1930 in succession to Robert Bridges ?
(A) Walter de La Mare
(B) John Masefield
(C) Arthur Waugh
(D) Wyndham Lewis

1063. Eliot's *The Waste Land* appeared first in the quarterly magazine,
(A) *Imagists*
(B) *The Criterion*
(C) *Blast*
(D) *Life*

1064. Whose most innovative novel *Tarr* is set in an artist-dominated Paris in which a frantic bohemianism has assumed a political and sexual arrogance in the face of bourgeois "sentimentalism" ?
(A) Ezra Pound
(B) Arthur Waugh
(C) Wydham Lewis
(D) Masefield

1065. In which of Lewis's political and artistic manifestoes, he has argued that society had been inevitably revolutionized by mechanical change and that both change and revolution ought to be embraced by the artist ?
(A) *The Art of Being Ruled*
(B) *The Human Age*
(C) *The Apes of God*
(D) *Malign Fiesta*

1066. Who wrote the novel *Death of a Hero*, which deals with both the frustrations of pre-war English society and "the false ideals, the unintelligent ideas.... the humbug, the hypocrisy, the stupidity" of those who waged the war ?
(A) D.H. Lawrence
(B) James Joyce
(C) Aldington
(D) Joseph Conrad

1067. Which two novelists collaborated on the novels *The Inheritance* of 1901 and *Romance* of 1903 ?
(A) Madox Ford and Aldington
(B) Aldington and Joseph Conrad
(C) Joseph Conrad and Madox Ford
(D) None of the above

1068. Christopher Tietjens, an unhappy lover, a largely unsuccessful soldier, and a rootless, passive and neurotic survivor after 1918, is the protagonist of Ford Madox Ford's tetralogy,
(A) *The Good Soldier*
(B) *Parade's End*
(C) *The Fifth Queen*
(D) *The Inheritors*

1069. The earlier poets who had great influence on T.S. Eliot's poetry include
(A) Boudelaire
(B) Dante
(C) Laforgue
(D) All of the above

1070. When in *Ash-Wednesday* and *Four Quartets* Eliot attempted to explore 'beyond the frontiers of ordinary consciousness', his immediate prompting and much of his reference reflected the influence of
(A) Boudelaire

1141. "Never-Never Land" is depicted in
(A) *The Pigeon* by John Galsworthy
(B) *Peter Pan* by J.M. Barrie
(C) *The Apple Cart* by G.B. Shaw
(D) *Pillars of Society* by Henrick Ibsen

1142. Human nature does not change. This theme runs in
(A) J.M. Barrie – *Dear Brutus*
(B) Somerset Maugham – *Sheppey*
(C) John Galsworthy – *Strifie*
(D) James Bridie – *The Angel*

1143. Who says, "Godot will come and we will be saved. If we drop him He will punish us." ?
(A) Estragon
(B) Vladimir
(C) Pozzo
(D) Lucky

1144. Who is the author of these poetic plays, *The Countess Cathleen*, *Deidre*, *The Green Helmet*, *A Full Moon in March* ?
(A) W.B. Yeats
(B) T.S. Eliot
(C) J.M. Barrie
(D) John M. Synge

1145. One of J.M. Synge's play depicts the tragedy of the fisher community by the story of the pathetic Maurya. Name it.
(A) *The Playboy of the Western World*
(B) *Riders to the Sea*
(C) *The Shadow of the Glen*
(D) *The Well of the Saints*

1146. The concept of the Absurd was originated by Albert Camus, the French existential philosopher, novelist. But it was popularized by
(A) Samuel Beckett
(B) Ionesco
(C) N.F. Simpson
(D) James Saunders

1147. Ionesco's Jack is the funniest example of nonconformity. Jack, the protagonist refuses to marry the girl because she is not ugly enough. How many noses does this girl have ?
(A) One (B) Three
(C) Two (D) No nose at all

1148. In the play *Chairs*, Ionesco shows emptiness of existence by representing
(A) Two people on a chair
(B) Empty chairs
(C) Hollow chairs
(D) Legless chairs

1149. Who are the exponents of the theatre of total cruelty ?
(A) Jean Genet
(B) Peter Weiss
(C) Jose Triana
(D) All of the above

1150. These writers have had a sad past which made them bitter. Identify the writer correctly matched with the circumstances of his life.

(A) Jean Genet	1.	Child of Castro's revolution
(B) Dostoevsky	2.	A jailbird of Russia
(C) Jose Triana	3.	German refugee
(D) James Bridie	4.	The Angel

1151. In which of Woolf's novels Ms. La Trobbe appears ?.
(A) *To the Lighthouse*
(B) *Mrs. Dalloway*
(C) *Between the Acts*
(D) *Orlando*

1152. Who of the following continental authors influenced English drama considerably ?
(A) Turgenev (B) Ibsen
(C) Baudelair (D) Bergson

1153. Who employed stream-of-consciousness?
(A) Jane Austen
(B) George Eliot
(C) Virginia Woolf
(D) Thomas Hardy

(B) Emily Dickinson
(C) Edith Sitwell
(D) Elizabeth Jennings

1167. In which work does W.B. Yeats pay a tribute to Lady Gregory and Anne Gregory and reminiscences the old glory of his ancestors ?
(A) *A Full Moon in March*
(B) *The Tower*
(C) *Stream and Sun*
(D) *The Winding Stair*

1168. Who wrote the poem *Lapis-Lazuli* ?
(A) Robert Browning
(B) W.B. Yeats
(C) Ezra Pound
(D) Stephen Spender

1169. Who evokes supernatural atmosphere in his poems like, *The Listeners, Peacock Pie and The Veil* ?
(A) S.T. Coleridge
(B) Mrs. Radcliffe
(C) Walter de la Mare
(D) None of the above

1170. Who of the following was never a Poet Laureate?
(A) John Masefield
(B) Robert Bridges
(C) Lord Tennyson
(D) Sir Henry Newbolt

1171. Which poem of John Masefield contains a sinner's confession ?
(A) *Lollingdon Downs*
(B) *Enslaved*
(C) *The Everlasting Mercy*
(D) *Right Royal*

1172. Who wrote the popular poem *Sea-Fever* ?
(A) Walter de la Mare
(B) W.H. Davies
(C) John Masefield
(D) W.B. Yeats

1173. Name the author of *The Day of the Triffids*, an improbable scientific fantasy of the future, which describes lethal plants which uproot themselves and walk.
(A) H.G. Wells
(B) John Wyndham
(C) Nevil Shute
(D) None of the above

1174. Three of the following have distinguished themselves as short story writers. Identify the one who does not fall in this category.
(A) H.E. Bates
(B) Katherine Mansfield
(C) Iris Murdoch
(D) V.S. Pritchett

1175. This boy's book rejected by 56 publishers was finally accepted by Faber and Faber. Now, it has been widely acclaimed and is on the school/college syllabi in U.S.A., England, India and many other countries. Identify the book.
(A) William Golding – *Lord of The Flies*
(B) J.R.R. Tolkien – *The Lord of the Rings*
(C) R.M. Ballantyne – *The Coral Island*
(D) R.L. Stevenson – *Kidnapped*

1176. One of Shaw's plays ridicules the popular romantic conception of the professional soldier's courage and incidentally the pretensions of the aristocracy. Identify it.
(A) *Candida*
(B) *Arms and the Man*
(C) *The Apple Cast*
(D) *Man and Superman*

1177. Who is the author of plays : *The Silver Box* and *Strife* ?
(A) John Osborne
(B) John Galsworthy
(C) G.B. Shaw
(D) Samuel Beckett

1178. Who said, "A human being is the best plot there is .... " ?
(A) John Galsworthy
(B) T.S. Eliot
(C) G.B. Shaw
(D) Henrick Ibsen

1179. In which novel a girl wearing a scarlet sash means that she is a member of the Junior Anti-Sex League ?

(A) William Golding – *The Inheritors*
(B) George Orwell's – *1984*
(C) George Moore's – *Confessions of a Young Man*
(D) H.G. Well's – *Kipps*

1180. In which novel Aldous Huxley depicts a scientific utopia of the Wellsian conception?

(A) *Brave New World Revisited*
(B) *Island*
(C) *Eyeless in Gaza*
(D) *Brave New World*

1181. Arthur Conan Doyle, Edgar Wallace, Ian Fleming, Erle Stanley Gardner are all known for their detective novels. But, who was the first English novelist to take up detection of crime ?

(A) John Buchan, Lord Tweedsmuir
(B) Dr. Watson
(C) William Wilkie Collins
(D) E.C. Bentley

1182. What 20th century novel has as its epigraph the words "only connect" ?

(A) Conrad – *Almayer's Folly*
(B) F.M. Forster – *Howards End*
(C) D.H. Lawrence – *Sons and Lovers*
(D) Virginia Woolf – *Mrs. Dalloway*

1183. Name the unfinished autobiography of William MacNeice.

(A) *Holes in the Sky*
(B) *Plant and Phantom*
(C) *The Strings are False*
(D) *Overtures to Death*

1184. Auden moved from a conspicuous Marxist alignment in his early poetic career to the Christian existentialism of

(A) Nietzse (B) Hobbes
(C) Rousseau (D) Kierkegard

1185. Whose painting of the fall of Icarus Auden refers to in his poem *Musee des Beaux Arts* ?

(A) Brueghel (B) Raphael
(C) Da Vinci (D) None of these

1186. Auden's *The Sea and the Mirror* is a response to

(A) Milton (B) Shakespeare
(C) Freud (D) Yeats

Match the following lists using the codes given below.

1187.

List I	List II
a. *The Portrait of a Lady*	1. H.G. Wells
b. *An Outcast of the Islands*	2. Henry James
c. *Marriage*	3. Joseph Conrad

Codes:

	a	b	c
(A)	1	3	2
(B)	1	2	3
(C)	2	3	1
(D)	3	2	1

1188.

List I	List II
a. *The Invisible Man*	1. H.G. Wells
b. *The Voyage Out*	2. Samuel Butler
c. *The Way of All Flesh*	3. Virginia Woolf

Codes:

	a	b	c
(A)	1	3	2
(B)	1	2	3
(C)	3	1	2
(D)	3	2	1

1189.

List I	List II
a. *Jacob's Room*	1. Joseph Conrad
b. *Spring Rays*	2. George Moore
c. *The Shadow Line*	3. Virginia Woolf

Codes:

	a	b	c
(A)	2	3	1
(B)	3	2	1
(C)	2	1	3
(D)	1	3	2

1190.

List I	List II
a. *Clayhanger*	1. E.M. Forster

b. *The Longest Journey* 2. Arnold Bennett
c. *Ledan* 3. Aldous Huxley

Codes:

	a	b	c
(A)	3	1	2
(B)	2	3	1
(C)	2	1	3
(D)	3	2	1

1191. List I **List II**

a. *The Author's Craft* 1. G.H. Gissing
b. *By the Ionian sea* 2. George Moore
c. *Confessions of a Young Man* 3. Arnold Bennet

Codes

	a	b	c
(A)	3	2	1
(B)	1	2	3
(C)	1	3	2
(D)	3	1	2

1192. List I

a. *Hilda Lessways*
b. *Tales from the Hills*
c. *Time must Have a Stop*
d. *Two Cheers for Democracy*

List II

1. Aldous Huxley 2. Arnold Bennett
3. E.M. Forster 4. Rudyard Kipling

Codes:

	a	b	c	d
(A)	2	4	1	3
(B)	3	2	4	1
(C)	1	3	2	4
(D)	4	1	3	2

1193. List I **List II**

a. *Arbinger Harvest* 1. E.M. Forster
b. *The Five Nations* 2. Rudyard Kipling
c. *The Burning Wheel* 3. V.S. Naipaul
d. *The Mimic Man* 4. Aldous Huxley

Codes:

	a	b	c	d
(A)	3	4	2	1
(B)	2	3	1	4
(C)	4	2	3	1
(D)	1	2	4	3

1194. List I **List II**

a. *A Burnt Out Case* 1. C.P. Snow
b. *The Mystic Masseur* 2. Kingsley Amis
c. *Lucky Jim* 3. V.S. Naipaul
d. *Strangers and Brothers* 4. Graham Greene

Codes:

	a	b	c	d
(A)	4	2	3	1
(B)	4	3	2	1
(C)	4	1	3	2
(D)	1	2	3	4

1195. List I **List II**

a. Graham Greene 1. *The Anathemata*
b. W.G. Golding 2. *Pincher Martin*
c. David Jones 3. *May We Burrow Your Husband?*
d. Kingsley Amis 4. *I Like it Here*

Codes:

	a	b	c	d
(A)	4	1	2	3
(B)	3	2	1	4
(C)	1	3	4	2
(D)	2	4	3	1

1196. List I **List II**

a. Anthony Powell 1. *The Great Tradition*
b. F.R. Leavis 2. *The Music of Time*
c. W.G. Golding 3. *Our Man in Havana*
d. Graham Greene 4. *The Spire*

Codes:

	a	b	c	d
(A)	2	1	4	3
(B)	3	4	1	2
(C)	1	4	3	2
(D)	4	2	1	3

1197. List I **List II**

a. *The Scorpion God* 1. F.R. Leavis
b. *Revaluation* 2. I.A. Richards
c. *The Meaning of Meaning* 3. William Golding

Codes:

	a	b	c
(A)	1	2	3
(B)	3	2	1
(C)	3	1	2
(D)	2	3	1

1198. List I **List II**

a. *Room at the Top* 1. George Orwell
b. *Nineteen Eighty Four* 2. John Braine
c. *Time for a Tiger* 3. Anthony Burgess

Codes:

	a	b	c
(A)	1	2	3
(B)	2	1	3
(C)	2	3	1
(D)	3	2	1

1199. List I **List II**

a. *Under the Net* 1. Irish Murdock
b. *The Shadowy Waters* 2. W.B. Yeats
c. *The Siege of Krishnapur* 3. J.G. Ferrell

Codes:

	a	b	c
(A)	3	2	1
(B)	1	2	3
(C)	3	1	2
(D)	2	3	1

1200. List I **List II**

a. *God's Grandeur* 1. W.B. Yeats
b. *The Winding Stair* 2. G.M. Hopkins
c. *The Orators* 3. W.H. Auden

Codes:

	a	b	c
(A)	2	3	1
(B)	3	2	1
(C)	1	2	3
(D)	2	1	3

1201. List I **List II**

a. *Responsibilities* 1. T.S. Eliot
b. *The Winhover* 2. G.M. Hopkins
c. *The Hollow Men* 3. W.B. Yeats

Codes:

	a	b	c
(A)	3	2	1
(B)	1	2	3
(C)	2	3	1
(D)	3	1	2

1202. List I **List II**

a. *Harry Ploughman* 1. W.H. Auden
b. *Ash Wednesday* 2. G.M. Hopkins
c. *Look Stranger* 3. T.S. Eliot

Codes:

	a	b	c
(A)	1	2	3
(B)	3	2	1
(C)	2	3	1
(D)	2	1	3

1203. List I **List II**

a. *The Rock* 1. T.S. Eliot
b. *The Poet's Tongue* 2. Dylan Thomas
c. *The Map of Love* 3. W.H. Auden

Codes:

	a	b	c
(A)	3	2	1
(B)	3	1	2
(C)	1	2	3
(D)	1	3	2

1204. List I **List II**

a. W.H. Auden 1. *Vienna*
b. Stephen Spender 2. *New Year Letter*
c. Dylan Thomas 3. *Twenty-Five poems*

Codes:

	a	b	c
(A)	2	3	1
(B)	2	1	3
(C)	1	2	3
(D)	1	3	2

1205. List I **List II**

a. *The Sleeping Beauty* 1. Stephen Spender
b. *The Pisan Cantos* 2. Ezra Pound
c. *Ruins and Visions* 3. Edith Sitwell

Codes:

	a	b	c
(A)	3	2	1
(B)	1	3	2
(C)	2	1	3
(D)	3	1	2

1206. List I **List II**

a. *The Earth Compels* 1. Dylan Thomas
b. *Transitional Poem* 2. Louis MacNeice
c. *18 Poems* 3. C. Day Lewis

Codes:

	a	b	c
(A)	1	3	2
(B)	3	1	2
(C)	2	1	3
(D)	2	3	1

1207. List I

a. *The Growth of Love*
b. *Reynard the Fox*
c. *Peacock Pie*
d. *The Heart's Journey*

List II

1. Masefield
2. Robert Bridges
3. Siegfried Sassoon
4. Walter de la Mare

Codes:

	a	b	c	d
(A)	2	1	4	3
(B)	2	1	3	4
(C)	4	3	1	2
(D)	4	3	2	1

1208. List I

a. Brian Friel
b. Shelagh Stephenson
c. Dennis Potter
d. Ted Hughes

List II

1. *The Singing Detective*
2. *The Memory of Water*
3. *Dancing at Lughnasa*
4. *The Bull Moses*

	a	b	c	d
(A)	2	3	4	1
(B)	3	2	1	4
(C)	2	1	4	3
(D)	3	4	1	2

1209. List I

a. *Tales from Ovid*
b. *The Triumph of Love*
c. *Field Work*
d. *Courtyard in Delft*

List II

1. Ted Hughes
2. Derek Mahon
3. Seamus Heany
4. Geoffrey Hill

	a	b	c	d
(A)	1	2	3	4
(B)	2	1	4	3
(C)	3	2	1	4
(D)	1	4	3	2

1210. List I **List II**

a. Tom Sharpe 1. *The Cement Garden*
b. Malcolm Bradbury 2. *Rates of Exchange*
c. Gaskell 3. *North and South*
d. Ian McEwan 4. *The Wild Alternative*

Codes:

	a	b	c	d
(A)	2	3	4	1
(B)	1	4	3	2
(C)	4	2	3	1
(D)	3	1	2	4

1211. Who ended her highly romantic and impressively wide ranging survey, *Pleasure of Ruins* (1953) with 'A Note on New Ruins' in which she was fascinated with the 'catastrophic tipsy chaos' of a British bomb-site ?

(A) Rose Macaulay
(B) Compton-Burnett
(C) Heany
(D) Anita Desai

1212. Elizabeth Bowen took as her theme the loss of innocence in the face of shallow sophistication and the flashy glamour of metropolitan values in her most Jamesian novel,

(A) *The Last September*
(B) *The Little Girls*
(C) *The Death of the Heart*
(D) *Look at all those Roses*

1213. Stella Rodney and Rober Kelway appear as lovers in Bowen's

(A) *Demon Lover*
(B) *Heat of the Day*
(C) *The Little Girls*
(D) *The Death of the Heart*

1214. *The Fountain overflows* is a novel whose first-person narrator tells the story with a subtle combination of adult knowingness and a sense of lost, or never-achieved, content. Who is its author ?

(A) Rebecca West
(B) Elizabeth Bowen
(C) Compton-Burnett
(D) Rose Macaulay

1215. Rebecca West wrote a searching historical novel about the ideological divisions of pre-revolutionary Russia in 1966, entitled

(A) *A Train of Powder*
(B) *Black Lamb and Gray Falcon*
(C) *Harriet Hume*
(D) *The Birds Fall Down*

1216. Who wrote in his autobiographical memoir *A Sort of Life* that "success is only a delayed failure" ?

(A) Graham Greene
(B) Elizabeth Bowen
(C) John Osborne
(D) Rebecca West

1217. Against which novel of Graham Greene the Haitian Government had brought a case in France, claiming that it had damaged the Republic's tourist trade ?

(A) *Brighton Rock*
(B) *The Power and the Glory*
(C) *The Comedians*
(D) *The Ministry of Fear*

1218. Which novel of Graham Greene bore as its epigraph a quotation from Sir Thomas Brown : "There is another man within me that is angry with me" ?

(A) *The Power and the Glory*
(B) *The Man Within*
(C) *The End of the Affair*
(D) *The Heart of the Matter*

1219. The catholic boy-gangster, Pinkie, is fascinated by the idea of "Hell, Flames and damnation" in Greene's eighth novel

(A) *The Third Man*
(B) *The Heart of the Man*
(C) *The Comedians*
(D) *Brighton Rock*

1220. What is Anthony Powell's sequence of 12 novels collectively known as ?

(A) *The Soldiers Art*
(B) *A Dance to the Music of Time.*
(C) *A la reherche du temps perdu*
(D) *Hearing Secret Harmonies*

1221. It was assumed at the time and continues to be assumed that the play *Look Back in Angers* (1956) marked either a 'revolution' or a 'watershed' in the history of the modern British theatre. Who was its author ?

(A) G.B. Shaw (B) Agatha Christie
(C) John Osborne (D) George Orwell

1222. Who is the author of successful comedies such as *A Phoenix too Frequent*, *The Lady's Not for Burning* and *Venus Observed* is

(A) Terence Rattigan
(B) Christopher Fry
(C) Arthur Rowe
(D) Anthony Powell

1223. Which of the following plays is not written by Arthur Miller ?

(A) *Death of a Salesman*
(B) *The Crucible*

(C) *A View from the Bridge*
(D) *Mother Courage*

1224. Who is the author of *The Glass Menagerie, A Streetcar Named Desire* and *Cat on a Hot Tin Root* ?
(A) Brecht
(B) Greene
(C) Tennessee Williams
(D) Samuel Beckett

1225. The most famous of Beckett's works has been his mysterious but innovative play
(A) *Waiting for Gadot*
(B) *Happy Days*
(C) *Endgame*
(D) *Embers*

1226. In which of his plays Beckett uses blindness of Hamm as a mode of suggesting that one kind of deprivation may alert audiences to the force of alternative ways of perceiving ?
(A) *Film*
(B) *Endgame*
(C) *Happy Days*
(D) *Krapp's Last Tape*

1227. Who is the protagonist in Osborne's *Look Back in Anger* ?
(A) Martin
(B) Luther
(C) Jimmy Porter
(D) Murphy

1228. In 1992, a middle-aged Jimmy porter returned to the stage in Osborne's
(A) *Luther*
(B) *Footfalls*
(C) *That Time*
(D) *Deja Vu*

1229. Osborne's pungently observant and equally pungently spiteful autobiography was named
(A) *More Pricks than Kicks*
(B) *A Better Class of Person*
(C) *That Time*
(D) *The Unnamable*

1230. Samuel Beckett's biology, published together in 1959 under the English titles *Molloy*, *Malone Dios* and *The Unnamable*, was first written in
(A) Greek
(B) German
(C) French
(D) Portuguese

1231. The writer, deeply influenced by the American novelist Henry Miller, born in India and the author of the overtly erotic *The Black Book : an Agon,* is
(A) Lawrence Durell
(B) D.H. Lawrence
(C) William Golding
(D) Eric Seagal

1232. William Golding's first and most enduringly popular novel, set on a desert island on which a marooned party of school boys gradually falls away from civilization, is
(A) *The Pyramid*
(B) *The Coral Island*
(C) *Lord of the Flies*
(D) *The Spire*

1233. Which novel of Golding moves back to an anthropological pre-history in which the talented and brutish progenitors of *Homo Sapiens* exterminate their simpler-minded Neanderthal precursors ?
(A) *Pincher Martin*
(B) *The Inheritors*
(C) *Free Fall*
(D) *The Pyramid*

1234. Which novel of Golding has as its central character, Joceline, the ambitious Dean of an unnamed English Cathedral ?
(A) *The Pyramid*
(B) *Free Fall*
(C) *Darkness Visible*
(D) *The Spire*

1235. Golding's *The Pyramid* (1967) was followed by what appeared to be a period of abstention from fiction, an abstention broken in 1979 by
(A) *Free Fall*

(B) *Darkness Visible*
(C) *Rites of Passage*
(D) *The Paper Men*

1236. Who began his literary career with two volumes of short stories. *The Wrong Set* (1919) and *Such Darling Dodos* (1950) ?
(A) Emile Zola
(B) Moupassant
(C) Angus Wilson
(D) Iris Murdoch

1237. Angus Wilson's works do not include
(A) *Late Call*
(B) *Bruno's Dream*
(C) *As if By Magic*
(D) *Setting the World on Fire*

1238. Who is the author of philosophical studies such as *The Sovereignty of Good* (1970) and *Metaphysics as a Guide to Morals* (1992) ?
(A) Angus Wilson
(B) William Golding
(C) Muriel Spark
(D) Iris Murdoch

1239. Iris Murdoch read Beckett's *Murphy* as an undergraduate at Oxford and paid homage to it in her first novel
(A) *Bruno's Dream*
(B) *Under the Net*
(C) *The Bell*
(D) *The Sea, The Sea*

1240. Bradley Pearson, a novelist, is the narrator of Murdoch's most experimental novel
(A) *The Philosopher's Pupil*
(B) *The Black Prince*
(C) *The Flight from the Enchanter*
(D) *Under the Net*

1241. Whose first novel, *The Comforters*, is concerned with a neurotic woman writer, Caroline Rose, having to come to terms with her new-found Catholicism, with her hallucinations and with her God-like status as a creator ?
(A) Muriel Spark
(B) Iris Murdoch
(C) L.P. Hartley
(D) Agatha Christie

1242. What is Muriel Spark's autobiography entitled as ?
(A) *Vox Ego Sum Amoris*
(B) *Curriculum Vitae*
(C) *A Fairly Honourable Defeat*
(D) *Memento Mori*

1243. The most notable of Leslie Poles Hartley's novels include
(A) *Eustace and Hilda*
(B) *The Hireling*
(C) *The Go-Between*
(D) All of the above

1244. The poems *Redimiculum Matellarum* and *Briggflatts* were written by
(A) Philip Larkin
(B) Ted Hughes
(C) Basil Bunting
(D) John Betjman

1245. Larkin's first volume of poetry which was published in 1945 was
(A) *The Whitsun Weddings*
(B) *The North Ship*
(C) *High Windows*
(D) None of the above

1246. What has since become Larkin's most quoted line, "They fuck you up, your mum and dad", opens the poem
(A) *Annus Mirabilis*
(B) *This Be the Verse*
(C) *To the Sea*
(D) *Church Going*

1247. A poet who was phenomenally successful in terms selling by 1960 became the Poet Laureate in 1972. Identify him among the following :
(A) Philip Larkin
(B) Ted Hughes
(C) John Betjeman
(D) None of the above

1248. Whose two volumes of verse *A Good time was Had by All* and *Tender only to One* had received relatively little attention in their own time but achieved belated celebrity in 1957?
(A) Edith Sitwell
(B) Stevie Smith
(C) John Betjeman
(D) Iris Murdoch

1249. The dissenting, anarchic, constantly shifting youth culture in the 1950's have been preliminarily delineated in his novels *City of Spades* and *Absolute Beginners* by
(A) Colin MacInnes
(B) Philip Barking
(C) E. M. Forster
(D) Graham Greene

1250. Who is the author of *The Female Eunuch* that provided a stimulus to the development of a newly outspoken and often provocative feminism in the 1970s ?
(A) Harold Pinter
(B) Germaine Greer
(C) Stevie Smith
(D) Alan Sillitoe

1251. Whose five-volume sequence *Children of Violence* deals with the developing political commitment, and the later political disillusion, of Martha Quest ?
(A) Doris Lessing,
(B) Germaine Greer
(C) Anthony Burgess
(D) John Fowles

1252. Who wrote the *Wide Sargasso Sea* (1966) which can be said partly to be a rethinking of Mr. Rochester's account of his courtship and marriage as given in *Jane Eyre* ?
(A) Barbara Pym
(B) Jean Rhys
(C) Angela Carter
(D) John Fowle

1253. Two men and two women who work together in a London office, are observed as they divide, briefly celebrate and privately decay in Barbara Pym's notable novel,
(A) *A Glass of Blessing*
(B) *Jane and Prudence*
(C) *Quartet in Autumn*
(D) *Excellent Women*

1254. *Nights at the Circus* (1984), the story of Fevers, a cockney bird-woman, was written by
(A) Barbara Pym
(B) Angela Carter
(C) Anthony Burgess
(D) John Arden

1255. Charles Smithson and Sarah Woodruff are the central characters in the most popular novel of John Fowles,
(A) *The Collector*
(B) *Montissa*
(C) *The Magus*
(D) *The French Lieutenant's Woman*

1256. The autobiographical narrator of Anthony's *Earthly Powers,* who strikes up acquaintances with Joyce, Lewis, Ford Madox Ford, and Kipling, is
(A) Alex (B) Toomey
(C) Mozart (D) Mooney

1257. Which of the following, written by Anthony Burgess, is a sharply anti-utopian vision of the technical future, told from the point of view of Alex ?
(A) *Earthly Powers*
(B) *A Clockwork Orange*
(C) *The Wanting Seed*
(D) None of the above

1258. *The Ice Age* (1977), a novel centred on a series of interlinked relationships all of which humorously suggest something of the shabby and disappointed state of contemporary England, is the most suggestive of novels by
(A) Anthony Burgess
(B) Margaret Drabble
(C) J.B. Priestley
(D) Angela Carter

1259. Who is the author of *Live Like Pigs*, a play about the resettlement of gypsies in a housing-estate, which explores anti-social behaviour ?
(A) Arnold Wesker
(B) Harold Pinter
(C) Joe Orton
(D) John Arden

1260. *The Room*, *The Dumb Waiter*, *The Birthday Party* and *The Caretaker* are the first four plays of
(A) John Arden
(B) Joe Orton
(C) Harold Pinter
(D) Arnold Wesker

1261. Harold Pinter's later plays which leave a residual sense of sourness and negativity include
(A) *The Homecoming*
(B) *Old Times*
(C) *Betrayal*
(D) *All of the above*

1262. Pinter's relatively recent plays *One for the Road* (1984) and *Mountain Language* (1988) are insistently concerned with acts of interrogation and with
(A) adultery
(B) language
(C) pettiness of values
(D) All of the above

1263. The playwright took to writing to the press and to the theatre managers under the *nom de plume* Mrs. Edna Wethorpe and died in 1967 at the young age of thirty-four. Who is being referred to here ?
(A) Joe Orton
(B) Tom Stoppard
(C) Caryl Churchill
(D) Harold Pinter

1264. Joe Orton's comedies that had been completed before his untimely death include
(A) *Loot* (1966, published 1967)
(B) *The Ephingam Camp* (1967)
(C) *What the Butler Saw* (1969)
(D) All of the above

1265. Henry Carr is the dim-witted central figure of what is perhaps Tom Stoppard's most sustainedly witty inventive play,
(A) *Travesties*
(B) *Jumpers*
(C) *The Real Inspector Hound*
(D) *If You're Glad I'll be Frank*

1266. Stoppard's most subtle and allusive later play, which in 1998 was accorded the singular honour of being the first play of a living playwright to be produced in translation at the Sale Richelieu at the Comedie Francasse, is
(A) *Hapgood*
(B) *Professional Foul*
(C) *The Invention of Love*
(D) *Arcadia*

1267. The author of *The Pope's Wedding* and *Saved*, his first plays, who sees anger and violence as the only means of self-expression open to the socially deprived, is
(A) Tom Stoppard
(B) Howard Brenton
(C) Edward Bond
(D) None of the above

1268. In which play of Edward Bond, Shakespeare, in his complacent bourgeois retirement, is complicity in the economic oppression of the poor, but silent whom it comes to effective social protest ?
(A) *Lear* (B) *Bingo*
(C) *The Bundle* (D) *The Fool*

1269. The early years of Margaret Thatcher's primeministership were remarkable for the theatrical protest against Government policies, philosophies and philistinism. Which of the following is one such instance ?
(A) Hare's *The Great Exhibition*
(B) Griffith's *Comedians*
(C) Griffith's *The Party*
(D) Both (A) and (C)

1270. *Plenty*, the study of an intelligent and corrupted woman, was written by
(A) David Hare
(B) David Edgar
(C) Trevor Griffith
(D) Howard Brenton

1271. Who is the author of the plays *Owners* and *Cloud Nine* ?
(A) David Hare
(B) Trevor Griffith
(C) Caryl Churchill
(D) Howard Brenton

1272. There is an implicit parallel between the manipulation of information in the Soviet Union and the corrupt control of the British press by an ambitious and unscrupulous newspaper tycoon in Hare and Brenton's collaborative play
(A) *Top Girls*
(B) *Pravda : A Fleet Street Comedy*
(C) *The Great Exhibition*
(D) *The Romans in Britain*

1273. In which of her plays Caryl Churchill explores the superficial 'liberation' of women in the Thatcherite in 1980's by contrasting the lifestyle of Marlone, a pushy, urban woman executive, with that of her articulate, rural stay-at-home sister ?
(A) *Owners*
(B) *Cloud Nine*
(C) *Serious Money*
(D) *Top Girls*

1274. Which play of Caryl Churchill is the outcome of her work with a group of British drama students in immediate aftermath of the Romanian revolution ?
(A) *Blue Heart*
(B) *Mad Forest*
(C) *Blue Kettle*
(D) None of the above

1275. The most distinctive and sharp-witted playwright of the 1990's, whose first play *The Memory of Water* was written for Hampstead Theatre in London in 1996, is
(A) Shelagh Stephenson
(B) Caryl Churchill
(C) Alan Ayckbourn
(D) Brian Friel

1276. *Translations*, premiered in 1980, and *Making History*, in 1988, were written by
(A) Caryl Churchill
(B) Brian Friel
(C) Shelagh Stephenson
(D) Alam Ayckbourn

1277. Friel's questioning of assumptions, manners and inherited prejudices is evident in his subtlest and densest play, premiered at the Abbey Theatre in Dublin in 1990,
(A) *Making History*
(B) *Translations*
(C) *Philadelphia, Here I come*
(D) *Dancing at Lughnasa*

1278. The immensely popular dramatist who in 1976 managed to have five plays running simultaneously in London is
(A) Dennis Potter
(B) Bennett
(C) Alan Ayckbourn
(D) Brian Friel

1279. Name the poet whose first two volumes *The Hawk in the Rain* and *Lupercal* express a rapt fascination with animal energy and independence ?
(A) Philip Larkin
(B) Seamus Heany
(C) Ted Hughes
(D) Louis MacNiece

1280. "Two eyes serve a movement, that now
And again now, and now, and now
Sets neat prints in the snow,
Between trees..."
This is an extract from Ted Hughes's
(A) *The Thought Fox*
(B) *Wodwo*
(C) *Hawk Roosting*
(D) *The Bull Moses*

1281. *Tales from Ovid : Twenty-four Passages from the Metamarphoses* of Ted Hughes was published in
(A) 1993 (B) 1995
(C) 1997 (D) 1999

1282. Which work of Ted Hughes published in 1998 describes a continuing relationship with a restless wife and fellow poet Sylvia Plath, who committed Suicide in 1963 ?
(A) *Tales from Ovid*
(B) *Birthday Letters*
(C) *Wodwo*
(D) *Sir Gawain and the Green Knight*

1283. Who wrote *For the Unfallen* and *King Log*, which so dextrously play what is called, "Funeral Music" ?
(A) Seamus Heany
(B) Derek Mahon
(C) Geoffrey Hill
(D) None of the above

1284. Hill's tortured lyricism of "Funeral Music" has been eschewed in favour of a poor Modernist play in
(A) *The Triumph of Love*
(B) *Mercian Hymns*
(C) *King Log*
(D) *Tenebrae*

1285. The Irish poet who recalls and reconstants a familiar childhood landscape peopled by farmers, labourers and fishermen, in his poems *Death of a Naturalist* and *Door into the Dark* ?
(A) Derek Mahon
(B) Seamus Heany
(C) Tony Harrison
(D) Malcolm Muggeridge

1286. Who is the poet, a fellow Irishman of Heany, of volumes such as *Night-Crossing, Lives, The Snow Party*, etc. ?
(A) Charlemagne
(B) Caryl Churchill
(C) Derek Mahon
(D) None of the above

1287. Who in a prefatory lyric to his own work *The School of Eloquence* wrote:
"How you became a poet's a mystery !
Wherever did you get your talent from ?
I say : I had two uncles, Joe and Harry–
One was a stammerer, the other dumb"?
(A) Derek Mahon (B) Tony Harrison
(C) Geoffrey Hill (D) Ted Hughes

1288. In which year was the annual Booker Prize established ?
(A) 1959 (B) 1969
(C) 1979 (D) 1989

1289. Who literally exploded the unresolved frictions within a corrupt Cambridge college and its members in *Porterhouse Blue* (1974) ?
(A) Malcolm Bradbury
(B) Kingsley Amis
(C) Malcolm Muggeridge
(D) Tom Sharpe

1290. Campus novels, *Changing Places : A Tale of Two Campuses, Small World : An Academic Romance* and *Nice Work* all loosely centred on the University of Rummidge, were written by
(A) Ian McEwan
(B) David Lodge
(C) Malcolm Bradbury
(D) Alasdair Gray

1291. *Amsterdam*, a somewhat diagrammatic and dispiriting study of euthanasia, published in 1998, was authored by
(A) Ian McEwan (B) David Lodge
(C) Alasdair Gray
(D) James Hogg

1292. Whose two most ambitious novels, *A Life in Four Books* and *Poor Things*, fantastically reimagine Glasgow, drawing from the English and Scots Gothic traditions ?
(A) Alasdair Gray
(B) Ian McEwan
(C) David Lodge
(D) Irvine Welsh

1293. The violent, hallucinatory world of *Trainspotting* (1993) has a youthful cult following largely based on verbal and vernacular freneticism and exaggerated impressions of a reeling Edinburgh drug culture. Who is its author ?
(A) Irvine Welsh
(B) David Lodge
(C) Ian McEwan
(D) Alasdair Gray

1294. The acclaimed *London Fields* (1989) and *Times Arrow* (1991) are written by one who has been called the most self-consciously "American writer of his generation',
(A) Jeanette Winterson
(B) Martin Amis
(C) David Lodge
(D) Julian Barne

1295. Who began her career in 1985 with *Oranges Are Not the Only Fruit*, a witty, bitingly perceptive study of a provincial childhood passed within the narrow, women-dominated confines of an evangelical Christian sect?
(A) Allan Hollinghurst
(B) Julian Barnes
(C) Jeanette Winterson
(D) Charles Palliser

1296. The novels of Jeanette Winterson do not include
(A) *The Passion*
(B) *Possession*
(C) *Sexing the Cherry*
(D) *Written on the Body*

1297. *Possession* (1990) and *The Virgin in the Garden* (1978) are the two most substantial and demanding novels of
(A) Neil Bartlett
(B) Allan Hollinghurst
(C) Antonia Susan Byatt
(D) Julian Barnes

1298. *The Swimming Pool Library* (1988) and *The Folding Star* (1994) were the first two fictional works of an avowedly 'gay' fiction writer,
(A) Neil Bartlett
(B) Allan Hollinghurst
(C) Julian Barnes
(D) Charles Palliser

1299. *Mr. Clive and Mr. Page* (1996) has been called the most subtle and well-designed recent study of homoerotic obsession, written by
(A) Julian Barnes
(B) Charles Palliser
(C) Neil Bartlett
(D) Allan Hollinghurst

1300. Charles Palliser's historical novel *The Quincunx* (1989) scrupulously recreates a Victorian narrative, shaping it according to a precise five-fold pattern. Name his second historical novel, published in 1999, which returns to the idea of an older and equally dark murder story.
(A) *Dan Leno*
(B) *The Unburried*
(C) *Hawksmoor*
(D) *Flaubert's Parrot*

1301. The author of historical novels *Hawksmoor* and *Chatterton* also wrote biographies of T.S. Eliot, Dickens and Blake. Identify him among the following :
(A) M.R. James
(B) Ian Pears
(C) Julian Barnes
(D) Peter Ackroyd

1302. The idea of juxtaposing supposedly contradictory narratives, each of which explores a historical murder mystery from a different angle, has been taken up with real learning and panache by Ian pears in his novel, published in 1998,
(A) *Flaubert's Parrot*
(B) *An Instance of the Fingerpost*
(C) *Dan Leno and Limehouse Golem*
(D) *The Name of the Rose*

1303. Who is the author of *Flaubert's Parrot* (1984), a peculiar blend of ingenuity, literary detective work, and biographical reconstruction ?
(A) Julian Barnes
(B) Ian Pears
(C) M.R. James
(D) Pat Barker

1304. Who has scrupulously recreated a Victorian Narrative shaping it according to a precise fivefold pattern, in his historical novel 'The Quincunx (1989) ?
(A) Umberto Eco
(B) Julian Barnes
(C) Alan Hollinghurst
(D) Charles Palliser

1305. Who is the author of the so called *Flashman Papers*, dealing with the supposed career of the ex-villain of *Tom Brown's Schooldays*, three of which variously deal with the Afghan War of 1842, with the British acquisition of the Punjab, and with the Mutiny of 1857 ?
(A) G.M. Fraser
(B) W.H.R. Rivers
(C) J.G. Farrell
(D) Billy Prior

1306. Who is the author of *The Siege of Krishnapur* an account of British common sense, British eccentricity, and British arrogance in a besieged and crumbling residency during the Sepoy Rebellion ?
(A) Paul Scott
(B) J.G. Farrell
(C) Pat Barker
(D) Graham Swift

1307. Whose four novels known collectively as the 'Raj Quartet' deal broadly with India during the Second World War and with its uneasy progress towards independence and partition ?
(A) J.G. Farrell
(B) Ian Pears
(C) G.M. Fraser
(D) Paul Scott

1308. Whose *Regeneration* triology suggests a return to the 'classic' made of historical fiction, intermixing real historical figures with invented ones ?
(A) G.M. Fraser (B) Paul Scott
(C) Pat Barker (D) Tolkien

1309. Paul Scott's last novel deals with two ageing minor characters from the earlier sequence, the 'Raj Quartet' who are obliged to adjust to the circumstances of the disconcertingly new, independent India. Name of the novel.
(A) *The Eye in the Poor*
(B) *Staying on*
(C) *The Ghost Road*
(D) *Sour Sweet*

1310. Name the work by Salman Rushdie which is the most striking and inventive single novel to discuss India's transition from Raj to Republic.
(A) *The Satanic Verses*
(B) *The Moor's Last Sigh*
(C) *Midnight's Children*
(D) *Sour Sweet*

1311. Who is the central character in Rushdie's *Midnight's Children* ?
(A) Saleem Sinai
(B) Abdual Gaffur
(C) Meera Menon
(D) None of the above

1312. Which novel of Rushdie interfuses time and destiny, good and evil, the secular and the religious, the material and the spiritual in so dangerous and inventive a phantasmagoria that many Muslims have interpreted it as deliberate blasphemy ?
(A) *The Moor's Last Sigh*
(B) *An Insular Possession*
(C) *Satanic Verses*
(D) *The Ground Beneath her Feet*

1313. Timothy Mo, Rushdie's narrator, born in Hongkong in 1950 of an English mother and a Cantonese father, has deftly described the closed, protective, alienated and opportunistic society of the London Chinese in

(A) *An Insular Possession*

(B) *Sour Sweet*

(C) *The Moor's Last Sigh*

(D) *The Ground Beneath her Feet*

1314. Who is the author of the novel *An Artist of the Floating World*, a delicate fictional study of an ageing painter's awareness of, and detachment from, the political development of twentieth century Japan ?

(A) Salman Rushdie

(B) Kazuo Ishiguro

(C) Louis de Bernieres

(D) Irvine Welsh

1315. *Captain Corelli's Mandolin* (1994) is the most widely applauded novel of

(A) Kazuo Ishiguro

(B) Louis de Bernieres

(C) Irvine Welsh

(D) Billy Prior

1316. Which of the following is not written by Louis de Bernieres ?

(A) *The War of Emmanuel's Nether Parts*

(B) *Senor Vivo and the Coca Lord*

(C) *The Troublesome Offspring of Cardinal Gazman*

(D) *The Golden Notebook*

1317. In January 1997 a chain of British Booksellers and an independent television channel announced the results of a survey in which some 25,000 people had been asked to assist in drawing up a list of the 100 best books of the century. What place James Joyce's *Ulysses* had in the final list?

(A) First

(B) Second

(C) Fourth

(D) Fifth

1318. In 1999 which literary personality was chosen as the 'British Personality of the Millennium' by listeners to a popular news programme ?

(A) Shakespeare (B) Wordsworth

(C) Dickens (D) G.B. Shaw

Match the following lists using the codes given below.

1319. List I

a. *The World My Wilderness*

B. *The Fountain Overflows*

c. *The Comedians*

d. *The Ministry of Fear*

List II

1. Elizabeth Bowen
2. Cecily Isabel Fairchild
3. Rose Macaulay
4. Graham Greene

Codes:

	a	b	c	d
(A)	1	3	4	2
(B)	3	2	4	1
(C)	1	2	3	4
(D)	3	4	1	2

1320. List I

a. *The Birds Fall Down*

b. *King Solomon's Mines*

c. *A Dance to the Music of Time*

d. *Brief Lives*

List II

1. John Aubrey 2. Anthony Powell

3. Rider Haggard 4. Rebecca West

Codes:

	a	b	c	d
(A)	1	2	3	4
(B)	2	3	4	1
(C)	3	4	1	2
(D)	4	3	2	1

1321. List I

a. *Brideshead Revisited*

b. *Nineteen Eighty-four*

c. *Look Back in Anger*

d. *Mousetrap*

List II

1. John Osborne 2. George Orwell
3. Agatha Christie 4. Evelyn Waugh

Codes:

	a	b	c	d
(A)	2	3	1	4
(B)	3	2	4	1
(C)	4	2	1	3
(D)	4	1	3	2

1322. List I **List II**

a. Rattigan 1. *Happy Days*
b. Arthur Miller 2. *Mother Courage*
c. Brecht 3. *French Without Tears*
d. Beckett 4. *Death of a Salesman*

Codes:

	a	b	c	d
(A)	1	4	2	3
(B)	2	4	3	1
(C)	1	2	4	3
(D)	3	4	2	1

1323. List I **List II**

a. *Embers* I. John Osborne
b. *Luther* 2. Samuel Beckett
c. *The Spire* 3. Angus Wilson
d. *Hemlock and After* 4. William Golding

Codes:

	a	b	c	d
(A)	1	2	4	3
(B)	2	1	4	3
(C)	1	2	3	4
(D)	2	1	3	4

1324. List I **List II**

a. *Bruno's Dream* 1. Philip Larkin
b. *Memento Mori* 2. Muriel Spark
c. *Briggflats* 3. Iris Murdoch
d. *Jill* 4. Basil Bunting

Codes:

	a	b	c	d
(A)	3	2	4	1
(B)	2	4	1	3
(C)	1	2	3	4
(D)	4	1	2	3

1325. List I **List II**

a. *The Less Deceived* 1. Philip Larkin
b. *Coming Home* 2. John Betjeman
c. *Terry Street* 3. Douglas Dunn
d. *The Frog Prince* 4. Stevie Smith

Codes:

	a	b	c	d
(A)	1	2	3	4
(B)	4	3	2	1
(C)	3	2	1	4
(D)	2	1	4	3

1326. List I

a. *Saturday Night and Sunday Morning*
b. *The Female Eunuch*
c. *The Golden Note Book*
d. *Wide Sargasso Sea*

List II

1. Jean Rhys 2. Allam Sillitoe
3. German Greer 4. Doris Lessing

	a	b	c	d
(A)	2	3	1	4
(B)	2	3	4	1
(C)	4	1	2	3
(D)	3	1	4	2

1327. List I

a. Angela Carter
b. John Fowles
c. Anthony Burgess
d. Margaret Drabble

List II

1. *A Clockwork Orange*
2. *The Bloody Chamber*
3. *The Ice Age*
4. *The French Lieutenant's Woman*

	a	b	c	d
(A)	2	4	1	3
(B)	4	2	3	1
(C)	1	3	2	4
(D)	1	4	2	3

1328. List I

a. *The Birthday Party*
b. *Loot*

c. *The Real Inspector Hound*
d. *The Great Exhibition*

List II

1. Joe Orton 2. Harold Pinter
3. Stoppard 4. David Hare

	a	b	c	d
(A)	3	4	2	1
(B)	2	1	4	3
(C)	2	1	3	4
(D)	1	3	2	4

1329. List I **List II**

List I	List II
a. David Hare	1. *The Romans in Britain*
b. Brenton	2. *Cloud Nine*
c. Griffith	3. *The Party*
d. C. Churchill	4. *Plenty*

Codes:

	a	b	c	d
(A)	4	2	3	1
(B)	1	3	2	4
(C)	4	1	3	2
(D)	2	3	4	1

1330. List I **List II**

List I	List II
(a) *Catch-22*	1. Albert Camus
(b) *War is Kind*	2. Joseph Heller
(c) *Raj*	3. Stephen Crane
(d) *The Plague*	4. Geeta Mehta

Codes:

	a	b	c	d
(A)	2	3	4	1
(B)	3	4	1	2
(C)	4	1	2	3
(D)	1	2	3	4

1331. Who wrote the famous American play *The Iceman Cometh* ?
(A) John Osborne
(B) Eugene O'Neill
(C) Earnest Hemingway
(D) Walt Whitman

1332. Bob Smith is the central figure in which of the following plays of O'Neill ?
(A) *The Iceman Cometh*
(B) *The Farewell to Arms*
(C) *The Hairy Ape*
(D) *None of the above*

1333. How does Yank, the central character in *The Hairy Ape* differ from Aristotelean tragic heroes ?
(A) He doesn't meet a sad end despite his flaws
(B) He meets a sad end without having any tragic flaw
(C) There is a sudden reversal of fate at the end which is different from Aristotelean tragedy.
(D) None of the above

1334. Who wrote the *Leaves of Grass*, one of the classics of world poetry ?
(A) Walt Whitman
(B) Robert Frost
(C) T.S. Eliot
(D) Emily Dickinson

1335. In which of his poems given below do we witness Whitman's uninhibited treatment of sex ?
(A) *Children of Adam*
(B) *Spontaneous Me*
(C) *A Woman Waits for Me*
(D) *All of the above*

1336. Who wrote *I Felt a Funeral in My Brain* ?
(A) Walt Whitman
(B) Eugene O'Neill
(C) Emily Dickinson
(D) Robert Frost

1337. Which of the following poems is written by Robert Frost ?
(A) *Calamus*
(B) *Blueberries*
(C) *A Light Exists in Spring*
(D) *Modern Age Man*

1338. Which of the following is an elegy on the death of Abraham Lincoln ?
(A) *O Captain! My Captain*
(B) *I Hear America Singing*
(C) *Because I Could Not Stop for Death*
(D) *Stopping by Woods*

1339. The *Old Man and The Sea* recounts the 84 days' adventure of
(A) Matadors
(B) Santiago
(C) the author
(D) Philip

1340. Steinbeck's novel *Grapes of Wrath* is the story of
(A) Quentin family
(B) The Negro community
(C) Joad family
(D) Colonialism in Africa

1341. Roderick Hudson is written by
(A) James Joyce
(B) Henry James
(C) Tobias Smollett
(D) Henry Fielding

1342. Who is the author of *Caleb William* and *St. Leon* ?
(A) Hanah More
(B) Mrs. Inchbald
(C) Horace Walpole
(D) William Godwin

1343. "Lives of greatmen all remind us
We can make our life sublime
And departing leave behind us
Footprints on the sands of time."
Who wrote these lines ?
(A) Lord Tennyson
(B) H.W. Longfellow
(C) Walt Whitman
(D) Robert Browning

1344. *The Scarlet Letter* is written by
(A) Mark Twain
(B) Charles Dickens
(C) Virginia Woolf
(D) Nathaniel Hawthorne

1345. Who of the following is known as the pioneer of the modern detective stories ?
(A) Edgar Allan Poe
(B) Sir Arthur Conan Doyle
(C) Agatha Christie
(D) Anna K. Green

1346. The *Autobiography of an Unknown Indian* is written by
(A) V.S. Naipaul
(B) Nirad C. Chaudhary
(C) S. Radhakrishanan
(D) Manohar Malgonkar

1347. *Age of Innocence* is
(A) a book of verse by William Blake
(B) a novel by Edith Wharton
(C) a play by Eugene O'Neil
(D) an absurd drama by Edward Albee

1348. Mr. Zero is the main character in
(A) Elmer Rice's *Adding Machine*
(B) Samuel Beckett's *Waiting for Godot*
(C) Edward Albee's *The Sandbox*
(D) Robert Penn Warren's *All The King's Men*

1349. Isaac Asimove invented the Three Laws of Robotics in his stories which are given below. Identify the first law.
(A) A robot must obey the orders given by human beings
(B) A robot may not injure a human being, or, through inaction, allow a human being to come to harm.
(C) A robot must protect its own existence

1350. *Tender is The Night* is written by
(A) William Faulkner
(B) F.Scott Fitzgerald
(C) Ernest Hemingway
(D) Walt Whitman

1351. Sister Carrie is
(A) the name of a nun
(B) the heroine of Edith Wharton's novelette summer
(C) a novel by Dresier T.
(D) a play by O'Neill

1352. Who received the Commonwealth Writers Prize, 1994 ?

(A) Amit Chaudhary – *A Strange and Sublime Address*
(B) Sashi Tharoor - *Show Business*
(C) Upamanyu Chatterjee - *English August*
(D) Vikram Seth – *A Suitable Boy*

1353. Isabel Archer is the romantic heroine of
(A) *The Portrait of a Lady* – Henry James
(B) *Herzog* – Saul Bellow
(C) *Catch-22* – Joseph Heller
(D) *Roderick Hudson* – Henry James

1354. *Tales of the Grotesque and Arabesque* is a collection of stories by
(A) O' Henry
(B) Anton Tchekov
(C) Edgar Allan Poe
(D) Sylvia Plath

1355. Which one is Sylvia Plath's novel ?
(A) *Ariel*
(B) *The Colossus*
(C) *The Bell Jar*
(D) *Catch-22*

1356. What is the name of Walt Whitman's poem celebrating the completion of the Suez Canal and the Transcontinental Railroad ?
(A) *A Passage to India*
(B) *Passage to India*
(C) *Train to Pakistan*
(D) *Indian Wonderland*

1357. *Grapes of Wrath* is written by
(A) John Steinbeck
(B) F.Scott. Fitzgerald
(C) Gertrude Stein
(D) Nathaniel Hawthorne

1358. An Indian-born Canadian poet and novelist received one of the following awards in 1993. Identify the award.
(A) Poet of Peace
(B) Encore Prize
(C) Kothavale Award
(D) Asan Prize

1359. Joan Brady, a former ballet dancer received one of the following prizes for her book *Theory of War*. She is the first woman to get this prize. Name the prize.
(A) Asan Prize
(B) Whitebread Book of the Year
(C) National Book Award, USA
(D) Encore Prize

1360. Name the Indian-English writer who got the Austrian State Prize for European Literature in 1993.
(A) Vikram Seth
(B) Amitav Ghose
(C) Salman Rushdie
(D) Nirad C. Chaudhary

1361. Who wrote under the pen-name Saki ?
(A) H.H. Munro
(B) N.E. McNeile
(C) William Forter
(D) K.A. Abbas

1362. V.S. Naipaul's *The Mimic Man* is about
(A) an exiled Roman king
(B) an exiled Caribbean politician
(C) an Indian living in Trinidad
(D) an expatriate

1363. *The Naked and the Dead* is written by
(A) Ernest Hemingway
(B) Norman Mailer
(C) Arthur Miller
(D) P.G. Wodehouse

1364. *Finnegans Wake* is
(A) a poem by Robert Browning
(B) a prose work by Jonathan Swift
(C) a novel by Henry James
(D) a prose work by James Joyce

1365. Who translated *Omar Khayyam* into English?
(A) Edward Fitzgerald
(B) Scott Fitzgerald
(C) Edgar Fawcet
(D) Ford Madox Ford

1366. Name the mathematician and philosopher who was awarded the Nobel Prize for Literature in 1950
(A) Bertrand Russell
(B) Aldous Huxley
(C) William James
(D) James Joyce

1367. Which one of the following is a verse novel?
(A) *Golden Gate*
(B) *The Great Indian Novel*
(C) *Music for Mohini*
(D) *Ulysses*

136 Kenaburo Oe of Japan received the Nobel Prize for literature 1994 for creating an imaginary world where life and myth condense to give a picture of the human situation. What kind of a world does he imagine ?
(A) Utopian – ideal like Sir Thomas More's *Utopia*
(B) Arcadian – an earthly paradise as in Sir Philip Sidney's *Arcadia*
(C) Totally disconcerting picture of human predicament
(D) Selfish as described by Hobbes in *Leviathan*

1369. *Who's Afraid of Virginia Wolf* ? is a
(A) novel by Melville
(B) play by Edward Albee
(C) critical study on Virginia Woolf's novels
(D) a poem by Toru Dutt

1370. Who wrote under the pseudonym Mark Twain?
(A) Washington Irving
(B) Samuel Langhorne Clemens
(C) Walt Whitman
(D) Arthur Conan Doyle

1371. *The Prophet* is written by
(A) Salman Rushdie
(B) Franz Kafka
(C) Khalil Gibran
(D) Abul Fazal

1372. Albert Camus was a French existentialist. Given below is the list of his novels. Identify the novels not written by him.
(A) *The Trial*
(B) *The Plague*
(C) *The Outsider*
(D) None of the above

1373. "I think I could turn and love with animals." These are the opening lines of a poem. Who is the poet ?
(A) Walt Whitman
(B) Robert Frost
(C) William Wordsworth
(D) Ted Hughes

1374. The author of *Portrait of India* is
(A) V.S. Naipaul
(B) N.C. Chaudhary
(C) Ved Mehta
(D) E.M. Forster

1375. Who wrote *My True Faces*, *Azadi*, *Into Another Dawn*, *The Crown* and *The Loincloth*?
(A) Sudhir Ghose
(B) Khushwant Singh
(C) Manohar Malgaonkar
(D) Chaman Nahal

1376. Which of the following is not Anita Desai's work ?
(A) *In Custody*
(B) *Vices in The City*
(C) *A Silence of Desire*
(D) *Clear Light of Day*

1377. Edwin Markham once saw Millet's painting of a bowed, broken toiler. Making the French painting a symbol for the workers, he wrote a poem. Identify it.
(A) 'Song of the Shirt'
(B) 'Two Tramps in Mud Time'
(C) 'The Man With the Hoe'

1378. Only one of the following is not a collection of short stories. Identify it.
(A) *The Policeman And the Rose*
(B) *Into Another Dawn*

(C) *Games at Twilight*
(D) *Bombay Beware*

1379. Which of the following is V.S. Naipaul's comic novel of colonial politics ?
(A) *A House for Mr. Biswas*
(B) *The Mystic Masseur*
(C) *The Mimic Men*
(D) *In a Free State*

1380. *Too Long in the West* is written by
(A) V.S. Naipaul
(B) Kamala Markandaya
(C) Nirad C. Chaudhary
(D) Balachandra Rajan

1381. V.S. Naipaul's the *Mystic Masseur* received a prestigious prize. Name it.
(A) Booker's
(B) Commonwealth
(C) Pulitzer
(D) Rhys Memorial

1382. Where is R.K. Narayan's imaginary town Malgudi located ?
(A) In the territory of the Nizam of Hydrabad
(B) In Madras Presidency
(C) In Cochin
(D) In Mysore State

1383. When *A Beginning*, his first book of verse appeared, the poet was just 199. He received the Hawthornden prize the next year and became the youngest poet to get it. Name him.
(A) Keki N. Daruwala
(B) Dom Moraes
(C) Frank Moraes
(D) A.K. Ramanujan

1384. Who wrote *Tughlaq*, a successful stage play?
(A) Girish Karnad
(B) Badal Sirkar
(C) Mohan Rakesh
(D) Vijay Tendulkar

1385. In one of his novels Manohar Malgaonkar writes the story from the point of view of a Pakistani captain placed in Bangla Desh (then East Pakistan). Name it.
(A) *Distant Drums*
(B) *Cactus Country*
(C) *Combat of Shadow*
(D) *A Bend in the Ganges*

1386. Who is the author of *Raj* ?
(A) Geeta Mehta
(B) Rama Mehta
(C) Shobha De
(D) Nargis Dalal

1387. Dominique Lapierre wrote an appealing account of the sordid squalor of an Indian city. Identify the city.
(A) Calcutta (B) Bombay
(C) Udaipur (D) Delhi

1388. Who is the author of following poems : "The Gift of India", "Bangle-seller", "The Anthem of Love", "Palanquin Bearers"?
(A) Kamala Das
(B) Sarojini Naidu
(C) Toru Dutt
(D) Nissim Ezekiel

1389. Who wrote the hard-hitting poem "Sita Speak" indicating the society for the injustice meted out to women down the ages ?
(A) Bina Agarwal
(B) Kamala Das
(C) P. Lal
(D) Sarojini Naidu

1390. In which of the following poems of Ezekiel do we get a moving picture of a mother's suffering ?
(A) '*The Couple*'
(B) '*Night of the Scorpion*'
(C) '*The Visitor*'
(D) '*Philosophy*'

1391. Who is the author of *Two Virgins* ?
(A) Kamala Markandaya
(B) Kamala Das
(C) Anita Desai
(D) Shastri Deshpande

1392. Name the Indo-English novelist who wrote *A Suitable Boy*.
(A) Vikram Seth
(B) Amitav Ghose
(C) Upamanyu Chatterjee
(D) Anita Desai

1393. Two Indian writers living abroad created furore – one was Vikram Seth who got an unprecedented amount as an advance for his novel, the other who came under 'fatwa', for one of his controversial novels, issued by Muslim countries, was
(A) Amitav Ghose
(B) Bharati Mukherjee
(C) Anita Desai
(D) Salman Rushdie

1394. Name Salman Rushdie's latest Novel.
(A) *The Moor's Last Sigh*
(B) *Fury*
(C) *The Ground Beneath Her Feet*
(D) *Satanic Verses*

1395. Of the following novels one does not portray the Gandhian Age and the impact of Gandhi. Which one ?
(A) K.A. Abbas's *Inquilab*
(B) Venu Chitale's *In Transit*
(C) R.K. Narayan's *The Dark Room*
(D) K. Nagarajan's *Chronicles of Kedaram*

1396. Who is the author of the following books : *The Foreigner*, *The Apprentice*, *The Last Labyrinth*, *The City and the River* ?
(A) Ruth P. Jhabvala
(B) Amitav Ghose
(C) Dom Moraes
(D) Arun Joshi

1397. Whose collections of poems are these : *A Time to Change*, *Sixty Poems*, *The Third*, *The Unfinished Man* ?
(A) P. Lal
(B) Nissim Ezekiel
(C) Kamala Das
(D) Bina Aggarwal

1398. Listed below are the works of Bhabani Bhattacharya of which only one is his collection of short stories. Identify it.
(A) *So Many Hungers*
(B) *A Dream in Hawaii*
(C) *Sea Hawk*
(D) *Shadow from Ladakh*

1399. *Baumgartner's Bombay* is a novel about a German Jew who remains an outsider all his life, in his country because he is a Jew and in India, where he is a *firangi*. Who wrote this moving novel ?
(A) Vikram Seth
(B) Anita Desai
(C) Nayantara Sehgal
(D) Ruth P. Jhabvala

1400. In which novel does R.K. Narayan focus on family planning ?
(A) *The Guide*
(B) *Mr. Sampath*
(C) *Bachelor of Arts*
(D) *The Painter of Signs*

1401. In *The Guide* we come across a dancer. What is her name ?
(A) Daisy (B) Bharati
(C) Rosie (D) Savitri

1402. Who wrote these lines :
" Woman is the earth, air, ether, sound; woman is the microcosm of the mind....."?
(A) Raja Rao
(B) R.K. Narayan
(C) Kamala Markandaya
(D) Kamala Das

1403. Arthur Symons wrote about this person, "All the life of the tiny figure seemed to concentrate itself in the eyes: they turned towards beauty as the sunflower turns towards the sun." Who is the person referred to ?
(A) Toru Dutt (B) Aru Dutt
(C) Sarojini Naidu
(D) Rabindra Nath Tagore

1404. H.A.L. Fisher wrote about this person, ".... this child of the green valley of the Ganges has by sheer force of native genius earned for herself the right to be enrolled in the great fellowship of English poets." Who is the poet?
(A) Sarojini Naidu
(B) Toru Dutt
(C) Michael Madhusudan
(D) Manmohan Ghose

1405. An Indo-English poet once remarked that his disciplines (*i.e.*, linguistics and anthropology) and his education give him his "Outer" form, whereas his Indian origin, first thirty years in India and knowledge of Kannada and Tamil give him his "inner" form. Who said this ?
(A) A.K. Ramanujan
(B) Kamala Das
(C) Gieve Patel
(D) Raja Gopal Parthasarathy

1406. Who wrote *Jejuri* the Commonwealth Poetry Prize winner work ?
(A) Shiv K. Kumar (B) Arun Kolatkar
(C) Keki N. Daruwala
(D) Jayant Mahapatra

1407. In which of Anita Desai's novel an insane wife kills her husband ?
(A) *Voices in The City*
(B) *In Custody*
(C) *Cry, The Peacock*
(D) *Baumgartner's Bombay*

1408. In which novel does the hero sing the refrain:
"This is the machine age, sons
This is the machine age
We are the men who will master it" ?
(A) The Big Heart
(B) The Sword and The Sickle
(C) Two Leaves and a Bud
(D) The Road

1409. Who was the first recipient of the Sahitya Academi Award for English literature ?
(A) Mulk Raj Anand
(B) Nayantara Sehgal
(C) R.K. Narayan
(D) Raja Rao

1410. Following novels except one, describe the condition of Westners living in India. Mark the one which does not.
(A) *Heat and Dust*
(B) *The Princess*
(C) *Coffer Dam*
(D) *A Passage to India*

1411. Which of the following novels focuses on the question of rape ?
(A) *The Bending Vine*
(B) *Voices in The City*
(C) *Some Inner Fury*
(D) *A Time to Be Happy*

1412. Who is the author of the following novels : *A Bend in The Ganges*, *The Princes*, *Distant Drums*, *Devil's Wind*, *A Combat of Shadows* ?
(A) Mulk Raj Anand
(B) Bhabani Bhattacharya
(C) Manohar Malgaonkar
(D) Salman Rushdie

1413. Who wrote "*Our Casuarina Tree*" a splendid Keatsian poem ?
(A) Toru Dutt
(B) Romesh Chander Dutt
(C) Swami Vivekanand
(D) Sri Aurobindo

1414. To whom do we assign following works – *The Lake of Palms*, *A History of Civilization of Ancient India*, *The Slave-Girl of Agra*?
(A) Manmohan Ghose
(B) Romesh Chander Dutt
(C) Bankim Chandra Chatterjee
(D) Sharat Chandra

1415. Which one of the following is a collection of Anita Desai's short stories ?
(A) *Voices in the City*

(B) *Games at Twilight*
(C) *Village by the Sea*
(D) *Cry, the Peacock*

1416. Browning's *The Ring and the Book* is a long poem having about 21,000 lines, but Aurobindo's *Savitri* is longer. How many lines does the epic contain ?
(A) 24,000 (B) 21,500
(C) 30,000 (D) 22,000

1417. Toru Dutt, Romesh Chander Dutt and Aurobindo, all wrote on one common theme taken out from the *Mahabharata*. Identify the story which the tree found irresistible.
(A) Karna and Kunti
(B) Nal-Damyanti
(C) Savitri
(D) Gandhari

1418. Who of the following was highly influenced by French Romanticism, French language and literature ?
(A) Romesh Chander Dutt
(B) Michael Madhusudan Dutt
(C) Toru Dutt
(D) Govind Dutt

1419. About an Indian poet writing in English, a critic, George Sampson says that a reader of his poems, "Would readily take them as the work of an English poet trained in the classical tradition." An Indian critic feels that his poetry has no imagery or sentiment that can be termed as Indian. Who was this poet?
(A) Michael Madhusudan Dutt
(B) Romesh Chander Dutt
(C) Aurobindo Ghose
(D) Manmohan Ghose

1420. *The Fakir of Jhungheera* was written by one of the first Indo-Anglian poets. The poem is often hailed as a "Competent narrative verse with Byronic echoes." Identify the writer.
(A) Toru Dutt
(B) Henry Derozio
(C) Michael Madhusudan Dutt
(D) Hasan Ali

1421. He was the first Indian poet to have published a regular volume of English verse. He also edited an English Weekly *The Hindu Intelligence*. Name him.
(A) Michael Madhusudan Dutt
(B) Mohan Lal
(C) Romesh Chander Dutt
(D) Kashiprasad Ghose

1422. Paying a tribute to a Bengali poet who wrote in English also, Sri Aurobindo said, "The God himself took up thy pen and wrote." Who was he ?
(A) Michael Madhusudan Dutt
(B) Henry Derozio
(C) Romesh Chander Dutt
(D) Kashiprasad Ghose

1423. One of the following works is written by Michael Madhusudan Dutt. Identify which one ?
(A) *The Shair and Other Poems*
(B) *The Captive Ladie*
(C) *Bianca*
(D) *Lays of Ancient India*

1424. Name the poet of "Kali, the Mother."
(A) Swami Vivekanand
(B) Subramaniam Bharathi
(C) Swami Ramakrishna Paramhans
(D) Sri Aurobindo

1425. He is a Sahitya Akademi Award Winner and he loves to write for children. Who is he ?
(A) R. K. Narayan
(B) Manohar Malgaonkar
(C) Ruskin Bond
(D) Upamanyu Chatterjee

1426. Whose autobiography is entitled *My Father's Son* ?
(A) Dom Moraes (B) Frank O' Connor
(C) Nirad Chaudhury
(D) V.S. Naipaul

1427. Mulk Raj Anand, about one of his female characters says, "Gauri is my tribute to Indian womanhood." In which novel does Gauri appear ?
(A) *The Road*
(B) *The Old Woman and The Cow*
(C) *Untouchable*
(D) *The Sword and The Sickle*

1428. Read the following passage and identify the novel and its author : "Lago, I am as meek as Moses, but I have just heard that you have been mishandled by that Bhatta Govinda. Whip me, ye devils! Roast me in sulphur ! Gall, worse than gall ! A rascally Yea-for-smooth knave ! Three Judases, each one thrice worse than Judas ! Falstaff speaking. I am as subject to heat as butter."
(A) *In Custody* by Anita Desai
(B) *Midnight's Children* by Salman Rushdie
(C) *All About H. Hatter* by G.V. Desani
(D) *Vermillion Boat* by Sudhir Ghosh

1429. Name the author who has been described by a critic as an "outsider inside."
(A) Anita Desai
(B) Salman Rushdie
(C) Nirad C. Chaudhary
(D) Ruth Jhabvala

1430. Following novels, except one, describe the condition of Indians settled abroad. Mark the one which does not.
(A) *The Nowhere Man*
(B) *Bye-Bye, Blackbird*
(C) *The Serpent And The Rope*
(D) *The Guide*

1431. *The Angel of Misfortune* is a poem of about 5000 lines, written by Nagesh Vishwanath Pai. Whose story is narrated in this book?
(A) Saturn, the Dark Angel
(B) King Arthur of the Holy Grail
(C) King Vikramaditya
(D) Kamadeva

1432. Name the author of *The Gardener*, *The Fugitive*, *Chitra*, *Sacrifice*, *The Post Office*.
(A) Rabindra Nath Tagore
(B) Bankim Chandra
(C) Aurobindo Ghose
(D) Romesh Chander Dutt

1433. Name the two prizes, one in literature and another in History, awarded to young Aurobindo while studying in England.
(A) Pulitzer Prizes in Literature and Bedford Prize in History
(B) Bookers in Literature and Butterworth in History
(C) Butterworth in Literature and Bedford in History

1434. Name Sarojini Naidu's last collection of poems.
(A) *The Broken Wing*
(B) *The Golden Threshold*
(C) *The Bird of Time*
(D) *The Temple*

1435. What is the full title of Aurobindo's *Savitri*?
(A) *Savitri – An Epic*
(B) *Savitri*
(C) *Savitri – A Legend and a Symbol*
(D) *Savitri – A Poem in Three Parts*

1436. Who wrote *Murugan, The Tiller and Kandan, the Patriot*, *Jatadharan* and *The Next Rung*?
(A) K.S. Venkataramani
(B) Shanker Ram
(C) Humayun Kabir
(D) K. Subba Rao

1437. *The Devil's Wind* depicts the events of our First War of Independence (1857 mutiny). Who is the author of this novel ?
(A) Shanker Ram
(B) Manohar Malgaonkar
(C) R.K. Narayan
(D) Sasthi Brata

1438. Which novel highlights the Bengal famine?
(A) *So Many Hungers*

(B) *A Handful of Rice*
(C) *A Time to be Happy*
(D) *Athawar House*

1439. Who wrote *Ilion* ?
(A) Virgil
(B) Aurobindo
(C) Homer
(D) Rabindra Nath Tagore

1440. Who is the author of *Love of Dust* ?
(A) Ruth P. Jhabvala
(B) Humayun Kabir
(C) Shanker Ram
(D) K.S. Venkataramani

Match the following lists using the codes given below.

1441. List I
(a) Aurobindo Ghose
(b) Rabindra Nath Tagore
(c) Gujarat and Gujaratis
(d) Toru Dutt

List II
1. *Red Oleanders*
2. *Savitri*
3. *Le Journal de Mademoisellers d'Arvers*
4. *Behramji Malabari*

Codes:

	a	b	c	d
(A)	4	1	2	3
(B)	1	3	4	2
(C)	1	4	2	3
(D)	2	1	3	4

1442. List I / **List II**
(a) *Mahatma* — 1. D.F. Karaka
(b) *Mahatma Gandhi* — 2. Hiren Mukherjee
(c) *Gandhiji* — 3. P.A. Wadia
(d) *Out of Dust* — 4. D.G. Tendulkar

Codes:

	a	b	c	d
(A)	4	3	2	1
(B)	4	1	3	2
(C)	1	4	3	2
(D)	3	2	1	4

1443. List I
(a) *The Well of the People*, Bharati Sarabhai
(b) *The House at Adampur*, Anand Lall
(c) *Savitri*, Aurobindo
(d) *Reminiscences*, Tagore

List II
1. Prose (Autobiography)
2. Poetry (Epic)
3. Fiction (Novel)
4. Drama (Play)

Codes:

	a	b	c	d
(A)	1	2	3	4
(B)	4	3	2	1
(C)	3	4	1	2
(D)	2	1	4	3

1444. List I
(a) *The Golden Gate*
(b) *The Golden Honey Comb*
(c) *Herzog*
(d) *Tiger's Daughter*

List II
1. Bharati Mukherjee
2. Saul Bellow
3. Vikram Seth
4. Kamala Markandaya

Codes:

	a	b	c	d
(A)	2	3	1	4
(B)	1	4	3	2
(C)	3	4	2	1
(D)	4	2	1	3

1445. List I / **List II**
a. *Catylus* — 1. Zeno
b. *De Oratore* — 2. Cicero
c. *Homeric Problems* — 3. Plato
d. *Epistle to Augustus* — 4. Horace

Codes:

	a	b	c	d
(A)	3	2	1	4
(B)	2	1	4	3
(C)	4	2	1	3
(D)	3	2	4	1

1446. **List I** **List II**

a. *Convivio* 1. Boileau

b. *Confessions* 2. Tasso

c. *Discorsi* 3. Dante

d. *Art Poetique* 4. St. Augustine

Codes:

	a	b	c	d
(A)	1	2	3	4
(B)	4	3	2	1
(C)	3	4	2	1
(D)	2	1	3	4

1447. **List I**

a. *Defense of Poesie*

b. *A Defence of Rhyme*

c. *Discourse of Poesie*

d. *Observations in the Art of English Poesie*

List II

1. Webbe 2. Sidney

3. Daniel 4. Campion

Codes:

	a	b	c	d
(A)	2	3	1	4
(B)	2	1	4	3
(C)	3	2	1	4
(D)	1	4	3	2

1448. **List I**

a. *On the Composition of Romances*

b. *Discourses on the Heroic Poem*

c. *Compendium of Tragicomic Poetry*

d. *Poetics*

List II

1. Cinthio 2. Guarini

3. Scalinger 4. Tasso

Codes:

	a	b	c	d
(A)	3	4	2	1
(B)	4	2	1	3
(C)	2	1	3	4
(D)	1	4	2	3

1449. **List I**

a. Association of ideas

b. Objective Correlative

c. Synaesthetics

d. Primary imagination

List II

1. T.S. Eliot 2. I.A. Richards

3. Coleridge 4. John Locke

Codes:

	a	b	c	d
(A)	3	2	1	4
(B)	4	1	2	3
(C)	4	3	1	2
(D)	3	4	2	1

1450. **List I**

a. *Hamburg Dramaturgy*

b. *Conservations*

c. *Philosophy of Fine Art*

d. *Critique of Judgement*

List II

1. Kant 2. Goethe

3. Lessing 4. Hegel

Codes:

	a	b	c	d
(A)	1	4	2	3
(B)	3	2	1	4
(C)	2	1	4	3
(D)	3	2	4	1

1451. The earliest piece of extended literary criticism which survives from classical antiquity is an agon or debate in the *Frogs* of

(A) Homer (B) Plato

(C) Aristophanes (D) Euripides

1452. Who is the special literary target of Aristophanes in *Frogs* ?

(A) Homer

(B) Plato

(C) Euripides

(D) Aeschylus

1453. In Plato's *Ion* as in *Frogs* of Aristophanes, literary criticism takes the form of a dramatic

(A) monologue

(B) dialogue

(C) debate by a group of philosophers

(D) None of the above

1454. Which English poet translated the *Ion* and was deeply impressed by it ?
(A) Shelley (B) Byron
(C) Sydney (D) Pope

1455. In which of the following works of Plato, a useful kind of "right opinion" is conceded to all poetic persons ?
(A) *Ion* (B) *Republic*
(C) *Phaedrus* (D) *Meno*

1456. What should be the ideal age of the poet according to Plato in *Laws* ?
(A) Less than thirty
(B) More than thirty
(C) Less than fifty
(D) More than fifty

1457. Plato's brilliant use of allegorical imagery like that of the soul as the charioteer and the higher and the lower passions as his pair of horses in
(A) *The Republic*
(B) *Phaedrus*
(C) *Ion*
(D) *Meno*

1458. Which are the two major categories into which Plato divided 'Art' ?
(A) Acquisitive and Productive
(B) Divine and Human
(C) Real and Imaginary
(D) Of likeneses and of semblances

1459. Into which category of 'Art' did Plato put reflections, dreams and shadows ?
(A) Human (B) Divine
(C) Acquisitive (D) None of these

1460. A rhapsode as mentioned by Plato was a sort of
(A) actor
(B) college teacher of literature
(C) a combination of the above two
(D) a singer and actor

1461. Which of the following is not one of the works of Aristotle ?
(A) *Metaphysics*
(B) *Ethics*
(C) *Poetics*
(D) *Symposium*

1462. Which work of Aristotle has been called "achromatic" by Aristotelians, *i.e.*, to be interpreted only with the help of other and larger works ?
(A) *Metaphysics* (B) *Ethics*
(C) *Poetics* (D) *Symposium*

1463. In which of his works Aristotle has distinguished between faults which affect a poem as such and those which do not ?
(A) *Politics* (B) *Poetics*
(C) *Metaphysics* (D) *Rhetoric*

1464. In *Poetics*, Aristotle argued that poetry is more philosophic and more serious than
(A) Metaphysics
(B) Biology
(C) Visual Art
(D) History

1465. According to Aristotle
(A) Art finishes the job that nature leaves undone
(B) Art counteracts nature
(C) Art imitates the crude aspects of nature
(D) None of the above

1466. Regarding which of the following Aristotle said in *Poetics* that in "having passed through many phases, reached its natural form, and there it stopped" ?
(A) Poetry
(B) Philosophy
(C) Tragedy
(D) Comedy

1467. In *Poetics*, Aristotle writes, "In a simpler and restrictive sense the action of a tragedy is not longer than"
(A) twelve hours
(B) eighteen hours
(C) one day
(D) thirty-six hours

1468. Which of the following terms, as used by Aristotle, means a sudden turn ?
(A) *Peripeteia*
(B) *Anagnorisis*
(C) *Nemesis*
(D) *Megethos*

1469. What is meant by *anagnorisis* in Aristotelian Vocabulary ?
(A) Ignorance
(B) Recognition
(C) Magnitude
(D) Change of fortune

1470. Which of the following in Aristotelian vocabulary means the plot ?
(A) *Megethos*
(B) *Mythos*
(C) *Ethos*
(D) *Phobou*

1471. Which of the following is not a part of *Hamartia* ?
(A) Error and punishment
(B) Fate
(C) Human Will
(D) Tragic consequence

1472. Which of the following types of *Anagnorisis* is most effective according to Aristotle?
(A) The scar discovered in the bath by Odysseous
(B) When Orestes makes himself known to Iphigenia
(C) The messenger in Oedipus
(D) All of the above

1473. According to Aristotle the comedy consists of some defect or ugliness which is
(A) painful
(B) not painful
(C) necessary
(D) unnecessary

1474. Whose *Characters* is a further development of Aristotelian division of the tragedy and the comedy ?
(A) Socrates
(B) Theophrastus
(C) Aristophanes
(D) None of the above

1475. According to Aristotle, 'Imagination', 'Symbol' and 'Paradox' are the characteristics of
(A) Tragedy (B) Comedy
(C) Poetry (D) Art

1476. According to Aristotle, 'Reason', 'Concept' and 'Contrast' are the characteristics of
(A) Tragedy (B) Comedy
(C) Poetry (D) Art

1477. Aristotle's *Rhetoric* opens with the statement:Rhetoric is a counterpart of
(A) Ethic
(B) Dialectic
(C) Didactic
(D) Reality

1478. In *Poetics* and *the Rhetoric* as well oft-quoted statement is that the greatest poetic gift is to be master of the
(A) Onometopoeia
(B) Metaphor
(C) Simile
(D) Paradox

1479. Who wrote in his *De Oratore* that if an orator is distinguished from a philosopher, the philosopher would be inferior ?
(A) Aristotle (B) Quintilian
(C) Cicero (D) Augustine

1480. Which of the following, a slick piece of writing by Horace, was dubbed *Ars Poetica* by Quintilian in the next century ?
(A) *Epodes*
(B) *Satires*
(C) *Epistola and Pisones*
(D) *Epistles*

1481. Which of the following is not one of the explicit instructions for literary genres given by Horace in *Ars Poetica* ?
(A) Give three acts, no more, no less
(B) No scene off the stage, good or ugly

(C) Only three speakers at a time
(D) Hexameter verse for war poems

1482. Which emotion should be expressed in iambs according to *Ars Poetica* ?
(A) Pleasure (B) Fear
(C) Sorrow (C) Anger

1483. The power of forming great conceptions, inspired and vehement passion, formation of figures, noble diction, and dignified and elevated composition are the five sources of "elevation" according to
(A) Aristotle (B) Horace
(C) Longinus (D) Plotinus

1484. Who in his youthful summation of Hellenistic doctrine, the *De Inventione,* prescribed five parts of speech ?
(A) Horace
(B) Aristotle
(C) Demetrius
(D) Cicero

1485. Who, in the earlier of his two essays, written on beauty, *Ennead*, strongly inclined to depreciate physical beauty ?
(A) Quintilian
(B) Cicero
(C) Plotinus
(D) None of the above

1486. The 13th century vernacular poem which has been called the earliest literary criticism is
(A) *Teiresias*
(B) *Ennead*
(C) *The Owl and the Nightingale*
(D) *Ulixes*

1487. Who wrote a Latin essay about 1300 A.D. defending vernacular poetry, the *De Vulgari Eloquentia* ?
(A) *Dante* (B) *Demetrius*
(C) *Quintilian* (D) *Cicero*

1488. Who attacked the rhyme in his *Observations in the Art of English Poesie ?*
(A) Puttenham
(B) Campion
(C) Daniel
(D) Dyer

1489. Who answered Campion's attack on rhyme in *A Defence of Rhyme* in 1603 ?
(A) Sidney (B) Daniel
(C) Webbe (D) Dryden

1490. Who is the author of *An Essay on Unnatural Flights in Poetry* (1701)
(A) Boileau (B) Tasso
(C) Pope (D) Granville

1491. Who wrote in his *Proficience and Advancement of Learning* that poetry "doth raise and erect the Minde, by submitting the shows of things to the desires of the mind."?
(A) Sidney (B) Jonson
(C) Dr. Johnson (D) Bacon

1492. In which of his works Jonson wrote that poetry requires not only "goodness of natural wit", but "exercise", "imitation", "study" and "art" ?
(A) *Timber*
(B) *Discourses*
(C) *Examens*
(D) None of the above

1493. Dryden's dialogue, published in 1668 that is considered the most important for his general literary theory, was entitled
(A) *An Essay of Dramatic Poesy*
(B) *Defence of an Essay of Dramatic Poesy*
(C) *Essay of Heroic Plays*
(D) *Aurangzebe*

1494. Who is a representation of Dryden himself in *An Essay of Dramatic Poesy* ?
(A) Crites (B) Eugenius
(C) Neander (D) Lisideius

1495. Crites in *An Essay of Dramatic Poesy* is the fictional person representing Dryden's brother-in-law'
(A) Sir Robert Howard

(B) Dr. Samucl Johnson
(C) John Donne
(D) Ben Jonson

1496. The first attempt at critical resistance to heroic insensibility of Dryden and others was made by Buckingham and his friends in
(A) *The Tragedy of Tragedies*
(B) *The Rehearsal*
(C) *The Conquest of Granada*
(D) *None of the above*

1497. According to Dryden, comedy begets
(A) divine pleasure
(B) irresistible pleasure
(C) malicious pleasure
(D) critical pleasure

1498. Dryden's theory of satire appeared in the long essay entitled *The Origin and Progress of Satire* (1693) prefixed to his translation of
(A) Horace
(B) Juvenal
(C) Persius
(D) Both (B) and (C)

1499. Dryden distinguished between three types of translation: metaphrase, paraphrase and imitation. Which of the following means turning an author word by word, and line by line, from one language to another ?
(A) Paraphrase
(B) Metaphrase
(C) Imitation
(D) None of the above

1500. Which of the following, according to Dryden, is translation with latitude, where the author is kept in view by the translator, so as never to be last, but his words are never so strictly followed as his sense ?
(A) Paraphrase
(B) Metaphase
(C) Imitation
(D) None of the above

1501. In which of his works Dryden wrote, "... the definition of Wit.... is only this : that it is a propriety of thoughts and words; or, in other terms, thoughts and words elegantly adapted to the subject" ?
(A) *An Essay of Dramatic Poesy*
(B) *Defence of An Essay of Dramatic Poesy*
(C) *Apology for Heroic Poetry*
(D) *Defence of the Epilogue*

1502. Who wrote in *Leviathan* that "In a good poem, whether it be *Epique* or *Dramatique* ... both judgement and fancy are required?
(A) Locke (B) Hobbes
(C) Pope (D) Bacon

1503. Locke referred to wit in his *Essay concerning Human Understanding,* as a faculty of seeing
(A) differences
(B) resemblances
(C) both differences and resemblances
(D) beyond differences and resemblances

1504. Whose view on wit was supported by Addison in one of his spectator essays, No. 62 ?
(A) Dryden's (B) Hobbes's
(C) Locke's
(D) All of the above

1505. Which work of Pope, written squarely on the tradition of the Horatian *Ars Poetica,* is considered his most ambitious critical work?
(A) *Essay on Criticism*
(B) *Peri Bathous*
(C) *Essay on Man*
(D) None of the above

1506. Who, in an *Essay on Pope's Odyssey*, invoked the statement by Quntilian as a classical sanction for the same thing ?
(A) Joseph Warton
(B) Spence
(C) Lord Kames
(D) George Campbell

1507. Which of the following critical works is not by Dr. Johnson ?
(A) *Rasselas*
(B) *Preface to Shakespeare*
(C) *Life of Cowley*
(D) None of the above

1508. What was the view of Dr. Johnson on Shakespeare ?
(A) A ruthless, urban and sublime poet
(B) A pathetic, tender and domestic poet
(C) A rhapsodic, violent and exuberant poet
(D) None of the above

1509. Which kind of poetry was simply "unsatisfactory" according to Johnson ?
(A) Didactic
(B) Sentimental
(C) Secular
(D) Devotional

1510. Surblimity, according to Johnson, was not within the reach of metaphysical poets, for great thoughts are always
(A) divine
(B) particular
(C) general
(D) serious

1511. Johnson didn't like Milton's *Samson Agonistes* on the Aristotelian grounds, because
(A) it had a beginning and a middle but no end
(B) it had a middle and an end but no beginning
(C) it had a beginning and an end but no middle
(D) None of the above

1512. What did Dr. Johnson think about "general opinion" or "common voice" ?
(A) That it was usually wrong
(B) That it was usually right
(C) That it was always at the border that separates right from wrong
(D) None of the above

1513. What was Dr. Johnson's opinion on language of poetry ?
(A) It should be the language of the learned
(B) It should be an universal language
(C) It should be a sublime poetic language
(D) None of the above

1514. Johnson had nine conditions for generality of an idea. Which of the following is not one of them ?
(A) An idea is general in a more special way if it is viable for a great many persons.
(B) An idea is general when it is applicable to several individuals.
(C) An idea is general if it refers to objects which generally exist, *i.e.*, which are statistically common.
(D) An idea is general if it was not conceived by Aristotle at the substantive level.

1515. "If I am not deceived, a play is supposed to be the work of the poet, imitating or representing the conversation of several persons." Who has been quoted here ?
(A) Thomas Browne
(B) John Dryden
(C) Samuel Johnson
(D) Philip Sidney

1516. "The task of an author is, either to teach what is not known, or to recommend known truths by his manner of adorning them." Who has been quoted here ?
(A) John Dryden
(B) George Granville
(C) Dr. Samuel Johnson
(D) D.B. Shelley

1517. Who among the following opined that "a poet should take particular care to guard himself against idiomatic ways of speaking" ?
(A) Richard Steele
(B) Joseph Addison
(C) Francis Bacon
(D) Samuel Johnson

1518. Who used the term "diction" in the high Augustan era as an apology for Latinism, in the preface to Sylvae ?
(A) Pope
(B) Johnson
(C) Dryden
(D) Addison

1519. Who among the following was apparently the first to use the term "Poetic diction" in his *Advancement and Reformation of Modern Poetry* ?
(A) Dennis
(B) Granville
(C) Pope
(D) Dryden

1520. In which of his works Wordsworth gave the famous statement. "All good poetry is spontaneous overflow of powerful feelings"?
(A) *Advertisement*
(B) *Preface to Lyrical Ballads*
(C) *The Prelude*
(D) None of the above

1521. Who opined that "it is exactly as wasteful for a poet to do what has been done already, as for a biologist to rediscover Mendel's discoveries " ?
(A) Addison
(B) T.S. Eliot
(C) W.B. Yeats
(D) W.H. Auden

1522. A.W. Schlegel devoted the first of his *Vienna lectures on Dramatic Art and Literature* to rebuking neoclassic exclusiveness and pleading for a universality of
(A) true poetry
(B) true poetic language
(C) true criticism
(D) true art

1523. Who in a late polemical statement aimed against the French romantics said, "I call the classic *healthy*, the romantic *sickly*" ?
(A) Rousseau
(B) Boudelair
(C) Goethe
(D) Schlegel

1524. Who opined that imagination "draws all things to one .... it makes things animate or inanimate, beings with their attributes, subjects with their accessories, take one colour and serve to one effect" ?
(A) William Taylor
(B) Coleridge
(C) Wordsworth
(D) Charles Lamb

1525. The primary imagination differed from the secondary imagination, as per Coleridge's distinction,
(A) only in the degree
(B) in the method of its operation
(C) in the kind of its agency
(D) Both (A) and (B)

1526. Which of the following was defined by Coleridge as "a mode of Memory emancipated from the order of time and space" ?
(A) Fancy
(B) Primary imagination
(C) Secondary imagination
(D) All of the above

1527. Who said that "No man was ever yet a great poet, without being at the same time a profound philosopher" ?
(A) Wordsworth
(B) Coleridge
(C) Arnold
(D) T.S. Eliot

1528. Who among the following wrote, "The appropriate business of poetry, ... and her duty, is to treat of things not as they are, but as they appear" ?
(A) Coleridge
(B) Wordsworth
(C) Shelley
(D) Keats

1529. Who wrote in his *Salon de* (1767), "Poetry always contains a pinch of untruth" ?
(A) Diderot

(B) Fontenelle
(C) Macaulay
(D) Maurice Morgann

1530. Whose philosophic career can be traced from French naturalism and necessitarianism, through a Platonic or ontologic idealism to the psychologic or epistemologic idealism in the *Poems* of 1822 ?
(A) Byron
(B) Shelley
(C) Keats
(D) None of the above

1531. Who said that poetry is feigning "notable images of virtues, vices or what else, with..... delightful teaching" ?
(A) Sidney
(B) Coleridge
(C) Shelley
(D) Arnold

1532. Who among the following said, "I hold that a long poem does not exist. I maintain that the phrase, 'a long poem' is simply a flat contradiction in terms" ?
(A) Victor Huge
(B) W.H. Auden
(C) Edgar Alan Poe
(D) Geoffrey Tillotson

1533. "For a literary masterpiece two powers must concur, the power of the man, and the power of the moment, and the man is not enough without the moment." Who has been quoted in these lines ?
(A) Bacon
(B) Johnson
(C) Coleridge
(D) Arnold

1534. Who, according to Arnold, was an imperfect disciple of Shakespeare, for he had an excess of natural magic, not enough moral profundity, while Shakespeare had both qualities to the full ?
(A) Wordsworth
(B) Keats
(C) Tennyson
(D) All of the above

1535. What was the lacuna in Chaucer's poetry according to Arnold ?
(A) Truth
(B) Fluidity of movement
(C) High seriousness
(D) Heroic subject matter

1536. Who are the two great "classics of our prose" according to Arnold ?
(A) Bacon and Johnson
(B) Addison and Lamb
(C) Pope and Johnson
(D) Dryden and Pope

1537. Which of the following ideas was supported by Tolstoy ?
(A) Art for art's sake
(B) Art as a monitor and propagandist for the social process
(C) Art as a record of reality in space and time
(D) None of the above

1538. "Most false ideas about the beautiful arise from the false idea of morality current during the 18th century". Which French critic has been quoted above ?
(A) Kant (B) Schlegel
(C) Schelling (D) Baudelaire

1539. "We hate poetry that has a palpable design upon us". Who has been quoted here?
(A) Keats (B) Shakespeare
(C) Gautier (D) Kant

1540. Who held that "Form is everything. It is the secret of life" ?
(A) Eliot (B) Wilde
(C) Shaw (D) Auden

1541. Who wrote in the preface to his *Renaissance Studies*, "What is more important..... is not that the critic should possess a correct abstract definition of beauty for the intellect, but a certain kind of temperament, the power of being deeply moved by the presence of beautiful objects" ?

(A) Keats (B) Wilde
(C) de la Mare (D) Pater

1542. Who argued in his brilliant essay on *The Birth of Tragedy* that tragedy is profoundly musical ?
(A) Nietzsche (B) Kant
(C) Diderot (D) Schopenhauer

1543. The main line of succession of the French symbolist movement, it is generally agreed, runs from
(A) Baudelaire to Valery and then to Mallarme
(B) Mallarme to Baudelaire and then to Valery
(C) Baudelaire to Mallarme and then to Valery
(D) Valery to Baudelaire and then to Mallarme

1544. What did W.B. Yeats refer to as the "greatest of all powers whether they are used consciously by the masters of magic, or half unconsciously by their successors, the poet, the musician and the artist" ?
(A) Metaphors (B) Alliteration
(C) Rhyme (D) Symbols

1545. Who argued in *The Sense of Beauty* (1896), that the beauty that we attribute to objects is merely the objectification of our own emotions ?
(A) Max Eastman
(B) George Santayana
(C) I.A. Richards
(D) T.S. Eliot

1546. What did I.A. Richards mean by synaesthesis?
(A) The peculiar organization of our impulses in a manner that harmonizes them
(B) The highest point of aesthetic pleasure
(C) The simultaneous consciousness of beauty in so many things
(D) None of the above

1547. Who are the authors of the critical work *The Meaning of Meaning ?*
(A) I.A. Richards and W.B. Stanford
(B) W.B. Stanford and Edgar Alan Poe
(C) Edgar Alan Poe and C.K. Ogden
(D) C.K. Ogden and I.A. Richards

1548. Who wrote the famous critical work, *Seven Types of Ambiguity ?*
(A) Robert Graves (B) I.A. Richards
(C) Empson (D) Ogden

1549. I.A. Richards is not associated with
(A) *Principles of Literary Criticism*
(B) *The Meaning of Meaning*
(C) *The Symbolist Movement in Literature*
(D) *The Philosophy of Rhetoric*

1550. Eliot made it plain in his essay entitled *"The Perfect Critic"* that he did not consider that the proper alternative to moralization was
(A) Symbolism
(B) Impressionism
(C) Expressionism
(D) Imagism

1551. In which of his critical works Eliot wrote that "the poet has, not a personality to express, but a particular medium, which is only a medium and not a personality, in which impressions and experiences combine in peculiar and unexpected ways" ?
(A) *The Sacred Wood*
(B) *The Metaphysical Poets*
(C) *Speculations*
(D) *Tradition and the Individual Talent*

1552. Who had said that the Metaphysical Poets "yoked by violence together" the most heterogeneous ideas" ?
(A) Eliot (B) Richards
(C) Johnson (D) Bacon

1553. Who found in the bold and often strenuous figurative language of the metaphysical poets the necessary fears for achieving "a direct sensuous apprehension of thought, or a recreation of thought into feeling" ?
(A) Coleridge (B) Arnold
(C) Eliot (D) Richards

1554. In his doctrine of the "objective correlative" Eliot follows the theory and practice of the

(A) Classicists (B) Romanticists
(C) Symbolists (D) Naturalists

1555. Who attacked T.S. Eliot saying that *The Waste Land* betrays in its "Limp" rhythms his own "spiritual limpness" ?

(A) Ransom (B) Empson
(C) Tate (D) Winters

1556. Which of the following is true regarding Eliot's opinion on poetry ?

(A) Poetry is an extension of the poet's personality
(B) Poetry has a life of its own independent of poet's personality
(C) The line between the poet's life and the life of his poetry is thin and hazy
(D) Poetry is the antithesis of the poet's personality

1557. Who declared in his *The Art of Fiction* that "A novel is in its broadest definition a personal, a direct impression of life" ?

(A) E.M. Forster
(B) Henry James
(C) Ford Madox Ford
(D) Joseph Conrad

1558. In, *Poetry and Drama* Eliot opined that

(A) All poetry has natural drama
(B) Poetry and drama must be kept separate
(C) Drama in verse is the ideal
(D) Drama in verse is rarely exciting

1559. The poet is only the *efficient* cause of the poem, but the poem, having form, has a formal cause that is to be sought. On examination, Northop Frye finds this formal cause to be

(A) the myth
(B) the archetype
(C) the universal emotion
(D) none of the above

1560. Who held that poetry and myth arise out of the same human needs represent the same kind of symbolic structure and succeed in investing experience with the same kind of awe and magical wonder ?

(A) Northop Frye
(B) Fergusson
(C) Mrs. Langer
(D) Richard Chase

Match the following lists using the codes given below.

1561.

List I	List II
a. *Poetics*	1. Plotinus
b. *Symposium*	2. Longinus
c. *Peri Hupsous*	3. Plato
d. *Enneads*	4. Aristotle

Codes:

	a	b	c	d
(A)	2	3	1	4
(B)	4	2	3	1
(C)	4	3	2	1
(D)	3	2	1	4

1562.

List I	List II
a. *Mimesis*	1. *Faith*
b. *Pistis*	2. *Imitation*
c. *Cikasia*	3. *Sensory Imaging*
d. *Cide*	4. *Idea*

Codes:

	a	b	c	d
(A)	1	2	3	4
(B)	2	1	3	4
(C)	3	2	1	4
(D)	4	3	2	1

1563.

List I	List II
a. *Nemesis*	1. Complication
b. *Metabosis*	2. Denouement
c. *Lusis*	3. Fate
d. *Desis*	4. Change of fate

Codes:

	a	b	c	d
(A)	1	2	3	4
(B)	3	1	2	4
(C)	3	4	2	1
(D)	4	3	1	2

1564. List I **List II**

a. End 1. *Teleute*
b. Beginning 2. *Arche*
c. Middle 3. *Meson*

Codes:

	a	b	c
(A)	3	2	1
(B)	1	2	3
(C)	2	3	1
(D)	2	1	3

1565. Which form of sonnet falls into two main parts: an octave and a sestet ?
(A) Petrarchan
(B) Shakespearean
(C) Spenserian
(D) All of the above

1566. The seven line, iambic pentameter stanza rhyming *ababbcc* is called
(A) *ottava rima* (B) *terza rima*
(C) *sonnet* (D) *rhyme royal*

1567. Of the three stock characters of old Greek comedy *Alazon* was
(A) an imposter and self-deceiving braggart
(B) a self-deprecating but understanding character
(C) a buffoon whose antics were for unmixed laughter
(D) a sober and intelligent man of wit

1568. Who among the following is a self-deprecating but understanding character whose contest with the braggart was central to the Greek comic plot ?
(A) *Alazon*
(B) *Eiron*
(C) *Bomolochos*
(D) *None of the above*

1569. According to Northop Frye the style which is modelled on the language, rhythms and associations of ordinary speech is the
(A) hieratic style
(B) demotic style
(C) colloquial style
(D) middle style

1570. The style in which the members within a sentence or else a sequence of complete sentences, are put one after the other without any expression of their connection or relations except the noncommittal connective "and", is called
(A) periodic
(B) nonperiodic
(C) paratactic (D) hypotactic

1571. An extended narrative which carries a second meaning alongwith its surface story would be called
(A) Symbol (B) Allegory
(C) Exposition (D) Conceit

1572. Which one of the following terms is applied to a character type or plot pattern or description which recurs frequently in literature and is thought to evoke profound emotional responses in the reader by evoking an image already existing in his unconscious mind ?
(A) Myth
(B) Oedepeus complex
(C) Archetype
(D) Anagnorisis

1573. Baroque means
(A) Hilarious and sarcastic literature
(B) Luxurious and extravagant literature
(C) Dull and unenthusiastic literature
(D) Serious and pedantic literature

1574. *Belles lettres* means
(A) beautiful letter writing
(B) beautiful handwriting
(C) lighter writings in prose
(D) chief works or masterpieces

1575. Bathos means
(A) intentional, ludicrous descent from the exalted to the commonplace
(B) unintentional, ludicrous descent from the exalted to the commonplace
(C) Both (A) and (B)
(D) Sudden rise to an exalted style from the commonplace

1576. In case of metaphysical poetry, the term is used to designate an ingenious and fanciful notion or conception, usually expressed through analogy, and pointing to a striking parallel between two seemingly dissimilar things. Identify the term from among the following

(A) Conceit (B) Wit

(C) Cliche (D) Axiom

1577. What is meant by *denouement* in drama?

(A) The final unravelling of the plot

(B) The anticlimax

(C) The expected consequence or end

(D) None of the above

1578. What do you mean by *deus ex machina* ?

(A) The contrived plot and its gradual opening

(B) The main theme or subject in the story

(C) The sudden and unexpected turn in fortune

(D) The supernatural agency in an epic poem

1579. What is a caesura in poetry ?

(A) A pause in a line of verse dictated by the metres

(B) A pause in a line of verse not dictated by the metres but by the natural rhythm of the language

(C) A pause after every stanza inbuilt into the rhythm of the language and matter

(D) Any pause in poetry

1580. Dithyramb is an emotional choral hymn in honour of

(A) Apollo

(B) Saturn

(C) Dionysius

(D) None of the above

1581. Who was the pioneer of the idea of deconstruction that holds that "no work of literature whatsoever has been able to express exactly what it wanted to say" ?

(A) Northop Frye

(B) Daniel Deronda

(C) T.S. Eliot

(D) Jacques Derrida

1582. What is an eclogue ?

(A) A poem expressing lament or sorrow

(B) A short pastoral poem in which shepherds converse with one another

(C) A short lyric describing an incident of deep sorrow like death

(D) None of the above

1583. Epistle is a

(A) letter in verse

(B) story in verse

(C) play in verse

(D) essay in verse

1584. The chief four types of composition are : argumentation, description, narration and

(A) expression

(B) summation

(C) exposition

(D) extension

1585. The school of poetry which flourished under the leadership of Ezra Pound in the second decade of the twentieth century is

(A) symbolism

(B) imagism

(C) expressionism

(D) impressionism

1586. What is the device called by which a writer expresses almost the opposite meaning to what he ostensibly speaks ?

(A) Paradox

(B) Conceit

(C) Irony

(D) Understatement

1587. Malapropism, which means ridiculous misuse of words, is derived from Mrs. Malaprop in Sheridan's novel,

(A) *Life of Romulus*

(B) *Roderick Random*

(C) *Book of Nonsense*

(D) *The Rivals*

1588. Lampoon is a crude, defamatory satire usually attacking a/an

(A) race (B) country
(C) religion (D) individual

1589. A miracle play is one in which

(A) improbable and sensational characters are shown
(B) supernatural theme and characters are displayed
(C) sacred subjects are represented
(D) medieval set up and theme are dealt with

1590. What is a monody ?

(A) A poem of mourning, spoken by one person only
(B) A poem regarding praise of one individual by another
(C) A poem about oneself, one's own thoughts and ideas
(D) A poem written with a singular metrical pattern

1591. Limerick is a special, often ribald, species of light verse, first popularized by

(A) Fitzgerald
(B) Edward Lear
(C) John Donne
(D) Pope

1592. What is the term used by Emile Zola and other French writers to distinguish their methods from the realism of Balzac and Flaubert ?

(A) Naturism
(B) Naturalism
(C) Surrealism
(D) Humanism

1593. Who coined the term "dissociation of sensibility ?

(A) I.A. Richards
(B) Matthew Arnold
(C) S.T. Coleridge
(D) T.S. Eliot

1594. To get the complete meaning of a poem ontological criticism puts emphasis on

(A) The texture
(B) The structure
(C) The narrator
(D) Both (A) and (B)

1595. Panegyric is a formal written or oral composition

(A) deriding a person
(B) lauding a person
(C) lamenting the death of a person
(D) celebrating the marriage of a person

1596. Which of the following is a nuptial song, praying for the joy and prosperity of the bride and the bridegroom ?

(A) Elegy
(B) Epistle
(C) Epithalamion
(D) Eclogue

1597. Irving Babbit, Paul Elmer More and Norman Foerter started a reactionary movement against the excess of Romantic individualism and realistic naturalism of the 1920s. What was the movement called ?

(A) New Humanism
(B) Neo-Platonism
(C) Neologism
(D) New Realism

1598. What is the device called by which non-human and non-living nature is credited with human emotions ?

(A) Parody
(B) Pathetic fallacy
(C) Objective correlation
(D) Unification of sensibility

1599. Purple passage means

(A) a sudden heightening of style, which makes a section of work stand out among the rest
(B) a sudden fall in style which reverses the tone of all the foregone passages
(C) a passage written in grand and heightened style and treating a ridiculous theme for comic effect

(D) a passage expressing a delicate and amorous theme or emotion creating an emotional effect on the reader

1600. What is the term used to mean a sudden change of fortune in a play or story ?
(A) Hamartia
(B) Anagnorisis
(C) Peripeteia
(D) Nemesis

1601. Which of the following means a song, usually of love sung by night under a lady's window ?
(A) Threnody
(B) Bathos
(C) Doggerel
(D) Serenade

1602. "You will leave at once by the town drain." The transposition of initial sounds such as this is called
(A) Malapropism
(B) Spoonerism
(C) Solecism
(D) Sarcasm

1603. The movement in art and literature emphasizing the expression of the imagination as realized in dreams and presented without conscious control, which developed in France under the leadership of Andre Breton, is
(A) Symbolism
(B) Imagism
(C) Surrealism
(C) Mysticism

1604. "Kill the boys and the luggage" — this statement, in which "kill" is incorrectly related to the second object is a
(A) solecism
(B) spoonerism
(C) pun
(D) zeugma

1605. The feet of two syllables in which the unstressed syllable precedes the stressed one is called
(A) trochaic
(B) dactylic
(C) anapaestic
(D) iambic

1606. In the trochaic
(A) two stressed syllables follow one unstressed syllable
(B) two unstressed syllables follow one stressed syllable
(C) a stressed syllable is followed by an unstressed syllable
(D) an unstressed syllable follows two stressed syllables

1607. What is the feet of three syllables called in which two unstressed syllables precede the stressed one ?
(A) Anapaestic (B) Dactylic
(C) Amphibrachic (D) Trochaic

1608. The pattern of two unaccented syllables following the accented one is called
(A) Anapaestic
(B) Dactylic
(C) Amphibrachic
(D) Trochaic

1609. In the amphibrachic
(A) the accented syllable comes between the two unaccented
(B) the unaccented syllable comes between the two accented
(C) two accented syllables are followed by two unaccented syllables
(D) two unaccented syllables are followed by two accented syllables

1610. Spondaic foot contains two
(A) stressed syllables
(B) unstressed syllables
(C) stressed or unstressed syllables
(D) different syllables

1611. What is the rhyming pattern of Pope's *Essay on Man* ?
(A) *aa* (B) *abab*
(C) *ab* (D) *ababc*

1612. What is the rhyming pattern of the quatrain used by Keats in *La Belle Dame Sans Merci?*
(A) *aabb* (B) *abab*
(C) *abcb* (D) *abac*

1613. Identify the Spenserian stanza from the rhyming patterns given below :
(A) *abcabacbc*
(B) *ababbcbcc*
(C) *abccbabac*
(D) *abcaabbcc*

1614. Byron in his *Beppo* and Keats in *Isabella* used an eight lined stanza with the rhyming scheme of *abababcc* which is called the
(A) Spenserian stanza
(B) Italian stanza
(C) Petrarchan stanza
(D) Chaucerean stanza

1615. The 'heroic' couplet is written in
(A) trochaic tetrameter
(B) spondaic hexameter
(C) iambic tetrameter
(D) iambic pentameter

1616. What is the meter in Longfellow's *Evangeline*, Kingsley's *Andromeda* and Clough's *Bothic of Tober-na-Vuolich* ?
(A) Iambic pentameter
(B) Trochaic tetrameter
(C) Dactylic hexameter
(D) Spondaic hexameter

1617. Wilde's novel *The Picture of Dorian Gray* and his play *Salome* are representative literary products of the
(A) Renaissance of wonder
(B) Decadent movement
(C) Impressionist school
(D) Edwardian period

1618. Which of the following is alternatively known as the Age of Sensibility ?
(A) The Age of Pope
(B) The Age of Milton
(C) The Age of Johnson
(D) The Age of Wordsworth

1619. "Affective fallacy" was first defined as the error of evaluating a poem by its effects in an essay published in 1946 by
(A) W.K. Wimsatt, Jr.
(B) Monroe C. Beardsley
(C) A.C. Bradley
(D) Both (A) and (B)

1620. In Dryden's *Absalom and Achitophel* King David represents Charles II, Absalom represents his natural son the Duke of Monmouth and the biblical plot allegorizes a political crisis in contemporary England. This is an example of
(A) Symbolism
(B) Allegory
(C) Chronicle play
(D) Melodrama

1621. Which of the following is a short narrative presented so as to stress the implicit but detailed analogy between its component parts and a lesson or moral that the narrator is trying to bring home to the readers?
(A) Parable
(B) Fable
(C) Exemplum
(D) Allegory

1622. An extremely popular device in the Middle Ages was a story told as a particular instance of the general text of a sermon. What is it called ?
(A) Fable
(B) Parable
(C) Exemplum
(D) Ballad

1623. "Thou st*i*ll unrav*i*shed br*i*de of qu*i*etness
Thou foster child of silence and slow time"
The repetition of the '*i*' sound in the above lines is an instance of
(A) alliteration
(B) consonance

(C) assonance
(D) None of the above

1624. W.H. Auden's "O where are you going?' said reader to rider" makes prominent use of
(A) alliteration
(B) consonance
(C) assonance
(D) None of the above

1625. Alliteration is the repetition of speech sounds in a sequence of nearby words, usually applied to
(A) consonants only
(B) vowels only
(C) both consonants and vowels
(D) unstressed syllables

1626. Allusion in a work of literature is a brief, explicit or indirect reference to
(A) a person
(B) a place or event
(C) another literary work
(D) any of the above

1627. What is meant by *portmanteau,* a term introduced by Humpty Dumpty in Lewis Caroll's *Through the Looking Glass* ?
(A) A word opposite in meaning to its sound
(B) A word used in its original meaning
(C) A word coined by fusing together two or more words
(D) A word with very complex meaning

1628. Alexander Pope's description of Atticus in his *Epistle to Dr. Arbuthnot*, "Willing to wound, yet afraid to strike" is an example of
(A) irony
(B) antithesis
(C) paradox
(D) ambiguity

1629. The deliberate use of words and expressions that have become obsolete in common speech is called
(A) archaism (B) archetype
(C) allusion
(D) anachronism

1630. Who among the following was the first to employ in literary criticism the theory of archetype ?
(A) Richard chase
(B) Maud Bodkin
(C) Northop Frye
(D) G. Wilson Knight

1631. The most common stanza form in popular ballads is a *quatrain* in alternate four and three-stress iambic lines, in which only the
(A) first and third lines rhyme
(B) first and fourth lines rhyme
(C) second and fourth lines rhyme
(D) third and fourth lines rhyme

1632. What is meant by a bowdlerized text ?
(A) one that pretends to terrify the reader by horrific images
(B) one full of bombast and euphuism
(C) one improvised in style and language upon the original text by another writer
(D) One from which passages considered off- ending or indecent have been expurgated.

1633. A *mock epic* or *mock-heroic* poem imitates the elaborate form and ceremonious style of the epic genre, and applies it to a commonplace subject matter, while a *parody* imitates the serious materials and manner of a
(A) particular work
(B) particular author
(C) both (A) and (B)
(D) particular genre

1634. The Hudibrastic poem is named after *Hudibras* (1863) of
(A) Spenser
(B) Samuel Butler
(C) John Donne
(D) None of the above

1635. Which of the following is a variety of low burlesque which, like parody, mocks a par-

ticular work by treating its lofty subject in a jocular and undignified manner ?
(A) Hudibrastic poem
(B) Mock epic
(C) Travesty
(D) Doggerel

1636. Which of the following is the name for a very common literary motif, especially in lyric poetry, emphasizing that life is short and time is fleeting and exhorting the addressee, often a reluctant virgin, to make the most of present pleasures ?
(A) Cavalier
(B) *Carpe diem*
(C) *Deus ex machina*
(D) Prothalamion

1637. What is meant by a *choral character* in modern criticism ?
(A) The central character in a play
(B) The central character in the chorus in a play
(C) A character within the play itself who stands apart from the action and by his comments and provides the audience with a special perspective
(D) A character who interferes in the play at times to interpret the action and characters for the audience

1638. Mimetic criticism views literary work as an imitation, or reflection of
(A) previous authors
(B) myths and legends
(C) the world and human life
(D) dreams and reveries

1639. The phrase "dissociation of sensibility" was introduced by T.S. Eliot with reference to
(A) the Romantic poets
(B) Shakespeare
(C) Milton
(D) the metaphysical poets

1640. What is a closet drama ?
(A) A drama though written in the dramatic form, intended to be read rather than to be performed in the theater
(B) A drama intended to be performed within a closet and not on stage
(C) A drama set in a closet or a single room with characters coming into and out of it
(D) None of the above

1641. The dirge also expresses grief on the occasion of death, but differs from the elegy in that it is
(A) long and less formal
(B) short and more formal
(C) long and more formal
(D) short and less formal

1642. Which of the following is not a characteristic feature of a postoral elegy ?
(A) The lyric speaker begins by invoking the muses
(B) There is a procession of appropriate mourners
(C) The mourner charges with negligence the nymphs or other guardians of the dead shepherd
(D) The soul of the dead shepherd realizes at the end that death in this world is the entry to a higher life

1643. Keat's expression that he becomes "a part of all he sees" reflects his intense
(A) sensuousness
(B) empathy
(C) sympathy
(D) romanticism

1644. What is the meaning of epiphany ?
(A) A religious text in verse meant for preaching
(B) A sudden radiance or revelation while observing a commonplace object
(C) A mock revelation used for comic effect at the sight of a trivial object
(D) A letter written by an anonymous writer for public reading

1645. Replacing a supposedly offensive or disagreeable term by a less direct or less colloquial term is termed as
(A) euphuism

(B) euphemism
(C) bowdlerization
(D) spoonerism

1646. Language which seems smooth, pleasant and musical to the ear is termed as
(A) euphony
(B) cacophony
(C) melody
(D) harmony

1647. The artistic movement which began in Germany at the start of the twentieth century, under the strong influence of the Swedish dramatist Strindberg is
(A) impressionism
(B) expressionism
(C) decadence
(D) imagism

1648. Which of the following is a medieval form: a short comic or satiric tale in verse dealing realistically with middle-class or lower-class characters and delighting in the ribald and the obscene ?
(A) Ballad (B) Parable
(C) Fabliau (C) Fable

1649. What is meant by "tropes" in rhetoric ?
(A) figures of speech
(B) language loaded with metaphors
(C) indirect saying
(D) a decided extension or change in the standard meaning of words.

1650. Burns's "O my love's like a red, red rose" is an example of
(A) simile
(B) metaphor
(C) dead metaphor
(D) symbol

1651. "The leg of the table" and "the heart of the matter" are examples of
(A) implicit metaphor
(B) mixed metaphor
(C) dead metaphor
(D) simple metaphor

1652. What is the term used to denote the use of one term to mean another with which it has become closely associated as 'the crown' stands for 'the king' ?
(A) Synecdoche
(B) Onometopoeia
(C) Prosopopeia
(D) Metonymy

1653. What is meant by Synecdoche ?
(A) A part of something used to signify the whole
(B) The whole of something used to signify a part
(C) An inanimate object endowed with human feelings
(D) The terms with a pronunciation similar to their meaning

1654. The Greek term *meiosis* stands for
(A) a hyperbole
(B) an understatement
(C) moderation in style
(D) improper treatment of subject

1655. A special form of understatement, which asserts an affirmative by negating the contrary is
(A) meiosis (B) litotes
(C) irony (D) variorum

1656. The error of interpreting or evaluating a work by reference to the plan or design of the author is termed as
(A) pathetic fallacy
(B) affective fallacy
(C) intentional fallacy
(D) None of the above

1657. The kind of irony the intention of which is shared by the author and the reader or audience but not by the speaker is a case of
(A) verbal irony
(B) socratic irony
(C) cosmic irony
(D) structural irony

1658. Socratic irony is a pretention to
(A) ignorance in place of knowledge
(B) admiration in place of contempt
(C) affection in place of disgust
(D) enthusiasm in place of disinterestedness

1659. What sort of irony do we find in *Tristam Shandy* and *Don Juan* ?
(A) Invective irony
(B) Romantic irony
(C) Cosmic irony
(D) Socratic irony

1660. Two successive syllables with approximately equal light stresses constitute a
(A) spondee
(B) pyrrhic
(C) trochaic
(D) dactylic

1661. What is meant by a feminine ending of a line of verse ?
(A) closing with an extra light syllable
(B) closing with an extra stressed syllable
(C) closing with an extra syllable
(D) closing without any extra syllable

1662. The *ubi sunt motif* in poetry means the formula for lamenting
(A) the irony of fate
(B) the death of a friend
(C) the past that is no more
(D) the general degradation of human world

1663. According to the theory of Northop Frye the four main narrative genres of literature are comedy, romance, tragedy and
(A) autobiography
(B) poetry
(C) myth
(D) irony

1664. The Pindaric Ode stanza pattern was in sets of three: the strophe, the antistrophe and
(A) the interlude
(B) the trophe
(C) the epode
(D) the antipode

1665. Onomatopoeia means
(A) echoing the same sound repeatedly
(B) echoing of the sense by the sound, shape, size or movement
(C) echoing of the same sense or meaning in different words
(D) none of the above

1666. *A Woman Killed with Kindness* — this title is an instance of
(A) onomatopoeia
(B) synecdoche
(C) paradox
(D) irony

1667. If the paradoxical utterance combines two terms that in ordinary usage are contraries, such as "pleasing pains" and "burning chill", it is called a/an
(A) oxymoron
(B) conceit
(C) cliche
(D) equivoque

1668. Pun is a play on words that are similar
(A) in sound but diverse in meaning
(B) in meaning but diverse in sound
(C) both in sound and meaning but with different spellings
(D) None of the above

1669. Refrain is
(A) a short pause between lines
(B) the concluding line of a stanza in verse
(C) a line or group of lines which is repeated throughout the course of the poem
(D) the pause between stanzas

1670. Out of three main categories of oratory distinguished by Aristotelian critics which one stands for 'display rhetoric', used on ceremonial occasions to amplify the praise of a person ?
(A) Deliberative
(B) Epideictic

(C) Forensic
(D) None of the above

1671. Which of the following is a direct address either to an absent person or to an abstract or inanimate entity ?
(A) Ode
(B) Epode
(C) Zeugma
(D) Apostrophe

1672. *Roman a Clef* is a French term which literally means
(A) a romantic novel
(B) a work of fiction
(C) a novel with a key
(D) a romantic satire

1673. Which of the following is a sequence of two phrases or clauses which are parallel in syntax, but with a reversal in the order of the words ?
(A) Chiasmus
(B) Zeugma
(C) Tercet
(D) Lai

1674. Name the literary device in which a single word stands in the same grammatical relation to two or more other words, but with some alteration in its meaning from one instance to the next.
(A) Cliche (B) Zeugma
(C) Epithet (D) Conceit

1675. *Gone with the Wind* shows
(A) futility of romantic love
(B) how true love is nearby while one struggles to find it elsewhere as scarlet realized that Rhett was her true love while she thought it to be Ashley
(C) human relationship is supreme
(D) romantic love completes the mission of life

1676. What happens after Wang Lung's death in *The Good Earth?*
(A) the sons remain wealthy and powerful through inheritance
(B) the sons divorce their lives from the soil and lose their pre-eminence for they lacked the vigour and intensity
(C) the sons join other ways of livelihood and lose contact with reality
(D) the good earth is neglected

1677. *Lolita* became famous because
(A) it presents an unusual sexual story
(B) it presents a story of a mature man's sexual fantasy – which attracts as well as repels
(C) it tells of Humbert seducing his own step daughter
(D) a unique story of love and sex between 13 year old girl and her step father of 56 years

1678. What happens in *A Doll's House* (1879)?
(A) a woman declares independence
(B) Nora awakens to her responsibility and leaves her husband to be herself
(C) it deals with woman emancipation
(D) new-world order

1679. What is God's plan for man in *Faust?*
(A) man may be tempted and beguiled but he cannot be misled forever because he retains the instinct for the one true divine way
(B) man errs
(C) man falls but is capable of arising
(D) man created in the image of God, so basically he is good

1680. *The Wild Duck* is based on
(A) the idea of a wild a goose chase
(B) the legend that when a wild duck is wounded it does not return to the flock but dives deep and fastens itself to seaweed
(C) the belief that a wild duck can never be tamed or caged
(D) the spirit of wilderness, freedom

1681. Words from which language began to enter English vocabulary around the time of the Norman Conquest in 1066?

(A) French (B) Norwegian
(C) Spanish (D) Hungarian

1682. Which hero made his earliest appearance in Celtic literature before becoming a staple subject in French, English, and German literatures?
(A) Beowulf
(B) Arthur
(C) Caedmon
(D) Augustine of Canterbury

1683. Toward the close of which century did English replace French as the language of conducting business in Parliament and in court of law?
(A) tenth (B) twelfth
(C) thirteenth (D) fourteenth

1684. Who would be called the English Homer and father of English poetry?
(A) Bede
(B) Sir Thomas Malory
(C) Geoffrey Chaucer
(D) Caedmon

1685. What was vellum?
(A) parchment made of animal skin
(B) the service owed to a lord by his peasants ("villeins")
(C) unrhymed iambic pentameter
(D) a prized ink used in the illumination of prestigious manuscripts

1686. Only a small proportion of medieval books survive, large numbers having been destroyed in:
(A) the Anglo-Saxon Conquest beginning in the 1450s.
(B) the Peasant Uprising of 1381.
(C) the Dissolution of the Monasteries in the 1530s.
(D) the wave of contempt for manuscripts that followed the beginning of printing in 1476.

1687. What is the first extended written specimen of Old English?
(A) Boethius's *Consolidation of Philosophy*
(B) Saint Jerome's translation of the Bible
(C) Bede's *Ecclesiastical History of the English People*
(D) a code of laws promulgated by King Ethelbert

1688. In Anglo-Saxon heroic poetry, what is the fate of those who fail to observe the sacred duty of blood vengeance?
(A) banishment to Asia
(B) everlasting shame
(C) conversion to Christianity
(D) being buried alive

1689. Christian writers like the Beowulf poet looked back on their pagan ancestors with:
(A) nostalgia and ill-concealed envy.
(B) bewilderment and visceral loathing.
(C) admiration and elegiac sympathy.
(D) bigotry and shallow triumphalism.

1690. The use of "whale-road" for sea and "life-house" for body are examples of what literary technique, popular in Old English poetry?
(A) Symbolism
(B) Metonymy
(C) Keening
(D) Appositive expression

1691. Which of the following statements is not an accurate description of Old English poetry?
(A) Romantic love is a guiding principle of moral conduct.
(B) Its formal and dignified use of speech was distant from everyday use of language.
(C) Irony is a mode of perception, as much as it was a figure of speech.
(D) Its idiom remained remarkably uniform for nearly three centuries.

1692. Which of the following best describes litote, a favorite rhetorical device in Old English poetry?
(A) embellishment at the service of Christian doctrine

(B) ironic understatement
(C) stress on every third diphthong
(D) a compound of two words in place of a single word

1693. Which of the following languages did not coexist in Anglo-Norman England?
(A) Latin (B) Dutch
(C) French (D) Celtic

1694. Which twelfth-century poet or poets were indebted to Breton storytellers for their narratives?
(A) Geoffrey Chaucer
(B) Marie de France
(C) Chrétien de Troyes
(D) B and C only

1695. To what did the word the roman, from which the genre of "romance" emerged, initially apply?
(A) a work derived from a Latin text of the Roman Empire
(B) a story about love and adventure
(C) a work written in the French vernacular
(D) a series of short stories

1696. Popular English adaptations of romances appealed primarily to
(A) the royal family and upper orders of the nobility
(B) the lower orders of the nobility
(C) agricultural laborers
(D) the clergy

1697. What is the climax of Geoffrey of Monmouth's *The History of the Kings of Britain?*
(A) the reign of King Arthur
(B) the coronation of Henry II
(C) King John's seal of the *Magna Carta*
(D) the marriage of Henry II to Eleanor of Aquitaine

1698. *Ancrene Riwle* is a manual of instruction for
(A) translators of French romances
(B) women who have chosen to live as religious recluses
(C) knights preparing for their first tournament
(D) witch-hunters and exorcists

1699. The styles of *The Owl and the Nightingale and Ancrene Riwle* show what about the poetry and prose written around the year 1200?
(A) They were written for sophisticated and well-educated readers.
(B) Writing continued to benefit only readers fluent in Latin and French.
(C) Their readers' primary language was English.
(D) A and C only

1700. In addition to Geoffrey Chaucer and William Langland, the "flowering" of Middle English literature is evident in the works of which of the following writers?
(A) Geoffrey of Monmouth
(B) the Gawain poet
(C) the Beowulf poet
(D) Chrétien de Troyes

1701. Which influential medieval text purported to reveal the secrets of the afterlife?
(A) Dante's *Divine Comedy*
(B) Boccaccio's *Decameron*
(C) *The Dream of the Rood*
(D) Chaucer's *Legend of Good Women*

1702. Who is the author of Piers Plowman?
(A) Sir Thomas Malory
(B) Margery Kempe
(C) William Langland
(D) Geoffrey of Monmouth

1703. Which literary form, developed in the fifteenth century, personified vices and virtues?
(A) the short story
(B) the heroic epic
(C) the morality play
(D) the romance

1704. Which of the following statements about Julian of Norwich is true?

(A) She sought unsuccessfully to restore classical paganism.
(B) She was a virgin martyr.
(C) She is the first known woman writer in the English vernacular.
(D) She made pilgrimages to Jerusalem, Rome, and Santiago.

1705. Which of the following authors is considered a devotee to chivalry, as it is personified in Sir Lancelot?
(A) Julian of Norwich
(B) Margery Kempe
(C) William Langland
(D) Sir Thomas Malory

1706. Which of the following statements accurately reflects the status of England, its people, and its language in the early sixteenth century?
(A) English travelers were not obliged to learn French, Italian, or Spanish during their explorations of the Continent.
(B) English was fast supplanting Latin as the second language of most European intellectuals.
(C) English travelers often returned from the Continent with foreign fashions, much to the delight of moralists.
(D) Intending his Utopia for an international intellectual community, Thomas More wrote in Latin, since English had no prestige outside of England.

1707. Which of the following sixteenth-century works of English literature was translated into the English language after its first publication in Latin?
(A) Christopher Marlowe's *Doctor Faustus*
(B) William Shakespeare's *King Lear*
(C) Thomas More's *The History of King Richard III*
(D) Thomas More's *Utopia*

1708. Which royal dynasty was established in the resolution of the so-called War of the Roses and continued through the reign of Elizabeth I?
(A) Tudor
(B) Windsor
(C) York
(D) Lancaster

1709. From which of the following Italian texts might Tudor courtiers have learned the art of intrigue and the keys to gaining and keeping power?
(A) Dante's "Divine Comedy"
(B) Boccaccio's "Decameron"
(C) Machiavelli's "The Prince"
(D) Ariosto's "Orlando Furioso"

1710. Who authored *Il Cortigiano* (The Courtier), a book that was highly influential in the English court, providing subtle guidance on self-display?
(A) Castiglione
(B) Pirandello
(C) Boccaccio
(D) Machiavelli

1711. Who introduced the art of printing into England?
(A) Elizabeth Eisenstein
(B) Johannes Gutenberg
(C) Henry VIII
(D) William Caxton

1712. To what does the phrase "the stigma of print" refer?
(A) lead poisoning contracted from handling printer's ink
(B) the brutal punishment for printing without a license
(C) the perception among court poets that printed verses were less exclusive
(D) all of the above

1713. Which of the following sixteenth-century poets was not a courtier?
(A) George Puttenham
(B) Philip Sidney
(C) Thomas Wyatt
(D) all of the above

1714. Which of the following statements is not an accurate reflection of education during the English Renaissance?
(A) It was aimed primarily at sons of the nobility and gentry.
(B) Its curriculum emphasized ancient Greek, the language of diplomacy, professions, and higher learning.
(C) It was conducted by tutors in wealthy families or in grammar schools.
(D) It was ordered according to the medieval trivium and quadrivium.

1715. What impulse probably accounts for the rise of distinguished translations of works, such as Homer's *Iliad* and *Odyssey*, into English during the sixteenth century?
(A) human reverence for the classics
(B) the belief that the English were direct descendants of the ancient Greeks
(C) pride for the vernacular language
(D) a and c only

1716. What was the only acknowledged religion in England during the early sixteenth century?
(A) Atheism (B) Protestantism
(C) Catholicism
(D) Judaism

1717. Who began to ignite the embers of dissent against the Catholic church in November 1517 in a movement that came to be known as the Reformation?
(A) Anne Boleyn
(B) Martin Luther
(C) Ulrich Zwingli
(D) John Calvin

1718. Expressed in Elizabethan poetry as well as court rituals and events, a cult of ______ formed around Elizabeth and dictated the nature of relations between herself and her court.
(A) ignominy
(B) unwarranted abuse
(C) odium
(D) love

1719. Which of the following describes the chief system by which writers received financial rewards for their literary production?
(A) charity (B) patronage
(C) censorship
(D) subscription

1720. *In the Defense of Poesy,* what did Sidney attribute to poetry?
(A) a magical power whereby poetry plays tricks on the reader
(B) a divine power whereby poetry transmits a message from God to the reader
(C) a moral power whereby poetry encourages the reader to emulate virtuous models
(D) a defensive power whereby poetry and its figurative expressions allow the poet to avoid censorship

1721. Which of the following might be addressed/ represented by pastoral poetry?
(1) an exaltation of the city life over the boring country life
(2) shepherd and shepherdesses who fall in love and engage in singing contests
(3) heroic stories in epic form
(4) a celebration of the humility, contentment, and simplicity of living in the country

Codes :
(A) 1 and 2 only (B) 2 and 4 only
(C) 1, 2 and 4 (D) all the above

1722. The churchyard of St. Paul's Cathedral was well-known for its
(A) ruinous condition.
(B) graffiti.
(C) wine bars.
(D) bookshops.

1723. Who owned the rights to a theatrical script?
(A) the playwright(s)
(B) the patron of the acting company, e.g., the Lord Chamberlain
(C) the printer
(D) the acting company

1724. Short plays called ________-staged dialogues on religious, moral, and political themes-were performed by playing companies before the construction of public theaters.
(A) interludes (B) spectacles
(C) mysteries (D) vaudeville

1725. To what subgenre did the Senecan influence give rise, as evidenced in the first English tragedy Gorboduc, or Ferrex and Porrex?
(A) villain tragedy
(B) poetic tragedy
(C) heroic tragedy
(D) revenge tragedy

1726. What is blank verse?
(A) iambic pentameter in rhyming couplets
(B) free verse, without rhyme or regular meter
(C) alliterative iambic tetrameter
(D) unrhymed iambic pentameter

1727. Which of the following is true about public theaters in Elizabethan England?
(A) They relied on admission charges, an innovation of the period.
(B) They were located outside the city limits of London.
(C) The seating structure was tiered, with placement correlating to ticket cost.
(D) all of the above

1728. Which was not an objection raised against the public theaters in the Elizabethan period?
(A) They caused excessive noise and traffic.
(B) They charged too much.
(C) They excited illicit sexual desires.
(D) They drew young people away from work.

1729. Which writer was not active under both Elizabeth I and James I?
(A) William Shakespeare
(B) John Donne
(C) Francis Bacon
(D) John Milton

1730. Which of the following was not one of the four bodily humours?
(A) choler
(B) blood
(C) cholesterol
(D) phlegm

1731. Which poet was a member of the powerful and culturally influential Sidney family?
(A) Aemilia Lanyer
(B) Samuel Daniel
(C) Mary Wroth
(D) George Herbert

1732. What was the licensing system?
(A) Poets were required to have a university diploma (the original "poetic license").
(B) All books had to be dedicated to a noble or royal patron.
(C) Books could be recalled and burned on the basis of anonymous complaints.
(D) All books had to be submitted for official approval before publication.

1733. Which was not among the genres promoted by poets such as Jonson, Donne, and Herbert?
(A) the Petrarchan sonnet
(B) the classical satire
(C) the country-house poem
(D) the epigram

1734. Which of the following plays was not authored by Shakespeare in the Jacobean period?
(A) *Othello*
(B) *Volpone*
(C) *The Tempest*
(D) *Antony and Cleopatra*

1735. Which poem testifies to the profound doubts and uncertainties attending Donne's conversion from Catholicism to Protestantism?

(A) "Air and Angels"
(B) "Satire 3"
(C) "The Apparition"
(D) "You Don't Change Horses in the Middle of the Stream"

1736. What major new prose genre emerged in the Jacobean era?
(A) the novel
(B) the sermon
(C) the familiar essay
(D) the intimate essay

1737. Which of the following female authors of the Jacobean era wrote a work that became the "first" of its kind to be published by an English woman?
(A) Rachel Speght
(B) Elizabeth Cary, Lady Falkland
(C) Lady Mary Wroth
(D) all of the above

1738. Which group of radicals got their name from their penchant for rambling prophecy?
(A) the Fifth Monarchists
(B) the Roarers
(C) the Quakers
(D) the Ranters

1739. What was one of the first acts of Parliament after the outbreak of hostilities in the First Civil War?
(A) the abolishment of public plays and sports
(B) the conversion of the English church to Catholicism
(C) the adoption of English as the official language
(D) the consolidation of power in an absolute monarch

1740. Which of the following themes or subjects was not common in the works of Cavalier poets, such as Thomas Carew, Sir John Denham, Edmund Walter, Sir John Suckling, James Shirely, Richard Lovelace, and Robert Herrick?
(A) courtly ideals of the good life
(B) *carpe diem*
(C) loyalty to the king
(D) pious devotion to religious virtues

1741. What was the general subject of the Welsh poet Katherine Philips's work?
(A) celebrations of the transience of all life and beauty
(B) celebrations of lesbian sexuality in terms that did not imply a male readership
(C) celebrations of religious ecstasy and divine inspiration
(D) celebrations of female friendship in Platonic terms normally reserved for male friendships

1742. What was the title of Thomas Hobbes's defense of absolute sovereignty based on a theory of social contract?
(A) *The Litany in a Time of Plague*
(B) *Leviathan*
(C) *The Advancement of Learning*
(D) *The Obedience of a Christian Man*

1743. What is the delicate balancing act of Marvell's "Horatian Ode"?
(A) praising feminine virtue whilst mocking the fixation on chastity
(B) celebrating Cromwell's victories whilst inviting sympathy for the executed king
(C) celebrating the Restoration whilst regretting the frivolity of the new regime
(D) satirizing John Milton whilst appearing to praise him

1744. Which of the following did Milton not advocate in print in the 1640s and 1650s?
(A) the disestablishment of the church and the removal of bishops
(B) the free circulation of ideas without prior censorship
(C) the right to divorce on the grounds of incompatibility
(D) the restoration of the monarchy

1745. Who authored the scholarly biography, *Life of Donne?*

(A) Izaak Walton
(B) Katherine Philips
(C) John Skelton
(D) Isabella Whitney

1746. What is the title to Milton's blank-verse epic that assimilates and critiques the epic tradition?
(A) *Lycidas*
(B) *Paradise Lost*
(C) *The Divine Comedy*
(D) *The Beggar's Opera*

1747. What literary work best captures a sense of the political turmoil, particularly regarding the issue of religion, just after the Restoration?
(A) Gay's *Beggar's Opera*
(B) Butler's *Hudibras*
(C) Pope's *Dunciad*
(D) Dryden's *Absalom and Achitophel*

1748. In the late seventeenth century, a "battle of the books" erupted between which two groups?
(A) round-earthers and flat-earthers
(B) the Welsh and the Scots
(C) champions of ancient and modern learning
(D) Oxfordians and Baconians

1749. Which of the following best describes the doctrine of empiricism?
(A) All knowledge is derived from experience.
(B) Human perceptions are constructed and reflect structures of political power.
(C) The search for essential or ultimate principles of reality.
(D) God is the center of an ordered and just universe.

1750. Against which of the following principles did Jonathan Swift inveigh?
(A) Theoretical science
(B) Metaphysics
(C) Abstract logical deductions
(D) A, B, and C

1751. Whose great Dictionary, published in 1755, included more than 114,000 quotations?
(A) William Hogarth
(B) Jonathan Swift
(C) Samuel Johnson
(D) James Boswell

1752. What drove William Cowper to break down and become a recluse?
(A) the conviction that he was damned forever
(B) the loss of his fortune in the "South Sea Bubble"
(C) condemnation of his work by Jeremy Collier
(D) his skewering in Pope's Dunciad

1753. According to Samuel Johnson, "No man but a blockhead ever wrote except for
(A) love." (B) honor."
(C) money." (D) fun."

1754. Which of the following women exposed themselves to scandal by writing racy stories for the popular press?
(A) Charlotte Perkins Gilman, Mary Wroth, and Elizabeth Cary
(B) Aphra Behn, Delarivier Manley, and Eliza Haywood
(C) Anne Finch, Anne Killigrew, and Lady Mary Wortley Montagu
(D) Rachel Speght, Katherine Philips, and Frances Burney

1755. What name is given to the English literary period that emulated the Rome of Virgil, Horace, and Ovid?
(A) Augustan
(B) Metaphysical
(C) Romantic
(D) Neo-Romantic

1756. Horace's doctrine "ut pictura poesis" was interpreted to mean:
(A) A picture is worth a thousand words.
(B) Poetry is the supreme artistic form.
(C) Art should hold a mirror up to nature.
(D) Poetry ought to be a visual as well as a verbal art.

1757. What was most frequently considered a source of pleasure and an object of inquiry by Augustan poets?
(A) civilization (B) woman
(C) alcohol (D) nature

1758. What word did writers in this period use to express quickness of mind, inventiveness, a knack for conceiving images and metaphors and for perceiving resemblances between things apparently unlike?
(A) wit
(B) sprezzatura
(C) naturalism
(D) gusto

1759. Which of the following was probably not a stock phrase in eighteenth-century poetry?
(A) checkered shade
(B) simian rivalry
(C) shining sword
(D) bounding main

1760. Which metrical form was Pope said to have brought to perfection?
(A) the heroic couplet
(B) blank verse
(C) the ode
(D) the spondee

1761. Which poet, critic and translator brought England a modern literature between 1660 and 1700?
(A) Addison
(B) Crabbe
(C) Dryden
(D) Equiano

1762. Which of the following is not an example of Restoration comedy?
(A) Etherege's *The Man of Mode*
(B) Wycherley's *The Country Wife*
(C) Behn's *The Rover*
(D) Marlowe's *Doctor Faustus*

1763. Which group of intellectual women established literary clubs of their own around 1750 under the leadership of Elizabeth Vesey and Elizabeth Montagu?
(A) the Behnites
(B) the bluestockings
(C) the coteries of plenty
(D) the tattlers and spectators

1764. Which work exposes the frivolity of fashionable London?
(A) Swift's *Gulliver's Travels*
(B) Behn's *Oroonoko*
(C) Richardson's *Clarissa*
(D) Pope's *The Rape of the Lock*

1765. With its forbidden themes of incest, murder, necrophilia, atheism, and torments of sexual desire, Horace Walpole's *Castle of Otranto,* created which literary genre?
(A) the revenge tragedy
(B) the Gothic romance
(C) the epistolary novel
(D) the comedy of manners

1766. Which of the following is not indebted to the Gothic genre?
(A) William Beckford's *Vathek*
(B) Matthew Lewis's *The Monk*
(C) Tobias Smollett's *Roderick Randsom*
(D) Ann Radcliffe's *The Italian*

1767. While compiling what sort of book did Samuel Richardson conceive of the idea for his Pamela, or Virtue Rewarded?
(A) a history of everyday life
(B) an instructional manual for manners
(C) a book of devotion
(D) a book of model letters

1768. Who was the ancient Gaelic warrior-bard considered by Napoleon and Thomas Jefferson to have been greater than Homer?
(A) Merlin (B) Decameron
(C) Taliesin (D) Ossian

1769. Who wrote *The Life and Opinions of Tristram Shandy*, a novel that abandons clock time for psychological time?
(A) Henry Fielding
(B) Laurence Sterne

(C) Samuel Richardson
(D) Tobias Smollett

1770. Which social philosophy, dominant during the Industrial Revolution, dictated that only the free operation of economic laws would ensure the general welfare and that the government should not interfere in any person's pursuit of their personal interests?
(A) economic independence
(B) the Rights of Man
(C) laissez-faire
(D) enclosure

1771. What served as the inspiration for Percy Bysshe Shelley's poems to the working classes A Song: "Men of England" and England in 1819?
(A) the organization of a working class men's choral group in Southern England
(B) the Battle of Waterloo
(C) the Peterloo Massacre
(D) the storming of the Bastille

1772. Who applied the term "Romantic" to the literary period dating from 1785 to 1830?
(A) Wordsworth because he wanted to distinguish his poetry and the poetry of his friends from that of the ancien régime, especially satire
(B) English historians half a century after the period ended
(C) "The Satanic School" of Byron, Percy Shelley, and their followers
(D) Oliver Goldsmith in *The Deserted Village* (1770)

1773. Which poets collaborated on the Lyrical Ballads of 1798?
(A) Mary Wollstonecraft and William Blake
(B) Mary Wollstonecraft Shelley and Percy Bysshe Shelley
(C) William Wordsworth and Samuel Taylor Coleridge
(D) Dorothy Wordsworth and Sally Ashburner

1774. Which of the following became the most popular Romantic poetic form, following on Wordsworth's claim that poetic inspiration is contained within the inner feelings of the individual poet as "the spontaneous overflow of powerful feelings"?
(A) the lyric poem written in the first person
(B) doggerel rhyme
(C) the political tract
(D) the ode

1775. Looking to the ancient past, many Romantic poets identified with the figure of the
(A) troubadour (B) skald
(C) minstrel (D) bard

1776. What did Byron deride with his scathing reference to "'Peddlers,' and 'Boats,' and 'Wagons'!"?
(A) the neo-classical influence of Pope and Dryden
(B) the clumsiness of Shakespeare's plots
(C) the Orientalist fantasies of Coleridge
(D) Wordsworth's devotion to the ordinary and everyday

1777. Wordsworth described all good poetry as
(A) the rhythmic expression of moral intuition
(B) the spontaneous overflow of powerful feelings
(C) the polite patter of a corrupted age
(D) the divine gift of grace

1778. Which poet asserted in practice and theory the value of representing rustic life and language as well as social outcasts and delinquents not only in pastoral poetry, common before this poet's time, but also as the major subject and medium for poetry in general?
(A) William Blake
(B) Alfred Lord Tennyson
(C) Samuel Johnson
(D) William Wordsworth

1779. Horace Walpole's *The Castle of Otranto* initiated which literary tradition?
(A) Gothic fiction
(B) epistolary novel
(C) meta-novel
(D) medieval romance

1780. Which of the following was a typically Romantic means of achieving visionary states?
(A) opium
(B) dreams
(C) childhood
(D) A, B and C

1781. Which of the following texts published in the 1790s did not epitomize the radical social thinking stimulated by the French Revolution?
(A) Wollstonecraft's *Vindication of the Rights of Men*
(B) Godwin's *Enquiry Concerning Political Justice*
(C) Burke's *Reflections on the Revolution in France*
(D) none of the above.

1782. Which philosopher had a particular influence on Coleridge?
(A) Aristotle
(B) David Hume
(C) Immanuel Kant
(D) Bertrand Russell

1783. Which of the following was not considered a type of the alienated, romantic visionary?
(A) Prometheus (B) Cain
(C) Napoleon (D) George III

1784. Which of the following factors did not contribute to the growth of the reading public in 19th century?
(A) The notoriety of the "Lake School"
(B) Technological developments, such as the steam-driven printing press
(C) Innovations in retailing, such as the cut-price sale of remaindered books
(D) Increased literacy, thanks in large part to Sunday schools

1785. Which of the following periodical publications (reviews and magazines) first appeared in the Romantic era?
(A) London Magazine
(B) The Spectator
(C) The Edinburgh Review
(D) (A) and (C) only

1786. According to a theater licensing act, repealed in 1843, what was meant by "legitimate" drama?
(A) All of the actors were male.
(B) All of the actors were British.
(C) The play was spoken.
(D) The play had to be a full musical or produced in full pantomime.

1787. Which of the following plays was actually performed on stage?
(A) Byron's *Manfred*
(B) Coleridge's *Remorse*
(C) Shelley's *Prometheus Unbound*
(D) all of the above

1788. Which of the following charges were commonly levelled at the novel by its detractors at the dawn of the Romantic era?
(A) Too many of its readers were women.
(B) It required less skill than other genres.
(C) It lacked the classical pedigree of poetry and drama.
(D) all of the above

1789. Which two writers can be described as writing historical novels?
(A) Mary Shelley and Percy Bysshe Shelley
(B) William Wordsworth and Samuel Taylor Coleridge
(C) Sir Walter Scott and Maria Edgeworth
(D) Jane Austen and Charlotte Brontë

1790. Which chilling novel of surveillance and entrapment had the alternative title Things as They Are?
(A) Jane Austen's *Emma*

(B) Mary Shelley's *Frankenstein*
(C) William Godwin's *Caleb Williams*
(D) Horace Walpole's Castle of Otranto

1791. Thomas and Henrietta Bowdler's edition of The Family Shakespeare gave rise to the verb "bowdlerize." What does it mean?
(A) The expurgation of indelicate language
(B) The modernization of archaic vocabulary
(C) The expansion of female characters
(D) The misspelling of simple words like "the" and "and"

1792. Which of the following is a typically Romantic poetic form?
(A) The fractal (B) The figment
(C) The fragment (D) The aubade

1793. Who exemplified the role of the "peasant poet"?
(A) John Clare
(B) John Keats
(C) Robert Burns
(D) a and c only

1794. Who in the Romantic period developed a new novelistic language for the workings of the mind in flux?
(A) Maria Edgeworth
(B) Sir Walter Scott
(C) Thomas De Quincey
(D) Jane Austen

1795. Which ruler's reign marks the approximate beginning and end of the Victorian era?
(A) King Henry VIII
(B) Queen Elizabeth I
(C) Queen Victoria
(D) all of the above, in that order, with Victoria's reign marking the most pivotal period for England's colonial efforts in India, Africa, and the West Indies

1796. What did Thomas Carlyle mean by "Close thy Byron; open thy Goethe"?
(A) Britain's preeminence as a global power will depend on mastery of foreign languages.
(B) Even a foreign author is better than a homegrown scoundrel.
(C) Abandon the introspection of the Romantics and turn to the higher moral purpose found in Goethe.
(D) In a carefully veiled critique of the monarchy, Byron and Goethe stand in symbolically for Queen Victoria and Charles Darwin respectively.

1797. Elizabeth Barrett's poem *The Cry of the Children* is concerned with which major issue attendant on the Time of Troubles during the 1830s and 1840s?
(A) child labor
(B) chartism
(C) the prudishness and old-fashioned ideals of her fellow Victorians
(D) insurrection in the colonies

1798. Who were the "Two Nations" referred to in the subtitle of Disraeli's *Sybil* (1845)?
(A) the rich and the poor
(B) Anglicans and Methodists
(C) England and Ireland
(D) the industrial north and the agrarian south

1799. Which of the following novelists best represents the mid-Victorian period's contentment with the burgeoning economic prosperity and decreased restiveness over social and political change?
(A) Anthony Trollope
(B) Charles Dickens
(C) John Ruskin
(D) Friedrich Engels

1800. What does the phrase "White Man's Burden," coined by Kipling, refer to?
(A) Britain's manifest destiny to colonize the world
(B) the moral responsibility to bring civilization and Christianity to the peoples of the world
(C) the British need to improve technology and transportation in other parts of the world

(D) the importance of solving economic and social problems in England before tackling the world's problems

1801. Which of the following best defines Utilitarianism?

(A) A farming technique aimed at maximizing productivity with the fewest tools

(B) A moral arithmetic, which states that all humans aim to maximize the greatest pleasure to the greatest number

(C) A critical methodology stating that all words have a single meaningful function within a given piece of literature

(D) A philosophy dictating that we should only keep what we use on a daily basis.

1802. Which of the following terms is defined as the application of a scientific attitude of mind toward studying the Bible, seen as a mere text of history and not an infallibly sacred document?

(A) Critical Inquiry

(B) Scientific Bibliology

(C) Higher Criticism

(D) New Historicism

1803. Which of the following authors promoted versions of socialism?

(A) William Morris

(B) John Ruskin

(C) Edward FitzGerald

(D) all but C

1804. Which best describes the general feeling expressed in literature during the last decade of the Victorian era?

(A) studied melancholy and aestheticism

(B) raucous celebration mixed with self-congratulatory sophistication

(C) paranoid introspection and cryptic dissent

(D) all of the above

1805. Which contemporary discussions on women's rights did Tennyson's *The Princess* address?

(A) The debate on women's suffrage

(B) The need to enlarge and improve educational opportunities for women, resulting in the establishment of the first women's college in London

(C) The question of monarchical succession and if a woman should hold royal power

(D) The establishment of a civil divorce court

1806. What did Victorian journalists mean by terming certain women "surplus" or "redundant"?

(A) They remained unmarried due to a population imbalance between the sexes.

(B) Their willingness to work for low wages resulted in a surplus of textiles, causing them to drop in price.

(C) They were women writers who wrote frequently about similar topics.

(D) They prostituted themselves as a way to make money in a market economy that didn't provide extensive job opportunities to women.

1807. Fill in the blanks from Tennyson's *The Princess*.

Man for the field and woman for the _____:
Man for the sword and for the _____ she:
Man with the head and woman with the _____:
Man to command and woman to _____.

(A) crop; scabbard; foot; agree

(B) throne; scepter; soul; decree

(C) school; scalpel; pen; set free

(D) hearth; needle; heart; obey

1808. Which of the following Victorian writers regularly published their work in periodicals?

(A) Thomas Carlyle

(B) Charles Dickens

(C) Elizabeth Barrett Browning

(D) all of the above: In addition to short fiction, most Victorian novels appeared serialized in periodicals.

1809. What best describes the subject of most Victorian novels?

(A) The representation of a large and comprehensive social world in realistic detail

(B) A surrealist exploration of alternate states of consciousness

(C) The attempt of a protagonist to define his or her place in society

(D) A and C

1810. Why did the novel seem a genre particularly well-suited to women?

(A) It did not carry the burden of an august tradition like poetry.

(B) It was seen as a frivolous form where one shouldn't make serious statements about society.

(C) It often concerned the domestic world with which women were familiar.

(D) all but c

1811. What was the relationship between Victorian poets and the Romantics?

(A) The Victorians were disgusted by the immorality and narcissism of the Romantics.

(B) The Romantics were seen as gifted but crude artists belonging to a distant, semi-barbarous age.

(C) The Victorians were strongly influenced by the Romantics and experienced a sense of belatedness.

(D) The Victorians were aware of no distinction between themselves and the Romantics; the distinction was only created by critics in the twentieth century.

1812. Experimentation in which of the following areas of poetic expression characterize Victorian poetry and allow Victorian poets to represent psychology in a different way?

(A) the use of pictorial description to construct visual images to represent the emotion or situation of the poem

(B) perspective, as in the dramatic monologue

(C) all of the above

(D) none of the above: Victorians were not experimental in their poetry.

1813. What type of writing did Walter Pater define as "the special and opportune art of the modern world"?

(A) the novel

(B) nonfiction prose

(C) the lyric

(D) comic drama

1814. What factors contributed to the increased popularity of nonfiction prose?

(A) a new market position for nonfiction writing and an exalted sense of the didactic function of the writer

(B) theforbiddinglyhighcostofthree-volume novelsandthedifficultyoffindingpoetry inbookshopsoutsideofLondon

(C) the deconstruction of the truth-fiction dichotomy and an accompanying relativistic sense that every opinion was of equal value

(D) B and C

1815. For what do Matthew Arnold's moral investment in nonfiction and Walter Pater's aesthetic investment together pave the way?

(A) a renewed secularism in the twentieth century

(B) modern literary criticism

(C) late–nineteenth-century and early–twentieth-century satirical drama

(D) none of the above: Victorian prose was mostly forgotten until recently and had little impact on literature of or after its time.

1816. Which of the following comic playwrights made fun of Victorian values and pretensions?

(A) W. S. Gilbert and Arthur Sullivan

(B) George Bernard Shaw

(C) Robert Corrigan

(D) all but C

1817. Which of the following phrases best characterizes the late-nineteenth century aesthetic movement which widened the breach between artists and the reading public, sowing the seeds of modernism?
(A) art for intellect's sake
(B) art for the masses
(C) art for art's sake
(D) art for sale

1818. What was the impact on literature of the Education Act of 1870, which made elementary schooling compulsory?
(A) the emergence of a mass literate population at whom a new mass-produced literature could be directed
(B) a new market for basic textbooks which paid better than sophisticated novels or plays
(C) a popular thirst for the "classics," driving contemporary writers to the margins
(D) none of the above

1819. Which text exemplifies the anti-Victorianism prevalent in the early twentieth century?
(A) Eminent Victorians
(B) Philistine Victorians
(C) The Way of All Flesh
(D) both a and c

1820. With which enormously influential perspective or practice is the early-twentieth-century thinker Sigmund Freud associated?
(A) eugenics
(B) psychoanalysis
(C) phrenology
(D) all of the above

1821. Which thinker had a major impact on early-twentieth-century writers, leading them to reimagine human identity in radically new ways?
(A) Sigmund Freud
(B) Sir James Frazer
(C) Immanuel Kant
(D) all but C

1822. Which best describes the imagist movement, exemplified in the work of T. E. Hulme and Ezra Pound?
(A) a poetic aesthetic vainly concerned with the way words appear on the page
(B) an effort to rid poetry of romantic fuzziness and facile emotionalism, replacing it with a precision and clarity of imagery
(C) an attention to alternate states of consciousness and uncanny imagery
(D) a neoplatonic poetics that stresses the importance of poetry aiming to achieve its ideal "form"

1823. What characteristics of seventeenth-century Metaphysical poetry sparked the enthusiasm of modernist poets and critics?
(A) its intellectual complexity
(B) its union of thought and passion
(C) its uncompromising engagement with politics
(D) A and B

1824. In the 1930s, younger writers such as W. H. Auden were more _______ but less _______ than older modernists such as Eliot and Pound.
(A) popular; reverenced
(B) brash; confident
(C) radical; inventive
(D) anxious; haunting

1825. Which poet could be described as part of "The Movement" of the 1950s?
(A) Thom Gunn
(B) Dylan Thomas
(C) Philip Larkin
(D) both A and C

1826. Which of the following writers did not come from Ireland?
(A) W. B. Yeats
(B) Seamus Heaney
(C) Oscar Wilde
(D) none of the above; all came from Ireland

1827. Which phrase indicates the interior flow of thought employed in high-modern literature?
(A) automatic writing
(B) confused daze
(C) total recall
(D) stream of consciousness

1828. Which of the following is not associated with high modernism in the novel?
(A) stream of consciousness
(B) free indirect style
(C) irresolute open endings
(D) narrative realism

1829. Which novel did T. S. Eliot praise for utilizing a new "mythical method" in place of the old "narrative method" and demonstrates the use of ancient mythology in modernist fiction to think about "making the modern world possible for art"?
(A) Virginia Woolf's *The Waves*
(B) Joseph Conrad's *Heart of Darkness*
(C) E. M. Forster's *A Passage to India*
(D) James Joyce's *Ulysses*

1830. Who wrote the dystopian novel *Nineteen-Eighty-Four* in which Newspeak demonstrates the heightened linguistic self-consciousness of modernist writers?
(A) George Orwell
(B) Virginia Woolf
(C) Evelyn Waugh
(D) Orson Wells

1831. Which of the following novels display post-war nostalgia for past imperial glory?
(A) Jean Rhys's *Wide Sargasso Sea*
(B) Joseph Conrad's *Heart of Darkness*
(C) Paul Scott's *Staying On*
(D) B and C

1832. Which of the following would be considered post-colonial novelists, defined as coming historically after the era of England's large-scale imperialism?
(A) Salman Rushdie
(B) Joseph Conrad
(C) Rabindranath Tagore
(D) A and C

1833. When was the ban finally lifted on D.H. Lawrence's novel *Lady Chatterley's Lover*, written in 1928.
(A) 1945 (B) 1960
(C) 2000
(D) The ban has not yet been formally lifted.

1834. Which of the following was originally the Irish Literary Theatre?
(A) the Irish National Theatre
(B) the Independent Theatre
(C) the Abbey Theatre
(D) both A and C

1835. What did T. S. Eliot attempt to combine, though not very successfully, in his plays *Murder in the Cathedral* and *The Cocktail Party?*
(A) religious symbolism and society comedy
(B) iambic pentameter and sexual innuendo
(C) witty paradoxes and feminist diatribe
(D) all of the above

1836. How did one critic sum up Samuel Beckett's *Waiting for Godot*?
(A) "nothing happens-twice"
(B) "political correctness gone mad"
(C) "kitchen sink drama"
(D) "better than Cats"

1837. In what decade did the "angry young men" come to prominence on the theatrical scene?
(A) 1910s (B) 1930s
(C) 1950s (D) 1970s

1838. What event allowed mainstream theater companies to commission and perform work that was politically, socially, and sexually controversial without fear of censorship?
(A) the abolition of the Lord Chamberlain's office in 1968

(B) the illegal performance of work by Howard Brenton and Edward Bond

(C) the collapse of liberal humanist consensus in the late 1960s

(D) the foundation of the Field Day Theater Company in 1980

1839. Which events in and after the 1960s contributed significantly to the decentralization of England from London to a more regional focus, ultimately also making way for a less homogenous vision of England and the popularity of post-colonial fiction?

(A) Radio announcers were permitted to speak in regional dialects and multicultural accents.

(B) The Arts Council designated many of its resources to supporting regional arts councils.

(C) Regional radio and television stations appeared throughout the country.

(D) all of the above

1840. What did Henry James describe as "loose baggy monsters"?

(A) novels (B) plays

(C) the English (D) publishers

1841. Into how many periods can we divide Chaucer's works?

(A) Two - French and English

(B) Three - French, English and Italian

(C) Four - French, English, Italian and Latin

(D) One - English only

1842. Who in Shakespeare's Hamlet mumbles a song from the "Book of Songs and Sonnets" known as Total's Miscellany ?

(A) Hamlet himself

(B) One of the two clowns, a grave-digger

(C) Polonius

(D) Gertrude

1843. Name the castle where Spenser lived and finished the first three books of Fairy Queen.

(A) Leicester House

(B) Kilcolman

(C) Lord Grey's Castle

(D) Harvey House

1844. William Shakespeare was born on

(A) 26 April 1563

(B) 23 April 1564

(C) 23 April 1563

(D) 3 May 1564

1845. Identify the first English comedy written by a headmaster of Eton.

(A) *Grammar Gorton's Needle*

(B) *Ralph Roister Roister*

(C) *The Pour Ps*

(D) *Wit and Science*

1846. Who wrote the introductory Sonnet to Spencer's Fairy Queen?

(A) Spencer himself

(B) Leicester

(C) Sir Philip Sidney

(D) Sir Walter Raleigh

1847. He was a musician in the court of Henry VIII. His aim was to amuse and not moralise. His interludes were hilarious and they paved the way for comedy. Name the writer and his work.

(A) Bishop Bale - *King John*

(B) John Heywood - *The Four Ps*

(C) Skeleton - *Magnificence*

(D) Lindsay - *Satire of the Three Estates*

1848. Name the dramatist of *Campuses, Edition, Love's Metamorphoses.*

(A) John Lyly

(B) Robert Greene

(C) Thomas Lodge

(D) Thomas Nash

1849. "The fault, dear Brutus, is not in our stars, But in ourselves that we are underlings." Who said this and in which play?

(A) Cassius in *Julius Caesar*

(B) Antony in *Julius Caesar*

(C) Cali ban in *The Tempest*

(D) Antony in *Antony and Cleopatra*

1850. Whom would you assign the line "Drink to me only with thane eyes."?
(A) John Lyly
(B) William Shakespeare
(C) Ben Jonson
(D) Thomas Nash

1851. One contemporary of Jonson had a bitter and extravagant style. In his Poetaster Jonson gives him a purge which makes him vomit his learned and bombastic words. Who is this poet?
(A) George Chapman
(B) Thomas Dekker
(C) Marston
(D) Fournier

1852. About whom these words are uttered: "Cover her face; mine eyes dazzle: She died young."
(A) Juliet in *Romeo and Juliet* (Shakespeare)
(B) Duchess in *The Duchess of Mali* (Webster)
(C) *Cordelier in King Lear* (Shakespeare)
(D) *Anne in A Woman Killed with Kindness* (Thomas Heywood)

1853. Name the famous pair of writers who gained popularity by their joint ventures.
(A) Ben Jonson and George Chapman
(B) George Chapman and Marston
(C) Fournier and Webster
(D) Beaumont and Fletcher

1854. "Farewell ! Othello's occupation's gone", What does this cry signify?
(A) There were no dramatists left after Ben Jonson
(B) The dramatists were taking other occupations
(C) The British Parliament closed the theatre as Puritans came to power
(D) People preferred poetry

1855. Name the play in which Shakespeare and Fletcher collaborated.
(A) *Henry VIII*
(B) *Griselda*
(C) *The Two Noble Kinsmen*
(D) *The Maid's Tragedy*

1856. How would you classify *The Knight of the Burning Pestle* by Beaumont and Fletcher?
(A) Comedy (B) Tragedy
(C) Tragic-comedy (D) Farce

1857. This public place was made famous and immortal by Shakespeare, Seldon, Donne, Beaumont, Fletcher and Ben Jonson. Name it.
(A) The Friday Street Club
(B) Mermaid Tavern
(C) Bread Street Tavern
(D) Will's Coffee House

1858. Who wrote the book *England from Noah to Elizabeth*?
(A) Daniel
(B) Michael Drayton
(C) William Warner
(D) Christopher Marlowe

1859. In the first three plays of Marlowe each of the heroes is consumed by a burning passion which leads to his doom. In *The Jew of Malta,* it is the greed for riches; in *Dr. Faustus* it is inordinate thirst for knowledge. Which passion is depicted in his *Tamburlaine?*
(A) Thirst for bloodshed
(B) Homicidal instinct
(C) Lust
(D) Thirst for power

1860. Barabbas is ruined by Christians. He plans a revenge by resorting to incredible cruelties until he falls into a cauldron of boiling water prepared for his enemies. This is in short, the story of a play by Marlowe. Identify the play.
(A) *Edward II*
(B) *The Jew of Malta*
(C) *The Massacre of Paris*
(D) *Dido*

1861. How many books are contained in *The Shepherd's Calendar?*
(A) 12 (B) 10
(C) 7 (D) 11

1862. In *The Shepherd's Calendar*, England is represented as a big sheep-farm ruled by
(A) Queen Elizabeth
(B) Shepherd Queen Lisa
(C) Shepherded Queen Elisa
(D) Mother Nature

1863. Which poem of Spenser was praised by' Coleridge for its "Swan-Like Movement"?
(A) *Epithalamion* (B) *Prothalamion*
(C) *Amoretti*
(D) *Strophe*

1864. Edmund Spenser is considered the best poet of Elizabethan age. Identify his period,
(A) 1551-1560 (B) 1552-1599
(C) 1557-1590 (D) 1552-1596

1865. When did Spenser's *Shepherd's Calendar* appear?
(A) 1579 (B) 1580
(C) 1570 (D) 1596

1866. In which of Shakespeare's plays the following lines appear:
"Blow, blow, thou winter wind Thou art not so unkind As man's ingratitude..." ?
(A) *All's Well That Ends Well*
(B) *As You Like It*
(C) *Antony and Cleopatra*
(D) *King Lear*

1867. Which work records Spenser's experiences of his first visit to England in 1589-90 when he was introduced by Sir Walter Raleigh to the Queen?
(A) *Strophes*
(B) *Colin Clout's Come Home Again*
(C) *Prothalamion*
(D) *Amoretti*

1868. Who wrote the romance Rosalinda which supplied the plot for Shakespeare's *As You Like It?*
(A) Greene (B) Lodge
(C) Lyly (D) Nash

1869. Edmund Spenser dedicated his *Shepherd's Calendar* to his friend describing him as "the distinguished and virtuous gentleman most worthy of all titles both of learning and chivalry." Who was this friend?
(A) Sir Walter Raleigh
(B) Leicester
(C) Harvey
(D) Sir Philip Sidney

1870. Arcadia, a pastoral romance, was written by its author to entertain
(A) The queen
(B) His friend Spenser
(C) His daughter
(D) His sister, the Countess of Pembroke

1871. Given below are some of early tragedies. Out of these one was full of "horror". However, it became popular and remained so till the end of the century. Ben Jonson refers to it in his Everyman in his Humor Ide ify it.
(A) *Dr. Faustus* by Marlowe
(B) *The Jew of Malta* by Marlowe
(C) *Spanish Tragedy* by Kyd
(D) *Gorboduc* by Thomas Norton and Thomas Sackville

1872. The first printed collection of William Shakespeare's plays was brought out by Heming and Condell who asserted that they did the work "in order to keep the memory of so worthy a friend and fellow alive." What is this first edition now called?
(A) *Heming and Condell's Edition*
(B) *Everyman's Shakespeare*
(C) *First Folio*
(D) *Authentic Shakespeare*

1873. How many plays are attributed to Shakespeare in toot?
(A) 37 (B) 36
(C) 21 (D) 154

1874. Which of the following books marks the beginning of Shakespeare's success?
(A) *Love's Labor Lost*
(B) *The Merchant of Venice*
(C) *Venus and Adonis*
(D) *Sonnets*

1875. In 1609 an unusual event took place which gave a theme to Shakespeare for one of his enchanting plays. An English ship disappeared, and all aboard were given up for lost. However, a year later the sailors came back. They had been ship-wrecked on the unknown Bermudas and were terrified by mysterious noises which they thought came from the devils. This account was used by Shakespeare in
(A) *The Tempest*
(B) *The Winter's Tale*
(C) *As You Like It*
(D) All of the above

1876. Name the theatre in which Shakespeare had shares.
(A) The Black friars
(B) The Theatre
(C) The Universe
(D) The Rose

1877. Shakespeare depended primarily on two sources for his legendary and historical plays. Which is the most important one?
(A) King Arthur's legend
(B) Holinshed's Chronicles
(C) Plutarch Lives
(D) Legends of Charlemagne

1878. How many sonnets has Shakespeare written in total?
(A) 150 (B) 154
(C) 120 (D) 130

1879. Name the romance which is considered by some critics as the first Elizabethan novel.
(A) *Rosalinda* by Lodge
(B) *Euphuism's Golden Legacy* by Lodge
(C) *Jack of Newbury* by Delaney
(D) *Jack Wilton or The Unfortunate Traveler* by Nash

1880. Queen Elizabeth, it is said, desired to see Falstaff in Love. So at her behest Shakespeare wrote a comedy entitled.
(A) *Taming of the Shrew*
(B) *Comedy of Errors*
(C) *Merry Wives of Windsor*
(D) *Measure for Measure*

1881. In which play does Shakespeare introduced us to the world of fairies, with the roguish imp of folklore, Puck?
(A) *The Tempest*
(B) *As You Like It*
(C) *Twelfth Night*
(D) *A Midsummer Night's Dream*

1882. Name the writer of the Elizabethan period who completed Marlowe's *Hero and Leander* and collaborated with Jonson and Marston in *Eastward Ho I*
(A) Thomas Dekker
(B) George Chapman
(C) John Webster
(D) Thomas Heywood

1883. Which of Ben Jonson's work is a seething satire on false poets of the age?
(A) *Vulpine, The Fox*
(B) *Poetaster*
(C) *Cynthia's Revel*
(D) *Epicene or The Silent Woman*

1884. Who among the following was a friend of Edmund Spenser and offered hints for the perpetration of Spenser's *The Fairies Queen* indicating a plan of 12 books in all that was never completed?
(A) Bacon (B) Daniel
(C) Drayton (D) Raleigh

1885. Philoclea and Pamela in *The Arcadia'* are the daughters of
(A) Proclus (B) Basilisk
(C) Musidorus (D) Earaches

1886. Tennyson's poem 'In Memoriam' was written in memory of?
(A) A. H. Hallam (B) Edward King
(C) Wellington (D) P. B. Shelley

1887. Identify the work by Ruskin which began as a defence of contemporary landscape artist especially Turner?
(A) *The Stones of Venice*
(B) *The Two Paths*
(C) *The Seven Lamps of Architecture*
(D) *Modem Painters*

1888. Identify the writer who first used blank verse in English poetry?
(A) Sir Thomas Wyatt
(B) William Shakespeare
(C) Earl of Surrey
(D) Milton

1889. The epigraph of *The Waste Land* is borrowed from?
(A) Virgil (B) Fetronius
(C) Seneca (D) Homer

1890. Who called *'The Waste Land'* a music of ideas'?
(A) Allen Tate
(B) J. C. Ransom
(C) I. A. Richards
(D) F. R Leavis

1891. T. S. Eliot has borrowed the term 'Unreal City' in the first and third sections from?
(A) Baudelaire
(B) Irving Babbit
(C) Dante
(D) Laforgue

1892. Which of the following myths does not figure in *The Waste Land?*
(A) Oedipus
(B) Grail Legend of Fisher King
(C) Philomela
(D) Sysyphus

1893. Joe Gargery is Pip's?
(A) brother
(B) brother-in-Jaw
(C) guardian
(D) cousin

1894. Estella is the daughter of?
(A) Joe Gargery
(B) Abel Magwitch
(C) Miss Havisham
(D) Bentley Drumnile

1895. Which book of John Ruskin influenced Mahatma Gandhi?
(A) *Sesame and Lilies*
(B) *The Seven Lamps of Architecture*
(C) *Unto This Last*
(D) *Fors Clavigera*

1896. Graham Greene's novels are marked by?
(A) Catholicism
(B) Protestantism
(C) Paganism
(D) Buddhism

1897. One important feature of Jane Austen's style is?
(A) boisterous humour
(B) humour and pathos
(C) subtlety of irony
(D) stream of consciousness

1898. The title of the poem 'The Second Coming' is taken from?
(A) The Bible
(B) The Irish mythology
(C) The German mythology
(D) The Greek mythology

1899. The main character in *Paradise Lost* Book I and Book II is?
(A) God (B) Satan
(C) Adam (D) Eve

1900. In *Sons and Lovers,* Paul Morel's mother's name is?
(A) Susan (B) Jane
(C) Gertrude (D) Emily

1901. The twins in *Lord of the Flies* are?
(A) Ralph and Jack
(B) Simon and Eric

(C) Ralph and Eric
(D) Simon and Jack

1902. Mr. Jaggers, in *Great Expectations,* is a
(A) lawyer (B) postman
(C) Judge
(D) School teacher

1903. What does 'I' stand for in the following line?
'To Carthage then I came'
(A) Buddha
(B) Tiresias
(C) Smyrna Merchant
(D) Augustine

1904. The following lines are an example of __________ image.
'The river sweats Oil and tar'
(A) visual (B) kinetic
(C) erotic (D) sensual

1905. Which of the following novels has the sub-title 'A Novel Without a Hero'?
(A) *Vanity Fair*
(B) *Middlemarch*
(C) *Wuthering Heights*
(D) *Oliver Twist*

1906. In 'Leda and the Swan', who wooes Leda in guise of a swan?
(A) Mars (B) Hercules
(C) Zeus (D) Bacchus

1907. Who invented the term 'Sprung rhythm'?
(A) Hopkins (B) Tennyson
(C) Browning (D) Wordsworth

1908. Who wrote the poem 'Defence of Lucknow'?
(A) Browning (B) Tennyson
(C) Swinburne (D) Rossetti

1909. Which of the following plays of Shakespeare has an epilogue?
(A) *The Tempest*
(B) *Henry IV, Pt I*
(C) *Hamlet*
(D) *Twelfth Night*

1910. Hamlet's famous speech 'To be, or not to be; that is the question' occurs in?
(A) Act II, Scene I
(B) Act III, Scene III
(C) Act IV, Scene III
(D) Act III, Scene I

1911. Identify the character in *The Tempest* who is referred to as an honest old counselor
(A) Alonso (B) Ariel
(C) Gonzalo (D) Stephano

1912. What is the sub-title of the play *Twelfth Night?*
(A) Or, What is you Will
(B) Or, What you Will
(C) Or, What you Like It
(D) Or, What you Think

1913. Which of the following plays of Shakespeare, according to T. S. Eliot, is 'artistic failure'?
(A) *The Tempest*
(B) *Hamlet*
(C) *Henry IV, Pt I*
(D) *Twelfth Night*

1914. Who is Thomas Percy in *Henry IV, Pt I?*
(A) Earl of Northumberland
(B) Earl of March
(C) Earl of Douglas
(D) Earl of Worcester

1915. *Paradise Lost* was originally written in?
(A) ten books (B) eleven books
(C) nine books (D) eight books

1916. In *Pride and Prejudice,* Lydia elopes with?
(A) Darcy
(B) Wickham
(C) William Collins
(D) Charles Bingley

1917. Who coined the phrase 'Egotistical Sublime'?
(A) William Wordsworth
(B) P. B. Shelley
(C) S. T. Coleridge
(D) John Keats

1918. Who is commonly known as 'Pip' in Great Expectations?

(A) Philip Pirrip
(B) Filip Pirip
(C) Philip Pip
(D) Philips Pirip

1919. The novel *The Power and the Glory* is set in?
(A) Mexico
(B) Italy
(C) France
(D) Germany

1920. Which of the following is Golding's first novel?
(A) *The Inheritors*
(B) *Lord of the Flies*
(C) *Pincher Martin*
(D) *Pyramid*

1921. Identify the character who is a supporter of Women's Rights in *Sons and Lovers?*
(A) Mrs. Morel
(B) Annie
(C) Miriam
(D) Clara Dawes

1922. *Vanity Fair* is a novel by?
(A) Jane Austen
(B) Charles Dickens
(C) W. M. Thackeray
(D) Thomas Hardy

1923. Shelley's *Adonais* is an elegy on the death of?
(A) Milton (B) Coleridge
(C) Keats (D) Johnson

1924. Which of the following is the first novel of D. H. Lawrence?
(A) *The White Peacock*
(B) *The Trespasser*
(C) *Sons and Lovers*
(D) *Women in Love*

1925. In the poem 'Tintern Abbey', 'dearest friend' refers to?
(A) Nature (B) Dorothy
(C) Coleridge (D) Wye

1926. Who, among the following, is not the second generation of British Romantics?
(A) Keats
(B) Wordsworth
(C) Shelley
(D) Byron

1927. Which of the following poems of Coleridge is a ballad?
(A) Work Without Hope
(B) Frost at Midnight
(C) The Rime of the Ancient Mariner
(D) Youth and Age

1928. Identify the writer who was expelled from Oxford for circulating a pamphlet—
(A) P. B. Shelley
(B) Charles Lamb
(C) Hazlitt
(D) Coleridge

1929. Keats's *Endymion* is dedicated to?
(A) Leigh Hunt
(B) Milton
(C) Shakespeare
(D) Thomas Chatterton

1930. The second series of *Essays of Elia* by Charles Lamb was published in?
(A) 1823 (B) 1826
(C) 1834 (D) 1833

1931. Which of the following poets does not belong to the 'Lake School'?
(A) Keats
(B) Coleridge
(C) Southey
(D) Wordsworth

1932. Who, among the following writers, was not educated at Christ's Hospital School, London?
(A) Charles Lamb
(B) William Wordsworth
(C) Leigh Hunt
(D) S. T. Coleridge

1933. Which poem ends 'I shall but love thee better after death'?

(A) How do I love thee
(B) Ode to a Grecian urn
(C) In faith I do not love thee with mine eyes
(D) Let me not to the marriage of true minds

1934. Which poet is considered a national hero in Greece?
(A) John Keats (B) Lord Byron
(C) Solan (D) Sappho

1935. Which kind of poem is Edward Lear associated with?
(A) Nature (B) Epics
(C) Sonnets (D) Nonsense

1936. In Coleridge's poem 'The rime of the Ancient Mariner' where were the three gallants going?
(A) A funeral (B) A wedding
(C) Market (D) To the races

1937. Harold Nicholson described which poet as 'Very yellow and glum. Perfect manners'?
(A) E. E. Cummings
(B) T. S. Elliot
(C) John Greenleaf Whittier
(D) Walt Whitman

1938. What was strange about Emily Dickinson?
(A) She rarely left home
(B) She wrote in code
(C) She never attempted to publish her poetry
(D) She wrote her poems in invisible ink

1939. Rupert Brooke wrote his poetry during which conflict?
(A) Boer War
(B) Second World War
(C) Korean War
(D) First World War

1940. Which Poet Laureatewrote about a church mouse?
(A) Betjeman
(B) Hughes
(C) Marvel
(D) Larkin

1941. Which American writer published 'A brave and startling truth' in 1996?
(A) Robert Hass
(B) Jessica Hagdorn
(C) Maya Angelou
(D) Micheal Palmer

1942. Who wrote about the idyllic 'Isle of Innisfree'?
(A) Dylan Thomas
(B) Ezra Pound
(C) W. B. Yeats
(D) E. E. Cummings

1943. A pattern of accented and unaccented syllables in lines of poetry
(A) rhyme scheme (B) meter
(C) alliteration (D) assonance

1944. The repetition of similar ending sounds
(A) alliteration
(B) onomatopoeia
(C) rhyme
(D) assonance

1945. Applying human qualities to non-human things
(A) personification
(B) onomatopoeia
(C) alliteration
(D) inversion

1946. The repetition of beginning consonant sounds
(A) rhyme (B) onomatopoeia
(C) alliteration (D) assonance

1947. A comparison of unlike things without using a word of comparison such as like or as
(A) metaphor
(B) simile
(C) personification
(D) analogy

1948. The comparison of unlike things using the words like or as
(A) metaphor
(B) simile

(C) personification
(D) analogy

1949. Using words or letters to imitate sounds
(A) alliteration
(B) simile
(C) onomatopoeia
(D) phonetics

1950. A description that appeals to one of the five senses
(A) imagery
(B) personification
(C) metaphor
(D) visualization

1951. A poem that tells a story with plot, setting, and characters
(A) lyric (B) free verse
(C) narrative (D) ode

1952. A poem with no meter or rhyme
(A) lyric (B) free verse
(C) narrative (D) ode

1953. A poem that generally has meter and rhyme
(A) lyric (B) free verse
(C) narrative (D) ode

1954. Carl Sandburg 'Planked whitefish' contains what kind of imagery?
(A) Sea scenes
(B) Rural Idyll
(C) War
(D) Innocent childhood

1955. In 1960 'The Colossus' was the first book of poems published by which poetess?
(A) Elizabeth Bishop
(B) Sylvia Plath
(C) Marianne Moore
(D) Laura Jackson

1956. In his poem Kipling said 'If you can meet with triumph and _______ '?
(A) Glory (B) Ruin
(C) Disaster (D) victory

1957. Which of the following is not a literary device used for aesthetic effect in poetry?
(A) Assonance
(B) Onomatopoeia
(C) Rhyme
(D) Grammar

1958. True or false: Writing predates poetry.
(A) True
(B) False
(C) No evidence
(D) Both evolved at around the same time

1959. What is the earliest surviving European poem?
(A) The Homeric epic
(B) The Gilgamesh epic
(C) The Deluge epic
(D) The Hesiodic ode

1960. Which of the following is not a poetic tradition?
(A) The Epic (B) The Comic
(C) The Occult (D) The Tragic

1961. What is the study of poetry's meter and form called?
(A) Prosody
(B) Potology
(C) Rheumatology
(D) Scansion

1962. Shakespeare composed much of his plays in what sort of verse?
(A) Alliterative verse
(B) Sonnet form
(C) Iambic pentameter
(D) Dactylic hexameter

1963. Which poet invented the concept of the variable foot in poetry?
(A) William Carlos Williams
(B) Emily Dickinson
(C) Gerard Manly Hopkins
(D) Robert Frost

1964. Who wrote this famous line: 'Shall I compare thee to a summer's day/ Thou art more lovely and more temperate...'
(A) TS Eliot
(B) Lord Tennyson

(C) Charlotte Bronte
(D) Shakespeare

1965. From what century does the poetic form the folk ballad date?
(A) The 12th (B) The 14th
(C) The 17th (D) The 19th

1966. From which of Shakespeare's plays is this famous line: 'Did my heart love til now?/ Forswear it, sight/ For I never saw a true beauty until this night'
(A) *A Midsummer Night's Dream*
(B) *Hamlet*
(C) *Othello*
(D) *Romeo and Juliet*

1967. What is a poem called whose first letters of each line spell out a word?
(A) Alliterative
(B) Epic
(C) Acrostic
(D) Haiku

1968. *Auld Lang Syne* is a famous poem by whom?
(A) Sir Walter Scott
(B) William Butler Yeats
(C) Henry Longfellow
(D) Robert Burns

1969. How has Stephen Dunn been described in 'the Oxford Companion to 20th Century Poetry?
(A) A poet of middleness
(B) Capturing a sense of spiritual maroonness
(C) One of the leading prairie poets
(D) Has some distinction as a critic

1970. 'The Cambridge school' refers to a group who emerged when?
(A) The 1900's (B) The 1960's
(C) The 1920's (D) The 1930's

1971. Which of the following words describe the prevailing attitude of High-Modern Literature?
(A) Skeptical
(B) Authoritative
(C) Impressionistic
(D) Both (A) & (C)

1972. Which Welsh poet wrote "Under Milk Wood?"
(A) Anthony Hopkins
(B) Richard Burton
(C) Tom Jones
(D) Dylan Thomas

1973. Who wrote *Canterbury Tales?*
(A) Geoffrey Chaucer
(B) Dick Whittington
(C) Thomas Lancaster
(D) King Richard II

1974. Who wrote "The Hound of the Baskervilles"?
(A) Agatha Christie
(B) H Ryder-Haggard
(C) P D James
(D) Arthur Conan Doyle

1975. William Shakespeare is not the author of:
(A) *Titus Andronicus*
(B) *Taming of the Shrew*
(C) *White Devil*
(D) *Hamlet*

1976. ___________ is a late 20th century play written by a woman?
(A) *Queen Cristina*
(B) *Top Girls*
(C) *Camille*
(D) *The Homecoming*

1977. Which of the following writers wrote historical novels?
(A) Jane Austen and Charlotte Bronte
(B) Sir Walter Scott and Maria Edgeworth
(C) William Wordsworth and Samuel Taylor Coleridge
(D) Mary Shelley and Percy Bysshe Shelley

1978. Who wrote "Ten Little Niggers?"
(A) Sir Arthur Conan Doyle

(B) Irvine Welsh
(C) Agatha Christie
(D) None of above

1979. Which of the following is not a work of John Keats?
(A) Endymion
(B) To some ladies
(C) To hope
(D) None of above

1980. Who wrote the poems, "On death" and "Women, Wine, and Snuff?"
(A) John Milton
(B) John Keats
(C) P. B. Shelley
(D) William Wordsworth

1981. "Of Man's first disobedience, and the fruit Of that forbidden tree whose mortal taste Brought death into the world, and all our woe, With loss of Eden."

This is an extract from:
(A) *Paradise Lost*
(B) *Paradise Regained*
(C) *Samson Agonistes*
(D) *Divorce Tracts*

1982. Which of the following is not a Shakespeare tragedy?
(A) *Titus Andronicus*
(B) *Othello*
(C) *Macbeth*
(D) None of the above

1983. Who wrote 'The Winter's Tale?'
(A) George Bernard Shaw
(B) John Dryden
(C) Christopher Marlowe
(D) William Shakespeare

1984. What is the difference between a simile and a metaphor?
(A) No difference. Simply two different ways in referring to the same thing.
(B) A simile is more descriptive.
(C) A simile uses as or like to make a comparison and a metaphor doesn't.
(D) A simile must use animals in the comparison.

1985. What is the word for a "play on words"?
(A) pun (B) simile
(C) haiku (D) metaphor

1986. Which represents an example of alliteration?
(A) Language Arts
(B) Peter Piper Picked Peppers
(C) I like music.
(D) A beautiful scenery with music

1987. What is the imitation of natural sounds in word form?
(A) Personification
(B) Hyperboles
(C) Alliteration
(D) Onomatopoeia

1988. The theme is ...?
(A) a plot.
(B) an character
(C) an address
(D) the point a writer is trying to make about a subject.

1989. Concentrate on these elements when writing a good poem.
(A) characters, main idea, and theme
(B) purpose and audience
(C) theme, purpose, form, and mood
(D) rhyme and reason

1990. Which is not a poetry form?
(A) epic (B) tale
(C) ballad (D) sonnet

1991. Which is an example of a proverb?
(A) Get a "stake" in our business.
(B) You can't have your cake and eat it, too
(C) The snow was white as cotton.
(D) You're driving me crazy.

1992. Which is an exaggeration?
(A) Alliteration
(B) Haiku

(C) Hyperbole
(D) Prose

1993. Which of the following is not a poet?
(A) William Shakespeare
(B) Terry Saylor
(C) Elizabeth B. Browning
(D) Emily Dickinson

1994. Who has defined 'poetry' as a fundamental creative act using languages?
(A) H. W. Longfellow
(B) Ralph Waldo Emerson
(C) Dylan Thomas
(D) William Wordsworth

1995. What is a sonnet?
(A) A poem of six lines
(B) A poem of eight lines
(C) A poem of twelve lines
(D) A poem of fourteen lines

1996. What is study of meter, rhythm and intonation of a poem called as?
(A) Prosody
(B) Allegory
(C) Scansion
(D) Assonance

1997. Which figure of speech is it when a statement is exaggerated in a poem?
(A) Onomatopoeia
(B) Metonymy
(C) Alliteration
(D) Hyperbole

1998. There was aware of her true love, at length come riding by - This is a couplet from the Bailiff's Daughter of Islington. What figure of speech is used by the poet?
(A) Metaphor
(B) Synecdoche
(C) Euphemism
(D) Irony

1999. Which culture is known for their long, rhymic poetic verses known as Qasidas?
(A) Hindu
(B) Celtic
(C) Arabic
(D) Arameic

2000. Complete this Shakespearean line - Let me not to the marriage of true minds bring:
(A) Impediments
(B) Inconveniences
(C) Worries
(D) Troubles

2001. Which of the following is a Japanese poetic form?
(A) Jintishi
(B) Villanelle
(C) Ode
(D) Tanka

2002. What is the title of the poem that begins thus - 'What is this life, if full of care, we have no time to stand and stare'?
(A) Comfort
(B) Leisure
(C) Relaxation
(D) Tranquility

2003. Which of the following is not an English poet (i.e. from England)?
(A) Victor Hugo
(B) Alexander Pope
(C) John Milton
(D) Samuel Taylor Coleridge

2004. Who was often called as the Romantic Poet as most of his poems revolved around nature?
(A) William Blake
(B) William Shakespeare
(C) William Morris
(D) William Wordsworth

2005. What is a funny poem of five lines called?
(A) Quartet
(B) Limerick
(C) Sextet
(D) Palindrome

2006. How did W. H. Auden describe poetry?
(A) An awful way to earn a living

(B) A game of knowledge
(C) The soul exposed
(D) An explosion of language

2007. Sassoon and Brooke wrote what kind of poetry?
(A) Light verse (B) Romantic
(C) Political satire (D) War poems

2008. Ted Hughes was married to which American poetess?
(A) Carolyn Kizer
(B) Mary Oliver
(C) Sylvia Plath
(D) Marianne Moore

2009. In what form did Dylan Thomas's 'Under Milk Wood' first become known?
(A) Book of poetry
(B) A radio play
(C) A stage play
(D) a short film

2010. The magazine 'Contemporary Poetry and Prose' was inspired by which exhibition?
(A) The Festival of Britain
(B) The Surrealist Exhibition
(C) People of the 20th Century
(D) Drawing the 20th Century

2011. Why did 'Poetry Quarterly' cease publication in 1953?
(A) Owner convicted of fraud
(B) Fall in Sales
(C) Rise in taxation on magazines
(D) Shortage of paper

2012. Aldous Huxley was a poet, but was better known as what?
(A) Politician (B) Dramatist
(C) Novelist (D) Architect

2013. Of which poet was it said 'Even if he's not a great poet, he's certainly a great something'?
(A) Elliot (B) Kipling
(C) Cummings (D) Brooke

2014. "The Everlasting Yea" is associated with
(A) Browning
(B) Carlyle
(C) Ruskin
(D) Macaulay

2015. In which Shakespearean play do you find the lines? Men must endure Their going hence, even as their coming hither: Ripeness is all.
(A) Horatio in *Hamlet*
(B) Brutus in *Julius Caesar*
(C) Edgar in *King Lear*
(D) Enobarbus in *Antony* and *Cleopatra*

2016. "Marius, the Epicurean" was written by
(A) A.C. Ward
(B) Walter Pater
(C) T.S. Eliot
(D) Saintsbury

2017. Whose philosophy is the following? "The Moving Finger writes; and, having writ, Moves on: nor all your Piety nor Wit Shall lure it back to cancel half a Line, Nor all your Tears wash out a Word of it."
(A) Epicure
(B) Aristotle
(C) Russel
(D) Omar Khayyam

2018. *Kunstleroman* is a novel on the development of
(A) an individual
(B) an artist
(C) a thief
(A) a woman

2019. The Georgian poets are called after
(A) George IV (B) George V
(C) George VI (D) George Eliot

2020. *Ladies Coupe* is a novel by
(A) Anita Nair
(B) Jhumpa Lahiri
(C) Amrita Pritam
(D) Anita Desai

2021. Whom does Dryden's *Eugenius* take up the case for?
(A) the French

(B) the Medievals
(C) the Moderns
(D) the Ancients

2022. Which of the following writers is associated with the concept of 'tension' in poetry?
(A) Robert Penn Warren
(B) John Crowe Ransom
(C) Cleanth Brooks
(D) Allen Tate

2023. Who called Shelley 'A beautiful but ineffectual angel beating in a void his luminous wings in vain'?
(A) T.S. Eliot
(B) Cleanth Brooks
(C) Arnold
(D) Lockhart

2024. Who criticized *Paradise Lost* for its lack of human interest?
(A) Pope (B) Johnson
(C) Arnold (D) Eliot

2025. *Asolando* was written by
(A) Keats (B) Scott
(C) Shelley (D) Browning

2026. Which of the following novels ends with the word "Tomorrow"?
(A) God of Small Things
(B) The Portrait of the Artist as a Young Man
(C) Lady Chatterley's Lover
(D) Jude the Obscure

2027. Morose and Cutbeard are characters in
(A) *Volpone*
(B) *Everyman in His Humour*
(C) *The Silent Woman*
(D) *The Alchemist*

2028. *The Gunny Sack* was written by
(A) Rohinton Mistry
(B) M.G. Vassanji
(C) V.S. Naipaul
(D) Vikram Seth

2029. Eric Blair wrote under the pen name
(A) O. Henry
(B) William Golding
(C) Oscar Wilde
(D) George Orwell

2030. Who of the following did not belong to the "Lost Generation"?
(A) Ernest Hemingway
(B) Ezra Pound
(C) F. Scott Fitzgerald
(D) Henry James

2031. __________ introduced the concept of 'defamiliarization'.
(A) Mikhail Bakhtin
(B) Viktor Shklovsky
(C) Jan Mukarovsky
(D) Roland Barthes

2032. Who introduced Rabindranath Tagore to European readers?
(A) W.B. Yeats
(B) T.S. Eliot
(C) Ezra Pound
(D) Harold Bloom

2033. Who wrote *A Tale of a Tub?*
(A) Dickens (B) Defoe
(C) Swift (D) Hardy

2034. Which school of critics have been called Neo-Aristotleians?
(A) Myth Criticism
(B) New Historicism
(C) New Criticism
(D) Chicago Critics

2035. Who made this statement "An aged man is a paltry thing"?
(A) W.B. Yeats (B) T.S. Eliot
(C) W.H. Auden (D) Philip larkin

2036. Who is the author of *Raj*?
(A) Geeta Mehta
(B) Rama Mehta
(C) Shobha De
(D) Nargis Dalai

2037. Dominique Lapierre wrote an appealing account of the sordid squalor of an Indian city. Identify the city.

(A) Calcutta (B) Bombay
(C) Udaipur (D) Delhi

2038. Who is the author of following poems? "The Gift of India", "Bangle-seller", "The Anthem of Love", "Palanquin Bearers"

(A) Kamala Das
(B) Sarojini Naidu
(C) Toru Dutt
(D) Nissim Ezekiel

2039. Who wrote the hard-hitting poem "Sita Speak" indicating the society for the injustice meted out to women down the ages?

(A) Bina Agarwal
(B) Kamala Das
(C) P. Lai
(D) Sarojini Naidu

2040. In which of the following poems of Ezekiel do we get a moving picture of a mother's suffering ?

(A) 'The Couple'
(B) 'Night of the Scorpion'
(C) 'The Visitor'
(D) 'Philosophy'

2041. Who is the author of *Two Virgins*?

(A) Kamala Markandaya
(B) Kamala Das
(C) Anita Desai
(D) Shastri Deshpande

2042. Name the Indo-English novelist who wrote *A Suitable Boy.*

(A) Vikram Seth
(B) Amitav Ghose
(C) Upamanyu Chatterjee
(D) Anita Desai

2043. Two Indian writers living abroad created furor - one was Vikram Seth who got an unprecedented amount as an advance for his novel, the other who came under 'fatwa', for one of his controversial novels, issued by Muslim countries, was

(A) Amitav Ghose
(B) Bharati Mukherjee
(C) Anita Desai
(D) Salman Rushdie

2044. Name Salman Rushdie's latest Novel.

(A) *The Moor's Last Sigh*
(B) *Fury*
(C) *The Ground beneath Her Feet*
(D) *Satanic Verses*

2045. Of the following novels one does not portray the Gandhian Age and the impact of Gandhi. Which one?

(A) K.A. Abbas's *Inquilab*
(B) Venu Chitale's *In Transit*
(C) R.K. Narayan's *The Dark Room*
(D) K. Nagarajan's *Chronicles of Kedaram*

2046. Who is the author of the following books: *The Foreigner, The Apprentice, The Last Labyrinth, The City and the River?*

(A) Ruth P. Jhabvala
(B) Amitav Ghose
(C) Dom Moraes
(D) Arun Joshi

2047. Whose collections of poems are these: *A Time to Change, Sixty Poems, The Third, The Unfinished Man?*

(A) P. Lai
(B) Nissim Ezekiel
(C) Kamala Das
(D) Bina Aggarwal

2048. Listed below are the works of Bhabani Bhattacharya of which only one is his collection of short stories. Identify it.

(A) *So Many Hungers*
(B) *A Dream in Hawaii*
(C) *Sea Hawk*
(D) *Shadow from Ladakh*

2049. *Baumgartner's Bombay* is a novel about a German Jew who remains an outsider all his life, in his country because he is a Jew and in India, where he is a firangi. Who wrote this moving novel?

(A) Vikram Seth
(B) Anita Desai
(C) Nayantara Sehgal
(D) Ruth P. Jhabvala

2050. In which novel does R.K. Narayan focus on family planning?
(A) *The Guide*
(B) *Mr. Sampath*
(C) *Bachelor of Arts*
(D) *The Painter of Signs*

2051. In the *Guide* we come across a dancer. What is her name?
(A) Daisy (B) Bharati
(C) Rosie (D) Savitri

2052. Who wrote these lines?
"Woman is the earth, air, ether, sound; woman is the microcosm of the mind "?
(A) Raja Rao
(B) R.K. Narayan
(C) Kamala Markandaya
(D) Kamala Das

2053. Arthur Symons wrote about this person, "All the life of the tiny figure seemed to concentrate itself in the eyes: they turned towards beauty as the sunflower turns towards the sun." Who is the person referred to?
(A) Toru Dutt
(B) Aru Dutt
(C) Sarojini Naidu
(D) Rabindra Nath Tagore

2054. H.A.L. Fisher wrote about this person,".... this child of the green valley of the Ganges has by sheer force of native genius earned for herself the right to be enrolled in the great fellowship of English poets." Who is the poet?
(A) Sarojini Naidu
(B) Toru Dutt
(C) Michael Madhusudan
(D) Manmohan Ghose

2055. An Indo-English poet once remarked that his disciplines (i.e., linguistics and anthropology) and his education give him his "Outer" form, whereas his Indian origin, first thirty years in India and knowledge of Kannada and Tamil give him his "inner" form. Who said this?
(A) A. K. Ramanujan
(B) Kamala Das
(C) Gieve Patel
(D) Raja Gopal Parthasarathy

2056. Who wrote Jejurithe Commonwealth Poetry Prize winner work?
(A) Shiv K. Kumar
(B) Arun Kolatkar
(C) Keki N. Daruwala
(D) Jayant Mahapatra

2057. In which of Anita Desai's novel an insane wife kills her husband?
(A) *Voices in The City*
(B) *In Custody*
(C) *Cry, The Peacock*
(D) *Baumgartner's Bombay*

2058. In which novel does the hero sing the refrain?
"This is the machine age, sons
This is the machine age
We are the men who will master it"?
(A) *The Big Heart*
(B) *The Sword and The Sickle*
(C) *Two Leaves and a Bud*
(D) *The Road*

2059. Who was the first recipient of the Sahitya Academi Award for English literature?
(A) Mulk Raj Anand
(B) Nayantara Sehgal
(C) R.K. Narayan
(D) Raja Rao

2060. Following novels except one, describe the condition of Westerners living in India Mark the one which does not.
(A) *Heat and Dust*
(B) *The Princess*
(C) *Coffer Dam*
(D) *A Passage to India*

2061. Which of the following novels focuses on the question of rape?
(A) *The Bending Vine*
(B) *Voices in The City*
(C) *Some Inner Fury*
(D) *A Time to Be Happy*

2062. Who is the author of the following novels: *A Bend in The Ganges, The Princes, Distant Drums, Devil's Wind, A Combat of Shadows?*
(A) Mulk Raj Anand
(B) Bhabani Bhattacharya
(C) Manohar Malgaonkar
(D) Salman Rushdie

2063. Who wrote *"Our Casuarina Tree"* a splendid Keatsian poem?
(A) Toru Dutt
(B) Romesh Chander Dutt
(C) Swami Vivekanand
(D) Sri Aurobindo

2064. To whom do we assign following works - *The Lake of Palms, A History of Civilization of Ancient India, The Slave-Girl of Agra?*
(A) Manmohan Ghose
(B) Romesh Chander Dutt
(C) Bankim Chandra Chatterjee
(D) Sharat Chandra

2065. Which one of the following is a collection of Anita Desai's short stories?
(A) *Voices in the City*
(B) *Games at Twilight*
(C) *Village by the Sea*
(D) *Cry, the Peacock*

2066. Browning's *The Ring and the Book* is a long poem having about 21,000 lines, but Aurobindo's *Savitri* is longer. How many lines does the epic contain?
(A) 24,000 (B) 21,500
(C) 30,000 (D) 22,000

2067. Toru Dutt, Romesh Chander Dutt and Aurobindo, all wrote on one common theme taken out from the *Mahabharata* Identify the story which the three found irresistible.
(A) Kama and Kunti
(B) Nal-Damyanti
(C) Savitri
(D) Gandhari

2068. Who of the following was highly influenced by French Romanticism, French language and literature?
(A) Romesh Chander Dutt
(B) Michael Madhusudan Dutt
(C) Toru Dutt
(D) Govind Dutt

2069. About an Indian poet writing in English, a critic, George Sampson says that a reader of his poems "Would readily take them as the work of an English poet trained in the classical tradition." An Indian critic feels that his poetry has no imagery or sentiment that can be termed as Indian. Who was this poet?
(A) Michael Madhusudan Dutt
(B) Romesh Chander Dutt
(C) Aurobindo Ghose
(D) Manmohan Ghose

2070. *The Fakir of Jhungheera* was written by one of the first Indo-Anglian poets. The poem is often hailed as a "Competent narrative verse with Byronic echoes." Identify the writer.
(A) Toru Dutt
(B) Henry Derozio
(C) Michael Madhusudan Dutt
(D) Hasan Ali

2071. He was the first Indian poet to have published a regular volume of English verse. He also edited an English Weekly *The Hindu Intelligence*. Name him.
(A) Michael Madhusudan Dutt
(B) Mohan Lai
(C) Romesh Chander Dutt
(D) Kashiprasad Ghose

2072. Paying a tribute to a Bengali poet who wrote in English also, Sri Aurobindo said, "The God himself took up thy pen and wrote." Who was he?
(A) Michael Madhusudan Dutt
(B) Henry Derozio
(C) Romesh Chander Dutt
(D) Kashiprasad Ghose

2073. One of the following works is written by Michael Madhusudan Dutt. Identify which one?
(A) *The Shair and Other Poems*
(B) *The Captive Ladie*
(C) *Bianca*
(D) *Lays of Ancient India*

2074. Name the poet of *"Kali, the Mother."*
(A) Swami Vivekanand
(B) Subramaniam Bharathi
(C) Swami Ramakrishna Paramhans
(D) Sri Aurobindo

2075. He is a Sahitya Akademi Award Winner and he loves to write for children. Who is he?
(A) R. K. Narayan
(B) Manohar Malgaonkar
(C) Ruskin Bond
(D) Upamanyu Chatterjee

2076. Whose autobiography is entitled *My Father's Son*?
(A) Dom Moraes (B) Frank Moraes
(C) Nirad Chaudhury
(D) V.S. Naipaul

2077. Mulk Raj Anand, about one of his female characters says, "Gauri is my tribute to Indian womanhood" In which novel does Gauri appear?
(A) *The Road*
(B) *The Old Woman and The Cow*
(C) *Untouchable*
(D) *The Sword and The Sickle*

2078. Read the following passage and identify the novel and its author: "Lago, I am as meek as Moses, but I have just heard that you have been mishandled by that Bhatta Govinda Whip me, ye devils! Roast me in sulphur! Gall, worse than gall! A rascally Yea-for-smooth knave! Three Judases, each one thrice worse than Judas! Falstaff speaking. I am as subject to heat as butter."
(A) *In Custody* by Anita Desai
(B) *Midnight's Children* by Salman Rushdie
(C) *All About H. Hatter* by G.V. Desani
(D) *Vermillion Boat* by Sudhir Ghosh

2079. Name the author who has been described by a critic as an "outsider inside."
(A) Anita Desai
(B) Salman Rushdie
(C) Nirad C. Chaudhary
(D) Ruth Jhabvala

2080. Following novels, except one, describes the condition of Indians settled abroad Mark the one which does not.
(A) *The Nowhere Man*
(B) *Bye-Bye, Blackbird*
(C) *The Serpent And The Rope*
(D) *The Guide*

2081. *The Angel of Misfortune* is a poem of about 5000 lines, written by Nagesh Vishwanath Pai. Whose story is narrated in this book?
(A) Saturn, the Dark Angel
(B) King Arthur of the Holy Grail
(C) King Vikramaditya
(D) Kamadeva

2082. Name the author of *The Gardener, The Fugitive, Chitra, Sacrifice, The Post Office.*
(A) Rabindra Nath Tagore
(B) Bankim Chandra
(C) Aurobindo Ghose
(D) Romesh Chander Dutt

2083. Name the two prizes, one in literature and another in History, awarded to young Aurobindo while studying in England
(A) Pulitzer Prizes in Literature and Bedford Prize in History
(B) Bookers in Literature and Butterworth in History

(C) Butterworth in Literature and Bedford in History

2084. Name Sarojini Naidu's last collection of poems.
(A) *The Broken Wing*
(B) *The Golden Threshold*
(C) *The Bird of Time*
(D) *The Temple*

2085. What is the full title of Aurobindo's Savitri?
(A) *Savitri - An Epic*
(B) *Savitri*
(C) *Savitri - A Legend and a Symbol*
(D) *Savitri - A Poem in Three Parts*

2086. Who wrote *Murugan, The Tiller* and *Kandan, the Patriot, Jatadharan* and *The Next Rung?*
(A) K.S. Venkataramani
(B) ShankerRam
(C) Humayun Kabir
(D) K. Subba Rao

2087. *The Devil's Wind* depicts the events of our First War of Independence (1857 mutiny). Who is the author of this novel?
(A) Shanker Ram
(B) Manohar Malgaonkar
(C) R.K. Narayan
(D) Sasthi Brata

2088. Which novel highlights the Bengal famine?
(A) *So Many Hungers*
(B) *A Handful of Rice*
(C) *A Time to be Happy*
(D) *Athawar House*

2089. Who wrote *Ilion*?
(A) Virgil (B) Aurobindo
(C) Homer
(D) Rabindra Nath Tagore

2090. Who is the author of *Love of Dust?*
(A) Ruth P. Jhabvala
(B) Humayun Kabir
(C) Shanker Ram
(D) K.S. Venkataramani

2091. Which is Ngugi wa Thoingo's novel written against the backdrop of Mau Mau Rebellion?
(A) *A Grain of Wheat*
(B) *Weep Not, Child*
(C) *Petals of Blood*
(D) All of these

2092. The Great Indian Novel is a reworking of
(A) *The Ramayana*
(B) *The Mahabharata*
(C) *Kathasaritsagara*
(D) *Panchatantra*

2093. The rhyme scheme of a Spenserian stanza is
(A) abbcabbcc (B) ababbcbcd
(C) ababbcbcc (D) abbaabbaa

2094. Who called Kyd "Sporting Kyd"?
(A) Ben Jonson
(B) Dr. Johnson
(C) T.S. Eliot
(D) Dryden

2095. *Angry Young Man* is the autobiography of
(A) John Osborne
(B) Kingsley Amis
(C) John Wain
(D) Leslie Paul

2096. *Caesar and Cleopatra* is a play by
(A) Shakespeare
(B) Bernard Shaw
(C) Dryden
(D) Drinkwater

2097. Esemplastic in Coleridge's theory refers to
(A) fancy
(B) flexible
(C) shaping power
(D) force of imagination

2098. The term 'stream-of-consciousness' was first used by
(A) James Joyce
(B) Virginia Woolf

(C) T.S. Eliot
(D) William James

2099. "Milton" is a symbolic poem by
(A) Blake (B) Gray
(C) Yeats (D) Auden

2100. Arrange the following chronologically: i. Henry VIII ii. Hamlet iii. Measure for Measure iv. Macbeth
(A) iii—ii—iv—i
(B) iii—iv—ii—i
(C) i—iii—ii—iv
(D) iii—iv—i—ii

2101. "And I am dumb to tell the lover's tomb How at my sheet goes the same crooked worm." These lines occur in a poem by
(A) Dylan Thomas
(B) Philip Larkin
(C) R.S. Thomas
(D) Robert Graves

2102. The setting of Hardy's *The Dynasts* is
(A) World War I
(B) Spanish Civil War
(C) Napoleanic wars
(D) American Civil War

2103. Where do you find these lines, "When composition begins, inspiration is already on the decline"?
(A) *Biographia Literaria*
(B) Shelley's *A Defence of Poetry*
(C) Arnold's *Essays in Criticism*
(D) F.R. Leavis's *The Great Tradition*

2104. Millament is the heroine in
(A) *She Stoops to Conquer*
(B) *The Rivals*
(C) *The White Devil*
(D) *The Way of the World*

2105. The line "My mistress' eyes are nothing like the sun" is an example for
(A) Simile
(B) Hyperbole
(C) Euphemism
(D) Personification

2106. Existentialism in its religious aspect goes back to ________.
(A) Sartre
(B) Camus
(C) Hegel
(D) Kierkegaard

2107. Match the following:

(a) Terry Eagleton	i. Reader Response
(b) Louis Althusser	ii. Postcolonialism
(c) Geoffrey Hartman	iii. New Historicism
(d) Louis Montrose	iv. Post-structuralism
(e) Aijaz Ahmed	v. Marxism

(A) a-v, b-iv, c-i, d-iii, e-ii
(B) a-v, b-iii, c-iv, d-i, e-ii
(C) a-iv, b-v, c-iii, d-i, e-ii
(D) a-iv, b-v, c-ii, d-iii, e-i

2108. *The Dark Lady of the Sonnets* is a one-act play by
(A) W.B. Yeats
(B) J. M. Synge
(C) Galsworthy
(D) Bernard Shaw

2109. The last (sixth) book of *The Faerie Queene* deals with
(A) The adventures of Redcrosse Knight
(B) The legend of Chastity
(C) The adventures of Sir Calidore
(D) The adventures of the Knight of Temperance

2110. Which of the following classical writers did Chaucer translate into English?
(A) Homer
(B) Aristotle
(C) Boethius
(D) Bede

2111. Which classical writer was Pope's Epistle to Dr. Arbuthnot modelled on?
(A) Homer
(B) Boccaccio
(C) Theophrastus
(D) Horace

2112. __________ was the founder editor of the periodical *The Examiner.*
(A) Leigh Hunt (B) Lockhart
(C) Johnson (D) Hazlitt

2113. Who wrote the verse drama *Becket*?
(A) Oscar Wilde
(B) Tennyson
(C) Osborne
(D) Yeats

2114. "That praises are without reason lavished on the dead, and that the honors due only to excellence are paid to antiquity, is a complaint likely to be always continued by those, who, being able to add nothing to truth, hope for eminence from the heresies of paradox; or those, who: being forced by disappointment upon consolatory expedients, are willing to hope from posterity what the present age refuses, and flatter themselves that the regard which is yet denied by envy, will be at last bestowed by time." Who wrote this, and in which work?
(A) Longinus -- *On The Sublime*
(B) Sir Philip Sidney -- *An Apology For Poetry*
(C) Samuel Johnson – *Preface To Shakespeare*
(D) John Dryden – *An Essay Of Dramatic Poesy*

2115. Match I with II

I	II
a. *The Friar*	1. Theseus
b. *The Host*	2. Nicholas
c. *The Knight's Tale*	3. Hubert
d. *The Miller's Tale*	4. Harry Bailey

(A) a-3, b-4, c-2, d-1
(B) a-1, b-4, c-3, d-2
(C) a-2, b-3, c-4, d-1
(D) a-3, b-4, c-1, d-2

2116. The following are extracts from the works of literary critics and theorists. Find out the titles of the works from the options given.

a. "But criticism, real criticism is essentially the exercise of this very quality. It obeys an instinct prompting it to try to know the best that is known and thought in the world, irrespectively of practice, politics, and everything of the kind; and to value knowledge and thought as they approach this best, without the intrusion of any other considerations whatever. [...]Its business is, as I have said, simply to know the best that is known and thought in the world, and by in its turn making this known, to create a current of true and fresh ideas."

b. "The all-important fact for the study of literature-or any other mode of communication-is that there are several kinds of meaning. Whether we know and intend it or not, we are all jugglers when we converse, keeping the billiard balls in the air while we balance the cue on our nose. Whether we are active, as in speech or writing, or passive, as readers or listeners, the total meaning we are engaged with is, almost always, a blend, a combination of several contributory meanings of different types."

c. "FANCY, on the contrary, has no other counters to play with, but fixities and definites. The Fancy is indeed no other than a mode of Memory emancipated from the order of time and space; and blended with, and modified by that empirical phenomenon of the will, which we express by the word CHOICE. But equally with the ordinary memory it must receive all its materials ready made from the law of association."

d. "One remark in passing: when semiology becomes organized as a science, the question will arise whether or not it properly includes modes of expression based on completely natural signs, such as pantomime. Supposing that the new science welcomes them, its main concern will still be the whole group of systems grounded on the arbitrariness of the sign."

1. Practical Criticism
2. Course in General Linguistics
3. The Function of Criticism at the Present Time
4 Biographia Literaria

Code :

(A) a-1, b-3, c-4, d-2
(B) a-2, b-1, c-4, d-3
(C) a-3, b-1, c-4, d-2
(D) a-4, b-3, c-2, d-1

2117. Find the related terms from the options given below.

a. "... is, when man is capable of being in uncertainties, mysteries, doubts, without any irritable reaching after fact and reason."
b. A term applied to language which strikes the ear as smooth, pleasant, and musical.
c. "at the bridal chamber"
d. "seize the day"

1. Carpe Diem
2. Euphony
3. Negative Capability
4. Epithalamion

Code :

(A) a-3, b-2, c-4, d-1
(B) a-3, b-1, c-4, d-2
(C) a-3, b-2, c-1, d-4
(D) a-2, b-3, c-4, d-1

2118. The following statements are about *The Faerie Queene*. Find out the statements that are TRUE.

1. *The Faerie Queene* addresses itself to 12 great virtues, which are anatomized in 12 books, arranged in 6 Cantos per book.
2. *Britomart* is the embodiment of 'true Christianity'.
3. Malbecco is the protective husband of the lascivious Hellenore.
4. Duessa represents the 'False' Catholic Church.
5. The Red Crosse Knight bears the emblem of Saint Patrick.

Code :

(A) 1, 2, 3 and 4 (B) 3 and 4
(C) 1, 2 and 3 (D) 2, 3, 4 and 5

2119. Match I and II

I	II
a. Daniel Defoe	1. Dr.Slop
b. Samuel Richardson	2. Squire Allworthy
c. Henry Fielding	3. Friday
d. Laurence Sterne	4. Mr. B

Code:

(A) a-3, b-4, c-2, d-1
(B) a-4, b-3, c-2, d-1
(C) a-1, b-2, c-3, d-4
(D) a-2, b-1, c-4,d-3

2120. Who is the author of the passage given below?

"He shows, however, in the Odyssey (and this further observation deserves attention on many grounds) that, when a great genius is declining, the special token of old age is the love of marvelous tales. It is clear from many indications that the Odyssey was his second subject. A special proof is the fact that he introduces in that poem remnants of the adventures before Ilium as episodes, so to say, of the Trojan War. And indeed, he there renders a tribute of mourning and lamentation to his heroes as though he were carrying out a long-cherished purpose. In fact, the Odyssey is simply an epilogue to the Iliad."

(A) Aristotle
(B) Longinus
(C) Sir Philip Sidney
(D) Matthew Arnold

2121. Match I with II

I	II
a. Lake Poets	1. Richard Lovelace
b. Cavalier Poets	2. Sylvia Plath
c. Metaphysical Poets	3. Robert Southey

d. Confessional Poetry — 4. Andrew Marvell

Code :

(A) a-4, b-1, c-3, d-2
(B) a-3, b-1, c-4, d-2
(C) a-1, b-3, c-4, d-2
(D) a-3, b-4, c-2, d-1

2122. "Courage!" he said, and pointed toward the land,
"This mounting wave will roll us shoreward soon."
In the afternoon they came unto a land
In which it seemed always afternoon.
All round the coast the languid air did swoon,
Breathing like one that hath a weary dream.
These lines are taken from which of the following poems?

(A) *The Lotos Eaters*
(B) *Idylls of the King*
(C) *Tithonus*
(D) *The Eagle*

2123. Find out the sources of the quotes.

a. "Time shall unfold what plaited cunning hides."
b. Frailty, thy name is woman!
c. O! beware, my lord, of jealousy; It is the green-ey'd monster which doth mock The meat it feeds on.
d. Full fathom five thy father lies;
Of his bones are coral made;
Those are pearls that were his eyes;
Nothing of him that doth fade,
But doth suffer a sea-change
Into something rich and strange.

1. *Hamlet*
2. *The Tempest*
3. *Othello*
4. *King Lear*

Code :

(A) a-4, b-1, c-3, d-2
(B) a-2, b-3, c-1, d-4
(C) a-3, b-2, c-1, d-4
(D) a-3, b-2, c-4, d-1

2124. That moment she was mine, mine, fair,
Perfectly pure and good: I found A thing to do, and all her hair
In one long yellow string I wound
Three times her little throat around,
And strangled her. No pain felt she;
I am quite sure she felt no pain.
These lines stand for the speaker's:

(A) true love
(B) dilemma
(C) pride
(D) abnormal psychology

2125. But oh! that deep romantic chasm which slanted
Down the green hill athwart a cedarn cover!
A savage place! as holy and enchanted
As e'er beneath a waning moon was haunted
By woman wailing for her demon lover!
These line are taken from:

(A) *Christabel*
(B) *Dejection: An Ode*
(C) *The Rime Of The Ancient Mariner*
(D) *Kubla Khan*

2126. In his story Sarrasine Balzac, describing a castrato disguised as a woman, writes the following sentence: 'This was woman herself, with her sudden fears, her irrational whims, her instinctive worries, her impetuous boldness, her fussings, and her delicious sensibility.' Who is speaking thus? Is it the hero of the story bent on remaining ignorant of the castrato hidden beneath the woman? Is it Balzac the individual, furnished by his personal experience with a philosophy of Woman? Is it Balzac the author professing 'literary' ideas on femininity? Is it universal wisdom? Romantic psychology? We shall never know, for the good reason that writing is the destruction of every voice, of every point of origin. Writing is that neutral, composite, oblique space where our subject slips away, the negative where all identity is lost, starting with the very identity of the body writing.

This paragraph advocates:
(A) Structuralism
(B) Post-structuralism
(C) Formalism
(D) Expressionism

2127. Match I with II

I	II
a. Eugenius	1. Speaks for the French drama
b. Crites	2. Speaks for the English drama
c. Lisideius	3. Speaks for the ancient drama
d. Neander	4. Speaks for the modern drama

(A) a-4, b-2, c-1, d-3
(B) a-1, b-2, c-4, d-3
(C) a-4, b-3, c-1, d-2
(D) a-2, b-3, c-4, d-1

2128. Match I with II

I	II
a. Surrealism	1. Lord Byron
b. Stream of Consciousness	2. T.S. Eliot
c. Romanticism	3. Dylan Thomas
d. Modernism	4. James Joyce

(A) a-1, b-3, c-4, d-2
(B) a-3, b-4, c-2, d-1
(C) a-3, b-4, c-1, d-2
(D) a-1, b-2, c-3, d-4

2129. " Hence all original religions are allegorical, or susceptible of allegory and, like Janus, have a double face of false and true. Poets, according to the circumstances of the age and nation in which they appeared, were called, in the earlier epochs of the world, legislators, or prophets: a poet essentially comprises and unites both these characters."
This is from:
(A) *Art of Poetry*
(B) *An Apology for Poetry*
(C) *An Essay on Criticism*
(D) *A Defense of Poetry*

2130. Match the lines with the authors.
a. The curfew tolls the knell of parting day.
The lowing herd winds slowly o'er the lea,
The ploughman homeward plods his weary way,
And leaves the world to darkness and to me.
b. The vale funereal, the sad cypress gloom;
The land of apparitions, empty shades!
c. Wild shrieks have issued from the hollow tombs;
Dead men have come again, and walked about;
And the great bell has tolled, unrung and untouched
d. "When men my scythe and darts supply
How great a King of Fears am I!"

1. Robert Blair 2. Thomas Parnell
3. Thomas Grey 4. Edward Young

Code :
(A) a-3, b-1, c-2, d-4
(B) a-3, b-4, c-1. d-2
(C) a-3, b-1, c-2, d-4
(D) a-1, b-2, c-4, d-3

2131. "But though it is in terms of structure that we must describe poetry, the term structure is certainly not altogether satisfactory as a term. One means by it something far more internal than the metrical pattern, say, or than the sequence of images. The structure meant is certainly not formed in the conventional sense in which we think of form as a kind of envelope which "contains" the "content." The structure obviously is everywhere conditioned by the nature of the material which goes into the poem."
The author is:
(A) John Crowe Ransome
(B) William Empson

(C) Cleanth Brooks
(D) I.A.Richards

2132. It will be convenient at this point to introduce two definitions. In a full critical statement which states not only that an experience is valuable in certain ways, but also that it is caused by certain features in a contemplated object, the part which describes the value of the experience we shall call the critical part. That which describes the object we shall call the technical part.

This is taken from:
(A) *Seven Types of Ambiguity*
(B) *The Heresy of Paraphrase*
(C) *The Principles of Literary Criticism*
(D) *The New Criticism*

2133. The loveliest and the last,

The bloom, whose petals nipped before they blew

Died on the promise of the fruit.

The context is:
(A) The death of Edward Young
(B) The death of Mary Shelley
(C) The death of Fanny Brawne
(D) The death of Keats

2134. "Racial memory, animal instinct and poetic imagination all flow into one another with an exact sensuousness."

Who said this about Ted Hughes?
(A) Paul de Man
(B) Richard Rorty
(C) Seamus Heaney
(D) W.H. Auden

2135. "As for the having of them obnoxious to ruin; if they be of fearful natures, it may do well; but if they be stout and daring, it may precipitate their designs, and prove dangerous. As for the pulling of them down, if the affairs require it, and that it may not be done with safety suddenly, the only way is the interchange, continually, of favors and disgraces; whereby they may not know what to expect, and be, as it were, in a wood."

This is taken from Bacon's:
(A) Of Friendship
(B) Of Ambition
(C) Of Revenge
(D) Of Love

2136. "To anyone in the habit of thinking with his ears, the words 'cultural criticism' (Kulturkritik) must have an offensive ring, not merely because, like 'automobile,' they are pieced together from Latin and Greek. The words recall a flagrant contradiction. The cultural critic is not happy with civilization, to which alone he owes his discontent. He speaks as if he represented either unadulterated nature or a higher historical stage."

The Author is:
(A) Theodor W. Adorno
(B) Charles Baudelaire
(C) Walter Pater
(D) Mikhail Bakhtin

2137. Find out the authors of the following extracts.

a. "Because, if I am not mistaken, we shall have to say that about men poets and story-tellers are guilty of making the gravest misstatements when they tell us that wicked men are often happy, and the good miserable; and that injustice is profitable when undetected, but that justice is a man's own loss and another's gain-these things we shall forbid them to utter, and command them to sing and say the opposite."

b. "Our next subject will be the style of expression. For it is not enough to know, what we ought to say; we must also say it as we ought; much help is thus afforded towards producing the right impression of a speech. The first question 'to receive attention was naturally the one that comes first naturally-how persuasion can be produced from the facts themselves. The second is how to set these facts out in language. A third would be the proper method of delivery; this is a thing that affects the success of a speech greatly; but hitherto the subject has been neglected."

c. And first, truly, to all them that professing learning inveigh against poetry may justly be objected, that they go very near to ungratefulness, to seek to deface that which, in the noblest nations and languages that are known, hath been the first light-giver to ignorance, and first nurse, whose milk by little and little enabled them to feed afterwards of tougher know ledges.

d. "For the second unity, which is that of place, the ancients meant by it, that the scene ought to be continued through the play, in the same place where it was laid in the beginning: for the stage on which it is represented being but one and the same place, it is unnatural to conceive it many; and those far distant from one another."

1. Sidney 2. Dryden
3. Plato 4. Aristotle

(A) a-2, b-3, c-1, d-4
(B) a-3, b-2, c-1, d-4
(C) a-4, b-1, c-3, d-2
(D) a-3, b-4, c-1, d-2

2138. Who are the Trench poets?

1. Siegfried Sassoon 2. Rupert Brooke
3. Issac Rosenberg 4. Wilfred Owen
5. W.H. Auden

(A) Only 1,2 and 3
(B) Only 3, 4 and 5
(C) Only 3 and 5
(D) Only 1,2,3 and 4

2139. "Yo! We have heard tell of the majesty of the Speardanes, of the Folk-kings, how the princes did valorous deeds."

These lines are taken from:

(A) Beowulf
(B) Canterbury Tales
(C) Caedmon's Hymn
(D) Piers Plowman

2140. Donne's poem "The Sun Rising" reveals:

1. His knowledge of Ancient Greek Mythology
2. His knowledge of Metaphysics
3. His knowledge of Ptolemaic system of astronomy
4. His knowledge of Platonic doctrine of archetypal ideas

(A) Only 1 and 2
(B) Only 2, 3 and 4
(C) Only 3 and 4
(D) Only 1, 2 and 4

2141. Match I with II

I		II
(A) Thomas Kyd	1.	*The Passionate Shepherd to His Love*
(B) Marlowe	2.	*The Poetaster*
(C) Ben Johnson	3.	*She Stoops to Conquer*
(D) Oliver Goldsmith	4.	*The Spanish Tragedy*

Code :

(A) a-2, b-4, c-1, d-3
(B) a-4, b-1, c-2, d-3
(C) a-1, b-3, c-2, d-4
(D) a-4, b-1, c-2, d-3

2142. Who completed Marlowe's unfinished poem "Hero and Leander"?

(A) John Marston
(B) Sir Philip Sidney
(C) George Chapman
(D) Richard Marriot

2143. According to Coleridge Primary Imagination is:

1. Superior to secondary imagination
2. Inferior to Secondary imagination
3. God's revelation
4. Demands no active response from the poet

Code :

(A) Only 1, 2 and 3
(B) Only 2, 3 and 4

(C) Only 2 and 4
(D) Only 1 and 3

2144. "Hudibras" is:

1. an English mock heroic and narrative poem
2. from the 17th century
3. written by Samuel Butler
4. from the 18th century

Code :

(A) Only 1, 3 and 4
(B) Only 1 and 3
(C) Only 1, 2 and 3
(D) Only 1 and 4

2145. Match I with II

	I		II
a.	*The Prelude*	1.	T.S. Eliot
b.	*Preludes*	2.	Wordsworth
c.	*Ode On The Nativity*	3.	Matthew Arnold
d.	*Tristram and Iscult*	4.	Milton

Code :

(A) a-4, b-3, c-1, d-2
(B) a-3, b-1, c-4, d-2
(C) a-3, b-2, c-1, d-4
(D) a-2, b-1, c-4, d-3

2146. "Our sight is the most perfect and most delightful of all our senses. It fills the mind with the largest variety of ideas, converses with its objects at the greatest distance, and continues the longest in action without being tired or satiated with its proper enjoyments. The sense of feeling can indeed give us a notion of extension, shape, and all other ideas that enter at the eye, except colors; but at the same time it is very much straitened and confined in its operations, to the number, bulk, and distance of its particular objects."

This is taken from:

(A) *The Study of Poetry*
(B) *The Salon of 1859*
(C) *Studies in the History of the Renaissance*
(D) *On the Pleasures of the Imagination*

2147. Match I with II

	I		II
a.	*Thyrsis*	1.	Elegy on John Keats
b.	*In Memoriam*	2.	Elegy on Hugh Clough
c.	*Adonias*	3.	Elegy on Edward King
d.	*Lycidas*	4.	Elegy on Henry Hallam

Code :

(A) a-1, b-4, c-2, d-3
(B) a-2, b-4, c-3, d-1
(C) a-3, b-1, c-4, d-1
(D) a-2, b-4, c-1, d-3

2148. Match I with II

	I		II
a.	Autolycus	1.	Aldous Huxley
b.	Mark Twain	2.	Samuel Cemens
c.	George Eliot	3.	Mary Ann Evans
d.	Elia	4.	Charles Lamb

Code :

(A) a-1, b-2, c-3, d-4
(B) a-2, b-1, c-4, d-3
(C) a-3, b-2, c-1, d-4
(D) a-4, b-3, c-2, d-1

2149. Cynewulf is :

1. one of the 12 Anglo-Saxon poets
2. an epic
3. a parody of Beowulf
4. the author of 'Juliana' and 'Elene'

Code :

(A) Only 1
(B) Only 1, 2 and 3
(C) Only 3
(D) Only 1 and 4

2150. "Having thus explained a few of my reasons for writing in verse, and why I have chosen subjects from common life, and endeavored to bring my language near to the real language of men, if I have been too minute in pleading my own cause, I have at the same time been treating a subject of general interest; and for this reason a few words shall be added with reference solely to these particular poems, and to some defects which will probably be found in them. I am sensible that my associations must have sometimes been particular instead of general, and that, consequently, giving to things a false importance, I may have sometimes written upon unworthy subjects; but I am less apprehensive on this account, than that my language may frequently have suffered from those arbitrary connections of feelings and ideas with particular words and phrases, from which no man can altogether protect himself."

This is taken from:

(A) *An Essay on Criticism*
(B) *Preface to the Second Edition of Lyrical Ballads*
(C) *Biographia Literaria*
(D) *A Defense of Poetry*

2151. According to Longinus which are the sources of sublimity that cannot be cultivated?

1. Dignity of Composition
2. Appropriate use of Figures
3. Capacity for strong emotion
4. Nobility of Diction
5. Grandeure of Thought

Code :

(A) Only 1, 2, and 5
(B) Only 3 and 4
(C) Only 2, 4 and 5
(D) Only 3 and 5

2152. According to S.T. Coleridge:

1. Primary imagination has the "esemplastic" power.
2. On the way to the supernatural from natural if the poet fails to carry on he ends up as a "materialist".
3. Allegory is superior to symbol.
4. Being an 'organic whole' is the quality of good poetry.

Code :

(A) Only 2, 3 and 4
(B) Only 1, 2 and 3
(C) Only 2 and 4
(D) 1, 2, 3 and 4

2153. Who translated the "Seafarer"?

(A) A.L. Tennyson
(B) Ezra Pound
(C) T.S.Eliot
(D) Sylvia Plath

2154. Marlowe's tragedies are:

(A) tragedies of noble men
(B) love tragedies
(C) one-man tragedies
(D) revenge plays

2155. Who coined the phrase, "Marlowe's mighty line"?

(A) Ben Jonson
(B) Samuel Johnson
(C) R.L. Stevenson
(D) Richard Steele

2156. Out of the four chief dialects that flourished in the pre-Chaucerian period, the one that became the standard English in Chaucer's time is:

(A) the Northern
(B) the East-Midland
(C) the West-Midland
(D) the Southern

2157. Which of the following statements is incorrect regarding medieval literature?

(A) Allegory was frequent and usual
(B) The dream-vision convention was prevalent
(C) Chaucer exploited the dream-vision convention in *The Canterbury Tales.*
(D) There was often an undercurrent of moral and dialectic strain.

2158. In *Prologue* and *Canterbury Tales* Chaucer employed the

(A) Ottawa Rhyme (B) Rhyme Royal
(C) Heroic Couplet (D) Both A and C

2159. Chaucer has been criticized for presenting an incomplete picture of his times, because

(A) he overemphasizes the rights of the lower class
(B) he exaggerates the courtly benevolence
(C) he writes for the court and cultivated classes and neglects the suffering of the poor
(D) he supports the Lolland and the Peasant Revolution too fervently

2160. Which of the following are correctly matched?

a.	Captain Singleton	1.	a sailor
b.	Moll Flanders	2.	a prostitute
c.	Colonel Jack	3.	a valiant solider
d.	Cavalier	4.	a prince

Code :
(A) Only a-1 and b-2
(B) Only b-2
(C) Only c-3 and d-4
(D) Only d-4

2161. " Lunatics, lovers, and poets all are ruled by their overactive imaginations. " These words of Shakespeare are taken from:

(A) *Love's Labor Lost*
(B) *Hamlet*
(C) *Henry IV*
(D) *Midsummer Night's Dream*

2162. An author sums up the human condition thus, "human life is everywhere a state, in which much is to be endured and little to be enjoyed" Who said this and where?

(A) Alexander Pope - *Essay on Man*
(B) Oliver Goldsmith - *The Vicar of Wakefield*
(C) Albert Camus - *The Stranger*
(D) Dr. Johnson – *Rasselas*

2163. "Yet if the only form of tradition, of handing down, consisted in following the ways of the immediate generation before us in a blind or timid adherence to its successes, "tradition" should positively be discouraged. We have seen many such simple currents soon lo.st in the sand; and novelty is better than repetition. Tradition is a matter of much wider significance. Ii cannot be inherited, and if you want it you must obtain it by great labor."

(A) T.S.Eliot
(B) Alexander Pope
(C) P.B. Shelley
(D) Matthew Arnold

2164. "…the error of evaluating a poem by its effects—especially its emotional effects—upon the reader" is:

(A) Affective Fallacy
(B) Intentional Fallacy
(C) Both A and B
(D) Pathetic Fallacy

2165. Match I with II

	I		II
a.	Robert Penn Warren	1.	*Ode to the Confederate Dead*
b.	Allen Tate	2.	*Understanding Poetry*
c.	John Crowe Ransom	3.	*Literary Criticism: A Short History*
d.	W.K. Wimsatt	4.	*The New Criticism*

Code :
(A) a-4, b-3, c-1, d-2
(B) a-2, b-4, c-3, d-1
(C) a-2, b-1, c-4, d-3
(D) a-1, d-4, c-2, d-3

2166. Marlowe's all four great tragedies share two features in common. Which are they?

1. Magic Realism
2. Theme of overreaching
3. Blank Verse
4. Romantic presentation

Code :

(A) Only 1, 2 and 3

(B) Only 3 and 4

(C) Only 2, 3 and 4

(D) Only 2 and 3

2167. Who said that the writer should be "outside the whale", because otherwise, the state or society could swallow the writer up, as the whale had swallowed Jonah.

(A) Andrew Marvell

(B) S.T.Coleridge

(C) T.S.Eliot

(D) George Orwell

2168. "I have used similitude." Who said this about his which work?

(A) Thomas Hobbes about 'Leviathan'.

(B) Bunyan about 'The Pilgrim's Progress'

(C) Milton about 'Paradise Lost'

(D) Alexander Pope about 'The Dunciad'

2169. Which of the following is wrong?

(A) Jonathan Swift—A Modest Proposal—Pamphlet—1728

(B) Samuel Johnson—The Vanity of Human Wishes—Imitation of Juvenal's 10th satire

(C) Robinson Crusoe—Friday—Colonialism

(D) Henry Feilding—Tom Jones—Story of a foundling

2170. The two gentlemen in the Two Gentlemen of Verona are

(A) Douglas and Calvin

(B) Valentine and Protons

(C) Henry Bailey and Davenant

(D) Lovelace and Herrick

2171. Who popularized the inductive method for arriving at a conclusion through his Novum Organum?

(A) Ben Jonson

(B) Francis Bacon

(C) Addison and Steele

(D) Dr. Johnson

2172. Thomas Hardy's life and career are obliquely depicted in:

(A) The Return of the Native

(B) Jude the Obscure

(C) Tess of the d' Urbervilles

(D) The Mayor of Casterbridge

2173. Which of the following statements is/are wrong based on the novel "Heart of Darkness"?

1. Kurtz pretends to be mad
2. The novel opens on the mouth of the Thames.
3. Marlow is the hero-narrator of the tale
4. Chinu Achebe denounced this novel as "bloody racist".

Code :

(A) Only 1 (B) Only 2

(C) Only 3 and 4 (D) Only 4

2174. "The humblest craftsman over near the Aemilian school will model fingernails and imitate waving hair in bronze; but the total work will be unhappy because he does not know how to represent it as a unified whole. I should no more wish to be like him, if I desired to compose something, than to be praised for my dark hair and eyes and yet go through life with my nose turned awry. You who write, take a subject equal to your powers, and consider at length how much your shoulders can bear. Neither proper words nor lucid order will be lacking to the writer who chooses a subject within his powers. The excellence and charm of the arrangement, I believe, consists in the ability to say only what needs to be said at the time, deferring or omitting many points for the moment. The author of the long-promised poem must accept and reject as he proceeds."

Horace here:

(A) Gives advice

(B) Criticises

(C) Evaluates

(D) Inspires

2175. Read the following statement and the reason given for it. Choose the right response.

Assertion (A) : *Gulliver's Travels* earned Jonathan Swift the bad name of being a misanthrope.

Reason (R) : Swift in the novel was neutral to the image of man.

(A) Both (A) and (R) are true, and (R) is the correct explanation.
(B) Both (A) and (R) are true, but (R) is not the correct explanation.
(C) (A) is true, but (R) is false.
(D) (A) is false, but (R) is true.

2176. "I had not a dispute but a disquisition with Dilke on various subjects; several things dovetailed in my mind, and at once it struck me what quality went to form a man of achievement especially in literature and which Shakespeare possessed so enormously-I mean negative capability, that is when a man is capable of being in uncertainties, mysteries, doubts, without any irritable reaching after fact and reason-Coleridge, for instance, would let go by a fine isolated verisimilitude caught from the penetralium of mystery, from being incapable of remaining content with half-knowledge."

This is taken:

(A) from Letter to Benjamin Bailey.
(A) from Letter to George and Thomas Keats.
(B) from Letter to John Taylor .
(C) from Letter to Richard Woodhouse.

2177. Assertion (A) : "Tam O' Shanter" by John Clare is about the experience of an ordinary human being and became quite popular during that time.

Reason (R) : John Clare, having suffered bouts of madness, could really feel for the misery of common man.

In the context of the two statements, which of the following is correct ?

(A) Both (A) and (R) are true and (R) explains (A).
(B) Both (A) and (R) are true, but (R) does not explain (A).
(C) (A) is true but (R) is false.
(D) (A) is false but (R) is true.

2178. Or, after dark, will dubious women come
To make their children touch a particular stone;
Pick simples for a cancer; or on some
Advised night see walking a dead one?
Power of some sort will go on
In games, in riddles, seemingly at random;
But superstition, like belief, must die,
And what remains when disbelief has gone?

This is taken from Philip Larkin's

(A) *The Less Deceived*
(B) *An Arundel Tomb*
(C) *Church Going*
(D) *Toads*

2179. Which of the following statements in the context of Virgil's *Aenid* is not correct?

(A) Goddess Juno persuades the wind God, Aeolus, to bring on a storm and scatter the Trojan fleet.
(B) God Neptuen is persuaded by Venus to intervene and quells the storm.
(C) Fidus Achates was faithful follower of Aneeas
(D) Dido, the Tyrian princess, does not accord a hospitable welcome to Aeneas

2180. In Homer's *Iliad* Achilles refuses to take further part in a war. Which of the following may be the cause for it?

(A) Achilles felt tired
(B) Agamemnon, the commander-in-chief of the Achaean Army had seized Briseis, the slave concubine of Achilles
(C) Achillies knew that the army was very strong
(D) none of the above

2181. In the context of Homer's *Obyssey* which of the following statements is not correct?

(A) the *Iliad* and the *Odyssey* are epics describing the exploits of the heroes Achilles and Odysseus. But no attempt is made to tell everything about these heroes.

(B) One specific action in the life of Odysseus is taken as the theme or subject

(C) In *Odyssey* the homecoming of Odysseus after the fall of Troy is the theme

(D) Odysseus does not possess enough courage to endure his manifold difficulties.

2182. In the context of Aeschylus' *Agamemnon* which of the following statement is true?

(A) Agamemnon was the king of Argos. He married Clytemnestra and was elected commander of the Greek Host that went to Troy to recover Helen

(B) Helen was the wife of Agamemnon's brother Menelaus

(C) Helen was carried off by Paris

(D) All the above statements are true

2183. In the context of Sophocles *Oedipus, the King* which of the following statements may be true?

(A) Oedipus was the son of Laius, king of Thebes and Jocasta

(B) Oedipus' father was informed by an oracle that he must perish at his son's hands

(C) in ignorance of his parentage, Oedipus slew Lais, his father and married his mother, Jocasta

(D) all the above statements may be true

2184. In the tragedy *Antigone* what may be called the tragic flaw in the character of Antigone?

(A) she was over-ambitious like Macbeth

(B) she was too suspicious like Othelo

(C) Antigone's tragic flaw lies in an uncalled for insolence towards civil authority, her determination not merely to do her duty for her brother but also to be put to death for it

(D) she had a hesitant nature

2185. What is the meaning of the word 'testament'?

(A) The word 'testament' comes from the Latin, and is a translation of the Greek word meaning covenant

(B) The word 'testament' comes from the Greek language and it means a religious story

(C) The word 'testament' means words of God

(D) None of the above

2186. Which of the following statements may be correct?

(A) Koine language reflects the influence of Aramaic, the language that was the common tongue of the Palestinian Jews and which Jesus himself employed

(B) "Revelation" is the first book in *The Bible*

(C) Jesus Christ is the author of *The New Testament*.

(D) None of the above

2187. Which of the following statements is correct in the context of More's *Utopia?*

(A) All the cities in *Utopia* are built on the same plan and are of about the same size

(B) the streets are very dirty, not well-drained

(C) the houses are built without any planning

(D) in *Utopia* nobody is required to work on the farms or in trade

2188. How "The Bridge" acquired such great significance for Hart Crane?

(A) the greatest suspension Brooklyn bridge was an engineering feat and for Crane it became a symbol of integration between machine and man, past and present

(B) a myth which made Absolute intelligible to Americans

(C) logo of a new dawn

(D) embodiment of an exile's quest

2189. Which of the following incidents have not been mentioned in Tolstoy's *War and Peace?*

(A) Napoleon had been proclaimed Emperor of the French

(B) Napoleon had annexed Genoa, seized Hanover from the British

(C) England was Napoleon's enemy

(D) Russia was friend of Napoleon

2190. Which of the following statements may not be true about Tolstoy's *War and Peace?*

(A) the scene shifts continually, from one family to another from a scintillating ball to a quiet conversation between two people, from love affairs to hunting scenes

(B) the novel is full of apparently disjointed scenes all taking place in the interlocking aristocratic circles

(C) the plot of the novel is loose and complex. It creates a facsimile of real life: its untidiness its disjointedness, its extreme variety, its crowed of struggling, lonely human beings and its seemingly lack of purpose

(D) the novel is very compact. The plot of the novel is organic. There is a causal relationship between the incidents of the novel

2191. Which of the following sentences may be an extract from Machiavellis's *The Princes?*

(A) the truly capable ruler must combine the qualities of the lion and the fox, striving to be as brave as the one and as crafty as the other

(B) now the Lord had said unto Abraham get thee out of the country and from thy kindred and from thy father's house unto land that I will show thee

(C) Ful wel she sang the services divine, Entuned in her nose ful seemly; And French she spake ful faire and sweetly

(D) none of these

2192. *The Prince* advocates that

(A) a state should run strictly on the principles of truth and non-violence

(B) a state is free to do anything necessary to strengthen itself

(C) a state should perish but never adopt unfair means even though the unfair means may be for the welfare of the state

(D) none of these

2193. Which of the following statements may be true in the context of Maupassant's *Pierre Et Jean?*

(A) Madame Rosenilly is a neighbour of Monsieur Roland

(B) Monsieur Marechal of Paris is a former friend of the Rolands

(C) Monsieur Marechal has died and has left all his money to jean

(D) all the above statements are true

2194. In Maupassant's *Pierre Et Jean* what was the suspicion in the mind of Pierre?

(A) his younger brother Jean was conspiring to kill him

(B) his younger brother Jean was conspiring to kill him

(C) his younger brother was not his father's son

(D) none of these

2195. In the context of Cervantes's *Don Quixote* which of the following statements may be true?

(A) Don Quixote had decided to become a great philosopher and preacher

(B) Don Quixote was moving about here and there to preach his religious beliefs

(C) Don Quixote had decided to become a knight-errant, He would travel the globe in shining armour, mounted on a steed, in search of adventure

(D) none of these

2196. Which of the following, statements may be true in the context of Cervantes' *Don Quixote?*

(A) Don Quixote is one of the most pathetic, laughable and lovable characters in all fiction

(B) Don Quixote would travel the globe in shining armour, mounted on a mettlesome steed, in search of adventure righting wrongs rescuing maids in distress

(C) in Don Quixote adventure succeeds adventure and in almost all of the them Quixote is the loser

(D) all the above statements may be true

2197. Which of the following statements is true about Pasternak's *Doctor Zhivago?*

(A) the novel gives an account of the Crimean War

(B) the novel presents a graphic panorama of life in Russia during the Russian Revolution, the Provisional Government and the Civil War

(C) the novel presents the discoveries of a scientist Doctor Zhivago

(D) none of these

2198. The main thread of *Doctor Zhivago* is provided by

(A) the political events during the Russian Revolution and after it

(B) the private world of two characters–Yuri Zhivago and Larissa Guishar

(C) the story of the two characters–Yuri Zhivago and Larissa Guishar runs parallel to and is influenced by political events of the Russian revolution

(D) none of these

2199. In the context of Synge's *The Playboy of the Western World* which of the following statements may be correct?

(A) Christy is a young weakling who flees away to an isolated public house after a family quarrel

(B) Christy is accepted as a dashing figure by all the country folk, on the basis of his boast that he had just killed his father

(C) Christy becomes the local hero, centre of female admiration and attention, especially pursued by a widow

(D) all the above statements are correct

2200. Which of the following statements in Synge's *The Playboy of the Western World* may not be true?

(A) Christy said that he had killed his father, but his father appeared alive

(B) Christy had killed his father

(C) Christy was engaged to Pegeen

(D) Mahon, Christy's father, is proud to be led off by the son who has become a man

2201. Which of the following statements may be true in the context of Dante's *The Divine Comedy?*

(A) *The Divine Comedy* is a description of the Trojan War

(B) *The Divine Comedy* is a description of heaven, hell and purgatory

(C) *The Divine Comedy* is a mock epic presenting the war between man and woman

(D) *The Divine Comedy* is a mock epic presenting the war between man and women

2202. What was the ultimate result of the moral bankruptcy of the Stuart kings of England?

(A) Famine (B) Revolts

(C) Riots

(D) Puritan dictatorship

2203. Which play of Shakespeare was left out in the first collection of his plays ?

(A) *Pericles* (B) *Twelfth Night*

(C) *The Tempest* (D) *Winter's Tale*

2204. 'This was due, first, to the growth of religious controversies; secondly, to the desire of introducing into English literature the critical and philosophical ideas newly absorbed from the Greek Plato, Aristotle with the neo-Platonists; and the Roman

Cicero, Seneca, Boetheus and other thinkers; and thirdly, to the desire to analyse literary, ethical and philosophical concepts as they affected the renascent human mind.' These views are expressed

(A) for the maturity of English prose during Elizabethan Era
(B) for translations
(C) as personal views of critic
(D) None of the above

2205. P.B. Shelley was deeply impressed by one of Keats' poems. Which poem was it ?

(A) *Hyperion*
(B) *Ode to a Nightingale*
(C) *Ode on the Poets*
(D) *Ode to Autumn*

2206. Sidney's *Arcadia* is a/an

(A) long poem (B) prose romance
(C) moral discussion (D) epic

2207. Middleton's *Women Beware Women* and the fantasies and imagination of the poets and dramatists of his time showed marked similarity. Such darkening of mood was due to

(A) rising prices of foodstuff
(B) england's defeat in wars
(C) mounting problems and tensions of the time due to fall of morality
(D) aggravating social problems

2208. When was '*Anatomy of Wit*' published ?

(A) 1599 (B) 1580
(C) 1560 (D) 1571

2209. "Among others his book his book contains Strachey's account of the ship-wreck on the Bermudas which was the background of Shakespeare's *The Tempest*. But he is generally inferior to his master. He was the source of Coleridge's dream-poem *Kubla Khan.*" Above lines are about :

(A) Sir Walter Raleigh
(B) Sir Richard Grenville
(C) Samuel Purchas
(D) Coryate

2210. What was the title of the Anthology of William Painter's translations ?

(A) *Pleasant Histories*
(B) *The Palace of Pleasure*
(C) *Excellent Stories*
(D) None of the above

2211. Which of the following was Thomas Paine's work that he wrote in reply to Burke?

(A) *Beyond the Melting Pot*
(B) *The Rights of Man*
(C) *Whither Liberty*
(D) *Can Man be Free*

2212. "Her whose gentle will have changed my fate and made my life a perfumed altar flame." To whom are these lines dedicated by Tennyson ?

(A) Elizabeth Barrett Browning
(B) Emily Sellwood
(C) Queen Victoria
(D) None of the above

2213. Which poem of Miss Barrett impressed Browning greatly ?

(A) *The Cry of the Children*
(B) *Lady Geraldine's Courtship*
(C) *Sonnets from the Portuguese*
(D) *Casa Guidi Windows*

2214. Which poem of Browning describes the strength and weakness of a painter ?

(A) An Epistle
(B) Andrea Del Sart
(C) The Bishop Orders his Tomb
(D) Faultless Painter

2215. Who wrote '*The Christian Year*', a book of devotional verse ?

(A) Frederic William Faber
(B) John Keble
(C) Christina Rossetti
(D) William Rossetti

2216. Which poet was a leader of the Pre-Raphaelite Movement in Art and Literature?

(A) Morris
(B) Everett Millais

(C) Thomas Woolney
(D) Dante Gabriel Rossetti

2217. William Makepeace Thackeray's work '*The Four Georges*' is a
(A) Social novel (B) Social comedy
(C) Satire (D) Tragedy

2218. Dante's 'Divina Comedia' became known to the people in
(A) 1310 (B) 1420
(C) 1286 (D) 1395

2219. Who was chosen as King of England around the year of death of Chaucer, by the England's Parliament ?
(A) Henry IV (B) Henry V
(C) Henry VII (D) Richard III

2220. Which of the followinng is an elegy ?
(A) *Paradise Lost* of Milton
(B) *Seige* of *Corianth*
(C) Shelley's *Adonais*
(D) Grey's *The Bard*

2221. Which of the following was an epic ?
(A) Wordsowrth's *Daffodil*
(B) Milton's '*Paradise Lost*'
(C) Coleridge's *Kubla Khan*
(D) Keat's *Hyperion*

2222. Name the event that followed *Pier's Plowman* (1362)
(A) The Hundred Year's War
(B) The War of Roses
(C) The Peasant Rebellion of 1381
(D) The Battle of Agincourt

2223. Who succeeded Richard III ?
(A) The Tudors (B) Richard IV
(C) Normans (D) Henry V

2224. When did Julius Caesar invade England ?
(A) 105 A.D. (B) 55 B.C.
(C) 200 A.D. (D) 200 A.C.

2225. After Shakespeare, Massinger and Ford
(A) strove to increase sensationalism in their plays
(B) produced licentious scenes for their own sake
(C) wrote tragedies
(D) None of the above

2226. Marlowe's drama *Edward II* Act I scene I opens with Gaveston in London. He has come from
(A) France (B) Spain
(C) Germany (D) Rome

2227. The famous work *History of Dramatic Literature* is written by-
(A) Dr. Arbuthnot (B) Ward
(C) Swinburne (D) Dryden

2228. When was the present version of 'Beowulf' brought out ?
(A) 8th century (B) 16th century
(C) 15th century (D) 9th century

2229. The writer of *Ars Poetica* is
(A) Virgil (B) Horace
(C) Plato (D) Aristotle

2230. When was the expedition to Guyana taken up by Sir Walter Raleigh ?
(A) 1590 (B) 1618
(C) 1681 (D) 1716

2231. When Charles Dickens was middle aged his name was linked with an actress, a girl twenty five years younger than him. What is her name ?
(A) Mary Hogarth
(B) Maria Beadnell
(C) Emily Sellwood
(D) Ellen Ternan

2232. There was in 16th century a Renaissance of mathematical knowledge. It was developed and polished in 17th century. Leibnitz, Newton, and Pascal were some of the contributors. What particular field of mathematics did Descartes apply himself to ?
(A) Logarithms (B) Geometry
(C) Algebra (D) Trigonometry

2233. 'Political Arithmetic' was also developed in the 17th century. What is the new name given to it today ?
(A) Statistics (B) Analysis
(C) Dynamics (D) New Statics

2234. There was the author of several Homilies, in one of which he describes the desolation caused by the Danes and castigates the English people for their vices. His prose may not have the grace, but it has a far more popular appeal. Who was this author?

(A) Dr. Arbuthnot
(B) Wulfstan
(C) Alfred the great
(D) Boethius

2235. The story of this epic poem is told in great detail and vigorous language. In pure literary excellence or human appeal it cannot of course be compared with the Homeric epics. It is the epic or saga of a rude age and a rough people. It presents a picture common enough in the early history of all countries which embodies the fierce struggle between the savages and their conquerors belonging to a superior race, (such as is depicted in the Mahabharat between the Aryan Princes and the *Rakshasas* inhabiting the forests). It is also a folk-tale in the truest sense because it is based on, and is a sublimation of, the actual experiences of a primitive people, working their way towards a civilised life. Identify this epic poem ?

(A) *Mahabharat* (B) *Beowulf*
(C) *Odyssey*
(D) None of the above

2236. "A thing of beauty is a joy forever." In which of the following Keats poems do we find this line ?

(A) *Ode to a Grecian Urn*
(B) *Endymion*
(C) *Ode to West Wind*
(D) *Eve of St. Agnes*

2237. Which of the following persons translated Ariosto into English in 1591 ?

(A) George Chapman
(B) Philip Sydney
(C) John Harrington
(D) Herbert Spenser

2238. Who wrote 'Sianus' ?

(A) Bekker (B) Ben Jonson
(C) Middleton (D) Webster

2239. Who was the author of 'The Rival Ladies' which was published in 1664 ?

(A) Dryden (B) Racine
(C) Sydney (D) Pope

2240. When was Comeille's *Le Cid*, published ?

(A) 1587 (B) 1637
(C) 1687 (D) 1837

2241. Identify the authority who had written, "Putting all this together, with much more of the same kind, which has only been indicated here, we should certainly gather, that while there are manifest tokens preserved in our language of the Saxon having been for a season an inferior and even an oppressed race, the stable elements of Anglo-Saxon life, however overlaid for a while, had still made good their claim to be the solid ground work of the after nation as of the after language; and to the justice of this conclusion all other historic records, and the present social condition of England, consent in bearing witness."

(A) Arthur Compton Ridert
(B) Trench
(C) Ben Jonson
(C) Samuel Johnson

2242. Who translated the classic 'Ovid' (in Elizabethan Era) ?

(A) Chapman (B) Golding
(C) Harrington (D) Fairfax

2243. What was the writing for which P.B. Shelley was expelled from the university ?

(A) '*The Necessity of Atheism*'
(B) '*Alastor*'
(C) '*Adonais*'
(D) None of the above

2244. Who translated The Old Testament from Greek ?

(A) William Tyndale (1484-1536)
(B) Wycliffe

(C) Miles Coverdale
(D) None of the above

2245. '*Tale of a Tub*' was published in :
(A) 1701 (B) 1702
(C) 1704 (D) 1707

2246. Who is the central character of Marlowe's *The Jew of Malta* ?
(A) Shylock (B) Abraham
(C) Barabas (D) None of these

2247. What was his age when Christopher Marlowe died of a stab wound sustained during a drunken brawl ?
(A) Twenty seven years
(B) Thirty two years
(C) Forty four years
(D) Twenty nine years

2248. In *Julius Caesar* and in another play Shakespeare is said to have depicted Romans better than the Roman writers themselves have done. Which is that play ?
(A) *Troilus and Cressyde*
(B) *Two Gentlemen of Verona*
(C) *Coriolanus*
(D) *Romeo and Juliet*

2249. Of far greater poetic merit is the translation of *Homer* to which Keats paid tribute in a memorable sonnet. Seven books of the *Iliad* appeared in 1598; the rest being completed in the next reign. He also used the "long swinging' fourteen syllabled line for his translation of the *Iliad*. The choice of the heroic couplet for the Odyssey was not so happy." Who was this translator ?
(A) Sir Thomas North
(B) George Chapman
(C) Philemon Holland
(D) William Langland

2250. In which of Ben Jonson's plays do we find the characters Morose and Cutbeard ?
(A) *The Alchemist*
(B) *The Silent Woman*
(C) *Volpone*
(D) *Every Man in his Humour*

2251. One of the best-plays, *The Tempest* is the last of Shakespeare's plays. He was inspired to write it by the incident of
(A) sinking of a ship
(B) the defeat of Armada
(C) return of the sailors of a ship that had disappeared
(D) None of the above

2252. He wrote plays that belong to the horror school of tragedy. His plots are horrible and fantastic. He uses all the conventions of this type of drama, and is the last word in all that is morbid and melodramatic. His two famous plays are *The Revenger's Tragedy* (1600) and *The Atheist's Tragedy* (1607-11). He is weakest where Webster is strongest.
Who is this writer ?
(A) Cyril Tourneur
(B) Thomash Kyd
(C) Phillip Massinger
(D) None of these

2253. He brought into English poetry the dignity and elevation of classical poetry by his high moral fervour, his wealth of classical learning and his lofty tone. But his chief contribution is the noble rhythm of his blank verse. Shakespeare and the Elizabethan playwrights gave to Surrey's blank verse an energy of movement that simulated the freedom of animated conversation while retaining its poetic nuances. But this poet gave his verse the rare quality, the swing and movement of impassioned thought. It not only consists of 'apt numbers and fit quantity of syllables'. but also of 'sense variously drawn from line to line.' The essence of this lies in varying the middle pause (*caesura*) artfully to suit the nuances of thought.
About whose contribution to English poetry the above has been said ?
(A) Dryden (B) Milton
(C) Pope (D) Spenser

2254. The characters are well drawn and the style is animated but not extravagant. What it lacks is Shakespeare's imaginative boldness and poetic fire, which of course is not to be expected in the age in which he wrote. Any further comparison with *Antony and Cleopatra* is profitless, for Shakespeare's is a moving drama of life while he wrote a competent play for the stage.
In whose criticism the above has been observed while comparing him with Shakespeare ?
(A) Thomas Otway
(B) John Dryden
(C) Ben Johnson
(D) None of the above

2255. Spenser's poetry is important to the growth of the English language and literature for the following reasons. Which reason is not correct ?
(A) Spenser's poetry shows the melody and variety of English poetry
(B) He was the first to write pastoral poetry in English
(C) It was the beginning of the outburst of Elizabethan poetry
(D) It proved the inferiority of the poetry of Chaucer.

2256. One of the most worthwhile exponents of this particular tradition is he who died too early to fulfil the high promise. Of his two plays "*The Orphan*" and "*Venice Preserved*", the former is still read; the other is sometimes acted. He is capable of ardent passion, usually love. Leigh Hunt has called him the poet of sensual pathos, for 'affecting though he sometimes is, he knows no way to the heart but through the sense.' In these tragedies he made much of sentiment and pathos. Who is being described here ?
(A) Dryden (B) Thomas Otway
(C) Pope
(D) George Etherage

2257. 'These were restless years unfavourable to the concentration needed for producing real work of art. Added to his emotional troubles was his inability to secure a means of livelihood due to his revolutionary associations. His humanitarian sympathies or his love of nature also brought him no peace. He even confessed that 'cataracts and mountains are good occasional society but will not do for constant companions.'
The above observation pertains to :
(A) Walter Scott
(B) William Wordsworth
(C) Coleridge
(D) Lord Byron

2258. He, who had written so ardently on the superiority of the heroic couplet as a vehicle for drama, now took to blank verse, and produced his tragedy "*All for Love*" which was based on Shakespeare's *Antony and Cleopatra*. This is certainly his masterpiece. Though he follows the outline of Shakespeare's play, he never imitates it, and the result is on the whole satisfactory. He observes the Unities of Time and Place, and this certainly has a cramping effect on his art. The human problem underlying Shakespeare's play is reduced to a social problem, – the fatal consequence of unlawful love.
In whose appreciation the above has been said ?
(A) Dryden (B) Johnson
(C) Thomas Otway (D) None of these

2259. 'He made himself the leader of the Romantic movement, first, because he issued in his *preface* to the *Lyrical Ballads* what may be called the manifesto of the movement, in which he demanded a change both in the subject and the form of poetry that was truly revolutionary; and *secondly* because the theme of his great poem *The Prelude* is the apotheosis of the Self which lies at the root of Romanticism. In *The Prelude* he has recorded his boyhood experiences among the mountains and lakes of

Cumberland which established a new relation between the poet and Nature of mutual intercommunication.

About whom the above observation has been made ?

(A) William Wordsworth
(B) Coleridge
(C) Keats
(D) Shelley

2260. Then happened the most significant event in his life-his meeting with the Wordsworths. Under the moderating influence of Wordsworth's remarkable sister Dorothy, the two poets turned from frustrating politics, from the influence of Rousseau and Godwin, to Poetry and to Nature. The association bore fruit in the poems of the *Lyrical Ballads*, to which he contributed four poems in blank verse and the incomparable. *Rime of the Ancient Mariner.*'

The above observation has been made about:

(A) Byron (B) Keats
(C) Shelley (D) Coleridge

2261. 'He was tutor to Queen Elizabeth and Lady Jane Grey. Curiously enough, his first important work *Taxophilus* (1548) was written in the form of a Socratic dialogue in defence of archery and its value as an ideal sport. He urges the use of English in scholarly writing and the acquisition of knowledge both from books and personal experience. Like most of the prose-writers of the period he favours the balanced structure with a marked preference for alliteration and assonance. His second work, *The Scholemaster* (1570), is the first book in English on education : It was published posthumously and the somewhat graceless style shows that it had not the advantage of revision. He says that for teaching children, gentle and persuasive methods are more efficacious than the use of the birch rod then in vogue.' To whom the above lines refer ?

(A) William Tyndale
(B) Roger Ascham (1515)
(C) Richard Hooker
(D) John Foxe

2262. 'His interest in geography and in travels to distant lands was insatiable; not only did he lecture on these subjects at Oxford, but he interviewed seamen and mechantmen, collected letters and log-books and thus compiled what may be described as first-hand records of adventures abroad. His *Navigation, Voyages, Discoveries, etc.* was finally completed in 1598-1600 and combines something of the vision of the poet with the curiosity of a modern newspaper reporter. No book gives us a more vivid idea of the spirit that inspired the Elizabethans'.

These lines refer to :

(A) Richard Hakluyt
(B) Robert Green
(C) Thomas Nash
(D) Thomas Malory

2263. He was the most versatile and prolific writer of the age: he wrote plays, romances, pamphlets. He is not a great playwright, but he did some fine work in certain directions of English drama. He excels in the art of plot construction to create supense in the spectator. The influence of classical drama is hardly noticeable in his plays. On the other hand, he shows great skill in weaving the many threads of his complicated plots into a close-knit design. Who is he ?

(A) John Lyly
(B) Morlowe
(C) Kyd
(D) Ascham

2264. "We take cunning for a sinister and crooked wisdom. And certainly there is a great difference between a cunning man and a wise man, not only in point of honesty, but in point of ability. There he that can touch the cords, and yet cannot play well; so there are some that are good in canvasses and factories that are otherwise weak men.

Again, it is one thing to understand persons, and another thing to understand matters; for many are perfect in men's humours, that are not greatly capable of the real part of business; which is the constitution of one that hath studied men more than books. Such men are fitter for practice than for counsel; and they are good but in their own alley; turn them to new men and they have lost their aim."

Above lines have been written by

(A) Sidney

(B) Francis Bacon

(C) Dryden

(D) Lyly

2265. His contributions to the development of English drama are notable, the most outstanding being the creation of genuine blank verse and genuine tragedy in the English language. "After his arrival, the way was prepared, the path was made straight for Shakespeare" (*Swinburne*). Identify the playwright being referred to.

(A) Christopher Marlowe

(B) George Peele

(C) Robert Greene

(D) Thomas Kyde

2266. 'He was an Italian Protestant refugee who was educated at Oxford and was a university teacher of French and Italian. His translation of *Montaigne's* 'Essays' deserves high praise. Shakespeare knew him and freely borrowed from his translation in many of his plays. He was a master in the use of words as is testified by his book on the "World of Words' (1598), and his translation must have satisfied the Elizabethan love for the beauty of words for their own sake.'

About whom is this appreciation ?

(A) Francis Bacon

(B) Giovanni Florio

(C) Arthur Golding

(D) None of these

2267. The play is said to be a command performance meant for the old Queen who wanted to see Falstaff in love. The play is not Shakespearean in quality. It is a farce comedy of his own invention; it partakes of the topicality of Dekker and shows traces of Jonson's comedy of 'humour' and realistic satire. The characterisation is slight and sketchy. Sir Hugh Evans, Dr. Caius, Nym and Ford are distinctly in the manner of Jonson, whose early comedies were just then being sponsored by Shakespeare's company. The play bears all the traces of hasty composition, and there are many inconsistencies. The Falstaffian episodes are skilfully handled. It is :

(A) '*Merry Wives of Windsor*'

(B) '*Merchant of Venice*'

(C) '*As You Like It*'

(D) *Henry V*

2268. He is as subtle, learned and original in his own way as Burton was. *Religio Medici* breathed a spirit of tolerance and geniality rare in that age, and was quickly translated into Latin and other languages. Himself a medical man, his attitude was both scientific and religious. His manner is humorous and irionical, while his sentences, have a rhythm that charmingly sustains the eloquence of more inspired passages. The Latinised vocabulary adds dignity to the language while the condensed epigrams give it force. It is a highly personal style. Who is this writer of the Jacobean period?

(A) Thomas Browne

(B) Burton

(C) Bunyan

(D) None of these

2269. 'He was learned and broad-minded, and used his reasoning with the calm dignity of a scholar. His great contribution is that he introduced in English literature the Ciceronian style, the flowing periodic structure in English prose. In the periodic style clauses branch out from the stem in abundance, but they are always subordinated to it and bound to it. In every sentence again the subordinate clauses balance one another to sustain the whole, the total effect being greatly enhanced by internal correspondence and assonance.' The above lines are about :

(A) John Foxe
(B) Richard Hooker
(C) John Lyly
(D) Sir Philip Sydney

2270. 'He was a scholar who rose to the highest offices in the State by a rare combination of learning and worldly wisdom. He was a lawyer, statesman, scholar and philosopher, and, above all, he systematised the logical basis of experimental science. In literature he made his mark with his *Essays* (1597-1626). They reveal an acute intellect, the faculty of observation of men and affairs, and deep practical wisdom. They have often been compared with Montaigne, but are more concentrated in expression and economical in treatment. He cultivated to perfection the art of saying notable things with the utmost of economy and clearness. Like Montaigne, he strung his reflections with quotations from the Bible and the classics, and he enlivened his arguments with illustrative anecdotes and allusions.' The above words refer to

(A) Robert Burton
(B) Sir Fancis Bacon
(C) Thomas Campion
(D) Stephen Gosson

2271. 'The structure, however elaborate is designed to hold the reader's attention from beginning to end. Hooker's magnificent sentences move on majestically and musically, and with a smooth harmonious cadence that carries the reader along as in a flowing current with almost effortless ease. The influence of this style on Donne and Taylor, Milton and Browne, the great seventeenth century masters of prose, is obvious. It introduced a healthy reaction against the affectations of *Euphues and Arcadia* and the artificialities of a purely rhetorical prose.'

About whom the above words have been written ?

(A) Sir Phillip Sidney
(B) Francis Bacon
(C) Gosson
(D) None of these

2272. The *Tragical History of Doctor Faustaus* (1588-89) is a great tragedy but suffers from loose dramatic structure and lack of proportion. The theme is based on the well-known medieval legend of the magician Faustus, who sold his soul to the Devil to obtain his heart's desire, – knowledge through experience — a theme treated also by Calderon in the 17th and Goethe in the 19th century. Who is the author of above tragedy ?

(A) Shakespeare
(B) Marlowe
(C) Calderon
(D) Jonson

2273. It is a dramatic adaptation of a pastoral story by Lodge. The interweaving of the minor plots shows Shakespeare's high skill in workmanship. The device of women disguising themselves as men, so successfully begun in *The Merchant of Venice,* is used in this and the next play with greater effect and irony. Rosalind as a heroine is superior to both Portia and Beatrice, and yields only to Viola in depth. The most interesting character is Jaques. The name of the play is:

(A) *The Twelfth Night*
(B) *As You Like It*
(C) *Henry V*
(D) None of these

2274. He belonged to the *Tribe of Ben*, and imitated the classical lyricists Horace, Catullus and Martial. He is the best of the Cavalier poets, who excelled in passionate love-lyrics. The best of them are contained in the *Hesperides* (1648), which is marked by a delicate fancy, Arcadian grace, pagan sensuousness, and simple expression. The pastoral note appears more exquisitely than in the Spenserians in his love of summer-time flowers which are delicately woven into the amatory motive. His apparent spontaneity conceals a most careful workmanship. Identify the poet

(A) Richard Herrick
(B) Richard Crashaw
(C) Herbert
(D) None of these

2275. It is based on an Italian story. This romantic comedy has a depth beyond any of the others. Viola is the loveliest of Shakespeare's romantic heroines, tactful, and wistful, yet full of kindly and readywitted humour. She is contrasted with the sentimental and somewhat affected lady. The title of the play :

(A) *Twelfth Night*
(B) *Julius Ceaser*
(C) *Hamlet*
(D) None of these

2276. He is Shakespeare's Problem King. Some (Hazlitt, Bradley), characterise him as an ill-bred egoist, whereas others (Ruskin, Dowden) look upon him as Shakespeare's conception of an ideal king and a great man of courage and common-sense.

The criticism pertains to the play :

(A) Hamlet (B) Henry V
(C) King Lear (D) None of these

2277. He was a disciple of Herbert, but with strong mystical note and intensity of feeling and language. He emphasised the manifestation of God in nature. His *The Retreat* influenced Wordsworth's 'Immortality Ode' both in thought and language, while the poem, *The World* ("I Saw Eternity in an Hour") has a far reaching depth of thought and suggestion.

He was:

(A) Crashaw
(B) Henry Vaughan
(C) Andrew Marvell
(D) None of these

2278. 'A much more pretentious work is his *Advancement of Learning* (1605), a philosophical treatise in defence of learning and to show the methods of advancing knowledge. He here initiates a movement against mere Rhetoric and Imagination and in favour of Logic and Reason. Of his other works in English *Henry II* (1622) is a philosphical history written with understanding and insight; while *New Atlantis* (1624) is a picture of an ideal commonwealth suggested by Plato's *Republic* and More's *Utopia*; he here outlined a society based on scientific knowledge and in a way anticipated the methods and achievements of modern science. In all his writings he showed the qualities of logical and lucid thinking expressed with an economy of words rare in that age of exuberance and enthusiasm. At his best he is undoubtedly one of the greatest masters of English prose.

The appreaciation refers to

(A) Richard Hooker
(B) Roger Aschm
(C) Francis Bacon
(D) John Lyly

2279. 'It is possibily a recast of an older play, which may have been the *Love's Labour Won* mentioned by Meres in 1598. The source is Boccaccio. The tone is a continuation of Troilus and Cressyde. The foul-mouthed Lavache and the contemptible Parolles may be said to act as chorus in an unpleasant story. The character of Helena has been as much praised as condemned. She is the only heroine of Shakespeare who belongs to the middle-class. Hazlitt thought her sweet; Shaw Charming; Masefield despicable. The hero Bertram is an ordinary young man of unimaginative prejudices.'

The above qualities are found in :

(A) *Henry V*

(B) *All is Well that Ends Well*

(C) *King Lear*

(D) *Love's Labour Lost*

2280. He is a greater poet than Cowley, and combines metaphysical conceits with rare lyric grace. He is the last poet to labour under the influence of Donne. He wrote charming poems in praise of the country side, as well as some effective satires. His imagery is nearly always rich and fanciful. His best known poem is the *Horatian Ode on Cromwell's Return from Ireland* (1650) which has been called the most truly classic poem in the language. The four-lined stanza (two pentametric lines followed by two trimeters) is his own adaptation of Horace.

Which poet is he ?

(A) George Herbert

(B) Andrew Marvell

(C) Henry Vaughan

(D) None of these

2281. "*The Maid's Tragedy* is a very well constructed play with a high tragic motive. The characterisation is excellent. But the plot is one of 'brutal grossness.' It rises to moments of high tragic passion, but the decadent note is clear. A better play is *Philaster*, acted about the same time. It is a tragic-comedy, with a heroine who suggests Shakespeare's Viola in *Twelfth Night*. The plot is impossible but well-managed; the characters brilliant but shallow. There are spectacular scenes with a mixture of humour and seriousness."

Who was the writer of the plays mentioned here ?

(A) Fletcher and Beaumont

(B) Francis Beaumont

(C) Philip Massinger

(D) John Fletcher

2282. "The writings", said Lamb of him, "are usually designated by the title of *quaint*, and with sufficient reason, for such was his natural bias to conceits that I doubt not upon most occasions it would have him going out of his way to have expressed himself out of them. His conceits are oftentimes deeply steeped in human feeling and passion." He has been described as "original, humorous, vivacious, erudite, but not pedantic." He is often garrulous, but has a something of Bacon's terseness of manner.

Who is this writer ?

(A) Jeremy Taylor

(B) Thomas Fuller

(C) Issac Walton

(D) None of the above

2283. He spoke nobly of his resolve to write a great poem which was 'not to be raised with the heat of youth or the vapour of wine', but by devout prayer to the Eternal Spirit who can enrich all utterance and all knowledge, and sends out his Seraphim with the hallowed fire of his altar 'to touch and purify the lips of whom he pleases.' It is significant that at this moment he was already revolving within his mind the suitability for epic and drama of certain high themes.

Identify the poet about whom the above lines have been written

(A) Dryden

(B) Shakespeare

(C) Milton

(D) Edward Spencer

2284. He has insight into the mind of women, and of men labouring under a sense of guilt. His choice of violence, horror and forbidden themes and erotic situations indicate his decadent role in the history of English drama. His best play from the standpoint of plot-structure and development of character is the tragedy *The Broken Heart* (1633). The denouement is particularly well-managed. '*Tis Pity She's a Whore* is a powerful psychological study of guilty passion. His *Chronicle of Perkin Warbeck* (1634) is regarded by some as the best

historical play after Shakespeare. Who was this writer ?
(A) James Shirley
(B) John Ford
(C) Fletcher
(D) Webster

2285. He is a disciple of Fletcher and a link between the Jacobeans and the Restoration play-wrights. *His The Lady of Pleasure* is a typical comedy of manners based on intrigues in fasionable society which he depicts with a touch of satire. The plot is well-constructed and the dialogue is regular. In spite of an element of grossness, his purpose is moral. He has also more than a spark of genuine humour.
Who one is this author ?
(A) John Ford
(B) James Shirley
(C) Fletcher
(D) Webster

2286. This is a playwright who has evoked widely different responses from different critics. There is no doubt that his technical competence as a playwright is of a very high order, both in command over language and in the management of plot. But his characterisation is unequal and he has neither humour nor pathos.
Which one of the following is this author ?
(A) John Fletcher
(B) Cyril Tourneur
(C) Phillip Massinger
(D) None of these

2287. He is chiefly remembered for his charming book, *Compleat Angler* (1653). It is, as the subtitle describes it, "the contemplative man's recreation." It is a discourse on the joy of fishing expressed in the form of a conference between an angler (the author himself), a falconer and a hunter. It is written in a simple, quick and naive style, and combines odd bits of learning with the mellow wisdom of the countryside.
Who is this author ?
(A) Isaac Walton
(B) Cyril Torneur
(C) Thomas Fuller
(D) None of these

2288. He is regarded by many as the greatest tragic dramatist in England after Shakespeare. As a matter of fact, he is what Shakespeare would have been had he continued the *Titus Andronicus* vein, and remained a disciple of Kyd and Sencea. He has a finer sense of language than any of his Jacobean contemporaries. He has not only a powerful imagination but also true insight into human psychology.
Who is this dramatist ?
(A) Phillip Massinger
(B) John Webster
(C) John Fletcher
(D) Francis Beaumont

2289. "He is one of the greatest masters of English prose. His language is rich, embroidered, colourful and rhetorical. His prose has the majesty of Milton; while his mind has an almost Shakespearean tolerance. His two most memorable works are *Holy Living* (1650) and *Holy Dying* (1651). They are marked by ripe wisdom and deep earnestness of tone. The rhetorical beauties of his prose are expressed in sentences that have both melody and majesty. His manner compensates for his lack of profundity."
Which of the following is this prose writer?
(A) Jeremy Tylor
(B) Thomas Fuller
(C) Issac Walton
(D) John Marston

2290. He brought into the discussion of political questions the passionate pulpit manner of the church. His earliest prose tracts were entirely devoted to the problems of the Church and religion. They were mostly anonymous contributions to religious controversies. He spoke on behalf of freedom of opinion, 'the liberty of free speech.' In the last of these occurs a grand auto-biographical passage in which the poet rises indignantly from the quagmire of controversy into which he had been drawn to look back on his self-dedicated past with justifiable pride.

To whose works the above discussion shall apply ?

(A) Alexander Pope
(B) John Milton
(C) Dryden
(D) None of these

2291. He was educated at Oxford, and was actively associated with the theatre for only a few years. But within these years he made his presence felt both by his merits as a playwright, and for his pugnacity. He took part in the War of Theatres by collaborating with Dekker in the *Satiromastix*, and was himself satirised by Jonson in *The Poetaster* in the character of Crispinus. He shares all the general deficiencies of most of his contemporaries in the construction of his plots and inconsistency in characterisation. His faults are those of exaggeration and excess.

Which one of the following is the author ?

(A) Thomas Heywood
(B) John Marston
(C) Phillip Massinger
(D) None of these

2292. Known as his best work, *The History of the Worthies of England* was published in the year after his death. It contains a well known account of Shakespeare's encounter with Ben Jonson, whom he likens to the Spanish galleon, "built far higher in learning; solid, but slow in his performance; Shakespeare, like the English man-of-war, lesser in bulk but lighter in sailing, could turn with all tides, tack about and take advantage of all winds, by the quickness of his wit and invenion."

Who is this writer ?

(A) John Marston
(B) Thomas Fuller
(C) Geremy Taylor
(D) Isaac Walton

2293. 'He followed the romantic tradition set by Lyly and Sidney, though his narrative skill was much greater. His Romance *Rosalynde* not only supplied Shakespeare with the plot of "*As You Like it*", but something also of its golden Arcadian atmosphere. The story shows excellent narrative skill, and is told with wit and charm.'

These lines refer to :

(A) Fletcher
(B) Thomas Lodge
(C) Marlowe
(D) None of these

2294. 'He was not a University man, but he belonged to the group. In many ways he was the most influential play-wright of the time; he knew how to construct plots. He may be given the credit of creating fullblooded characters and devising stage situations. The Senecan form of tragedy with all its thrills and horrors was introduced by him in the Elizabethan stage."

The above words refer to

(A) John Lyly
(B) Thomas Kyd
(C) Geene
(D) Nashe

2295. The humour of the comedy is provided by some of Shakespeare's most original characters, the irrepressible Sir Toby, inferior only to Falstaff in humour; Sir Andrew Aguecheek, the country gull, Malvolio, a type of humourless egoist who is a butt of ridicule for the others, and Feste who is the most penetrating of Shakespeare's court-jesters. Both the style and the action have a natural and easy vitality. "It is Shakespeare's best high romantic comedy, supreme in its blend of mirth and beauty, romance, realism and satire."

The above lines refer to which play of Shakespeare ?

(A) *Tempest*

(B) *Twelfth Night*

(C) *Hamlet*

(D) None of these

2296. He had a pretty poetic fancy which he used delightfully in his dialogues and songs. Indeed it is poetry and a sense of humour that gave some distinction to his plays which are otherwise weak, both in plot and characterisation. He did the same service to English comedy that the writers of pastoral plays did to Italian comedy. His characters are decent well-bred men and women. His court-allegories are witty and ingenious. In *Endymion* (1588) his most representative play he introduced Queen Elizabeth as Cynthia.

(A) Robert Greene

(B) Jonson

(C) Lyly

(D) Keats

2297. He was a contemporary of Ben Jenson. He was said to have led the way in forming a more spontaneous style which others followed and improved. His *Anatomy of Melancholy* (1612) was one of the most influential books of the age and treated a fashionable convention of the age with much erudition and widom. He analyses the causes and the use of melancholy, and distinguishes among others, between love-melancholy and religious melancholy. Burton's manner is a strange mixture of learning and whimsical fancy, and exercised marked fascination over minds so different as Dr. Johnson and Charles Lamb. Which writer was he ?

(A) Robert Burton

(B) Andrew Marvell

(C) Sir Thomas Browne

(D) None of these

2298. 'He differed from the other University Wits in that he used the prose of which he was a master in preference to verse in all his plays except one, and he excelled in high comedy where the others preferred Senecan tragedies. He was essentially a court poet; he intended his plays to be "very pleasant for gentlemen to read". His plays reflected the court of Elizabeth, found ample scope for flirtatious and witty dialogues. His eccentricities of language have been criticised.

The above is the apt criticism of

(A) Robert Greene

(B) John Lyly

(C) Thomas Kyd

(D) Christopher Marlowe

2299. He is inferior in quality though his lyrics to Lucasta have a delicate, if somewhat laboured charm. "The two – 'Stonewalls Do Not a Prison Make', and 'I Could Not Love Thee, Dear, So Much Loved I Not Honor More'– are found in every anthology."

Who is this poet ?

(A) Lovelace (B) Suckling

(C) Herrick (D) None of these

2300. He has been praised somewhat extravagantly by Charles Lamb as a 'prose Shakespeare'. He is, like Dekker, a dramatist who is concerned chiefly with London life. "His works epitomise the bourgeois ideals of his age." His best play is the domestic tragi-comedy *A Woman Killed With Kindness* (1603). Who is this writer ?

(A) John Marston'

(B) Thomas Heywood

(C) Phillip Massinger

(D) John Lyly

2301. He wrote lyrics marked by religious piety, simple language and colloquial rhythms. The 'metaphysical' element is seen in his use of striking imagery drawn from church ritual, farming, trade and even household pursuits. All his poems were published posthumously, the best being contained in *The Temple* (1633).

Who was he ?

(A) George Herbert
(B) Crashaw
(C) Vaughman
(D) Herrick

2302. 'A dialect used by only one particular class of people' is called
(A) Jargon
(B) Slang
(C) Epithet
(D) Tapinosis

2303. Which book of Hardy is not pessimistic ?
(A) *Jude the Obscure*
(B) *The Return of the Native*
(C) *A Pair of Blue Eyes*
(D) Tess of D'verbervilles

2304. *Confession Amantis* is attributed to
(A) Gower (B) Lydgate
(C) Campion (D) None of these

2305. 'Edda' is the name given to a collection of ancient plays discovered by scholars in the 17th century. They are old stories about gods and heroes of
(A) Germany
(B) Rome
(C) Scandinavia
(D) Greece

2306. Even more poignant is his *The Song of the Shirt* with the dull thud of its refrain conveying the hopelessness of the sweated women workers of London, employed to stitch clothes for the rich for a bare pittance : where each dagger-pointed line is a stab at our conscience:
"With finger weary and worn,
With eyelids heavy and red,
A woman sat in unwomanly rags,
Plying her needle and thread–
Stitch ! Stitch ! Stitch !
In poverty hunger and dirt,
Sewing at once with a double thread
A shroud as well as a shirt"
Who is this poet ?
(A) Lelgh Hunt
(B) Thomas Hood
(C) P.B. Shelley
(D) Samuel Rager

2307. His political writings appeared in his own journal *The Review* which proved to be short-lived. They reveal his power of original thought; for example, he advocated income tax, higher education of women, national highways, and a more humane treatment of the insane, at a time when no one thought of these questions. From the literary standpoint, the importance of these lies in his style – his sharp, quick, clear style represents the emergency of a language of practical utility suited to all purposes.
Who is this writer ?
(A) Oliver Goldsmith
(B) Jonathan Swift
(C) Daniel Defoe
(D) Henry Fielding

2308. His experience as a journalist stood him in good stead here. Given the broad facts of an incident, a journalist had to fill it in with details to make his narrative vivid and credible. In *robinson Crusoe,* the reported shipwreck of one Alexander Selkirk in a lonely Pacific island provided him with the bare outline of an adventure, which he filled in magnificently with realistic details, making them logically possible and completely believable.
Which one of the following authors has been referred to in the above passage ?
(A) Daniel Defoe
(B) Richardson
(C) Fielding
(D) Swift

2309. Herman Melville's *Magnum Opus*' has an enigma about it. Who among the following critics does not consider his *Moby Dick* to be an allegory ?
(A) Ellergy Sedgwick
(B) Somerset Maugham

(C) Lewis Mumford
(D) Compton Rickett

2310. His poem *Campaign* is a versified account of events with Marlborough as a hero. It is a mere catalogue of names and places in heroic couplets, and has, not unaptly, been called a 'rhymed gazette'. No one reads it now, but it brought him profit and fame and high credit with his party. His only other poem is the one-time favourite of anthologists, the pompous lyric. "*The Spacious Firmament on High*."
Who is this poet ?
(A) Swift
(B) Addison
(C) Goldsmith
(D) Steele

2311. Walter Savage Lander died in the year :
(A) 1864 (B) 1865
(C) 1866 (D) 1867

2312. John Skelton has been described as '*Lumen-et-decus*' of English letters. Who gave him this title ?
(A) Goethe (B) Dryden
(C) Erasmus (D) None of these

2313. Of his great poems the first that appeared in the *Lyrical Ballads* was 'The Rime of the Ancient Mariner.' Written in ballad style, the poem deals with the supernatural punishment undergone by a sailor in the only South Seas for his crime against the sanctity of life which he incurred for killing a sea-bird (Albatross) who had come to the ship 'as if it was Christian soul'. The story is told to a Wedding Guest by the Ancient Mariner himself, who makes an unforgettable impression by his 'long grey beard and glittering eyes.' Which poet has been referred in the above observation ?
(A) Wordsworth (B) Coleridge
(C) Byron (D) keats

2314. "We know not where to look in history or letters, for a more commanding picture of man, as he might be than in the Arthur of this volume. Wherever he appears, it is as the great pillar of the moral order and the resplendent top of human excellence."
Who made this comment ?
(A) Johnson
(B) Gladstone
(C) Arnold
(D) W.B. Yeats

2315. *The Ode to France* was composed by Coleridge in :
(A) 1788 (B) 1798
(C) 1792 (D) 1796

2316. When was the unfinished dream poem 'Kubla Khan' published ?
(A) 1816 (B) 1810
(C) 1820 (D) 1821

2317. Coleridge has been called a 'muddle headed metaphysician" by :
(A) Matthew Arnold
(B) William Morris
(C) Compton Ricketts
(D) I.A. Richards

2318. 'More popular perhaps is *The Lady of the Lake*, a romantic story set amidst the picturesque scenery of the Trossachs. The description of the wild mountain scenery around Loch Katrine contains some of his best nature poetry. The character of Roderick Dhu is the most finished among all the characters in the poems. Unlike *Marmion,* all its interest is confined to the earlier parts; the last canto is insipid by comparison.'
Who is this romantic poet ?
(A) Walter Scott
(B) Wordsworth
(C) Coleridge
(D) Byron

2319. This poet had in common with Landor his strongly republican sympathies, for in other respects he was Landor's antithesis. His *Story of Rumini* (1816) retold the story of Paolo and Francesca in loose rambling couplets; its worst vice, that of excessive sentimentalism, was imitated by Keats in his immaturity. He lacked restraint which spolit his otherwise felicitous imagination. Who is this poet ?

(A) Leigh Hunt
(B) Wordsworth
(C) Shelley
(D) Byron

2320. Lady Charlotte Guest gave the name *Mabinoglon* to a set of folk stories translated by her. Original language was

(A) Scottish (B) Irish
(C) Welsh (D) Latin

2321. T.S. Eliot was born in the year

(A) 1886 (B) 1887
(C) 1888 (D) 1889

2322. He is a typical product of the age. he was one of the first to depend for his livelihood on his penmanship. His clear-sightedness made it impossible for him to be a fanatic, and like so many men of his time, he seemed to trim his sails the way the wind happened to be blowing at the time. This attitude put him in the wrong with both parties and he suffered imprisonment, pillory and other similar indignities.
Who is this writer ?

(A) Daniel Defoe
(B) Swift
(C) Henry Fielding
(D) Francis Bacon

2323. From the sophistication of high-bred life, the two poets turned to common things, and by the magic power of imagination, they brought mystery into these and rendered them supernatural and significant. They also threw off the trappings of poetical diction and showed the poetic possibilities inherent in common words if used with true sensibility and imagination – as the medieval balladists had done. Who were these two ?

(A) Shelley and Keats
(B) Wordsworth and Coleridge
(C) Keats and Byron
(D) Byron and Shelley

2324. Ulysses, the hero of Homer's *Odyssey* was the king of,

(A) Sparta and Athens
(B) Athens alone
(C) Macedonia
(D) Ithaca

2325. Daniel Defoe was born in the year:

(A) 1658 (B) 1659
(C) 1670 (D) 1671

2326. He is third of these English 'Lakers'. His reputation has steadily declined, and may without injustice be relegated to the minor dignity of a footnote. In his own time, his reputation was perhaps greater than that of his friends, and for thirty years, he was Poet Laureate of England. He is to-day remembered more for his shorter pieces, like *The Inchcape Rock* and *The Battle of Blenheim* than for his more ambitious narrative poems.
Who is this Lake poet ?

(A) Walter Savage Lander
(B) Robert Southey
(C) Wordsworth
(D) Walter Scott

2327. *Omoo, Mardi, Purre and White Jacket* are books by

(A) Nathaniel Hawthorne
(B) Herman Melville
(C) Raymond Weaver
(D) Robert Louis Stevenson

2328. One poem of Rudyard Kipling is in Cockney dialect. Identify it.

(A) *Danny Deever*
(B) *Fuzzy Wuzzy*
(C) *Mandalay*
(D) *If*

2329. His themes were romantic, and his style was simple and straightforward, but without a touch of genuine poetic feeling. It may be that readers will remember him as the

unenvied hero of Byron's *Vision of Judgement* than the poet of his own vision. It was he however who started the vogue of writing romantic tales in verse which was to be taken up by Walter Scott and Lord Byron, each of them far surpassing him in the art.
Who was this Lake Poet ?
(A) Robert Southey
(B) Walter Savage Lander
(C) William Wordsworth
(D) Walter Scott

2330. In some respects he is superior to Addison-his humour is more warm, his emotions more lively, his personality more endearing. It is he who, through Goldsmith, looks forward to the essayists of the Romantic period. But he lacks Addison's wit, irony and many-sidedness. He has not the subtleties of Addison's observation of life. He realised, however, earlier than Addison did, the influence that woman might exercise in social life, and regarded women as an instrument in the moral elevation of man.
Who has been referred to here as superior to Addison ?
(A) Defoe
(B) Steele
(C) Goldsmith
(D) Hazlitt

2331. The most readable of all of H.G. Wells' books for being least scientific is-
(A) *The Soul of a Bishop*
(B) *Joan and Peter*
(C) *The Time Machine*
(D) None of these

2332. On whom was the character of Sherlock Holmes and his uncanny methods of deduction based ?
(A) The author himself
(B) Dr. Bell
(C) Conan Doyle's friend James
(D) Imagination

2333. "Unlike his English contemporaries, he was from the very beginning thoroughly anti-revolutionary. His sympathies were all with the feudal virtues and ideals. HIs romanticism was essentially historical. Percy's Reliques had touched his imagination, and the heroic tales of Border warfare and chivalry stirred him deeply. On the other side was the appeal of the Gothic which came to him through the German poet Burger's *Lencre* which he translated in 1796. A compilation of *Border Minstrelsy* helped him discover his literary forte, the telling of old-time tales in spirited verse."
Who is this writer ?
(A) Walter Scott
(B) Walter Savage Lander
(C) Leigh Hunt
(D) Sir Walter Raleigh

2334. This poem is an English version of an Indian lullaby :
(A) *The Cricket and the Grasshopper*
(B) *The Feet of the Young Men*
(C) *Mother O'mine*
(D) *Shiva and the Grasshopper*

2335. Foremost among these, was he who embodied in himself both the virtues and the defects of his class. Consciousness of unmerited poverty gave him a kind of rugged strength and defiance; forthright convictions made him prejudiced and hostile to new ideas. They combined to give him a unique personality which he imposed upon his contemporaries. He was an honest man with strong commonsense and human feeling who took pride in his personal independence which he never failed to assert. The writer was :
(A) Steele
(B) Samuel Johnson
(C) Bacon
(D) Sterne

2336. Which Dickensian character exposes the inner greatness of man ?

(A) Sydney Carton
(B) Betsy Trotwood
(C) Min Havinsham
(D) None of these

2337. During whose reign were most of Tennyson's poems published ?
(A) William IV
(B) George IV
(C) Queen Victoria
(D) Elizabeth I

2338. He began his literary career, however, as a poet and a disciple of Pope. As the master had imitated Horace in his satires, he wrote imitations of the Latin Satirist Juvenal. As a poet he is known by his two poems : the first, *London* (1738) imitated Juvenal's Third Satire, and the other, *The Vanity of Human Wishes* (1749) imitated the Tenth Satire. *London* expresses the poet's disgust at the vices. Who is this disciple of Pope ?
(A) Goldsmith
(B) Samuel Johnson
(C) Samuel Richardson
(D) None of these

2339. 'Satirical composition with the purpose of ridicule' is called
(A) Allegory
(B) Innuendo
(C) Epigram
(D) Chiasmus

2340. 'Treat abstractions as if they were human beings' is
(A) Personification
(B) Simile
(C) Paradox
(D) Metaphor

2341. He was a greater poet than Johnson and a more versatile writer; he left his mark on poetry, novel, drama and essay of the period. He was an Irishman of a lovable but unstable character, who after a varied experience in the Continent settled down, with a medical degree of unknown origin, to make what money he could as a writer and to spend it as much in extravagance as in charity. This poet was :
(A) Browne (B) Goldsmith
(C) Milton (D) Gray

2342. 'Terms of comparison changed in intentionally for a humorous purpose' is called
(A) Metaphor
(B) Mixed Metaphor
(C) Dead Metaphor
(D) Metonymy

2343. 'Which of Huxley's novels has borrowed its title from a phrase occuring in Shakespeare's play 'The Tempest' ?
(A) *After Many a Summer*
(B) *Time Must Stope*
(C) *A Brave New World*
(D) None of these

2344. Who among the following talks of 'the rhetorical theory of tropes' in criticism ?
(A) Horace
(B) Michael Fou Cault
(C) Lacan
(D) Northop Frye

2345. 'Besides Dryden through his work 'An Essay of Dramatic Poesy,' who else replied to the uncomplimentary remarks of Samuel Sorbiere about the English stage ?
(A) Dr. Johnson
(B) Thomas Spat
(C) Philip Sidney
(D) None of the above

2346. This great prose work, printed in English appeared in 1485. What was it ?
(A) *Sayings of Philosophers*
(B) *Tyndale'sh Bible*
(C) *Book of Courtesy*
(D) Malory's *Morte D' Arthur*

2347. He wrote the *Lay of the Last Minstrel* in Coleridge's *Christabel* metre, but without its delicate verbal witchery. Into the composition of the prose poem have gone His historical sense, medieval magic and knowledge of local scenery and manners. But his real excellence lies in his power of animating poetry with the vitality of life and movement. It has the speed of the ballad style and is displayed against a swiftly changing natural background. He shows himself here that he was a born story-teller, recovering something of what English poetry had lost since Chaucer wrote. The style is vigorous but in no way distinguished.

Which one of the following is this great poet ?

(A) Wordsworth
(B) Walter Scott
(C) Southey
(D) Shelley

2348. *Tender is the Night* is a novel by

(A) Maugham
(B) Marrie Correlli
(C) James Joyce
(D) F. Scott Fitzgerald

2349. Name the person who proposed that the function of a critic to be "the elucidation of works of art and the correction of taste."

(A) Matthew Arnold
(B) T.S. Eliot
(C) I.A. Richards
(D) Samuel Johnson

2350. In expressing the pathos underlying social wrongs, in such poems as *The Bridge of Sighs* and *The Song of the Short,* he achieves a quality of intensity that is not inferior to any. The suicide of a woman betryaed by a man's falseness leads the poet to cry out against religion as professed and as practised-

Alas for the rarity
Of Christian charity
Under the sun!
O it was pitiful,
Near a whole cityful-
Home she had none !

Which of the following is this poet ?

(A) Thomas Hood
(B) Robert Southey
(C) William Wordsworth
(D) P.B. Shelley

2351. He is remembered chiefly for the lyric qualities of his *Irish Melodies* whose music attracted Rabindranath Tagore when he was first in England. His lyrics are charming and sentimental trifles but without any depth or intensity. The patriotic note of his *Pro Patria More* entitles him to be called the earliest of the Irish lyrists. His narrative poem *Lalla Rookh* is an oriental story in verse in the manner of Byron, and enjoyed a reputation that seems to us fantastic today.

This poet is

(A) Thomas Moore
(B) Samuel Roger
(C) Walter Scott
(D) Thomas Hood

2352. Who was the first one to attack Restoration Comedy of Manners for its immorality?

(A) Jeremy Collier
(B) Macaulay
(C) Dr. Johnson
(D) None of the above

2353. Name the real life prototype of Achitophel in *Absalom and Achitophel* ?

(A) Shaftesbury
(B) Arbuthnot
(C) Monmouth
(D) None of the above

2354. Identify the one which is not carried by the devil in a morality play.

(A) A hairy vest
(B) Horns
(C) A wooden sword or dagger
(D) He carried all of these

2355. Given below are the names of the novels by Dickens. Uriach appears in which of them?

(A) *Great Expectations*
(B) *David Copperfield*
(C) *Hard Times*
(D) None of the above

2356. Madam Defarge is a character in a novel by Dickens. Name the novel.
(A) *Great Expectations*
(B) *The Old Curiosity Shop*
(C) *Hard Times*
(D) None of the above

2357. *Grammer Gurton's Needle* was written by
(A) John Still
(B) Nashe
(C) William Stevenson
(D) Backett

2358. Select the year in which for the first time printing was started in England.
(A) 1545 (B) 1476
(C) 1425 (D) None of these

2359. How would you describe *Tottel's Miscellany*?
(A) An anonymous collection of ballads and folk lore.
(B) Collection of poems by Sir Thomas Wyatt and the Earl of Surrey
(C) Collection of random prose writings inspired by the Renaissance.
(D) None of the above

2360. Who is a Cavalier Poet ?
(A) Suckling (B) Lovelace
(C) Herrick (D) All of these

2361. *Uncle Tom's Cabin* was written by
(A) Cotton Mather
(B) John Osborne
(C) Harriet Beecher Stowe
(D) None

2362. The most prominent and influential of the New Critics is :
(A) I.A. Richards
(B) Cleanth Brooks
(C) John Crowe Ransom
(D) None of the above

2363. Who was the editor of 'Daily News' ?
(A) Robert Browning
(B) Keats
(C) Hardy
(D) Addison

2364. For the first time where did Wordsworth present his views on the nature and function of poetry ?
(A) In the "preface" to the *Lyrical Ballads*.
(B) In a separate supplement.
(C) In an "advertisement" appended to the first edition of *Lyrical Ballads*.
(D) None of the above.

2365. With Thomas Kyd began the tradition of
(A) political play
(B) domestic tragedy
(C) poetic drama
(D) revenge play

2366. Who, of the mentioned ones, is not a metaphysical poet ?
(A) Donne
(B) Dryden
(C) Cowley
(D) Herbert

2367. "Ideal work is one where the artist is invisible, remains out of existence, indifferent". Who defined ideal work in this manner ?
(A) James Joyce
(B) T.S. Eliot
(C) Virginia Woolf
(D) Richards

2368. The idea of 'Decorum' in poetry, is associated with
(A) Dryden (B) Horace
(C) Johnson (D) None of these

2369. Who out of the following gave the first "affective" theory of literature in the real sense?
(A) Longinus (B) Horace
(C) Aristotle (D) Plato

2370. The characters of Henry James' novels are
(A) illiterates
(B) intellectuals

(C) middle class workers
(D) None of the above

2371. Charles Lamb, the great essayist, also wrote a play named :
(A) *Dream Children*
(B) *John Woodwill*
(C) *South Sea-house*
(D) None of the above

2372. Identify the period in which Aristotle's poetics was written ?
(A) It cannot be precisely dated.
(B) 5th Century B.C.
(C) 6th Century B.C.
(D) 10th Century B.C.

2373. "He is the greatest comic novelist in English, he is also the most truly poetic novelist". About whom has this been said by Walter Allen ?
(A) Fielding (B) Dickens
(C) Goldsmith (D) None

2374. "A poetry of revolt against moral ideas is a poetry of revolt against life; a poetry of indifference towards moral ideas is a poetry of indifference towards life."
Who has been quoted here ?
(A) F.R. Leavis
(B) Eliot
(C) Arnold
(D) None of the above

2375. An anti-novel is one in which there is
(A) no dialogue
(B) no characterisation
(C) no relations of Times and Space
(D) All the above

2376. Who among the following said of *Paradise Lost* that "Milton was in the Devil's party without knowing it" ?
(A) Arnold (B) Lamb
(C) Coleridge (D) None of these

2377. '*Alton Locke*', the novel by Charles Kingsley, expresses his views concerning
(A) Political Idealism
(B) Radical Humanism
(C) Christian Socialism
(D) None of these

2378. Written against the background of the partition of India, '*A Train to Pakistan*' is a novel, by :
(A) K.A. Abbas
(B) Khushwant Singh
(C) E.M. Forster
(D) V.S. Naipaul

2379. Among the following who can be considered to be the first practitioner of sonnets?
(A) Dante
(B) Shakespeare
(C) Petrarch
(D) None of the above

2380. Identify that period of British history which is called the Jacobean age ?
(A) 1625–1660
(B) 1620–1700
(C) 1603–1625
(D) None of the above

2381. "I am a dial's hand, still walking hand, you are the compass." Name the poet of these lines.
(A) Carew (B) Marvell
(C) Donne (D) None of these

2382. Who Lamented :
"Oh two vexine, contraries meet in one,
Inconstancy naturally hath begot,
A constant habit."
(A) Marvel (B) Cowley
(C) Carew (D) Vaughan

2383. Alfred Tennyson's *In Memoriam* was written in memory of :
(A) Arthur Hallam
(B) Arnold
(C) A.H. Clough
(D) None of the above

2384. The first recipient of the Nobel Prize for Literature was :
(A) Theodor Mommsen
(B) Leo Tolstoy

(C) Rudyard Kipling
(D) Sully-Pradhomme

2385. Thomas Love Peacock in his *Nightmare Abbey* satirised :
(A) Coleridge
(B) Shelley
(C) Both Coleridge and Shelly
(D) Keats

2386. The neoclassical writers propounded that
(A) man is limited being
(B) the human pride needs to be suppressed
(C) man has to follow a natural hierarchy
(D) all these three

2387. A memorable character, Gradgrind figures in which of the following ?
(A) *Pickwick Papers*
(B) *Hard Times*
(C) *A Tale of Two Cities*
(D) None of these

2388. Identify the correct one that describes the form of Petrarchan sonnet ?
(A) It has the endings of alternate lines rhyming with each other
(B) It has three quatrains and a couplet
(C) It has an octave and a sestet.
(D) It has an integrated form with no such division

2389. Which of the following statements is false?
(A) Sir Thomas More wrote *Utopia* in Latin.
(B) Sir Roger Ascham wrote *Scholemaster* presenting a Renaissance ideal of education.
(C) Erasmus, the writer of *The Praise of Jolly* was a Dutchman.
(D) All the above are true.

2390. Who was the person to bring in the idea of the three unities for the first time in English literary criticism ?
(A) Johnson (B) Dryden
(C) Arnold (D) None of these

2391. In which year did the Hundred Years War with France begin ?
(A) 1358 (B) 1305
(C) 1338
(D) None of the above

2392. Identify the one which is not a "novel of terror".
(A) *The Mysteries of Udolpho*
(B) *Vathek*
(C) *Castle of Otranto*
(D) *Castle of Indolence*

2393. Define the term 'Nature' in the 18th century context.
(A) The external phenomena of animal and vegetable life
(B) What comes naturally to man, viz., feelings, anotians
(C) A national and intelligible moral order in the universe
(D) All the above

2394. While describing Romanticism who used term "liberalism in literature" ?
(A) Schlegel
(B) Victor Hugo
(C) Walter Pater
(D) None of the above

2395. Name the author of *The Decline and Fall of the Romantic Ideal* ?
(A) Lionel Trilling
(B) F.L. Lucas
(C) L.C. Knights
(D) None of the above

2396. Out of the following in which does Lady Booby appear as a character ?
(A) *Pamela*
(B) *Joseph Andrews*
(C) *Clarissa*
(D) None of the above

2397. Name the poet whose poetry was criticised by Dr. Johnson in the following lines:
"The fault of pursuing his thoughts to their last remification by which he loses the grandeur of generality."
(A) Donne (B) Cowley
(C) Marvel (D) All of these

2398. Who among the following wrote these lines"
"The general purpose of this paper is to expose the false arts of life, to pull off the disguises of cunning, vanity and affectation and to recommend a general simplicity in our dress, our discourse, and our behaviour."
(A) Goldsmith
(B) Addison
(C) Steele
(D) None of the above

2399. Name the subtitle of Dryden's *The Medal*?
(A) *A satire against seditions*
(B) *A satire*
(C) There was no subtitle
(D) *A poem*

2400. Out of the following who did not form part of the French literature which inlfuenced the Neo-classicals in England ?
(A) Racine
(B) Corneille
(C) Moliere
(D) All formed part

2401. "I describe not men but manners not an individual but the species": who said the above lines ?
(A) Addison (B) Dickens
(C) Fielding (D) Swift

2402. "Pity would be no more, if we did not make somebody poor." Who wrote these lines ?
(A) Wordsworth (B) Blake
(C) Shelley (D) None of these

2403. When was Tagore's *Gitanjali* published in English
(A) 1905 (B) 1912
(C) 1919 (D) 1921

2404. Huxley's *Brave New World* is about
(A) The courageous emerging world
(B) The satire on the influence of science in future
(C) The life in future free from disease and devoid of emotion and spiritual life too
(D) Both (A) and (B)

2405. Who is the writer of the poem *Village* ?
(A) Goldsmith
(B) Congreve
(C) Cradle
(D) None of the above

2406. Which critical work has been written by Sidney ?
(A) *An Apologie for Poetrie*
(B) *A Defence of Rhyme*
(C) *The Defence of Poetry*
(D) None

2407. Milly Theale is a prominent character in Henry Jame's novel :
(A) *The Golden Bowl*
(B) *The Wings of the Dove*
(C) *The Princess*
(D) *None of these*

2408. Bacon's essays are regarded as compendiums of
(A) Wordly-wisdom
(B) Diplomatic matters
(C) State affairs
(D) Morality

2409. Who is the writer of *Euphues* ?
(A) Marlowe
(B) Lyly
(C) Greene
(D) Bungan

2410. Charles Darwin is chiefly known for his work
(A) *The Wealth of Nations*
(B) *On the Origin of Species*
(C) *Leviathan*
(D) None of the above

2411. Thomas Gray's Poems 'The Bard' and 'The Progress of Poesy' belong to the category of;

(A) Pastoral Elegy
(B) Pindaric Ode
(C) Horatian Ode
(D) None of these

2412. Graham Greene's *Our Man in Havana* is a satire on

(A) religion (B) spy Novels
(C) education (D) All of these

2413. *Paradise Lost* is the greatest _____ in the English Language.

(A) Allegory (B) Epic
(C) Ode (D) Poem

2414. "Shelley dismissed Keats' Poetry by saying "Inspite of his transcendental genius Keats never was, nor ever will be, a popular poet". Shelly disliked Keats' poetry because :

(A) Keats' poetry is irrelevant
(B) Keats' poetry is devoid of the revolutionary spirit
(C) Keats died young
(D) None of these

2415. Pope's *Essay on Criticism* is written in

(A) Prose
(B) Elegiac Quatrains
(C) Heroic Couplet
(D) Blank Verse

2416. Walter Pater's book *Appreciation* begins with an essay on

(A) Study of poetry
(B) Style
(C) Lamb
(D) Renaissance

2417. Who was the ruler of England when Pope's *The Rape of the Lock* was published ?

(A) George III
(B) George II
(C) Queen Anne
(D) None of these

2418. Just as Hardy is a novelist of the region Wessex, Arnold Bennett is novelist of

(A) Essex
(B) Five Towns (Potteries)
(C) The Midlands
(D) All of the above

2419. The romantic comedy *The Spanish Gipsy* by Thomas Middleton bears some similarities with Shakespeare's

(A) *Twelfth Night*
(B) *As You Like it*
(C) *All's Well that Ends Well*
(D) None of these

2420. Milton's poetic style is usually regarded as

(A) plain
(B) classical
(C) grand
(D) ornamental

2421. In which novel of his Trollope has parodied Carlyle and Dickens ?

(A) *Barchester Towers*
(B) *The Warden*
(C) *The Prime Minister*
(D) None of these

2422. The Royal Society of Science is the result of _____ emphasis on the collection of facts.

(A) Bacon's
(B) Thomas More's
(C) Nash's
(D) None of the above

2423. Browning, as a poet, is basically an

(A) Organist
(B) Optimist
(C) Occultist
(D) None of these

2424. *Life of Samuel Johnson* is written by
(A) Goldsmith (B) Gibbon
(C) Addison (D) Boswell

2425. Bacon's *Essays* first appeared in
(A) 1618 (B) 1622
(C) 1625 (D) 1597

2426. What is *The Mousetrap* ?
(A) A play by Ben Jonson
(B) A play by Marlowe
(C) The name of the play within the play in Hamlet
(D) All of the above

2427. Charles Morgans 'survived the impact of modern scientific investions upon the soul of humanity.'
Which work is being referred to ?
(A) *The Guinea Pig*
(B) *The Burning Glass*
(C) *The River Line*
(D) None of these

2428. Hardy's is his epic drama of the Napoleanic wars.
(A) *The Woodlanders*
(B) *The Dynasts*
(C) *Life's Little Ironies*
(D) None of these

2429. The line 'I am not Prince Hamlet, nor was meant to be' belongs, to T.S. Eliot's poem
(A) *Gerontion*
(B) *The Wasteland*
(C) *Love Song of J. Alfed Prufrock*
(D) None of these

2430. Who among the following revolted against the contemporary artistic principles ?
(A) John Donne
(B) Ben Jonson
(C) Both (A) and (B)
(D) Thomas Dekker

2431. Virginia Woolf belonged to a group of eminent literary figures known as
(A) Angry Young Men
(B) Avant Garde
(C) Bloomsbury Group
(D) None of the above

2432. Which epithet cannot be applied to Robert Frost's poetry ?
(A) Regional
(B) Dramatic
(C) Conversational
(D) Neo-classical

2433. The critical essays of Walter Pater are collected in the form of a book under the title:
(A) *Critical Essays*
(B) *Essays in Criticism*
(C) *Appreciations*
(D) None of these

2434. The period from 1830 to 1890 is known as
(A) The Romantic Revival
(B) Neo-Classical Age
(C) Victorian Age
(D) None of the above

2435. William Golding's preoccupation in many of his novels is with
(A) modern predicament
(B) political corruption
(C) instinctive desire of men to destroy the good
(D) All of the above

2436. Swift's *A Tale of the Tub* is allegory which is
(A) religous
(B) political
(C) literary
(D) All of these

2437. Which of the poems mentioned below is not by Browning ?
(A) *Pippa Passes*

(B) *Sordello*

(C) *Empedocles on Etna*

(D) None of the above

2438. Who is said to be the "Greatest Commonwealth Poet of the 19th Century" ?

(A) Sarojini Naidu

(B) Aurobindo

(C) Tagore

(D) None of these

2439. *The MIll on the Floss* is the story of Maggie Tulliver and her brother

(A) Tom (B) Philip

(C) Dr. Kenn (D) Fred

2440. Which historical event forms the background of Hardy's *The Dynasts* ?

(A) World War I

(B) Spanish Civil War

(C) Napoleanic Wars

(D) None of the above

2441. Who wrote *Desire Under the Elms* ?

(A) Arthur Miller

(B) Tennessee Williams

(C) Eugene O'Neill

(D) None of the above

2442. Which critic made this statement "Mr. Henry James writes, fiction as if it is a painful duty"?

(A) Virginia Woolf

(B) F.R. Leavis

(C) G.B. Shaw

(D) Oscar Wilde

2443. *Bartholomew Fair* is a play by

(A) Marlowe

(B) Sheridan

(C) Ben Jonson

(D) None of these

2444. In the *Preface to Lyrical Ballads*, Wordsworth propounded his theory of

(A) Fancy

(B) Imagination

(C) Prose

(D) Poetic Diction

2445. The remark, "There is sometimes a greater judgment shown in deviating from the rules of art than in adhering to them" has been made by

(A) Samuel Johnson

(B) Dryden

(C) Pope

(D) Joseph Addison

2446. *Rich Like Us* is a Sahitya Academy Award winning novel by

(A) Anita Desai

(B) Kamla Markandeya

(C) Nayantara Sehgal

(D) None of the above

2447. Which metre has Marlowe used in his plays ?

(A) Blank verse

(B) Heroic couplet

(C) Hexametre

(D) None of these

2448. *Inscape* and *Instress* and *Sprung Rhythm* are associated with

(A) G.M. Hopkins

(B) Ezra Pound

(C) Dryden

(D) None of these

2449. Who among the following was the admirer of Emile Zola ?

(A) George Gissing

(B) George Moore

(C) Both Gissing and Moore

(D) None of these

2450. Maya is the central character in Anita Desai's novel

(A) *Bye, Bye, Blackbird*

(B) *Voices in the City*

(C) *Cry, the Peacock*
(D) None of these

2451. Which of these novels is written by John Wain?
(A) *Jacob's Room*
(B) *A Room with a View*
(C) *Strike the Father Dead*
(D) None of these

2452. Stuart Hall's original argument in Cultural Studies was that the media were tools to:
(A) persuade people
(B) keep the powerful in control
(C) promote understanding among people
(D) reduce uncertainties

2453. Hall drew many of his ideas from:
(A) Marxism
(B) Communism
(C) Socialism
(D) democratic ideals

2453. A key assumption of Cultural Studies is that people are part of a hierarchical structure of
(A) culture
(B) mediated communication
(C) power
(D) ideology

2455. According to Cultural Studies, _______ in our culture is strongly affected by the media.
(A) industry
(B) hierarchy
(C) advertising
(D) meaning

2456. _________ refers to the dominant culture and its power over other co-cultures present in a nation.
(A) Hegemony
(B) Theatre of struggle
(C) Culture wars
(D) Dominance

2457. ________ refers to an audience resisting the messages of the dominant group.
(A) Theatre of struggle
(B) Resistance phase
(C) Social struggle
(D) Counter hegemony

2458. Cultural Studies suggests that mediated messages must be ___________ by the mass audience.
(A) accepted
(B) resisted
(C) decoded
(D) encoded

2459. Audience members may engage in a(n) _________ position, which occurs when they substitute an alternative code for the code supplied by the media.
(A) negotiated
(B) communicated
(C) oppositional
(D) dominant

2460. Cultural Studies has been criticized for its insistence on a(n) ________ audience.
(A) active
(B) passive
(C) knowledgeable
(D) intuitive

2461. The New Critics were:
(A) Formalist critics
(B) Marxist critics
(C) Feminist critics
(D) Psychological Critics

2462. What approach to literary criticism requires the critic to know about the author's life and times?
(A) Historical
(B) Formalist
(C) Mimetic
(D) All of these

2463. Formalist critics believe that the value of a work cannot be determined by the author's intention. What term do they use when speaking of this belief?

(A) The intentional fallacy
(B) The affective fallacy
(C) The pathetic fallacy
(D) The objective correlative

2464. Who originated the term "objective correlative," which is often used in formalist criticism?

(A) T.S. Eliot
(B) Matthew Arnold
(C) C.S. Lewis
(D) Virginia Woolf

2465. In a Freudian approach to literature, concave images are usually seen as

(A) Male symbols
(B) Female symbols
(C) Phallic symbols
(D) Evidence of an Oedipus complex

2466. He was an influential force in archetypal criticism.

(A) Tate (B) Freud
(C) Jung (D) Richards

2467. Seven is an archetype associated with:

(A) Evil (B) Death
(C) Birth (D) Perfection

2468. This feminist critic proposed that all female characters in literature are in at least one of the following stages of development: the feminine, feminist, or female stage.

(A) Virginia Woolf
(B) Elaine Showalter
(C) Mary Wolstencraft
(D) Ellen Mores

2469. A critic argues that in John Milton's "Samson Agonistes," the shearing of Samson's locks is symbolic of his castration at the hands of Delilah. What kind of critical approach is this critic using?

(A) Mimetic approach
(B) Formalist approach
(C) Historical approach
(D) Psychological approach

2470. One archetype in literature is the scapegoat. Which of these literary characters serves that purpose?

(A) Billy Budd
(B) Hamlet
(C) Captain Ahab
(D) Ophelia

2471. One of the disadvantages of this school of criticism is that it tends to make readings too subjective.

(A) Historical Criticism
(B) These are all equally subjective
(C) Formalist Criticism
(D) Reader Response Criticism

2472. This literary critic coined the term "fancy."

(A) Matthew Arnold
(B) Carl Jung
(C) Virginia Woolf
(D) Samuel Taylor Coleridge

2473. Michael Foucault was the major practitioner of this school of criticism.

(A) Structuralism
(B) Mimetic Criticism
(C) Deconstructionism
(D) Formalist Criticism

2474. This critical approach assumes that language does not refer to any external reality. It can assert several, contradictory interpretations of one text.

(A) Structuralism
(B) Deconstructionism
(C) Formalist Criticism
(D) Mimetic Criticism

2475. A critic examining John Milton's "Paradise Lost" focuses on the physical description of the Garden of Eden, on the symbols of hands, seed, and flower, and on the characters of Adam, Eve, Satan, and God. He pays special attention to the epic similes and metaphors and the point of view from which the tale is being told. He looks for meaning in the text itself, and does not refer to any biography of Milton. He is most likely a ____ critic.

(A) Feminist
(B) Reader Response
(C) Formalist
(D) Mimetic

2476. This literary critic warned: "We must remember that the greater part of our current reading matter is written for us by people who have no real belief in a supernatural order . . . And the greater part ________ is coming to be written by people who not only have no such belief, but are even ignorant of the fact that there are still people in the world so 'backward' or so 'eccentric' as to continue to believe."

(A) T.S. Eliot
(B) G.K. Chesterton
(C) C.S. Lewis
(D) Matthew Arnold

2477. A critic of Thomas Otway's "Venice Preserv'd" wishes to know why the play's conspirators, despite the horrible, bloody details of their obviously brutish plan, are portrayed in a sympathetic light. She examines the author's life and times and discovers that there are obvious similarities between the conspiracy in the play and the Popish Plot. She is most likely a _________ critic.

(A) Tory
(B) Psychological
(C) Feminist
(D) Historical

2478. This poet might be described as a moral or philosophical critic for arguing that works must have "high seriousness."

(A) T.S. Eliot
(B) Virginia Woolf
(C) Elizabeth Browning
(D) Matthew Arnold

2479. A critic examining Pope's "An Essay on Man" asks herself: How well does this poem accord with the real world? Is it accurate? Is it moral? She is most likely a _____ critic.

(A) Mimetic
(B) Formalist
(C) Feminist
(D) Reader Response

2480. One of the potential disadvantages of this approach to literature is that it can reduce meaning to a certain time frame, rather than making it universal throughout the ages.

(A) Historical (B) Feminist
(C) Formalist (D) Mimetic

2481. The method of teaching English adopted at present in school curriculum is

(A) Formative Correlation Approach
(B) Foncatunal Communicative Approach
(C) Function Corrective Approach
(D) Figurative Comprehensive Approach

2482. FCA is a opposition to

(A) Structural Approach
(B) Comprehensive Approach
(C) Translation and grammar Method
(D) Fictional Approach

2483. Communicative Language Teaching replaces basically...

(A) Natural Language Processing
(B) Structural Teaching
(C) Situational Language Teaching
(D) Motivational Teaching

2484. Direct Method is also known as

(A) Natural Method
(B) Indirect Approach

(C) Inductive Approach
(D) All the above

2485. Grammer Transilation Method Stresses on
(A) Accuracy
(B) Fluency
(C) Appropriateness
(D) Listening skill

2486. Grammer Transilation Method is basically used to teach
(A) Grammar
(B) Foreign language
(C) Rules of any language usage
(D) Classical language

2487. The objective of Direct Method is
(A) To increase power of Comprehension
(B) To increase communicative power
(C) To develop a command over the target language
(D) To develop personality

2488. Traditional method goes against the
(A) Prescriptive grammar
(B) Simulation
(C) Pedagogic principles
(D) Generalization

2489. The incidental or Corrective method is known as
(A) Inductive
(B) Deductive
(C) Structural
(D) Reference method

2490. Journey from Example to generalization is
(A) Inductive
(B) Deductive
(C) Incidental
(D) All of above

2491. One of the principles of materials preparation for language learning is that
(A) Complex material should be chosen
(B) Graded of material should be chosen
(C) Any kind of materials can be chosen
(D) A small amount of material should be introduced

2492. Correct pronunciation of individual sound of related to
(A) Accuracy
(B) Fluency
(C) Both accuracy and fluency
(D) Neither accuracy nor fluency

2493. Language accusation occurs only when
(A) The child is taught the rules of grammar
(B) The child is given a reward
(C) The child has exposure to the language
(D) The child absorbs the language without conscious attention

2494. When a child is asked to recite a poem, it can help the teacher to test
(A) Knowledge of literature
(B) Proficiency of speaking
(C) Acting talent
(D) Comprehension

2495. The structure "he goes to school" is often produced by learners due to
(A) Failure of literature
(B) Mother tongue interference
(C) Overgeneralization of rules
(D) Wrong teaching

2496. For teaching grammar, the best grammar that a teacher can use is
(A) Traditional grammar
(B) Modern grammar
(C) Pedagogic grammar
(D) No grammar is needed

2497. "Brain storming" means
(A) collect all kinds of ideas on a tropic
(B) To do some mental exercise
(C) To make efforts to understand something

(D) To give some kinds of stimulus to the brain

2498. "Interactive" listening is
(A) Listening and responding
(B) Listening for mode of tone
(C) Listening for word stress and emphasis
(D) Listening for finding out speaker's attitude

2499. Which of the following is an incorrect assumption in language teaching
(A) Learners acquire language by trying to use it in real situations
(B) Learner's first language plays a important role in learning
(C) Language teaching should have a focus in communicative activities
(D) Language teaching should give importance to writing rather than speech

2500. Reading skill can be developed best by
(A) Writing answers to questions on text
(B) Focusing on the use of words from context in the text
(C) Doing vocabulary exercises
(D) Doing quizzes and playing word games

2501. Practice of grammatical structures in a controlled manner can be done by
(A) Correcting wrong sentence produced by Learners
(B) Gap filling grammar exercises
(C) Writing paragraphs and essays
(D) Explaining the use of particular structures

2502. A test which is administered at the end of a language course is
(A) Diagnostic test
(B) Placement test
(C) Achievement test
(D) Memory test

2503. Study of meaning in a language is known as
(A) Syntax
(B) Semantics
(C) Morphology
(D) Linguistics

2504. While writing a notice, the writer should prefer
(A) Active voice
(B) Passive voice
(C) Any voice
(D) None of these

2505. Phonetics is basically associated with
(A) Sounds
(B) Sentences
(C) Grammar
(D) Of all these

2506. /m/ sound in the word 'make' is...
(A) Labio dental
(B) Dental
(C) Bilabial
(D) Alveolar

2507. Remedial teaching
(A) Fills the gap that creeps into a pupil's learning
(B) Rectifies the concepts which have been misunderstood
(C) Helps in retaining homogeneity in the class
(D) All of above

2508. Identify the correct passive voice of the sentence: obey me.
(A) I should be obeyed
(B) Let be obeyed
(C) Both a and b
(D) None of these

2509. Find the word nearest in meaning to 'REMORSE'
(A) Obdurate

(B) Hard
(C) Penitent
(D) None of these

2510. Which of the following organs of speech is also known as 'VELUM'
(A) Hard palate
(B) Voice box
(C) Alveolar ridge
(D) Soft palate

2511. Find the appropriate preposition to fill in the sentence: She lives ________ Mumbai.
(A) At (B) In
(C) Into (D) An

2512. The major deference between 'ARTICLE' and 'SPEECH' is
(A) Speech is more formal
(B) Speech is more informal
(C) Speech is more descriptive
(D) All of these

2513. When a teacher uses lessons in Science and Social Science to teach language, such an approach can be termed as
(A) Objective language teaching
(B) Pluralistic language teaching
(C) Discipline wise language teaching
(D) Language across the curriculum

2514. A teacher gives many sentences and asks her students to arrange them into a letter using appropriate connectors. The skill then is chiefly involved in this task is
(A) Collecting information
(B) Expanding notice
(C) Organizing
(D) Rewriting

2515. After reading a story on fish, if a teacher asks children to answer "Imagine you are a fish in a pond. What do you see around you"? This is an Example of
(A) Comprehension question
(B) Close type question
(C) Open end question
(D) Multiple choice question

2516. The language skill that cannot be assessed through a traditional pen paper test are
(A) Listening and speaking
(B) Reading and speaking
(C) Writing and listening
(D) Reading and listening

2517. A teacher uses a report from a news paper to teach writing. The material used thus for teaching is referred to
(A) External material
(B) Realistic material
(C) Natural material
(D) Authentic material

2518. When student learn a language for bright employment opportunities, their motivation is
(A) Extrinsic (B) Intrinsic
(C) Exotic (D) Eccentric

2519. A children entered class room is characterized by
(A) A variety of learning activities for the learners
(B) Children sitting in the centre of the classroom
(C) Children teaching other children under the super vision of the teacher
(D) Very passive teachers and active learners

2520. Constructive approach to language teaching experts the teacher to
(A) Give pre constructed knowledge to learner
(B) Contract his own curriculum
(C) Make learner prepare their own text book
(D) Help construct knowledge using their experience

2521. When a test item experts the learners to use the tense forms, voice connectors, prepositions and articles accurately, such an approach can be called
(A) Improper grammar testing
(B) Integrated grammar testing
(C) Asserted grammar practice
(D) Mixed grammar task

2522. Comprehensive Evaluation refers to assessment of
(A) Co curricular activities
(B) Academic subjects
(C) Both scholastic and co scholastic areas
(D) Summative assessment tests

2523. A mixed ability group is heterogeneous in
(A) Economic status
(B) Gender and age
(C) Social strata
(D) Knowledge and skill

2524. Teacher should not give corporal punishment to learners because
(A) It makes parents very angry
(B) It is risky
(C) It create stress and fear in learner
(D) It is only an emotional realization for the teacher

2525. Pre reading tasks are meant for
(A) Evaluating the reading skill of the learners
(B) Giving the meaning of difficult words and phrases
(C) Introducing the mean idea and motivating the learners
(D) Explaining the grammatical items used in the reading text

2526. When a teacher asks her students to write a letter after having a group discussion, she is
(A) Adopting the Direct Method of language teaching
(B) Integrating different language skill
(C) Following a traditional method
(D) Likely to confuse the student

2527. Speaking skill can be best developed by enabling the learners to
(A) Read challenging and difficult texts
(B) Communicate in real life situation
(C) Listen to the model provided by the teacher
(D) Avoid all errors while speaking

2528. Curriculum is an educational programme which does not state
(A) The lesson –planning details of the topics
(B) The educational purpose of the programme
(C) The content(meterial etc. teaching Strategies and learning experiences which will be necessary to achieve this purpose
(D) The means of evaluating where those educational ends have been achieve or not

2529. A good test on reading comprehension will have questions
(A) That focus primarily on the structure and words used in the text
(B) That test the textual knowledge thoroughly
(C) That encourage learners to write answers without errors
(D) That test inference, interpretation and evaluation besides comprehension

2530. Teaching grammar is useful to improve
(A) Accuracy (B) Fluency
(C) Literacy (D) Numeracy

2531. The most important feature of an effective language classroom is opportunity for learners to
(A) Relax (B) Interact
(C) Evaluate (D) Imitate

2532. In learning a new language multilingualism is
(A) A methodology
(B) An asset
(C) An interference
(D) A burden

2533. Which of the following will help learners take greater responsibility for theirown learning
(A) Controlled writing tasks
(B) Peer Assessment
(C) Summative assessment
(D) Supervised Assessment

2534. The main purpose of assessment is
(A) To give practice in writing
(B) To improve the teaching learning process
(C) To decide pass and fail
(D) To measure achievement of learners

2535. When young learners are taught to improve their spelling and punctuation, they will
(A) Nature their creativity
(B) Sharpen their listening skill
(C) Improve their accuracy
(D) Enhance their fluency

2536. Instead of asking questions and getting answers from her learners, a teacher gives some short text and asks her learners to frame questions. Her primary objective to
(A) Make the learners realize the difficulties faced by teacher in preparing question papers
(B) Enhance the learners' analytical and critical thinking
(C) Train the learners and good question paper setters
(D) Help during examinations

2537. Correct speech habits can be developed most effectively through
(A) Vocabulary practice
(B) Quizzes
(C) Dictations
(D) Pronunciation practice

2538. After reading a poem, a teacher involves the learners in group work. One group writes the summary of the poem, another draws a picture to depict the main theme and yet another sets the poem to music. This activity
(A) Caters to diverse abilities and interests
(B) Is aimed at preparing the learners for assessment
(C) Will distract the learners from the lesson
(D) Is a sheer waste of time

2539. Young learners will enjoy a play included in the text book when they
(A) Enact the play
(B) Get detailed explanations about the play from the teacher
(C) Read the play silently
(D) Listen to the teacher reading the play

2540. Under Constructivist Approach to language learning, learners are encouraged to
(A) Avoid errors completely
(B) Practice language drills mechanically
(C) Learn the grammar rule by rote
(D) Discover the rules of grammar from examples

2541. The primary objective of using role play is
(A) To promote the reading habit
(B) To improve the communicative skill
(C) Competence
(D) To evaluate dialogue writing skill

2542. Language skills are best learnt
(A) If They are taught in an integrated manner
(B) With the help of challenging and mechanical language drills
(C) When they are introduced in isolation one skill at a time

(D) Only through written tests and assignment

2543. Substitution table drill helps teachers in
(A) Improving the fluency of learners
(B) Evaluating the listening skill
(C) Giving controlled language practice
(D) Developing free writing skills

2544. Telling interesting stories to young learners is primarily meant for improving their
(A) Writing skills
(B) Speaking Skills
(C) Listening skills
(D) Reading skills

2545. The best way to sensitize young learners to rhythm and intonation is
(A) By reading out poems in different meters and explaining them
(B) By making the learners listen to nursery rhymes and recite them effectively
(C) By making the learners copy out simple poems in neat handwriting
(D) By explaining the rules of phonetics in simple words

2546. An effective language teacher
(A) Will make children learn all the answers to the questions given in the text book
(B) Will use the text book as well as other material and resource for teaching
(C) Will prepare questions papers using only the questions given in the text book
(D) Will rely entirely on the prescribed book

2547. The most effective tool to assess values and attitude of learners is
(A) Anecdotal record
(B) Portfolio
(C) Unit test
(D) Summative

2548. A teacher engages her learners in a fun activity before beginning a new lesson. The purpose of this activity is to
(A) Discipline the learners before the lesson
(B) Divert the attention of the learners
(C) Reduce the workload of the teacher
(D) Motivate and energize the learners

2549. The main purpose of using oral drill is
(A) To access the comprehension skills of learners
(B) To improve pronunciation and accuracy
(C) To enhance the speaking skills of learners
(D) To improve the retention capacity of learners

2550. Continuous and comprehensive Evaluation should be adopted by all schools because
(A) It is the latest development in the field of education
(B) Traditional pen paper tests do not assess and enhance all the attributes and abilities of learners
(C) It frees the learners from studies and hard work
(D) It affords teachers opportunities to test learners frequently

2551. Knowledge of more than one language
(A) Becomes a burden to the teacher in the language classroom
(B) Configures the learners while leaning a new classroom
(C) Is very helpful in teaching and learning a new language
(D) Comes interference in learning a new language

2552. Setting management should be fixable so
(A) Many group, pair and whole class activates can be conducted easily
(B) Children do not form permanent friendship
(C) The teacher ensures equality prevails in the class
(D) Children have the freedom to move their seats wherever they want

2553. Curriculum is an educational programme which does not state
(A) The number of lessons to be taught in a term
(B) The means of evaluating whether the educational objectives have been achieved or not
(C) The content (material etc.) teaching and learning experiences which will be necessary to achieve the purpose
(D) The educational purpose of a programme

2554. Which of the following is an important stage in the writing process
(A) Editing
(B) Memorization
(C) Calligraphy
(D) Comprehension

2555. Scanning means darting over much of a text to search for
(A) The opinion of the author
(B) Difficult words
(C) A specific item or piece of information that we wish to discover
(D) The central idea

2556. We use real objects to teach young learners new words because
(A) It helps in teaching the correct spelling of words
(B) We can teach vocabulary only through objects
(C) Young learners are not capable of abstract thinking
(D) It helps learners associate words with objects they see in real life

2557. A good introduction to a text should be
(A) Telling the students anything that they can find out for themselves by reading the text
(B) A details explanation of the meaning of the text
(C) Blocking the students' active involvement by means of questioning
(D) Short and to the point

2558. Fluency in English can be developed through
(A) Creating opportunities to use the target language for communication
(B) The teacher talking freely most of the time
(C) The teacher being alert to spot the errors and correct them
(D) Allowing students who are not conf

2559. An effective lesson for teaching a language begins with
(A) Listening the learning objective of the lesson
(B) Presenting the content of the lesson
(C) Recapitulation and motivation through fun activity
(D) Writing on the blackboard

2560. Some noise in the language class indicates
(A) Indiscipline of learners
(B) Incompetence of the teacher
(C) Constructive activities with learners engaged in language learning
(D) Lack of interest among the learners

2561. Enquiry based learning
(A) Dose not place students in thorough provoking situations
(B) Encourages quiet learners
(C) Does not nurture creative thinking in learners
(D) Allows learners to raise questions

2562. Effective learning takes place when learners are
(A) Passive
(B) Interactive
(C) Quiet
(D) Good at preparing for examinations

2563. Which of the following is best studies for improving the speaking skills of learners

(A) Recitation of poetry

(B) Reading a prose and drama aloud

(C) Oral language drill

(D) Debates and group discussions followed by role play

2564. Which of the following will be most effective to remove conventional beliefs about gender roles?

(A) Showing a picture in which the mother is seen cooking and the father is seen reading a newspaper

(B) Teaching all the learners to sweep, wash and sew in the craft class without any gender discrimination

(C) Encouraging girls to developed interest in household chores from a young age

(D) Telling the girls that talking freely is not the trait of a good girl

2565. A play can be best taught by

(A) Making the students read it silently a number of times to understand the story

(B) Encouraging the students to stage the play after working in groups to understand the plot, characters etc.

(C) Asking a number of questions to test the comprehension of the students

(D) Conducting a test with specific questions on the story and grammars

2566. The Constructive Approach to learning means

(A) Involving the students in a variety of activities to encourage them to learn new words and structures by accommodating them with those that they have already learnt through a process of discovery

(B) Teaching rules of grammar and consolidating through rigorous practice

(C) Helping learners acquire new vocabulary by studying literature intensively

(D) Teaching new words and structures using a variety of audio visual aids following by practice through drill

2567. "Schools need to become centers that prepare children for life and ensure that all children, especially the differently able children from marginalized sections, and children in difficult circumstances get the maximum benefit of these critical areas of education." This observation found in the National Curriculum Framework 2005 is related to

(A) Inclusive education

(B) Constructivist learning

(C) Gender quality

(D) Critical pedagogy

2568. What is the skill among the ones given below that cannot be tested in a formal written examination?

(A) Reading for information

(B) Meaning for words and phrases

(C) Extensive reading for pleasure

(D) Analyzing texts

2569. Which of the following is suitable for making students responsible for their own learning?

(A) Discouraging students from making decision about how they learn best

(B) Using technology to chat and network

(C) Encouraging students to ask more and more questions

(D) Giving a lot of homework, project work and assignments to improve language skills of students

2570. A teacher, while teaching paragraph construction, should draw attention to

(A) A large variety of ideas

(B) Originality of ideas

(C) Topic sentence, supporting details and connectors

(D) A range of vocabulary

2571. Communicative language teaching is concerned with
(A) Teaching of vocabulary and grammar through rules of spelling and language
(B) Teaching language to learners for written tests
(C) Interpreting grammar rules to suit the audience
(D) Enhancing receptive and productive skills such as speaking, listening, reading and writing.

2572. Formative assessment is assessment of learning
(A) Of learning
(B) At learning
(C) In learning
(D) For learning

2573. The term 'comprehensive' in continuous and comprehensive evaluation means
(A) Scholastic development
(B) Co scholastic development
(C) Academic skills
(D) Scholastic and co scholastic development

2574. When learners are engaged in a pair activity, taking on roles of a doctor and patient, the activity is called
(A) Real activity
(B) Declamation
(C) Simulation
(D) Exchanging notes

2575. Essays or long writing tasks especially on a discursive issue should
(A) Help students development their literary skills
(B) Help students with grammar
(C) Help them to improve their hand writing
(D) Help them discuss the different points of view and justify them with illustrative.

2576. Using a word bank and brainstorming helps to build
(A) Vocabulary
(B) Ideas
(C) Writing skills
(D) Reading comprehension

2577. Gender stereotypes and bias among learners can be discouraged by
(A) Enabling all learners to cook and sew irrespective of gender
(B) Using text books which do not perpetuate such beliefs
(C) Creating an open and encouraging atmosphere in a mixed class
(D) Pressuring girls to learn cooking

2578. The spoken skill in a language teaching classroom can be developed through
(A) Engaging in small talk as confident aggressive learners
(B) Emotionally connecting with learners
(C) Enabling activities with a focus on conversation skill leading to communicative competence
(D) Group activities where learners can talk in whichever language they would like to

2579. Ritu often makes errors in Subject Verb concord. The teacher can help her by
(A) Talking up many examples for the entire class and paying special attention to Ritu
(B) Explaining to her the rules of grammar
(C) Asking Ritu to learn the rules and scolding her
(D) Asking Ritu to write the rules ten times in her notebook

2580. How will a teacher best teach 'writing' skill to a class
(A) By brainstorming ideas and asking students to write in their own words
(B) By asking students to write neatly

(C) Through dictation

(D) By asking students to learn articles and rewrite them

2581. Mary, a young teacher, believes in personalized learning because she thinks that

(A) Every person must be exposed to learning

(B) Every learner is unique and needs to be given a change to developed to the best of their ability

(C) All learners must learn on their own

(D) Children must enjoy their learning

2582. Grammar should be taught by

(A) Asking students to learn rules

(B) Making learners do written assignments

(C) Giving clear explanations

(D) Enabling practice in context

2583. A teacher uses Big Reading Book in her language classes to

(A) Allow students to read at home

(B) Ensure books carry a lot of information

(C) Use these illustrated colorful books for reading together

(D) Use them for big students of different ages

2584. A teacher can cater to learning styles of all the children by

(A) Teaching every lesson thoroughly and revising the lessons

(B) Testing the children frequently

(C) Advising the children to join drawing/dance/music classes

(D) Employing a variety of teaching methods and modes of assessment which cater to diversity among learners

2585. Reading for comprehension can be best achieved through

(A) Helping learners speak words softly while reading

(B) Learners reading silently and asking comprehension questions

(C) Teaching learners to run a finger or pencil under the line being read

(D) Asking the children to read the text aloud

2586. Remedial teaching as part of Formative Assessment means

(A) Extra coaching by partners

(B) Teaching for gifted students

(C) Diagnosing and addressing gaps in learning

(D) Teaching beyond the textbook

2587. What types of questions promote thinking skills in children?

(A) Personal response questions

(B) Closed ended questions

(C) Factual questions

(D) Questions based purely on the reading text

2588. Which of the following is a value associated with an inclusive classroom?

(A) Sympathy

(B) Collaboration

(C) Competition

(D) Envy

2589. Which of the following is an instance of non formal learning?

(A) Children learning through correspondence lessons

(B) Children learning to draw from their art teacher

(C) Children learning to cook from their parents

(D) Children learning a new game from friends

2590. Listening, Speaking, Reading, writing are

(A) Motor skills

(B) Verbal skills

(C) Formal skills

(D) Language skills

2591. Examples are
(A) More effective than using a blackboard
(B) More effective than mere teaching
(C) Less effective than explanation
(D) Not needed in a language class

2592. The aim of mechanical drills is to
(A) Improve the fluency of the learners
(B) Improve the accuracy of the learners
(C) Strengthen the role learning capacity of the learners
(D) Encourage creative use of language among the learners

2593. Teachers help learners 'construct' their knowledge in English by
(A) Giving extensive language drills in which learners practice language items mechanically
(B) Enabling them to see the relationship between their prior knowledge and the new knowledge
(C) Giving the learners a lot of assignments and projects that will lead to much practice
(D) Correcting every mistake a learner makes and giving the relevant rule of grammar as immediate feedback

2594. Learners are involved in individual activities, pair work, group work and whole class work because these
(A) Enable the already ever worked teacher to preserve her energy thereby becoming more effective
(B) Afford the learners opportunities to use the language in a focused manner for real life interaction
(C) Provide the learners enough opportunities to relax in a language classroom
(D) Have the sole aim of introducing variety in a language classroom

2595. Which of the following statements is true?
(A) While all formative tasks are meant for improving teaching learning, some are used for assessment too.
(B) Formative assessment helps us to grade students into good, average and poor.
(C) All formative tasks are meant for assessment
(D) Formative assessment, to be effective, must be conducted only after teaching a lesson.

2596. Group project helps in developing
(A) Competition
(B) Good memory in the young
(C) A high level of ambition to achieve
(D) Collaboration, critical thinking and problems solving

2597. The founder of structural grammar was
(A) Newfield
(B) Chapman
(C) Chomskey
(D) C.C. Fries

2598. In the traditional method of teaching grammar
(A) Language fluency is to be required
(B) Black boards are essential
(C) Text book is must
(D) All the above

2599. Method of teaching grammar is
(A) Deductive
(B) Inductive
(C) Incidental
(D) All the above

2600. Mention the point which negates the idea of modern grammar teaching
(A) Study of use
(B) Study of rules
(C) Contextualize grammar with situation
(D) Integrate grammar with the text

2601. Mixed ability group of learners mean
(A) Learners coming from different cultures
(B) Learners coming from the different parts of the state
(C) Learners with different cognitive levels
(D) Learners coming from the different levels of the society

2602. The curriculum should ideally
(A) Connect knowledge outside
(B) Do away with assessment
(C) Provide overall development of children
(D) Address social need

2603. Students in FCA are allowed
(A) No freedom
(B) To learn the rules first
(C) Much freedom
(D) To learn according to their own will

2604. At the initial stage FCA focuses on
(A) Listening
(B) Speaking
(C) Writing
(D) Listening and speaking

2605. Grammar Translation method does
(A) Not give importance to grammar
(B) Not encourage learning through mother tongue
(C) Not encourage a student's communicative skills
(D) All of the above

2606. In the Grammar Translation Method little importance is given to
(A) Vocabulary
(B) Punctuation
(C) Spelling
(D) Pronunciation

2607. In Grammar Translation Method
(A) The teacher is dominating
(B) The students are not interactive
(C) Extensive use of mother tongue is advocated
(D) All of the above

2608. A language teacher following Grammar Translation Method in classroom will give less emphasis on
(A) Reading proficiency
(B) Grammar
(C) Oral use
(D) Mother tongue usage

2609. The Direct Method was popularized by
(A) The International Phonetic Association
(B) The International Semantic Association
(C) German Linguists
(D) American linguists

2610. Direct Method prohibits
(A) Communicability
(B) Fluency
(C) Vocabulary
(D) Memorization

2611. Direct Method is an attempt to
(A) Minimize the use of mother tongue
(B) Activate the skill of writing
(C) Minimize errors in vocabulary
(D) All of the above

2612. In speaking a language the role of grammar is
(A) Most important
(B) Not at all important
(C) Liberal
(D) None of these

2613. Teaching a second language must
(A) Allow use of mother tongue
(B) Avoid use of mother tongue
(C) Ban using mother tongue
(D) Allow legitimate use of mother tongue

2614. Language learning needs
(A) Reinforcement

(B) Review
(C) Feedback
(D) All of the above

2615. When a person is using language to express his feelings and meanings he is employing the
(A) Regulatory function
(B) Interactional function
(C) Personal function
(D) Expressive function

2616. A poem can be best taught by
(A) Making the students recite it
(B) Oral language drill
(C) Reaction and then explanation
(D) Group discussion

2617. An essay can be best taught by
(A) Making the student read it loudly
(B) Giving an ideal reading and translation the meaning
(C) Oral language drill
(D) Explaining the main idea and allowing group discussion

2618. Noise in a language class indicates
(A) Indiscipline of the learners
(B) Incompetence of the teacher
(C) Constructive activities going on
(D) Disinterested learners

2619. The material used by the teacher to make his teaching very effectively is called
(A) Teaching Methods
(B) Teaching strategies
(C) Teaching Learning material
(D) None of these

2620. A project work does not test
(A) Creativity
(B) Memory
(C) Writing skill
(D) adaptability

2621. Culture is
(A) collective
(B) ahistorical
(C) undisputed
(D) individual

2622. Bourdieu's concept of cultural capital means
(A) the mass production of cultural icons.
(B) the ways in which culture is marketed to increase the sale of nationally produced goods.
(C) the ways in which culture is marketed to increase tourism.
(D) the idea that schools are not neutral and that scholastic success requires certain cultural understandings.

2623. Why is culture relevant to the study of politics?
(A) Because it pertains to differences between countries.
(B) Because it pertains to differences between countries and questions of democracy and justice.
(C) Because it pertains to differences between countries, relations of power, challenges to the status quo, and questions of democracy and justice.
(D) Culture is not relevant to the study of politics.

2624. What are the three types of attitudes people have about their own role in the political process as identified by Almond and Verba?
(A) parochial, passive, and participant
(B) parochial, subject, and participant
(C) parochial, subject, and representative
(D) liberal, conservative, and revolutionary

2625. Which or who of the following is not associated with the cultural studies approach?
(A) David Easton
(B) Louis Althusser

(C) Centre for Contemporary Cultural Studies

(D) Richard Hoggart

2626. Difference blindness holds that

(A) Quebec must be recognized as a distinct society.

(B) certain groups should be extended special recognition.

(C) everyone should be treated equally and exactly the same.

(D) distinctions should be drawn between citizens because of their cultural, social, or religious background.

2627. What was Gramsci's term for cultural consensus supporting capitalism?

(A) hegemony

(B) discourse

(C) ideological state apparatuses

(D) universalism

2628. From what does the cultural identity approach stem?

(A) the economic determinism of Marx.

(B) U.S.'s desire to win the Cold War against the Soviet Union.

(C) the branch of political science known as political philosophy.

(D) the branch of political science known as political sociology.

2629. The political culture approach of Almond and Verba

(A) advocated for a change in power relations.

(B) built on the normative concerns of political philosophy.

(C) was historical and interdisciplinary.

(D) studied the issue of cultural hegemony.

2630. What are the three approaches to the study of culture and politics reviewed in this chapter?

(A) political science, political sociology, and historical materialism

(B) political culture, cultural studies, and cultural identity

(C) political culture, civic culture, and cultural studies

(D) cultural hegemony, cultural identities, and political philosophy

2631. Teaching and learning is a journey from

(A) Concrete to abstract

(B) Simple to complex

(C) Known to unknown

(D) All the above

2632. The method of teaching English adopted at present in school curriculum is

(A) Formative Correlational Approach

(B) Functional Communicative Approach

(C) Function Corrective Approach

(D) Figurative Comprehensive Approach

2633. FCA is in opposition to

(A) Structural Approach

(B) Comprehensive Approach

(C) Translation and Grammar Method

(D) Functional Approach

2634. Communicative Language Teaching replaced basically ...

(A) Natural Language Processing

(B) Structural Teaching

(C) Situational Language Teaching

(D) Motivational Teaching

2635. Direct Method is also known as

(A) Natural Method

(B) Indirect Approach

(C) Inductive Approach

(D) All the above

2636. Grammar-Translation Method stresses on

(A) Accuracy

(B) Fluency

(C) Appropriateness

(D) Listening skill

2637. Grammar-Translation Method is basically used to teach
(A) Grammar
(B) Foreign language
(C) Rules of any language usage
(D) Classical language

2638. The objective of Direct Method is
(A) To increase power of comprehension
(B) To increase communicative power
(C) To develop a command over the target language
(D) To develop personality

2639. Grammar-Translation Method does not
(A) Encourage learning through mother tongue
(B) Give importance to grammar
(C) Enhance a student's communicative skill
(D) Enable the student too use the language fluently

2640. Traditional method goes against the
(A) Prescriptive grammar
(B) Simulation
(C) Pedagogic principles
(D) Generalization

2641. The incidental or Correlative Method is known as
(A) Inductive
(B) Deductive
(C) Structural
(D) Reference method

2642. Journey from example to generalization is
(A) Inductive
(B) Deductive
(C) incidental
(D) All the above

2643. Inductive method proceeds from
(A) Heavy materials to light ones
(B) Known to unknown
(C) Simple to complex
(D) Both (B) & (C)

2644. Deductive method proceeds from
(A) Law and rule to observation
(B) Observation
(C) Generalization to specification
(D) Examples and illustrations

2645. One of the principles of materials preparation for language learning is that
(A) Complex material should be chosen
(B) Grading of materials should be done
(C) Any kind of material can be chosen
(D) A small amount of material should be introduced

2646. Correct pronunciation of individual sound is related to
(A) Accuracy
(B) Fluency
(C) Both accuracy and fluency
(D) Neither accuracy nor fluency

2647. Language accusation occurs only when
(A) The child is taught the rules of grammar
(B) The child is given a reward
(C) The child has exposure to the language
(D) The child absorbs the language without conscious attention

2648. When a child is asked to recite a poem, it can help the teacher to test
(A) Knowledge of literature
(B) Proficiency of speaking
(C) Acting talent
(D) Comprehension

2649. The structure 'he goes to school' is often produced by learners due to
(A) Failure of intelligence
(B) Mother tongue interference
(C) Overgeneralization of rules
(D) Wrong teaching

2650. For teaching grammar, the best grammar that a teacher can use is
(A) Traditional grammar
(B) Modern grammar
(C) Pedagogic grammar
(D) No grammar is needed

2651. A test of listening comprehension is a test of
(A) Receptive skill
(B) Productive skill
(C) Hearing skill
(D) Phonology

2652. Organization of arguments and ideas in paragraphs is an important aspect of
(A) Writing essays
(B) Writing memos
(C) Writing stories
(D) Writing personal letters

2653. 'Brain storming' means
(A) To collect all kinds of ideas on a topic
(B) To do some mental exercise
(C) To make efforts to understand something
(D) To give some kind of stimulus to the brain

2654. 'Interactive' listening is
(A) Listening and responding
(B) Listening for mood and tone
(C) Listening for word stress and emphasis
(D) Listening for finding out speaker's attitude

2655. Which of the following is an incorrect assumption in language teaching
(A) Learners acquire language by trying to use it in real situations
(B) Learners' first language plays an important role in learning
(C) Language teaching should have a focus in communicative activities
(D) Language teaching should give importance to writing rather than speech

2656. Reading skill can be developed best by
(A) Writing answers to questions on text
(B) Focusing on the use of words from context in the text
(C) Doing vocabulary exercises
(D) Doing quizzes and playing word games

2657. Mother tongue influence can be effectively minimized in the classroom by
(A) Using the mother tongue more often
(B) Giving examples from the mother tongue
(C) Giving a lot of exposure in the target language
(D) Giving inputs from the target language in a simple, graded manner

2658. Practice of grammatical structures in a controlled manner can be done by
(A) Correcting wrong sentences produced by learners
(B) Gap-filling grammar exercises
(C) Writing paragraphs and essays
(D) Explaining the use of particular structures

2659. A test which is administered at the end of a language course is
(A) Diagnostic test
(B) Placement test
(C) Achievement test
(D) Memory test

2660. Study of meaning in a language is known as
(A) Syntax
(B) Semantics
(C) Morphology
(D) Linguistics

2661. Who is the author of Raj?
(A) Geeta Mehta
(B) Rama Mehta

(C) Shobha De
(D) Nargis Dalai

2662. Dominique Lapierre wrote an appealing ac-count of the sordid squalor of an Indian city. Identify the city.
(A) Calcutta
(B) Bombay
(C) Udaipur
(D) Delhi

2663. Who is the author of following poems? "The Gift of India", "Bangle-seller", "The Anthem of Love", "Palanquin Bearers"
(A) Kamala Das
(B) Sarojini Naidu
(C) Toru Dutt
(D) Nissim Ezekiel

2664. Who wrote the hard-hitting poem "Sita Speak" indicating the society for the injus-tice meted out to women down the ages
(A) Bina Agarwal
(B) Kamala Das
(C) P. Lai
(D) Sarojini Naidu

2665. In which of the following poems of Ezekiel do we get a moving picture of a mother's suffering ?
(A) 'The Couple'
(B) 'Night of the Scorpion'
(C) 'The Visitor'
(D) 'Philosophy'

2666. Who is the author of Two Virgins?
(A) Kamala Markandaya
(B) Kamala Das
(C) Anita Desai
(D) Shastri Deshpande

2667. Name the Indo-English novelist who wrote A Suitable Boy.
(A) Vikram Seth
(B) Amitav Ghose
(C) Upamanyu Chatterjee
(D) Anita Desai

2668. Two Indian writers living abroad created furor - one was Vikram Seth who got an unprec-edented amount as an advance for his novel, the other who came under 'fatwa', for one of his controversial novels, issued by Muslim countries, was
(A) Amitav Ghose
(B) Bharati Mukherjee
(C) Anita Desai
(D) Salman Rushdie

2669. Name Salman Rushdie's latest Novel.
(A) The Moor's Last Sigh
(B) Fury
(C) The Ground beneath Her Feet
(D) Satanic Verses

2670. Of the following novels one does not por-tray the Gandhian Age and the impact of Gandhi. Which one?
(A) K.A. Abbas's Inquilab
(B) Venu Chitale's In Transit
(C) R.K. Narayan's The Dark Room
(D) K. Nagarajan's Chronicles of Kedaram

2671. Who is the author of the following books: The Foreigner, The Apprentice, The Last Labyrinth, The City and the River?
(A) Ruth P. Jhabvala
(B) Amitav Ghose
(C) Dom Moraes
(D) Arun Joshi

2672. Whose collections of poems are these: A Time to Change, Sixty Poems, The Third, The Unfinished Man?
(A) P. Lai
(B) Nissim Ezekiel
(C) Kamala Das
(D) Bina Aggarwal

2673. Listed below are the works of Bhabani Bhattacharya of which only one is his col-lection of short stories. Identify it.

(A) So Many Hungers
(B) A Dream in Hawaii
(C) Sea Hawk
(D) Shadow from Ladakh

2674. Baumgartner's Bombay is a novel about a German Jew who remains an outsider all his life, in his country because he is a Jew and in India, where he is a firangi. Who wrote this moving novel?

(A) Vikram Seth
(B) Anita Desai
(C) Nayantara Sehgal
(D) Ruth P. Jhabvala

2675. In which novel does R.K. Narayan focus on family planning?

(A) The Guide
(B) Mr. Sampath
(C) Bachelor of Arts
(D) The Painter of Signs

2676. In the Guide we come across a dancer. What is her name?

(A) Daisy (B) Bharati
(C) Rosie (D) Savitri

2677. Who wrote these lines?

"Woman is the earth, air, ether, sound; woman is the microcosm of the mind "?

(A) Raja Rao
(B) R.K. Narayan
(C) Kamala Markandaya
(D) Kamala Das

2678. Arthur Symons wrote about this person, "All the life of the tiny figure seemed to concen-trate itself in the eyes: they turned towards beauty as the sunflower turns towards the sun." Who is the person re-ferred to?

(A) Toru Dutt
(B) Aru Dutt
(C) Sarojini Naidu
(D) Rabindra Nath Tagore

2679. H.A.L. Fisher wrote about this person,".... this child of the green valley of the Ganges has by sheer force of native genius earned for herself the right to be enrolled in the great fellowship of English poets." Who is the poet?

(A) Sarojini Naidu
(B) Toru Dutt
(C) Michael Madhusudan
(D) Manmohan Ghose

2680. An Indo-English poet once remarked that his disciplines (i.e., linguistics and anthropol-ogy) and his education give him his "Outer" form, whereas his Indian ori-gin, first thirty years in India and knowl-edge of Kannada and Tamil give him his "inner" form. Who said this?

(A) A.K. Ramanujan
(B) Kamala Das
(C) Gieve Patel
(D) Raja Gopal Parthasarathy

2681. Who wrote Jejurithe Commonwealth Po-etry Prize winner work?

(A) Shiv K. Kumar
(B) Arun Kolatkar
(C) Keki N. Daruwala
(D) Jayant Mahapatra

2682. In which of Anita Desai's novel an insane wife kills her husband?

(A) Voices in The City
(B) In Custody
(C) Cry, The Peacock
(D) Baumgartner's Bombay

2683. In which novel does the hero sing the re-frain?

"This is the machine age, sons
This is the machine age
We are the men who will master it"?

(A) The Big Heart

(B) The Sword and The Sickle
(C) Two Leaves and a Bud
(D) The Road

2684. Who was the first recipient of the Sahitya Academi Award for English literature?
(A) Mulk Raj Anand
(B) Nayantara Sehgal
(C) R.K. Narayan
(D) Raja Rao

2685. Following novels except one, describe the condition of Westners living in India. Mark the one which does not.
(A) Heat and Dust
(B) The Princess
(C) Coffer Dam
(D) A Passage to India

2686. Which of the following novels focuses on the question of rape?
(A) The Bending Vine
(B) Voices in The City
(C) Some Inner Fury
(D) A Time to Be Happy

2687. Who is the author of the following novels: A Bend in The Ganges, The Princes, Dis-tant Drums, Devil's Wind, A Combat of Shadows?
(A) Mulk Raj Anand
(B) Bhabani Bhattacharya
(C) Manohar Malgaonkar
(D) Salman Rushdie

2688. Who wrote "Our Casuarina Tree" a splen-did Keatsian poem?
(A) Toru Dutt
(B) Romesh Chander Dutt
(C) Swami Vivekanand
(D) Sri Aurobindo

2689. To whom do we assign following works - The Lake of Palms, A History of Civiliza-tion of Ancient India, The Slave-Girl of Agra?
(A) Manmohan Ghose
(B) Romesh Chander Dutt
(C) Bankim Chandra Chatterjee
(D) Sharat Chandra

2690. Which one of the following is a collection of Anita Desai's short stories?
(A) Voices in the City
(B) Games at Twilight
(C) Village by the Sea
(D) Cry, the Peacock

2691. Browning's The Ring and the Book is a long poem having about 21,000 lines, but Aurobindo's Savitri is longer. How many lines does the epic contain?
(A) 24,000 (B) 21,500
(C) 30,000 (D) 22,000

2692. Toru Dutt, Romesh Chander Dutt and Aurobindo, all wrote on one common theme taken out from the Mahabharata. Identify the story which the tree found irresistible.
(A) Kama and Kunti
(B) Nal-Damyanti
(C) Savitri
(D) Gandhari

2693. Who of the following was highly influenced by French Romanticism, French language and literature?
(A) Romesh Chander Dutt
(B) Michael Madhusudan Dutt
(C) Toru Dutt
(D) Govind Dutt

2694. About an Indian poet writing in English, a critic, George Sampson says that a reader of his poems "Would readily take them as the work of an English poet trained in the classical tradition." An Indian critic feels that his poetry has no imagery or senti-ment that can be termed as Indian. Who was this poet?
(A) Michael Madhusudan Dutt
(B) Romesh Chander Dutt

(C) Aurobindo Ghose
(D) Manmohan Ghose

2695. The Fakir of Jhungheera was written by one of the first Indo-Anglian poets. The poem is often hailed as a "Competent narrative verse with Byronic echoes." Identify the writer.
(A) Toru Dutt
(B) Henry Derozio
(C) Michael Madhusudan Dutt
(D) Hasan Ali

2696. He was the first Indian poet to have pub-lished a regular volume of English verse. He also edited an English Weekly The Hindu Intelligence. Name him.
(A) Michael Madhusudan Dutt
(B) Mohan Lai
(C) Romesh Chander Dutt
(D) Kashiprasad Ghose

2697. Paying a tribute to a Bengali poet who wrote in English also, Sri Aurobindo said, "The God himself took up thy pen and wrote." Who was he?
(A) Michael Madhusudan Dutt
(B) Henry Derozio
(C) Romesh Chander Dutt
(D) Kashiprasad Ghose

2698. One of the following works is written by Michael Madhusudan Dutt. Identify which one?
(A) The Shair and Other Poems
(B) The Captive Ladie
(C) Bianca
(D) Lays of Ancient India

2699. Name the poet of "Kali, the Mother."
(A) Swami Vivekanand
(B) Subramaniam Bharathi
(C) Swami Ramakrishna Paramhans
(D) Sri Aurobindo

2700. He is a Sahitya Akademi Award Winner and he loves to write for children. Who is he?
(A) R. K. Narayan
(B) Manohar Malgaonkar
(C) Ruskin Bond
(D) Upamanyu Chatterjee

2701. Whose autobiography is entitled My Father's Son?
(A) Dom Moraes
(B) Frank Moraes
(C) Nirad Chaudhury
(D) VS. Naipaul

2702. Mulk Raj Anand, about one of his female characters says, "Gauri is my tribute to Indian womanhood." In which novel does Gauri appear?
(A) The Road
(B) The Old Woman and The Cow
(C) Untouchable
(D) The Sword and The Sickle

2703. Read the following passage and identify the novel and its author: "Lago, I am as meek as Moses, but I have just heard that you have been mishandled by that Bhatta Govinda. Whip me, ye devils! Roast me in sulphur! Gall, worse than gall! A rascally Yea-for-smooth knave! Three Judases, each one thrice worse than Judas! Falstaff speaking. I am as subject to heat as butter."
(A) In Custody by Anita Desai
(B) Midnight's Children by Salman Rushdie
(C) All About H. Hatter by G.V. Desani
(D) Vermillion Boat by Sudhir Ghosh

2704. Name the author who has been described by a critic as an "outsider inside."
(A) Anita Desai
(B) Salman Rushdie
(C) Nirad C. Chaudhary
(D) Ruth Jhabvala

2705. Following novels, except one, describes the condition of Indians settled abroad. Mark the one which does not.

(A) The Nowhere Man
(B) Bye-Bye, Blackbird
(C) The Serpent And The Rope
(D) The Guide

2706. The Angel of Misfortune is a poem of about 5000 lines, written by Nagesh Vishwanath Pai. Whose story is narrated in this book?

(A) Saturn, the Dark Angel
(B) King Arthur of the Holy Grail
(C) King Vikramaditya
(D) Kamadeva

2707. Name the author of The Gardener, The Fu-gitive, Chitra, Sacrifice, The Post Of-fice.

(A) Rabindra Nath Tagore
(B) Bankim Chandra
(C) Aurobindo Ghose
(D) Romesh Chander Dutt

2708. Name the two prizes, one in literature and another in History, awarded to young Aurobindo while studying in England.

(A) Pulitzer Prizes in Literature and Bedford Prize in History
(B) Bookers in Literature and Butterworth in History
(C) Butterworth in Literature and Bedford in History

2709. Name Sarojini Naidu's last collection of po-ems.

(A) The Broken Wing
(B) The Golden Threshold
(C) The Bird of Time
(D) The Temple

2710. What is the full title of Aurobindo's Savitri?

(A) Savitri - An Epic
(B) Savitri
(C) Savitri - A Legend and a Symbol
(D) Savitri - A Poem in Three Parts

2711. Who wrote Murugan, The Tiller and Kandan, the Patriot, Jatadharan and The Next Rung?

(A) K.S. Venkataramani
(B) ShankerRam
(C) Humayun Kabir
(D) K. Subba Rao

2712. The Devil's Wind depicts the events of our First War of Independence (1857 mutiny). Who is the author of this novel?

(A) Shanker Ram
(B) Manohar Malgaonkar
(C) R.K. Narayan
(D) Sasthi Brata

2713. Which novel highlights the Bengal famine?

(A) So Many Hungers
(B) A Handful of Rice
(C) A Time to be Happy
(D) Athawar House

2714. Who wrote Ilion?

(A) Virgil
(B) Aurobindo
(C) Homer
(D) Rabindra Nath Tagore

2715. Who is the author of Love of Dust?

(A) Ruth P. Jhabvala
(B) Humayun Kabir
(C) Shanker Ram
(D) K.S. Venkataramani

2716. How should we seek deliverance as per the poem 'Leave This Chanting' by Rabindranath Tagore?

(A) By incessant prayers
(B) By going to the temple regularly
(C) By being pious and righteous-minded
(D) By helping our fellow beings who are in need

2717. What should we do to meet God as per the poem 'Leave This Chanting' the Rabindranath Tagore?
(A) Mediate on God
(B) Have true faith in God
(C) Offer flowers and incense
(D) Stand by God in toil and in sweat

2718. Arthur Symons wrote about this person, "All the life of the tiny figure seemed to concentrate itself in the eyes: they turned towards beauty as the sunflower turns towards the sun." Who is the person referred to?
(A) Toru Dutt
(B) Aru Dutt
(C) Sarojini Naidu
(D) Rabindranath Tagore

2719. 'The Gift of India', 'Bangle-Seller', 'The Autumn of Love', 'Palanquin Bearers'. Identify the author from the following.
(A) Sarojini Naidu (B) Anita Desai
(C) Vikram Seth (D) None of these

2720. Hal Fisher wrote about this person, ". . . this child of the green valley of the Ganges has by sheer force of native genius earned for herself the right to be enrolled in the great fellowship of English poets." Who is the poet?
(A) Sarojini Naidu
(B) Toru Dutt
(C) Michael Maclhusudan
(D) Manmohan Ghose

2721. Toru Dutt, Romesh Chunder Dutt and Aurobindo, all wrote on one common theme taken out from the Mahabhrata. Identify the story which the three found irresistible.
(A) Kama and Kunti
(B) Nal-Damyanti
(C) Savitri
(D) Gandhari

2722. The Fakir of Jhungheera was written by one of the first Indo-Anglian poets. The poem is often hailed as a "Competent narrative verse with Byronic echoes." Identify the writer.
(A) Toru Dutt
(B) Henry Derozio
(C) Michael Madhusudan Dutt
(D) Hassan Ali

2723. Paying a tribute to a Bengali poet who wrote in English also, Sri Aurobindo said, "The God himself took up thy pen and wrote." Who was he?
(A) Michael Madhusudan Dutt
(B) Henry Derozio
(C) Romesh Chunder Dutt
(D) Kashiprasad Ghose

2724. To whom do we assign following works — The Lake of Palms, A History of Civilisation of Ancient India, The Slave-Girl of Agra?
(A) Manmohan Ghose
(B) Romesh Chunder Dutt
(C) Bankim Chandra Chatterjee
(D) Sharat Chandra Chatterjee

2725. About an Indian poet writing in English, a critic, George Sampson says that a reader of his poems
"Would readily take them as the work of an English poet trained in the classical tradition."
An Indian critic feels that his poetry has no imagery or sentiment that can be termed as Indian. Who was this poet?
(A) Michael Madhusiidan Dutt
(B) Romesh Chunder Dutt
(C) Aurobindo Ghose
(D) Manmohan Ghose

2726. Following novels, except one, describe the condition of Indians settled abroad. Mark the one which does not.

(A) The Nowhere Man
(B) Bye-Bye, Blackbird
(C) The Serpent And The Rope
(D) The Guide

2727. R.K. Narayan is one of the most widely read Indian novelists. He wrote for more than fifty years including travelogues, English translations of Indian epics and his memoirs 'My Days'. Which of these is a fictional town created by him?
(A) Alleypey
(B) Malgudi
(C) Udipi
(D) Coimbatore

2728. Read the following passage and identify the novel and its author.
"Lago, I am as meek as Moses, but I have just heard that you have been mishandled by that Bhatta Govinda. Whip me, ye devils! Roast me in sulphur! Gall, worse than gall! A rascally Yea-for-smooth knave! Three Judases, each one thrice worse than Judas! Falstaff speaking. I am as subject to heat as butter."
(A) In Custody by Anita Desai
(B) Midnight's Children by Salman Rushdie
(C) All About H Hatterr by G.V. Desani
(D) Vermillion Boat by Sudhir Ghosh

2729. Identify the author from the following, who has written 'The Devil's Wind' which depicts the events of India's First wax; of Independence, (1857) Mutiny.
(A) K. Subba Rao
(B) Manohar Malgonkar
(C) K.S. Venkatramani
(D) None of the above

2730. Who among the following was first Indian poet to have published a regular volume of English verse? He also edited an English weekly, 'The Hindu Intelligence'?
(A) Mohan Lal
(B) Kashiprasad Ghosh
(C) R.K. Narayan
(D) None of the above

2731. In his poem 'A Morning Walk' Nissim Ezekiel talks about a 'Barbaric City sick with slums/Deprived of seasons, blessed with rains/Its hawkers, beggars, iron-lunged/Processions led by frantic drums.' Identify the city.
(A) Kolkata
(B) Banaras
(C) Mumbai
(D) Agra

2732. In Indo-English poet once remarked that his disciplines (i.e., linguistics and anthropology) and his education give him his Outer form, Whereas his Indian origin, first thirty years in India and knowledge of Kannada and Tamil give him his inner form. Who said this?
(A) A.K. Ramanujan
(B) Kamala Das
(C) Gieve Patel
(D) Raja Gopal Parthasarathy

2733. In which novel does the hero sing the refrain?
"This is the machine age, sons
This is the machine age"
Which of the following novels focuses on the question of rape?
(A) The Bending Vine
(B) Voices in The City
(C) Some Inner Fury
(D) A Time to Be Happy

2734. Baumgartner's Bombay is a novel about a German Jew who remains an outsider all his life in his country because he is a Jew and in India, where he is a firangi. Who wrote this moving novel?
(A) Vikram Seth
(B) Anita Desai

(C) Nayantara Seghal

(D) Ruth P Jhabvala

2735. This author has been short-listed for the Booker Prize thrice as of 2007 but is yet to win it, however, her daughter won the Booker Prize in 2006 for her second novel. Name this mother-daughter duo.

(A) Sooni and Farida Taraporewala

(B) Kinari and Vidya Sharma

(C) Depa and Rashmi Mehta

(D) Anita and Kiran Desai

2736. Who is the author of the following books: The Foreinger, The Apprentice, The Last Labyrinth The City and the River?

(A) Ruth P Jhabvala

(B) Amitav Ghosh

(C) Dom Moraes

(D) Arun Joshi

2737. Two Indian writers living abroad created furore-one was Vikram Seth who got an unprecedented among as an advance for his novel, the other who came under 'fatwa', for one of his controversial novels, issued by Muslim countries, was

(A) Amitav Ghose

(B) Bharati Mukherjee

(C) Anita Desai

(D) Salman Rushdie

2738. Salman Rushdie is a British-Indian author who has won numerous awards including the Booker Prize for Fiction and the Whitbread Novel Award. Which of his books caused Ayatollah Khomeini, the then leader of Iran, to pronounce a fatwa (death sentence) on him?

(A) Midnight's Children

(B) Shalimaar the Clown

(C) The Satanic Verses

(D) The Moor's Last Sigh

2739. This author's novels include 'The Hungry Tide 'The Glass Palace' and "The Shadow Lines'. He refused the Eurasian Commonwealth Writers Prize in 2001.

(A) Amitav Ghosh

(B) Suketu Mehra

(C) Vikram Chandra

(D) David Davidar

2740. Name this Indo-Canadian writer who has won the Commonwealth Writers Prize twice for 'Such A Long Journey (1992) and 'A Fine Balance' (1996).

(A) Rohinton Mistry

(B) Kiran Nagarkar

(C) Bapsi Sidhwa

(D) Chitra Banrgerjee

2741. Shashi Tharoor was in the news when he campaigned to succeed Kofi Anna as the Secretary-General of the United Nations. However, he lost to Ban Ki-moon of South Korea.
Which of the following is not a book written by him?

(A) The Great Indian Novel

(B) The Argumentative Indian

(C) Show Business

(D) Riot

2742. "13th December, a Reader : The Stranger Case of the Attack on the Indian Parliament", is written by

(A) Aundhati Roy

(B) Anita Desai

(C) Amrita Pritam

(D) Amitav Ghosh

2743. In which Year The New York Times Cited Bhagat as 'The Biggest Selling English Language Novelist in India's History'?

(A) 2009 (B) 2010

(C) 2008 (D) 2011

2744. "There are times in life you wish dinosaurs weren't extinct and could be whistled to come and gulp you down. I went motionless, fingers in mid-air."

In which of Chetan Bhagat's novels are the above mentioned mood and sentiments expressed?

(A) Five Point Someone

(B) Half Girlfriend

(C) 2 States : The Story of My Marriage

(D) One Night @ the Call Center

2745. Examine the following statements and identify one of them which is not correct?

(A) Rudyard Kipling died in the year 1936

(B) He was born in India, but schooled in England

(C) He returned to India as a police constable in Burma

(D) He is the author of Jungle Book and Barrack Room Ballads

2746. Which of the following statements is not correct for Swami Vivekanand?

(A) His childhood name was Vishweshwar Dutt

(B) He founded Ram Krishna Mission

(C) He was a critic of doctrines of Buddhism

(D) He believed in the philosophy of 'Advaitvad'

2747. Assertion (A). Language plays a very pivotal role in human life.

Reason (R). It is the medium through which views are conveyed from one person to another.

Codes:

(A) Both A and R are true and R is the correct explanation

(B) Both A and R are true, but R is not the correct explanation of A

(C) A is true, but R is false

(D) A is false, but R is true

2748. Assertion (A). Modern Indian literature has been greatly influenced by English Literature.

Reason (R). English has become an important element of contemporary Indian culture.

Codes:

(A) Both A and R are true and R is the correct explanation

(B) Both A and R are true, but R is not the correct explanation of A

(C) A is true, but R is false

(D) A is false, but R is true

2749. Assertion (A). Raja Ram Mohan Roy initiated movements to introduce western scientific education through English.

Reason (R). Lord macaulay was the chairman of the committee which was formed to take a decision regarding replacement of Sanskrit and Persian by English.

Codes:

(A) Both A and R are true and R is the correct explanation

(B) Both A and R are true, but R is not the correct explanation of A

(C) A is true, but R is false

(D) A is false, but R is true

2750. Assertion (A). In 1958, The Central Institute of English was started in Hyderabad. Regional institute were established in Bangalore and Chandigarh.

Reason (R). Officially, English has the status of main (prime) language in India.

Codes:

(A) Both A and R are true and R is the correct explanation

(B) Both A and R are true, but R is not the correct explanation of A

(C) A is true, but R is false

(D) A is false, but R is true

2751. Which is the correct sequence of the novels of V.S. Naipaul?

(A) The Mystic Masseur, Miguel Street, The Suffrage of Elvira, A House for Mr Biswas

(B) Miguel Street, The Mystic Masseur, A House for Mr Biswas, The Suffrage of Elvira

(C) The Suffrage of Elvira, Miguel Street, The Mystic Masseur, A house for Mr. Biswas

(D) The Mystic Masseur, The Suffrage of Elvira, Miguel Street, A House for Mr Biswas

2752. Which of the following Anita Desai's works is in correct chronological order?

(A) Cry the Peacock, Voices in the City, Bye-Bye Black Bird, In Custody

(B) Voices in the City, Bye-Bye Black Bird, In Custody, Cry the Peacock

(C) Bye-Bye Black Bird, In Custody, Cry the Peacock, Voices in the City

(D) In Custody, Cry the Peacock, Voices in the City, Bye-Bye Black Bird

2753. Consider the following statements about Rabindranath Tagore

1. was called Gurudev by Mahatma Gandhi
2. founded the Viswabharati University.
3. rejected the title of Knighthood in protest against Quit India Movement.
4. was not a poet.

Which of the statements given above are correct?

(A) 1 and 2 (B) 1 and 4
(C) 3 and 2 (D) 3 and 4

2754. Consider the following statement about Sarojini Naidu

1. was called the Nightingale of India.
2. was not a poet, who wrote on different aspects of Indian life.
3. was not in touch with Symons and Edmund Gosse while in England.
4. was a poet and a great lyric writer, who emoted through her poem.

Which of the statements given above are correct?

(A) 1 and 2 (B) 1 and 4
(C) 3 and 2 (D) 3 and 4

2755. Consider the following statements about Khushwant Singh

1. did not write political commentary and contemporary satire.
2. did not translate Urdu poetry.
3. column contains message of peace.
4. was elected a member of the Rajya Sabha.

Which of the statements given above are correct?

(A) 1 and 2 (B) 1 and 4
(C) 3 and 2 (D) 3 and 4

2756. Given below are some of the famous works Tick the one which is not written by Salman Rushdie.

1. The Enchantress of Florence.
2. The Ground Beneath her Feet.
3. Midnight's Children.
4. Nehru : The Invention of India.

Select the correct answer using the codes given below.

(A) 1 and 2 (B) Only 4
(C) Only 3 (D) Only 1

2757. Consider the following statements Raja Rao .....

1. did not come into content with professor Dickinson.
2. did not go to France to study French literature.
3. wrote the novel 'Kanthapura'.
4. was a great philosopher and novelist.

Which of the statements given above are correct?

(A) 1 and 2 (B) 1 and 4
(C) 3 and 2 (D) 3 and 4

2758. Consider the following statements Anita Desai

1. always tries to explore the psychological state of her characters.
2. uses symbols and images to describe the suffering of the mind.

3. is not affected by domestic men and woman relationship.
4. thinks that the outer life of man or woman decides his or her character.

Which of the statements given above are correct?

(A) 1 and 2 (B) 1 and 4
(C) 3 and 2 (D) 3 and 4

2759. What is common to the following works? Identify of correct description below.

Malgudi Days,
The Swami and Friends,
The Dark Room, The Guide.

Codes:

(A) All these are works by R.K. Narayan
(b All these are works by Shashi Deshpande
(C) All these are works by Mulk Raj Anand
(D) All these are works by Raja Rao

2760. What is common to the following writer? Identify the correct description below.

Jayati
Hayavadana
Tughlaq
Naga Mandal

Codes:

(A) All these are plays by Arun Joshi
(B) All these are names of famous folk tales of Karnataka
(C) All these are famous plays of Karnad Girish
(D) All these are characters from contemporary Kannada literature

2761. Match the following Indian English works with their Indian authors

Indian English Work	**Indian Author**
1. Relationship	a. Khushwant Singh
2. A Sangam City	b. Kamala Da
3. Inheritance of Loss	c. Jayant Mahapatra
4. A rain Rites	d. Kiran Desai

Codes:

(A) 1-a, 2-b, 3-c, 4-d
(B) 1-d, 2-a, 3-d, 4-c
(C) 1-c, 2-d, 3-a, 4-b
(D) 1-d, 2-c, 3-b, 4-a

2762. Match the following

List-1	**List-2**
a. The Interior Landscape	1. 1927
b. Mrinalini	2. 1869
c. Anandmath	3. 1866
d. His Poems and Plays	4. 1967

Codes:

	a	**b**	**c**	**d**
(A)	1	2	3	4
(B)	4	2	1	3
(C)	4	3	2	1
(D)	4	1	3	2

2763. Match the following awards with their recipient Indian Writers.

Awards	**Recipient Indian Writer**
1. Padma Shri	a. A K Ramanujan
2. Padma Shree	b. Kiran Desai
3. Fiction Award	c. Jayant Mahapatra
4. A rain of Rites	d. Kiran Desai

Codes:

(A) 1-a, 2-b, 2-c, 4-d
(B) 1-d, 2-c, 3-b, 4-a
(C) 1-a, 2-c, 3-b, 4-d
(D) 1-c, 2-a, 3-d, 4-d

2764. Match the following Indian English writers with their works

Indian English Writers	**Literary Work**
1. H.N. Chattopadhyaya	a. The Coffin
2. Arundhati Roy	b. The Algebra of Indefinite Justice
3. Anita Desai	c. Fire on the Mountain
4. Amitav Ghosh	d. The Incendiary Circumstances

Codes:

(A) 1-a, 2-b, 3-c, 4-d

(B) 1-d, 2-c, 3-b, 4-a

(C) 1-b, 2-d, 3-a, 4-c

(D) 1-c, 2-a, 3-d, 4-b

2765. In the given series, which one has all the religious texts matched correctly with their Indian English Composers?

(A) The Ramayana—AK Ramanujan, The Bhagvad Gita- Marimathanath Dutt, The Mahabharata-Mohini Chatterjee, Speaking of Shiva-Romesh Chander Dutt

(B) The Ramayana-Romesh Chander Dutt, The Bhagwat Gita-Mohini Chatterjee, The Mahabharata-Manmathanath Dutt, Speaking of Shiva-AK Ramanuj an.

(C) The Ramayana-Mohini Chatterjee, The Bhagwat Gita- AK Ramanujan, The Mahashtra-Romesh Chander Dutt, Speaking of Shiva-Manmathanath Dutt

(D) The Ramyana-Manmathanath Dutt, The Mahashtra-Romesh Chander Dutt, The Bhagwat Gita-AK Ramanujan, Speaking of Shiva-Mohini Chatterjee

2766. In the given series, which one has all the Indian English authors matched correctly with their mood and style of writing?

(A) V.S. Naipaul-Memoirist, Vikram Seth-Elizabethan Style, Sri Aurobindo-Pessimistic, T.P. Kailsam-Humorous Plays

(B) V.S. Naipaul-Humorous Plays, Vikram Seth-Pessimistic, Sri Aurobindo-Elizabethan Style, T.P. Kailsam-Memoirist

(C) V.S. Naipaul-Pessimistic, Vikram Seth-Memoirist, Sri Aurobindo-Elizabethan Style, T.P. Kailsam-Humorous Plays

(D) V.S. Naipaul-Elizabethan Style, Vikram Seth-Humorous Plays, Sri Aurobindo-Memoirist, T.P. Kailsam-Pessimistic

2767. "Where the mind is without fear
And the head in held high
where knowledge is free
Where the world has not been broken into fragments by narrow domestic walls."

(A) This is Amrita'Pritam in 'Kat Canvas'

(B) This is Rabindranath Tagore in 'Gitanjali'

(C) This is Vikram Seth in 'The Golden Gate'

(D) This is Jayanta Mahapatra in 'Life Signs'

2768. "The best and noblest gifts of humanity cannot be the monopoly of a particular race or country; its scope may not be limited nor may it be regarded as the miser's hoard buried underground."

Which Indian English author in which of his/ her works has used the above lines?

(A) Anita Desai, Fasting and Feasting

(B) Jawaharlal Nehru, The Descovery of India

(C) Kiran Desai, The Inheritance of Loss

(D) Mulk Raj Anand, Untouchable

2769. "Gandhiji was not born in freedom. All his life, except for a few months. lay within the framework of colonial rule. A good part of that life lay buried in prison cells. Yet he was always the free man, while those who held him imprisoned were the unfree ones."

Which Indian writers in which of his/ her works has quoted the above lines?

(A) Khushwant Singh, The End of India

(B) Salman Rushdie, The Satanic Verses

(C) Bhabani Bhattacharya, Shadow from Ladakh

(D) Ruskin Bond, Scenes From a Writer's Life

2770. "It is stimulating to live in a society that is not standardised or mechanised, and is free from monotony".

Which of the Indian writers in which of his/ her works has quoted the above lines?

(A) Anita Desai, The Village by the Sea

(B) Khushwant Singh, Khushwant Singh on Women, Sex, Love and Lust

(C) R.K. Narayan, Malgudi Days

(D) Vijay Tendulkar, The Court is in Session

2771. What is the textual Research

(A) Establishment of an authoritative text

(B) Corrections of past edition

(C) Genuineness of the text

(D) All of the above

2772. Which of the following expressions is used when two or more successive footnote refer to the same work?

(A) Et.al (B) Ob.cit:

(C) Loc.cit. (D) Ibid

2773. Which of the following is a parameter for judging the depth of any research?

(A) Funding of the research

(B) Time period of the research

(C) Aims and objectives of the research

(D) Heading of the research

2774. The qualities of a researcher are

(A) a specialist rather than a generalist

(B) diligent and determined in his study

(C) Both (a) and (b)

(D) None of the above

2775. Sin qua non of a good research is

(A) Null Hypothesis

(B) Research supervisor who is good

(C) Well stocked library

(D) A good funding organization

2776. Pre-requisites of a researcher in subject of Humanities and Social Science are

(A) Archives, Supervisor, Topic, Knowledge

(B) Patience, Critical Analysis, Topic, Supervisor

(C) Flexible Thinking, Records Topic, Supervisor

(D) Good Behaviour, Honesty, Supervisor, Topic, Biased Assumptions

2777. Which of the following statements is incorrect? while conducting a literary Research involves

(A) the concerned person can work randomly

(B) Researcher must have a thorough knowledge about the work and critical reviews about the concerned author

(C) the discovery of new facts and fresh interpretation

(D) advancing one's explanation of facts which were previously overlooked.

2778. The main aim of interdisciplinary research is

(A) to reduce the importance of single subject in research domain

(B) to make the research problem more simple

(C) to give a new direction to research methodology

(D) to bring out integrated approach to research

2779. The term 'phenomenology' is related to the process of

(A) ANOVA or Analysis of Variance

(B) probability sampling

(C) qualitative research

(D) None of the above

2780. A team of experts in a specific area of knowledge collected at a place and prepared a study

content for a new stream. This may be termed as

(A) seminar

(B) conference

(C) symposium

(D) workshop

2781. Archival method of research involves

(A) Study of history

(B) quantitative methods

(C) seeking information from historical documents or records
(D) None of the above

2782. "Frequency of occurrence of words, phrases of imagery" is an example of
(A) Discourse Analysis
(B) Quantitation Analysis in English Studies
(C) Textual Analysis
(D) Ethnography studies

2783. An Interviw
(A) is a conversation where questions are asked to extract information
(B) requires a series of pratical skills
(C) Both the above
(D) None of the above

2784. Josephine Miles and Roberto Busa, English Professors did pioneering work in this field. Identify the field.
(A) Archival Method
(B) Digital Humanities
(C) Ethnography
(D) Textual Analysis

2785. The collection, preservation, and dissemination of historical data obtained through planned in-depth, life history interviews can be termed as
(A) ethographical research
(B) auto-biographical research
(C) oral history method of research
(D) None of the above

2786. In English Studies,
(A) Only qualitative methods are used
(B) Only quantitative methods are used
(C) Both qualitative and quantitative method are used
(D) None of the above mentioned methods are used

2787. August Ludwig von Schlözer and Christoph Wilhelm jacob Gatterer of the University of Gottingen introduced this term in the academic discourse. Identify this term.
(A) Ethnography
(B) Discourse
(C) Digital humanities
(D) None of these

2788. Identify the correct statement
(A) Zellig Harris published a series of papers from 1952
(B) These papers reported on work from which he developed transformational grammar in the late 1930's
(C) The term discourse analysis first came into general use following the publication of these papers by Zelling Harris
(D) All of the above

2789. Ethnography is an important methodology used in disciplines such as
(A) social science (B) anthropology
(C) psychology (D) sociology

2790. Identify the correct statement
(A) Interviewing is a quantitative research method
(B) Interviewing includes other research methods like oral history and autodiographical methods
(C) Interviewing does not include ethnographic methods
(D) All of the above

2791. Which of the following are methods of research used in English Literature?
(A) Archival Methods. Oral History, Visual Methodologies
(B) Ethnographic Studies, Discourse Analysis, Textual Analysis
(C) Interviewing, Autobiographical Methods
(D) All of the above

2792. Image is never a 'mere' reflection of reality, but rather a multi-layered text. This statement can be rewritten as
(A) Image is a refection method
(B) Image is a speaking picture
(C) Images is sometimes as reflection of reality
(D) None of the above

2793. Ethnographic research technique can be categorized into categories such as
(A) travel writings
(B) reading groups
(C) audience response criticism
(D) All of the above

2794. Discourse analysis and text linguistics are closely related with an essential difference
(A) True (B) False
(C) Partially True (D) Partially False

2795. Textual analysis on a text means making an educated guess at some of the most likely

interpretations that might be made of that text.
(A) True (B) False
(C) Partly false (D) Partly true

2796. Creative writing
(A) Is an important element within English department
(B) Represents the inventions and generation of ideas images and performances
(C) Both of the above
(D) None of the above

2797. Research in conducted
(A) to generate new knowledge
(B) to develop a theory
(C) not to obtain research degree
(D) reinterpret existing knowledge
Which of the above is correct?
(A) 1, 3, and 2 (B) 3, 2 and 4
(C) 2, 1 and 3 (D) 1, 2 and 4

2798. The review of Research reports should be done in context of
(A) investigator bias
(B) cultural context
(C) methodological factors
Which one of the following is correct?
(A) 1 and 3 (B) Only 1
(C) Only 3 (D) 1, 2 and 3

2799. Which of the following options are the main tasks of research in modern society?
(A) To add on to the existing knowledge
(B) To explore new facts
(C) To conduct a systematic examination and analyse the data collected in an objective manner
(D) To evaluate the earlier writings
which of the following options is correct?
(A) 1, 2 and 3
(B) 4, 2 and 3
(C) 2 and 3
(D) 2, 3 and 4

2800. Select the most suitable option
A. Discourse analysis and text linguistics have an essential difference
B. Discourse analysis aims at revealing the socio-psychological characteristics of a person rather than text structure.

Codes:
(A) Both A and B are correct.
(B) Both A and B are false
(C) Only A is correct
(D) Only B is correct

2801. Which of the following is true about Cultural studies? Cultural Studies believes literary texts are symptomatic of
1. The authors' response/ reaction to their social dynamics.
2. The imaginative faculties of their authors.
3. A close reading of the works of canonical writers.
4. A nostalgia for the bygone era/ or a vision for a utopian society.

(A) 1 and 2 (B) 1 and 3
(C) 1 and 4 (D) 2 and 4

2802. Which of the following is in the correct order?
(A) Drama in Performance – Modern Tragedy – May Day Manifesto — Writing in Society
(B) Modern Tragedy – May Day Manifesto – Writing in Society — Drama in Performance

(C) May Day Manifesto – Writing in Society – Drama in Performance — Modern Tragedy
(D) Drama in Performance – May Day Manifesto – Modern Tragedy — Writing in Society

2803. Match the following works with their Authors.

Works
1. Language and Literature
2. Continuing Education
3. Notes towards The Definition of Culture
4. Situating Marx

Authors
5. Stuart Hall
6. T. S Eliot
7. Richard Hoggart
8. Raymond Williams

(A) 1-8, 2-7, 3-6, 4-5
(C) 1-8, 2-5, 3-6, 4-7
(B) 1-5, 2-7, 3-6, 4-8
(D) 1-6, 2-5, 3-8, 4-7

2804. Who among the following is considered to be founding figures of Feminism in the United States academia?
(A) Virginia Woolf
(B) Elaine Showalter
(C) Helen Cixous
(D) Sandra Gilbert and Susan Gubar

2805. Arrange the following works by Elaine Showalter sequentially.
1. Inventing Herself
2. Speaking of Gender
3. Teaching Literature
4. Sexual Anarchy

(A) 2-4-1-3 (B) 1-3-2-4
(C) 4-3-2-1 (D) 3-4-1-2

2806. What is not true about Mary Wollstonecraft?
(A) She was a twentieth century advocate of Women's rights.
(B) She was posthumously regarded as a feminist
(C) A Vindication of the Rights of Women is her most notable contribution.
(D) Her daughter was a great writer, Mary Shelley.

2807. Which among the following is in correct sequence?
(A) Thoughts on the Education of Daughter — Mary — A Vindication of the Roghts of Woman — Maria
(B) Thoughts on the Education of Daughter — Maria — A Vindication of the Roghts of Woman — Mary
(C) Mary — A Vindication of the Roghts of Woman — Maria - Thoughts on the Education of Daughter
(D) Thoughts on the Education of Daughter — Maria - Mary — A Vindication of the Roghts of Woman

2808. Arrange the following works by Julia Kristeva in their correct sequence.
1. Power of Horror
2. Semiotike
3. Revolution in Poetic Language
4. The Samurai

(A) 2-3-1-4 (B) 1-3-2-4
(C) 4-3-2-1 (D) 3-4-1-2

2809. Which among the following is not correctly matched?
(A) This Sex Which is not One : 1966
(B) Ethics of Sexual Difference : 1982
(C) To Be TV : 1994
(D) Forgetting of Air : 1999

2810. Which among the following is in the chronological order?
(A) The Newly Born Woman — Stigmata — Three Steps on the Ladder of Writing - Dream I Tell You
(B) The Newly Born Woman - Dream I Tell You - Stigmata – Three Steps on the Ladder of Writing

(C) The Newly Born Woman— Three Steps on the Ladder of Writing — Dream I Tell You— Stigmata

(D) Stigmata - Three Steps on the Ladder of Writing — Dream I Tell You - The Newly Born Woman

2811. Match the following works with their authors

Works

1. Angst
2. Everyday Prayers
3. Possessions
4. Parting Ways

Authors

5. Luce Irigaray
6. Helen Cixous
7. Julia Kristeva
8. Judith Butler

(A) 1-6, 2-5, 3-7, 4-8

(B) 1-5, 2-7, 3-6, 4-8

(C) 1-7, 2-5, 3-8, 4-6

(D) 1-6, 2-8, 3-5, 4-7

2812. Match the following works to their dates of publication

1. In Other Worlds
2. A Critique of Postcolonial Reason
3. Can the Subaltern Speak?
4. The Postcolonial Critic

Dates

5. 2008
6. 1990
7. 1999
8. 1987

(A) 1-8, 2-7, 3-5, 4-6

(B) 1-5, 2-8, 3-7, 4-6

(C) 1-5, 2-6, 3-7, 4-8

(D) 1-7, 2-6, 3-8, 4-5

2813. Identify the essay from which the following quote has been taken:

"The class which has the means of material production at its disposal, has control at the same time over the means of mental production, so that thereby, generally speaking, the ideas of those who lack the means of mental production are subject to it."

(A) The German Ideology

(B) When Goods Get Together

(C) Value, Price and Profit

(D) Sur La Reproduction

2814. Assertion. In a capitalist society, the proletariat are exploit.

Reason. The bourgeoise amasses the surplus production and this leads to unequal distribution of profit.

(A) Both A and R are true.

(B) Both A and R are false.

(C) Both A and R are true, but R is not the correct explanation of (A)

(D) Both A and R are true and R is the correct explanation (A).

2815. Which of these is in the correct sequence?

(A) The Communist Manifesto- The Civil War in the United States — Karl Marx on India— Notes on James Mill

(B) The Communist Manifesto - Notes on James Mill - The Civil War in the United States — Karl Marx on India

(C) The Communist Manifesto — The Civil War in the United States — Notes on James Mill — Karl Marx on India

(D) Notes on James Mill - The Communist Manifesto - The Civil War in the United States — Karl Marx on India

2816. Arrange the following works by Louis Althusser in chronologicaliorder.

1. How to be a Marxist in Philosophy
2. The Humanist Controversy and Other Writings
3. Essays in Self Criticism
4. Montesquieu, Rousseau, Marx

(A) 1-2-3-4 (B) 4-3-2-1

(C) 2-4-1-3 (D) 1-3-2-4

2817. Assertion. Gramsci's theory of hegemony reveals that bourgeoise use cultural institutions to maintain their power.

Reason. The bourgeoise ideology is emanated as 'common sense' and becomes the belief system in a capitalist economy.

(A) Both A and R are true.

(B) Both A and R are false.

(C) Both A and R are true and R is the correct explanation of A.

(D) Both A and R are true but R is not the correct explanation of A.

2818. Which of the following is not true for post structuralism?

(A) Post-structuralism critiqued structuralism.

(B) It emphasised the plurality and multiplicity of the meanings in language

(C) It analysed the effects of post war trauma on human brains

(D) It refused to construct a subject within the comprehensibility of language.

2819. Arrange the following works by Roland Barthes in chronological order.

1. Mythologies
2. Camera Lucida
3. The Death of the Author
4. A Lover's Discourse

(A) 1-3-4-2

(B) 1-4-2-3

(C) 3-4-2-1

(D) 2-4-1-3

2820. Which of the following is in the correct sequence?

(a) Margins of Philosophy - Glas — The Gift of Death - Archive Fever

(B) Margins of Philosophy - The Gift of Death - Glas — Archive Fever

(C) Margins of Philosophy – The Gift of Death — Archive Fever- Glas

(D) Glas — Margins of Philosophy - The Gift of Death - Archive Fever

2821. Match the following works with their authors.

Works

1. S/Z
2. The Beast and the Sovereign
3. The Order of Things
4. Antologia

Authors

5. Antonio Gramsci
6. Michael Foucault
7. Jacques Derrida
8. Roland Barthes

Codes:

(A) 1-8, 2-7, 3-6, 4-5

(B) 1-7, 2-8, 3-6, 4-5

(C) 1-6, 2-8, 3-5, 4-7

(D) 1-5, 2-6, 3-7, 4-8

2822. Consider the point of commonality between the following works?

1. In a Materialist Way
2. The Object of Literature
3. Theory of Literary Production
4. Reading Capital

Codes:

(A) These are all works by Pierre Bourdieu

(B) These are all works by Pierre Macherey

(C) These are all works by Umberto Eco

(D) These are all works by Raymond Williams

2823. In the field of Dalit studies, which of these cannot contribute to theorizing or contextualizing Dalit literature?

(A) Gail Omvedt's Seeking Begumpura

(B) Arjun Dangle's Poisoned Bread

(C) B. R. Ambedkar's The Annihilation of Caste

(D) Raja Rao's Kanthapura

2824. "No, we don't believe that any woman should have this choice. No woman should be authorised to stay at home to bring up her children. Society should be totally different. Women should not have that choice, too many women will make that one. It is a way of forcing women in a certain direction."

Identify the speaker of the above lines.

(A) Simon de Beauvoir

(B) Julia Kristeva
(C) Elaine Showalter
(D) Gayatri Spivack

2825. In the following series, which of the set is correctly matched?
(A) Karl Marx - Critique of Political Economy, Theodor Adorno — The Cultural Industry, Terry Eagleton — Marxism and Literary Criticism, Raymond Williams — The Country and the City
(B) Karl Marx - The Cultural Industry, Theodor Adorno — Critique of Political Economy, Terry Eagleton — Marxism and Literary Criticism, Raymond Williams — The Country and the City
(C) Karl Marx — Critique of Political Economy, Theodor Adorno - The Country and the City, Terry Eagleton —i The Cultural Industry, Raymond Williams — Marxism and Literary Criticism
(D) Karl Marx — The Country and the City, Theodor Adorno — Critique of Political Economy, Terry Eagleton — Marxism and Literary Criticism, Raymond Williams — The Cultural Industry

2826. Match the following works to their authors,

Works
a. The Madwoman in the Attic
b. Language and Sexual Difference
c. Simon de Beauvoir: A Re-reading
d. The Second Sex

Authors
1. Susan Gubar and Sandra Gilbert
2. Simone de Beauvoir M
3. Judith Okely
4. Susan Sellers

Codes:

	a	b	c	d
(A)	2	3	4	1
(B)	4	1	2	3
(C)	1	2	3	4
(D)	1	4	3	2

2827. Which of the following is true about the 'Two Treatises of Government'
1. It was published anonymously by John Locke
2. It was published anonymously by Sir Robert Filmer.
3. It is a treatise stating Filmer's contestations against the paternalistic view of the government.
4. It was published in 1689.

Codes:
(A) 1 and 4
(B) 2 and 4
(C) 2 and 3
(D) 1 and 3

2828. What is not true about cultural studies?
(A) Cultural studies is an inter-disciplinary field.
(B) Cultural studies reads the different ways in which texts are read
(C) Cultural studies is dependent on canonical writers' perspectives.
(D) Cultural studies examines various socio-political and economic factors of the authors as well as the characters of a given text.

2829. A researcher conducts a research on finding out which leadership style contributes more to institutional effectiveness. This will be an example of
(A) Basic research
(B) Action research
(C) Applied research
(D) None of the above

2830. In this research, the field study the laws to draw more and more clear ideas about the problem. Identify this research
(A) Applied research
(B) Action research
(C) Philosophical research
(D) All of the above

2831. Identify the work below that does not belong to the literature of the eighteenth century
(A) *Advancement of Learning*
(B) *Gulliver's Travels*
(C) *The Spectator*
(D) *An Epistle to Dr. Arbuthnot*

2832. Which, among the following, is a place through which John Bunyan's Christian does NOT pass ?
(A) The Slough of Despond
(B) Mount Helicon
(C) The Valley of Humiliation
(D) Vanity Fair

2833. The period of Queen Victoria's reign is
(A) 1830–1900
(B) 1837–1901
(C) 1830–1901
(D) 1837–1900

2834. Which of the following statements about *The Lyrical Ballads* is NOT true ?
(A) It carried only *one* ballad proper, which was Coleridge's The Rime of the Ancient Mariner.
(B) It also carried pastoral and other poems.
(C) It carried a "Preface" which Wordsworth added in 1800.
(D) It also printed from Gray's Elegy Written in a Country Churchyard.

2835. One of the following texts was published earlier than 1955. Identify the text
(A) William Golding, *The Inheritors*
(B) Philip Larkin, *The Less Deceived*
(C) William Empson, *Collected Poems*
(D) Samuel Becket, *Waiting for Godot*

2836. Who among the poets in England during the 1930s had left–leaning tendencies ?
(A) T. S. Eliot, Ezra Pound, Richard Aldington
(B) Wilfred Owen, Siegfried Sassoon, Rupert Brooke
(C) W. H. Auden, Louis MacNeice, Cecil Day Lewis
(D) J. Fleckner, W. H. Davies, Edward Marsh

2837. Match the following :
1. The Sage of Concord
2. The Nun of Amherst
3. Mark Twain
4. Old Possum
5. Emily Dickinson
6. R.W. Emerson
7. T.S. Eliot
8. Samuel L. Clemens
(A) 1–6; 2–5; 3–8; 4–7
(B) 1–5; 2–6; 3–7; 4–8
(C) 1–8; 2–7; 3–6; 4–5
(D) 1–7; 2–8; 3–5; 4–6

2838. Name the theorist who divided poets into "strong" and "weak" and popularized the practice of misreading
(A) Alan Bloom
(B) Harold Bloom
(C) Geoffrey Hartman
(D) Stanley Fish

2839. In *The Rape of the Lock* Pope repeatedly compares Belinda to
(A) the sun
(B) the moon
(C) the north star
(D) the rose

2840. Which of the following awards is not given to Indian–English writers ?
(A) The Booker Prize
(B) The Sahitya Akademi Award
(C) The Gyanpeeth
(D) Whitbread Prize

2841. Identify the correct statement below
(A) *Gorboduc* is a comedy, while Ralph Roister Doister and *Gammer Gurton's Needle* are tragedies.
(B) *Gorboduc* is a tragedy, while Ralph Roister Doister and *Gammer Gurton's Needle* are comedies.

(C) All of them are problem plays.
(D) All of them are farces.

2842. W.M. Thackeray's *Vanity Fair* owes its title to
(A) Browning's *Fifine at the Fair*
(B) Shakespeare's *Merchant of* Venice
(C) Goldsmith's *Vicar of Wakefield*
(D) Bunyan's *Pilgrim's Progress*

2843. The Puritans shut down all theaters in England in
(A) 1642 (B) 1640
(C) 1659 (D) 1660

2844. Who of the following was **not** a contemporary of Wordsworth and Coleridge ?
(A) Robert Southey
(B) Sir Walter Scott
(C) William Hazlitt
(D) A. C. Swinburne

2845. Which of the following statements about *Waiting for Godot* is NOT true ?
1. It carries a subtitle: "a tragicomedy in two acts".
2. It carries a subtitle: "a tragicomedy in two scenes".
3. It carries a subtitle: "a tragicomedy in two parts".
4. It does not carry a subtitle.

(A) 4 (B) 2
(C) 3 (D) 1

2846. The Bloomsbury Group included British intellectuals, critics, writers and artists. Who among the following belonged to the Bloomsbury Group ?
I. John Maynard Keynes, Lytton Strachey
II. E.M. Forster, Roger Fry, Clive Bell
III. Patrick Brunty, Paul Haworth
IV. Thomas Hardy, Henry James, Walter Pater

(A) I and II (B) I
(C) II and III (D) IV

2847. Who, among the following is credited with the making of the first authoritative *Dictionary of the* English Language ?
(A) Bishop Berkeley
(B) Samuel Johnson
(C) Edmund Burke
(D) Horace Walpole

2848. In Dryden's *Essay of Dramatic Poesy* (1668), who opens the discussion on behalf of the ancients ?
(A) Lisideius (B) Crites
(C) Eugenius (D) Neander

2849. The term *invective* refers to
(A) the abusive writing or speech in which there is harsh denunciation of some person or thing.
(B) an insulting writing attack upon a real person, in verse or prose, usually involving caricature and ridicule.
(C) a written or spoken text in which an apparently straightforward statement or event is undermined in its context so as to give it a very different significance.
(D) the chanting or reciting of words deemed to have magical power.

2850. Which of the following novels depicts the plight of the Bangladeshi immigrants in East London ?
(A) *How far can you go*
(B) *The White Teeth*
(C) *An Equal Music*
(D) *Brick Lane*

ANSWERS

1. (A) 2. (C) 3. (B) 4. (C) 5. (D) 6. (C) 7. (B) 8. (A) 9. (D) 10. (C)
11. (B) 12. (A) 13. (A) 14. (C) 15. (B) 16. (D) 17. (B) 18. (A) 19. (C) 20. (D)
21. (B) 22. (C) 23. (C) 24. (A) 25. (B) 26. (B) 27. (C) 28. (C) 29. (C) 30. (A)
31. (D) 32. (B) 33. (B) 34. (C) 35. (C) 36. (C) 37. (D) 38. (B) 39. (B) 40. (A)
41. (B) 42. (D) 43. (B) 44. (B) 45. (C) 46. (A) 47. (A) 48. (D) 49. (D) 50. (B)
51. (C) 52. (B) 53. (D) 54. (C) 55. (A) 56. (A) 57. (D) 58. (D) 59. (C) 60. (C)
61. (B) 62. (C) 63. (D) 64. (B) 65. (A) 66. (C) 67. (B) 68. (C) 69. (B) 70. (A)
71. (C) 72. (D) 73. (B) 74. (A) 75. (C) 76. (B) 77. (C) 78. (D) 79. (B) 80. (D)
81. (D) 82. (A) 83. (B) 84. (A) 85. (C) 86. (C) 87. (D) 88. (A) 89. (D) 90. (B)
91. (A) 92. (D) 93. (B) 94. (C) 95. (C) 96. (D) 97. (B) 98. (C) 99. (B) 100. (A)
101. (C) 102. (D) 103. (B) 104. (C) 105. (A) 106. (D) 107. (C) 108. (B) 109. (D) 110. (C)
111. (C) 112. (A) 113. (D) 114. (B) 115. (C) 116. (D) 117. (A) 118. (B) 119. (D) 120. (C)
121. (B) 122. (C) 123. (D) 124. (B) 125. (B) 126. (A) 127. (B) 128. (C) 129. (B) 130. (D)
131. (C) 132. (B) 133. (A) 134. (A) 135. (B) 136. (A) 137. (C) 138. (D) 139. (B) 140. (C)
141. (A) 142. (C) 143. (D) 144. (B) 145. (C) 146. (B) 147. (C) 148. (D) 149. (B) 150. (D)
151. (A) 152. (D) 153. (B) 154. (C) 155. (C) 156. (A) 157. (B) 158. (D) 159. (C) 160. (A)
161. (B) 162. (C) 163. (D) 164. (C) 165. (B) 166. (D) 167. (A) 168. (D) 169. (C) 170. (A)
171. (D) 172. (B) 173. (C) 174. (A) 175. (C) 176. (D) 177. (C) 178. (D) 179. (B) 180. (D)
181. (A) 182. (C) 183. (D) 184. (B) 185. (A) 186. (B) 187. (C) 188. (C) 189. (A) 190. (A)
191. (A) 192. (B) 193. (C) 194. (C) 195. (C) 196. (A) 197. (C) 198. (B) 199. (A) 200. (A)
201. (C) 202. (B) 203. (B) 204. (B) 205. (B) 206. (D) 207. (B) 208. (A) 209. (A) 210. (C)
211. (C) 212. (B) 213. (D) 214. (C) 215. (A) 216. (D) 217. (B) 218. (C) 219. (D) 220. (B)
221. (A) 222. (C) 223. (B) 224. (B) 225. (A) 226. (B) 227. (B) 228. (B) 229. (D) 230. (D)
231. (C) 232. (C) 233. (A) 234. (C) 235. (A) 236. (A) 237. (B) 238. (A) 239. (D) 240. (C)
241. (D) 242. (C) 243. (B) 244. (A) 245. (B) 246. (B) 247. (D) 248. (B) 249. (C) 250. (B)
251. (D) 252. (A) 253. (A) 254. (B) 255. (C) 256. (A) 257. (D) 258. (B) 259. (C) 260. (A)
261. (D) 262. (A) 263. (C) 264. (C) 265. (A) 266. (C) 267. (B) 268. (A) 269. (D) 270. (B)
271. (D) 272. (C) 273. (B) 274. (C) 275. (B) 276. (D) 277. (D) 278. (A) 279. (B) 280. (A)
281. (B) 282. (C) 283. (A) 284. (D) 285. (A) 286. (B) 287. (D) 288. (C) 289. (B) 290. (B)
291. (D) 292. (D) 293. (A) 294. (B) 295. (C) 296. (C) 297. (B) 298. (C) 299. (B) 300. (C)
301. (D) 302. (A) 303. (C) 304. (A) 305. (D) 306. (B) 307. (C) 308. (C) 309. (B) 310. (C)
311. (B) 312. (A) 313. (C) 314. (D) 315. (B) 316. (B) 317. (A) 318. (C) 319. (D) 320. (B)
321. (C) 322. (A) 323. (D) 324. (B) 325. (A) 326. (C) 327. (B) 328. (A) 329. (C) 330. (D)
331. (C) 332. (B) 333. (C) 334. (A) 335. (B) 336. (C) 337. (D) 338. (B) 339. (D) 340. (B)
341. (C) 342. (B) 343. (A) 344. (B) 345. (D) 346. (C) 347. (C) 348. (C) 349. (D) 350. (B)
351. (B) 352. (B) 353. (A) 354. (C) 355. (D) 356. (A) 357. (C) 358. (C) 359. (D) 360. (A)
361. (D) 362. (D) 363. (C) 364. (B) 365. (D) 366. (A) 367. (A) 368. (C) 369. (C) 370. (B)
371. (C) 372. (B) 373. (C) 374. (D) 375. (D) 376. (B) 377. (A) 378. (B) 379. (D) 380. (B)
381. (D) 382. (B) 383. (C) 374. (D) 385. (C) 386. (B) 387. (A) 388. (D) 389. (D) 390. (A)

391. (B)	392. (A)	393. (B)	394. (A)	395. (B)	396. (D)	397. (C)	398. (C)	399. (C)	400. (D)
401. (B)	402. (A)	403. (C)	404. (C)	405. (C)	406. (D)	407. (B)	408. (A)	409. (C)	410. (D)
411. (A)	412. (C)	413. (B)	414. (D)	415. (A)	416. (B)	417. (C)	418. (A)	419. (B)	420. (C)
421. (C)	422. (C)	423. (B)	424. (D)	425. (C)	426. (D)	427. (D)	428. (A)	429. (B)	430. (B)
431. (A)	432. (C)	433. (D)	434. (A)	435. (A)	436. (C)	437. (B)	438. (B)	439. (D)	440. (C)
441. (C)	442. (B)	443. (D)	444. (A)	445. (B)	446. (D)	447. (C)	448. (B)	449. (A)	450. (C)
451. (B)	452. (C)	453. (D)	454. (C)	455. (C)	456. (D)	457. (A)	458. (D)	459. (B)	460. (C)
461. (D)	462. (B)	463. (B)	464. (D)	465. (D)	466. (B)	467. (A)	468. (D)	469. (C)	470. (B)
471. (B)	472. (A)	473. (C)	474. (C)	475. (A)	476. (C)	477. (D)	478. (B)	479. (C)	480. (D)
481. (C)	482. (C)	483. (B)	484. (A)	485. (B)	486. (B)	487. (C)	488. (C)	489. (B)	490. (D)
491. (A)	492. (C)	493. (A)	494. (D)	495. (A)	496. (B)	497. (C)	498. (B)	499. (C)	500. (D)
501. (B)	502. (C)	503. (B)	504. (D)	505. (C)	506. (C)	507. (A)	508. (B)	509. (D)	510. (B)
511. (A)	512. (C)	513. (B)	514. (C)	515. (A)	516. (B)	517. (A)	518. (C)	519. (D)	520. (D)
521. (D)	522. (C)	523. (B)	524. (B)	525. (A)	526. (C)	527. (D)	528. (D)	529. (C)	530. (D)
531. (B)	532. (B)	533. (A)	534. (C)	535. (B)	536. (D)	537. (C)	538. (B)	539. (C)	540. (A)
541. (A)	542. (A)	543. (C)	544. (B)	545. (A)	546. (C)	547. (B)	548. (D)	549. (C)	550. (D)
551. (B)	552. (A)	553. (B)	554. (C)	555. (C)	556. (B)	557. (C)	558. (C)	559. (D)	560. (B)
561. (A)	562. (D)	563. (D)	564. (D)	565. (B)	566. (C)	567. (A)	568. (C)	569. (B)	570. (D)
571. (B)	572. (B)	573. (C)	574. (A)	575. (C)	576. (D)	577. (C)	578. (D)	579. (C)	580. (C)
581. (B)	582. (C)	583. (C)	584. (A)	585. (C)	586. (C)	587. (B)	588. (A)	589. (C)	590. (D)
591. (C)	592. (B)	593. (A)	594. (D)	595. (C)	596. (D)	597. (B)	598. (B)	599. (D)	600. (B)
601. (A)	602. (B)	603. (D)	604. (A)	605. (B)	606. (D)	607. (A)	608. (D)	609. (B)	610. (D)
611. (B)	612. (C)	613. (D)	614. (A)	615. (D)	616.(B)	617. (C)	618. (B)	619. (C)	620. (A)
621. (D)	622. (A)	623. (C)	624. (B)	625. (B)	626. (D)	627. (A)	628. (B)	629. (D)	630. (D)
631. (C)	632. (C)	633. (B)	634. (A)	635. (D)	636. (D)	637. (C)	638. (B)	639. (D)	640. (C)
641. (B)	642. (D)	643. (C)	644. (B)	645. (C)	646. (B)	647. (C)	648. (C)	649. (A)	650. (D)
651. (B)	652. (D)	653. (C)	654. (B)	655. (C)	656. (A)	657. (C)	658. (C)	649. (B)	660. (B)
661. (C)	662. (B)	663. (C)	664. (C)	665. (B)	666. (B)	667. (A)	668. (A)	669. (C)	670. (D)
671. (C)	672. (D)	673. (B)	674. (D)	675. (C)	676. (D)	677. (A)	678. (C)	679. (D)	680. (D)
681. (A)	682. (B)	683. (D)	684. (C)	685. (D)	686. (A)	687. (A)	688. (B)	689. (C)	690. (D)
691. (C)	692. (B)	693. (A)	694. (B)	695. (D)	696. (A)	697. (C)	698. (B)	699. (D)	700. (C)
701. (B)	702. (C)	703. (A)	704. (B)	705. (B)	706. (A)	707. (D)	708. (D)	709. (A)	710. (D)
711. (B)	712. (B)	713. (C)	714. (B)	715. (C)	716. (D)	717. (C)	718. (A)	719. (D)	720. (A)
721. (D)	722. (B)	723. (A)	724. (C)	725. (A)	726. (D)	727. (A)	728. (D)	729. (C)	730. (C)
731. (D)	732. (B)	733. (D)	734. (D)	735. (C)	736. (B)	737. (C)	738. (B)	739. (A)	740. (B)
741. (B)	742. (A)	743. (C)	744. (B)	745. (B)	746. (C)	747. (D)	748. (C)	749. (D)	750. (A)
751. (A)	752. (B)	753. (B)	754. (C)	755. (B)	756. (A)	757. (A)	758. (A)	759. (C)	760. (B)
761. (B)	762. (C)	763. (B)	764. (B)	765. (D)	766. (C)	767. (D)	768. (C)	769. (B)	770. (A)
771. (C)	772. (C)	773. (B)	774. (C)	775. (A)	776. (C)	777. (A)	778. (C)	779. (B)	780. (B)
781. (A)	782. (A)	783. (B)	784. (C)	785. (D)	786. (D)	787. (C)	788. (A)	789. (C)	790. (B)
791. (C)	792. (D)	793. (B)	794. (D)	795. (A)	796. (B)	797. (D)	798. (C)	799. (D)	800. (B)
801. (A)	802. (B)	803. (C)	804. (D)	805. (A)	806. (C)	807. (B)	808. (D)	809. (A)	810. (B)

811. (C)	812. (A)	813. (B)	814. (C)	815. (D)	816. (B)	817. (D)	818. (B)	819. (A)	820. (B)
821. (B)	822. (C)	823. (C)	824. (B)	825. (D)	826. (C)	827. (A)	828. (B)	829. (D)	830. (C)
831. (D)	832. (A)	833. (C)	834. (D)	835. (D)	836. (D)	837. (B)	838. (A)	839. (D)	840. (B)
841. (C)	842. (D)	843. (C)	844. (B)	845. (D)	846. (B)	847. (D)	848. (C)	849. (A)	850. (B)
851. (B)	852. (D)	853. (A)	854. (C)	855. (A)	856. (C)	857. (B)	858. (D)	859. (C)	860. (D)
861. (B)	862. (C)	863. (D)	864. (A)	865. (C)	866. (D)	867. (B)	868. (C)	869. (B)	870. (A)
871. (B)	872. (A)	873. (C)	874. (D)	875. (B)	876. (A)	877. (B)	878. (D)	879. (D)	880. (A)
881. (C)	882. (B)	883. (C)	884. (B)	885. (A)	886. (C)	887. (D)	888. (B)	889. (A)	890. (B)
891. (C)	892. (B)	893. (D)	894. (C)	895. (D)	896. (A)	897. (B)	898. (C)	899. (D)	900. (B)
901. (A)	902. (C)	903. (B)	904. (C)	905. (D)	906. (B)	907. (A)	908. (C)	909. (A)	910. (C)
911. (A)	912. (B)	913. (A)	914. (C)	915. (C)	916. (A)	917. (D)	918. (C)	919. (C)	920. (A)
921. (A)	922. (B)	923. (D)	924. (B)	925. (C)	926. (B)	927. (B)	928. (C)	929. (D)	930. (A)
931. (C)	932. (B)	933. (C)	934. (B)	935. (A)	936. (A)	937. (B)	938. (B)	939. (B)	940. (B)
941. (B)	942. (A)	943. (D)	944. (A)	945. (B)	946. (D)	947. (A)	948. (C)	949. (B)	950. (B)
951. (D)	952. (C)	953. (B)	954. (C)	955. (B)	956. (D)	957. (B)	958. (A)	959. (C)	960. (C)
961. (A)	962. (B)	963. (A)	964. (B)	965. (A)	966. (C)	967. (B)	968. (B)	969. (C)	970. (D)
971. (B)	972. (A)	973. (A)	974. (C)	975. (D)	976. (C)	977. (B)	978. (C)	979. (A)	980. (A)
981. (D)	982. (C)	983. (C)	984. (B)	985. (D)	986. (A)	987. (D)	988. (C)	989. (B)	990. (A)
991. (B)	992. (B)	993. (A)	994. (C)	995. (C)	996. (D)	997. (B)	998. (C)	999. (B)	1000. (A)
1001. (A)	1002. (C)	1003. (C)	1004. (D)	1005. (A)	1006. (C)	1007. (D)	1008. (B)	1009. (C)	1010. (A)
1011. (D)	1012. (B)	1013. (C)	1014. (D)	1015. (C)	1016. (A)	1017. (A)	1018. (D)	1019. (B)	1020. (D)
1021. (B)	1022. (C)	1023. (D)	1024. (B)	1025. (A)	1026. (B)	1027. (B)	1028. (B)	1029. (C)	1030. (C)
1031. (A)	1032. (D)	1033. (C)	1034. (B)	1035. (D)	1036. (B)	1037. (A)	1038. (C)	1039. (B)	1040. (A)
1041. (B)	1042. (B)	1043. (D)	1044. (C)	1045. (C)	1046. (B)	1047. (D)	1048. (A)	1049. (D)	1050. (C)
1051. (D)	1052. (C)	1053. (C)	1054. (B)	1055. (D)	1056. (B)	1057. (A)	1058. (C)	1059. (B)	1060. (D)
1061. (D)	1062. (B)	1063. (B)	1064. (C)	1065. (A)	1066. (C)	1067. (C)	1068. (B)	1069. (D)	1070. (B)
1071. (B)	1072. (A)	1073. (C)	1074. (D)	1075. (D)	1076. (C)	1077. (B)	1078. (D)	1079. (B)	1080. (B)
1081. (C)	1082. (A)	1083. (D)	1084. (D)	1085. (B)	1086. (A)	1087. (C)	1088. (B)	1089. (C)	1090. (D)
1091. (B)	1092. (D)	1093. (B)	1094. (A)	1095. (A)	1096. (C)	1097. (D)	1098. (C)	1099. (B)	1100. (A)
1101. (C)	1102. (D)	1103. (B)	1104. (C)	1105. (B)	1106. (D)	1107. (C)	1108. (A)	1109. (B)	1110. (C)
1111. (D)	1112. (D)	1113. (B)	1114. (A)	1115. (B)	1116. (D)	1117. (C)	1118. (C)	1119. (B)	1120. (B)
1121. (B)	1122. (D)	1123. (C)	1124. (A)	1125. (C)	1126. (D)	1127. (C)	1128. (C)	1129. (A)	1130. (C)
1131. (C)	1132. (D)	1133. (B)	1134. (D)	1135. (D)	1136. (C)	1137. (B)	1138. (A)	1139. (D)	1140. (B)
1141. (B)	1142. (A)	1143. (B)	1144. (A)	1145. (B)	1146. (B)	1147. (C)	1148. (B)	1149. (D)	1150. (B)
1151. (C)	1152. (B)	1153. (C)	1154. (C)	1155. (B)	1156. (D)	1157. (B)	1158. (C)	1159. (B)	1160. (A)
1161. (C)	1162. (C)	1163. (C)	1164. (B)	1165. (B)	1166. (C)	1167. (B)	1168. (B)	1169. (C)	1170. (D)
1171. (C)	1172. (C)	1173. (B)	1174. (C)	1175. (A)	1176. (B)	1177. (B)	1178. (A)	1179. (B)	1180. (D)
1181. (C)	1182. (B)	1183. (C)	1184. (D)	1185. (A)	1186. (B)	1187. (C)	1188. (A)	1189. (B)	1190. (C)
1191. (D)	1192. (A)	1193. (D)	1194. (A)	1195. (B)	1196. (A)	1197. (C)	1198. (B)	1199. (B)	1200. (D)
1201. (A)	1202. (C)	1203. (D)	1204. (B)	1205. (A)	1206. (D)	1207. (A)	1208. (B)	1209. (D)	1210. (C)
1211. (A)	1212. (C)	1213. (B)	1214. (A)	1215. (D)	1216. (A)	1217. (C)	1218. (B)	1219. (D)	1220. (B)
1221. (C)	1222. (B)	1223. (D)	1224. (C)	1225. (A)	1226. (B)	1227. (C)	1228. (D)	1229. (B)	1230. (C)

1231. (A) 1232. (C) 1233. (B) 1234. (D) 1235. (B) 1236. (C) 1237. (B) 1238. (D) 1239. (B) 1240. (B)
1241. (A) 1242. (B) 1243. (D) 1244. (C) 1245. (B) 1246. (B) 1247. (C) 1248. (B) 1249. (A) 1250. (B)
1251. (A) 1252. (B) 1253. (C) 1254. (B) 1255. (D) 1256. (B) 1257. (B) 1258. (B) 1259. (D) 1260. (C)
1261. (D) 1262. (B) 1263. (A) 1264. (D) 1265. (A) 1266. (D) 1267. (C) 1268. (B) 1269. (D) 1270. (A)
1271. (C) 1272. (B) 1273. (D) 1274. (B) 1275. (A) 1276. (B) 1277. (D) 1278. (C) 1279. (C) 1280. (A)
1281. (C) 1282. (B) 1283. (C) 1284. (C) 1285. (B) 1286. (C) 1287. (B) 1288. (B) 1289. (D) 1290. (B)
1291. (A) 1292. (A) 1293. (A) 1294. (B) 1295. (C) 1296. (B) 1297. (C) 1298. (B) 1299. (C) 1300. (B)
1301. (D) 1302. (B) 1303. (A) 1304. (D) 1305. (A) 1306. (B) 1307. (D) 1308. (C) 1309. (B) 1310. (C)
1311. (A) 1312. (C) 1313. (B) 1314. (B) 1315. (B) 1316. (D) 1317. (C) 1318. (A) 1319. (B) 1320. (D)
1321. (C) 1322. (D) 1323. (B) 1324. (A) 1325. (A) 1326. (B) 1327. (A) 1328. (C) 1329. (C) 1330. (A)
1331. (B) 1332. (C) 1333. (B) 1334. (A) 1335. (D) 1336. (C) 1337. (B) 1338. (A) 1339. (B) 1340. (C)
1341. (B) 1342. (D) 1343. (B) 1344. (D) 1345. (A) 1346. (B) 1347. (B) 1348. (A) 1349. (B) 1350. (B)
1351. (C) 1352. (D) 1353. (A) 1354. (C) 1355. (C) 1356. (A) 1357. (A) 1358. (B) 1359. (B) 1360. (C)
1361. (A) 1362. (B) 1363. (B) 1364. (D) 1365. (A) 1366. (A) 1367. (A) 1368. (C) 1369. (B) 1370. (B)
1371. (C) 1372. (A) 1373. (A) 1374. (C) 1375. (D) 1376. (C) 1377. (A) 1378. (B) 1379. (B) 1380. (C)
1381. (D) 1382. (B) 1383. (B) 1384. (A) 1385. (B) 1386. (A) 1387. (A) 1388. (B) 1389. (A) 1390. (B)
1391. (A) 1392. (A) 1393. (D) 1394. (B) 1395. (C) 1396. (D) 1397. (B) 1398. (C) 1399. (B) 1400. (D)
1401. (C) 1402. (A) 1403. (C) 1404. (B) 1405. (A) 1406. (B) 1407. (C) 1408. (A) 1409. (C) 1410. (B)
1411. (A) 1412. (C) 1413. (A) 1414. (B) 1415. (A) 1416. (A) 1417. (C) 1418. (C) 1419. (D) 1420. (B)
1421. (D) 1422. (A) 1423. (B) 1424. (A) 1425. (C) 1426. (B) 1427. (B) 1428. (C) 1429. (D) 1430. (D)
1431. (C) 1432. (A) 1433. (A) 1434. (A) 1435. (C) 1436. (A) 1437. (B) 1438. (A) 1439. (B) 1430. (C)
1441. (D) 1442. (A) 1443. (B) 1444. (C) 1445. (A) 1446. (C) 1447. (A) 1448. (D) 1449. (B) 1450. (D)
1451.(C) 1452. (C) 1453. (B) 1454. (A) 1455. (D) 1456.(C) 1457. (B) 1458. (A) 1459. (B) 1460. (C)
1461. (D) 1462. (C) 1463. (B) 1464. (D) 1465. (A) 1466. (C) 1467. (C) 1468. (A) 1469. (B) 1470. (B)
1471. (C) 1472. (D) 1473. (B) 1474. (B) 1475. (A) 1476. (B) 1477. (B) 1478. (B) 1479. (C) 1480. (C)
1481. (B) 1482. (C) 1483. (C) 1484. (D) 1485. (C) 1486. (C) 1487. (A) 1488. (B) 1489. (B) 1490. (D)
1491. (D) 1492. (A) 1493. (A) 1494. (C) 1495. (A) 1496. (B) 1497. (C) 1498. (D) 1499. (B) 1500. (A)
1501. (C) 1502. (B) 1503. (B) 1504. (C) 1505. (A) 1506. (B) 1507. (D) 1508. (C) 1509. (D) 1510. (C)
1511. (C) 1512. (B) 1513. (B) 1514. (D) 1515. (B) 1516. (C) 1517. (B) 1518. (C) 1519. (A) 1520. (B)
1521. (B) 1522. (C) 1523. (C) 1524. (D) 1525. (D) 1526. (A) 1527. (B) 1528. (B) 1529. (A) 1530. (B)
1531. (A) 1532. (C) 1533. (D) 1534. (B) 1535. (C) 1536. (D) 1537. (B) 1538. (D) 1539. (A) 1540. (B)
1541. (D) 1542. (A) 1543. (C) 1544. (D) 1545. (B) 1546. (A) 1547. (D) 1548. (C) 1549. (C) 1550. (B)
1551. (D) 1552. (C) 1553. (C) 1554. (C) 1555. (D) 1556. (B) 1557. (B) 1558. (C) 1559. (B) 1560. (D)
1561. (C) 1562. (B) 1563. (C) 1564. (B) 1565. (A) 1566. (D) 1567. (A) 1568. (B) 1569. (B) 1570. (C)
1571. (B) 1572. (C) 1573. (B) 1574. (C) 1575. (B) 1576. (A) 1577. (A) 1578. (D) 1579. (B) 1580. (C)
1581. (D) 1582. (B) 1583. (A) 1584. (C) 1585. (B) 1586. (C) 1587. (A) 1588. (D) 1589. (C) 1590. (A)
1591. (B) 1592. (B) 1593. (D) 1594. (D) 1595. (B) 1596. (C) 1597. (A) 1598. (B) 1599. (A) 1600. (C)
1601. (D) 1602. (B) 1603. (C) 1604. (D) 1605. (D) 1606. (C) 1607. (A) 1608. (B) 1609. (A) 1610. (A)
1611. (A) 1612. (C) 1613. (B) 1614. (B) 1615. (D) 1616. (C) 1617. (B) 1618. (C) 1619. (D) 1620. (B)
1621. (A) 1622. (C) 1623. (C) 1624. (B) 1625. (A) 1626. (D) 1627. (C) 1628. (B) 1629. (A) 1630. (B)
1631. (C) 1632. (D) 1633. (C) 1634. (B) 1635. (C) 1636. (B) 1637. (C) 1638. (C) 1639. (D) 1640. (A)
1641. (D) 1642. (D) 1643. (B) 1644. (B) 1645. (B) 1646. (A) 1647. (B) 1648. (C) 1649. (D) 1650. (A)

1651. (C) **1652.** (D) **1653.** (A) **1654.** (B) **1655.** (B) **1656.** (C) **1657.** (D) **1658.** (A) **1659.** (B) **1660.** (B)

1661. (A) **1662.** (C) **1663.** (D) **1664.** (C) **1665.** (B) **1666.** (C) **1667.** (A) **1668.** (A) **1669.** (C) **1670.** (B)

1671. (D) **1672.** (C) **1673.** (A) **1674.** (B) **1675.** (B) **1676.** (B) **1677.** (B) **1678.** (B) **1679.** (A) **1680.** (B)

1681. (A) **1682.** (B) **1683.** (D) **1684.** (C) **1685.** (A) **1686.** (C) **1687.** (D) **1688.** (B) **1689.** (C) **1690.** (C)

1691. (A) **1692.** (B) **1693.** (B) **1694.** (D) **1695.** (C) **1696.** (B) **1697.** (A) **1698.** (B) **1699.** (D) **1700.** (B)

1701. (A) **1702.** (C) **1703.** (C) **1704.** (C) **1705.** (D) **1706.** (D) **1707.** (D) **1708.** (A) **1709.** (C) **1710.** (A)

1711. (D) **1712.** (C) **1713.** (A) **1714.** (B) **1715.** (D) **1716.** (C) **1717.** (B) **1718.** (D) **1719.** (B) **1720.** (C)

1721. (B) **1722.** (D) **1723.** (D) **1724.** (A) **1725.** (D) **1726.** (D) **1727.** (D) **1728.** (B) **1729.** (D) **1730.** (C)

1731. (C) **1732.** (D) **1733.** (A) **1734.** (B) **1735.** (B) **1736.** (C) **1737.** (D) **1738.** (D) **1739.** (A) **1740.** (D)

1741. (D) **1742.** (B) **1743.** (B) **1744.** (D) **1745.** (A) **1746.** (B) **1747.** (D) **1748.** (C) **1749.** (A) **1750.** (D)

1751. (C) **1752.** (A) **1753.** (C) **1754.** (B) **1755.** (A) **1756.** (D) **1757.** (D) **1758.** (A) **1759.** (B) **1760.** (A)

1761. (C) **1762.** (D) **1763.** (B) **1764.** (D) **1765.** (B) **1766.** (C) **1767.** (D) **1768.** (D) **1769.** (B) **1770.** (C)

1771. (C) **1772.** (B) **1773.** (C) **1774.** (A) **1775.** (D) **1776.** (D) **1777.** (B) **1778.** (D) **1779.** (A) **1780.** (D)

1781. (C) **1782.** (C) **1783.** (D) **1784.** (A) **1785.** (D) **1786.** (C) **1787.** (B) **1788.** (D) **1789.** (C) **1790.** (C)

1791. (A) **1792.** (C) **1793.** (D) **1794.** (D) **1795.** (C) **1796.** (C) **1797.** (A) **1798.** (A) **1799.** (A) **1800.** (A)

1801. (B) **1802.** (C) **1803.** (D) **1804.** (A) **1805.** (B) **1806.** (A) **1807.** (D) **1808.** (D) **1809.** (D) **1810.** (D)

1811. (C) **1812.** (C) **1813.** (B) **1814.** (A) **1815.** (B) **1816.** (D) **1817.** (C) **1818.** (A) **1819.** (D) **1820.** (B)

1821. (D) **1822.** (B) **1823.** (D) **1824.** (C) **1825.** (D) **1826.** (D) **1827.** (D) **1828.** (D) **1829.** (D) **1830.** (A)

1831. (C) **1832.** (A) **1833.** (B) **1834.** (D) **1835.** (A) **1836.** (A) **1837.** (C) **1838.** (A) **1839.** (D) **1840.** (A)

1841. (C) **1842.** (B) **1843.** (B) **1844.** (B) **1845.** (B) **1846.** (D) **1847.** (B) **1848.** (A) **1849.** (A) **1850.** (C)

1851. (C) **1852.** (B) **1853.** (D) **1854.** (C) **1855.** (A) **1856.** (D) **1857.** (B) **1858.** (C) **1859.** (D) **1860.** (B)

1861. (A) **1862.** (C) **1863.** (B) **1864.** (B) **1865.** (A) **1866.** (B) **1867.** (B) **1868.** (B) **1869.** (D) **1870.** (D)

1871. (C) **1872.** (C) **1873.** (A) **1874.** (C) **1875.** (A) **1876.** (A) **1877.** (B) **1878.** (B) **1879.** (D) **1880.** (C)

1881. (D) **1882.** (B) **1883.** (B) **1884.** (D) **1885.** (B) **1886.** (A) **1887.** (D) **1888.** (C) **1889.** (D) **1890.** (A)

1891. (C) **1892.** (D) **1893.** (C) **1894.** (A) **1895.** (C) **1896.** (A) **1897.** (B) **1898.** (A) **1899.** (B) **1900.** (C)

1901. (A) **1902.** (A) **1903.** (D) **1904.** (C) **1905.** (A) **1906.** (D) **1907.** (A) **1908.** (C) **1909.** (A) **1910.** (D)

1911. (C) **1912.** (B) **1913.** (B) **1914.** (A) **1915.** (D) **1916.** (B) **1917.** (C) **1918.** (C) **1919.** (A) **1920.** (B)

1921. (A) **1922.** (C) **1923.** (C) **1924.** (A) **1925.** (B) **1926.** (B) **1927.** (C) **1928.** (A) **1929.** (D) **1930.** (D)

1931. (A) **1932.** (A) **1933.** (A) **1934.** (B) **1935.** (D) **1936.** (B) **1937.** (B) **1938.** (A) **1939.** (D) **1940.** (A)

1941. (C) **1942.** (C) **1943.** (B) **1944.** (C) **1945.** (A) **1946.** (C) **1947.** (A) **1948.** (B) **1949.** (C) **1950.** (A)

1951. (C) **1952.** (B) **1953.** (A) **1954.** (C) **1955.** (B) **1956.** (C) **1957.** (D) **1958.** (B) **1959.** (A) **1960.** (C)

1961. (A) **1962.** (C) **1963.** (A) **1964.** (D) **1965.** (A) **1966.** (D) **1967.** (C) **1968.** (D) **1969.** (A) **1970.** (B)

1971. (D) **1972.** (D) **1973.** (A) **1974.** (D) **1975.** (C) **1976.** (C) **1977.** (B) **1978.** (C) **1979.** (D) **1980.** (B)

1981. (A) **1982.** (D) **1983.** (D) **1984.** (C) **1985.** (A) **1986.** (B) **1987.** (D) **1988.** (D) **1989.** (C) **1990.** (B)

1991. (B) **1992.** (C) **1993.** (B) **1994.** (C) **1995.** (D) **1996.** (A) **1997.** (D) **1998.** (B) **1999.** (C) **2000.** (A)

2001. (A) **2002.** (B) **2003.** (A) **2004.** (D) **2005.** (B) **2006.** (B) **2007.** (D) **2008.** (C) **2009.** (B) **2010.** (B)

2011. (A) **2012.** (C) **2013.** (B) **2014.** (B) **2015.** (C) **2016.** (B) **2017.** (D) **2018.** (B) **2019.** (B) **2020.** (A)

2021. (C) **2022.** (D) **2023.** (C) **2024.** (B) **2025.** (D) **2026.** (A) **2027.** (C) **2028.** (B) **2029.** (D) **2030.** (D)

2031. (B) **2032.** (A) **2033.** (C) **2034.** (D) **2035.** (A) **2036.**(A) **2037.**(A) **2038.**(B) **2039.**(A) **2040.** (B)

2041. (A) **2042.** (A) **2043.** (D) **2044.** (B) **2045.** (C) **2046.**(D) **2047.** (B) **2048.** (C) **2049.** (B) **2050.**(D)

2051. (C) **2052.** (A) **2053.** (C) **2054.** (B) **2055.** (A) **2056.** (B) **2057.** (C) **2058.**(A) **2059.** (C) **2060.** (B)

2061. (A) **2062.** (C) **2063.** (A) **2064.** (B) **2065.** (A) **2066.**(A) **2067.** (C) **2068.** (C) **2069.** (D) **2070.**(B)

2071. (D) 2072. (A) 2073. (B) 2074. (A) 2075. (C) 2076. (A) 2077. (B) 2078. (C) 2079. (D) 2080. (D)
2081. (C) 2082. (A) 2083. (A) 2084. (A) 2085. (C) 2086. (A) 2087. (B) 2088. (A) 2089. (B) 2090. (C)
2091. (A) 2092. (B) 2093. (C) 2094. (A) 2095. (D) 2096. (B) 2097. (C) 2098. (D) 2099. (A) 2100. (A)
2101. (A) 2102. (C) 2103. (B) 2104. (D) 2105. (A) 2106. (D) 2107. (A) 2108. (D) 2109. (C) 2110. (C)
2111. (D) 2112. (A) 2113. (B) 2114. (C) 2115. (D) 2116. (C) 2117. (A) 2118. (B) 2119. (A) 2120. (B)
2121. (B) 2122. (A) 2123. (A) 2124. (D) 2125. (D) 2126. (B) 2127. (C) 2128. (C) 2129. (D) 2130. (B)
2131. (C) 2132. (C) 2133. (D) 2134. (C) 2135. (B) 2136. (A) 2137. (D) 2138. (D) 2139. (A) 2140. (C)
2141. (B) 2142. (C) 2143. (B) 2144. (C) 2145. (D) 2146. (D) 2147. (D) 2148. (A) 2149. (D) 2150. (B)
2151. (D) 2152. (C) 2153. (B) 2154. (C) 2155. (B) 2156. (B) 2157. (C) 2158. (C) 2159. (C) 2160. (A)
2161. (D) 2162. (D) 2163. (A) 2164. (A) 2165. (C) 2166. (D) 2167. (D) 2168. (B) 2169. (A) 2170. (B)
2171. (B) 2172. (B) 2173. (A) 2174. (A) 2175. (B) 2176. (B) 2177. (B) 2178. (C) 2179. (D) 2180. (B)
2181. (D) 2182. (D) 2183. (D) 2184. (C) 2185. (A) 2186. (A) 2187. (A) 2188. (A) 2189. (D) 2190. (D)
2191. (A) 2192. (B) 2193. (D) 2194. (C) 2195. (C) 2196. (D) 2197. (B) 2198. (C) 2199. (D) 2200. (B)
2201. (C) 2202. (D) 2203. (A) 2204. (B) 2205. (C) 2206. (B) 2207. (B) 2208. (B) 2209. (C) 2210. (A)
2211. (B) 2212. (B) 2213. (B) 2214. (B) 2215. (B) 2216. (D) 2217. (C) 2218. (A) 2219. (A) 2220. (C)
2221. (B) 2222. (C) 2223. (A) 2224. (B) 2225. (B) 2226. (A) 2227. (B) 2228. (A) 2229. (B) 2230. (C)
2231. (C) 2232. (B) 2233. (A) 2234. (B) 2235. (B) 2236. (B) 2237. (C) 2238. (B) 2239. (A) 2240. (B)
2241. (C) 2242. (B) 2243. (A) 2244. (B) 2245. (B) 2246. (B) 2247. (D) 2248. (C) 2249. (B) 2250. (B)
2251. (C) 2252. (A) 2253. (B) 2254. (B) 2255. (D) 2256. (B) 2257. (B) 2258. (A) 2259. (A) 2260. (D)
2261. (B) 2262. (A) 2263. (A) 2264. (B) 2265. (A) 2266. (B) 2267. (A) 2268. (A) 2269. (B) 2270. (B)
2271. (B) 2272. (B) 2273. (B) 2274. (A) 2275. (A) 2276. (B) 2277. (B) 2278. (C) 2279. (B) 2280. (B)
2281. (A) 2282. (B) 2283. (C) 2284. (B) 2285. (A) 2286. (C) 2287. (A) 2288. (B) 2289. (A) 2290. (B)
2291. (B) 2292. (B) 2293. (B) 2294. (B) 2295. (B) 2296. (C) 2297. (A) 2298. (B) 2299. (A) 2300. (B)
2301. (A) 2302. (A) 2303. (C) 2304. (A) 2305. (C) 2306. (B) 2307. (C) 2308. (A) 2309. (B) 2310. (B)
2311. (A) 2312. (C) 2313. (B) 2314. (B) 2315. (B) 2316. (A) 2317. (B) 2318. (A) 2319. (A) 2320. (C)
2321. (C) 2322. (A) 2323. (B) 2324. (D) 2325. (B) 2326. (B) 2327. (B) 2328. (B) 2329. (A) 2330. (B)
2331. (B) 2332. (B) 2333. (A) 2334. (D) 2335. (B) 2336. (A) 2337. (C) 2338. (B) 2339. (B) 2340. (A)
2341. (B) 2342. (B) 2343. (C) 2344. (B) 2345. (B) 2346. (D) 2347. (B) 2348. (D) 2349. (B) 2350. (A)
2351. (A) 2352. (A) 2353. (A) 2354. (C) 2355. (B) 2356. (D) 2357. (C) 2358. (B) 2359. (B) 2360. (D)
2361. (C) 2362. (A) 2363. (A) 2364. (C) 2365. (D) 2366. (B) 2367. (A) 2368. (B) 2369. (A) 2370. (B)
2371. (B) 2372. (B) 2373. (C) 2374. (C) 2375. (D) 2376. (D) 2377. (C) 2378. (B) 2379. (C) 2380. (C)
2381. (A) 2382. (B) 2383. (B) 2384. (D) 2385. (C) 2386. (B) 2387. (B) 2388. (C) 2389. (D) 2390. (D)
2391. (C) 2392. (D) 2393. (C) 2394. (B) 2395. (B) 2396. (B) 2397. (C) 2398. (C) 2399. (A) 2400. (D)
2401. (C) 2402. (B) 2403. (B) 2404. (D) 2405. (D) 2406. (A) 2407. (B) 2408. (A) 2409. (B) 2410. (B)
2411. (B) 2412. (B) 2413. (B) 2414. (B) 2415. (C) 2416. (B) 2417. (C) 2418. (B) 2419. (B) 2420. (C)
2421. (B) 2422. (A) 2423. (B) 2424. (D) 2425. (D) 2426. (C) 2427. (B) 2428. (B) 2429. (C) 2430. (C)
2431. (C) 2432. (D) 2433. (C) 2434. (C) 2435. (C) 2436. (A) 2437. (C) 2438. (B) 2439. (A) 2440. (C)
2441. (C) 2442. (C) 2443. (C) 2444. (D) 2445. (D) 2446. (C) 2447. (A) 2448. (A) 2449. (B) 2450. (C)
2451. (C) 2452. (B) 2453. (A) 2454. (C) 2455. (D) 2456. (A) 2457. (D) 2458. (C) 2459. (C) 2460. (A)
2461. (A) 2462. (A) 2463. (A) 2464. (A) 2465. (B) 2466. (C) 2467. (D) 2468. (B) 2469. (D) 2470. (A)
2471. (D) 2472. (D) 2473. (A) 2474. (B) 2475. (C) 2476. (A) 2477. (D) 2478. (D) 2479. (A) 2480. (A)
2481. (B) 2482. (A) 2483. (B) 2484. (A) 2485. (A) 2486. (D) 2487. (C) 2488. (C) 2489. (D) 2490. (A)

2491. (B) **2492.** (A) **2493.** (C) **2494.** (D) **2495.** (C) **2496.** (C) **2497.** (A) **2498.** (A) **2499.** (D) **2500.** (B)
2501. (B) **2502.** (A) **2503.** (A) **2504.** (B) **2505.** (A) **2506.** (C) **2507.** (D) **2508.** (A) **2509.** (C) **2510.** (D)
2511. (B) **2512.** (B) **2513.** (D) **2514.** (C) **2515.** (C) **2516.** (A) **2517.** (A) **2518.** (A) **2519.** (A) **2520.** (D)
2521. (B) **2522.** (C) **2523.** (A) **2524.** (C) **2525.** (C) **2526.** (B) **2527.** (B) **2528.** (A) **2529.** (D) **2530.** (A)
2531. (B) **2532.** (B) **2533.** (C) **2534.** (B) **2535.** (C) **2536.** (B) **2537.** (D) **2538.** (A) **2539.** (A) **2540.** (D)
2541. (A) **2542.** (C) **2543.** (C) **2544.** (B) **2545.** (B) **2546.** (B) **2547.** (D) **2548.** (B) **2549.** (B) **2550.** (C)
2551. (C) **2552.** (A) **2553.** (A) **2554.** (D) **2555.** (C) **2556.** (D) **2557.** (D) **2558.** (D) **2559.** (D) **2560.** (A)
2561. (C) **2562.** (D) **2563.** (B) **2564.** (D) **2565.** (B) **2566.** (B) **2567.** (A) **2568.** (B) **2569.** (C) **2570.** (C)
2571. (D) **2572.** (A) **2573.** (D) **2574.** (C) **2575.** (D) **2576.** (A) **2577.** (A) **2578.** (C) **2579.** (A) **2580.** (A)
2581. (B) **2582.** (D) **2583.** (B) **2584.** (D) **2585.** (B) **2586.** (D) **2587.** (B) **2588.** (C) **2589.** (A) **2590.** (B)
2591. (A) **2592.** (D) **2593.** (B) **2594.** (B) **2595.** (A) **2596.** (D) **2597.** (D) **2598.** (C) **2599.** (D) **2600.** (B)
2601. (C) **2602.** (A) **2603.** (C) **2604.** (D) **2605.** (C) **2606.** (D) **2607.** (D) **2508.** (C) **2609.** (A) **2610.** (D)
2611. (A) **2612.** (C) **2613.** (D) **2614.** (B) **2615.** (C) **2616.** (C) **2617.** (D) **2518.** (C) **2619.** (C) **2620.** (B)
2621. (A) **2622.** (D) **2623.** (C) **2624.** (B) **2625.** (A) **2626.** (C) **2627.** (A) **2528.** (C) **2629.** (D) **2630.** (B)
2631. (D) **2632.** (B) **2633.** (A) **2634.** (B) **2635.** (A) **2636.** (A) **2637.** (D) **2638.** (C) **2639.** (C) **2640.** (C)
2641. (D) **2642.** (A) **2643.** (D) **2644.** (A) **2645.** (B) **2646.** (A) **2647.** (C) **2648.** (D) **2649.** (C) **2650.** (C)
2651. (A) **2652.** (A) **2653.** (A) **2654.** (A) **2655.** (D) **2656.** (B) **2657.** (D) **2658.** (B) **2659.** (A) **2660.** (A)
2661. (A) **2662.** (A) **2663.** (B) **2664.** (A) **2665.** (B) **2666.** (A) **2667.** (A) **2668.** (D) **2669.** (B) **2670.** (C)
2671. (D) **2672.** (B) **2673.** (C) **2674.** (B) **2675.** (D) **2676.** (C) **2677.** (A) **2678.** (C) **2679.** (B) **2680.** (A)
2681. (B) **2682.** (C) **2683.** (A) **2684.** (C) **2685.** (B) **2686.** (A) **2687.** (C) **2688.** (A) **2689.** (B) **2690.** (A)
2691. (A) **2692.** (C) **2693.** (C) **2694.** (D) **2695.** (B) **2696.** (D) **2697.** (A) **2698.** (B) **2699.** (A) **2700.** (C)
2701. (A) **2702.** (B) **2703.** (C) **2704.** (D) **2705.** (D) **2706.** (C) **2707.** (A) **2708.** (A) **2709.** (A) **2710.** (C)
2711. (A) **2712.** (B) **2713.** (A) **2714.** (B) **2715.** (B) **2716.** (D) **2717.** (D) **2718.** (C) **2719.** (A) **2720.** (B)
2721. (C) **2722.** (B) **2723.** (A) **2724.** (B) **2725.** (D) **2726.** (D) **7727.** (B) **2728.** (C) **2729.** (B) **2730.** (B)
2731. (C) **2732.** (A) **2733.** (A) **2734.** (B) **2735.** (D) **2736.** (D) **2737.** (D) **2738.** (C) **2739.** (A) **2740.** (A)
2741. (B) **2742.** (A) **2743.** (C) **2744.** (A) **2745.** (C) **2746.** (C) **2747.** (A) **2748.** (A) **2749.** (B) **2750.** (C)
2751. (D) **2752.** (A) **2753.** (A) **2754.** (B) **2755.** (D) **2756.** (B) **2757.** (D) **2758.** (A) **2759.** (A) **2760.** (C)
2761. (B) **2762.** (C) **2763.** (C) **2764.** (A) **2765.** (B) **2766.** (C) **2767.** (B) **2768.** (B) **2769.** (C) **2770.** (C)
2771. (B) **2772.** (D) **2773.** (C) **2774.** (C) **2775.** (B) **2776.** (B) **2777.** (A) **2778.** (D) **2779.** (C) **2780.** (D)
2781. (C) **2782.** (B) **2783.** (C) **2784.** (B) **2785.** (C) **2786.** (C) **2787.** (A) **2788.** (D) **2789.** (A) **2790.** (B)
2791. (D) **2792.** (B) **2793.** (D) **2794.** (A) **2795.** (A) **2796.** (C) **2797.** (D) **2798.** (C) **2799.** (C) **2800.** (A)
2801. (C) **2802.** (A) **2803.** (A) **2804.** (B) **2805.** (A) **2806.** (A) **2807.** (A) **2808.** (A) **2809.** (A) **2810.** (A)
2811. (A) **2812.** (A) **2813.** (A) **2814.** (D) **2815.** (B) **2816.** (B) **2817.** (C) **2818.** (C) **2819.** (A) **2820.** (A)
2821. (A) **2822.** (B) **2823.** (D) **2824.** (A) **2825.** (A) **2826.** (D) **2827.** (A) **2828.** (C) **2829.** (C) **2830.** (A)
2831. (A) **2832.** (B) **2833.** (B) **2834.** (D) **2835.** (C) **2836.** (C) **2837.** (A) **2838.** (B) **2839.** (A) **2840.** (C)
2841. (B) **2842.** (D) **2843.** (A) **2844.** (D) **2845.** (D) **2846.** (A) **2847.** (B) **2848.** (B) **2849.** (A) **2850.** (D)

LITERARY TERMS

Abstract idea. A general statement about a quality or state, about a class of persons, objects, ideas. It is opposed to a specific fact or concrete statement. *Example* : Wealth corrupts the soul.

Abstract noun. Refers to a quality or state. It is opposed to a concrete noun that refers to a specific object or person. *Examples* : *love, honor, courtesy.*

Adage. A proverb or wise saying. Early to bed, early to rise. Makes a man healthy, wealthy, and wise.

Allegory. A literary form in which some or all the characters are embodiments of abstract ideas. It is a story which carries a second meaning along with its surface story: Bunyan's *Pilgrim's Progress.*

Alliteration. Repetition of the initial sound in words. This device, is most effective in poetry and polyphonic prose. *Example* : To sit in solemn silence.

Allusion. A casual reference to some character, person, fact, idea, or event. The reader is expected to see the application of the allusion to the thought being expressed. *Example* : He sees himself as another. Hercules assigned to clean out the rubbish of the centuries.

Ambiguity. When used as a derogatory term, refers to the lack of clarity that makes meaning vague when more than one interpretation is highly possible. Ambiguity may also be used to describe the richness in poetry that "gives room for alternative reactions to the same piece of poetry." William Epsom referred to the seven types of ambiguity in literature.

Anachronism. A device describing something placed in an inappropriate period of time. It may be an unintentional error, or it may be used deliberately for effect. *Example* : Sir Patrick Rafter brandished his antic shotgun at the mass of attacking renegades.

Analogy. A comparison of two things in certain aspects. Analogies are often dangerous because we tend to assume that since two people or things are similar in one or more respects, they should necessarily be similar in others. *Example* : Since we both come from the same country, we should have similar choices.

Anapest. The anapestic foot begins with two unaccented syllables which are followed by the accented syllable.

Anecdote. A brief, pointed, or humorous story sometimes as a part of in a larger whole. It lacks the complicated plot of a short story. It is an effective device for beginning a speech or driving home a universal truth.

Antagonist. The main character opposed to the author's principal character, the protagonist. The antagonist need not be villain. In a story dealing with Satan, the protecting angel could be the antagonist.

Anthology. A collection of selected pieces of essays, short-stories or poetry. Many of the textbooks used in English courses in literature are anthologies.

Anticlimax. The arrangement of details in such an order that the unimportant suddenly appears at the point where the critical or serious detail should be found. Anticlimax is an unexpected twist in a story, usually at the end, in which the hero has an unpredicted allergy attack just when he is to lead his troops into battle. It can be an effective device in humorous material.

Antithesis. A rhetorical device in which contrasted words, clauses, or ideas are balanced. *Example*: Love and hate, desire and fulfilment make our lives purposeful and tumultuous. Antithesis must be used sparingly; too many sentences containing this dramatic approach gives the material a heavy, artificial tone.

Antonomasia. The use of a proper noun as a common name. It is a type of allusion in which the reader must see the relationship between the person referred to and the present subject. Beware of him! He is another Hitler!

Aphorism. A short, pithy statement of universal principle or precept. *Example*: All that glitters is not gold.

Apostrophe. A rhetorical device used in prose because of the intensity it generates. *Example : Poverty, touch not his hopes !* This device is restricted in its use to prose.

Apostrophe. The figure of speech in which the absent are addressed as though they were present, the living as well as the dead, objects as well as human beings. Again, this can be a device highly charged with emotion. *Example* : Blow, blow thou winter wind | Thou art not so unkind | As man's ingratitude. This device can be easily abused, leading to overcharged words that fail to arouse the reader's imagination.

Archaism. A word or phrase no longer used in contemporary speech. *Example* : methinks this is a facile, often too facile, device for dating a speech or work.

Argument. Refers, as a literary device, to the summary of the plot placed at the beginning of a section or chapter. *Paradise Lost* contains an argument summarizing the main lines of action at the beginning of each Book.

Assonance. Repetition of vowel sounds, the pairing of the same vowel sounds without regard for consonants. This is a device used to give tonal values to lines. It is difficult to introduce and not easily sensed by the reader. *Example* : 'Where are you going ?' said the reader to a rider.

Atmosphere. The tone and mood established by a literary work as a whole. The atmosphere of comedy is light while that of a tragedy tends to be heavy.

Autobiography. A literary work in which the author describesthe real story of his own past. A *diary* emphasizes inner rather than outward manifestations. *Memoirs* stress reactions, impressions and people met. A *journal* is more private and more episodic.

Bathos. A kind of anticlimax, a sudden descent from the heights of greater significance, a going from the sublime to the ridiculous. Bathos can be evidenced in action or words.

Biography. The account of the life of a real, usually important, person.

Blank Verse. Each line contains ten syllables. The predominant beat is iambic. The lines are unrhymed. Blank verse is written in unrhymed iambic pentameter. This has been most popular among the best of the poetic technicians. If each line is a complete thought, then it is *end stop.* If the ideas flow from one line to the next, then it is *enjambed.* The pause within the line is called the *caesura.*

Bombast. Grandiloquent, artificial and extravagant language. *Example* : From the depths of sincerity and honesty, we decry, with all the lymphatic force at our command, the scurrilous, unfounded accusations brought forth as so obvious an attempt to obfuscate the truth in our just and modest claims.

Burlesque. The type of humorous writing which satirizes and imitates a literary convention, style, or attitude. *Don Quixote* was written as a burlesque of the medieval romance so popular in Cervantes' Spain.

Cacophony. Harsh combinations of sound. The experienced writer may use cacophony as a device to emphasize action related to his dialogue, but in expository writing, one should avoid having the sound of his words interfere with the flow of meaning. Cacophony is the antonym of *euphony.*

Caricature. A character or action exaggerated for sarcapic or humorous effect. A limited number of personal qualities is usually selected for such an exaggeration.

Circumlocution. A roundabout expression, one that avoids a direct label. "He is a man who avoids telling or revealing in direct terms any item that may put him in a bed light, despite the needs of the listener!" "Simply then, he's liar!"

Cliche. An expression which the author or reader feels has been so overused that it has lost its forcefulness. *Example* : As smart as a whip.

Climax. (1) An arrangement in which the chief point of interest is at the end. (2) The moment in the plot at which a crisis reaches its highest intensity and is resolved. Narrative and expository literature benefits from being planned towards reaching a climax.

Coherence. A work has coherence when the relationship of one part to another is clear and intelligible. Words, phrases, clauses, sentences, paragraphs, and chapters are the units which should show coherence through progressive and logical arrangement. Illogical arrangement results in lack of coherence.

Colloquial. Such expressions as are used in everyday conversation. Expressions labelled as belonging to the colloquial speech are avoided in Standard and Formal writings.

Comedy. 1. Any light-hearted presentation usually with a happy ending 2. Any literary work with a happy ending 3. Any literary work dealing with satire or humor. Note that humor is not essential under definition (2).

Comic relief. A humorous scene inserted in a serious or tragic work to relieve tension and so heighten the tragic emotion by contrast. The porter scene in *Macbeth,* following the slaying of the king, is the classic example of comic relief at its most effective level.

Conceit. A complex or far-fetched comparison. *Example* : Shut out the sun from your eyes. Because of the time such comparisons take for analysis, they have long fallen into disrepute. However, many modern writers attempting to evoke the complexities of present-day living have revived the conceit. When the comparison is startling and appropriate, the effect is commendable; when the comparison confuses the reader or leads to too great an overrefinement, then it may sound toppish or shallow.

Concrete noun. It stresses the tangible, that which can be seen, heard, felt. It is close to the specific, the particular. The concrete has actual existence and can be experienced through senses. Concrete terms are the converse of abstract nouns: *Honesty* is an abstract term. Effective writing tends to be concrete.

Confidant. A character to whom another reveals his most intimate feelings and intentions. *Confidante* is the feminine form. Hamlet's friend, Horatio, was his *confidant.*

Conflict. The struggle which grows out of the interplay of opposing forces in a plot.

Connotation. The implications or suggestions evoked by a word. *Connotation* is distinguished from denotation, which refers to the direct, objective meaning only. Scientific writing stresses denotative values. The scientist avoids using terms that have differing connotations for his readers. The literary artist uses connotation richness and emotive effect.

Convention. Any generally accepted literary device or form. The soliloquy in which a character expresses his innermost thoughts and feelings to the audience was an Elizabethan convention.

Dactyl. The dactylic foot begins with an accented syllable which is followed by two unaccented syllables.

Denotation. A word's most literal and limited meaning, the person, thing, or idea to which a word refers irrespective of attitudes or feelings which the writer or speaker may have. The denotation of *cow* is its dictionary definition of the mature female of cattle. When *cow* is used to describe a humble and docile human being, then the connotative values of the word are being used. The propagandist specializes in manipulating a word for its various connotations. *Example* : *national pride, one hundred percent patriot* !

Denouement. The events following the final climax of a story, the final unraveling and setting straight, the solution of the mystery, the explanation of all misunderstandings.

Deus ex machina. The term in Latin, means literally *god from the machine.* In Greek drama, one of the conventions allowed a god to be lowered onto the stage to rescue one of the characters. The term today is used critically, referring to any artificial device for resolving difficulties. Serious writers avoid such a device since the resolution of difficulties should grow from the action itself. The story line is weakened and the reader's faith is strained when an unexpected and improbable fucist is employed to make things turn out "right".

Diction. The choice and arrangement of words. The kind of diction used must be appropriate to the literary form, the subject, and the style of the period. Formal diction is inappropriate in a play set in a crude farm or in a city slum. Slang and colloquial expressions are inappropriate when interspersed in writing that calls for standard or formal usage. Sometimes the term is used derogatorily for the artificial and rhetorical language used in poetry by the neo-classical school.

Didactic. A label applied to a literary work when its principal aim is to counsel or educate in moral, ethical, or religious matters. Didactic is a neutral term when applied by those who accept teaching as the purpose of the material. Didactic becomes a derogatory term when the reader feels that the writer overemphasizes the moral values to the detriment of art.

Digression. Unrelated material inserted in a discussion. It is a violation of unity in formal essays. It is a standard device in the personal essay. Sometimes a digression is most effectively used in narratives to bring home a point.

Dramatic irony. When the words or acts of a character carry a meaning contrary to what he means to say or do and unperceived by him, but understood by the audience or reader. The irony lies in the contrast between the speaker's intended meaning and the realization of the others. *Example* : The character who, unknown to himself, is dying, makes elaborate plans for his future with his bride-to-have-been.

Dynamic character. One who changes as the result of the plot. Usually the protagonist is dynamic, and his growth and development as he reacts to circumstance create the central interest in the plot. Macbeth is dynamic in that they change. Dynamic characters are contrasted with static, stereotyped characters who remain dominated by a single quality throughout the story.

Economy of expression. A term of approval, implying the use of the minimum possible number of words for clarity and emphasis.

Empathy. The feeling of identity that a reader has when he becomes so involved with a character in a play or novel that he experiences the emotions that the character is going through. With *sympathy* we feel for the other; with *empathy* we feel as the other feels.

Emphasis. The planning of elements so that the important items, ideas, facts, personalities are stressed.

Epigram. A witty, pointed, terse saying. *Example* : Corruption is something that only others do.

Epilogue. (1) A concluding statement at the end of a speech or play. (2) An appendix added after the conclusion of a play or story. An epilogue may be the conclusion of a speech, the final remarks of an actor addressed to the audience, or a scene added after the main action of a drama has ended. An epilogue is the opposite of a prologue.

Epithet. A word or group of words used to characterize a person. *Example* : Jude the *Obscure.*

Essay. A short prose work emphasising the author's opinion on one topic. The personal essay stresses revelation of personal reactions. The formal essay develops an idea or expresses a point of view.

Euphemism. A rhetorical device for conveying a harsh or unpalatable idea pleasantly or indirectly. *Example* : *pass away* instead of *die.*

Euphony. The juxtaposition of words and sounds that combine together harmoniously. Writers use assonances, phrase rhythms, and alliterations as the principal rhetorical devices to achieve euphony. When used in excess, such devices can result in bombast or insincerity.

Exposition. The type of writing in which explanations are emphasized. Narrative writing tells a story; descriptive writing has as its purpose description of a scene, person, or process; in argumentation, the writer either attacks or defends a point of view. Expository writing tells how something works out or how something is done. For example, *Streamlining* by C. Bevers is an expository essay.

Fable. A short moral tale usually having animals as its characters. *Example* : The stories of Aesop, La Fontaine.

Farce. A humorous play based on exaggerated, improbable situations. The humour is based on horseplay, coarse wit and gross incogruities. *Example* : The typical Three Stooges' television movie.

Fiction. A narrative writing based on the author's free use of experience and imagination rather than on history or fact. Novels and short stories are examples of fiction.

Figurative language. Writing that includes one or more of the various figures of speech: simile, metaphor, apostrophe. The literal meaning of the words is avoided in favour of the connotative significance. Figurative language is the basis of poetry; overuse of this type of writing makes prose vague and difficult to understand.

Figures of speech. Those forms of expression that are different from the ordinary modes in order to emphasize or make the significance more effective or rich. These devices are most effective when used sparingly in prose, lest the reader's attention would be caught by the device rather than its purpose.

Flashback. A device whereby the reader or audience views scenes or incidents that occurred prior to the opening scene: For example, a play opens with a man walking toward the gallows. The next scene is a flashback to his the action that led to his present plight.

Free Verse. The rhythm is determined by the subject matter. The lines do not follow a regular meter but vary from thought. Rhyme is scarcely used. Walt Whitman and Carl Sandburg have helped to popularize this as a staple in the repertory of modern poetry. Free verse is a modern form and therefore the images and the language used by the poet tend to be modern.

Fustian. Bombastic or pompously ornate language.

Genre. A literary type classified by form and technique: novel, formal essay, short storyetc.

Heroic Couplet. Two lines of rhymed iambic pentameter. We think our fathers fools so wise we grow; our wiser sons no doubt will think us so.

Homily. A literary term used to describe a work which lectures its readers and urges them to adhere to high moral standards: a typical Sunday sermon.

Hyperbole. A rhetorical term for conscious exaggerations. *Example* : There were thousands of people packed into that little carriage.

Iambus. The iambic foot contains an unaccented first syllable and an accented second syllable.

Interior Monologue. A recording of the thoughts and emotional experiences of a character on one or more levels of consciousness. It is the technique employed by James Joyce in *Ulysses.* In a *soliloquy,* the revelations are limited to one level of consciousness, to one thought process.

Inversion. The figure of speech in which words are presented in a distorted syntax, out of their natural or expected order. Of arms and a man I sing.

Irony. The expression of the opposite of what is intended. You are truly kind to me !. Irony is more restrained and less bitter than sarcasm. Moreover irony may be inbuilt into a story or a situation without any express use of it as a device.

Litotes. The denial of the opposite to achieve intensity and emphasis. Litotes is a form of under statement. *Example* : She is not *stupid* to emphasize she is clever.

Malapropism. An error in diction caused by the substitution of one word for another similar in sound but different in meaning. Malaproprisms result from the misuse of formal or bombastic words intended to impress.

Maxim. A short, pithy statement based on experience and giving some pragmattic advice. If you cannot beat them, join them ! Maxims are often used as the opening sentence or summary sentence in expository writing.

Melodrama. A play based on a sensational, romantic plot with emotional jolts for the audience. The melodrama has a happy ending achieved over a course of improbable events in which the good are rewarded and the wicked are punished. Soap operas and typical television drama are prime examples of this genre.

Metaphor: A comparison which is implied rather than stated. It does not use the words *like* or *as.* Trite metaphor : pearly teeth, icy stare, clammy hands. Exaggerated Metaphor : Nehru was *the right hand of India.* Appropriate Metaphor: The Lord is my shephered. Mixed Metaphor: The bitterness of her remarks acted as a fuse that set off my anger.

Mis-en-scene. The stage setting of a play: scenery, costumes, properties of a theatrical production.

Mood. The tone of a literary work. *Example* : *Thoughtful, light, somber.*

Nonfiction. Literature based on actual occurrences, on facts. It is the term associated with diaries, biographies, textbooks, etc.

Novel. A long story, extended fictional prose narrative. It is a representation of life in fictional narrative.

Omniscient Author. An author who shifts from the objective exterior world into the subjective interior world of any number of characters. He feels free to comment at any time on the significance of events or reactions. That is, he rejects the mode of narrating from the point of view of any individual in particular.

Onomatopoeia. Formation of words to represent natural sounds. A most effective device in appealing to the sense of sound. *Example* : Flapping of wings, tinkling of coins etc.

Oxymoron. The figure of speech describing seemingly contradictory terms used to create a paradox. *Example* : Exuberant passimist, kind cruelty of a surgeon, *conspicuous by his absence.*

Parable. A short, simple story containing a moral lesson. The parable of the *Greedy Lion* is one of the best known examples of this genre.

Paradox. A seemingly contradictory or absurd statement which may actually contain a basic truth. It is a rhetorical device used for emphasis. *Example* : I have never felt so happy as I feel today to be icolded by you

Parallelism. The balancing of similar items: word against word, clause against clause, sentence against sentence. It is the device that leads to balanced sentences.

Paraphrase. A restatement in different words. The paraphrase, unlike a precis or summary, may be as long as the original.

Parody. A satirical imitation of a poem or other writing. The devices employed by Poe in his poems are so theatrical that his style has led to the many parodies that have been published in imitation of his most famous works.

Pathetic fallacy. A projection in which inanimate objects are shown as feeling emotions like human beings. *Example* : The trees wept with her in that dark night.

Pedantry. A derogatory term used to label a display of learning for its own sake. It is applied to a style in which the author uses an excess of allusions, quotations, exotic phrases, illusions, name-dropping, etc. to show off his learning.

Periodic sentence. A sentence in which the meaning is suspended until the end of the sentence, in which the main clause appears last. The periodic sentence when used exclusively gives a heavy tone to writing. It is best employed when interspersed with simple short sentences to gain variety.

Personification. The device in which inanimate objects and abstraction are referred to as having life or personality. *Example* : Thou unruly, pedantic sun. Personification has fallen into disfavour in modern prose writing.

Personification: The figure of speech in which we attribute human qualities to non-human things or beings.

Platitude. An overused generalization uttered as though it were fresh and original. Polonius' advice to Laertes is the classic example: *Neither a borrower nor lender be.*

Pleonasm. The label applied when more words than necessary are used to convey an idea: *write it down, cold white ice walk on foot,* the misery of misfortune.

Poetic justice. The good are rewarded and the evil punished. Poetic justice becomes pedantic when the author applies its principles with a heavy brush to the action in a plot.

Poetic language: This is use of old-fashioned words that were once considered elegant and poetic. Some such words are *ope* for open *oft* for *often.*

Poetic licence. It refers to the freedom of expression attributed to a poet or, more generally, any writer of literature, which may go beyond conventional morals, ideas or uses of language.

Precis. A summary or abstract which doesn't miss any of the important points conveyed in the original. A precis usually contains less than half number of words found in the original.

Prologue. A preface or introduction, usually to a play.

Protagonist. The main character around whom the plot revolves. The protagonist is not necessarily a *hero* or *villain.* He may be the thief or the protecting officer of the law, depending upon the choice of the author.

Pseudonym. A fictitious name assumed by a writer: George Eliot (Mary Ann Evans)

Purple Patch. A selection in which the author seems to overstrain for effect, relying heavily on rhetorical devices and emotive phrases. A purple patch is usually more rhythmic than most prose. It contains a strongly emotional tone marked by figures of speech and poetic diction. *Purple patch* is used as a derogatory term in modern criticism.

Quatrain. Any four-lined stanza. The best known of the quatrains is in the old English ballads. The most frequent ballad quatrain consisted of alternating iambic tetrameter and iambic trimeter lines rhyming *abcb*; that is, the second and fourth lines only would usually rhyme.

Rhetorical figure. A specific arrangement of words for emphasis: *inversions, rhetorical question, apos trophes.* Rhetorical figures do not alter the meaning of the words employed as do figures of speech (similes, metaphors).

Rhetorical question. A question that is asked, not to elicit information, but to achieve a stylistic effect. It is often used by a speaker to add dramatic emphasis at the introduction of a thought unit. *Example* : Why can't our politicians be honsest ? Because power corrupts, and absolute power corrupts absolutely.

Rhyme. The words with similar end-sounds occurring at the end of lines. To the seas and the *streams*

Sarcasm. A statement of the opposite of what is meant, a bitter, derisive statement of disapproval. I am so glad to see that you are not stupid when you interfere with my plans! Sarcasm is caustic, intended to hurt.

Satire. A type of writing which ridicules or denounces human vices and frailties. Horatian satire stresses a sophisticated, amused comment on vice or folly. Juvenalian satire is bitter, vehement, scathing in its denunciation.

Simile : A directly expressed comparison usually using the words *like* or *as*. The successful simile can evoke an ever-expanding vivid image in the mind of the reader. An effective simile must have an element of surprise in it; it must be appropriate; it should realize the emotional reaction anticipated by the poet as idle as "a painted ship upon a painted ocean. Similes, however, may be misused.

Slapstick. Comedy involving physical action such as throwing point on somebody or falling into the swimming pool in formal clothing.

Static character. A character centering about a single quality; one that does not grow or change during the action of the plot. Such characters usually surround the more complex, dynamic characters around whom the plot evolves. Othello is dynamic; lago is static.

Stereotype. The too usual, the customary, a generalized pattern applied in a specific instance. *A stereotyped character* or *stereotype* is a stock character. The hardboiled detective, the sweet, self-sacrificing mother and the friend who is an impostor are such stereotyped characters.. A *stereotyped solution* is one that is found in most stories in a particular instance. A *stereotyped plot* is one that contains no surprises for the audience. A *stereotyped idea* is a facile generalization. *Stereotype* and *stereotyped* are usually terms of disapproval.

Stock character. Stereotypes that appear regularly in certain literary forms. The drunkard, the malicious uncle, the rival in love, the forgetful professor are such stock characters in prose fiction.

Style. (1) The verbal pattern that characterizes a writer or writings. Bacon had a distinctive style. (2) Excellence. He has style !

Subjective. Personal, limited to one person's standards, reactions, feelings, impressions, evaluations. *Subjective* is opposed to *objective,* which stresses external, verifiable and accepted standards. The personal essay is subjective; the formal essay tends to be objective. One's impressions of an adolsescent heartbreak is are subjective; an evaluation of the advantages and disadvantages of city living in statistical terms would be objective.

Suspension. The basic device in the periodic sentence in which the meaning is suspended until the end of the sentence. Line by line with infinite patience and with complete disregard of time, she repainted the entire scenery on her canvass.

Synopsis. A summary, a condensation of a work. The synopsis should contain fewer words than the original.

Thesis. A formal essay, longer than a theme and resulting from research. It also means a proposition to be defended or proved formally: The thesis of the author is that intelligence is mainly the result of environmental factors.

Tirade. A long uninterrupted speech usually condemnatory.

Tone. A quality of a work of art which reveal in the attitude of the writer toward his material or his readers: *formal, ironic, condescending, etc.*

Tragedy. A dramatic plot that follows the classic or Aristotelian definition: disaster in the life of a ruler brought about inevitably as a result of a flaw in his character. It also means a plot that follows the contemporary definition: an important series of related events in the life of a person significant to the audience, leading to an unhappy ending. The protagonist may be the victim of a flaw in his own character, forces of society, or forces of nature.

Tragic flaw. The flaw or demerit in the protagonist which leads to his downfall despite his other noble qualities.

Trochee. The trochaic foot contains an accented first syllable and an unaccented second syllable.

Unity. Oneness. Each element and each larger part of a work should produce one wholesome effect. All the parts should be so inter-related that the work appears as an organic whole. The introduction of irrelevant detail destroys unity.

Universality. The ability of a work to appeal to a wide segment of the reading public, all over the world and to people of all generations.

Verisimilitude. The quality of semblance reality possessed by plot, episode, setting or character. The reader is willing to accept as representation of truth those elements that possess verisimilitude.

The lines of poetry. Poetry lines are named according to the number of feet they contain. The most common ones are given below.

Dimeter	A line of two feet.
Trimeter	A line of three fet.
Tetrameter	A line of four feet.
Pentameter	A line of five feet.
Hexameter	A line of six feet.

The lines of poetry are usually named after the type of foot that is found most frequently in it. Therefore we speak of an iambic pentameter or a trochaic trimeter. The most commonmetre in English poetry is the iambic pentameter. The dactylic hexameter, while much used in Latin and French, has never been a favourite of the English.

MODEL PAPERS – Revised Pattern

SET-1

Note : This paper contains **hundred** (100) Objective type questions, each question carrying **two** (2) marks. Attempt all of them.

1. Literary Research studies
(A) Literary text
(B) Literary writers
(C) Both Literary text and writer
(D) None of the above

2. Which among the following is not a critical theory in the development of Cultural Studies?
(A) Frankfurt Theory
(B) Psychoanalytic Theory
(C) Leavisite Criticism
(D) Mass Communication Theory

3. The literary movement that began in response to structuralism was
(A) Romanticism
(B) Colonialism
(C) Post-structuralism
(D) Post-colonialism

4. Defining creative writing is a difficult task in context of
(A) Society
(B) Individuality
(C) Humanities Computing
(D) None of the above

5. Consider the following works.
1. The Cow of Barricades
2. The Cat and Shakespeare
3. The Suicide
4. The Maggots

Which of the abqve works belongs to Raja Ras /Rao ?
(A) 1 and 2 (B) Only 2
(C) 2 and 4 (D) 1 and 3

6. "Provincializing Europe" is a concept propounded by
(A) Edward Said
(B) Paul Gilroy
(C) Abdul R. Gurnah
(D) Dipesh Chakravarty

7. The earliest tract on feminism is
(A) Simone de Beauvoir's *The Second Sex*
(B) Virginia Woolf's *A Room of One's Own*
(C) Mary Wollstonecraft's *A Vindication of the Rights of Woman*
(D) Mary Astell's *A Serious Proposal to the Ladies*

8. Match the imaginary location with its creator:
1. Emily Bronte
2. Thomas Hardy
3. Lowood Parsonage
4. Charles Dickens
5. Wessex
6. Egdon Heath
7. Coketown
8. Charlotte Bronte

(A) 1-7 2-5 4-6 3-8
(B) 1-6 2-5 3-8 4-7
(C) 1-5 2-6 3-8 4-7
(D) 2-5 1-7 3-4 6-8

9. Which Chaucerian text parodies Dante's The Divine Comedy ?
(A) *The Canterbury Tales*
(B) *The Book of the Duchess*
(C) *The House of Fame*
(D) *Legend of Good Women*

10. *Essays of Elia* was published in
(A) 1800 (B) 1823
(C) 1827 (D) 1850

11. Which of the following is an example of homosexual fiction ?
(A) *The Well of Loneliness*
(B) *Maurice*
(C) *Orlando*
(D) *The Ballad of the Reading Gaol*

12. W.B. Yeat's "Easter 1916" is
(A) a response to a major political uprising
(B) a reminiscence of his visit to a nursery school
(C) a love poem for Maud Gonne
(D) an ode to his native country

13. William Empson's *Seven Types of Ambiguity* is
(A) A structuralist study of narrative
(B) A piece of psychoanalytic criticism
(C) A study of the media
(D) An analysis of poetic ambivalence

14. Who among the following is associated with the ideology of Utilitarianism ?
(A) J.A. Froude
(B) Charles Kingsley
(C) J.S. Mill
(D) Cardinal Newman

15. The 'Condition of England' literature refers to
(A) The literature written by the labour class.
(B) The literature of England extolling living conditions.
(C) The literature of England depicting the vulnerability of labour classes.
(D) The literature of England depicting the imperial projects abroad.

16. Philip Sidney wrote *An Apology for Poetry* in immediate response to
(A) Plato's *Republic*
(B) Aristotle's *Poetics*
(C) Stephen Gosson's *The School of Abuse*
(D) Jeremy Collier's *Immorality and Profaneness of the English Stage.*

17. Silence ! *The Court is in Session* is a ________ play translated into English.
(A) Gujarati (B) Bengali
(C) Marathi (D) Kannada

18. Arrange the following in ascending order in terms of size :
1. epic 2. epigram
3. stanza 4. sonnet
(A) 1 2 3 4 (B) 2 1 3 4
(C) 2 3 4 1 (D) 1 3 4 2

19. "Fail I alone in words and deeds ?/Why, all men strive and who succeeds ?" These lines are from
(A) "Rabbi Ben Ezra"
(B) "Fra Lippo Lippi"
(C) "Caliban upon Setebos"
(D) "The Last Ride Together"

20. Dr. Johnson's "The Vanity of Human Wishes" expresses
(A) Epicureanism
(B) Humanism
(C) Stoicism
(D) Cynicism

21. "A trivial comedy for serious people" was the subtitle for
(A) *Everyman in His Humour*
(B) *Blythe Spirit*
(C) *The Way of the World*
(D) *The Importance of Being Earnest.*

22. Which famous elegy closes with the following lines ?
"In the deserts of the heart/Let the healing fountain start,/In the prison of his days,/ Teach the free man how to praise."
(A) *In Memoriam*
(B) *Thyrsis*
(C) "In Memory of W.B. Yeats"
(D) "Verses on the Death of T.S. Eliot"

23. *The Temple* is a collection of poems by
(A) Thomas Carew
(B) Robert Herrick
(C) George Herbert
(D) Richard Crashaw

24. Ben Jonson's comedies are
(A) Volpone, Bartholomew Fair, The Shoemaker's Holiday
(B) *Volpone, The Alchemist, Epicoene*
(C) *Volpone, The Alchemist, The Knight of the Burning Pestle*
(D) *Volpone, Epicoene, The Shoemaker's Holiday*

25. What is 'L' Allegro's' companion piece called ?
(A) *Lamia* (B) *Hyperion*
(C) *Il Penseroso* (D) *Thyrsis*

26. Match the character with the novel :
1. Caddy
2. Lennie
3. Jake Barnes
4. Tommy Wilhelm
5. *The Sound and the Fury* 6. *Of Mice and Men*
7. *The Sun Also Rises* 8. *Seize the Day*

Codes :
(A) 1-5 2-6 3-7 4-8 (B) 2-7 1-8 3-5 4-6
(C) 3-5 4-6 2-8 1-7 (D) 4-5 3-8 2-7 1-8

27. Who among the following writers belonged to the American Beat Movement ?
(A) Allen Ginsberg (B) Mark Beard
(C) Isaac McCaslih (D) Charles Beard

28. "The Lost Generation" is a name applied to the disillusioned intellectuals and aesthetes of the years following the First World War. Who called them "The Lost Generation" ?
(A) H.L. Mencken (B) Willa Cather
(C) Jack London (D) Gertrude Stein

29. Hyperbole is
1. an extravagant exaggeration
2. a racist slur
3. a metrical skill
4. a figure of speech
(A) 1 is correct
(B) 1 and 4 are correct
(C) 1 and 3 are correct
(D) 3 is correct

30. "Imagined Communities" is a concept propounded by
(A) Benedict Anderson
(B) Homi Bhabha
(C) Aijaz Ahmed
(D) Partha Chatterjee

31. The New Historicists include
(A) Greenblatt, Showalter, Montrose
(B) Greenblatt, Sinfield, Butler
(C) Greenblatt, Montrose, Goldberg
(D) Williams, Greenblatt, Belsey

32. Wallace Stevens' "The Man with the Blue Guitar" may be linked to the work of the following artist :
(A) Modigliani (B) Chagall
(C) Picasso (D) Cezanne

33. The author of *Gender Trouble* is
(A) Elaine Showalter
(B) Helene Cixous
(C) Michele Barrett
(D) Judith Butler

34. The structural analysis of signs was practised by
(A) Michel Foucault
(B) Jacques Lacan
(C) Julia Kristeva
(D) Roland Barthes

35. Which of the following is a spoof of a Gothic novel ?
(A) *Frankenstein*
(B) *Northanger Abbey*
(C) *Castle of Otranto*
(D) *Mysteries of Udolfo*

36. The "madwoman in the attic" is a specific reference to
(A) The narrator of "Goblin Market"
(B) Augusta Egg's 1858 narrative painting
(C) The Heroine of *The Yellow Wallpaper*
(D) Bertha Mason of *Jane Eyre*

37. "Recessional : A Victorian Ode", Kipling's well-known poem,
I. laments the end of an Era

II. marks a new commitment to scientific knowledge

III. expresses the sincerity of his religious devotion

IV. was occasioned by Queen Victoria's 1897 Jubilee Celebration

The correct combination for the statement, according to the code, is

(A) I, II and III are correct.

(B) III and IV are correct.

(C) I and IV are correct.

(D) I, III and IV are correct.

38. What is the correct chronological sequence of the following ?

(A) *Moll Flanders, Pamela, Joseph Andrews, Tristram Shandy*

(B) *Joseph Andrews, Tristram Shandy, Pamela, Moll Flanders*

(C) *Tristram Shandy, Moll Flanders, Pamela, Joseph Andrews*

(D) *Pamela, Moll Flanders, Joseph Andrews, Tristram Shandy*

39. "How can what an Englishman believes be heresy ? It is a contradiction in terms." This means

1. An Englishman does not know what heresy is.
2. An Englishman has no beliefs.
3. And, therefore, there is no question of his heresy.
4. And, therefore, there cannot be any question of his acting his beliefs.

(A) 1 and 4 are correct

(B) 2 and 1 are correct

(C) 1 and 3 are correct

(D) ? and 4 are correct

40. Which of the following is an essentially Freudian concept ?

(A) Archetype (B) The Uncanny

(C) The Absurd

(D) The Imaginary

41. He wrote an essay called "Conrad's Darkness" where he praises the earlier writer for offering him a vision of the world's "half-made societies'. Identify the writer.

(A) Chinua Achebe

(B) V.S. Naipaul

(C) Salman Rushdie

(D) Ngugi wa Thiongo

42. "Magic Realism" is closely associated with

(A) Italo Calvino

(B) Gabriel Garcia Marquez

(C) Anita Desai

(D) Rohinton Mistry

43. Who among the following combines anthropology, history and fiction ?

(A) Kamala Markandya

(B) Mulk Raj Anand

(C) Upmanyu Chatterjee

(D) Amitav Ghosh

44. Which of the following is NOT a Partition novel ?

(A) *Train to Pakistan*

(B) *Sunlight on a Broken Column*

(C) *The Shadow Lines*

(D) *In Custody*

45. Which of the following options is correct ?

(i) Transcendentalism was a philosophical and literary movement.

(ii) It flourished in the Southern States of America in the 19th century.

(iii) It was a reaction against 18th century rationalism and the skeptical philosophy of Locke.

(iv) Among the major texts of Transcendentalist thought are the essays of Emerson, Thoreau's Walden and the writings of Margaret Fuller.

(A) (i) and (iv) are correct.

(B) (ii) and (iii) are correct.

(C) (iii) and (iv) are correct.

(D) (iv) is correct.

Read the following passage carefully, and select the right answers from the alternatives given below in the question 46 to 50 :

It would be more accurate to say that discourse, rather than language, plays a crucial part in structuring our experience. The whole idea of 'language' is something of a fiction : what we normally refer to as 'language' can more realistically be seen as heterogeneous collection of discourses. Each of us has access to a range of discourses, and it is these different discourses which give us access to, or enable us to perform, different 'selves'. A discourse can be conceptualized as a 'system of statements which cohere around common meanings and values'. So, for example, in contemporary Britain there are discourses which can be labelled 'conservative' – that is, discourses which emphasize values and meanings where the status quo is cherished : and there are discourses which can be labelled 'patriarchal' – that is, discourses which emphasize meanings and values which assume the superiority of males. Dominant discourses such as these appear 'natural' : they are powerful precisely because they are able to make invisible the fact that they are just one among many different discourses.

Theorizing language in this way is still new in linguistics (to the extent that many linguists would not regard analysis in terms of discourses as being part of linguistics). One of the advantages of talking about discourses rather than about language is that the concept 'discourse' acknowledges the value-laden nature of language. There is no neutral discourse : whenever we speak we have to choose between different systems of meaning, different sets of values. This process allows us to show how language is implicated in our construction of different 'selves' : different discourses position us in different ways in relation to the world.

46. Which of the following is True in the light of this passage ?
(A) Language is inaccurate.
(B) Discourse is accurate.
(C) Language comprises discourse.
(D) Discourse comprises language.

47. What words/phrases suggest the *plurality* of discourse in this passage ?
I. different selves
II. range
III. system of statements
IV. heterogeneous collection
(A) II and IV (B) II and III
(C) III and IV (D) I

48. Having called language "something of a fiction", how does the author suggest its opposite ?
By using the phrase
(A) conceptualized as a system
(B) more accurate to say
(C) range of discourses
(D) more realistically be seen

49. Which among the following statements is NOT true ?
(A) Conservative discourses plead for the status quo.
(B) Patriarchal discourses privilege male values.
(C) Dominant discourses are natural.
(D) Dominant discourses seem natural.

50. What does this passage plead for ?
(A) Theorizing language in a new way.
(B) Theorizing language in terms of discourses.
(C) Studying language as discourse.
(D) Studying discourse as language.

51. The epithet "a comic epic in prose" is best applied to
(A) Richardson's *Pamela*
(B) Sterne's *A Sentimental Journey*
(C) Fielding's *Tom Jones*
(D) Defoe's *Robinson Crusoe*

52. Muriel Spark has written a dystopian novel called
(A) *Memento Mori*
(B) *The Prime of Miss Jean Brodie*
(C) *Robinson*
(D) *The Ballad of Peckham Rye*

53. Samuel Butler's Erewhon is an example of
(A) Feminist Literature
(B) Utopian Literature
(C) War Literature
(D) Famine Literature

54. The line "moments of unageing intellect" occurs in Yeats's
(A) Byzantium
(B) Among School Children
(C) Sailing to Byzantium
(D) The Circus Animals' Desertion

55. In his 1817 review of Coleridge's *Biographia Literaria*, Francis Jeffrey grouped the following poets together as the 'Lake School of Poets':
(A) Keats, Wordsworth and Coleridge
(B) Wordsworth, Byron and Coleridge
(C) Blake, Wordsworth and Coleridge
(D) Wordsworth, Coleridge and Southey

56. Which of the following novels is not by Patrick White ?
(A) *The Vivisector*
(B) *The Tree of Man*
(C) *Voss*
(D) *Oscar and Lucienda*

57. The famous line "....... where ignorant armies clash by night" is taken from a poem by
(A) Wilfred Owen
(B) W.H. Auden
(C) Siegfried Sassoon
(D) Matthew Arnold

58. Which among the following novels is not written by Margaret Atwood ?
(A) *Surfacing*
(B) *The Blind Assassin*
(C) *The Handmaid's Tale*
(D) *The Stone Angel*

59. The term 'theatre of cruelty' was coined by
(A) Robert Brustein
(B) Antonin Artaud
(C) Augusto Boal
(D) Luigi Pirandello

60. The verse form of Byron's *Childe Harold* was influenced by
(A) Milton (B) Spenser
(C) Shakespeare (D) Pope

61. Tennyson's *Ulysses* is
(I) a poem expressing the need for going forward and braving the struggles of life
(II) a dramatic monologue
(III) a morbid poem
(IV) a poem making extensive use of satire
The right combination for the above statement, according to the code, is
(A) I & IV (B) II and III
(C) III and IV (D) I and II

62. Which post-war British poet was involved in a disastrous marriage with Sylvia Plath ?
(A) Philip Larkin (B) Ted Hughes
(C) Stevie Smith (D) Geoffrey Hill

63. Chaucer's *Parliament of Fowls* is in part
(I) a puzzle
(II) a debate
(III) a threnody
(IV) a beast fable
The correct combination for the above statement, according to the code, is
(A) I, II & IV (B) II, III & IV
(C) I & IV (D) II & IV

64. Who among the following wrote a book with the title *The Age of Reason* ?
(A) William Godwin
(B) Edmund Burke
(C) Thomas Paine
(D) Edward Gibbon

65. The Restoration comedy has been criticized mainly for its
(A) excessive wit and humour
(B) bitter satire and cynicism
(C) indecency and permissiveness
(D) superficial reflection of society

66. *Ideology and Ideological State Apparatuses* is an essay by
(A) Terry Eagleton (B) Karl Marx
(C) Raymond Williams
(D) Louis Althusser

67. Sexual possessiveness is a theme of Shakespeare's

(A) Coriolanus
(B) Julius Caesar
(C) Henry IV Part – I
(D) A Midsummer Night's Dream

68. The term 'Cultural Materialism' is associated with
(A) Stephen Greenblatt
(B) Raymond Williams
(C) Matthew Arnold
(D) Richard Hoggart

69. Which of the following authorbook pair is correctly matched ?
(A) Muriel Spark – *Under the Net*
(B) William – *Girls of Golding Slender Means*
(C) Angus Wilson – *Lucky Jim*
(D) Doris Lessing – *The Grass is Singing*

70. Who among the following is a Canadian critic ?
(A) I.A. Richards
(B) F.R. Leavis
(C) Cleanth Brooks
(D) Northrop Frye

71. Sethe is a character in
(A) *The Colour Purple*
(B) *The Women of Brewster Place*
(C) *Beloved*
(D) *Lucy*

72. Imagined Communities is a book by
(A) Aijaz Ahmad
(B) Edward Said
(C) Perry Anderson
(D) Benedict Anderson

73. Who among the following is a Cavalier poet ?
(A) Henry Vaughan
(B) Richard Crashaw
(C) John Suckling
(D) Anne Finch

74. Which play of Wilde has the subtitle, *A Trivial Comedy for Serious People* ?
(A) *A Woman of No Importance*
(B) *Lady Windermere's Fan*
(C) *The Importance of Being Earnest*
(D) *An Ideal Husband*

75. Which of the following plays is not written by Wole Soyinka ?
(A) *The Lion and the Jewel*
(B) *The Dance of the Forests*
(C) *Master Harold and the Boys*
(D) *Kongi's Harvest*

76. Which of the following plays by William Wycherley is in part an adaptation of Moliere's *The Misanthrope* ?
(A) *The Plain Dealer*
(B) *The Country Wife*
(C) *Love in a Wood*
(D) *The Gentleman Dancing Master*

77. 'Inversion' is the change in the word order for creating rhetorical effect, e.g. *this book I like*. Another term for inversion is
(A) Hypallage (B) Hubris
(C) Haiku (D) Hyperbaton

78. The phrase 'the willing suspension of disbelief' occurs in
(A) *Biographia Literaria*
(B) *Preface to Lyrical Ballads*
(C) *In Defence of Poetry*
(D) *Poetics*

79. The religious movement Methodism in the 18th century England was founded by
(A) John Tillotson
(B) Bishop Butler
(C) Bernard Mandeville
(D) John Welsey

80. *My First Acquaintance with Poets*, an unforgettable account of meeting with literary heroes, is written by
(A) Charles Lamb
(B) Thomas de Quincey
(C) Leigh Hunt
(D) William Hazlitt

81. The figure of the Warrior Virgin in Spenser's *Faerie Queene* is represented by the character

(A) Britomart (B) Gloriana
(C) Cynthia (D) Duessa

82. The book Speech Acts is written by
(A) John Austin (B) John Searle
(C) Jacques Derrida
(D) Ferdinand de Saussure

83. Which among the following is not a sonnet sequence ?
(A) Philip Sydney – *Astrophel and Stella*
(B) Samuel Daniel – *Delia*
(C) Derek Walcott – *Omeroos*
(D) D.G. Rossetti – *The House of Life*

84. 'Incunabula' refers to
(A) books censured by the Roman Emperor
(B) books published before the year 1501
(C) books containing an account of myths and rituals
(D) books wrongly attributed to an author

85. The most notable achievement in Jacobean prose was
(A) Bacon's Essays
(B) King James' translation of the Bible
(C) Robert Burton's *Anatomy of Melancholy*
(D) None of the above

86. The Court of Chancery is a setting in Dickens'
(A) *Little Dorrit*
(B) *Hard Times*
(C) *Dombey and Son*
(D) *Bleak House*

87. Which romantic poet coined the famous phrase 'spots of time' ?
(A) John Keats
(B) William Wordsworth
(C) S.T. Coleridge
(D) Lord Byron

88. The statement 'I think, therefore, I am' is by
(A) Schopenhauer (B) Plato
(C) Descartes (D) Sartre

89. Verse that has no set theme – no regular meter, rhyme or stanzaic pattern is
(I) open form
(II) flexible form
(III) free verse
(IV) blank verse
The correct combination for the statement, according to the code, is
(A) I, II and III are correct
(B) III and IV are correct
(C) II, III and IV are correct
(D) I and III are correct

90. Which is the correct sequence of publication of Pinter's plays ?
(A) The Room, One for the Road, No Man's Land, The Homecoming
(B) The Homecoming, No Man's Land, The Room, One for the Road
(C) The Room, The Homecoming, No Man's Land, One for the Road
(D) One for the Road, The Room, The Homecoming, No Man's Land

91. Johnson's *Dictionary of the English Language* was published in the year
(A) 1710 (B) 1755
(C) 1739 (D) 1759

92. The literary prize, Booker of Bookers, was awarded to
(A) J.M. Coetzee
(B) Nadine Gordimer
(C) Martin Amis
(D) Salman Rushdie

93. In Keats' poetic career, the most productive year was
(A) 1816 (B) 1817
(C) 1820 (D) 1819

94. Pope's *The Rape of the Lock* was published in 1712 in
(A) three cantos (B) four cantos
(C) five cantos (D) two cantos

95. Stephen Dedalus is a fictional character associated with
I. A Portrait of the Artist as a Young Man
II. Sons and Lovers
III. Ulysses
IV. The Heart of Darkness

The correct combination for the above statement according to the code is

(A) I & II (B) I, II & III
(C) III & IV (D) I & III

96. In Moby Dick Captain Ahab falls for his

(A) ignorance (B) pride
(C) courage (D) drunkenness

97. The first complete printed English Bible was produced by

(A) William Tyndale
(B) William Caxton
(C) Miles Coverdale
(D) Roger Ascham

98. Elizabeth Gaskell's novel Mary Barton is sub-titled

(A) *The Two Nations*
(B) *A Tale of Manchester Life*
(C) *A Story of Provincial Life*
(D) *The Factory Girl*

99. Some of the Jacobean playwrights were prolific. One of them claimed to have written 200 plays. The playwright is

(A) John Ford
(B) Thomas Dekker
(C) Philip Massinger
(D) Thomas Heywood

100. The concept of "Star-equilibrium" in connection with man-woman relationship appears in

(A) *Women in Love*
(B) *Maurice*
(C) *Mrs. Dalloway*
(D) *The Old Wives' Tales*

✔ ANSWERS

1. (C)	**2.** (B)	**3.** (C)	**4.** (C)	**5.** (A)	**6.** (D)	**7.** (D)	**8.** (B)	**9.** (C)	**10.** (B)
11. (B)	**12.** (A)	**13.** (A)	**14.** (C)	**15.** (C)	**16.** (C)	**17.** (C)	**18.** (C)	**19.** (D)	**20.** (B)
21. (D)	**22.** (C)	**23.** (C)	**24.** (B)	**25.** (C)	**26.** (A)	**27.** (A)	**28.** (D)	**29.** (B)	**30.** (A)
31. (C)	**32.** (C)	**33.** (D)	**34.** (D)	**35.** (B)	**36.** (D)	**37.** (B)	**38.** (A)	**39.** (A)	**40.** (B)
41. (B)	**42.** (B)	**43.** (D)	**44.** (D)	**45.** (C)	**46.** (D)	**47.** (A)	**48.** (D)	**49.** (D)	**50.** (B)
51. (C)	**52.** (B)	**53.** (B)	**54.** (C)	**55.** (D)	**56.** (D)	**57.** (D)	**58.** (D)	**59.** (B)	**60.** (B)
61. (D)	**62.** (B)	**63.** (C)	**64.** (C)	**65.** (C)	**66.** (D)	**67.** (D)	**68.** (B)	**69.** (D)	**70.** (D)
71. (C)	**72.** (D)	**73.** (C)	**74.** (C)	**75.** (C)	**76.** (A)	**77.** (D)	**78.** (A)	**79.** (D)	**80.** (D)
81. (A)	**82.** (A)	**83.** (C)	**84.** (B)	**85.** (B)	**86.** (D)	**87.** (B)	**88.** (C)	**89.** (D)	**90.** (C)
91. (B)	**92.** (D)	**93.** (D)	**94.** (D)	**95.** (D)	**96.** (B)	**97.** (C)	**98.** (B)	**99.** (D)	**100.** (A)

MODEL PAPER

SET-2

Note : This paper contains **hundred** (100) Objective type questions, each question carrying **two** (2) marks. Attempt all of them.

1. Who among the following was key witness in the British trial of D.H. Lawrence's novel, "Lady Chatterly's Lover"?
(A) Raymond Williams
(B) Stuart Hall
(C) Richard Hoggart
(D) Mathew Arnold

2. What do Wimsatt and Beardsley rail against in 'The Intentional Fallacy'?
(A) The idea that authors are the ultimate source of meaning
(B) Close reading
(C) Reading poems as poems
(D) Watching movie adaptations of novels

3. "All love is expansion, all selfishness is contraction. Love is therefore the only law of life. He who loves lives, he who is selfish is dying. Therefore love for love's sake, because it is the only law of life, just as you breathe to live."
Which of the Indian writers in which of his/ her works has quoted the above lines?
(A) Rabindranath Tagore, Stray Birds
(B) Arundhati Roy, The God of Small Things
(C) Swami Vivekananda, Letters of Swami Vivekananda
(D) Raja Rao, The Cat and Shakespeare

4. _____ is associated with the phrase, "Ain't I a Woman"?
(A) Toni Morrison (B) Maya Angelou
(C) Sojourner Truth
(D) Paul Gilroy

5. "The best poetry will be found to have a power of forming, sustaining and delighting us". This assertion implies
(A) Poetry is more useful than other arts
(B) All other arts including poetry have their limitations
(C) Poetry has multiple functions to perform
(D) Poetry has no role to play

6. Although Nobel Laureate Seamus Heaney writes in English, in voice and subject matter, his poems are
(A) Welsh (B) Scottish
(C) Irish (D) Polish

7. To whom is Mary Shelley's famous work *Frankenstein* dedicated ?
(A) Lord Byron (B) Claire Clairmont
(C) William Godwin
(D) P.B. Shelley

8. Which among the following poems by Philip Larkin records his impressions while travelling to London by train ?
(A) "Aubade"
(B) "Church Going"
(C) "The Whitsun Wedding"
(D) "An Arundel Tomb"

9. The English satirist who used the sharp edge of praise to attack his victims was
(A) Ben Jonson (B) John Donne
(C) John Dryden (D) Samuel Butler

10. One of the most famous movements of direct address to the reader – "Reader, I married him" – occurs in
(A) Henry Fielding's *Tom Jones*

(B) Charlotte Bronte's *Jane Eyre*
(C) Laurence Sterne's *Tristram Shandy*
(D) George Eliot's *Middlemarch*

11. Langland's *Piers Plowman* is a satire on
(A) aristocracy (B) chivalry
(C) peasantry (D) clergy

12. Which of the following thinker-concept pair is correctly matched ?
(A) I.A. Richards – Archetypal Criticism
(B) Christopher – Mysticism Frye
(C) Jacques – Deconstruction Derrida
(D) Terry – Psychological Eagleton Criticism

13. Sexual jealousy is a theme in Shakespeare's
(A) *The Merchant of Venice*
(B) *The Tempest*
(C) *Othello* (D) *King Lear*

14. The title, *The New Criticism*, published in 1941, was written by
(A) Cleanth Brooks
(B) John Crowe Ransom
(C) Robert Penn Warren
(D) Allan Tate

15. Which of the following is not a Revenge Tragedy ?
(A) *The White Devil*
(B) *The Duchess of Malfi*
(C) *Doctor Faustus*
(D) *The Spanish Tragedy*

16. Who of the following playwrights rejects the Aristotelian concept of tragic play as imitation of reality ?
(A) G.B. Shaw (B) Arthur Miller
(C) Bertolt Brecht (D) John Galsworthy

17. The label 'Diasporic Writer' can be applied to
I. Meena Alexander
II. Arundhati Roy
III. Kiran Desai
IV. Shashi Deshpande
The correct combination for the statement, according to the code, is
(A) I and IV are correct.
(B) II and III are correct.
(C) I, II and IV are correct.
(D) I and III are correct.

18. The letter 'A' in *The Scarlet Letter* stands for
I. Adultery II. Able
III. Angel IV. Appetite
The correct combination for the statement, according to the code, is
(A) I and II are correct.
(B) II and III are correct.
(C) I, II and IV are correct.
(D) I, II and III are correct.

19. A monosyllabic rhyme on the final stressed syllable of two lines of verse is called
(A) monorhyme
(B) feminine rhyme
(C) masculine rhyme
(D) eye rhyme

20. A fatwa was issued in Salman Rushdie's name following the publication of :
(A) *Midnight's Children*
(B) *Shame*
(C) *Satanic Verses* (D) *Grimus*

21. "There is nothing outside the text" is a key statement emanating from
(A) Feminism
(B) New Historicism
(C) Deconstruction
(D) Structuralism

22. The Augustan Age is called so because
(A) King Augustus ruled over England during this period
(B) The English writers imitated the Roman writers during this period
(C) The English King was born in the month of August
(D) This was an age of sensibility

23. One of the important texts of Angry Young Man Movement is
(A) *Time's Arrow* by Martin Amis
(B) *A Portrait of the Artist as a Young Man* by James Joyce

(C) *Lucky Jim* by Kingsley Amis
(D) *The French Lieutenant's Woman* by John Fowles

24. Whom does Alexander Pope satirise in the portrait of Sporus ?
(A) Lady Wortley Montague
(B) Joseph Addison
(C) Lord Shaftsbury
(D) Lord Harvey

25. The hero of Marlowe's *Tamburlaine* was born as a
(A) carpenter
(B) goldsmith
(C) shepherd
(D) fisherman

26. In a letter to his brother George in September 1819, John Keats had this to say about a fellow romantic poet : "He describes what he sees – I describe what I imagine – Mine is the hardest task." The poet under reference is
(A) Wordsworth
(B) Coleridge
(C) Byron
(D) Southey

27. A sequence of repeated consonantal sounds in a stretch of language is
(A) alliteration
(B) acrostic
(C) assent
(D) syllable

28. Reformation was predominantly a movement in
(A) politics (B) literature
(C) religion
(D) education

29. The motto "only connect" is taken from
(A) Joseph Conrad's *Nostromo*
(B) Rudyard Kipling's *Kim*
(C) H.G. Wells' *The History of Mr. Polly*
(D) E.M. Forster's *Howards End*

30. English Iambic Pentameter was brought to its first maturity in
(A) sonnet
(B) dramatic verse
(C) lyric
(D) elegy

31. Who among the following was not a member of the Bloomsbury Group ?
(A) Lytton Strachey
(B) Clive Bell
(C) E.M. Forster
(D) Winston Churchill

32. The concept of human mind as *tabula rasa* or blank tablet was propounded by
(A) Bishop Berkley
(B) David Hume
(C) Francis Bacon
(D) John Locke

33. The terms 'resonance' and 'wonder' are associated with
(A) Stephen Greenblatt
(B) Terence Hawkes
(C) Terry Eagleton
(D) Ronald Barthes

34. The rhetorical pattern used by Chaucer in *The Prologue to Canterbury Tales* is
(A) ten-syllabic line
(B) eight-syllabic line
(C) rhyme royal
(D) ottava rima

35. Charles Darwin's *Origin of the Species* was published in the year
(A) 1859
(B) 1879
(C) 1845
(D) 1866

36. Who of the following is the author of *Juno and the Paycock* ?
(A) Lady Gregory
(B) W.B. Yeats
(C) Oscar Wilde
(D) Sean O'Casey

37. The title of William Faulkner's *The Sound and the Fury* is taken from a play by
(A) Christopher Marlowe

(B) William Shakespeare
(C) Ben Jonson
(D) John Webster

38. "Silverman has never read Browning." This is an example of
(A) chiasmus
(B) conceit
(C) zeugma
(D) metonymy

39. The term 'Intentional Fallacy' is first used by
(A) William Empson
(B) Northrop Frye
(C) Wellek and Warren
(D) Wimsatt and Beardsley

40. "Recessional : A Victorian Ode", Kipling's well-known poem,
I. laments the end of an Era
II. marks a new commitment to scientific knowledge
III. expresses the sincerity of his religious devotion
IV. was occasioned by Queen Victoria's 1897 Jubilee Celebration
The correct combination for the statement, according to the code, is
(A) I, II and III are correct.
(B) III and IV are correct.
(C) I and IV are correct.
(D) I, III and IV are correct.

41. Who among the following is not a Restoration playwright ?
(A) William Congreve
(B) William Wycherley
(C) Ben Jonson
(D) George Etherege

42. Which famous Romantic poem begins with the line : 'Hail to thee, blithe spirit ! / Bird thou never wert" ?
(A) "Ode to a Nightingale"
(B) "To the Cuckoo"
(C) "To a Skylark"
(D) "To the Daisy"

43. Who among the following Victorian poets disliked his middle name ?
(A) Arthur Hugh Clough
(B) Dante Gabriel Rossetti
(C) Gerard Manley Hopkins
(D) Algernon Charles Swinburne

44. Aston is a character in Pinter's
(A) *The Birthday Party*
(B) *The Caretaker*
(C) *The Dumb Waiter*
(D) *The Homecoming*

45. Byron's *English Bards and Scottish Reviewers* is about
I. the survey of English poetry
II. satire in English poetry
III. contemporary literary scene
IV. the early English travellers
The correct combination for the statement, according to the code, is
(A) III and IV are correct.
(B) II, III and IV are correct.
(C) I and II are correct.
(D) I and III are correct.

46. Which Eliotian character utters the question – "Do I eat a peach" ?
(A) Marina
(B) Prufrock
(C) Sweeney
(D) Stetson

47. Which among the following works by Daniel Defoe landed him in prison and the pillory ?
(A) The True-Born Englishman
(B) Captain Singleton
(C) The Shortest Way with Dissenters
(D) Moll Flanders

48. The arrival of printing in fifteenth century England was engineered by
(A) Sir Thomas Malory
(B) John Gower
(C) John Barbour
(D) William Caxton

49. About which nineteenth century English writer was it said that "He had succeeded as a writer not by conforming to the *Spirit of the Age*, but in opposition to it" ?
(A) Lord Byron on Coleridge
(B) Coleridge on Keats
(C) Hazlitt on Lamb
(D) De Quincey on Crabbe

50. The Restoration comedy, *The Double Dealer* was written by
(A) John Dryden
(B) William Wycherley
(C) William Congreve
(D) George Etherege

51. Little Nell is a character in Dickens's
(A) *Hard Times*
(B) *Great Expectations*
(C) *Oliver Twist*
(D) *The Old Curiosity Shop*

52. Who, among the following Indian writers in English, has created an identifiable imagined locale ?
(A) Mulk Raj Anand
(B) RajaRao
(C) R.K. Narayan
(D) Anita Desai

53. Who among the following is not a formalist critic ?
(A) Allen Tate
(B) Cleanth Brooks
(C) Stanley Fish
(D) William Empson

54. The rhyme scheme of the Spenserian sonnet is
(A) abab bcbc cdcd ee
(B) abab cdcd efef gg
(C) abba cddc effe gg
(D) abba abba cde cde

55. Who among the following Marlovian characters is consumed by greed?
(A) *Barabas*
(B) *Tamburlaine*
(C) *Doctor Faustus*
(D) *Mephistopheles*

56. The plan of Arthurian stories has influenced the composition of Tennyson's
(A) *In Memo riam*
(B) Idylls
(C) "Maud"
(D) "Locksley Hall"

57. There are two lists given below. Match the authors in List - I with their nationality in List - II by choosing the right option against the code.

List - I (Author)	**List - II (Nationality)**
(I) Patrick White	(1) Canada
(II) Nadine Gordimer	(2) New Zealand
(III) Margaret Atwood	(3) Australia
(IV) Ken Hulme	(4) South Africa

Code:

(A)	(2)	(1)	(4)	(3)
(B)	(4)	(3)	(2)	(1)
(C)	(3)	(4)	(1)	(2)
(D)	(3)	(2)	(4)	(1)

58. A Shakespearean sonnet has the following rhyme scheme:
(A) ABBA, ABBA, CDCDCD
(B) ABAB, BCBC, CD CD EE
(C) ABAB, CDCD, EFEF, GG
(D) ABBA, ABBA, CDCD, EE

59. "The future of poetry is immense, because in poetry.... our race, as time goes on, will find an ever surer and surer stay." — This claim for poetry is made in
(A) Arnold's "The Study of Poetry"
(B) Shelley's "A Defence of Poetry"
(C) Sidney's "An Apology for Poetry"
(D) Eliot's of Poetry and Poets

60. Which of the following is not about a dystopia?
(A) George Orwell's Nineteen Eighty-Four
(B) Aldous Huxley's Brave New World

(C) William Golding' s Lord of the Flies
(D) R.M. Ballantyne's The Coral Island

61. Who among the following is not associated with the translation of the Bible?
(A) Miles Coverdale
(B) William Tyndale
(C) John Wycliffe
(D) Thomas Browne

62. Arrange the following stages in a sequence in which all Shakespearean tragedies are structured. Use the code given below:
I. Denouement
II. Conflict
III. Exposition
IV. Climax

Code:
(A) III, II, IV, I
(B) III, IV, II, I
(C) II, IV, III, I
(D) II, IV, I, III

63. The term, 'curtal sonnet', was coined by
(A) John Milton
(B) William Blake
(C) Gerald Manley Hopkins
(D) Matthew Arnold

64. The author of the pamphlet *Short View of Immorality and Profaneness of the English Stage* (1698) was
(A) John Bunyan
(B) Jeremy Collier
(C) William Wycherley
(D) John Vanbrugh

65. Identify a play in the following list that is not written by Oscar Wilde:
(A) *A Woman of No Importance*
(B) *The Importance of Being Earnest*
(C) *Saints and Sinners*
(D) *An Ideal Husband*

66. Put the following novels by Charles Dickens in a sequential order with the help of the code:
1. Great Expectations
2. Hard Times
3. Bleak House
4. A Tale of Two Cities

Code:
(A) 3,2,4,1 (B) 2,4,3,1
(C) 1,2,4,3 (D) 4,2,1,3

67. Thomas Kyd's *The Spanish Tragedy* was influenced by
(A) Seneca
(B) Tertullian
(C) Virgil
(D) Plautus

68. In its final published version, Eliot's *The Waste Land* contains a total of
(A) 334 lines (B) 433 lines
(C) 373 lines (D) 423 lines

69. Jean Rhys's *Wide Sargasso Sea* is set in
(A) The Congo region
(B) The Niger Delta
(C) The Caribbean
(D) The African Savannah

70. Hamlet, lying wounded, says to his friend, "Horatio, I am dead." This is an example of
(A) protasis
(B) anacrusis
(C) prolepsis
(D) pun

71. *The Castle of Otranto* is an example of
(A) Gothic fiction
(B) Romance
(C) Comic fiction
(D) Bildungsroman

72. "The City of Dreadful Night", a long poem depicting the late Victorian sense of gloom and despondency, is written by
(A) Matthew Arnold
(B) Robert Browning
(C) James Thomson
(D) John Davidson

73. Which of the following novels by V.S. Naipaul is set in Africa and carries echoes of Joseph Conrad ?
(A) *The Mystic Masseur*
(B) *A Bend in the River*

(C) *A House for Mr. Biswas*
(D) *The Mimic Men*

74. In *The Rape of the Lock, Belinda's* lapdog is named
(A) Luck (B) Shock
(C) Pluck (D) Muck

75. *You Can 't Do Both* is a novel by
(A) John Fowles (B) Doris Lessing
(C) Kingsley Amis (D) Irish Murdoch

76. The character, Nathan Zuckerman, is associated with the fiction of
(A) Norman Mailer (B) Saul Bellow
(C) Philip Roth
(D) Bernard Malamud

77. Plato censured poetry because he believed it
(A) eliminates the ego.
(B) promotes sensuality.
(C) distorts reality.
(D) cripples the imagination.

78. Which of the following Tennyson poems is a dramatic monologue?
(A) *In Memoriam*
(B) *"The Charge of the Light Brigade"*
(C) *"Crossing the Bar"*
(D) *"Tithonus"*

79. The character Giovanni features in one of the following texts
(A) John Cleland' s Fanny Hill Memoirs of a Woman of Pleasure
(B) John Ford's 'Tis Pity She's a Whore
(C) John Braine's Room at the Top
(D) John Evelyn's Diaries

80. Which of the following poems features the phrase, "the still, sad music of humanity"?
(A) "Ode: Intimations of Immortality from Recollections of Early Childhood"
(B) "Michael: A Pastoral Poem"
(C) "The Solitary Reaper"
(D) "Tintern Abbey"

81. Molly Bloom is a character in James Joyce's
(A) *A Portrait of the Artist as a Young Man*
(B) *Dubliners*
(C) *Ulysses*
(D) *Exiles*

82. Eliot uses the term "objective correlative" in his essay.
(A) "The Metaphysical Poets"
(B) "Hamlet"
(C) "Tradition and the Individual Talent"
(D) "Dante"

83. Seamus Heaney was awarded the Nobel Prize for literature in the year
(A) 1995 (B) 1996
(C) 1997 (D) 1998

84. The pamphlet on the Irish condition, "An Address to the Irish People" was composed by
(A) W.B. Yeats (B) P.B. Shelley
(C) Jonathan Swift (D) G.B. Shaw

85. Which of the following arrangements of English novels is in the correct chronological sequence ?
(A) *Kim, A Passage to India, Sons and Lovers, Brave New World*
(B) *Sons and Lovers, A Passage to India, Kim, Brave New World*
(C) *Kim, Sons and Lovers, A Passage to India, Brave New World*
(D) *Brave New World, Kim, Sons and Lovers, A Passage to India*

86. "Verses on the Death of Dr. Swift" is written by
(A) Alexander Pope
(B) Samuel Johnson
(C) John Gay
(D) Jonathan Swift

87. *Widowers' Houses* was written by
(A) Oscar Wilde
(B) T.S. Eliot
(C) John Galsworthy
(D) G.B. Shaw

88. Who among the following Marxist critics has reconsidered the classic problem of 'base and superstructure" in relation to literature?

(A) Edmund Wilson
(B) Raymond Williams
(C) Lucien Goldmann
(D) Walter Benjamin

89. "Heteroglossia" refers to

(A) the multiple readings of a text.
(B) the juxtaposition of multiple voices in a text.
(C) the comments on the margins of a text.
(D) the gloss or commentary relating to a text.

90. Margaret Drabble is the author of

(A) *The Memoirs of a Survivor*
(B) *The Witch of Exmoor*
(C) *The Service of Clouds*
(D) *The Godless in Eden*

91. *MacFlecknoe* is an attack on Dryden' s literary rival,

(A) Richard Flecknoe
(B) Thomas Shadwell
(C) John Wilmot
(D) Matthew Prior

92. Eighteenth century writers used satire frequently for

(A) attacking human vices and follies.
(B) inciting the reading public.
(C) glorifying the culture of the upper classes.
(D) pleasing their women readers.

93. Byron's "The Vision of Judgement" is a satire directed against

(A) Charles Lamb
(B) John Keats
(C) Henry Hallam
(D) Robert Southey

94. Tom Paine's *The Rights of Man* was published in

(A) 1790 (B) 1791
(C) 1792 (D) 1793

95. Andrew Marvell' s "An Horatian Ode upon Cromwell's Return from Ireland" was written in

(A) 1647 (B) 1649
(C) 1650 (D) 1648

96. "The Rime of Ancient Mariner" is about

(A) a perilous adventure in the sea
(B) the accidental killing of an octopus
(C) the curse of a sea God
(D) the guilt and expiation of the Ancient Mariner

97. "To Daffodils" is a poem, written by

(A) Robert Heffick
(B) William Wordsworth
(C) John Keats
(D) P.B. Shelley

98. Which of the following novels reconstructs the historical events of the Indian Mutiny?

(A) *The Jewel in the Crown*
(B) *The Siege of Krishnapur*
(C) *The Day of the Scorpion*
(D) *The Towers of Silence*

99. "England, my England" is a poem by

(A) W.E. Henley
(B) A.E. Housman
(C) R.L. Stevenson
(D) Rudyard Kipling

100. Shelley was expelled from the Oxford University due to the publication of

(A) *The Revolt of Islam*
(B) *The Necessity of Atheism*
(C) *The Triumph of Life*
(D) *The Masque of Anarchy*

ANSWERS

1. (C)	**2.** (A)	**3.** (C)	**4.** (C)	**5.** (C)	**6.** (C)	**7.** (C)	**8.** (C)	**9.** (B)	**10.** (B)
11. (D)	**12.** (C)	**13.** (C)	**14.** (B)	**15.** (C)	**16.** (B)	**17.** (D)	**18.** (D)	**19.** (C)	**20.** (C)
21. (C)	**22.** (B)	**23.** (C)	**24.** (D)	**25.** (C)	**26.** (C)	**27.** (A)	**28.** (C)	**29.** (D)	**30.** (A)
31. (D)	**32.** (D)	**33.** (A)	**34.** (A)	**35.** (A)	**36.** (D)	**37.** (B)	**38.** (D)	**39.** (D)	**40.** (C)
41. (C)	**42.** (C)	**43.** (B)	**44.** (B)	**45.** (C)	**46.** (B)	**47.** (C)	**48.** (D)	**49.** (C)	**50.** (C)
51. (D)	**52.** (C)	**53.** (C)	**54.** (A)	**55.** (A)	**56.** (B)	**57.** (C)	**58.** (C)	**59.** (A)	**60.** (D)
61. (D)	**62.** (A)	**63.** (C)	**64.** (B)	**65.** (C)	**66.** (A)	**67.** (A)	**68.** (B)	**69.** (C)	**70.** (C)
71. (A)	**72.** (C)	**73.** (B)	**74.** (B)	**75.** (C)	**76.** (C)	**77.** (C)	**78.** (D)	**79.** (B)	**80.** (D)
81. (C)	**82.** (B)	**83.** (A)	**84.** (B)	**85.** (C)	**86.** (D)	**87.** (D)	**88.** (B)	**89.** (B)	**90.** (B)
91. (B)	**92.** (A)	**93.** (D)	**94.** (B)	**95.** (C)	**96.** (D)	**97.** (A)	**98.** (B)	**99.** (A)	**100.** (B)

PREVIOUS YEARS' PAPERS

June, 2014

ENGLISH LITERATURE

PAPER-II

Note : This paper contains **fifty (50)** objective type questions, each question carrying **two (2)** marks. Attempt **all** the questions.

1. "The just man justices. What kind of foregrounding do you find in these lines?
(A) Syntactic (B) Semantic
(C) Collocation (D) None of the above

2. Match the items in List – I with items in List – II according to the code given :

List – I	List – II
i. Lambic	1. An unstressed syllable followed by a stressed syllable
ii. Anapaestic	2. A stressed is followed by two unstressed syllables.
iii. Dactylic	3. An unstressed syllable is followed by a stressed syllable
iv. Trochaic	4. A stressed syllable is followed by an unstressed syllable

Codes :

	i	ii	iii	iv		i	ii	iii	iv
(A)	2	1	3	4	(B)	3	2	1	4
(C)	4	1	2	3	(D)	3	1	2	4

3. The separation of styles in accordance with class appears more consistently in ______ than in medieval works of literature and art.
(A) Ben Jonson (B) Shakespeare
(C) Philip Sidney (D) Edmund Spenser

4. "Had we but world enough, and time, This coyness, lady, were no crime." This statement is an example of
(A) Irony (B) Paradox
(C) Hyperbole (D) Euphemism

5. A Spenserian stanza has
(A) four iambic pentameters
(B) six iambic pentameters
(C) eight iambic pentameters
(D) ten iambic pentameters

6. Match the items in List – I with items in List – II according to the code given below :

List – I (Critic)	List – II (Theory)
i. Cleanth Brooks	1. Ambiguity
ii. William Empson	2. Paradox
iii. Mark Schorer	3. Archetypal patterns in poetry
iv. Maud Bodkin	4. Techniques as discovery

Codes :

	i	ii	iii	iv		i	ii	iii	iv
(A)	2	1	4	3	(B)	3	2	1	4
(C)	1	2	3	4	(D)	2	3	4	1

7. "The artist may be present in his work like God in creation, invisible and almighty, everywhere felt but nowhere seen." Henry James is talking here about the artist's
(A) impersonality (B) absence
(C) presence (D) creativity

8. Match the items in List – I with items in List – II according to the code given below :

List – I (Theorist)	List – II (Book)
i. Michel Foucault	1. *Gender Trouble*
ii. Judith Butler	2. *Epistemology of the Closet*
iii. Alan Sinfield	3. *History of Sexuality*
iv. Eve Kosofsky Sedgwick	4. *Cultural Politics-Queer Reading*

Which is the correct combination according to the code :

Codes :

	i	ii	iii	iv		i	ii	iii	iv
(A)	3	1	2	4	(B)	3	1	4	2
(C)	4	2	1	3	(D)	4	3	1	2

9. "The greatness of a poet", Arnold says, "lies in his powerful and beautiful application of ideas to life". But a critic pointed out it was "not a happy way of putting it, as if ideas were a lotion for the inflamed skin of suffering humanity". Who was this critic ?

(A) T.S. Eliot (B) F.R. Leavis
(C) David Lodge (D) Allen Tate

10. Derrida's American disciples were

(A) Geoffrey Hartman, Paul de Man, J. Hills Miller
(B) Gertrude Stein, Barbara Johnson, Michael Ryan
(C) Barbara Johnson, Michael Ryan, Mary Ellman
(D) Jean Baudrillard, Gilles Deleuze, Felix Guattari

11. Identify the correct group of playhouses in late sixteenth century London from the following groups :

(A) Curtain, Rose, Swan, Globe, Hope
(B) Curtain, Rose, Swan, Globe, Sejanus
(C) Hope, Curtain, Rose, Swan, Globe
(D) Swan, Curtain, Rose, Globe, Thames

12. "Keep up your bright swords, for the dew will rust them. Good Signior, you shall more command with years. Than with your weapons." The above lines are addresses by Othello to

(A) Roderigo and officers
(B) Brabantio, Roderigo and Officers
(C) The Duke and Senators
(D) Montano and Cassio

13. Act V of Marlowe's *Edward the Second shows* the murder of the king. Where does it take place ?

(A) Westminster, a room in the palace
(B) A room in Berkeley Castle
(C) A room in Killingworth Castle
(D) Within the Abbey of Neath

14. Identify the correctly matched set :

(A) *"The Shepheards Calender"* – 1579
Tottels Miscellany – 1557
Astrophel and Stella – 1591
The Spanish Tragedie – about 1585

(B) *"The Shepheards Calender"* – 1559
Tottels Miscellany – 1579
Astrophel and Stella – 1585
The Spanish Tragedie – about 1591

(C) *"The Shepheards Calender"* – 1585
Tottels Miscellany – 1591
Astrophel and Stella – 1579
The Spanish Tragedie – about 1557

(D) *"The Shepheards Calender"* – 1579
Tottels Miscellany – 1591
Astrophel and Stella – about 1585
The Spanish Tragedie – about 1557

15. Match the items in the List – I with items in List – II according to the code given below :

List – I (Authors)	List – II (Works)
i. Lucy Hutchinson	1. *The Life and Death of Mr. Badman*
ii. John Bunyan	2. *Sylva : or a Discourse of Forest Trees*
iii. John Evelyn	3. *Natures Pictures*
iv. Margaret Cavendish	4. *Memoirs of the Life of Colonel Hutchinson*

Codes :

	i	ii	iii	iv		i	ii	iii	iv
(A)	2	3	1	4	(B)	4	3	2	1
(C)	4	1	2	3	(D)	4	2	1	3

16. "But deeds, and language, such as men do use;
And persons, such as comedy would choose,
When she would show an image of the time,
and sport with human follies, not with crime."

In the above lines Jonson

I. Opposes the artificiality of the romantic tragic-comedy.
II. Initiates the use of realism.
III. Considers analysis of moral short comings more important
IV. Encourages the use of farce with melodrama.

Find out the correct combination according to the code :
(A) I, II and III are correct
(B) I, II and IV are correct
(C) I, III and IV are correct
(D) II, III and IV are correct

17. "And if no peece of chronicle we prove,
We'll build in ________ pretty roomes."
(A) lyrics (B) epics
(C) sonnets (D) stanzas

18. "That glory never shall his wrath or might extort from me." (*Paradise Lost*, Book I) What 'glory' is being referred to by Satan ?
(A) The courage never to submit or yield
(B) To reign in Hell
(C) To defeat God (D) To spread evil

19. It has been described as a "novel without predecessors", the product of an original mind and became immediately popular. It is a peculiar blend of pathos and humour, though the pathos is sometimes overdone to the point of becoming offensively sentimental.
The novel was published in 1760. What is the name of the novel ?
(A) *Gulliver's Travels*
(B) *The Castle of Otranto*
(C) *Tristram Shandy* (D) *A Tender Husband*

20. The son of a joiner, he was apprenticed as a printer. He remained a printer throughout his life. He was asked to prepare a series of modern letters for those who could not write for themselves. This humble task taught him the art of expressing himself in letters. Who is the novelist ?
(A) Daniel Defoe (B) Samuel Richardson
(C) Henry Fielding (D) Tobias Smollett

21. "Where ignorance is Bliss Tis folly to be wise."
Who wrote the following lines ?
(A) Pope (B) Gray
(C) Collins (D) Southey

22. Which of the following works is not actually a prose essay ?
(A) *Essay of Dramatic Poesy*
(B) *Essay on Man*
(C) *An Essay Concerning Human Understanding*
(D) *An Essay Towards a New Theory of Vision*

23. Whom does Mirabell deceive into believing that he loves her in *The Way of the World* ?
(A) Millamant (B) Lady Wishfort
(C) Mrs. Marwood (D) Mrs. Fainall

24. "Competence to age is supplementary to youth, a sorry supplement indeed, but I fear the best that is to be had. We must ride where we formerly walked : live better and be softer and shall be wise to do so – than we had means to do in the good old days you speak of."
Who speaks these words and to whom ?
(A) Lamb to Bridget
(B) Wordsworth to Dorothy
(C) Dorothy to Bridget
(D) Lamb to Dorothy

25. *The Prelude* although begun as early as 1799 and finished in its first version in 1805, was not published until ________.
(A) 1815 (B) 1820
(C) 1830 (D) 1850

26. "A rosy sanctuary will I dress With the wreathed trellis of a working brain." The above lines are quoted from
(A) 'Adonais' (B) 'Ode to Psyche'
(C) 'Eve of St. Agnes' (D) 'Endymion'

27. "Love seeketh only self to please, To bind another to its delight." This selfish and possessive nature of love is illustrated in Blake's
(A) 'The Clod and the Pebble'
(B) 'The Sick Rose'
(C) 'A Poison Tree' (D) 'Ah Sunflower'

28. Who is the author of *Mary*, and the unfinished *The Wrongs of Woman* ?
(A) Mary Wollstonecraft
(B) William Godwin
(C) Mary Hay
(D) Elizabeth Inchbald

29. Identify the incorrect factor in Henry James' theory of the novel :
(A) It should be sentimental
(B) It should be objective

(C) It should be realistic

(D) It should be viewed as an artistic form

30. Match the items in List – I with items in List – II according to the code given below :

List – I (Novels)	List – II (Characters)
i. *Ulysses*	1. Mrs. Moore
ii. *A Passage to India*	2. Molly Bloom
iii. *To the Lighthouse*	3. Gerald Crich
iv. *Women in Love*	4. Lily Briscoe

Codes :

	i	ii	iii	iv
(A)	3	1	2	4
(B)	2	1	4	3
(C)	4	2	1	3
(D)	1	3	2	4

31. Which among the following novels was not written in 1922 ?

(A) *Ulysses* (B) *Jacob's room*

(C) *Aaron's Rod* (D) *A Passage to India*

32. "A sudden blow : the great wings beating still
Above the staggering girl, her thighs caressed
By the dark webs, her nap caught in his bill,
He holds her helpless breast upon his breast."

Who is the author of the above lines ?

(A) W.B. Yeats (B) T.S. Eliot

(C) W.H. Auden (D) D.H. Lawrence

33. "Consume my heart away; sick with desire
And fastened to a dying animal."

The above lines are taken from

(A) "Felix Randal"

(B) "Sailing to Byzantium"

(C) "Coole and the Ballylee, 1931"

(D) "The Second Coming"

34. Who among the following is not a surrealist poet ?

(A) Hugh Sykes Dykes

(B) David Gascoyne

(C) Kenneth Allot (D) C. Day Lewis

35. The protagonist returns with an admonition, the diamond sent to him for smuggling out a packet of diamonds as bribe. This scene occurs in one of the novels of Graham Greene – Identify the novel

(A) *The End of the Affair*

(B) *The Heart of the Matter*

(C) *The Ministry of Fear*

(D) *Our Man in Havana*

36. Samuel Beckett's trilogy published together in London in 1959 under the English titles is

(A) *More Pricks than Kicks, Murphy, Molloy*

(B) *B. Molloy, Malone Dies, The Unnamable*

(C) *Molloy, Murphy, Malone Dies*

(D) *The Unnamable, More Pricks than Kicks, Murphy*

37. Among the following playwrights, who was awarded the Pulitzer prize in 1920 ?

(A) Eugene O'Neill (B) Sean O'Casey

(C) William Somerset Maugham

(D) J.B. Priestly

38. D.H. Lawrence popularized the concept of ________ in his novels.

(A) Realism (B) Naturalism

(C) Primitivism (D) Expressionism

39. Who among the following is not an American modernist poet ?

(A) William Carlos Williams

(B) Ezra Pound

(C) William Ellery Channing, the younger

(D) Marianne Moore

40. An important poet and playwright who in the 1960s led the Black Arts Movement, in the spirit of negritude, posited a 'Black Aesthetic' that expressed a pan-African, organic and whole sensibility.

(A) Henry Louis Gates Jr.

(B) Amiri Baraka

(C) Ishmael Reed (D) Bell Hooks

41. Match List – I with List – II according to the code given below :

List – I (Authors)	List – II (Books)
i. V.S. Naipaul	1. Foe
ii. Jean Rhys	2. Indigo or Mapping the Waters
iii. Marina Warners	3. Wide Sargasso Sea
iv. J.M. Coetzee	4. Mimic Men

Codes :

	i	ii	iii	iv		i	ii	iii	iv
(A)	4	2	3	1	(B)	4	1	2	3
(C)	4	3	2	1	(D)	1	3	4	2

42. Yasmine Gooneratne's *The Pleasures of Conquest* termed as a postcolonial novel of the nineties is ironically enough set in the tropical island nation of

(A) Sri Lanka (B) Fiji
(C) The Caribbean (D) Amnesia

43. Which of the following is not an Asian – Canadian writer ?

(A) Shauna Singh Badlwin
(B) Himani Banerjee
(C) Joy Kogawa (D) Meena Alexander

44. Which of the following is true ?

(A) 'Aurora Leigh' is a poem in nine books
(B) 'Aurora Leigh' is a collection of sonnets from the Portuguese
(C) 'Aurora Leigh' is a nursery rhyme book
(D) 'Aurora Leigh' is "the Seeds and Fruits of English Poetry"

45. "The old order changeth yielding place to new,
And God fulfils himself in many way."
In which of the following poems do these lines appear ?

(A) 'Locksley Hall' (B) 'Two Voices'
(C) 'Morte d'Arthur' (D) 'Ulysses'

46. George Eliot's attempt to write a historical novel of the Italian Renaissance was not successful. Which was this novel ?

(A) *Adam Bede* (B) *Felix Holt*
(C) *Silas Marner* (D) *Romola*

47. In which novel, does the hero, driven by passion and revenge, add a new dimension to the concept of suffering ?

(A) *Wuthering Heights* (B) *Jude the Obscure*
(C) *Mill on the Floss* (D) *Hard Times*

48. From the following women characters in Hardy's novels choose the odd one out :

(A) Bathsheba Everdene (B) Eustacia Vye
(C) Elizabeth Jane (D) Lucetta

49. "Out of the gosple he tho wordes caughte
And this figure he added eek therto, That if gold ruste, what shal iren do ?"
In the Prologue the Parson is represented as a man :

1. who loved money
2. who criticized the corrupt clergy
3. who practiced what he preached
4. who was a poor but honest clerk

Find the correct combination according to the code :

(A) 1, 2 and 3 are correct
(B) 1, 2 and 4 are correct
(C) 2, 3 and 4 are correct
(D) 1, 3 and 4 are correct

50. Match the items in List – I with items in List – II according to the code given below :

List – I (Plays)	**List – II (Characters)**
i. *White Devil*	1. Hieornimo
ii. *Maids Tragedy*	2. Old Knowell
iii. *Every Man in his Humour*	3. Vittoria Corombona
iv. *The Spanish Tragedie*	4. Aspatia

Codes :

	i	ii	iii	iv		i	ii	iii	iv
(A)	4	3	1	2	(B)	2	1	3	4
(C)	3	4	2	1	(D)	4	3	2	1

✓ ANSWERS

1. (AB)	**2.** (*)	**3.** (B)	**4.** (A)	**5.** (C)	**6.** (A)	**7.** (A)	**8.** (B)	**9.** (A)	**10.** (A)
11. (AC)	**12.** (B)	**13.** (B)	**14.** (A)	**15.** (C)	**16.** (A)	**17.** (C)	**18.** (A)	**19.** (C)	**20.** (B)
21. (B)	**22.** (B)	**23.** (B)	**24.** (A)	**25.** (D)	**26.** (B)	**27.** (A)	**28.** (A)	**29.** (A)	**30.** (B)
31. (D)	**32.** (A)	**33.** (B)	**34.** (D)	**35.** (B)	**36.** (*)	**37.** (A)	**38.** (C)	**39.** (C)	**40.** (B)
41. (C)	**42.** (D)	**43.** (D)	**44.** (A)	**45.** (C)	**46.** (D)	**47.** (A)	**48.** (C)	**49.** (*)	**50.** (C)

* Denotes marks given to all candidates.

June, 2014

ENGLISH LITERATURE

PAPER-III

Note : This paper contains seventy **five (75)** objective type questions of **two (2)** marks each. All questions are compulsory.

1. Where Sir Thomas Wyatt adapted Petrarch and Petrarchanism to English sounds and metres, Survey's verse tends to look back beyond Petrarch to the

(A) French verse (B) Italian verse

(C) Spanish verse (D) Latin verse

2. Here are some characteristics of Morality Plays :

1. They are dramatized allegories of the life of man.
2. They depict man's temptation and sinning, his quest for salvation and his confrontation with Death.
3. Though the hero represents Mankind, the other characters are by no means personifications, of virtues, vices and death.
4. A character known as the Vice often plays the role of the hero, a predecessor of the Villainhero in Elizabethan drama.

Find the correct combination according to the code :

(A) Only 1 and 2 are correct.

(B) Only 1 and 3 are correct.

(C) Only 1 and 4 are correct.

(D) Only 2 and 3 are correct.

3. In Spenser's Re Faerie Queene there are the allegorized moral and religious virtues with their counterparts in the vices. Identify the correctly matched set :

(A) Una – Truth
Guyon – Temperance
Duessa – Deceit
Orgoglio – Pride

(B) Una – Pride
Guyon – Deceit
Duessa – Temperance
Orgoglio – Truth

(C) Una – Deceit
Guyon – Pride
Duessa – Temperance
Orgoglio – Truth

(D) Una – Temperance
Guyon – Truth
Duessa – Pride
Orgoglio – Deceit

4. "Fop at the toilet, flatt'rer at the board
Now trips a lady, a now struts a lord."

The above lines are quoted from

(A) McFlecknoc

(B) The Rape of the Lock

(C) Epistle to Dr. Arbuthnot

(D) Absalom and Achitrphel

5. Which of the following arrangements is in the correct chronological sequence ?

(A) Every Man in His Humour
The Shoemaker's Holiday
Antonio's Revenge
The Changeling

(B) The Shoemaker's Holiday
Every Man in his Humour
The Changeling
Antonia's Revenge

(C) The Changeling
Antonio's Revenge
Every Man in His Humour
The Shoemaker's Holiday

(D) Antonio's Revenge
Every Man in His Humour
The Changeling
The Shoemaker's Holiday

6. Though Coleridge refers to "Motivehunting of a motiveless malignity", the "human villain" Iago is far from "motiveless". His motives are

I. He has been disappointed of military promotion.
II. He suspects Othello of cuckolding him
III. He has been in love with Desdemona
IV. He wants to become Othello.

Find the most appropriate combination according to the code :

(A) I and II are correct
(B) I and III are correct
(C) I and IV are correct
(D) II and IV are correct

7. In 'The Prologue' to Dr. Faustus, the chorus proposes that the theme should be –

I. "cursed necromancy"
II. "audacious deeds"
III. "dalliance of love"
IV. "self-conceit"

The correct combination according to the code is

(A) I and II are correct
(B) II and III are correct
(C) I and IV are correct
(D) III and IV are correct

8. The centre of his plays is a proud character on Marlowe's model, with a bold licence in speech and action, full of elaborate metaphors, phrase tumbling after phrase, as he asserts himself in the French Court. Dryden unjustly described his style as "a dwarfish thought, dressed up in gigantic words". Who is this Jacobean playwright ?

(A) John Fletcher
(B) John Webster
(C) George Chapman
(D) John Marston

9. In Paradise Lost BK IX Milton writes that Adam was overcome with "______" and so ate the forbidden fruit against his "better knowledge".

(A) "female charm"
(B) "exceeding love"
(C) "faithful love"
(D) "taste so divine"

10. In which poem of Donne's is the lover's face reflected in the eyes of his beloved ?

(A) "The Good Morrow"
(B) "The Canonization"
(C) "The Apparition"
(D) "A Valediction : Forbidding Mourning"

11. Match List – I with List – II according to the code given below :

List – I (Dramatists)	**List – II (Plays)**
i. Thomas Otway	1. The Provok'd Husband
ii. William Wycherley	2. The Recruiting Officer
iii. Colley Cibber	3. The Country Wife
iv. George Farquhar	4. The Orphan, or the unhappy marriage

Codes :

	i	ii	iii	iv
(A)	4	3	1	2
(B)	3	2	1	2
(C)	4	2	3	1
(D)	3	1	2	4

12. "Thou wast no born for death immortal Bird."

In what sense is the Bird "immortal" as compared to mortal man ?

I. Here man as an individual is unfairly compared to a bird as a species.
II. The word "Bird" stands for the nightingale's song.
III. When considered as a species man is equally "immortal" as the "Bird".
IV. The "Bird" is "Immortal" because songs of birds have given pleasure to man through the ages.

Find the correct combination according to the code :

(A) Only I and III are correct
(B) Only IV is incorrect
(C) Only II and IV are correct
(D) Only I and IV are incorrect

13. Coleridge's "The Rime of the Ancient Mariner" is a poem in ________ .
(A) 8 parts (B) 9 parts
(C) 7 parts (D) 6 parts

14. Scott is known for the creation of mad, irrational witch-like women characters. From the following list pick the odd one out :
(A) Madge Wildfive
(B) Meg Murdockson
(C) Euphemia Deans
(D) Meg Merrilees

15. Joseph Addison called him "The Miracle of the present age" and Alexander Pope wrote the epitaph for the monument erected in his memory. Who is he ?
(A) John Locke (B) Isaac Newton
(C) Ashley Cooper (D) Christopher Wren

16. The play was first performed in 1773. The author asked a friend "Did it make you laugh ?" and getting the answer "Exceedingly" said then that was all he required. He used for plot a reputed experience of his own as a schoolboy when he lost his way and asked to be directed to an inn but was shown the gateway to the local squire's house. Which play is this ?
(A) Sheridan's The Rivals
(B) Sheridan's The School for Scandal
(C) Goldsmith's She Stoops to Conquer
(D) Goldsmith's The Good Natured Man

17. What is Johnson's opinion regarding the "Violation" of the three unities in the plays of Shakespeare ?
I. Shakespeare should have followed the Unities.
II. Shakespeare followed the important Unity of Action satisfactorily.
III. Shakespeare's plays suffered because they did not follow the Unities.
IV. Unity of Time and Place arise from false assumptions.

The correct combination according to the code is
(A) I and II are correct.
(B) II and IV are correct.
(C) III and IV are correct.
(D) I and III are correct

18. The Tatler appeared thrice a week
(A) On Tuesdays, Thursdays and Saturdays
(B) On Sundays, Tuesdays and Thursdays
(C) On Mondays, Wednesdays and Fridays
(D) On Wednesdays, Thursdays and Fridays

19. "No man is truly great, who is great only in his lifetime. The test of greatness is the page of history. Nothing can be said to be great that has a distinct limit, or that borders on something evidently greater than itself. Besides, what is shortlived and pampered into mere notoriety, is of a gross and vulgar quality in itself."

This passage describing the quality of greatness is taken from
(A) "Of studies" by Francis Bacon
(B) "The Indian Jugglers" by William Hazlitt
(C) Preface to Shakespeare by Samuel Johnson
(D) An Essay of Dramatic Poesy by John Dryden

20. In Blake's "The Human Abstract", the fragmented world of Experience is symbolized in the image of the
(A) Caterpillar (B) Fly
(C) Raven (D) Fruit of Deceit

21. Here are sentences labelled Assertion (A) and Reason (R) :

Assertion (A) : While referring to Charlotte Bronte's claim that she has excluded public interest from her novels Graham Greene writes : 'Public interest in her day was surely more separate from public life... with us, however consciously unconcerned we are, it obtrudes through the cracks of our stories terribly persistent like grass through cement'.

Reason (R) : The decade of the "thirties was bristling with recurring economic and political crisis like the Great Depression, Wall Street Crash, Unemployment, rise of Hitler and Mussolini, series of murders, invasions and tensions; writers could not remain unaffected.

In the light of (A) and (R) which of the following is correct ?

(A) Both (A) and (R) are true and (R) is the correct explanation of (A).

(B) Both (A) and (R) are true, but (R) is not the correct explanation of (A).

(C) (A) is true but (R) is false.

(D) (A) is false, but (R) is true.

22. Match the titles of the books with their authors :

List – I	List – II
i. Psychology and Art Today	1. John Strachey
ii. Revolution in Writing	2. W.H. Auden
iii. The Coming Struggle for Power	3. C. Day Lewis
iv. Arrow in the Blue	4. Arthur Koestler

Codes :

	i	ii	iii	iv
(A)	3	1	2	4
(B)	4	2	3	1
(C)	2	3	1	4
(D)	1	2	4	3

23. George Meredith's first novel was banned by Mudie's Circulating Library for its supposed moral offence.

Identify the novel :

(A) The Egoist

(B) Evan Harrington

(C) Diana of the Crossways

(D) The Ordeal of Richard Feverel

24. Match the titles of the following poems by Tennyson with their opening lines according to the code given below :

List – I (Titles of poems)	List – II (Opening Lines)
i. "Tithonus"	1. "'Courage' he said, and pointed towards the land. The mounting wave will roll us shoreward soon."
ii. "The Lotos-Eaters"	2. "The woods decay, the woods decay and fall, The vapours weep their burthen to the ground."
iii. 'Ulysses'	3. "On either side the river lie Long fields of barley and of rye."
iv. 'The Lady of Shalott'	4. "It little profists that an idle king, By this still hearth, among these barren crags, Matched with an aged wife, I mete and dole Unequal laws unto a savage race."

Codes :

	i	ii	iii	iv
(A)	2	1	4	3
(B)	3	2	1	4
(C)	4	3	2	1
(D)	2	4	3	1

25. Why are Elizabeth Barrett Browning's Sonnets called "From Sonnets from the Portuguese" ?

(A) She wrote the whole in Portugal

(B) The sonnets were translated from the Portuguese.
(C) She presented it under the guise of a translation from the Portuguese language.
(D) The sonnets were narrated by a Portuguese.

26. Yeast's "Sailing to Byzantium" is about
(A) Irish Culture
(B) The art and culture of Byzantium in general
(C) Irish revolutionaries
(D) Regenerating the art and culture that existed in Byzantium

27. "She had _______ lilies in her hand And the stars in her hair were ______."
(Rossetti's "The Blessed Damozel")
(A) 7 and 3 (B) 3 and 7
(C) 6 and 4 (D) 4 and 6

28. Which of the following arrangements is in the correct chronological sequence ?
(A) Adam Bede – Wuthering Heights – North and South – Villette
(B) Wuthering Heights – Villete – North and South – Adam Bede
(C) Villettee – North and South – Wuthering Heights – Adam Bede
(D) North and South – Wuthering Heights – Adam Bede – Villette

29. In which of the following novels by canrod do the Gould couple and Decoud appear as characters with Costaguana as the setting ?
(A) Victory
(B) Under Western Eyes
(C) Nostromo
(D) The Nigger of the Narcissus

30. Match the following plays with their authors according to the code given below :

List – I (Plays)	List – II (Authors)
i. Heartbreak House	1. John Galsworthy
ii. Loyalties	2. Bertolt Brecht
iii. In the Jungle of Cities	3. T.S. Eliot
iv. The Family Reunion	4. George Bernard Shaw

Codes :

	i	ii	iii	iv
(A)	3	4	2	1
(B)	1	2	3	4
(C)	2	1	4	3
(D)	4	1	2	3

31. In November 1910 in an exhibition organized by Roger Fry, the paintings of three painters were displayed. Identify the painters :
(A) Duncan Grant, Vanessa Bell, Clive Bell
(B) Cezanne, Van Gogh, Gauguin
(C) Matisse, Picasso, Braque
(D) Cezanne, Van Gogh, Matisse

32. Why did Phaedra, wife of Theseus, commit suicide by hanging herself ?
(A) Theseus hated her
(B) Her stepson, Hippolytus rejected her love
(C) Hippolytus wanted to marry her
(D) She was lonely and depressed

33. Identify the poet in whose verse rural Ulster figures prominently
(A) Tony Harrison
(B) Ted Hughes
(C) Seamus Heaney
(D) Louis MacNeice

34. Match the pairs of authors and their works according to the code given :

List – I (Authors)	List – II (Works)
i. Alexander Dumas	1. Remembrance of Things Past
ii. Honore de Balzac	2. Madame Bovary
iii. Gustav Flaubert	3. The Human Comedy
iv. Marcel Proust	4. The Count of Monte Christo

Codes :

	i	ii	iii	iv
(A)	4	3	2	1
(B)	1	2	3	4
(C)	2	1	4	3
(D)	3	4	1	2

35. Which of the following statements best applies to Anna Karenina ?

1. Among her most prominent qualities are her passionate spirit and determination to live life on her own terms.
2. She accepts the exile to which she has been condemned.
3. She is a victim of Russian patriarchal system.
4. Anna is deeply devoted to her family and children.

Codes :

(A) 1 and 2 are correct
(B) 2 and 3 are correct
(C) 1 and 3 are correct
(D) 1, 3 and 4 are correct

36. Match the pairs of authors and their works according to the code given :

List – I (Authors)	List – II (Works)
i. Vladimir Nabokov	1. Germinal
ii. Italo Calvino	2. Foucault's Pendulum
iii. Umberto Eco	3. If on a Winter's Night a Traveller
iv. Emile Zola	4. Lolita

Codes :

	i	ii	iii	iv
(A)	3	1	4	2
(B)	4	3	2	1
(C)	1	2	3	4
(D)	2	4	1	3

37. Which among the following plays by Aristophanes is an attack on 'modern' education and morals as imparted and taught by the radical intellectuals known as The Sophists ?

(A) Clouds (B) Wasps
(C) Acharnians (D) Knights

38. In which novel of Virginia Woolf does a painter in the act of painting actually figure as a character ?

(A) The Voyage Out
(B) The Waves
(C) Jacob's Room
(D) To the Lighthouse

39. Religious controversies in England particularly during the 15th century led to the promotion of

(A) English prose
(B) The British Empire
(C) Naval power
(D) The Missionary Movement

40. Fill in the blanks with a suitable word from the list below :

In his fiction, Ian McEwan more than often suggests the ________ of love

(A) Fragility (B) Madness
(C) Completeness (D) Security

41. Match List – I with List – II according to the code given below :

List – I (Dramatists)	List – II (Plays)
i. Arnold Wesker	1. Jumpers
ii. Harold Pinter	2. What the Butler Saw
iii. Joe Orton	3. The Room
iv. Tom Stoppard	4. Roots

Codes :

	i	ii	iii	iv
(A)	3	2	4	1
(B)	1	2	4	3
(C)	4	3	2	1
(D)	4	3	1	2

42. Modern English emerged from the

(A) South Midland dialect
(B) East Midland dialect
(C) French language
(D) Northumbrian dialect

43. Most culinary terms in English are derived from
(A) Exotic cooking (B) French cooking
(C) Native sources (D) Arabic cooking

44. "Blended learning" is a mode of instruction/learning in which
(A) the learner's mother tongue and the target language are blended
(B) learning is accessed through the mother tongue
(C) a variety of instructional modes are integrated
(D) learning of a language is mediated by humanistic approaches

45. 'Risk-taking' is one of the traits of a good
(A) language learner
(B) language teacher
(C) teacher of grammar rules
(D) printer of books and authors

46. A teaching method advocated by Dr. Georgia Lozanav which is based on the principle of 'joy and easiness' is called
(A) Suggesto paedia
(B) Total physical response
(C) The Direct Method
(D) The audio-lingual method

47. Albert Camus, in his essay, 'The Myth of Sisyphus' conveys :
1. The concept of Naturalism
2. The Absurdity of Human Existence
3. The Futility of all Human Endeavour
4. The concept of Existentialism
(A) 1, 2 and 3 are correct
(B) 2, 3 and 4 are correct
(C) 1, 2 and 4 are correct
(D) 1, 3 and 4 are correct

48. In The Portrait of a Lady Gilbert Osmond marries Isabel Archer because
1. Osmond wanted to get hold of Isabel's property.
2. He loved her
3. Though he did not like her moral ideas about many things in life, he had hoped to win her over.
4. He realized that her moral ideas were quite deep-rooted.

Find the correct combination according to the code :
(A) only 1 and 2 are correct
(B) only 1, 2 and 3 are correct
(C) only 3 and 4 are correct
(D) only 1 is correct

49. Pick out the two relevant and correct descriptions of U.R. Ananthamurthy's Samskara.
1. The novel is written in English
2. The novel is concerned with the progressive ideas of the times.
3. The novel is set in Malgudi
4. The novel is a satire on the representatives of a decadent Brahmin society.
5. Samskara is a regional novel
6. Praneschacharya does not atone for his sin.
(A) 4 and 5 are correct
(B) 1 and 4 are correct
(C) 5 and 6 are correct
(D) 3 and 2 are correct

50. Willy in Arthur Miller's play Death of a Salesman compares Biff and Happy to the mythic characters/figures
(A) Venus and Adonais
(B) Adonais and Hercules
(C) Jupiter and Hercules
(D) Venus and Hercules

Question Nos **51** to **55** are based on a poem. Read the poem carefully and pick out the most appropriate answers.

A Valediction Forbidding Mourning

My swirling wants, your frozen lips.
The grammar turned and attacked me.
Themes, written under duress.
Emptiness of the notations.

They gave me a drug that slowed the healing of wounds.

I want you to see this before I leave :
the experience of repetition as death
the failure of criticism to locate the pain

the poster in the bus that said :
my bleeding is under control
A red plant in a cemetary of plastic wreaths.
A last attempt : the language is a dialect called metaphor.
These images go unglossed : hair, glacier, flashlight.
When I think of a landscape I am thinking of a time.
When I talk of taking a trip I mean forever.
I could say : those mountains have a meaning but further than that I could not say.
To do something very common, in my own way.

Adrienne Rich

51. How does the poet suggest that the lover has not left ?

(A) The words "a last attempt" indicate that she is trying her best to leave.

(B) The words "before I leave" suggest that the speaker has not left yet.

(C) The speaker talks of a trip 'forever' which means she will never return.

(D) A drug she takes slows the healing of her wounds perhaps indicating that she may be able to leave sometime in future.

52. Why does the speaker/lover in Rich's poem plan to leave ?

I. Because her love has not been returned.

II. Because of the pain she has suffered in the relationship.

III. Because the lover has criticized her so much.

IV. Because though the pain has been located, the bleeding continues.

The right combination according to the code is

(A) I and II are correct

(B) I and IV are correct

(C) I, II and III are correct

(D) I and III are correct

53. What does Rich imply when she says "The grammar turned and attacked me" ?

(A) Language that has been used to hurt her.

(B) Her lover has beaten her.

(C) The person she is leaving is not the source of pain but something else.

(D) The pain she has herself inflicted through language.

54. How would you compare Rich's poem and Donne's poem with the same title ?

(A) Rich is recreating Donne's poem

(B) Rich is eulogising Donne's poem

(C) Rich's poem is a scathing attack on Donne's poem.

(D) Rich is defining Donne's concept of love

55. What is the theme of the poem ? Identify the false statement in the list below :

It is

(A) about the difficulty of actually saying goodbye.

(B) about not having the strength to leave though one might want to.

(C) about the pain suffered in relationship.

(D) a Classical love poem like Donne's where the speaker dominates the addressee.

56. Why does Girish Karnad base his play Hayavadana on Thomas Mann's Transposed Heads ?

(A) It is a mock-heroic transcription of the original Sanskrit tales.

(B) It is concerned with materialism.

(C) It deals with domestic strife.

(D) It deals with ancient times.

57. The collected poems of A.K. Ramanujan has been divided into four sections. Arrange them in their chronological order :

(A) The striders – The Relations – Second Sight – the Black Hen

(B) The Relations – The Striders – The Black Hen – Second Sight

(C) Second Sight – The Relations – The Black Hen – Striders

(D) The Black Hen – Second Sight – The Striders – The Relations

58. In one of her novels, Margaret Atwood demonstrated the potentially 'Cannibalistic' nature of human relationships. Identify the novel :

(A) Surfacing (B) Lady Oracle
(C) Life Before Man
(D) The Edible Woman

59. Match the characters with the novels of Amitav Ghosh in which they appear according to the code given below :

List – I (Characters)	List – II (Novels)
i. Fakir	1. The Glass Palace
ii. Tridip	2. The Hungry Tide
iii. Rajkumar	3. The Calcutta Chromosome
iv. Murugan	4. Shadow Lines

Codes :

	i	ii	iii	iv
(A)	2	4	1	3
(B)	2	4	3	1
(C)	1	3	1	4
(D)	3	2	4	1

60. Which of the following is not a play by Badal Sircar ?
(A) Bhooma
(B) Evam Indrajeet
(C) That Other History
(D) Agra Bazar

61. Who is the protagonist of Shashi Deshpande's That Long Silence ?
(A) Mohan (B) Jaya
(C) Rati (D) Kamat

62. In Derek Walcott's Dream on Monkey Mountain, Makak's vision of freedom for his people is
(A) through money
(B) through violence
(C) through black power
(D) through a decolonisation of the mind

63. Given below are two statements, one labelled as Assertion (A) and the other as Reason (R).
Assertion (A) : To give a text an author is to impose a limit on that text, to furnish it with a final signified, to close the writing.
Reason (R) : A text is made up of multiple meanings drawn from many sources, and this multiplicity is focused on the reader.
In the context of the two statements, which one of the following is correct :
(A) Both (A) and (R) are true and (R) is the correct explanation of (A).
(B) Both (A) and (R) are true and (R) is not the correct explanation of (A).
(C) (A) is true but (R) is false.
(D) (A) is false but (R) is true.

64. Given below are two statements, one labelled as Assertion (A) and the other as Reason (R).
Assertion (A) : Spivak sees the project of colonialism as characterized by what Foucault had called 'epistemic violence', the imposition of a given set of beliefs over another.
Reason (R) : Spivak suggests that participation in the political process – access to citizenship, becoming a voter – will help to mobilize the subaltern on "the long road to hegemony."
In the context of the two statements, which one of the following is correct :
(A) Both (A) and (R) are true and (R) is the correct explanation of (A).
(B) Both (A) and (R) are true and (R) is not the correct explanation of (A).
(C) (A) is true but (R) is false.
(D) (A) is false but (R) is true.

65. Match the following authors with their works from the given below :

List – I (Authors)	List – II (Works)
i. Buchi Emecheta	1. Burger's Daughter
ii. Ama Ata Aidoo	2. Joy of Motherhood
iii. Nadine Gordimer	3. Devil on the Cross
iv. Nqugi Wa Thiongo	4. Our Sister Killjoy

Find the correct combination according to the code :

Codes :

	i	ii	iii	iv
(A)	1	2	3	4
(B)	2	4	1	3
(C)	3	1	4	2
(D)	4	3	2	1

66. Match the following authors with their plays from the lists given below :

List – I (Authors)	List – II (Plays)
i. Langston Hughes	1. Dutchman
ii. Lorraine Hansberry	2. Clara's Ole Man
iii. Ed Bullins	3. Don't You want to be Free
iv. Amiri Baraka	4. Raisin in the Sun

Find the correct combination according to the code :

Codes :

	i	ii	iii	iv
(A)	3	4	2	1
(B)	1	2	3	4
(C)	2	1	4	3
(D)	4	3	1	2

67. Identify the critics and their respective works:

(A) Horace – Ars Poetica
Aristotle – Poetics
Quintillian – Institutio Oratoria
Ben Jonson – Discoveries
Sidney – An Apology for Poetry
Dryden – An Essay of Dramatic Poesy

(B) Horace – Poetics
Aristotle – Ars Poetica
Quintillian – On the sublime
Longinus – Discoveries
Ben Jonson – Institutio Oratoria
Sidney – An Essay of Dramatic Poesy
Dryden – An Apology for Poetry

(C) Horace – On the sublime
Aristotle – Poetics
Quintillian – Discoveries
Longinus – Institutio Oratoria
Ben Jonson – An Essay of Dramatic Poesy
Sidney – Ars Poetica
Dryden – An Apology for Poetry

(D) Horace – Ars Poetica
Aristotle – Poetics
Quintillian – Institutio Oratoria
Longinus – On the Sublime
Ben Jonson – An Apology for Poetry
Sidney – An Essay of Dramatic Poesy
Dryden – Discoveries

68. Which of the following is **not** true of Imagist poetry ?

(A) The poet spreads his language across the page as though language were sensation, to reproduce the mental effect of 'image'.

(B) The image is itself an instrument of vision, or lens, as well as an expression of imagination

(C) The imagist like a scientist learns from history and uses it, and like a scientist does not deal in emotions.

(D) The new artist as scientist focuses vision through image as against the symbol which resorts to reduction to simplicity.

69. Who among the following is not a myth critic?

(A) Robert Graves
(B) Raymond Williams
(C) Francis Fergusson
(D) Northrop Frye

70. According to Northrop Frye there are four main narrative genres associated with the seasonal cycle of spring, summer, autumn and winter. They are comedy, ________, tragedy and irony (satire). Which is the second one ?

(A) Romance (B) Epic
(C) Fiction (D) Novel

Questions No. 71 – 75 are based on the following passage :

Read the passage carefully and select the most appropriate option.

The town belonging to the colonized people, or at least the native town, the negro village, the medina, the reservation, is a place of ill fame, peopled by men of evil repute. They are born there, it matters little where or how; they die there, it matters not where, nor how. The native town is a hungry town, starved of bread, of meat, of shoes, of coal, of light. The native town is a crouching village, town on its knees, a town wallowing in the mire. The look that the native turns on the settler is a look of lust, of envy.... The colonized man is an envious man. And this the settler knows very well... It is true, for there is no native who does not dream atleast once a day of setting himself up in the settler's place.

(From Frantz Fanon's The Wretched of The Earth)

71. To Frantz Fanon, the 'Negro' village is
   1. the worst face of apartheid
   2. a protected area
   3. a place of moral and physical degradation
   4. a special village with its own amenities.

   (A) 1 and 3 are correct
   (B) 1 and 2 are correct
   (C) only 3 is correct (D) only 4 is correct

72. Why is the 'native town' a hungry town?
   1. it did not have agricultural farms
   2. it did not have markets
   3. the blacks were steeped in poverty
   4. they were denied their fundamental rights by the Whites.

   (A) 1 and 2 are correct
   (B) 3 and 4 are correct
   (C) only 1 is correct (D) only 4 is correct

73. What does the term 'crouching village' indicate?
   1. The latent aggressiveness of the blacks
   2. The defenselessness of the people
   3. Hopelessness and despair
   4. Overflowing filth

   (A) 1 and 2 are correct
   (B) 2 and 3 are correct
   (C) only 1 is correct (D) only 2 is correct

74. Why does the native look at the settler's town with envy?
   1. it arises from a sense of desperation
   2. he has no other option in his life
   3. he wants to occupy a position of power.
   4. he wants to be the colonizer instead of the colonized.

   (A) only 1 is correct (B) 3 and 4 are correct
   (C) only 2 is correct (D) 1 and 4 are correct

75. What is the settler's attitude towards the blacks?
   1. the settler is not afraid
   2. the settler considers the blacks to be harmless
   3. the settler is contemptuous of the blacks.
   4. the settler feels resentment because he knows that his position is never safe.

   (A) only 1 is correct (B) 2 and 3 are correct
   (C) only 4 is correct (D) 3 and 4 are correct

ANSWERS

1. (*)	2. (A)	3. (A)	4. (C)	5. (A)	6. (A)	7. (C)	8. (C)	9. (A)	10. (A)
11. (A)	12. (C)	13. (C)	14. (C)	15. (B)	16. (C)	17. (B)	18. (A)	19. (B)	20. (D)
21. (A)	22. (C)	23. (*)	24. (A)	25. (C)	26. (D)	27. (B)	28. (B)	29. (C)	30. (D)
31. (B)	32. (B)	33. (C)	34. (A)	35. (D)	36. (B)	37. (A)	38. (D)	39. (A)	40. (A)
41. (C)	42. (B)	43. (B)	44. (C)	45. (A)	46. (A)	47. (B)	48. (*)	49. (A)	50. (B)
51. (B)	52. (C)	53. (AD)	54. (A)	55. (D)	56. (A)	57. (A)	58. (D)	59. (A)	60. (D)
61. (B)	62. (D)	63. (B)	64. (B)	65. (B)	66. (A)	67. (A)	68. (C)	69. (B)	70. (A)
71. (A)	72. (B)	73. (C)	74. (B)	75. (C)					

* Denotes marks given to all candidates.

December, 2014

ENGLISH LITERATURE

PAPER-II

Note : This paper contains **fifty (50)** objective type questions, each question carrying **two (2)** marks. Attempt **all** the questions.

1. Two of the following list are "Angry Young Men" of the 1950's British literary scene.

I. John Osborne II. C.P. Snow
III. Anthony Powell IV. Kingsley Amis

The right combination, according to the code

(A) I & II (B) II & IV
(C) I & IV (D) I & III

2. Laurence Sterne's Tristram Shandy contains

(A) Six volumes (B) Nine volumes
(C) Ten volumes (D) Four volumes

3. Which of the following statement is NOT true of Areopagitica ?

(A) It was published in 1644.
(B) It argues for the liberty of Unlicensed Printing.
(C) It pleads for British privileges regarding Free Trade.
(D) It is a speech addressed to the Parliament of England.

4. Thomas Hardy's last major novel was ___.

(A) *Tess of the D'urbervilles*
(B) *Jude the Obscure*
(C) *The Return of the Native*
(D) *The Trumpet Major*

5. *The Hind and the Panther Transvers'd to the Story of the Country Mouse and the City Mouse* is a satire on

(A) Alexander Pope (B) Jonathan Swift
(C) John Dryden (D) Samuel Butler

6. Match the columns :

Terms	Theorists
I. Apollonian – Dionysian	1. Matthew Arnold
II. Fancy – Imagination	2. Friedrich Nietzsche
III. Hellenism – Hebraism	3. G.H. Hopkins
IV. Inscape – Instress	4. S.T. Coleridge

	I	II	III	IV
(A)	2	4	1	3
(B)	2	4	3	1
(C)	1	4	2	3
(D)	4	2	1	3

7. In *King Lear* who among the following speaks in the voice of Poor Tom ?

(A) Kent (B) Edgar
(C) Edmund (D) Gloucester

8. In Wordsworth's *Prelude* the Boy of Winander is affected by

(A) Blindness (B) Deafness
(C) Muteness (D) Lameness

9. Which of the following is NOT mentioned as part of the London locale in *The Waste Land* ?

(A) St. Magnus Martyr
(B) King Arthur Street
(C) St. Mary Woolnoth
(D) Lower Thames Street

10. Which of the following novels is NOT written by Jean Rhys ?

(A) *After Leaving Mr. Mackenzie*
(B) *Good Morning, Midnight*
(C) *The Quiet American*
(D) *Wide Sargasso Sea*

11. The first official royal Poet Laureate in English literary history was ______.

(A) Ben Jonson
(B) William Davenant
(C) John Dryden
(D) Thomas Shadwell

12. Who does Alexander Pope refer to in the following lines ?

"Born to no pride; inheriting no strife,
Nor marrying discord in a noble wife,
Stranger to civil and religious rage,
The good man walked innoxious through his age."

(A) Pope's father (B) Pope himself
(C) Dr. Arbuthnot
(D) The Duke of Marlborough

13. The Theory of Natural Selection is attributed to ________.

(A) Arthur Schopenhauer
(B) Charles Darwin
(C) A.N. Whitehead
(D) Aldous Huxley

14. Which character in William Golding's *Lord of the Flies* maintains, "Life is scientific" ?

(A) Simon (B) Piggy
(C) Ralph (D) Jack

15. Match the authors under List – I with the titles under List – II :

List – I	List – II
I. Claude Levi-Strauss	1. *Of Grammatology*
II. Jacques Derrida	2. *The Archaeology of Knowledge*
III. Northrop Frye	3. *Structural Anthropology*
IV. Michel Foucault	4. *Anatomy of Criticism*

	I	II	III	IV
(A)	1	3	4	2
(B)	3	1	2	4
(C)	3	1	4	2
(D)	2	1	3	4

16. How did Chaucer's Pardoner make his living ?

(A) By selling stolen cattle from the neighbourhood ottery
(B) By selling indulgences to those who committed sins
(C) By pardoning those who stole property or committed other crimes
(D) By assisting the Friar in Church services

17. From among the following, identify Coleridge's companion in a fanciful scheme to establish a Utopian community of free love on the banks of the Susquehaina river ?

(A) Lord Byron (B) Robert Southey
(C) William Hazlitt
(D) William Wordsworth

18. Which of the following novels by H.G. Wells is about the condition of England as Empire?

(A) *The Island of Dr. Moreau*
(B) *The War of the Worlds*
(C) *Tono-Bungay*
(D) *The Invisible Man*

19. *Joothan* by Om Prakash Valmiki is

(A) a collection of poems
(B) a play
(C) an autobiography (D) a novel

20. Listed below are some English plays across several centuries :

Twelfth Night, She Stoops to Conquer, The Importance of Being Earnest, Pygmalion and *Blithe Spirit.*

What is common to them ?

(A) All problem plays; scheming and intrigue
(B) All tragedies; sin and redemption
(C) All ideologically framed; class and gender
(D) All romantic comedies; love and laughter

21. Who among the following wrote a poem comparing a lover's heart to a hand grenade?

(A) John Donne (B) Abraham Cowley
(C) Wilfred Owen (D) Robert Graves

22. The Uncertainty Principle is attributed to

(A) William James (B) John Dewey
(C) Werner Heisenberg
(D) Charles Darwin

23. "Jabberwocky" is a creation in ________.

(A) Edward Lear's poetry
(B) Lewis Carroll's work
(C) Charles Dickens's *Martin Chuzzlewit*
(D) Thomas Hardy's *Woodlanders*

24. Who are Didi and Gogo ?
(A) They are two characters in *Endgame.*
(B) They are nicknames, respectively, for Lucky and Pozzo.
(C) They are nicknames, respectively, for Vladimir and Estragon.
(D) They are two characters in *Breath.*

25. Who among the following theorists talks about "the circulation of social energy" ?
(A) Raymond Williams
(B) Stephen Greenblatt
(C) Antonio Gramsci
(D) Haydon White

26. How many legends of good women could Chaucer complete in his *The Legend of Good Women* ?
(A) Six (B) Seven
(C) Eight (D) Nine

27. *The Round Table* is a collection of essays jointly written by ________.
(A) Charles Lamb and William Hazlitt
(B) Charles Lamb and Leigh Hunt
(C) William Hazlitt and Leigh Hunt
(D) William Hazlitt and Thomas de Quincey

28. Dylan Thomas is associated with the group ________.
(A) The New Apocalypse
(B) The Black Arts
(C) The Movement
(D) Deep Image Poetry

29. Which of the following writers writes from Canada ?
(A) V.S. Naipaul (B) Margaret Atwood
(C) Derek Walcott (D) James Joyce

30. "The boast of heraldry, the pomp of power,
And all that beauty, all that wealth e'er gave,
Awaits alike the inevitable hour
The paths of glory lead but to the grave."
What is the subject of *awaits* ?
(A) Hour
(B) The things mentioned in the first 2 lines.
(C) "And all that beauty, all that wealth e'er gave"
(D) Grave

31. "Heav'n has no rage, like love to hatred turn'd / Nor Hell a fury, like a woman scorn'd."
Identify the text in which the above quote occurs :
(A) *The Double-Dealer*
(B) *The Way of the World*
(C) *The Mourning Bride*
(D) *Love for Love*

32. *A Young Lady's Entrance into the World* is the sub-title of ________.
(A) *Belinda* (B) *Cecilia*
(C) *Evelina* (D) *Camilla*

33. "The old order changeth, yielding place to new" is from ________.
(A) "Morte d'Arthur"
(B) "Idylls of the King"
(C) "Paracelsus"
(D) "Asolando"

34. Which of the following cannot be classified as fantasy fiction ?
(A) *The Inheritors* (William Golding)
(B) *The Magus* (John Fowles)
(C) *The Lord of the Rings* (J.R.R. Tolkein)
(D) *The History Man* (Malcolm Bradbury)

35. *Philosophy of Symbolic Forms* is a work associated with ________.
(A) Wilhelm von Humboldt
(B) Ernst Cassirer
(C) Immanuel Kant (D) Battista Vico

36. Which of the following facts is NOT true of Spenser ?
(A) He is a kind of English Homer, telling stories of heroic confrontations.
(B) He fashioned an original verse form : The Spenserian Stanza.
(C) He opposed England's break with the Roman Catholic Church.
(D) He is a Christian poet.

37. William Blake developed the ideas of "Prolifics" and "Devourers" in
(A) *Jerusalem* (B) *Milton*
(C) *Marriage of Heaven and Hell*
(D) *Songs of Innocence and Songs of Experience*

38. Surrealism is associated with
(A) Ernst Cassirer (B) Tristan Tzara
(C) Henrik Ibsen (D) Andre Breton

39. "And miles to go before I sleep" is a line from a poem by
(A) Emily Dickinson (B) Walt Whitman
(C) Ralph Waldo Emerson
(D) Robert Frost

40. What common link do you find among "The Disquieting Muses" by Sylvia Plath, "The Starry Night" by Anne Sexton, "Mourning Picture" by Adrienne Rich, and "Musee des Beaux Arts" by W.H. Auden ?
(A) They inspired paintings.
(B) They are confessional poems.
(C) They are all inspired by paintings.
(D) They are all inspired by Van Gogh's paintings.

41. "All Rising to *Great Place* is by a ________ staire." (Francis Bacon)
(A) Murky (B) Winding
(C) Crooked (D) Sinister

42. In Jeremy Collier's 1698 pamphlet attacking the immorality and profaneness of the English stage, who among the following was the principal target ?
(A) William Congreve
(B) John Dryden
(C) John Vanbrugh
(D) William Wycherley

43. Charles Dickens's visit to the United States produced ________.
(A) *Hard Times*
(B) *Nicholas Nickleby*
(C) *Martin Chuzzlewit*
(D) *Oliver Twist*

44. Who among the following is a working-class poet ?
(A) John Betjeman (B) Tony Harrison
(C) Thom Gunn (D) Robert Graves

45. *New Science* is a work associated with ______.
(A) Ernest Cassirer
(B) Wilhelm von Humboldt
(C) G. Battista Vico
(D) Immanuel Kant

46. Identify Petrarch's sonnet sequence from among the following :
(A) *Rine Sparse* (B) *Astrophel and Stella*
(C) *Amoretti* (D) *Delia*

47. The island setting of Latmos figures in Keats's
(A) *Endymion* (B) *The Eve of St. Agnes*
(C) *Lamia* (D) *Hyperion*

48. The Artist Hero is a theatrical creation emphasized by ________.
(A) W.B. Yeats (B) Charles Baudelaire
(C) Oscar Wilde (D) Andre Gide

49. Which of the following African writers won the Nobel Prize for Literature ?
(A) Chinua Achebe
(B) Nadine Gordimer
(C) Ngugi wa Thiong'o
(D) Bessie Head

50. "My lute, be as thou wert when thou didst grow With thy green mother in some shady groove" – William Drummond
The above quote is an example of ______.
(A) End-stopped rhyme
(B) Alliteration
(C) Run-on line (D) Tercet

✓ ANSWERS

1. (C)	**2.** (B)	**3.** (C)	**4.** (B)	**5.** (C)	**6.** (A)	**7.** (B)	**8.** (C)	**9.** (B)	**10.** (C)
11. (C)	**12.** (A)	**13.** (B)	**14.** (C)	**15.** (C)	**16.** (B)	**17.** (B)	**18.** (C)	**19.** (C)	**20.** (D)
21. (B)	**22.** (C)	**23.** (B)	**24.** (C)	**25.** (B)	**26.** (D)	**27.** (C)	**28.** (A)	**29.** (B)	**30.** (AD)
31. (C)	**32.** (C)	**33.** (B)	**34.** (D)	**35.** (B)	**36.** (C)	**37.** (C)	**38.** (D)	**39.** (D)	**40.** (C)
41. (B)	**42.** (C)	**43.** (C)	**44.** (B)	**45.** (C)	**46.** (A)	**47.** (A)	**48.** (*)	**49.** (B)	**50.** (C)

* All option are correct.

December, 2014

ENGLISH LITERATURE

PAPER-III

Note : This paper contains seventy **five (75)** objective type questions of **two (2)** marks each. All questions are compulsory.

1. This work was a satire in Ottava rima, attacking George III and Robert Southey. Identify the poem :
   (A) *Dunciad*
   (B) *The Vision of Judgment*
   (C) *Childe Harold's Pilgrimage*
   (D) *Alastor*

2. Here's a famous exchange from Arthur Conan Doyle's *Silver Blaze* :
   'Is there any point to which you would wish to draw my attention ?'
   'To the curious incident of the dog in the night-time.'
   'The dog did nothing in the night-time.'
   What was Sherlock Holmes' response ?
   (A) 'Nothing ? Nothing at all ? Rather unbelievable.'
   (B) 'That was the curious incident.'
   (C) 'Anything else, at all ?'
   (D) 'That sounds rather curious, don't you think ?'

3. "The shrill, demented choirs of waiting shells,
   And bugles calling for them from sad shires."
   These lines are from Wilfred Owen's :
   (A) "Strange Meeting"
   (B) "Futility"
   (C) "Anthem for Doomed Youth"
   (D) "Duke et Decorum Est"

4. In Aphra Behn's *Oronooko*, how does the titular character die ?
   (A) He disembowels himself.
   (B) He is whipped to death.
   (C) He is hanged in the public square.
   (D) He is cut to pieces slowly by the executioner.

5. The narrative of this novel is a meticulous, present-tense account of a woman with a death-wish who plots the circumstances of her own violent murder.
   Identify the novel.
   (A) Iris Murdoch's *A Fairly Honourable Defeat*
   (B) Muriel Spark's *The Driver's Seat*
   (C) Doris Lessing's *Children of Violence*
   (D) Angela Carter's *The Passion of the New Eve*

6. The library where the "Battle of Books" takes place is ________.
   (A) St. James' Library
   (B) King's Library
   (C) Sir William's Library
   (D) Christ Church Library

7. In Sophocles' *Oedipus Rex* the first scene finds Oedipus
   (A) in conversation with a priest
   (B) in consultation with a general
   (C) giving audience to an ambassador
   (D) in consultation with a minister

8. Who among Shakespeare's contemporaries did not write tragedies ?
   (A) Thomas Kyd
   (B) John Lyly
   (C) Christopher Marlowe
   (D) Ben Jonson

9. *The Kite Runner*, a novel by Khaled Hosseini tells the story of ________.

(A) Ahmed (B) Nadira
(C) Amir (D) Amourrah

10. Thomas Babington Macaulay, the writer of the infamous Minute of 1835, finds a mention in Salman Rushdie's
(A) *Midnight's Children* (B) *Shame*
(C) *The Moor's Last Sigh* (D) *Fury*

11. The issue of privileging speech over writing was taken up for discussion in Plato's :
(A) *Ion* (B) *Republic* Book III
(C) *Republic* Book X (D) *Phaedrus*

12. 'The Medium is the Message' is a concept given by
(A) Ernest Hemingway
(B) Sylvia Plath
(C) Seymour Hersh
(D) Marshal McLuhan

13. Seamus Heaney's famous poem "Digging" forms a part of his celebrated collection called
(A) *North*
(B) *Death of a Naturalist*
(C) *Field Work*
(D) *Door into the Dark*

14. The first major report on *The Teaching of English in England* was published in 1921. It is known as ________, named after the Chair, Board of Education, ________.
(A) the Newbolt Report; Sir Henry Newbolt
(B) the Wood's Despatch; Charles Wood, Lord Halifax
(C) the Chatham Report; Earl John Chatham
(D) the Landow Document; Sir George Landow

15. Who first developed the notion of 'competence' in language studies ?
(A) Dell Hymes
(B) Noam Chomsky
(C) Leech and Svartvik
(D) Henry Sweet

16. The fruit *was eaten.*
The fruit *is ripening.*
Which of the following statement(s) is/are correct ?
(1) English has two kinds of participle : the present and the past.
(2) English has three kinds of participle : the present, the past and the future.
(3) The first sentence here is an example of a verb in past participle.
(4) The first sentence here is an example of a verb in the perfect tense.
(5) The second sentence here is an example of a verb in present participle.
(6) The second sentence here is an example of a verb in the continuous tense.
(A) 2, 4, 6 are correct.
(B) 1, 5, 6 are correct.
(C) 1, 3, 5 are correct.
(D) 3, 4, 5 are correct.

17. In 1722 the Crown awarded a certain English merchant a patent to manufacture copper coins for Ireland. Jonathan Swift intervened by way of composing a series of letters in response, better known as *The Drapier's Letters*. Who was the merchant ?
(A) Isaac Bickerstaff
(B) William Bickerstaff
(C) William Wood
(D) William Sacheverell

18. "While the world moves In appentency on its metalled way Of time past and time future"
These lines are from :
(A) "Little Gidding" (B) "Dry Salvages"
(C) "Burnt Norton" (D) "East Coker"

19. The following is the stage-description of an opening scene of a famous modern play :
A basement room. Two beds, flat against the back wall. A serving hatch, closed, between *the beds. A door to the kitchen and lavatory, left. A door to a passage, right.*
Identify the play :
(A) *The Importance of Being Earnest*
(B) *Travesties*
(C) *The Dumb Waiter*
(D) *Look Back in Anger*

20. 'Homonyms' are words that ______
(A) are pronounced differently but have the same meaning.
(B) refer to both the male and female of the human species.
(C) are spelt similarly but have different meanings.
(D) refer to people who live in houses with similar structures.

21. Match the columns :

Shakespearean	Actors Period
I. David Garrick	1. The 19th century
II. John Gielgud	2. The 18th century
III. Henry Irving	3. The Restoration
IV. Thomas Betterton	4. The 20th century

	I	II	III	IV
(A)	2	4	1	3
(B)	4	2	1	3
(C)	3	4	1	2
(D)	2	3	4	1

22. In his "Structure, Sign, and Play in the Discourse of the Human Sciences," Derrida is all praise for the *bricoleur* whom Levi-Strauss sees as a supreme methodologist, "someone who uses 'the means at hand'."
Who does Levi-Strauss contrast *bricoleur* with in terms of method and approach ?
(A) The Botanist
(B) The Anthropologist
(C) The Engineer
(D) The Semiotician

23. Heinrich Böll has something to say, and not of course merely something about the Germans. He says it several times. A common weakness of writers with something to say is their inability to understand that saying it four times is not necessarily four times as effective as saying it once. But to have something to say – how rare this is ! – D. J. Enright, "Three New Germans".
From a reading of the above, the reader can deduce :
I. Enright mildly disapproves of Heinrich Böll's saying not merely something about Germans.
II. Enright is disappointed that Heinrich Böll has practically nothing to say about people other than Germans.
III. Enright agrees that Heinrich Böll shares a weakness with writers who prefer saying something four times to saying it once.
IV. Enright does not believe that saying something four times will necessarily make the same effective.
The right combination, according to the code, is
(A) I and II
(B) II and III
(C) III and IV
(D) I and IV

24. Michel Foucault's earlier "archaeological" study is found in
(A) *Power/Knowledge*
(B) *Social Theory and Transgression*
(C) *The Birth of the Clinic*
(D) *Beyond Structuralism and Hermeneutics*

25. *Invisible Man* by Ralph Ellison is widely recognized as a masterpiece. It is also one of the finest examples of
(A) science fiction
(B) picaresque novel
(C) coming-of-age novel
(D) crime thriller

26. Match the following correctly :

List – I	List – II
I. Mulk Raj Anand	1. *Premashram*
II. Raja Rao	2. *The Cat and Shakespeare*
III. Prem Chand	3. *Coolie*
IV. Girish Karnad	4. *Nagamandala*

	I	II	III	IV
(A)	3	2	4	1
(B)	2	3	1	4
(C)	3	2	1	4
(D)	4	3	2	1

27. From which of Sheridan's plays the following extract is taken ?
Lady Sneerwell : Why truly Mrs. Clackitt has a very pretty talent and a great deal of industry.

Snake : True, Madam, and has been tolerably successful in her day. To my knowledge she has been the cause of six matches being broken off and three sons disinherited, of four forced elopements ....

Lady Sneerwell : She certainly has talents but her manner is gross.

(A) *The Rivals*

(B) *The School for Scandal*

(C) *St. Patrick's Day*

(D) *The Critic*

28. Who, from among the following, has NOT been discussed by Simon-de-Bevoir in "The Myth of Woman in Five Authors" in *The Second Sex* ?

(A) Montherlant (B) Lawrence

(C) Stendhal (D) Kafka

29. In a collection of essays Orhan Pamuk shares how he writes his novels, tells about his friendship with his daughter, talks about his loneliness and happiness.

Identify the text :

(A) *Other Colors* (B) *The Silent House*

(C) *The Black Book* (D) *The White Castle*

30. Two of the following plays won the Sultan Padamsee Prize for Indian plays in English:

I. *Princes*

II. *Where There's a Will*

III. *Larins Sahib*

IV. *Doongaji House*

The right combination according to the code is :

(A) III and IV (B) I and III

(C) II and III (D) I and IV

31. Who among the following is NOT an Australian writer ?

(A) Morris West

(B) Patrick White

(C) Thomas Keneally

(D) Bill Pearson

32. After Independence, Mulk Raj Anand, wrote a number of semi-autobiographical works to narrate chunks of his own life through a fictional persona. The name he gave this persona is _______.

(A) Lal Singh (B) Krishan Chander

(C) Puran Singh (D) Rahul Singh

33. What a mockery this.

Of history, the past and that to come !

Now do I feel how all men are deceived,

Reading of nations and their, in faith,

Faith given to vanity and emptiness ...

The prelude

The above extract is from

(A) Book 9 Residence in France

(B) Book 7 Residence in London

(C) Book 3 Residence in Cambridge

(D) Book 4 Summer Vacations

34. While foregrounding the marginal presence of women in history in *A Room of One's Own*, Virginia Woolf refers to ______ *History of England*.

(A) Campbell's (B) Trevelyan's

(C) Sander's (D) Carter's

35. *Salonie* is a play written by Oscar Wilde written in

(A) English (B) Irish

(C) French (D) Italian

36. In More's *Utopia*, the fictional traveller Raphael Hythloday's second name in Greek means

(A) Dispenser of Justice

(B) Dispenser of Nonsense

(C) Dispenser of Grace

(D) Dispenser of Mercy

37. "You do not dwell in me nor I in you however much I pander to your name"

These lines from Geoffrey Hill's "Lachrimae" address

(A) Christ

(B) The Devil

(C) The poet's beloved

(D) The poet's enemy

38. The author of *Black Skin, White Masks* is

(A) Ngugi wa Thiong'o

(B) Frantz Fanon

(C) Richard Wright
(D) Martin Luther King (Jr.)

39. Match the following :

Poet	Bird
I. John Keats	1. Hawk
II. P.B. Shelley	2. Falcon
III. G.H. Hopkins	3. Skylark
IV. Ted Hughes	4. Nightingale

	I	II	III	IV
(A)	4	3	2	1
(B)	4	3	1	2
(C)	3	4	2	1
(D)	3	4	1	2

40. Who of the following has written the novel *The Return* ?
(A) Bapsi Sidhwa (B) V.S. Naipaul
(C) K. S. Maniam (D) Pankaj Mishra

41. Who among the following is a well-known Neo-Aristotelian critic ?
(A) R.P. Blackmur
(B) John Crowe Ranson
(C) R.S. Crane
(D) Lionel Trilling

42. **Assertion (A) :** The act of reading a text is both determinate and indeterminate.
Reason (R) : Since our reading includes both a sense of the unity of the narrative held in place at the end and the different wishes and guesses made along the way.
(A) Both (A) and (R) are true and (R) is the true explanation of (A).
(B) Both (A) and (R) are true, but (R) is not the true explanation of (A).
(C) (A) is true, but (R) is false.
(D) (A) is false, but (R) is true.

43. Girish Karnad's *Hayavadana*, originally in Kannada, has been translated into English by
(A) U.R. Ananthamurthy
(B) By the playwright himself
(C) G.S. Amur
(D) A.K. Ramanujan

44. Edward Said's well-known book *Orientalism* was published in
(A) 1978 (B) 1968
(C) 2008 (D) 1988

45. "To the Memory of my Beloved, the Author Mr. William Shakespeare : And What He Hath Left Us" is an ode composed by
(A) John Milton
(B) Ben Jonson
(C) Andrew Marvell
(D) John Suckling

46. *Call me Ishmail Tonight* is written by
(A) A.K. Ramanujan
(B) Agha Shahid Ali
(C) Saleem Peeradina
(D) Nissim Ezekiel

47. "All fiction for me is a kind of magic or trickery – a confidence trick." The statement has been made by
(A) Angus Wilson (B) Anthony Powell
(C) John Fowles (D) George Orwell

48. Here is a list of American words and word-makers. Match the following :

I. H.L. Mencken	1. Babbit
II. Philip Wylie	2. Yes man
III. Jack Conway	3. Bible belt
IV. Sinclair Lewis	4. Monism

	I	II	III	IV
(A)	4	3	2	1
(B)	3	4	1	2
(C)	3	4	2	1
(D)	4	3	1	2

49. Which of the following in Jacques Derrida's epigraph to his "Structure, Sign and Play in the Discourse of the Human Sciences" ?
(A) *More body, hence more writing.*
.... Helene Cixous.
(B) *We need to interpret interpretations more than to interpret things.*
.... Michel Eyquem de Montaigne.
(C) *But unlike philosophical reflection, ... the reflections we are dealing with here concern rays whose only source is hypothetical*
... Claude Levi-Strauss

(D) *If Cleopatra's nose had been shorter the whole history of the world would have been different.* .... Blaise Pascal.

50. In Mann's *Death in Venice*, death of the protagonist occurs

(A) in a bar (B) in a beach
(C) in a church (D) on the highway

51. Two among the following poets wrote the "Village" poems that address the perennial theme of rural poverty:

I. Oliver Goldsmith
II. William Collins
III. Samuel Johnson
IV. George Gabbe

The right combination according to the code is

(A) I and III (B) II and III
(C) I and IV (D) I and II

52. In which of the following works Yeats developed his theory of 'gyres'?

(A) "A Vision"
(B) "The Secret Rose"
(C) "John Sherman and Dhoya"
(D) "The Celtic Twilight"

53. Mystery and Miracle plays in English were based on ______.

(A) English folklore
(B) English legends
(C) Biblical stories
(D) Anglo-Saxon myths

54. When we rewrite a piece of discourse from one script into another, it is called ______.

(A) Translation (B) Transliteration
(C) Transcreation (D) Transformation

55. "No wonder then." Explain.

(A) No wonder that the words here begin to mean.
(B) No wonder that you now find the words menacing.
(C) No wonder that the words find you menacing.
(D) No wonder the words still mean and are tame.

56. The term "womanism" was first used by

(A) Helene Cixous (B) Gayatri Spivak
(C) Kate Millet (D) Alice Walker

57. Two among the following critics have dealt with the reproduction of motherhood in feminist theory:

I. Nancy Chodorow
II. Judith Fetterley
III. Catherine R. Stimpson
IV. Carol Gilligan

The right combination according to the code is

(A) I and II (B) II and IV
(C) I and IV (D) III and IV

58. *Flowers* is a short play written by

(A) Mahesh Dattani
(B) Asif Currimbhoy
(C) Girish Karnad
(D) Paoli Sengupta

59. Match the columns:

Character	Novel
I. Lady Dedlock	1. *Vanity Fair*
II. Lady Bertram	2. *Wives and Daughters*
III. Lady Harriet	3. *Mansfield Park*
IV. Lady Jane	4. *Bleak House*

	I	II	III	IV
(A)	4	2	3	1
(B)	3	2	1	4
(C)	4	3	2	1
(D)	3	4	1	2

60. "The Books You Needn't Read, the Books Made For Purposes Other Than Reading, Books Read Before You Open Them Since They Belong To The Category of Books Read Before Being Written ..."

The above extract is taken from

(A) Jorge Luis Borges's "The Library of Babel"
(B) Italo Colvino's *If on a Winter's Night a Traveller*
(C) Umberto Eco's *The Name of the Rose*
(D) Francis Bacon's "Of Studies"

61. Listed below are the titles of novels and the sources to which they are aligned by readers. Match them appropriately :

List – I	List – II
I. Peter Carey's *Jack Maggs*	1. *Daniel Defoe's Robinson Crusoe*
II. J.M. Coetzee's *Foe*	2. Charlotte Bronte's *Jane Eyre*
III. Jean Rhys's *Wide Sargasso Sea*	3. R.M. Ballantyne's *The Coral Island*
IV. William Golding's *Lord of the Flies*	4. Charles Dickens's *Great Expectations*

	I	II	III	IV
(A)	4	1	3	2
(B)	4	3	1	2
(C)	4	1	2	3
(D)	4	2	1	3

62. Identify the right chronological sequence :
(A) *The Game of Chess – Volpone – The Duchess of Malfi – The City Madam*
(B) *The City Madam – The Duchess of Malfi – Volpone – A Game of Chess*
(C) *Volpone – The Duchess of Malfi – A Game of Chess – The City Madam*
(D) *The Duchess of Malfi – Volpone – A Game of Chess – The City Madam*

63. 'Nasal tone' in speech is a distinguishing feature of _______.
(A) British English
(B) Scottish English
(C) Australian English
(D) American English

64. Which of the following writers did NOT receive the Nobel Prize for Literature ?
(A) Wole Soyinka
(B) Chinua Achebe
(C) J. M. Coetzee
(D) Nadine Gordimer

65. *The Decline and Fall of the Roman Empire* by Edward Gibbon is a significant work in _____ volumes.
(A) 3 (B) 4
(C) 5 (D) 6

66. The first novel written by Graham Greene is
(A) *Stamboul Train*
(B) *England Made Me*
(C) *The Heart of the Matter*
(D) *The Man Within*

67. From among the Canterbury pilgrims, which group would qualify as the 'upper class' ?
(A) The Pardoner, The Miller, The Nun's Priest
(B) Franklin, Parson, Wife of Bath
(C) The Knight, The Squire, The Prioress
(D) The Reeve, The Manciple, The Clerk

68. Plagiarism is a well-known word and concept in academic circles. The word *plagiarius* in Latin, however, meant
(A) a trickster, a cheat
(B) a quack, a swindler
(C) a loafer, a lout
(D) a torturer, a plunderer

69. What superstition around the Eve of St. Agnes is crucial to an understanding John Keat's famous poem ?
(A) If a virgin performed the proper ritual on St. Agnes' Eve, she would dream of her future husband.
(B) If a virgin performed the proper ritual on St. Agnes' Eve, she would marry her lover.
(C) If a married woman performed the proper ritual on St. Agnes' Eve, she would be reunited with her husband.
(D) If a woman performed the proper ritual on St. Agnes' Eve, she would dream of her future lover.

70. Identify the person who sets himself up as the 'Knight' with a pestle rather than a sword in the play *The Knight of the Burning Pestle* :
(A) Ralph (B) Tim
(C) George (D) Squire

71. Works like *The Earthly Paradise, Dante and His Circle, Goblin Market and Other Poems* and the journal, *The Germ* are associated with _______.

(A) the Pre-Raphaelites
(B) Higher Criticism
(C) the Cavalier Poets
(D) the Pre-Romantics

Read the following poem and answer questions (72 to 75):

A Bird came down the Walk –
He did not know I saw –
He bit an Angleworm in halves
And ate the fellow, raw,
And then he drank a Dew
From a convenient Grass –
And then hopped sidewise to the Wall
To let a Beetle pass –
He glanced with rapid eyes
That hurried all around –
They looked like frightened Beads,
I thought –
He stirred his Velvet Head
Like one in danger, Cautious,
I offered him a Crumb
And he unrolled his feathers
And rowed him softer home –
Than Oars divide the Ocean,
Too silver for a seam –
Or Butterflies, off Banks of Noon
Leap, plashless as they swim.

72. Is "a convenient Grass" an example of "transferred epithet"?
(A) Yes, it is. The "convenience" of grass is transferred from the bird to the poet who finds grass convenient of access.
(B) Yes, it is. The grass is not "convenient", but is transferred from the bird who finds the grass convenient of access.
(C) No. It is a regular epithet.
(D) No. It is not an epithet in the strict sense.

73. Which of the following is NOT an example of kinetic imagery?
(A) "unrolled his feathers"
(B) "hopped sidewise"
(C) "Velvet Head"
(D) "rowed him"

74. The poem stages an encounter between:
(A) the human and the non-human
(B) distrust of the non-human about the humans
(C) two old friends
(D) two old enemies

75. "Like one in danger ..." Who is in danger?
(A) The Bird
(B) The Poet
(C) The Angleworm
(D) Frightened Beads

✓ ANSWERS

1. (B)	**2.** (B)	**3.** (C)	**4.** (D)	**5.** (B)	**6.** (B)	**7.** (A)	**8.** (B)	**9.** (C)	**10.** (C)
11. (D)	**12.** (D)	**13.** (B)	**14.** (A)	**15.** (B)	**16.** (C)	**17.** (C)	**18.** (C)	**19.** (C)	**20.** (C)
21. (A)	**22.** (C)	**23.** (C)	**24.** (C)	**25.** (C)	**26.** (C)	**27.** (B)	**28.** (D)	**29.** (A)	**30.** (A)
31. (D)	**32.** (B)	**33.** (A)	**34.** (B)	**35.** (*)	**36.** (B)	**37.** (A)	**38.** (B)	**39.** (A)	**40.** (C)
41. (C)	**42.** (A)	**43.** (B)	**44.** (A)	**45.** (B)	**46.** (B)	**47.** (A)	**48.** (*)	**49.** (B)	**50.** (B)
51. (*)	**52.** (A)	**53.** (C)	**54.** (B)	**55.** (*)	**56.** (D)	**57.** (C)	**58.** (C)	**59.** (C)	**60.** (B)
61. (C)	**62.** (C)	**63.** (D)	**64.** (B)	**65.** (D)	**66.** (D)	**67.** (C)	**68.** (*)	**69.** (A)	**70.** (A)
71. (A)	**72.** (B)	**73.** (C)	**74.** (AB)	**75.** (A)					

* All option are correct.

June, 2015

ENGLISH LITERATURE

PAPER-II

Note : This paper contains **fifty (50)** objective type questions, each question carrying **two (2)** marks. Attempt **all** the questions.

1. Matthew Arnold's "touchstones" were "short passages, even single lines" of classic poetry beside which the lines of other poets may be placed in order to detect the presence or absence of high poetic quality. In his "Study of Poetry" Arnold cited "touchstones" from such non-English poets as Homer and Dante and also from the English poets, Shakespeare and Milton. Which English poet did he disapprovingly call "not one of the great classics" in the list below ?

(1) Chaucer (2) Sidney
(3) Spenser (4) Donne

2. Samuel Pepys began his diary on

(1) New Year's Day 1660
(2) All Saints' Day 1662
(3) Thanksgiving Day 1665
(4) New Year's Day 1667

3. On which of the following authors has Peter Ackroyd NOT written a biography ?

(1) Charles Dickens
(2) William Blake
(3) T. S. Eliot
(4) W. B. Yeats

4. Which group of the following poets was called the Auden Group because they developed a style and viewpoint similar to that of W. H. Auden ?

(1) Louis MacNeice, C. D. Lewis, Stephen Spender
(2) John Masefield, Edwin Muir, Norman McCaig
(3) MacDiarmid, G. M. Hopkins, Edwin Muir
(4) W. H. Davies, Robert Bridges, John Masefield

5. When one line of poetry runs into the next, with no punctuation to slow the reading, it is a case of________.

(1) caesura (2) consonance
(3) enjambment (4) hyperbole

6. Which of the following is NOT a characteristic of the Victorian Age ?

(1) The rise of a highly competitive industrial technology
(2) An emphasis on strictly controlled social behaviour
(3) A romantic focus on home and family
(4) The growth of rural traditions and movement from large cities

7. In *The Heart of Midlothian,* Walter Scott deals with real political and personal details, but notable among his characters is the depiction of______.

(1) Queen Anne
(3) Queen Caroline
(2) Queen Victoria
(4) Queen Elizabeth

8. Chaucer's first work, *The Book of the Duchess* is a dream poem on the death of

(1) Duchess of Malfi
(2) Duchess of Lancaster
(3) Duchess of Scotland
(4) Duchess of Paris

9. What was Charles Lamb's connection with India ?

(1) He was fascinated by the Indian jugglers and trades-people in London and wrote an essay on them
(2) He was fascinated by Eastern mystical religions, especially Buddhism
(3) He was a clerk for thirty three years in the East India Company
(4) He was clerk in South Sea House that prepared patents and documents for British trading companies in India

10. Find the odd one among the Marxist critics below
(1) Georg Lukacs
(2) Louis Althusser
(3) Raymond Williams
(4) Northrop Frye

11. In the lines "With gold jewels cover every part, / And hide with ornaments their want of art" *(Essay on Criticism)*, Pope rejects
(1) the 'Follow Nature' fallacy
(2) artificiality
(3) aesthetic order
(4) poor taste

12. The opposite of hyperbole is________
(1) meiosis (2) inversion
(3) anagnorisis (4) synecdoche

13. What significance do we attach to the publication of *I Am an Indian* in Canada ?
(1) The title refers to the autobiography of an unknown Indian writer longing for the South Asian countryside
(2) The first ever account of ethnic conflicts within Canada
(3) The first anthology of Native Canadian writing following the Civil Rights Movement of the 1960s
(4) The first anthology of writers afflicted by class and gender differences in Canada of the late 1970s

14. What is the moral of "The Nun's Priest's Tale" ?
(1) Slow and steady wins the race.
(2) Greed is the root of all evil.
(3) Beauty lies within.
(4) Never trust a flatterer.

15. The author of the essay "Silly Novels by Lady Novelists" is
(1) George Eliot
(2) Henry James
(3) Oscar Wilde
(4) Richard Steele

16. The unquenchable spirit of Robinson Crusoe struggling to maintain a substantial existence on a lonely island reflects____.
(1) man's desire to return to nature
(2) the author's criticism of colonization
(3) the ideal of rising bourgeoisie
(4) the aristocrat's disdain for the harsh social reality

17. Who is the author of the collection *The Celtic Twilight* ?
(1) J. M. Synge (2) Sean O'Casey
(3) W. B. Yeats (4) Lady Gregory

18. In medieval England a________was understood to be a trained craftsman, one who worked under a master who owned the business.
(1) pardoner (2) summoner
(3) journeyman (4) manciple

19. Christopher Marlowe's heroes are said to be larger than life, exaggerated both in their faults and in their qualities. They have a desire for everything in extreme. In one of his plays the hero wants to conquer the whole world. The name of the play is_____.
(1) *The Jew of Malta*
(2) *Doctor Faustus*
(3) *Tamburlaine the Great*
(4) *Edward II*

20. With what does the speaker claim to be half in love in "Ode to a Nightingale" ?
(1) the nightingale's haunting melody
(2) the scented flavour of early summer
(3) the night sky and all the stars
(4) the peace that comes with death

21. In which chapter of *Poetics* does Aristotle use the word 'catharsis' in his definition of tragedy ?

(1) Chapter IV (2) Chapter VI
(3) Chapter III (4) Chapter V

22. Match the following :

(a) "The Function of Criticism" (i) Terry Eagleton
(b) "The Function of Criticism at the Present Time" (ii) Richard Ohmann
(c) The Function of Criticism : From *'The Spectator' to Poststructuralism* (iii) Matthew Arnold
(d) "The Function of English at the Present Time" (iv) T. S. Eliot

The right matching according to the code is

Codes :

	(a)	(b)	(c)	(d)
(1)	(iv)	(iii)	(i)	(ii)
(2)	(i)	(ii)	(iii)	(iv)
(3)	(iii)	(iv)	(i)	(ii)
(4)	(ii)	(iii)	(iv)	(i)

23. Identify the TRUE statement on Thomas More's *Utopia.*

(1) *Utopia* is divided into four parts, each dealing with Raphael Hythloday's adventures in the four suburbs of Antwerp.
(2) *Utopia* is divided into two parts; the first records a conversation between Thomas More and Raphael Hythloday, and the second is Hythloday's discourse on the institutions and practices of Utopia.
(3) *Utopia* is divided into two parts; the first is Thomas More's discourse on the institutions and practices of Utopia, and the second a conversation between More and Hythloday.
(4) *Utopia* is divided into four parts, each dealing with the ordered patterns of towns and cities in Antwerp.

24. In "The Rime of the Ancient Mariner" what disaster befalls the ship and the crew ?

(1) The ship is caught in ice and breaks into pieces.
(2) A fierce storm batters the ship and drowns the crew.
(3) "Slimy things with legs" attack the ship and kill many of the crew.
(4) The ship is becalmed and the crew dies of thirst.

25. Falstaff is a character in______.

(a) *Henry IV Part I*
(b) *The Merry Wives of Windsor*
(c) *The Comedy of Errors*
(d) *Titus Andronicus*

The right combination according to the code is

(1) (a) and (b) (2) (a) and (c)
(3) (c) and (d) (4) (a) and (d)

26. In her essay "Professions for Women" Virginia Woolf finds an analogy between the act of writing and______.

(1) driving a motor car
(2) riding a horse
(3) fishing
(4) gardening

27. The ascension of King James I in __________inaugurated the Jacobean age.

(1) 1600 (2) 1601
(3) 1603 (4) 1609

28. Which of the following is NOT true of the Byronic hero ?

(1) moody (2) passionate
(3) repentant (4) remorse-torn

29. Like many other novelists, Hardy employed language variation (dialect and standard) with a purpose. In this respect which of the following statements is correct ?

(1) His major characters such as Tess and Jude always speak in local dialects, as per their social positions.
(2) His major characters such as Tess and Jude rarely speak in local dialects, in spite of their social positions.
(3) His major characters such as Tess and Jude rarely speak in standard language in spite of their social positions.

(4) His major characters such as Tess and Jude rarely speak in a mixture of a dialect and standard.

30. "It used to be said," began a famous English writer, "everyone had a novel in them ... Just now, though, in 1999, you would probably be obliged to doubt the basic proposition: What everyone has in them, these days, is not a novel but a memoir". Identify the source
(1) Martins Amis, *Experience*
(2) Michel Butor, *Passing Time*
(3) John Fowles, *The French Lieutenant's Woman*
(4) Julian Barnes, *Flaubert's Parrot*

31. The opening sixteen lines of *Paradise Lost* comprise
(1) One sentence (2) Two sentences
(3) Three sentences (4) Four sentences

32. Who among the following poets compared human tears to "love's wine"?
(1) Ben Jonson
(2) John Donne
(3) Andrew Marvell
(4) John Suckling

33. Ernest Pontifex is a character in
(1) *Tono Bungay*
(2) *The Man of Property*
(3) *The Way of All Flesh*
(4) *Nostromo*

34. In which of the following stories does Rudyard Kipling present a newspaper editor who recounts his dealings with a couple of "loafers"?
(1) "His Chance in Life"
(2) "Thrown Away"
(3) "Lispeth"
(4) "The Man Who Would Be King"

35. Trying to capture the upbeat mood of 1964-65, the poet Thorn Gunn said: "They stood for a great optimism, barriers seemed to be coming down all over, it was as if World War II had finally drawn to close, there was an openness and high-spiritedness and relaxation of mood". Who were "they"?
(1) The Beatles
(3) The New Left
(2) The Rolling Stones
(4) The Arts Council folks

36. In *Paradise Lost* Milton presents the action of the fall of man in two stages in Books
(1) IV and IX (2) IV and VIII
(3) III and IX (4) V and X

37. In *Gulliver's Travels* Struldbruggs are
(1) people replete with abstract learning.
(2) people exempt from natural death.
(3) people persecuted by pets and servants.
(4) people lured by a new ideal.

38. Margaret Atwood has tried a revisionist writing of a crucial scene in Hamlet called 'Gertrude Talks Back'. The scene in Atwood opens with a reference to the name of an implied listener. Who is this implied listener?
(1) Hamlet (2) Ophelia
(3) Polonius (4) Claudius

39. Samuel Johnson wrote *London* in imitation of______.
(1) Horace (2) Ovid
(3) Juvenal (4) Moschus

40. Which of the following is NOT written by Buchi Emecheta?
(1) *The Joys of Motherhood*
(2) *Second-Class citizen*
(3) *A Question of Power*
(4) *Kehinde*

41. Samuel Johnson's use of the term "metaphysical" in a piece of criticism was
(1) approving (2) disapproving
(3) positive (4) accidental

42. "I am not an angel and I will not be one till I die: I will be myself." This is
(1) Maggie Tulliver in *Mill on the Floss*
(2) Aurora Leigh in the eponymous poem
(3) Jane Eyre in the eponymous novel
(4) Betty Higdon in *Our Mutual Friend*

43. Who among the following playwrights was the son of a gardener ?

(1) Harold Pinter (2) Joe Orton
(3) Tom Stoppard (4) Edward Bond

44. "He is the very pineapple of politeness!" This sentence is an example of

(1) paronomasia (2) spoonerism
(3) malapropism (4) anaphora

45. Ferdinand de Saussure argued that meaning is generated through

(1) a system of structured differences in language
(2) a system of random differences in language
(3) a system of structured references in language
(4) a system of random references in language

46. Identify the group known as "The Wesker Trilogy" ?

(1) *The Growth of the Soil, Game of Life, In the Grip of Life*
(2) *Chicken Soup with Barley, Roots, I'm Talking about Jerusalem*
(3) *The Four Seasons, Chips with Everything, Golden City*
(4) *Lunatics and Lovers, The Patriots, Dead End*

47. Who is the central character of Derek Walcott's *Dream on the Monkey Mountain* ?

(1) Diana Guinness, one of the Mitford Sisters
(2) Jordan, a fantasist
(3) Makak, a charcoal burner
(4) Eva Smith, a seamstress

48. The phrase "darkness visible" (Paradise Lost, 1.63) is an example of______.

(1) periphrasis (2) pun
(3) oxymoron (4) transposition

49. What is common to writers such as Sam Selvon *(The Lonely Londoners)*, Timothy Mo *(Sour Sweet)*, and Hanif Kureishi *(The Black Album)* ?

(1) All of them are brilliant writers of autobiographies who tell stories and write poetry.
(2) They use Standard English with some Creole inflections peculiar to the Caribbean.
(3) They are diasporic writers who depict postcolonial London very different from its colonial representations.
(4) They contrast the 'First Nations' with local populations of their respective countries.

50. F. R. Leavis and Q. D. Leavis launched a critical journal devoted to the moral centrality of English Studies. Name the Journal.

(1) *The English Historical Review*
(2) *The Criterion*
(3) *Scrutiny*
(4) *The Edinburgh Review*

✔ ANSWERS

1. (1)	**2.** (1)	**3.** (4)	**4.** (1)	**5.** (3)	**6.** (4)	**7.** (3)	**8.** (2)	**9.** (4)	**10.** (4)
11. (2)	**12.** (1)	**13.** (3)	**14.** (4)	**15.** (1)	**16.** (3)	**17.** (3)	**18.** (3)	**19.** (3)	**20.** (4)
21. (2)	**22.** (1)	**23.** (2)	**24.** (4)	**25.** (1)	**26.** (3)	**27.** (3)	**28.** (3)	**29.** (2)	**30.** (1)
31. (1)	**32.** (2)	**33.** (3)	**34.** (4)	**35.** (1)	**36.** (1)	**37.** (2)	**38.** (1)	**39.** (3)	**40.** (3)
41. (2)	**42.** (3)	**43.** (2)	**44.** (3)	**45.** (1)	**46.** (2)	**47.** (3)	**48.** (3)	**49.** (3)	**50.** (3)

June, 2015

ENGLISH LITERATURE

PAPER-III

Note : This paper contains seventy **five (75)** objective type questions of **two (2)** marks each. All questions are compulsory.

1. When Luigi Pirandello's *Six Characters in Search of an Author* opens the audience find the producer attempting to stage a play. What is the title of this play ?

(1) "Rites of Performance"
(2) "Rules of the Game"
(3) "Tonight We Stage a Play"
(4) "Modes of Acting"

2. Which Canterbury pilgrim carries a brooch inscribed with the Latin words meaning "Love Conquers All" ?

(1) The Prioress
(2) The Monk
(3) The Wife of Bath
(4) The Squire

3. In his Introduction to *The Oxford Book of Twentieth-Century English Verse* (1973), Philip Larkin underlines the importance of a native tradition with________seen as the major poet of the Modern Period.

(1) William Butler Yeats
(2) T.S. Eliot
(3) Thomas Hardy
(4) D.H. Lawrence

4. Philip Sidney defended poetry against such descriptions of it as "the mother of lies" and "the nurse of abuse." His main argument here is

(1) The poet is no conjuror or illusionist and represents a world.
(2) The poet cannot lie because he is not claiming to tell us the truth.
(3) The poet cannot speak the truth because he is not representing the real world.
(4) The poet is a philosopher for whom truth is a lie, and lie truth, in an imaginary world.

5. Chapter III of *Oliver Twist* opens with a narratorial remark about Oliver being punished for "the commission of the impious and profane offence of asking for more." What did Oliver ask for more ?

(1) More time to play
(2) More food to eat
(3) More books to read
(4) More money to spend

6. Edmund Spenser's *Epithalamion* is a carefully structured poem carrying corresponding to the________.

(1) twelve stanzas; months of the year
(2) three hundred and sixty five lines; days of the year
(3) fourteen stanzas; two week-long bridal ceremonies
(4) eleven stanzas; eleventh month, November

7. Choose the right chronological sequence below

(1) Victorian Period - Jacobean Period - Tudor Period - Restoration Period
(2) Edwardian Period - Tudor Period - Jacobean Period - Victorian Period
(3) Tudor Period - Jacobean Period - Restoration Period - Edwardian Period

(4) Jacobean Period - Tudor Period - Restoration Period - Edwardian Period

8. "That woman's days were spent
In ignorant good - will,
Her nights in argument
Until her voice grew shrill" (W. B. Yeats : "Easter 1916") Who is the poet referring to ?

(1) Maud Gonne
(2) Lady Augusta Gregory
(3) Kathleen Pilcher
(4) Constance Gore - Booth Markievicz

9. Which of the following was replaced by Communicative Language Teaching ?

(1) Motivational Approach
(2) Situational Language Teaching
(3) Natural Language Processing
(4) Structural Approach

10. To whom does Francis Bacon offer the following piece of advice ?

"Let him sequester himself from the Company of his Countrymen, and diet in such Places, where there is good company of the Nation... Let him upon his Removes, ... procure. Recommendation, to some person of Quality, residing in the Place, whither he removeth..."

(1) The Beaux (2) The Peddler
(3) The Traveller (4) The Stationer

11. In his masterpiece, *Of the Lawes of Ecclesiasticall Politie*, Richard Hooker affirmed the Anglican tradition as that of a "threefold cord not quickly broken." He specifically referred to the following EXCEPT______.

(1) tradition (2) scripture
(3) community (4) reason

12. Match the following :

List - I	List-II
(a) Christina Rossetti: *Goblin Market*	(i) The tale of a father who inadvertently destroys his son
(b) Matthew Arnold : *Sohrab and Rustom*	(ii) Gently satiric account of an Oxford student on vacation
(c) Robert Browning : *The Ring and the Book*	(iii) Story of pleasure-seeking Laura and the conventionally moral Lizzie who resists temptations
(d) Arthur Hugh Clough : *The Bothie of Tober-na-Vuolich*	(iv) A sensational 17* century murder presented through multiple dramatic monologues

The right matching according to the code is:

Codes :

	(a)	(b)	(c)	(d)
(1)	(iii)	(iv)	(i)	(ii)
(2)	(ii)	(iv)	(iii)	(i)
(3)	(iii)	(i)	(iv)	(ii)
(4)	(iv)	(ii)	(iii)	(i)

13. "Beneath them sit the aged men, wise guardians of the poor;
Then cherish pity, lest you drive an angel from your door."

These concluding lines of William Blake's *Innocence* poem called "Holy Thursday" allude to a Biblical passage. Identify the passage.

(1) The angel of the Lord encampeth round about those who fear Him and delivereth them. Psalms 34.7
(2) Suffer not thy mouth to cause thy flesh to sin; neither say thou before the angel, that it was an error. Ecclesiastes 5.6
(3) And they said unto her, Thou art mad. But she constantly affirmed that it was even so. Then said they, It is his angel. The Acts 12.15
(4) Be not forgetful to entertain strangers for thereby some have entertained angels unawares. Hebrews 13.2

14. Direct Method of Language Teaching involves

(a) the use of Target Language only
(b) repetition of exercises
(c) linguistic correctness
(d) problem solving exercises

In relation to the above which of the following is correct ?

(1) (c) and (d) only
(2) (a), (b) and (d)
(3) (a), (b) and (c)
(4) (a), (b), (c) and (d)

15. In which of the following works does the narrator proclaim, "either I'm nobody, or I'm the nation" ?

(1) George Lamming's *In the Castle of My Skin*
(2) Derek Walcott's "The Schooner Flight"
(3) Jamaica Kincaid's "Girl"
(4) Kamau Braithwaite's "Nation Language"

16. Like Cordelia, the Fool in *King Lear* is____.

(1) killed by Goneril's troops.
(2) referred to by Lear as his child.
(3) disliked by Regan and Cornwall.
(4) punished for not telling the truth.

17. Sindi Oberoi, the narrator hero in Arun Joshi's *The Foreigner* says : "My foreignness lay within me and I couldn't leave myself behind wherever I went." Identify the countries which Sindi Oberoi went to.

(1) Kenya, Uganda, England, America, India
(2) Kenya, Uganda, New Zealand, England, India
(3) Kenya, England, Canada, India
(4) Kenya, America, England, Australia, India

18. **Assertion (A)** : The world does not become raceless or will not become unracialized by assertion. The act of enforcing racelessness in literary discourse is itself a racial act.

Reason (R) : Pouring rhetorical acid on the fingers of a black hand may indeed destroy the prints, but not the hand. Besides, what happens, in that violent, self-serving act of erasure, to the hands, the fingers, the fingerprints of the one who does the pouring ? Do they remain acid-free ? The literature itself suggests otherwise.

In the context of the statements above,

(1) (A) makes complete sense in the light of (R).
(2) (A) makes complete sense regardless of (R).
(3) Neither (A) nor (R) makes complete sense.
(4) (R) challenges the view advanced in (A).

19. A poet laureate said "I do not think that since Shakespeare there has been such a master of the English language as I." Who is the poet ?

(1) Stephen Spender
(2) John Dryden
(3) Alfred Lord Tennyson
(4) Ted Hughes

20. Who among the following was a contemporary of John Milton and wrote *The Worthy Communicant* ? It is said that his prose "can be read easily, when Milton's must be studied."

(1) Jeremy Taylor
(2) John Bunyan
(3) Andrew Marvell
(4) George Herbert

21. In 1668, Dryden wrote *Of Dramatic Poesie* : An Essay which uses_____separate characters to dramatise the conflicting viewpoints which new theatrical activity had produced.

(1) three
(2) two
(3) four
(4) six

22. Writing his most influential play, August Strindberg called it "My most beloved drama, the child of my greatest suffering." The play is

(1) *A Dream Play*

(2) *Miss Julie*

(3) *The Bridal Crown*

(4) *The Dance of Death*

23. In which essay does Virginia Woolf observe that "if a writer were a free man [sic] and not a slave" to the conventions of the literary market-place, there would be "no plot, no comedy, no tragedy, no love interest, or catastrophe in the accepted style, and perhaps not a single button sewn on as the Bond Street tailors would have it" ?

(1) "How it Strikes a Contemporary"

(2) 'Modern Fiction"

(3) "The Russian Point of View"

(4) 'Mr. Bennett and Mr. Brown"

24. In his famous letter to Benjamin Bailey (November 22,1817) John Keats wrote : "I am certain of nothing but the holiness of the Heart's affections and the truth of Imagination - What the imagination seizes as Beauty must be truth." Which of the following sentences follows this passage ?

(1) Now I am sensible all this is a mere sophistication, however it may neighbour to any truths, to excuse my own indolence...

(2) The Imagination may be compared to Adam's dream - he woke and found it true.

(3) This however I am persuaded of, that nothing beside Imagination can give us sweet sensations and pleasurable thoughts.

(4) My pains at last some respite shall afford, while I behold the battles Imagination maintains.

25. Which of the following pair best describes the characteristic features of Marlowe's portrait of Tamburlaine ?

(a) ambition

(b) apathy

(c) cruelty

(d) sympathy

The right combination according to the code is__________.

(1) (a) and (b)

(2) (a) and (d)

(3) (a) and (c)

(4) (b) and (c)

26. Who is the author of the statement: "The nineteenth century dislike of Realism is the rage of Caliban seeing his own face in the glass" ?

(1) Arthur Symons

(2) Benjamin Disraeli

(3) W. B. Yeats

(4) Oscar Wilde

27. Which of the following statements about Thomas Mann's novels is true ?

(a) *Buddenbrooks* is a family saga set in the early decades of the twentieth century.

(b) Aschenbach, the writer protagonist in *Death in Venice,* is preoccupied with classicism, especially with classical ideals of male beauty.

(c) In his second winter at the sanatorium, Hans Castorp, protagonist of *The Magic Mountain* gets lost in a blizzard during a solitary skiing expedition.

(d) Adrian Leverkuhn, the modern day Faustus in Mann's *Doctor Faustus* is a musician.

The right combination according to the code is :

(1) Only (a) and (c) are correct

(2) Only (b) and (d) are correct

(3) (b), (c) and (d) are correct

(4) (a), (b) and (d) are correct

28. To whom did Raja Ram Mohan Roy write in 1823 his letter seeking the introduction of English education in India ?

(1) Lord Amherst
(2) Lord Bentinck
(3) Lord Cunningham
(4) Lord Hastings

29. Listed below are the seemingly friendly characters in *The Pilgrim's Progress* who give Christian dangerous advice. Among them is one who does not belong to this group. Identify this odd character.
(1) Mr. Worldly Wiseman
(2) Evangelist
(3) Ignorance
(4) Talkative

30. Aristotle argued that poetry provides a/an _______ outlet for the release of intense emotions.
(1) safe
(2) dangerous
(3) uncertain
(4) unreliable

31. The direct French influence on the English language during the Middle English period was in the form of______.
(1) loss of inflections.
(2) intake of French words into English.
(3) both the loss of inflections and intake of French words into English.
(4) addition of inflections.

32. A significant development in 1662 was the establishment of The Royal Society in England. The main purpose of the society was______..
(1) to set the rules for the royal court and governance
(2) to guide and promote the development of science and scientific exploration
(3) to set norms for civil society
(4) to promote theatre

33. William Cowper wrote in *The Task* (IV. 681-82) about those who "Build factories with blood, conducting trade/At the sword's point ..." These lines allude to :
(1) Turkish militant traders across Europe
(2) Nordic conquerors across East Asia
(3) West Indian slave-plantation owners and the East India Company 'nabobs'
(4) Exploiters of child labour in the London suburbs

34. The *commedia dell'arte* originated in Italy in the sixteenth century. Which of the following descriptions are the most appropriate ?
(a) Tears alternating with crude laughter
(b) Comedy of the guild or by the professionals in the "art"
(c) Plautine comedy alternating with ritualistic manoeuvres
(d) Improvised comedy that follows a scenario rather than written dialogue

The right combination according to the code is
(1) (a) and (b)
(2) (b) and (d)
(3) (a) and (c)
(4) (b) and (c)

35. "Nature and Nature's Laws lay hid in Night,
God said Let Newton be! And all was Light."

Alexander Pope's famous couplet impressively captures_______.
(1) Newton's confirmation of the Genesis passage where God ordains Light
(2) Newton's empirical observations of *Philosophiae Naturalis Principia Mathematica*
(3) Newton's application of principles of motion to account for many natural phenomena
(4) Newton's discovery that all colours are contained in white light

36. What was the name of the experimental theatre group founded in 1915 by Susan Glaspell, Eugene O'Neill and other dramatists in order to challenge Broadway's control over American drama ?

(1) The Wall Street Theatre Group
(2) The Washington Square Players
(3) The Actor's Studio
(4) The Provincetown Players

37. After his return from the land of Houyhnhnms, Gulliver refused to let his wife and children
(1) show disrespect to English horses.
(2) ride horse-drawn carriages.
(3) touch his bread, or drink out of his cup.
(4) communicate with him in English tongue.

38. In which of the following volumes do you find a charming appreciation of the Wordsworth household by Thomas de Quincey ?
(1) *The Confessions of an English Opium-Eater*
(2) *Lives and Letters, Far Away and Long Ago*
(3) *Notes on My Lake Country Evenings*
(4) *Reminiscences of the English Lake Poets*

39. One of the most highly revered, scholarly, and passionate interpreters of English and world literatures, he was appointed the Lord Northcliffe Professor of Modern English Literature at University College, London in 1967, and later as King Edward VII Professor of English Literature at Cambridge in 1974, an appointment made by the Crown at the suggestion of the Prime Minister of the United Kingdom. He was knighted by Queen Elizabeth in 1991. Entitled to designate himself as "Sir," he never did, but wrote and autobiography entitled *Not Entitled* in 1995. The epigraph to this book came from *Coriolanus* : "He was a kind of nothing, titleless."

Who among the following is this writer/critic ?
(1) F. R. Leavis
(2) I. A. Richards
(3) Frank Kermode
(4) David Lodge

40. Which of the following provided theoretical basis for Audio-Lingual Method of Language Teaching ?
(1) Transformational Generative Linguistics
(2) Congnitive Psychology and Structural Linguistics
(3) Behaviourist Psychology and Bloomfieldian Structural Linguistics
(4) Systemic Functional Linguistics

41. Who among the following characters of *The Cherry Orchard* by Anton Chekhov dies in the final scene ?
(1) Anya
(2) Firs
(3) Varya
(4) Lopakhin

42. In tracing the history of English poetry, Thomas Gray's "Progress of Poesy" invokes a major poet as follows :
"Nor second He, that rode sublime
Upon the seraph-wings of Extasy,
The secrets of th' Abyss to spy."
Who is "He" ?
(1) William Shakespeare
(2) Edmund Spenser
(3) John Milton
(4) John Dryden

43. "I suffered from impaired eye-sight, depression and poverty and left Oxford without a degree.

After a period as a teacher and my marriage to a widow twice my age, I left for London, to begin writing for a magazine, I produced my own journal." Choose the correct answer, identifying the writer, the magazine and the journal.
(1) John Milton, *The Examiner's Magazine, London Magazine*
(2) Joseph Addison, *The Freeholder, The Tatler*
(3) Richard Steele, *The Guardian, The Spectator*

(4) Samuel Johnson, *The Gentlemen's Magazine, The Rambler*

44. Which of the American novelists is associated with the series of five books about Natty Bumppo, an old hunter, also called Leatherstocking ?

(1) Stephen Crane
(2) James Fennimore Cooper
(3) Herman Melville
(4) Jack London

45. In John Dryden's *Essay on Dramatic Poesy* Neander defends the English invention of

(1) romantic comedy
(2) action tragedy
(3) tragi-comedy
(4) morality plays

46. Who wrote *The History of Australian Literature* in 1961 ?

(1) Randolph Stow
(2) H. M. Green
(3) Handel Richardson
(4) Francis Adam

47. Match the following :

Theorist	**Theories**
(a) Bharata	(i) Vakrokti
(b) Kuntaka	(ii) Riti
(c) Bhamaha	(iii) Dhvani
(d) Anandavardhana	(iv) Rasa

The right matching according to the code is:

Codes :

	(a)	**(b)**	**(c)**	**(d)**
(1)	(i)	(iv)	(ii)	(iii)
(2)	(ii)	(iii)	(i)	(iv)
(3)	(iv)	(i)	(ii)	(iii)
(4)	(iii)	(ii)	(iv)	(i)

48. What is "Forster Collection" ?

(1) Memorabilia and documents related to the Scottish War of Independence (1296-1328) housed in Glasgow Museum
(2) The special collection of E. M. Forster effects housed in King's College, Cambridge
(3) The largest collection of Charles Dickens manuscripts and proofs curated by John Forster
(4) The collection of political and military documents named after the liberal M. P., W. E. Forster reputed for the Forster Education Act

49. What was remarkable about the poet F. T. Marinetti's first Futurist Manifesto in *Le Figaro* ?

(1) It resounded like the monotonous beating of a big drum that filled the air with muffled shocks and lingering vibration.
(2) It proclaimed that someone must go on writing for those who were still convinced of the future for which they had taken up arms.
(3) It blasted the dead weight of "museums, libraries, and academics," glorifying "the beauty of speed."
(4) It declared that man, the individual, is an infinite reservoir of possibilities; and if man can so rearrange society by the destruction of oppressive disorder, then the possibilities have a future.

50. How would one best describe Thomas Carlyle's *Sartor Resartus* (1833) ?

(1) A combination of journal, fashion-book, and tips for advertisers
(2) A lyrical novel *a la* Marcel Proust
(3) A combination of novel, autobiography, and essay
(4) A satire on sartorial fashions and feibles of medieval Europe

51. An Indian English poet once remarked that his discipline and education gave him his "outer" whereas his Indian origin gave him "inner" form. Reflecting a part of this claim is a famous essay he called .

(1) "Is There a Native Way of Thinking ?"

(2) "Can the Subaltern Speak ?"
(3) "Where Do We Go from Here : Some Speculations"
(4) "Is There an Indian Way of Thinking ?"

52. In the remarkably crucial courtroom scene of *Their Eyes Were Watching God*, Janie is called upon to speak. Whose voice do we hear in the narrative ?
(1) Tea Cake's voice
(2) Janie's first-person voice
(3) Pheoby's voice
(4) The omniscient third-person voice

53. Who is the author of the statement "A prophet is a Seer, not an Arbitrary Dictator"?
(1) Salman Rushdie
(2) Kahlil Gibran
(3) William Blake
(4) Oscar Wilde

54. The word order in Modern English became relatively fixed because
(1) it developed its inflectional system.
(2) it lost its highly developed inflectional system.
(3) it lost its derivational system of word formation.
(4) it developed its derivational system of word formation

55. Julia Kristeva's 'intertextuality' derives from______
(a) Noam Chomsky's deep structure
(b) Mikhail Bakhtin's dialogism
(c) Jacques Derrida's differance
(d) Ferdinand de Saussure's sign
The right combination according to the code is
(1) (a) and (b)
(2) (b) and (c)
(3) (c) and (d)
(4) (a) and (d)

56. Dylan Thomas's famous poem "Fern Hill," is named after
(1) a countryside in Austria to which he paid occasional visits.
(2) a childhood haunt of the poet's family in Devonshire.
(3) the Welsh farmhouse where the poet spent summer holidays as a boy
(4) The Welsh Anglican church to which the young poet used to be taken by his mother.

57. "In the seventeenth century," writes T. S. Eliot in "The Metaphysical Poets," "a dissociation of sensibility set in, from which we have never recovered; and this dissociation, as is natural, was aggravated by the influence of the two most powerful poets of the century,________and________.
(1) Ben Jonson and Abraham Cowley
(2) George Herbert and Henry Vaughan
(3) John Donne and Andrew Marvell
(4) John Milton and John Dryden

58. The label 'material feminism' refers to the work of those thinkers who study inequality in terms of________.
(1) gender differences.
(2) class differences.
(3) both gender and class differences.
(4) female consumerism.

59. Who among the following displays in her best work the dual influence of feminism and magic realism ?
(1) Pat Barker
(2) Muriel Spark
(3) Angela Carter
(4) J. K Rowling

60. Identify the group of British poets who evidently draw upon new trends in literary theory (such as poststructuralism) and wrote poems that reflect on themselves and the language used in/by them.
(1) Seamus Heaney, Michael Longley, Derek Mahon
(2) Medbh McGuckian, Denise Riley, Wendy Cope

(3) Christopher Middleton, Roy Fisher, J. H. Prynne
(4) Donald Davie, Charles Tomlinson, Thorn Gunn

61. In Old English other grammatical classes also had the four cases that nouns had. Which were these grammatical classes ?
(1) Pronouns and verbs only
(2) Pronouns and adjectives only
(3) Definite article and verbs only
(4) Pronouns, adjectives and definite article

62. Which of the following novels opens with the description of an accident to a hot-air balloon ?
(1) John Fowles's *The Magus*
(2) Ian McEwan's *Enduring Love*
(3) James Kelman's *How Late It Was, How Late*
(4) Irvine Welsh's *Trainspotting*

63. Azizun, a courtesan from Kanpur in *A Tale from the Year 1857 : Azizun Nisa* by Tripurari Sharma undergoing self-actualisation says : "Yes, I must complete what I've set out to do.
I'm not a mere woman." In order to make her impact by her attitudinal shift, she____.
(1) challenges the codifiers of the Shariat.
(2) forsakes her profession to become a soldier.
(3) becomes a political leader.
(4) becomes a successful dancer.

64. The *hermeneutics of suspicion* is a term coined by Paul Ricoeur________.
(a) to designate the postcolonial tendency to see theory and related reading manoeuvres as a global conspiracy.
(b) to describe interpretive bids that challenge and seek to overcome compartmentalized cultural experiences.
(c) who, following Marx, Nietzsche, and Freud, held that textual appearances are deceptive and texts do not gracefully relinquish their meanings.
(d) to describe a mode of interpretation that adopts a distrustful attitude towards texts in order to elicit otherwise inaccessible meanings or implications.

The right combination according to the code is :
(1) (a) and (b)
(2) (a) and (d)
(3) (c) and (d)
(4) (b) and (c)

65. Which of the following is not a feminist novel?
(1) Ashapurna Debi's *Subarnalata*
(2) Rajam Krishnan's *Lamp in the Whirlpool*
(3) Chudamani Raghavan's *Yamini*
(4) Bani Basu's *The Enemy Within*

66. The term 'poetic justice' was coined by___
(1) Samuel Taylor Coleridge
(2) Thomas Rymer
(3) Samuel Johnson
(4) William Wordsworth

67. Which of the following novels deals with the Biafran War ?
(1) *July's People*
(2) *Waiting for the Barbarians*
(3) *Half of a Yellow Sun*
(4) *Arrow of God*

68. Which of the following is not true in Dalit aesthetics as given by Sharan Kumar Limbale ?
(1) The agony, assertion, resistance, anger and protest of the dalits should be expressed.
(2) Dalit *anubhava* (experience) should take precedence over *anuman* (speculation).
(3) Sympathy for the dalits should be generated.
(4) Ungrammatical language, different from the standard norms of expression, should be used.

69. Which of the following is **not** a critical study by William Empson ?

(1) *Seven Types of Ambiguity*
(2) *The Dyer's Hand*
(3) *Milton's God*
(4) *Some Versions of the Pastoral*

70. This was a path-breaking feminist essay written in the 1970s which used hybrid terms like "sext" and "chaosmos." Identify the author.
(1) Luce Irigaray
(2) Helene Cixous
(3) Julia Kristeva
(4) Simon de Beauvoir

Read the poem and answer the questions that follow (71 - 75) :

The Voice

Woman much missed, how you call to me, call to me,
Saying that now you are not as what you were
When you had changed from the one who was all to me
But as first, when our day was fair
Can it be you that I hear ? Let me view you, then
Standing as when I drew near to the town Where you would wait for me : yes, as I knew you then,
Even to the original air-blue gown!
Or is it only the breeze, in its listlessness
Travelling across the wet mead to me here,
You being ever dissolved to wan wistlessness
Heard no more again far or near ?
Thus I; faltering forward,
Leaves around me falling,
Wind oozing thin through the thorn from norward
And the woman calling.

71. What suggestion does the opening stanza give of a woman won or a woman lost ?
(1) The contrast between 'now' and 'then'
(2) The continuity between 'now' and 'then'
(3) The phrase "had changed"
(4) The phrase "our day was fair"

72. What is tantalizing about the speaker's experience in stanza 2 ?
(1) the disappearance of the lady and the echo of the voice
(2) the indistinct voice heard by the speaker and the absence of woman
(3) The uncertainty of the voice and the speaker's inability to see the woman
(4) the woman disappearing before her voice is fully heard

73. What phrase in the poem suggests the possibility of the woman as "dead" ?
(1) "You had changed .... to me"
(2) "I knew you then"
(3) "You being ever dissolved"
(4) "Woman much missed"

74. Identify the special sound effect in the line given : Wind oozing thin through the thorn from norward...
(1) Alliteration
(2) Onomatopoeia
(3) Assonance
(4) The use of sibilants

75. What longing does the speaker voice ?
(1) longing for reunion in the other world
(2) longing for physical union in the present
(3) longing for physical union in the town where they used to meet
(4) longing for a return to the town where they used to meet

✓ ANSWERS

1. (2)	**2.** (1)	**3.** (3)	**4.** (2)	**5.** (2)	**6.** (2)	**7.** (3)	**8.** (4)	**9.** (2,4)	**10.** (3)
11. (3)	**12.** (3)	**13.** (4)	**14.** (*)	**15.** (2)	**16.** (2)	**17.** (1)	**18.** (1)	**19.** (3)	**20.** (1)
21. (3)	**22.** (1)	**23.** (2)	**24.** (2)	**25.** (3)	**26.** (4)	**27.** (3)	**28.** (1)	**29.** (2)	**30.** (1)
31. (2)	**32.** (2)	**33.** (3)	**34.** (2)	**35.** (4)	**36.** (4)	**37.** (3)	**38.** (4)	**39.** (3)	**40.** (3)
41. (2)	**42.** (3)	**43.** (4)	**44.** (2)	**45.** (3)	**46.** (2)	**47.** (3)	**48.** (3)	**49.** (3)	**50.** (3)
51. (4)	**52.** (4)	**53.** (3)	**54.** (2)	**55.** (*)	**56.** (3)	**57.** (4)	**58.** (3)	**59.** (3)	**60.** (3)
61. (4)	**62.** (2)	**63.** (2)	**64.** (3)	**65.** (4)	**66.** (2)	**67.** (3)	**68.** (3)	**69.** (2)	**70.** (2)
71. (1,3)	**72.** (3)	**73.** (3)	**74.** (1)	**75.** (3)					

* No option is correct.

December, 2015

ENGLISH LITERATURE

PAPER-II

Note : This paper contains **fifty (50)** objective type questions, each question carrying **two (2)** marks. Attempt **all** the questions.

1. Who, among the following, advanced the theory that the mind is a *tabula rasa* at birth, and acquires all ideas by experience ?
(1) John Locke (2) John Wesley
(3) Isaac Watts (4) Denis Diderot

2. Which of the following authors wrote *Studies in the History of the Renaissance* ?
(1) Walter Pater (2) Oscar Wilde
(3) Thomas Carlyle (4) John Ruskin

3. Whom does Harriet Smith finally marry in one of Jane Austen's novels ?
(1) Knightley (2) Darcy
(3) Collins (4) Mr. Martin

4. A poet once referred to an old man as "A tattered coat upon a stick". That is an example of
(1) Metonymy (2) Sarcasm
(3) Simile (4) Metaphor

5. Which of these is **NOT** a pastoral elegy ?
(1) *Lycidas* (2) *In Memoriam*
(3) *Thyrsis* (4) *Adonais*

6. In Beckett's *Waiting for Godot* the characters often use dislocated, repetitious and cliched speech primarily to :
(1) illustrate the essentially illogical, purposeless nature of the human condition
(2) re-create the workings of the subconscious
(3) mock the exaggerated dignity and wisdom of modern, self-professed intellectuals
(4) reinforce the comic action of farcical plots

7. Which of the following sixteenth-century poets was **NOT** a courtier ?
(1) George Puttenham
(2) Philip Sidney
(3) Walter Raleigh
(4) Thomas Wyatt

8. Patrick White published two novels in the 1950s giving the eras of pioneering and exploration in Australian history an epic, ironic and psychological dimension.
The novels are :
(a) *A Fringe of Leaves*
(b) *The Tree of Man*
(c) *Voss*
(d) *The Aunt's Story*
The right combination according to the code is :
(1) (a) and (b) (2) (b) and (c)
(3) (c) and (a) (4) (c) and (d)

9. In which of the following works did Bakhtin propose his widely cited concept of the 'Carnivalesque' ?
(1) "Discourse in the novel"
(2) *Dialogic Imagination*
(3) *Rabelais and his world*
(4) "Forms of Time and of the Chronotope in the Novel"

10. Match the columns :

(Author)	**(Text)**
(a) Sebastian Faulks	(i) *Amsterdam*
(b) Peter Ackroyd	(ii) *Changing Places*
(c) Ian McEwan	(iii) *Hawksmoor*
(d) David Lodge	(iv) *Birdsong*

Codes :

	(a)	(b)	(c)	(d)
(1)	(i)	(ii)	(iii)	(iv)
(2)	(ii)	(iii)	(i)	(iv)
(3)	(iv)	(iii)	(i)	(ii)
(4)	(iii)	(iv)	(ii)	(i)

11. In New Criticism, the key term 'tension' is associated with :

(1) Cleanth Brooks
(2) John Crow Ransom
(3) Austin Warren
(4) Allen Tate

12. While compiling what sort of book did Samuel Richardson conceive of the idea for his *Pamela or Virtue Rewarded* ?

(1) an account of the plague in London
(2) an instruction manual for manners
(3) a book of devotion
(4) a book of model letters

13. Who among the war Poets gained notoriety in 1917, when disenchanted with the way the war was being conducted he drafted his letter of "wilful defiance of the military authority" which captured attention in the House of Commons, and was forcibly admitted to the war hospital at Craiglockhart, primarily to avoid his being court-martialled ?

(1) Rupert Brooke
(2) Siegfried Sassoon
(3) Wilfred Owen
(4) Isaac Rosenberg

14. If you cannot understand an argument and remark, "It's Greek to me", you are quoting

(1) John Milton
(2) Samuel Johnson
(3) William Shakespeare
(4) John Donne

15. Which of the following works did Walter Scott compile ?

(1) *The Lay of the Last Minstrel*
(2) *Marmion*
(3) *Ivanhoe*
(4) *The Minstrelsy of Scottish Border*

16. Which of the following is **NOT** written by Wole Soyinka ?

(1) *Home and Exile*
(2) *Kongi's Harvest*
(3) *The interpreters*
(4) *The Swamp Dwellers*

17. In the *Defense of Poesy* Sidney says : " Now as in geometry the oblique must be known as well as right and in arithmetic, the odd as well as the even, so in the actions of our life who seeth not the filthiness of evil wanteth a great foil to perceive the beauty of virtue". Which of the following forms of poesy offers a foil that helps us perceive the beauty of virtue ?

(1) Pastorals
(2) Parody
(3) Comedy
(4) Tragedy

18. John Dry den described a major English poet as "a rough diamond, and must first be polished ere he shines" Identify him :

(1) Geoffrey Chaucer
(2) John Gower
(3) George Herbert
(4) Robert Herrick

19. In a remarkably proleptic insight, a critic wrote the following, anticipating Benedict Anderson's definition of the nation as "an imagined political community" :

"Most novels are in some sense knowable communities. It is part of a traditional method -an underlying stance and approach - that a novelist offers to show people and their relationships in essentially knowable and communicable ways". Name the critic and the reference :

(1) Van Wyck Brooks, *The writer in America*
(2) Raymond Williams, *The country and the city*
(3) Joseph Wood Krutch, *The Modern Temper*
(4) T.S. Eliot, *Notes Towards a Definition of culture*

20. "Fair is my love, and cruel as she's fair; Her brow-shades frown, although her eyes are sunny". The above lines are characterized by :

(1) circumlocution (2) antithesis
(3) anticlimax (4) bathos

21. In his "Epistle to Dr. Arbuthnot" Pope tells us that as a poet he had benefited from "This saving counsel, 'keep your piece nine years'" - which enjoins on writer's patience and great care before they rush to print. Whose "counsel" is Pope referring to ?
(1) Longinus's in *On the Sublime*
(2) Horace's in *Ars Poetica*
(3) Quintilian's *Institutio Oratoria*
(4) Aristotle's *Poetics*

22. An English architect and stage-designer - Beginning 1605, joined Jacobean court to design masques - contributed significantly to the spectacular theatre which succeeded the commonwealth after his death - the first designer to use revolving screens to indicate scene-changes on the English stage. Identify this artist/designer.
(1) Henry Irving
(2) Inigo Jones
(3) Henry Arthur Jones
(4) William Inge

23. ______ may be defined as any departure from the rules of pronunciation or diction, for the sake of rhyme or metre, or an unjustifiable departure from fact.
(1) Poetic license (2) Poetic justice
(3) Poetic deviance (4) Poetic diction

24. That Humanities and the sciences were in fact "two cultures" was suggested by
(1) Aldous Huxley in his oxford lectures on poetry
(2) W.H. Anden in his oxford lectures on poetry
(3) F.R. Leavis in his book, *The Great Tradition*
(4) C.P. Snow in his Rede lecture

25. Chaueer satirizes the Monk because the Monk:
(1) is too concerned with courtesy and matters of etiquette
(2) cheats the poor peasants by selling them false religious relics
(3) courts favour of wealthy people but spends no time with poor people
(4) spends too much time hunting and too little time on religious duty

26. Divided into three sections this groundbreaking work published in 1953 uses as the frame of the spiritual and moral awakening of a fourteen-year-old during a Saturday night service in a Harlem church. Identify the work.
(1) Zora Neale Hurston's *Their Eyes Are Watching God*
(2) James Baldwin's *Go Tell it on the Mountain*
(3) Toni Morrison's *Song of Solomon*
(4) Richard Wright's *Native Son*

27. Chartism, a political movement that took its name from the People's Charter had six points. Identify the one point on the following list that was **NOT** Chartist :
(a) universal manhood sufferage
(b) equal electoral districts
(c) comprehensive insurance scheme for labour
(d) vote by secret ballot
(e) payment of MPs
(f) no property qualifications for MPs
(g) Annual parliaments

Codes :
(1) (e) (2) (g)
(3) (c) (4) (d)

28. These beauteous forms,
Through a long absence, have been to me
As is a landscape to a blind man's eye...
("Tintern Abbey Lines")
Which of the following rhetorical terms best suits these lines ?
(1) Apostrophe (2) Litotes
(3) Hyperbole (4) Catachresis

29. The 'monster' in *Frankenstein* is **NOT** responsible for the death of :
(1) Clerval (2) Justine
(3) Elizabeth
(4) Alphonse Frankenstein

30. Which of the following plays of William Shakespeare is **NOT** directly referred to in T.S. Eliot's *The Waste Land* ?
(1) *Hamlet* (2) *King Lear*
(3) *Coriolanus* (4) *The Tempest*

31. Identify the group below which is known as the "Sons of Ben".
(1) Noel Coward, E.G. Craig, William Macready, Matheson, Lang
(2) John Dryden, the Earl of Rochester, Samuel Butler
(3) William Cartwright, Richard Corbett, Thomas Randolph
(4) William Holman Hunt, John E. Millais, D.G. Rossetti, William Morris

32. Christopher Marlowe was one of the first major writers to affirm what can be identified as a clearly homosexual sensibility. Which drama of his deals with it ?
(1) *Edward II*
(3) *Doctor Faustus*
(2) *The Jew of Malta*
(4) *Dido, Queen of Carthage*

33. "When true silence falls we are still left with echo but are nearer nakedness. One way of looking at speech is to say that it is a constant stratagem to cover nakedness". Identify the playwright who underlines the significance of silence thus.
(1) Samuel Beckett
(2) Harold Pinter
(3) Luigi Pirandello
(4) Joe Orton

34. The determining feature of *syllabic verse* is neither ____ nor____ but the number of syllables in a line.
(1) number, numbers
(2) sounds, silences
(3) stress, quantity
(4) gists, piths

35. In Robert Browning's dramatic monologue, which painter does Andrea del Sarto compare himself to ? What does he find lacking in his own work in comparison ?
(1) Fra Lippo Lippi - humour
(2) Raphael - Soul
(3) Leonardo da Vinci - Verisimilitude
(4) Botticelli - liveliness

36. In which of the following does Robert Southey detail the Indian superstitions as an idolatry to be suppressed by a civilizing protestant form of colonialism ?
(1) "Thalaba"
(2) *The Curse of Kehama*
(3) "Pitying the wolves"
(4) *Country Horrors !*

37. The following is the classic ending of a celebrated novella in English :
"I kept on creeping just the same, but I looked at him over my shoulder. 'I've got out at last', said I, "in spite of you and Jane. And I've pulled off most of the papers, so you can't put me back !"
Now why should that man have fainted ? But he did, and right across my path by the wall, so that I had to creep over him every time !"
(1) *Yellow Woman* (Leslie Mormon Silko)
(2) *The Yellow Wallpaper* (Charlotte P.Gilman)
(3) *Johny Panic and the Bible of Dreams* (Sylvia Plalth)
(4) *Where Are You Going, Where Have You Been ?* (Joyce C. Oates)

38. Harriet B. Stowe had wanted to write a work based on the life of an Afro-American writer which was later published as :
(1) *Uncle Tom's Cabin*
(2) *Incidents in the Life of a Slave Girl*
(3) *Cry, The Beloved Country*
(4) *Narrative of the Life of Frederick Douglass*

39. Samuel Johnson's "Dissertation upon Poetry" is part of which of his following works?
(1) the final section of his preface to Shakespeare
(2) a chapter of his novel *Rasselas*
(3) the epilogue of his *Lives of Poets*
(4) one of his *Rambler* essays

40. A new series called "New Accents" was launched by Methuen in 1977. The first title to be published in the series was :
(1) *Deconstruction : Theory and Practice*
(2) *Formalism and Marxism*
(3) *Structuralism and Semiotics*
(4) *Making and Difference : Feminist Literary criticism*

41. "Humble and rustic life was generally chosen, because, in that condition, the essential passions of the heart find a better soil in which they can attain their maturity, are less under restraint, and speak a plainer and more emphatic language... The language, too, of these men has been adopted... because such men hourly communicate with the best objects from which the best part of language is originally derived". Which of the following groups of the author's poems in the *Lyrical Ballads* (1800) contradict this statement in the "Preface to the Lyrical Ballads", as pointed out by S.T. Coleridge ?
(1) "Ode on the Intimations of Immortality", *Prelude.*
(2) *The Tasks, Seasons.*
(3) "Michael", "Ruth", "The Brothers".
(4) "Elegy Written in a country churchyard", "Ode on the Popular Superstitions of the Highlands".

42. A remarkable novelist of the English Modernist phase who wrote a short book on what the novel is (and why it matters) remarked, "Oh dear, yes - the novel tells a story". Identify the novelist:
(1) Virginia Woolf (2) James Joyce
(3) E.M. Forster (4) D.H. Lawrence

43. What is the name of the angel, who, of those who owed allegeance to Satan, dared to protest against his impious doctrine and left his company to return to God (*Paradise Lost*, Book V) ?
(1) Michael (2) Abdiel
(3) Uriel (4) Gabriel

44. Which of the following is NOT a school associated with Romantic period in English literature ?
(1) The Cockney School
(2) The Fireside School
(3) The Lake School
(4) The Satanic School

45. The idea of "new ethnicities" in post-war Britain was advanced by
(1) Donald Hall (2) Stuart Hall
(3) Paul Gilroy (4) Hanif Kureishi

46. Virginia Woolf s *To the Lighthouse* begins in a piece of dialogue :
"Yes, of course, if it's fine tomorrow", said Mrs. Ramsay. "But you'll have to be up with lark", she added.
Present among the listeners of her remark is

47. Match the phrase with character :

(a) "motiveless malignity"	(i) Macbeth
(b) "Reason in Madness"	(ii) Hamlet
(c) "Supp'd full of horrors"	(iii) Lear
(d) "To be, or not to be"	(iv) Iago

Codes :

	(a)	(b)	(c)	(d)
(1)	(i)	(iii)	(ii)	(iv)
(2)	(iv)	(ii)	(iii)	(i)
(3)	(iv)	(iii)	(i)	(ii)
(4)	(iii)	(i)	(ii)	(iv)

48. In *Tristram Shandy* the narrator's presentation of his life and opinions is
(1) linear (2) digressive
(3) chronological (4) rounded

49. The famous sonnet of John Milton beginning "When I consider how my light is spent..." ends with
(1) Before me stares a wolfish eye, Behind me creeps a groan or sigh
(2) They also serve who only stand and wait
(3) And - which is more - you'll be a Man, my son !
(4) And bless him for the sake of him that's gone

50. Her vision was of several caves. She saw herself in one, and she was also outside it, watching its entrance, for Aziz to pass in. She failed to locate him. It was the doubt that had often visited her, but solid and attractive, like the hills. "I am not -" speech was more difficult than vision. "I am not quite sure".

The above extract from *A Passage to India* is about Adela's cave experience. Who is questioning Adela ?

(1) Mrs. Moore
(2) Mr. McBryde
(3) Fielding
(4) Ronney Heaslop

✔ ANSWERS

1. (1)	**2.** (1)	**3.** (4)	**4.** (4)	**5.** (2)	**6.** (1)	**7.** (1)	**8.** (2)	**9.** (3)	**10.** (3)
11. (4)	**12.** (4)	**13.** (2)	**14.** (3)	**15.** (4)	**16.** (1)	**17.** (3)	**18.** (1)	**19.** (2)	**20.** (2)
21. (2)	**22.** (2)	**23.** (1)	**24.** (4)	**25.** (4)	**26.** (2)	**27.** (3)	**28.** (*)	**29.** (4)	**30.** (2)
31. (3)	**32.** (1)	**33.** (2)	**34.** (3)	**35.** (2)	**36.** (2)	**37.** (2)	**38.** (2)	**39.** (2)	**40.** (3)
41. (3)	**42.** (3)	**43.** (2)	**44.** (2)	**45.** (2)	**46.** (3)	**47.** (3)	**48.** (2)	**49.** (2)	**50.** (2)

* No option is correct.

December, 2015

ENGLISH LITERATURE

PAPER-III

Note : This paper contains seventy **five (75)** objective type questions of **two (2)** marks each. All questions are compulsory.

1. Thomas and Henrietta Bowdler's edition of *The Family Shakespeare* gave rise to the word "Bowdlerize". What does it mean ?

(1) the expurgation of indelicate language
(2) the modernization of archaic vocabulary
(3) the insertion of bawdy songs
(4) the expansion of female characters

2. First follow ______ and your judgement frame. By her just ______, which is still the same. Supply the appropriate words to fill in the blanks.

(1) wit, law (2) reason, rule
(3) nature, standard
(4) sense, criterion

3. Preparation of vocabulary list for the purpose of English language teaching was carried out by

(1) Otto Jespersen (2) Noam Chomsky
(3) N.S. Prabhu (4) Michael West

4. Michael Hardt and Antonio Negri prefer to use "Empire" rather than imperialism. According to them :

(1) There is only one empire and we had better recognize it. Hence the Empire with E upper case.
(2) There may be many empires but only one is patently visible and operational. That is denoted by Empire with E upper case.
(3) The present day empire does not have an identifiable location or centre. Hence we ought to differentiate this view of Empire with E upper case.
(4) The culturally dominant global empire is the only one that really matters. We signify that Empire with E upper case.

5. Who among the following critics discerned in the Shelley an Lyric the signs "of adolescence" ?

(1) F.R. Leavis (2) T.S. Eliot
(3) Cleanth Brooks (4) LA. Richards

6. Two among the following critical journals became strongly associated with New Criticism.

(a) *Partisan Review* (b) *Southern Review*
(c) *Kenyon Review* (d) *Hudson Review*

The right combination according to the code is :

(1) (a) and (b) (2) (a) and (d)
(3) (b) and (c) (4) (c) and (d)

7. Match the columns :

(a) Robert Burton (i) *Urn Burial*
(b) Richard Hooker (ii) *The Unfortunate Traveller*
(c) Thomas Browne (iii) *The Anatomy of Melancholy*
(d) Thomas Nashe (iv) *Of the Laws of Ecclesiastical Politie*

Codes :

	(a)	(b)	(c)	(d)
(1)	(iii)	(i)	(ii)	(iv)
(2)	(iv)	(ii)	(i)	(iii)
(3)	(iii)	(iv)	(i)	(ii)
(4)	(i)	(iii)	(iv)	(ii)

8. Which of the following characters in *The White Devil* describes the glory of great men as :

"Glories, like glow worms a far off shine bright / But looked to near have neither heat nor light".

(1) Vittoria (2) Lodovico
(3) Flamineo (4) Cornelia

9. In which of Philip Larkin's poem does he refer to "long uneven lines" of men waiting to be enlisted for the war ?

("Never such innocence again" concludes the poem)

(1) "Mr. Bleaney" (2) "Me MXIV"
(3) "Ambulances" (4) "Sad Steps"

10. In Franz Kafka's *Metamorphosis,* Gregor Samsa one morning found himself changed in his bed to a monstrous kind of vermin. The most difficult thing for Samsa was :

(1) to look at his image in the mirror
(2) to remember what happened the day before
(3) to communicate with anyone
(4) to brush his teeth

11. Identify the individual who is a nihilist from the following :

(1) Pechorin in *A Hero of Our Times*
(2) Bazarov in *Fathers and Sons*
(3) Levin in *Anna Karenina*
(4) Oblomov in *Oblomov*

12. Which of these works in nineteenth-century Russian fiction originated the type of a Superfluous Man ?

(1) *The Diary of a Superfluous Man*
(2) *A Hero of our Own Times*
(3) *Eugene Onegin*
(4) *Dead Souls*

13. What is *Gilgamesh* ?

(a) a Babylonian epic poem
(b) a series of gnomic verses
(c) a classical play
(d) the story of a harsh ruler

(1) (a) and (b) (2) (c)
(3) (a) and (d) (4) (b)

14. *American Dictionary of the English Language* was the work of published in

(1) Merriam Webster, 1903
(2) H.L. Mencken, 1930
(3) Noah Webster, 1828
(4) Benjamin Franklin, 1768

15. Which of the following texts of Amitav Ghosh is based on the refugee occupation of an island in the Sundarvans ?

(1) Sea of Poppies
(2) The Hungry Tide
(3) River of Smoke
(4) The Glass Palace

16. Which of the following is described by Robert Browning as "A Child's Story" ?

(1) "Bells and Pomegranates"
(2) "Pauline"
(3) "Fifine at the Fair"
(4) "The Pied Piper of Hamelin"

17. Identify the New Critic who served as the cultural attache at the American Embassy in London from 1964 to 1966 :

(1) John Crowe Ransom
(2) Cleanth Brooks
(3) Allen Tate
(4) Robert Penn Warren

18. *"The Gilded Age"* refers to a period of American history between 1870 and the first decades of the twentieth century.

Who among the following American writers is credited with the coining of the term ?

(1) F. Scott Fitzgerald
(2) Mark Twain
(3) William Dean Howells
(4) Theodore Dreiser

19. *The Decline and Fall of the Roman Empire* in six volumes was a great achievement by Edward Gibbon. It was published between 1776 and 1788, two significant dates that.

(1) Signalled the end of the Napoleonic wars and the rise of Feudalism.
(2) Signalled the American Revolution and the French Revolution.
(3) Covered the fall of peasantry and the rise of bureaucracy in England.

(4) Suggest the period of Queen Anne's reign.

20. Being so caught up, so mastered by the brute _____ of the air, Did she put on his knowledge with his power, Before the _____ beak could let her drop.
Yeats, "Leda and the Swan".
Choose the right words for the blanks :
(1) beast, shiny (2) force, animal
(3) blood, indifferent (4) thrust, irate

21. Match the following

Terms	**Description**
(a) Ambiguity	(i) A term coined by Julia Kristeva to refer to the fact that texts are constituted by a "tissue of citations".
(b) Aporia	(ii) A term used by Mikhail Bakhtin to describe the variety of languages and voices within a novel.
(c) Intertextuality	(iii) An irresolvable internal contradiction or logical disjunction in a text, usually associated with deconstructive thinking.
(d) Heteroglossia	(iv) A term made famous by William Empson to indicate that a word, phrase, or text can be interpreted in more than one way.

	(a)	(b)	(c)	(d)
(1)	(iv)	(i)	(ii)	(iii)
(2)	(ii)	(iii)	(iv)	(i)
(3)	(iv)	(iii)	(i)	(ii)
(4)	(iii)	(iv)	(i)	(ii)

22. Did I request thee, Maker, from my clay To mould me man ? Did I solicit thee From darkness to promote me ? Which nineteenth-century work bears these lines from *Paradise Lost* as epigraph ?
(1) *Wuthering Heights*
(2) *Frankenstein*
(3) *Don Juan*
(4) *Jude the Obscure*

23. A literary researcher now faced with choosing between a print text and its digital counterpart chooses the latter mostly to :
(1) facilitate the consultation of an exhaustive bibliography
(2) avoid the expense of buying books
(3) look for specific words and phrases and lines
(4) enhance his/her understanding of textual variants, if any, between the two media

24. Which of the following statements on *Hudibras* are true ?
(a) It is a novel written by Matthew Prior.
(b) It is a satirical poem published in 3 parts.
(c) *Hudibras* was written by Samuel Butler.
(d) *Hudibras* discusses complex issues of justice, politics and religion.
(1) (c) and (d) are true
(2) (a) and (d) are true
(3) (b) and (c) are true
(4) (a) and (b) are true

25. The formalist critic _____ mocked the character - based criticism of _____ posing a famous question, "How many children had Lady Macbeth" ?
(1) F.R. Leavis, E.K. Chambers
(2) Cleanth Brooks, F.L. Lucas
(3) Monroe Beardsley, Kenneth Burke
(4) L.C. Knights, A.C. Bradley

26. Which of the following pair of words does not have two different vowel glides ?
(1) care, pure (2) write, freight
(3) caught, court (4) eight, ate

27. Assertion (A): Arts will often work obliquely, by myth or symbol. They may make their best 'criticism of life' simply by being; they may best state by not stating.

Reason (R): It follows, if even only part of all this is true, that the arts do have an important social function. [...] Arts can give greater depth to a society's sense of itself. [...] A country without great art might be a powerful collection of thriving earthworms but would be a sorry society.

(1) Reason (R) is perfectly aligned with **Assertion (A)**
(2) Assertion (A) is unrelated to **Reason (R)**
(3) Assertion (A) hardly reflects **Reason (R)**'s elaboration
(4) Reason (R), in fact, contradicts **Assertion (A)**

28. Which of the following is **NOT** an example of derivational morpheme ?
(1) friend - friendship
(2) courage - courageous
(3) rely - reliable
(4) climate - climactic

29. Which of these statements is **incorrect** about presentism and its basic premises ?
(1) Hugh Grady is its principal proponent.
(2) Our knowledge of works from the past is conditioned by and dependent upon the ideologies of the present.
(3) Presentism does not contextualize cultural production in the same way or make use of the theorists that New Historicism does.
(4) Historicism itself necessarily produces an implicit allegory of the present in its configuration of the past.

30. "Where there is leisure for fiction, there is little grief", was Samuel Johnson's criticism of a famous poem. Which poem was it ?
(1) P.B. Shelley's "Adonais"
(2) Philip Sidney's "Astrophel and Stella"
(3) Thomas Gray's "Elegy Written on a Country Churchyard"
(4) John Miltion's "Lycidas"

31. The story is grounded in the forbidden nature of Aschenbach's Obsession with a young boy; its author ultimately links the obsession with death, disease and esthetic disintegration.
The author of the story is :
(1) Goethe (2) Mann
(3) Borges (4) Proust

32. Which of the following novels of Joseph Conrad is set in Malay ?
(1) *Nigger of the Narcissus*
(2) *Lord Jim*
(3) *Nostromo*
(4) *Heart of Darkness*

33. Nuruddin Farah's *Maps* tells the story of
(1) Abida (2) Abu
(3) Askar (4) Andy

34. One of the most quoted statements on poetry by John Keats is reproduced with blanks below. Complete the statement with correct words.
"If Poetry ______ as naturally as the leaves to a tree, it ______ at all".
(1) does not come; had better not come
(2) comes not; might come not
(3) come not; had better not come
(4) come not; did not come

35. Manohar Malgonkar was a hunter, a lieutenant colonel in the British army, and a tea-planter. He also wrote a memorable novel about the Sepoy Mutiny, especially Peshwa Baji Rao II. What is that novel ?
(1) *A Distant Drum*
(2) *A Combat of Shadows*
(3) *A Bend in the Ganges*
(4) *The Devil's Wind*

36. Who wrote the screenplay for the film version of John Fowles's novel *The French Lieutenant's Woman* ?
(1) Harold Pinter (2) Tom Stoppard
(3) David Mamet (4) Caryl Phillips

37. "How all their plays be neither right tragedies, nor right comedies, mingling kings and elowns, not because the matter so carrieth it, but thrust in the clown by head and shoulders to play a part in majestical matters".

What term does Philip Sidney use to characterize such plays and which of the unities of Aristotle do they violate ?

(1) mongrel tragicomedy; unity of action
(2) mixed tragedies; unity of action
(3) multi-plot drama; unity of time
(4) mingled yarn; unity of place

38. There is a large number of religious poems in Old English Poetry. One of the finest is the *Dream of the Rood.* The words 'the Rood' in the title means :

(1) the Cross (2) the Christian
(3) the Infidel (4) the Cardinal

39. Identify from among the following, the one *incorrect* statement on M. Anantanarayanan's *Silver Pilgrimage* (1961) :

(1) M. Anantanarayanan modelled this narrative on the well-known picaresque novels in English.
(2) *The Silver Pilgrimage* is M. Anantanarayanan's only foray into fiction.
(3) This novel is mainly an account of the adventures of Jayasurya, a Sri Lankan prince of the sixteenth century.
(4) Among the literary texts quoted by the novel are lines from Shakespeare, Donne and Rilke and classical Tamil poets.

40. Listed below are the titles of some influential books by Frank Kermode. Identify which one of the titles that does **NOT** belong to the set.

(1) *The Sense of an Ending*
(2) *Not Entitled - A Memoir*
(3) *The Genesis of Secrecy*
(4) *The Great Code : The Bible and Literature*

41. Identify the one *erroneous* statement on Neoclassicism listed below :

(1) Lodovico Castelvetro and Torquato Tasso greatly influenced English writers like Milton and Dryden.
(2) Neoclassicism took its final form during the reign of Louis XIV (1638-1715).
(3) Boilean's *L'Art poetique* influenced Pope's *Essay on Criticism.*
(4) The English relation to Neoclassicism was one of dialogue. Most literally, this dialogue is effected in Addison's *An Essay on Dramatic Poesy.*

42. In his *Poems of Love and War*, a collection of classic Indian poems in English translation, A.K. Ramanujan sought to revive an ancient _______ poetic tradition. Choose the right word.

(1) Tamil (2) Sanskrit
(3) Kannada (4) Pali

43. Arrange the following sentences in the order in which they appear in Emerson's "Self-Reliance" :

(a) To be great is to be misunderstood.
(b) Pythagoras was misunderstood, and Socrates, and Jesus, and Luther, and Copernicus, and Galileo, and Newton, and every pure and wise spirit that ever took flesh.
(c) If it so bad then to be misunderstood!
(d) It is a right fool's word.
(e) Misunderstood!

(1) (a), (e), (d), (c), (b)
(2) (e), (a), (b), (c), (d)
(3) (c), (d), (a), (b), (e)
(4) (e), (d), (c), (b), (a)

44. X ... Do you know it is nearly seven ?
Y (irritably) Oh! it always is nearly seven.
X well, I'm hungry.
Y I never knew you when you weren't ...
X What shall we do after dinner ? Go to a theatre ?
Y Oh no! I loathe listening.
X Well, let us go to the club ?
Y Oh no! I hate talking.
X Well, we might trot round to the Empire at ten ?
Y Oh no! I can't bear looking at things. It is so silly.

X Well, what shall we do ?

Y Nothing!

X It is awfully hard work doing nothing. However, I don't mind hard work where there is no definite object of any kind. Identify the speakers in this dialogue :

(1) Aston (X) to Mick (Y) *The Caretaker*
(2) Algernon (X) to Jack (Y) *The Importance of Being Earnest*
(3) Lucky (X) to Pozzo (Y) *Waiting for Godot*
(4) Man (X) to the Woman (Y) *The Waste Land*

45. Which of these Greek plays was a source for *The Winter's Tale* ?

(1) *Iphigeneia at Aulis*
(2) *Alcestis*
(3) *Medea*
(4) *Iphigeneia at Tauris*

46. Sweet is the lore which nature brings;
Our meddling intellect
Mis-shapes the beauteous forms of things :
We murder to dissect.

- Word sworth

Which of the following best summarises the speaker's position ?

(1) Nature is incomplete without a human witness to attest to its beauty.
(2) Human endeavours will succeed only if the laws of nature are taken into account.
(3) Nature yields a pleasure superior to that derived from intrusive human inquiry
(4) The flaws inherent in human nature are also evident in the natural world.

47. (a) Jean Baudrillard tells us that postmodern societies are marked by simulacra.

(b) By simulacra he means non-representations of reality.

(c) Simulacra artificially produce a mediated world masquerading as authenticity.

(d) It was not Jean Baudrillard but his interpreters who coined the term "simulacra".

Which of the above statements are true ?

(1) (b), (c) and (d) (2) (a) and (c)
(3) (c) and (d) (4) (b) and (c)

48. Which of the following is correct as the natural order of language acquisition ?

(1) Listening - Reading - Speaking - Writing
(2) Writing - Reading - Listening - Speaking
(3) Listening - Speaking - Reading - Writing
(4) Reading - Listening - Speaking - Writing

49. Which of the following statements is **NOT** TRUE regarding the poems of Derek Walcott?

(1) His poem "Goats and Monkeys" has an epigraph from Shakespeare's *Othello*
(2) In "The Sadhu of Couva" Walcott refers to Diwali, Hanuman and the Ramayana
(3) Walcott has written a poem entitled "Jean Rhys"
(4) In "A Far Cry From Africa" Walcott depicts his divided loyalties in the context of the Changuna Uprising

50. In Shakespeare's time who owned the rights to a theatrical script ?

(1) the playwright(s)
(2) the patron of the acting company
(3) the printer
(4) the acting company

51. Which of the following sentences uses more than three cohesive devices ?

(1) At that time a person could drive for miles without seeing a house.
(2) All of them could recite the poem yesterday.
(3) You can use a pencil, though not a pen, to write your name.
(4) As soon as Mohan entered the stadium the crowd cheered.

52. Match the columns :

Indian Text	English Translator
(a) The love of Kamarupa and Kamalata	(i) William Jones
(b) Ramayana	(ii) Nathaniel Halhed

(c) *Upanishads* (iii) W. Franklin
(d) Abhijnan Sakuntalam (iv) T.H. Griffith

	(a)	(b)	(c)	(d)
(1)	(iv)	(iii)	(ii)	(i)
(2)	(iii)	(iv)	(ii)	(i)
(3)	(ii)	(iv)	(iii)	(i)
(4)	(iv)	(ii)	(iii)	(i)

53. Which of the following is **NOT** TRUE of the New Bolt Report, "The Teaching of English in England" ?
(1) It was commissioned in 1919.
(2) It urged the teaching of the national literature.
(3) It proposed the teaching of English Literature at the university level.
(4) It aimed at uniting divided classes after the war.

54. This revenge tragedy opens with the long soliloquy of the protagonist carrying the skull of his poisoned fiance' and swearing vengeance for the old Duke who has committed the vicious act. Identify the play.
(1) *The Spanish Tragedy*
(2) *The Revenger's Tragedy*
(3) *The Duchess of Malfi*
(4) *The Changeling*

55. What did Anthony Trollope seek to criticize through the character Mr. Slope ?
(1) Methodism
(2) Low Churchmen
(3) High Church doctrine
(4) Anglicanism

56. "To refer to symbols as 'Lacanian symbols', to dub self-doubt as 'Lacanian self-doubt', and to call reflections in a mirror 'Lacanian reflections' is not to read the mind from a perspective informed by Lacan. Nor do parenthetical references to Barthes' hermeneutic code and Foucault's analysis of sexual discourse constitute an interpretation necessarily different from that of traditional humanist criticism".
The author of the passage is objecting to critics who ______.
(1) try to force a parallel between recent critical approaches and traditional humanist criticism.
(2) decoratively apply the names and terminology of recent critical theories without employing the methodology.
(3) attempt to reduce the study of literature to a hunt for coded messages and symbols.
(4) stubbornly maintain a traditional notion of the role of criticism while refusing to acknowledge new theoretical developments.

57. Peter Ackroyd's first novel, *The Great Fire of London*, picks up the historical echoes and artfully deploys a Dickens novel as an intertext. Identify the source Dickens text.
(1) *Great Expectations*
(2) *Little Dorrit*
(3) *Martin Chuzzlewit*
(4) *Old Curiosity Shop*

58. Which of the following plays by Henrik Ibsen deals with the perils that await the emancipated woman in a society which is not ready to accept her ?
(1) *A Doll's House*
(2) *An Enemy of the People*
(3) *Hedda Gabler*
(4) *Pillars of Society*

59. "Yet it is the masculine values that prevail", observed a famous writer "Speaking cruelly", she continued, "football and sport are 'important', the worship of fashion, the buying of clothes 'trivial'."
Name the author and the text.
(1) Mary Wollstonecraft, *A Vindication of the Rights of Woman*
(2) Audre Lorde "Age, Race, Class..."
(3) Virginia Woolf, *A Room of One's Own*
(4) Jean Rhys, *After Leaving Mr. Mackenzie*
(4) dissociates

60. According to coleridge, the "secondary imagination" "dissolves, diffuses, ______, in order to recreate...".
Choose the right word for the blank.

(1) disintegrates (2) dissipates
(3) displaces (4) dissociates

61. Beginning 1996, an Indian publisher commenced the publication of a series of modern Indian novels in English translation. By 2003, it had published eighty novels of repute from almost all Indian languages. Identify the publisher.
(1) Asia Publishing House
(2) Macmillan India
(3) Jaico
(4) Arnold Heinemann

62. William Dunbar's *Lament for the makers* is about :
(1) kings (2) priests
(3) poets (4) peasants

63. Who among the following protagonists of Thomas Hardy feels his lot as akin to Job's ?
(1) Clym Yeo bright
(2) Angel Clare
(3) Jude (4) Troy

64. Edward Brathwaite's poem "Calypso" assumes that you are familiar with
(1) the business of Calypso during the Middle Passage
(2) the West Indian music in syncopated African rhythm
(3) the folk ways and mores of Trinidadian merchants
(4) the operatic performance of Banjos

65. Which of the modern plays by a British playwright actually puts Shakespeare as character on stage ?
(1) Edward Bond's *Bingo*
(2) Harold Pinter's *Mountain Language*
(3) Terence Rattigan's *Inspector calls*
(4) Joe Orton's *Loot*

66. A famous challenge to the Neoclassical tenets of form and reason in aesthetic considerations came from Edmund Burke. His work was titled :
(1) *An Enquiry into the Philosophical Origin of, Our Ideas of the sublime and the Beautiful*
(2) *Philosophical Enquiry into the Origin of Our Ideas of the Sublime and the Beautiful*
(3) *An Enquiry into the Philosophical Origin of Our Ideas of the Beautiful and the Sublime*
(4) *Philosophical Enquiry into Our Original Ideas of the Beautiful and the Sublime*

67. Match the following

	List-A		List-B
(a)	The Grammar - Translation Method	(i)	comprehensible input
(b)	The Direct Method	(ii)	strategic use of mother tongue
(c)	Total Physical Response	(iii)	shuns mother tongue
(d)	The Natural Approach	(iv)	oral input

	(a)	(b)	(c)	(d)
(1)	(ii)	(iii)	(iv)	(i)
(2)	(ii)	(iv)	(i)	(iii)
(3)	(iv)	(ii)	(i)	(iii)
(4)	(iii)	(i)	(ii)	(iv)

68. Which of these works by Indian writers does **NOT** have the Naxalite Movement as a background ?
(1) *Mother of 1084*
(2) *The Lives of Others*
(3) *The Shadow Lines*
(4) *The Lowland*

69. "So when the last and dreadful hour
This crumbling pageant shall devour,
The trumpet shall be heard on high,
The dead shall live, the living die,
And music shall untune the sky"
These are the closing lines of a famous poem. Identify the poem.
(1) *Il penseroso*
(2) "Song for St. Cecilia's Day"
(3) "The Good - Morrow"
(4) "Song : The Year's at the Spring"

70. This eighteenth-century English poem imitates Spenser in stanza form and in allegorical narrative : passers - by are lured by an enchanter with promises of ease, luxury, and aesthetic delight, then consigned to a dungeon where they languish in apathy and impotence until the Knight of Arts and Industry dissolves the spell. Identify the poem.

(1) *The Vanity of Human Wishes*
(2) *The Seasons*
(3) *The Castle of Indolence*
(4) *The Task*

71. Which of the following statements on the Hogarth press is FALSE ?

(1) The Hogarth press was founded in 1917 by Leonard and Virginia Woolf
(2) Its location was their home, called Hogarth House
(3) The press was solely devoted to publishing international classics in translation
(4) The press published translations of Gorky, Chekhov, Tolstoy, Dostoevsky, Rilke, Svevo and others

Read the below passage and answer questions 72 to 75 that follow :

THE ANTIGUA THAT I knew, the Antigua in which I grew up, is not the Antigua you, a tourist, would see now. That Antigua no longer exists. That Antigua no longer exists partly for the usual reason, the passing of time, and partly because the bad-minded people who used to rule over it, the English, no longer do so. (But the English have become such a pitiful lot these days, with hardly any idea what to do with themselves now that they no longer have one quarter of the earth's human population bowing and scraping before them. They don't seem to know that this empire business was all wrong and they should, at least, be wearing sackcloth and ashes in token penance of the wrongs committed, the irrevocableness of their bad deeds, for no natural disaster imaginable could equal the harm they did. Actual death might have been better. And so all this fuss over empire - what went wrong here, what went wrong there - always makes me quite crazy, for I can say to them what went wrong : they should never have left their home, their precious England, a place they loved so much, a place they had to leave but could never forget. And so everywhere they went they turned it into England; and everybody they met they turned English. But no place could ever really be England, and nobody who did not look exactly like them would ever be English, so you can imagine the destruction of people and land that came from that. The English hate each other and they hate England, and the reason they are so miserable now is that they have no place else to go and nobody else to feel better than.)

72. To whom is the passage directly addressed?

(1) readers (2) non-antiguans
(3) tourists (4) the English

73. The English feel extremely miserable because :

(1) Their political supremacy is over
(2) They do not have anyone else to feel superior to
(3) They have been reduced to a state of non-entity
(4) They have no lands to colonise

74. Do the British realize that colonizing countries was a bad practice, according to the narrator ?

(1) Yes; they do
(2) No; they don't
(3) The narrator is rather unsure they do
(4) The narrator is rather unsure they don't

75. Which of the following best describes the content of the extract ?

(1) The speaker fervently desires better understanding between the English and the colonized people in post colonial times
(2) The speaker is interested in nostalgic tours of emigre antiguans to their childhood home
(3) The speaker whose childhood was spent in Antigua reports the great change currently evident in the pungent irony
(4) The speaker is making a case for the penance of the English, the erstwhile rulers of Antigua.

ANSWERS

1. (1)	**2.** (3)	**3.** (4)	**4.** (3)	**5.** (2)	**6.** (3)	**7.** (3)	**8.** (3)	**9.** (2)	**10.** (3)
11. (2)	**12.** (3)	**13.** (3)	**14.** (3)	**15.** (2)	**16.** (4)	**17.** (2)	**18.** (2)	**19.** (2)	**20.** (3)
21. (3)	**22.** (2)	**23.** (3)	**24.** (3)	**25.** (4)	**26.** (4)	**27.** (1)	**28.** (4)	**29.** (3)	**30.** (4)
31. (2)	**32.** (2)	**33.** (3)	**34.** (3)	**35.** (4)	**36.** (1)	**37.** (1)	**38.** (1)	**39.** (1)	**40.** (4)
41. (4)	**42.** (1)	**43.** (4)	**44.** (2)	**45.** (2)	**46.** (3)	**47.** (2)	**48.** (3)	**49.** (4)	**50.** (4)
51. (3)	**52.** (2)	**53.** (3)	**54.** (2)	**55.** (2)	**56.** (2)	**57.** (2)	**58.** (3)	**59.** (3)	**60.** (2)
61. (2)	**62.** (3)	**63.** (3)	**64.** (2)	**65.** (1)	**66.** (2)	**67.** (1)	**68.** (3)	**69.** (2)	**70.** (3)
71. (3)	**72.** (3)	**73.** (2)	**74.** (3)	**75.** (3)					

July, 2016

ENGLISH LITERATURE

PAPER-II

Note : This paper contains **fifty (50)** objective type questions, each question carrying **two (2)** marks. Attempt **all** the questions.

1. Which British University figures in William Wordsworth's Prelude ?
(1) Durham (2) Glasgow
(3) Cambridge (4) Oxford

2. Who is the author of A Woman Killed with Kindness ?
(1) John Marston
(2) Thomas Middleton
(3) John Fletcher
(4) Thomas Heywood

3. In William Congreve's The Way of the World identify the speaker of the line : "One's cruelty is one's power, and when one parts with one's cruelty, one parts with one's power."
(1) Mirabell (2) Witwoud
(3) Millamant (4) Mincing

4. T.S. Eliot found spiritual support in
(1) Christianity (2) Hinduism
(3) Buddhism (4) Judaism

5. By what name is Gulliver known in Brobdingnag ?
(1) Grildrig (2) Glumdalclitch
(3) Splacknuck (4) Mannikin

6. Who among the following was born in India ?
(1) Paul Scott (2) Lawrence Durrell
(3) E.M. Forster (4) V.S. Naipaul

7. What metaphor does Edmund Spenser employ (Faerie Queene Book 1 Canto 12) to frame his tale and to describe the relationship between the tale and its readers ?
(1) That of a caravan of lost souls, traversing a desert.
(2) That of a stagecoach, which picks up diverse passengers along the way.
(3) That of a ship filled with jolly mariners.
(4) That of a riderless horse, following his own direction.

8. Who among the following is not associated with Russian formalism ?
(1) Roman Jakobson
(2) Georges Poulet
(3) Boris Eichenbaum
(4) Victor Shklovsky

9. Which character in Dickens keeps on hoping that "something will turn up" ?
(1) Barkis (2) Micawber
(3) Uriah Heep (4) Miss Havisham

10. What is the name of the boat that rescues Ishmael in Herman Melville's Moby Dick ?
(1) Pequod (2) Rachel
(3) Hagar (4) Sphinx

11. Northanger Abbey is a parody of the _______ romance.
(1) Oriental (2) French
(3) Gothic (4) Popular

12. Who among the following authors were greatly influenced by Thomas Carlyle's writings ?
I. Charles Dickens
II. Elizabeth Gaskell
III. Emily Bronte IV. Oscar Wilde
The right combination according to the code is
(1) I and II (2) II and III
(3) I and IV (4) I and III

13. Which of the following is another term to describe "art for art's sake"?
(1) Aestheticism (2) Didacticism
(3) Realism (4) Neo-realism

14. The statement that there are "none so credulous as infidels" is an illustration of
(1) Oxymoron (2) Antithesis
(3) Paradox (4) Metonomy

15. Who narrates Heart of Darkness?
(1) Marlow
(2) Director of Companies
(3) Kurtz
(4) An unnamed narrator

16. The Mistakes of a Night is the subtitle of
(1) The Conscious Lovers
(2) The Good Natur'd Man
(3) She Stoops to Conquer
(4) The Rivals

17. Identify the first novel written by Patrick White:
(1) The Living and the Dead
(2) The Tree of Man
(3) Happy Valley
(4) The Aunt's Story

18. In King Lear for what reason does Kent assume a disguise?
(1) To continue to serve Lear, though Lear has banished him.
(2) To spy on Edmund.
(3) To antagonize Goneril and Regan.
(4) To revenge upon Lear for banishing him.

19. What is a feminine rhyme?
(1) A rhyme on two syllables in which the last syllable is unstressed.
(2) A rhyme on two syllables.
(3) A rhyme on three syllables.
(4) A poem in which every third syllable rhymes.

20. Identify two of the following written by Christopher Fry:
I. French Without Tears
II. The Lady's Not for Burning
III. Venus Observed
IV. The Deep Blue Sea

The right combination according to the code is
(1) II and III (2) I and III
(3) II and IV (4) I and IV

21. In "Tradition and Individual Talent", according to T.S. Eliot, the term "Traditional" usually means
(1) something positive
(2) something negative
(3) something historical
(4) something old

22. Who of the following is a Cavalier poet?
(1) George Herbert (2) John Donne
(3) Robert Herrick (4) Andrew Marvell

23. Which of the following is not Jacques Derrida's work?
(1) Of Spirit : Heidegger and the Question
(2) The Transcendence of the Ego
(3) Of Grammatology
(4) The Work of Mourning

24. In Paradise Lost which character narrates the story of the making of Eve from a rib in Adam's side?
(1) Adam (2) Eve
(3) Raphael (4) God

25. A.S. Byatt's Possession attempts the imitation of the work of two Victorian poets, loosely based on
I. Alfred Tennyson
II. Robert Browning
III. Christina Rossetti
IV. William Morris

The right combination according to the code is
(1) I and II (2) II and IV
(3) II and III (4) III and IV

26. The Dark Lady of the Sonnets is a short comedy by
(1) Bernard Shaw (2) W.B. Yeats
(3) J.M. Synge (4) John Osborne

27. John Milton's description of gold as a "precious bane" (Paradise Lost, Book II) is best described as
(1) a dactyl (2) an oxymoron
(3) enjambment (4) zeugma

28. There is a play on the name of Machiavelli in the prologue to Christopher Marlowe's
(1) Doctor Faustus
(2) The Jew of Malta
(3) Tamburlaine, the Great
(4) Edward II

29. Shakespeare famously neglects to observe Aristotle's rules concerning the three dramatic unities, and Samuel Johnson undertakes to defend Shakespeare from these criticisms in his Preface to Shakespeare. Which of the Aristotelian dramatic unities does Johnson believe Shakespeare to observe most successfully ?
(1) Time (2) Place
(3) Action
(4) Johnson does not feel that the Aristotelian dramatic unities are important

30. Who among the following was praised and patronized as a "Ploughman Poet" ?
(1) John Clare (2) George Crabbe
(3) Robert Burns (4) Walter Scott

31. Which novel of Doris Lessing ends with a projection forward in time after a devastating atomic war ?
(1) The Grass is Singing
(2) The Golden Notebook
(3) The Four-Gated City
(4) A Proper Marriage

32. Name the dominant meter of the following quatrain :
The curfew tolls the knell of parting day,
The lowing herd winds slowly o'er the lea,
The plowman homeward plods his weary way,
And leaves the world to darkness and to me.
(1) Iambic Hexameter
(2) Trochaic Pentameter
(3) Iambic Pentameter
(4) Terza Rima

33. Which two novels of Buchi Emecheta provide a fictionalized portrait of poor, young Nigerian women struggling to bring up their children in London ?
I. The Slave Girl
II. The Joys of Motherhood
III. Second Class Citizen
IV. In the Ditch
The right combination according to the code is
(1) I and II (2) II and III
(3) III and IV (4) I and IV

34. In John Bunyan's Pilgrim's Progress who keeps Christian's head above water in the River of Death ?
(1) Hopeful (2) Helpful
(3) Faithful (4) Cheerful

35. Childe Harold's Pilgrimage is a
(1) religious allegory (2) fairy tale
(3) long poem (4) Utopian novel

36. In Thomas More's Utopia which of the following leisure pastimes is not a favourite among Utopians ?
(1) Music (2) Public lectures
(3) Conversation (4) Dicing and cards

37. Which of the following statements does not describe Michel Foucault's position ?
(1) In Foucault's work sexuality is literally written on the body.
(2) Power operates through discourse.
(3) There is connection between power and knowledge.
(4) Where there is power, it is possible to find resistance.

38. In which year did the Great Exhibition take place ?
(1) 1851 (2) 1857
(3) 1861 (4) 1871

39. When Fidessa says, "O but I fear the fickle freakes ..../ Of fortune false, and oddes of armes in field" (Faerie Queene, Book I, Canto 5), this is a fine example of
(1) Alliteration (2) Allegory
(3) Assonance (4) Antithesis

40. Match the work with author :
I. "The Excursion" A. S.T. Coleridge
II. "Christabel" B. P.B. Shelley
III. Milton C. William Wordsworth
IV. Queen Mab D. William Blake

	I	II	III	IV
(1)	C	A	B	D
(2)	C	A	D	B
(3)	B	C	A	D
(4)	B	A	C	D

41. Which of the following phrases is not found in Thomas Gray's "Elegy written in a Country Churchyard" ?
(1) "Far from the madding crowd"
(2) "A youth to Fortune and Fame unknown"
(3) "Full many a flower is born to blush unseen"
(4) "All nature is but art, unknown to thee"

42. Robert Browning's "Rabbi Ben Ezra" is a defence of
(1) youth against old age
(2) old age against youth
(3) power against knowledge
(4) knowledge against power

43. In Geoffrey Chaucer's Canterbury Tales, the pilgrims, like the medieval society of which they are a part, are made up of three social groups or 'estates'. What are the three estates ?
(1) Nobility, church and commoners
(2) Royalty, nobility and peasantry
(3) Royalists, republicans and peasants
(4) Country, city and commons

44. Which novel of Toni Morrison tells the wrenching story of a protagonist who murders her child rather than to allow him/her to live as a slave ?
(1) Sula (2) Tar Baby
(3) Song of Solomon
(4) Beloved

45. Who among the following translated Homer ?
(1) Thomas Gray (2) Samuel Johnson
(3) Oliver Goldsmith
(4) Alexander Pope

46. Shyam Selvadurai's Funny Boy is a
(1) Picaresque novel
(2) Epistolary novel
(3) Diary novel
(4) Coming-of-age novel

47. When was the English ban on James Joyce's Ulysses lifted ?
(1) 1924 (2) 1945
(3) 1936 (4) 1962

48. Who among the following is not an imagist ?
(1) Ezra Pound (2) W.B. Yeats
(3) Amy Lowell (4) T.E. Hulme

49. Thomas Carew's Poems appeared in print in 1640 and contain a variety of amorous addresses to and reflections on, a fictional mistress known as
(1) Celia (2) Julia
(3) Anne (4) Melanie

50. Match the novelists with their work :
I. William Golding A. Grimus
II. Salman Rushdie B. Hawksmoor
III. Graham Swift C. Darkness Visible
IV. Peter Ackroyd D. Waterland

	I	II	III	IV
(1)	D	A	C	B
(2)	C	A	D	B
(3)	B	C	A	D
(4)	B	A	C	D

ANSWERS

1. (3)	**2.** (4)	**3.** (3)	**4.** (1)	**5.** (1)	**6.** (2)	**7.** (3)	**8.** (2)	**9.** (2)	**10.** (2)
11. (3)	**12.** (1)	**13.** (1)	**14.** (3)	**15.** (4)	**16.** (3)	**17.** (3)	**18.** (1)	**19.** (1)	**20.** (1)
21. (2)	**22.** (3)	**23.** (2)	**24.** (1)	**25.** (3)	**26.** (1)	**27.** (2)	**28.** (2)	**29.** (3)	**30.** (3)
31. (3)	**32.** (3)	**33.** (3)	**34.** (1)	**35.** (3)	**36.** (4)	**37.** (1)	**38.** (1)	**39.** (1)	**40.** (2)
41. (4)	**42.** (2)	**43.** (1)	**44.** (4)	**45.** (4)	**46.** (4)	**47.** (3)	**48.** (2)	**49.** (1)	**50.** (2)

July, 2016

ENGLISH LITERATURE

PAPER-III

Note : This paper contains seventy **five (75)** objective type questions of **two (2)** marks each. All questions are compulsory.

1. Which of W.M. Thackeray's novel's closing sentence is this ?
"Which of us is happy in this world ? Which of us has his desire ? Or, having it, is satisfied ?"
(1) The History of Henry Esmond
(2) Vanity Fair
(3) The Luck of Barry Lyndon
(4) Pendennis

2. Why does Lovewit in Ben Jonson's play The Alchemist leave his house, setting the stage for his servant Face, alongwith Subtle, a fake alchemist to fleece people ?
(1) To visit his father who left him long ago.
(2) To find out new sources of minting money.
(3) Because of an epidemic of plague.
(4) To make a pilgrimage.

3. By the end of the nineteen fifties novelists like Stan Barstow, Sid Chaplin, Alan Sillitoe and David Storey were routinely lumped together as representatives of "Kitchen-sink realism". Who in 1954 wrote the article "The Kitchen Sink", calling attention to the gritty and direct realism ?
(1) Martin Harrison (2) Stan Smith
(3) David Sylvester (4) Philip Callow

4. Which of the following is not an allegorical character in the play Everyman ?
(1) Kindred (2) Strength
(3) Christian (4) Discretion

5. Who among the following translators is notable as the first translator of Bhagavad Gita into English ?
(1) Charles Wilkins
(2) Nathaniel Halhead
(3) William Jones
(4) Barbara Stoler Miller

6. In Biographia Literaria S.T. Coleridge defines the imagination as the faculty by which
(1) the soul perceives the phenomenal diversity of the universe.
(2) the soul perceives the spiritual unity of the universe.
(3) the mind acquires images by its associative power.
(4) the mind separates images by its discriminatory power.

7. Why do the Houyhnhnms have so few words in their language ?
(1) Their wants and passions are fewer than human wants and passions, and they need fewer words.
(2) They consider language to be morally corrupt and prefer to remain silent.
(3) They find speech difficult because they are horses.
(4) They prefer action to words.

8. Identify the title of A.D. Hope's first published book of poems.
(1) Native Companions
(2) The Wandering Islands
(3) A Midsummer Eve's Dream
(4) The Cave and the Spring

9. Which of the following is an incorrect assumption in language teaching ?
(1) Learners acquire language by trying to use it in real situations.
(2) Learners' first language plays an important role in learning.
(3) Language teaching should have a focus on communicative activities.
(4) Language teaching should give importance to writing rather than speech.

10. The Bhasmasura myth is used in R.K. Narayan's ________.
(1) The Man-Eater of Malgudi
(2) The Financial Expert
(3) The English Teacher
(4) The World of Nagaraj

11. During the Middle English period, many words were borrowed from two languages :
I. Celtic II. Latin
III. French IV. Old Norse
The right combination according to the code is
(1) I and II (2) II and III
(3) II and IV (4) III and IV

12. Select the right chronological sequence of the date of Bible translations.
(1) King James Version – Tyndale –Revised Standard Version – Holman Christian Standard Bible
(2) Revised Standard Version – King James Version – Tyndale – Holman Christian Standard Bible
(3) Tyndale – King James Version – Revised Standard Version – Holman Christian Standard Version
(4) Revised Standard Version – Holman Christian Standard Bible – King James Version – Tyndale

13. The last word in James Joyce's Finnegans Wake is
(1) No (2) The
(3) Morning ! (4) Jaysus

14. **Assertion (A) :** In so far as we are taught how to read, what we engage are not texts but paradigms.
Reason (R) : We appropriate meaning from a text according to what we need or desire, or, in other words, according to the critical assumptions or predispositions that we bring to it.
(1) Both (A) and (R) are true and (R) is the correct explanation of (A).
(2) Both (A) and (R) are true but (R) is not the correct explanation of (A).
(3) (A) is true, but (R) is false.
(4) (A) is false, but (R) is true.

15. One of the key terms in Michel Foucault's work is discourse. This is best described as
(1) the power of persuasion in all articulations.
(2) the selective language powerful people use.
(3) conceptual frameworks which enable some mode of thought and deny or severely constrain certain others.
(4) the ability to suggest transcendental levels of meaning in an utterance.

16. The narrators of Oroonoko are
I. a woman II. Oroonoko
III. a purported eyewitness of the events described
IV. Trefy
The right combination according to the code is
(1) I and IV (2) I and III
(3) II and III (4) II and IV

17. Which character of Henrik Ibsen speaks the following lines : "The life of a normally constituted idea is generally about seventeen or eighteen years, at the most twenty ?"
(1) Nora in A Doll's House
(2) Dr. Thomas Stockman in An Enemy of the People
(3) John Rosmer in Rosmerscholm
(4) Oswald in Ghosts

18. In literary studies structuralism promotes
(1) new interpretations of literary works.
(2) the view that literature is one signifying practice among others.
(3) a systematic account of literary archetypes.
(4) unstable structures of systems of signification.

19. P.B. Shelley's Julian and Maddalo is a conversation between Julian and Count Maddalo.
Who do these two characters represent ?
(1) Julian represents Keats and Count Maddalo, Byron
(2) Julian represents Shelley and Count Maddalo, Byron
(3) Julian represents Shelley and Count Maddalo, William Godwin
(4) Julian represents Mary Shelley and Count Maddalo, William Godwin

20. What is practical criticism ?
(1) The close analysis of literary texts in such a way as to bring out their political meaning.
(2) A movement which wished to make literary criticism more relevant.
(3) The close analysis of poems without taking account of any external information.
(4) The study of ambiguity.

21. Which of the following does not describe some of the practices/beliefs of feminist literary criticism ?
(1) Feminist criticism recuperates female writers ignored by the canon.
(2) Feminist literary critics offer a criticism of the construction of gender.
(3) Feminist literary critics argue that the traditional canon is justified.
(4) Feminist literary critics mostly reject the essentialising of 'male' and 'female'.

22. Which work by Franz Kafka is also known as The Man Who Disappeared ?
(1) The Castle (2) "Metamorphosis"
(3) "In the Penal Colony"
(4) Amerika

23. Towards the end of Evelyn Waugh's A Handful of Dust the protagonist Tony Last is trapped in the jungle by the calculating crazy Mr. Todd who forces him to read and reread the novels of a particular author. Waugh has also written a short story dealing with Tony's singular experience in the jungle. Who is the novelist referred to and what is the title of the short story ?
(1) Rudyard Kipling, "Revisiting the Jungle"
(2) Joseph Conrad, "Shadows of the Dark Trees"
(3) Charles Dickens, "The Man Who Liked Dickens"
(4) Henry Fielding, "Tom Jones's Journey into the Wild"

24. At the beginning of the Restoration period, there was a seismic shift in the social, political and religious attitudes of the English. Which of the following statements best describes that shift ?
(1) England shifted from an aristocratic Catholic monarchy to a parliamentary democracy.
(2) England shifted from an atheistic oligarchy to a deistic squirearchy.
(3) England shifted from a Republican Puritan Commonwealth to an aristocratic Anglican monarchy.
(4) England shifted from a parliamentary democracy to an aristocratic Catholic tyranny.

25. The Grammar-Translation Method in English Language Teaching stresses on
(1) Fluency (2) Accuracy
(3) Appropriateness (4) Listening Skill

26. "[They] then heaved out,/ away with a will in their wood-wreathed ship." This line describing Beowulf's departure from Geatland, is typical of the poem's form and Old English poetic technique because
I. it features alliteration
II. it rhymes
III. it features onomotopoeia
IV. it has four strong stresses
The right combination according to the code is
(1) I and II (2) II and III
(3) I and IV (4) II and IV

27. Identify the poet, translator, publisher and essayist who founded a press in the 1950s called Writers' Workshop and provided a publishing outlet for Indians writing in English.
(1) P. Lal (2) A.K. Mehrotra
(3) Vinay Dharwadkar
(4) A.K. Ramanujan

28. Antagonised by what he considered to be the provinciality of the Lake Poets, Byron wrote the preface to which of his works as a rebuke to Wordsworth's own introduction to "The Thorn" ?
(1) The Prisoner of Chillon
(2) Don Juan
(3) Childe Harold's Pilgrimage
(4) The Vision of Judgement

29. Which of the following theoretical movements claimed that "the device is the only hero of literature" ?

(1) Russian formalism (2) New Criticism
(3) Phenomenology (4) Deconstruction

30. In Jean Francois Lyotard's works the term "language games", sometimes also called "phrase regimens" denotes :
   I. the multiplicity of communities of meaning.
   II. the breakdown of communities of meaning.
   III. the innumerable and incommensurable separate systems in which meanings are produced.
   IV. the singular system in which meanings are dispersed and displaced.
   The right combination according to the code is
   (1) I and IV (2) I and III
   (3) II and IV (4) II and III

31. What part of Canada is Alice Munro most famous for depicting ?
   (1) Vancouver (2) Montreal
   (3) Ontario (4) Quebec

32. In John Gay's Beggar's Opera what is Peachum's occupation ?
   I. Pimp II. Lawyer
   III. Fencer of stolen goods, and master of a gang of thieves
   IV. Impeader of less powerful criminals
   The right combination according to the code is
   (1) III & IV (2) II & III
   (3) I & IV (4) II & IV

33. In the opening stanza of "Song of Myself", Whitman begins his spiritual awakening at the age of ______.
   (1) 37 (2) 15
   (3) 24 (4) 61

34. In which of the following poems does Tennyson describe and condemn the spirit of aestheticism whose sole religion is the worship of beauty and of knowledge for their own sake and which ignores human responsibility and obligations of one's fellowmen ?
   (1) "The Princess"
   (2) "The Lady of Shalott"
   (3) "The Palace of Art"
   (4) "Tithonus"

35. Luigi Pirandello's Six Characters in Search of an Author deliberately blurs the boarder lines between the world of the theatre and the world of 'real life' by carefully chiselled dialogues like :
   "Don't you feel the ground beneath your feet as you reflect that this 'you' which you feel today, all this present reality of yours, is destined to seem a mere illusion to you tomorrow ?"
   Who is the speaker ? Who is it addressed to ?
   (1) Stepdaughter to Father
   (2) Father to Stage Manager
   (3) Stage Manager to Director
   (4) Mother to Director

36. In a poem in memory of Major Robert Gregory, Lady Gregory's son, W.B. Yeats mentions an Irish writer who had found his inspiration "In a most desolate stony place" that he came "Towards nightfall upon a race / passionate and simple like his heart." Who is the writer ?
   (1) J.M. Barrie (2) J.M. Synge
   (3) Isaac Bickerstaffe (4) Thomas More

37. Jacques Derrida's work received some criticism from analytical philosophers. Who below was a critic of Derrida ?
   (1) John Searle
   (2) Jean-Francois Lyotard
   (3) Emmanuel Levinas
   (4) Paul de Man

38. Who among the following bought and renovated the house of the Anglican poet, George Herbert, near Salisbury, England, in 1996 ?
   (1) Daljit Nagra (2) Vikram Seth
   (3) Amitava Kumar (4) Arundhati Roy

39. Which pair of novels by Anita Desai take as their subject the suppression and oppression of Indian women ?
   I. Where Shall We Go This Summer ?
   II. The Zigzag Way
   III. Cry, the Peacock
   IV. Baumgartner's Bombay
   The right combination according to the code is
   (1) I and II (2) I and III
   (3) II and III (4) III and IV

40. From among the following identify the two Indian English authors who received appreciation and encouragement from their British counterparts :

I. R.K. Narayan, Graham Greene
II. Nirad C. Chaudhuri, Evelyn Waugh
III. Mulk Raj Anand, E.M. Forster
IV. Raja Rao, Iris Murdoch

The right combination according to the code is

(1) I and II (2) II and IV
(3) I and III (4) III and IV

41. Match the character with the work :

I. Count Fosco — A. Villette
II. Margaret — B. Adam Bede
III. Lucy Snowe — C. The Woman in White
IV. Maggie Tulliver — D. North or South

Codes :

	I	II	III	IV
(1)	C	D	A	B
(2)	D	C	A	B
(3)	C	A	D	B
(4)	C	A	B	D

42. This poet was accidently killed in Burma by a pistol shot in 1944. His posthumously published collection of poems Ha ! Ha ! Among the Trumpets is divided into three sections.

The first section describes a tense, waiting England and the second the voyage to the East.

In the third section he uncomfortably comes to terms with the alien contours, the harsh light and the dry wastes of India as evident in poems like "The Maratta Ghats", "Indian Day" and "Observation Post : Forward Area". Who is the poet ?

(1) Keith Douglas (2) Sidney Keyes
(3) David Gascoyne (4) Alun Lewis

43. As Adam and Eve leave Paradise, "hand in hand with wand'ring steps and slow" (Book XII, Paradise Lost) what is their consolation ?

(1) They are comforted by their love for one another.
(2) They are comforted by their foreknowledge of the coming of Christ as Redeemer of mankind.
(3) They are comforted by God, who travels before them in the form of a pillar of fire.
(4) They are comforted by the angel, who holds each of them by the hand.

44. In An Essay of Dramatic Poesy to whom does Dryden refer with the phrase "he needed not the spectacles of books to read Nature" ?

(1) Ben Jonson (2) Ovid
(3) William Shakespeare
(4) Geoffrey Chaucer

45. Emily Dickinson's use of "open form" or "free verse" is comparable to her contemporary American poet,

(1) Anne Bradstreet (2) Robert Lowell
(3) Walt Whitman (4) Sylvia Plath

46. In "A Letter of the Authors" Edmund Spenser writes that two characters in Faerie Queene represent Queen Elizabeth. Who are they ?

I. Britomart II. Cynthia
III. Belphoebe IV. The Faerie Queene

The right combination according to the code is

(1) III and IV (2) I and IV
(3) I and III (4) II and III

47. Who among the following African novelists was a student of philosophy and literature in India ?

(1) Nuruddin Farah (2) Ben Okri
(3) Helon Habila (4) Benjamin Kwakye

48. In particular William Blake was influenced by the religious writings of

I. Martin Luther II. Jacob Boehme
III. Emanuel Swedenborg
IV. Confucious

The right combination according to the code is

(1) I and IV (2) I and II
(3) II and III (4) III and IV

49. Which British King, having defeated the Viking invaders, consciously used the English language to create a sense of national identity and retain political control over independent countries ?

(1) Alfred the Great (2) Edward the Elder
(3) King Arthur (4) Ethelbert of Kent

50. In "Politics and the English Language" George Orwell provides a list of rules to aid in curing the English language. What is the final rule ?
(1) Never use a metaphor, simile or other figure of speech which you are used to seeing in print.
(2) Never use a long word where a short one will do.
(3) If it is possible to cut a word out, always cut it out.
(4) Break any of these rules sooner than say anything outright barbarous.

51. In his Defence of Poesy what is the "best and most accomplished kind of poetry" in Sidney's estimation ?
(1) Heroical, or epic poetry
(2) Lyric poetry
(3) Pastoral poetry (4) Elegiac poetry

52. Which writer of the Romantic period makes the following comment : "The poet is far from dealing only with these subtle and analogical truths. Truth of every kind belongs to him, provided it can bud into any kind of beauty, or is capable of being illustrated and impressed by poetic faculty" ?
(1) Wordsworth in Preface to the Lyrical Ballads
(2) William Hazlitt in "On the Feeling of Immortality in Youth"
(3) Leigh Hunt in What is Poetry ?
(4) Keats in one of his letters to his brother

53. In his poem "Whispers of Immortality" T.S. Eliot says that a dramatist "was much possessed by death/And saw the skull beneath the skin" and a poet "knew the anguish of the marrow/The ague of the skeleton." Who are the dramatist and the poet referred to by Eliot ?
(1) Christopher Marlowe and Andrew Marvell
(2) John Webster and John Donne
(3) Seneca and Homer
(4) Thomas Kyd and Henry Vaughan

54. Functional Communicative Approach in English Language Teaching is in opposition to
(1) Structural Approach
(2) Comprehensive Approach
(3) Translation and Grammar Method
(4) Functional Approach

55. According to Julia Kristeva, it is the eruption of the ______ within the ______ that provides the creative and innovative impulse of modern poetic language.
(1) individual, tradition
(2) specific, generic
(3) semiotic, symbolic
(4) particular, general

56. In Crime and Punishment which character speaks the following words. Who/what are they addressed to ?
"I waited for you impatiently. all this blasted psychology is a double-edged weapon."
(1) Svidrigailov to the pistol with which he shoots himself
(2) Katherine Ivanovna to Marmeladov
(3) Porfiry Petrovich to Raskolnikov
(4) Raskolnikov to the Bible he finds in the prison cell in Siberia

57. What three Germanic tribes invaded Britons in the fifth century AD, bringing with them the roots of modern English ?
(1) The Danes, Saxons and Celts
(2) The Celts, Jutes and Saxons
(3) The Saxons, Danes and Angles
(4) The Jutes, Angles and Saxons

58. Which of the following is not a part of the series of poems called Jejuri, written by Arun Kolatkar ?
(1) "Yeshwant Rao" (2) "Chaitanya"
(3) "The Priest" (4) "An Old Man"

59. Bertolt Brecht's concept of alienation was a rejection of the idea that realism was the only mode of art a critique of capitalist society should produce. Alienation is best described as
(1) making the audience feel that they do not belong.
(2) distancing artistic conventions to prevent an emotional catharsis.
(3) scripting unnatural behaviour on stage.
(4) a rejection of capitalism or the market.

60. Ngugi wa Thiongo changed the medium of his writing from English to ______.
(1) Swahili (2) Yoruba
(3) Xhosa (4) Gikuyu

61. Which of the following ancient critics does Alexander Pope commend as exemplary in

Essay on Criticism ?
(1) Aristotle, Quintilian, Dryden, Dionysius, Horace
(2) Aristotle, Longinus, Quintilian, Durfey, Dryden
(3) Aristotle, Horace, Dionysius, Quintilian, Longinus
(4) Aristotle, Horace, Durfey, Quintilian, Longinus

62. Which of the following poems by Philip Larkin is best described as a self-elegy, anticipating the poet's death ?
(1) "The Old Fools" (2) "Aubade"
(3) "Ambulances" (4) "Faith Healing"

63. In John Bunyan's Pilgrims Progress what is the first obstacle encountered by Christian on his progress ?
(1) The Slough of Despond
(2) Vanity Fair
(3) The River of Death
(4) The Swamp of Despair

64. Identify the correct chronological sequence of publication of the four parts of The Four Quartets.
(1) Burnt Norton – The Dry Salvages – East Coker – Little Gidding
(2) Burnt Norton – Little Gidding – The Dry Salvages – East Coker
(3) Burnt Norton – East Coker – The Dry Salvages – Little Gidding
(4) Little Gidding – Burnt Norton – The Dry Salvages – East Coker

65. Which of the following is not true of the novels of Charles Dickens ?
(1) They deal with the problems of the discontents of an urban civilization.
(2) The plots are strikingly tight-knit.
(3) They share a sense of fun and determining optimism.
(4) They incorporate elements of popular contemporary culture.

66. Published in 1604, the first monolingual English Dictionary was
(1) Nathaniel Bailey's Universal Etymological Dictionary of the English Language
(2) Samuel Johnson's Dictionary of the English Language
(3) Robert Cawdrey's Table Alphabetical
(4) Thomas Blount's Glossographia

67. Which of the following statements best describe the narrative perspective employed in Thomas More's Utopia ?
I. First-person narration by Raphael Hythloday
II. Third-person narration by a narrator named Thomas More
III. First-person narration by a narrator named Thomas More
IV. Third-person narration by Raphael Hythloday

The right combination according to the code is
(1) I and III (2) II and IV
(3) II and III (4) I and II

68. In the opening pages of one of Thomas Mann's novels we can see space itself becoming a form of time : "Space, like time, engenders forgetfulness but it does so by setting us bodily free from our surroundings and giving us back our primitive unattached state." Which is the novel ?
(1) Doctor Faustus
(2) Death in Venice
(3) The Confessions of Felix Krull
(4) The Magic Mountain

69. Match the lines with the titles of the poems :

I. The boa-constrictor's coil/ Is a fossil	A. "Thrushes"
II. My manners are tearing off heads / The allotment of death	B. "The Jaguar"
III. More coiled steel than living	C. "Relic"
IV. Time in the sea eats its tail	D. "Hawk Roosting"

Code:

	I	II	III	IV		I	II	III	IV
(1)	A	D	A	C	(2)	B	D	A	C
(3)	C	D	B	A	(4)	D	B	C	A

70. Which one of Joseph Conrad's novels expresses the contrast between the solidarity of shipboard life and the profound underlying loneliness of existence thus : "loneliness impenetrable and transparent, elusive and everlasting.... that surrounds, envelops, clothes every human soul from the cradle to the grave, and perhaps beyond" ?
(1) The Heart of Darkness

(2) The Nigger of the Narcissus
(3) Lord Jim (4) Nostromo

71. John Dryden's two philosophico-religious poems are
I. Absalom and Achitophel
II. A Layman's Faith
III. Annus Mirabilis
IV. The Hind and the Panther
The right combination according to the code is
(1) I and II (2) III and I
(3) II and III (4) II and IV

Read the following poem and answer the questions, 72 to 75 :

Stray Cats
They are not exactly homeless.
They are dissidents who have lost their faith
in furnished interiors, morning walks,
the cake and the cutlery.
When you have nine lives to live
you learn to take things in your stride.
You learn to stretch your body
at full length and yawn at domestic
fictions. And for this reason
you figure in horror films
in the mandatory moment
between the flash of lightning
and the appearance of the ghost.
The light is darkish blue and you see
yourself in the iris of the burning
eye. The horror is in the seeing.
What you see is altered by the act
of seeing. The mystery does not stop
there. The seer is in turn altered
by what he sees. Having known this,
stray cats jump from roof to roof.
They monitor the world from treetops
and hold their weekly meetings
in the graveyard, like wandering mendicants.
And when they walk out of the mirror
of the sun and cross the crowded road
in a flash, for a shining moment,
they lurk in the light like a giant shadow
of doubt. Ill-omens to those who cannot
see beyond what they see.

72. The poem constructs its account of stray cats by way of a contrast with
(1) wild cats (2) ominous cats
(3) domestic cats (4) mysterious cats

73. In the overall context, what do "furnished interiors, morning walks,/ the cake and the cutlery" represent ?
(1) Ordinary life
(2) "Domestic fictions"
(3) "A giant shadow of doubt"
(4) Creaturely comforts

74. The last two lines suggest that cats crossing the crowded road
(1) is an unexceptionable superstition.
(2) is not necessarily the ill-omen it is held out to be.
(3) is an example of human obsession.
(4) is indicative of the homelessness of stray cats.

75. From among the following select two words that help accentuate the enigmatic character of stray cats :
I. Doubt II. Mandatory
III. Faith IV. Mystery
The right combination according to the code is
(1) I and II (2) I and IV
(3) II and IV (4) III and IV

✔ ANSWERS

1. (2)	**2.** (3)	**3.** (3)	**4.** (3)	**5.** (1)	**6.** (2)	**7.** (1)	**8.** (2)	**9.** (4)	**10.** (1)
11. (2)	**12.** (3)	**13.** (2)	**14.** (1)	**15.** (3)	**16.** (2)	**17.** (2)	**18.** (2)	**19.** (2)	**20.** (2)
21. (3)	**22.** (4)	**23.** (3)	**24.** (3)	**25.** (2)	**26.** (3)	**27.** (1)	**28.** (2)	**29.** (1)	**30.** (2)
31. (3)	**32.** (1)	**33.** (1)	**34.** (3)	**35.** (2)	**36.** (2)	**37.** (1)	**38.** (2)	**39.** (2)	**40.** (3)
41. (1)	**42.** (4)	**43.** (2)	**44.** (3)	**45.** (3)	**46.** (1)	**47.** (1)	**48.** (3)	**49.** (1)	**50.** (4)
51. (1)	**52.** (3)	**53.** (2)	**54.** (1)	**55.** (3)	**56.** (3)	**57.** (4)	**58.** (4)	**59.** (2)	**60.** (4)
61. (3)	**62.** (2)	**63.** (1)	**64.** (3)	**65.** (2)	**66.** (3)	**67.** (1)	**68.** (4)	**69.** (2)	**70.** (*)
71. (4)	**72.** (3)	**73.** (2)	**74.** (2)	**75.** (2)					

* All option are correct.

January, 2017

ENGLISH LITERATURE

PAPER-II

Note : This paper contains **fifty (50)** objective type questions, each question carrying **two (2)** marks. Attempt **all** the questions.

1. Identify from the following the work Nirad C. Chaudhuri called "the finest novel in the English language with an Indian theme".
(1) *Kim* (2) *A Passage to India*
(3) *Train to Pakistan*
(4) *Private Life of an Indian Prince*

2. Who is the author of the poem "The Defence of Lucknow" dealing with the siege of Lucknow, one of the terrible incidents of the Indian Mutiny ?
(1) Rudyard Kipling (2) Edward Lear
(3) Alfred Lord Tennyson
(4) Robert Browning

3. Who among the following theorists holds that metaphor and metonymy are the two fundamental structures of language ?
(1) Ferdinand de Saussure
(2) J.L. Austin
(3) Roman Jakobson (4) Victor Shklovsky

4. From among the following, who are the Dashwood sisters in Jane Austen's *Sense and Sensibility* ?
I. Elinor II. Marianne
III. Mary IV. Amanda
The right combination according to the code is
(1) I and III (2) I and II
(3) II and III (4) III and IV

5. Which among the following texts can be characterised as a lesbian Bildungsroman?
(1) Angela Carter, *The Magic Toyshop*
(2) Sylvia Plath, *The Bell Jar*
(3) Jeanette Winterson, *Oranges Are Not the Only Fruit*
(4) Ruth Pawar Jhabvala, *Heat and Dust*

6. Identify the correct chronological sequence of publication :
(1) *Paradise Lost – The Advancement of Learning – An Essay Concerning Human* Understanding – MacFlecknoe
(2) *The Advancement of Learning – An Essay Concerning Human Understanding* – MacFlecknoe – Paradise Lost
(3) *The Advancement of Learning – Paradise Lost – MacFlecknoe – An Essay* Concerning Human Understanding
(4) *Paradise Lost – MacFlecknoe – The Advancement of Learning – An Essay* Concerning Human Understanding

7. Poe's "The Raven" mourns the death of Poe's
(1) lost Lenore (2) lost Abigail
(3) pet animal (4) lost heritage

8. In Shakespeare's *Macbeth* who was "untimely ripped" from his mother's womb ?
(1) Macbeth (2) Macduff
(3) Duncan (4) Malcolm

9. Alexander Pope revised *The Rape of the Lock* three times. In the final revision of the poem in 1717 he inserted a speech by
(1) Belinda (2) Clarissa
(3) Betty (4) Thalestris

10. Identify, from the following list, two plays written by John Webster :
I. *A Woman Killed with Kindness*
II. *The Revenger's Tragedy*
III. *The White Devil*
IV. *The Ducchess of Malfi*
The right combination according to the code is
(1) I & IV (2) II & IV
(3) III & IV (4) I & III

11. Which of the following works by David Malouf tells the story of the Roman poet, Ovid, during his exile in Tomis ?
(1) *Remembering Babylon*

(2) *The Great World*
(3) *The Conversations at Curlow Creek*
(4) *An Imaginary Life*

12. In his *Defence of Poesy* which of the following works does Sidney commend as good examples of English Poesy ?
I. *The Mirror of Magistrates*
II. *The Shepherd's Calendar*
III. *Lament for the Makers*
IV. *Ballad of Scottish King*
The right combination according to the code is
(1) I and III (2) I and IV
(3) I and II (4) II and III

13. Who among the following dismissed *Ulysses* as "a misfire" ?
(1) Virginia Woolf (2) Wyndham Lewis
(3) E.M. Forster (4) D.H. Lawrence

14. Which of the following works Daniel Defoe offered his readers as a collection of "Strange Surprising Adventures" ?
(1) *Moll Flanders* (2) *Robinson Crusoe*
(3) *Roxana* (4) *Captain Singleton*

15. In Charlotte Bronte's *Jane Eyre,* what does Mr. Brocklehurst accuse Jane of when he visits Lowood School ?
(1) Laziness (2) Stealing
(3) Lying (4) Spying

16. William Faulkner's *As I Lay Dying* contains one of the shortest chapters in literary history. Which of these sentences is the chapter in its entirety ?
(1) "For the love of God, where is my hat ?"
(2) "My mother is a fish."
(3) "Addie Bundren was dead, to begin with."
(4) "Apricot jam is the worst sort of jam."

17. The prelude to *Middlemarch* makes a reference to the particular history of a remarkable woman, ____.
(1) St. Agnes (2) St. Theresa
(3) St. Joan (4) St. Carmel

18. "O, for a draught of vintage ! that hath been
Cooled a long age in the deep-delved earth,
Tasting of Flora and the country green,
Dance, and Provencal song, and sunburnt mirth !"

The above description is an example of
(1) Paronomasia (2) Synaesthesia
(3) Aphaeresis (4) Synecdoche

19. The term, "poetic justice," to designate the idea that the good are rewarded and the evil punished, was devised by
(1) Aristotle (2) John Dryden
(3) Thomas Rhymer (4) Ben Jonson

20. ______ is the producer of the first complete printed English Bible.
(1) Jerome (2) William Tyndale
(3) Miles Coverdale (4) Bede

21. In *The Fall of Hyperion : A Dream* Keats sees a ladder leading upwards and is addressed by a prophetess in the following words : "None can usurp this height ... / But those to whom the miseries of the world / Are misery, and will not let them rest." Who is the prophetess ?
(1) Urania (2) Moneta
(3) Melete (4) Mneme

22. Virginia Woolf's *To the Lighthouse* has a tripartite structure. The three parts are named the following EXCEPT :
(1) The Sky (2) The Window
(3) Time Passes (4) The Lighthouse

23. Which novel by Patrick White is based on the story of Ludwig Leichhardt, the Prussian naturalist who explored Australia in the mid-1840s, in which White's fictional hero says when asked about navigation – "The Map? I will first make it" ?
(1) *The Tree of Man* (2) *Voss*
(3) *Riders in the Chariot*
(4) *The Solid Mandala*

24. Who among the following is not a character in William Golding's *Lord of the Flies* ?
(1) Ralph (2) Piggy
(3) Peter (4) Jack

25. Dante Gabriel Rossetti founded the Pre-Raphaelite Brotherhood which included
I. Holman Hunt
II. Arthur Hugh Clough
III. Gerald Manley Hopkins
IV. John Millais
The right combination according to the code is

(1) II and III (2) I and IV
(3) I and III (4) II and IV

26. The seven deadly sins are sought to be portrayed in Chaucer's *Canterbury Tales*. Which of the following sins is not covered by Chaucer ?

I. Jealousy II. Envy
III. Lust IV. Homicide

The right combination according to the code is

(1) I & II (2) I & III
(3) I & IV (4) III & IV

27. Richardson's *Pamela* had its origin in

(1) the real case of a woman born to lower-middle-class parents
(2) an elementary letter-writing manual
(3) the general plight of English women
(4) the suggestion of a friend to defend middle-class values

28. *The Medall*, a poem written by John Dryden in 1681, is sub-titled

(1) *A Satire against Sedition*
(2) *A Satire against Tyranny*
(3) *A Satire against Greed*
(4) *A Satire against Apostasy*

29. "Full fathom five thy father lies" is an example of

(1) assonance (2) alliteration
(3) apostrophe (4) enjambment

30. What is a trochee ?

(1) A two syllable foot of verse with two heavy stresses
(2) A two syllable foot of verse in which the stress falls on the first syllable
(3) Three successive heavy stresses
(4) A six line stanza in which the rhyme sounds are all identical

31. Keats's "La Belle Dame Sans Merci" combines two poetic forms

I. Lyric II. Dramatic Monologue
III. Ballad IV. Sonnet

The right combination according to the code is

(1) II and III (2) I and IV
(3) I and III (4) II and IV

32. ______ narrator highlights the problem of narrative authority.

(1) First person (2) Self-conscious
(3) Third person (4) Participant

33. Who among the following modern writers is associated with the quote, "Only connect"?

(1) D.H. Lawrence (2) Virginia Woolf
(3) James Joyce (4) E.M. Forster

34. Which of the following images does not figure in Auden's "Musee des Beaux Arts"?

(1) a boy falling out of the sky
(2) children ... skating on a pond at the edge of wood
(3) ranches of isolation and the busy griefs
(4) the dogs go on with their doggy life

35. Feste is a clown in

(1) *Twelfth Night* (2) *As You Like It*
(3) *The Taming of the Shrew*
(4) *Much Ado About Nothing*

36. Which play by Tom Stoppard has a play within the play ?

(1) *Enter a Free Man*
(2) *The Real Inspector Hound*
(3) *Jumpers* (4) *Night and Day*

37. Which of the following is not true of free verse?

(1) Characterised by short, irregular lines.
(2) No rhyme pattern.
(3) Written in iambic pentameter
(4) A dependence on the effective and more intense use of pauses

38. James Thomson's long poem, *The Seasons*, revised and expanded all his life, began in the first instance as a poem entitled

(1) *Spring* (2) *Summer*
(3) *Winter* (4) *Autumn*

39. Two cantos from the seventh book of *The Faerie Queene* appeared posthumously. They are known as

(1) Mutability cantos (2) Friendship cantos
(3) Justice cantos (4) Courtesy cantos

40. Foucault believes that the facts of history will protect us from

(1) repeating mistakes (2) totalitarianism
(3) deconstructionism (4) historicism

41. What is the occupation of Max's son, Lenny, in Harold Pinter's *The Home Coming* ?
(1) boxer (2) butcher
(3) pimp (4) cab driver

42. Which Byron poem begins in the following manner : "I want a hero : an uncommon want, when every year and month sends forth a new one" ?
(1) *Beppo*
(2) *Childe Harold's Pilgrimage*
(3) *Don Juan*
(4) *The Vision of Judgement*

43. In the second ending of John Fowles's *The French Lieutenant's Woman* Charles Smithson's lawyer finds that Sarah has been living in the house of
(1) William Morris
(2) William Holman Hunt
(3) D.G. Rossetti (4) James Collinson

44. In 1692 William Congreve published *Incognita*, a work of fiction which is dubbed a 'novel' on its title-page. What is the sub-title?
(1) *Love and Duty Reconcil'd*
(2) *Beauty in Distress*
(3) *Virtue Rewarded* (4) *Love in Excess*

45. In "Tradition and the Individual Talent" T.S Eliot uses the analogy of the catalyst to elucidate his theory of impersonal poetry. He cites the example of a filament of platinum and, in the poetic process this is equivalent to
(1) the language of the poet
(2) the mind of the poet
(3) the soul of the poet
(4) the life of the poet

46. Match the character with the work :
A. Pip I. *Middlemarch*
B. Causaubon II. *Great Expectations*
C. Becky Sharp III. *Wuthering Heights*
D. Heathcliff IV. *Vanity Fair*
The right combination according to the code is

	I	II	III	IV		I	II	III	IV
(1)	B	C	D	A	(2)	D	A	C	B
(3)	B	A	D	C	(4)	C	B	A	D

47. Samuel Johnson's *Lives of the English Poets* combines the following except
(1) analytical criticism
(2) literary history
(3) personal biography
(4) Socratic dialogue

48. Which two works of JM Coetzee won Booker Prize on two occasions ?
I. *In the Heart of the Country*
II. *Life and Times of Michael K.*
III. *Disgrace*
IV. *Waiting for the Barbarians*
The right combination according to the code is
(1) II and III (2) II and IV
(3) III and IV (4) I and III

49. Who among the following Greek Philosophers has a bearing on the composition of Shelley's "Adonais" ?
(1) Miletus (2) Socrates
(3) Plato (4) Aristotle

50. Match the author with the work :
A. John Locke I. *A Short View of the Immorality and Profanity of the Stage*
B. William Dampier II. *Two Treatises on Government*
C. Jeremy Collier III. *A Short View of Tragedy*
D. Thomas Rhymer IV. *Voyages*

	A	B	C	D		A	B	C	D
(1)	II	I	IV	III	(2)	III	IV	I	II
(3)	II	IV	I	III	(4)	IV	III	II	I

✓ ANSWERS

1. (1)	**2.** (3)	**3.** (3)	**4.** (2)	**5.** (3)	**6.** (3)	**7.** (1)	**8.** (2)	**9.** (2)	**10.** (3)
11. (4)	**12.** (3)	**13.** (1)	**14.** (2)	**15.** (3)	**16.** (2)	**17.** (2)	**18.** (2)	**19.** (3)	**20.** (3)
21. (2)	**22.** (1)	**23.** (2)	**24.** (3)	**25.** (2)	**26.** (3)	**27.** (2)	**28.** (1)	**29.** (2)	**30.** (2)
31. (3)	**32.** (2)	**33.** (4)	**34.** (3)	**35.** (1)	**36.** (2)	**37.** (3)	**38.** (3)	**39.** (1)	**40.** (4)
41. (3)	**42.** (3)	**43.** (3)	**44.** (1)	**45.** (2)	**46.** (3)	**47.** (4)	**48.** (1)	**49.** (3)	**50.** (3)

January, 2017

ENGLISH LITERATURE

PAPER-III

Note : This paper contains seventy **five (75)** objective type questions of **two (2)** marks each. All questions are compulsory.

1. Who among the following is not a diasporic writer ?
(1) Beryl Bainbridge (2) Timothy Mo
(3) Hanif Kureishi (4) Sam Selvon

2. "A text is not a line of words releasing a single 'theological' meaning (the 'message' of the Author-God) but a multi-dimensional space in which a variety of writings, none of them original, blend and clash. The text is a tissue of quotations drawn from the innumerable centres of culture."
Which of the following best expresses the position stated above ?
(1) A text is a tissue of lies that has no referential and cultural validity.
(2) A text is a communication from the Author-God with multiple meanings.
(3) A text is a force field of ambiguity where meanings collapse in the face of opposition.
(4) A text is a linguistic construct without any unity of meaning and is linked to multiple sources of language and culture.

3. In William Congreve's *The Way of the World* Fairall is Lady Wishfort's
(1) Son (2) Son-in-law
(3) Nephew (4) Servant

4. Match the periodical with the founder/s :

List – I	List – II
A. *The Egoist*	I. Wyndham Lewis and Ezra Pound
B. *The English Review*	II. Harriet Monroe
C. *Blast*	III. Harriet Weaver and Dora Marsden
D. *Poetry : A Magazine of Verse*	IV. Ford Madox Ford

Codes :

	A	B	C	D
(1)	II	III	I	IV
(2)	III	I	IV	II
(3)	III	IV	I	II
(4)	III	II	I	IV

5. Which statement best expresses the theme of Coleridge's "The Rime of the Ancient Mariner" ?
(1) To kill a living creature is immoral.
(2) People should honour and respect all living things.
(3) Prayer can accomplish miracles.
(4) True harmony is achieved only through cooperative effort.

6. "The Comprehensible Output Hypothesis" was proposed by
(1) Stephen Krashen (2) M.A.K. Halliday
(3) Merrill Swain (4) Gertrude Buck

7. In *Tristram Shandy* Corporal Trim's brother Tom describes the oppression of a black servant in a sausage shop in Lisbon that he visited. This episode is inspired by a letter Laurence Sterne received from a black man. Sterne's reply became an integral part of 18th century abolitionist literature.
Name the person who wrote the aforementioned letter to Sterne.
(1) William Wilberforce
(2) Ignatius Sancho
(3) William Blackstone
(4) John Hawkins

8. In Bertolt Brecht's *Mother Courage and Her Children,* which song does Yvette sing to Mother Courage and Kattrin ?
(1) "The Song of the Great Souls of the Earth"
(2) "The Fraternization Song"
(3) "The Song of the Great Capitulation"
(4) "The Memorial Song"

9. In Gustave Flaubert's *Madame Bovary,* under what pretext does Emma go every week for her clandestine meeting with Leon in Rouen ?
(1) Under the pretext of going to the church for weekly confession.
(2) Under the pretext of meeting her blind friend who lives alone.
(3) Under the pretext of weekly shopping.
(4) Under the pretext of taking piano lessons.

10. Identify the two books by C.S. Lakshmi (Ambai) published in English translation :
I. *Astride the Wheel* II. *Going Home*
III. *A Purple Sea*
IV. *In a Forest, A Deer*
The right combination according to the code is
(1) III and II (2) I and II
(3) I and IV (4) III and IV

11. Elizabeth Barrett Browning's *Sonnets from the Portuguese* is
I. a sequence of forty four Petrarchan sonnets.
II. a rewriting of Popean didactic verse.
III. a depiction of a contemporary setting and small events of ordinary life.
IV. a scathing criticism of the British colonial enterprise.
The right combination according to the code is
(1) I and II (2) I and III
(3) II and IV (4) I and IV

12. In *The Story of My Experiments with Truth,* M.K. Gandhi covers the narrative of his life from early childhood through to
(1) 1925 (2) 1929
(3) 1921 (4) 1927

13. In a writing system the minimal unit that can cause a difference of meaning is called
(1) phoneme (2) grapheme
(3) morpheme (4) jargon

14. Nnu Ego is a character in
(1) Chinua Achebe's *Anthills of Savannah*
(2) Chimamanda Ngozi Adichie's *Half of a Yellow Sun*
(3) Buchi Emecheta's *The Joys of Motherhood*
(4) Ben Okri's *The Famished Road*

15. Match the word with definition :

List – I	List – II
A. Etymon	I. Changing from one language variety to another in discourse
B. Code switching	II. Rules governing the social use of language
C. Cognate	III. Etymological source of a word
D. Pragmatics	IV. Words with a common ancestor

Codes :

	A	B	C	D		A	B	C	D
(1)	IV	I	III	II	(2)	III	II	IV	I
(3)	III	I	IV	II	(4)	IV	I	II	III

16. What would help a reader recognize Keats's "To Autumn" as a poem from the Romantic period ?
(1) Its logical succession of images
(2) Its concise use of couplets
(3) Its lavish natural imagery
(4) Its use of iambic pentameter

17. Which of the following is an accurate description of 'heteroglossia' ?
(1) Heteroglossia makes the job of the novelist easier by incorporating diversity into the novelistic structure.
(2) Heteroglossia functions in a novel in alliance with its stylistic system incorporating multiple voices inscribed in social language and differentiated components of a writer's ideological position.
(3) Heteroglossia creates concrete conceptualisations through language in

association with the singular view of the artistic effort resulting in the unified world of the novel.

(4) Heteroglossia enters the linguistic universe of the novel to homogenize its multiple differences and voices in a singular vision of accomplished structure.

18. In *Ulysses* Leopold Bloom works for a Dublin

(1) bar (2) park
(3) newspaper (4) bank

19. Which pair of plays belongs to the early career of Harold Pinter ?

I. *The Caretaker* II. *One for the Road*
III. *Celebration* IV. *The Room*

The right combination according to the code is

(1) I and III (2) II and III
(3) I and IV (4) II and IV

20. Who among the following contemporaries of John Donne wrote the following lines on his death : "Here lies a king, that ruled as he thought fit/The universal monarch of wit"?

(1) George Herbert (2) Henry King
(3) Thomas Carew (4) Henry Crashaw

21. In his poem "Australia" A.D. Hope says that

I. Australia is "without songs, architecture, history".
II. "Her five cities are like five dry rivers."
III. The poet turns to her "to find/The Arabian desert of the human mind/Hoping if still from deserts prophets come."
IV. "She is the first of lands, the warmest."

Codes :

(1) I and III (2) II and III
(3) III and IV (4) I and IV

22. Basic English, a simplified and fundamental framework of English, was formulated by

I. A. Richards II. Alastair Fowler
III. William Empson IV. C.K. Ogden

The right combination according to the code is :

(1) I and II (2) II and III
(3) I and IV (4) I and III

23. "Britons will never be slaves !" – felt proud Britons in the eighteenth century. A great many Britons, though, had no qualms about owning slaves and profiting from them. Who among the following British authors self-consciously engaged with the issue of slavery in some poems ?

I. Hannah More II. Mary Collier
III. Anna Seward IV. Anna Yearsley

The right combination according to the code is

(1) I and III (2) I and IV
(3) II and III (4) III and IV

24. Match the Novelist with the work :

List – I	List – II
A. Anita Desai	I. *Rich Like Us*
B. Nayantara Sahgal	II. *The Nowhere Man*
C. Arun Joshi	III. *In Custody*
D. Kamala Markandaya	IV. *The Last Labyrinth*

Codes :

	A	B	C	D		A	B	C	D
(1)	III	II	IV	I	(2)	III	I	IV	II
(3)	II	I	IV	III	(4)	III	IV	I	II

25. Identify the right chronological sequence :

(1) *The American Pastoral – Sister Carrie – The Great Gatsby – Beloved*
(2) *The Great Gatsby – Sister Carrie – Beloved – The American Pastoral*
(3) *Sister Carrie – The Great Gatsby – Beloved – The American Pastoral*
(4) *Sister Carrie – The Great Gatsby – The American Pastoral – Beloved*

26. In which of the following senses did Marx and Engels originally use the term "ideology" in *The German Ideology* ?

(1) Something that mystifies the actual material conditions of society, a sort of false consciousness.
(2) The elaborate structures and institutions that mark the bourgeoise society.
(3) The concepts of base and superstructure that govern the economic relations of the society.
(4) The fundamental class consciousness of the proletariat which leads to their awakening.

27. The plot of this Coetzee novel unravels the narrative of a poor man of colour trying to survive in a civil-war situation, never taking sides. Identify the novel.
    (1) *Disgrace* (2) *Age of Iron*
    (3) *Waiting for the Barbarians*
    (4) *Life and Times of Michael K.*

28. Which of the following lines of T.S. Eliot is used by Anita Desai as the epigraph for her novel, *Baumgartner's Bombay* ?
    (1) "I will show you fear in a handful of dust," *The Waste Land*
    (2) "In my beginning is my end", "East Coker"
    (3) "Human kind cannot bear very much reality", "Burnt Norton"
    (4) "I have measured out my life with coffee spoons," "Love Song of J. Alfred Prufrock"

29. In the General Prologue to *The Canterbury Tales* which two characters are examples of deep Christian goodness ?
    I. the Summoner II. the Parson
    III. the Ploughman IV. the Pardoner
    The right combination according to the code is
    (1) I and II (2) II and IV
    (3) II and III (4) I and IV

30. Identify Falstaff's first words in *Henry IV, Part I* :
    (1) "Now, Harry, what time of day is it, lad ?"
    (2) "Now, Hal, what time of day is it, lad ?"
    (3) "Now, Harry, what time of night is it, lad ?"
    (4) "Now, Hal, what time of night is it, lad ?"

31. Anna Barbauld, Laetitia Elizabeth London, Charlotte Smith, Mary Robinson and Felicia Hemans are
    (1) first wave feminists
    (2) women poets of the Romantic period
    (3) Victorian writers of popular fiction
    (4) nineteenth century stage artists

32. Ray Bradbury has titled one of his short story collections – *Golden Apples of the Sun* – after the last line of a W.B. Yeats poem. Which poem ?
    (1) "The Death of Cuchulain"
    (2) "The Peacock"
    (3) "The Hour Before Dawn"
    (4) "The Song of Wandering Aengus"

33. Which play by Tom Stoppard set in Zurich during the First World War presents a character's interactions with James Joyce as he was writing *Ulysses*, Tristran Zara during the rise of Dadaism, and Lenin leading up to the Russian Revolution, all of whom were living in Zurich at that time ?
    (1) *After Magritte* (2) *Dirty Linen*
    (3) *Artist Descending a Staircase*
    (4) *Travesties*

34. "Most blameless is he, centered in the sphere
    Of common duties, decent not to fail
    In offices of tenderness..."
    In these lines from "Ulysses", what does Ulysses suggest about Telemachus ?
    (1) He shows heroic qualities.
    (2) He is patient and selfless.
    (3) He is very much like his father.
    (4) He may be too tender-hearted to be king.

35. In Restoration comedies the following is true EXCEPT
    (1) the London life of hedonistic young men is portrayed.
    (2) names encapsulate traits.
    (3) unchaste women, widows and cuckolds scarcely make an appearance.
    (4) the heroines seek a say in the choice of a marriage partner.

36. What happens to the character Boy at the end of Luigi Pirandello's play *Six Characters in* Search of an Author ?
    (1) He drowns in the fountain.
    (2) He is shot dead by the Father.
    (3) He leaves the stage alone.
    (4) He commits suicide.

37. Which of the following adjectives will not apply to Becky Sharp, a major character in *Vanity Fair* ?

(1) ambitious (2) energetic
(3) wellborn (4) scheming

38. Which character in Anton Chekhov's play, *The Cherry Orchard*, first suggests the selling of the orchard ?
(1) Trofimov (2) Yephikodov
(3) Lopakhin (4) Varya

39. Identify the correct chronological sequence of the founding of the following 18th century English periodicals :
(1) *Tatler – Spectator – The Gentleman's Magazine – Rambler*
(2) *Spectator – Tatler – The Gentleman's Magazine – Rambler*
(3) *Rambler – Tatler – Spectator – The Gentleman's Magazine*
(4) *Tatler – Spectator – Rambler – The Gentleman's Magazine*

40. Who identified "strangled articulateness" as a theme in Canadian writing ?
(1) Margaret Atwood (2) Northrop Frye
(3) Michael Ondaatjee (4) Joy Kogawa

41. Identify the gynocritics in the following list:
I. Alice Jardine II. Elaine Showalter
III. Sandra Gilbert IV. Kate Millett
The right combination according to the code is
(1) I and II (2) II and IV
(3) II and III (4) III and IV

42. Identify the character who is not part of the group of three protagonists in Girish Karnad's *Hayavadana* :
(1) Padmini (2) Gautama
(3) Kapila (4) Devadatta

43. Aurobindo Ghosh, author of *'Savitri'*, taught for some time at Baroda College after his return from England in 1893. Which subject did he teach ?
(1) English (2) French
(3) Sanskrit (4) Bengali

44. Christopher Marlowe's *Hero and Leander* can be classified as a/an
(1) complaint (2) stichomythia
(3) epyllion (4) pasturelle

45. Which among the following does not belong to Indo-European language family ?
(1) English (2) German
(3) Scandinavian (4) Finnish

46. What, among the following, is ruled out by Longinus as a way of achieving the sublime?
(1) great thoughts
(2) immoderate emotion
(3) noble diction
(4) dignified and elevated word arrangement

47. Who among the following is not a beat writer?
(1) Jack Kerouac (2) Allen Ginsberg
(3) Robert Lowell
(4) William Burroughs

48. This was a masque written by Ben Jonson, staged on Twelfth Night and it was the first masque in which Prince Charles took part.
(1) *Masque of Blankness*
(2) *The Masque of Queens*
(3) *Pleasure Reconciled to Virtue*
(4) *The Gypsies Metamorphed*

49. Elizabeth Bishop's poems are best remembered for their
(1) conversational intimacy
(2) intellectual tenor
(3) astringent satire
(4) urban topography

50. Which chilling novel of surveillance and entrapment had the alternative title *Things as They Are* ?
(1) Horace Walpole's *Castle of Otranto.*
(2) Matthew Gregory Lewis's *The Monk.*
(3) Thomas Love Peacock's *Nightmare Abbey.*
(4) William Godwin's *Caleb Williams.*

51. In "My Last Duchess" which of the following is not one of the Duchess's misdemeanours, according to the Duke ?
(1) She was flattered by compliments from Fra Pandolf.
(2) She enjoyed the sunset as much as she enjoyed her husband's favour.
(3) She wouldn't listen to her husband when he tried to correct her behaviour.
(4) She was equally grateful for all acts of kindness, regardless of their source.

52. In his essay "From Work to Text" Roland Barthes says the following about the text :

I. The text is singular.

II. The text can be held in the hand.

III. The text is held in language.

IV. The text is a methodological field.

The right combination according to the code is

(1) I and III (2) II and IV

(3) III and IV (4) III and II

53. Seamus Heaney's "Digging" in his first volume of poetry, *Death of a Naturalist*, illustrates all the following EXCEPT

(1) his preoccupation with his roots

(2) his obsession with Irish legend and folklore

(3) his respect for the natural world of the farming community and the labour of his ancestors

(4) his displaced vocation of digging with a pen

54. Here is a list of Indian writers who have translated their work into English. Match the writer with his source language :

List – I	List – II
A. O.V. Vijayan	I. Kannada
B. Vilas Sarang	II. Malayalam
C. Krishna Baldev Vaid	III. Marathi
D. Girish Karnad	IV. Hindi

Codes :

	A	B	C	D		A	B	C	D
(1)	II	IV	III	I	(2)	I	III	IV	II
(3)	II	III	IV	I	(4)	II	III	I	IV

55. In Book 8, *Paradise Lost* Adam identifies his chief flaw or weakness to Raphael. What is this flaw ?

(1) gluttony

(2) pride in his superiority to Eve

(3) overconfidence in his free will

(4) passion for Eve

56. Identify the correct chronological sequence of the following early English texts :

(1) *Troilus and Criseyde – The Owl and The Nightingale – Utopia – Morte d'Arthur*

(2) *Troilus and Criseyde – Utopia – Morte d'Arthur – The Owl and the Nightingale*

(3) *The Owl and the Nightingale – Troilus and Criseyde – Morte d'Arthur – Utopia*

(4) *The Owl and the Nightingale – Morte d'Arthur – Troilus and Criseyde – Uttopia*

57. In Sophocles's play *King Oedipus* Laius, the erstwhile ruler of Thebes, was murdered

(1) at the edge of the forest on his way to Delphi

(2) at the edge of the forest as he returned from Delphi

(3) at the crossroads as he returned from Delphi

(4) at the crossroads on his way to Delphi

58. The quintessentially metafictional novel, *If On a Winter's Night a Traveller* by Italo Calvino has alternate chapters with chapter numbers and titles. Which of the following are the titles of the chapters in the novel?

I. Looks Down in the Gathering Shadow

II. In a Network of Lines that Enlace

III. In a Network of Lines that Interface

IV. What Story there Awaits its End ?

The right combination according to the code is

(1) I and II (2) I and IV

(3) III and IV (4) II and IV

59. The novel *Maurice* by E.M. Forster appeared posthumously in 1971. It had a homosexual theme, so Forster considered its subject matter too indelicate for publication during his life time. It was influenced by a writer who was a socialist and open homosexual. Identify the writer.

(1) Oscar Wilde (2) Edward Carpenter

(3) W.H. Auden (4) E.F. Benson

60. Who among the following has elaborated on the "Indianisation" of English ?

(1) L.M. Khubchandani

(2) B. Kumaravadivelu

(3) B.B. Kachru (4) Rajendra Singh

61. These are four models of relating literature to history. Which of the following is associated with formalism ?

(1) Literary texts are universal and transcend history : the historical context of their production and reception has no

bearing on the literary work which is aesthetically autonomous, having its own laws, being a world into itself.

(2) The historical context of a literary work is integral to a proper understanding of it : the text is produced within a specific historical context but in its literariness it remains separate from that context.

(3) Literary works can help us to understand the time in which they are set : realist texts in particular provide imaginative representations of specific historical moments, events or periods.

(4) Literary texts are bound up with other discourses and rhetorical structures : they are part of a history that is still in the process of being written.

62. As Gunter Grass's novel *The Tin Drum* opens we find Oskar Matzerath

(1) on the war front entertaining the soldiers as part of a band of dwarfs.

(2) in a mental hospital writing his story.

(3) admitted in a hospital after his fatal fall in the wine cellar.

(4) watching a ball in which the young ladies ignore his presence.

63. D.H. Lawrence's 1926 novel *The Plumed Serpent* is set in which country ?

(1) Egypt (2) South Africa
(3) Mexico (4) Peru

64. Which two writers can be described as writing historical novels ?

I. Sir Walter Scott II. Charlotte Bronte
III. Maria Edgeworth IV. Jane Austen

The right combination according to the code is

(1) I and II (2) II and III
(3) I and III (4) III and IV

65. Which of Kazuo Ishiguro's novels are set mostly in Japan ?

I. *The Unconsoled*
II. *The Remains of the Day*
III. *An Artist of the Floating World*
IV. *A Pale View of Hills*

The right combination according to the code is

(1) I and III (2) II and III
(3) III and IV (4) I and IV

66. In *The Advancement of Learning* Bacon noted the need for more studies of

I. moral knowledge
II. forbidden knowledge
III. civil knowledge
IV. spiritual knowledge

The right combination according to the code is

(1) I and III (2) I and IV
(3) II and III (4) II and IV

67. Which among the following texts purports to be the autobiography of a mad German philosopher edited by an equally fictitious editor ?

(1) *Sartos Resartus*
(2) *The Dream of Gerontius*
(3) *The Professor* (4) *Felix Holf*

68. As Sidney argues in *A Defence of Poesy* which discipline is more useful and praiseworthy – history or poetry ?

(1) History "being captivated to truth" is more useful than poetry.

(2) Poetry where man can see "virtue exalted and vice punished" is more useful than history.

(3) History is more useful for poetry is "an encouragement to unbridled wickedness".

(4) History and poetry are synonymous, and so both are useful.

69. In Bunyan's *Pilgrim's Progress* Christian and his friend faithful cause a commotion at the Vanity Fair for many reasons. Which of the following statements is not true of their appearance at the fair ?

(1) They are dressed differently than the other fair-goers.

(2) They speak the language of the Bible at the fair.

(3) They sample every entertainment at the fair.

(4) They refuse to look at the merchandise at the fair.

70. What does the title *Morte d'Arthur* mean ?
(1) Arthur mortified (2) Death of Arthur
(3) Castle of Arthur (4) Burial of Arthur

71. **Assertion (A) :** Characters in novels are people whose secret lives are visible or might be visible. We are people whose secret lives are invisible.
Reason (R) : Even when novels are about wicked people, they can solace us; they suggest a more manageable human race, they give us the illusion of seeing clearly and of power.
In the light of the statements above
(1) Both (A) and (R) are correct and (R) is the correct explanation of (A).
(2) Both (A) and (R) are correct but (R) is not the correct explanation of (A).
(3) (A) is right, but (R) is wrong.
(4) (A) is wrong, but (R) is right

Read the following poem and answer the questions, 72 to 75 :

Dead Fox

We pretended to know nothing about it.
I withdrew to my childhood training: stay out
of swampy undergrowth, choked edges.
This was around the time
we were too cruel to kill the mice we caught,
leaving them in the Have-a-Heart trap
under the sun-burning bramble of rugosa.
But moving up the trail, we caught a glimpse
right at the start: the fox just over the hillock
on the dune-side slope, spoiling
the grass-inscribed sand. Neither of us looked –
it seemed best to back away.
On the dune's steep side
we surveyed what we'd come for : ocean's
snaking blue beyond the meadow, the silvered
blade-like wands lying down. Lovely enough
to hold ourselves to that view.
But the currents of an odor wafted in and out,
until the sweep of smell grew wider, wilder.
The heat compounded, and ugliness
settled its cloud over us, profound as human speech,
although by then we were not speaking.

72. The "We" of the opening line indicates
(1) a group (2) two persons
(3) the speaker and an imaginary listener
(4) an unspecified crowd

73. The dead animal was sighted
(1) at the end of the trail
(2) on the dune's steep side
(3) on the dune's sloping side
(4) in the swampy undergrowth

74. The reaction evoked in response to a glimpse of the dead fox is best described as
I. evasive II. angry
III. bizarre IV. muted
The right combination according to the code is
(1) I and II (2) II and III
(3) I and IV (4) III and IV

75. At the close of the poem, which of the following senses overpowers and renders the visitors speechless ?
(1) sight (2) touch
(3) sound (4) smell

✔ ANSWERS

1. (1)	**2.** (4)	**3.** (2)	**4.** (3)	**5.** (2)	**6.** (3)	**7.** (2)	**8.** (2)	**9.** (4)	**10.** (4)
11. (2)	**12.** (3)	**13.** (2)	**14.** (3)	**15.** (3)	**16.** (3)	**17.** (2)	**18.** (3)	**19.** (3)	**20.** (3)
21. (1)	**22.** (3)	**23.** (2)	**24.** (2)	**25.** (3)	**26.** (1)	**27.** (4)	**28.** (2)	**29.** (3)	**30.** (2)
31. (2)	**32.** (4)	**33.** (4)	**34.** (2)	**35.** (3)	**36.** (4)	**37.** (3)	**38.** (3)	**39.** (1)	**40.** (2)
41. (3)	**42.** (2)	**43.** (1,2)	**44.** (3)	**45.** (4)	**46.** (2)	**47.** (3)	**48.** (3)	**49.** (1)	**50.** (4)
51. (3)	**52.** (3)	**53.** (2)	**54.** (3)	**55.** (4)	**56.** (3)	**57.** (4)	**58.** (1)	**59.** (2)	**60.** (3)
61. (1)	**62.** (2)	**63.** (3)	**64.** (3)	**65.** (3)	**66.** (1)	**67.** (1)	**68.** (2)	**69.** (3)	**70.** (2)
71. (2)	**72.** (2)	**73.** (3)	**74.** (3)	**75.** (4)					

November, 2017

ENGLISH LITERATURE

PAPER-II

Note : This paper contains **fifty (50)** objective type questions, each question carrying **two (2)** marks. Attempt **all** the questions.

1. In Frances Burney's novel, Evelina, the eponymous heroine comes out in society in two locations. They are :

(a) Bath (b) Bristol

(c) Leeds (d) London

The right combination according to the code is :

(1) (a) and (b) (2) (b) and (c)

(3) (a) and (d) (4) (b) and (d)

2. Which of the following lines by Shakespeare is repeated several times in Virginia Woolf's novel Mrs. Dalloway ?

(1) "If music be the food of love, play on".

(2) "Fear no more the heat of the sun, Nor the furious winter's rages".

(3) "Those are pearls that were his eyes".

(4) "There is a tide in the affairs of man".

3. Identify the important theatres of the Elizabethan period :

(a) Peacock (b) Globe

(c) Swan (d) Grand

The right combination according to the code is :

(1) (a) and (b) (2) (b) and (c)

(3) (b) and (d)

(4) (a) and (d)

4. In which poem does Matthew Arnold express the dilemma of :

"Wandering between two worlds, one dead, The other powerless to be born" ?

(1) "Self - Dependence"

(2) "Stanzas from the Grande Chartreuse"

(3) "To a Republican Friend"

(4) "Dover Beach"

5. Who made the comment that, "All modern American literature comes from one book by Mark Twain called Huckleberry Finn" ?

(1) Henry James

(2) William Faulkner

(3) Jack London

(4) Ernest Hemingway

6. The Emblem is a poetic genre containing a symbolic picture with a text and a verse exposition popular in the early 17th century. Who popularised this kind of poetry through the work *Emblems [1635]* ?

(1) Robert Southwell

(2) Francis Quarles

(3) John Davies

(4) Joseph Sylvester

7. Which Byron work begins thus :

"I want a hero : an uncommon want, when every year and month sends forth a new one ...." ?

(1) Beppo (2) Cain

(3) Manfred (4) Don Juan

8. The title of Sir Thomas Browne's famous treatise, *Religio Medici* means :

(1) Religion of a Doctor

(2) Religion of Magician

(3) Religion of Divinity

(4) Religion of Meditation

9. Which among the following recent novels is a retelling of Sophocles's *Antigone* ?

(1) Kamila Shamsie, *Home Fire*

(2) Fiona Mozley, *Elmet*

(3) Zadie Smith, *Swing Time*

(4) Mohsin Hamid, *Exit West*

10. Identify the two important works of Paul de Man from the following list :
 (a) *Blindness and Insight*
 (b) *Allegories of Reading*
 (c) *Theoretical Essays*
 (d) *Criticism and Ideology*
 The right combination according to the code is :
 (1) (a) and (b) (2) (a) and (c)
 (3) (b) and (c) (4) (b) and (d)

11. Samuel Johnson denounced the metaphysical poets saying, "About the beginning of the seventeenth century appeared a race of writers that may be termed the metaphysical poets". In the biography of which of the following poets in his *Lives of Poets* did Johnson make this remark ?
 (1) John Dryden
 (2) Thomas Parnell
 (3) Abraham Cowley
 (4) Alexander Pope

12. The terms of the contract are not disagreeable to me.
 The above sentence contains an example of:
 (1) enumeratio
 (2) litotes
 (3) anaphora
 (4) metonymy

13. Who is the author of the following lines ?
 "To see a World in a Grain of Sand
 And a Heaven in a Wild Flower
 Hold Infinity in the palm of your hand
 And Eternity in an hour...".
 (1) Thomas Gray
 (2) William Blake
 (3) William Collins
 (4) William Cowper

14. *In Women in Love* what is Winifred's pekinese dog called ?
 (1) Bismarck
 (2) Looloo
 (3) Lucky
 (4) Buddy

15. Which of the following New Critics put forward the idea of the 'heresy of paraphrase'?
 (1) Allen Tate
 (2) Cleanth Brooks
 (3) W.K. Wimsatt
 (4) Monroe C Beardsley

16. Edmund Spenser's *Colin Clout's Come Home Again* is a fine example of :
 (1) carpe diem
 (2) sonnet sequence
 (3) georgic poetry
 (4) pastoral eclogue

17. In *An Essay of Dramatic Poesy* whom does John Dryden refer to as "the most learned and judicious Writer which any Theater ever had" ?
 (1) John Webster
 (2) Christopher Marlowe
 (3) Ben Jonson
 (4) William Shakespeare

18. This Australian poet was raised in New South Wales and grew up in rural Australian landscape. In 1946 she published her first book of poems. In 1962, she became co-founder and president of the Wild Life Preservation Society of Queensland and served as its president several times thereafter. Identify the poet.
 (1) Dorothy Hewett
 (2) Nettie Palmer
 (3) Judith Wright
 (4) Amy Witting

19. Aphra Behn's *Oroonoko* is set in
 (1) Surinam
 (2) Abyssinia
 (3) Egypt
 (4) Assyria

20. Who published the first collected edition of Gerard Manley Hopkins's poems in 1918 ?
 (1) Robert Bridges
 (2) Coventry Patmore
 (3) John Betjeman
 (4) Stephen Spender

21. Samuel Richardson named his heroine Pamela after one of the characters in ______.
(1) Edmund Spenser's *Faerie Queene*
(2) William Shakespeare's *Venus and Adonis*
(3) Philip Sidney's *Arcadia*
(4) Geoffrey Chaucer's *Canterbury Tales*

22. Pinter once admitted that he first became aware of the dramatic power of the pause from seeing a popular American comedian. Which one ?
(1) Bob Hope
(2) W. C. Fields
(3) Jack Benny
(4) Charlie Chaplin

23. Charles Dickens's *Bleak House* is pointedly critical of England's :
(1) Privy Council
(2) Court of Appeal
(3) Court of Chancery
(4) military courts

24. Which of the following is NOT true of the ideal state in Thomas More's *Utopia* ?
(1) Personal property, money and vice are effectively abolished.
(2) The root causes of crime, ambition and political conflict, are eliminated.
(3) There is only one religion guided by the principle of a benevolent Supreme Being.
(4) Its priesthood, which includes some women, is limited in number.

25. Which character created by Coleridge makes the following account of her harrowing experience ?
"Five warriors seized me yestermorn,
Me, even me, a maid forlorn :
They choked my cries with force and fright,
And tied me on a palfrey white".
(1) Geraldine
(2) Christabel
(3) Christabel's mother
(4) The maid who appeared in Christabel's dream

26. Which novel of Thomas Hardy begins with the sombre description of Egdon Heath ?
(1) *Jude the Obscure*
(2) *The Return of the Native*
(3) *Far from the Madding Crowd*
(4) *Under the Greenwood Tree*

27. The metrical form of Gower's *Confessio Amantis* is :
(1) iambic pentameter
(2) anapestic trimeter
(3) octosyllabic couplets
(4) trochaic tetrameter

28. What happens to the lock of hair at the end of Alexander Pope's *The Rape of the Lock* ?
(1) It is given back to its rightful owner.
(2) It is preserved in a monument.
(3) It turns into a star.
(4) It is presented to the poet as a token of gratitude

29. The Bard. The Iron Lady. The King.
The above are examples of :
(1) anacoluthon
(2) aposiopesis
(3) asyndenton
(4) antonomasia

30. Which of the following novels by Margaret Atwood depicts the historical event of the notorious murders committed in 1843 ?
(1) *The Blind Assassin*
(2) *Alias Grace*
(3) *Cats Eye*
(4) *Oryx and Crake*

31. Which of the following poems by W. B. Yeats repudiates the sensual world in favour of "the artifice of eternity" ?
(1) "Under Ben Bulben"
(2) "Among School Children"
(3) "Sailing to Byzantium"
(4) "After Long Silence"

32. Which of the following characters in *Moby Dick* falls overboard and turns insane as a result ?

(1) Pip (2) Queequeg
(3) Starbuck (4) Tashtego

33. Which of the following poems by Seamus Heaney is dedicated to the Irish poet Paul Muldoon ?
(1) "The Loaning"
(2) "The Sandpit"
(3) "A Migration"
(4) "Widgeon"

34. In William Golding's *Lord of the Flies* which of the following characters is put to death ?
(1) Piggy (2) Ralph
(3) Simon (4) Jack

35. In *Canterbury Tales* who has a red face full of sores ?
(1) the Summoner
(2) the Shipman
(3) the Yeoman
(4) the Reeve

36. The pace of speech is called :
(1) syllable (2) loudness
(3) tempo (4) pitch

37. Match the title with the author :

(a) *Sexual Politics*	(i) Mary Ellman
(b) *A Literature of Their Own*	(ii) Elaine Showalter
(c) *Thinking About Women*	(iii) Helene Cixous
(d) *The Laugh of the Medusa*	(iv) Kate Millet

Code :

	(a)	(b)	(c)	(d)
(1)	(iv)	(iii)	(i)	(ii)
(2)	(iv)	(ii)	(i)	(iii)
(3)	(iii)	(iv)	(i)	(ii)
(4)	(iv)	(i)	(ii)	(iii)

38. Which of the following historical events does Tennyson's poem "The Charge of the Light Brigade" describe ?
(1) The Battle of Hastings
(2) The Wars of the Roses
(3) The Battle of Waterloo
(4) The Crimean War

39. Northrop Frye's influential work, *Anatomy of Criticism* includes, as the subtitle indicates, four essays. Which of the following is NOT one among them?
(1) "Archetypal Criticism : Theory of Myths"
(2) "Typological Criticism : Theory of Types"
(3) "Historical Criticism : Theory of Modes"
(4) "Ethical Criticism : Theory of Symbols"

40. In Robert Browning's "Andrea del Sarto", with which of the following painters does Andrea NOT compare himself with ?
(1) Michelangelo
(2) Leonardo da Vinci
(3) Rembrandt
(4) Raphael

41. In Jonathan Swift's *Gullivers Travels* Gulliver refers to William Dampier, the famous writer of two voyages, as :
(1) master (2) brother
(3) cousin (4) uncle

42. Who among the following is NOT a character in *Pride and prejudice* ?
(1) Mr. Darcy
(2) Miss Bingley
(3) Miss Bates
(4) Mr. Collins

43. "All the world's a stage,
And all the men and women merely players",
occurs in Shakespeare's *As You Like It*. Which character says the line ?
(1) Jacques
(2) Celia
(3) Rosalind
(4) Touchstone

44. Which of the following rivers are mentioned in Andrew Marvell's poem "To His Coy Mistress" ?
(1) Thames and Rhine

(2) Thames and Ganges
(3) Ganges and Humber
(4) Thames and Humber

45. "The truth, the whole truth, and nothing but the truth".
The above is an example of :
(1) ploce
(2) epizeuxis
(3) plurisignation
(4) diaeresis

46. Which of the following images is NOT part of W.H. Auden's poem "In Memory of W.B. Yeats" ?
(1) Mercury sinking in the mouth of the dying day
(2) Wolves running through evergreen forests
(3) Silence invading the suburbs
(4) Memory scattering like the beads

47. Who among the following is the author of *Steps to the Temple* ?
(1) John Donne
(2) Richard Crashaw
(3) George Herbert
(4) Henry Vaughan

48. Match the character with the work :

(a) Jim Dixon	(i) *Room at the Top*
(b) Jimmy Porter	(ii) *Hurry on Down*
(c) Joe Lampton	(iii) *Look Back In Anger*
(d) Charles Lumley	(iv) *Lucky Jim*

Code :

	(a)	(b)	(c)	(d)
(1)	(iv)	(iii)	(i)	(ii)
(2)	(iv)	(iii)	(ii)	(i)
(3)	(iii)	(iv)	(i)	(ii)
(4)	(iii)	(i)	(ii)	(iv)

49. In the opening book of *The Prelude* Wordsworth mentions famously that he was "fostered alike by ________ and ________". Pick out the right pair.
(a) nature (b) fear
(c) imagination (d) beauty
The right combination according to the code is :
(1) (a) and (c) (2) (d) and (b)
(3) (d) and (c) (4) (a) and (d)

50. The title of Ngugi wa Thiong'o's *Petals of Blood* is derived from a poem by Derek Walcott. Identify the poem.
(1) "A Far Cry from Africa"
(2) "The Swamp"
(3) "Goats and Monkeys"
(4) "Midsummer"

✔ ANSWERS

1. (4)	**2.** (2)	**3.** (2)	**4.** (2)	**5.** (4)	**6.** (2)	**7.** (4)	**8.** (1)	**9.** (1)	**10.** (1)
11. (3)	**12.** (2)	**13.** (2)	**14.** (2)	**15.** (2)	**16.** (4)	**17.** (3)	**18.** (3)	**19.** (1)	**20.** (1)
21. (3)	**22.** (3)	**23.** (3)	**24.** (3)	**25.** (1)	**26.** (2)	**27.** (3)	**28.** (3)	**29.** (4)	**30.** (2)
31. (3)	**32.** (1)	**33.** (4)	**34.** (1,3)	**35.** (1)	**36.** (3)	**37.** (2)	**38.** (4)	**39.** (2)	**40.** (3)
41. (3)	**42.** (3)	**43.** (1)	**44.** (3)	**45.** (1)	**46.** (4)	**47.** (2)	**48.** (1)	**49.** (2)	**50.** (2)

November, 2017

ENGLISH LITERATURE

PAPER-III

Note : This paper contains seventy **five (75)** objective type questions of **two (2)** marks each. All questions are compulsory.

1. This Byron work revolves around a wife whose husband is presumed lost at sea and she takes a lover in his absence. Everybody behaves agreeably on the husband's return. Byron's technical skills in verse is in display here as the work counterpoints the colloquial and the formal. Identify the work :

(1) *Manfred*
(2) *Don Juan*
(3) *Beppo*
(4) *The Bride* of Abydos

2. Who is the author of the poem, "Our Casuarina Tree" ?

(1) *Sarojini Naidu*
(2) *Toru Dutt*
(3) *Rabindranath Tagore*
(4) *Kamala Das*

3. In this Jacobean play the Black King and his men, representing Spain and the Jesuits, are checkmated by the White Knight, Prince Charles. This political satire drew crowds to the Globe Theatre until the Spanish ambassador protested and James I suppressed the play. Identify the play :

(1) The Wonderful Yeare
(2) A Game at Chess
(3) A King and No King
(4) The Knight of the Burning Pestle

4. Frederic Jameson associated postmodern culture with __________ capitalism.

(1) market
(2) monopoly
(3) imperialist
(4) multinational

5. Early in Evelyn Waugh's *A Handful of Dust*, while Tony and his young son, John Andrew, walk to the church, John tells his father a story he has heard from the stable manager, Ben about a mule "who had drunk his company's rum ration" in the First World War and subsequently died. What is the mule named ?

(1) Peppermint (2) Dopey
(3) Dynamo (4) Pookey

6. The *Oxford English Dictionary* was published in twelve volumes with its current title in the year :

(1) 1928 (2) 1930
(3) 1933 (4) 1915

7. *The Life and Opinions of Tristram Shandy, Gentleman* is notorious for its many digressions across nine volumes and its failure to deliver a complete autobiography. In which volume does Tristram Shandy finally recount his birth ?

(1) Volume III
(2) Volume V
(3) Volume VIII
(4) Volume IX

8. Miguel de Cervantes's inimitable *Don Quixote*, foreshadows metafictional moorings when the novelist,

(a) says that the first chapters of the narrative are recreated from the Archive of La Mancha

(b) says that it is a faithful rendering of a Catalan text in Spanish
(c) says that part of it has been translated from the Arabic by the Moorish author Cide Hamete Benengeli
(d) says that he is rewriting the history of a medieval knight altering the heroic vein with a farcical mode

The right combination according to the code is :
(1) (a) and (b)
(2) (b) and (c)
(3) (a) and (c)
(4) (b) and (d)

9. In his theory of Mimesis, Plato says that all art is mimetic by nature; art is an imitation of life.
To argue his case he gives the example of a :
(1) cloud (2) chair
(3) tree (4) river

10. The translation of Geeta into English in 1784 called *Bhagvit - Geeta* marked, in William Jones's opinion, an "event that made it possible for the first time to have a reliable impression of Indian Literature". Who was the translator ?
(1) Charles Wilkins
(2) H. J. Colebrooke
(3) Rammohan Roy
(4) Nathaniel Halhed

11. One of the plays among the following contains the characters Coll, Gib, Dan and Mak. Identify the play :
(1) *Everyman*
(2) *The Castle of Perseverance*
(3) *The Second Shepherd's Play*
(4) *The Marshals*

12. Tereza, in Milan Kundera's novel *The Unbearable Lightness of Being*, troubled by Tomas's promiscuity, falls an easy prey to jealousy, fear and nightmares. Which of the following are the terrible dreams she has ?
(a) She dreams of cats attacking her.
(b) She dreams of wolves attacking her.
(c) She dreams that she is dead and buried in a common grave where she lies with the corpses of strangers.
(d) She dreams that she is dead, stripped of her clothes and plagued by other naked corpses.

The right combination according to the code is :
(1) (a) and (c)
(2) (a) and (d)
(3) (b) and (c)
(4) (b) and (d)

13. The opening lines of Wordsworth's "Immortality Ode":

"There was a time when meadow, grove, and stream,
The earth , and every common sight,
To me did seem
Apparelled in celestial light
The glory and freshness of a dream",

closely resembles Coleridge's lines :

"There was a time when earth, and sea, and skies,
The bright green vale, and the forest's dark recess,
With all things, lay before mine eyes
In steady loveliness".

Identify the Coleridge poem :
(1) "Fears In Solitude"
(2) "The Mad Monk"
(3) "To William Wordsworth"
(4) "Dejection : An Ode"

14. Christina Rossetti's "Goblin Market", a rare blend of allegory and fairytale world presents the story of two sisters, Laura and Lizzie. Which of the following is NOT true about the enchanted world that the poem unravels ?
(1) Laura buys fruits from the goblins in exchange of her "golden lock" of hair and a "tear more rare than pearl"

(2) Jeanie, a girl who ate the goblins' fruits, "pined away" and "sought them by night and day"
(3) Laura, who goes to the market again, does not see the goblins but hears only "their shrill cry piercing the air"
(4) Laura's hair "grew thin and grey" and she wanes like the full moon to "swift decay"

15. In which of these prisons is Defoe's character, Moll Flanders born ?
(1) Gatehouse
(2) King's Bench
(3) Newgate
(4) Ludgate

16. In which poem does Judith Wright lament the erasure of native culture in the following lines ?
"The song is gone; the dance
Is secret with the dancers in the earth,
The ritual useless, and the tribal story
Lost in an alien tale".
(1) "The Five Senses"
(2) "Legend"
(3) "Bullocky"
(4) "Bora Ring"

17. Years before, Winston Smith, the protagonist of George Orwell's dystopia, *Nineteen Eighty-Four* got an evidence of the party's dishonesty. What is it ?
(1) Emmanuel Goldstein's confession that he is a party operative; not an enemy of the party.
(2) O' Brien's diary entry hinting at the non-existence of Big Brother.
(3) A photograph which proves that some citizen accused of a crime was out of the country while it was committed.
(4) A colleague's revelation that the Inner Party members have systematically destroyed all historical documents and created false documents.

18. *The Indian Queen* is :
(1) a heroic tragedy in rhymed couplets by John Dryden
(2) a long poem in free verse by Keki Daruwalla
(3) an autobiography of an Indian princess in exile
(4) a fictional account of the Life of Maharani Gayatri Devi

19. In J. M. Coetzee's *Disgrace* David Lurie is working on an opera on the life of one of the Romantic poets. Who is the poet ?
(1) Blake (2) Shelley
(3) Byron (4) Coleridge

20. **Assertion (A) :** There is no unity or absolute source of the myth.
Reason (R) : The focus or the source of the myth are always shadows and virtualities which are elusive, unactualizable, and non-existent in the first place. Any search for the discursive unity in the myth is, therefore, misplaced.
In the context of the above statements :
(1) Both (A) and (R) are true and (R) is the correct explanation of (A)
(2) Both (A) and (R) are true but (R) is not the correct explanation of (A)
(3) (A) is true but (R) is false
(4) (A) is false, but (R) is true

21. Which of the following landscapes of England figures prominently in the poetry of Ted Hughes ?
(1) Cornish cliffs
(2) Dorset moors
(3) Yorkshire moors
(4) Chesil Beach

22. The title of M.C. Chagla's autobiography is:
(1) *Memoirs of my Working Life*
(2) *Without Fear or Favour*
(3) *Roses in December*
(4) *The Pen as My Sword*

23. Who/Which among the following gave the expression, "a leopard can't change its spots," to English language ?
(1) The King James Bible
(2) Geoffrey Chaucer
(3) Shakespeare
(4) The Royal Society

24. Which of the following is NOT true about Albert Camus's novel, *The Plague* ?
(1) Dr. Rieux describes the phenomenon of dying rats using the metaphors of disease, especially the bubonic plague.
(2) Paneloux interprets the plague in his first sermon as a sign of the Apocalypse.
(3) M. Michel is the first victim of the plague.
(4) Tarrou thinks that the plague symbolizes human indifference.

25. John Lydgate begins his *Siege of Thebes* with a prologue of 176 lines in which he imagines himself joining Chaucer's pilgrims in Canterbury, where he speaks with the Host and agrees to tell the first tale on homeward journey. The story that Lydgate tells as the pilgrims depart from Canterbury is meant to be a companion piece to :
(1) The Pardoner's Tale
(2) The Wife of Bath's Tale
(3) The Knight's Tale
(4) The Miller's Tale

26. Stephen Krashen's theory of second language acquisition consists of six main hypotheses. Which of the following is NOT one of them ?
(1) The Input Hypothesis
(2) The Affective Filter Hypothesis
(3) The Monitor Hypothesis
(4) The Writing Hypothesis

27. Among Derek Walcott's plays, which one is an exploration of colonial relationships through the Robinson Crusoe story ?
(1) *Pantomime*
(2) *Dream on Monkey Mountain*
(3) *Ti-Jean and His Brothers*
(4) *The Charlatan*

28. 'Anti - foundationalism' holds that :
(1) Every theory poses different questions and, therefore, what counts as 'fact' and 'truth' differs in every case.
(2) All truth claims can be judged true or false, usually against empirical facts.
(3) Causal statements about the relationship between dependent and independent variables can be made.
(4) Truth is the foundation of all representational experience.

29. The interaction hypothesis is a theory of second language acquisition which states that the development of language proficiency is promoted by face-to-face interaction and communication. The idea is usually credited to :
(1) David Nunan
(2) Michael Long
(3) Alastair Pennycook
(4) Claire Kramsch

30. In Pinter's *Birthday Party* Stanley is terrorised by two visitors to a seaside boarding house.
Identify the two
(a) McGrath
(b) Goldberg
(c) McCann
(d) Robinson
The right combination according to the code is :
(1) (a) and (b)
(2) (b) and (c)
(3) (a) and (d)
(4) (b) and (d)

31. Match the phrase to the ode :

(a) beechen green	(i) "Ode on a Grecian Urn"
(b) gathering swallows	(ii) "Ode on Melancholy"

(c) globed peonies (iii) "Ode to a Nightingale"

(d) green altar (iv) "To Autumn"

Code:

	(a)	(b)	(c)	(d)
(1)	(iii)	(ii)	(iv)	(i)
(2)	(iv)	(ii)	(iii)	(i)
(3)	(iv)	(iii)	(ii)	(i)
(4)	(iii)	(iv)	(ii)	(i)

32. Which 19th century novelist expressed a wish to "exterminate the race" of Indians following the 1857 Mutiny in India ?

(1) William Makepeace Thackeray
(2) Charles Dickens
(3) George Eliot
(4) Anthony Trollope

33. The second part of *Pilgrim's Progress* deals with the pilgrimage of Christian's wife, Christiana. She has a companion and a guide in this journey. Pick out the pair's names from the following list.

(a) Patience
(b) Tenderheart
(c) Mercy
(d) Greatheart

The right combination according to the code is :

(1) (c) and (d)
(2) (b) and (c)
(3) (a) and (d)
(4) (b) and (d)

34. In which play by Eugene Ionesco do you find the grotesque image of the leg of a corpse thrusting onto the stage, and, which begins to grow larger as the play progresses in a menacing manner ?

(1) *The Bald Soprano*
(2) *Amede or How to Get Rid of It*
(3) *Exit the King*
(4) *The Lesson*

35. Which of the following characters finds that complete happiness is elusive and that "while you are making the choice of life, you neglect to live" ?

(1) Lovelace in Samuel Richardson's *Clarissa*
(2) Rasselas in Samuel Johnson's *Rasselas*
(3) Matthew Bramble in Tobias Smollett's *Humphry Clinker*
(4) Harley in Henry Mackenzie's *The Man of Feeling*

36. Arrange the following in the chronological order of publication :

(1) *In Memoriam - A Christmas Carol - Men and Women - Henry Esmond*
(2) *A Christmas Carol - In Memoriam - Men and Women - Henry Esmond*
(3) *A Christmas Carol - In Memoriam - Henry Esmond - Men and Women*
(4) *In Memoriam - A Christmas Carol - Henry Esmond - Men and Women*

37. Which one of Alice Munro's short stories is about the domestic erosions of Alzheimer's disease ?

(1) "Dear Life"
(2) "Runaway"
(3) "The Bear Came Over the Mountain"
(4) "Dance of the Happy Shades"

38. What work begins thus : "It befell in the days of Uther Pendragon, when he was king of all England, and so reigned, that there was a mighty duke in Cornwall that held war against him long time" ?

(1) *Sir Gawain and the Green Knight*
(2) *Le Morte D'arthur*
(3) *Confessio Amantis*
(4) *Piers Plowman*

39. ________ is the subject of Asif Currimbhoy's play, *Inquilab*.

(1) The Naxalite movement
(2) The Freedom movement
(3) The Non-Cooperation movement
(4) The Khilafat movement

40. Tom Stoppard's play *Rosencrantz and Guildenstern are Dead*, being metatheatrical, lays bare the constructed nature of theatrical performance. In referring to *Hamlet's* end and the Elizabethan stage conditions lacking curtains one of the characters of Stoppard's play says :

"No one gets up after death - there is no applause - there is only silence and some second hand clothes, and that's death". Who makes this statement ?

(1) Rosencrantz
(2) Guildenstern
(3) The Player
(4) Hamlet

41. Who among the following, has translated the classic Malayalam novel, Chemmeen ?

(1) A. K. Ramanujan
(2) Anita Nair
(3) Nandini Nopany
(4) Gita Krishnankutty

42. Which Victorian poet is the author of the following lines ?

"God himself is the best Poet,
And the Real is His song."

(1) Lord Tennyson
(2) Robert Browning
(3) Matthew Arnold
(4) Elizabeth Barrett Browning

43. "You are your words. Your listeners see
Written on your face the poems they hear
Like letters carved in a tree's bark
The sight and sounds of solitudes endured".

These are lines from a poem by ___________ on the death of ___________.

(1) T. S. Eliot ; Robert Frost
(2) Siegfried Sassoon ; Wilfred Owen
(3) Stephen Spender ; W. H. Auden
(4) Dylan Thomas ; Robert Bridges

44. Allen Ginsberg's "Howl", a key work of the Beat Movement, was dedicated to

(1) Lucien Carr
(2) Carl Solomon
(3) Herbert Huncke
(4) Jack Kerouac

45. In his views on the death of Cordelia in *King Lear*, which is the ground NOT specifically cited by Samuel Johnson ?

(1) It is contrary to the natural ideas of justice.
(2) It is contrary to neoplatonic idea of decorum.
(3) It is contrary to the hope of the reader.
(4) It is contrary to the faith of chronicles.

46. Which of the following plays by David Hare is NOT part of a trilogy of 'state of the nation' plays ?

(1) *The Absence of War*
(2) *Racing Demon*
(3) *The Power of Yes*
(4) *Murmuring Judges*

47. Chimamanda Adichie's last novel, *Americanah* (2013) centres on the romantic and existential struggles of a young Nigerian woman studying in the United States and finding success as a blogger. What is her blogging about ?

(1) poverty
(2) development
(3) race
(4) religion

48. Why does Father Dolan punish Stephen with the pandybat in Joyce's *Portrait of the Artist as a young Man* ?

(1) Stephen is talking to another student to get the answer to a Latin problem.
(2) Stephen is not doing his work because his glasses are broken.
(3) Stephen is looking out of the window towards the infirmary.
(4) Stephen is lost in remembering his mother's farewell and cannot hear Father Dolan calling out his name.

49. Using a non-linear narrative, this American novel explores the psychic damage to a veteran of World War II and shows how a measure of healing is attained through his acceptance of Laguna myths and rituals. Identify the work :

(1) *Dred*
(2) *Beloved*
(3) *Ceremony*
(4) *End Zone*

50. What illusion does Lyuba Ranevsky in Anton Chekhov's play *The Cherry Orchard* have as she looks at the orchard ?

(1) She sees it gleaming with a bluish aura.
(2) She sees her dead mother walking through the orchard.
(3) She sees it full of ripe fruits without a trace of leaves.
(4) She sees her childhood friends playing in the orchard.

51. From which source did Swift get the idea of writing "Verses on the Death of Dr. Swift" ?

(1) In a conversation with John Gay
(2) After a reading of a maxim by la Rochefoucauld
(3) While taking a walk near Dublin's St. James's graveyard
(4) After reading Richard Burton's *Anatomy of Melancholy*

52. Two of the following words were borrowed from French after the Norman Conquest.

(a) mutton
(b) pork
(c) sheep
(d) swine

The right combination according to the code is :

(1) (a) and (b)
(2) (a) and (c)
(3) (b) and (d)
(4) (c) and (d)

53. Which of the following is NOT true regarding the *Oresteia* trilogy by Aeschylus ?

(1) Cassandra, cursed by Apollo predicts the death of Agamemnon, though her prophecy is ignored.
(2) Aegisthus's vengeful feelings for Agamemnon results from their rivalry for the hand of Clytemnestra.
(3) Orestes, who has come back with the intention of murdering Clytemnestra unexpectedly meets her, and pretending to be a stranger, tells her that Orestes is dead.
(4) Orestes, pursued by the Furies, flees from them when they fall asleep. Then, Clytemnestra's ghost appears to wake them up.

54. The first instance of female cross-dressing with the disconcerting nuances of a boy actor dressing as a boy while playing the role of a woman in the dramatic world of Shakespeare occurs in ________.

(1) *The Two Gentlemen of Verona*
(2) *As you Like It*
(3) *Twelfth Night*
(4) *A Midsummer Night's Dream*

55. For Coleridge, our power to perceive symbols gleaned from the world about us is related to the category of :

(1) primary imagination
(2) secondary imagination
(3) fancy
(4) intuition

56. After independence, although English was not an Indian language, it was accorded the status of an :

(1) Additional language
(2) Ancilliary language
(3) Associate language
(4) Administrative language

57. Which English journal announced that it was "principally intended for the use of Politick Persons who are so publick - spirited as to neglect their own Affairs to look into Transactions of State" but failed to live

up to this and amused readers with "accounts of Gallantry, Pleasure and Entertainment"?
(1) *The Spectator*
(2) *The Tatler*
(3) *The Daily Courant*
(4) *The Review*

58. The grammar-translation method of language teaching does NOT include :
(1) focus on grammar rules
(2) vocabulary memorization
(3) inductive teaching
(4) focus on written language

59. Who is the narrator in Kamala Markandaya's *Nectar in a Sieve*?
(1) Premala
(2) Saroja
(3) Rukmani
(4) Mira

60. How would a New Historicist critic interpret Derrida's statement, "there is nothing outside the text"?
(1) historicist critics should restrict their attention to a culture's literary productions, all other data is irrelevant to the critic's task
(2) language conditions the way we see the world, and there is no reality beyond the 'prison house' of language
(3) there is no meaning outside of textual meaning (contrary to the mimeticist's position)
(4) "literature" encompasses all cultural artifacts and all the values, power relations, and ways of seeing reflected in those artifacts; there is nothing outside of the "text" broadly conceived

61. Pick out two Austen heroines from the following list who are right-minded but neglected in the beginning but gradually are acknowledged to be correct by characters who have previously looked down on them.
(a) Elizabeth Bennet
(b) Fanny Price
(c) Emma Woodhouse
(d) Anne Elliot
The right combination according to the code is :
(1) (a) and (c)
(2) (b) and (d)
(3) (c) and (d)
(4) (a) and (d)

62. The variety of English used between non-native speakers who do not share a first language is called :
(1) English for specific purposes
(2) English for basic purposes
(3) English as a lingua Franca
(4) English as a language tool

63. Identify the story for which E. M. Forster wrote the libretto for its opera version :
(1) *Heart of Darkness*
(2) *The Man Who Would Be the King*
(3) *Billy Budd*
(4) *Death in Venice*

64. Who, among the following Prem Chand translators has NOT translated Godan ?
(1) Jai Ratan
(2) P. Lal
(3) Gordon C. Roadarmel
(4) Christopher R. King

65. "When Fred got into debt, it always seemed to him highly probable that something or other - he did not necessarily conceive what - would come to pass enabling him to pay in due time". Why is Fred Vincy in debt in *Middle march*?
(1) He takes out a large loan to enable him to woo Mary Garth.
(2) He is an inveterate gambler.
(3) He is paying off a blackmailer.
(4) He runs a charity that has got into trouble.

66. William Blake has a rare elan to provide telling images in arresting phrases. Match the phrases with the poems they belong to :

(a) "mind forg'd manacles" (i) "The Tyger"

(b) "eternal winter" (ii) "The Sick Rose"

(c) "fearful symmetry" (iii) "London"

(d) "crimson joy" (iv) "Holy Thursday"

Code :

	(a)	(b)	(c)	(d)
(1)	(ii)	(iv)	(i)	(iii)
(2)	(iii)	(i)	(iv)	(ii)
(3)	(iii)	(iv)	(i)	(ii)
(4)	(iv)	(i)	(ii)	(iii)

67. In the debate between the two birds in the Middle English poem The Owl and the Nightingale who acts as the arbiter ?

(1) Master Henry of Shrewsbury
(2) Master William of Hereford
(3) Master Freeman of Stamford
(4) Master Nicholas of Guildford

68. In the first scene in which Goethe's Faust appears he is dejected by the study of Philosophy, Law, Medicine and Theology, turns to Magic art to acquire infinite knowledge. But he fails and in desperation attempts to commit suicide, but refrains at the final moment. What prevents Faust from committing suicide ?

(1) The intervention of archangel Gabriel
(2) His attendant Wagner persuades him to revoke the decision
(3) The chirning of the bells announcing Easter festivities
(4) Mephistopheles appears and offers to initiate him into magic art

69. Which novel by Joseph Conrad presents a young captain who like Coleridge's Ancient Mariner is haunted by the "vision of a ship drifting in calm and swinging in light airs, with all the crew dying slowly about her decks" and who feels "the sickness of my soul... the weight of my sins... my sense of unworthiness" ?

(1) *Under Western Eyes*
(2) *The Shadow Line*
(3) *Victory*
(4) *The Rescue*

70. "Our almost-instinct almost true :
What will survive of us is love."
Identify the poem by Philip Larkin that ends with the above lines :

(1) "This Be the Verse"
(2) "An Arundel Tomb"
(3) "High Windows"
(4) "Next, Please"

71. In the epilogue to Congreve's *Way of the World* there is a warning :

Others there are whose malice we'd prevent,
Such, who watch plays, with scurrilous intent
To mark out who by characters are meant.
. . . .
These, with false glosses feed their own ill-nature,
And turn to libel, what was meant a satire.

What does this warning mean ?

(1) Critics should not be ill-natured and malicious.
(2) Critics should not look for portrait of real people in the play's characters and remember that the play is a social satire.
(3) Critics should avoid writing malicious reviews, lest they be charged with libel.
(4) Critics should try to identify the real-life equivalent for each character.

72. Which of the following is an elegy on John Donne's wife, who died in 1617 ?

(1) "Death, be not proud"
(2) "Thou hast made me"
(3) "Holy Sonnet 17"
(4) "At the round earth's imagined corners"

Read the following poem and answer questions, 73 to 75 :

Bored

Margaret Atwood

All those times I was bored
out of my mind. Holding the log
while he sawed it. Holding
the string while he measured, boards,
distances between things, or pounded
stakes into the ground for rows and rows
of lettuces and beets, which I then (bored)
weeded. Or sat in the back
of the car, or sat still in boats,
sat, sat, while at the prow, stern, wheel
he drove, steered, paddled. It
wasn't even boredom, it was looking,
looking hard and up close at the small
details. Myopia. The worn gunwales,
the intricate twill of the seat
cover. The acid crumbs of loam, the granular
pink rock, its igneous veins, the sea-fans
of dry moss, the blackish and then the graying
bristles on the back of his neck.
Sometimes he would whistle, sometimes
I would. The boring rhythm of doing
things over and over, carrying
the wood, drying
the dishes. Such minutiae. It's what
the animals spend most of their time at,
ferrying the sand, grain by grain, from their tunnels,
shuffling the leaves in their burrows. He pointed
such things out, and I would look
at the whorled texture of his square finger, earth under
the nail. Why do I remember it as sunnier
all the time then, although it more often
rained, and more birdsong?
I could hardly wait to get
the hell out of there to
anywhere else. Perhaps though
boredom is happier. It is for dogs or
groundhogs. Now I wouldn't be bored.
Now I would know too much.
Now I would know.

73. "All those times" - the opening words of the poem locate the speaker in :
(1) a city suburb
(2) a mountain resort
(3) a natural environment
(4) a highway motel

74. Which pair of words best describes the repetitive tenor of the speaker's unpretentious yet oppressive life ?
(a) details
(b) the car
(c) the wood
(d) the minutae

The right combination according to the code is :
(1) (a) and (b)
(2) (a) and (d)
(3) (b) and (c)
(4) (c) and (d)

75. Which of the following approximates closely a thematic statement of the poem ?
(1) Dogs or groundhogs lead a better life than men or women
(2) Irrespective of the place, the boring rhythm of doing things over and over in human life cannot be escaped
(3) Myopia is the result if you live life in the lap of nature
(4) Knowledge cures existential boredom

ANSWERS

1. (3)	**2.** (2)	**3.** (2)	**4.** (4)	**5.** (1)	**6.** (3)	**7.** (1)	**8.** (3)	**9.** (2)	**10.** (1)
11. (3)	**12.** (2)	**13.** (2)	**14.** (3)	**15.** (3)	**16.** (4)	**17.** (3)	**18.** (1)	**19.** (3)	**20.** (1)
21. (3)	**22.** (3)	**23.** (1)	**24.** (2)	**25.** (3)	**26.** (4)	**27.** (1)	**28.** (1)	**29.** (2)	**30.** (2)
31. (4)	**32.** (2)	**33.** (1)	**34.** (2)	**35.** (2)	**36.** (3)	**37.** (3)	**38.** (2)	**39.** (1)	**40.** (2)
41. (2)	**42.** (4)	**43.** (3)	**44.** (2)	**45.** (2)	**46.** (3)	**47.** (3)	**48.** (2)	**49.** (3)	**50.** (2)
51. (2)	**52.** (1)	**53.** (2)	**54.** (1)	**55.** (1)	**56.** (3)	**57.** (2)	**58.** (3)	**59.** (3)	**60.** (4)
61. (2)	**62.** (3)	**63.** (3)	**64.** (4)	**65.** (2)	**66.** (3)	**67.** (4)	**68.** (3)	**69.** (2)	**70.** (2)
71. (2)	**72.** (3)	**73.** (3)	**74.** (2)	**75.** (2)					

July, 2018

ENGLISH LITERATURE

PAPER-II

Note : This paper contains **hundred (100)** objective type questions of **two (2)** marks each. **All** questions are **compulsory**.

1. Which narrative poem by Lord Tennyson presents the story of a fisherman turned merchantsailor who, after a shipwreck, is marooned on a desert island ?
(1) "Crossing the Bar" (2) "Tithonus"
(3) "Enoch Arden" (4) "Maud"

2. In "Memorial Verses" Matthew Arnold pays tribute to three great poets. Who are they ?
(1) Goethe, Shakespeare, Wordsworth
(2) Goethe, Shakespeare, Milton
(3) Shakespeare, Milton, Wordsworth
(4) Goethe, Wordsworth, Byron

3. Who among the following English playwrights wrote screenplays on novels such as Marcel Proust's *In Search of Lost Time*, John Fowles's *French Lieutenant's Woman*, and Margaret Atwood's *Handmaid's Tale* ?
(1) John Arden (2) Edward Bond
(3) Harold Pinter (4) David Hare

4. The years in English literary history between 1649 and 1660 are known as ________.
(1) the Neo-classical period
(2) the Commonwealth period
(3) the Stuart period
(4) the Jacobean period

5. In R.K. Narayan's Swami and Friends, which game offers Swami the best kind of emotional release from the strains and pressures of disagreeable circumstances ?
(1) cricket (2) football
(3) tennis (4) hockey

6. William Blake expressed the importance of the particular when he said that "To Generalize is to be ________. To particularize is the alone Distinction of Merit." Fill in the blank.
(1) an idiot (2) a poet
(3) a dreamer (4) a skunk

7. Which of the following was not a dialect of Old English ?
(1) Irish (2) Northumbrian
(3) Mercian (4) Kentish

8. Anthony Burgess's last novel, published in 1993, is called A Dead Man in Deptford. Who is the central character to whom the title refers ?
(1) Sir Walter Raleigh (2) Sir Philip Sidney
(3) Christopher Marlowe
(4) Earl of Southampton

9. Choose the correct chronological order :
(1) William Caxton prints the first English book - William Shakespeare's First Folio - John Milton's *Areopagitica* - "Tottel's Miscellany" (*Songs and Sonnets*).
(2) "Tottel's Miscellany" (*Songs and Sonnets*) - William Shakespeare's First Folio - William Caxton prints the first English book - John Milton's *Areopagitica*.
(3) William Caxton prints the first English book - "Tottel's Miscellany" (*Songs and Sonnets*) - William Shakespeare's First Folio - John Milton's *Areopagitica*.
(4) William Shakespeare's First Folio - John Milton's *Areopagitica* - William Caxton prints the first English book - "Tottel's Miscellany" (*Songs and Sonnets*).

10. What does the phrase ut pictura poesis from *Horace's Art of Poetry* mean ?
(1) "as in painting, so in poetry".
(2) "poetry beggars pictorial description".
(3) "as in poetry, so in painting".
(4) "picture above all poetry".

11. Who among the following is the author of Account of the *Augustan Age in England* (1759) ?

(1) John Gay (2) William Hazlitt
(3) Oliver Goldsmith
(4) Samuel Johnson

12. In how many parts did Cervantes publish his novel, *Don Quixote* ?

(1) three (2) five
(3) two (4) twelve

13. Lytton Strachey's *Eminent Victorians* carries biographical sketches of writers and public figures. Identify the list below that correctly mentions those Eminent Victorians.

(1) Cardinal Manning, Florence Nightingale, Thomas Arnold and General Gordon.
(2) A.E.W. Mason, Sir Arthur Quiller Couch, Matthew Arnold, Robert Bridges.
(3) E.F. Benson, Cardinal Manning, Lord Tennyson, Beatrice Webb.
(4) George Harding, General Gordon, Robert Browning, Mrs Humphrey Ward.

14. One of the following statements about the eponymous saint of Dryden's "Song for St. Cecilia's Day" is incorrect. Identify that statement.

(1) St. Cecilia was a Roman lady, an early Christian martyr.
(2) St. Cecilia was an Armenian devotee of the Christian faith.
(3) St. Cecilia's festival is celebrated on 22 November in England.
(4) St. Cecilia was a patroness of music who was fabled to have invented the organ.

15. Which of the statements on Michael Roberts's Faber Book of Modern Verse (1936) is not true ?

(1) His anthology canonized modern poetry and poets for quite some decades.
(2) The collection begins with the poems of Robert Bridges.
(3) Roberts omitted the Georgian poets in his anthology.
(4) Yeats, Eliot and Pound find a place in the Faber Book of 1936.

16. Who among the following proposed that the First Gulf War had never taken place, it was simply a hyperreal, media-generated spectacle ?

(1) Richard Rorty
(2) Jean-Francois Lyotard
(3) Jean Baudrillard (4) Umberto Eco

17. Sir Thomas Browne's *Urn Burial* was prompted by __________.

(1) the discovery of ancient burial-urns near Norwich.
(2) the contemporary researches on burial rites in Norway.
(3) the death of St. Francis of Assissi and his burial.
(4) the publication of the *English Book of Common Prayer*.

18. Identify from among the following list those that cannot be called War Fiction.

(a) *A Modern Instance*
(b) *Catch - 22*
(c) *The Age of Innocence*
(d) *The Naked and the Dead*

(1) (a) and (d) (2) (b) and (c)
(3) (a) and (c) (4) (b) and (d)

19. Who among the following writers was not the one identified with The Movement of the 1950's England ?

(1) Roy Fuller (2) Kingsley Amis
(3) Philip Larkin (4) Donald Davie

20. Which of the following novels does not belong to Nuruddin Farah's Blood In the Sun Trilogy ?

(1) *Maps* (2) *Knots*
(3) *Gifts* (4) *Secrets*

21. In the following series, which one has all the poets correctly matched with their poems ?

(1) Ezekiel, "Poet, Lover, Birdwatcher"; Ramanujan, "Small-scale Reflections on a Great House"; Dutt, "Sunset at Puri"; Mahapatra, "Our Casuarina Tree".
(2) Ezekiel, "Sunset at Puri"; Ramanujan, "Small-scale Reflections on a Great House"; Dutt, "Our Casuarina Tree"; Mahapatra, "Poet, Lover, Birdwatcher".

(3) Ezekiel, "Poet, Lover, Birdwatcher"; Ramanujan, "Sunset at Puri"; Dutt, "Our Casuarina Tree"; Mahapatra, "Small-scale Reflections on a Great House".

(4) Ezekiel, "Poet, Lover, Birdwatcher"; Ramanujan, "Small-scale Reflections on a Great House"; Dutt, "Our Casuarina Tree"; Mahapatra, "Sunset at Puri".

22. From among the following, identify the incorrect observation regarding Ferdinand de Saussure's seminal distinction between langue and parole.

(1) Parole is the particular language system, the elements of which we learn as children, and which is codified in our grammars and dictionaries, whereas langue is the language-occasion (what A says to B).

(2) A language consists in the interrelationship between langue and parole.

(3) Saussure made this crucial distinction in a study called A Course in General Linguistics (1916).

(4) Langue is the particular language-system, the elements of which we learn as children, and which is codified in our grammars and dictionaries, whereas parole is the language-occasion (what A says to B).

23. John Heywood wrote a farcical interlude called *The Four P's*. Who were the Four P's?

(1) a Palmer, a Pedlar, a Pothecary, a Packer
(2) a Printer, a Pedlar, a Pothecary, a Palmer
(3) a Pedlar, a Parson, a Palmer, a Pothecary
(4) a Palmer, a Pardoner, a Pothecary, a Pedlar

24. In the mechanical drill method of second language acquisition :

(a) The learner has the freedom to choose from many responses.
(b) The learner's response is totally controlled.
(c) Comprehension of the item by the learner is not required.
(d) Comprehension of the item by the learner is obligatory.

The right combination according to the code is :

(1) (a) and (d) (2) (a) and (c)
(3) (b) and (c) (4) (b) and (d)

25. Thou wilt not wake
Till I thy fate shall overtake;
Till age, or grief, or sickness must
Marry my body to that dust
It so much loves; and fill the room
My heart keeps empty in thy Tomb.
Stay for me there; I will not fail
To meet thee in that hollow Vale.
And think not much of my delay;
I am already on the way.

Which of the following readings do you find appropriate to the spirit of the lines above ?

(1) In that interspace between the lines, the ending of one and the beginning of another, there is a silent internal language, the poem's language-within-language, tacitly signalled through the deployment of rhymed space.

(2) Ageing and dying are of course helplessly passive; but here love makes them as though they were now also willing things in the husband eager to join his dead wife. Through simple intimate tones of their shared earthly life - stay for me, wait for me, I will not fail - he not only imagines her but imagines her thinking of him.

(3) The lyric voice here can feel the poem speaking back to him - in the cold lineal stare of 'there was nothing in my belief' - even as his dead wife did not. It is as though the poem itself then demands his response, in order to be able to move from one line to another. To attempt that movement in keeping the poem's space alive, the lyric voice asserts, "I will not fail/To meet there in that hollow Vale."

(4) My whole nature was so penetrated with grief and humiliation of such considerations, that, even now, famous and caressed and happy as I am, I often forget in my dream that I have a dear wife who died, leaving me alone in this world. Even that I am a man, and now I wander desolately back to that time of

our lives when my wife and I shared moments of bliss.

26. Match the characters with the novels :

(a) Arthur Seaton (i) Top Girls

(b) Marlene (ii) The Golden Note-book

(c) Anna Wulf (iii) The Swimming Pool Library

(d) Beckwith (iv) Saturday Night and Sunday Morning

Code :

	(a)	(b)	(c)	(d)		(a)	(b)	(c)	(d)
(1)	(ii)	(iii)	(i)	(iv)	(2)	(iv)	(i)	(ii)	(iii)
(3)	(iii)	(iv)	(ii)	(i)	(4)	(ii)	(iv)	(iii)	(i)

27. The very last passage of a novel is given below. Identify the novel.

"Welcome, O life, I go to encounter for the millionth time the reality of experience and to forge in the smithy of my soul the uncreated conscience of my race.

April 27. Old father, old artificer, stand me now and ever in good stead."

(1) *To the light house*
(2) *A Portrait of the Artist as a Young Man*
(3) *Maurice*
(4) *Almayer's Folly*

28. Francis Bacon's New Atlantis is about a utopian state called ________.

(1) Asgard (2) Avalon
(3) Bensalem (4) Baltia

29. The 1950's saw the rise of backlash against modernism and against New Romanticism that became known as The Movement. Which of the following little magazines came to be associated with The Movement ?

(a) *Departure* (b) *New Verse*
(c) *London Mercury* (d) *New Poems*

The right combination according to the code is :

(1) (a) and (b) (2) (c) and (d)
(3) (a) and (d) (4) (b) and (d)

30. The error of interpreting a literary work by referring to evidence outside of itself, such as the design and purpose of the author is called ________.

(1) Affective fallacy
(2) Intentional fallacy
(3) Authorial fallacy
(4) Synecdochic fallacy

31. A.R. Ammons parodies a famous poem in his "Swoggled"

I'd rather
be
suckled by
an
outworn pagan
than
get my horn
wreathed in
an
old triton.

Which poet, which poem ?

(1) John Keats, "On First Looking into Chapman's Homer"
(2) John Milton, "On His Blindness"
(3) William Wordsworth, "The World is Too Much with Us"
(4) Elizabeth B. Browning, "How do I Love Thee... ?"

32. Fanny Burney's Evelina carries the subtitle:

(1) *or a Naive Lady's Entrance into the World*
(2) *or a Young Lady's Entrance into the World*
(3) *or a Young Lady's Exit from the World*
(4) *or a Bold Lady's Entrance into the Hall*

33. What does Philip Sidney call poet-haters in his *Defence of Poesie* ?

(1) misogynists (2) misanthropes
(3) misnomers (4) mysomousoi

34. Who, among the following, raises the following painful question of longing and belonging ? "Where shall I turn, divided to the vein ?
I who have cursed
The drunken officer of British rule, how choose
Between this Africa and the English tongue I love ?"

(1) Derek Walcott (2) Louise Bennett
(3) Kamau Brathwaite (4) Wole Soyinka

35. In the 1940's, a critic and a philosopher produced two influential and controversial

papers called "The Intentional Fallacy" and "The Affective Fallacy". Identify them.

(a) Cleanth Brooks
(b) Monroe C. Beardsley
(c) William K. Wimsalt Jr.
(d) R.P. Blackmur

The right combination according to the code is :

(1) (a) and (b) (2) (b) and (d)
(3) (b) and (c) (4) (c) and (d)

36. Philip Larkin's "Sad Steps" notices "The way the moon dashes through clouds that blow
Loosely as cannon-smoke to stand apart...."
The poem alludes to :

(1) Coleridge's "Dejection : An Ode"
(2) The moonlit scenes in *A Midsummer Night's Dream*
(3) Philip Sidney's *Astrophel and Stella*
(4) T.S. Eliot's *"Morning at the Window"*

37. Match the following opening lines with their respective titles :

(a) "I leant upon a coppice gate"	(i) "Thirteen Blackbirds"
(b) "A sudden blow: the great wings beating still...."	(ii) "Sympathy"
(c) "Among twenty snowy mountains"	(iii) "The Darkling Thrush"
(d) "I know what the caged bird feels, alas..."	(iv) "Leda and the Swan"

Code :

	(a)	(b)	(c)	(d)		(a)	(b)	(c)	(d)
(1)	(iv)	(iii)	(ii)	(i)	(2)	(iii)	(iv)	(i)	(ii)
(3)	(ii)	(i)	(iii)	(iv)	(4)	(i)	(ii)	(iv)	(iii)

38. Identify the titles that were published in the 1920's.

(a) *Look, Stranger!* (b) *The Tower*
(c) *The Waste Land*
(d) *The Road to Wigan Pier*

Code :

(1) (a) and (c) (2) (b) and (c)
(3) (b) and (d) (4) (c) and (d)

39. This novel is dedicated "To the railroad of bones" and has as its epigraph the line, "I am the woman they give dead women's clothes to" from Christine Gelineau's "Inheritance".
Identify the novel.

(1) *African Psycho* by Alain Mabanckou
(2) *The Chibok Girls* by Helon Habila
(3) *The Underground Railroad* by Colson Whitehead
(4) *The Book of Night Women* by Marlon James

40. An English poet couldn't help the excitement that an historical event caused in his life-time :
Bliss was it in that dawn to be alive,
But to be young was very heaven.
Which poet ? What "dawn" ?

(1) W.H. Auden ; the Spanish Civil War
(2) Lord Tennyson ; the Jubilee of Queen Victoria's reign
(3) William Wordsworth ; the French Revolution
(4) William Blake ; the Industrial Revolution

41. Which novel by John Banville tells the story of a group of travellers who arrive on a small island and stumble upon the house of Prof. Kreutznaer whose relationship to a painting entitled *The Golden World* by a fictional Dutch artist named Vaublin plays a central role ?

(1) *Ghosts* (2) *The Sea*
(3) *The Ark* (4) *Eclipse*

42. Identify the two plays, usually paired for their critique of the politics of language and acts of police interrogation.

(1) *Earthly Powers, The Wanting Seed*
(2) *Chicken Soup with Barley, Roots*
(3) *Left-handed Liberty, The Hero Rises*
(4) *One for the Road, Mountain Language*

43. Semiotics originated mainly in the works of two theorists. They are :

(a) Charles Sanders Peirce
(b) Mikhail Bakhtin

(c) Ferdinand de Saussure
(d) Valentin Voloshinov

The right combination according to the code is ________.

(1) (a) and (b) (2) (b) and (c)
(3) (a) and (c) (4) (c) and (d)

44. Robert Burton's Anatomy of Melancholy was published in 1621 and expanded and altered in ________ subsequent editions.

(1) two (2) four
(3) six (4) five

45. Which of the following magazines self-consciously created an identity for Vorticists, a group of painters, sculptors and writers ?

(1) Blast (2) The Egoist
(3) The Criterion (4) New Age

46. "In every cry of every Man,
In every Infant's cry of fear,
In every voice, in every ban..."

The figure of speech characterized by repetition of words or group of words at the beginning of consecutive sentences is called ________.

(1) apostrophe (2) anaphora
(3) incremental repetition
(4) alliteration

47. At whose behest does the Redcrosse Knight undertake his quest in *The Faerie Queene* ?

(1) Gloriana's (2) Una's
(3) Duessa's (4) Prosperine's

48. In which city did John Ruskin see a paradigm for Victorian Britain ?

(1) Vienna (2) Venice
(3) Rome (4) Paris

49. Which novel of Kazuo Ishiguro is narrated by a Japanese widow living in England and draws on the destruction and rehabilitation of Nagasaki ?

(1) *An Artist of the Floating World*
(2) *The Unconsoled*
(3) *A Pale View of Hills*
(4) *When We Were Orphans*

50. Which novel opens thus :
"Whether I shall turn out to be the hero of my own life, or whether that station will be held by anyone else, these pages must show."

(1) *Tristram Shandy*
(2) *Lady Audley's Secret*
(3) *David Copperfield*
(4) *Fitz-Boodle's Confessions*

51. Traces of the Morality plays are discernible in a play like Dr. Faustus, traces such as __.

(1) vernacular songs adapting secular themes
(2) its soliloquizing protagonist, Good and Bad Angels and its final moral
(3) its refrains from the Corpus Christi Carol, the complaint of Christ, the lover of mankind
(4) its rhythmical prose, and the presence of a larger narrative rhythm in the Morality plays

52. The branch of philosophy that asks the question, 'How do we know what we know ?' is ________.

(1) ontology (2) epistemology
(3) eschatology (4) phenomenology

53. The eighteenth century practice in England of bookselling was midway between direct patronage and impersonal sales. A patron paid half the cost of a book before publication and half on delivery. The author of the book received these payments directly. The patron's name appeared in the preface for the book published in this manner.
This practice was known as ________.

(1) Subscription (2) Contribution
(3) Pre-publication (4) Remaindering

54. Oxford India has published a volume of Premchand translations in English, The Oxford India Premchand. Who among the following is not one of the translators ?

(1) David Rubin (2) Alok Rai
(3) Gillian Wright (4) Christopher King

55. Which of the two novels of Jane Austen have the spa town of Bath as a primary location ?

(a) *Emma* (b) *Pride and Prejudice*
(c) *Northanger Abbey* (d) *Persuasion*

The right combination according to the code is :

(1) (a) and (d) (2) (b) and (c)
(3) (c) and (d) (4) (a) and (b)

56. In the communicative approach to ELT, the development of language learning or teaching involves a shift :

(a) from form-based to a meaning-based approach.
(b) from an eclectic approach to a rigid method.
(c) from teacher-centred to learner-centred classes.
(d) from broad-based competence to specific needs.

The right combination, according to the Code is :

(1) (b) and (d) (2) (a) and (d)
(3) (b) and (c) (4) (a) and (c)

57. The four *Moral Essays* of Alexander Pope are addressed to carefully selected figures. Identify the correct group.

(1) Timons, Newton, Martha Blount, Wellington
(2) Lord Cobham, Robert Walpole, Houghton Hall, Chandos
(3) Martha Blount, Lord Cobham, Bathurst, Burlington
(4) William III, John Haydn, Joseph Addison, John Dennis

58. Bertolt Brecht's *Mother Courage and Her Children* presents the war-torn Europe as its protagonist as she follows troops with her canteenwagon.

What is the real name of Mother Courage ?

(1) Paula Danckert (2) Anna Fierling
(3) Jane Vanstone (4) Jani Lauzon

59. From among the following, identify the journal that publishes articles on English language teaching and learning.

(1) *University of Toronto Quarterly*
(2) *Agenda*
(3) *TESOL Quarterly*
(4) *English Language Notes*

60. Arrange the following elegies in English in chronological order.

(1) "Elegy Written in a Country Churchyard" - "Adonais" - "Thyrsis" - "In Memoriam"
(2) "Elegy Written in a Country Churchyard" - "Adonais" - "In Memoriam" - "Thyrsis"
(3) "Elegy Written in a Country Churchyard" - "In Memoriam" - "Adonais" - "Thyrsis"
(4) "Adonais" - "Elegy Written in a Country Churchyard" - "In Memoriam" - "Thyrsis"

61. Who is the only one of Milton's contemporaries to be mentioned by name in *Paradise Lost* ?

(1) Francis Bacon (2) Johannes Vermeer
(3) Gallileo (4) King Charles 1

62. K.S. Maniam is a major writer of Indian origin, writing in English, born and living in Malaysia. Identify two of his novels from the following list.

(a) *The Rice Mother* (b) *The Return*
(c) *Touching Earth* (d) *Between Lives*

The right combination according to the code is :

(1) (a) and (d) (2) (b) and (c)
(3) (c) and (d) (4) (b) and (d)

63. What did Thomas Percy collect in his Reliques ?

(1) medieval folklore and lyrics of the Midlands
(2) old songs, ballads, and romances in English and Scots
(3) Highland lore, mostly oral wisdom of the Scots
(4) Romantic idylls, sonnets and odes

64. Nirad Chaudhuri's *Autobiography of an Unknown Indian* concludes with an essay on the course of Indian history. But in the penultimate chapter Chaudhuri concludes the account of events in his life. How does this narrative end ?

(1) Chaudhuri ties the knot with his childhood sweetheart and moves from Calcutta to Delhi
(2) Chaudhuri obtains a job in the military accounts department and gives it up because he finds it soul-destroying
(3) Chaudhuri joins the editorial team of a Calcutta newspaper and is upset over the drudgery of a reporter's life.

(4) Chaudhuri rushes to his ancestral village Bangram on receiving the news of the death of his uncle and recalls his past life.

65. In John Gower's Confessio Amantis, Amans, the lover makes his confession to the priest named ________.

(1) Verito (2) Genius
(3) Amor (4) Phoebe

66. In Eugene Ionesco's Chairs, the absurdity is not so much in the banal words that are uttered as ________.

(1) in the large scale use of frightening stage props and lightning effects.
(2) in the absurdist interpretation of them by character after character.
(3) in the fact that they are spoken to an ever-growing number of empty chairs.
(4) in the fact that they are spoken time and again by members of the audience.

67. A half-sentence in *Purchas his Pilgrimage* triggered off "Kubla Khan". Whose work was *Purchas his Pilgrimage*?

(1) Robert Herrick, the poet's
(2) John Hakluyt's, the collector of traveller's tales
(3) Samuel Purchas, the London Parson's
(4) Edward Purchas, the globe-trotter's

68. Based on the life of a thirteenth-century troubadour, from among the following identify the work, that marked a catastrophic failure in Robert Browning's poetic career, earning him a reputation for impenetrable difficulty?

(1) *Paracelsus* (2) *Sordello*
(3) *The Ring and The Book*
(4) *Pauline*

69. In Tristram Shandy, the Author's preface__

(1) is hawked to the highest bidder.
(2) appears in-between chapters 13 and 14 in Volume II.
(3) is printed in italics in all editions.
(4) appears in-between chapters 10 and 11 in Volume I.

70. Evelyn Waugh once complained that T.S. Eliot's Poems, 1909-1925 was "marvellously good, but very hard to understand." The most pessimistic novel Waugh wrote was called ______ and he owed the title to _____.

(1) *Black Mischief* - "Sweeney among the Nightingales"
(2) *Scoop* - "Morning At the Window"
(3) *Prancing Nigger* - *Ash Wednesday*
(4) *A Handful of Dust* - *The Waste Land*

71. During the years 1830 to 1850, the illusion of peace in Victorian England was broken by such incidents as ______.

(1) the Revolution in France and the Chartist Movement in England
(2) the General Strike of 1835 and the Rail Tragedy of 1847
(3) the visionary libertarianism of poets and the lawless embodiment of revolution
(4) the disaster of the Indian Mutiny and the incompetent bungling of the Crimean War

72. Gulliver receives the following response when he boasts about his countrymen:
"... the most pernicious race of little odious vermin that nature ever suffered to crawl upon the face of the earth." Whose response?

(1) The King of Lilliput's
(2) The King of Brobdingnag's
(3) The Governor of Glubbdubrib's
(4) The first of the Houyhnhnms's he meets

73. In the *Inferno* Dante, as he travels through the various circles of the hell finds Judas who is unable to speak. What is the reason behind this?

(1) His tongue is transformed into a coiled snake.
(2) His head is battered and so he cannot open his mouth.
(3) Lucifer is chewing on his head.
(4) His tongue is pulled out and nailed on the tree of sin.

74. **Assertion (A) :** Our reality is linguistic, a language mediated reality.

Reason (R) : Our perception and understanding of reality are largely constructed by the words and other signs we use.

In the light of the statements above,

(1) Both (A) and (R) are true and (R) is the correct explanation of (A).
(2) Both (A) and (R) are true, but (R) is not the correct explanation of (A).
(3) (A) is true but (R) is false.
(4) (A) is false but (R) is true.

75. In his book, In Theory, Aijaz Ahmed works out the relations between the three entities :
(1) Classes, Nations, Literatures
(2) Regions, Nation, Languages
(3) State, Religions, Gender
(4) Literature, Print, Theory

76. In 1660, a group of 12 people including Robert Boyle and Christopher Wren formed what they called the Royal Society. In 1663, it became The Royal Society of London for Improving Natural Knowledge. What was the Society's motto ?
(1) "In Him we trust"
(2) "In the words of no one"
(3) "Lighted to lighten"
(4) "Love conquers all"

77. Of whom did W.B. Yeats say that "We were the last Romantics" ?
(1) The Pre-Raphaelite Brotherhood
(2) The Imagiste poets
(3) His Friends in the Irish Literary Revival
(4) Himself and his lady love, Maud Gonne

78. Who wrote *The Wandering Jew*, a poem in four cantos and the short lyric, "The Wandering Jew's Soliloquy" ?
(1) S.T. Coleridge (2) Lord Byron
(3) Thomas Gray (4) P.B. Shelley

79. Where, according to T.S. Eliot, are we likely to find "not only the best, but the most individual parts of a poet's work" ?
(1) in the poet's juvenilia or rejected drafts.
(2) in the best anthologies and scrap-books.
(3) in those parts where the dead poets assert their immortality.
(4) in those parts where the living poets depart from their ancestors.

80. Which of the following is true of *The Canterbury Tales* ?
(1) Chaucer, the pilgrim, narrates *Sir Thopas' Tale* only.
(2) Chaucer, the pilgrim, narrates *The Tale of Melibee* only.
(3) Chaucer, the pilgrim, narrates both *Sir Thopas' Tale* and *The Tale of Melibee.*
(4) Chaucer, the pilgrim does attempt to narrate an unnamed tale but abruptly stops due to the intervention of the other pilgrims.

81. During the reign of Norman Kings, it was fashionable to speak __________ in upper-class circles in England.
(1) Norse (2) Latin
(3) Danish (4) French

82. Who, among the following, collaborated with Purohit Swami in translating the Ten Principal Upanishads into English ?
(1) Christopher Fry (2) Aldous Huxley
(3) Lawrence Durrell (4) W.B. Yeats

83. What unique distinction does Ben Jonson's "To Penshurst" have in the English literary canon ?
(1) It is the only distinguished poem in English addressed to the Lords of Penshurst.
(2) It celebrates Philip Sidney's elevation to knighthood, Sidney being the youngest scion of the family.
(3) It is one of the first English poems celebrating a specific place, a forerunner to *Cooper's Hill* and *Windsor-Forest*.
(4) It is the first poem in an elegiac series that late Elizabethan poets began on the demise of the Lord of Penshurst.

84. It is well known that in many of his plays, Tom Stoppard has consciously drawn upon earlier, often reputed, works. Match the following Stoppard plays with earlier works whose spirit seems to have informed them.

(a) *Rosencrantz and Guildenstern Are Dead* (i) *Hamlet*
(b) *Indian Ink* (ii) *A Passage to India*
(c) *Inspector Hound* (iii) *The Mousetrap*

(d) *Travesties* (iv) *Importance of Being Earnest*

Code :

	(a)	(b)	(c)	(d)		(a)	(b)	(c)	(d)
(1)	(iii)	(ii)	(i)	(iv)	(2)	(i)	(ii)	(iv)	(iii)
(3)	(iv)	(iii)	(i)	(ii)	(4)	(ii)	(i)	(iv)	(iii)

85. After discovering the truth about his heinous crimes committed in the past, what does Oedipus request as his punishment ?
(1) exile (2) castration
(3) decapitation (4) blindness

86. How does *Women in Love* open ?
(1) Rupert Birkin, Lawrence's alter ego, is taking a walk in the English Countryside.
(2) The Brangwen sisters, Ursula and Gudrun, are "working and talking."
(3) The wedding party gathers at shortlands, the Criches's home.
(4) The last lesson is in progress, "peaceful and still" in Ursula's classroom.

87. Samuel Johnson has the following to say about an English poet :
"These images are marked by glittering accumulations of ungraceful ornaments : they strike, rather than please. The images are magnified by affectation : the language is laboured into harshness. The mind of the writer seems to work with unnatural violence - 'Double, double, toil and trouble'. He has a kind of strutting dignity, and is tall by walking on tiptoe. His art and his struggle are too visible, and there is too little appearance of ease and nature." Identify the poet.
(1) Thomas Gray (2) John Dryden
(3) John Milton (4) Thomas Wyatt

88. "Take the smoking disclaimer issue" begins Vishal Bharadwaj. "Putting a disclaimer every time somebody smokes on screen is not an answer. If M.F. Hussain had painted a man with a cigar, would you have asked him to put the disclaimer, 'Cigarette smoking is injurious to health' on the painting" ? The point Bharadwaj makes with his rhetorical question is the following :
(1) The smoking disclaimer is ineffectual because M.F. Hussain's painting wouldn't have carried it.
(2) The smoking disclaimer on objects perceived as 'art' is simply superfluous.
(3) The smoking disclaimer is ineffectual because 'art' entertains but does not instruct.
(4) The smoking disclaimer on screen or on an M.F. Hussain painting distracts us from enjoying art.

89. According to ________, certain verbs actually 'perform' an act when they are uttered.
(1) Speech Act theorists such as Austin and Searle.
(2) Russian Formalists such as Shklovsky and Propp.
(3) Language theorists such as Sapir and Whorf.
(4) Cognitive linguists such as Lakoff and Johnson.

90. Haunted castles, strange noises, and an acceptance of the supernatural with all its trappings mark ________.
(1) metafiction
(2) fantasy fiction
(3) epistolary fiction
(4) gothic fiction

91. .... sure it waits upon
Some god o' th' island. Sitting on a bank,
Weeping again the King my father's wrack,
This music crept by me upon the waters,
Allaying both their fury and my passion
With its sweet air. Thence I have followed it,
Or it hath drawn me rather....

Which of the following statements on this passage are **true** ?
(a) These lines, spoken by *Edgar in King Lear*, are part of a long speech delivered on the heath.
(b) These lines, spoken by Ferdinand in *The Tempest*, describe Ariel's music.
(c) The passage reappears in an altered and ironic version in T.S. Eliot's *Waste Land*.

(d) The passage reappears verbatim in W.H. Auden's *Sea and the Mirror*.

The correct answer according to the code is:

(1) (a) and (d) (2) (b) and (c)
(3) (c) and (d) (4) (a) and (c)

92. Arrange the following plays of Shakespeare according to their periods (early, middle, late...) of composition.

(1) *As You Like It, Love's Labours Lost, Antony and Cleopatra, The Tempest, Midsummer Night's Dream.*
(2) *Antony and Cleopatra, The Tempest, Midsummer Night's Dream, Love's Labours Lost, As You Like It.*
(3) *Love's Labours Lost, Midsummer Night's Dream, As You Like It, Antony and Cleopatra, The Tempest.*
(4) *Midsummer Night's Dream, Antony and Cleopatra, The Tempest, As You Like It, Love's Labours Lost.*

93. Who among the following is not a reader-response critic ?

(1) Maud Bodkin
(2) Hans-Robert Jauss
(3) Stanley Fish (4) Wolfgang Iser

94. Leo Tolstoy's *Anna Karenina's* closing lines present...

(1) a sad reflection on the unfortunate suicide of Anna which should have been averted.
(2) the enlivening freshness of a rain which has been threatening to break out.
(3) Levin's affirmation that whatever happens to him, life is not meaningless but unquestionably meaningful.
(4) Vronsky's lament over the death of Anna which ends on a positive note, affirming the human tendency to pass over the tragic events with hope.

95. Which of the following novels begins with a Prologue under the title "The Storming of Seringapatam", saying "I address these lines written in India - to my relatives in England" ?

(1) *The Siege of Krishnapur* by J.G. Farell
(2) *The Moonstone* by Wilkie Collins
(3) *The Sign of Four* by Sir Arthur Conan Doyle
(4) *The Jewel in the Crown* by Paul Scott

96. In "Gerontion", T.S. Eliot says :

"__________ has many cunning passages, contrived corridors / And issues, deceives with whispering ambitions, / Guides us by vanities."

What is Eliot's subject ?

(1) History (2) Politics
(3) State (4) Religion

Read the following poem and answer questions 97 to 100.

THE MOUNTAIN

My students look at me expectantly.
I explain to them that the life of art is a life
of endless labor. Their expressions
hardly change; they need to know
a little more about endless labor.
So I tell them the story of Sisyphus,
how he was doomed to push
a rock up a mountain, knowing nothing
would come of this effort
but that he would repeat it
indefinitely. I tell them
there is joy in this, in the artist's life,
that one eludes
judgment, and as I speak
I am secretly pushing a rock myself,
slyly pushing it up the steep
face of a mountain. Why do I lie
to these children? They aren't listening,
they aren't deceived, their fingers
tapping at the wooden desks -
So I retract
the myth; I tell them it occurs
in hell, and that the artist lies
because he is obsessed with attainment,
that he perceives the summit
as that place where he will live for ever,
a place about to be
transformed by his burden: with every breath,
I am standing at the top of the mountain.
Both my hands are free. And the rock has added
height to the mountain.

(Louise Gluck)

97. Whose poetic voice is triggered right from the beginning ?
(1) of student's (2) of teacher's
(3) of critics' (4) of an observer's

98. The speaker brings up the story of Sisyphus specifically by way of glossing ________.
(1) art in life (2) life in art
(3) endless labor (4) poetic expectation

99. In its context, the words "their fingers / tapping at the wooden desks", best represent the students' ________.
(1) lack of protest
(2) lack of interest
(3) show of disrespect
(4) show of impatience

100. Why does the speaker say that "the rock has added height to the mountain" ?
(1) because the speaker is already on the top of the mountain.
(2) because both the hands of the speaker are now free.
(3) because the mountain now seems largely incomprehensible.
(4) because she feels that the immensity of the problem has grown.

✓ ANSWERS

1. (3)	**2.** (4)	**3.** (3)	**4.** (2)	**5.** (1)	**6.** (1)	**7.** (1)	**8.** (3)	**9.** (3)	**10.** (1)
11. (3)	**12.** (3)	**13.** (1)	**14.** (2)	**15.** (2)	**16.** (3)	**17.** (1)	**18.** (3)	**19.** (1)	**20.** (2)
21. (4)	**22.** (1)	**23.** (4)	**24.** (3)	**25.** (2)	**26.** (2)	**27.** (2)	**28.** (3)	**29.** (3)	**30.** (2)
31. (3)	**32.** (2)	**33.** (4)	**34.** (1)	**35.** (3)	**36.** (3)	**37.** (2)	**38.** (2)	**39.** (4)	**40.** (3)
41. (1)	**42.** (4)	**43.** (3)	**44.** (4)	**45.** (1)	**46.** (2)	**47.** (*)	**48.** (2)	**49.** (3)	**50.** (3)
51. (2)	**52.** (2)	**53.** (1)	**54.** (3)	**55.** (3)	**56.** (4)	**57.** (3)	**58.** (2)	**59.** (3)	**60.** (2)
61. (3)	**62.** (4)	**63.** (2)	**64.** (3)	**65.** (2)	**66.** (3)	**67.** (3)	**68.** (2)	**69.** (*)	**70.** (4)
71. (4)	**72.** (2)	**73.** (3)	**74.** (1)	**75.** (1)	**76.** (2)	**77.** (3)	**78.** (4)	**79.** (3)	**80.** (3)
81. (4)	**82.** (4)	**83.** (3)	**84.** (*)	**85.** (1)	**86.** (2)	**87.** (1)	**88.** (2)	**89.** (1)	**90.** (4)
91. (2)	**92.** (3)	**93.** (1)	**94.** (3)	**95.** (2)	**96.** (1)	**97.** (2)	**98.** (3)	**99.** (4)	**100.** (4)

* The marks have been awarded to all the Candidates against the question(s)

December, 2018

ENGLISH LITERATURE

PAPER-II

Note : This paper contains **hundred (100)** objective type questions of **two (2)** marks each. **All** questions are **compulsory**.

1. Match the following concepts with their definitions :

(Concepts)	**(Definitions)**
(a) Collocation	(i) A semantic relationship of one-to-many
(b) Corpus	(ii) A grid used in lexical analysis
(c) Hyponymy	(iii) A combination of two lexical items in a grammatical pattern
(d) Matrix	(iv) A large body of texts

Code:

(1) (a)–(iii), (b)–(i), (c)–(ii), (d)–(iv)
(2) (a)–(iii), (b)–(iv), (c)–(i), (d)–(ii)
(3) (a)–(iv), (b)–(ii), (c)–(iii), (d)–(i)
(4) (a)–(i), (b)–(iii), (c)–(iv), (d)–(ii)

2. What is the delicate balancing act of Andrew Marvell's "Horatian Ode"?

(1) Celebrating Cromwell's victories while inviting sympathy for the executed King.
(2) Praising feminine virtues while mocking the fixation on chastity.
(3) Praising Roman virtues while endorsing Christian beliefs.
(4) Celebrating the Restoration while regretting the frivolity of the new regime.

3. The en-ending to denote the plural nouns (as in oxen, children, brethren) has survived from the

(1) Anglo-Norman case of making plural nouns
(2) Old English practice of making plural nouns
(3) Odd Middle-English pronouncing custom of plurals
(4) Middle English hymnals and chants in English parishes

4. In Thomas Moore's Utopia (Book II), the reader is told that in this new world there are few mistakes in marriage because

(1) There is a community get together where prospective husbands and wives announce wedding plans endorsed by elders.
(2) There is an extensive courtship period preceding the actual wedding.
(3) The family gods are invoked before finalising the nuptials.
(4) Prospective husbands and wives see one another naked before agreeing to the match.

5. Which Walter Scott novel is set in France in the fifteenth century ?

(1) Quentin Durward
(2) The Antiquarry
(3) Ivanhoe
(4) Redgauntlet

6. "Search the heads of the greatest rivers in the world, you shalt find them but bubbles of water."

Who is the author of this line ?

(1) John. Webster
(2) Francis Bacon
(3) Oscar Wilde
(4) R.B. Sheridan

7. Which of the following had the alternative title Things as They Are?
   (1) William Godwin's Caleb Williams
   (2) Sir Walter Scott's Waverley
   (3) Horace Walpole's The Castle of Otranto
   (4) Mary Shelley's Frankenstein

8. Which of the following acts were not passed during the Victorian Era ?
   (1) The Custody Act
   (2) A series of Factory Acts
   (3) The Married Women's Property Rights Act
   (4) The Women's Suffrage Act

9. The fault of Cowley and perhaps of all the writers of the metaphysical race is that of pursuing his thoughts to their ramifications, by which he loses the grandeur of generality; for of the greatest things the parts are little; what is little can be but pretty, and by claiming dignity becomes ridiculous. Thus all the power of description is destroyed by a scrupulous enumeration; and the force of metaphors is lost, when the mind by the mention of particulars is turned more upon the original than the secondary sense, more upon that from which the illustration is drawn than that to which it is applied.
   (Life of Cowley, 1779)
   What Dr. Johnson actually faults here is :
   (1) The metaphysical poets' tendency to saunter away.
   (2) The force of metaphors that blunts description.
   (3) The mind that goes astray toward the original.
   (4) The metaphysical insistence on the particular than the general.

10. As a boy growing up in Squire Allworthy's estate, Tom gets one of the following characters into trouble. Identify the character.
    (1) Nightingale
    (2) Black George
    (3) Blifil
    (4) Partridge

11. Which ancient Greek writer's name is directly mentioned in Lord Byron's poem "The Isles of Greece" ?
    (1) Euripides (2) Sophocles
    (3) Sappho (4) Aeschylus

12. This poet was of the Auden generation and was only briefly a member of the Communist party. In his poem, "The Pylons", he averred that the Pylons are "Bare like nude giant girls that have no secrets". This prompted the label, Pylon Poets, for the new generation of poets who were happy to use the gas works or pistons of a steam-engine as poetic imagery. (Name this poet.)
    (1) Louis MacNeice
    (2) Christopher Isherwood
    (3) Cecil DayLewis
    (4) Stephen Spender

13. Which of the following is not indebted to the Gothic genre ?
    (1) Matthew Lewis's The Monk
    (2) William Beckford's Vathek
    (3) Ann Radcliffe's The Italian
    (4) Tobias Smolletes Roderick Random

14. In which work does William Blake say that Milton was "a true poet and of devil's party without knowing if' ?
    (1) "The Chimney Sweeper"
    (2) "The Marriage of Heaven and Hell"
    (3) "Songs of Innocence"
    (4) "London"

15. I, Allan Sealy's The Trotter-Nama traces the history of the Anglo-Indian community in a chronicle of seven generations of the Trotter family, told by the seventh Trotter. This narrator is
    (1) a collector of rare manuscripts.
    (2) a quack in the Indian outback.
    (3) an accountant in the Indian army.
    (4) a forger of Indian miniatures.

16. Which of the following is the most accurate description of Butler English ?
    (1) A minimal pidgin that emerged during colonial times in the Madras Presidency.

(2) Any non-grammatical variety of English used by menials in Commonwealth countries.

(3) A dialect of English spoken by the descendants of Anglo-Indians.

(4) A pidgin, also called "Kitchen English" spoken by South Asians in Europe.

17. Alas ! what boots it with uncessant care
To tend the homely, slighted Shepherd's trade,
And strictly meditate the thankless Muse ?
Were it not better done, as others use,
To sport with Amaryllis in the shade,
Or with the tangles of Neaera's hair ?

Who are Amaryllis and Neaera in the above extract from John Milton's "Lycidas"?

(1) Amaryllis is a shepherdess mentioned in Shakespeare's romantic comedies; Neaera, a minor character in Love's Labour's Lost.

(2) Amaryllis is a shepherdess mentioned in ancient pastoral poetry, notably in Virgil's Eclogues; Neaera, a nymph who appears in Virgil's Eclogues.

(3) Both were one-time lovers of Lycidas, the dead shepherd.

(4) Both were goddesses of love and war respectively appearing in Greek pastoral poetry.

18. Match the following authors with the novels :

(Name of Author)	**(Name of Novel)**
(a) Chitra Banerjee Divakaruni	(i) Inheritance
(b) Anita Rau Badami	(ii) Listening Now
(c) Anjana Appacliana	(iii) Sister of My Heart
(d) Indira Ganesan	(iv) The Hero's Walk

Code:

(1) (a)–(iv), (b)–(i), (c)–(iii), (d)–(ii)

(2) (a)–(iv), (b)–(ii), (c)–(i), (d)–(iii)

(3) (a)–(iii), (b)–(iv), (c)–(ii), (d)–(i)

(4) (a)–(i), (b)–(iii), (c)–(ii), (d)–(iv)

19. The following epitaph was written by Rudyard Kipling during the War of 1914-18.

HINDU SEPOY IN FRANCE

This man is his own country prayed we know not to what Powers.

We pray Them to reward him for his bravery in ours.

"Powers" here refers to__________"Them" to_____and "ours" to______.

(1) the Hindus, the French, the British

(2) authorities, his compatriots, our country

(3) the divine, Powers, our country

(4) the military, the Hindu sepoys, Powers

20. The titular figure of Federico Garcia Lorca's elegy "Lament for Ignacio Sanchez Mejfas" was

(1) a popular matador and writer

(2) a revolutionary who was associated with Che Guevara

(3) a popular priest and poet

(4) a spy who helped the revolutionaries during the Spanish Civil War

21. Match the writer with the work :

(Writer)	**(Name of work)**
(a) George Puttenham	(i) Leviathan
(b) Thomas Sprat	(ii) The Practice of Piety
(c) Lewis Bayly	(iii) The Art of English. Poesy
(d) Thomas Hobbes	(iv) The History of the Royal Society

Code:

(1) (a)–(iii), (b)–(iv), (c)–(ii), (d)–(i)

(2) (a)–(iv), (b)–(iii), (c)–(ii), (d)–(i)

(3) (a)–(iii), (b)–(iv), (c)–(i), (d)–(ii)

(4) (a)–(iii), (b)–(ii), (c)–(iv), (d)–(i)

22. What attitude towards death would you find in such poems as Tennyson's "Crossing the Bar," Whitman's "Death Carol," and Kipling's "L'Envoi" ?

(1) Protest

(2) Hope

(3) Resignation
(4) Despair

23. Given below are two statements, one labelled as Assertion (A) and the other labelled as Reason (R). Read the statements and choose the correct answer using the code given below :

Assertion (A) : Gender studies do not see an urgent need to help us navigate the various pitfalls of racism, ethnocentrism, cultural relativism, and plain ignorance that flow from using "culture" as an explanatory tool.

Reason (R) : Issues relating to women's rights, gender roles, sexuality and family obligations are centrally implicated in the so-called clash of civilisations between Christianity or Secularism, and Islam.

Code:
(1) (R) does not follow logically from (A).
(2) (A) and (R) are most logically related.
(3) (A) is only ply addressed in (R).
(4) (R) is (A) and vice versa.

24. In an ode, William Collins lamented the passing of a contemporary poet. The ode began with the line: "In yonder grave a Druid lies. "Name the poet whose passing Collins laments.
(1) Alexander Pope
(2) James Thomson
(3) Thomas Gray
(4) William Cowper

25. Mango Souffle, India's first major gay themed film, is an adaptation of Mahesh Dattani's play
(1) Do the Needful
(2) Dance like a Man
(3) On a Muggy Night in Mumbai
(4) Bravely Fought the Queen

26. The term 'Rigger' is associated with a group of agrarian communists who flourished in England in 1649–50 and were led by
(1) Gerrard Winstanley
(2) John Lilburne
(3) Laurence Clarkson
(4) George Fox

27. Which of the following statements on Rajmohan's Wife is not true ?
(1) His vivid descriptions of the routine of Bengali households reveal a lot about the nineteenth century.
(2) The novel was serialized in 1864 in a short-lived magazine in Calcutta.
(3) Bankim Chandra published it soon after serialization and was elated in seeing its first copy.
(4) By common consent, Raimohan's Wife is the first novel in English published by an Indian.

28. In Marlow's Doctor Faustus, what books does Valdes counsel Faustus to study in preparation for conjuring up spirits ?
(i) The works of Bacon and Abanus
(ii) The Hebrew Psalter and New Testament
(iii) The works of Ovid and Homer
(iv) The works of Baxter and Horst
The right combination according to the code is

Code:
(1) (ii) and (iii)
(2) (i) and (ii)
(3) (i) and (iii)
(4) (i) and (iv)

29. Early African-American texts like slave narratives were often described as told to narratives as their 'authors' dictated their experiences. The persons who noted down these experiences are
(1) Slave-drivers
(2) Abolitionists
(3) Translators
(4) Amanuenses

30. The enigmatic castle which attempts to reach in vain in Franz Kafka's The Castle belongs to
(1) Count Westwest
(2) Count Strangewest
(3) Count Eastwest
(4) Count Aloofwest

31. Braj Kachru has observed a tendency among Indian-English speakers and writers to use hybridized lexical items. One example of this is

(1) Chaywalllah
(2) Lathi-charge
(3) Jugarh
(4) Ping-pong

32. In the spring of 1941, Nikos Kazantzakis embarked on one of his most ambitious projects, a play known as Yangtze. What English/Greek title is it now known as ?

(1) Brobdingnag
(2) Buddha
(3) Zorba
(4) Zoroaster

33. In imitation of which classical poet did Samuel Johnson write his Lcitdon and The Vanity of Human Wishes?

(1) Horace
(2) Tasso
(3) Homer
(4) Juvenal

34. During the Raj, the British viewed their rule in terms of a thankless duty to uplift the downtrodden and inculcate order into Oriental minds. The mission to civilize the "silent, sullen peoples" of the East was a burden imposed upon them by destiny.
The last observation is a fairly obvious allusion to

(1) Rudyard Kipling's "The White Man's Burden"
(2) Maud Diver's The Englishwoman in India
(3) Flora Annie Steel's The Garden of Fidelity"
(4) J.R. Ackerley's Hindoo Holiday : An Indian Journal

35. Which of the following would not be invoked to describe a form of new Historicist criticism ?

(1) Archaeology of social constructs
(2) Cultural materialism
(3) Post-structural recovery of authorial intent
(4) Geneology of patriarchal discourse

36. It was the first narrative on the life of a black woman slave to be published in England in 1831. It has profound influence on the abolition movement in Britain. Identify the book and its author

(1) Elizabeth – Memoir of Old Elizabeth, a Coloured Woman
(2) Mary Prince – The History of Mary Prince
(3) Harriet Jacobs – Incidents in the Life of a Slave Girl
(4) Mattie Jane Jackson – The Story of Mattie J. Jackson

37. What comes "After great pain" in the famous Emily Dlickindon poem ?

(1) Substantial light
(2) The letting go
(3) A formal feeling
(4) A concrete simplicity

38. The Romantic period produced a fair amount of dramatic criticism. A notable example is "On the Knocking at the Gate in Macbeth."
Who is the author ?

(1) William Hazlitt
(2) William Charles Macready
(3) Thomas de Quincey
(4) Edmund Kean

39. There are helpers and harmers among fellow-pilgrims in Christian's journey in Pilgrim's Progress. Who among the following is not a helper ?

(1) The Interpreter
(2) The Evangelist
(3) Mr. Worldly Wiseman
(4) Good Will

40. "Reality is that nothing happens. How many of the events of history have occurred, ask yourselves, for this and for that reason, but for no other reason, fundamentally, than the desire to make things happen ? I present to you History, the fabrication, the diversion, the reality-obscuring drama."

Which postmodern novel thus subverts the truth claims of traditional historiography ?

(1) John Fowles's The French Lieutenant's Woman.
(2) Graham Swift's Waterland
(3) Michael Ondaatje's The English Patient
(4) A.S. Byatt's Possession

41. One of the less noticed and acknowledged distinction of The Canterbury Tales is that

(1) it married domesticity to divinity, the baker's loaf with the bread of life.
(2) it upheld the idea that we cannot divorce poetry from knowledge because poetry itself is an object of knowledge.
(3) instead of revealing England's divisions, it revelled in its diversity.
(4) it alerted us to the term auctor, someone who is both 'an originator, or one who gives increase', the best description for Chaucer himself.

42. "Tomorrow, and tomorrow, and tomorrow, _______in this petty pace from day to day, To the last__________of recorded time; And all our yesterdays have lighted fools The way to dusty death. Out, out brief candle! Life's but a walking shadow, a poor player, That_______and frets his hour upon the stage, And then is_______no more: it is a tale Told by an idiot, full of sound and fury, Signifying nothing."

Fill in the blanks. Choose the set that carries the correct words.

(1) Creeps, moment, struts, seen
(2) Moves, syllable, frowns, heard
(3) Walks, breath, creeps, shown
(4) Creeps, syllable, struts, heard

43. In his Practical Criticism I.A. Richards suggests that there are several kinds of meanings and that the "total meaning" is a blend of contributory meanings which are of different types. He identified four kinds of meaning, or the total meaning of a word depends upon four factors. Choose the right combination as proposed by Richards.

(1) Sense, Feeling, Tone and Matter
(2) Sound, Sense, Tone and Matter
(3) Image, Feeling, Tone and Intention
(4) Sense, Feeling, Tone and Intention

44. The Norman Conquest was a significant landmark in English history. What French did the Normans speak and what was it known as ?

(1) They spoke Norman French (Anglo-Norman). Theirs was certainly not the standard French.
(2) They spoke normal French, rather distinct from Anglo-Norman, another standard language.
(3) They spoke a dialectal French (also called Anglo-Frisian), somewhat closer to the Parisian.
(4) They spoke standard French (of mainland France). Their French was very sweet and musical.

45. Which of the following is the most accurate statement by W.E.B. Du Bois's famous articulation of the 'twoness' of black Americans ?

(1) "Through the eyes of others, this sense of always Looking at one's self, we acquiré the double-consciousness."
(2) "This sense of always looking at one's self, a peculiar sensation through the eyes of others, is double consciousness."
(3) "It is a peculiar sensation, this double-consciousness, this sense of always looking at one's self through the eyes of others."
(4) "This double consciousness, this sense of always looking at one's self through the eyes of others, is a peculiar sensation."

46. Which of the following statements is true of The Way of the World ?

(1) The Way of the World was performed and published in 1702.
(2) The Way of the World failed on stage.
(3) Millamant and Mirabell fail to obtain the consent of Millamant's aunt for their marriage.

(4) The Way of the World presents a heroine pretending to love an older man.

47. What is an "implied reader" ?

(1) A reader who embodies all those predispositions necessary for a literary work to exercise its effect.

(2) The ideal audience envisioned by the author and to whom the work of literature is supposedly addressed.

(3) The ideal reader of a work of literature which is approximated over time by successive responses of generations of actual readers.

(4) The ideal "average" reader who can approach a work of literature with no preconceived ideas about the author's life, the time of composition, etc.

48. Which of the following poems is quoted as the epigraph to A Raisin in the Sun by Lorraine Hansberry ?

(1) "Harlem (A Dream Deferred)"

(2) "I, too, Sing America"

(3) "The Negro Speaks of Rivers"

(4) "The Big Sea."

49. Who viewed Wordsworth, Southey and Coleridge as representatives of a "sect of poets ... dissenters from the established systems in poetry and criticism" who constituted "the most formidable conspiracy against sound judgement in matters political" ?

(1) Henry Vaughan

(2) Francisco Franco

(3) Ralph Vaughan

(4) Francis Jeffrey

50. 1992 demolition of the disputed structure in Ayodya produced two controversial literary responses. Identify them.

(1) The Moor's Last Sigh, Lajja

(2) Chronicles of a Riot Foretold, Shame

(3) Out of Place, The Algebra of Infinite Justice

(4) Annals and Antiquities, Between Sunlight and Shadows

51. ________read Adam Bede with such pleasure that she not only keenly recommended it to her relatives but also commissioned two paintings of scenes from the novel.

(1) Queen Victoria

(2) Horace Nightingale

(3) Margaret Cavendish

(4) George Eliot

52. Adherents of the fourteenth century religious movement associated with vernacular preaching, translation of New Testament into English, and challenges to the authority of priests and bishops were called

(1) Agnostics

(2) Levellers

(3) Deists

(4) Collards

53. Deconstructionist critics argue that texts are never free from

(1) the interpretations bestowed by the totalizing critic.

(2) the equivocal and ironically unstable worldview of the author.

(3) the material conditions that determine the production and reception.

(4) distortions inherent in the rhetoricity of language.

54. In this novel by Graham Greene a double agent uses classic works of fiction to encode secret information. He put Clarissa Harlowe back in the bookcase" is the first clue to his treachery. Then he draws on War and Peace and The Way We Live Now as matrices for secretly transmitting information. Identify the novel.

(1) The Human Factor

(2) The Man Within

(3) The Confidential Agent

(4) Our Man in Havana

55. What tone will be best suited to the following poem ?

THE COMING OF WISDOM WITH AGE

Though leaves are many, the root is one;
Through all the lying days of my youth

I swayed my leaves and flowers in the sun;
Now I may wither into the truth.

(1) Excitement
(2) Revulsion
(3) Exultation
(4) Regret

56. Identify the character, a black-eyed dwarf who "constantly revealed a few discoloured fangs that were yet scattered in his mouth, and gave him the aspect of a panting dog".

(1) Mulberry Hawk in Nicholas Nickleby
(2) Mr. Crook in Bleak House
(3) Daniel Quilp in The Old Curiosity Shop
(4) Rig and in Little Dorrit

57. Who among the following exemplified the role of the "peasant poet" ?

(i) John Clare
(ii) John Keats
(iii) William Cobbett
(iv) Robert Burns

The right combination according to the code is :

Code :

(1) (i) and (iv)
(2) (i) and (ii)
(3) (ii) and (iii)
(4) (iii) and (iv)

58. Match the author with the title :

(Author)	**(Title)**
(a) Alan Paton	(i) Open City
(b) Ngugiwa Thiong'o	(ii) Cry, the Beloved Country
(c) Teju Cole	(iii) A Grain of Wheat
(d) Wole Soyinka.	(iv) The Interpreters

Code.

(1) (a)–(iii), (b)–(i), (c)–(iv), (d)–(ii)
(2) (a)–(ii), (b)–(iii), (c)–(i), (d)–(iv)
(3) (a)–(i), (b)–(iii), (c)–(iv), (d)–(ii)
(4) (a)–(iii), (b)–(ii), (c)–(iv), (d)-(i)

59. Arnold Wesker is associated with "kitchen-sink drama", a rather condescending title applied to the then new-wave realistic drama depicting the family lives of working-class characters, on stage and in broadcast plays. Two of the following plays begin with one character doing the dishes in a kitchen sink. Identify the pair.

(i) The Kitchen
(ii) Chicken Soup with Barley
(iii) Roots
(iv) Menace

The right combination according to the code is :

Code :

(1) (i) and (ii)
(2) (ii) and (iv)
(3) (ii) and (iii)
(4) (i) and (iv)

60. "What is honour ? A word. What is that word honour ? Air. A trim reckoning ! Who hath it ?
He that died o' Wednesday. Doth he feel it ? No. Doth he hear it ? No. Is it insensible, then ?
Yea, to the dead. But will it not live with the living ? No. Why ? Detraction will not suffer it.
– therefore, I'll none of it: Honour is a mere scutcheon; and so ends my catechism."
Which character in the following Shakespeare's dramas made this statement about honour ?

(1) Hamlet in Hamlet, the Prince of Denmark
(2) Claudius in Hamlet, the Prince of Denmark
(3) Hotspur in King Henry IV-Part I
(4) Falstaff in King Henry IV-Part I

61. Nicholas Nickleby firmly established Charles Dickens as a dominant novelist of his time and the book as an unrivalled literary phenomenon. To celebrate the completion of the book, a painter noted that there had been nothing comparable to him since the days of Samuel Richardson. Identify the painter.

(1) Ernest Dawson
(2) Leonard Woolf

(3) David Wilkie
(4) John Cruickshank

62. "Full many a lady
I have eye'd with best regard: and many a time
The harmony of their tongues hath into bondage
Brought my too diligent ear; for several virtues
Have I liked several women; never any
With so full soul, but some defect in her
Did quarrel with the noblest grace she ow'd,
And put it to the foil. But you, 0 you,
So perfect and so peerless, are created
Of every creature's best."

This passage admiring the perfect matching of inner and outward beauty of a woman is taken from

(1) Marlowe's Dr. Faustus
(2) Shakespeare's Tempest
(3) John Webster's The Duchess of Malfi
(4) Thomas Middleton's Women Beware Women

63. "The good thing about words, "Hand Kureishi remarks in "Loose Tongues", "is that their final effect is incalculable. [...] You can never know what your words might turn out to mean for yourself or for someone else; or what the world they make will be like. Anything could happen. The problem with silence is that we know exactly what it will be like."

Kureishi, in sum, suggests :

(i) There is always some risk involved in writing/speaking.
(ii) It is better to avoid using words than to risk miscommunication.
(iii) Words being predictable, are always open to misinterpretation.
(iv) The unpredictable, in deed, is the strength of words.

Determine the correct combination according to the code :

Code :

(1) (i) and (iii)
(2) (i) and (iv)
(3) (ii) and (iv)
(4) (ii) and (iii)

64. Which interpretation of Keats's "Beauty is truth, truth beauty" best represents the mimetic perspective ?

(1) The line is an ironic quotation, the equation of "beauty" and "truth" as "all we know on earth" suggests that reality is an illusory concept and that the primary function of art is to construct a world within an aesthetic reality of its own.
(2) The author's arbitrary imposition of order upon the chaotic impressions of reality constitutes the only "truth" in a work of art.
(3) A work of literature is "beautiful" insofar as it offers an accurate representation of its subject matter, with fully realized characters and vivid description of events.
(4) Those aspects of reality which we perceive to be "beautiful" are the only worthy subject matter of the artist, and it is the artist's job to observe closely and isolate those sublime elements from the flux of the mundane.

65. In which of his novels does Italo Calvino construct his narrative through a tarot pack of cards and re-interpret the Western canon providing new versions of Oedipus Rex, Faust, Hamlet, Macbeth and King Lear ?

(1) Invisible Cities
(2) The Castle of Crossed Destinies
(3) The Path to the Nest of Spiders
(4) Our Ancestors

66. One of the most flexible metres, ______ is a five foot line. It was introduced by Geoffrey Chaucer in the fourteenth century and has since then become the commonest of metres in English poetry.

(1) Hexameter (2) Trochaic
(3) Iambic (4) Pentameter

67. The following lines are W.B. Yeats's metaphor for an old man :

A tattered coat upon a stick, unless
Soul clap its hands and sing, and louder sing
For every tatter in its mortal dress.
Here, the aged man is________, and his "soul...in its mortal dress," is_______.

(1) vehicle, tenor
(2) point, counterpoint
(3) analogy, analogue
(4) tenor, vehicle

68. S.T. Coleridge's "Dejection : An Ode" opens with an epigraph which is a reference to a ballad. Identify the ballad.

(1) "Ballad of Sir Patrick Spence"
(2) 'Ballad of the Gibbet'
(3) "La Belle Dame Sans Merci"
(4) "Ballad of the Goodly Fere"

69. Ah, what a trifle is a heart,
If once into love's hands it come!
All other griefs allow a part
To other griefs, and ask themselves but some;
They come to us, but us love draws;
He swallows us and never chaws;
By him, as by chain'd shot, whole ranks do die;
He is the tyrant pike, our hearts the fry.

– John Donne, 1633

Which sentence best paraphrases line 5 of the passage above ?

(1) Emotions can damage us, but none as severely as love.
(2) Distress comes in many forms, but none lasts as long as heartache.
(3) Unbidden pain afflicts us, but we are lured by love.
(4) Love tends to grab us and never let go.

70. Jonathan Swift arrived in London in 1710 and confronted a rapidly changing world in the new Tory ministry. His reactions to this world are vividly recorded in his Journal to Stella, a series of letters addressed to

(i) Hester Vanhomrigh
(ii) Esther Johnson
(iii) Rebecca Dingley
(iv) Lady Mary Montagu

The right combination according to the code is :

Code :

(1) (i) and (ii)
(2) (iii) and (iv)
(3) (ii) and (iii)
(4) (ii) and (iv)

71. Match the poem with the opening lines :

(a) "Ode to Psyche"	(i) "My heart aches, and a drowsy numbness pains My sense, as though of hemlock I had drunk,"
(b) "Ode on a Grecian Urn"	(ii) "No, no, go not to Lethe, neither twist Wolfs-bane, tight-rooted, for its poisonous wine,"
(c) "Ode to a Nightingale"	(iii) "Thou still unravish'd bride of quietness, Thou foster-child of silence and slow time,"
(d) "Ode on Melancholy"	(iv) "O Goddess ! hear these tuneless num bers, wrung By sweet enforcement and remembrance dear,"

Code:

(1) (a)–(iv), (b)–(iii), (c)–(i), (d)–(ii)
(2) (a)–(iv), (b)–(i), (c)–(iii), (d)–(ii)
(3) (a)–(i), (b)–(iii), (c)–(ii), (d)–(iv)
(4) (a)–(iii), (b)–(iv), (c)–(ii), (d)–(i)

72. Who among the following are referred to as the "Scottish Chaucerians" ?

(i) Thomas Hoccleve
(ii) Robert Henryson
(iii) John Lydgate
(iv) William Dunbar

The right combination according to the code is :

Code :

(1) (ii) and (iii) (2) (iii) and (iv)
(3) (ii) and (iv) (4) (i) and (ii)

73. What is peculiar about the reference in the following to some poets' names in the plural ?

"It is a freezing, bleak day in January, and I am looking for poetry. I see a few Chaucers, a few Shakespeares, and a hardcover, three-dollar History of Modern Poetry published in 1987."

(1) usually refer to biographies of the poets in question.
(2) Synecdochic use; names for their respective works.
(3) Unusual; awkward metaphors no longer in use.
(4) standard reference to more texts of one poet/author.

74. The title of Dylan Thomas's Deaths and Entrances was taken from

(1) John Donne's "Death's Duell"
(2) T.S. Eliot's Murder in the Cathedral
(3) Rudyard. Kipling's "A Death-Bed"
(4) William Shakespeare's Macbeth

75. The "grammar bullies" – you read them in places like the New York Times – and they tell you what is correct.

You must never use 'hopefully". "Hopefully, we will be going there on Thursday," That is incorrect and wrong and you are basically an ignorant pig if you say it.

This is judgementalism. The game that is being played there is a game of social class. It has nothing do with the morality of writing and speaking and thinking clearly, of which George Orwell, for instance, talked so well.

To which famous essay of Orwell does the author refer here ?

(1) "Inside the Whale"
(2) "Politics and the English Language"
(3) "Reflections on Gandhi"
(4) "Why I Write"

76. Identify the Fireside poets of the US.

(1) Amy Lowell, Emily Dickinson, Phillis Wheatley
(2) William Cullen Bryant, H.W. Longfellow, Oliver Wendell Holmes
(3) T.S. Eliot, Wallace Stevens, William Carlos Williams
(4) Marianne Moore, Elizabeth Bishop, Anne Seaton

77. Albert Camus borrows the following epigraph to his novel The Plague from

"It is as reasonable to represent one kind of imprisonment by another, as it is to represent anything that really exists by that which exists not."

(1) James Hogg's The Confessions of a Justified Sinner
(2) Robert Burton's The Anatomy of Melancholy
(3) Daniel Defoe's Robinson Crusoe
(4) Jeremy Bentham's The Principles of Morals and Legislation

78. Match the plays to their setting :

(a) *Krapp's Last Tape*	(i) A country road; A tree.
(b) *Happy Days*	(ii) Bare interior; Two small windows high up; grey light.
(c) *Waiting for Godot*	(iii) Expanse of scorched grass forming a low mound; blinding light.
(d) *Endgame*	(iv) A late evening in future; white light.

Code:

(1) (a)–(ii), (b)–(iv), (c)–(iii), (d)–(i)
(2) (a)–(iii), (b)–(iv), (c)–(i), (d)–(ii)
(3) (a)–(ii), (b)–(iii), (c)–(i), (d)–(iv)
(4) (a)–(iv), (b)–(iii), (c)–(i); (d)–(ii)

79. Thomas Nashe's The Unfortunate Traveller is narrated by

(1) Ben Lyte, a coarse Papist
(2) Jack Wilton, an English page

(3) Philip Foxe, an English highwayman
(4) Peter Marston, a sworn Calvinist

80. Which post-War British poet ends a poem with the line, "Get Stewed : Books are a load of crap" ?
(1) Thom Gunn
(2) Ted Hughes
(3) Philip Larkin
(4) Craig Raine

81. Evelina was published in 1778
(1) under a pseudonym
(2) posthumously
(3) using the name Fanny Burney
(4) anonymously

82. Which of the following themes was not common to the works of Cavalier poets such as Thomas Carew, Sir John Denham, Edmund Waller, Sir John Suckling, James Shirley, Richard Lovelace, and Robert Herrick ?
(1) Courtly ideals of the good life
(2) Carpe diem.
(3) Loyalty to the king
(4) Pious devotion to religious virtues

83. What type of writing did Walter Pater define as "the special and opportune art of the modern world" ?
(1) The novel
(2) Nonfiction prose
(3) The lyric
(4) Connie drama

84. Match the Character with the Play :

(Character)	**(Play)**
(a) Dorimant	(i) The Plain Dealer
(b) Lady Fidget	(ii) The Man of Mode
(c) Malevole	(iii) The Country Wife
(d) Vernish	(iv) The Malcontent

Code :
(1) (a)–(ii), (b)–(iii), (c)–(iv), (d)-(i)
(2) (a)–(iv), (b)–(i), (c)–(iii), (d)–(ii)
(3) (a)–(ii), (b)–(iv), (c)–(iii), (d)–(i)
(4) (a)–(iv), (b)–(iii), (c)–(i), (d)–(ii)

85. Why did Plato banish the poet from his ideal state ?
(1) Poetry deals with form, to the neglect of content.
(2) The poet can never produce a completely accurate replica of the reality it seeks to represent, and (moreover) the purpose of art is not to describe reality but to change it.
(3) Poetry makes an artificial distention between form and content.
(4) In representing the sensual aspects of reality, the poet fails to discern the transcendent reality behind mere appearance.

86. "Why don't we have a little game ? Lees pretend that we're human beings, and that we are actually alive."
This passage forms part of
(1) Samuel Beckett's Whiting for Godot
(2) Harold Pinter's The Birthday Party
(3) Agatha Christie's The Mousetrap
(4) John Osborne's Look Back in. Anger

87. Match the Term with the Theorist :

(Term)	**(Theorist)**
(a) Negritude	(i) Alice Walker
(b) Womanisnm	(ii) Jurgen Habermas
(c) Interpellation	(iii) Aime Cesaire
(d) Public Sphere	(iv) Louis Althusser

Code :
(1) (a)–(i), (b)–(ii), (c)–(iv), (d)–(iii)
(2) (a)–(iii), (b)–(i), (c)–(iv), (d)–(ii)
(3) (a)–(ii), (b)–(i), (c)–(iv), (d)–(iii)
(4) (a)–(iii), (b)–(ii), (c)–(iv), (d)–(i)

88. I have carried the manuscript of these translations about with me for days, reading it in railway trains, or on the top of omnibuses and in restaurants, and I have often had to close it lest some stranger would see how much it moved me. These lyrics – which are in the original, my...(Indian friends) tell me, full of subtlety of rhythm, of untranslatable delicacies of colour, of metrical invention – display in their thought a world I have dreamed of all my life long. The work of a supreme culture, they yet appear as much a growth of the common soil as the grass and the rushes. A tradition, where poetry and religion are the same thing, has passed through the centuries, gathering from learned and unlearned metaphor and emotion, and carried back again to the multitude the thought of the scholar and the noble. If the civilization of Bengal remains unbroken, if that common mind which - as one divines - runs through all, is not, as with us, broken into a dozen minds that know nothing of each other, something even of what is most subtle in these verses will have come, in a few generations, to the beggar on the roads.

– W.B. Yeats, from Introduction to Rabindranath Tagore's Gitanjaii

In this passage, Yeats praises Indian culture primarily because it

(1) reflects a marvellous eclecticism in drawing from many disparate cultures.
(2) is accessible to Westerners though it is rooted in a different religious tradition.
(3) embodies values and gives rise to art that can be shared by people of all classes.
(4) has been flexible enough to survive a transition into the modern world.

89. David Maloufs novel Ransom is based on
(1) a war memoir by Edmund Blunden
(2) a war poem by Yevgeny Yevtushenko
(3) an episode in The Mahabharata
(4) an episode in the Trojan War

90. "We know now that a text is not a line of words releasing a single "theological" meaning (the "message" of the Author-God) but a multidimensional space in which a variety of writings, none of them original, blend and clash. . . . Literature . . . by refusing to assign a "secret", an ultimate meaning, to the text (and to the world as text) liberates what may be called an anti-theological activity, an activity that is truly revolutionary since to refuse to fix meaning is in the end to refuse God and his hypostases – reason, science, law."

The passage conies from which of the following essays?
(1) 'What is an Author ?" by Michel Foucault
(2) "Discourse in the Novel" by Mikhail Bakhtin
(3) The Death of the Author" by Roland. Barthes
(4) "Tradition and Individual Talent" by T.S. Eliot

91. The chapter on the Fall of the Rupee you may omit. It is somewhat too sensational. Even these metallic problems have their melodramatic side." The fall of the Indian rupee in the final decades of 19th century is referred to in one of Oscar Wilde's plays. Identify the play.
(1) Lady Windermere's Fan
(2) The Importance of Being Earnest
(3) A Woman of No Importance
(4) An Ideal Husband

92. Allen Tate once made a useful distinction between structure and texture. The distinction referred to
(1) objects and materials on which a narrative casts light, and the devices employed to enlighten them respectively.
(2) the rhetorical, stylistic, metaphorical and other devices, and the main line of a narrative, argument, etc., respectively.
(3) the main line of a narrative, argument, etc., and the rhetorical, stylistic, metaphorical and other devices respectively.
(4) the devices employed to enlighten objects and materials in a narrative, and the objects and material themselves, respectively.

93. Match the character with the work :

(Characters)	**(Name of work)**
(a) Rupert Birkin	(i) Sons and Lovers
(b) Lydia Lensky	(ii) Kangaroo
(c) Miriam Leivers	(iii) Women in Love
(d) Richard Somers	(iv) The Rainbow

Code :

(1) (a)–(ii), (b)–(iii), (c)–(iv), (d)–(i)
(2) (a)–(iii), (b)–(iv), (c)–(i), (d)–(ii)
(3) (a)–(i), (b)–(ii), (c)–(iv), (d)–(iii)
(4) (a)–(iv), (b)–(i), (c)–(ii), (d)–(iii)

94. Herr God, Herr Lucifer
Beware
Beware.
Out of the ash
I rise with my red hair
And I eat men like air.

Lines 4 and 5 in the above evoke :

(1) Christ's resurrection
(2) The legend of the Lady of the Lake
(3) The fairy-tale of a girl in the woods
(4) The myth of the phoenix

95. In traditional ELT methods and materials, the native speaker is elevated and idealized against stereotyped non-native speakers. This tendency is dubbed____________by Adrian Holliday.

(1) The near-native fallacy
(2) Native speakerism
(3) The native-speaker bias
(4) The non-native fallacy

96. Who among the ancients prescribed that poetry should both instruct and delight ?

(1) Horace (2) Aristotle
(3) Longinus (4) Plotinus

97. In his essay "The Function of Criticism at the Present Time" (1864) Matthew Arnold contended that

(1) Creative power should be ranked higher than critical power
(2) Critical power should be ranked higher than creative power
(3) Creative and critical powers are not comparable in any way
(4) Creative and critical powers should be ranked equally

Directions (Q. 98-100). The following is an extract from a famous play. Read it carefully to answer questions that follow.

MAID : [*From the hall doorway.*] Ma'am, a lady to see you –

NORA : All right, let her come in.

[... The MAID shows in MRS. LINDE, *dressed in travelling clothes, and shuts the door after her.*]

MRS. LINDE : [*In a dispirited and somewhat hesitant voice.*] Hello, Nora.

NORA : [Uncertain.] Hello –

MRS. LINDE : You don't recognise me.

NORA : No, I don't know – but wait, I think – (Exclaiming.] What What ! Is it really you?

MRS. LINDE : Yes, It's me.

NORA : Kristine ! To think I didn't recognize you. But then, how could I ? [*More quietly.*]

How you've changed, Kristine !

MRS. LINDE : Yes, no doubt I have. In nine–ten long years.

NORA : It is so long since we met ! Yes, it's all of that. Oh, these last eight years have been a happy time, believe me. And so now you've come in to town, too. Made the long trip in the winter. That took courage.

MRS. LINDE : I just got here by ship this morning.

NORA : To enjoy yourself over Christmas, of course. Oh, how lovely ! Yes, enjoy ourselves, we'll do that. But take your coat off. You're not still cold ? [*Helping her.*] There now, let's get cozy here by the stove. No, the easy chair there ! I'll take the rocker here. [*Seizing her hands.*] Yes, now you have your old look again; it was only in that first moment. You're a bit more pale, Kristine – and maybe a bit thinner.

MRS. LINDE : And much, much older, Nora.

NORA : Yes, perhaps a bit older; a tiny, tiny bit; not much at all. [*Stopping short, suddenly serious.*] Oh, but thoughtless me, to sit here, chattering away. Sweet, good Kristine, can you forgive me ?

MRS. LINDE : What do you mean, Nora ?

NORA : [*Softly.*] Poor Kristine, you've become a widow.

MRS. LINDE : Yes, three years ago.

NORA : Oh, I knew it, of course; I read it in the papers. Oh, Kristine, you must believe me; I often thought of writing you then, but kept postponing it, and something always interfered.

MRS. LINDE : Nora, dear, I understand completely.

NORA : No, it was awful of me, Kristine. You poor thing, how much you have gone through. And he left you nothing ?

MRS. LINDE : No.

NORA : And no children ?

MRS. LINDE : No.

NORA : Nothing at all, then ?

MRS. LINDE : Not even a sense of loss to feed on.

NORA : [*Looking incredulously at her.*] But Kristine, how could that be ?

MRS. LINDE : [*Smiling wearily and smoothing her hair.*] Oh, sometimes it happens, Nora.

NORA : So completely alone. How terribly hard that must be for you. I have three lovely children. You can't see them now; they're out with the maid.

(....)

98. "Not even a sense of loss to feed on" implies that

(1) Mrs. Linde is completely devoid of all feeling.
(2) Mrs. Linde is given over to feeding on sorrow.
(3) Mrs. Linde's severance from her tragic pair is total.
(4) Mrs. Linde is sentimentally attached to an irretrievable past.

99. Identify the play of which this section is an excerpt.

(1) The Cherry Orchard by Anton Chekhov
(2) The Importance of Being Earnest by Oscar Wilde
(3) A Doll's House by Henrik Ibsen
(4) Wit by Margaret Edson

100. Which of the following descriptions best applies to the above extract ?

(1) A meeting of two friends – one married, the other unmarried after a gap of years.
(2) The sense of loss inevitable with the passage of time and the imperceptible dissolution solution of the conventional marriage.
(3) A chance meeting between old friends which leaves one puzzling over the inexplicable losses the other suffered.
(4) Friends comparing notes and counting losses in a meeting sudden and unanticipated

✔ ANSWERS

1. (2)	**2.** (1)	**3.** (2)	**4.** (4)	**5.** (1)	**6.** (1)	**7.** (1)	**8.** (4)	**9.** (1)	**10.** (2)
11. (3)	**12.** (4)	**13.** (4)	**14.** (2)	**15.** (4)	**16.** (1)	**17.** (2)	**18.** (3)	**19.** (3)	**20.** (1)
21. (1)	**22.** (2)	**23.** (1)	**24.** (2)	**25.** (3)	**26.** (1)	**27.** (3)	**28.** (2)	**29.** (4)	**30.** (1)
31. (2)	**32.** (2)	**33.** (4)	**34.** (1)	**35.** (3)	**36.** (2)	**37.** (3)	**38.** (3)	**39.** (3)	**40.** (2)
41. (3)	**42.** (4)	**43.** (4)	**44.** (1)	**45.** (3)	**46.** (2)	**47.** (1)	**48.** (1)	**49.** (4)	**50.** (1)
51. (1)	**52.** (4)	**53.** (4)	**54.** (1)	**55.** (4)	**56.** (3)	**57.** (1)	**58.** (2)	**59.** (3)	**60.** (4)
61. (3)	**62.** (2)	**63.** (2)	**64.** (3)	**65.** (2)	**66.** (4)	**67.** (4)	**68.** (1)	**69.** (3)	**70.** (3)
71. (1)	**72.** (3)	**73.** (2)	**74.** (1)	**75.** (2)	**76.** (2)	**77.** (3)	**78.** (4)	**79.** (2)	**80.** (3)
81. (4)	**82.** (4)	**83.** (2)	**84.** (1)	**85.** (4)	**86.** (4)	**87.** (2)	**88.** (3)	**89.** (4)	**90.** (3)
91. (2)	**92.** (3)	**93.** (2)	**94.** (4)	**95.** (2)	**96.** (1)	**97.** (1)	**98.** (3)	**99.** (3)	**100.** (3)

June, 2019

ENGLISH LITERATURE

PAPER-II

Note : This paper contains **hundred (100)** objective type questions of **two (2)** marks each. **All questions are compulsory.**

1. In which of the following paired terms, the relationship between the active and passive forms of a sentence can be best established?

(1) Deep structure – Surface structure
(2) Signifier – Signified
(3) Metaphor – etonymy
(4) Syntagmatic – Paradigmatic

2. For which one of the following reasons, in Oscar Wilde's novel, The Picture of Dorian Gray, Gray breaks down when he sees his finished portrait?

(1) Overwhelmed by the beauty of the portrait
(2) Overjoyed by the feeling that his beauty will be known to all
(3) Distraught by the fact that his beauty will fade while the portrait stays beautiful
(4) Distraught by the badly drawn portrait

3. By which two of the following processes, according to Michel Foucault, does power operate?

(a) By right rather than technique
(b) By normalization rather than law
(c) By control rather than punishment
(d) By repression rather than agreement

Choose the correct option :

(1) (a) and (c) (2) (b) and (c)
(3) (b) and (d) (4) (a) and (d)

4. Identify the two names from the following who are associated with Hermeneutics :

(a) Edmund Husserl
(b) E.D. Hirsch
(c) Martin Heidegger
(d) Stephen Greenblat

Choose the correct option :

(1) (a) and (c)
(2) (a) and (b)
(3) (b) and (c)
(4) (b) and (d)

5. "He that is not with us is against us. He that is not against us is with us." Who said this?

(1) Charles Lamb
(2) Samuel Johnson
(3) Francis Bacon
(4) R. W. Emerson

6. In Eliot's *Love Song of J. Alfred Prufrock* who among the following painters is the subject of conversation among the perambulating women?

(1) da Vinci
(2) Raphael
(3) Michelangelo
(4) Donatello

7. Who is the author of the essay, The Rationale of the Copy-Text?

(1) Fredson Bums
(2) W. W. Greg
(3) R.B. McKerrow
(4) Paul Maas

8. In Which of Anita Desai's novels does an insane wife kill her husband?

(1) Voices in the City
(2) In Custody
(3) Cry, The Peacock
(4) Baumgartner's Bombay

9. Which one of the following novels of Jane Austen was abandoned unfinished?

(1) Northanger Abbey

(2) Persuasion
(3) The Watsons
(4) Emma

10. "Culture is ordinary: that is the first fact." Which one of the following is the source of this statement?
(1) The Country and the City
(2) Resources of Hope
(3) The Long Revolution
(4) Keywords

11. Which of the following books is written by an Englishman in universal Latin, is further added to by the Flemish Peter Giles, is revised by the Dutch Erasmus, is printed at Louvain in 1516, later at Paris, still later at Basie, where it was illustrated by two woodcuts from the hand of the German Holbein?
(1) The Golden Legend
(2) Confessio Amantis
(3) Utopia
(4) Erewhon

12. Which of the following two points Were emphasised by 'Wood's Despatch of 1854'?
(a) Teaching of the English language along with the study of vernacular language
(b) Compulsory inclusion of Christianity in the curriculum
(c) The gradual Withdrawal of government patronage from Indian languages
(d) The importance of female education
Choose the correct option :
(1) (a) and (d)
(2) (a) and (b)
(3) (a) and (c)
(4) (b) and (c)

13. What is the name of the poetic style characterized by short staccato rhymed lines, as shown below?
What can it avayle
To dryve forth a snayie,
Or to make a sayle
Of a heryngestayle?
(1) Cranmerish
(2) Wolseyan
(3) Chaucerian
(4) Skeltonic

14. Which one of the following is the right definition of 'peer review"?
(1) A post-publication process in which the work is submitted to a panel of reviewers for ascertaining quality
(2) A pre-publication process in which work submitted for publication is evaluated for quality by experts in the field
(3) A pre-publication process in which work submitted for publication is accompanied by recommendation of other experts in the field
(4) A post-publication process in which the work is submitted for a professional review

15. What is the meaning of 'langue' in Saussurean linguistics?
(1) Individual speech acts
(2) An organized system of differences
(3) The dialectic between thought and speech
(4) Language in the abstract sense

16. "The great English novelists are Jane Austen, George Eliot, Henry James and Joseph Conrad." Which one of the following critical texts begins with the above assertion?
(1) Walter Allen, The English Novel
(2) Terry Eagleton, The English Novel
(3) F.R. Leavis, The Great Tradition
(4) Ian Watt, Rise of the Novel

17. "The last temptation is the greatest treason To do the right deed for the wrong reason." (T.S. Eliot, Murder in the Cathedral) Why is the 'temptation', 'treason' for the speaker of the lines?
(1) It is only self-serving
(2) It is not intended
(3) It violates a norm
(4) It is conspiratorial

18. Match the works with authors :

Works

(a) Image-Music-Text
(b) Why Marx was Right
(c) Mirror and the Lamp
(d) Culture and Society

Authors

(i) M.H. Abrams
(ii) Raymond Williams
(iii) Roland Barthes
(iv) Terry Eagleton

Choose the correct option from those given below :

(1) (a)-(i); (b)-(ii); (c)-(iv); (d)-(iii)
(2) (a)-(iv); (b)-(iii); (c)-(ii); (d)-(i)
(3) (a)-(ii); (b)-(i); (c)-(iii); (d)-(iv)
(4) (a)-(iii); (b)-(iv); (c)-(i); (d)-(ii)

19. What was Gramsci's term for cultural consensus supporting capitalism?

(1) Monopoly
(2) Ideology
(3) Discourse
(4) Hegemony

20. Which one of the following paired terms is correct in its explication?

(1) Phonology—Sound system
(2) Semiology—Ordering of speech sounds
(3) Etymology—Sign system
(4) Morphology—Evolution of words

21. From among the following, identify the two correct statements in Johnson's criticism of Shakespeare :

(a) His Athenians are not sufficiently Greek and his kings not completely royal.
(b) He sacrifices virtue to convenience and is more careful to please than to instruct.
(c) He adheres to strict chronology and gives to one age or nation only its own customs and opinions.
(d) He sacrifices reason, property and truth to pursue even a poor and barren quibble.

Choose the correct option:

(1) (a) and (b)
(2) (a) and (c)
(3) (c) and (d)
(4) (b) and (d)

22. Who among the following analysed the naturalizing of connotative meanings into myths?

(1) Michel Foucault
(2) Roman Ingarden
(3) J. Hillis Miller
(4) Ronald Barthes

23. Match the following items/ideas with the writers who first used/popularized them :

(a) *The Frontier Thesis* (i) Raymond Williams
(b) *The Lost Generation* (ii) HomiBhabha
(c) *Third Space* (iii) F. J. Turner
(d) *Structure of Feeling* (iv) Gertrude Stein

Choose the correct option from those given below :

(1) (a)-(iv); (b)-(i); (c)-(ii); (d)-(iii)
(2) (a)-(iii); (c)-(i); (c)-(iv); (d)-(ii)
(3) (a)-(iii); (b)-(iv); (c)-(ii); (d)-(i)
(4) (a)-(i); (b)-(iii); (c)-(iv); (d)-(ii)

24. Which of the following plays 18 characterized by the exclusivity of a Single character talking to himself?

(1) A Streetcar Named Desire
(2) Equus
(3) The Misanthrope
(4) Krapp's Last Tape

25. Which of the following aptly names the language resulting from the contact of two mutually unintelligible language systems?

(1) Creole
(2) Dialect
(3) Colloquial
(4) Pidgin

26. What, according to Raymond Williams, is the right description of the term 'Cultural Materialism'?

(1) The cultural effect that religion has in social life
(2) The political effect that matter has in social lives
(3) The material effect that culture has in wider social life
(4) The effect of social life in cultural situations of uncertainty

27. Which one of the following is the source of the passage given below?
"I have observed with growing anxiety the career of this word culture during the past six of seven years. We may find it natural, and significant, that during a period of unparalleled destructiveness, this word should come to have an important role. . ."
(1) F. R Leavis, Mass Civilization and Minority Culture
(2) T. S. Eliot, Notes Towards the Definition of Culture
(3) Raymond Williams, Culture and Society
(4) Stuart Hall, Cultural Representations and Signifizing Practice

28. Which of the following sociologists' ideas on the practice of receiving and giving gifts are used by J. Hillis Miller to reinforce her arguments in the essay, Critic as Host
(1) Emile Durkheim
(2) Max Weber
(3) Marcel Mauss (4) Daniel Bell

29. What is the meaning of Ziauddin Sardar's statement? "Cultural studies started as a dissenting intellectual tradition outside academia, dedicated to exposing power in all its cultural forms. But it has now become a discipline and a part of the academic establishment and its power structure."
(1) Devolution
(2) Displacement
(3) Instuitionalization
(4) Dissension

30. Which artistic technique best describes the interplay of light and shade in the following lines?
"I have looked at it so long
I think it is part of my heart. But it flickers.
Faces and darkness separate us over and over
A woman bends over me,
Searching my reaches for what she really is
Then she turns to those liars, the candles or the moon.
I see her back, and reflect it faithfully."
(1) Collage
(2) Flashback
(3) Montage (4) Chiaroscuro

31. Identify the stage that falls between the imaginary and symbolic stages according to Jacques Lacan :
(1) Middle stage
(2) Minor stage
(3) Medieval stage
(4) Intermediate stage

32. Who's the author of the short story, *The Ghost of Firozsha Bang*?
(1) Vikram Seth
(2) V.S. Naipaul
(3) Kiran Desai
(4) Rohinton Mistry

33. Which one of the following correctly describes the meaning of Macbeth's words 'Life is but a walking shadow'?
(1) Life is just devoid of light
(2) Life is just devoid of substance
(3) Life is just devoid of spirit
(4) Life is just devoid of stability

34. Who among the following is celebrated in John Keats's *Lines on the Mermaid Tavern*?
(1) Jack, the Ripper
(2) Bryson of the Park
(3) Jack, the Giant-Killer
(4) Robin Hood

35. Who among the following is mourned in Walt Whitman's *O Captain? My Captain*?
(1) R. W. Emerson
(2) John Keats
(3) P. B. Shelley
(4) Abraham Lincoln

36. Which type of textual copy is concerned With an assessment of the physical details of the books and their exact relationship to the condition in which the book was planned to appear at the time of its initial publication?
(1) Real copy
(2) Ideal copy
(3) Initial copy
(4) Base copy

37. Which of the following works is reviewed in George Orwell's essay, Inside the Whale?
(1) Henry Miller's Tropic of Cancer
(2) James Joyce's Ulysses
(3) D.H. Lawrence's Lady Chatterley's Lover
(4) Anais Nin's Delta of Venus

38. Which novel by J.G. Farrell describes the experiences of a polio Victim?
(1) *Troubles*
(2) *The Singapore Grip*
(3) *The Lung*
(4) *The Hill Station*

39. Which two writers have written essays on the defence of poetry?
(a) Sir Philip Sidney
(b) P. B. Shelley
(c) Mathew Arnold
(d) T. S. Eliot
Choose the correct option:
(1) (a) and (d) (2) (a) and (c)
(3) (c) and (d) (4) (a) and (b)

40. Considering the story of the novel, what does the title Dombey and Son stand for?
(1) It suggests the choice between a son and a daughter
(2) It suggests the commercial aspect of life
(3) It suggests the opposition between a father and a son
(4) It suggests the importance of a dynasty

41. What term used by Ferdinand de Saussure corresponds to Noam Chomsky's term 'performance'?
(1) Difference (2) Parole
(3) Paradigm (4) Langue

42. While looking for publication details of a book, a researcher may consult the book's copyright page, which may appear
(1) just after the cover
(2) usually the reverse of the title page
(3) invariably the reverse of the title page
(4) just before the title page

43. Match each of the following concepts/objects with the corresponding description:
List-I
(a) Farce (b) Props
(c) Music hall (d) Closet drama
List-II
(i) Articles and objects used on the stage
(ii) Drama written to be read rather than acted
(iii) Characterized by broad humour, wild antics, slapsticks etc.
(iv) Variety entertainment of songs, comic turns that flourished in England through the late 19th Century
Choose the correct option from those given below:
(1) (a)-(iv); (b)-(ii); (c)-(i); (d)-(iii)
(2) (a)-(iii);(b)-(i); (c)-(iv); (d)-(ii)
(3) (a)-(i); (b)-(iii); (c)-(ii); (d)-(iv)
(4) (a)-(ii) (b)-(iv); (c)-(iii); (d)-(i)

44. From which Greek word does the term 'comedy' derive and what does it mean?
(1) Comedia, largeness of heart
(2) Komoidia, revel-song
(3) Comedies, commodious
(4) Komedieon, light foolery

45. Identify the author in whose works the character Ashenden appears many times:
(1) Dorothy Sayers
(2) Daniel Defoe
(3) D. H. Lawrence
(4) Somerset Maugham

46. What, in sum, is Sidney's point in the following?

"Nature never set forth the earth in so rich tapestry as divers poets have done; neither with pleasant rivets, fruitless trees, sweet—smelling flowers, not what so ever else may make the too-much-loved earth more lovely. Her world is brazen, the poets only deliver a golden" (Philip Sidney)

(1) Works of art are superior to the natural world they represent
(2) Works of art can often compete with the natural world represented by them
(3) Neither the poets nor the natural world they set forth equal nature's rich tapestry
(4) The natural world is far superior to the works of art that represent it

47. Which one of the following groups of novelists has, in the given order, Captain Ahab, Hester Prynne, Roderick Usher and Daisy Miller as characters in their novels?
(1) Henry James, Edgar A. Poe, Nathaniel Hawthorne, Herman Melville
(2) Herman Melville, Nathaniel Hawthorne, Edgar A. Poe, Henry James
(3) Edgar A. Poe, Henry James, Nathaniel Hawthorne, Herman Melville
(4) Nathaniel Hawthorne, Edgar A. Poe, Henry James, Herman Melville

48. Which version of the Lyrical Ballads was the first one to have the Preface by Wordsworth?
(1) 1798 (2) 1800
(3) 1802 (4) 1804

49. In which play, other than *Julius Caesar*, has Shakespeare depicted the Romans better than the Roman writers themselves have done?
(1) *Troilus and Cressida*
(2) *Coriolanus*
(3) *Romeo and Juliet*
(4) *Two Gentlemen of Verona*

50. Given below are two statements – one is labelled as Assertion (A) and the other is labelled as Reason (R) :
Assertion (A): Instances of beliefs triggering action are present in social life and may give rise to problems in determining 'causality'.
Reason (R): Beliefs may not be accompanied by or give rise to logically appropriate actions, and actions may occur which are consistent with motivations and intentions, but they often, if not usually, also have unanticipated outcomes.
In the light of the above two statements choose the correct option :
(1) Both (A) and (R) are true and (R) is the correct explanation of (A)
(2) Both (A) and (R) are true and (R) is not the correct explanation of (A)
(3) (A) is true, but (R) is false
(4) (A) is false, but (R) is true

51. Read the following lines :
IN A STATION OF THE METRO
The apparition of these faces in the crowd :
Petals on a wet, black bough.
Which of the following poetic programmes is illustrated by the above lines?
(1) The Movement (2) Naturalism
(3) Symbolism (4) Imagism

52. Who of the following are being talked about in the following lines?
"... you seem to misunderstand me,
By each at once her choppy finger laying
Upon her skinny lips: you should be women,
And yet your beards forbid me to interpret
That you are so."
(1) The plebeians in *Coriolanus*
(2) The sisters in *King Lear*
(3) The Witches in *Macbeth*
(4) The players in *Hamlet*

53. Which of the following novels by Iris Murdoch tells the story of an ageing theatre celebrity who withdraws into a life of seclusion and writes a diary/journal/novel?
(1) The Sandcastle
(2) Under the Net
(3) The Sea, the Sea
(4) Flight from the Enchanter

54. What does 'Harlem Renaissance' refer to?

(1) A scientific and rational ethos, including freedom from superstition, in 18th century Europe

(2) The flourishing of African American literature in the 19205 and 19305

(3) A church system, overseen by a governing hierarchy of four courts, championed by the English Puritans

(4) The revelation of Christ to the Gentiles in the persons of the Magi

55. "To see him act is like reading Shakespeare by fiashes of lighting." About which Shakespearean actor Coleridge wrote the above line?

(1) David Garrick

(2) Richard Burbage

(3) John Philip Kemble

(4) Edmund Kean

56. What is 'euphmism'?

(1) Eulogical and adulatory style of writing

(2) Discursive and hortatory style of writing

(3) Pompous and affected style of writing

(4) Exalted and gland style of writing

57. What is the Priest's entreaty to Oedipus in the opening scene of *Oedipus Rex*?

(1) To liberate Thebes from the domination of the Sphinx

(2) To rid Thebes of the plague that afflicts its people

(3) To afford the Thebans the luxury of newer forms of worship

(4) To send Creon to seek advice from the oracle of Delphi oracle

58. Match the following journals with their distinguishing aims and methods of scholarship:

List-I

(a) *Obsidian* (b) *Clio*

(c) *Interventions* (d) *Sign*

List-II

(i) Literature, history and the philosophy of history

(ii) Literature and arts in the African diaspora

(iii) Feminist writing

(iv) Postcolonial Writing

Choose the correct option from those given below :

(1) (a)-(ii); (b)-(i); (c)-(iv); (d)-(iii)

(2) (a)-(iv); (b)-(iii); (c)-(i); (d)-(ii)

(3) (a)-(ii); (b)-(iv); (c)-(i); (d)-(iii)

(4) (a)-(iii); (b-i); (c)-(iv); (d)-(ii)

59. Who among the following established and popularised the concept of 'Cardinal Vowels"?

(1) A. S. Homby (2) E. V. Lucas

(3) Danial Jones (4) C. J. Dodson

60. Which one of the following arrangements of poets is in the correct chronological order?

(1) William Langland, William Dunbar, Layamon

(2) William Langland, Layamon, William Dunbar

(3) Layamon, William Langland William Dunbar

(4) William Dunbar, Layamon, William Langland

61. Who speaks the following lines and to whom?

"O, look upon me, sir,
And hold your hands in benediction o'er me.
No, sir, you must not knee

(1) Kent to Lear

(2) Cordelia to Lear

(3) Goneril to Lear

(4) Regan to Kent

62. Match the Novelist with the Publisher :

(a) Laurence Sterne (i) Thomas Lowndes

(b) Henry Fielding (ii) Andrew Millar

(c) Frances Burney (iii) William Taylor

(d) Daniel Defoe (iv) Robert Dodsley

Choose the correct option from those given below :

(1) (a)-(iii); (b)-(i); (c)-(ii); (d)-(iv)

(2) (a)-(ii); (b)-(iv); (c)-(i); (d)-(iii)

(3) (a)-(iv); (b)-(ii); (c)-(i); (d)-(iii)
(4) (a)-(ii); (b)-(iii); (c)-(iv); (d)-(i)

63. All in the world know the beauty of the beautiful, and in doing this they have (the idea of) what ugliness is; they all know the skill of the skillful, and in doing this they have (the idea of) what the want of the skill is. So it is that existence and non-existence gave birth to (the idea of) the other; that difficulty and ease produce (the idea of) the other; that the length and shortness fashion out the one figure of the other; that (the idea of) height and lowness arise from the contrast of one with the other; that the musical notes and tones become harmonious through the relation of one with another; and that: being before and behind give the idea of one following another.

Which one of the following is the correct meaning of the ominous little phrase 'the idea of in the first sentence of the passage?

(1) Prior Knowledge
(2) Prior imagination
(3) Prior confirmation
(4) Prior rejection

64. Why did T. S. Eliot assert that Virgil, not Homer, is the poet of Europe?

(1) There are some initial moral concerns in Virgil
(2) Virgil belongs to the Roman period
(3) Homer was a pagan who was a renegade
(4) Virgil wrote in Latin while Homer wrote in Greek

65. Match the critics and their works :

Critics
(a) Edward Said
(b) Terry Eagleton
(c) Francis Mulhern
(d) K. M. Newton

Works
(i) *The Illusion: of Postmodernism*
(ii) *Contemporary Marxist Criticism*
(iii) *Theory into Practice*
(iv) *Culture and Imperialism*

Choose the correct option from those given below :

(1) (a-iv); (b-i); (c-ii); (d-iii)
(2) (a-iv); (b-i); (c-iii); (d-ii)
(3) (a-ii); (b-i); (c-iv); (d-iii)
(4) (a-i); (b-ii); (c-iii); (d-iv)

66. Which of the following combinations correctly defines the phonological system of Indian English in relation to Standard English?

(a) Absence of aspirated consonants
(b) Simplified vowel system
(c) Similar international pattern
(d) Presence of voiced aspirated consonants

Choose the correct option :

(1) (a) and (b) (2) (b) and (d)
(3) (c) and (a) (4) (b) and (c)

67. Which of the following is the accurate description of 'dramatic irony"?

(1) A character's knowledge or expectation is contradicted by what the audience knows, or by the outcome of events
(2) An audience knows or expects something to happen but the events on stage turn out to be different
(3) Ironic events and expectations of actual actions and results converge in drama and the audience feels rewarded
(4) A dramatist's irony reinforces his actors' performance, thereby fulfilling audience expectations

68. What is being described by Wordsworth in the following lines from his poem, The Thorn?

I've measured it from side to side;
'Tis three feet long and two feet wide.

(1) Fallen bough
(2) A cradle
(3) A small cot
(4) An Infant's grave

69. Which of the following poets does William Hazlitt call 'Don Quixote-like' in his essay, My First Acquaintance with Poets?

(1) William Wordsworth
(2) Samuel Taylor Coleridge
(3) William Cowper
(4) Lord Byron

70. Which of the following poems by Thomas Hardy was originally titled By the Century's Deathbed?
(1) *The Minute Before Meeting*
(2) *Neutral Tones*
(3) *The Darkling Thrush*
(4) *The Oxen*

71. The medieval English university organised its studies based on the seven liberal arts Three of these, the trivium, referred to the study of
(1) arithmetic, geometry, music
(2) astronomy, music, logic
(3) geometry, grammar, music
(4) grammar, logic, rhetoric

72. Given below are two statements – one is labelled as Assertion (A) and the other is labelled as Reason (R) :
Assertion (A): The dialects of English that have resulted from the regional separation of English-speaking communities have not acquired the status of languages.
Reason (R): The Germanic dialects that are now Dutch, English, German, Swedish etc., have become distinct owing to geographical dispersion.
In the light of the above two statements choose the correct option:
(1) Both (A) and (R) are true and (R) is the correct explanation of (A)
(2) Both (A) and (R) are true but (R) is not the correct explanation of (A)
(3) (A) is true, but (R) is false
(4) (A) is false, but (R) is true

73. Which of the following statements best describes T.S. Eliot's assertion that Shakespeare's Hamlet is an 'artistic failure"?
(1) Hamlet's emotion is not adequately objectified
(2) Hamlet's feelings far outweigh the release of his emotions
(3) Hamlet's obsession should have been within representational limits
(4) Hamlet's indecisiveness slows the steady progress of action

74. Which of the following correctly describes 'black humour' as a morbid and provocative treatment of
(1) old age and disease
(2) youth and passionate love
(3) death and disease
(4) childhood and accident

75. Which of the following statements is true in terms of distribution of metrical feet?
(1) *Anapaestic is to Dactylic as Trochaic is to Iambic*
(2) *Trochaic is to Anapaestic as Dactylic is to Iambic*
(3) *Iambic is to Trochaic as Anapaestic is to Dactylic*
(4) *Dactylic is to Trochaic as Iambic is to Anapaestic*

76. Which two titles from among the following deal with issues related to the institutionalization of English in post-independence India?
(a) Provocations
(b) Professing Literature
(c) The Lie of the Land
(d) The Muse Unchained
The right combination according to the code is
(1) (a) and (d) (2) (a) and (c)
(3) (b) and (c) (4) (c) and (d)

77. Which of the following propositions refers to the recommendations of Charles Grant?
(1) The introduction of English as the medium of instruction in an Indian system of education that included literature, art and craft
(2) The introduction of English as the medium of instruction from lower levels in a few states as an experiment

(3) The introduction of English as the medium of instruction in a Western system of education that included literature, natural sciences and mechanical inventions

(4) The introduction of English as the medium of instruction in regional medium institutions that included only literature

78. Which writer applied the term 'cultural poetics' to his own critical contribution to make literature and arts as part of social practice?

(1) Stephen Greenblatt
(2) Mikhail Bakhtin
(3) Jonathan Dollimore
(4) Raymond Williams

79. Who says the following lines and to whom?
"If it be aught toward the general good,
Set honor in one eye and death i' th' other,
And I will look on both indifferently."

(1) Octavius to Antony
(2) Hamlet to Claudius
(3) Brutus to Cassius
(4) Casca to Calpumia

80. Who among the following explored the shifting and contested power-relations, knowledge and the human body?

(1) Louis Althusser (2) Clifford Geertz
(3) Jacques Lacan (4) Michel Foucault

81. Match the character with the novel :

Character

(a) Kate (b) Florence
(c) Miss Havisham (d) Agnes

Novel

(i) *Great Expectations*
(ii) *Nicholas Nickleby*
(iii) *David Copperfield*
(iv) *Dombey and Son*

Choose the correct option from those given below :

(1) (a)-(i); (b)-(iii); (c)-(iv); (d)-(ii)
(2) (a)-(ii); (b)-(iv); (c)-(i); (d)-(iii)
(3) (a)- (iii); (b)-(i); (c)-(ii); (d)-(iv)
(4) (a-iv); (b)-(ii); (c)-(iii); (d)-(i)

82. The Sadler Commission Report (1917-1919) was critical of the quality of students graduating harm the university and had very perceptive remarks on English and the use of mother tongue in Indian education. What was this Commission appointed for?

(1) To examine the functioning of the Directorate of Public Instruction in Delhi
(2) To study the problems of Calcutta University
(3) To investigate and recommend teaching methods of languages generally
(4) To evolve a three-language formula for the Indian schools

83. Who wrote a guide called *How to Write a Doctoral Thesis : The Humanistic Subjects*, considered equal in standard to the *American MLS Handbook or The Chicago Manual of Style*?

(1) Alain Robbe-Grillet
(2) Cesare Pavese
(3) Umberto Eco (4) Leo Spitzer

84. Which of the following descriptions fits the unit of verse, Dacyl?

(1) One stressed syllable followed by three unstressed syllables
(2) One stressed syllable followed by two unstressed syllables
(3) Two stressed syllables followed by one unstressed syllable
(4) Two stressed syllables followed by two unstressed syllables

85. Match the books with the writers :

List-I

(a) *The Madwoman in the Attic*
(b) *The Wretched of the Earth*
(c) *Shakespearean Negotiations*
(d) *Is There a Text in This Class?*

List-II

(i) Frantz Fanon
(ii) Stephen Greenblatt
(iii) Stanley Fish
(iv) Sandra M. Gilbert and Susan Gubar

Choose the correct option from those given below :

(1) (a)-(iii); (b)-(iv); (c)-(i); (d)-(ii)
(2) (a)-(i); (b)-(ii); (c)-(iii); (d)-(iv)
(3) (a)-(iv); (b)-(i); (c)-(ii); (d)-(iii)
(4) (a)-(ii); (b)-(iii); (c)-(iv); (d)-(i)

86. Who is referred to as 'beast' in the quote 'Kill the beast! Cut his throat! Spill his blood' in William Golding's *Lord of the Flies?*

(1) Ralph (2) Piggy
(3) Simon (4) Roger

87. Which among the following clusters matches the prose style that came to be known as 'Calylese'?

(1) Capital letters, exclamation marks, phrases in German
(2) Question marks, long sentences, phrases in French
(3) Frequent ellipses, Latin sayings, comic non-sequitors
(4) Biblical phrases, capital letters, missing letters

88. Which one of the following of Plato's beliefs/acts was Shelley countering by saying that 'poets are the acknowledged legislators of mankind"?

(1) Banishment of poets from the republic
(2) Distrust of value of poetry for mankind
(3) Preference for legislatórs over poets
(4) Description of poets as mad men

Directions (Q. 89 to 90). Read the passage and answer the question below:

It is an axiom in mental philosophy, that we can think of nothing which we have not perceived. When I say that we can think of nothing, I mean we can imagine nothing, we can reason of nothing, we can remember nothing, we can foresee nothing. The most astonishing combinations of poetry, the subtlest deductions of logic and mathematics, are no other than combinations Which the intellect makes of sensations according to its own laws. A catalogue of all the thoughts of the mind, and of all their possible modifications, is a cyclopaedic history of the universe.

89. According to the writer, perception is the basic epistemology. Which one of the following is the other accepted epistemology?

(1) Language (2) Experience
(3) Inference (4) Simile

90. According to the passage given, which of the following correctly captures the meaning of 'a cyclopaedic history of the universe'?

(1) The knowledge about the universe from its beginning to its possible end
(2) A catalogue of rivers, mountains and continents
(3) Statements about the universe based on logic and mathematics
(4) A published encyclopaedia of the universe

91. Which of the following correctly list the two novels figuring the writer as a public figure, as a celebrity and as grist for the academic mill?

(1) *Rabbit Redux and Rabbit, Run*
(2) *Rabbit is Rich and The Coup*
(3) *Of the Farm and The Centaur*
(4) *Bech: A Book and Bech is Back*

92. Which one of the following words best describes the heroes of Cervantes' *Don Quixote*, Mark Twain's *The Adventure of Tom Sawyer* and Thomas Mann's *The Confessions of Felix Krull?*

(1) Ficelle (2) Picaro
(3) Mannequin (4) Philanderer

93. Given below are two statements – one is labelled as Assertion (A) and the other is labelled as Reason (R):

Assertion (A): Language constructs meaning.

Reason (R): Language structures meanings depending on the speaking subjects' perception, context and auditor(s).

In the light of the above two statements choose the correct option:

(1) Both (A) and (R) are true and (R) is the correct explanation of (A)

(2) Both (A) and (R) are true but (R) is not the correct explanation of (A)
(3) (A) is true, but (R) is false
(4) (A) is false, but (R) is true

94. Who among the following is one of the University Wits?
(1) Thomas Hooker
(2) Thomas Nashe
(3) Michael Drayton
(4) William Harvey

95. In the study of Anglo-American literatures, certain distinguished names in critical/editorial scholarship become synonymous with famous writers and periods of literary history.
Match the following names with their respective areas of scholarship :

(a) Edward Mendelson	(i) John Milton
(b) Jerome McGann	(ii) Ezra Pound
(c) Stanley Fish	(iii) W. H. Auden
(d) Hugh Kenner	(iv) Textual Scholarship

Choose the correct option from those given below :
(1) (a)-(ii); (b)-(i); (c)-(iv); (d)-(iii)
(2) (a)-(iii); (b)-(iv); (c)-(i); (d)-(ii)
(3) (a)-(iv); (b-iii); (c)-(ii); (d)-(i)
(4) (a)-(iii); (b)-(ii); (c)-(iv); (d)-(i)

96. Match the play with the subject matter of the play :

List-I
(a) *The Doctor's Dilemma*
(b) *You Never Can Tell*
(c) *Candida*
(d) *Arms and the Man*

List-II
(i) Flouting of stage conventions
(ii) Satire on military heroes
(iii) Devaluation of social traditions
(iv) Mockery of physicians' ignorance

Choose the correct option from those given below :
(1) (a)-(ii); (b)-(iii); (c)-(iv); (d)-(i)
(2) (a)-(iii); (b)-(i); (c)-(iv); (d)-(ii)
(3) (a)-(i); (b)-(ii); (c)-(iii); (d)-(iv)
(4) (a)-(iv); (b)-(iii); (c)-(i) (d)-(ii)

Directions (Q. 97 to 100). Read the Comprehension and answer the question below it:

THE GROCER'S CHILDREN

The grocer's children
eat day-old bread,
moldy cakes and cheese,
soft black bananas
on stale shredded wheat,
weeviled rice, their plates
heaped high with wilted
greens, bruised fruit,
surprise treats
from unlabelled cans,
tainted meat.
The grocer's children
never go hungry.

97. Which of the following words best describes the last sentence of the poem?
(1) Ironic (2) Paradoxical
(3) Pathetic (4) Disdainful

98. Whose point of view seems to have been stated in the poem?
(1) The Grocer's (2) The children's
(3) The narrator's (4) The poet's

99. What is suggested by the word 'tainted' in line 11?
(1) Tinctured (2) Cooked
(3) Spoiled (4) Boiled

100. How does the poem achieve its effect?
(1) It lists a number of grocery items which do not have any tangible nutritive benefit
(2) It presents a series of inedible fare in the face of the basic need to eat
(3) It strays away from the tongue-in–cheek beginning to state the obvious
(4) It posits the circumspect existence of a reasonable plan to alleviate hunger

ANSWERS

1. (1) **2.** (3) **3.** (2) **4.** (1) **5.** (3) **6.** (3) **7.** (2) **8.** (3) **9.** (3) **10.** (2)
11. (3) **12.** (1) **13.** (4) **14.** (2) **15.** (*) **16.** (3) **17.** (1) **18.** (4) **19.** (4) **20.** (1)
21. (4) **22.** (4) **23.** (3) **24.** (4) **25.** (4) **26.** (3) **27.** (2) **28.** (3) **29.** (3) **30.** (4)
31. (3) **32.** (4) **33.** (2) **34.** (4) **35.** (4) **36.** (2) **37.** (1) **38.** (3) **39.** (4) **40.** (1)
41. (2) **42.** (2) **43.** (2) **44.** (2) **45.** (4) **46.** (1) **47.** (2) **48.** (2) **49.** (2) **50.** (1)
51. (4) **52.** (3) **53.** (3) **54.** (2) **55.** (4) **56.** (3) **57.** (2) **58.** (1) **59.** (3) **60.** (3)
61. (2) **62.** (3) **63.** (1) **64.** (1) **65.** (1) **66.** (2) **67.** (1) **68.** (4) **69.** (1) **70.** (3)
71. (4) **72.** (2) **73.** (1) **74.** (3) **75.** (3) **76.** (2) **77.** (3) **78.** (1) **79.** (3) **80.** (4)
81. (2) **82.** (2) **83.** (3) **84.** (2) **85.** (3) **86.** (3) **87.** (3) **88.** (3) **89.** (3) **90.** (1)
91. (4) **92.** (2) **93.** (1) **94.** (2) **95.** (2) **96.** (4) **97.** (1) **98.** (3) **99.** (3) **100.** (2)

December, 2019

ENGLISH LITERATURE

PAPER-II

Note : This paper contains **hundred (100)** objective type questions of **two (2)** marks each. **All** questions are **compulsory**.

1. Match the author with the story:

List-I

(a) Edgar Allan Poe

(b) E. M. Forster

(c) Katherine Mansfield

(d) Sahnan Rushdie

List-II

i. The Fall of the House of Usher

ii. The Prophet's Hair

iii. The Garden Party

iv. The Celestial Omnibus

Choose the correct option:

	(a)	(b)	(c)	(d)		(a)	(b)	(c)	(d)
(1)	iii	ii	i	iv	(2)	iv	iii	i	ii
(3)	i	iv	iii	ii	(4)	ii	i	iv	iii

2. Who among the following theorists believes that the proliferation of television images is producing a cultural condition akin to 'historical amnesia' ?

(1) Jean Baudrillard

(2) Ihab Hassan

(3) Frederic Jameson

(4) Daniel Bell

3. Which three of the following writers are associated with 'Kitchen sink drama'?

(a) Amold Wesker

(b) John Arden

(c) Shelagh Delaney

(d) John Osborne

Choose the most appropriate option:

(1) (a), (b) and (d) (2) (a), (b) and (c)

(3) (b), (c) and (d) (4) (a), (c) and (d)

4. Which of the following characters in Shakespeare's Love's Labour Lost over uses formal Latinate diction ?

(1) Holofemes (2) Dull

(3) Costard (4) Moth

5. Match the works with authors:

List-I

(a) Bodies that Matter

(b) A World of Difference

(c) A Literature of their Own

(d) Vamps and Tramps

List-II

i. Camille Paglia

ii. Elaine Showalter

iii. Barbara Johnson

iv. Judith Butler

Choose the correct option:

	(a)	(b)	(c)	(d)		(a)	(b)	(c)	(d)
(1)	i	ii	iii	iv	(2)	ii	iii	iv	i
(3)	iv	iii	ii	i	(4)	iii	iv	i	ii

6. Who among the following prose writers of the Romantic period authored "On Murder Considered as one of the Fine Arts" ?

(1) Charles Lamb

(2) Walter Savage Lander

(3) Thomas De Quincey

(4) Arme Radcliffe

7. Which two of the following poems can be categorized as poems belonging to the neo-classical period of English literature.

(a) The Ring and the Book.

(b) The Vanity of Human Wishes

(c) Cato

(d) Lamia

Choose the correct option:

(1) (a) and (b) (2) (b) and (c)

(3) (c) and (d) (4) (a) and (d)

8. Who among the following proposed that the English language is "man made", not 'woman made'?
   (1) Mary Haas
   (2) Dorothy L. Sayers
   (3) Dale Spender
   (4) Carol Chomsky
9. Given below are two statements:
   Assertion (A) : Only actual research develops research skills.
   Reason (R) : Information is discrete, whereas knowledge consists of a network of connections.
   In the light of the above two statements choose the correct option:
   (A) Both (A) and (R)are true and (R) is the correct explanation of (A).
   (B) Both (A) and (R) are true but (R) is not the correct explanation of (A).
   (C) (A) is true but (R) is false.
   (D) (A) is false but (R) is true.
10. Who are the co-editors of Chutneyfying English:
   The Phenomenon of English?
   (a) 'Jamuna-Kachru
   (b) Rita Kothari
   (c) Rupert Snell
   (d) Alastair Pennycook
   Choose the correct option:
   (1) (a) and (d) (2) (a) and (b)
   (3) (b) and (c) (4) (b) and (d)
11. Match the characters with the play:
   List-I
   (a) Donalbain (b) Claudio
   (c) Nerissa (d) Goneril
   List-II
   i. King Lear
   ii. Macbeth
   iii. Merchant of Venice
   iv. Measure for Measure
   Choose the correct option:

	(a)	(b)	(c)	(d)		(a)	(b)	(c)	(d)
(1)	iv	iii	ii	i	(B)	ii	iv	iii	i
(3)	iii	i	ii	iv	(D)	i	iv	ii	iii

12. Which of the following plays by T.S. Eliot is in the correct chronological order of publication?
   (1) Murder in the Cathedral–The Family Reunion-The Cocktail Party–The Confidential Clerk.
   (2) The Cocktail Party–The confidential Clerk-The Family Reunion–Murder in the Cathedral
   (3) The Family Reunion–The Cocktail Party-Murder in the Cathedral–The Confidential Clerk
   (4) The Confidential Clerk–Murder in the Cathedral–The Cocktail Party–The Family Reunion
13. Which combination in the following constitutes the trilogy Oresteia?
   (1) Agamemnon, The Persians, Eumenides
   (2) The Persians, The Suppliants, Agamemnon
   (3) Agamemnon, Choephoroe, Eumenides
   (4) Seven Against Thebes, Agamemnon, The Suppliants.
14. Which two names from R.M. Ballantyne's Coral Island are repeated in William Golding's reworking of the same text as Lord of the Flies?
   (a) Ralph (b) Roger
   (c) Jack (d) Simon
   The correct option is:
   (1) (a) and (d) (2) (a) and (c)
   (3) (c) and (d) (4) (b) and (d)
15. Which of the following set of characters in Charles Dickens' novels is in the right chronological order'?
   (1) Mr. Bounderby–David Copperfield–Mrs. Mann–Nathaniel Winkle
   (2) David Copperfield–Mr. Bounderby–Nathaniel Winkle–Mrs. Mann
   (3) Nathaniel Winkle-Mrs. Mann–David Copper-field–Mrs. Bounderby
   (4) Mrs. Mann–David Copperfield-Nathaniel Winkle–Mr. Bounderby
16. Which of the following periods of English Literature is also called 'Puritan Interregnum'?

(1) The Neoclassical Period
(2) The Caroline Age
(3) The Restoration
(4) The Commonwealth Period

17. Who made the remark: "Great literature is simple language charged with meaning to the utmost possible degree"?
(1) Rabindranath Tagore
(2) Ezra Pound
(3) W. B. Yeats (4) T.S. Eliot

18. Which of the following work by Henry Fielding begins as a parody of Samuel Richardson's Pamela?
(1) Tom Jones (2) Don Quixote
(3) Amelia (4) Joseph Andrews

19. Which of the following arrangements of prose-pamphlets is in the right chronological order'?
(1) The Shortest Way with Dissenters–A Modest Proposal–Areopagitica–Reflections on the Revolution in France
(2) A Modest Proposal–The Shortest Way with Dissenters–Areopagitica–Reflection on the Revolution in France
(3) Areopagitica–The Shortest Way with Dissenters–A Modest Proposal–Reflections on the Revolution in France
(4) Areopagitica-Reflections on the Revolution in France–The Shortest Way with Dissenters- A Modest Proposal

20. Match the theorist with the text:
List-I
(a) John Fiske (b) Michel de Certeau
(c) Pierre Bourdieu
(d) Jean Francois Lyotard
List-II
i. Distinction
ii. The Postmodem Condition
iii. Reading the Popular
iv. The Practice of Everyday Life
Choose the correct option:

	(a)	(b)	(c)	(d)		(a)	(b)	(c)	(d)
(1)	iii	iv	i	ii	(3)	iv	iii	ii	i
(3)	ii	i	iv	iii	(4)	ii	iv	iii	i

21. Who among of following are associated with the 'Jazz Age'?
(1) Ernest Hemingway and Scott Fitzgerald
(2) Scott Fitzgerald and John Dos Passos
(3) John Dos Passos and Sherwood Anderson
(4) Ernest Hemingway and Sherwood Anderson

22. From whose Work did John Milton take the epigraph to his Areopagitica?
(1) Sophocles (2) Euripides
(3) Plato (4) More

23. In Paradise Lost Milton invokes his 'Heavenly Muse', 'Urania', at the beginning of which two books'?
(a) Book I (b) Book IV
(c) Book IX (d) Book VII
Choose the correct option:
(1) (a) and (d) (2) (b) and (c)
(3) (c) and (d) (4) (b) and (d)

24. Which two aspects of cultural diffusion in the Age of Globalization need to be addressed by pedagogy of language in general and English in particular?
(a) Uni directionality
(b) Multidirectionality
(c) Complex and extensive
(d) Simplistic and abbreviated
Choose the correct option:
(1) (a) and (b) (2) (b) and (c)
(3) (c) and (d) (4) (d) and (a)

25. Which of the following is the proper explanation of the concept of "Freytag's Pyramid"?
(1) Analysis of the plot of a drama
(2) Analysis of the characters of a drama
(3) Analysis of the theme of conflict between a woman and two men in drama
(4) Analysis of the different types of drama

26. What is the chronological order of the appearance of the following periodicals?
(a) The Tatler (b) The Spectator
(c) The Examiner (d) The Reflector

Choose the correct option:

(1) (b), (a), (d), (c) (2) (c), (b), (a), (d)
(3) (a), (b), (c), (d) (4) (d), (a), (b), (c)

27. Given below are two statements : Assertion (A) and Reason (R):

Assertion (A) : Many modern British writers infused their works with an extreme sense of uncertainty, disillusionment and despair.

Reason (R) : The Waste Land ends in a flurry of random allusions.

In the light of the above two statements choose the correct option:

(A) Both (A) and (R) are true and (R) is the correct explanation of (A)
(B) Both (A) and (R) are true but (R) is not the correct explanation of (A)
(C) (A) is true, but (R) is false
(D) (A) is false, but (R) is true

28. In the UNESCO definition, a 'Pamphlet' is an unbound publication that is not a periodical and contains:

(1) No fewer than 5 and no more than 48 pages
(2) No fewer than 10 and no more than 68 pages
(3) No fewer than 15 and no more than 64 pages
(4) No fewer than 20 and no more than 80 pages

29. Which one of W. M. Thackeray's novels has the following as the closing sentence? "Which of us in happy in this world? Which of us has his desire? or, having it, is satisfied"?

(1) The Luck of Bary Lyndon
(2) Pendennis
(3) Vanity Fair
(4) The History of Henry Esmond

30. The following is a list of key critical terms. Which is the right chronological order of their formulation ?

(1) Langue–the unconscious–difference–heresy of paraphrase
(2) The unconscious–langue–heresy of paraphrase–difference
(3) Difference–langue–heresy of paraphrase–the unconscious
(4) Langue–difference–the unconscious–heresy of paraphrase

31. Which two of the following are autobiographical narratives?

(a) Kanthapura (b) Meatless Days
(c) Prison and Chocolate Cake
(d) The God of Small Things

The Correct option is:

(1) (a) and (b) (2) (b) and (c)
(3) (a) and (c) (4) (c) and (d)

32. Given below are two statements–Assertion (A) and Reason (R):

Assertion (A) : The Primary component in novelistic forms is a plot that evolves coherently from its beginning to an end in which all complications are resolved.

Reason (R) : The novel is constituted by a multiplicity of divergent and contending social voices that achieve their full significance only in the process of their dialogic interaction both with each other and with the voice of the narrator.

In the light of the above two statements choose the correct option:

(A) Both (A) and (R) are true and (R) is the correct explanation of (A).
(B) Both (A) and (R) are true but (R) is not the correct explanation of (A).
(C) (A) is true, but (R) is false.
(D) (A) is false, but (R) is true.

33. Which British administrator passed a resolution for the "Promotion of European literaters and Science among the natives of India" ?

(1) Lord Hastings (2) Lord Cornwallis
(3) Lord Bentick (4) Lord Hardinge

34. In which one of the following Middle English poems in Hector a character ?

(1) Troilus and Cressida
(2) Piers Plowman
(3) The Seafarer (4) Beowulf

35. Match the periodicals with their writers/contributors:

List-I

(a) The Rambler
(b) Macmillan's Magazine
(c) The Guardian
(d) Bentley's Miscellany

List-II

i. Charles Dickens
ii. Samuel llolmson
iii. David Masson iv. Richard Steele

Choose the correct option:

	(a)	(b)	(c)	(d)		(a)	(b)	(c)	(d)
(1)	iii	iv	i	ii	(2)	i	ii	iii	iv
(3)	ii	iii	iv	i	(4)	iv	i	ii	iii

36. How often did Richard Steele's Tatler appear every week and how many issues of Tatler in total were published ?

(1) Two times a week; 171 issues
(2) Once a week; 151 issues
(3) Three times a week; 271 issues
(4) Three times a week; 261 issues

37. Which of the following plays by Ben Jonson ends with the performance of a puppet play in mutation of Marlowe's Hero and Leander?

(1) The Alchemist (2) Volpone
(3) Bartholomew Fair
(4) Every Man in His Humour

38. Which one of the following observations of 'Lost Generation', a term coined by Gertude Stein is correct ?

(1) German Jews who survived the Second World War and went to Israel
(2) The American expatriates in Europe after the First World War
(3) The Irish Freedom fighters of the early Twentieth Century
(4) The Europeans living in America

40. Which of the following stylistic features characterise spoken discourse?

(a) Greater use of explicit connectives.
(b) Greater dependence on non-verbal connectives.
(c) Greater syntactic embedding.
(d) Greater use of fillers and repetitions.

Choose the correct option:

(1) (a) and (b) (2) (b) and (c)
(3) (c) and (d) (4) (b) and (d)

41. Which of the following movements was Arthur Symons was referring to as 'an interesting disease' and 'an over-subtilizing refinement upon refinement' ?

(1) Celtic Revival
(2) Romantic Movement
(3) Decadence
(4) Feminism

42. Which of the following descriptions delineate Roman a Clef (Novel with key) ?

(1) A novel depicting the life of an artist from childhood to maturity
(2) A novel using the altered names of the actual people of the time
(3) A novel describing historical incidents with fictional characters
(4) A novel giving the effect of realism by high-lighting the social problems of the time

43. Which of the following is true of Aristotle's Critical Position ?

(1) Writers are likely to be mere entertainers who appeal to the emotions and passions of the audience
(2) Tests created by poets are almost inevitably inaccurate and defective as imitations
(3) The best artitistic tests will be both complex and unified every part of the work will be essential to it and will be linked to every other part
(4) Texts should be judged on the basis of how accurately they imitate philosophical truth

44. Match the works with authors–

List-I

(a) Homi Bhabha (b) Geoffrey Hartman
(c) Edward Said
(d) Julia Kristeva

List-II

i. Saving the Text
ii. The Location of Culture
iii. Desire in Language
iv. Culture and Imperialism

Choose the correct option:

	(a)	(b)	(c)	(d)		(a)	(b)	(c)	(d)
(1)	i	ii	iv	iii	(2)	ii	i	iv	iii
(3)	iv	iii	i	ii	(4)	iii	ii	i	iv

44. Which two concepts, developed by the French sociologist Pierre Bourdieu, have become increasingly influential in cultural studies?

(a) Dissemination (b) Gynesis
(c) Cultural Capital (d) Habitus

Choose the correct option:

(1) (a) and (c) (2) (b) and (c)
(3) (c) and (d) (4) (b) and (d)

45. Match the type of writing with their descriptions:

List-I

(a) Exegesis (b) Invective
(c) Hagiography (d) Apology

List-II

i. Writing about saints' lives
ii. Detailed explanation of a passage
iii. A defence or justification of one's actions and beliefs
iv. A bitterly critical attack of something

Choose the correct option:

	(a)	(b)	(c)	(d)		(a)	(b)	(c)	(d)
(1)	ii	iv	i	iii	(2)	iv	ii	iii	i
(3)	i	iii	iv	ii	(4)	iii	i	ii	iv

46. Which two aspects of cultural diffusion in the Age of Globalization need to be addressed by pedagogy of language in general and of English in particular ?

(a) Uni directionality
(b) Multidirectionality
(c) Complex and extensive
(d) Simplistic and abbreviated

Choose the correct option:

(1) (a) and (b) (2) (b) and (c)
(3) (c) and (d) (4) (d) and (a)

47. Which two principal kinds of melancholy are proposed by Robert Burton in Volume III of Anatomy of Melancholy ?

(a) Love (b) Religious
(c) Morbid (d) Psychic

The Correct option is:

(1) (a) and (b) (2) (a) and (c)
(3) (b) and (d) (4) (c) and (d)

48. Following Plato, which two of the following statements about 'Phantasm' and 'Semblance' are correct ?

(a) Phantasm is an image, while Semblance is the real object
(b) Phantasm is the real object while Semblance is only a resemblance
(c) Phantasm unlike semblance has the same proportions as the object
(d) Semblance is 'unreal' but looks 'real as compared to phantasm

Choose the correct option:

(1) (b) and (c) (2) (c) and (d)
(3) (a) and (b) (4) (d) and (a)

49. Match the poet with the opening line of the poem.

List-I

(a) Shelley (b) Coleridge
(c) Keats (d) Wordsworth

List-II

i. I cry your mercy–pity love ! aye, love !
ii. The world is too much with us
iii. O world, O life, O time
iv. When true love burns desire is Love's pure flame

Choose the correct option:

	(a)	(b)	(c)	(d)		(a)	(b)	(c)	(d)
(1)	iii	iv	i	ii	(2)	iv	iii	ii	i
(3)	ii	iii	iv	i	(4)	1	ii	iii	iv

50. Which two of the following works were published after 1947 ?

(a) The Dark Room
(b) Mr. Sampath : A Printer of Malgudi
(c) Seven Summers
(d) The Big Heart

Choose the correct option:
(1) (a) and (b) (2) (b) and (c)
(3) (c) and (d) (4) (a) and (d)

51. Of the five conditions of the Sublime, according to Longinus, the most important condition is–
(1) Vigorous treatment of passions
(2) Majesty of the structure
(3) A lofty cast of mind
(4) A wide range of thoughts

52. Which arrangement of D.H. Lawrence's novels is in the correct chronological sequence?
(1) Kangaroo–The Plumed Serpent–Sons and Lovers–The Ranbow
(2) Sons and Lovers–The Rainbow–Kangaroo–The Plumed Serpent
(3) The Rainbow–The Plumed Serpent–Kangaroo–Sons and Lovers
(4) The Rainbow–Kangaroo–The Plumed Serpent–Sons and Lovers

53. Which of the following describes Foucault's views on knowledge ?
(a) Knowledge is not metaphysical or transcendental
(b) Knowledge is not a matter of perspective
(c) Knowledge is not pure or neutral but is always from a point of view
(d) Knowledge is unconstrained by regimes of power
Choose the correct option:
(1) (a) and (d) (2) (b) and (c)
(3) (a) and (c) (4) (b) and (d)

54. Which one of the following has two heroes with the same name?
(1) The Island of the Mighty
(2) The German Goddess
(3) Animal Farm
(4) Annadale

55. Which of the following fictional characters is in the right Chronological order ?
(1) Uncle Toby–Man Friday–Stephen Dedalus–Miss Havisham
(2) Stephen Dedalus–Man Friday–Uncle Toby–Miss Havisham
(3) Man Friday–Uncle Toby–Miss Havisham-Stephen Dedalus
(4) Miss Havisham–Uncle Toby–Stephen Dedalus–Man Friday

56. Which two of the following statements are applicable to feminist criticism ?
(a) Recuperate the female writers ignored by the canon
(b) Fully endorse the social construction of gender
(c) Valorize the traditional canon uncritically
(d) Mostly reject the essentialising of 'male' and 'female'
Choose the correct option:
(1) (a) and (b) (2) (b) and (c)
(3) (a) and (d) (4) (a) and (c)

57. Which two of the following plays were written by Thomas Heywood ?
(a) Gorboduc
(b) The Play Called the Four P. P.
(c) The Play of the Weather
(d) The Spanish Tragedy
Choose the correct option:
(1) (a) and (b) (2) (a) and (c)
(3) (b) and (c) (4) (c) and (d)

58. Which one of the following titles of Robert Browing's works means, 'to disport in the open air, to amuse oneself at random ?'
(1) Jocoseria (2) Andreadel Sarto
(3) Abt Vogler (4) Asolando

59. What does Scrates mean when in Plato's Ion, he says "Poets are nothing but the interpreters of gods" ?
(1) The poets are the markers of their poems
(2) The poets are acutely aware of gods in composing their poems
(3) The poets are divinely possessed when they compose their poems
(4) The poets first hear what gods say then put that into words

60. Match the following technological advancements impacting learning and teaching of language with their corresponding years

List-I

(a) Hypertext Markup Language (HTML)
(b) Streaming of Video on the Internet
(c) My Space. com
(d) Fecebook

List-II

I. 2004 II. 2003
III. 1991 IV. 1997

Choose the correct option–

	(a)	(b)	(c)	(d)		(a)	(b)	(c)	(d)
(A)	III	IV	II	I	(B)	II	IV	I	III
(C)	III	II	IV	I	(D)	IV	III	I	II

61. Which among the following group of writers is labelled as 'University Wits' ?

(1) Thomas Lodge, Thomas Wilson, Walter Raleigh
(2) John Fletcher, Ben Jonson, George Peele
(3) Thomas Kyd, Francis Beaumont, John Lyly
(4) Christopher Marlowe, Robert Greene, Thomas Nashe

62. In the following list, which two actors belong to the Elizabethan period ?

(a) Richard Burbage
(b) Will Kempe
(c) David Garrick
(b) John Kemble

Choose the correct option:

(1) (a) and (c) (2) (b) and (d)
(3) (a) and (b) (4) (c) and (d)

63. Which term among the following will be applicable to a situation in which a character initiates a scheme which depends for its success on the ignorance of the person against whom it is directed ?

(A) Conflict (B) Intrigue
(C) Ally (D) Foil

64. Examples of poetic compounding are found in the work of which two modemist writers?

(a) Graham Greene
(b) James Joyce
(c) Gerard Manley Hopkins
(d) Stephen Spender

Choose the correct option:

(1) (c) and (d) (3) (a) and (b)
(3) (b) and (c) (4) (a) and (c)

65. In the following list, which two journals relate to the field of post-colonial literature?

(a) Kunapipi (b) Interventions
(c) Daedalus (d) Clio

Choose the correct option–

(1) (a) and (c) (2) (b) and (c)
(3) (c) and (d) (4) (a) and (b)

66. What is the order of publication of the following books of Noam Chomsky?

(a) Problems of Knowledge and Freedom
(b) Aspects of the Theory of Syntax
(c) Syntactic Structures
(d) Knowledge of Language

Choose the correct option:

(1) (d), (c), (b), (a) (2) (b), (c), (d), (a)
(3) (c), (b), (a), (d) (4) (a), (b), (c), (d)

67. The key figures in the development of British Cultural Studies are:

(a) Richard Hoggart
(b) Raymond Williams
(c) Stuart Hall
(d) Lawrence Grossberg

The most appropriate option is:

(1) (a) and (b) (2) (b) and (c)
(3) (a), (b) and (c) (4) (d), (b), (c) and (d)

68. Given below are two statements–Assertion (A) and Reason (R).

Assertion (A): Cultural Studies is simply the study of culture as a discrete entity divorced from its social and political context.

Reason (R) : Cultural Studies aim to understand Culture in all its complex forms and to analyse the Social and Political context with in which it manifests itself.

In the light of the above two statements choose the correct option

(A) Both (A) and (R) are true and (R) is the correct explanation of (A).
(B) Both (A) and (R) are true but (R) is not the correct explanation of (A).
(C) (A) is true but (R) is false.
(D) (A) is false but (R) is true.

69. Which three of the following poets figure in William Dunbar's Lament for the Makers ?
(a) Geoffrey Chaucer
(b) John Gower
(c) Robert Henryson
(d) William Langland
Choose the most appropriate option:
(1) (a), (b) and (d) (2) (a), (b) and (c)
(3) (b), (c) and (d) (4) (a), (c) and (d)

70. In which of the following essays did Charles Lamb first use the pseudonym./persona. Elia?
(1) My First Play
(2) The Two Races of Men
(3) New Year's Eve
(4) The South-Sea House

71. How many tales and pilgrims are there is Chaucer's The Caunterbury Tales '?
(1) 24 pilgrims and 23 tales
(2) 23 pilgrims and 24 tales
(3) 22 pilgrims and 24 tales
(4) 24' pilgrims and 22 tales

72. Who said the following ? "Discursive practices are not purely and simply modes of manufacture of discourse. They take shape in technical ensembles, in institutions, in behavioural schemes, in types of transmission and dissemination, in pedagogical forms that both impose and maintain them"-
(1) Roland Barthes
(2) Michel Foucault
(3) Homi K. Bhabha
(4) Gayatri Chakravorty Spivak

73. How many syllables are there in the word intransigently ?
(1) Three (2) Six
(3) Five (4) Four

74. Which one of the following novels by Kingsley Amis represents its protagonist as an 'angry young man'?
(1) I Like it Here
(2) Lucky Jim a
(3) The Biographer's Moustache
(4) The Great Man

75. Which of the following tales in Chaucer's Canterbury Tales deals with the murder of a child by Jews ?
(1) The Monk's Tale
(2) The Second Nun's Tale
(3) The Prioress's Tale
(4) The Shipman's Tale

76. Which cultural analyst has combined the study of different dimensions of youth culture with commentary on developments in cultural theory and politics ?
(1) Angela Mc. Robbie
(2) Donna Horraway
(3) Linda Hutcheon
(4) Julia Kristeva

77. Which of the following books carried the additional title Sermon on the Sea ?
(1) The Religion of Man by Tagore
(2) Essay on the Gita by Aurobindo
(3) Hind Swaraj or Indian Home Rule by Gandhi
(4) Christ and Satyagraha by Elwin

78. Which two of the following are associated with Deconstruction ?
(a) Jacques Derrida
(b) Raymond Williams
(c) Paul de Man
(d) Jonathan Dolli more
Choose the correct option:
(1) (a) and (b) (2) (a) and (c)
(3) (a) and (d) (4) (b) and (d)

79. In which of the following works is the character 'Ariel' an exclusion ?
(1) The Tempest (2) Paradise Lost
(3) The Rape of the Lock
(4) The Rime of the Ancient Mariner

80. Which two of the following novels belong to the Victorian Age in English Literature '?
(a) Pendennis
(b) The Way of All Flesh
(c) The Battle of the Books
(d) Barchester Towers
Choose the correct option:
(1) (a) and (c) (2) (b) and (d)
(3) (c) and (d) (4) (a) and (d)

81. Which two of the following novels deal with the theme of apartheid ?
(a) Purple Hibiscus
(b) July's People
(c) Cry, The Beloved Country
(d) The Mimic Men
Choose the correct option:
(1) (a) and (c) (2) (b) and (d)
(3) (b) and (C) (4) (a) and (d)

82. Given below are two statements–Assertion (A) and Reason (R):
Assertion (A) : Dialects are the broad range of social as well as regional varieties.
Reason (R) : A dialect describes variation not only at the phonological level, but also at the levels of laxis and syntax.
In the light of the above two statements choose the correct option:
(1) Both (A) and (R) are true and (R) is the correct explanation of (A).
(2) Both (A) and (R) are true but (R) is not the correct explanation of (A).
(3) (A) is true but (R) is false.
(4) (A) is false but (R) is true.

83. Which of the following is the correct chronological order of publication of the following poems ?
(1) Lamia–Paradise Lost–Alastor–The Dunciad
(2) The Dunciad–Alastor–Lamia–Paradise Lost
(3) Alastor–The Dunciad–Paradise Lost–Lamia
(4) Paradise Lost–The Dunciad–Alastor–Lamia

84. Which of the following statements is correct?
(1) Langue is the language system, and Parole, the individual usage
(2) Langue is the language usage, and Parole, the individual system .
(3) Langue is the language in abeyance, and Parole, the individual application
(4) Langue is the language collective, and Parole, the individual deviation

85. Match the author with the text:
List-I
(a) Rita Kothari
(b) Probal Dasgupta
(c) Braj B. Kachru
(d) Baljinder K. Mahal
List-II
i. The Queen's English
ii. The Indianization of English
iii. Translating India
iv. The Othemess of English
Choose the correct option:

	(a)	(b)	(c)	(d)		(a)	(b)	(c)	(d)
(1)	iv	iii	i	ii	(2)	iii	iv	ii	i
(3)	iv	ii	i	iii	(4)	iii	i	ii	iv

86. What is the correct chronological order of the publication of the following ?
(a) German Grammar (Jacob Grimm)
(b) Comparative Grammar of Sanskrit, Zend, Greek Latin, Lithuanian, Gothic and German (Franz Bopp)
(c) An Investigation into the Origin of Old Norse or Icelandic Language (Rasums Rask)
(d) Concerning the Conjugation System of the Sanskrit Language in Comparison with those of the Greek, Latin, Persian and German Languages (Franz Bopp)
(1) (a), (b), (c), (d) (2) (b), (c), (d), (a)
(3) (c), (d), (a), (b) (4) (d), (c), (b), (a)

87. Which of the following is a collaborative work of W. H. Auden and Christopher Isherwood?
(1) Letters from Iceland

(2) The Dance of Death

(3) The Ascent of F6 (4) The Orators

88. Which two of the following correctly describe the features of Wuthering Heights?

(1) Flash backs and time shifts

(2) Oedipal obsessions

(3) Magic and ritual

(4) Acute evocation of place

89. Who among the following has written a series of poems entitled, 'Very Indian Poems in Indian English'?

(1) Vikram Seth (2) Arun Kolatkar

(3) Nissim Ezekiel (4) Keki N. Daruwalla

90. Which of the following combinations best describes the typical methodology of literary research ?

(1) Direct, empirical and quantitative

(2) Phenomenological, speculative and abstract

(3) Textual, critical and historical

(4) Synoptic, conceptual and speculative

COMPREHENSION

Direction–*(Q. 91 to 94).* Read the following poem answer the questions:

Home Is So Sad

Home is so sad. It stays as it was left, Shaped to the comfort of the last to go As if to win them back. Instead, bereft of anyone to please, it withers so, Having no heart to put aside the theft.

And turn again to what is started as, A joyous shot at how things ought to be, Long fallen wide. You can see how it was : Look at the pictures and the cutlery.

The music in the piano stool. That Vase.

91. There is a 'thief in the poem. Who is that thief'?

(1) The time that ticks away

(2) The fate that overpowers

(3) The tenant who leaves

(4) The past that beckons

92. Why is the 'Home' 'Sad' ?

(1) Because it has waited in vain

(2) Because it remains unchanged

(3) Because its joy has faded

(4) Because it is devoid of residents

93. How was the home before it became 'sad'?

(1) It was as it would be

(2) It was as it shall be

(3) It was as it should be

(4) It was as it could be

94. Why has the 'home' 'withered' ?

(1) Because everything has to fade sooner or later

(2) Because it has no longer the reason to be what it was

(3) Because it is an organic entity in any case

(4) Because it has been betrayed categorically

Direction–(Q. 95 to 98). Read the following poem and answer the questions:

Lying is an accursed vice. It is only our words which bind us together and make us human. If we realized the horror and weight of lying, we would see that is more worthly of the stake than other crimes. I find that people normally waste time quite inappropriately punishing children for innocent misdemeanors fomenting them for thoughtless actions which lead nowhere and leave no trace. It seems to me that the only faults which we should vigorously attack as soon as they arise and start to develop are lying and, a little below that, stubbornness. Those faults grow up with the children. Once let the tongue acquire the habit of lying and it is astonishing how impossible it is to make it give it up. That is why some otherwise decent men are object slaven to it. One of my tailors is a good enough fellow, but I have never heard him once speak the truth, not even when it would help him, if he did so.

95. How does 'lying' affect human relationship?

(1) It makes the relationship 'human'

(2) It reduces the affinity among people

(3) It promotes togetherness among diverse people

(4) It does not affect at all as it is merely words

96. 'Lying' is a fault that should be punished only
(1) When the first lie is uttered
(2) When it becomes convenient
(3) When it becomes stubborn
(4) When it begins to turn into a habit

97. According to the author "thoughless actions"?
(1) Torment others
(2) Are strictly not misdemeanours
(3) Mean nothing and are soon forgotten
(4) Are punishments for children

98. It is suggested in the passage that the tailor does never speak the truth because
(1) He cannot keep the word he gives
(2) He does not know lying is a crime
(3) He thinks lying will help him
(4) He is a slave of his profession

99. Read the following passage from Antigone and answer question:
Creon: And yet wert bold enough to break the law.
Antigone:
Yea, for these laws were not ordained by Zeus.
And she who sits enthroned with gods below,
Justice, enacted not these human laws.
Nor did I deem that thou, a mortal man,
Could," by a breath annual and override'
The immutable unwritten laws of Heaven.
The three kinds of laws implicit in Antigone's response are:
(1) Human unwritten, written
(2) Of Gods, of Zeus, of Justice
(3) Of Gods, of Justice, of Man
(4) Of Man, of Heaven, of Zeus

100. Read the following passage and answer the questions:
It was the best of times, it was the worst of times, it was the age of wisdom, it was the age of foolishness, it was the epoch of belief, it 'was the epoch of incredulity, it was the season of light, it was the season of Darkness, it was the spring of hope, it was the winter of despair, we had everything before us, we had nothing before us, we were all going direct to Heaven, we were all going direct the other way–in short, the period was far like the present period, that some of its noisiest authorities insisted on its being received, for good or for evil, in the superlative degree of comparison only.
The Age described in the above passage is best described as the Age of:
(1) Parallelisms (2) Inconsistencies
(3) Contraries (4) Anomalies

ANSWERS

1. (3)	**2.** (3)	**3.** (4)	**4.** (1)	**5.** (3)	**6.** (3)	**7.** (2)	**8.** (3)	**9.** (2)	**10.** (3)
11. (2)	**12.** (1)	**13.** (3)	**14.** (2)	**15.** (3)	**16.** (4)	**17.** (2)	**18.** (4)	**19.** (3)	**20.** (1)
21. (1)	**22.** (2)	**23.** (1)	**24.** (2)	**25.** (1)	**26.** (3)	**27.** (2)	**28.** (1)	**29.** (3)	**30.** (2)
31. (2)	**32.** (2)	**33.** (3)	**34.** (1)	**35.** (3)	**36.** (3)	**37.** (3)	**38.** (2)	**39.** (4)	**40.** (3)
41. (2)	**42.** (3)	**43.** (2)	**44.** (3)	**45.** (1)	**46.** (*)	**47.** (1)	**48.** (2)	**49.** (1)	**50.** (2)
51. (2)	**52.** (2)	**53.** (3)	**54.** (4)	**55.** (3)	**56.** (3)	**57.** (3)	**58.** (4)	**59.** (3)	**60.** (1)
61. (4)	**62.** (3)	**63.** (2)	**64.** (3)	**65.** (4)	**66.** (3)	**67.** (3)	**68.** (4)	**69.** (2)	**70.** (4)
71. (*)	**72.** (2)	**73.** (3)	**74.** (2)	**75.** (3)	**76.** (1)	**77.** (3)	**78.** (2)	**79.** (4)	**80.** (4)
81. (3)	**82.** (2)	**83.** (4)	**84.** (1)	**85.** (2)	**86.** (3)	**87.** (3)	**88.** (3)	**89.** (3)	**90.** (3)
91. (4)	**92.** (1)	**93.** (3)	**94.** (2)	**95.** (2)	**96.** (4)	**97.** (3)	**98.** (1)	**99.** (3)	**100.** (3)

October, 2020

ENGLISH LITERATURE

PAPER-II

Note : This paper contains **hundred (100)** objective type questions of **two (2)** marks each. **All** questions are **compulsory**.

1. The deductive method differs from the inductive method in drawing its conclusions from

(1) verification
(2) particular instances
(3) applications
(4) general truths

2. Which one of the following journals publishes articles related to critical theory exclusively?

(1) *Salmagundi* (2) *Diacritics*
(3) *Callaloo* (4) *Grand Street*

3. Which one of the following assumptions best expresses the position of Post-Structuralist criticism?

(1) Definite structures underlie empirical events.
(2) Language is representational.
(3) Apprehension of reality is a construct.
(4) Knowledge operates according to procedures that are axiomatic.

4. Which one of the following is correct about Saussure's analysis of language?

(1) *La langue* is the system of a language.
(2) *Parole* focuses on language as a system at a particular time.
(3) *La langue* is the particular instance of speech and writing.
(4) *Parole* is the study of language over a period of time.

5. Who among the following theorists particularly emphasized the social and historical dimensions of a text's reception?

(1) Wolfgang Iser
(2) Stanley Fish
(3) Hans Robert Jauss
(4) Pierre Bourdieu

6. Which one among the following is a set of the Metaphysical Poets?

(1) John Dryden, George Herbert, and Alexander Pope
(2) Henry Vaughan, John Dryden, and John Donne
(3) John Donne, Henry Vaughan, and Andrew Marvell
(4) Samuel Johnson, T.S. Eliot and Herbert Grierson

7. Which one of the following statements is true about Aristotle's poetics?

(1) He asserted the value of poetry by integrating rhetoric and imitation (mimesis).
(2) He asserted the value of poetry by focusing on both rhetoric and imitation (mimesis).
(3) He asserted the value of poetry by giving preference to rhetoric over imitation (mimesis).
(4) He asserted the value of poetry by focusing on imitation (mimesis) rather than rhetoric.

8. Who said of the blank verse, quoting an unnamed critic, that it is 'Inverse only to the eye", adding further that it "has neither the easiness of prose, nor the melody of numbers"?

(1) John Dryden
(2) Alexander Pope
(3) Samuel Taylor Coleridge
(4) Samuel Johnson

9. Poetry according to Sir Philip Sidney is of three kinds. They are:
(1) religious, dramatic, romantic
(2) classical, romantic, neo-classical
(3) philosophical, imaginative, narrative
(4) religious, philosophical, imaginative

10. In *Anxiety of Influence* which of the following definitions is given by Harold Bloom to explain the term, 'clinamen'?
(1) poetic hyperbole
(2) poetic misprision
(3) poetic sublime
(4) poetic supplement

11. Who among the following is known to have popularized the term 'globalization'?
(1) Ronald Robertson
(2) Francis Fukuyama
(3) John Urry
(4) John Tomlinson

12. Who among the following coined the dictum, "the medium is the message"?
(1) Raymond Williams
(2) Erving Goffman
(3) Marshall McLuhan
(4) John Fiske

13. Who among the following presented the concept of 'multi-accentuality' of the sign, saying that signs possess an 'inner dialectical quality' and 'evaluative accent'?
(1) Roland Barthes
(2) Stuart Hall
(3) Jacques Derrida
(4) Valentin Voloshinov

14. On December 11, 1823, Rammohan Roy addressed a letter to the British authority which pleaded for modern western education and is considered historically important for the introduction of English education in India. Who was the letter addressed to?
(1) Lord Amherst
(2) Lord Minto
(3) Lord Macaulay
(4) Lord Bentick

15. Which British administrator sought "to make everything as English as possible in a country which resembles England in nothing", as recorded by Sir Thomas Munro?
(1) Lord Bentick
(2) Lord Hastings
(3) Lord Cornwallis
(4) Lord Wellesley

16. Who among the following was the first Director of the Central Institute of English and Foreign Languages, Hyderabad (now EFL University)?
(1) Prof V.K. Gokak
(2) Prof C. D. Narasimhaiah
(3) Prof C. J. Daswani
(4) Prof K. R. S. Iyengar

17. Which one of the following best explains the term 'paralanguage'?
(1) The ways in which people mask what they mean by the words they use
(2) The ways in which people show what they mean other than by the words they use
(3) The ways in which words carry meanings unintended by the speaker
(4) The ways in which the silence underlying speech communicates wrong meanings

18. Which two of the following oppositions are best evoked by Hamlet's utterance - "To be or not to be"?
A. between life and death
B. between action and emotion
C. between affirmation and confirmation
D. between doing and abstaining from doing

Choose the correct answer from the options given below:

(1) A and D only
(2) B and D only
(3) C and A only
(4) D and C only

19. Who among the following linguists proposed the terms, 'competence' and 'performance'?

(1) Noah Webster
(2) Steven Pinker
(3) Roman Jakobson
(4) Noam Chomsky

20. Which one of these statements defines the scope of semiotics?

(1) Semiotics studies the sound systems of a language.
(2) Semiotics is a study of sign systems.
(3) Semiotics studies human sign system only.
(4) Semiotics is a study of non-human sign systems only.

21. Which according to Thomas Hobbes is the only 'science' God has bestowed on mankind, that informs the structure of his monumental work, *Leviathan*?

(1) Astronomy
(2) Architecture
(3) Occult sciences
(4) Geometry

22. As mentioned in "My First Acquaintance with Poets" which poet does William Hazlitt describe as the "only person I ever knew who answered the idea of a man of genius"?

(1) Coleridge
(2) Wordsworth
(3) Byron
(4) Shelley

23. Which one of the following essays holds that "As a method, realism is a complete failure"?

(1) Virginia Woolf, "The Mark on the Wall"
(2) Oscar Wilde, "The Decay of Lying"
(3) D.H. Lawrence, "Why the Novel Matters"
(4) Mary McCarthy, "My Confession"

24. Which of the following novels is structured into a poem of 999 lines, preceded by a Foreword, followed by a Commentary and an Index?

(1) *Ragtime*
(2) *Pale Fire*
(3) *The Inner Side of the Wind*
(4) *Hourglass*

25. Which among the following novels includes a questionnaire for the reader such as "Do you like the story so far? Yes () No ()"?

(1) *Mantissa* by John Fowles
(2) *Waterland* by Graham Swift
(3) *Snow White* by Donald Barthelme
(4) *If on a Winter's Night a Traveller* by Italo Calvino

26. What is the subject of Ivan's controversial essay in Brothers Karamazov?

(1) Transubstantiation
(2) The evils of clergy
(3) The Eucharist
(4) Ecclesiastical courts

27. Which one of the following Sherlock Holmes stories refers to a significant event in English history?

(1) "The Musgrove Ritual"
(2) "The Speckled Band"
(3) "The Solitary Cyclist"
(4) "The Red-Headed League"

28. Harold Skimpole is a character in:

(1) *Bleak House*
(2) *Dombey and Son*
(3) *Great Expectations*
(4) *Oliver Twist*

29. Who is the author of A Fragment (1819) one of the earliest vampire stories in English?

(1) P. B. Shelley
(2) Lord Byron

(3) Bram Stoker
(4) Mary Shelley

30. Lala Kanshi Ram is a character in:
(1) Arun Joshi's *The Apprentice*
(2) Chaman Nahal's *Azadi*
(3) Anita Desai's *Fire on the Mountain*
(4) Kamala Markandayas *A Handful of Rice*

31. Which of the following poems by Philip Larkin deals with the trauma of a rape victim who saws "Even so distant, I can taste the grief"?
(1) "Deceptions"
(2) "Faith Healing"
(3) "Sad Steps"
(4) "Wild Oats"

32. In which of the Bog poems does Seamus Heaney speak about the "perishable treasure" of a body "Murdered, forgotten, nameless, terrible"?
(1) "Bog Queen"
(2) "Grauballe Man"
(3) "Punishment"
(4) "Strange Fruit"

33. Which book of *Paradise Lost* incorporates the speech rhythms of Adam and Eve's marital quarrel?
(1) Book 4 (2) Book 6
(3) Book 7 (4) Book 9

34. Who among the following wrote *Marzeppa*, a long narrative poem about a seventeenth-century military leader of Ukraine?
(1) William Cowper
(2) Lord Byron
(3) P. B. Shelley
(4) S. T. Coleridge

35. Which one of the following statements is appropriately true of Harold Pinter's plays?
(1) Menace is in the air and it leads to bloody violence.
(2) Menace is in the air and it is realized through the female characters.
(3) Menace is in the air, but it is not pinned down, or explained.
(4) Menace is in the air and anarchy follows in a systematic manner.

36. To which mythological character is Faustus compared in the Prologue of Dr. Faustus?
(1) Perseus
(2) Theseus
(3) Icarus
(4) Achilles

37. Who makes the following speech in Samuel Becketts *Waiting for Godot*?
"Astride of a grave and a difficult birth. Down in the hole, lingeringly, the grave-digger puts on the forceps."
(1) Estragon
(2) Lucky
(3) Vladimir
(4) Pozzo

38. Which of the following are the major themes in William Congrexe's *The Way of the World*?
(1) jealousy and revenge
(2) love and intrigue
(3) intrigue and death
(4) love and loyalty

39. What game do the characters play in Act II of Harold Pinter's *The Birthday Party*?
(1) A game of chess
(2) A game of cards
(3) Blind man's buff
(4) Musical chairs

40. *The Duchess of Malfi* is based on :
(1) a French romance
(2) an Italian novella
(3) a Geman fable
(4) a Scottish chronicle

41. Which two of the following strictly follow the parameters of documentation prescribed by the eighth edition of the MLA Handbook?
A. Nunberg, Geoffrey editor, *The Future of the Book*, U of California P, 1996

B. Puig, Manuel, *Kiss of the Spider Woman*, Trans. Thomas Colchie, London Vintage, 1991

C. Nunberg, Geoffrey, ed. *The Future of the Book*. Berkeley: U of California P, 1996

D. Puig, Manuel, *Kiss of the Spider Woman*, Translated by Thomas Colchie, Vintage Books 1991

Choose the correct answer from the options given below

(1) A and B only
(2) A and C only
(3) A and D only
(4) B and C only

42. A research hypothesis is :

A. a proposition which is always true
B. a provisional explanation of anything
C. a theory which will be disproved by evidence
D. a statement which is assumed to be true for the sake of argument

Choose the most appropriate answer from the options given below:

(1) A and B only
(2) B and C only
(3) B and D only
(4) A and C only

43. Which two of the following aspects are to be scrupulously followed to avoid the trap of plagiarism?

A. subjectivity
B. acknowledgment
C. citation
D. interpretation

Choose the most appropriate answer from the options given below:

(1) A and B only
(2) A and C only
(3) C and D only
(4) B and C only

44. Which two texts among the following are linked to literary feminism?

A. *A Small Place*
B. *The Yellow Wallpaper*
C. *Emma*
D. *A Room of One's Own*

Choose the correct answer from the options given below:

(1) A and D only
(2) C and D only
(3) B and D only
(4) A and C only

45. Who among the following feminist theorists posted a separate realm of female experience captured in a style of writing different from men's?

A. Elaine Showalter
B. Luce Irigaray
C. Kate Millett
D. Simone de Beauvoir
E. Helene Cixous

Choose the correct answer from the options given below:

(1) A, C and D only
(2) B and D only
(3) C, D and E only
(4) B and E only

46. Which of these statements describe correctly the basic assumption of Structuralism?

A. Structuralism is concerned with signs and signification.
B. A structuralist theory considers only verbal conventions and codes.
C. Structuralism began in the works of Jacques Derrida that influenced the 20th-centuly literary criticism.
D. Structuralism challenges the long-standing belief that literature reflects a given reality.
E. All signs are arbitrary but without them we cannot comprehend reality.

Choose the correct answer from the options given below:

(1) A, C and E only

(2) A, D and E only
(3) A, B and C only
(4) A, B and E only

47. Which two terms among the following are associated with formalist criticism?

A. aura
B. actant
C. narratee
D. defamiliarization
E. foregrounding

Choose the correct answer from the options given below:

(1) A and C only
(2) B and D only
(3) B and C only
(4) D and E only

48. Who among the following believed that rhyme is not an integral part of poetry?

A. William Wordsworth
B. Horace
C. Samuel Daniel
D. Philip Sidney

Choose the most appropriate answer from the options given below:

(1) A and C only
(2) B and D only
(3) A and D only
(4) D and C only

49. Who among the following are the two great masters of the French language that T.S. Eliot contrasts with Dryden and Milton in "The Metaphysical Poets"?

A. Francois Villon
B. Jean Racine
C. Charles Baudelaire
D. Arthur Rimbaud

Choose the correct answer from the options given below:

(1) A and C only
(2) A and D only
(3) B and C only
(4) B and D only

50. Which two terms from among the following are specifically linked to the work of Pierre Bourdieu?

A. habitus
B. consciousness
C. desire
D. distinction

Choose the correct answer from the options given below:

(1) A and C only
(2) A and D only
(3) B and D only
(4) C and D only

51. Macaulay's Minute of 1835 sought to

A. promote European literature and science among the natives
B. impart knowledge of English literature and science through translated texts
C. encourage branches of native learning by more useful studies
D. stop expenditure on the publication of oriental works and spend funds only on English education.

Choose the correct answer from the options given below:

(1) A and D only
(2) B and D only
(3) A and C only
(4) B and C only

52. Which two of the following statements are applicable to 'metalanguage'?
It is :

A. a technical language which describes the properties of language.
B. known as a 'first-order' language.
C. a 'second-order' language that replaces a 'first-order' language with metaphors.
D. a 'second-order' language.

Choose the correct answer from the options given below:

(1) A and B only
(2) C and D only

(3) A and D only
(4) B and C only

53. "Hari wrote a poem on the mountains". Which two of the following are admissible statements about the above sentence?

A. The sentence is an example of lexical ambiguity
B. The sentence is an example of structural ambiguity
C. The sentence involves two deep structures
D. The sentence involves two surface structures

Choose the correct answer from the options given below

(1) A and B only
(2) B and C only
(3) B and D only
(4) C and D only

54. Which two of the following events are described in Samuels Pepys s Diary?

A. The Plague in London
B. The Great Fire of London
C. The War of Spanish Succession
D. Essex Rebellion

Choose the correct answer from the options given below:

(1) A and B only
(2) A and C only
(3) B and C only
(4) B and D only

55. Which two of the following inspired the rise of the periodical essay?

A. Robert Burton
B. Francois Rabelais
C. Francis Bacon
D. Michel de Montaigne

Choose the most appropriate answer from the options given below

(1) C and A only
(2) A and B only
(3) C and D only
(4) B and D only

56. Which two of the following works does Walter Pater regard as examples of "great art" in his essay "Style"?

A. *Iliad*
B. *The Divine Comedy*
C. *Les Miserables*
D. *Faust*

Choose the most appropriate answer from the options given below:

(1) A and B only
(2) A and D only
(3) B and C only
(4) B and D only

57. According to his essay Civil Disobedience what two things did Thoreau learn from the night he spent in jail?

A. He concluded that the State is ultimately weak
B. He realized that captivity inspires courage
C. He realized that the neighbours are only friends during good times
D. He concluded that captivity brings wisdom about human affairs

Choose the correct answer from the options given below

(1) A and B only
(2) A and C only
(3) A and D only
(4) C and D only

58. Which two of the following are the titles of the sections in Thomas De Quincey's "The English Mail – Coach"?

A. The Glory of Mobility
B. The Vision of Sudden Death
C. The Glory of Motion
D. The Vision of Unexpected Truth

Choose the correct answer from the options given below:

(1) A and B only
(2) A and D only
(3) B and C only
(4) B and D only

59. Which two of the following books are explorations of the art of the novel by novelists?
A. *The Brief Compass*
B. *The Naive and the Sentimental Novelist*
C. *The Visionary Company*
D. *Testaments Betrayed*
Choose the most appropriate answer from the options given below:
(1) A and B only
(2) A and C only
(3) B and C only
(4) B and D only

60. The lives of which of the following writers have been the subject matter of novels by Anthony Burgess?
A. Milton B. Marlowe
C. Shelley D. Keats
Choose the correct answer from the options given below:
(1) A and B only
(2) A and D only
(3) B and C only
(4) B and D only

61. Which two rivers are mentioned by Andrew Marvell at the beginning of "To Hrs Coy Mistress"?
A. The Ganges
B. Thames
C. Humber
D. The Jhelum
Choose the correct answer from the options given below
(1) A and D only
(2) A and B only
(3) A and C only
(4) B and C only

62. Which two poems in the following list are examples of dramatic monologue?
A. Alfred Tennyson, "Ulysses"
B. Philip Larkin, "Church Going"
C. Carol Ann Duffy, "Medusa"
D. Katherine Philips, "A Married State"
Choose the correct answer from the options given below:
(1) A and D only
(2) B and C only
(3) C and D only
(4) A and C only

63. Which two of the following poems are by Robert Browning?
A. "Locksley Hall"
B. "The Pied Piper of Hamelin"
C. "The Lady of Shalott"
D. "Two in the Campagna?
Choose the correct answer from the options given below:
(1) A and D only
(2) B and C only
(3) A and C only
(4) B and D only

64. Which two of the following dramatists are associated with the Epic Theatre?
A. Fernando Arrabal
B. Bertolt Brecht
C. Arnolt Bronnen
D. James Saunders
Choose the correct answer from the options given below:
(1) A and B only
(2) B and C only
(3) A and D only
(4) B and D only

65. Which two characters/speakers among the following exhibit the studious abstraction of scholars?
A. Shylock
B. Hamlet

C. Il Penseroso
D. Mosca

Choose the correct answer from the options given below:

(1) A and D only
(2) B and C only
(3) C and D only
(4) A and C only

66. Match List I with List II

List I Terms	List II Theorists
A. arche-ecriture	I. Julia Kristeva
B. cyborg	II. Donna Haraway
C. genotext	III. Friedrich Schleiermacher
D. hermeneutic circle	IV. Jacques Derrida

Choose the correct answer from the options given below:

(1) A-IV, B-II, C-I, D-III
(2) A-III, B-I, C-II, D-IV
(3) A-III, B-II, C-IV, D-I
(4) A-IV, B-I, C-II, D-III

67. Match List I with List II

List I Terms	List II Theorists
A. Superreader	I. Michel Foucault
B. Biopower	II. Mikhail Bakhtin
C. Bricolage	III. Michael Riffaterre
D. Chronotope	IV. Claude Levi-Strauss

Choose the correct answer from the options given below:

(1) A-III, B-II, C-IV, D-I
(2) A-III, B-I, C-IV, D-II
(3) A-IV, B-I, C-III, D-II
(4) A-II, B-I, C-IV, D-III

68. Match List I with List II

List I Critics	List II Text
A. Horace	I. *A Defence of Rhyme*
B. John Dryden	II. *Timber: or, Discoveries*
C. Samuel Daniel	III. *Ars Poetica*
D. Ben Jonson	IV. *Of Dramatic Poesy*

Choose the correct answer from the options given below:

(1) A-II, B-I, C-IV, D-III
(2) A-III, B-IV, C-II, D-I
(3) A-III, B-IV, C-I, D-II
(4) A-II, B-IV, C-I, D-III

69. Match List I with List II

List I Author	List II Text
A. Michel de Certeau	I. *Distinction*
B. John Fiske	II. *Reading the Romance*
C. Pierre Bourdieu	III. *Understanding Popular Culture*
D. Janice Radway	IV. *The Practice of Everyday Life*

Choose the correct answer from the options given below:

(1) A-IV, B-I, C-II, D-III
(2) A-III, B-IV, C-I, D-II
(3) A-IV, B-III, C-I, D-II
(4) A-III, B-I, C-IV, D-II

70. Match List I with List II

List I Linguist	List II Concept
A. Paul Grice	I. language death
B. Edward Sapir	II. linguistic signs
C. Ferdinand de Saussure	III. linguistic relativity
D. Nancy Dorian	IV. cooperative principle

Choose the correct answer from the options given below:

(1) A-I, B-III, C-II, D-IV
(2) A-IV, B-III, C-II, D-I
(3) A-III, B-IV, C-I, D-II
(4) A-III, B-IV, C-II, D-I

71. Match List I with List II

List I Word Borrowed	List II Source Indian Language
A. mongoose	I. Tamil
B. loot	II. Malayalam
C. curry	III. Hindi/Urdu
D. betel	IV. Marathi

Choose the correct answer from the options given below:

(1) A-IV, B-III, C-I, D-II
(2) A-IV, B-II, C-I, D-III
(3) A-II, B-III, C-IV, D-I
(4) A-II, B-I, C-IV, D-III

72. Match List I with List II

List I Essayist	List II Essay
A. George Orwell	I. "On the Artificial Comedy of the Last Century"
B. Michel de Montaigne	II. "Why I Write"
C. Charles Lamb	III. "A Modest Proposal"
D. Jonathan Swift	IV. "On the Cannibals"

Choose the correct answer from the options given below:

(1) A-III, B-IV, C-II, D-I
(2) A-II, B-IV, C-I, D-III
(3) A-IV, B-III, C-II, D-I
(4) A-II, B-III, C-I, D-IV

73. Match List I with List II

List I Author	List II Text
A. Thomas Pynchon	I. G.
B. Howard Jacobson	II. V
C. Anthony Burgess	III. J
D. John Berger	IV. M/F

Choose the correct answer from the options given below:

(1) A-II, B-IV, C-I, D-III
(2) A-II, B-III, C-IV, D-I
(3) A-II, B-III, C-I, D-IV
(4) A-IV, B-III, C-I, D-II

74. Match List I with List II

List I Lines	List II Poems
A. "Monuments of unaging intellect"	I. "Leda and the Swan"
B. "In the foul rag-and-bone shop of the heart"	II. "Adam's Curse"
C. "So mastered by the brute blood of the air"	III. "Sailing to Byzantium"
D. "As weary hearted as that hollow moon"	IV. "The Circus Animals' Desertion"

Choose the correct answer from the options given below:

(1) A-III, B-IV, C-II, D-I
(2) A-III, B-I, C-IV, D-II
(3) A-III, B-IV, C-I, D-II
(4) A-II, B-I, C-IV, D-III

75. Match List I with List II

List I Author	List II Work
A. John Keats	I. Alastor
B. William Wordsworth	II. Songs of Experience
C. P. B. Shelley	III. Lamia
D. William Blake	IV. The Excursion

Choose the correct answer from the options given below:

(1) A-III, B-I, C-IV, D-III
(2) A-III, B-IV, C-I, D-II
(3) A-I, B-IV, C-III, D-II
(4) A-IV, B-II, C-I, D-III

76. Arrange the following terms in the chronological order of emergence

A. Heresy of Paraphrase
B. Stream of Consciousness

C. Practical Criticism
D. Defamiliarization

Choose the correct answer from the options given below:

(1) D, B, C, A
(2) B, D, A, C
(3) B, D, C, A
(4) D, C, B, A

77. Arrange the following critical works in their chronological order of publication:

[illegible] Ballads"
C. "Life of Cowley"
D. "The Frontiers of Criticism"

Choose the correct answer from the options given below:

(1) A, C, B and D
(2) B, A, C and D
(3) B, C, A and D
(4) C, A, D and B

78. Arrange the following in the chronological order of publication:

A. Aspects of the Theory of Syntax
B. Course in General Linguistics
C. Semiotics and the Philosophy of Language
D. How to Do Things with Words

Choose the correct answer from the options given below:

(1) D, B, A, C
(2) C, B, A, D
(3) B, D, A, C
(4) B, A, D, C

79. Arrange the following an the chronological order of publication

A. *Advancement of Learning*
B. *The Origin of Species*
C. *On Heroes and Hero Worship*
D. *The Lives of the Poets*

Choose the correct answer from the options given below

(1) D, A, C, B
(2) D, A, B, C
(3) A, D, C, B
(4) A, D, B, C

80. Arrange the following 18th-century magazines in the chronological order of publication:

A. *The Critical Review*
B. *The Monthly Review*
C. *The Gentleman's Magazine*
The Rambler

Choose the correct answer from the options given below:

(1) A, D, B, C
(2) D, A, B, C
(3) B, A, C, D
(4) C, B, D, A

81. Arrange the following in the chronological order of publication

A. *Crome Yellow*
B. *Sons and Lovers*
C. *Mrs Dalloway*
D. *A Portrait of the Artist as a Young Man*

Choose the correct answer from the options given below

(1) B, A, D, C
(2) A, B, D, C
(3) A, C, B, D
(4) B, D, A, C

82. Arrange the following women novelists in the chronological order (by date of birth)

A. Anne Bronte
B. Jane Austen
C. Ann Radcliffe
D. Fanny Burney
E. Maria Edgeworth

Choose the correct answer from the options given below:

(1) B, A, D, C, E
(2) C, D, B, E, A
(3) D, C, E, B, A
(4) A, B, C, E, D

83. Arrange the following authors in the chronological order of their birth:

A. Oscar Wilde

B. William Langland

C. Geoffrey Chaucer

D. John Dryden

E. Alexander Pope

Choose the correct answer from the options given below:

(1) B, C, D, E, A

(2) A, B, C, E, D

(3) B, C, D, A, E

(4) C, B, A, D, E

84. Arrange the following plays in their chronological order:

A. *The Country Wife*

B. *Cymbeline*

C. *The Spanish Tragedy*

D. *The Rivals*

Choose the correct answer from the options given below:

(1) B, A, C, D

(2) B, C, D, A

(3) C, B, A, D

(4) C, A, B, D

85. Arrange the following plays in the chronological order of publication:

A. *All for Love*

B. *Venice Preserved*

C. *The School for Scandal*

D. *The Country Wife*

Choose the correct answer from the options given below:

(1) B, C, A, D (2) D, A, B, C

(3) C, B, D, A (4) A, D, C, B

86. Given below are two statements: one is labelled as Assertion A and the other is labelled as Reason R.

Assertion A: Research methods are a range of tools that are used for different types of inquiry.

Reason R: The tools used in research are products of the situations in which they are applied.

In light of the above statements, choose the correct answer from the options given below:

(1) Both A and R are true and R is the correct explanation of A

(2) Both A and R are true and [illegible] correct explanation [illegible]

(3) A is [illegible]

(4) A is false but R is true

87. Given below are two statements: one is labelled as Assertion A and the other is labelled as Reason R

Assertion A: Signs are never neutral or innocent.

Reason R: In all cases signs are organized into systems that convey some meaning.

In light of the above statements, choose the correct answer from the options given below

(1) Both A and R are true and R is the correct explanation of A

(2) Both A and R are true but R is NOT the correct explanation of A

(3) A is true but R is false

(4) A is false but R is true

88. Given below are two statements

Statement I: Consumption is an outcome of self-interest and a maximization of personal pleasure.

Statement II: There are strong correlations between social status and such things as housing styles, musical tastes and food preferences

In light of the above statements, choose the correct answer from the options given below

(1) Both Statement I and Statement II are true

(2) Both Statement I and Statement II are false

(3) Statement I is correct but Statement II is false

(4) Statement I is incorrect but Statement II is true

89. Given below are two statements:

Statement I: The Orientalists in British India were not sympathetic towards India's ancient learning.

Statement II: William Jones thought that in "imagination", "ratiocination", and philosophy, Indians were by no means inferior to Europeans.

In light of the above statements, choose the correct answer from the options given below

(1) Both Statement I and Statement II are true

(2) Both Statement I and Statement II are false

(3) Statement I is correct but Statement II is false

(4) Statement I is incorrect but Statement II is true

90. Given below are two statements: one is labelled as Assertion A and the other is labelled as Reason R

Assertion A: The introduction of English in India was primarily for the benefit and consolidation of British power.

Reason R: English catered to the social and economic aspirations of the emerging middle class and urban elites in India.

In light of the above statements, choose the correct answer from the options given below

(1) Both A and R are true and R is the correct explanation of A

(2) Both A and R are true but R is NOT the correct explanation of A

(3) A is true but R is false

(4) A is false but R is true

Question Numbers : (91 to 93)

Question Label : Comprehension

Read the given passage and answer the questions that follow

Daybreak

At dawn she lay with her profile at that angle
Which, sleeping, seems the stone face of an angel:
Her hair a harp the hand of a breeze follows
To play, against the white cloud of the pillows.
Then in a flush of rose she woke, and her eyes were open,
Swimming with blue through the rose flesh of dawn.
From her dew of lips, the drop of one word
Fell, from a dawn of fountains, when she murmured
Darling, ' — upon my heart the song of the first bird.
'My dream glides in my dream,' she said, 'come true.
I waken from you to my dream of you.'
O, then my waking dream dared to assume
The audacity of her sleep. Our dreams
Flowed into each other's arms, like streams.

– Stephen Spender

91. Which among the following best describes the lady's face as "At dawn she lay..." asleep?

(1) Her face appears to be that of a stone sculptures.

(2) The side-view of her face appears to be that of a sculpted angels.

(3) Her face appears to be that of a stone-angel.

(4) The side-view of her face appears to be that of an angel's.

92. Match List I with List II

List I The Item	List II What it is an example of
A. 'Her hair'	I. player
B. 'pillows'	II. 'a harp'

C. 'breeze' III. 'rose'
D. 'cheeks' IV. 'cloud'

Choose the correct answer from the options given below:

(1) A-I, B-II, C-IV, D-III
(2) A-III, B-I, C-II, D-IV
(3) A-II, B-IV, C-I, D-III
(4) A-IV, B-III, C-I, D-II

93. Match List I with List II

List I Item	List II What it is an example of
A. 'Her hair a harp'	I. Simile
B. 'the hand of a breeze'	II. Metaphor
C. 'seems the stone face'	III. Oxymoron
D. 'my waking dream'	IV. Synecdoche

Choose the correct answer from the options given below:

(1) A-II, B-IV, C-I, D-III
(2) A-IV, B-II, C-III, D-I
(3) A-IV, B-III, C-II, D-I
(4) A-I, B-IV, C-II, D-III

Question Numbers : (94 to 95)
Question Label : Comprehension
Read the given passage and answer the questions that follow

Logic cannot have any empirical part; that is, a part in which the universal and necessary laws of thought should rest on grounds taken from experience; otherwise it would not be logic, i.e., a canon for the understanding or the reason, valid for all thought, and capable of demonstration. Natural and moral philosophy, on the contrary, can each have their empirical part, since the former has to determine the laws of nature as an object of experience; the latter, the laws of the human will, so far as it is affected by nature: the former, however, being laws according to which everything does happen; the latter, laws according to which everything ought to happen. Ethics, however, must also consider the conditions under which what ought to happen frequently does not. *–Immanuel Kant*

94. "Logic cannot have any empirical part", because

A. laws of thought are subjective.
B. it propounds laws whose applicability can be shown
C. its laws are valid for all thought
D. its laws are valid for everyone's experience

Choose the most appropriate answer from the options given below:

(1) A and D only
(2) B and C only
(3) A and C only
(4) B and D only

95. Based on the given passage which two of the following statements are correct?

A. For natural philosophy nature influences the laws
B. For moral philosophy nature is to be experienced
C. Natural philosophy does not describe how things actually do happen
D. Moral philosophy accounts for what should be

Choose the correct answer from the options given below:

(1) A and C only
(2) B and D only
(3) C and D only
(4) A and D only

Question Numbers : (96 to 98)
Question Label : Comprehension
Read the given passage and answer the questions that follow

And the creature run from the cur?
There thou mightst behold the great image of authority: a dog's obeyed in office. —
Thou rascal beadle, hold thy bloody hand!
Why dost thou lash that whore? Strip thine own back:
Thou hotly lust'st to use her in that kind
For which thou whipp'st her. The usurer hangs the cozener.

Through tatter'd clothes small vices do appear;
Robes and furr'd gowns hide all. Plate sin with gold,
And the strong lance of justice hurtless breaks;
Arm it in rags, a pigmy's straw doth pierce it.

– *King Lear*

96. Who speaks these lines and to whom?

(1) Edgar to Lear
(2) Goneril to Edgar
(3) Lear to Gloucester
(4) Gloucester to Lear

97. In the passage, the church officer is asked to whip his own back rather than the prostitutes because:

(1) as a religious man he should punish himself for others' sins.
(2) he at one time had lusted after her.
(3) men like him make them prostitutes.
(4) he does not have the authority to whip a woman.

98. The two sentences in the lines from "Through tatter'd clothes..." to "...straw doth pierce it" deal with two foibles, (i) *vice* and (ii) *sin*. About these two, the speaker says that

(1) Vice afflicts all but sin afflicts only the weak.
(2) Sin afflicts all but vice afflicts only the strong.
(3) Sin and vice are seen in both the weak and the strong.
(4) Sin and vice are palpable in the weak and impalpable in the strong.

Question Numbers : (99 to 100)

Question Label : Comprehension

Read the given passage and answer the questions that follow

The surgeon deposited it in her arms. She imprinted her cold, white lips passionately on its forehead; passed her hands over her face; gazed wildly around; shuddered; fell back— and died. They chafed her breast, hands, temples; but the blood had stopped forever. They talked of hope and comfort. They had been strangers too long. 'It's all over, Mrs. Thingummy!', said the surgeon at last.

Dickens, *Oliver Twist*

99. In the expression, "passed her hands over her face", the 'face' is of:

(1) the lady surgeon
(2) the child
(3) the nurse
(4) the patient

100. The implication of "they had been strangers too long" is:

(1) Those who spoke of 'hope and comfort' had been strangers too long.
(2) 'Hope' had been stranger to 'comfort' for too long.
(3) 'Hope and comfort' had been stranger to the patient too long.
(4) 'Hope and comfort' had been strangers to the surgeon, nurse and the patient too long.

ANSWERS

1. (4)	**2.** (2)	**3.** (3)	**4.** (1)	**5.** (3)	**6.** (3)	**7.** (4)	**8.** (4)	**9.** (4)	**10.** (2)
11. (1)	**12.** (3)	**13.** (4)	**14.** (1)	**15.** (3)	**16.** (1)	**17.** (2)	**18.** (1)	**19.** (4)	**20.** (2)
21. (4)	**22.** (1)	**23.** (2)	**24.** (2)	**25.** (3)	**26.** (4)	**27.** (1)	**28.** (1)	**29.** (2)	**30.** (2)
31. (1)	**32.** (4)	**33.** (4)	**34.** (2)	**35.** (3)	**36.** (3)	**37.** (3)	**38.** (2)	**39.** (3)	**40.** (2)
41. (3)	**42.** (3)	**43.** (4)	**44.** (3)	**45.** (4)	**46.** (2)	**47.** (4)	**48.** (2)	**49.** (3)	**50.** (2)
51. (1)	**52.** (3)	**53.** (2)	**54.** (1)	**55.** (3)	**56.** (3)	**57.** (2)	**58.** (3)	**59.** (4)	**60.** (4)
61. (3)	**62.** (4)	**63.** (4)	**64.** (2)	**65.** (2)	**66.** (1)	**67.** (2)	**68.** (3)	**69.** (3)	**70.** (2)
71. (1)	**72.** (2)	**73.** (2)	**74.** (3)	**75.** (2)	**76.** (3)	**77.** (3)	**78.** (3)	**79.** (3)	**80.** (4)
81. (4)	**82.** (3)	**83.** (1)	**84.** (3)	**85.** (2)	**86.** (2)	**87.** (1)	**88.** (1)	**89.** (4)	**90.** (2)
91. (2)	**92.** (3)	**93.** (1)	**94.** (2)	**95.** (4)	**96.** (3)	**97.** (3)	**98.** (4)	**99.** (4)	**100.** (3)

❖❖❖

November, 2021

ENGLISH LITERATURE

PAPER-II

Note : This paper contains **hundred (100)** objective type questions of **two (2)** marks each. **All questions are compulsory.**

Question Numbers : (1 to 3)

Read the following passage and answer the questions that follow:

What can be the use of a poetry that has no true subject except the poet's own selfhood? The traditional use of poetry in the Western world has been instruction through delight, where teaching has meant the common truths or common deceptions of societal tradition, and where esthetic pleasure has meant a fulfillment of expectations founded upon past joys of the same design.

But an individual psyche has its own accidents, which it needs to call truths, and its own necessity for self-recognition, which requires the pleasures of originality, even if those pleasures depend upon a kind of lying against time, and against the achievements of the past. The use of such poetry demands to be seen in a deidealized way, if it is to be seen more truly.

–Harold Bloom, "The Use of Poetry"

1. In the context of the above which is closest to being true?

(1) There can be no use of poetry.
(2) Poetry can have no true subject.
(3) Man may be the true subject of poetry.
(4) The poet himself may be the subject.

2. What is meant by 'traditional use of poetry'?

(1) Promoting serious ideas
(2) Promoting doubtful pleasure
(3) Promoting joyous expectations
(4) Promoting social honesty in life

3. If 'selfhood' of a poet is the subject of poetry, then 'originality' shall spring from:

(1) some truth of untruths.
(2) truth of self-recognition.
(3) creating ideal pleasures.
(4) re-living the past joys.

Question Numbers : (4 to 6)

Read the following poem and answer the questions that follow:

No worst, there is none.
No worst, there is none. Pitched past pitch of grief,
More pangs will, schooled at forepangs, wilder wring.
Comforter, where, where is your comforting?
Mary, mother of us, where is your relief?
My cries heave, herds-long; huddle in a main, a chief
Woe, world-sorrow; on an age-old anvil wince and sing.
Then lull, then leave off. Fury had shrieked 'No lingering!
Let me be fell: force I must be brief."'
O the mind, mind has mountains; cliffs of fall
Frightful, sheer, no-man-fathomed. Hold them cheap
May who ne'er hung there. Nor does long our small
Durance deal with that steep or deep. Here! creep,
Wretch, under a comfort serves in a whirlwind: all
Life death does end and each day dies with sleep.

– Gerard Manley Hopkins

4. Which of the following best describes the meaning of the title of the poem, 'No worst, there is none.'?

(1) It is not worst because there is nothing.
(2) Nothing can be so much bad as this.
(3) No it is worst as nothing is there.
(4) It is very bad as no one is there.

5. Beyond the intensity of known grief, there can be
   (1) no grief than being experienced.
   (2) only a new pain more painful.
   (3) only the twisted known pains.
   (4) the griefs beyond limits of pain.
6. Which two of the following are true?
   A. Not all know the intensity or depth of suffering.
   B. Death does not put an end to our sufferings.
   C. Suffering is seen as winds that hinder comfort.
   D. Suffering's intensity or depth is in the mind.

   Choose the correct answer from the options given below:
   (1) A and B only (2) C and D only
   (3) A and D only (4) B and D only

Question Numbers : (7 to 8)

Read the following extract and answer the questions that follow:

'Justice' was done, and the President of the Immortals, in Aeschylean phrase, had ended his sport with Tess. And the D'Urberville knights and dames slept on in their tombs unknowing.

The two speechless gazers bent themselves down to the earth, as if in prayer, and remained thus a long time, absolutely motionless; the flag continued to wave silently. As soon as they had enough strength they arose, joined hands again, and went on.

– Thomas Hardy, Tess of the D'Urbervilles

7. How did the 'sport with Tess' end?
   (1) She was hanged.
   (2) She was expelled from Wintoncester.
   (3) The tormentor married her.
   (4) She died an untimely death.
8. Who are the 'two speechless gazers'?
   (1) Reverend James Clare and Mrs. Brooks
   (2) 'Liza-Lu and Angel Clare
   (3) Tess's two parents
   (4) Parson Tringham and Mrs. d'Urberville

Question Numbers : (9 to 10)

Read the following extract and answer the questions that follow:

The solemn temples, the great globe itself,
Yea, all which it inherit, shall dissolve
And, like this insubstantial pageant faded,
Leave not a rack behind. We are such stuff
As dreams are made on, and our little life
Is rounded with a sleep.

– Shakespeare, The Tempest

9. '[T]his insubstantial pageant' refers to:
   (1) the shutdown of Globe theatre.
   (2) a non-real performance.
   (3) the destroyed mother earth.
   (4) enactment with support structure.
10. 'We are such stuff as dreams are made on' means:
   (1) Human life is full of imaginary colours.
   (2) Our life is a text of what happened.
   (3) We are a bundle of past reality.
   (4) There is no substance to human life.
11. In "An Apology for Poetry" Sidney discusses the didactic function of poetry by comparing it to philosophy and
   (1) religion (2) aesthetics
   (3) history (4) ethics
12. According to Longinus which two of the following qualities apply to 'great poetry'?
   A. It must be the work of genius, an inspired person.
   B. It must cause a feeling of melancholy in the reader.
   C. It must employ devices of rhetoric.
   D. It must please selectively and on special occasions.

   Choose the correct answer from the options given below:
   (1) A and B only (2) A and C only
   (3) B and D only (4) C and D only
13. In "The Function of Criticism" T.S. Eliot attacked J. Middleton Murry and similar critics for being devotees of what he called
   (1) "the Inner Voice".
   (2) "the Romantic Impulse".
   (3) "the Symbol Hunt".
   (4) "the Muse's Mystery".

14. Who among the following compared 'the mind in creation' to 'a fading coal'?
(1) Wordsworth (2) Coleridge
(3) Shelley (4) Keats

15. Who among the following considered paraphrase as 'a heresy'?
(1) Percy Lubbock (2) Edmund Wilson
(3) I.A. Richards (4) Cleanth Brooks

16. Empiricist linguistics is concerned with
(1) investigation of the human mind.
(2) directly observable sense-data.
(3) reason as a determinant of enquiry.
(4) innate language knowledge

17. In Noam Chomsky's definition of grammar which two features are drawn from mathematics?
A. complexity B. abstraction
C. transformation D. generation
Choose the correct answer from the options given below:
(1) A and B only (2) A and C only
(3) B and D only (4) C and D only

18. 'Potato' is a sixteenth-century borrowing into English from
(1) Spanish (2) French
(3) German (4) Norwegian.

19. Who among the following represents the global spread of English diagrammatically as three concentric circles?
(1) David Crystal (2) Jenny Cheshire
(3) Braj B. Kachru (4) Salikoko Mufwene

20. Who among the following is the founder of the Survey of English Usage (SEU)?
(1) Randolph Quirk
(2) Henry Watson Fowler
(3) Michael Swan (4) Bryan Garner

21. Who is the author of the short story, "Beethoven Was One-Sixteenth Black"?
(1) J. M. Coetzee (2) Nadine Gordimer
(3) Andre Brink (4) Bessie Head

22. Arrange the following texts in the chronological order of publication.
A. *This Bridge Called My Back*
B. *Sexual Politics*
C. *Gender Trouble*
D. *The Feminine Mystique*
Choose the correct answer from the options given below
(1) B, D, A, C (2) D, B, A, C
(3) D, A, B, C (4) B, D, C, A

23. Who is the author of the essay "Lear, Tolstoy and the Fool"?
(1) Aldous Huxley (2) George Orwell
(3) Virginia Woolf
(4) Somerset Maugham

24. Which of the following poems by Robert Browning contains the lines, "Our interest's on the dangerous edge of things. / The honest thief, the tender murderer, / The superstitious atheist. . ."?
(1) "A Death in the Desert"
(2) "Count Gismond"
(3) "Bishop Blougram's Apology"
(4) "Love Among the Ruins"

25. Who among the following edited *The Cornhill Magazine*?
(1) Charles Dickens
(2) Lewis Carroll
(3) William Makepeace Thackeray
(4) Anthony Trollope

26. Which of the following novels has its epigraph taken from the *Katha Upanishad*?
(1) *The Island of Doctor Moreau* by H. G. Wells
(2) *The Razor's Edge* by Somerset Maugham
(3) *Point Counter Point* by Aldous Huxley
(4) *A Room with a View* by E. M. Forster

27. Who is the author of the essay, "What Isn't Literature?"?
(1) E. D. Hirsch Jr. (2) Paul Ricoeur
(3) Hans-Georg Gadamer
(4) Terry Eagleton

28. Erich Auerbach's *Mimesis* (1946) ends with a chapter on
(1) Virginia Woolf's *To the Lighthouse.*
(2) Wyndham Lewis's *The Apes of God.*
(3) James Joyce's *Ulysses.*
(4) George Eliot's *Middlemarch*

29. Which of the following clusters is associated with what Julia Kristeva terms the 'semiotic'?
(1) Authority, order and patriarchy

(2) Displacement, slippage and condensation
(3) Repression, control and normalcy
(4) Logic, reason and power

30. Which two works in the following list are written by Aphra Behn?
A. *Rover* B. *Oroonoko*
C. *Soldier's Fortune*
D. *The Princess of Cleve*
Choose the correct answer from the options given below:
(1) A and B only (2) B and C only
(3) B and D only (4) A and C only

31. Which two of the following are works by Gustave Flaubert?
A. The Temptation of Saint Anthony
B. Old Goriot
C. Therese Raquin
D. Sentimental Education
Choose the correct answer from the options given below:
(1) A and C only (2) B and C only
(3) A and D only (4) B and D only

32. Which two of the following conform to liberal humanist thought?
A. Literature transcends the limits of the age of its origin and so is timeless.
B. Literature is untouched by the essential human nature which is unchanging.
C. Literature is devoid of any purpose to enhance life or promote human values.
D. Identity is a unique essence unaffected by environment and society.
Choose the correct answer from the options given below:
(1) A and C only (2) B and C only
(3) A and D only (4) B and D only

33. Which two of the following conform to Northrop Frye's typology of literature?
A. Mythos of spring: Comedy
B. Mythos of summer: Satire
C. Mythos of autumn: Tragedy
D. Mythos of winter: Romance
Choose the correct answer from the options given below:
(1) A and B only (2) B and D only
(3) A and C only (4) B and D only

34. Which two of the following writers does A. D. Hope address through his poetic responses in *A Book of Answers*?
A. Tolstoy B. Dostoevsky
C. Mallarme D. Goethe
Choose the correct answer from the options given below:
(1) A and D only (2) B and C only
(3) B and D only (4) A and C only

35. Which two of the following are true according to the documentation style prescribed by the eighth edition of the *MLA Handbook*?
A. If the title page of a book contains an imprint as well as the publisher's name, omit the imprint and use the publisher's name.
B. While giving a URL copy it from the Web browser but omit http:// or https://.
C. If a quotation extends to more than five lines set it off from the text as block indented an inch from the left margin.
D. Long titles should be abbreviated using the first letter of key words typed in upper case without intervening space.
Choose the correct answer from the options given below:
(1) A and B only (2) A and C only
(3) B and C only (4) B and D only

36. Which two of the following are highlighted in relation to specific historical moments by Stephen Greenblatt?
A. crisis of meaning
B. circulation of meaning
C. production of meaning
D. deferral of meaning
Choose the correct answer from the options given below:
(1) A and B only (2) B and C only
(3) C and D only (4) B and D only

37. Who among the following belong to the Chicago School of critics?
A. R. S. Crane B. E. M. W. Tillyard
C. Elder Olson D. Allen Tate
Choose the correct answer from the options given below:
(1) A and C only (2) A and D only
(3) B and C only (4) B and D only

38. Which of the following poems contains John Donne's famous conceit bringing a parallel between lovers and the hands of a compass?
(1) "Negative Love"
(2) "Lovers Infinitenesse"
(3) "A Valediction: Forbidding Mourning"
(4) "A Valediction: Of Weeping"

39. Arrange the following essays in the chronological order of publication.
A. T. S. Eliot, "The Function of Criticism"
B. Edgar Allan Poe, "The Philosophy of Composition"
C. Henry James, "The Art of Fiction"
D. Virginia Woolf, "Modern Fiction"
Choose the correct answer from the options given below
(1) C, B, A, D (2) C, B, D, A
(3) B, C, D, A (4) B, C, A, D

40. Arrange the following journals in the chronological order in which they started publication.
A. The Tatler B. The Examiner
C. The Review D. The Spectator
Choose the correct answer from the options given below
(1) A, D, C, B (2) B, A, D, C
(3) C, A, B, D (4) C, A, D, B

41. Given below are two statements, one is labelled as Assertion A and the other is labelled as Reason R
Assertion A : Postmodern narratives focus on the indeterminate and unstable nature of textuality and subjectivity.
Reason R : Postmodern narrative acts regard narratives and characters as tentative representations of writing and identity.
In light of the above statements, choose the correct answer from the options given below
(1) Both A and R are true and R is the correct explanation of A
(2) Both A and R are true but R is NOT the correct explanation of A
(3) A is true but R is false
(4) A is false but R is true

42. Given below are two statements
Statement I: In Waiting for Godot, it is Vladimir who questions the Boy who comes from Godot towards the end of the two Acts.
Statement II: In Waiting for Godot, it is Estragon who says, "Nothing happens, nobody comes, nobody goes, it's awful."
In light of the above statements, choose the correct answer from the options given below
(1) Both Statement I and Statement II are true
(2) Both Statement I and Statement II are false
(3) Statement I is true but Statement II is false
(4) Statement I is false but Statement II is true

43. Given below are two statements
Statement I: New Historicism stipulates that teleological connotations of history have to be eschewed.
Statement II: New Historicism neither denies nor accepts totalizing explanations of historical events.
In light of the above statements, choose the correct answer from the options given below
(1) Both Statement I and Statement II are true
(2) Both Statement I and Statement II are false
(3) Statement I is true but Statement II is false
4. Statement I is false but Statement II is true

44. What was poor Yorick in Hamlet?
(1) Jester (2) Actor
(3) Soldier (4) Gravedigger

45. Which of the following words refers to a sound that is associated with a particular meaning?
(1) phoneme (2) phonic substance
(3) phonestheme (4) phonemoid

46. Who among the following Dickens characters appears as a ghost?
(1) Daniel Quilp (2) Dora Spenlow
(3) Esther Summerson (4) Jacob Marley

47. Virginia Woolf's Orlando opens in 1588 and Orlando, a sixteen-year-old boy, writes a poem called:
(1) "The Evergreen Tree".
(2) "The Poison Tree".
(3) "The Oak Tree".
(4) "The Magic Tree".

48. What function of English is exemplified by the use of English in India as a "link language" along with a first language by stable bilinguals in well-defined social contexts?
(1) complementary (2) supplementary
(3) auxiliary (4) equative

49. Who among the following is said to have believed that the Persian Gulf War (1990-91) never happened?
(1) Zygmunt Bauman
(2) Jean Baudrillard
(3) Jacques Derrida
(4) Jurgen Habermas

50. What 19th-century philosophical term of Russian origin did Friedrich Nietzsche use to describe the disintegration of traditional morality in western society?
(1) absolutism (2) cynicism
(3) nihilism (4) anarchism

51. Which of the following statements is true of the working group set up by the University Grants Commission in 1978 to study the medium of instruction in higher education?
(1) It recommended a quicker switchover of the medium of instruction from English to Indian languages.
(2) It observed that English need not be displaced as the medium of instruction although regional languages were quite ready to take over its functions.
(3) It argued that English as a highly developed language was best suited for India's industrial and scientific progress.
(4) It asserted that English had the potential to further polarize an already-divided nation along socio-economic and intellectual fault lines.

52. In comparative philology and sometimes in modern phonology, what is the term used to refer to the deletion of a vowel within a word?
(1) Aphaeresis (2) Equi-deletion
(3) Paradigm (4) Syncope

53. Which of the following statements best describes Terry Eagleton's views on literature?
(1) It is involved in the reproduction of the dominant social order.
(2) Its raison d'être is to reflect social reality directly.
(3) Its primary purpose is to produce beauty and pleasure.
(4) It is closely allied to religion in its significance and seriousness.

54. Which of the following are true of 'performance', as used in linguistic theory?
A. It is analogous to the Saussurean concept of langue.
B. It refers to the specific utterances of individual native speakers in actual situations.
C. It is an innate grammar that suggests humans' universal ability to use language.
D. It includes hesitations and unfinished structures arising out of psychological difficulties acting upon the speaker.
Choose the correct answer from the options given below:
(1) A and B only (2) B and C only
(3) A and C only (4) B and D only

55. Which among the following are the works of George Gissing?
A. New Grub Street
B. Agnes Grey
C. The Odd Women D. Mary Barton
Choose the correct answer from the options given below:
(1) A and C only (2) B and D only
(3) A and B only (4) C and D only

56. Which of the following are novels by Ian McEwan?
A. Atonement
B. The Man with Two Left Feet
C. The Child in Time
D. The Rachel Papers

Choose the correct answer from the options given below:

(1) A and C only (2) B and D only
(3) C and D only (4) D and A only

57. Which of the following are poems by Nissim Ezekiel that make fun of Indians' use of English?

A. "Goodbye Party for Miss Pushpa T.S."
B. "Philosophy"
C. "Very Indian Poem in Indian English"
D. "Jewish Wedding in Bombay"
E. "Poet, Lover, Birdwatcher"

Choose the correct answer from the options given below:

(1) A and C only (2) B and D only
(3) A, B and D only (4) A, C and E only

58. Match List I with List II

List I (Author)	**List II (Text)**
A. Sean O'Casey	I. *I'm Talking About Jerusalem*
B. Dylan Thomas	II. *The Winslow Boy*
C. Terence Rattigan	III. *Juno and the Paycock*
D. Arnold Wesker	IV. *In the Shadow of the Glen*
E. J.M. Synge	V. *Under Milk Wood*

Choose the correct answer from the options given below:

(1) A-II, B-I, C-III, D-V, E-IV
(2) A-V, B-IV, C-II, D-I, E-III
(3) A-III, B-V, C-II, D-I, E-IV
(4) A-IV, B-II, C-III, D-V, E-I

59. Match List I with List II

List I (First line)	**List II (Poet)**
A. "Courage!" he said, and pointed toward the land...	I. G.M.Hopkins
B. I am poor brother Lippo, by your leave!	II. Alfred Tennyson
C. I caught this morning morning's minion...	III. D.G. Rossetti
D. Look in my face; my name is Might-have-been...	IV. Matthew Arnold
E. The sea is calm tonight...	V. Robert Browning

Choose the correct answer from the options given below:

(1) A-II, B-III, C-I, D-V, E-IV
(2) A-IV, B-V, C-I, D-III, E-II
(3) A-III, B-IV, C-V, D-I, E-II
(4) A-II, B-V, C-I, D-III, E-IV

60. Match List I with List II

List I (Character)	**List II (Novel)**
A. Winston Smith	I. Sons and Lovers
B. Paul Morel	II. Ulysses
C. 'whiskey priest'	III. Nineteen Eighty-four
D. Leopold Bloom	IV. Decline and Fall
E. Paul Penny-feather	V. The Power and the Glory

Choose the correct answer from the options given below:

(1) A-III, B-I, C-V, D-II, E-IV
(2) A-I, B-V, C-II, D-III, E-IV
(3) A-IV, B-III, C-V, D-II, E-I
(4) A-V, B-I, C-IV, D-II, E-III

61. Arrange the following language areas of the human brain in the order in which they involve in hearing, understanding and saying a word:

A. arcuate fasciculus
B. anterior speech cortex
C. motor cortex
D. posterior speech cortex

Choose the correct answer from the options given below:

1. A, C, D, B 2. B, A, D, C
3. C, B, A, D 4. D, A, B, C

62. Choose the right chronological sequence of the publication of the following books:

A. Margaret Atwood, The Handmaid's Tale
B. Alice Walker, The Color Purple
C. Doris Lessing, The Golden Notebook
D. Toni Morrison, The Bluest Eye

Choose the correct answer from the options given below:

1. A, B, D, C   2. B, A, D, C
3. C, D, B, A   4. D, C, B, A

63. Arrange the following terms in the chronological order of their use in literary theory:

A. gynesis   B. *scriptible*
C. *negritude*   D. paratext

Choose the correct answer from the options given below:

(1) D, A, C, B   (2) A, B, C, D
(3) C, A, D, B   (4) B, C, D, A

64. Given below are two statements:

Statement I: Unlike scientific research, literary research does not have specific materials for investigation and scientific tools for reaching a conclusion and formulating a theory.

Statement II: Literary research consists of critical interpretations of an author's work to the exclusion of biography and editing of texts.

In the light of the above statements, choose the most appropriate answer from the options given below:

(1) Both Statement I and Statement II are correct.
(2) Both Statement I and Statement II are incorrect.
(3) Statement I is correct but Statement II is incorrect.
(4) Statement I is incorrect but Statement II is correct.

65. Given below are two statements:

Statement I: Linguists, being primarily interested in the scientific study of language, approach language dispassionately.

Statement II: Linguists are necessarily polyglots who bring their own biases to language study.

In the light of the above statements, choose the most appropriate answer from the options given below:

(1) Both Statement I and Statement II are correct.
(2) Both Statement I and Statement II are incorrect.
(3) Statement I is correct but Statement II is incorrect.
(4) Statement I is incorrect but Statement II is correct.

66. Which of the following are features of the 'Theatre of the Absurd'?

A. emphasis on the central role of God in the universe
B. presentation of futile actions devoid of any goal
C. portrayal of situations that point to the meaningfulness of life
D. lacking in conflicts and dramatic tensions
E. presenting players in a stasis or drift without definite roles

Choose the correct answer from the options given below:

(1) A, C and E only (2) B, D and E only
(3) A, B and D only (4) B, C and D only

67. Who, among the following, is known to have used elements from the Yakshagana tradition in his theatre?

(1) Badal Sircar
(2) Girish Karnad
(3) Mohan Rakesh
(4) Mahesh Dattani

68. Match List I with List II

List I (Writer)	**List II (Book)**
A. Bankimchandra Chatterjee	I. Untouchable
B. Mulk Raj Anand	II. Rajmohan's Wife
C. Panchkouree Khan	III. Stories from Indian Christian Life
D. Kamala Sathianadhan	IV. The Revelations of an Orderly

Choose the correct answer from the options given below:

(1) A - II, B - I, C - IV, D - III
(2) A - I, B - III, C - II, D - IV
(3) A - III, B - IV, C - II, D - I
(4) A - IV, B - I, C - II, D - III

69. Which of these UK universities saw the first institutional incorporation of Cultural Studies?

(1) Bath Spa University
(2) Oxford University
(3) University of Birmingham
(4) Cambridge University

70. Which of these poets wrote a poem that served to inspire W B Yeats to write his own poem, "When you are Old"?
(1) Francois Villon (2) Pierre de Ronsard
(3) Edmund Spencer
(4) Heinrich Heine

71. Which of these does Meenakshi Mukherjee propose as the possible target readership of early Indian English novel?
A. A pan-Indian readership
B. A localized Indian readership
C. A British readership
D. The colonial administrator in India
Choose the correct answer from the options given below:
(1) A and B only (2) B and C only
(3) C and D only (4) A and D only

72. Match List I with List II

List I (Poet)	List II (Language)
A. Charles Baudelaire	I. French
B. Heinrich Heine	II. German
C. Sylvia Path	III. English
D. Jose Marti	IV. Spanish

Choose the correct answer from the options given below:
(1) A - I, B - II, C - III, D - IV
(2) A - II, B - III, C - IV, D - I
(3) A - III, B - IV, C - I, D - II
(4) A - IV, B - I, C - II, D - III

73. Which of these constitute the preoccupations of the protagonist of Upamanyu Chatterjee's English, August?
A. Marijuana B. Magic
C. Monotheism D. Marcus Aurelius
Choose the correct answer from the options given below:
(1) A and B only (2) A and D only
(3) B and C only (4) B and D only

74. What was the name of the journal published from Bowling Green University beginning 1969, which carried essays on amusement parks, comics and detective films?
(1) *Journal of Mass Culture*
(2) *Journal of Popular Culture*
(3) *Journal of Public Culture*
(4) *Journal of Culture Studies*

75. Which of these best describes Shyam Selvadurai's novel, Funny Boy?
(1) Novel of manners
(2) Sentimental novel
(3) Coming-of-age novel
(4) Picaresque novel

76. Which of these questions would Cultural Studies be most interested in asking?
A. Who decides what is to be produced?
B. Who can afford the artifact?
C. How is the artifact marketed?
D. What is the register of speech in the artifact?
Choose the correct answer from the options given below:
(1) A, B and C only (2) A, C and D only
(3) B, C and D only (4) A, B and D only

77. Who, among the following, played the most significant role in mobilizing the concept of 'cultural intermediaries'?
(1) Luis Althusser (2) Karl Marx
(3) Pierre Bourdieu (4) Jurgen Habermas

78. From whom does Gayatri Chakravorty Spivak borrow the term 'subaltern'?
(1) Karl Marx (2) Friedrich Engels
(3) Louis Althusser (4) Antonio Gramsci

79. Which of the following does the Subaltern Studies project contend?
A. Traditional historiography celebrated the role of the subalterns.
B. Traditional history of India's freedom movement celebrates the contribution of select icons.
C. Traditional historiography highlights the dominant strands of India's freedom struggle.
D. Subaltern Studies historiography highlights the dominant strands of India's freedom struggle.

Choose the correct answer from the options given below:

(1) A and B only (2) B and C only
(3) A and C only (4) B and D only.

80. Which of these did the Wood's Despatch (1854) seek to propagate?

A. Impart Western knowledge to Indians
B. Restrict access to English learning in India
C. Educate British officers in Sanskrit and Persian
D. Create a class of public servants

Choose the correct answer from the options given below:

(1) A and B only (2) B and C only
(3) A and C only (4) A and D only

81. Arrange the following periodicals in the chronological order in which they started publication:

A. The Spectator B. The Tatler
C. The Rambler D. The Critical Review

Choose the correct answer from the options given below:

(1) A, B, C, D (2) B, A, C, D
(3) B, C, D, A (4) A, D, B, C

82. Who, among these, does Gabriel Garcia Marquez name right in the beginning of his Nobel Prize address?

A. Ferdinand Magellan
B. Christopher Columbus
C. Marco Polo
D. Antonio Pigafetta

Choose the correct answer from the options given below:

(1) A and B only (2) B and C only
(3) C and D only (4) A and D only

83. Which of these constitutes the only extant trilogy from ancient Greek tragedy?

(1) King Oedipus, Oedipus at Colonus, Antigone
(2) Agamemnon, Choephori, The Eumenides
(3) Agamemnon, Orestes, The Eumenides
(4) King Oedipus, Orestes, Antigone

84. Match List I with List II

List I (Author)	List II (Form)
A. Pindar	I. Epinicia
B. Menander	II. Old Comedy
C. Sappho	III. Lyric poetry
D. Aristophanes	IV. New Comedy

Choose the correct answer from the options given below:

(1) A - I, B - III, C - II, D - IV
(2) A - I, B - IV, C - III, D - II
(3) A - II, B - I, C - IV, D - III
(4) A - III, B - IV, C - I, D - II

85. Which of these does the book How to read Donald Duck identify as an important element in its analysis of imperialist ideology in the Walt Disney comicbook?

(1) impoverished royalty
(2) noble savage
(3) scientific magic
(4) heartless civilisation

86. Match List I with List II

List I (Play)	List II (Playwright)
A. Bertolt Brecht	I. Cat on a Hot Tin Roof
B. Tennessee Williams	II. Life of Galileo
C. Vaclav Havel	III. Miss Julie
D. August Strindberg	IV. Temptation

Choose the correct answer from the options given below:

(1) A - I, B - II, C - IV, D - III
(2) A - III, B - II, C - I, D - IV
(3) A - IV, B - III, C - I, D - II
(4) A - II, B - I, C - IV, D - III

87. Which of these plays by Girish Karnad shares its theme with Thomas Mann's The Transposed Heads?

(1) Hayavadana (2) *Yayati*
(3) *Nagamandala* (4) *Tale Danda*

88. With which of these is Ngugi wa Thiongo generally associated?

(1) Decolonising the State
(2) Decolonising the Mind

(3) Decolonising the Body
(4) Decolonising the Polity

89. Match List I with List II

List I (Novel)	List II (Author)
A. Don Quixote	I. Machado de Assis
B. Sorrows of Young Werther	II. Honore de Balzac
C. Lost Illusions	III. Goethe
D. Epitaph of a Small Winner	IV. Miguel de Cervantes

Choose the correct answer from the options given below:
(1) A - I, B - III, C - II, D - IV
(2) A - II, B - I, C - III, D - IV
(3) A - IV, B - III, C - II, D - I
(4) A - III, B - I, C - IV, D - II

90. Charles Lamb used the pseudonym Elia for writing in which of the following periodicals?
(1) *London Magazine*
(2) *The Edinburg Review*
(3) *The Quarterly Review*
(4) *Athenaeum*

91. In "Mr Bennett and Mrs Brown" Virginia Woolf
(1) responds to E.M. Forster's remarks on character in fiction.
(2) criticises book buying preferences of the educated English class.
(3) analyses the state of modern fiction by contrasting two generations of writers.
(4) presents modernity as a stable and coherent project uniting all artists.

92. In "Politics and the English Language" which two of the following 'tricks' are mentioned by George Orwell as 'bad habits' of English use?
A. obsolete words
B. pretentious diction
C. dying metaphors
D. false modifiers

Choose the correct answer from the options given below:
(1) A and B only (2) B and C only
(3) B and D only (4) C and D only

93. Match List I with List II

List I (Essay)	List II (Essayist)
A. "The Tory Fox-Hunter	I. Francis Bacon
B. "What I Believe"	II. Joseph Addison
C. "The Death of the Moth"	III. E.M. Forster
D. "Of Ambition"	IV. Virginia Woolf

Choose the correct answer from the options given below:
(1) A - I, B - III, C - IV, D - II
(2) A - III, B - IV, C - II, D - I
(3) A - II, B - III, C - IV, D - I
(4) A - IV, B - I, C - II, D - III

94. Arrange the following characters in their chronological sequence of appearance:
A. A. Mirabell
B. Shylock
C. Jimmy Porter
D. Sir Epicure Mammon

Choose the correct answer from the options given below
(1) D, B, A, C (2) B, D, A, C
(3) D, B, C, A (4) B, D, C, A

95. Which two of the following concepts are deployed in the work of Frederic Jameson?
A. Pastiche B. Hyperreal
C. Schizophrenia D. Habitus

Choose the correct answer from the options given below:
(1) A and B only (2) C and D only
(3) B and D only (4) A and C only

96. Arrange the following plays in their chronological sequence:
A. *Sergeant Musgrave's Dance*
B. *The Playboy of the Western World*
C. *Look Back in Anger*
D. *Man and Superman*

Choose the correct answer from the options given below
(1) D, B, A, C (2) B, D, A, C
(3) D, B, C, A (4) B, D, C, A

97. Match List I with List II

List I (Text)	List II (Author)
A. Modernity at Large	I. J. Urry
B. The Tourist Gaze	II. E.W. Said
C. Culture and Imperialism	III. C.L.R. James
D. The Black Jacobins	IV. A. Appadurai

Choose the correct answer from the options given below:

(1) A - IV, B - III, C - II, D - I
(2) A - III, B - IV, C - II, D - I
(3) A - II, B - III, C - IV, D - I
(4) A - IV, B - I, C - II, D - III

98. What might the speaker mean when he addresses 'Time' in a Shakespearean sonnet and declares that "I will be true, despite thy scythe and thee"?

A. Time preserves human life.
B. With time comes change.
C. Time creates opportunities.
D. Time removes human life.

Choose the correct answer from the options given below:

(1) A and B only (2) C and D only
(3) B and D only (4) A and C only

99. Which two of the following stage directions are from Harold Pinter's *The Birthday Party?*

A. *The living-room of a house on a seaside town.*
B. *A garbage pail on the ground next to the porch steps.*
C. *A light shows from upstairs bedroom, lower floor windows being dark.*
D. *He hangs the drum around his neck, taps it gently with the sticks, then marches round the table, beating it regularly.*

Choose the correct answer from the options given below:

(1) A and D only (2) C and D only
(3) B and C only (4) A and C only

100. Arrange the following lines of poetry in their chronological sequence:

A. "An aged man is but a paltry thing."
B. "The world is too much with us."
C. "Daddy, I have had to kill you."
D. "After great pain, a formal feeling comes-"

Choose the correct answer from the options given below

(1) B, D, A, C (2) D, B, A, C
(3) D, B, C, A (4) B, D, C, A

ANSWERS

1. (4)	**2.** (3)	**3.** (1)	**4.** (2)	**5.** (3)	**6.** (3)	**7.** (1)	**8.** (2)	**9.** (2)	**10.** (4)
11. (3)	**12.** (2)	**13.** (1)	**14.** (3)	**15.** (4)	**16.** (2)	**17.** (4)	**18.** (1)	**19.** (3)	**20.** (1)
21. (2)	**22.** (2)	**23.** (2)	**24.** (3)	**25.** (3)	**26.** (2)	**27.** (1)	**28.** (1)	**29.** (2)	**30.** (1)
31. (3)	**32.** (3)	**33.** (3)	**34.** (4)	**35.** (1)	**36.** (2)	**37.** (1)	**38.** (3)	**39.** (3)	**40.** (3,4)
41. (1)	**42.** (1)	**43.** (3)	**44.** (1)	**45.** (3)	**46.** (4)	**47.** (3)	**48.** (1)	**49.** (2)	**50.** (3)
51. (3)	**52.** (4)	**53.** (1)	**54.** (4)	**55.** (1)	**56.** (1)	**57.** (1)	**58.** (3)	**59.** (4)	**60.** (1)
61. (4)	**62.** (3)	**63.** (*)	**64.** (2)	**65.** (3)	**66.** (2)	**67.** (2)	**68.** (1)	**69.** (3)	**70.** (2)
71. (3)	**72.** (1)	**73.** (2)	**74.** (2)	**75.** (3)	**76.** (1)	**77.** (3)	**78.** (4)	**79.** (2)	**80.** (4)
81. (2)	**82.** (4)	**83.** (3)	**84.** (2)	**85.** (2)	**86.** (4)	**87.** (1)	**88.** (2)	**89.** (3)	**90.** (1)
91. (3)	**92.** (2)	**93.** (3)	**94.** (2)	**95.** (4)	**96.** (3)	**97.** (4)	**98.** (3)	**99.** (1)	**100.** (1)

October, 2022

ENGLISH

PAPER-II

Note : This paper contains **hundred (100)** objective type questions of **two (2)** marks each. **All questions are compulsory**.

1. Identify the one that has not been paired correctly.
(1) Criticism in Wilderness – Geoffrey Hartman
(2) Madness and Civilization – Roland Barthes
(3) Poetry and Regression – Harold Bloom
(4) Strangers to Ourselves – Julia Kristeva

2. Which of the following Articles of the Indian Constitution made the provision for use of English, alongside Hindi, for official purposes, for fifteen years?
(1) Article 351 (2) Article 344
(3) Article 343 (4) Article 358

3. What is meant by "Corporate author" in research?
(1) A writer who belongs to a corporate company
(2) A writer who writes on matters of corporate affairs
(3) A work produced by an institution, an association or a government agency
(4) A renowned author

4. Which of the following theorists identifies "metonymy" and "metaphor" as two fundamental structures of language?
(1) Ferdinand de Sassure
(2) Roland Barthes
(3) J.L. Austin
(4) Roman Jacobson

5. Which of the following is not true about "Lyrical Ballads"?
(1) It is a manifesto of Romantic poetry
(2) It turns English Poetry away from the social and intellectual sophistication of the seventeenth and the eighteenth century poetry
(3) It takes poetry out of the confines of reason and intellect to the unravished and unspoilt beauties of nature
(4) It is very particular about the form and structure of a poem

6. J Hillis Miller, one of the leading exponents of deconstruction, makes a deconstructionist reading of which of the following poems of P.B. Shelley?
(1) "The Triumph of Life"
(2) "Ode to the West Wind"
(3) "Revolt of Islam"
(4) "The Witch of Atlas"

7. The Deserted Village by Oliver Goldsmith
(1) Critiques the rural institutions
(2) Voices revolt of the individual man against institutions
(3) Reflects upon different views on the human soul
(4) Advocates urbanism over rural backwardness

8. A. L. Tennyson in the following lines :
"Yet I doubt not through the ages one increasing purpose runs.
And the thoughts of men are widen'd with the process of the suns"
(1) Reflects upon secularism
(2) Reflects upon evolutionary faith
(3) Reflects upon utilitarianism
(4) Reflects upon materialism

9. Philip Sidney's Arcadia was influenced by
(1) The Spanish Romance of Montemayor
(2) The Italian Paintings of Veronese
(3) The Arthurian Legends
(4) The Metaphysical Poetry

10. Who among the following has authored The Revenge's Tragadie?
(1) Cyril Tourneur
(2) John Webster
(3) John Fletcher
(4) Thomas Heywood

11. Besides being a playwright, who among the following has translated Homer?
(1) Ben Johnson
(2) Thomas Dekker
(3) Thomas Heywood
(4) George Chapman

12. Who among the following in the article. "Fleshly School of Poetry", attacked the Pre-Raphaelites, especially D.G. Rossetti?
(1) Robert Browning
(2) William Holeman Hunt
(3) Robert Buchanan
(4) Christina Rossetti

13. Which among the following is an incomplete poem by P.B. Shelley?
(1) "The Triumph of Life"
(2) "Ode to the West-wind"
(3) "Queen Mab"
(4) "The Daemon of the World"

14. Who among the following attached himself to the Earl of Nottingham's theatrical company?
(1) William Shakespeare
(2) Christopher Marlowe
(3) George Peele
(4) Ben Johnson

15. When was Haruki Murkami's Men Without Women published?
(1) 2017 (2) 2018
(3) 2014 (4) 2019

16. Who is the author of the essay 'Three Women's Texts and a Critique of Imperialism" (1985)?
(1) Ania Loomba
(2) Meenakshi Mukherjee
(3) Susan Meyer
(4) Gayatri Chakravorty Spivak

17. Who among the following critics appropriates the following statement by Karl Marx? "They cannot represent themselves : they must be represented".
(1) Ruth Vanita
(2) Kamla Bhasin
(3) Flaria Agnes
(4) Chandra Talpade Mohanty

18. Under the Net (1954) written by
(1) John Fowles
(2) Iris Mudroch
(3) Edmund Goose
(4) William Cooper

19. Who among the following is not a recipient of the Nobel Prize for Literature?
(1) Winston Churchill
(2) T.S. Eliot
(3) W.H. Auden
(4) Madam Curie

20. Find out the correct sequence of the publications of the following books
(1) India : An Area of Darkness: India : A Wounded Civilization: India : A Million Mutinies Now: A House for Mr. Biswas
(2) A House for Mr. Biswas: India : A Million Mutinies Now: India : An Area of Darkness: India : A Wounded Civilization
(3) A House for Mr. Biswas: India : An Area of Darkness: India : A Wounded Civilization: India : A Million Mutinies Now
(4) India : A Wounded Civilization: A House for Mr. Biswas: India : An Area of Darkness: India : A Million Mutinies Now

21. The "Ancient and Modern Quarrel" in Western Literacy Criticism appears during
(1) 100 BC
(2) Fifth Century CE
(3) Sixteenth Century CE
(4) Twentieth Century CE

22. In which year Miles Coverdale translated The Old Testament of The Bible?
(1) 1533 (2) 1534
(3) 1535 (4) 1536

23. Who is the author of the poem "House of Fame"?
(1) William Langland
(2) Geoffrey Chaucer
(3) Thomas Moore
(4) Philip Sidney

24. The heroic couplet is a pan of
(1) Twelve-syllable lines that rhyme
(2) Ten-syllable lines that rhyme
(3) Eight-syllable lines that do not rhyme
(4) Eight-syllable lines that rhyme

25. The book Women Beware Women was published in the year
(1) 1612 (2) 1620
(3) 1621 (4) 1622

26. Which of the following is not a part of Amitav Ghosh's Ibis Trilogy?
(1) Sea of Poppies
(2) River of Smoke
(3) Flood of Fire
(4) The Calcutta Chromosome

27. A man can be destroyed but not defeated". Which of the following texts glorifies this as it predominant theme?
(1) The Old Man and the Sea
(2) War and Peace
(3) A Farwell to Alms
(4) For whom the Bell Tolls

28. Which of the following critics is associated with the term "contrapuntal reading"?
(1) Mikhail Bakhtin
(2) Edward Said
(3) Roland Barthes
(4) Jacques Derrida

29. Who is the author of A literature of their Own?
(1) Sandra Gilbert and Susan Gubar
(2) Elaine Showalter
(3) Virginia Woolf
(4) Sylvia Plath

30. Who said, "There is, there can be and there ought to be the difference between the language of prose and metrical composition"?
(1) John Dryden
(2) William Wordsworth
(3) S.T. Coleridge
(4) T.S. Eliot

31. Stuart Hall belongs to ______ schools of cultural studies.
(1) Oxford
(2) Cambridge
(3) Birmingham
(4) American

32. Tolkappiyam is a book of grammar and poetics written in the _____ language.
(1) Telugu
(2) Tamil
(3) Kannada
(4) Malayalam

33. Gaiutra Bahadur wrote an autobiographic novel titled
(1) An Era of Darkness
(2) Dauka Puran
(3) The Collie Woman
(4) Rama's Banishment

34. Subramani's Fantasy Eaters (1988) is a
(1) novel
(2) collection of short stories
(3) collection of essays
(4) poem

35. Canadian Multiculturalism Act was passed in the year

(1) 1958 (2) 1968
(3) 1978 (4) 1988

36. The Writer and the World by V.S. Naipaul is a
(1) novel
(2) travelogue
(3) collection of essays
(4) non-fiction

37. "It is significant that the productive capacities of this Third Space have a colonial or post colonial provenance". The above lines have been written by
(1) Salman Rushdie
(2) Edward Said
(3) Benedict Anderson
(4) Homi K. Bhabha

38. Find the correct explanation of the term "Aporia"
(1) It denotes a speakers or characters deliberation on an irresolvable question
(2) It is an address to something inanimate
(3) It is applied to a work of art fraught with inherent tension
(4) It refers to a form of denial of existence

39. Which writer does not belong to the Angry Young Men Movement?
(1) John Osborne
(2) Kingsley Amis
(3) Seamus Heaney
(4) Philip Larkin

40. Should poets bicycle-pump the human heart or squash it flat?
Mans love is of man's life a thing apart:
Girls aren't like that.
The above lines are written by :
(1) Philip Larkin
(2) Kingsley Amis
(3) Donald Davie
(4) John Wain

41. Which of the collections of poems are not written by Meena Alexander
A. River and Bride
B. Articulate Silence
C. Raw Silk
D. Stone Roots
E. A Time to Change
Choose the correct answer from the options given below :
(1) A and B only (2) B and D only
(3) C and E only (4) B and E only

42. Which of these are not forms of flash fiction?
A. Drabble
B. Postcard fiction
C. Novelette
D. Short Story
E. Nanofiction
Choose the most appropriate answer from the options given below :
(1) A and E only
(2) A, B and E only
(3) D and E only
(4) C, D and E only

43. Identify the poems termed as "pastoral elegies" :
A. Lycidas
B. In Memory of W.B. Yeats
C. Adonais
D. Thyrsis
E. In Memoriam
Choose the most appropriate answer from the options given below
(1) A, B and C only
(2) B, C and E only
(3) A, C and D only
(4) C, D and E only

44. Identify the correct combination among the following :

A.	Demons	–	Novel
B.	Landlady	–	Novella
C.	The Crocodile	–	Short-Story
D.	A Writers Diary	–	Essay
E.	Marv Stuart	–	Translation

Choose the most appropriate answer from the options given below

(1) A, B and E only

(2) C, D and E only

(3) B, C and E only

(4) B, C and D only

45. Identify the correct ones among the following :

A. Arun Kolatkar uses colloquial speech in his poems

B. Kolatkar envisions abstract qualities to paint a picture of life of his own kind

C. The poem Boatride by Kolatkar talks about a ride in the Ganges

D. Private Poems in Public Garden is composed by Dilip Chitre

E. 'In Ethiopia' is a poem on Africa by Arun Kolatkar

Choose the most appropriate answer from the options given below :

(1) A, B and C only

(2) B, D and E only

(3) A, B and D only

(4) C, B and E only

46. Which of these are correct combination of the works by Doris Lessing and their respective themes?

A.	The Golden Notebook	deals with Johor travelling to Rohonda
B.	The Good Terrorist	is about a doomed love affair
C.	Shikasta	is about a planet, which is out-off due to the advanced influence of civilization
D.	Alfred and Emily	explores the life of her parents
E.	The Grass is Singing	draws from her experiences in Africa

Choose the correct answer from the options given below :

(1) B, A and D only

(2) A, B and E only

(3) C, D and E only

(4) E, B and A only

47. Identify the correct combination among the following:

A.	Spondee	:	It consists of three stressed syllables
B.	Pyrrhic	:	It consists of two unstressed syllables
C.	Amphimacer	:	It is a metrical foot of three syllables
D.	Choriambus	:	It is a foot of verse consisting of two stressed syllables enclosing two unstressed syllables
E.	Trochaic	:	It has a stressed syllable followed by an unstressed one.

Choose the most appropriate answer from the options given below :

(1) A, B and C only

(2) B, C and E only

(3) B, C and D only

(4) C, D and E only

48. Which of the following observations are true about Roland Barthes contributions to literary Theory?

A. He rejected the model for structural analysis of narratives

B. He perceived "meaning" as an effect of various interconnections among linguistic codes

C. He identified the various codes found in the process of structuration

D. He played a significant role in the development of 'semiology'

E. He questioned the concept of literary criticism as an act of uncovering some hidden truth intended by the "Author"

Choose the correct answer from the options given below :

(1) A, B and C only
(2) C. D and E only
(3) B, C, D and E only
(4) A, B, C, D and E only

49. Which among the following is true about the Tractarian Movement?

A. It was widespread across the world
B. The other leaders of the movement were Paul Newman and RH. Fronde
C. The movement began with a sermon by John Keble in 1833
D. Pusey gave the movement cohesion, fame and a name
E. The ideal of the Christian Church was praised by Oxford Convocation

Choose the most appropriate answer from the options given below :

(1) A, B and C only
(2) A, C and E only
(3) C, D and E only
(4) B, C and D only

50. Which of the following denote the three phases of literary feminism according to Elain Showalter?

A. Feminine
B. Gynic
C. Womanish
D. Feminist
E. Female

Choose the most appropriate answer from the options given below :

(1) A, B and C only
(2) A, D and E only
(3) A, B and E only
(4) B, C and D only

51. Consumerism is a major theme in which of the following works'?

A. Loyalties
B. Saint Joan of Stockyards
C. Death of a salesman
D. Candida
E. Waiting for Godot

Choose the most appropriate answer from the options given below :

(1) A and B only
(2) D and A only
(3) B and C only
(4) A and E only

52. Which of these statements are true in the context of Neuro-Linguistic programming?

A. 'Neuro' in NLP means that our behaviour is determined by our sensory experiences
B. Grammatical Knowledge is a matter of practice
C. NLP was developed by Richard Bandler and John Grinder in the 1970s
D. Neuro covers "invisible thoughts and visible physiological reactions"
E. All of the above

Choose the most appropriate answer from the options given below :

(1) E only
(2) A, C and D only
(3) A and D only
(4) B, C and D only

53. Kimberle Crenshaw's term "intersectionality" is widely used for

A. academic deterioration
B. racial justice
C. peace formation
D. complex construction of power
E. identity politics

Choose the most appropriate answer from the options given below :

(1) B, D and E only
(2) A, C and E only
(3) B, D and C only
(4) C, D and E only

54. Identify the combination(s) that belong to the genre of sci-fi/speculative fiction.

A. Vandana Singh – The Woman Who Thought She was Planet

B. Tehmina Durrani – Blasphemy

C. Salman Rushdie – The Satanic Verses

D. Priya Sarukkai Crabria – Generation 14

E. Gautam Bhatia – The wall

Choose the most appropriate answer from the options given below :

(1) A, B and D only

(2) A, D and E only

(3) A, C and D only

(4) D, A and C only

55. Choose the right chronological sequence of publication of the following novels by Margaret Atwood.

A. Lady Oracle

B. The Blind Assassin

C. The Handmaid's Tale

D. The Testaments

E. Alias Grace

Choose the most appropriate answer from the options given below:

(1) A, B, C, D, E

(2) A, C, E, B, D

(3) E, A, D, B, C

(4) C, A, D, E, B

56. Which among the following is appropriate about Ngugi Wa Thiongo's article "Literature in schools"?

A. The article discusses the relevance and adequacy of the present education system.

B. It advocates teaching of European texts and literature to the students of the third world countries

C. It reflects negatively upon the literature taught to the Kenyan students in National Schools

D. It argues that cultural imperialism distorts peoples vision of history

E. It observes that European teachers are better equipped to teach literature to the Kenyan students

Choose the most appropriate answer from the options given below :

(1) A, B and C only

(2) C, D and E only

(3) B, C and D only

(4) A, C and D only

57. Which of the following concepts are associated with Bhartrhari's theory of 'Sphota'?

A. Rasa

B. Alankara

C. Dhvani

D. Vakrokti

E. Shabda Brahman

Choose the most appropriate answer from the options given below :

(1) A and E only

(2) C and E only

(3) D and B only

(4) A and C only

58. Which of these graphic narratives depict political crisis?

A. Amruta Patil – Kari

B. Joe Sacco – Footnotes in Gaza

C. Art Spiegelman – Maus

D. Sarnath Banerjee – Corridor

E. Phoebe Gloeckner – The Diary of a Teenage Girl

Choose the most appropriate answer from the options given below:

(1) A, B and C only

(2) C, D and E only

(3) B and C only

(4) B, C and D only

59. Anglo-Irish relations in the 20th Century have been represented in which of the following novels?

A.	Elizabeth Bowen	–	The Last September
B.	May Sinclair	–	The Divine Fire
C.	JG Farewell	–	Troubles
D.	J G Farewll	–	The Siege of Krishnapur
E.	Jeffer Farnol	–	Black Bartlemy's Treasure

Choose the most appropriate answer from the options given below :

(1) A, B and C only
(2) A and C only
(3) D, E and B only
(4) B, C and A only

60. Identify the novels that were published in the 1980s and the 1990s

A. Red Earth and Pouring Rain
B. The Circle of Reason
C. The Ghosts of Vasu Master
D. Miguel Street
E. The Siege of Babylon

Choose the correct answer from the options given below :

(1) B, C, D and E only
(2) A, B and C only
(3) B, A and D only
(4) A, C and E only

61. Which among the following are appropriate about Latin American Literature?

A. There has been racial coherence and unity in literary representations of Latin America
B. The Latin American Literary tradition draws analogy between plant growth and human movement
C. Dzul Poot's stories depict the geography of the Chilam Balam Towns
D. Quechua had a wider popularity and presence across different nations
E. The Latin American Literature is unitary and refrains from intextuality of any land

Choose the most appropriate answer from the options given below :

(1) A, D and E only
(2) C, B and E only
(3) B, C and E only
(4) B, C and D only

62. According to Roland Barthes, which of the following "Codes" are common to all narratives'?

A. Synthetic code
B. Proairctic code
C. Semic Code
D. Hermeneutic code
E. Symbolic code

Choose the correct answer from the options given below :

(1) A and B only
(2) B and C only
(3) A, B and C only
(4) B, C, D and E only

63. What does Aristotle mean by the phrase "language with pleasurable accessories" in his definition of tragedy?

A. A language full of pompous vocabulary
B. An embellished language
C. A language full of rhythm and harmony
D. A language superadded with song
E. Emotive language

Choose the correct answer from the options given below :

(1) A and B only
(2) B and E only
(3) C and D only
(4) A, B and D only

64. Which among the following are true about Harold Pinter?

A. Harold Pinter was born in the year 1925.

B. He was influenced by Samuel Beckett and the Theatre of the Absurd.

C. The Caretaker and The Alchemist are his famous plays.

D. Stanley is a character in The Birthday Party.

E. Betrayal is a story of a married couple.

Choose the correct answer from the options given below :

(1) A, D and E only
(2) B, D and E only
(3) B, C and D only
(4) A, C and D only

65. Which of the following are Plato's main objections against poetry?

A. The poet is an imitator.

B. The poet is incapable of bravery.

C. The poet, by fueling passions and emotions, weakens the reasoning capacity of the citizens.

D. The poet is less responsible.

E. The poet has no knowledge of the world

Choose the correct answer from the options given below:

(1) A, C and E only
(2) A and B only
(3) B and D only
(4) E and D only

66. Match List I with List II

List I	List II
A. Donald Davie	I. Against Romanticism
B. Philip Larkin	II. Hurry on Down
C. Kingsley Amis	III. The Shires
D. John Wain	IV. The North Ship

Choose the correct answer from the options given below:

(1) A - IV, B - I, C - II, D - III
(2) A - I, B - III, C - IV, D - II
(3) A - II, B - I, C - III, D - IV
(4) A - III, B - IV, C - I, D - II

67. Match List I with List II

List I	List II
A. Salim Ali	I. Wild Beauty
B. Jim Corbett	II. The Fall of a Sparrow
C. Kailash Sankhala	III. Night and Days: My Book of Indian Wildlife
D. M. Krishnan	IV. My India

Choose the correct answer from the options given below:

(1) A - II, B - IV, C - I, D - III
(2) A - III, B - II, C - IV, D - I
(3) A - I, B - III, C - IV, D - II
(4) A - II, B - III, C - IV, D - I

68. Match List I with List II

List I	List II
A. "Willing to wound, and yet afraid to strike."	I. Irony
B. "It is a truth universally acknowledged that a single man in possession of good fortune must be in want of a wife."	II. Simile
C. "Thou still unravished bride of quietness. / Thou foster child of silence and slow time."	III. Antithesis
D. "And ice, mast-high, come floating by, as green as emerald."	IV. Assonance

Choose the correct answer from the options given below:

(1) A - II, B - III, C - I, D - IV
(2) A - III, B - I, C - IV, D - II
(3) A - III, B - II, C - IV, D - I
(4) A - I, B - IV, C - II, D - III

69. Match List I with List II

List I	List II
A. Malcolm Bradbury	I. Masters
B. David Lodge	II. Lucky Jim
C. Kingsley Amis	III. The History Man

D. C P Snow IV. Changing places

Choose the correct answer from the options given below:

(1) A - I, B - II, C - III, D - IV
(2) A - III , B - IV, C - II, D - I
(3) A - II , B - III, C - IV, D - I
(4) A - IV, B - III, C - I, D - II

70. Match List I with List II

List I	List II
A. The Poetics of Prose	I. Stanley Fish
B. Problems of Dostoevsky's Poetics	II. Tzvetan Todrov
C. Surprised by Sin	III. Mikhail Bakhtin
D. The Way Women Write	IV. Mary Hiatt

Choose the correct answer from the options given below:

(1) A - IV, B - II, C - I, D - III
(2) A - II, B - IV, C - II, D - I
(3) A - II, B - III, C - I, D - IV
(4) A - II, B - IV, C - III, D - I

71. Match List I with List II

List I	List II
A. "Faces along the bar/cling to their average day	I. Wilfred Owen
B. "The awful daring of a moments surrender."	II. T.S. Eliot
C. "Bent double, like old beggars under sacks."	III. Allen Ginsberg
D. "I saw the best minds of my generation	IV. W.H. Anden

Choose the correct answer from the options given below:

(1) A - IV, B - II, C - I, D - III
(2) A - III, B - I, C - IV, D - II
(3) A - I, B - IV, C - II, D - III
(4) A - II, B - IV, C - I, D - III

72. Match List I with List II

List I	List II
A. Gender and Nation	I. Catherine Belsey
B. Greek Homosexuality	II. K.J. Dover
C. The Subject of Tragedy	III. W.E.B. Du Bois
D. The Souls of Black Folk	IV. Nira Yuval-Davis

Choose the correct answer from the options given below:

(1) A - I, B - IV, C - III, D - II
(2) A - III, B - II, C - IV, D - I
(3) A - II, B - IV, C - III, D - I
(4) A - IV, B - II, C - I, D - III

73. Match List I with List II

List I	List II
A. Hamlet	I. 1606
B. Macbeth	II. 1599
C. Julius Caesar	III. 1604
D. Othello	IV. 1600

Choose the correct answer from the options given below:

(1) A - III, B - IV, C - II, D - I
(2) A - I, B - II, C - IV, D - III
(3) A - II, B - I, C - III, D - IV
(4) A - IV, B - I, C - II, D - III

74. Match List I with List II

List I	List II
A. To the Light house	I. 1913
B. Sons and Lovers	II. 1927
C. Finnegans Wake	III. 1939
D. The Waste Land	IV. 1922

Choose the correct answer from the options given below:

(1) A - I, B - II, C - IV, D - III
(2) A - IV, B - II, C - I, D - III
(3) A - III, B - IV, C - I, D - II
(4) A - II, B - I, C - III, D - IV

75. Match List I with List II

List I	List II
A. O' Henry	I. The Last Suttee
B. Rudyard Kipling	II. Beauty
C. Oscar Wilde	III. At Verona
D. Ralph Waldo Emerson	IV. Hard to Forget

Choose the correct answer from the options given below:

(1) A - III, B - I, C - IV, D - II
(2) A - II, B - IV, C - III, D - I
(3) A - IV, B - I, C - III, D - II
(4) A - I, B - III, C - II, D - IV

76. Identify the correct pairs :

A. The Boyfriend – Juliette Banerjee
B. Nude Therapy – Margaret Chatterjee
C. The Other woman and Other Stories – Dina Mehta
D. The Yankee and the Yogi – B.G. Siddarth
E. Prejudice of Ages – Vera Sharma

Choose the correct answer from the options given below:

(1) (A), (B) and (C)
(2) (A), (C) and (D)
(3) (B), (C) and (E)
(4) (C), (D) and (E)

77. Identify the correct combinations :

A. Dadaism – Tristan Tzara
B. Super Realism – Guillanne Apollinaire
C. Surrealism – Filipo Marinetti
D. Futurism – Andre Breton
E. Nihilism – Ivan Sergeyevich Turgenev

Choose the correct answer from the options given below:

(1) (A), (C) and (E)
(2) (A), (B) and (E)
(3) (B), (C) and (D)
(4) (C), (D) and (E)

78. Who among the following were poet Laureates of England?

(A) Alfred Austin
(B) Robert Bridges
(C) Watts-Dunton
(D) Oscar Wilde

Choose the correct answer from the options given below :

(1) (A) and (C) only
(2) (A) and (D) only
(3) (B), (C) and (D) only
(4) (A), (B) and (C) only

79. Match the following works of Edward Braithwaite according to their year of publication:

A. Rights of Passage	I. 1973
B. Islands	II. 1969
C. Masks	III. 1967
D. The Arrivants	IV. 1968

Choose the correct answer from the options given below:

(1) A - II, B - I, C - III, D - IV
(2) A - I , B - III, C - IV, D - II
(3) A - IV , B - II, C - I, D - III
(4) A - III, B - IV, C - II, D - I

80. What is the correct sequence of the following feminist texts?

A. Sexual Politics
(B) A World of Difference
(C) The Female Imagination
(D) Thinking About Women
(E) A Room of One's Own

Choose the correct answer from the options given below:

(1) (A), (B), (C), (D), (E)
(2) (E), (B), (D), (A), (C)
(3) (E), (D), (A), (C), (B)
(4) (B), (C), (D), (E), (A)

83. Given below are two statements :

Statement I: According to W.H. Auden. The Importance of Being Earnest is the purest example in English Literature of a 'Verbal Opera'.

Statement II: Oscar Wilde possessed profound insight into the range of the arts that in a combined form make theatre performance possible.

In the light of the above statements, choose the correct answer from the options given below :

(1) Both Statement I and Statement II are true
(2) Both Statement I and Statement II are false
(3) Statement I is true but Statement II is false
(4) Statement I is false but Statement II is true

82. Given below are two statements :

Statement I: The teaching of non-native literature to the students of English Language Teaching is arid.

Statement II: The negative responses in ELT classroom can create an interesting classroom situation.

In the light of the above statements, choose the correct answer from the options given below :

(1) Both Statement I and Statement II are correct
(2) Both Statement I and Statement II are incorrect
(3) Statement I is correct but Statement II is incorrect
(4) Statement I is incorrect but Statement II is correct

83. Given below are two statements :

Statement I: ".....he who discovers no God Whatever, how shall he discover Heroes, the Visible Temples of God" is a statement by Thomas Carlyle.

Statement II: "It is not that men are ill fed, but that they have no pleasure in the work by which they make their bread, and therefore look to wealth as the only means of pleasure" is a statement made by John Ruskin.

In the light of the above statements, choose the correct answer from the options given below:

(1) Both Statement I and Statement II are true
(2) Both Statement I and Statement II are false
(3) Statement I is true but Statement II is false
(4) Statement I is false but Statement II is true

84. Given below are two statements :

Statement I: Hannah Arendt's "defactualization" is very close to the concept of "Post-truth".

Statement II: Post-truth relies on absolute lies.

In the light of the above statements, choose the correct answer from the options given below :

(1) Both Statement I and Statement II are correct
(2) Both Statement I and Statement II are incorrect
(3) Statement I is correct but Statement II is incorrect
(4) Statement I is incorrect but Statement II is correct

85. Given below are two statements :

Statement I: Comparative Literature is a study of different cultures, nations and genres, and it explores the inherent relationship between literature and other forms of cultural exploration.

Statement II: In the study of literature and culture, the importance of methodology is secondary.

In the light of the above statements, choose the correct answer from the options given below :

(1) Both Statement I and Statement II are true

(2) Both Statement I and Statement II are false
(3) Statement I is true but Statement II is false
(4) Statement I is false but Statement II is true

86. Given below are two statements : One is labelled as Assertion A and the other is labelled as Reason R.

Assertion (A): In 19th century, Charlotte Perkins Gilman asserted economic independence over voting rights.

Reason (R): The representation of women as power-seekers was not socially acceptable in 19th century America.

In the light of the above statements, choose the most appropriate answer from the options given below :

(1) Both (A) and (R) are correct and (R) is the correct explanation of (A)
(2) Both (A) and (R) are correct but (R) is NOT the correct explanation of (A)
(3) (A) is correct but (R) is not correct
(4) (A) is not correct but (R) is correct

87. Given below are two statements : One is labelled as Assertion A and the other is labelled as Reason R.

Assertion (A): Roland Barthes describes two basic categories of text as "the readerly" and "the writerly".

Reason (R): Language is the window through which one sees the world.

In the light of the above statements, choose the most appropriate answer from the options given below :

(1) Both (A) and (R) are correct and (R) is the correct explanation of (A)
(2) Both (A) and (R) are correct but (R) is NOT the correct explanation of (A)
(3) (A) is correct but (R) is not correct
(4) is not correct but (R) is correct

88. Given below are two statements : One is labelled as Assertion A and the other is labelled as Reason R.

Assertion (A): The Marxists represent Marxism as a scientific account of social change.

Reason (R): The Marxist ideology believes that culture is a mirror of social life and the artist is an engineer of the human soul educating the working classes.

In the light of the above statements, choose the most appropriate answer from the options given below :

(1) Both (A) and (R) are correct and (R) is the correct explanation of (A)
(2) Both (A) and (R) are correct but (R) is NOT the correct explanation of (A)
(3) (A) is correct but (R) is not correct
(4) (A) is not correct but (R) is correct

89. Given below are two statements : One is labelled as Assertion A and the other is labelled as Reason R.

Assertion (A): Jacques Lacan was radically critical of the esistium psychoanalytical theory.

Reason (R): Lacan was expelled from the International Psychoanalytical Association in 1959.

In the light of the above statements, choose the most appropriate answer from the options given below :

(1) Both (A) and (R) are true and (R) is the correct explanation of (A)
(2) Both (A) and (R) are true but (R) is NOT the correct explanation of (A)
(3) (A) is true but (R) is false
(4) (A) is false but (R) is true

90. Given below are two statements : One is labelled as Assertion A and the other is labelled as Reason R.

Assertion (A): In so far as we are taught how to read, what we engage are not texts but paradigms.

Reason R: We appropriate meaning from a text according to what we need or desire, or, in other words, according to the critical assumptions of the predispositions that we bring to it.

In the light of the above statements, choose the most appropriate answer from the options given below :

(1) Both (A) and (R) are correct and (R) is the correct explanation of (A)

(2) Both (A) and (R) are correct but (R) is NOT the correct explanation of (A)

(3) (A) is correct but (R) is not correct

(4) (A) is not correct but (R) is correct

Read the following passage, and answer the questions that follow : (91-95)

However, faced with this world of faithful and complicated objects, the child can only identify himself as owner, as user, never as creator, he does not invent the World, he uses it: there are, prepared for him, actions without adventure. Without wonder, without joy. He is turned into a little stay-at-home householder who does not even have to invent the mainsprings of adult causality: they are supplied to him ready-made: he has only to help himself, he is never allowed to discover anything from start to finish. The merest set of blocks, provided it is not too refined, implies a very different learning of the world: then, the child does not in any way create meaningful objects, it matters little to him whether they have an adult name: the actions he performs are not those of a user but those of a demiurge. He creates forms which walk, which roll, he creates life, not property: objects now act by themselves, they are no longer an inert and complicated material in the palm of his hand.

Roland Barthes "Toys"
(Excerpt from Mythologies)

91. The world of objects makes the child

(1) Imaginative (2) Inventor

(3) Actant (4) Creator

92. In the context of the above passage, which is the closest to being true :

(1) Children actively learn while playing.

(2) Children are objects for toy makers.

(3) Toys affect the cognitive abilities of the children.

(4) Children recreate meaning from the toys.

93. The adult causality is about

(1) Sensual and sexual knowledge of the world.

(2) Cognitive and logical structure of the world.

(3) Nihilistic recreation of the world.

(4) Linguistic structure of the objects.

94. Which of the following is a correct interpretation?

(1) The child claims the object as his property.

(2) The objects that the child holds are obscure and useless.

(3) The child cannot understand the design of the object.

(4) In touching the object, the child creates dynamic forms of life.

95. The word "demiurge" connotes

(1) cognitive inactiveness of the children.

(2) their sensational realisation of the objects.

(3) their creative abilities.

(4) their sudden discovery.

Read the following poem, and answer the questions that follow : (96-100)

Mr Bleaney

'This was Mr Bleaney's room. He stayed
The whole time he was at the Bodies, till
They moved Flowered curtains, thin and frayed.
Fall to within five inches of the sill.

Whose window shows a strip of building land.
Tussocky, littered, 'Mr Bleaney took
My bit of garden properly in hand.'
Bed, upright chair, sixty-Watt bulb, no hook

Behind the door, no room for books or bags -
'I'll take it.' So it happens that I lie
Where Mr Bleaney lay, and stub my fags
On the same saucer-souvenir, and try

Stuffing my ears with cotton-wool, to drown
The jabbering set he egged her on to buy.
I know his habits - What time he came down.
His preference for sauce to gravy, why

He kept on plugging at the four aways –
Likewise their yearly frame: the Frinton folk
Who put him up for summer holidays.
And Christmas at his sister's house in Stoke.

But if he stood and watched the frigid wind
Tousling the clouds, lay on the fusty bed
Telling himself that this was home, and grinned.
And shivered, without shaking off the dread

That how we live measures our own nature.
And at his age having no more to show
Than one hired box should make him pretty sure
He warranted no better. I don't know.

Philip Larkin

96. The poem, "Ur. Bleaney", is written in a ____ form.
(1) Satirical
(2) Lyrical
(3) Dramatic
(4) Philosophical

97. Mr. Bleaney was the ________ of the house.
(1) Owner
(2) Tenant
(3) Master
(4) Possessor

98. In the third line 'They' refers to
(1) Workers
(2) Owners
(3) Master
(4) Manufacturers

99. According to the speaker Mr. Bleany was
(1) a humorous person
(2) a social and fun-loving person
(3) a hard working person
(4) a sad and dull person

100. The poem 'Mr. Bleaney" deals with the portrayal of ____________.
(1) richness
(2) extravagance
(3) luxuriousness
(4) ordinariness

ANSWERS

1. (2)	**2.** (3)	**3.** (3)	**4.** (4)	**5.** (4)	**6.** (1)	**7.** (2)	**8.** (2)	**9.** (1)	**10.** (1)
11. (4)	**12.** (3)	**13.** (1)	**14.** (2)	**15.** (3)	**16.** (4)	**17.** (4)	**18.** (2)	**19.** (3,4)	**20.** (3)
21. (3,4)	**22.** (3)	**23.** (2)	**24.** (2)	**25.** (*)	**26.** (4)	**27.** (1)	**28.** (2)	**29.** (2)	**30.** (*)
31. (3)	**32.** (2)	**33.** (3)	**34.** (2)	**35.** (4)	**36.** (3)	**37.** (4)	**38.** (*)	**39.** (3,4)	**40.** (2)
41. (1,4)	**42.** (*)	**43.** (3)	**44.** (*)	**45.** (3)	**46.** (3)	**47.** (*)	**48.** (3)	**49.** (4)	**50.** (2)
51. (3)	**52.** (2)	**53.** (1)	**54.** (2)	**55.** (2)	**56.** (4)	**57.** (2)	**58.** (3)	**59.** (2)	**60.** (2)
61. (4)	**62.** (4)	**63.** (3)	**64.** (2)	**65.** (1)	**66.** (4)	**67.** (1)	**68.** (2)	**69.** (2)	**70.** (3)
71. (1)	**72.** (4)	**73.** (*)	**74.** (4)	**75.** (3)	**76.** (2)	**77.** (2)	**78.** (*)	**79.** (*)	**80.** (3)
81. (1)	**82.** (1)	**83.** (1)	**84.** (3)	**85.** (3)	**86.** (1)	**87.** (2)	**88.** (1)	**89.** (2)	**90.** (1)
91. (3,4)	**92.** (3)	**93.** (2)	**94.** (4)	**95.** (3)	**96.** (3)	**97.** (2)	**98.** (*)	**99.** (4)	**100.** (4)

❖❖❖

March, 2023

ENGLISH

PAPER-II

Note : This paper contains **hundred (100)** objective type questions of **two (2)** marks each. **All** questions are **compulsory**.

1. "When nature prompted and no law denied
Promiscuous use of concubine and bride;
Then Israel's monarch after Heaven's own heart,
His vigorous warmth did variously impart
To wives and slaves."

From which poem are these lines taken?

(1) Absalom and Achitophel: A Poem

(2) MacFlecknoe

(3) A Song for St. Cecilia's Day

(4) Alexander's Feast

2. Which of the following poems is written by Oliver Goldsmith?

(1) A Deserted Village

(2) A Deserted Villa

(3) The Deserted Village

(4) A Deserted City

3. Tribute to Papa is a book of poems written by

(1) Kamala Das

(2) Mamta Kalia

(3) Suniti Namjoshi

(4) Meena Alexander

4. Which of the following poems is not written by Sylvia Plath?

(1) Lady Lazarus

(2) Ariel

(3) Daddy

(4) To Ariel

5. Robert Burns was born in

(1) Scotland

(2) England

(3) Ireland

(4) America

6. Who among the following characters personifies necessity in P.B. Shelley's Prometheus Unbound?

(1) Prometheus

(2) Demogorgon

(3) Jove

(4) Jeus

7. Who among the following, after watching the performance of William Shakespeare's play, A Midsummer Night's Dream, observed that "it is the most insipid, ridiculous play that I ever saw in my life."

(1) John Evelyn

(2) Samuel Pepys

(3) John Dryden

(4) Robert Greene

8. Name the playwright who wrote the play Epicene, or the Silent Woman?

(1) William Congreve

(2) Thomas Kyd

(3) Ben Jonson

(4) Thomas Farquhar

9. Abhijnansakuntalam makes use of the following four languages

(1) Sanskrit, Shauraseni, Tamil and Maharshtri

(2) Sanskrit, Shauraseni, Pali and Oriya

(3) Sanskrit, Brajabuli, Maharashtri and Magdhi

(4) Sanskrit, Shauraseni, Maharashtri and Magdhi

10. Choose from the following options the correct combination of playwrights who contributed to the movement called "Kitchen Sink Drama".

(1) John Osborne, Arnold Wesker, Shelagh Delaney and John Arden

(2) John Osborne, Arnold Wesker, Harold Pinter and Shelagh Delaney

(3) John Osborne, Arnold Wesker, Antonin Artaud and John Arden

(4) John Osborne, Harold Pinter, Shelagh Delaney and John Arden

11. Choose from the following options the correct combination of the plays which made significant use of expressionistic techniques:

(1) The Hairy Ape, Machinal, All My Sons, Waiting for Lefty

(2) The Hairy Ape, The Crucible, Rapid Transit, The Adding Machine

(3) The Hairy Ape, Rapid Transit, All My Sons, The Adding Machine

(4) The Hairy Ape, The Emperor Jones, Rapid Transit, The Adding Machine

12. Apart from Bertolt Brecht others who have influenced Epic theatre are:

(1) Erwin Piscator and Antonin Artaud

(2) Martin Esslin and Max Reinhardt

(3) Erwin Piscator and Max Reinhardt

(4) Constantin Stanislavski and Max Reinhardt

13. The theological treatise Ecclesiastical Polity was written by

(1) Richard Hakluyt

(2) Francis Bacon

(3) Raphael Holinshed

(4) Richard Hooker

14. Who wrote the popular instruction manual for fishermen titled The Compleat Angler, or The Contemplative Man's Recreation?

(1) Isaac Walton

(2) Jeremy Taylor

(3) Richard Baxter

(4) Thomas Hobbes

15. What did Matthew Arnold imply by the term "Hebraism" in his Culture and Anarchy?

(1) Moral education

(2) Intellectual autonomy

(3) Rational outlook

(4) Pragmatic attitude

16. The journal Scrutiny was founded in 1932 by

(1) I. A. Richards

(2) F. R. Leavis

(3) Cleanth Brooks

(4) John Crowe Ransom

17. Samuel Pepys' claim to fame rests on his

(1) Biography

(2) Autobiography

(3) Diary

(4) Speculative Fiction

18. Dr Primrose is a character in

(1) Nicholas Nickleby

(2) Adam Bede

(3) The Vicar of Wakefield

(4) Joseph Andrews

19. "So the baby was carried in a small deal box, under an ancient woman's shawl, to the churchyard that night, and buried by lantern-light, at the cost of a shilling, and a pint of beer to the sexton, in that shabby corner of God's allotment where He lets the nettles grow, and where all unbaptized infants, notorious drunkard, suicides and others of the conjecturally damned are laid." From which novel is this excerpt taken?

(1) Wuthering Heights by Emily Bronte

(2) Tess by Thomas Hardy

(3) Great Expectation by Charles Dickens

(4) Mill on the Floss by George Eliot

20. Which of the following novels is written by Patrick White?

(1) Cry, the Beloved Country
(2) The Vivisector
(3) The Handmaid's Tale
(4) The Stone Angel

21. Which among the following is NOT written by Kamala Markandaya?
(1) Some Inner Fury
(2) The Nowhere Man
(3) A Time to be Happy
(4) The Golden Honeycomb

22. Who among the following were revaluing 'the masses' as sources and subjects of literature?
(1) Richard Hoggart and Raymond Williams
(2) Penny Summerfield and Gillian Rose
(3) Rachel Alsop and Catherine Belsey
(4) Ion Cook and Marilyn Deegan

23. Who among the following theorists has written on narrative empathy?
(1) Michael Ryan
(2) Suzanne Keane
(3) Toni Morrison
(4) Sara Ahmed

24. The science that systematically studies the function of signs is known as
(1) Semantics
(2) Scriptoria
(3) Sismograhpy
(4) Serniology

25. Who among the following first framed a theory of general hermeneutics?
(1) Wilhelm Dilthey
(2) Ferdinand de Saussure
(3) Friedrich Schleiermacher
(4) E.D. Hirsch

26. Roland Barthes Image, Music, Text was published in
(1) 1968 (2) 1977
(3) 1979 (4) 1969

27. Who among the following distinguished the 'constatives' from the 'performatives'?
(1) John Austin
(2) Judith Butler
(3) Stanley Fish
(4) Mary Louise Pratt

28. Who among the following coined the phrase 'soft capitalism'?
(1) Louis Althusser
(2) Slavoj Zizek
(3) Nigel Thrift
(4) Terry Eagleton

29. To whom is the term 'thick description' attributed?
(1) John Storey
(2) Clifford Geertz
(3) Deleuze and Guattari
(4) James Clifford

30. The subject matter of Cultural Studies as it emerged as a 'proto-discipline' in the 1960s, was predominantly exploration of
(1) High Culture
(2) Popular Culture
(3) Subaltern History
(4) Contemporary Politics

31. What does the abbreviated term CCCS stand for in the context of cultural studies?
(1) Consortium of Cooperative Culture and Society
(2) Conference on Contemporary Culture and Society
(3) Centre for Contemporary Cultural Studies
(4) Conclave for Collective Consciousness and Socialisation

32. According to Stuart Hall, the concept of played a seminal role in Cultural Studies.
(1) Interpellation
(2) Dispositive
(3) Hegemony
(4) Society

33. The book Political Shakespeare: Essays in Cultural Materialism was jointly edited by
(1) Gilles Deleuze and Felix Guattari
(2) Alan Sinfield and Ionathan Dollimore
(3) Bill Ashcroft and Helen Tiffin
(4) Theodor Adorno and Max Horkheimer

34. Identify the work which has NOT been authored by the famous cultural critic Raymond Williams:
(1) The Country and the City
(2) Culture and Society
(3) Modern Tragedy
(4) The Making of the English Working Class

35. Second Language is
(1) The Language Second In Importance In Terms Of The Use Of Languages By A Learner.
(2) The Language Used By A Second-Generation Learner.
(3) Any Language Other Than The Learner's Native Language Or Mother Tongue.
(4) The Language Which Is The Learner's Native Language But Not The Mother Tongue.

36. When a learner's second language learning system seems to freeze or get stuck at some more or less deviant stage, that phenomenon is known as
(1) Freezer
(2) Fossilization
(3) Language Learning Blockade
(4) Language Scaffolding

37. Integrative motivation refers to
(1) Language Learning For Immediate Goals.
(2) Language Learning For Practical Goals.
(3) Language Learning For Personal Growth and Cultural Enrichment.
(4) None of these

38. In 1835, which of the following languages was replaced by English as the official language of the East India Company?
(1) Sanskrit
(2) Persian
(3) Arabic
(4) Hindi

39. Choose the correct option from the following options:
(1) The "Magna Carta" of Indian Education in the colonial period refers to "The Missionary Clause 1698".
(2) The "Magna Carta" of Indian Education in the colonial period refers to "Indian Education Commission in 1882".
(3) The "Magma Carta" of Indian Education in the colònial period refers to "Macaulay's Minute 183 5".
(4) The "Magna Carta" of Indian Education in the colonial period refers to "Wood's Education Despatch of 1854".

40. Which of the following plays of William Shakespeare was translated into Bengali and directed by Girish Chandra Ghosh.
(1) The Tempest
(2) Hamlet
(3) Macbeth
(4) King Lear

41. Which of the following works of Browning are pure dramas?
(A) Strafford
(B) The Last Ride Together
(C) A Blot in the Scutcheon
(D) Pippa Passes
(E) Porphyria's Lover
Choose the correct answer from the options given below:
(1) A and C
(2) B and E
(3) C and D
(4) B and C

42. Who among the following poets have lived in Australia?

(A) Judith Wright

(B) Yusef Komunyakaa

(C) Kath Walker

(D) Thomas Kinsella

(E) T. S. Eliot

Choose the correct answer from the options given below:

(1) A and B

(2) A, B and C

(3) A, B and D

(4) A and E

43. An Essay on Criticism, Pope

(A) analyses the causes of faulty criticism and praises the great critics of the past.

(B) analyses the causes of faulty criticism and characterises the good critic.

(C) analyses the structure of a good essay and praises the great critics of the past.

(D) analyses the structure of a good essay and suggest how such an essay could be converted into good criticism.

(E) analyses the merits of the poetry of Wordsworth and praises the great critics of the past.

Which of the above statements are correct?

(1) A and B

(2) A, B, and C

(3) C, D and E

(4) A and D

44. Which of the following are plays written by Harold Pinter?

(A) Family Voices

(B) A Moon for the Misbegotten

(C) The Room

(D) No Man's Land

(E) Krapp's Last Tape

Choose the correct answer from the options given below:

(1) A, B and E

(2) B, C and D

(3) A, C and D

(4) C, D and E

45. Which of the following have NOT been written by Mahesh Dattani?

(A) Dance Like a Man

(B) Fire and the Rain

(C) On A Muggy Night in Mumbai

(D) A Touch of Brightness

(E) Bravely Fought the Queen

Choose the correct answer from the options given below:

(1) A and C

(2) B and D

(3) C and E

(4) B and E

46. Name the dramas which fall within the category of the Theatre of the Absurd.

(A) The Birthday Party

(B) Endgame

(C) Mrs. Warren's Profession

(D) The Rhinoceros

(E) Riders to the Sea

Choose the correct answer from the options given below:

(1) A, B and E

(2) B, C and D

(3) A, B and D

(4) C, D and E

47. Which of the playwrights have been correctly matched with their works?

(A) William Wycherly - The Rivals

(B) Ben Ionson - Volpone, or the Fox

(C) William Congreve - The Country Wife

(D) Aphra Behn - The Dutch Lover

(E) Richard Sheridan < A School for Scandal

Choose the correct answer from the options given below:

(1) C, D and E

(2) B, C and D
(3) A, C and E
(4) B, D and E

48. Choose the plays written by Lord Byron
(A) Sardanapalus
(B) Hellas
(C) Cain
(D) The Two Foscari: An Historical Tragedy
(E) The Cenci
Choose the correct answer from the options given below:
(1) A, B and C
(2) B, C and E
(3) A, B and D
(4) A, C and D

49. John Bunyan authored the following:
(A) The Pilgrim's Progress
(B) Grace Abounding
(C) Short View
(D) The Holy War
(E) Thoughts on Education
Choose the correct answer from the options given below:
(1) A, B and C
(2) A, C and D
(3) A, D and E
(4) A, B and D

50. Which of the following works have been authored by Thomas De Quincey?
(A) Confessions of An English Opium Eater
(B) The French Revolution
(C) Hudibras
(D) Autobiography
(E) Suspiria De Profoundis
Choose the correct answer from the options given below:
(1) A, B and C
(2) A, C and D
(3) A, D and E
(4) A, B and D

51. Which of the following works have been written by Thomas Carlyle?
(A) Of Heroes and Hero-Worship
(B) The French Revolution
(C) Of Human Bondage
(D) The Hour and the Man
(E) Hudibras
Choose the correct answer from the options given below:
(1) A and B
(2) A and C
(3) A and D
(4) A and E

52. Which of the following books are written by Iulia Kristeva?
(A) Desire in Language: A Semiotic Approach to Literature and Art
(B) Illuminations
(C) Syntax and Semantics
(D) La revolution du language poétique
(E) The Madwoman in the Attic
Choose the correct answer from the options given below:
(1) A and C
(2) B and A
(3) A and D
(4) B and E

53. To which of the following theories New Historicism is indebted?
(A) Marxism
(B) Formalism
(C) Reader-response Theory
(D) Existentialism
(E) Hermeneutics
Choose the correct answer from the options given below:
(1) A and C
(2) B and A
(3) A and E
(4) B and C

54. Which of the following statements are true about cyberpunk?

(A) It is a kind of science fiction.
(B) It uses postmodernist techniques and posthumanist themes.
(C) Events in this novel usually take place within the virtual reality.
(D) It is a kind of fiction written using online platforms.
(E) The first cyberpunk was written by Thomas Sterne.

Choose the most appropriate answer from the options given below:
(1) A, B and D
(2) A, C and D
(3) A, B and C
(4) A, C and E

55. Identify the correct pairs:
(A) Gabriel Garcia Marquez - The Feast of the Goat
(B) Jorge Luis Borges - The Autumn of the Patriarch
(C) Salman Rushdie - The Enchantress of Florence
(D) E.L. Doctorow - Ragtime
(E) A.S. Byatt - Possession

Choose the correct answer from the options given below:
(1) A, B and C
(2) A, B and E
(3) B, C and D
(4) C, D and E

56. Which of the following books are written by Aravind Adiga?
(A) The Blue Bedspread
(B) Between the Assassinations
(C) The House of the Blue Mangoes
(D) Last Man in Tower
(E) The White Tiger

Choose the correct answer from the options given below:
(1) A, B and C
(2) B, D and E
(3) B, C and D
(4) A, C and D

57. Which among the following are correct?
(A) JM Coetzee - South Africa
(B) Margaret Atwood - Canada
(C) Philip Roth - Australia
(D) Orhan Pamuk - Turkey
(E) Graham Swift - New Zealand

Choose the correct answer from the options given below:
(1) A, B and C
(2) A, B and D
(3) B, C and E
(4) B, D and E

58. Which among the following is correct in the context of R.K. Narayan?
(A) His The Guide is an open-ended novel.
(B) Most of the characters of his novels are from elite section of society.
(C) He wrote a short story titled "The Martyr's Corner."
(D) He received the Booker's prize for his novel The Vendor of Sweets.
(E) Malgudi is a real-life city in Karnataka.

Choose the correct option given below:
(1) A, B, and C
(2) A and C
(3) A, C and D
(4) A, C and E

59. Identify the correct pairs:
(A) J. C. Ransom - Criticism, Inc.
(B) William Empson - Seven Types of Ambiguity
(C) C. Brooks and R. P. Warren - Understanding Poetry
(D) R. P. Blackmur - In Search of the New Criticism
(E) Allen Tate - The New Apologists for Poetry

Choose the correct answer from the options given below:

(1) A, B and C
(2) A, B and D
(3) B, C and E
(4) B, D and E

60. Thomas Rymer coined the term 'poetic justice' to imply the following:
(A) the distribution of earthly rewards and punishments in proportion to the virtue or vice of the various characters
(B) literary work governed by decorum and morality
(C) literary work guided by random ways things often work out in the actual world
(D) the metaphysical nature of poetic experience
(E) the justification of poetry to be an integral part of the Ideal republic
Choose the correct answer from the options given below:
(1) A and B
(2) B and C
(3) C and D
(4) D and E

61. Which among the following are written by Roland Barthes:
(A) Allegories of Reading
(B) Mythologies
(C) The Pleasure of the Text
(D) Some Versions of Pastoral
(E) What is an Author?
Choose the correct option given below:
(1) B and C
(2) A and C
(3) A, C and D
(4) A, C and E

62. Which of the following are correctly matched:
(A) Jonathan Culler - Culture and Society
(B) Raymond Williams - Literary Theory: A Very Short Introduction
(C) Terry Eagleton - Criticism and Ideology
(D) Walter Benjamin - Illuminations
(E) Stanley Fish - The Implied Reader
Choose the correct option:
(1) B, C and E
(2) C and D
(3) A, C and D
(4) B, C and D

63. Which among the following are true in the context of methods and methodologies in literary research?
(A) Both are identical in nature.
(B) Methods are concerned with how one conducts a given piece of research.
(C) Methodologies are concerned with how one conducts a given piece of research.
(D) Methodologies are concerned with the perspectives one brings to bear on one's work.
(E) Methods are concerned with the perspectives one brings to bear on one's work.
Choose the correct option:
(1) A, D and E
(2) B, C and E
(3) A and C
(4) B and D

64. According to the English Subject Centre report, skills needed for postgraduate work in English include
(A) Searching skills in libraries
(B) Editorial skills
(C) Bibliographic skills
(D) Peer management skills
(E) IT skills
Choose the correct option:
(1) A, C and D
(2) B, C, D and E
(3) A, B and D
(4) A, B, C and E

65. Which of the following are possible ways of turning a topic into an argument?

(A) An argument for or against an existing critic (or critical position) in relation to the author or group of works one is studying.

(B) An argument about the value of a new theoretical approach to a text or set of texts.

(C) An argument about some historical or literary-historical aspect of literature.

(D) An argument showing how a particular theme or concept is not at all related to a group of texts.

(E) An argument about the significance of only well-known author/work.

Choose the correct option:

(1) A, B and C
(2) B, C, D and E
(3) A, C and D
(4) A, B, C and D

66. Match List I with List II

List I	List II
(A) SriAurobindo	I. Other Poems
(B) Kamala Das	II. Calcutta: A Long Poem
(C) P. Lal	III. A Sheaf Gleaned in French
(D) Toru Dutt	IV. Savitri

Choose the correct answer from the options given below:

(1) (A)-(III), (B)-(II), (C)-(I), (D)-(IV)
(2) (A)-(IV), (B)-(I), (C)-(II), (D)-(III)
(3) (A)-(II), (B)-(III), (C)-(IV), (D)-(I)
(4) (A)-(II), (B)-(III), (C)-(I), (D)-(IV)

67. Match List I with List II

List I	List II
(A) Walt Whitman	I. Howl
(B) A.D. Hope	II. A Far Cry From Africa
(C) Derek Walcott	III. Beat! Beat! Drums!
(D) Allen Ginsberg	IV. Australia

Choose the correct answer from the options given below:

(1) (A)-(II), (B)-(III), (C)-(I), (D)-(IV)
(2) (A)-(I), (B)-(II), (C)-(III), (D)-(IV)
(3) (A)-(III), (B)-(IV), (C)-(II), (D)-(I)
(4) (A)-(III), (B)-(II), (C)-(I), (D)-(IV)

68. Match List I with List II

List I	List II
(A) Come what come may, Time and the hour runs through the roughest day.	I. Othello
(B) When sorrows come they come not single spies, But in battalions!	II. King Lear
(C) I am a man more sinned against than sinning.	III. Macbeth
(D) But I will wear my heart upon my sleeve For Daws to peck at: I am not what I am.	IV. Hamlet

Choose the correct answer from the options given below:

(1) A-IV, B-III, C-II, D-I
(2) A-II, B-HI, C-I, D-IV
(3) A-III, B- IV, C-II, D-I
(4) A-I, B-II, C-IV, D-III

69. Match List I with List II

List I	List II
(A) You can't eat the orange and throw the peel away- a man is not a piece of fruit.	I. Man, and Superman
(B) Liberty means responsibility, That is why most men dread it.	II. A Doll's House
(C) Nobody thinks nobody cares, No beliefs, no convictions and no enthusiasm. Just	III. Death of a Salesman

another Sunday evening.

(D) Our home has been nothing but a playroom, I have been your doll-wife, just as at home I was papa's doll-child; and here the children have been my dolls, — IV. Look Back in Anger

Choose the correct answer from the options given below:

(1) A-I, B-III, C-II, D-I
(2) A-II, B-III, C-IV, D-I
(3) A-I, B-IV, C-II, D-III
(4) A-III, B-I, C-IV, D-II

70. Match List I with List II

List I	List II
(A) Anthropology	I. Edward Soja
(B) Postmodern Geography	II. Martin Heidegger
(C) Diaspora Space	III. Claude Lévi-Strauss
(D) Dasein	IV. Avtar Brah

Choose the correct answer from the options given below:

(1) (A)-(III), (B)-(II), (C)-(I), (D)-(IV)
(2) (A)-(IV), (B)-(I), (C)-(II), (D)-(III)
(3) (A)-(III), (B)-(I), (C)-(IV), (D)-(II)
(4) (A)-(II), (B)-(III), (C)-(III), (D)-(IV)

71. Match List I with List II

List I	List II
(A) The Poetics of Prose	I. Wolfgang Iser
(B) Structuralist Poetics	II. Tzvetan Todorov
(C) The Implied Reader	III. Stanley Fish
(D) Is There a Text in This Class?	IV. Ionathan Culler

Choose the correct answer from the options given below:

(1) (A)-(II), (B)-(III), (C)-(I), (D)-(IV)
(2) (A)-(II), (B)-(IV), (C)-(I), (D)-(III)
(3) (A)-(III), (B)-(IV), (C)-(II), (D)-(I)
(4) (A)-(III), (B)-(II), (C)-(I), (D)-(IV)

72. Match List I with List II

List I	List II
(A) Plato	I. Rhetoric
(B) Aristotle	II. Symposium
(C) P. B. Shelley	III. Apology of Poetry
(D) Philip Sydney	IV. Defence of Poetry

Choose the correct answer from the options given below:

(1) A-I, B-II, C-III, DIV
(2) A-III, B-II, C-IV, D-I
(3) A-IV, B-III, C-II, D-I
(4) A-II, B-I, C-IV, D-III

73. Match List I with List II

List I	List II
(A) Bertrand Russell	I. The Verbal Icon
(B) Thomas Stearns Eliot	II. The Well Wrought Urn
(C) W.K. Wimsatt	III. History of Western Philosophy
(D) Cleanth Brooks	IV. The Sacred Wood

Choose the correct answer from the options given below:

(1) A-III, B-IV, C-I, D-II
(2) A-III, B-I, C-IV, D-II
(3) A-III, B-II, C-I, D-IV
(4) A-III, B-I, C-II, D-IV

74. Match List I with List II

List I	List II
(A) "Negative Capability"	I. Matthew Arnold
(B) "Sweetness and light"	II. Samuel Taylor Coleridge
(C) "Esemplastic"	III. T.S. Eliot
(D) "Dissociation of Sensibility"	IV. John Keats

Choose the correct answer from the options given below:

(1) A-II, B-IV, C-I, D-III

(2) A-II, B-I, C-IV, D-III

(3) A-IV, B-III, C-II, D-I

(4) A-IV, B-I, C-II, D-III

75. Match List I with List II

List I	List II
(A) Munira	I. Things Fall Apart
(B) Nnu Ego	II. Petals of Blood
(C) Ikemefuna	III. July's People
(D) Maureen	IV. The Joys of Motherhood

Choose the correct answer from the options given below:

(1) A-II, B-IV, C-I, D-III

(2) A-III, B-II, C-IV, D-I

(3) A-IV, B-III, C-II, D-I

(4) A-III, B-IV, C-I, D-II

76. Choose the correct chronological sequence in which the following texts were written,

(A) Lycidas

(B) Hero and Leander

(C) Masque of Comus

(D) Paradise Lost

(E) The Waste Land

(1) A, B, D, E, C

(2) B, C, A, D, E

(3) B, A, E, C, D

(4) B, E, D, C, A

77. Arrange the following poets in accordance with their years of birth,

(A) Rudyard Kipling

(B) Robert Browning

(C) John Masefield

(D) A.E. Housman

(E) John Donne

(1) E, A, B, D, C

(2) E, B, A, C, D

(3) E, B, A, D, C

(4) A, D, B, C, E

78. Arrange the works in chronological sequence:

(A) Rajmohan's Wife

(B) A Bend in the Ganges

(C) Kanthapura

(D) Untouchable

(E) Distant Drum

Choose the correct answer from the options given below

(1) A, B, C, D, E

(2) A, C, D, E, B

(3) A, D, C, B, E

(4) A, E, D, C, B

79. Find the chronological order of publication of Charles Dickens's novels:

(A) Oliver Twist

(B) Dombey and Sons

(C) Pickwick Papers

(D) Bleak House

(E) David Copperfield

Choose the correct answer from the options given below

(1) A, D, C, B, E

(2) D, E, B, C, A

(3) B, D, C, A, E

(4) C, A, B, D, E

80. Arrange the works in the chronological order of the staging/publication of the following plays:

(A) A Woman Killed with Kindness

(B) John Bull's Other Island

(C) The Double Dealer

(D) The Shoemaker's Holiday

(E) The Conscious Lovers

Choose the correct answers from the options given below:

(1) B, D, C, A and E

(2) D, A, C, E and B

(3) C, D, A, B and E

(4) E, B, D, C and A

81. Arrange the works in chronological sequence:

(A) The Theatre of Revolt by Robert Brustein
(B) The Theater of the Absurd by Martin Esslin
(C) The Playwright as Thinker by Eric Bentley
(D) Modern American Drama by C.W.E Bigsby
(E) Modern Drama in Theory and Practice by L.N. Styan

Choose the correct answers from the options given below:

(1) A, D, C, D and E
(2) E, C, D, A and B
(3) B, D, A, E and C
(4) C, B, A, E and D

82. Choose the correct chronological sequence in which the following texts were published:

(A) Madness and Civilization
(B) The Archaeology of Knowledge
(C) The Language of the Self: The Function of Language in Psychoanalysis
(D) The Birth of the Clinic
(E) Culture and Anarchy

(1) E, B, D, C, A
(2) E, A, C, B, D
(3) E, B, D, A, C
(4) C, A, B, D, E

83. Choose the correct chronological sequence in which the following theories appeared.

(A) Structuralism
(B) Psychoanalysis
(C) Ecocriticism
(D) Orientalisrn
(E) New Criticism

(1) E, B, D, C, A
(2) E, A, C, B, D
(3) B, E, D, A, C
(4) B, E, A, D, C

84. Arrange the works in chronological sequence:

(A) Matthew Arnold's Culture and Anarchy
(B) Thomas Browne's The Anatomy of Melancholy
(C) Thomas Hobbes' Leviathan
(D) Walter Pater's Studies in the History of the Renaissance
(E) P.B. Shelley's Defense of Poesie

Choose the correct answer from the options given below:

(1) B, C, E, A, D
(2) A, B, C, D, E
(3) C, D, E, A, B
(4) D, C, B, A, E

85. Arrange the works in chronological sequence:

(A) Structuralist Poetics
(B) Course in General Linguistics
(C) The Pursuit of Signs
(D) The Pleasure of the Text
(E) The Implied Reader

Choose the correct answer from the options given below

(1) A, C, D, E, B
(2) B, D, E, A, C
(3) C, D, A, B, E
(4) D, E, A, C, B

86. Given below are two statements:

Statement I: The Book The Theatre of Revolt was written by Robert Brustein.

Statement II: The Book The Theatre of Revolt is written in the context of French Revolution.

In the light of the statements given above choose the correct answer given below:

(1) Both Statement I and Statement II are true
(2) Both Statement I and Statement II are false

(3) Statement I is true and Statement II is false

(4) Statement I is false and Statement II is true

87. Given below are two statements:

Statement I: Constantin Stanislavski collaborated with Anton Chekhov to stage dramas on Stage.

Statement II: The book My Life in Art was written by Constantin Stanislavski.

In the light of the statements given above choose the correct answer given below:

(1) Both Statement I and Statement II are false

(2) Both Statement I and Statement II are true

(3) Statement I is true and Statement II is false

(4) Statement I is false and Statement II is true

88. Given below are two statements:

Statement I: Human bodies, like those of other living organisms, are only 'sexed' from a particular narrow perspective.

Statement II: Most of the reproductions that we undertake in our lifetimes has nothing to do with sex.

In the light of the above statements, choose the correct answer given below:

(1) Both Statement I and Statement II are true.

(2) Both Statement I and Statement II are false.

(3) Statement I is true but Statement II is false.

(4) Statement I is false but Statement II is true.

89. Given below are two statements, One is labelled as Assertion A and the other is labelled as Reason R.

Assertion (A): Co-operative learning activities are those in which students must work together in order to complete a task or solve a problem.

Reason (R): These techniques are used to identify a weak learner and to separate him/her from the rest of the members of the group for taking special care of him/ her.

In the light of the above statements, choose the most appropriate answer from the option given below:

(1) Both (A) and (R) are correct and (R) is the correct explanation of (A).

(2) Both (A) and (R) are correct and (R) is not the correct explanation of (A).

(3) (A) is correct but (R) is not correct.

(4) (A) is not correct but (R) is correct.

90. Given below are two statements, One is labelled as Assertion A and the other is labelled as Reason R.

Assertion (A): In second language learning, in the same classroom setting, some students progress rapidly through the initial stages of learning a new language while others struggle making very slow progress.

Reason (R): Some learners never achieve native-like command of a second language.

In the light of the above statements, choose the most appropriate answer from the option given below:

(1) Both (A) and (R) are correct and (R) is the correct explanation of (A).

(2) Both (A) and (R) are correct and (R) is not the correct explanation of (A).

(3) (A) is correct but (R) is not correct.

(4) (A) is not correct but (R) is correct.

Read the following poem and answer the question:

Talking in Bed

Talking in bed ought to be easiest,

Lying together there goes back so far, An emblem of two people being honest,

Yet more and more time passes silently, Outside, the wind's incomplete unrest Builds and disperses clouds about the sky,

And dark towns heap up on the horizon. None
of this cares for us, Nothing shows why At this
unique distance from isolation
It becomes still more difficult to find
Words at once true and kind,
Or not untrue and not unkind.

Philip Larkin

91. Which of the following statements is true?
(1) The poet says that talking in bed is very easy.
(2) The poet says that talking in bed is not very easy.
(3) The poet says that talking in bed should be easy but it is not.
(4) The poet says that talking in bed can never be easy.

92. The poet says that when two people are lying together, they look like
(1) Two Pure Human Beings
(2) Two Hypocrites
(3) Two Innocent Fellows
(4) None of These

93. The poet says that while lying in bed he and his companion pass time
(1) By Talking Between Themselves
(2) By Observing The Trees Outside The Window
(3) Silently
(4) By Playing Cards

94. The poet and his companion are
(1) In A Hotel In The Middle Of A Town
(2) In A Room Of A Hotel On The Margin Of The Town
(3) In The Corridor Of A Hotel Far Away From The Towns
(4) In A Place Away From The Towns

95. The poet says that while lying in bed with one's companion it is difficult to find words which are
(1) At Once Honest And Caring
(2) At Once True And Unkind
(3) At Once Pure And Impure
(4) At Once Honest And Touching

Read the following passage and answer the questions that follows:

Poetry in its use of language continually distorts and denies the structure of reality to exalt the structure of the self. By means of rhyme, assonance or alliteration it couples together words which have no rational connection, that is, no nexus through the world of external reality, It breaks the word up into lines of arbitrary length, cutting across their logical construction, It breaks down their associations, derived from the world of external reality, by means of inversion and every variety of artificial stressing and counterpoint, Thus the world of external reality recedes and the world of instinct, the affective emotional linkage behind the words, becomes the world of reality. In the novel, too, the subjective elements are valued for themselves, and rise to view, but in a different way, The novel blots out external reality by substituting a more or less consistent mock reality which has sufficient 'stuff' to stand between the reader and reality, This means that in the novel the emotional associations attach not to words but to the moving current of mock reality symbolised by the words, This is why rhythm, 'preciousness', and style are alien to the novel; why the novel translates so well; why novels are not composed of words, They are composed of scenes, actions, stuff, people, just as plays are.

96. In the above passage, Christopher Caudwell's statement, "Poetry in its use of language continually distorts and denies the structure of reality to exalt the structure of the self' implies:
(1) The pragmatic function of poetry that reflects the social reality through expressive language
(2) The capacity of poetry to draw attention to itself as an aesthetic object or artefact

(3) Poetry exalts the "structure of the self" by privileging the notion of the 'egotistical sublime

(4) The mimetic function of poetry that alludes to the world of external reality in simple, clear language

97. What does the word "assonance" mean?

(1) Repetition Of Identical Or Similar Consonants

(2) Repetition Of Identical Or Similar Vowels

(3) Repetition Of Identical Or Similar Phrases

(4) Repetition Of Identical Or Similar Clauses

98. What does Caudwell imply by the statement: "The novel blots out external reality by substituting a more or less consistent mock reality which has sufficient 'stuff' to stand between the reader and reality"?

(1) The implication is that the reality of fiction has no existence independent of the words, and our emotional responses are directed by the words

(2) The implication is that the reality of fiction is not dependent on the words, and our affective states are not triggered by the words

(3) The mock reality subverts the external reality so obtrusively that readers become conscious of the writer's strategy

(4) The novel is different from poetry in the sense that it is metonymic in its mode of linear progression, while poetry is metaphoric relying on subject-privileging

99. What do you understand by "mock reality" in context of the usage in the above passage?

(1) The reality contrived into existence by novelists through strategic use of words

(2) The reality evoked through figurative devices

(3) The quasi reality effected through the use of poetic devices

(4) The reality which is approximate to the external reality

100. If rhythm, 'preciousness', and style are alien to the novel, in which genre are they distinctive features?

(1) Drama

(2) Poetry

(3) Prose

(4) Non-fiction

ANSWERS

1. (1)	**2.** (3)	**3.** (2)	**4.** (4)	**5.** (1)	**6.** (2)	**7.** (2)	**8.** (3)	**9.** (4)	**10.** (1)
11. (4)	**12.** (3)	**13.** (4)	**14.** (1)	**15.** (1)	**16.** (2)	**17.** (3)	**18.** (3)	**19.** (2)	**20.** (2)
21. (3)	**22.** (1)	**23.** (2)	**24.** (4)	**25.** (3)	**26.** (2)	**27.** (1)	**28.** (3)	**29.** (2)	**30.** (2)
31. (3)	**32.** (3)	**33.** (2)	**34.** (4)	**35.** (3)	**36.** (2)	**37.** (3)	**38.** (2)	**39.** (4)	**40.** (3)
41. (1)	**42.** (2)	**43.** (1)	**44.** (3)	**45.** (2)	**46.** (3)	**47.** (4)	**48.** (4)	**49.** (4)	**50.** (3)
51. (1)	**52.** (3)	**53.** (1)	**54.** (3)	**55.** (4)	**56.** (2)	**57.** (2)	**58.** (2)	**59.** (1)	**60.** (1)
61. (1)	**62.** (2)	**63.** (3)	**64.** (3)	**65.** (1)	**66.** (2)	**67.** (3)	**68.** (3)	**69.** (4)	**70.** (3)
71. (2)	**72.** (4)	**73.** (1)	**74.** (4)	**75.** (1)	**76.** (2)	**77.** (3)	**78.** (3)	**79.** (4)	**80.** (2)
81. (4)	**82.** (2)	**83.** (4)	**84.** (1)	**85.** (2)	**86.** (3)	**87.** (2)	**88.** (1)	**89.** (3)	**90.** (2)
91. (3)	**92.** (1)	**93.** (3)	**94.** (4)	**95.** (1)	**96.** (2)	**97.** (2)	**98.** (1)	**99.** (1)	**100.** (2)

December, 2023

ENGLISH

PAPER-II

Note : This paper contains **hundred (100)** objective type questions of **two (2)** marks each. **All** questions are **compulsory**.

1. Sharankumar Limbale argues that Dalit literature is unique because:

(A) This brings out the Dalit reality which is liminal in time and space.

(B) This has unique historical and ideological concerns.

(C) This offers literary and cultural representations of marginalised and dispossessed people.

(D) This brings out narratives and discourses of pity.

(E) It uses disrespectful and offensive language towards revered figures.

Choose the most appropriate answer from the options given below:

(1) (A), (B) and (C) Only
(2) (B), (C) and (D) Only
(3) (A), (B) and (D) Only
(4) (A), (C) and (E) Only

2. Edgar Allan Poe is often called as the originator of the short story as an established genre. He defined 'the prose tale' as:

(1) A narrative which can be read at one sitting of from half an hour to two hours.
(2) A narrative which can be read within five minutes or less.
(3) A narrative that can be read at one sitting of from one hour to four hours.
(4) A narrative that may be concluded and enjoyed in the single spell of less than half an hour.

3. "An Introduction" by Kamla Das is:

(1) A short story on the theme of people's rights and freedom
(2) An introduction to her autobiography My Story
(3) An essay on the theme of gender rights
(4) A poem of resistance and protest

4. Which of the following statements/concepts are relevant for understanding of Postmodernism?

(A) Postmodernism and Postcolonialism are mutually dependent in responding to colonial experience.

(B) Lyotard argues that the Postmodern condition is characterised by a deeply felt scepticism towards metanarratives.

(C) Edward W. Said has been instrumental in postmodern theory and criticism.

(D) Jean Baudrillard's Simulacra and Simulations is a seminal postmodern text.

(E) Fredric Jameson argues that parody has been replaced by pastiche in postmodernism.

Choose the most appropriate answer from the options given below:

(1) (B), (D) and (E) Only
(2) (A), (B) and (D) Only
(3) (B), (C) and (E) Only
(4) (C), (D) and (E) Only

5. All writers since Chaucer have come from the middle class... have had good, at least expensive education...."
Where has Virginia Woolf explained it?

(1) Mrs. Dalloway
(2) To the Lighthouse
(3) The Leaning Tower
(4) A Room of One's Own

6. What is the correct order of publication of the novels of Charles Dickens?

(A) Great Expectations
(B) Hard Times
(C) Oliver Twist
(D) David Copperfield
(E) A Tale of Two Cities

Choose the correct answer from the options given below:
(1) (E), (C), (A), (B), (D)
(2) (C), (D), (B), (E), (A)
(3) (B), (A), (D), (C), (E)
(4) (D), (B), (C), (A), (E)

7. Which among the following writers are popular for partition narratives?
(A) Krishna Sobti
(B) Shashi Deshpande
(C) Saros Cowasjee
(D) Bharti Mukherjee
(E) Rahi Masoom Raza

Choose the correct answer from the options given below:
(1) (A), (B) and (C) Only
(2) (B), (C) and (D) Only
(3) (A), (C) and (E) Only
(4) (C), (D) and (E) Only

8. Arrange the chronological sequence in which the following works were published:
(A) Culture and Society
(B) Culture and Anarchy
(C) To Hell with Culture
(D) Studies in Dying Culture
(E) Notes towards the Definition of Culture

Choose the correct answer from the options given below:
(1) (E), (B), (A), (D), (C)
(2) (C), (E), (D), (B), (A)
(3) (A), (D), (E), (B), (C)
(4) (B), (A), (D), (C), (E)

9. Match List – I with List – II.

List – I (Character)	List – II (Novel)
(A) Sethe	(I) The Handmaid's Tale
(B) Okonkwo	(II) Beloved
(C) Offred	(III) Things Fall Apart
(D) Winston Smith	(IV) Nineteen Eighty-Four

Choose the correct answer from the options given below:
(1) (A)-(II), (B)-(III), (C)-(I), (D)-(IV)
(2) (A)-(III), (B)-(II), (C)-(IV), (D)-(I)
(3) (A)-(I), (B)-(III), (C)-(II), (D)-(IV)
(4) (A)-(IV), (B)-(1), (C)-(III), (D)-(II)

10. Which among the following statements are true?
(A) Miscegenation is a sexual relationship or marriage between the people of the same race
(B) Creole is a language that has evolved from a pidgin but serves as the native language of a speech community
(C) Indian tribal people are popularly termed as aboriginals
(D) Mulatto is a person of mixed white and black ancestry
(E) Australian indigenous population is termed as Red Indians

Choose the most appropriate answer from the options given below:
(1) (A) and (E) Only
(2) (B) and (C) Only
(3) (C) and (D) Only
(4) (B) and (D) Only

11. Which of the following is true of Edward Said's Orientalism?
(A) It was published in 1979.
(B) Utilises the concept of discursive formulation as argued by Foucault.
(C) He has taken up the detailed analysis of imaginative geography and representation of the Orient.
(D) It is one of the foundational texts of Postcolonial theory.
(E) It puts to use Barthes' concept of 'death of the author'.

Choose the most appropriate answer from the options given below:
(1) (A), (B) and (E) Only
(2) (A), (B) and (C) Only

(3) (A), (C) and (E) Only
(4) (B), (C) and (D) Only

12. Given below are two statements: one is labelled as Assertion (A) and the other is labelled as Reason (R).

Assertion (A): Culture is one of the two or three most complicated words in the English language.

Reason (R): This is mainly because of several different though related meanings have emerged at particular moments throughout its long history.

In the light of the above statements, choose the most appropriate answer from the options given below

(1) Both (A) and (R) are true and (R) is the correct explanation of (A).
(2) Both (A) and (R) are true but (R) is NOT the correct explanation of (A).
(3) (A) is true but (R) is false.
(4) (A) is false but (R) is true.

13. Use of broader principles of research underscored by philosophical rationales is termed as:

(1) Research Methods
(2) Research Tools
(3) Research Techniques
(4) Research Methodology

14. Who among the following declared in 1920 that "there is no longer any intellectual life in England"?

(1) Dorothy Richardson
(2) Virginia Woolf
(3) Ezra Pound
(4) T.S. Eliot

15. Identify the poet of the following poems:

(a) The Skylark
(b) The Badger
(c) The Gypsy Camp
(d) First Love

(1) P.B. Shelley (2) John Clare
(3) Lord Byron (4) Robert Burns

16. The term 'simulacra' in postmodern discourse is about:

(A) Absence of vivid representation of reality
(B) Artificially produced reality dubbed as authentic
(C) A rejection of modernistic view of reality
(D) The gap between the perception and reality
(E) The psychological interplay at the level of subconscious

Choose the correct answer from the options given below:

(1) (C) and (E) Only
(2) (D) and (E) Only
(3) (A) and (B) Only
(4) (B) and (C) Only

17. Which two cities are referred in Charles Dickens' *A Tale of Two Cities*?

(1) Paris and Venice
(2) Venice and Florence
(3) London and Paris
(4) London and Birmingham

18. Transcendental Club was a group of American intellectuals for philosophical discussions. Which text among the following is taken as a short treatise on Transcendentalism?

(1) Emerson's Nature
(2) Thoreau's Walden
(3) Whitman's Leaves of Grass
(4) Thoreau's Civil Disobedience

19. Match List – I with List – II.

List – I (Text)	List – II (Author)
(A) The Collaborator	(I) Amandeep Sandhu
(B) The Garden of Solitude	(II) Shahnaz Bashir
(C) Roll of Honour	(III) Siddhartha Gigoo
(D) The Half Mother	(IV) Mirza Waheed

Choose the correct answer from the options given below:

(1) (A)-(IV), (B)-(III), (C)-(I), (D)-(II)
(2) (A)-(I), (B)-(II), (C)-(III), (D)-(IV)

(3) (A)-(II), (B)-(III), (C)-(IV), (D)-(I)
(4) (A)-(III), (B)-(I), (C)-(II), (D)-(IV)

20. Name the author/writer who is not associated with British Cultural Studies.
(1) I.A. Richards
(2) Richard Hoggart
(3) Raymond Williams
(4) Stuart Hall

21. Given below are two statements:
Statement (I): Non-fictional narrative Follow the Rabbit-Proof Fence by Doris Pilkington is based on the real-life experiences of three aboriginal girls who fled from the Moore River Native Settlement.
Statement (II): The names of the three girls are- Molly, Daisy and Mary.
In the light of the above statements, choose the most appropriate answer from the options given below:
(1) Both Statement (I) and Statement (II) are correct
(2) Both Statement (I) and Statement (II) are incorrect
(3) Statement (I) is correct but Statement (II) is incorrect
(4) Statement (I) is incorrect but Statement (II) is correct

22. Arrange the chronological sequence in which the following works of Richard Hoggart were published:
(A) An Imagined Life
(B) The Uses of Literacy
(C) Higher Education: Demand and Response
(D) A Local Habitation
(E) A Sort of Clowning
Choose the correct answer from the options given below:
(1) (A), (B), (D), (E), (C)
(2) (D), (B), (C), (A), (E)
(3) (B), (E), (A), (C), (D)
(4) (B), (C), (D), (E), (A)

23. Match List – I with List – II.

List – I (Character)	List – II (Work)
(A) Christophine	(I) Wuthering Heights
(B) Zillah	(II) Wide Sargasso Sea
(C) Estella	(III) Things Fall Apart
(D) Ekwefi	(IV) Great Expectations

Choose the correct answer from the options given below:
(1) (A)-(IV), (B)-(III), (C)-(II), (D)-(I)
(2) (A)-(I), (B)-(II), (C)-(III), (D)-(IV)
(3) (A)-(II), (B)-(I), (C)-(IV), (D)-(III)
(4) (A)-(III), (B)-(IV), (C)-(I), (D)-(II)

24. Which of the following characteristics of She Stoops to Conquer is not correct?
(1) It is endowed with an ingenious and lively plot.
(2) It does not cast excellent characters.
(3) It has a vivacious and delightful style.
(4) It lacks the Restoration grossness.

25. Antonio Gramsci's Prison Notebooks primarily deals with:
(1) Pain of a prisoner during colonial times
(2) Recollections of love, romance and blissful life
(3) Philosophy, culture, literature and the role of intellectuals
(4) Exploitation of blacks during the colonial times

26. Given below are two statements:
Statement (I): A Room of One's Own is a feminist essay about women's education, exclusion and writing by Virginia Woolf.
Statement (II): In Other Worlds is a collection of essays written by Edward W. Said on contemporary ideas such as psychoanalysis and social theory.
In the light of the above statements, choose the most appropriate answer from the options given below
(1) Both Statement (I) and Statement (II) are true

(2) Both Statement (I) and Statement (II) are false
(3) Statement (I) is true but Statement (II) is false
(4) Statement (I) is false but Statement (II) is true

27. Which of the following is true about Tennessee Williams' A Street Car Named Desire?
(A) It is set in New Orleans.
(B) The protagonist is a Mississippi landowner.
(C) It ends with Blanche's defeat and departure.
(D) Tom Wingfield is the narrator.
(E) Laura and Stella are cousins.
Choose the correct answer from the options given below:
(1) (A) and (D) Only
(2) (A) and (C) Only
(3) (B) and (C) Only
(4) (B) and (E) Only

28. Prose romances preceded the emergence of novel as a popular literary genre. Which texts among the following fall under the category of Prose Romance?
(1) The Pilgrim's Progress and The Spectator
(2) Oroonoko and The Fair Jilt
(3) Pamela and Clarissa
(4) Amelia and Ferdinand, Count Fathom

29. Which of the following statement(s) best describe Anna Karenina's situation and worldview?
(A) Anna is deeply committed to the family and children
(B) Anna's choices were more an outcome of passion and instinct
(C) Anna accepted the exile to which she was condemned
(D) Anna's passionate spirit and determination to live life at her own terms make her so unique
(E) She became a victim of rampant patriarchal forces
Choose the most appropriate answer from the options given below:
(1) (A), (C) and (D) Only
(2) (A), (B) and (E) Only
(3) (A), (D) and (E) Only
(4) (A), (B) and (D) Only

30. Which of the following assumptions are true in the context of New Criticism?
(A) The new movement in literature popularised closed reading of the text.
(B) The leading critics of New Criticism are Allen Tate, Robert Penn Warren, R.P. Blackmur and Kenneth Burke.
(C) The critical approach is extensively used in the study of novels and plays.
(D) This critical approach tends to discredit historical, social and political contexts of a work of literature.
(E) J.C. Ransom published a book New Criticism wherein he appreciates I.A. Richards, William Empson and T.S. Eliot.
Choose the correct answer from the options given below:
(1) (A), (B) and (C) Only
(2) (B), (C) and (D) Only
(3) (C), (D) and (E) Only
(4) (A), (B) and (D) Only

31. Roland Barthes in his "Introduction to the Structural Analysis of Narratives" (1966) proposed three levels of narrative structure. Which among the following are the narrative structures proposed by him:
(A) Functions (B) Actions
(C) Grammar (D) Narration
(E) Coherence
Choose the correct answer from the options given below:
(1) (A), (E) and (C) Only
(2) (A), (B) and (D) Only
(3) (B), (C) and (E) Only
(4) (A), (C) and (D) Only

32. Which of the following is not true about Raymond Williams' views on culture?

(1) Culture is ordinary
(2) Culture is a whole way of life
(3) The masses do not participate in the creation of cultural values
(4) There exists at least three layers of a culture at a given point of time in a society- dominant, residual and emergent

33. The Calcutta Chromosome (1995) is a novel exploring past and future. It has been written by:
(1) Rabindranath Tagore
(2) Amitav Ghosh
(3) Raja Rao
(4) Mulkraj Anand

34. Identify the correct order of the publications given below:
(A) Simon Gikandi's Maps of Englishness: Writing Identity in the Culture of Colonialism
(B) Frantz Fanon's The Wretched of the Earth
(C) Homi K. Bhabha's Nation and Narration
(D) Ernest Gellner's Nations and Nationalisms
(E) Robert Young's Colonial Desire: Hybridity in Theory, Culture and Race
Choose the correct answer from the options given below:
(1) (B), (D), (E), (C), (A)
(2) (A), (B), (C), (D), (E)
(3) (A), (C), (D), (E), (B)
(4) (B), (D), (C), (E), (A)

35. Who of the following was the immediate predecessor of the drama proper?
(1) The Interlude
(2) The Morality Play
(3) The Miracle Play
(4) The Liturgical Play

36. Which of the following is true about Samuel Beckett's Waiting for Godot?
(A) It illustrates vanity of human kind.
(B) It has uncompromising views on humanitarian communism.
(C) It projects self-deception, striving to disguise failure.
(D) It is a static representation without structure or development.
(E) Its incoherent dialogue suggests despair of a society.
Choose the correct answer from the options given below:
(1) (A) and (C) Only
(2) (C) and (D) Only
(3) (A) and (B) Only
(4) (D) and (E) Only

37. What is the correct chronological order pf publication of the texts given under?
(A) R.K. Narayan's The Financial Expert
(B) Manohar Malgonkar's A Bend in the Ganges
(C) Raja Rao's Kanthapura
(D) Shashi Tharoor's The Great Indian Novel
(E) Arundhati Roy's The God of Small Things
Choose the correct answer from the options given below:
(1) (D), (A), (B), (C), (E)
(2) (A), (D), (C), (B), (E)
(3) (C), (A), (B), (D), (E)
(4) (E), (D), (C), (B), (A)

38. Who among the following is the earliest available Indian dramatist?
(1) Bhavabhuti (2) Kalidas
(3) Bhasa (4) Rajashekhar

39. Which of the following statements are valid for postcolonial theory and literature?
(A) Abrogation, resistance and assertion form the basis of postcolonial thought.
(B) Postcolonial theory defends binaries of Master and Slave, White and Black, and Coloniser and Colonised.
(C) Weep Not, Child is the first novel in English by an East African Writer, Ngugi Wa Thiong'o.
(D) Wide Sargasso Sea by Jean Rhys is based on the experiences of colonized African population.

(E) Homi K. Bhabha, Edward W. Said and Gayatri Spivak are important postcolonial thinkers.

Choose the most appropriate answer from the options given below:

(1) (A), (B) and (D) Only
(2) (B), (D) and (E) Only
(3) (A), (C) and (E) Only
(4) (C), (D) and (E) Only

40. Indicate the correct chronological order of publication of the following literary works:

(A) Beowulf
(B) Divina Commedia
(C) Summa Theologica
(D) Le Morte d' Arthur
(E) Canterbury Tales

Choose the correct answer from the options given below:

(1) (B), (A), (C), (D), (E)
(2) (A), (C), (B), (E), (D)
(3) (C), (A), (D), (E), (B)
(4) (D), (A), (E), (C), (B)

41. Chronologically arrange the following works of Sri Aurobindo in accordance with their year of publication:

(A) The Hour of God
(B) The Mother
(C) The Life Divine
(D) The Future Poetry
(E) The Synthesis of Yoga

Choose the correct answer from the options given below:

(1) (B), (D), (C), (A), (E)
(2) (A), (B), (C), (D), (E)
(3) (E), (C), (D), (A), (B)
(4) (C), (A), (D), (B), (E)

42. Which among the following are not mentioned as the aspects of the novel by E.M. Forster?

(A) Tory (B) Imagination
(C) Plot (D) Harmony
(E) Prophecy

Choose the correct answer from the options given below:

(1) (A) and (C) Only
(2) (C) and (E) Only
(3) (A) and (E) Only
(4) (B) and (D) Only

43. Match List – I with List – II.

List – I (Novel)	List – II (Writer)
(A) Waiting for the Mahatama	(I) Bhabani Bhattacharya
(B) So Many Hungers	(II) R.K. Narayan
(C) The Sword and the Sickle	(III) Manohar Malgonkar
(D) Distant Drum	(IV) Mulk Raj Anand

Choose the correct answer from the options given below:

(1) (A)-(II), (B)-(I), (C)-(IV), (D)-(III)
(2) (A)-(I), (B)-(III), (C)-(II), (D)-(IV)
(3) (A)-(IV), (B)-(II), (C)-(I), (D)-(III)
(4) (A)-(III), (B)-(IV), (C)-(II), (D)-(I)

44. What does aptly define minor literature, according to Giles Deleuze?

(1) Deconstruction of Material Reality
(2) Deterritorialisation of language
(3) Heteroglossia
(4) Metanarrative

45. Which one of these is not a literary journal/ magazine?

(1) The Egoist
(2) The Criterion
(3) The English Review
(4) The Hundred and One Dalmatians

46. "All happy families are alike; every unhappy family is unhappy in its own way." It is the opening line of the novel:

(1) Anna Karenina
(2) War and Peace
(3) Nineteen Eighty-Four
(4) Jane Eyre

47. How many major forms of drama have been described by Bharata in his manual of dramaturgy?

(1) Seven (2) Three
(3) Four (4) Ten

48. Given below are two statements: one is labelled as Assertion (A) and the other is labelled as Reason (R).

Assertion (A): Toni Morrison and Adrienne Rich have contributed to a distinctive style.

Reason (R): Feminism, Adrienne Rich observes, is the field where "subjectivity and politics have to come together" in the most natural way.

In the light of the above statements, choose the most appropriate answer from the options given below:

(1) Both (A) and (R) are correct and (R) is the correct explanation of (A).
(2) Both (A) and (R) are correct but (R) is NOT the correct explanation of (A).
(3) (A) is correct but (R) is not correct.
(4) (A) is not correct but (R) is correct.

49. Identify the correct option(s) in the theorisation of nation by Homi K. Bhabha.

(A) Nation arises from similarities among people.
(B) Nationalist representation is defined by ambivalence.
(C) Nationalist representation engages with two contradictory modes of representation.
(D) Nationalist discourses are split by a disruptive double-narrative movement.
(E) Nation is a stable and fixed category.

Choose the most appropriate answer from the options given below:

(1) (A), (B) and (C) Only
(2) (B), (C) and (E) Only
(3) (B), (C) and (D) Only
(4) (C), (D) and (E) Only

50. The term 'Gynocriticism' refers to :

(1) Feminist consciousness
(2) Production of writings on women by men
(3) Analysis of Andro texts
(4) Production and analysis of writings by women on women

51. Arrange the following texts chronologically:

(A) Bharat's Natyashastra
(B) Kshemendra's Aucityavicharacharcha
(C) Bhamah's Kavyalankara
(D) Kuntak's Vakroktijivitam
(E) Anandavardhan's Dhvanyaloka

Choose the correct answer from the options given below:

(1) (A), (E), (C), (D), (E)
(2) (A), (C), (D), (E), (B)
(3) (A), (C), (E), (D), (B)
(4) (B), (A), (C), (E), (D)

52. A portmanteau is:

(1) A word which sounds the same but have different meanings.
(2) A word that results from blending two or more words or part of words.
(3) Creation of new words without reference to the existing morphological resources.
(4) Copying a word that originally belonged to one language into another language.

53. Who among the following described drama in the following words?

"A true play is three dimensional; it is literature that walks and talks before our eyes."

(1) Marjorie Boulton
(2) Allardyce Nicoll
(3) G.B. Shaw
(4) Arthur Miller

54. What among the following is not true about Anna Karenina?

(1) The novel was published in 1872.
(2) The novel is written in eight parts.
(3) It tells the story of two major characters, Anna and Konstantin Levin.
(4) The novel is revolutionary in its treatment of women.

55. Which among the following statement is not true about NEP-2020?

(1) NEP-2020 recommends that there should be high quality learning and print material in Indian languages

(2) The Policy recommends early implementation of three-language formulae to promote multilingualism
(3) The Policy recommends that English language should be the only medium of instruction at elementary level
(4) The Policy recommends teaching in local language wherever possible

56. 'Panopticism' is a concept that refers to external spying. Who among the following coined this term?
(1) Antonio Gramsci
(2) Michel Foucault
(3) Slavoj Zizek
(4) Roland Barthes

57. Match List – I with List – II.

List – I (Story)	List – II (Author)
(A) "A Simple Heart"	(I) Joseph Conrad
(B) "An Outpost of Progress"	(II) Gustave Flaubert
(C) "Six Feet of the Country"	(III) R.K. Narayan
(D) "A Horse and Two Goats"	(IV) Nadine Gordimer

Choose the correct answer from the options given below:
(1) (A)-(I), (B)-(IV), (C)-(III), (D)-(II)
(2) (A)-(II), (B)-(I), (C)-(IV), (D)-(III)
(3) (A)-(III), (B)-(II), (C)-(I), (D)-(IV)
(4) (A)-(IV), (B)-(III), (C)-(II), (D)-(I)

58. According to Sigmund Freud, civilisation is to some extent the cumulative product of our psychology. Choose the correct option(s):
(A) The purpose of human life is the pursuit of happiness.
(B) Man is wholly good.
(C) Abolition of private property will remove ill-will and hostility among men.
(D) Creative art reflects the purpose of human life.
(E) Civilisation is analogous with the human psyche.
Choose the most appropriate answer from the options given below:
(1) (C), (D) and (E) Only
(2) (B), (C) and (D) Only
(3) (A), (D) and (E) Only
(4) (A), (B) and (C) Only

59. Match List – I with List – II.

List – I (Term)	List – II (Coined by)
(A) Heteroglossia	(I) William Empson
(B) Structures of Feeling	(II) Raymond Williams
(C) Ambiguity	(III) Mikhail Bakhtin
(D) Discourse	(IV) Michel Foucault

Choose the correct answer from the options given below:
(1) (A)-(III), (B)-(II), (C)-(I), (D)-(IV)
(2) (A)-(I), (B)-(IV), (C)-(III), (D)-(II)
(3) (A)-(IV), (B)-(II), (C)-(I), (D)-(III)
(4) (A)-(II), (B)-(IV), (C)-(III), (D)-(I)

60. Which of the following novels of Thomas Hardy was first published in an abridged form as Hearts Insurgent?
(1) The Mayor of Casterbridge
(2) Jude the Obscure
(3) Far From the Madding Crowd
(4) The Return of the Native

61. Which work of Francis Bacon explains the new logic or inductive method of reasoning?
(1) Apophthegms
(2) The History of Henry VII
(3) Novum Organum
(4) De Augmentis Scientiarum.

62. Match List – I with List – II.

List – I (Term)	List – II (Definition)
(A) Ambivalence	(I) Rejection of a normative concept of 'correct' or 'standard' English
(B) Magic Realism	(II) Marriage or cohabitation by persons of different race
(C) Abrogation	(III) Complex mix of attraction and repulsion

(D) Miscegenation (IV) Inclusion of fantastic or mythical elements into seemingly realistic fiction

Choose the correct answer from the options given below:

(1) (A)-(I), (B)-(II), (C)-(IV), (D)-(III)
(2) (A)-(II), (B)-(III), (C)-(I), (D)-(IV)
(3) (A)-(IV), (B)-(I), (C)-(III), (D)-(II)
(4) (A)-(III), (B)-(IV), (C)-(I), (D)-(II)

63. Which among the following is not a character from Jane Austen's novel Persuasion?

(1) Sir Walter Elliot
(2) Lady Russell
(3) Miss Crawford
(4) Frederick Wentworth

64. Name the poet who has composed the following poems:

(a) The Divine Image
(b) The Holy Thursday
(c) The Little Boy Lost
(d) The Little Boy Found

(1) William Shakespeare
(2) William Blake
(3) William Collins
(4) Samuel Johnson

65. According to Greek Mythology, who is a Psyche in John Keats' "Ode to Psyche"?

(1) A mortal woman
(2) Cupid
(3) An immortal woman
(4) Venus

66. Match List I with List II.

List – I (Literary Device)	List – II (Definition)
(A) Hyperbole	(I) Referring to something by the name of something else that is closely connected with it
(B) Metonymy	(II) A roundabout or indirect manner of writing or speaking
(C) Synecdoche	(III) A figure of speech in which a part represents the whole
(D) Periphrasis	(IV) An intentional exaggeration for emphasis or comic effect

Choose the correct answer from the options given below:

(1) (A)-(II), (B)-(III), (C)-(IV), (D)-(I)
(2) (A)-(I), (B)-(II), (C)-(IV), (D)-(III)
(3) (A)-(III), (B)-(IV), (C)-(II), (D)-(I)
(4) (A)-(IV), (B)-(I), (C)-(III), (D)-(II)

67. Which among the following is not written by a sportsperson?

(1) Open: An Autobiography
(2) Unbreakable: An Autobiography
(3) Playing It My Way: My Autobiography
(4) A Country Called Childhood: A Memoir

68. Match List – I with List – II.

List – I (Work)	List – II (Author)
(A) The Wretched of the Earth	(I) Benedict Anderson
(B) Nation and Narration	(II) Homi K. Bhabha
(C) Culture and Imperialism	(III) Edward W. Said
(D) Imagined Communities	(IV) Frantz Fanon

Choose the correct answer from the options given below:

(1) (A)-(I), (B)-(III), (C)-(IV), (D)-(II)
(2) (A)-(II), (B)-(I), (C)-(III), (D)-(IV)
(3) (A)-(IV), (B)-(II), (C)-(III), (D)-(I)
(4) (A)-(II), (B)-(IV), (C)-(I), (D)-(III)

69. What is not true about D.H. Lawrence's Sons and Lovers?

(A) Sons and Lovers is a semi-autobiographical novel.

(B) It is a psychological study of the familial and love relationships of a working-class English family.
(C) The film adaptation of the novel was directed by Jack Cardiff.
(D) The storyline traces three generations of Brangwen family.
(E) The novel narrates the story of Paul Morel whose love for his beloved overshadows the affectionate bond with his mother.

Choose the correct answer from the options given below:
(1) (A) and (C) Only
(2) (B) and (D) Only
(3) (D) and (E) Only
(4) (C) and (E) Only

70. Which among the following poems has not been composed by P.B. Shelley?
(1) To Wordsworth
(2) Mutability
(3) Hymn to Intellectual Beauty
(4) When We Two Parted

71. Given below are two statements: one is labelled as Assertion (A) and the other is labelled as Reason (R).

Assertion (A): Discourses are cultural and social practices rooted in psychic and physical reality.

Reason (R): Foucault defines discourse as the material manifestation of thought which shapes our subjectivity.

In the light of the above statements, choose the most appropriate answer from the options given below:
(1) Both (A) and (R) are correct and (R) is the correct explanation of (A).
(2) Both (A) and (R) are correct but (R) is NOT the correct explanation of (A).
(3) (A) is correct but (R) is not correct.
(4) (A) is not correct but (R) is correct.

72. Arrange the following in the chronological order of the date/year of publication:
(A) Chitra Banerjee Divakaruni's The Mistress of Spices
(B) Anand Giridhar Das's India Calling: An Intimate Portrait of a Nation's Remaking
(C) V.S. Naipaul's India: A Wounded Civilisation
(D) Bharati Mukherjee's Desirable Daughters
(E) Salman Rushdie's Midnight's Children

Choose the correct answer from the options given below:
(1) (A), (B), (C), (D), (E)
(2) (B), (C), (D), (A), (E)
(3) (C), (E), (A), (D), (B)
(4) (E), (D), (C), (B), (A)

73. Which of the following is true about Arthur Miller's plays?
(A) After the Fall is a semi-autobiographical play.
(B) Incident of Vichy deals with Nazi prosecution of the Jews.
(C) The Price anticipates economic crash.
(D) The Creation of the World is not a serio-comic re-writing of the story of Jesus.
(E) The Crucible uses a specific setting to consider the responsibilities of the artist.

Choose the most appropriate answer from the options given below:
(1) (E) and (A) Only
(2) (A) and (C) Only
(3) (A) and (B) Only
(4) (D) and (E) Only

74. Identify the correct option in Julia Kristeva's definition of 'chora':
(A) Liminal Space
(B) Space of the marginalised
(C) Non-expressive totality created by the bodily drives
(D) The chora has no fixed identity
(E) It precedes the linguistic sign

Choose the most appropriate answer from the options given below:
(1) (A), (B) and (E) Only
(2) (C), (D) and (E) Only

(3) (A), (C) and (D) Only
(4) (A), (B) and (C) Only

75. "Being a white man, in short, was a very concrete manner of being-in-the-world, a way of taking hold of reality, language and thought."
What does the theorist signify by the term 'white man' here?
(1) A dominating man
(2) A megalomaniac
(3) A man with double consciousness
(4) A form of colonial authority

76. "I am a sick man... I am a spiteful man. I am an unattractive man. I think my liver is diseased."
These are the opening lines of:
(1) Gabriel Garcia Marquez's Love in the Time of Cholera
(2) Dostoevsky's Notes from Underground
(3) Albert Camus The Plague
(4) Daniel Defoe's A Journal of the Plague Year

77. Who among the following is not associated with Cultural Imperialism?
(1) Jonathan Dollimore
(2) Alan Sinfield
(3) Raymond Williams
(4) Stanley Fish

78. "Did not Shakespeare hate and despise Iago and Edmund?"
Identify the book in which this question has been mentioned.
(1) An Apology for Poetry
(2) Kings of Norway
(3) Fool of Quality
(4) Aspects of Poetry

79. Choose the correct option(s) in the New Historicist reading of Dalit writing:
(A) Dalit writing does not essentialise Indian society, culture and identity.
(B) Dalit writing has inflected the immanent metanarratives.
(C) There is no single location of Dalit writing.
(D) Dalit writing is only a political category.
(E) Dalit writing is not grounded in history.
Choose the most appropriate answer from the options given below:
(1) (A), (B) and (C) Only
(2) (A), (C) and (D) Only
(3) (C), (D) and (E) Only
(4) (B), (D) and (E) Only

80. Which of the following qualities of heroic treatment was not needed in the plays of the University Wits?
(1) Splendid descriptions
(2) Long swelling speeches
(3) The handling of violent incidents and emotions
(4) Lives of common figures

81. Which among the following writers remarked that "I know of no more encouraging fact than the unquestionable ability of man to elevate his life by a conscious endeavour"?
(1) Henry David Thoreau
(2) Ralph Waldo Emerson
(3) Henry James
(4) Emily Dickinson

82. Choose the correct option in the light of the following statement:
"The fact that I am a black working-class man will determine my worldview just as much, and perhaps far more than I consciously learn in the domain of ideas."
(A) Man is capable of making free choices in the sphere of intellection and morality.
(B) The unconscious determines human thought and behaviour
(C) Man is condemned to be free
(D) We bear a form of "otherness" within ourselves
(E) We can no longer talk unequivocally of a writer's intention.
Choose the most appropriate answer from the options given below:

(1) (B), (D) and (E) Only
(2) (A), (B) and (C) Only
(3) (C), (D) and (E) Only
(4) (A), (B) and (E) Only

83. Arrange the following in the chronological order of the dates of publication:
(A) Michel Foucault's The Order of Things
(B) M.K. Gandhi's Hind Swaraj or The Indian Home rule
(C) Stephen Greenblatt's The Swerve: How the World Became Modern
(D) Donna Harraway's When Species Meet
(E) Tony Bennett's Formalism and Marxism

Choose the correct answer from the options given below:
(1) (A), (B), (C), (E), (D)
(2) (B), (A), (E), (D), (C)
(3) (C), (D), (E), (B), (A)
(4) (D), (C), (A), (E), (B)

84. Which among the following statements are true about Emily Bronte's Wuthering Heights?
(A) This novel was published in 1847.
(B) Emily Bronte published this novel under the pseudonym Ellis Bell.
(C) Lockwood and Catherine Linton are the main narrators of the story.
(D) The novel is unique for its abstention from authorial intrusion, unusual structure and narrative technique.
(E) Wuthering Heights was the third novel of Emily Bronte.

Choose the correct answer from the options given below:
(1) (B), (C) and (D) Only
(2) (A), (B) and (C) Only
(3) (A), (B) and (D) Only
(4) (C), (D) and (E) Only

85. Match List – I with List – II.

List – I (Novel)	**List – II (Subtitle)**
(A) The Castle of Otranto	(I) A Pure Woman
(B) Tess of the d'Urbervilles	(II) The Modern Prometheus
(C) Frankenstein	(III) A Novel without A Hero
(D) Vanity Fair	(IV) A Gothic Story

Choose the correct answer from the options given below:
(1) (A)-(IV), (B)-(I), (C)-(II), (D)-(III)
(2) (A)-(I), (B)-(II), (C)-(III), (D)-(IV)
(3) (A)-(II), (B)-(I), (C)-(IV), (D)-(III)
(4) (A)-(III), (B)-(IV), (C)-(II), (D)-(I)

86. Which of the following assertions is/are not true in the context of culture industry?
(A) The term 'culture industry' was used by the Frankfurt School to describe the operations of mass media.
(B) The dominant capitalist class instils its values and beliefs in the minds of the working-class people.
(C) The word 'industry' signifies the production of cultural products for mass consumption.
(D) The authentic culture arising from the working class is preserved and protected.
(E) The mass culture thus produced induces activism and critical thinking among the youth.

Choose the correct answer from the options given below:
(1) (D) and (A) Only
(2) (E) and (B) Only
(3) (B) and (C) Only
(4) (D) and (E) Only

87. Which among the following are the titles of the periodicals?
(A) Dickens' Household Words
(B) S.T. Coleridge' Friend
(C) Richard Steele's Guardian
(D) Franz Kafka's The Metamorphosis
(E) Leigh Hunt's Indicator

Choose the correct answer from the options given below:
(1) (A) and (B) Only

(2) (B) and (C) Only
(3) (A), (B), (C) and (E) Only
(4) (C), (D) and (E) Only

88. In Antonio Gramsci's definition of intellectual, which is the correct option?

(A) Every social group joining the world of production creates organically a stratum of intellectuals.
(B) Intellectuals give homogeneity and awareness of a social group's function in all the fields.
(C) Intellectuals do not work for consolidating the power of a social group.
(D) The category of ecclesiastics is organically bound to the bourgeoisie.
(E) The monopoly held by the ecclesiastics in the superstructural domain was not exercised without a contestation.

Choose the correct answer from the options given below:
(1) (A), (B) and (C) Only
(2) (B), (C) and (D) Only
(3) (A), (B) and (E) Only
(4) (C), (D) and (E) Only

89. The essay "Discourse in the Novel" discusses that the novel is constituted by a multiplicity of divergent and contending social voices. Who is the author of this essay?
(1) E.M. Forster
(2) Mikhail Bakhtin
(3) Dostoevsky
(4) Edgar Allan Poe

90. In Absurd Theatre, the characters often use disjointed, repetitive and clichéd speech to:
(A) Suggest that meaninglessness is also about a meaning.
(B) Suggest the working of the subconscious.
(C) Bring about the comic action and relief.
(D) Illustrate the illogical and purposelessness of human condition.
(E) Defy the self-professed 'modern' notion of dignity and wisdom.

Choose the correct answer from the options given below:
(1) (A) and (B) Only
(2) (B) and (C) Only
(3) (D) and (E) Only
(4) (A) and (D) Only

Read the following stanza and answer the questions that follow:

Shall I compare thee to a Summer's Day
Thou art more lovely and more temperate:
Rough winds do shake the darling buds of May'
And summer's lease hath all too short a date.
Sometimes too hot the eye of heaven shines,
And often is his gold complexion dimm'd.

91. Which of the following statements rightly shows the relationship of upameya with upamana in the poem:
(1) Upameya is superior to upamana
(2) Upamana is superior to upameya
(3) Both upamana and upameya are equal
(4) Both are governed by position and superimposition

92. The poem is an example of:
(1) Parampariterupaka (consequential metaphor) because here the superimposition, undermined by a resemblance, is the cause of another superimposition.
(2) Nirangarupaka (entire metaphor) because here upameya is superimposed by upamana together with its subordinate parts.
(3) Malarupaka (deficient metaphorserial) because here upameya is superimposed by serial of upamanas.
(4) Mishritarupaka (mixed metaphor) because here the common attribute, the words implying comparison, upamana and upameya, all are expressed.

93. What is the addressee in the poem?
(1) Feminine gender
(2) Masculine gender
(3) Common gender
(4) Neutral gender

94. What is upmana (object compared to) in the poem?
(1) Addressee
(2) Rough winds
(3) Buds of May
(4) Summer's Day

95. What is upmeya (object compared) in the poem?
(1) Addressee
(2) Rough winds
(3) Buds of May
(4) Summer's day

Read the following passage and answer the questions that follow:

Some sort of parallel may be found in the way logical connectives are usually unnecessary and often misleading, because too simple. Omitting an adjective one would need 'therefore' stressing the adjective 'although'; both logical connections are implied if the sentences are just put after another. In the same way, people are accustomed to judge automatically the forces that hold together a variety of ideas; they feel they know about the forces, if they have analysed the ideas; many forces, indeed, are covertly included within ideas; and so of the two elements, each of which defines the other, it is much easier to find words for the ideas than for the forces. Most of the ambiguities I have considered here seem to me beautiful; I consider, then, that I have shown by example, in showing the nature of the ambiguity, the nature of the forces which are adequate to hold it together. It would seem very artificial to do it the other way round, and very tedious to do it both ways at once. I wish only, then, to say here that such vaguely imagined 'forces' are essential to the totality of a poem and they cannot be discussed in terms of ambiguity, because they are complementary to it. But by discussing 'ambiguity', a great deal may be made clear about them. In particular, if there is contradiction, the greater the tension; in some way other than by the contradiction, the tension must be conveyed, and must be sustained.

96. What does the term "logical connectives" mean?
(1) The nature of ambiguity
(2) The logical content
(3) The statement of logical form in addition to logical context
(4) The statement of logical form

97. Why does the author say that "the tension must be conveyed and must be sustained"?
(1) Because it is unnecessary and often misleading
(2) Because it is too simple
(3) Because it is impregnated with adjectives
(4) Because tension is often an important clue to the meaning of a poem

98. It is easy to find words for ideas than for forces because:
(1) Ideas are embedded in forces
(2) Forces are embedded in ideas
(3) Two elements are synonymously defined
(4) Forces are abstract

99. Which of the following is not correct in relation to a poem?
(1) Forces are indispensable for the totality of a poem
(2) Forces can be discussed in terms of ambiguity
(3) Forces and ambiguity are complementary to it
(4) Many forces are included within the ideas

100. What is the possibility in the analysis of a poem, if the forces are included in the ideas?
(1) The ideas can be defined easily.
(2) The forces can be defined easily.
(3) Both the ideas and the forces can be defined easily.
(4) It is difficult to define both the ideas and the forces.

ANSWERS

1. (1)	**2.** (1)	**3.** (3)	**4.** (1)	**5.** (3)	**6.** (2)	**7.** (3)	**8.** (3)	**9.** (1)	**10.** (4)
11. (4)	**12.** (1)	**13.** (4)	**14.** (3)	**15.** (2)	**16.** (3)	**17.** (3)	**18.** (1)	**19.** (1)	**20.** (1)
21. (3)	**22.** (4)	**23.** (3)	**24.** (2)	**25.** (3)	**26.** (3)	**27.** (2)	**28.** (2)	**29.** (3)	**30.** (4)
31. (2)	**32.** (3)	**33.** (2)	**34.** (4)	**35.** (1)	**36.** (4)	**37.** (3)	**38.** (3)	**39.** (3)	**40.** (4)
41. (1)	**42.** (4)	**43.** (1)	**44.** (2)	**45.** (4)	**46.** (1)	**47.** (4)	**48.** (2)	**49.** (3)	**50.** (4)
51. (3)	**52.** (2)	**53.** (1)	**54.** (1)	**55.** (3)	**56.** (2)	**57.** (2)	**58.** (3)	**59.** (1)	**60.** (2)
61. (3)	**62.** (4)	**63.** (3)	**64.** (2)	**65.** (1)	**66.** (4)	**67.** (4)	**68.** (3)	**69.** (3)	**70.** (4)
71. (1)	**72.** (3)	**73.** (3)	**74.** (2)	**75.** (4)	**76.** (2)	**77.** (4)	**78.** (4)	**79.** (1)	**80.** (4)
81. (1)	**82.** (1)	**83.** (2)	**84.** (3)	**85.** (1)	**86.** (4)	**87.** (3)	**88.** (3)	**89.** (2)	**90.** (4)
91. (1)	**92.** (1)	**93.** (2)	**94.** (4)	**95.** (1)	**96.** (3)	**97.** (3)	**98.** (2)	**99.** (2)	**100.** (1)

❖❖❖

August, 2024

ENGLISH

PAPER-II

Note : This paper contains **hundred (100)** objective type questions of **two (2)** marks each. All questions are **compulsory**.

1. Which one of the following plays mock the Restoration drama of Dryden and Thomas Otway?
   (1) *The Beggar's Opera* by John Gay
   (2) *Tom Thumb* by Henry Fielding
   (3) *The Critic* by R.B. Sheridan
   (4) *The Rehearsal* by George Villiers

2. Identify the name of the essayist who made the following assertion:
   "If a man will begin with certainties, he shall end in doubts, but if will be content to begin with doubts, he shall end in certainties."
   (1) Richard Hooker
   (2) Sir Francis Bacon
   (3) Sir Richard Steele
   (4) Joseph Addison

3. From which book of John Milton's poem *Paradise Lost* the epigraph of Mary Shelley's novel *Frankenstein* taken when Adam asks God:
   "Did I request thee, maker from my clay to mould me man? Did I solicit thee. From darkness to promote me?"
   (1) Book I
   (2) Book II
   (3) Book X
   (4) Book XII

4. Three satirical stories by W.M. Thackeray portraying unhappy marriage and exploitation of one partner by the other, are titled as
   (1) *Men's Wives*
   (2) *Wives' Husbands*
   (3) *Wife and Husband*
   (4) *Wife without a Husband*

5. Who among the following wrote that - "Poetry is not a branch of authorship: it is 'the stuff of which one life is made'. The rest is 'mere oblivion', a dead letter: for all that is worth remembering in life, is the poetry of it."
   (1) Mary Shelley
   (2) Charles Lamb
   (3) William Hazlitt
   (4) S.T. Col

6. Who among the following wrote "Plan of a Novel"?
   (1) E.M. Forster
   (2) D.H. Lawrance
   (3) Jane Austen
   (4) Thomas Hardy

7. John Dryden's *Of Dramatick Poesy: An Essay* is written in the form of a dialogue between Eugenius, Crites, Lisideius and Neander, where Neander represents:
   (1) Alexander Pope
   (2) John Dryden
   (3) Sir Robert Howard
   (4) Charles Sackville

8. Which text is considered to be the first book of poetry published by an Aboriginal author?
   (1) Tracey Moffatt's *Night Cries: A Rural Tragedy'*
   (2) David Unaipon's *Native Legends*
   (3) Oodegroo Noonucal's *We Are Going*

(4) Doris Pilkington Garimara's *Caprice: A Stockman's Daughter*

9. Which among the following is said to be the first fiction magazine (created by Hugo Gernsback)?
(1) Time and the Conways
(2) Henceforward
(3) New Worlds
(4) Amazing Stories

10. Who wrote the poem "Poem in Praise of Menstruation"?
(1) Gloria Steinem
(2) Seamus Heaney
(3) Francis Thompson
(4) Lucille Clifton

11. Big Daddy is a fictional character in -
(1) the novel *Ninety Eighty Four* by George Orwell
(2) the play *Cat on a Hot Tin Roof* by Tennessee William
(3) the play *Look back in Anger* by John Osborne
(4) the novel *Brave New World* by Aldous Huxley

12. *Things as They Are* or *The Adventure of Caleb Williams* was written as a call to end
(1) The abuse of workers by the industrialists
(2) The abuse of masses by the Church
(3) The abuse of power by a tyrranical government
(4) The abuse of tenants by the landlords

13. *Absalom, Absalom!* is -
(1) a novel by William Faulkner
(2) a satirical poem by John Dryden
(3) a drama by G.B. Shaw
(4) a poem by P.B. Shelley

14. Sherlock Hohnes, the greatest of all fictional detectives, made his first appearance in which one of the following novels by Sir Arthur Conan Doyle?
(1) *Strand Magazine*
(2) *A Study in Scarlet*
(3) *The Adventures of Sherlock Holmes*
(4) *The Case-Book of Sherlock Holmes*

15. *Friendship's Garland* (1871) is a sequel to which one of the following works by Mathew Arnold?
(1) *Culture and Anarchy*
(2) *Essay's in Criticism*
(3) *On the Study of Celtic Literature*
(4) *Literature and Dogma*

16. Which one of the following novels by E.M. Forster is about 'homosexual love'?
(1) *Howards Had*
(2) *A Room with a View*
(3) *Maurice*
(4) *Where Angels Fear to Tread*

17. Which one of the following plays by Henrik Ibsen was described as 'an open sewer'?
(1) *A Doll's House*
(2) *An Enemy of the People*
(3) *Ghosts*
(4) *The Wild Duck*

18. *Women in Love* is a sequel to which one of the following novels by D.H. Lawrance?
(1) *Lady Chatterley's Lover*
(2) *The White Peacock*
(3) *Sons and Lovers*
(4) *The Rainbow*

19. The term 'Post-modernism' was used in 1917 by German philosopher Rudolf Pannwitz to describe:
(1) Nihilism of 20th century's western culture
(2) Communism as a system of Governance
(3) Decline of Oligarchies
(4) Epistemic Violence

20. In *The Post Modern Condition* Lyotard announced the eclipse of all grand narratives. The one whose death he above all sought to declare was...
(1) Hegelian Spirit
(2) Christian Redemption

(3) Keynesian Equilibrium
(4) Classical Socialism

21. Which of the following is considered to be the first Indian novel in English?
(1) Bankimchandra Chatterjee's *Rajamohan's Wife*
(2) Toru Dutt's *The Young Zamindar*
(3) K.K. Sinha's *Samjogita*
(4) K.K. Sinha's *The Star of Sikri*

22. In *Long Resolution,* Raymond Williams conducted a long-range study of 350 canonical writers drawn from the *Oxford Introduction to English Literature* for the period...
(1) 1789 - 1950
(2) 1764- 1939
(3) 1450 - 1914
(4) 1470 - 1920

23. Which of the following assertions is not true with respect to 'cultural intermediaries' ?
(1) The term 'cultural intermediaries' was introduced by the French cultural theorist Pierce Bourdieu.
(2) Cultural intermediaries mediate between the production of cultural events and its consumers
(3) Promotional materials do not constitute cultural intermediaries.
(4) Fan Clubs are cultural intermediaries.

24. Who made the following statements in defense *of Santarasa* "the eight rasas are like eight gods, and the sant is like their highest centre Siva"?
(1) Bharat
(2) Anandavardhan
(3) Dandhi
(4) Abhinavgupta

25. Which one of the following is not a screen adaptation of Shakespeare's The Comedy of Errors?
(1) *The Boys from Syracuse*
(2) *Angoor*
(3) *Do Dooni Char*
(4) *Love in a Wood*

26. *Akkarmasin (The Outcaste)* is an auto biograpgy of which one of the following Dalit writers?
(1) Annabhau Sathe
(2) Sharankumar Limbale
(3) Anand Teltumde
(4) Baby Kamble

27. Who among the following American writers was the first Black American to become the U.S. Poet Laureate and Consultant in Poetry at the Library of Congress?
(1) Kyra Davis
(2) Meri Nana-Ama Domquah
(3) Rita Francis Dove
(4) Lucille Clifton

28. Which one of the following English novels received Sahitya Academy Awards for the year 2023?
(1) *Requiem in Raga Janki* by Neehim Saran Gour
(2) *All the Lives We Never Lived* by Anuradha Roy
(3) *The Blind Lady's Descendants* by Anees Salim
(4) *Chronicles of a Corpse Bearer* by Cyrus Mistry

29. *Kai Po Che!* is the screen adaptation of which one of the following novels by Chetan Bhagat?
(1) *The 3 Mistakes of My Life*
(2) *Five Point Someone*
(3) *Half Girlfriend*
(4) *Two States*

30. Which of the following is not a Dalit narrative written by Perumal Murugan?
(1) *Tirukkural: The Book of Desire*
(2) *Poonachi*
(3) *One. Part Woman*
(4) *Pyre*

31. Who among the following women writers wrote the first female Dalit autobiography?
(1) Sharmila Rege
(2) Urmila Pawar

(3) Shantabai Krushnaji Kamble
(4) Meena Kandasamy

32. Who said that language is a system of signs whose parts can and must be considered in their synchronic solidarity?
(1) Saussure
(2) Bloomfield
(3) Roman Jakobson
(4) Sigmund Freud

33. Hypothesis made during or after the research work is over, is known as
(1) Inductive Hypothesis
(2) Deductive Hypothesis
(3) Null Hypothesis
(4) Internal Hypothesis

34. Who wrote the book *The History of European Languages?*
(1) Alexander Murrey
(2) A.S. Diamond
(3) William Jones
(4) Bloomfield

35. A manuscript having an overlap with earlier papers by the same authors or by some of the present authors is termed as:
(1) Plagiarism
(2) Self Plagiarism
(3) Intertextuality
(4) Multiple references

36. The property of research to replicate the same results using the same technique is termed as
(1) Validity
(2) Reliability
(3) Relevance
(4) Coherence

37. Who said that an author has no claim to original thought but only to apt presentation of what was already being thought by others?
(1) Alexander Pope
(2) Ezra Pound
(3) Max Muller
(4) Harold Bloom

38. Which research treats physical and social world as objects based on standardized data?
(1) Empirical
(2) Action
(3) Quantitative
(4) Qualitative

39. The key principles of research design brought together in material on measurement principles, sampling and case study, survey and experimentation is termed as -
(1) Research Methodology
(2) Research Methods
(3) Research Techniques
(4) Research Designs

40. Which one of the following statements about 'Booker Prize' is not correct?
(1) A prestigious British award given annually to a hill-length novel
(2) Eligible writers shall belong to the United Kingdom and the Commonwealth Countries
(3) It was established in 1968 by Booker McDonald, a multinational company.
(4) It was established to provide a counterpart to the Prix Goncourt in France.

41. Arrange the following plays by Shakespeare in order of their production publication
A. *Twelfth Night*
B. *The Taming of the Shrew*
C. *Much Ado About Nothing*
D. *Romeo and Juliet*
E. *The Winter's Tale*
Choose the *correct* answer from the options given below:
(1) D, C, B, A, E
(2) B, D, A, E, C
(3) A, D, C, B, E
(4) B, D, C, A, E

42. Chronologically arrange the following in order of their publication occurrence?
A. Caxton printed Malory's *Morte D'Arthur*

B. Establishment of Caxton's printing press
C. Gutenberg printed Bible in Mainz. Germany
D. Caxton's *History of Troy,* first book printed in English
E. First translation of the Christian Bible into English by Joint Wycliff

Choose the *correct* answer from the options given below:

(1) B, E, D, C, A (2) C, B, E, A, D
(3) E, C, D, B, A (4) D, A, B, C, E

43. Arrange the following Black American writers chronologically (in order of their birth)?

A. Maya Angelou
B. Toni Morrison
C. Alice Walker
D. Langston Hughes
E. James Baldwin

Choose the *correct* answer from the options given below:

(1) D, A, E, C, B
(2) D, E, A, B, C
(3) E, A, D, B, C
(4) E, A, D, C, D

44. Sequence the following works of Dostoyevsky in the order of their publication

A. *Notes from Underground*
B. *Crime and Punishment*
C. *The Idiot*
D. *The Brothers Karamazov*
E. *Poor Folk*

Choose the *correct* answer from the options given below:

(1) B, C, E, A, D
(2) E, A, B, C, D
(3) A, B, C, D, E
(4) C, A, D, B, E

45. Chronologically arrange the fictional writings of Margaret Atwood?

A. *Edible Woman*
B. *The Handmaid's Tale*
C. *The Blind Assassin*
D. *Lady Oracle*
E. *The Robbers Bride*

Choose the *correct* answer from the options given below:

(1) B, C, A, E, D
(2) D, B, C, A, E
(3) E, A, D, C, B
(4) A, D, B, E, C

46. Chronologically arrange the Anglo-Indian writers in order of their birth?

A. Sarojini Naidu
B. Michael Madhusudan Dutta
C. Manhoman Ghose
D. Henry Derozio
E. Toru Datt

Choose the *correct* answer from the options given below:

(1) C, E, A, B, D
(2) D, B, E, C, A
(3) B, D, C, E, A
(4) A, E, B, D, E

47. Chronologically arrange the fictional writings of R.K. Narayan in order of their publication?

A. *The Vendor of Sweets*
B. *The Bachelor of Arts*
C. *The English Teacher*
D. *The Guide*
E. *The Financial Expert*

Choose the *correct* answer from the options given below:

(1) A, D, B, E, C
(2) C, B, D, A, E
(3) B, C, E, D, A
(4) E, A, B, C, D

48. Chronologically arrange the following works in order of their publication

A. Aiiosto's *Orlando Furioso*
B. Martin Luther King's *95 Theses at Wittenberg*

C. *The first Book of Common Prayer* by Thomas Crammer
D. Thomas More's *Utopia*
E. Machiavelli's *The Prince*
Choose the **correct** answer from the options given below:
(1) E, D, B, A, C
(2) A, C, B, E, D
(3) E, B, C, A, D
(4) D, A, B, C, E

49. Arrange the following novels by Chinua Achebe in order of then publication.
A. *A Man of the People*
B. *Things Fail Apart*
C. *Arrow of God*
D. *Anthills of Savannah*
E. *No Longer at Ease*
Choose the **correct** answer from the options given below:
(1) C, B, E, D, A
(2) B, C, E, A, D
(3) B, E, C, A, D
(4) A, B, D, E, C

50. Chronologically arrange the Rudiom playwrights in order of their birth
A. Asif Currimbhoy
B. Nissim Ezekiel
C. Cyrus Mistry
D. Mahesh Dattani
E. Gurcharan Das
Choose the **correct** answer from the options given below:
(1) A, D, E, C, B
(2) D, B, C, E, A
(3) A, E, D, B, C
(4) B, A, E, C, D

51. Arrange the works of Toni Morrison in the order of chronology of their publication
A. *Jazz*
B. *Beloved*
C. *in Bluest Eye*
D. *Song of Solomon*
E. *Taf Baby*
Choose the **correct** answer from the options given below:
(1) A, E, C, D, B
(2) D, C, E, B, A
(3) C, D, E, B, A
(4) E, D, A, B, C

52. Chronologically arrange the novels of Salman Rushdie in order publication?
A. *Fury*
B. *Midnight's Children*
C. *The Ground Beneath Her Feet*
D. *The Moor's Last Sigh*
E. *Gritnus*
Choose the **correct** answer from the options given below:
(1) B, C, A, D, E
(2) E, B, D, C, A
(3) A, E, B, C, D
(4) D, C, B, E, A

53. Arrange the following partition based film in order of their release production
A. *Garm Hawa*
B. *Tanias*
C. *Khamosh Pant*
D. *Chinnamul*
E. *Subarnarekha*
Choose the **correct** answer from the options given below:
(1) D, E, A, B, C
(2) E, D, B, A, C
(3) A, B, D, E, C
(4) A, D, E, B, C

54. Arrange the following plays in order of their publication,
A. *Death of a Salesman* by Arthur Miller
B. *The Glass Menagerie* by Tennessee Williams
C. *Who is Afraid of Virginia Wolf?* by Edward Albee
D. *The Iceman Cometh* by Eugene O'Neil
E. *Twelve Angry Man* by Reginald Rose
Choose the **correct** answer from the options given below:

(1) A, D, E, B, C
(2) A, C, B, E, D
(3) D, C, B, A, E
(4) D, B, A, E, C

55. Place the following works in ascending order of their publication year,

A. *Diamond Dust* by Anita Desai
B. *Breast-Giver* by Mahashweta Devi
C. *Death and the King's Horseman* by Wole Soyinka
D. *Dream on Monkey Mountain* by Derek Walcott
E. *Exile and the Kingdom* by Albert Camus

Choose the *correct* answer from the options given below:

(1) A, B, C, D, E (2) E, D, C, B, A
(3) D, B, C, A, E (4) B, C, A, D, E

56. Plato viewed poetry as-

A. an imitation of reality
B. self-subsistent entity
C. distant from reality
D. manifestation of reality
E. life as experience in reality

Choose the *correct* answer from the options given below:

(1) A and C only
(2) B and D only
(3) D and E only
(4) A and E only

57. Greek word 'polis' refers to-

A. Social Structure
B. Political Structure
C. Legal Structure
D. City State
E. Barbarians

Choose the *correct* answer from the options given below:

(1) B and D only
(2) A and B only
(3) B and C only
(4) A and E only

58. The Latin epic *Aeneid* by Virgil?

A. incorporates various legends of Aeneas and makes him the founder of Roman greatness
B. Relates the story of the legendary founding of Rome,
C. relates the story of the legendary founding of Lavinium,
D. recounts the story of Aeneas journey in the first 6 books of the epic, and these 6 books are patterned after Homer's *Odyssey*
E. recounts the story of Aeneas journey in the last 6 books of the epic, and these 6 books are patterned after Homer's *Odyssey*

Choose the *correct* answer from the options given below:

(1) A, C and D only
(2) A, B and D only
(3) A, D and E only
(4) A, C and E only

59. Neo-Platonism was founded by-

A. Plato
B. Plotinus
C. Porphyry
D. Aristotle
E. Pythagoras

Choose the *correct* answer from the options given below:

(1) A and B only
(2) C and D only
(3) B and C only
(4) D and E only

60. Who among the following were not associated with Kit-Cat Club?

A. George Etherege
B. Richard Steele
C. Samuel Johnson
D. William Congreve
E. Joseph Addison

Choose the *correct* answer from the options given below:

(1) B and D only
(2) B and E only
(3) A and C only
(4) A and E only

61. Who among the following were associated with Metaphysical Society founded in 1869 by Sir James Knowles?
A. Robert Browning
B. T.H. Huxley
C. Alfred Tennyson
D. Mathew Arnold
E. William Gladstone
Choose the *correct* answer from the options given below:
(1) A, B and C only
(2) B, D and E only
(3) C, D and E only
(4) B, C and E only

62. The salient tendencies of Hellenistic Philosophy are:
A. Cynicism
B. Epicureanism
C. Stoicism
D. Surrealism
E. Expressionism
Choose the *correct* answer from the options given below:
(1) A, B and D only
(2) A, B and C only
(3) A, D and E only
(4) A, B and E only

63. Which among the following texts are not written by Mary Wollstonecraft?
A. The Wrongs of Man
B. Vindication of the Rights of Man
C. Thoughts on the Education of Sons
D. Vindication of the Rights of Woman
E. The Wrongs of Woman
Choose the *correct* answer from the options given below:
(1) B and D only
(2) B and E only
(3) D and E only
(4) A and C only

64. Who among the following are writers of wordless graphic narratives?
A. Roy Fuller
B. Orijit Sen
C. Anthony Hecht
D. George Mathew Appupen
E. George Monbiot
Choose the *correct* answer from the options given below:
(1) A and C only
(2) B and C only
(3) B and E only
(4) D and E only

65. Who among the following is not associated with lesbian and gay studies?
A. Jane Rule
B. Jonathan Dollimore
C. Joint Wain
D. Elizabeth Jennings
E. Richard Dyer
Choose the *correct* answer from the options given below:
(1) A and E only
(2) C and D only
(3) B and C only
(4) D and E only

66. The term 'abstract poem' -
A. was coined by Edith Sitwell
B. refers to a poem in which words are chosen for their aural quality
C. refers to a poem in which words are chosen for imagery and symbolism
D. was coined by W.H. Auden
E. refers to a poem in which words are not specifically used for their sense/meaning
Choose the *correct* answer from the options given below:
(1) B, C, D only
(2) A, B, E only

(3) A, C, E only
(4) C, D, E only

67. Which of the following assertions/assumptions are not true regarding cultures of space?

A. Space is about power to control access, representation and use.
B. Space is simply land or built-up area.
C. The Space influences social relations and communities.
D. Space is socially constructed through social relations.
E. Space has nothing to do with everyday activities of people.

Choose the *correct* answer from the options given below:

(1) A, B and C only
(2) E and D only
(3) B and E only
(4) A and E only

68. Which of the following assumption is not true with regard to Lacan's concept, theory' of standpoint?

A. It assumes that social position can provide privileged perspective on some relations and knowledge.
B. It argues that those who are marginalised or oppressed may have access to insights and perceptions that dominant group lacks.
C. It refers to a situation in which the oppressed class is destined to lose the class consciousness.
D. It suggests that the perspectives of those on the margins of society cannot help to understand social dynamics.
E. The theory is based on the idea that social contradictions and political struggle can shape counter-hegemonic norms.

Choose the *correct* answer from the options given below:

(1) A and C only (2) D and E only
(3) B and C only (4) C and D only

69. M.H. Abram's *The Mirror and the Lamp: Romantic Theory and the Critical Tradition-*

A. describes 18th century English Literature as 'mirror'.
B. describes 19th century English Literature as 'Lamp'.
C. describes 19th century English Literature as 'mirror'.
D. the metaphor of 'mirror' is used to describe literature as a cool intellectual reflection of outward realities.
E. the metaphor of 'mirror' is used to describe literature as an illumination shed by artists upon then inner and outer worlds.

Choose the *correct* answer from the options given below:

(1) C, D, E only
(2) C, D, A only
(3) A, B, D only
(4) A, B, E only

70. In his work, *The Dialogic Imagination,* Mikhail Bakhtin-

A. develops theory of Polyphony.
B. postulates that language is imaginary.
C. postulates that language evolves dynamically.
D. argues that language gets affected by the culture that produces it as it helps to shape that culture.
E. develops theory of imaginative language.

Choose the *correct* answer from the options given below:

(1) B, D, E only
(2) A, C, D only
(3) A, B, D only
(4) C, D, E only

71. The term "Collective Unconsciousness" -

A. was introduced by Sigmund Freud.
B. was introduced by Carl Jung.
C. contains archetypes or universal primordial images and ideas.

D. contains stereotypes and individual experiences stored in unconscious.

E. is used to describe the unconscious common to humanity as a whole that originates in the inherited structures of the brain.

Choose the *correct* answer from the options given below:

(1) A, C, E only
(2) B, C, E only
(3) B, D, E only
(4) C, D, E only

72. *The Birth of Tragedy from the Spirit of Music* by Friedrich Nietzsche-

A. Examines the origins and development of poetry, specifically Greek tragedy.

B. Argues that Socratic rationalism and optimism led to the death of Greek tragedy.

C. Examines the origin of music and dance in ancient Greece.

D. Argues that Greek tragedy arose out of the fusion of Apollonian and Dionysian elements.

E. Argues that the music is the spirit of tragedy.

Choose the *correct* answer from the options given below:

(1) A, B, D only (2) A, C, E only
(3) B, D,E only (4) B, C, D only

73. Wittgenstein's statement, 'Limits of language defines limits of thought', means,

A. The structure of language defines its meaning.

B. Intended meaning defines structure of language.

C. That which can be defined meaningfully, can be thought.

D. Structure and meaning are independent of each other.

E. Thought precedes language.

Choose the *correct* answer from the options given below:

(1) A and C only
(2) A and B only
(3) D and E only
(4) A and E only

74. Terms 'Social fact' and 'collective consciousness' in the context of language were used by

A. Franz Boas
B. Bloomfield
C. Emile Durkheim
D. Noam Chomsky
E. Saussure

Choose the *correct* answer from the options given below:

(1) C and E only
(2) A and B only
(3) B and C only
(4) D and B only

75. Phonetics refers to -

A. Production of speech sounds
B. Reception of speech sounds
C. Transmission of speech sounds
D. Pattern of speech sounds
E. Word formation

Choose the *correct* answer from the options given below:

(1) A and C only
(2) B and D only
(3) D and E only
(4) A and D only

76. Match the **List-I** with **List-II**

LIST I	LIST II
A. Langue	I. Meaning conveyed
B. Parole	II. Socially shared language
C. Signifier	III. speech
D. Signified	IV. word

Choose the *correct* answer from the options given below:

(1) A-II, B-III, C-IV, D-I

(2) A-I, B-III, C-III, D-II

(3) A-IIE B-II, C-I, D-IV

(4) A-IV, B-III, C-II, D-I

77. Match the **List-I** with **List-II**

LIST I **Rhyme**	**LIST II** **Author**
A. Twinkle, Twinkle Little Star	I. William Miller
B. Wee Willie Winkie	II. Jane and Ann Taylor
C. Mary had a Little Lamb	III. Sarah Catherine Martin
D. Old Mother Hubbard	IV. Sarah Josepha Hale

Choose the *correct* answer from the options given below:

(1) A-I, B-III, C-II, D-IV

(2) A II, B-IV, C-III, D-I

(3) A-III, B-II, C-I, D-IV

(4) A-II, B-I, C-IV, D-III

78. Match the **List-I** with **List-II**

LIST I **Postcolonial term**	**LIST II** **Coined Employed by**
A. 'othering'	I. The term employed by Robert Young
B. Ecological Imperialism	II. coined by Gayatri Spivak
C. Colonial Desire	III. Corned by Alfred W. Crosby
D. Third Space	IV. Corned by Homi K. Bhabha

Choose the *correct* answer from the options given below:

(1) A-IV, B-II, C-I, D-III

(2) A-III, B-I, C-IV, D-II

(3) A-I, B-III, C-II, D-IV

(4) A-II, B-III, C-I, D-IV

79. Match the **List-I** with **List-II**

LIST I	**LIST II**
A. Heteroglossia	I. deliberate foolishness nonsense for effect.
B. Homosociality	II. Diversity of languages used in Epics.
C. Mathnavi	III. Same-sex relationships which are not necessarily sexual.
D. Morology	IV. long narrative epic or heroic poem in rhyming couplets.

Choose the *correct* answer from the options given below:

(1) A-IV, B-I, C-III, D-II

(2) A-III, B-IV, C-I, D-II

(3) A-II, B-III, C-IV, D-I

(4) A-I, B-II, C-III, D-IV

80. Match the **List-I** with **List-II**

LIST I **Concept Theory**	**LIST II** **Developed by**
A. Polysystem Theory	I. Ernest August Gutt
B. Relevance Theory	II. Hans J. Vermeer
C. Skopos Theory	III. Itamar Enen Zohar
D. Covert Translation	IV. Juliane House

Choose the *correct* answer from the options given below:

(1) A-II, B-III, C-IV, D-I

(2) A-III, B-I, C-II, D-IV

(3) A-II, B-IV, C-III, D-II

(4) A-IV, B-II, C-I, D-III

81. Match the **List-I** with **List-II**

LIST I **Term**	**LIST II** **Meaning**
A. Catastrophe	I. the introductory part of a play or narrative poem

B. Epitasis	II. The final action that completes the unravelling of the plot in a play, especially a tragedy.
C. Protasis	III. The dramatic complication that immediately precedes the climax of the play.
D. Catastasis	IV. The part of the play that develops the main action and that lends to the catastrophe

Choose the ***correct*** answer from the options given below:

(1) A-IV, B-II, C-III, D-I
(2) A-IV, B-II, C-I, D-III
(3) A-II, B-IV, C-I, D-III
(4) A-II, B-I, C-IV D-III

82. Match the **List-I** with **List-II**

LIST I **Australian Aboriginal Text**	**LIST II** **Author**
A. *Wahngin Country*	I. Alexis Wright
B. *Plains of Promise*	II. Jack Davis
C. *My Place*	III. Anita Heiss
D. *Not Meeting Mr. Right*	IV. Sally Morgan

Choose the ***correct*** answer from the options given below:

(1) A-IV, B-III, C-II, D-I
(2) A-I, B-IV, C-III, D-II
(3) A-II, B-I, C-IV, D-III
(4) A-III, B-II, C-I, D-IV

83. Match the **List-I** with **List-II**

LIST I **Poem**	**LIST II** **Indian Poet**
A. Night of the Scorpion	I. Kamala Das
B. Unfinished Poem	II. A.K. Ramanujan
C. The Looking Glass	III. Eunice De Souza
D. To a Friend Far Away	IV. Nissim Ezekiel

Choose the ***correct*** answer from the options given below:

(1) A-III, B-II, C-IV, D-I
(2) A-II, B-I, C-III, D-IV
(3) A-IV, B-III, C-I, D-II
(4) A-II, B-IV, C-I, D-III

84. Match the **List-I** with **List-II**

LIST I **Disability Narrative**	**LIST II** **Writer**
A. *A Room Called Earth*	I. Won Pyung Sohn
B. *Tomorrow, and Tomorrow and Tomorrow*	II. Padma Venkaraman
C. *A Time to Dance*	III. Medeleine Ryan
D. *Almond: A Novel*	IV. Gabrielle Zevin

Choose the ***correct*** answer from the options given below:

(1) A-II, B-III, C-I, D-IV
(2) A-IV, B-II, C-I, D-III
(3) A-IIL B-IV, C-II, D-I
(4) A-I, B-II, C-IV, D-III

85. Match the **List-I** with **List-II**

LIST I **Text**	**LIST II** **Author**
A. *Critique of Judgement*	I. Martin Heidegger
B. *The Phenomenology of Spirit*	II. Sigmund Freud
C. *Group Psychology and the Analysis of the Ego*	III. Immanuel Kant
D. *The Role of the University in the New Reich*	IV G.W.F. Hegel

Choose the ***correct*** answer from the options given below:

(1) A-III, B-I, C-IV, D-II
(2) A-I, B-II, C-III, D-IV

(3) A-II, B-III, C-IV, D-I
(4) A-III, B-IV, C-II, D-I

86. Match the **List-I** with **List-II**

LIST I	LIST II
A. The Language Instinct	I. Steven Pinker
B. Reflections of Language	II. Noam Chomsky
C. Variety of language sending a specialized function in a multilingual community	III. Creole Creolization
D. Existence of a common variety of language for people from different cultures	IV. Diglossia

Choose the *correct* answer from the options given below:
(1) A-I, B-II, C-IV, D-III
(2) A-III, B-IV, C-II, D-I
(3) A-I, B-II, C-III, D-IV
(4) A-IV, B-III, C-I, D-II

87. Match the **List-I** with **List-II**

LIST I Event	LIST II Year
A. International year of the World's Indigenous People	I. 1998
B. Australian Parliament formally apologised to the stolen generation	II. 1993
C. Formal end of White Australian Policy	III. 1973
D. The first National Sorry Day	IV. 2008

Choose the *correct* answer from the options given below:
(1) A-I, B-III, C-IV, D-II
(2) A-III, B-I, C-II, D-IV
(3) A-IV, B-II, C-I, D-III
(4) A-II, B-III, C-III, D-I

88. Match the **List-I** with **List-II**

LIST I Work	LIST II Author
A. *On a Muggy Night in Mumbai*	I. R. Raj Rao
B. *The Golden Gate*	II. Mahesh Dutt
C. *The Boyfriend*	III. Vikram Chandra
D. *Love and Longing in Bombay*	IV. Vikram Seth

Choose the *correct* answer from the options given below:
(1) A-II, B IV, C-I, D-III
(2) A-IV, B-III, C-II, D-I
(3) A-I, B-II, C-IV, D-III
(4) A-III, B-I, C-II, D-IV

89. Match the **List-I** with **List-II**

LIST I Novel	LIST II Novelist
A. *Delinquent Chacha*	I. Rohinton Mistry
B. *Tales from Firozsha Baag*	II Ved Prakash Mehta
C. *Beethoven Among the Cows*	III. Gita Hariharan
D. *A Thousand Faces of Night*	IV. Rukun Advani

Choose the *correct* answer from the options given below:
(1) A-I, B-III, C-II, D-IV
(2) A-II, B-I, C-IV, D-III
(3) A-IV, B-II, C-III, D-I
(4) A-III, B-IV, C-II, D-I

90. Match the **List-I** with **List-II**

LIST I Author	LIST II Nobel Prize Year
A. Wole Soyinka	I. 1991
B. Nadine Gordimer	II. 1993
C. Derek Walcott	III. 2003
D. J.M. Coetzee	IV. 1986

Choose the *correct* answer from the options given below:

(1) A II, B-IV, C-III, D-I
(2) A-III, B-II, C-IV, D-I
(3) A-IV, B-I, C-II, D-III
(4) A-I, B-III, C-IV, D-II

Question Label : Comprehension

Leaning into the afternoons I cast my sad nets
towards your oceanic eyes.
There in the highest blaze my solitude lengthens
and flames
its aims turning a drowning man's.
I send out red signals across your absent eyes
that smell like the sea or the beach by a lighthouse.
You keep only darkness, my distant female
from your regard sometimes the coast of dread
emerges.
Leaning into the afternoons I fling my sad nets
to that sea that thrashed by your oceanic eyes.
The birds of night peck at the first stars
that flash like my soul when I love you
The night gallops on its shadowy mare
Shedding blue tassels over the land

91. Identify the mood of the poem -
(1) Sombre
(2) Sarcastic
(3) Exhilarating
(4) Nostalgic

92. What does the phrase 'red signals sent out' signify?
(1) Passion/zest for life
(2) Distress and desperation of speaker
(3) Threatening signals
(4) Hopefulness and warmth

93. The phrases 'oceanic eyes' and 'absent eyes' are the examples of
(1) Parallelism
(2) Consonance
(3) Anaphora
(4) Dissonance

94. Identify the type of imagery used in the poem?
(1) Natural Imagery
(2) War Imagery
(3) Urban Imagery
(4) Metaphysical imagery

95. What is the central theme of the poem?
(1) Search for self
(2) Love and longing
(3) Self-fulfilment
(4) Fate and destiny

Suspicion amongst thoughts are like bats amongst birds, they ever fly by twilight. Certainly they are to be repressed, or at the least well guarded: for they cloud the mind; they lease friends. And they check with business, whereby business cannot go on currently. They dispose Kings to tyranny, husbands to jealously, wise men to irresolution and melancholy. They are defects, not in the heart, but in the brain: for they take place in the stoutest natures; as in the example of Henry the seventh of England. There was not a more suspicious man, nor a more stout. And in such a composition they do small hurt. For commonly they are not admitted. But with examination, whether they be likely or not. But in fearful natures they gain ground too fast. There is nothing that makes a man suspect much, more than to know little; and therefore men should remedy suspicion by procuring to know more, and not to keep their suspicions in smother. What would men have? Do they not think they will have their own ends, and be truer to themselves than to them? Therefore there is no better way to moderate suspicions, than to account upon such suspicions as true, and yet to bridle them as false. For so far a man ought to make use of suspicions, as to provide, as if that should true that he suspects, yet it may do him no hurt. Suspicions that the mind of itself gathers are but buzzes; but suspicions: that are artificially nourished, and put into men's heads by the tales and whisperings of others, have strings. Certainly, the best mean to clear the way in this same wood of suspicion, is frankly to communicate them with the party that he suspects. For thereby he shall be sure to know more of the truth of them than he did before: and withal shall make that party more circumspect not to give further cease of suspicion. But this would not be done to men of base natures; for they. if they find themselves once suspected, will never be true. The situation says, suspicion gives license to faith; as if suspicion did give a passport to faith; but it ought rather to kindle it to discharge itself.

96. What helps in eliminating suspicion?
(1) Stout physique
(2) Discussion and knowledge
(3) Observation
(4) Eternal alliance

97. What does the word 'guarded' signify?
(1) to protect
(2) to possess
(3) to keep under control
(4) militaristic exercise

98. What tone does the passage predominantly convey?
(1) Nostalgic and sentimental
(2) Urgent and alarmed
(3) Detached and reflective
(4) Suspenseful and dramatic

99. What is the primary theme of the paragraph?
(1) the challenges of maintaining supremacy
(2) the importance of personal relationships
(3) perspectivising suspicion
(4) to contrast between fearful and stout people

100. Which among the following is true in the context of given paragraph?
(1) Henry the Seventh ruled ruthlessly for long time.
(2) Suspicion is a stepping stone to faith.
(3) Suspicion kills the layer of human spirit.
(4) Rulers should supress suspicion of all forms.

ANSWERS

1. (4)	**2.** (2)	**3.** (3)	**4.** (1)	**5.** (3)	**6.** (3)	**7.** (2)	**8.** (3)	**9.** (4)	**10.** (4)
11. (2)	**12.** (3)	**13.** (1)	**14.** (2)	**15.** (1)	**16.** (3)	**17.** (3)	**18.** (4)	**19.** (1)	**20.** (4)
21. (1)	**22.** (4)	**23.** (1,3)	**24.** (4)	**25.** (4)	**26.** (2)	**27.** (3)	**28.** (1)	**29.** (1)	**30.** (1)
31. (3)	**32.** (1)	**33.** (2)	**34.** (1)	**35.** (2)	**36.** (2)	**37.** (1)	**38.** (3)	**39.** (2)	**40.** (2,3)
41. (4)	**42.** (3)	**43.** (2)	**44.** (2)	**45.** (4)	**46.** (2)	**47.** (3)	**48.** (1)	**49.** (3)	**50.** (4)
51. (3)	**52.** (2)	**53.** (1)	**54.** (4)	**55.** (2)	**56.** (1)	**57.** (1)	**58.** (1)	**59.** (3)	**60.** (3)
61. (4)	**62.** (2)	**63.** (4)	**64.** (3)	**65.** (2)	**66.** (2)	**67.** (3)	**68.** (4)	**69.** (3)	**70.** (2)
71. (2)	**72.** (1)	**73.** (1)	**74.** (1)	**75.** (1)	**76.** (1)	**77.** (4)	**78.** (4)	**79.** (3)	**80.** (2)
81. (3)	**82.** (3)	**83.** (3)	**84.** (3)	**85.** (4)	**86.** (1)	**87.** (4)	**88.** (1)	**89.** (2)	**90.** (4)
91. (1)	**92.** (2)	**93.** (1)	**94.** (1)	**95.** (2)	**96.** (2)	**97.** (3)	**98.** (3)	**99.** (3)	**100.** (2)

December, 2024

ENGLISH

PAPER-II

Note : This paper contains **hundred (100)** objective type questions of **two (2)** marks each. **All questions are compulsory.**

1. Who among the following is credited with ending the system of patronage with his "Letter to Lord Chesterfield"?

(1) Bishop Berkeley (2) Samuel Johnson
(3) Edmund Burke (4) Horace Walpole

2. Match the **LIST-I** with **LIST-II**

LIST-I (Novel)	LIST-II (Novelist)
A. *The Childhood of Jesus*	I. L. P. Hartley
B. *The Go-Between*	II. Evelyn Waugh
C. *Brideshead Revisited*	III. J. M. Coetzee
D. *The Catcher in the Rye*	IV. J. D. Salhiger

Choose the **correct** answer from the options given below

(1) A-I, B-IV, C-III, D-II
(2) A-III, B-I, C-II, D-IV
(3) A-IV, B-II, C-I, D-III
(4) A-II, B-III, C-IV, D-I

3. Which of the following works of R. K. Narayan were published after independence?

A. *The Dark Room*
B. *The English Teacher*
C. *The Financial Expert*
D. *Swami and Friends*
E. *The Guide*

Choose the *correct* answer from the options given below:

(1) A and B only (2) B and D only
(3) C and E only (4) A and D only

4 Arrange the following in chronological order of then year of publication:

A. *Nation and Narration*
B. *The Dialogic Imagination*
C. *Anthropology and the Colonial Encounter*
D. *Discourse on Colonialism*
E. *Orientalism*

Choose the *correct* answer from the options given below:

(1) D, C, E, A, B (2) D, C, B, A, E
(3) C, E, B, A, D (4) A, B, C, D, E

5. The line "Thou still unravished bride of quietness" presents which of the following rhetorical figures?

(1) Anastrophe (2) Apostrophe
(3) Anaphora (4) Chiasmus

6. Which of the following is not an autobiography?

(1) *Patrick White : A Life*
(2) *Long Walk to Freedom*
(3) *My Experiments with Truth*
(4) *Akkarmashi (The Outcaste)*

7. Identify the statements which are correct.

A. The term Hanueur' is often associated with the poetry of Baudelaire.
B. The term Habitus' is associated with Pierre Bourdieu.
C. Michael Foucault is associated with the concept of 'Modernity : An Unfinished Project'
D. Frantz Fanon is associated with theterm 'Imagined Community'
E. The term 'Thick Description' is associated with Clifford Mentz.

Choose the *correct* answer from the options given below:

(1) A and B only (2) B and C only
(3) C and D only (4) A and E only

8. What does deductive method of reasoning refer to?
(1) From general to particular
(2) From particular to general
(3) From linear to circular
(4) From circular to linear

9. Which of the given statements are correct?
A. Omprakash Valmiki's *Joothan* is a novel.
B. *Joothan* represents the Dalit Vahniki community in critical light.
C. *Joothan* enumerates the difficulties of being a Dalit in independent India.
D. *Joothan* was translated into English by Arun Prabha Das.
E. *Joothan* critiques the upper castes.
Choose the *correct* answer from the options given below:
(1) A, B and C only (2) B, D and E only
(3) B, C and E only (4) C, D and E only

10. Identify the ones which are matched correctly.
A. Barbara Christian : "The Race for Theory"
B. Alfred W. Crosby : "Unhiding the Hidden"
C. Paul Carter : "Naming Place"
D. Graham Huggan : "Ecological Imperialism"
E. Thomas B Macaulay : "Minutes on Indian Education"
Choose the ***correct*** answer from the options given below:
(1) A and B only (2) A, C and E only
(3) C and D only (4) D and E only

11. Arrange the plays of William Shakespeare in the chronological order of their year of publication:
A. *The Tempest* B. *Love's Labour Lost*
C. *Twelfth Night*
D. *Much Ado About Nothing*
E. *A Mid Summer Night's Dream*
Choose the ***correct*** answer from the options given below:
(1) B, E, D, C, A (2) E, A, D, C, B
(3) A, B, C, D, E (4) A, C, D, B, E

12. Which of the statements given below are true?
A. The centre for contemporary Cultural Studies was established in Berkley in 1960.
B. Jurgen Habermas traces the rise of the public sphere to the rise of print culture.
C. Paul Gilroy introduced the concept of the Black Atlantic.
D. Adorno praises the alien nature of avant-garde modernist art such as the atonal music of Schoenberg.
E. Chutnification was a term used by Edward Soja.
Choose the *correct* answer from the options given below:
(1) A, B and C only (2) B, C and D only
(3) C, D and E only (4) A, B and D only

13. "Success is counted sweetest
By those who ne'er succeed.
To comprehend a nectar
Requires sorest need."
Who has composed the above lines?
(1) Christiana Rossetti
(2) Thomas Hardy
(3) Emily Dickinson
(4) Mathew Arnold

14. Arrange the following steps of 'Decision making' in the research process
A. The choice of a research topic or theme.
B. Data collection
C. Analysis and interpretation of data.
D. Formulating the research problem.
E. Conceptualization and operationalization.
Choose the *correct* answer from the options given below:
(1) A, B, D, C, B (2) A, B, C, D, E
(3) D, C, A, B, E (4) A, D, E, B, C

15. Chronologically arrange the following works according to the year of publication.
A. Gauri Viswanathan's *Masks of Conquests*.
B. Meenakshi Muklierjee's *The Twice Born Fiction*.
C. G. N. Dew's *After Amnesia*

D. M. K. Naik's *A History of Indian English Literature*

E. Harish Trivedi's *Colonial Transactions*

Choose the *correct* answer from the options given below:

(1) A, B, C, D,E (2) E, D, C, B, A

(3) C, A, D, B, A (4) B, D, A, C, E

16. Match the **LIST-I** with **LIST-II**

LIST-I (Poet)	**LIST-II (Poem)**
A. Edmund Spenser	I. "Whose List to Hunt"
B. Philip Sidney	II. "So Cruel Prison how could Betide"
C. Thomas Wyatt	III. "The Faerie Queene"
D. Henry Howard, Earl of Surrey	IV. "The Defense of Poesy"

Choose the **correct** answer from the options given below:

(1) A-IV, B-II, C-I, D-III

(2) A-III, B-IV, C-I, D-II

(3) A-I, B-III, C-IV, D-II

(4) A-II, B-IV, C-III, D-I

17. The first folio of Shakespeare's plays appeared in

(1) 1664 (2) 1650

(3) 1631 (4) 1623

18. Which of the following novels deal with the theme of apartheid?

A. *Purple Hibiscus* B. *July's People*

C. *Cry', the Beloved Country'*

D. *The Mimic Men* E. *My Son's Story*

Choose the *correct* answer from the options given below:

(1) C and E only (2) A, C and D only

(3) B. C and E only (4) A and B only

19. Who amongst the following was not a member of the Bloomsbury Group?

(1) Virginia Woolf (2) E. M. Forster

(3) Lytton Strachey (4) W. B. Yeats

20. Match the **LIST-I** with **LIST-II**

LIST-I (Author)	**LIST-II (Text)**
A. Manohar Malgaonkar	I. *The Weird Dance and Other Stories*
B Chaman Nahal	II. *The Survivor*
C. Ruskin Bond	III. *Rumble Tumble*
D. Arun Joshi	IV. *Neighbour's Wife and Other Stories*

Choose the **correct** answer from the options given below

(1) A-III, B-I, C-IV, D-II

(2) A-I, B-II, C-III, D-IV

(3) A-III, B-II, C-I, D-IV

(4) A-II, B-III, C-IV, D-I

21. Which of the following is not a character in William Congreve's *The Way of the World*?

(1) Fainall (2) Mirabell

(3) Waitwell (4) Peachum

22. From which poem are the following lines extracted?

"Once more the storm is hauling and half hid
Under this cradle-hood and coverlid,
My child sleeps on. There is no obstacle.
But Gregory's wood and one bare hill."

(1) "The Second Coming"

(2) "The Cold Heaven"

(3) "A Prayer for My Daughter"

(4) "Among School Children"

23. The author of "The Politics of Translation" and translator of Mahashweta Devi's "Standayini" is:

(1) Homi Bhabha (2) Jhumpa Lahiri

(3) Gayatri C. Spivak

(4) Tejaswini Niranjana

24. Match the **LIST-I** with **LIST-II**

LIST-I (Text)	**LIST-II(Author)**
A. *Autobiography of an Unknown Indian*	I. Dom Moraes
B. *My Son's Father*	II. A. S. lyenger
C. *All through the Gandhian Era*	III. Sasthi Brata
D. *M' God Died Young*	IV. Nirad C. Chaudhary

Choose the **correct** answer from the options given below:

(1) A-I, B-II, C-III, D-IV

(2) A-III, B-II, C-I, D-IV
(3) A-IV, B-I, C-II, D-III
(4) A-II, B-III, C-IV, D-I

25. From the statements given below, what is true about the Gothic Novel?

A. It appeared in 14th Century American Literature.
B. It often uses the medieval form of architecture as setting.
C. It is a form of baroque art.
D. It represents a style of mosaic and fresco wall painting.
E. It aims at evoking chilling terror by exploiting mystery and a variety of horrors.

Choose the *correct* answer from the options given below:

(1) A and D only (2) C and E only
(3) B and D only (4) B and E only

26. Identify the poet who has composed the following lines:

"Ganga was sunken, and the limp leaves
Waited for rain, while the black clouds
Gathered far distant, over Himavant.
The Jungle crouched, humped in silence."

(1) Ralph Waldo Emerson
(2) T. S. Eliot
(3) Emily Dickinson
(4) Sri Aurobindo

27. Arrange the following works of literature chronologically based on their year of publication:

A. *The English Patient*
B. *The Swinging Bridge*
C. *Lives of Girls and Women*
D. *Family Matters* E. *Birnam Wood*

Choose the *correct* answer from the options given below:

(1) D, B, A, C, E (2) B, A, D, C, E
(3) C, B, D, A, E (4) C, A, D, B, E

28. Arrange the following works of Francis Bacon in the chronological order of their year of publication:

A. *Advancement of Learning*
B. *De Augmentis Scientiarum*
C. *Novum Organum*
D. *The New Atlantis*
E. *History of Henry VII*

Choose the *correct* answer from the options given below:

(1) A, C, E, B, D (2) C, A, B, E, D
(3) A, B, E, D, C (4) E, D, C, A, B

29. The Grammar Translation Method in English Language Teaching stresses on:

(1) Fluency (2) Accuracy
(3) Appropriateness (4) Listening Skill

30. Which among the following is the last novel of George Eliot?

(1) *Middlemarch* (2) *Daniel Deronda*
(3) *Silas Marner*
(4) *The Mill on the Floss*

31. Choose the correct sequence of the following works of Pablo Neruda in chronological order:

A. *Spain in the Heart*
B. *Works and Book of Turlights*
C. *The Inhabitant and His Hope*
D. *Twenty Love Poems and a Song of Despair*
E. *The Trying of Infinite Man*

Choose the *correct* answer from the options given below:

(1) E, C, D, B, A (2) A, B, C, D, E
(3) E, D, B, C, A (4) B, D, E, C, A

32. Which of the following poems uses 'terza rima'?

(1) John Keats' "Ode to Nightingale"
(2) P. B. Shelley's "Ode to the West Wind"
(3) William Wordsworth's "The Solitary Reaper"
(4) Alfred Tennyson's "Ulysses"

33. Functional Communicative Approach in English Language Teaching is in opposition to the.

(1) Comprehensive Approach
(2) Grammar Translation Method
(3) Functional Approach
(4) Structural Approach

34. Match the **LIST-I** with **LIST-II**

LISTI (Text)	**LIST II (Author)**
A. *Bodies that Matter*	I. Barbara Johnson

B. *A World of Difference* II. Judith Butler

C. *A Literature of their Own* III. Camille Paglia

D. *Vamps and Tramps* IV. Elaine Showalter

Choose the **correct** answer from the options given below:

(1) A-I, B-II, C-III, D-IV
(2) A-III, B-II, C-I, D-IV
(3) A-II, B-I, C-IV, D-III
(4) A-IV, B-III, C-II, D-I

35. Arrange the following poems by W. B. Yeats in the chronological order of their year of publication:

A. "Adam's Curse"
B. "Among School Children"
C. "The Second Coming"
D. "The Wild Swans at Coole"
E. "Under Ben Bulben"

Choose the ***correct*** answer from the options given below:

(1) A, B, C, D, E (2) C, D, B, A, E
(3) E, B, D, C, A (4) A, D, C, B, E

36. "There is nothing outside the text" is a statement by

(1) Victor Shklovsky
(2) Jacques Derrida
(3) Roland Barthes
(4) Ferdinand de Saussure

37. Match the **LIST-I** with **LIST-II**

LIST-I	**LIST-II**
A. Mikhail Bakhtin	I. "Archaeology of the Human Sciences"
B. Michael Foucault	II. "Text can be either readerly or writerly"
C. Roland Barthes	III. "Dialogue as the intrinsic feature of language"
D. Sigmund Freud	IV. "Dreams end the unconscious"

Choose the **correct** answer from the options given below:

(1) A-I, B-II, C-III, D-IV
(2) A-III, B-II, C IV, D-I
(3) A-III, B-I, C-II, D-IV
(4) A-IV, B-II, C-III, D-I

38. Which among the following does not fall in the category of a Revenge Tragedy?

(1) *The Spanish Tragedy*
(2) *The Jew of Malta*
(3) *Hamlet* (4) *Cymbeline*

39. Which of the following statements are correct about 'Litotes'?

A. It contains an understatement for emphasis.
B. It is not opposite of hyperbole.
C. It is used with laconic intentions.
D. It is used with ironic intentions.
E. It is used in dramatic context.

Choose the ***correct*** answer from the options given below:

(1) B, C and D only (2) C, D and E only
(3) A, D and E only (4) A, C and D only

40. Match the **LIST-I** with **LIST-II**

LIST-I (Author)	**LIST-II (Text)**
A. Basudev Sunani	I. *Karukku*
B. Om Prakash Valmiki	II. *Weave of My Life*
C. Barna	III. *Cast Out*
D. Urmila Pawar	IV *Joothan*

Choose the **correct** answer from the options given below:

(1) A-III, B-I, C-II, D-IV
(2) A-III, B-IV, C-I, D-II
(3) A-IV, B-I, C-II, D-III
(4) A-I, B-II, C-III, D-IV

41. Arrange the following works in the chronological order of their year of publication:

A. S. Menon Marath's *The Wound of Spring*
B. Humayun Kabir's *Men and Rivers*
C. Anand Lall's *The House at Adampur*
D. Sudhindra N. Ghose's *The Vermillion Boat*
E. Ved Mehta's *Delinquent Chacha*

Choose the ***correct*** answer from the options given below:

(1) E, D, C, B, A (2) B, D, C, A, E
(3) A, B, C, D, E (4) D, C, B, A, E

42. Arrange the following works in the chronological order of their year of publication:
A. *Orientalism*
B. *Black Skin, White Masks*
C. *Masks of Conquest*
D. *The Wretched of the Earth*
E. *"Can the Subaltern Speak?"*
Choose the *correct* answer from the options given below:
(1) B, D, A, C, E (2) D, B, A, E, C
(3) C, B, D, A, E (4) A, C, B, E, A

43. Match the **LIST-I** with **LIST-II**

LIST-I (Term)	**LIST-II (Meaning)**
A. Antonomasia	I. Writings or statements of doubtful or spurious authorship.
B. Antiphrasis	II. A figure of speech in which some defining word or phrase is substituted for a person's proper name.
C. Apocrypha	III. A narrative of miraculous deeds of God or Hero.
D. Aretalogy	IV. Ironic or humorous use of words in senses opposite to the generally accepted meanings.

Choose the **correct** answer from the options given below:
(1) A-II, B-IV, C-I, D-III
(2) A-IV, B-II, C-III, D-I
(3) A-I, B-II, C IV, D-III
(4) A-II, B-I, C IV, D-III

44. Match the **LIST-I** with **LIST-II**

LIST-I (Author)	**LIST-II (Text)**
A. Paul Ehrlich	I. *The Environmental Imagination (1995)*
B. Lawrence Buell	II. *On the Beach (1957)*
C. Nevil Shute	III. *Silent Spring (1962)*
D. Rachel Carson	IV *The Population Bomb (1972)*

Choose the **correct** answer from the options given below:
(1) A-II, B-III, C-IV, D-I
(2) A-IV, B-I, C-II, D-III
(3) A-I, B-II, C-III, D-IV
(4) A-III, B-II, C-I, D-IV

45. Which of the following statements are true about A. K. Ramanujan?
A. He is a poet of the sixties.
B. His poetry draws his sustenance from his awareness of Hindu heritage,
C. He has poor sense of rhythm.
D. His verse poorly utilises Akam constructed techniques.
E. He utilises Akam constructed techniques in his poetry.
Choose the *correct* answer from the options given below:
(1) C, D and E only (2) A, B and E only
(3) B, C and D only (4) B, D and E only

46. Who said "The introduction of foreigners does not necessarily destroy the nation, they merge in it"?
(1) Frantz Farion (2) Leopold Senghor
(3) Sri Aurobindo (4) M. K. Gandhi

47. Which of the following is a Dramatic Monologue?
(1) "The Cannonization"
(2) "Tintern Abbey"
(3) "Andrea de Sarto" (4) "The Flea"

48. The famous short poem "Elegy on the Death of a Mad Dog" appears in which one of the following Eighteenth Century novels?
(1) *Roderick Random* by Tobias Smollet
(2) *Tristram Shandy* by Lawrence Sterne
(3) *The Vicar of Wakefield by Oliver Goldsmith*
(4) *The Castle of Otranto* by Horace Walpole

49. Which of the following is not correctly matched?
(1) Seamus Heaney : "Digging"
(2) Andre Lorde : "Coal"
(3) Dorn Moraes : "Kanheri Caves"
(4) John Updike : "The Swan"

50. In which year was Raja Rao's *Kanthapura* published?

(1) 1938 (2) 1960
(3) 1965 (4) 1947

51. Which of the following are correct according to the MLA Handbook. 9th edition?

A. One inch margin on all sides is compulsory in a research page.
B. Co-ordinating conjunctions are written in bold letters in the title of a research paper.
C. Slash is used between two norms paired as opposites.
D. 'Hanging indent' in the work cited entry is ½ inches.
E. Subordinating conjunctions are not written in bold letters in the title of the research paper.

Choose the *correct* answer from the options given below:

(1) A, C and D only (2) B, D and A only
(3) C, D and E only (4) B, C and E only

52. Arrange the following novels of D. H. Lawrence in chronological order of their year of publication:-

A. *Women in Love* B. *The White Peacock*
C. *Sons and Lovers* D. *The Rainbow*
E. *The Trespasser*

Choose the *correct* answer from the options given below:

(1) A, B, C, D, E (2) E,C, D, A, B
(3) B, E,C, D, A (4) C, A, E, D, B

53. Arrange the following in the chronological order of their year of publication:

A. "The Tyger"
B. "The Solitary Reaper"
C. "Adonais"
D. "The Rime of the Ancient Mariner"
E. "Ode to Autumn"

Choose the *correct* answer from the options given below:

(1) B, C, D, E, A (2) C, D, E, A, B
(3) A, D, B, E, C (4) D, A, E, B, C

54. Who is the author *of English in India : Its Present and Future* published in 1964?

(1) G. T. Garratt (2) Rameshwar Gupta
(3) V. K. Gokak (4) A. R. Chide

55. Match the **LIST-I** with **LIST-II**

LIST-I (Text)	**LIST-II (Author)**
A. *My Days with Gandhi*	I. D. K. Roy
B. *Among the Great*	II. N. K. Basu
C. *Life of Sri Aurobindo*	III. Krishna Kripalani
D. *Rabindranath Tagore*	IV. A. B. Purani

Choose the **correct** answer from the options given below:

(1) A-I, B-II, C-III, D-IV
(2) A-III, B-II, C-I, D-IV
(3) A-IV, B-III, C-II, D-I
(4) A-II, B-I, C-IV, D-III

56. Arrange the following in the chronological order of their year of publication.

A. *Deconstruction and Criticism*
B. *Multiculturalism : Roots and Realities*
C. *Literary Theory' and the Claims of History'*
D. *The Western Canon*
E. *An Appetite for Poetry'*

Choose the ***correct*** answer from the options given below:

(1) D, C, E, B, A (2) A, E, D, C, B
(3) A, B, C, D, E (4) C, D, B, A, E

57. Identify the correct options from the following statements:

A. Ecocriticism has often explained the 'human and non-human webs of inter-relation.
B. In Ecocriticism, human accountability to the environment is part of the text's ethical orientation.
C. Ecocriticism foregrounds the notion of an interplay between environment and the body.
D. There is only one wave of Ecocriticism.
E. Ecocriticism has not tackled the issue of gender.

Choose the ***correct*** answer from the options given below:

(1) A, B, C only (2) B, C, D only
(3) A, C, D only (4) A, B, D, E only

58. Who is the best known figure amongst the following for articulating the concept of 'Negritude'
(1) Edward Said (2) Aime Cesaire
(3) William Jones (4) Anna Rutherford

59. "O Sir, content you',
I follow him to serve my turn upon him.
We cannot all be masters, nor all masters cannot be truly followed."
The above lines were spoken by which of the following characters?
(1) Roderigo (2) Iago
(3) Caliban (4) Cassio

60. Langston Hughes' poem "I too Sing America" is a response to which of the following poets?
(1) Herman Melville
(2) Walt Whitman
(3) Henry David Thoreau
(4) Emily Dickinson

61. Which of the following options are true about the epistemological dimension of research?
A. Scientific realism
B. The search for truth
C. Critical theory
D. Certain and indubitable knowledge
E. Mechanism of social control
Choose the *correct* answer from the options given below:
(1) A and C only (2) B and D only
(3) D and A only (4) C, D and E only

62. When was 'International Phonetic Alphabet' (IPA) developed and promulgated?
(1) 1868 (2) 1878
(3) 1888 (4) 1978

63. Identify the one who was not a 'New Critic'
(1) Allen Tate
(2) Robert Penn Warren
(3) Cleanth Brooks
(4) Claude Levi-Strauss

64. Who among the following has written the poem. "Jejuri"?
(1) Michael Madhusudan Dutt
(2) Kamla Das
(3) Arun Kolatkar
(4) Toru DuttMatch the following concepts with the theorists

65. Match the **LIST-I** with **LIST-II**

LIST-I	**LIST-II**
A. Defamiliarization	I. Girgio Agamben
B. Uncanny	II. Bruno Latour
C. Actor Network Theory	III. Viktor Shlovsky
D. Homo Sacer	IV. Sigmund Freud

Choose the **correct** answer from the options given below:
(1) A-II, B-IV, C-III, D-I
(2) A-IV, B-I, C-II, D-III
(3) A-III, B-II, C-I, D-IV
(4) A-III, B-IV, C-II, D-I

66. Identify the statements which are true for Psychoanalytic Criticism.
A. The premises and procedures were established by Sigmund Freud.
B. Freud posited that artists are like neurotic patients.
C. Freud posited that 'Psychoanalysis' can be used to account for many developments and practices in the history of civilization.
D. A repressed wish does not become fantasy.
E. Freud proposed that literature and other arts manifest the repressed subconscious and unconscious drives of the artist.
Choose the *correct* answer from the options given below:
(1) A, B and D only (2) A, B and C only
(3) B, A and D only (4) A, C and E only

67. Match the **LIST-I** with **LIST-II**

LIST-I (Author)	**LIST-II (Text)**
A. Henry Miller	I. *The Grapes of Wrath*
B. John Steinback	II. *No Name in the Streets*

C. James Jones III. *Tropic of Cancer*
D. James Baldwin IV. *From Here to Eternity*

Choose the **correct** answer from the options given below:

(1) A-I, B-III, C-II, D-IV
(2) A-III, B-I, C-IV, D-II
(3) A-IV, B-II, C-I, D-III
(4) A-III, B-II, C-IV, D-I

68. Which of the following is an elegy on John Donne's wife who died in 1617?

(1) "Death be not Proud"
(2) "Thou Hast Made Me"
(3) "Holy Sonnet 17"
(4) "At the Round Earth's Imagined Corners"

69. Identify the correct statements concerning the respective genre:

A. An epistle is a literary' genre in the form of letter.
B. Epigraph is an inscription on funeral monument.
C. Epigram is a short, pithy poem wittily expressed.
D. Epitaph is a formal statement in the beginning of a literary' work E. Epyllion is a short poem in the meter of an epic poetry'.

Choose the *correct* answer from the options given below:

(1) A, B and C only (2) B, D and A only
(3) A, C and E only (4) D, C and E only

70. Which of the following statements are true about Modernism?

A. Modernism marked a break with formal conventions
B. Old ways of thought underwent cultural shift
C. Decline of liberal humanism
D. Modernism revived classical scholarship
E. Modernism promoted logocentric way of thoughts

Choose the *correct* answer from the options given below:

(1) C, D and E only (2) B, C and D only
(3) A, B and C only (4) A, D and E only

71. Which of the following texts has been written by Rabindranath Tagore?

(1) *Tiger-Claw* (2) *Chandalika*
(3) *A Touch of Brightness*
(4) *Image Breakers*

72. Arrange the following in chronological order of their year of publication:

A. *Fraser's Magazine* B. *The Spectator*
C. *The Westminster Review*
D. *The Quarterly Review*
E. *Edinburg Review*

Choose the *correct* answer from the options given below:

(1) A, B, C, D, E (2) C, D, E, A, B
(3) E, D, C, B, A (4) D, C, A, B, E

73. Shakespeare's *Much Ado About Nothing* is a

(1) Tragi Comedy
(2) Romantic Comedy
(3) Pastoral Play
(4) History Play

74. Who among the following illustrated the works of Thomas Gray and Robert Blair?

(1) Thomas Percy
(2) William Blake
(3) Robert Burns
(4) William Cowper

75. Match the **LIST-I** with **LIST-II**

LIST-I (Text)	LIST-II (Author)
A. *The Golden Light*	I. Torn Dutt
B. *The Lotus*	II. Sarojini Naidu
C. *Indian Dancers*	III. Henry Derozio
D. *The Harp of India*	IV. Sri Aurobindo

Choose the **correct** answer from the options given below:

(1) A-IV, B-II, C-I, D-III
(2) A-IV, B-III, C-II, D-I
(3) A-IV, B-II, C-III, D-I
(4) A-IV, B-I, C-II, D-III

76. Who is the critic associated with the term 'Blue Humanities'?

(1) Hannah Arendt (2) Stephan Hertz
(3) Thomas R. Cole (4) Nathan Carlin

77. What is 'Practical Critisism'?
(1) The close analysis of literary texts in such a way as to bring out their political meaning.
(2) A movement which wished to make literary criticism more relevant.
(3) The close analysis of poems without taking account of any external information.
(4) The study of ambiguity

78. Match the **LIST-I** with **LIST-II**

LIST-I (Author)	**LIST-II (Text)**
A. Kamla Markandeya	I. *The Grip of Change*
B. P. Sivakami	II. *The Enchanted Fruit*
C. Anita Desai	III. *Possession*
D. Raj Lakshmi Debi	IV. *Cry, the Peacock*

Choose the **correct** answer from the options given below:
(1) A-III, B-I, C-IV, D-II
(2) A-I, B-D, C-III, D-IV
(3) A-IV, B-II, C-III, D-I
(4) A-II, B-III, C-I, D-IV

79. Identify the correct statement on about 'Langue' and 'Parole' below:
A. Langue is the abstract language system, the grammar of a language.
B. Parole is the language actually produced by its users following Langue.
C. Langue is the language actually produced by its users following Parole.
D. Parole is the abstract language system, the grammar of a system.
E. Langue and Parole are not related to one language as concepts.
Choose the ***correct*** answer from the options given below:
(1) A and B only (2) A and C only
(3) B and C only (4) D and E only

80. An ideal research paper should include:
A. A statement that establishes the problem or controversial issue that the paper intends to examine.
B. Background information to establish past theories and current ideas on the topic.
C. Summarizing and paraphrasing.
D. Glorification of the paper writer himself.
E. A thesis to establish one's position.
Choose the ***correct*** answer from the options given below:
(1) A, C and D only (2) A and D only
(3) C and D only (4) A, B and E only

81. Identify all the Australian Aboriginal writers out of the following
A. Kim Scott B. Peter Carey
C. Oodgeroo Noonuccal
D. Kevin Gilbert E. Derek Walcott
Choose the ***correct*** answer from the options given below:
(1) B, C and D only (2) C, D and E only
(3) A, C and D only (4) B, A and E only

82. Which of the following novelists did not employ "Stream of Consciousness" technique?
(1) Virginia Wolf (2) James Joyce
(3) Dorothy Richardson
(4) Graham Greene

83. In which of the texts, the following lines occur?
"Of all the causes which conspire to blind
Man's erring judgement, and misguide the mind,
What the weak head with strongest bias rules,
Is pride, the never failing vice of fools."
(1) *An Essay on Criticism*
(2) *The Rape of the Lock*
(3) *An Essay on Man*
(4) *Epistle to Dr. Arbuthnot*

84. Which of the following is not matched correctly?
(1) Ira De: *The Hunt and Other Poems*
(2) Margaret Chatterjee: *The Spring and the Spectacle*
(3) Tapati Mookerji: *The Golden Road to Samerkhand*
(4) Tilottama Ranjan: *Poems of Govindagraj*

85. Which among the following novels is not written by Mary Shelley?

(1) *The Lost Woman* (2) *Frankenstein*
(3) *Faulkner* (4) *The Last Man*

86. Who has written *The Life Divine ?*
(1) Dante (2) Emerson
(3) Sri Aurobindo (4) Jayant Mahapatra

87. The incorrect works cited entries according to NILA Handbook, 9th edition are:
A. Jacobs, Alan. *The Pleasures of Reading in the Age of Destruction.* Oxford UP, 2011.
B. Charon. Rita, et al. *The Principles and Practice of Narrative Medicine.* Oxford UP. London, 2017.
C. Sabau, Ana. "The Perils of Ownership"'. *American Review,* vol. 10, no.2, 2007, pp. 1-27.
D. Riddle, Julie. "Shadow Animals."' *The Georgia Review,* 67.3, pp. 424-47.
E. Copeland, Edward. *The Cambridge Companion to Jane Austin.* Cambridge UP. 1997, 131-48.

Choose the *correct* answer from the options given below:
(1) A, B and C only (2) B, C and D only
(3) B, D and E only (4) D, E and A only

88. Arrange the following works in the chronological sequence of their year of publication:
A. Mathews Arnold's *Culture and Anarchy*
B. Thomas Browne's *The Anatomy of Melancholy*
C. P. B. Shelley's *Defence of Poetry'*
D. Thomas Hobbes' *Leviathan*
E. Walter Pater's *Studies in the History' of the Renaissance*

Choose the *correct* answer from the options given below:
(1) A, B, C, D, E (2) D, C, B, A, E
(3) B, C, E, A, D (4) B, D, C, A, E

89. Match the **LIST-I** with **LIST-II**

LIST-I	LIST-II
A. *Nala and Damayanti*	I. Sri Aurobindo
B. *Jayadeva*	II. Vasudeva Rao
C. *The Viziers of Bassora*	III. P.A. Krishnaswamy
D. *The Flute of Krishna*	IV. Harindranath

Choose the **correct** answer from the options given below:
(1) A-III, B-II, C-IV, D-I
(2) A-II, B-IV, C-I, D-III
(3) A-IV, B-III, C-II, D-I
(4) A-II, B-I, C-III, D-IV

90. Arrange the following texts in chronological order of their year of publication
A. *Coolie* B. *The Big Heart*
C. *The Village*
D. *Two Leaves and a Bud* E. *Seven Summers*

Choose the *correct* answer from the options given below:
(1) D, C, B, A, E (2) E, A, B, C, D
(3) A, B, C, D, E (4) A, D, C, B, E

Read the following passage and answer the questions that follows:-

One key development in the evolving discussion surrounding popular culture which occurred during the early twentieth century was the association of popular culture with the United States of America. Through Hollywood and associated modes of popular entertainment, USA was beginning to exercise international cultural influence. The term 'Mass culture' is particularly relevant in this context as it refers to both the effects of American culture as well as to a specific theoretical debate that emerged in America during the post-war period. Dominic Strinati contends in his *An Introduction to Theories of Popular Culture (1995)* that "mass culture refers to popular culture which is produced by the industrial techniques of mass production, and marketed for profit to a mass public of consumers.' Such a view of popular culture argues that the industrial revolution produces a series of atomised individuals who had not only lost touch with the communities of shared interest to which they once belonged but that they had also been subjected to the process of mechanisation and alienation. This rendered them ripe for systematic cultural manipulation through uniform, mass produced formulaic products designed to evoke frivolous, escapist and superficial pleasures.

91. "Mass Culture" refers to:
(1) Only the effects of American culture.
(2) Specific theoretical debate in America during post-war period.

(3) Theoretical debates in America during pre-war period.
(4) Both the effects of American culture and theoretical debates during post war period.

92. Systematic culture manipulation takes place through:
(1) Mass production of goods
(2) Mass production of culture
(3) Mass production of food
(4) Technological production

93. When did the popular culture get associated with U.S.A.?
(1) 19th Century (2) 20th Century
(3) Early 20th Century
(4) Early 21st Century

94. What is the core issue discussed in the above paragraph?
(1) Mass culture (2) Elite culture
(3) High culture (4) Low culture

95. What is the meaning of 'Atomised individuals' in the above paragraph?
(1) Mechanised individuals
(2) Organic individuals
(3) Scientific individuals
(4) Both mechanised and alienated individual

Read the following poem and answer the questions that follows:

In all my wand'rings round this world of care,
In all my griefs-and God has giv'n my share
I still had hopes, my latest hours to crown,
Amidst these humble bow'rs to lay me down;
To husband out life's taper at the close,
And keep the flame from wasting by repose;
I still had hopes, for pride attends us still,
Amidst the swains to show my book learn'd skill,
Around my fire an ev'ning group to draw,
And tell of all I felt, and all I saw.

96. What does the poet intend to do in life?
(1) To showcase his talent in singing
(2) To complain to God about his misery
(3) To complain to the king about injustice
(4) To share his life experience

97. What does the poem say about the nature of the world?
(1) It's full of joy
(2) It's full of care and hope
(3) Its full of desertion
(4) It's full of wonders

98. Identify the rhyme scheme in the poem.
(1) aa bb cc dd ee (2) abed abed ee
(3) aaab abca aa (4) abed ef ef gg

99. Identify the meter in the poem.
(1) Iambic trimeter (2) Iambic tetrameter
(3) Iambic pentameter
(4) Iambic hexameter

100. What is the mood of the poem?
(1) Pessimistic
(2) Optimistic and resolute
(3) Jovial (4) Envious

✓ ANSWERS

1. (2)	**2.** (2)	**3.** (3)	**4.** (4)	**5.** (2)	**6.** (1)	**7.** (4)	**8.** (1)	**9.** (3)	**10.** (2)
11. (1)	**12.** (2)	**13.** (3)	**14.** (4)	**15.** (4)	**16.** (2)	**17.** (4)	**18.** (3)	**19.** (4)	**20.** (1)
21. (4)	**22.** (3)	**23.** (3)	**24.** (3)	**25.** (4)	**26.** (2)	**27.** (4)	**28.** (1)	**29.** (2)	**30.** (2)
31. (4)	**32.** (2)	**33.** (4)	**34.** (3)	**35.** (4)	**36.** (2)	**37.** (3)	**38.** (4)	**39.** (4)	**40.** (2)
41. (2)	**42.** (4)	**43.** (1)	**44.** (2)	**45.** (2)	**46.** (4)	**47.** (3)	**48.** (3)	**49.** (4)	**50.** (1)
51. (1)	**52.** (3)	**53.** (3)	**54.** (3)	**55.** (4)	**56.** (2)	**57.** (1)	**58.** (2)	**59.** (2)	**60.** (2)
61. (2)	**62.** (3)	**63.** (4)	**64.** (3)	**65.** (4)	**66.** (4)	**67.** (2)	**68.** (3)	**69.** (3)	**70.** (3)
71. (2)	**72.** (3)	**73.** (2)	**74.** (2)	**75.** (4)	**76.** (4)	**77.** (3)	**78.** (1)	**79.** (1)	**80.** (4)
81. (3)	**82.** (4)	**83.** (1)	**84.** (4)	**85.** (1)	**86.** (3)	**87.** (3)	**88.** (4)	**89.** (2)	**90.** (4)
91. (4)	**92.** (2)	**93.** (3)	**94.** (1)	**95.** (4)	**96.** (4)	**97.** (2)	**98.** (1)	**99.** (3)	**100.** (2)

June, 2025

ENGLISH

PAPER-II

Note : This paper contains **hundred (100)** objective type questions of **two (2)** marks each. **All** questions are **compulsory**.

1. Choose the correct key points related to approach to Feminism and Gender Studies:

A. Feminism is concerned with the marginalization of women in a patriarchal culture.

B. Feminist critics explain how the subordination of women is reflected or challenged by literary texts.

They examine the experiences of women of all races, classes, sexual preferences, and cultures.

C. Mary Wollstonecraft defines four models of sexual difference: biological, linguistic, psychoanalytic, and cultural.

D. Feminist critics' goals: to expose patriarchal premises and resulting prejudices, to promote the discovery and reévaluation of literature by women, and to examine social, cultural, and psychosexual contexts of literature and literary criticism.

E. Simone de Beauvoir prefers "womanism" to "feminism."

Choose the **most appropriate** answer from the options given below:

(1) A, B and C Only
(2) A, B and D Only
(3) B, C and D Only
(4) B, D and E Only

2. Who said that "Shakespeare was the Homer, or father of our dramatic poets; Johnson was the Vergil, the pattern of elaborate writing"?

(1) Matthew Arnold
(2) John Dryden
(3) Samuel Johnson
(4) Ben Johnson

3. Read the following statements carefully and choose the correct ones:

A. Patrick White, Christina Stead and Robertson Davies are the famous Australian novelists.

B. The notion of "civilized barbarity" was anticipated in H. Rider Haggard's 1887 novel *Allan Quatermain,* in which "Civilization" is said to be "only savagery silver-gilt".

C. Novels like *French Lieutenant's Woman, Midnight's Children* and *Waterland* deconstruct traditional notions of history and subjectivity.

D. O'Brian's *Country Girls* trilogy and McGahern's *The Dark* which were banned in Ireland were published during 1950s.

E. The trauma of the mid-century years accounts for the prevalence of dystopian elements in novels like *A Clockwork Orange, Lanark* and *The Handmaid's Tate.*

Choose the most **appropriate** answer from the options given below:

(1) A, C and D Only
(2) A, B and D Only
(3) B, C and E Only
(4) B, C and D Only

4. The term "Trace", which refers to the trace of the other, has been borrowed by Jacques Lacan from

(1) Jacques Derrida
(2) Immanuel Levinas
(3) Sigmund Freud
(4) Christopher Norris

5. Who, amongst the following, attempted to reconcile discrepancies between various classical authors such as Plato and Aristotle, as well as between philosophy and poetry?
(1) Sir Philip Sidney
(2) Longinus
(3) The Neo-Platonists
(4) John Dryden

6. If the glide is distinct enough to be heard, the vowel + glide will be treated as
(1) A diphthong
(2) A monophthong
(3) A sequence of two vowels
(4) A sequence of two consonants

7. Match **List-I** with **List-II**

List-I	**List-II**
A. John Gross	I. *A History of English Prose Rhythm*
B. Wendy Martin	II. *The Oxford Book of Essays*
C. George Saintsbury	III. *Essays by Contemporary American Women*
D. Richard A Lalham	IV. *Analyzing Prose*

Choose the **correct** answer from the options given below:
(1) A-II, B-III, C-I, D-IV
(2) A-I, B-II, C-III, D-IV
(3) A-IV, B-III, C-I, D-ll
(4) A-IV, B-II, C-I, D-III

8. Match **List-I** with **List-II**

List-I	**List-II**
A. *Surprised by Sin: the Reader in "Paradise : Lost"*	I. Louise Rosenblatt
B. *Five Readers Reading*	II. Stanley Fish
C. *The Reader, the Text, the Poem*	III. Walter J Slatoff
D. *With Respect to Readers*	IV. Norman Holland

Choose the **correct** answer from the options given below:
(1) A-IV, B-I, C-II, D-III
(2) A-II, B-IV, C-I, D-III
(3) A-II, B-I, C-III, D-IV
(4) A-III, B-II, C-I, D-IV

9. Arrange the following novels in a chronological order as per their years of publication
A. *The Serpent and the Rope*
B. *Two Leaves and a Bud*
C. *A Bend in the Ganges*
D. *So Many Hungers*
E. *Waiting for the Mahatma*
Choose the correct answer from the options given below:
(1) A, E, B, D, C
(2) B, A, C, E, D
(3) C, D, B, E, A
(4) B, D, E, A, C

10. Match **List-I** with **List-II**

List-I	**List-II**
A. Thick description	I. Jacques Derrida
B. Transcendental signified	II. I A Richards
C. Vehicle, Tenor	III. Bertolt Brecht
D. Alienation Effect	IV. Clifford Geertz

Choose the **correct** answer from the options given below:
(1) A-IV, B-I, C-II, D-III
(2) A-I, B-III, C-II, D-IV
(3) A-II, B-I, C-III, D-IV
(4) A-III, B-II, C-I, D-IV

11. Match **List-I** with **List-II**

List-I (Author)	**List-II (Work)**
A. Lois Reynolds Kerr	I. *Dark Harvest*
B. Dorothy Livesay	II. *Guest of Honour*
C. Gwen Pharis Ringwood	III. *Red Emma*
D. Carol Bolt	IV. *Joe Derry*

Choose the **correct** answer from the options given below:
(1) A-II, B-IV, C-I, D-III
(2) A-I, B-II, C-III, D-IV

(3) A-III, B-I, C-IV, D-II
(4) A-IV, B-II, C-III, D-I

12. Match **List-I** with **List-II**

List-I (Line)	List-II (Author)
A. One day I wrote her name upon the strand/But came the waves and washed it away	I. Thomas Gray
B. Under the green-wood tree/ Who loves to lie with me,/ And turn his merry note/ Unto the sweet bird's note	II. William Shakespeare
C. The curfew tolls the knell of parting day,/ The lowing herd wind slowly o'er the lea	III. Ted Hughes
D. Remember how we picked the daffodils?/ Nobody else remembers, but I remember.	IV. Edmund Spenser

Choose the **correct** answer from the options given below:
(1) A-II, B-IV, C-I, D-III
(2) A-IV, B-II, C-I, D-III
(3) A-III, B-I, C-IV, D-II
(4) A-IV, B-III, C-II, D-I

13. Arrange the following commissions, committees, and events, which were important in the context of the history of English in India, in chronology:
A. Gokak Committee Report
B. Acharya Ramamurti Commission
C. All India Language Conference
D. Kothari Commission
E. The Officiai Language Act
Choose the correct answer from the options given below:
(1) B, E, D, C, A (2) C, E, D, A, B
(3) A, B, D, C, E (4) D, E, C, B, A

14. Who has described his criticism as a "by-product" of his "private poetry-workshop" and as "a prolongation of the thinking that went into the formation of my own verse"?
(1) S. T. Coleridge (2) Matthew Arnold
(3) Ezra Pound (4) T.S. Eliot

15. Who has written, "The two pillars upon which a theory of criticism must rest are an account of value and an account of communication"?
(1) William Empson (2) I. A. Richards
(3) Ezra Pound (4) J. C. Ransom

16. Which of the Schools of Criticism has strongly opposed Formalism, in both its European and American Varieties, rejecting the view that there is a sharp and definable division between ordinary language and literary language:
A. Marxism
B. Reader Response Criticism
C. Speech -Act Theory
D. New Historicism
E. Postcolonialism
Choose **the most appropriate** answer from the options given below:
(1) A, B and E Only
(2) A, C and E Only
(3) B, C and D Only
(4) A, D and E Only

17. Which of the following is not a distinct discourse analytical research tradition as suggested by Margaret Wetherall et al.?
(1) Discursive psychology
(2) Bakhtinian research
(3) Saussunan research
(4) Foucauldian research

18. Which of the following statements have been given by Barbara Johnson:
A. "Deconstruction is not synonymous with destruction..."
B. "The deconstruction of a text does not proceed by random doubt or arbitrary subversion..."
C. "Deconstruction is not a dismantling of the structure of a text but a demonstra-

tion that it has already dismantled itself."

D. "If anything is destroyed in a deconstructive reading, it is not the text, but the claim to unequivocal domination of one mode of signifying over another."

E. "Deconstruction as a mode of interpretation works by a careful and circumspect entering of each textual labyrinth..."

Choose the most **appropriate** answer from the options given below:

(1) A, B and D Only
(2) A, C and E Only
(3) B, C and D Only
(4) A, D and E Only

19. Match **List-I** with **List-II**

List-I	List-II
A. *Thinking About Women*	I. Betty Friedan
B. *The Female Eunuch*	II. Mary Ellman
C. *The Dialectic of Sex*	III. Shulamith Firestone
D. *The Feminine Mystique*	IV. Germaine Greer

Choose the **correct** answer from the options given below

(1) A-II, B-IV, C-III, D-I
(2) A-I, B-III, C-II, D-IV
(3) A-II, B-I, C-IV, D-III
(4) A-III, B-II, C-I, D-IV

20. "Territorialization" is a term given by-

(1) Gayatri C. Spivak
(2) Edward Said
(3) John Macleod
(4) Gilles Deleuze and Felix Guattari

21. Who has designed "Panopticon" and used the term as "a new mode of obtaining power of mind over mind"?

(1) Antony Easthope
(2) Jeremy Bentham
(3) Alan Sheridan
(4) Madan Sarup

22. Choose the correct statements amongst the following:

A. Macaulay was the practical man of affairs, helping and rejoicing in the progress of his beloved country.

B. Ruskin was like a Hebrew prophet just in from the desert, and the burden of his message was, "Woe to them that are at ease in Zion!"

C. Arnold was much like the cultivated Greek; his voice was soft, his speech suave, but he left the impression that you must be deficient in culture.

D. Newman was like the best French prose writers in expressing his thought with such naturalness and apparent ease that, without thinking of style, we received exactly the impression which he meant to convey.

Choose the most **appropriate** answer from the options given below:

(1) A, Band C Only
(2) A, C and D Only
(3) B, C and E Only
(4) C, D and E Only

23. Who described Raja Rammohan Roy as 'the inaugurator of the modern age in India'?

(1) Rabindranath Tagore
(2) Cavelly Venkata Boriah
(3) Mahatma Gandhi
(4) Jyotiba Phule

24. Which of the following critics are associated with Frankfurt School of German Intellectuals:

A. Waiter Benjamin
B. Luara Mulvey
C. Travis Henderson
D. Max Horkheimer
E. Leo Lowenthal

Choose the **most appropriate** answer from the options given below:

(1) A, D and E Only
(2) C, D and E Only
(3) B, C and D Only
(4) A, C and E Only

25. Match **List-I** with **List-II**

List-I	List-II
A. "Liberty of the Press"	I. Thomas de Quincey
B. "The Vision of Mirza: An Oriental Allegory"	II. John Ruskin
C. "On the Knocking at the Gate in Macbeth"	III. John Milton
D. "Mental Slavery of Modern Workmen"	IV. Joseph Addison

Choose the **correct** answer from the options given below:

(1) A-II, B-III, C-IV, D-I
(2) A-III, B-I, C-II, D-IV
(3) A-IV, B-II, C-III, D-I
(4) A-III, B-IV, C-I, D-II

26. Identify the poem in which the following lines occur:

"My babe so beautiful! It thrills my heart/ With tender gladness, thus to look at thee"

(1) "A Prayer for My Daughter"
(2) "Frost at Midnight"
(3) "Lucy Gray"
(4) "Ode on Melancholy"

27. Choose the correct match of play and playwright

A. *Hali* – Rabindranath Tagore
B. *Tiger Claw* – La khan Deb
C. *The Flute of Krishna* – P A Krishnaswami
D. *Nalini* – Gurucharan Das
E. *Hayavadana* – Girish Karnard

Choose the **most appropriate** answer from the options given below

(1) B, C and E Only
(2) A, D and E Only
(3) A, C and D Only
(4) B, C and D Only

28. Who wrote to the Committee of Public Instruction on introducing English as official language of the Government and that of education?

(1) Robert Clive
(2) Warren Hastings
(3) William Bentinck
(4) Zachary Macaulay

29. Who made the following remark?

"The Sanskrit language, whatever be its antiquity, is of a wonderful structure; more perfect than the Greek, more copious than the Latin, and more exquisitely refined than either, yet bearing to both of them a stronger affinity, both in the roots of verbs and in the forms of grammar, than could possibly have been produced by accident."

(1) Sir William Jones
(2) Patsy M Lightbown
(3) Ferdinand de Saussure
(4) Albert Sydney Hornby

30. Who among the following Mughal rulers carried out an experiment for newborn babies to be raised in silence, only to find that the children produced no speech at all?

(1) Akbar
(2) Bahadur Shah Zafar
(3) Aurangzeb
(4) Babur

31. Lord Curzon used the report of Indian Universities Commission of 1902 to

(1) decentralize school education.
(2) give representation to Indians in policy making.
(3) withdraw Indian Universities Act of 1904.
(4) centralize school education under a Director-General of Education.

32. Arrange the following works of Feminism in chronological order:

A. *The Female Imagination*
B. *The Madwoman in the Attic*
C. *A Literature of their Own*
D. *Women's Oppression Today: Problems in Marxist Feminist Analysis*
E. *Revolution in Poetic Language*

Choose the **correct** answer from the options given below:

(1) E, D, B, C, A (2) B, A, C, E, D
(3) E, A, C, B, D (4) A, B, C, D, E

33. Match **List-I** with **List-II**

List-I	List-II
A. Pidgin	I. The language special to an individual, sometimes described as a 'personal dialect'.
B. Creole	II. A language defined according to social use, such as scientific, formal, religious, and journalistic.
C. Idiolect	III. A contact language which draws on elements from two or more languages
D. Register	IV. A term relating to people and languages especially in the erstwhile colonial tropics and subtropics, in the Americas, Africa, the Indian Ocean, and Oceania

Choose the **correct** answer from the options given below:
(1) A-I, B-IV, C-III, D-II
(2) A-II, B-III, C-I, D-IV
(3) A-IV, B-11, C-III, D-I
(4) A-III, B-IV, C-I, D-II

34. Choose the correct statements.
A. English literature was first offered as a subject of study at King's College, London in 1831.
B. English was first offered as a subject of study in England only in 1828 in the universities of Oxford and Cambridge
C. Though taught as a medium of instruction and a subject of study in India since 1850s, Oxford and Cambridge did not allow the new subject of English literature to be taught till the end of the nineteenth century.
D. In 1931, English replaced the study of classics in Greek and Latin (the language of the Church) in Oxford and Cambridge.
E. Till the end of the nineteenth century literature meant only the study of great books in classical languages like Greek and Latin in Oxford and Cambridge.

Choose the most **appropriate** answer from the options given below:
(1) A, C and E Only
(2) B, C and D Only
(3) A, B and C Only
(4) B, D and E Only

35. Match **List-I** with **List-II**

List-I (Characters)	List-II(Novel)
A. Ursula-Skrebensky	I. *Women in Love*
B. Gudrun-Gerald	II. *Lady Chatterley's Lover*
C. Connie-Mellors	III. *Sons and Lovers*
D. Miriam-Paul	IV. *The Rainbow*

Choose the **correct** answer from the options given below:
(1) A-III, B-II, C-IV, D-I
(2) A II, B-IV, C-I, D-III
(3) A-IV, B-I, C-II, D-III
(4) A-III, B-IV, C-II, D-I

36. Who has coined the phrase "Bricolage"?
(1) Claude Levi Strauss
(2) Raymond Williams
(3) Martin Heidegger
(4) Michel Foucault

37. Identify the set of poems written by W. B. Yeats.
(1) "The Second Coming", "Death of Sohrab", "Lapis Lazuli", "Easter 1916"
(2) "The Home-Coming", "Among School Children", "Byzantium", "When You Are Old"
(3) "Sailing to Byzantium", "Leda and the Swan", "The Second Coming", "The House of Life"
(4) "No Second Troy", "Lapis Lazuli", "Easter 1916", "When You Are Old"

38. Which of the following works is not written by William Cooper?
(1) *Scenes from Provincial Life*
(2) *Scenes from Married Life*
(3) *The Field Marshal's Memoirs*
(4) *Memoirs of a New Man*

39. According to the 1991 census, _______ languages are considered scheduled languages.
(1) 17 (2) 18
(3) 20 (4) 22

40. Kipling's story "Mrs Bathurst" is set in
(1) India (2) South Africa
(3) Canada (4) Australia

41. Who is of the opinion that the concept of "ideology" is "the most important conceptual category in cultural studies"?
(1) James Carry
(2) Graeme Turner
(3) Raymond Williams
(4) Pavarotti

42. Arrange the following statements chronologically in order of their appearance in Aristotle's *Poetics:*
A. The plot is "the end at which tragedy aims".
B. Regarding the Plot, "A whole is what has a beginning and middle and end".
C. The plot of the tragedy should have a Unity: "the component incidents must be so arranged that if one of them be transposed or removed, the unity of the whole is dislocated and destroyed".
D. The character in question must occupy a mean between these extremes: he must be a man "who is not pre-eminently virtuous and just, and yet it is through no badness or villainy of his own that he falls into the misfortune, but rather through some flaw in him".
E. The function of the poet is to narrate "events such as might occur... in accordance with the laws of probability or necessity".

Choose the **correct** answer from the options given below:
(1) E, D, B, C, A (2) B, A, C, E, D
(3) C, D, A, B, E (4) A, B, C, E, D

43. The "notion of author' constitutes the privileged moment of individualization in the history of ideas, knowledge literature, philosophy and the sciences." Identify the critical essay in which the line occurs:
(1) "The Death of the Author"
(2) "What is an Author"
(3) "Heirs of the Living Body"
(4) "What is New Formalism"

44. Read the following statements carefully and find out the correct ones:
A. Charles Lamb was a lifelong friend of Coleridge and defender of the poetic creed of Wordsworth.
B. The London crowd, with its pleasures and occupations, never attracted Charles Lamb.
C. Charles Lamb gave us the best pen-portraits of Coleridge, Hazlitt, Landor, Hood, and many more of the interesting men and women of his age.
D. Charles Lamb wrote *Essays of Elia, Tales from Shakespeare* and *The Revolt of the Tartars.*
E. Lamb was especially fond of old writers, and was apparently unable to express his new thought without using their old quaint expressions.

Choose **the most appropriate** answer from the options given below:
(1) A, B and C Only
(2) B, C and D Only
(3) A, C and E Only
(4) C, D and E Only

45. Arrange the following works of John Storey in their chronological order of publication
A. *Inventing Popular Culture: From Folklore to Globalisation*
B. *Cultural Theory and Popular Culture: An Introduction*
C. *What is Cultural Studies: A Reader*
D. *Cultural Consumption and Everyday Life*

E. *Culture and Power in Cultural Studies: The Politics of Signification*

Choose the **correct** answer from the options given below:

(1) B, C, D, A, E (2) C, A, E, B, D
(3) E, D, A, C, B (4) E, A, C, B, D

46. Read the following statements carefully and choose the correct ones:

A. A mixed metaphor conjoins two or more obviously diverse metaphoric vehicles.
B. In metonymy, a part of something is used to signify the whole.
C. To scan a passage of verse is to go through it line by line to analyze its content, theme and diction.
D. The term 'kenning' denotes the recurrent use, in the poems written in old Germanic languages, of a descriptive phrase in place of the ordinary name for something.
E. Figurative language is often divided into two categories: Tropes and Schemes.

Choose the **most appropriate** answer from the options given below:

(1) A, D and E Only
(2) B, C and E Only
(3) B, C and D Only
(4) A, B and D Only

47. Which of the following rules are correct regarding formatting of date and time in the body of thesis writing according to MLA Handbook 9th Edition?

A. When using the month-day-year style in prose, a comma must be placed after the year unless another punctuation mark follows it.
B. Use a comma between month and year or between season and year.
C. Decades can be written out or expressed in numerals.
D. Spell out centuries in uppercase letters.
E. Numerals are used for most times of the day. Generally, use the twelve hour-clock system in prose

Choose the **most appropriate** answer from the options given below:

(1) A, B and C Only
(2) B, C and D Only
(3) A, C and E Only
(4) C, D and E Only

48. The term "Remainder" has been first used by-

(1) Giorgio Agamben
(2) Guy Debord
(3) Jacques Derrida
(4) J. Habermas

49. Who among the following is considered as "the father of South African English poetry"?

(1) Rider Hoggard (2) Thomas Pringle
(3) John Buchan (4) Percy Fitzpatrick

50. Erziehungsroman is a term which signifies:

(1) French Term signifies 'Novel of Manners'
(2) Greek Term signifies 'Novel of Love'
(3) Roman Term signifies 'Novel of Sentiments'
(4) German Term signifies 'Novel of Education'

51. Match **List-I** with **List-II**

List-I	**List-II**
A. He turned his back on the 'two decades of hypocrisy'.	I. Dylan Thomas
B. The Welsh traditions of the power of spoken word are present in his poetry.	II. John Betjeman
C. He is identified as a representative middle-brow voice of the present, adjusting to the past.	III. Philip Larkin
D. His poetry plays with and against Romantic tradition in poetry.	IV. W. H. Auden

Choose the **correct** answer from the options given below

(1) A-I, B-III, C-II, D-IV
(2) A-II, B-IV, C-I, D-III
(3) A-IV, B-I, C-II, D-III
(4) A-III, B-I, C-IV, D-II

52. Read the following statements carefully and choose the correct ones:

A. Mikhail Bakhtin traces the roots of the novel back into the imperial Rome and ancient Hellenistic romances.
B. Henry James considers the novel as the epic of a prosaic modern world.
C. Margaret Anne Doody locates novel's birthplace in the cultures of the ancient Mediterranean
D. F. R. Leavis defines novel as "one bright book of life".
E. Georg Lukacs Cails the novel "the epic of a world abandoned by God".

Choose the most **appropriate** answer from the options given below:
(1) A, C and E Only
(2) A, B and D Only
(3) B, C and D Only
(4) C, D and E Only

53. Match **List-I** with **List-II**

List-I	List-II
A. *Cynthia's Revels*	I. Thomas Middleton
B. *The Maid's Tragedy*	II. Ben Jonson
C. *Women Beware Women*	III. Thomas Dekker
D. *The Shoemakers' Holiday*	IV. Beaumont and Fletcher

Choose the **correct** answer from the options given below:
(1) A II, B-IV, C-I, D-III
(2) A-IV, B-II, C-I, D-III
(3) A-III, B-I, C-IV, D-II
(4) A-IV, B-II, C-III, D-I

54. Match **List-I** with **List-II**

List-I (Work)	List-II (Author)
A. *Poverty and Un-British Rule in India*	I. Romesh Chander Dutt
B. *The Slave Girl of Agra*	II. Dadabhai Naoroji
C. *Love Songs and Elegies*	III. Rabindranath Tagore
D. *Gora*	IV. Manmohan Ghosh

Choose the **correct** answer from the options given below:
(1) A-II, B-I, C-IV, D-III
(2) A-I, B-II, C-III, D-IV
(3) A-III, B-I, C-IV, D-II
(4) A-IV, B-II, C-III, D-I

55. Choose the correct events corresponding with their year

A. The Official Languages Commission submitted its report in 1936.
B. The first ELTI was established in Allahabad in 1954.
C. The Central Institute of English and Foreign Languages was established in Hyderabad in 1958
D. National Policy on Education came in 1960.
E. The NEP and POA came in 1986.

Choose the **most appropriate** answer from the options given below:
(1) B, C and E Only
(2) A, B and C Only
(3) B, C and D Only
(4) C, D and E Only

56. Match **List-I** with **List-II**

List-I	List-II
A. Collocation	I. A term borrowed in the 1960s from mathematics into linguistics by Noam Chomsky
B. Inflected	II. A term for the contrast between positive and negative in sentences, clauses, and phrases
C. Polarity	III. A habitual association between particular words

D. Generative IV. A term in which a word takes various forms to show its grammatical role

Choose the **correct** answer from the options given below:

(1) A-I, B-II, C-III, D-IV
(2) A-III, B-IV, C-II, D-I
(3) A-I, B-III C-IV, D-II
(4) A-IV, B-I, C-II, D-III

57. Arrange the following works of Criticism chronologically:

A. *More than Cool Reason*
B. *Death is the Mother of Beauty*
C. *Margins of Discourse*
D. *Meter in English: A Critical Engagement*
E. *The Rule of Metaphor*

Choose the **correct** answer from the options given below:

(1) B, D, C, A, E (2) C, A, E, D, B
(3) E, D, A, C, B (4) E, A, C, B, D

58. Read the following statements carefully and find out the correct ones:

A. Geoffrey Chaucer wrote *The Canterbury Tales, Troilus and Criseyde* and *Legend of Goode Women*
B. John Milton wrote the *Masque of Comus, Astophel and Stella* and *Paradise Lost.*
C. ST. Coleridge composed *The Rime of Ancient Mariner, Christabel and The Curse ofKehama.*
D. Shakespeare wrote *Two Gentlemen of Verona, Rape of Lucrece* and *Troilus and Cressida.*
E. Alexander Pope's works include *Dunciad, The Rape of the Lock* and *Epistle.*

Choose the **most appropriate** answer from the options given below:

(1) B, C and E Only (2) A, D and E Only
(3) A, B and D Only (4) C, D and E Only

59. Arrange the following steps of material collection according to hierarchy given by Delia da Sousa Correa and W.R. Owens in *The Handbook to Literary Research:*

A. Identify your nearest major research library
B. Visit your own university library
C. Identify what is available online
D. Visit your nearest major research library

Choose the correct answer from the options given below:

(1) D, A, C, B (2) A, B, C, D
(3) B, A, D, C (4) C, B, A, D

60. For Arnold, Culture is:

A. the ability to know what is best;
B. the ability to know what is worst
C. the mental and spiritual application of what is best
D. the pursuit of what is best
E. the pursuit of what is worst

Choose the **most appropriate** answer from the options given below:

(1) A, C and E Only
(2) B, C and E Only
(3) B, C and D Only
(4) A, C and D only

61. Choose the correct chronological order of the given works on Postcolonial Criticism

A. In Other Worlds
B. Postcolonial Literary Studies: First Thirty Years
C. Nation and Narration
D. The Protestant Ethnic and the Spirit of Acapitalism
E. Modernity at Large: Cultural Dimensions of Globalization

Choose the **correct** answer from the options given below:

(1) A, E, C, B, D (2) C, A, E, B, D
(3) E, D, A, C, B (4) A, C, E, D, B

62. Choose the correct statements regarding scope of linguistics from the following:

A. To describe and trace the history of all observable languages.
B. To determine the forces that are permanently and universally at work in all languages.

C. To study manifestations of civilized human speech only.

D. To consider only correct speech and flowery language.

E. To delimit and define itself.

Choose the most **appropriate** answer from the options given below:

(1) A, B and E Only
(2) B, C and D Only
(3) B, D and E Only
(4) A, C and D Only

63. Jacques Derrida's "Archive Fever: A Freudian Impression" is related to

(1) Archival Method
(2) Biographical Method
(3) Visual Method
(4) Creative Method

64. According to Ferdinand de Saussure, what is the minimum number necessary to complete the speaking-circuit?

(1) 1 (2) 2
(3) 3 (4) 4

65. Arrange the following books in chronological order:

A. G. N. Shuster's *The English Ode from Milton to Keats*

B. Paul H. Fry's *The Poet's Calling in the English Ode*

C. John Heath-Stubbs' *The Ode*

D. Carol Maddison's *Appollo and the Nine: A History of the Ode*

E. G.M. Foley's *Oral Traditional Literature*

Choose the **correct** answer from the options given below:

(1) C, A, D, E, B (2) A, B, C, E, D
(3) A, D, C, B, E (4) E, B, C, D, A

66. Which of the following works is written by Joseph Conrad?

(1) *Tales of Unrest*
(2) *The Madonna of the Future and other Tales*
(3) *The Two Magics*
(4) *The Spoils of Poynton*

67. Since the publication of Samuel Johnson's "Preface to Shakespeare" in 1765, which of the Unities have been regarded as optional devices, available as needed by playwrights in England to achieve special effects of dramatic concentration?

(1) Unities of Time and Action
(2) Unities of Place and Action
(3) Unities of Place and Time
(4) Unity of Place only

68. Choose the correct statements.

A. Miller's play *The Crucible* was first written in verse.

B. *The American Dream* is a play by Edward Albee about the absurd situation and immediate realities.

C. *The American Dream* is a novel by Ionesco about the problems of a middle aged professional.

D. Miller's play *The Price* is set in a baroque palace in eastern Europe teasing social and metaphysical sophistication that debates not only the responsibility of the writer but the extent to which reality is composed of a series of performed gestures.

E. Miller's play *The Price* explores the extent to which we retrospectively invent our own history.

Choose the most **appropriate** answer from the options given below:

(1) A, C and D Only
(2) B, D and E Only
(3) B, C and D Only
(4) A, Band E Only

69. Which group of the poets among the following is known as the Georgian Poets?

(1) Alfred Noyce, W. B. Yeats, W. H. Davis, W. W. Gibson
(2) Rupert Brooke, Walter de la Mare, John Drinkwater, James Elroy Flecker
(3) John Masefield, Roy Campbell, Robert Graves, Dylan Thomas
(4) W. B. Yeats, T. S. Eliot, Thomas Hardy, D. H. Lawrence

70. Name the theory which assumes that "culture is not separate from nature, and that there is no hierarchy of actants such that the human is more privileged".

(1) Actor Network Theory
(2) Posthumanism
(3) Cultural Materialism
(4) Adaptation Theory

71. Who has coined the term "Onto-Theology"?

(1) Jacques Derrida
(2) Felix Guattari
(3) Gilles Deleuze
(4) Ben Johnson

72. Identify the subtitle of Oliver Goldsmith's semi-autobiographical poem, "The Traveller:

(1) A Prospect of Society
(2) The Citizen of the World
(3) The Fashionable Lover
(4) An Ancient Epic Poem

73. Arrange the following works chronologically:

A. *The Heart of Hindustan*
B. *Occasional Speeches and Writings*
C. *Eastern Religions and Western Thought*
D. *Dhamnutpada*
E. *The Principal Upanishads*

Choose the **correct** answer from the options given below:

(1) D, C, A, B, E (2) C, A, E, B, D
(3) B, C, D, E, A (4) A, C, D, E, B

74. Match **List-I** with **List-II**

List-I (Term)	**List-II (Meaning)**
A. et sq.	I. the same
B. idem	II. in the place cited
C. loc. cit	III. everywhere
D. passim	IV. and the following

Choose the **correct** answer from the options given below

(1) A-III, B-II, C-I, D-IV
(2) A-II, B-III, C-IV, D-I
(3) A-IV, B-I, C-II, D-III
(4) A-I, B-IV, C-III, D-II

75. Arrange the following stages of first language acquisition schedule in its' chronological order:

A. The Two-Word Stage
B. Telegraphic Speech
C. The One-Word Stage
D. Cooing
E. Babbling

Choose the **correct** answer from the options given below:

(1) B, C, A, E, D (2) C, A, B, E, D
(3) C, A, D, E, B (4) D, E, C, A, B

76. Arrange the following statements in a chronological order:

A. Nissim Ezekiel founded Quest, a general intellectual review associated with liberal democratic politics.
B. *The illustrated Weekly of India* sponsored a short story competition and began publishing contemporary Indian English poetry.
C. The Writers Workshop began to publish volumes of poetry.
D. C. R. Mandy became editor of the *Illustrated Weekly of India.*

Choose the correct answer from the options given below:

(1) A, C, B, D (2) D, B, A, C
(3) B, C, A, D (4) B, A, D, C

77. Which of the following statements have been given by J S Mill in his *The Subjection of Women:*

A. "The husband was called the lord of the wife."
B. "She is a slave of any boy whose parents forces a ring upon her finger."
C. "Wives are in general no better treated than slaves."
D. "The wife is the actual bondservant of her husband."
E. "If all women are not the victim of actual rape, then all of them are the victims of the threat of rape.

Choose the most **appropriate** answer from the options given below:

(1) A, B and C Only
(2) A, C and D Only
(3) B, C and D Only
(4) B, D and E only

78. The term "Chronotope" has been coined by
(1) Mikhail Bakhtin
(2) Stephen Greenblatt
(3) Bertolt Brecht
(4) J H Miller

79. Arrange the following core elements of list of Work Cited according to MLA Handbook 9th edition
A. Publisher
B. Title of Source
C. Author
D. Title of Container
E. Publication Date
Choose the **correct** answer from the options given below:
(1) C, B, D, A, E (2) C, D, B, E, A
(3) C, B, E, A, D (4) C, B, D, E,

80. Identify the correct chronological order as per the publication years of the following works
A. *Characteristics of Men, Manners, Opinions and Times*
B. *The Advancement of Learning*
C. Inquiry into the Original of our Idea of Beauty and Virtues
D. *The Plan of a Dictionary of the English Language*
Choose the **correct** answer from the options given below:
(1) A, C, D, B (2) C, A, D, B
(3) D, B, A, C (4) B, A, C, D

81. Choose the statements given by Virginia Woolf about women:
A. "She is born stupid and can do nothing but stupidity."
B. "She dominates the lives of kings and conquerors in fiction."
C. "She pervades poetry from cover to cover; she is all but absent from history."
D. She criticized Shakespeare for being harsh and rude to his female characters in his plays.
E. "(I)n real life she could hardly read, could scarcely spell, and was the property of her husband".
Choose the **most appropriate** answer from the options given below:
(1) A, B and E Only
(2) B, C and E Only
(3) A, D and E Only
(4) A, Band C only

82. Who prepared the first blueprint on English education in India in 1792?
(1) William Carey (2) Charles Grant
(3) Lord Minto (4) William Pitt

83. Match **List-I** with **List-II**

List-I (Novel)	**List-II (Subtitle)**
A. *Silas Marner*	I. The Modern Prometheus
B. *Sybil*	II. The Parish Boy's Progress
C. *Frankenstein*	III. The Two Nations
D. *Oliver Twist*	IV. The Weaver of Raveloe

Choose the **correct** answer from the options given below:
(1) A-II, B-I, C-IV, D-III
(2) A-I, B-IV, C-II, D-III
(3) A-III, B-II, C-IV, D-I
(4) A-IV, B-III, C-I, D-II

84. Who developed the concept of the cultural circuit which is important to the study of the interactions of culture and memory in Oral History research method?
(1) Michael Holroyd and Roy Harrod
(2) Zygmunt Bauman and Robert Putnam
(3) Charles Taylor and Elizabeth Wilson
(4) Graham Dawson and Al Thomson

85. Choose the correct definitions of language:
A. Language uses symbols that are primarily vocal but may also be visual and its' subfields are phonetics, phonology, writing systems, orthography, and nonverbal communication.

B. Language is used for communication and its' subfields are sentence processing, pragmatics, discourse analysis, and conversation analysis.

C. Language uses symbols that have unconventionalized meanings and its' subfieids are universal grammar, innateness, emergentism, neurolinguistics and cross-cultural analysis.

D. Language is a systematic means of communicating ideas or feelings by the use of conventionalized signs, sounds, gestures, or marks having understood meanings.

E. Language has region specific characteristics and its' subfieids are phonetics, phonology, morphology, syntax, discourse analysis, and lexical analysis.

Choose the most **appropriate** answer from the options given below:

(1) A, B and C Only
(2) A, Band D Only
(3) B, C and D Only
(4) B, D and E Only

86. Arrange the following works of Criticism chronologically:

A. *Gender Trouble: Feminism and the Subversion of Identity*
B. *A History of Gay Literature: The Mole Tradition*
C. *History of Sexuality*
D. *New Lesbian Criticism: Literary and Cultural Readings*
E. *Bodies That Matter*

Choose the **correct** answer from the options given below:

(1) E, D, B, C, A (2) B, A, C, E, D
(3) C, A, D, E, B (4) C, B, A, D, E

87. Which bibliography is concerned with the close analysis of individual copies of books in the light of our knowledge of how books were produced in literary research?

(1) Descriptive bibliography
(2) Analytical bibliography
(3) Enumerative bibliography
(4) Historical bibliography

88. The study of how human beings acquire language and how we use language to speak and understand is called:

(1) Theoretical Linguistics
(2) Sociolinguistics
(3) Applied Linguistics
(4) Psycholinguistics

89. In how many volumes George Eliot's *Middlemarch* was first published?

(1) Five separate volumes
(2) Eight separate volumes
(3) Seven separate volumes
(4) Ten separate volumes

90. Which of the following is not a kind of literary research?

(1) Bibliography and textual criticism
(2) Biographical
(3) Experimental Research
(4) Interpretive

Read the following lines and give the answer of the questions

From thee, even from thy virtue!
What's this, what's this? Is this her fault or mine?
The tempter or the tempted, who sins most? Ha!
Not she: nor doth she tempt: but it is I
That, lying by the violet in the sun,
Do as the carrion does, not as the flower,
Corrupt with virtuous season. Can it be
That modesty may more betray our sense
Than woman's lightness? Having waste ground enough,
Shall we desire to raze the sanctuary
And pitch our evils there? O, fie, fie, fie!
What dost thou, or what art thou, Angelo?
Dost thou desire her foully for those things
That make her good? O, let her brother live!
Thieves for their robbery have authority
When judges steal themselves. What, do I love her,
That I desire to hear her speak again,
And feast upon her eyes? What is't I dream on?
O cunning enemy, that, to catch a saint,
With saints dost bait thy hook! Most dangerous

Is that temptation that doth goad us on
To sin in loving virtue: never could the strumpet,
With all her double vigour, art and nature,
Once stir my temper; but this virtuous maid
Subdues me quite. Even till now,
When men were fond, I smiled and wonder'd how.

91. What internal conflict does the speaker express?
(1) A desire to become a monk
(2) Regret over a political decision
(3) A struggle between his virtue and lust
(4) Fear of losing power

92. Seconding to the speaker how does temptation disguise itself?
(1) In riches and power
(2) As poverty and humility
(3) As a virtue
(4) In dreams"

93. Thieves for their robbery have authority / When judges steal themselves" implies what?
(1) Society is just.
(2) Theft is always punishable.
(3) Corruption among judges is hypocritical.
(4) Judges are above law.

94. What emotion is the speaker* feeling at the end of the passage?
(1) Pride and Joy
(2) Indifference
(3) Confusion and shame
(4) Joy only

95. What kind of temptation does the speaker say is most dangerous?
(1) That which disguises itself as pleasure
(2) That which appears in dreams
(3) That which urges one to sin in loving virtue
(4) That which comes from enemies

Read the following passage carefully and give the answer of the questions:

Painting, or art generally, as such, with all its technicalities, difficulties, and particular ends, is nothing but a noble and expressive language, invaluable as the vehicle of thought, but by itself nothing. He who has learned what is commonly considered the whole art of painting, that is, the art of representing any natural object faithfully, has as yet only learned the language by which his thoughts are to be expressed. He has done just as much towards being that which we ought to respect as a great painter, as a man who has learned how to express himself grammatically and melodiously has towards being a great poet. The language is, indeed, more difficult of acquirement in the one case than in the other, and possesses more power of delighting the sense, while it speaks to the intellect; but it is, nevertheless, nothing more than language, and all those excellences which are peculiar to the painter as such, are merely what rhythm, melody, precision, and force are in the words of the orator and the poet, necessary to their greatness, but not the tests of their greatness. It is not by the mode of representing and saying, but by what is represented and said, that the respective greatness either of the painter or the writer is to be finally determined.

96. What is the broader philosophical implication of the statement "It is not by the mode of representing and saying, but by what is represented and said..."?
(1) Aesthetic techniques are irrelevant.
(2) Ethical and thematic depth are the ultimate measure of artistic value.
(3) Abstract art is superior to representational art.
(4) The audience determines the value of a work.

97. The author s primary argument suggests that technical mastery in painting is
(1) The only thing that defines artistic genius
(2) A deceptive illusion of greatness in art
(3) A necessary foundation but not the essence of true art
(4) More important than content in the painting

98. What does the passage emphasize as the true measure of greatness in painting and writing?
(1) The material used
(2) The style and vocabulary
(3) The techniques applied
(4) The content expressed

99. What does the phrase "possesses more power of delighting the sense, while it speaks to the intellect" imply about visual art?
(1) It is primarily sensual and lacks depth.
(2) It uniquely blends sensual pleasure with intellectual engagement
(3) It fails to communicate abstract ideas through its art.
(4) It relies too much on technique and spectacle.

100. What implicit assumption about language and expression underpins the passage's argument?
(1) All forms of art must use written language to be effective.
(2) Expression without technical skill is more valuable.
(3) The medium of expression is secondary to the message conveyed.
(4) The value of grammar and melody lies in their aesthetic, not communicative power

✔ ANSWERS

1. (2)	**2.** (2)	**3.** (3)	**4.** (2)	**5.** (3)	**6.** (3)	**7.** (1)	**8.** (2)	**9.** (4)	**10.** (1)
11. (1)	**12.** (2)	**13.** (2)	**14.** (4)	**15.** (2)	**16.** (3)	**17.** (3)	**18.** (1)	**19.** (1)	**20.** (4)
21. (2)	**22.** (2)	**23.** (1)	**24.** (1)	**25.** (4)	**26.** (2)	**27.** (1)	**28.** (3)	**29.** (1)	**30.** (1)
31. (4)	**32.** (3)	**33.** (4)	**34.** (1)	**35.** (3)	**36.** (1)	**37.** (4)	**38.** (3)	**39.** (2)	**40.** (2)
41. (2)	**42.** (4)	**43.** (2)	**44.** (3)	**45.** (1)	**46.** (1)	**47.** (3)	**48.** (3)	**49.** (2)	**50.** (4)
51. (3)	**52.** (1)	**53.** (1)	**54.** (1)	**55.** (1)	**56.** (2)	**57.** (4)	**58.** (2)	**59.** (4)	**60.** (4)
61. (4)	**62.** (1)	**63.** (1)	**64.** (2)	**65.** (3)	**66.** (1)	**67.** (3)	**68.** (4)	**69.** (2)	**70.** (1)
71. (1)	**72.** (1)	**73.** (4)	**74.** (3)	**75.** (4)	**76.** (2)	**77.** (2)	**78.** (1)	**79.** (1)	**80.** (4)
81. (2)	**82.** (2)	**83.** (4)	**84.** (4)	**85.** (2)	**86.** (3)	**87.** (2)	**88.** (4)	**89.** (2)	**90.** (3)
91. (3)	**92.** (3)	**93.** (3)	**94.** (3)	**95.** (3)	**96.** (2)	**97.** (3)	**98.** (4)	**99.** (2)	**100.** (3)